ADVANCED ACCOUNTING

The Robert N. Anthony/Willard J. Graham Series in Accounting

ADVANCED ACCOUNTING

Charles H. Griffin, Ph.D.
University of Arizona

Thomas H. Williams, Ph.D.
University of Wisconsin, Madison

Kermit D. Larson, D.B.A.
The University of Texas at Austin

James R. Boatsman, Ph.D.
Oklahoma State University

Timothy B. Bell, Ph.D.
The University of Texas at Austin

1985   Fifth Edition

Homewood, Illinois   60430

Preface

In writing this fifth edition of *Advanced Accounting,* we have attempted to retain features from the fourth edition which adopters have found helpful. In the two units dealing with business combinations and consolidated financial statements, application of the "full" equity method continues to be the reference point for discussion. This approach reflects the fundamental principles underlying consolidation without the distraction of specific working paper techniques, and is presumed to be the dominant method encountered in practice. However, recognizing that the reader may encounter situations in which the investment is carried under the cost method, discussion of the changes in parent company entries and working paper techniques necessitated by application of this method has been continued.

In the explanation of consolidation techniques, we continue to highlight the distinctions between parent company entries and working paper eliminations. Although both are often presented in general journal entry format, the working paper eliminations are distinguished by showing them over a shaded screen.

A number of important changes have been incorporated. The first two chapters have been completely rewritten as one. This first chapter now contains an expanded discussion of the economic motivations for business combinations, including references to several actual transactions that illustrate these motivations. There is discussion of the various sequences of events that can lead to a business combination, as well as graphic presentations that highlight the relation between continuity of ownership and whether payment takes the form of cash or common shares. An introduction to the distinction between the purchase and pooling of interests methods naturally follows. Pricing of business combinations continues to be discussed. However, the discussion has been greatly simplified and centers on an example using actual data from the acquisition of Utah International shares by General Electric.

The second chapter dealing with consolidation at date of acquisition includes a more extensive treatment of purchase price allocation. Fair value determination when the tax basis of purchased assets differs from appraisal values has been included. In addition, the rationale and procedures of "push down" accounting are discussed. An appendix dealing with accounting for investments in corporate joint ventures, general and limited partnerships, and undivided interests has been added to the third chapter on accounting in periods following acquisition. The appendix also includes a discussion of proportionate consolidation.

At the end of Unit One is a new chapter which provides an introduction to professional accounting research. The reason for including this chapter is our belief, shared with many of our colleagues, that accounting education has placed too much emphasis on what might be termed "rule memorization." While some degree of familiarity with extant authoritative literature is essential, of at least equal importance is the ability to deal with ambiguous financial reporting situations. A successful practitioner must be able to *recognize issues, research* these issues in the authoritative literature, *make a decision* regarding how to account for transactions for which the authoritative literature provides no clear guidance, and *communicate* the conclusions and recommendations to an (often skeptical) audience. Chapter 6 is devoted to development of these skills. There is little textual material. For the most part, the textual material consists of an example of the process of deciding on an appropriate accounting for an actual transaction involving Conoco and Dome Petroleum, and a proposed transaction involving Conoco and Cities Service. The problem material accompanying this chapter consists solely of cases, the solutions to which require issue recognition, research, and decision making in varying levels of difficulty. All of these cases involve exclusively financial reporting issues, although in only a few instances are these related to business combinations. Solution of the cases will require access to an accounting library containing the reference sources described in the textual material.

There is no obvious placement of this chapter in an advanced accounting text. We have selected the end of Unit One to accommodate courses which do not include Unit Two. If both Unit One and Unit Two are included, it may be desirable to defer Chapter 6 in order to avoid breaking the continuity of the business combination subject matter. We do not believe placement is a matter of extreme importance. Rather, the important matter is that students' formal accounting education include *some* experience in dealing with the ambiguity characteristic of the contemporary accounting environment.

In Unit Two, accounting for international operations is now addressed in two chapters. Chapter 13 is devoted to accounting for foreign currency transactions and forward exchange contracts. Remeasurement and translation of foreign company financial statements are contained in Chapter 14. The expanded coverage provides a comprehensive treatment of this material, including several topics that have not previously been included in advanced accounting texts.

In recognition of the increased importance of government and other nonbusiness organizations, we have included two chapters on accounting for these entities. Accounting for governmental units is contained in Chapter 19. Accounting for colleges and universities, hospitals, voluntary health and welfare organizations, and other nonprofit organizations is contained in Chapter 20.

The teaching package accompanying *Advanced Accounting* includes a *Solutions Manual* (in transparency master format) for all questions, exercises, and problems in the book, a *Study Guide* written by C. Dwayne Dowell, a book of *Working Papers* designed to fit the problems and thereby reduce the amount of ''busy work'' often associated with consolidated statement working papers, a list of *Check Figures,* and a book of *Examination Materials* which includes a variety of items to assist in examination preparation.

We are appreciative of many suggestions made by the adopters of the fourth edition. Many of the changes in this fifth edition are the result of their suggestions. Particularly, we are grateful for the contributions of Professors James Theis, Jerry Trapnell, Glen Berryman, Saleha Krumawala, and Anna Fowler.

Finally, we also recognize that each of us remains in the debt of late Professor G. H. Newlove of the University of Texas at Austin for his pioneering work in many advanced accounting topics and life-long example of serious scholarship. We take special pride in dedicating this fifth edition to his memory.

CHARLES H. GRIFFIN
THOMAS H. WILLIAMS
KERMIT D. LARSON
JAMES R. BOATSMAN
TIMOTHY B. BELL

Contents

UNIT ONE
Accounting for Combined Corporate Entities   1

1. Economic and Accounting Issues in Business Combinations   **3**
   Motivations and Mechanisms for Business Combinations: *Economic Motivations for Business Combinations. Mechanisms for Business Combinations.* Accounting Methods for Business Combinations: *Offering Procedures.* Negotiations of Business Combinations: Publicly Traded Companies: *Exchange Ratio Negotiating Range. General Formulation of the Model. The Specific Exchange Ratio.* Negotiations of Business Combinations: Closely Held Companies: *Valuation of a Closely Held Company. Determining the Method of Payment.* Tax Factors Affecting Corporate Combinations: *Tax-Free Reorganizations. Criteria for Assessing Tax Status. Motives for Planning Tax Status. Tax Attribute Carryovers.*

2. Consolidated Financial Reports—Date of Acquisition   **35**
   Corporate Affiliations. Reasons for Corporate Affiliations. Consolidated Statements. Criteria for Inclusion in Consolidated Statements. Disclosure of Consolidation Policy. Precautions in the Evaluation of Consolidated Statements. Determining Cost of an Acquired Company. Consolidated Balance Sheet. Investment Cost per Share Equal to Book Value per Share of Subsidiary Stock. Investment Cost per Share Exceeds Book Value per Share of Subsidiary Stock. Investment Cost per Share Less than Book Value per Share of Subsidiary Stock. Disposition of Debit (Credit) Differentials. Push Down Accounting. Other Intercompany Transactions. Unpaid Subsidiary Dividends at Acquisition. Treasury Stock of the Subsidiary. Adjustments. Comprehensive Illustration.

3. **Consolidated Financial Reports—Postacquisition   79**
The Cost Method. The Equity Method. Entry Comparison. Statements of Consolidated Income and Retained Earnings. The Three-Division Working Paper—First Year Subsequent to Acquisition. Consolidated Statement Working Paper—Second Year Subsequent to Acquisition. Other Intercompany Transactions. Multicompany Affiliations. Reconsideration of Basic Definitions. Appendix A: Illustration of Consolidated Statement Working Paper Techniques when the Investment Account Is Carried under the Cost Method. Appendix B: Accounting for Investments in Joint Ventures.

4. **Consolidated Financial Reports—Postacquisition (continued)   129**
Treatment of Differentials Subsequent to Date of Acquisition. Realignment of Subsidiary's Shareholders' Equity. Interim Purchases. Income Tax Considerations. Combined and Parent Company Financial Statements. Statement of Changes in Financial Position. Appendix: Illustration of Consolidated Statement Working Paper Eliminating Entries for Differential Allocation and Amortization when the Investment Account Is Carried under the Cost Method.

5. **Interpretive Problems of Accounting for Business Combinations   181**
Purchase and Pooling of Interests Accounting: *Summary of the Criteria for Classifying Business Combinations. The Purchase Method of Accounting. The Pooling of Interests Method of Accounting. Comparative Summary of Purchase and Pooling of Interests Accounting. Historical Summaries and Trend Analysis of Combined Business Entities.* Earnings per Share Analysis: *Traditional Calculations. Primary Earnings per Share. Fully Diluted Earnings per Share. Earnings per Share Calculations Involving Affiliates. Changing Conversion Rates or Exercise Prices. Contingent Stock Issuances. Restatement of Prior Period's Earnings per Share. Other Problem Areas.* Segmental Reporting: *The Need for Segmental Reports. Identifying Significant Segments of a Firm. Intersegmental Transfer Pricing. Allocating Common Costs and Measuring Segmental Profitability. Identifying Segmental Assets. An Example of Segmental Reporting.*

6. **Accounting Research and Decision Making   235**
Financial Accounting Education and Practice. The Structure of Accounting Authority. Research Source Materials. The Research Process. A Comprehensive Example: *The Fact Situation. The Issues. Research.*

UNIT TWO
CONSOLIDATED STATEMENTS: AN EXPANDED
ANALYSIS   255

7. Consolidated Statements—Intercompany Profit on Asset
Transfers   **257**
*Overview of the Merchandise Transfer Problem. Determination of Amount of
Intercompany Profit. Elimination Principles for Unconfirmed Intercompany
Profit. Reported and Confirmed Incomes of Affiliates. Parent Company En-
tries for Intercompany Inventory Profits. Eliminating Intercompany Inven-
tory Profits in the Consolidated Statement Working Paper.*

8. Consolidated Statements—Intercompany Profit on Asset
Transfers (continued)   **309**
Intercompany Profit—Plant and Equipment. Intercompany Profits—
Related Topics: *Other Asset Transfers. Transfer Profits before Affiliation.
Deferral of Income Taxes Paid on Intercompany Profits.* Appendix: Two
Additional Intercompany Profit Elimination Methods.

9. Consolidated Statements—Preference Interests   **345**
Intercompany Bonds: *Intercompany Bonds and the Equity Method. Entries
and Eliminations at Date of Purchase. Analysis of Gain or Loss. Entries and
Eliminations after Date of Purchase. Interim Purchases of Intercompany
Bonds.* Preferred Stock: *Allocation of Earnings. Treatment in Consolidated
Statements—Nonparticipating, Cumulative, Preferred Stock. Definitional
Calculation of Consolidated Net Income.*

10. Consolidated Statements—Changes in Parent Company's
Equity   **391**
Incremental Purchases of Subsidiary Stock from the Public. Sales of
Subsidiary Stock to the Public. Subsidiary Stock Transactions: *Issuance
of New Subsidiary Shares. Subsidiary Repurchase of Treasury Shares. Effect
on Fundamental Definition of Consolidated Net Income.* Unconfirmed
Profit on Asset Transfers. Appendix: Restructuring the Form of the
Subsidiary Stock Transaction in Case 6.

11. Consolidated Statements—Special Ownership
Configurations   **445**
Multilevel Affiliations: *Effects of Differential Amortization. Chain Control
(Indirect) Less than 50 Percent. Intercompany Profit in Multilevel Affilia-
tions.* Bilateral Stockholdings—Traditional Allocation Method: *Bilat-
eral Stockholdings Not Involving Parent Company. Bilateral Stockholdings
Involving Parent Company. Intercompany Profit on Asset Transfers. Effects*

of Differential Amortization. Purchase of Shares in a Mutually Related Subsidiary. Recording Equity in Affiliates' Earnings. Investment Elimination Entry. Matrix Applications for Complex Affiliations. Bilateral Stockholdings—Treasury Stock Method.

12. **Consolidated Statements—Miscellaneous; Branch Accounting   485**
The Entity Theory: *Debit and Credit Differentials. Intercompany Profit. Minority Shareholder Interests and Consolidated Net Income. Illustrative Problem—Entity Theory.* The Trial Balance Working Paper. Consolidated Statements—A Review. Branch Accounting: *Agencies and Branches. Branch Accounts. Illustrative Entries. Combined Financial Statements. Branch Billing in Excess of Cost. Illustrative Problem. Reconciling Adjustments. Transshipments of Merchandise. Other Accounting Systems.*

13. **Accounting for International Operations   529**
Currency Exchange Rates. Foreign Currency Transactions: *Illustrative Import/Export Transactions. Exchange Gains and Losses. Forward Exchange Contracts—An Elaboration. Multiple Exchange Rates.*

14. **Accounting for International Operations (continued)   559**
Evolution of Translation Principles. The Functional Currency Concept: *Highly Inflationary Economies.* Initial Investment in Foreign Affiliate. Accounting Procedures for the Translation Process (Current Rate Method). Accounting Procedures for the Remeasurement Process (Temporal Method). Accounting for Differentials. Consolidating a Foreign Subsidiary. Consolidated Statement of Changes in Financial Position. Remeasuring Inventory Valued Using Lower of Cost or Market. Foreign Branches. Relevant Exchange Rates. Financial Statement Disclosures. Reporting on Foreign Affiliates.

**UNIT THREE
ACCOUNTING FOR PARTNERSHIPS   607**

15. **Formation and Operation of Partnerships   609**
Nature of a Partnership: *Aggregative versus Entity Concept. Partnership Agreement.* Partnership Formation: *Recording the Initial Contributions. Income Tax Considerations.* Partnership Operations: *Nature and Amount of Relative Interests. Allocating Net Income to Partners. Financial Statement Presentation.* Appendix: The Uniform Partnership Act.

16. Realignment of Ownership Structure **661**

Introduction: *Basic Legal Provisions. Types of Realignment.* Admission of a New Partner: *Admission with Payment to the Partnership. A Comparison of the Bonus and Goodwill Methods. Admission with Payment to the Existing Partner(s). Legal Status of a New Partner. Tax Basis of a New Partner.* Retirement or Death of a Partner: *Retirement of a Partner. Sale of an Interest to a New Partner. Sale of an Interest to Continuing Partners. Death of a Partner. Legal Status of a Retiring or Deceased Partner.*

17. Partnership Liquidation **695**

Introduction: *The Liquidation Process. Accounting Problems in Partnership Liquidation. Basic Dichotomy—Partnership Solvency and Insolvency.* Simple Liquidation: *Basic Distributive Rights. Partners' Debit Balances. Partners' Loans. Liquidation Expenses.* Installment (Periodic) Payments: *Basic Accounting Problem. Periodic Computation of Safe Payments to Partners. Partners' Loans. Liquidation Expenses and Unrecorded Liabilities. Cash Predistribution Plan.* Insolvent Partnership: *Basic Rights. Accounting Analysis of the Insolvent Partnership.* Comprehensive Illustration.

UNIT FOUR
FIDUCIARY AND INSTITUTIONAL ACCOUNTING **737**

18. Corporate Liquidation and Reorganization **739**

Liquidation: *Bankruptcy Reform Act of 1978. Assignment for Benefit of Creditors. The Statement of Affairs. Statement Annotations. Special Problems. Extended Usefulness of the Statement of Affairs.* Reorganization: *Nonjudicial Remedies. Judicial Remedies.* Trustee's Accounts. Realization and Liquidation Account: *Statement Annotations. Special Problems.*

19. Accounting for Estates and Trusts **783**

Administration by a Fiduciary: *Introduction. Role of the Fiduciary in Estate Administration. Inventory of Assets. Claims against the Estate. Bequests of Personal Property. Role of the Fiduciary in Trust Administration. Estate Planning.* Dual Bases of Accountability: *Principal (Corpus) and Income Distinguished. Special Problems.* Fiduciary Accounts and Reports: *Accounting Procedures and Entry Sequence for an Estate. Illustrative Problem. Charge and Discharge Statement. Closing Entries. Properties Transferred to Trustee.*

20. Accounting for State and Local Governmental Units **827**

Historical Perspective of Authoritative Pronouncements. Summary Statement of Principles of Governmental Accounting. Basic Concepts of Governmental Accounting for the General Fund: *The Nature of*

Funds. Expendable and Nonexpendable Funds. Allotments and Apportionments. Account Groups for General Fixed Assets and General Long-Term Debt. Budgetary Accounting. Modified Accrual Basis. Recognition of Grants, Entitlements, and Shared Revenue from Other Governments. Illustrations of Accounting for the General Fund: *Recording the Budget. Recording Actual Transactions. Recording Encumbrances. Closing the Budgetary and Proprietary Accounts. Other Reserves. Financial Statements for the General Fund. Comprehensive Illustrative Entries for General Fund.* Accounting for Other Governmental Funds and Account Groups: *Special Revenue Funds. Capital Projects Funds. Debt Service Funds. Special Assessment Funds.* Enterprise Funds: *Internal Service Funds. Trust and Agency Funds. General Fixed Assets—A Self-Balancing Group of Accounts. General Long-Term Debt—A Self-Balancing Group of Accounts. Annual Financial Reports of State and Local Governments.*

21. Accounting for Other Nonbusiness Organizations   **899**

Authoritative Pronouncements: *Distinguishing Characteristics of Nonbusiness Organizations.* Funds Used by Nonbusiness Organizations. Accounting for the Unrestricted Fund: *Accounting for Revenues. Donated Materials and Services. Pledges. Designated Funds. Mandatory and Nonmandatory Transfers. Expenses and Expenditures. Assets and Liabilities.* Accounting for Restricted Fund. Accounting for Plant Fund. Accounting for Loan Fund. Accounting for Endowment Fund. Accounting for Pooled Investments. Accounting for Agency Fund. Accounting for Annuity and Life Income Fund. Financial Statements of Nonbusiness Organizations.

Index   **959**

Accounting for Combined Corporate Entities (with an introduction to accounting research and decision making)

CHAPTER 1

Economic and Accounting Issues in Business Combinations

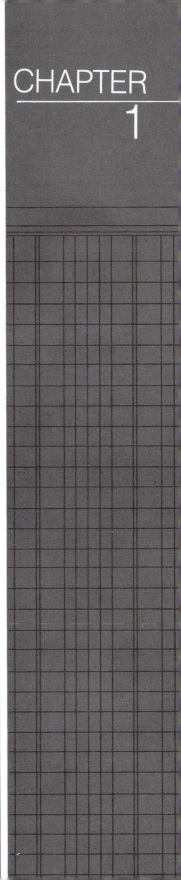

Motivations and Mechanisms for Business Combinations

There are a variety of mechanisms by which two or more corporations can be brought under common ownership. We will employ the term *business combination* to refer to all such transactions, regardless of the mechanism by which the transaction is executed. In virtually every year of recent history, hundreds of business combinations have occurred. In many of these transactions, at least one of the combining corporations is quite large. Because of the number of business combinations that occur and the size of the firms involved, accounting for business combinations is an important topic.

Economic Motivations for Business Combinations

At the outset, it will be helpful to reflect upon the economic motivations for a business combination. In principle, the decision to enter into a business combination is a special case of a more general class of capital budgeting decisions. The decision on the part of one firm to obtain the net assets of another in a business combination is not fundamentally distinct from the decision to obtain a single asset. Consider the decision to acquire a single asset, say, a machine. The decision to obtain a machine would normally be based on a net present value criterion, or some expedient approximation thereof.

Net present value is the result of subtracting the machine's cost from the discounted value of its estimated cash flows. Loosely speaking, the discounted value of the machine's cash flows is the value of the machine in the eyes of its "would be" purchaser. Similarly, its cost is the value of the machine in the collective eyes of the marketplace. Net present value, then, can be thought of as an incremental, or synergistic, value that is expected to be created by adding the machine to the "would be" purchaser's existing portfolio of assets. The net present value criterion states simply that the machine should be purchased if the value to its purchaser exceeds its value in the marketplace. In other words, the investment in a machine would be undertaken in an effort to produce synergistic value.

Similarly, the desire to create synergistic value is said to motivate business combinations. There is an incentive to combine two or more firms into one if the value of the combined firm exceeds the sum of the values of its constituents.

There are many reasons why a synergistic value might accompany a business combination. One possibility is the elimination of duplicate fixed costs. This would normally be expected when two companies with similar productive processes are combined. Recent examples are combinations involving Oscar Mayer and General Foods (two food producers) and Continental Air and Texas International Air (two air carriers). A second possibility is technical integration of successive phases of a productive process.

This would normally be expected with combinations involving one firm that produces another firm's input. Recent examples are Conoco (a petroleum producer) and Du Pont (a manufacturer of petroleum-based fiber).

A third possibility exists when one firm holds assets that are underutilized due to an enept management. A business combination, then, affords an opportunity for bringing such assets under the influence of a second firm's more efficient management. Such a situation was alleged in the recent unsuccessful attempt by Mesa Petroleum to acquire Cities Service Co. The chairman of Mesa was quoted in the *New York Times* as having said, "I would have to say that Cities management grades very low."[1] The context of this quotation was a discussion of 1981 losses on the part of Cities Service while the company held exploration rights on 10 million acres of undeveloped land, and the Mesa contention that this asset was underutilized. Lastly, a synergy may arise through utilization by one firm of another's soon-to-expire net operating loss carryforward.

The desire to create synergistic value may not be the exclusive motivation for business combinations. It is sometimes alleged that management compensation schemes play a role. Managers often receive compensation based on accounting earnings. A firm that acquires control of the net assets of another by issuing additional shares of its stock would normally expect accounting earnings to increase simply because of the expanded asset base. This is so even in the absence of any synergistic value brought about by the combination. Thus, managers whose compensation is based on accounting earnings have an incentive to engage in such transactions.

Mechanisms for Business Combinations

Business combinations are often achieved through an exchange of cash for common stock or common stock for common stock. Consider first the exchange of cash for common stock. Aspects of two combining firms, each owned by a single individual, prior to the combination are as follows:

Company A		Company B	
The Corporation	*Individual 1*	*The Corporation*	*Individual 2*
Cash	Share of A	Net assets	Share of B
Other net assets			

Prior to the combination, items in possession of A Corporation are cash to be used in the business combination and other net assets. The owner of A, individual 1, possesses a common share of A. Similarly, B Corporation possesses net assets, and its owner, individual 2, possesses a common

---
[1] "Mesa's Founder Takes on Big Foe," *New York Times*, June 7, 1982, p. 25.

share of B. A Corporation then acquires control of B's net assets by exchanging cash for the share of B in possession of individual 2. After the exchange, the above diagram would be altered as follows:

Company A		Company B	
The Corporation	*Individual 1*	*The Corporation*	*Individual 2*
Other net assets	Share of A	Net assets	Cash
Share of B			

B Corporation is now owned by A Corporation. Therefore, the net assets of B are under the control of a *different* individual, individual 1. Individual 2 now holds only cash and therefore is disenfranchised from the affairs of either corporation. In this situation, it is clear that the ownership of something, the net assets of B, has changed hands. A Corporation has *purchased* the net assets of B Corporation. The accounting for such a transaction is a matter to be discussed later in this chapter. For the moment, it is sufficient to note that the accounting for the purchase of net assets in such a fashion is consistent with purchases of all assets, i.e., the purchased assets are recorded at cost to the purchaser as of the date of purchase.

Now consider a business combination facilitated through a common stock for common stock exchange. Aspects of two combining firms, each of which are again owned by a single individual, are as follows:

Company A		Company B	
The Corporation	*Individual 1*	*The Corporation*	*Individual 2*
Net assets	Share of A	Net assets	Share of B
Share of A			

Items in possession of A Corporation include net assets and an unissued share (or treasury share). Other features of the scenario are identical to the scenario involving the cash for common stock exchange. A Corporation now acquires control of B's net assets by exchanging its unissued share (or treasury share) for the share of B in possession of individual 2. After the exchange, the diagram would appear as follows:

Company A		Company B	
The Corporation	*Individual 1*	*The Corporation*	*Individual 2*
Net assets	Share of A	Net assets	Share of A
Share of B			

As in the cash for common stock exchange, B Corporation is now owned by A Corporation. Moreover, individual 1 and B Corporation are in exactly the same position as they were following the cash for common stock exchange. Of profound significance, however, is the postcombination position of individual 2. Individual 2 has *not* been disenfranchised from the affairs of both corporations by virtue of receiving only cash. Instead, individual 2 remains involved by virtue of the ownership of half the outstanding shares of A Corporation. It is not obvious that something has been bought and sold. Before the transaction, the net assets of A and the net assets of B were owned by individuals 1 and 2. After the transaction, the net assets of A and the net assets of B are still owned by these same individuals. There is a *continuity of ownership*. It appears that individuals 1 and 2 have simply *pooled* their investments in net assets under the auspices of A Corporation.

Since it is not obvious that a purchase has taken place, the argument can be made that accounting for a common stock for common stock exchange should not result in a new asset valuation basis (as is the case with a purchase transaction). We will return to this matter shortly.

For purposes of terminology, both the cash for common stock and common stock for common stock exchanges illustrated above are termed an *acquisition*. The distinctive feature of an acquisition is that A Corporation and B Corporation persist as legal entities. B Corporation is termed a *subsidiary*, and an A Corporation is termed a *parent*. Each corporation would normally continue to operate its own distinct accounting system which produces financial statements at the ends of accounting periods. The accounting issues, then, for acquisitions are:

1. How should the separate statements of the parent reflect its investment in the subsidiary?
2. How should the separate statements of the subsidiary reflect the acquisition?
3. How should consolidated financial statements be prepared, i.e., how should the separate statements of the parent and subsidiary be aggregated together to produce a single set of financial statements reflecting the financial affairs of the combined economic entity?

A *merger* can be exemplified by slightly altering the circumstances of either the cash for common stock or common stock for common stock examples. Consider the affairs of A Corporation and B Corporation following the acquisition of B by A:

A Corporation	*B Corporation*
Net assets of A	Net assets of B
Share of B	

B Corporation now distributes its net assets to its owner (A Corporation) as a liquidating dividend. The outstanding share of B is retired, and B Corporation ceases to exist as a legal entity. The above diagram would then appear as:

A Corporation	B Corporation
Net assets of A	
Net assets of B	

The distinctive feature of a merger is that only one of the constituent firms in the business combination continues as a legal entity. Because of this, only one accounting system remains in operation, and the only financial statements produced are those of the surviving entity. The accounting issue, then, for a merger is simply, "How should the surviving entity account for net assets received from its merger partner?"

Now suppose that a new legal entity, C Corporation, is formed. In particular, A Corporation distributes all of its net assets, including those received from B Corporation, to C Corporation. This new corporation then issues shares of its stock to the owners of A Corporation (individuals 1 and 2 or just individual 1, depending on whether the initial transaction was a cash for common stock or common stock for common stock exchange). The A Corporation shares are then retired. A Corporation and B Corporation now cease to exist, and C Corporation is the surviving legal entity. This scenario illustrates a *consolidation*. Although there are more direct means of liquidating two (or more) corporations into a newly created corporation, the distinctive feature of a consolidation is that a new corporation is created that receives the net assets of its predecessors which cease to exist. Thus, as with a merger, there is but one surviving entity, one accounting system, and one set of financial statements. The accounting issue, then, for a consolidation is "How should the new corporation account for the net assets transferred to it by its predecessors?"

Recall that in all three cases (the acquisition, the merger, and the consolidation), individual 2 might have received cash or common stock. If cash were received, it is clear that there would be a *purchase* since ownership of net assets would have changed hands. If common stock were received, evidence of a purchase would be less obvious since a continuity of ownership on the part of individual 2 would be present. It should thus be clear at this point that the question of whether the substance of a business combination is more akin to a purchase of net assets or a mere pooling of investments with no change in ownership arises regardless of whether the combination is an acquisition, a merger, or a consolidation.

Accounting Methods for Business Combinations

In the United States there are two generally accepted methods of accounting for business combinations. These are termed the *purchase* method and the *pooling of interests* method. The two methods are not alternatives for one another. Rather, as we shall see, the pooling of interests method is only used when several quite restrictive circumstances are met. The purchase method is used in all other circumstances.

Appreciating the fundamental differences between the methods is simplified by considering a merger, such that any issues relating to the separate company statements of the parent and subsidiary do not arise.[2] (The only financial statements produced are those of the surviving firm.) If the combination is accounted for as a purchase, the financial statements of the surviving company will be identical to those that would be produced if the firm had simply made a "basket purchase" of net assets instead of entering into the merger. In the case of "basket purchases," the net assets acquired are recorded at fair value at date of acquisition (which may result in the recording of goodwill). In subsequent accounting periods, depreciation and amortization are based on these recorded values.[3] It is in this sense that business combinations in which ownership of net assets changes hands give rise to accounting consistent with that of any purchase of assets.

In contrast, the pooling of interests method of accounting ignores fair values of assets as of the date of the business combination. The financial statements of the surviving company will be identical to those that would have been produced if the constituent firms had been operating as a single company throughout their entire history. If the constituent companies had indeed been operating as one, the appropriate accounting basis of assets would clearly be the cost as of the date the assets had originally been acquired by this single company. In a pooling of interests, then, the basis of accounting for net assets acquired in a business combination remains at the basis used by the company that merges with the surviving entity. This basis is, of course, historical cost. In periods subsequent to the business combination, it is this historical cost upon which depreciation and amortization are based.

Thus, the fundamental distinction between the two methods lies in the accounting basis of net assets acquired in the business combination. The purchase method involves abandonment of historical cost in favor of fair value as of the date of the business combination. The pooling of inter-

---

[2] Moreover, in the case of an acquisition, the possibility of acquiring less than 100 percent of the outstanding shares of the subsidiary somewhat complicates a discussion of the difference between the two methods.

[3] For a discussion of "basket purchases" of net assets, see G. Welsch, C. Zlatkovich, and W. Harrison, *Intermediate Accounting*, 6th ed. (Homewood, Ill.: Richard D. Irwin, 1982).

ests method retains the historical cost basis. Because of inflation, fair values will tend to exceed historical costs. Therefore, the postcombination depreciation and amortization will tend to be higher (and income lower) when a transaction is accounted for as a purchase. Since managers of firms are often compensated on the basis of accounting income, other things equal, one would expect that managers would often prefer having a contemplated transaction accounted for as a pooling of interests. Or the management preference might be based on factors not directly related to their compensation. For example, higher earnings increases the "times interest earned" statistic. And this statistic might be a contractual benchmark used to determine whether a borrower is in technical default on debt covenants.

Historically, this tendency for managers to favor the pooling of interests method has been a source of some conflict between accountants and managers. Indeed, one often hears allegations about multimillion dollar transactions that would not have occurred had not the accountants consented to a pooling of interests accounting. The conflict has arisen because rarely are transactions as clear-cut as in our previous examples involving cash for common stock and common stock for common stock. It is obvious that when all the outstanding shares of one firm are acquired for cash, a purchase has taken place. Similarly, when all the stockholders of one firm surrender their common shares for common shares of another firm, the absence of a change of ownership of the combined firm's net assets is consistent with the "multiple entities operating as if they had always been one entity" notion inherent in the pooling of interests method.

However, between these two extremes lie a considerable number of more ambiguous possibilities. Many combinations involve acquisitions of less than 100 percent of the outstanding shares of a combining company. Many involve payment in the form of a mixture of cash and common stock. Others involve issuance of debt instruments and/or preferred stock in addition to cash and/or common stock. And the debt and/or preferred stock may or may not be convertible. In such exchanges, it is very difficult to ascertain whether or not a change in ownership has taken place. Because of the ambiguity of such transactions, accountants have been hard pressed to argue against the position often taken by managers that these exchanges be accounted for as a pooling of interests.

In 1970, the Accounting Principles Board (APB) clarified considerably the circumstances under which a pooling of interests is appropriate. In its *Opinion No. 16*, "Accounting for Business Combinations," the Board identified 12 rather restrictive conditions, all of which must be met, in order for a pooling of interests to be acceptable. All transactions failing to meet one or more of these conditions are to be accounted for as purchases. In short, the Board took a position consistent with a long-standing accounting tenet. That is, ambiguous cases are to be resolved in favor of the method of accounting that portrays the more conservative financial posture. And the

purchase method, with its higher depreciation and amortization, portrays a more conservative earnings posture.

The Board's 12 conditions are:

1. Each of the combining companies must be autonomous and must not have been a subsidiary or division of another corporation during the two-year period prior to the initiation of the combination plan. However, this does not exclude companies that were newly incorporated within the preceding two years, unless they were successors to part or all of a company that was not autonomous.

2. At the dates the plan of combination is initiated and consummated, none of the combining companies can hold as intercorporate investments more than 10 percent of the outstanding voting common stock of any combining company, unless the shares held were exchanged for shares that are issued to effect the combination plan. In other words, each of the combining companies must be independent of the other combining companies.[4]

3. The combination must be effected by a single transaction, or in accordance with a specific plan within one year after the plan is initiated.

4. The surviving (or resultant parent) corporation must issue *only* common stock with rights identical to those of the majority of its outstanding voting common stock, in exchange for "substantially all" of the voting common stock of the other (combining) companies outstanding at the date the plan of combination is consummated. *Opinion No. 16* specifies a detailed set of procedures for determining whether the requirement is satisfied that "substantially all" of the voting common stock be exchanged. The essence of the requirement is that 90 percent or more of the outstanding common stock of a combining company must be exchanged (between the dates the plan of combination is initiated and consummated) for the voting common stock issued by the surviving or parent (issuing) corporation.

5. Each of the combining companies must maintain substantially the same voting common stock interest; that is, none of the companies may change those interests by exchanges, retirements, or distributions to stockholders in contemplation of effecting the combination.

6. The combining companies may reacquire shares of voting common stock *only* for purposes other than business combinations, and no

---

[4] However, "Extension of 'Grandfather' Provisions for Business Combinations," *FASB Statement No. 10*, provides a permanent exception for companies which held a minority interest in other companies on October 31, 1970 (the date *APB Opinion No. 16* became effective), if the stockholder corporations eventually increase their investments to establish control. In these cases, the stockholder companies may have owned up to 50 percent of the investee's outstanding stock on October 31, 1970, and still qualify for a pooling of interests, so long as the other pooling of interest conditions are satisfied.

company may reacquire more than a normal number of shares after the date the plan of combination is initiated.

7. The ratio of the interest of an individual common stockholder to those of other common stockholders in a combining company must remain the same as a result of the exchange of stock to effect the combination.

8. The voting rights of the common stock interests in the resultant combined corporation must be exercisable by the stockholders; no mechanisms such as a voting trust can be used to deprive or restrict the common stockholders from exercising their voting rights.

9. The combination must be resolved at the date the plan is consummated, with no pending provision of the plan relating to the issue of securities or other consideration. As a consequence, the combined corporation cannot agree to contingent issuances of additional shares or other consideration to the former stockholders of a combining company.

10. The combined corporation must not agree directly or indirectly to retire to reacquire all or part of the common stock issued to effect the combination.

11. The combined corporation must not enter into other financial arrangements for the benefit of the former stockholders of a combining company, such as a guaranty of loans secured by stock issued in the combination.

12. The combined corporation must not intend to dispose of a significant part of the assets of the combining companies within two years after the combination, except to eliminate duplicate facilities or excess capacity and those assets that would have been disposed of in the ordinary course of business of the separate company.

Collectively, these conditions specify a situation in which there is little doubt that ownership interests in net assets have not been transferred from one group of owners to another, i.e., there is a clear continuity of ownership. Of the 12, condition 4 is especially revealing. It states that the surviving (or parent) corporation must issue *only* common stock, with rights identical to those of the majority of its outstanding voting common stock, in exchange for "substantially all" (defined to mean 90 percent or more) of the voting common stock of the other (combining) company. This means that the common stockholders of both combining companies will continue to be voting common stockholders of the combined company. Control of the combined company will be shared by the common stockholders of both combining companies. Since neither of the stockholder groups loses its ownership position, the combination does *not* involve the sale of one company to another. It is *not* a purchase/sale transaction. In one way or another, each of the 12 conditions contributes to the conclusion that neither company is being sold to the other and that the operations and ownership interests of each combining company in fact are continued through the combined company. For example, conditions 5, 6, and 10 prevent a circumvention of condition 4 through treasury stock transactions. Condition 5 rules out either firm buying shares from stockholders who may be disinclined to favor a forthcoming common stock for common stock exchange. Such a transaction would result in a change in ownership and thus smack of a purchase. Similarly, conditions 6 and 10 rule out an agreement by which shareholders initially receive common shares, and then sell these shares back to the issuing corporation after the combination.

Consider a recent transaction in which Crum and Forster acquired 750,000 of its own shares. The stated intent of this treasury stock transaction was to obtain shares to be issued in a common stock for common stock acquisition of Viking Insurance Co. The Viking acquisition would not qualify as a pooling of interests since the treasury stock transaction and common stock for common stock exchange together would result in an alteration of the ownership of Crum and Forster. At approximately the same time, Xerox announced an agreement to acquire Crum and Forster. The treasury stock transaction would similarly rule out a pooling of interests accounting for the Xerox acquisition of Crum and Forster. Others of the 12 conditions preclude any restrictions on the voting (and other rights) of the newly issued shares. Still others rule out the receipt of any significant additional compensation (besides newly issued shares) that might indicate that a sale has taken place.

Despite the specificity of *Opinion No. 16*, there still occur transactions that are difficult to classify as purchases or poolings of interests. Thus, accountants still are called upon to make hard decisions regarding the accounting for business combinations. Interestingly, the United States is virtually the only industrialized country in which the pooling of interests method is acceptable. The accounting principles of Canada, France, Germany, Japan, The Netherlands, Sweden, Switzerland, and the U.K. do not recognize the method at all.[5] Indeed, it is difficult to envision the possibility of an exchange in which there is, in truth, the continuity of ownership that is so critical to the pooling notion, particularly when the shares of the constituent firms are actively traded in an organized market. Ownership of such firms changes regularly. Nonetheless, many transactions between publicly traded companies meet the criteria specified by *Opinion No. 16* and are accounted for as a pooling of interests.

Offering Procedures

As a practical matter, it is difficult for one corporation to obtain at least 90 percent of the outstanding common shares of another without cooperation on the part of both firm managements. It is common for one manage-

---

[5] F. Choi and V. Bavishi, ''Diversity in Multinational Accounting,'' *Financial Executive*, August 1982, pp. 45–49.

ment to approach another with a proposal to exchange shares of one corporation for all the outstanding shares of the other. If the managements negotiate mutually satisfactory terms, the proposed exchange can be placed on the agenda for a stockholder meeting. Typically, a two-thirds favorable vote is sufficient to bind all stockholders to the transaction such that the 90 percent requirement for a pooling of interests can be met.

In many cases, however, the management of a "target" for acquisition may oppose the transaction. Refusal to place a proposed exchange before a vote of the stockholders leaves a "would be" acquiring firm only the option of dealing directly with the stockholders of the target firm. That is, the acquiring firm must make a tender offering for the shares of the target firm. And the target management can expend corporate resources in fighting a takeover attempt. For example, Marathon Oil Company disclosed in its fourth quarter 1980 report the expenditure of $11 million in fighting a takeover by Mobil Corporation. Because of the difficulty in acquiring at least 90 percent of the target firm shares in a tender offering, it is rare to observe a tender offer resulting in a pooling of interests.

Due to the tendency for managements to favor the income statement effects of a pooling of interest, availability of the method can have an important influence on management tactics in business combinations. In 1980, InterNorth, Inc., and Cooper Industries extended competing tender offers for Crouse-Hinds Co. common shares. Subsequently, InterNorth raised its offering price in an attempt to obtain slightly more than 10 percent of the Crouse-Hinds shares. Presumably, this was done in an effort to deny its rival bidder, Cooper Industries, the potential to account for any Cooper Industries/Crouse-Hinds combination as a pooling of interests, the result being that Cooper Industries would withdraw from the bidding. It had been estimated that purchase accounting would have increased by $12.5 million the annual depreciation of Cooper Industries.[6]

Negotiations of Business Combinations: Publicly Traded Companies

When a business combination is facilitated through an unopposed exchange of common shares for common shares, the principal issue to be negotiated is the *stock exchange ratio,* defined as the number of shares of the issuing firm to be given in exchange for one share of the other (nonissuing) firm. And even in cases where other forms of payment are employed, a stock exchange ratio might first be negotiated. Thereafter, an alternative payment form of equivalent value could be selected.

---

[6] "InterNorth Sets New Bid for Stock of Crouse-Hinds," *The Wall Street Journal,* December 18, 1980, p. 8.

If the common shares of each company are publicly traded, the market prices of these shares are important determinants of the stock exchange ratio. Presumably, neither the issuing nor nonissuing firm stockholders would agree to an exchange that results in a decline in the market value of their share investment. Moreover, the primary motive for a business combination presumably is to produce synergistic market value. Thus, negotiating a share exchange ratio can be conceived in terms of allocating the anticipated postcombination market value of the combined firm to the stockholders of the constituent firms in such a way that neither shareholder group suffers a decline in market value. In other words, negotiating a stock exchange ratio is a matter of agreeing on an allocation of anticipated synergistic market value.

Exchange Ratio Negotiating Range

It is relatively easy to derive upper and lower bounds between which the negotiated stock exchange ratio should fall. Consider the 1976 combination of General Electric and Utah International. At the time, this transaction was the largest in U.S. history. The combination was facilitated through an exchange of new General Electric shares for all the outstanding shares of Utah International. Data relating to these two companies prior to the exchange were as follows:

	General Electric	Utah International
Market value per share	$45.75	$47.50
Shares outstanding	182,855,000	31,540,000
Total market value	$8,365,616,000	$1,498,150,000

Shortly after the exchange, the market value of the combined firm's outstanding shares was $11,976,350,000. This amount exceeds the sum of the precombination values of the two firms by $2,112,584,000, a rather substantial synergistic effect. If we assume this actual combined firm value is a good approximation for what was anticipated, then the upper bound for the exchange ratio is the maximum that the General Electric stockholders would accept, i.e., the exchange ratio that awards all the anticipated synergistic market value of $2,112,584,000 to the Utah International stockholders and leaves the General Electric stockholders with only their original $8,365,616,000 in market value.

Let S_G' denote the additional shares of General Electric that are issued in exchange for the outstanding Utah International shares. The percentage ownership interest of the General Electric stockholders in the combined firm can then be written

$$\frac{182,855,000}{182,855,000 + S_G'}$$

and the market value associated with this ownership percentage can be written

$$\frac{182,855,000}{182,855,000 + S'_G} (11,976,350,000)$$

The value of S'_G which would leave the General Electric stockholders with only their original $8,365,616,000 in market value is given by the following equation:

$$\frac{182,855,000}{182,855,000 + S'_G} (11,976,350,000) = 8,365,616,000$$

The solution for S'_G is 78,923,000 additional General Electric shares. This implies the exchange ratio

$$\frac{78,923,000}{31,540,000} = 2.50$$

which is the largest price the General Electric stockholders would be willing to pay for the Utah International shares. With this exchange ratio, all the $2,112,584,000 in synergistic market value is awarded to the Utah International stockholders.

The lowest price the Utah International stockholders would be willing to accept can be similarly derived. The percentage ownership of the Utah International stockholders in the combined firm can be written

$$\frac{S'_G}{182,855,000 + S'_G}$$

and the market value associated with this ownership percentage can be written

$$\frac{S'_G}{182,855,000 + S'_G} (11,976,350,000)$$

The value of S'_G which would leave the Utah International stockholders with only their original $1,498,150,000 in market value is given by the following equation:

$$\frac{S'_G}{182,855,000 + S'_G} (11,976,350,000) = 1,498,150,000$$

The solution for S'_G is now 26,144,000 which implies the exchange ratio

$$\frac{26,144,000}{31,540,000} = .83$$

With this exchange ratio, all the $2,112,584,000 in synergistic market value is awarded to the General Electric stockholders.

According to the above analysis, the actual exchange ratio in the General Electric/Utah International exchange should have been between 2.50 and .83. Indeed it was: 41,002,000 additional General Electric shares were issued in exchange for the 31,540,000 outstanding Utah International shares. The actual exchange ratio was therefore

$$\frac{41,002,000}{31,540,000} = 1.30$$

General Formulation of the Model

The upper and lower bounds of the exchange ratio negotiating range can be expressed in terms of general formulas. Define:

ER_G = the maximum exchange ratio acceptable to the issuing firm stockholders

ER_U = the minimum exchange ratio acceptable to the nonissuing firm stockholders

S'_G = the additional shares of the issuing firm that are issued to facilitate the combination

S_G = the shares of the issuing firm that are outstanding prior to the combination

S_U = the shares of the nonissuing firm that are outstanding prior to the combination

W_G = the total market value of the issuing firm shares prior to the combination

W_U = the total market value of the nonissuing firm shares prior to the combination

W_{GU} = the anticipated total market value of the combined firm shares

The maximum exchange ratio acceptable to the issuing firm stockholders can be expressed

$$ER_G = \frac{S_G(W_{GU} - W_G)}{S_U W_G}$$

The minimum exchange ratio acceptable to the nonissuing firm stockholders can be expressed

$$ER_U = \frac{S_G W_U}{S_U(W_{GU} - W_U)}$$

Substitution of the data relating the General Electric/Utah International combination provides:

$$ER_G = 2.50 = \frac{182,855,000(11,976,350,000 - 8,365,616,000)}{31,540,000(8,365,616,000)}$$

$$ER_U = .83 = \frac{182,855,000(1,498,150,000)}{31,540,000(11,976,350,000 - 1,498,150,000)}$$

While these formulas are relatively simple, obtaining the requisite data may be quite difficult. Particularly troublesome is W_{GU}, the anticipated market value of the combined firm. Forecasting the value of an economic entity that does not yet exist is indeed a tricky affair. This forecasting problem might be simplified by decomposing it into forecasts of two components of W_{GU}. The value of the combined firm is the product of the price/earnings ratio of the combined firm and the earnings of the combined firm

$$W_{GU} = PE_{GU}(E_{GU})$$

where PE_{GU} is the price/earnings ratio of the combined firm, and E_{GU} is the earnings of the combined firm. Subsequent chapters of this text address various accounting issues related to the calculation of E_{GU}, termed *consolidated earnings*. These accounting issues can be quite complex. Thus, a contribution of accountants to negotiators is providing the expertise needed to calculate *consolidated earnings*.

The Specific Exchange Ratio

The difference between the upper and lower bounds of the exchange ratio negotiating range may be quite large. Recall that the determination of an exchange ratio is a matter of dividing any anticipated market value synergy between the stockholders of the constituent firms. The upper bound is the exchange ratio that awards all synergy to the nonissuing firm stockholders. The lower bound is the exchange ratio that awards all synergy to the issuing firm stockholders. When the synergy is large, the negotiating range will also be large.

Consider again the data relating to the combination of General Electric and Utah International. The synergistic market value was $2,112,584,000, and the model indicated only that the actual exchange ratio should fall between .83 and 2.50. Such a large negotiating range raises the question, "What determines where within the range the actual exchange ratio will fall?" The specific exchange ratio will depend on the relative bargaining power of the negotiants. More bargaining power in the hands of the nonissuing firm stockholders should drive the exchange ratio towards the upper bound. Conversely, more bargaining in the hands of the issuing firm stockholders should drive the exchange ratio towards the lower bound.

Unfortunately, the factors that give rise to bargaining power are not well understood. It is often suggested that the extent of competition among several "would be" issuing firms is an important factor in ascribing bargaining power to the nonissuing firm stockholders. That is, competition among several "would be" issuing firms in order to combine with the same nonissuing firm is said to drive the exchange ratio upward towards the point in which all anticipated gains in market value are captured by the nonissuing firm stockholders. However, several mitigating factors have also been mentioned in the literature. Evidence on the subject is mixed.[7]

Negotiations of Business Combinations: Closely Held Companies

In many business combinations, the shares of one or more of the constituent firms are not publicly traded, so that an observable market price of common shares is not available. Particularly frequent is a combination involving one large publicly traded company and one small closely held company. Negotiations involving closely held companies are not, in principle, different from negotiations involving only publicly traded companies. That is, the negotiating parties estimate the value of the combined firm, and allocate this value among the stockholders of the constituent companies in order to determine the terms of an exchange. Presumably, the combination will not take place if either of the constituent stockholder groups would stand to lose value. In a combination involving two companies, three numbers are especially relevant: the values of each of the two constituent companies in absence of the combination, and the value of the combined firm. These three numbers are sufficient to ascertain a range within which the negotiated allocation of combined firm value should fall. If the shares of both constituent companies are publicly traded, the values of each company are observable in the form of market prices. However, if

---

[7] The student interested in exploring this matter further should consult M. Bradley, "Interfirm Tender Offers and the Market for Corporate Control," *Journal of Business*, October 1980, pp. 345–76; R. Conn and J. Nielsen, "An Empirical Test of the Larson-Gonedes Exchange Ratio Determination Model," *Journal of Finance*, June 1977, pp. 749–60; P. Dodd, "Merger Proposals, Management Discretion and Stockholder Wealth," *Journal of Financial Economics*, June 1980, pp. 105–37; P. Dodd and R. Ruback, "Tender Offers and Stockholder Returns—An Empirical Analysis," *Journal of Financial Economics*, December 1977, pp. 351–73; D. Galai and R. Masulis, "The Option Pricing Model and the Risk Factor of Stock," *Journal of Financial Economics*, June 1976, pp. 53–81; K. Larsen and N. Gonedes, "Business Combinations: An Exchange Ratio Determination Model," *Accounting Review*, October 1969, pp. 720–28; S. Grossman and O. Hart, "Takeover Bids, the Free-Rider Problem, and the Theory of the Corporation," *Bell Journal of Economics*, Spring 1980, pp. 42–64; P. Halpern, "Empirical Estimates of the Amount and Distribution of Gains to Companies in Mergers," *Journal of Business*, October 1973, pp. 554–75; R. Haugen and T. Langetieg, "An Empirical Test for Synergism in Merger," *Journal of Finance*, September 1975, pp. 1003–14; R. Haugen and J. Udell, "Rates of Return to Stockholders of Acquired Companies," *Journal of Financial and Quantitative Analysis*, January 1972, pp. 1387–98; T. Langetieg, "An Application of a Three-Factor Performance Index to Measure Stockholder Gains from Merger," *Journal of Financial Economics*, December 1978, pp. 364–83; G. Mandelker, "Risk and Return: The Case of Merging Firms," *Journal of Financial Economics*, December 1974, pp. 303–35; and R. Smiley, "Tender Offers, Transaction Costs and the Theory of the Firm," *Review of Economics and Statistics*, February 1976, pp. 22–32.

the shares of either or both companies are not publicly traded, then a pseudo market value must be obtained.

Valuation of a Closely Held Company

Determining the price at which the shares of a closely held company would be traded if these shares were, in fact, actively traded in an organized market is a problem of immense practical difficulty. On the surface, the problem is straightforward. The value of an ownership interest is the present value of a claim to anticipated cash flow accruing to owners. The value of shares of a closely held company is therefore the present value of an anticipated series of cash flows accruing to owners. However, neither forecasting cash flows nor calculating their present value is simple.

Consider first the issues arising in the problem of forecasting cash flow for just one forthcoming period. Should the forecast be based solely on past cash flow data. If so, how much data? What statistical procedure should be used? If other historical data should be included as well, which data and how should they be incorporated? There are no agreed-upon answers to such questions?

Moreover, whatever forecast is obtained cannot be thought of as a single number, as if this single number will be realized with certainty. The future is decidedly uncertain, and a forecast can, at best, only take the form of a probability distribution. Calculating the present value of a single number is indeed straightforward. Calculating the present value of an entire probability distribution is not. Of course, one might reduce the probability distribution to a single number, say, its mean, and calculate the present value of this single number. But characterizing a probability distribution of cash flow with only its mean may suppress extremely important properties of the distribution. To see this, consider the following two scenarios involving the toss of a fair coin:

Outcome	First Scenario	Second Scenario
Heads..............	Receive $20	Receive $10,020
Tails	Pay $10	Pay $10,010

There is no forecasting problem in either scenario. The cash flows conditional upon both the heads and tails outcomes are known. Similarly, the probabilities of heads and tails are known. The problem is solely one of developing a single number that captures the value of the right to participate in each scenario.

In both scenarios, the mean cash flow is winning the sum of $5. But are the two scenarios equivalent, as a characterization in terms of means would imply? Would you feel equally comfortable about entering into each scenario? Probably not. Most individuals would be considerably more uneasy about participating in the second scenario in which one can win or lose a large sum. In this sense, the second scenario is more risky than the first. Thus, characterizing the two scenarios in terms of their means suppressed all consideration of risk.

How should risk be taken into account in order to calculate a present value? One might, for example, adjust the mean downward to reflect the disfunctional aspects of risk. Present value might then be calculated by discounting the resulting risk-adjusted mean at a riskless rate of interest. Alternatively, one might incorporate consideration of risk by discounting the unadjusted mean with an upwardly adjusted interest rate. Unfortunately, the precise fashions in which either of these two types of adjustments ought to be accomplished are not well understood.

The problems of valuing a claim to an uncertain amount of cash that will be received one period hence are even more perplexing if the forecasting horizon is extended beyond one period. Forecasting cash flow for several periods into the future is more arduous than forecasting for just one forthcoming period. In addition, the multiperiod forecast necessarily takes the form of a sequence of probability distributions, not just a sequence of numbers. Calculation of a present value therefore involves some form of risk adjustment for each distribution in the sequence.

In summary, thoughtful consideration of valuing a closely held company raises more unanswered questions than answered ones.[8] It is apparent that valuing a closely held company involves many subjective decisions that are beyond any precise description.

Determining the Method of Payment

Consider again the numerical example involving General Electric and Utah International. Suppose, however, that the shares of neither firm were publicly traded such that their precombination values of $8,365,616,000 and $1,498,150,000 had been determined subjectively. Assuming the same anticipated synergy of $2,112,584,000, we can still predict that the value of all consideration given the Utah International stockholders should fall between $1,498,150,000 and $1,498,150,000 + $2,112,584,000 = $3,610,734,000. Any amount less than $1,498,150,000 leaves the Utah International stockholders in a worsened position. Any amount greater than $3,610,734,000 leaves the General Electric stockholders in a worsened position.

---

[8] For a more involved discussion of valuing shares of a closely held company, see J. Boatsman and E. Baskin, "Asset Valuation with Incomplete Markets," *Accounting Review*, January 1981, pp. 38–53.

However, the presumption that both constituent companies are closely held raises an additional issue not present when shares of both constituent companies are publicly traded. In particular, it may not be equitable for the Utah International stockholders to receive payment only in the form of General Electric common shares. Preservation of equity may require that the combination take the form of a consolidation, in which both stockholder groups receive a mixture of common shares and preferred shares of the newly formed corporation.

As an example, suppose that the $8,365,616,000 value of General Electric is derived largely from goodwill. To be more specific, suppose that $5,000,000,000 of the total is due to goodwill and $3,365,616,000 is due to net severable assets.[9] Suppose further that the $1,498,150,000 value of Utah International is due to $98,150,000 in goodwill and $1,400,000,000 in net severable assets. Is it equitable for both stockholder groups to emerge from the combination holding only common shares of the combined entity? In one sense it is not.

By agreeing to the combination, the stockholders forego the alternative of selling the net severable assets piecemeal. Further, the cash receipts from such sales could have been reinvested in less risky securities, such as preferred shares. Because of this lost opportunity, the contribution of goodwill is a less significant commitment than is the contribution of net severable assets.[10] Therefore, a preferable position in return for the contribution of severable assets seems equitable. Preference positions in return for contributions of net severable assets can be achieved by forming a new entity that issues each stockholder group fully participating preferred shares with a value equal to the value of net severable assets contributed. Any remaining allocation of combined firm value takes the form of common shares. Illustration 1–1 contains such a distribution plan for the hypothetical example in which General Electric and Utah International are closely held companies.

The balance of $2,112,584,000 is the anticipated synergistic value. Additional common shares with this value would be distributed between the two stockholder groups. Distributing the entire amount to Utah International stockholders would make the total value of their new entity common and preferred shares equal to $3,610,734,000. Distribution of the entire amount to the General Electric stockholders would leave the Utah International stockholders with new entity common and preferred shares valued at $1,498,150,000, the value of their original investment.

---

[9] "Severable" assets include all tangible assets as well as intangibles that can be separately identified and offered for sale. It excludes goodwill, since goodwill cannot be disassociated from the collection of other assets. By implication, a "severable" asset can be individually offered for sale.

[10] This issue does not arise with publicly traded companies. Any stockholder can convert his or her entire investment to cash by selling shares at prevailing market prices. It is irrelevant whether or not the market value of shares is due partially to goodwill.

Illustration 1–1

Precombination values of constituent companies:

	General Electric	Utah International
Net severable assets	$3,365,616,000	$1,400,000,000
Goodwill	5,000,000,000	98,150,000
Total	$8,365,616,000	$1,498,150,000

Allocation of combined firm value:

Anticipated value of combined firm.................			$11,976,350,000
To General Electric stockholders:			
Value of preferred shares..........	$3,365,616,000		
Value of common shares	5,000,000,000	$8,365,616,000	
To Utah International stockholders:			
Value of preferred shares..........	$1,400,000,000		
Value of common shares	98,150,000	1,498,150,000	9,863,766,000
Balance			$ 2,112,584,000

Tax Factors Affecting Corporate Combinations

Tax consequences are significant in determining the methods to be used to pay for the acquired firm. In fact, the influence of taxes on one aspect of a combination often has a simultaneous impact on other aspects of the combination. For example, the tax implications of available payment methods may dominate the final decision as to whether a combination will be completed or abandoned. Furthermore, potential income tax benefits, such as operating loss carryforwards, may be a principal motivation underlying a proposed combination; and the transaction must therefore be carefully formulated to conform with relevant tax provisions.

Tax-Free Reorganizations

A critical tax factor in planning a corporate combination involves the taxable or tax-free status of the transaction between the acquiring corporation and the acquired corporation and/or its stockholders. In general, exchanges of assets (including securities such as stock) are recognized by the Internal Revenue Code as the appropriate point in time at which to assign new bases to the transferred items and to assess tax. However, corporate combinations may be either taxable or tax free, depending upon the nature of the agreement and the payments made to the combination participants (or their shareholders).

If a combination qualifies as a tax-free "reorganization," the acquired corporation may, in whole or in part, escape recognition of gain or loss on the transfer of its property to the acquiring corporation; and the existing bases of the assets are carried forward without change in amount to the acquiring corporation. The shareholders of the acquired corporation also may exchange their shares for stock of the acquiring corporation without the recognition of gain or loss. On the other hand, in a taxable combination, gain or loss is recognized by the selling party, and the acquiring corporation usually establishes new (current) bases in the assets acquired.[11]

Criteria for Assessing Tax Status

Tax-free acquisitions are usually effected under one of three basic forms of reorganization defined in Section 368 of the Internal Revenue Code. In general terms, the following alternatives are available:

1. Statutory mergers and consolidations, that is, a merger or consolidation consummated in accordance with a state statute (type A).
2. Acquisition of stock in exchange for *voting* shares of stock, subject to the requirement that the acquiring corporation must then hold a controlling interest (a minimum of 80 percent) in the acquired corporation (type B).
3. Acquisition of assets in exchange for *voting* stock where "substantially all" of the assets of the selling corporation are transferred to the purchasing corporation (type C).

The type A business combination refers to situations in which the acquiring and the acquired corporations are combined into one corporation (the acquiring, the acquired, or a new corporation), and the combination is effected in compliance with state statutes that specify the procedures to be followed. Such a transaction may qualify as a tax-free reorganization even if preferred stock and nonvoting stock are issued in payment for the acquired corporation. Depending on the relevant state statutes, the use of some limited amounts of cash and debt securities may also be permitted. However, an additional requirement imposed by the courts is that continuity of equity interests be maintained. For example, if debt regarded as excessive in amount is used as part payment, the courts may rule that a continuity of equity interests has not been maintained and accordingly refuse to accord tax-free status to the combination. Thus, it is possible for a combination to comply fully with the appropriate state merger laws and with the mechanics of the Code and yet be disallowed as a tax-free reorganization.

---

[11] B. I. Bittker and J. S. Eustice, *Federal Income Taxation of Corporations and Shareholders*, 4th ed. (Boston: Warren Gorham & Lamont, 1979), chap. 14.

To qualify as a type B reorganization, the means of payment is limited to voting stock of the acquiring corporation. However, cash purchases of the acquired corporation's stock in previous years do not necessarily disqualify the eventual tax-free status of the combination so long as at least 80 percent of the stock of the original corporation was acquired with voting stock of the acquiring corporation. Moreover, the *acquired* corporation may purchase (for cash) the shares of those stockholders who are unwilling to accept voting stock in the acquiring corporation.

Under a type C reorganization, the question as to what constitutes "substantially all" of the selling corporation's properties is subject to varied interpretation. Final determination depends on the nature of the assets (measured in terms of fair market value). In general, if the assets retained by the seller are not essential to the past operations of the seller, if retention is not for the purpose of continuing operations or for sales to another purchaser, and if the amount does not exceed the retained liabilities of the seller, the acquisition will satisfy type C requirements.

The type C requirement that payment be made with voting shares is not absolute. If at least 80 percent of the selling firm's assets are acquired in this manner, cash or other forms of consideration may be used to acquire the remaining 20 percent. Finally, the voting shares issued in payment may be shares in the acquiring firm's parent corporation.

Although the voting stock requirements of type B or C combinations are not absolute, it may be observed that the continuity of equity interests problem that may arise under a type A combination is always overcome as a natural consequence by the high voting stock requirements of types B and C reorganizations.

It should be noted that the distinguishable characteristics of the three reorganization types are difficult to isolate in many combination arrangements. What first appears as a type B reorganization may, if the acquired subsidiary is liquidated, have the substance of a type A or type C reorganization. This can be accomplished because the liquidation of a subsidiary into a parent is also tax-free. Also, types A and C reorganizations may be essentially equivalent in terms of their final equity arrangements.

Motives for Planning Tax Status

Whether a corporate combination will be deemed a taxable exchange or a tax-free reorganization is obviously susceptible to planning by combination participants. In this regard, a major concern of the acquiring corporation is the bases of the assets to be acquired. If the assets' current fair market values exceed their bases to the acquired corporation and the recognizable gain is long-term capital gain, a taxable transaction is desirable (other things being equal). Establishing a taxable status to the combination would permit the bases of the acquired corporation's assets to be stepped up to fair market value at a small tax cost relative to the decrease in future taxes available from increased tax deductions in future periods. Conversely, if current fair market values are less than the acquired corporation's bases in assets, the acquiring corporation should prefer a tax-free combination.

The acquired firm and/or its stockholders will generally prefer a tax-free combination status so long as the fair market value of securities received exceeds their bases in properties and/or shares given up. The general motive is, of course, to defer tax payments. Conversely, should the bases of properties and/or securities given up exceed their fair market value, a taxable exchange status would facilitate early recognition of losses.

Tax Attribute Carryovers

When a tax-free reorganization is accomplished as a type A or type C (as defined in Section 368), certain tax benefits, rights, and obligations of the acquired corporation may carry over to the surviving firm. Subject to specified conditions and limitations, the accounting methods employed by the acquired firm, net operating losses, unused investment credits, unexhausted capital loss carryforwards, and other tax attributes generally are applicable to the calculation of income tax for the surviving firm. However, numerous additional restrictions are imposed (e.g., Sections 269, 381, and 382) to prevent special advantages from carryforwards if the combination serves no sound business purpose other than to gain the benefit of the acquired corporation's favorable tax attributes.

If a combination involves the establishment of a parent-subsidiary relationship (type B), the tax attributes of the acquired subsidiary corporation typically remain with the subsidiary corporation. Should the constituents of the combination qualify for, and elect to file, a consolidated return, the subsidiary's unique attributes are generally applicable to that return only to the extent that they would be effective on a separate return. If the subsidiary is subsequently liquidated into the parent corporation, the same provisions that provide a carryforward (of tax attributes) in a type A or type C reorganization provide a carryforward of the liquidated subsidiary's attributes.

Questions

1. What are the economic motivations for business combinations? Are these, in principle, distinct from the motivation to acquire any asset?

2. Business combinations often result in synergistic market value. What are some reasons why this synergistic market value might materialize?

3. Explain the principal differences among business combinations that are classified as acquisitions, mergers, and consolidations.

4. Explain the relationship between the method of payment (cash or stock) and the issue of whether the ownership of the acquired company has changed hands. Also explain the relationship between changes in ownership and the methods of accounting for business combinations.

5. What are the balance sheet differences between a purchase and a pooling of interests? What are the income statement differences?

6. Explain the effect of treasury stock transactions on whether a business combination results in a change in ownership.

7. Explain how negotiation of a stock exchange ratio can be thought of as negotiating an allocation of the synergy anticipated from a forthcoming business combination.

8. Identify some practical problems in valuing a closely held company.

9. When one or both companies in a business combination are closely held, the combination often takes the form of a consolidation. Why is this so?

10. Briefly describe what is meant by type A, type B, and type C reorganizations under Section 368 of the Internal Revenue code.

Exercises

Exercise 1–1

Identify whether each of the following acquisitions appears to satisfy the criteria for a pooling of interests.

a. A Company acquired 95 percent of the outstanding common shares of B Company. Fifty-one percent of the B shares were acquired for cash. The remaining 44 percent were acquired in a common stock for common stock exchange.

b. A Company acquired all the outstanding common shares of B Company in a common stock for common stock exchange. A Company obtained the A shares given in the exchange as treasury shares shortly prior to the combination.

c. A Company acquired 95 percent of the outstanding common shares of B Company in exchange for shares of A Company's fully participating preferred stock.

d. A Company acquired 95 percent of the outstanding common shares of B Company in a common stock for common stock exchange.

e. B Company acquired 15 percent of its outstanding common shares shortly before its acquisition by A Company. These shares had been owned by C Company with the expectation that C Company would systematicly increase its ownership of B to 51 percent. The acquisition of B Company by A Company was achieved by A Company issuing its common shares in exchange for 95 percent of B Company's then outstanding common shares.

f. P Company acquired 100 percent interest in S Company on December 31, 19X0, by issuing 500,000 shares of P Company $1 par, common stock in exchange for S Company shares. The current market price of the P Company common stock is $40 per share. Additionally, P Company guaranteed that the market price of its shares will be at least $60 at the end of the second year succeeding the acquisition date. If at the end of the second year the market price of P Company stock is less than $60 per share, P Company will issue additional shares with a current market value equal to the difference between the total guaranteed value and the current market value of the shares previously issued.

g. A Company, a subsidiary of B Company, was acquired by C Company after it was spun off by B (by distributing the shares of A to the shareholders of B).

Exercise 1–2

Data relating to the acquisition of B by A appear below:

	A	B	Combined Entity
Net income	$ 2,000,000	$1,000,000	$ 3,000,000
Shares outstanding	7,000,000	2,000,000	?
Market value of common.	$10,000,000	$6,000,000	$20,000,000
Price/earnings ratio	5.00	6.00	6.67

Required:

a. Calculate the minimum stock exchange ratio of A shares to B shares acceptable to the owners of B.

b. Calculate the maximum stock exchange ratio of A shares to B shares acceptable to the owners of A.

Exercise 1–3

Company P has made a tender offering for all the common shares of S. The S management is opposed to P's offer and is aware that it is extremely important to P management that any P/S combination be accounted for as a pooling of interests. The S management identified a "white knight" company, X Company, willing to make a competing tender offer for 11 percent of the common shares of S. The S management encouraged the S owners to accept X Company's offer.

Required:

a. Explain why it might be important to the P management to have a P/S combination accounted for as a pooling of interests.

b. Explain why X Company's tender offer will be an effective tactic to fight the takeover of S by P.

Exercise 1–4

A Company and B Company are closely held and intend to combine by creating a new corporation that will issue a mixture of common and participating preferred shares to the current owners of A and B. Data relating to A and B are as follows:

	A	B
Value of net severable assets.......	$150,000	$300,000
Value of goodwill.................	50,000	10,000
Value of company	$200,000	$310,000

It is anticipated that the combined firm will have a value of $510,000, i.e., no synergy is anticipated.

Required:

a. Determine the value of common shares that will probably be distributed to the owners of A and B.

b. Determine the value of participating preferred shares that will probably be distributed to the owners of A and B.

c. Explain why your answers to *(a)* and *(b)* are equitable.

Exercise 1–5

A Company and B Company are considering a business combination. The precise way in which the combination is to be effected is being negotiated; however, it has been agreed that A will acquire B. B's net assets have a tax basis far below their fair value.

Required:

a. Would the owners of A likely prefer to structure the combination as a tax-free reorganization?

b. Would the owners of B likely prefer to structure the combination as a tax-free reorganization?

c. Assume that it has been determined that the B owners will receive cash for their shares (such that the exchange will be taxable). Will this fact likely bestow the B owners with any incremental bargaining power such that they can negotiate a higher cash price?

Problems

Problem 1–6

Howerton Company acquired 100 percent of the outstanding shares of Penney, Inc., for $500,000 cash. Immediately prior to the transaction, Howerton's balance sheet was as follows:

Cash....................................	$ 1,000,000
Other current assets........................	2,000,000
Plant and equipment........................	8,000,000
Total assets................................	$11,000,000

Current liabilities	$ 2,000,000
Long-term liabilities.......................	6,000,000
Total liabilities.......................	$ 8,000,000
Capital stock	$ 2,000,000
Retained earnings.........................	1,000,000
Total stockholders' equity..............	$ 3,000,000
Total liabilities and stockholders' equity........	$11,000,000

As of the date of acquisition, data relating to the net assets of Penney were as follows:

	Fair Value	Book Value
Cash............................	$ 200,000	$200,000
Other current assets...............	200,000	150,000
Plant and equipment...............	600,000	400,000
Total assets..................	$1,000,000	$750,000
Current liabilities	$ 100,000	$100,000
Long-term liabilities...............	450,000	500,000
Total liabilities..............	$ 550,000	$600,000
Total net assets	$ 450,000	$150,000

If the Howerton/Penney combination is accounted for as a purchase, the postcombination balance sheet of the combined entity would appear as follows:

Cash......................................	$ 700,000
Other current assets........................	2,200,000
Plant and equipment........................	8,600,000
Goodwill...................................	50,000
Total assets................................	$11,550,000
Current liabilities	$ 2,100,000
Long-term liabilities.......................	6,450,000
Total liabilities.......................	$ 8,550,000
Capital stock	$ 2,000,000
Retained earnings.........................	1,000,000
Total stockholders' equity..............	$ 3,000,000
Total liabilities and stockholders' equity........	$11,550,000

Required:
a. Assume that instead of purchasing Penney shares, Howerton purchased all of Penney's assets and assumed Penney's liabilities. Also assume that Howerton paid Penney's owners $500,000 cash in this transaction. Prepare the journal entry to record the transaction on the books of Howerton.
b. Under the assumptions above, prepare Howerton's balance sheet immediately after the purchase of Penney's net assets. Compare this balance sheet with postcombination balance sheet given earlier.

c. Is the purchase of net assets fundamentally different from the purchase of the shares of another company? If so, in what respect?

Problem 1–7

Howerton Company acquired 100 percent of the outstanding shares of Penney, Inc., by issuing 200,000 shares of its $1 par common stock ($1.10 market value). Immediately prior to the transaction, Howerton's balance sheet was as follows:

Current assets	$ 3,000,000
Plant and equipment	8,000,000
Total assets	$11,000,000
Current liabilities	$ 2,000,000
Long-term liabilities	6,000,000
Total liabilities	$ 8,000,000
Capital stock	$ 2,000,000
Retained earnings	1,000,000
Total stockholders' equity	$ 3,000,000
Total liabilities and stockholders' equity	$11,000,000

Penney was organized one year ago by issuing 200,000 shares of its $1 par common stock at $1 per share. The proceeds were invested in a savings account that has earned 10 percent interest. Immediately prior to its acquisition by Howerton, Penney's balance sheet was as follows:

Current assets	$220,000
Total assets	$220,000
Capital stock	$200,000
Retained earnings	20,000
Total stockholders' equity	$220,000

If the Howerton/Penney combination is accounted for as a pooling of interests, the postcombination balance sheet of the combined entity would appear as follows:

Current assets	$ 3,220,000
Plant and equipment	8,000,000
Total assets	$11,220,000
Current liabilities	$ 2,000,000
Long-term liabilities	6,000,000
Total liabilities	$ 8,000,000
Capital stock	$ 2,200,000
Retained earnings	1,020,000
Total stockholders' equity	$ 3,220,000
Total liabilities and stockholder's equity	$11,220,000

Required:

a. Assume that one year ago, Howerton issued 200,000 shares of its common stock at $1 per share. Also assume that the proceeds were invested in a savings account that has earned 10 percent interest during the past year. Prepare the journal entries to record the issuance of the 200,000 Howerton shares and investment of proceeds in the savings account.

b. Under the assumptions above, prepare the journal entry to record the collection of one year's interest on Howerton's investment in the savings account.

c. Under the assumptions above, prepare Howerton's balance sheet as of one year after the issuance of 200,000 shares and investment of proceeds in the savings account. Compare this balance sheet with the postcombination balance sheet given earlier.

Problem 1–8

Data relating to the acquisition of Bean Company by Adams Company appear below:

	Adams	Bean	Combined Entity
Net income	$ 100,000	$ 50,000	$ 200,000
Shares outstanding	1,000,000	2,000,000	?
Market value of common.	$3,000,000	$ 500,000	$4,000,000
Price/earnings ratio	30	10	20
EPS	$.10	$.03	?

Required:

a. Calculate the maximum stock exchange ratio acceptable to the owners of Adams.

b. Calculate the minimum stock exchange ratio acceptable to the owners of Bean.

c. Assume the actual negotiated stock exchange ratio is the one which divides the $500,000 anticipated synergy in proportion to the precombination firm sizes. That is, assume the owners of Adams are to receive a 3,000,000/(3,000,000 + 500,000) = .857 interest in the combined firm. Calculate the anticipated postcombination EPS.

Problem 1–9

Data relating to the combination of Chasteen Company and Armstrong Company (to be facilitated through an exchange of common shares) appear below:

	Chasteen	Armstrong	Combined Entity
Net income	$ 6,000,000	$ 4,000,000	$10,000,000
Shares outstanding	5,000,000	1,000,000	?
Market value of common.	$12,000,000	$20,000,000	$32,000,000
PE	2.00	5.00	3.20

Required:

Assuming one objective of the combination is to maximize the growth in EPS of the acquiring firm, would it be better for Chasteen to acquire Armstrong or vice versa?

Problem 1–10

Assume someone has offered you the opportunity to participate in a two-stage gamble. One year from now, a fair coin will be tossed. If the outcome is "heads," you will receive at that time the sum of $50. Otherwise, you will receive nothing. Two years from now, a fair coin will again be tossed. If the outcome is "heads," you will receive at that time the sum of $75. Otherwise, you will receive nothing.

Required:

a. How much would you be willing to pay today in exchange for the right to participate in this two-stage gamble?

b. How does the mental exercise in Requirement (*a*) correspond to the problem of placing a value on a closely held company in order to negotiate the terms of a business combination?

CHAPTER
2

Consolidated Financial Reports—Date of Acquisition

Corporate Affiliations

In Chapter 1, corporate combinations were categorized as *mergers, consolidations,* and *acquisitions.* In the present chapter (and Chapters 3 and 4), attention is focused on the financial reports of the economic entity which results from the *acquisition form* of combination. Following an acquisition, the acquiring company owns a majority of the acquired firm's voting stock. The acquiring company is frequently identified as the *parent;* the acquired company is described as a *subsidiary.* Their joint status is called a corporate *affiliation.* Of course, a corporate affiliation may include more than two corporations. The parent may hold a majority of the voting shares of many subsidiaries. Additionally, a chain of majority ownership may be established in which a parent *(P)* owns a majority interest in the stock of a subsidiary (S_1), which, in turn, owns a majority interest in another subsidiary (S_2), and so forth. Such multilevel affiliations commonly extend from three to five levels. In fact, the history of U.S. business evidences some multilevel affiliations that included up to 60 levels in the parent-subsidiary chain. It is not uncommon for some corporations at each level to engage in separate business operations in addition to holding stock in subsidiaries. Alternatively, other corporations are organized for the sole purpose of holding stock in subsidiaries, in which case the parent may be referred to as a *holding company.*

Reasons for Corporate Affiliations

There are numerous reasons why a corporate enterprise may select *acquisition* as a form of corporate combination, in contrast to mergers and consolidations. Stock acquisition is relatively simple, and it usually provides financial control with minimal difficulty. The continuity of legal life of each of the affiliated companies also serves to protect the group assets from possible attachment by creditors of individual subsidiaries. Acquisition may be achieved at substantially less cost than the processes of merger and consolidation. The latter forms of combination require 100 percent ownership by the acquiring firm, whereas the former permits the execution of control with any amount of voting stock in excess of 50 percent. Also, the legal and processing costs of mergers or consolidations are typically avoided by the acquisition method. Further, the asset acquired by the parent—subsidiary stock—may provide collateral to support additional debt financing above the traditionally acceptable levels that would apply to the combined entity existing in the form of one corporate structure. After a formal merger or consolidation, the subsidiary corporation stock that is acquired by the parent is retired or canceled, and therefore is not available for use as collateral. For these and other reasons, control achieved by stock acquisition may produce significant rewards for the parent company, frequently at less cost than would be possible through other forms of business amalgamation.

Consolidated Statements

According to *APB Statement No. 4*, "Basic Concepts and Accounting Principles Underlying Financial Statements of Business Enterprises," a basic feature of financial accounting is the concept of the *accounting entity*. This concept is described as follows: "Accounting information pertains to entities, which are circumscribed areas of interest. In financial accounting the entity is the specific business enterprise. The enterprise is identified in its financial statements" (para. 116). Choice of the circumscribed area of interest to report upon is motivated by the assumed decision needs of identifiable user groups. In many cases, the area of economic activity that is decision relevant coincides with the legally established boundary of a particular business unit—for example, a corporation. However, the existence of corporate affiliations raises the question: "What is the relevant area of economic activity that is of primary interest to the shareholders of a corporate entity (parent company) that exercises control over the resources and operations of another corporate entity (subsidiary company)?" In response to this question, accountants have decided that the primary financial reports of corporate affiliations, called *consolidated statements*, should reflect the group of companies as a single business enterprise—a single *economic* (accounting) entity. (See Illustration 2–1). Legal distinctions between the affiliates are ignored as being a matter of form rather than of substance.

Illustration 2–1

THE ECONOMIC ENTITY
(The Accounting Entity for Consolidated Statements)

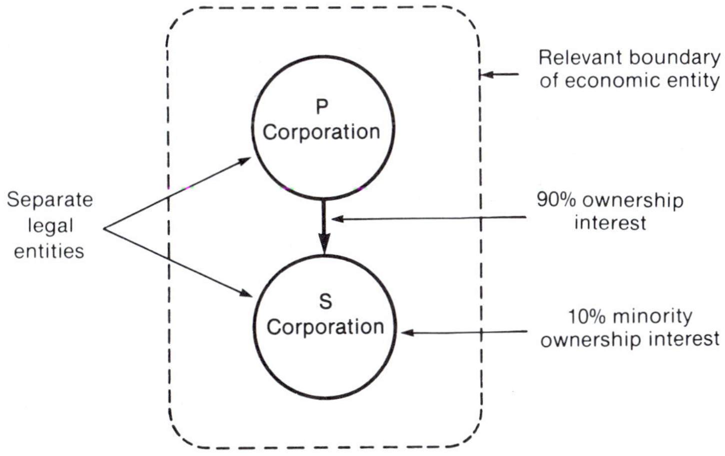

The consolidated financial statements of the economic entity are essentially summations of the assets, liabilities, revenues, and expenses of the individual affiliates, *calculated on the basis of transactions with nonaffiliates.* Intercompany investments, account balances, and operating transactions must be eliminated, or excluded, from the summation process in order to avoid double-counting of resources, obligations, or operating results. The statement formats and the account classifications parallel those of a single corporate entity. However, in the event that a minority portion of a subsidiary's stock is owned by parties that are unrelated to the parent, a special equity position—labeled *minority interest*—must be established in the consolidated statements so that the unique interest of these outside parties will be appropriately disclosed.

While consolidated statements constitute the primary source of financial information regarding corporate affiliations, they should not be viewed as the only source of such information. Some parties, such as "minority" shareholders in a subsidiary and the outside creditors of a subsidiary, are primarily concerned with the separate financial reports of the subsidiary company. Thus, the need for separate financial statements of each individual subsidiary corporation is not necessarily eliminated by the preparation of consolidated statements. Additionally, financial statement users whose primary interest is in the overall economic entity have found that consolidated statements do not always provide sufficient information for detailed analyses of operations. As a consequence, consolidated financial statements may be supplemented by information on defined segments of the consolidated entity. Further consideration of this segmental information is deferred until Chapter 5. The consolidated statements may also be supplemented (particularly in SEC filings) with summarized parent company financial statements. When there are material restrictions relating to the transfer of assets from the subsidiary to the parent, evaluations of parent company financial position (particularly liquidity) are easier made with parent-only statements. Such restrictions might arise because of subsidiary debt covenants, or when the subsidiary's activities are subject to government regulation.

Criteria for Inclusion in Consolidated Statements

The criteria for including a subsidiary in consolidated statements are typically stated in terms of the degree of control the parent exercises over the subsidiary. There are two essential attributes of this concept of control, neither of which alone provides sufficient ground for inclusion in the consolidated statement.

1. The parent corporation must have the ability to govern, or effectively regulate, the subsidiary corporation's managerial decisions.

2. The parent corporation must be so related to the subsidiary that the economic results of subsidiary operations will accrue to the parent, allowing, of course, for the necessity of making appropriate allocations to reflect the interests of minority (outside, noncontrolling) parties.

Reference has been made to the necessity for owning more than 50 percent of the voting stock of a subsidiary—either directly or indirectly—in order to justify inclusion in consolidated financial statements. Yet, in point of fact, effective *managerial* control may well exist short of this critical percentage. Accountants are generally agreed, however, that it is usually unwise to include in consolidated financial statements those corporations for which this majority ownership condition is not satisfied. On occasions, effective managerial control may exist without the ownership of *any* voting shares. For example, the presence of a lease arrangement, whereby the lessor retains control of leased property, may indicate effective managerial control. Normally, however, situations of this kind do not evidence sufficient control in terms of the second attribute stated above.[1]

Other factors that merit attention in determining the admissibility of a subsidiary in consolidated statements are (1) the expectation of continuity in control, (2) the degree of existing restrictions upon the availability of assets and earnings of a subsidiary (an item of special importance regarding foreign subsidiaries), and (3) the general coincidence of accounting periods. Historically, accountants were also concerned about consolidating affiliates with nonhomogeneous operations. Manufacturing parents have often not consolidated subsidiaries engaged in financing, banking, and insurance activities (and vice versa). However, current practice is not consistent on this issue. Subsidiaries whose operations are not homogeneous with those of their parents are sometimes consolidated; sometimes they are not. In those cases where significant subsidiaries are not consolidated, separate statements for the excluded subsidiaries are normally included as a supplement to the consolidated financial statements.

Disclosure of Consolidation Policy

The consolidation policy adopted by the parent company is important to a complete understanding of consolidated statements, and it should be disclosed in the financial reports. A statement of policy normally refers to such matters as the degree of stock control required of the parent company, the accounting methods that were used to record the acquisition of subsidiary stock (alternative methods are examined in Chapter 5), and the status of a subsidiary as either a domestic or a foreign corporate entity.

---

[1] The SEC specifically prohibits a registrant from consolidating any subsidiary that is not majority owned in filings with the Commission (see *Regulation S-X, Part 210—Form and Content of Financial Statements,* Article 4-02).

Since the adoption in 1972 of *APB Opinion No. 22*, "Disclosure of Accounting Policies," companies normally include their consolidation policy in the Summary of Significant Accounting Policies. An example from a recent General Motors annual report follows:

Principles of Consolidation

The consolidated financial statements include the accounts of the Corporation and all domestic and foreign subsidiaries which are more than 50% owned and engaged principally in manufacturing or wholesale marketing of General Motors products. General Motors' share of earnings or losses of nonconsolidated subsidiaries and of associates in which at least 20% of the voting securities is owned is generally included in consolidated income under the equity method of accounting. Intercompany items and transactions between companies included in the consolidation are eliminated and unrealized intercompany profits on sales to nonconsolidated subsidiaries and to associates are deferred.

Precautions in the Evaluation of Consolidated Statements

The summarizing character of consolidated statements provides them with special qualities of strength and usefulness; however, special precautions must be taken in evaluating these statements. Among the factors that require special care in the evaluation process are the following:

1. Some statistical analyses may be misleading. For example, ratios prepared from consolidated information are weighted averages. A weak position of one company may be balanced, in the process of summation, by an especially strong position of an affiliate. In such an instance, an average may for some purposes be an inaccurate descriptive index.

2. Differences in the bases of classification and valuation of accounts of the constituent companies may distort the meaning of composite statements. The unique accounting systems of the affiliates cannot easily be transformed so that the classifications and valuations of each affiliate will be entirely consistent. Further, the differing industry identifications of the affiliates limit the meaning that can be attributed to the aggregated account balances.

3. The monetary equities assigned to both creditors and owners may be misinterpreted in the evaluation of consolidated statements. This is particularly true in respect to the seeming availability of retained earnings for dividend distributions. The earnings of subsidiaries may not actually be available for parent company distributions until formally declared as dividends by the subsidiaries. In regard to liabilities, the result of summation often is to obscure the special legal status of those

individual creditors having liens on specific assets. Additionally, minority stockholders must continue to look to the subsidiary's separate financial statements to determine accurately the status of their investment. Their shareholder status relates *only* to the legal entity to which they have committed resources.

4. Consolidated statements involving foreign subsidiaries may be misleading if foreign exchange rates are subject to unusual fluctuations, or if foreign assets are unduly restricted as to their availability to a domestic parent company.

Notwithstanding these limitations, consolidated statements continue to grow in significance and number. Accumulating evidence suggests that they now assume a role of *primary* importance, with the separate statements of affiliates and other segmental reports relegated to a secondary or supplementary position.

Determining Cost of an Acquired Company

The valuation principles used to record the investment in an acquired company depend upon whether the combination is treated as a purchase or a pooling of interests (see Chapter 1). The specific criteria that control this choice and some important financial statement consequences of using one method vis-á-vis the other are discussed in Chapter 5. *At this point and through Chapters 2–4, we will treat all acquisitions as purchases.*

General Principle.   *Under the purchase method*, the acquisition of the stock of the subsidiary company is accounted for in accordance with the traditional principles of accounting for the acquisition of assets. The value of the stock acquired is measured by the fair value of the consideration given or the consideration received, whichever is more clearly evident. Note that the consideration given by the acquiring company may include cash, noncash assets, debt, and/or stock of the acquiring company.

Direct and Indirect Costs.   Only the direct, incremental costs of an acquisition are included in the cost of the investment. Indirect and general expenses related to acquisitions (for example, the costs of an "acquisitions" department) are expensed as incurred.[2]

Registration Costs.   When costs of registering and issuing equity securities used in an acquisition are incurred, the otherwise determinable fair market value of the securities should be reduced by the amount of these costs. The value assigned to the investment account then is the sum of these registration costs and the net value of the equity securities.[3] For example, assume that P Company issues 5,000 shares of its no-par com-

---

[2] AICPA, *Accounting Interpretation No. 33 of APB Opinion No. 16*, "Costs of Maintaining an 'Acquisitions' Department" (New York, 1971).

[3] APB, *APB Opinion No. 16*, "Business Combinations" (New York: AICPA, 1970), par. 76.

mon stock for all of the common stock of S Company and incurs registration costs (which it pays in cash) of $2,000. The estimated fair market value of the stock issued by P Company (when registered) is $30 per share. In this circumstance, the value of the stock issued by P Company is $150,000 (5,000 shares × $30), less registration costs of $2,000, or a net value of $148,000. The entry to record the purchase would be as follows:

Investment in S Company	150,000	
Cash		2,000
Capital Stock		148,000

If unregistered equity securities are issued in an acquisition with an agreement for subsequent registration, the estimated amount of these registration costs is accrued as a liability, and the net fair value of the share issued is determined as above.[4]

Contingent Consideration. The terms of a business combination may provide for additional consideration contingent on the occurrence of specified events or transactions in the future. When this situation exists, the following general measurement guidelines are applied:

> Contingent consideration should usually be recorded when the contingency is resolved and consideration is issued or becomes issuable. In general, the issue of additional securities or distribution of other consideration at resolution of contingencies *based on earnings* should result in an additional element of cost of an acquired company. In contrast, the issue of additional securities or distribution of other consideration at resolution of contingencies *based on security prices* should not change the recorded cost of an acquired company.[5]

Elaboration of these general guidelines is contained in paragraphs 77–86 of *APB Opinion No. 16*.

Acquisition Date. The cost of an acquired company (and the values assigned to assets acquired and liabilities assumed) is determined as of the date of acquisition. Normally, the date of acquisition is the date on which assets are received and other assets are given or securities are issued. However, the parties to the combination transaction may for convenience designate the effective date of the combination to be the end of an accounting period between the dates on which the combination is initiated and consummated. When this occurs, the cost of the investment should be reduced (and interest expense recognized) by the imputed interest on assets given, liabilities incurred, or preferred stock distributed from the acquisition date to the transfer date.[6]

---

[4] AICPA, *Accounting Interpretation No. 35 of APB Opinion No. 16*, "Registration Costs in a Purchase" (New York, 1972).

[5] *APB Opinion No. 16*, par. 79. (Emphasis supplied.)

[6] Ibid., pars. 93–94.

Consolidated Balance Sheet

Where the dates of investment in subsidiary stock and consolidated statement preparation coincide, attention may be confined to the consolidated balance sheet only. This financial report is a summary enumeration of the assets and liabilities of the various affiliates, calculated without regard to their separate corporate identities. Because majority stock ownership is tantamount to control over the assets of a subsidiary, it is meaningful to substitute the subsidiary's *net assets* for the stock investment account of the parent company. Traditionally, this substitution is accomplished in consolidated statement working papers (which have as their starting point the individual financial statements of the constituent companies) by eliminating the parent company's investment account against its equity in the stockholders' equity accounts of the subsidiary. Following this elimination, it is then appropriate to combine (sum) the assets and liabilities of the affiliate companies. It is, of course, important that the amounts of other accounts resulting from intercompany transactions, for example, intercompany receivable-payable balances, also be eliminated, in order that the consolidated balance sheet reflect the assets and equities of the affiliation perceived as a single economic entity.

It may be observed that the *total* net assets of the subsidiary are substituted for the contra investment account, notwithstanding the existence of minority shareholders. This accords with the accounting view that each group of shareholders has a fractional interest in the undivided net assets of the subsidiary. Accordingly, it is appropriate to measure the value of the *minority interest* in terms of the aggregate net assets of the subsidiary, rather than in terms of a fractional equity in specific assets and liabilities.

The form and arrangement of these accumulated data follow the usual statement classifications. Where minority shareholders exist, their rights must be clearly disclosed together with those of other claimants. Since consolidated statements are generally presumed to be oriented toward the parent company shareholders (the so-called *parent company concept* of consolidated statements[7]), the rights and equities of minority interests assume—at least partially—the character of liabilities. Yet, significantly, because the evidences of this type of equity are ownership certificates, they also have a certain quality of proprietorship. Accountants are not generally agreed as to the most appropriate balance sheet disposition of this category; often a compromise position is that of a separate identification between liabilities and stockholders' equity.

Procedural details for the preparation of consolidated balance sheet working papers are described and illustrated in the three sections that follow. In the first section, it is assumed that the parent company's invest-

---

[7] Chapter 12 contains a brief discussion of the alternative concept of consolidated statements—the *entity theory*.

ment cost per share is equal to the book value per share of the subsidiary's stock, and that the fair values of all subsidiary assets and liabilities are equal to book values. Two levels of investment are analyzed: (1) total (100 percent) acquisition of all of the subsidiary stock and (2) acquisition of a majority (90 percent) of the subsidiary's stock. In the following two sections, the 90 percent acquisition case is extended to cover those circumstances where (1) the investment cost per share exceeds the book value of the subsidiary stock and (2) the investment cost per share is less than the book value of the subsidiary stock. In each case that is analyzed, it is assumed that concurrent with the acquisition of a subsidiary's capital stock, a consolidated balance sheet is prepared.

Investment Cost per Share Equal to Book Value per Share of Subsidiary Stock

Case 1. Total (100 Percent) Acquisition of Subsidiary Stock. In this first case, it is assumed that P Company (the parent company) acquires 100 percent of the outstanding stock of S Company (the subsidiary company) for $50,000, and that the stockholders' equity account balances of S Company at the date of acquisition are capital stock, $40,000 (Cr.), and retained earnings, $10,000 (Cr.). Thus, the book value of the net assets of S Company on this date, $50,000, is equal to P Company's investment cost of $50,000; since P Company acquired all of the outstanding shares, this equivalence indicates that the book value per share is equal to the investment cost per share.

The substitution of S Company's net assets for the investment account of P Company is accomplished in the consolidated balance sheet working paper (Illustration 2–2) by "eliminating" P Company's investment account against its equity in S Company's stockholders' equity accounts and then combining (summing) the remaining account balances of the two companies. The amount of the elimination against each element (account) of the subsidiary company's stockholders' equity is determined by multiplying the parent company's percentage interest in the subsidiary (in this case, 100 percent) by the recorded balance in the account. The summation process relies upon the debit/credit properties of various account balances, and thus the eliminating entry, which is referred to as the *investment elimination entry*, is also expressed in a debit/credit format. For the data of this case, the investment elimination entry is as follows:

Capital Stock—S Company (100% × $40,000).....................	40,000	
Retained Earnings—S Company (100% × $10,000)...............	10,000	
Investment in S Company.....................................		50,000

Illustration 2–2

P COMPANY AND SUBSIDIARY S COMPANY
Consolidated Balance Sheet Working Paper
(Acquisition Date)

	P Company	S Company	Eliminations Dr.	Eliminations Cr.	Consolidated
Cash	15,000	4,000			19,000
Receivables	30,000	16,000			46,000
Inventory	25,000	35,000			60,000
Investment in S Company	50,000			(1) 50,000	–0–
	120,000	55,000			125,000
Payables	10,000	5,000			15,000
Capital stock:					
P Company	90,000				90,000
S Company		40,000	(1) 40,000		–0–
Retained earnings:					
P Company	20,000				20,000
S Company		10,000	(1) 10,000		–0–
	120,000	55,000	50,000	50,000	125,000

Although the investment elimination entry is traditionally expressed in the format of a "journal entry," it is an "entry" only on the consolidated working paper. *No entry is made on the books of either the parent or the subsidiary.*[8]

In the consolidated working paper (Illustration 2–2), it is useful to relate the contra elements of eliminating entries with some connective notation; in this instance, arabic numerals are used.

An examination of this consolidated working paper will confirm that the net assets of S Company have, in fact, been substituted for the investment account of P Company, and that the amounts extended to the Consolidated column are merely a result of a summation process. Since fair values are equal to book values, these net assets are stated at fair value. It may also be noted that consolidated capital stock and retained earnings at date of acquisition are the balances in the parent company's accounts, the total amount of the subsidiary's capital stock and retained earnings have been eliminated. Since none of the subsidiary's stock is held by outside parties, this result for consolidated capital stock is obviously appropriate. In respect to retained earnings, the result is in accord with the long-established accounting tenet that none of the preacquisition retained earnings (or defi-

---

[8] Shading will be used for all eliminating entries displayed in tables or the body of the text in order to distinguish these consolidated statement working paper entries from formal journal entries that are recorded on the books of the parent and/or subsidiary companies. We cannot emphasize too strongly the importance of keeping always clearly in mind the distinction between working paper entries and book entries.

cit) of a *purchased* subsidiary should be included in consolidated retained earnings.[9]

Although the stockholders' equity of S Company in this illustration was limited to capital stock and retained earnings accounts, no special problems would have arisen had there been other elements of stockholders' equity attributable to common shareholders (e.g., amounts of contributed capital in excess of par value and appropriations of retained earnings). Each of these elements would have been additional determinants in the calculation of book value, and subsequently eliminated in the investment elimination entry in the consolidation process. The existence of treasury stock does introduce several minor complications, and these are discussed in a subsequent section of this chapter. The more complex issues associated with the presence of more than one class of stock are however deferred to Chapter 9.

Case 2. Acquisition of a Majority (90 Percent) of Subsidiary Stock (Subsidiary Deficit).

This case illustrates the elimination procedures to be followed in the event the parent acquires a controlling interest in the voting shares of a subsidiary by purchasing less than 100 percent of the outstanding stock. Additionally, the case illustrates the effect on the investment elimination entry when the subsidiary has a retained earnings deficit (debit balance) at the acquisition date.

It is here assumed that 90 percent of the subsidiary's capital stock is acquired at a cost of $45,000. The stockholders' equity account balances of the subsidiary at the acquisition date are capital stock, $60,000 (Cr.), and retained earnings, $10,000 (Dr.), yielding a book value for the net assets of the subsidiary of $50,000. Since the parent company acquired a 90 percent interest in the subsidiary, the book value of the parent's purchased interest in the subsidiary is $45,000 (90 percent × $50,000), which is equal to the assumed investment cost. If the aggregate book value of the parent's acquired interest is equal to the aggregate investment cost, it follows that the book value per share is also equal to the investment cost per share. Henceforth, determination of the relationship between investment cost and book value is based upon aggregate values rather than per share values, but equivalent conclusions would be reached under either mode of analysis.

The investment elimination entry for this case is as follows:

Capital Stock—S Company (90% × $60,000)...................	54,000	
Retained Earnings—S Company (90% × $10,000)...........		9,000
Investment in S Company.................................		45,000

---

[9] AICPA, *Accounting Research Bulletin No. 51,* "Consolidated Financial Statements" (New York, 1959), par. 9. See, however, Chapter 5 for a different result when the combination is treated as a pooling of interests.

The deficit (debit balance) is eliminated by a credit to the retained earnings of S Company. It may be noted in Illustration 2–3 that the extended amounts of capital stock and retained earnings of S Company are marked with the letter "M" denoting that these amounts represent the interests of

Illustration 2–3

P COMPANY AND SUBSIDIARY S COMPANY
Consolidated Balance Sheet Working Paper
(Acquisition Date)

	P Company	S Company	Eliminations Dr.	Eliminations Cr.	Consolidated
Cash	15,000	4,000			19,000
Receivables	30,000	16,000			46,000
Inventory	25,000	35,000			60,000
Investment in S Company	45,000			(1) 45,000	–0–
	115,000	55,000			125,000
Payables	5,000	5,000			10,000
Capital stock:					
P Company	90,000				90,000
S Company		60,000	(1) 54,000		6,000 M
Retained earnings:					
P Company	20,000				20,000
S Company		[10,000]		(1) 9,000	[1,000]M
	115,000	55,000	54,000	54,000	125,000

[deduction]

minority shareholders in the net assets of the subsidiary. Such a notation serves as an appropriate reminder concerning the classification of these amounts in the preparation of formal statements. This working paper illustrates the importance of substituting the *total* net assets of the subsidiary for the investment account of the parent company (even though there are minority shareholders), and extending the interest of these minority shareholders on the basis of their fractional interest in the recorded stockholders' equity accounts of the subsidiary company. Since the book value of the net assets of the subsidiary is $50,000, the minority interest in the subsidiary is valued at $5,000 (10 percent of $50,000). This amount may be verified in Illustration 2–3—the sum of a $6,000 credit and a $1,000 debit. Although care must be exercised in dealing with debit balances in stockholders' equity accounts of the subsidiary, such balances do not introduce substantive complexities in either the investment elimination entry or the calculation of the minority interest.

Investment Cost per Share Exceeds Book Value per Share of Subsidiary Stock

Frequently, it will be necessary for the investing company to pay more than the book value of the subsidiary's capital stock. An investment in excess book value may be explained by an understatement of a subsidiary's recorded assets, the existence of unrecorded subsidiary assets, or for other less apparent reasons. Whatever the reason, it is necessary to recognize and identify this variation, or *differential*, in the consolidated statements.

Case 3.   The data of the previous case are repeated here, with the exception that the cost of P Company's 90 percent investment in the capital stock of S Company is now assumed to be $50,000. In this instance, the investment elimination entry indicates the presence of a *debt differential*.

Capital Stock—S Company	54,000	
Differential	5,000	
Retained Earnings—S Company		9,000
Investment in S Company		50,000

At this point the differential does not require more complete identification; it is sufficient to note that it represents the excess of the cost of the investment over the parent's acquired interest in the book value of subsidiary

Illustration 2–4

P COMPANY AND SUBSIDIARY S COMPANY
Consolidated Balance Sheet Working Paper
(Acquisition Date)

	P Company	S Company	Eliminations Dr.	Eliminations Cr.	Consolidated
Cash	15,000	4,000			19,000
Receivables	30,000	16,000			46,000
Inventory	25,000	35,000			60,000
Investment in S Company	50,000			(1) 50,000	–0–
Differential			(1) 5,000		5,000
	120,000	55,000			130,000
Payables	10,000	5,000			15,000
Capital stock:					
P Company	90,000				90,000
S Company		60,000	(1) 54,000		6,000 M
Retained earnings:					
P Company	20,000				20,000
S Company		[10,000]		(1) 9,000	[1,000]M
	120,000	55,000	59,000	59,000	130,000

[deduction]

stock at date of acquisition. The working paper treatment of a debit differential is given in Illustration 2–4.

Investment Cost per Share Less than Book Value per Share of Subsidiary Stock

In the event that the investment cost is less than the book value of a subsidiary's capital stock at acquisition, there exists a *credit* differential. This circumstance is illustrated in Case 4. The sources of debit and credit differentials will be developed more completely following this case illustration.

Case 4.   Using the basic data of Case 2, it is assumed that P Company acquires 90 percent of the capital stock of S Company at a cost of $40,000. The investment elimination entry follows:

Capital Stock—S Company	54,000	
Retained Earnings—S Company		9,000
Differential		5,000
Investment in S Company		40,000

These data confirm that there exists a credit differential, and that its amount is measured by the amount of the parent's interest in the book

Illustration 2–5

P COMPANY AND SUBSIDIARY S COMPANY
Consolidated Balance Sheet Working Paper
(Acquisition Date)

	P Company	S Company	Eliminations Dr.	Eliminations Cr.	Consolidated
Cash	25,000	4,000			29,000
Receivables	30,000	16,000			46,000
Inventory	25,000	35,000			60,000
Investment in S Company	40,000			(1) 40,000	–0–
Differential				(1) 5,000	[5,000]
	120,000	55,000			130,000
Payables	10,000	5,000			15,000
Capital stock:					
P Company	90,000				90,000
S Company		60,000	(1) 54,000		6,000 M
Retained earnings:					
P Company	20,000				20,000
S Company		[10,000]		(1) 9,000	[1,000]M
	120,000	55,000	54,000	54,000	130,000

[deduction]

value of subsidiary stock at date of acquisition which is in excess of the cost of the investment (see Illustration 2–5).

Disposition of Debit (Credit) Differentials

In the previous two cases, we have seen that the investment cost may exceed, or be less than, the parent's acquired interest in the book value of a subsidiary's net assets at date of acquisition. This difference occurs because the investment cost normally reflects the current economic values of the subsidiary's assets, and the recorded book values usually do not. In the investment elimination entry, the difference may simply be identified as a debit (or credit) differential, and recorded on the consolidated statement working paper in that fashion. However, it is then necessary to allocate this differential to the individual assets acquired and liabilities assumed in accordance with the valuation principles established in *APB Opinion No. 16*, "Business Combinations":

> First, all identifiable assets acquired, either individually or by type, and liabilities assumed in a business combination, whether or not shown in the financial statements of the acquired company, should be assigned a portion of the cost of the acquired company, *normally equal to their fair values at date of acquisition*. Second, the excess of the cost of the acquired company over the sum of the amounts assigned to identifiable assets acquired less liabilities assumed should be recorded as goodwill.[10]

Hence, the process of allocating the differential appears to be a process of restating the assets and liabilities of the acquired (subsidiary) company to their "fair values" as of the date of acquisition.[11] When all (100 percent) of the stock of the subsidiary is acquired, the allocation process will indeed restate the assets and liabilities of the subsidiary to their fair values. However, when less than 100 percent of the subsidiary's capital stock is purchased, the parent company concept of consolidated statements (which underlies much of current practice) is invoked to support recognition of only *the parent company's proportionate interest in the difference between the fair value and the recorded value of an asset (or liability)*. Under this procedure, the amount of the *difference* recognized is the amount of unrecorded value paid for by the parent company when it purchases the stock.[12] After these

---

[10] *APB Opinion No. 16*, par. 87. (Emphasis supplied.)

[11] See *APB Opinion No. 16*, par. 88, for general guidelines to be used in determining "fair value."

[12] In our discussion of the *entity theory* of consolidated statements in Chapter 12, a procedure for recording the *total* difference between fair and recorded values of identifiable assets and the *total* goodwill implicit in the purchase price, with concurrent recognition of the minority interest therein, will be explained. Although sound theoretically, this procedure is seldom applied in current practice. Additionally, paragraph 17 of *APB Opinion No. 6* would seem to preclude the subsidiary from recognizing the total difference in values by means of an entry on its books to write up its assets to their fair values.

allocations have been made to identifiable assets and liabilities, any remaining unallocated *debit* differential is classified as *goodwill*.

Reporting of subsidiary net assets at book value plus the parent company's share of the difference between fair value and book value is relevant to all business combinations treated as a purchase. That is, the investment cost per share might equal book value per share of subsidiary stock (such that no differential exists); but the fair value of subsidiary net assets equals book value only *in total*. (Fair values differ from book values for *individual* assets and liabilities; but *total* fair value equals *total* book value.) In such a case, the individual assets and liabilities are reported at book value plus parent's share of the difference between fair value and book value. Since such cases are expected to be extremely rare, all subsequent references to investment cost per share equaling book value per share implicitly presume that fair values equal book values for all individual assets and liabilities.

Case 5. Referring to the data of Case 3 (and Illustration 2–4), assume that a study of S Company's assets and liabilities produced the following estimates of fair values:

	Book Value	Fair Value	Excess of Fair Value over Book Value	P Company's 90% Interest in Excess
Receivables	$16,000	$16,000	—	—
Inventory	35,000	38,000	$3,000	$2,700
Payables	5,000	5,000	—	—

Given this information, the following additional elimination entry would be made to allocate the debit differential:

Inventory	2,700	
Goodwill.	2,300	
Differential.		5,000

Determining the disposition of differentials can be quite complex. This complexity centers on determining fair value. Paragraphs 88 and 89 of *APB Opinion No. 16* present general guidelines for assigning fair values to specific assets and liabilities. Noteworthy is the procedure utilized in the frequent instance when the market or appraisal value of an asset exceeds its tax basis. The value of such an asset to the parent company is less than the market or appraisal value since not all of the market or appraisal value is deductible for tax purposes. That is, market and appraisal values usually reflect the value of an asset if the asset is purchased separately. In most cases, the entire price of a separately purchased asset is eventually tax deductible and market and appraisal values reflect this fact. However, in certain business combinations the tax bases of acquired company assets are unaltered (see Chapter 1). The fair value of such assets is their market or appraisal value less the present value of all incremental tax payments arising because future tax deductions are limited to the original tax basis. Consider the following example.[13]

Case 6. An item of plant and equipment is appraised at $300,000. It has a tax basis of $100,000 and a remaining life of two years. Assuming straight-line depreciation for tax purposes, a discount rate of 10 percent, and a 46 percent tax rate, the fair value of the asset is:

Appraisal value	$300,000
Tax basis	100,000
Excess not deductible	$200,000
Annual amount not deductible (200,000/2)	$100,000
Tax rate	×.46
Annual incremental tax	$ 46,000
Present value of ordinary annuity of two rents (10% interest)	×1.7355
Present value of incremental tax payments	$ 79,835
Appraisal value	$300,000
Present value of incremental tax payments	79,835
Fair value	$220,165

The differential established in the investment elimination entry may be either a debit or a credit balance. Regardless of which type of balance results from this entry, the allocation process described and illustrated above is applied to give recognition to the fair values (or more precisely the parent's proportionate interest in the excess of fair value over book value) of the subsidiary's identifiable assets and liabilities. When the balance of the differential remaining after this elimination entry is a debit, it is, as illustrated above, classified as goodwill. However, where the allocation of the differential to identifiable assets and liabilities results in a residual (unallocated) *credit*, additional steps are required. In particular, this residual credit is reallocated proportionately among the subsidiary's noncurrent assets (except long-term investments in marketable securities). The rationale for this procedure is as follows. The presence of a residual credit implies one of two things:

a. The sum of the fair values of the subsidiary's net assets exceeds the price paid for the firm as a whole.

---

[13] For additional discussion, see E. Petri and C. Stickney, ''Business Combinations: Some Unresolved Issues,'' *Journal of Accountancy*, April 1982, pp. 64–79.

b. The fair values used in making the original differential disposition contained measurement error which biased them upward.

The first of these is unlikely. If the owners of a firm could have sold its assets piecemeal and obtained more than the price received for the firm as a whole, why did they not do so? The second is more likely. Estimating the fair values of noncurrent assets (except long-term investments in marketable securities) is often a very subjective process, and errors of overestimation are not particularly unusual. Therefore, the procedure assumes the residual credit is due to measurement error. Accordingly, the credit is eliminated by reducing the values of those assets for which fair value estimation is most subjective, i.e., noncurrent assets other than long-term investments in marketable securities. It is possible for such asset values to be reduced to zero without eliminating the entire residual credit. In such a case, any remaining residual credit is classified as a "deferred credit."[14]

There is some ambiguity regarding precisely how the residual credit should be allocated in reducing the values of noncurrent assets. One possibility is to perform an allocation in proportion to each of such asset's "first pass" valuation (book value plus parent's share of the excess of fair value over book value). Another is an allocation in proportion to each of such asset's full fair value. The two possibilities are, of course, equivalent when all of the subsidiary's stock has been acquired.

In view of the current interest in "fair value accounting," it is interesting to note that by means of these procedures for allocating the differential, the fair values of the assets and liabilities of a newly acquired subsidiary must be ascertained at the date of acquisition, and in consolidation these accounts are adjusted to values closely approximating their fair values (depending on the magnitude of the parent's percentage interest). The accounts of the parent company, of course, remain unadjusted for changes in values. Nonetheless, with the adoption of *APB Opinion No. 16* in 1970, accounting practice moved, albeit on an irregular and limited basis, into the realm of fair value accounting.

Push Down Accounting

The presence of a large differential raises a question of whether any adjustments of subsidiary assets and liabilities reflected in the consolidated statements ought also to be reflected in the separate company statements of the subsidiary. Separate company statements are issued under various circumstances, including when a minority interest exists and when debt of the subsidiary is publicly held. Data relating to fair values of subsidiary assets and liabilities will have been obtained in order to prepare the consolidated statements. Should such data be ignored when subsidiary state-

---

[14] *APB Opinion No. 16*, par. 87.

ments are prepared? Or should the subsidiary statements reflect these fair values?

Reporting subsidiary assets and liabilities at fair values in the separate company statements of the subsidiary is referred to as *push down accounting*. In addition, the term engenders utilization of these fair values in determining subsidiary net income. That is, depreciation and amortization are based upon fair value and not historical cost. And interest expense is based upon the current interest rate used in determining the fair value of subsidiary liabilities. In short, the consolidation adjustments are "pushed down" to the separate company statements of the subsidiary.

Proponents of push down accounting argue that the substantial change in ownership that occurs in a purchase transaction demands an accounting basis for assets and liabilities equivalent to that which would have been established had the parent merely purchased the net assets outright and established a new entity to continue the business. An argument against push down accounting is that the method impairs comparability of post-combination subsidiary statements with their prior year counterparts. In addition, push down accounting may place a subsidiary into technical default on debt convenants that are written in terms of financial statement data.

The method is rarely observed unless the change in ownership is indeed substantial, i.e., unless the parent has acquired virtually all of the outstanding shares of the subsidiary. The Securities and Exchange Commission currently requires push down accounting in situations wherein a subsidiary is "substantially wholly owned" by its parent.

Other Intercompany Transactions

Emphasis has thus far been directed to the intercompany transaction establishing the parent-subsidiary relationship. However, other intercompany transactions may be reflected in the accounts of the various affiliates, and their effects also must be eliminated in the consolidated statement working papers. All accounts classified as assets on one affiliate's books for which the originating transaction created a liability on the books of a second affiliate must be totally eliminated. The amount of the elimination is *not* dependent upon the percentage of stock control. Intercompany accounts receivable are eliminated against related accounts payable; intercompany notes receivable are eliminated against the related notes payable; and the intercompany portion of accrued expenses are eliminated against the corresponding accrued incomes. It is only necessary to establish the intercompany character of the originating transaction. Failure to eliminate the total amount of these accounts—whatever the percentage of stock ownership—will result in the consolidated balance sheet including claims to and from the same entity—the economic entity for which the consolidated balance sheet is prepared.

Unpaid Subsidiary Dividends at Acquisition

Should the parent become a stockholder of record after the declaration of subsidiary dividends but before the record date for payment, such dividends merely serve to reduce the cost of the investment shares. As such, they are classified as Dividends Receivable; the remainder of the investment outlay is debited to the Investment account. Subsequent collection of this receivable balance by the parent is recorded in the conventional manner.

For example, assume that P Company acquired 80 percent of the capital stock of S Company for $82,000, and that the purchase was made after the declaration date but before the record date for a cash dividend of $2,500 to be paid on the S Company shares. Since P Company purchased 80 percent of the capital stock of S Company, $2,000 (80 percent × $2,500) of the purchase price is attributable to the dividend. Thus, the entries that would be made by P Company to record the purchase of shares and the subsequent receipt of the dividend are as follows:

a. Purchase of shares:

Investment in S Company	80,000	
Dividends Receivable	2,000	
Cash		82,000

b. Receipt of dividend:

Cash	2,000	
Dividends Receivable		2,000

In the preparation of a consolidated balance sheet at the date of acquisition, the dividends receivable of $2,000 in P Company's balance sheet must be eliminated against dividends payable in S Company's balance sheet. As a consequence of this elimination, $500 will be extended to the Consolidated column for dividends payable—the amount payable to outside interests.

In the case where the record date for an unpaid subsidiary dividend occurs prior to the acquisition of subsidiary stock by the parent, the full amount of the dividend represents a liability to outside interests. Thus, the total purchase price for the shares is assignable to the investment account, and no intercompany payable-receivable relationship exists to be eliminated in the consolidated balance sheet as of the date of acquisition.

Treasury Stock of the Subsidiary

On some occasions, treasury stock may exist on the books of a subsidiary when its outstanding shares are acquired by a parent company. In such instances, the presence of these shares must be appropriately accounted for in the investment elimination entry. Consider the following example.

Case 7. P Company acquired 800 shares of the capital stock of S Company on January 1, 19X1, for $115,000 when the latter's net worth consisted of the following:

Capital stock (par, $100)	120,000
Treasury stock (recorded at par)	[20,000]
Retained earnings	40,000

Before considering the investment elimination entry details, two general observations are important. First, since P Company acquired 80 percent of S Company's 1,000 *outstanding* shares (800/1,000), the calculation of the purchased interest in S Company's net assets will be based upon this percentage. Second, the treasury stock of the subsidiary is not a meaningful item in the consolidated balance sheet (which is prepared from the point of view of the majority shareholders), and therefore it seems appropriate to treat these shares as having been constructively retired.

Given this perspective, a first elimination in the consolidated statement working paper is:

Capital Stock	20,000	
Treasury Stock		20,000

The investment elimination entry that follows is based upon the resulting account balances and takes the form:

Capital Stock	80,000	
Retained Earnings	32,000	
Differential	3,000	
Investment in S Company		115,000

Where the subsidiary's treasury shares are recorded at cost, and such cost is other than par value, an adjustment of its retained earnings accumulation and/or other contributed capital accounts is required before calculating the elimination elements. For example, if the treasury stock is carried at cost—$25,000—in the previous illustration, the first elimination is:

Capital Stock	20,000	
Retained Earnings	5,000	
Treasury Stock		25,000

The investment elimination necessarily relates to the adjusted balances *after* this entry and is calculated in the same manner as before.

The reader is referred to *Intermediate Accounting* in this series for a detailed discussion of accounting for treasury shares.

Adjustments

The accountant may occasionally discover during the preparation of consolidated statement working papers that one or more of the constituent companies has failed to properly record certain transactions in its books. In such cases, adjusting or correcting entries should be entered in the Eliminations column of the working paper before eliminations are determined and entered. Where appropriate, the adjustment or correction should also be entered on the books of the individual company. To distinguish adjusting and eliminating entries in the working paper, it is desirable to adopt some system of notation. The authors prefer to use numeral prefixes to identify eliminating entries, with lowercase letters used to indicate adjustments or corrections. The consolidated working paper in Case 8 uses this notation.

Comprehensive Illustration

Case 8. Assume the following data with respect to affiliate companies P, Y, and Z:

	January 1, 19X1		
	P Company	Y Company	Z Company
Capital stock (par, $100)............	$100,000	$50,000	$40,000
Retained earnings	54,000	5,000	4,000

On January 1, 19X1, P Company purchased 90 percent of the capital stock of Y Company for $70,000 and 80 percent of the capital stock of Z Company for $50,000. The notes receivable listed among the assets of Y Company (see Illustration 2–6) are the result of a loan to Z Company, on which the January 1, 19X1, accrued interest is $60. The interest is as yet unrecorded by Z Company.

The process of constructing a consolidated balance sheet should begin with the preparation of an affiliation diagram indicating percentages and directions of share ownership.

Affiliation Diagram

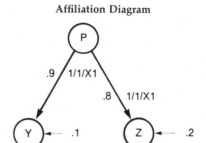

The investment elimination entries based upon the data given are:

Capital Stock—Y Company..	45,000	
Retained Earnings—Y Company	4,500	
Differential—Y Company.....................................	20,500	
Investment in Y Company.................................		70,000
Capital Stock—Z Company..	32,000	
Retained Earnings—Z Company	3,152	
Differential—Z Company.....................................	14,848	
Investment in Z Company.................................		50,000

It may be noted that the retained earnings of Z Company on January 1, 19X1, are overstated by the amount of the omission of accrued interest expense. Accordingly, the 80 percent elimination is made against the balance of this account *as adjusted* [80 percent of ($4,000 − $60), or $3,152].

Assume that an examination of the two subsidiaries indicated that all assets and liabilities were stated at their fair values except the inventories and the fixed assets, for which the following values were calculated:

	Book Value	Fair Value	Excess of Fair Value over Book Value	P Company's Interest in Excess
Company Y:				
Inventory...........................	$15,000	$18,000	$ 3,000	$ 2,700
Plant and equipment (net)............	25,000	35,000	10,000	9,000
Company Z:				
Inventory...........................	10,000	12,000	2,000	1,600
Plant and equipment (net)............	21,000	36,000	15,000	12,000

Based upon this information, the following allocations of the differentials are made:

Inventory...	2,700	
Plant and Equipment (net).............................	9,000	
Goodwill...	8,800	
Differential—Y Company.............................		20,500
Inventory...	1,600	
Plant and Equipment (net).............................	12,000	
Goodwill...	1,248	
Differential—Z Company.............................		14,848

Illustration 2–6

P COMPANY AND SUBSIDIARIES
Consolidated Balance Sheet Working Paper
January 1, 19X1

	P Company	Y Company	Z Company	Eliminations Dr.	Eliminations Cr.	Consolidated
Cash	4,000	4,940	3,000			11,940
Accounts receivable	5,000	19,000	15,000			39,000
Notes receivable		1,000			(5) 1,000	–0–
Inventory	25,000	15,000	10,000	(3) 2,700		54,300
				(4) 1,600		
Interest receivable		60			(6) 60	–0–
Investment in Y Company	70,000				(1) 70,000	–0–
Investment in Z Company	50,000				(2) 50,000	–0–
Plant and equipment (net)	15,000	25,000	21,000	(3) 9,000		82,000
				(4) 12,000		
Differential—Y Company				(1) 20,500	(3) 20,500	–0–
Differential—Z Company				(2) 14,848	(4) 14,848	–0–
Goodwill				(3) 8,800		10,048
				(4) 1,248		
	169,000	65,000	49,000			197,288
Accounts payable	5,000	10,000	4,000			19,000
Notes payable	10,000		1,000	(5) 1,000		10,000
Accrued interest payable				(6) 60	(a) 60	–0–
Capital stock:						
P Company	100,000					100,000
Y Company		50,000		(1) 45,000		5,000M
Z Company			40,000	(2) 32,000		8,000M
Retained earnings:						
P Company	54,000					54,000
Y Company		5,000		(1) 4,500		500M
Z Company			4,000	(a) 60		788M
				(2) 3,152		
	169,000	65,000	49,000	156,468	156,468	197,288

Explanations of adjustments and eliminations:
(a) Adjustment to record the accrual of interest expense by Z Company.
(1) Elimination of investment in Y Company.
(2) Elimination of investment in Z Company.
(3) Allocation of Y Company differential.
(4) Allocation of Z Company differential.
(5) Elimination of intercompany notes.
(6) Elimination of intercompany accrued interest.

Illustration 2–7

P COMPANY AND SUBSIDIARY COMPANIES Y AND Z
Consolidated Balance Sheet
January 1, 19X1

Assets		*Equities*		
Cash.........................	$ 11,940	Accounts payable ..		$ 19,000
Accounts receivable	39,000	Notes payable......		10,000
		Minority interest in—		
Inventory....................	54,300	Subsidiary Y		
Plant and equipment (net)	82,000	Company......	$ 5,500	
		Subsidiary Z		
Goodwill*	10,048	Company........	8,788	14,288
		Stockholders' equity:		
		Capital stock.....	$100,000	
		Retained earnings	54,000	154,000
Total assets	$197,288	Total equities		$197,288

* Terminology other than "goodwill" may be used in a company's formal financial statements. For example, one company labeled this term "Unamortized excess of cost of investment in subsidiary over net assets acquired." Other companies combine this asset with other assets into a class labeled "Intangible assets" or perhaps just "Other assets."

The consolidated working paper is shown in Illustration 2–6.

The preparation of the formal consolidated balance sheet is completed by recasting the account information from the Consolidated column of the working paper in traditional statement form (see Illustration 2–7). As mentioned earlier, these data are classified according to usual balance sheet arrangements, with the minority interest typically given separate status between the liability and owners' equity classifications. The equity of minority shareholders is sometimes presented together with that of the controlling interest; more frequently, however, it is interposed between the liabilities and the majority stockholders' equity. The traditional emphasis of consolidated statements on the dominant shareholder group would appear to support this latter position. Those who favor the *entity theory* of consolidated statements, about which more will be said later, would prefer to cite only one category of shareholders' equity, consisting of both majority and minority interest groups.

Questions

1. What is the appropriate designation of a company that is organized for the sole purpose of holding shares of stock in subsidiaries?

2. Why might a corporation prefer to use the acquisition form of corporate combination as opposed to the merger or consolidation forms?

3. What is the principal motivation in preparing consolidated financial statements of affiliated companies?

4. What are the essential elements of parental control over a subsidiary that must exist if consolidated statements are to be prepared?

5. Is it necessary to own 50 percent of a company's voting stock in order to maintain effective control over the company? Explain.

6. What factors (other than voting control) are important determinants in electing whether or not to include a specific subsidiary in consolidated statements?

7. Interpretation of consolidated statements requires careful consideration of the inherent limitations of these statements. What are some of these inherent limitations?

8. What is the general rule for determining the date of acquisition of a newly acquired subsidiary? Are there any exceptions to this general rule?

9. Given a situation in which a parent owns less than 100 percent of a subsidiary's stock, the consolidated balance sheet nevertheless includes 100 percent of the subsidiary's assets. Explain the reasoning that supports this principle.

10. After the differential has been allocated to identifiable assets and liabilities, any remaining unallocated debit differential is classified as goodwill. How would you justify this classification?

11. In the event a subsidiary has acquired treasury stock before its shares are acquired by a parent company, should the parent company's equity percentage in the subsidiary relate to the number of shares outstanding or to the total number of shares issued?

12. Describe what is meant by push down accounting. What arguments can be made for and against the method?

Exercises

Exercise 2–1

Select the best answer for each of the following:

1. Which of the following is the best theoretical justification for consolidated financial statements?
    a. In form the companies are one entity; in substance they are separate.
    b. In form the companies are separate; in substance they are one entity.
    c. In form and substance the companies are one entity.
    d. In form and substance the companies are separate.

2. Consolidated financial statements are prepared when a parent-subsidiary relationship exists in recognition of the accounting concept of—
    a. Materiality.
    b. Entity.
    c. Objectivity.
    d. Going concern.

3. In a business combination what is the appropriate method of accounting for an excess of fair value assigned to net assets over the cost paid for them?
    a. Record as negative goodwill.
    b. Record as additional paid-in capital from combination on the books of the combined company.
    c. Proportionately reduce values assigned to nonmonetary assets and record any remaining excess as a deferred credit.
    d. Proportionately reduce values assigned to noncurrent assets and record any remaining excess as a deferred credit.

    (AICPA adapted)

Exercise 2–2

Select the best answer in each of the following two situations.

1. On April 1, Bone Company paid $400,000 for all the issued and outstanding common stock of Dean Corporation in a transaction properly accounted for as a purchase. The assets and liabilities of Dean Corporation on April 1 follow:

Cash.......................................	$ 40,000
Inventory	120,000
Property and equipment (net of accumulated depreciation of $160,000)	240,000
Liabilities	[90,000]

On April 1, it was determined that the inventory of Dean had a fair value of $95,000 and the property and equipment (net) had a fair value of $280,000.

What would be the amount recognized as goodwill in a consolidated balance sheet prepared on April 1?
    a. $0.
    b. $25,000.
    c. $75,000.
    d. $90,000.

2. P Company purchased all of the outstanding stock of S Company for $80,000. On the date of purchase, S Company had no long-term investments in marketable securities and $10,000 (book and fair value) of liabilities. The fair values of S Company's assets on the date of purchase were as follows:

Current assets..............	$ 40,000
Noncurrent assets	60,000
	$100,000

How should the $10,000 difference between the fair value ($90,000) of S Company's net assets and the investment cost ($80,000) be handled in the consolidated balance sheet working paper prepared on the date of acquisition?
    a. The $10,000 difference should be credited to retained earnings.
    b. The noncurrent assets should be valued at $50,000.

    c. The current assets should be valued at $36,000, and the noncurrent assets should be valued at $54,000.

    d. A deferred credit of $10,000 should be established.

(AICPA adapted)

Exercise 2–3

Madison Company acquired 70 percent of the outstanding stock of Vail Corporation. The separate balance sheet of Madison immediately after the acquisition and the consolidated balance sheet are shown below.

Ten thousand dollars of the excess payment for the investment in Vail was allocated to undervaluation of its fixed assets; the balance of the excess payment was allocated to goodwill. Current assets of Vail included a $2,000 receivable from Madison which arose before they became related on an ownership basis.

The following two items relate to Vail's separate balance sheet prepared at the time Madison acquired its 70 percent interest in Vail. Select the best answer.

	Madison	*Consolidated*
Assets		
Current assets	$106,000	$146,000
Investment in Vail	100,000	—
Goodwill...................	—	8,100
Fixed assets (net)	270,000	370,000
Total assets................	$476,000	$524,100
Equities		
Current liabilities	$ 15,000	$ 28,000
Capital stock	350,000	350,000
Minority interest............	—	35,100
Retained earnings..........	111,000	111,000
Total equities..............	$476,000	$524,100

1. What was the total of the current assets on Vail's separate balance sheet at the time Madison acquired its 70 percent interest?
    a. $38,000.
    b. $40,000.
    c. $42,000.
    d. $104,000.
2. What was the total stockholders' equity on Vail's separate balance sheet at the time Madison acquired its 70 percent interest?
    a. $64,900.
    b. $70,000.
    c. $100,000.
    d. $117,000.

(AICPA adapted)

Exercise 2–4

P Company acquired a majority interest in S Company on 1/1/X1 by issuing 500,000 shares of no-par, common stock (current market price—$10 per share) for S Company shares. Treat each of the two situations below as independent cases, and select the best answer.

1. Assume that P Company guaranteed that if the market price of its shares fell below $10 per share at the end of one year, it would issue additional shares to restore the total market value of the consideration given to $5,000,000. Further assume that the market price at the end of the year was $5 per share, and that P Company issued an additional 500,000 shares to meet its obligation. Issuance of the additional 500,000 shares would be recorded by P Company:

    a. Investment in S Company............................   2,500,000
            Capital stock......................................   2,500,000
    b. Investment in S Company   5,000,000
            Capital Stock   5,000,000
    c. Goodwill   2,500,000
            Capital Stock   2,500,000
    d. Some other entry would be made.
    e. No entry would be made.

2. Assume P Company guaranteed that it would issue additional shares worth $1,000,000 (at 12/31/X1 market prices) if S Company's earnings for 19X1 exceeded a specific amount. Further assume that the condition was satisfied and P Company issued 50,000 additional shares (at a 12/31/XI market price of $20 per share). Issuance of the additional 50,000 shares at 12/31/X1 would be recorded by P Company:

    a. Investment in S Company   1,000,000
            Capital Stock......................................   1,000,000

    b. Investment in S Company   500,000
            Capital Stock......................................   500,000

    c. Goodwill   1,000,000
            Capital Stock......................................   1,000,000

    d. Some other entry would be made.
    e. No entry would be made.

(Hint: It may be helpful to review paragraphs 77–86 of *APB Opinion No. 16.*)

Exercise 2–5

On January 1, 19X1, Lincoln Corporation exchanged 10,000 shares of its own $20 par value common stock for 75 percent of the capital stock of the Juilliard Company.

Required:

a. An important limitation of consolidated financial statements is their lack of separate information about the assets, liabilities, revenues, and expenses of the individual companies included in the consolidation. List the problems that the reader of consolidated financial statements encounters as a result of the limitation.

b. The minority interest in Juilliard Company might be presented several ways on the consolidated balance sheet. Discuss the propriety of reporting the minority interest on the consolidated balance sheet—

(1) As a liability.

(2) As a part of stockholders' equity.

(3) In a separate classification between liabilities and the equity of the Lincoln Corporation.

(AICPA adapted)

Exercise 2–6

P Company acquired a majority interest in S Company on April 1, 19X1, by issuing 500,000 shares of unregistered P Company no-par, common stock and $1,500,000 cash in exchange for S Company shares. Additionally, P Company agreed to register these shares sometime within the next three months.

It is estimated that the fair value of the P Company shares on the date of exchange is $6 per share, and that total registration costs will amount to $200,000. Additionally, P Company maintains an "acquisitions" department, and P Company management estimates that this department devoted approximately 60 percent of its efforts during the first three months of 19X1 to the acquisition of S Company. This department incurs average monthly expenses of $10,000.

Required:
Prepare the journal entry on April 1, 19X1, to record P Company's investment in S Company. (Ignore the issue of discounting the liability for future registration costs.)

Exercise 2–7

In the preparation of the consolidated balance sheet of a parent corporation and its subsidiaries, a decision must be reached concerning the inclusion or exclusion of each of them as a member of the consolidated group. A common criterion is the percentage of voting stock owned by the parent company.

Required:
a. What is the significance of the percentage of voting stock ownership in justifying the inclusion of a subsidiary company in a consolidated statement?

b. List other criteria upon which the decision to consolidate or not may also rest.

(AICPA adapted)

Exercise 2–8

Prepare investment elimination entries for the Pacific Company and its subsidiary, Ocean Company, for each of the conditions listed below:

| | | | Ocean Capital Balances | |
| | | | | |
Acquired Interest	Amount Paid	Capital Stock	Other Contributed Capital	Retained Earnings [Deficit]
a. 100%	1,450,000	1,000,000	250,000	300,000
b. 90	1,125,000	1,000,000	325,000	[100,000]
c. 75	1,000,000	1,000,000	200,000	120,000

Exercise 2–9

An examination of the December 31, 19X1, balance sheet of S Company revealed the following account balances:

Capital stock (100,000 shares, $10 par)	$1,000,000
Other contributed capital	275,000
Donated capital.................................	125,000
Reserve for future inventory losses	100,000
Retained earnings...............................	300,000
Estimated 19X1 federal income tax liability	200,000

Prepare an investment elimination entry immediately following the December 31, 19X1, open-market purchases of S Company's capital stock by P Company in each of the following independent conditions:

a. 100,000 shares; per share cost, $20.
b. 100,000 shares; per share cost, $18.
c.   80,000 shares; total cost, $1,540,000.
d.   80,000 shares; total cost, $1,400,000.
e.   40,000 shares; per share cost, $20⅝.
f. 300,000 shares (authorized, but previously unissued) purchased *directly* from S Company; per share cost, $20.

Exercise 2–10

On December 1, 19X1, Valley-View Company declares a dividend of $2.50 per share on its outstanding 100,000 shares for shareholders of record, January 10, 19X2. On December 31, 19X1, Texton Company acquires 90,000 shares of Valley-View Company for a cash outlay of $2,000,000. Valley-View Company has the following balances in its capital accounts at December 31:

Capital stock ($10 par)...................	$1,020,000
Treasury stock (recorded at par)..........	20,000
Other contributed capital	500,000
Retained earnings......................	400,000

Required:

a. Prepare an investment elimination entry for Texton Company as of December 31, 19X1.
b. Give the journal entry Texton Company would make to record the acquisition.

Exercise 2–11

On January 1, 19X1, P Company purchased 90 percent of S Company for $124,000. At the time of the investment, the book values of all S Company's assets and liabilities were equal to their fair values. S Company's balance sheet on January 1, 19X1, was as follows:

S Company

Assets

Cash...	$ 10,000
Accounts receivable	5,000
Inventory...	50,000
Long-term investments in marketable securities	15,000
Plant and equipment (net)	50,000
Land...	60,000
Total assets...	$190,000

Equities

Accounts payable	$ 15,000
Notes payable	25,000
Capital stock...	50,000
Retained earnings	100,000
Total equities	$190,000

Required:
a. Prepare an investment elimination entry for P Company as of January 1, 19X1.
b. Give the elimination entry (entries) necessary to allocate the differential.

Exercise 2–12

P Company purchased an 80 percent interest in S Company for $84,800 on July 1, 19X1. S Company's balance sheet on that date was as follows:

S Company

Assets

Cash	$15,000
Receivables	20,000
Inventory...	30,000
Long-term investments in marketable securities	12,000
Plant and equipment (net).............................	11,000
Patents	4,000
Total assets..	$92,000

Equities

Payables..	$12,000
Capital stock...	30,000
Retained earnings	50,000
Total equities..	$92,000

A study of S Company's assets and liabilities revealed the following information:

	Fair Value
Inventory	$40,000
Long-term investments in marketable securities	15,000
Plant and equipment (net)	20,000
Patents	12,000

The fair values of the remainder of the assets and liabilities were equal to their book values.

Required:

a. Prepare the investment elimination entry at July 1, 19X1.
b. Give the elimination entry (entries) necessary to allocate the differential.

Exercise 2–13

P Company acquired a majority interest in S Company on December 31, 19X0, by issuing 500,000 shares of P Company $1 par, common stock in exchange for S Company shares. The current market price of the P Company common stock is $40 per share. Additionally, P Company guaranteed that the market price of its shares will be at least $60 at the end of the second year succeeding the acquisition date. If, at the end of the second year, the market price of P Company stock is less than $60 per share, P Company will issue additional shares with a current market value equal to the difference between the total guaranteed value and the current market value of the shares previously issued.

Required:

Assuming the market value of the P Company shares was $45 on December 31, 19X1, and $50 on December 31, 19X2, prepare the journal entries that P Company must make for this transaction on—

a. December 31, 19X0.
b. December 31, 19X1.
c. December 31, 19X2.

(Hint: It may be helpful to review paragraphs 77–86 of *APB Opinion No. 16.*)

Exercise 2–14

P Company acquired a majority interest in S Company on December 31, 19X0, by issuing 2,000,000 shares of P Company no-par, common stock in exchange for S Company shares. The current market price of the P Company common stock is $20 per share. Additionally, P Company guaranteed that if the market price of its shares has fallen below $20 at the end of four years, it will issue additional shares to restore the total market value of consideration given to $40,000,000 as of that date. P Company further guaranteed to pay a total purchase price equal to eight times S

Company's average annual earnings for the next four years (S Company's average annual earnings during the past four years were $5,000,000). If the guaranteed price, as calculated on December 31, 19X4, exceeds the December 31, 19X4, market value of shares previously issued, additional shares will be issued to make up the difference. In no case, however, can the total purchase price exceed $60,000,000.

Required:

a. Determine the cost of the investment on the date of acquisition.
b. Explain the economic and accounting implications of the various possible contingent outcomes on December 31, 19X4.

(Hint: It may be helpful to review paragraphs 77–86 of *APB Opinion No. 16.*)

Exercise 2–15

The annual report for the McLean Trucking Company for the year ended June 30, 19X2, included the following footnote:

Effective October 1, 19X1, all of the common stock of the Fort Worth Refining Company was purchased at an aggregate cost of $8,713,561 composed of cash of $2,000,000, notes in the amount of $5,988,452 and other costs of $725,109. Contingency payments representing 50% of cash profits above a certain amount, as defined in the agreement, are required to be paid to the sellers. A reduction in the purchase price results if certain cash profit levels are not attained. It is the Company's intention to charge contingency payments to operations and net contingency refunds (excess refunds over payments), should they arise, will be applied against the original purchase price. At June 30, 19X2, liability for estimated contingency payments under the Agreement amounted to approximately $209,000.

Required:

Comment on the propriety of this treatment of the contingent consideration. (Hint: It may be helpful to review paragraphs 77–86 of *APB Opinion No. 16.*)

Exercise 2–16

P Company acquired an 80 percent interest in S Company by issuing cash and other stock valued at $975,000. The investment elimination entry for this investment in P Company's consolidated statement working paper on the date of acquisition follows:

Capital Stock—S Company	80,000	
Retained Earnings—S Company	320,000	
Differential	575,000	
Investment in S Company		975,000

An analysis of the identifiable assets and liabilities of S Company produced the following data:

	Book Value	Fair Value
Cash............................	$ 50,000	$ 50,000
Receivables (net)...................	150,000	130,000
Inventory	250,000	310,000
Plant and equipment (net)..........	350,000	500,000
Patents	–0–	100,000
Land	100,000	150,000
Goodwill.........................	50,000	–0–
	$950,000	$1,240,000
Accounts and notes payable	$300,000	$ 280,000
Accruals	50,000	40,000
Deferred income tax liability	100,000	–0–
	$450,000	$ 320,000
	$450,000	$ 320,000
Net assets........................	$500,000	$ 920,000

Required:

a. Prepare the eliminating entry to allocate the differential to specific assets and liabilities.

b. The determination of "fair value" requires the application of different valuation bases (models) to different categories of assets and liabilities. Based upon the general guidelines established in paragraphs 88–89 of *APB Opinion No. 16*, indicate the probable valuation basis that was used to estimate the fair value for each asset and liability.

Exercise 2–17

Lacy Company purchased 1,000,000 common shares of Ireland Enterprises at $10 per share when Ireland's book value per share was $8. This investment represented a 90 percent ownership interest. Book values were equal to fair values for all Ireland's net assets except plant and equipment, which was appraised at $6,000,000 and had a book value of $4,000,000. The $4,000,000 book value will carry over as the tax basis of the plant and equipment. The plant and equipment is expected to have a remaining life of 10 years, and Lacy's marginal tax rate is 40 percent.

Required:

Determine the allocation of the debit differential assuming a 10 percent discount rate.

Problems

Problem 2–18

The following data relate to companies X, Y, and Z on February 1, 19X1:

	X Company	Y Company	Z Company
Capital stock (par, $100)..........	$10,000	$10,000	$10,000
Retained earnings [deficit]........	4,000	[2,000]	–0–

Prepare an investment elimination entry on February 2, 19X1, following the purchase of stock *from the subsidiary* as indicated in the following independent cases.

Case A: P Company purchased 800 shares of X Company stock; 100 shares were issued concurrently to minority shareholders. Sales price per share for each stockholder group in the following independent examples, was—
  (1) $140.
  (2) $160.
  (3) $120.

Case B: P Company purchased 800 shares of Y Company stock; 100 shares were issued concurrently to minority shareholders. Sales price per share for each stockholder group in the following independent examples, was—
  (1) $80 to P Company.
        $74 to minority shareholders.
  (2) $82 to P Company.
        $84 to minority shareholders.

Case C: P Company purchased 700 shares of Z Company stock; 200 shares were issued concurrently to minority shareholders. Sales price per share for each stockholder group in the following independent examples, was—
  (1) $102 to P Company.
        $105 to minority shareholders.
  (2) $93 to P Company.
        $91 to minority shareholders.

Problem 2–19

Given the following data, prepare an investment elimination entry for each of the following independent, open-market investment transactions:

January 1, 19X1, Balances

	Capital Stock (par value, $100)	Retained Earnings [deficit]	Other Contributed Capital	19X1 Net Income [loss]	19X1 Cash Dividends
M Company	$50,000	$10,000	$6,000	$20,000	$8,000
W Company	40,000	[5,000]		15,000	5,000
Z Company	30,000	12,000	2,000	[5,000]	

**For Consolidated Balance Sheet
January 1, 19X1**

P Company purchased on January 1, 19X1:
  Case A: 400 shares of M Company capital stock at book value.
  Case B: 300 shares of W Company capital stock at $90.
  Case C: 300 shares of M Company capital stock at $125.
  Case D: 200 shares of M Company capital stock at $130.

For Consolidated Balance Sheet
January 1, 19X2

P Company purchased on January 1, 19X2:
- Case E: 400 shares of M Company capital stock at $157.
- Case F: 300 shares of M Company capital stock at $150.
- Case G: 200 shares of Z Company capital stock at $125.
- Case H: 300 shares of W Company capital stock at book value and 200 shares of Z Company capital stock at $3 per share less than book value.

Problem 2–20

On November 1, 19X0, the Smith Company entered into negotiations with the King Corporation to purchase a controlling interest in its capital stock. On December 1, it was mutually agreed that the assets of the King Corporation should be appraised as a condition of final price determination. On December 31, the following data were available:

Long-lived assets:
Cost	$100,000
Accumulated depreciation (based upon a 20-year life)	50,000
Reproduction cost—new	200,000
Estimated remaining life	15 years
Straight-line depreciation is used.	
Capital stock (par, $100)	$ 50,000
Retained earnings [deficit]	[5,000]
Other contributed capital	10,000

Based on this information, the King Corporation recorded the appraisal on January 1, 19X1, after which the Smith Company purchased 1,500 shares of King Corporation's unissued capital stock at $300 per share.

Required:
a. Record the appraisal on the books of the King Corporation on January 1, 19X1.
b. Prepare an investment elimination entry for a consolidated balance sheet working paper as of January 1, 19X1.
c. Assuming that King Corporation did *not* record the new appraised value of its long-lived assets, prepare the investment elimination entry and the differential allocation entry (using the appraised values) for a consolidated balance sheet working paper as of January 1, 19X1.
d. Calculate the values that would be shown in the consolidated balance sheet for the subsidiary's long-lived assets, accumulated depreciation, and total minority interest under *(b)* and *(c)*.

Problem 2–21

On April 1, 19X1, the Pratt Company purchased a controlling interest in both the Trine Company and the Briski Corporation, after which the following balance sheet information was prepared:

	Pratt	Trine	Briski
Assets			
Cash..................................	$ 4,000	$ 1,500	$ 3,500
Accounts receivable......................	11,000	9,000	12,500
Other current assets......................	8,000	4,500	10,000
Investments:			
320 shares in Trine Company	50,000		
540 shares in Briski Corporation..........	51,000		
Long-lived assets (net)	30,000	41,000	54,000
Other assets............................	26,000	24,000	10,000
Total assets............................	$180,000	$80,000	$90,000
Equities			
Accounts payable........................	$ 14,000	$ 5,000	$15,000
Other current liabilities...................	6,000	12,000	8,000
Long-term debt..........................	15,000	3,000	11,000
Capital stock (par, $100)..................	100,000	40,000	60,000
Retained earnings [deficit]	41,000	18,000	[4,000]
Other contributed capital	4,000	2,000	
Total equities...........................	$180,000	$80,000	$90,000

Required:

Prepare a consolidated balance sheet working paper as of April 1, 19X1. Assume any differential is allocated to goodwill.

Problem 2–22

On October 1, 19X1, the Sydney Company purchased 960 shares of the Wood Company stock for $160,000 and $50,000 of Wood Company bonds at par plus accrued interest. Immediately after these transactions, the following trial balances were prepared:

	Sydney Company	Wood Company
Assets		
Cash ,,..	$ 19,250	$ 10,000
Accrued interest receivable	750	
Inventory...	120,000	100,000
Accounts receivable..................................	80,000	50,000
Long-lived assets (net)	100,000	160,000
Other assets..	20,000	10,000
Investment in Wood Company (stock)..................	160,000	
Investment in Wood Company (bonds).................	50,000	
Total assets	$550,000	$330,000

	Sydney Company	Wood Company
Equities		
Accounts payable.................................	$ 60,000	$ 21,500
Accrued interest payable		1,500
Accrued expenses	10,000	7,000
Bonds payable, 6%, payable January 1 and July 1........		100,000
Capital stock (par, $100).............................	300,000	150,000
Treasury stock (recorded at par).......................		[30,000]
Retained earnings	80,000	50,000
Other contributed capital............................	100,000	30,000
Total equities......................................	$550,000	$330,000

Additionally, a $4,000 balance remains in the respective trade accounts receivable and payable from previous trading between the two companies.

Required:

a. Prepare an investment elimination entry on October 1, 19X1.

b. Prepare a consolidated balance sheet working paper on October 1, 19X1.

Problem 2–23

The December 31, 19X1, trial balances of X Company, a petroleum refinery, and companies Y and Z, two of its crude oil suppliers, are as follows:

	X Company	Y Company	Z Company
Assets			
Cash.............................	$ 10,400,000	$ 570,000	$ 1,100,000
Marketable securities...............	27,300,000		
Accounts receivable	29,000,000	1,200,000	3,200,000
Notes receivable			1,500,000
Inventory	55,900,000	2,240,000	10,800,000
Long-lived assets (net)	187,000,000	3,900,000	14,600,000
Other assets.......................	4,320,000	100,000	200,000
Total assets........................	$313,920,000	$8,010,000	$31,400,000
Equities			
Accounts payable	$ 36,900,000	$1,200,000	$ 1,800,000
Notes payable, Z Company.........		1,500,000	
Dividends payable (Note 1)		100,000	
Accrued expenses..................	1,820,000	570,000	700,000
Bonds payable.....................	100,000,000		10,000,000
Capital stock:			
$100 par	100,000,000		
$10 par		2,000,000	
No par (100,000)			17,400,000
Other contributing capital	47,800,000	1,800,000	
Retained earnings..................	27,400,000	840,000	1,500,000
Total equities.....................	$313,920,000	$8,010,000	$31,400,000

Note 1: Cash dividends were declared December 28, 19X1, payable on January 25, 19X2, to stockholders of record, January 5, 19X2.

On January 1, 19X2, X Company purchased a controlling interest in the capital stock of companies Y and Z to assure continuity of supply of crude oil. The acquisition of stock was as follows:

1. Purchased 160,000 shares of Y Company's capital stock in the open market for $25⅝ per share. Payment was made by check.
2. Acquired 90,000 shares of Z Company's capital stock by issuing 80,000 shares of X Company's stock to the individual stockholders of Z Company. On January 1, 19X2, the capital stock of X Company was quoted at $250.

Required:

Prepare a consolidated balance sheet working paper as of January 1, 19X2. Assume any differential is allocated to goodwill.

Problem 2–24

The June 1, 19X1, balance sheets for A Company and B Company are as follows:

	A Company	B Company
Assets		
Cash.	$ 100,000	$ 52,000
Accounts receivable	200,000	125,000
Notes receivable	300,000	100,000
Merchandise inventory	375,000	225,000
Investment in B Company	800,000	
Long-lived assets (net).	825,000	700,000
Total assets.	$2,600,000	$1,202,000
Equities		
Accounts payable	$ 200,000	$ 150,000
Accrued interest payable.		2,000
Notes payable	500,000	300,000
Capital stock (par, $10)	1,500,000	500,000
Retained earnings.	400,000	250,000
Total equities	$2,600,000	$1,202,000

All of B Company's assets are recorded at their fair values except for the following:

	Book Value	Fair Value
Merchandise inventory	$225,000	$ 265,000
Long-lived assets (net)	700,000	750,000
	$925,000	$1,015,000

On June 1, 19X1, A Company purchased 80 percent of the capital stock of B Company for $800,000. Included in the accounts receivable for B Company is an account for $25,000 due from A Company. The notes receivable for A Company include a loan to B Company for $50,000 on which the June 1 accrued interest is $2,000. The interest is unrecorded by A Company.

Required:

Prepare a consolidated balance sheet for A Company and its subsidiary as of June 1, 19X1.

Problem 2–25

The Webster Company purchased 100 percent of the capital stock of the Reid Company on January 1, 19X1, for $61,000. Immediately following the investment, the statements of financial position for the constituent companies are as follows:

	Webster Company	Reid Company
Assets		
Cash..............................	$ 8,000	$ 5,000
Accounts receivable	16,000	15,000
Advances to Reid	5,000	
Investment in Reid Company	61,000	
Inventory	20,000	10,000
Other assets	53,000	40,000
Total assets........................	$163,000	$70,000
Equities		
Liabilities..........................	$ 8,000	$ 5,000
Due to Webster		5,000
Capital stock (par, $100)	100,000	50,000
Retained earnings...................	55,000	10,000
Total equities	$163,000	$70,000

Required:

Prepare a consolidated balance sheet working paper as of January 1, 19X1. Assume that the book values of all of Reid Company's assets and liabilities are equal to their fair values.

Problem 2–26

At December 31, 19X1, the balance sheet of A Company was as follows:

Assets		Equities	
Cash	$ 50,000	Payables....................	$1,750,000
Receivables (net).............	300,000	Accruals	450,000
Inventories..................	1,600,000	Common stock, 10,000 shares.	1,000,000
Current prepayments	47,000	Retained earnings	800,000
Long-lived assets (net)	2,003,000		
Total assets	$4,000,000	Total equities................	$4,000,000

An appraisal as of that date, which was carefully considered and approved by the boards of directors of A Company and B Company, placed a total replacement value, less sustained depreciation, of $3,203,000 on the long-lived assets of A Company.

B Company offered to purchase all the assets of A Company, subject to its liabilities, as of December 31, 19X1, for $3,000,000. However, 40 percent of the stockholders of A Company objected to the price on the ground that it did not include a consideration for goodwill, which they believed to be worth at least $500,000. A counterproposal was made, and final agreement was reached on the basis that B Company acquired 60 percent of the common stock of A Company at a price of $300 per share.

B Company's condensed balance sheet at December 31, 19X1, following the acquisition of A Company's stock, showed:

Assets		Equities	
Cash and investments		Payables	$ 7,872,000
(including stock of A)	$ 7,000,000	Accruals	1,615,000
Receivables (net)............	2,400,000	Common stock, 100,000	
Inventories..................	11,200,000	shares	10,000,000
Current prepayments	422,000	Retained earnings	20,513,000
Long-lived assets (net)	18,978,000		
Total assets	$40,000,000	Total equities..............	$40,000,000

Required:

Prepare a consolidated balance sheet working paper as of December 31, 19X1, for the two companies.

(AICPA adapted)

CHAPTER
3

Consolidated Financial
Reports—Postacquisition

The preparation of consolidated statements following a period of subsidiary operations is complicated, at least in part, by the introduction of two new variables: the elapsed time since the acquisition of subsidiary shares *and* the parent company's method of accounting for the investment. At date of acquisition, the investment is recorded at total purchase cost; subsequently, an election must be made by the parent as to whether this measurement should be preserved without change *or* periodically adjusted to reflect the activities and operations of the subsidiary. The former, more traditional, approach is the cost, or legal basis, method. The latter approach is referred to as the equity method. These two alternative methods of accounting for the parent company's investment have been covered in *Intermediate Accounting* and are summarized below. However, it may be noted at this point that regardless of which method is employed by the parent to account for its investment *in a subsidiary that is to be included in the consolidation,* the formal consolidated statements will remain unaffected. That is, only the separate company statements of the parent will differ. The working paper eliminations are designed to compensate for the differences between the two methods.

The Cost Method

The cost method of accounting for stock investments presumes that cost is an accurate reflection of the market value of the investment at date of acquisition, and that this valuation should remain undisturbed in most instances by the influence of subsequent operations of the company whose stock is held. Accordingly, under the cost method, subsidiary profits are not recorded by the parent when they are reported by the subsidiary. Similarly, the losses sustained by a subsidiary are not recorded by the parent *unless* there is convincing evidence that indicates the incurrence of a material and apparently permanent impairment of the value of the investment. Income is recognized by the parent company only when the subsidiary declares a cash dividend. At this time, the parent company debits Dividends Receivable and credits Dividend Income for its share of the subsidiary dividends.[1]

The Equity Method

Under the equity method, the parent company's equity in the postacquisition earnings of a subsidiary is recorded by debiting the investment account and crediting a suitably named account, such as Equity in Subsidi-

---

[1] If a cash dividend paid by a subsidiary is in excess of the accumulated, undistributed earnings of the subsidiary since the date the parent acquired the subsidiary, such excess is properly classified (from the point of view of the parent) as a *liquidating dividend*. Liquidating dividends received by the parent are credited to the investment account rather than Dividend Income.

ary Earnings. All or part of this "equity" may be in "undistributed" earnings, which emphasizes the unique *realization* criterion underlying the recognition of a subsidiary's contribution to the parent's net income. Historically, when the traditional realization concept was applied to stock investments, it was interpreted as a requirement that income not be recognized by the stockholder until declared as dividends by the issuing company. To the contrary, the equity method involves a significant relaxation of this traditional criterion. In essence, the equity method is based on the argument that the economic impact of a corporation's reported profits and losses immediately accrues to its stockholders, regardless of the timing of dividend declarations.

Postacquisition losses sustained by a subsidiary affiliate are recorded in a similar manner by the parent, that is, by a debit to Equity in Subsidiary Earnings with a corresponding credit to the investment account. Such losses result from a decrease in the underlying subsidiary net assets; consequently, the parent's entry is an effort to formally recognize the unfavorable economic circumstance.[2]

The parent company's receipt of a subsidiary cash dividend is recorded by debiting Cash and crediting the investment account. Such an entry reflects the financial realization of the parent's equity in subsidiary profits in the amount of the assets transferred; accordingly, the receipt of dividends is treated as a reduction in the reciprocal investment account balance. Since an antecedent entry has been made increasing the investment account for subsidiary profits, the parent's collection of subsidiary cash dividends is simply an act of conversion, or a partial recovery of the adjusted cost of the investment. The effect produced on the parent company's books is merely a transformation in asset form.

Entry Comparison

The entries made by the parent company using both the cost and equity methods are shown in Illustration 3–1. A comparison of these entries exposes some of the principal differences between the two methods. Please note that the entries shown in Illustration 3–1 are those recorded on the books of the parent company. They should not be confused with eliminating entries required for consolidated statement working papers.

The entries shown in Illustration 3–1 to record the parent's equity in subsidiary income under the equity method are based on the assumptions that (1) the cost of the parent's investment at date of acquisition is equal to its acquired equity in the subsidiary's recorded net assets, and (2) there are no transactions between the parent and the subsidiary that generate, from

---

[2] However, if the recording of losses would result in reducing the investment account below zero, the equity method is abandoned in favor of the cost method (unless the parent has guaranteed the obligations of its subsidiary).

Illustration 3–1

Cost Method		Equity Method	

A 90% investment in subsidiary stock is acquired for $50,000.

Investment in			Investment in		
Subsidiary Stock ...	50,000		Subsidiary Stock	50,000	
Cash		50,000	Cash		50,000

Cash dividends of $4,000 are paid by the subsidiary during the first year of its operations.

Cash	3,600		Cash	3,600	
Dividend income .		3,600	Investment in		
			Subsidiary Stock .		3,600

The subsidiary reports net income of $10,000 for the first year's operations.

No entry.			Investment in		
			Subsidiary Stock	9,000	
			Equity in Subsidiary		
			Earnings.........		9,000

Cash dividends of $3,000 are paid by the subsidiary during the second year.

Cash	2,700		Cash	2,700	
Dividend Income .		2,700	Investment in		
			Subsidiary Stock .		2,700

The subsidiary reports a net loss of $2,000 for the second year.

No entry.			Equity in Subsidiary		
			Earnings............	1,800	
			Investment in		
			Subsidiary Stock .		1,800

the point of view of the economic entity, unrealized gains or losses. In the event either, or both, of these assumptions are not valid, the calculations would be modified. Since these modifications are also necessary in preparing consolidated statements, they will be examined in subsequent chapters of the book. The procedure for giving effect to amortization of the difference between investment cost and the parent's equity in net assets is described in Chapter 4, and elimination of intercompany unrealized gains and losses is treated in Chapters 7, 8, and 9.

Although either method of accounting for the investment in the stock of the subsidiary may be used, many companies shifted from the cost method to the equity method following the adoption of *APB Opinion No. 18,* "The Equity Method of Accounting for Investments in Common Stock." Strictly speaking, this *Opinion* imposes a financial reporting requirement, not an accounting requirement, and it has an impact *in consolidated statements* only for investments in unconsolidated affiliates. Although the formal consolidated statements are unaffected by the choice of accounting method (cost or equity) for investments in subsidiaries that are consolidated, *the mechanics of consolidation are affected by the accounting method used.* Since the authors believe that the equity method is now the prevalent method (in practice and on the CPA Examination), we have elected to base the primary explanations and illustrations on the assumption that the parent company has employed the equity method. However, important differences in consolidated working paper techniques for investments carried under the cost method are presented, usually in chapter appendices or separately identified sections.

Statements of Consolidated Income and Retained Earnings

Following a period of subsidiary operations, it is important that consolidated statements of income and retained earnings be prepared in addition to the consolidated balance sheet. A consolidated income statement is essentially a summary enumeration of the revenues, expenses, gains, and losses of the allied companies after elimination of those account balances that result from transactions between the affiliates. The process of combination includes a deduction from the combined net incomes of all the affiliated companies, after eliminations, for the amounts of minority interests in the net incomes of the subsidiary affiliates. The residual, so determined, is then assignable to the majority (parent company) shareholders and is designated *consolidated net income*.

An alternative definition of consolidated net income is based on the argument that the amount of income allocated to minority interests should be treated as a *distribution* of consolidated net income rather than a *deduction necessary to determine* consolidated net income. This view emphasizes the single-entity concept of a corporate affiliation. It rests on the belief that the *determinants* of an entity's net income should not include allocations to any of the stockholders of the entity, notwithstanding the unique character of minority stockholders. This concept is further explored in Chapter 12.

It should be emphasized that the nature of consolidated net income is essentially a definitional problem. The authors support the first definition presented above primarily because it emphasizes the equity of parent company stockholders. The significance of consolidated statements clearly stems from the informational needs of parties that have interests in the parent company, that is, parent company creditors and stockholders. Defining consolidated net income as the portion of combined net income accruing to the parent is fully consistent with this dominant statement function. Thus, the preferred definition reflects the orientation of the principal users of consolidated statements. Subsequent development is based on this interpretation unless otherwise noted.

The consolidated statement of retained earnings is simply a sequential ordering of the consolidated retained earnings at the beginning of an accounting period, increased by consolidated net income, and reduced by the parent company's dividends declared; the algebraic sum of these amounts is the balance of consolidated retained earnings at the end of the accounting period.

In the preparation of a consolidated income statement, consolidated statement of retained earnings, and consolidated balance sheet, it is useful to select a working paper, the organization of which accommodates the preparation of all three statements in the series.

The Three-Division Working Paper—First Year Subsequent to Acquisition

The basic data for preparation of consolidated financial reports is contained in the financial statements of the separate affiliates. When the source information is conveniently prearranged in financial statement form, the three-division working paper is both an efficient and a logical basis for the development of consolidated statement information. On some occasions, however, the trial balances of the affiliates are more accessible. In these instances, the trial balances must be reclassified in financial statement form to accommodate the three-division working paper format. In the remaining discussion of consolidated statements, trial balances of affiliated companies are given as the source information for consolidated working papers in order to minimize the space devoted to underlying detail; nonetheless, the three-division working paper format will usually be employed because it provides a logical framework for analysis. The working paper techniques used with the "trial balance working paper" are discussed and illustrated in Chapter 12. Only very minor modifications are involved.

Case 1.   It is assumed that P Company acquired 90 percent of the capital stock of S Company on January 1, 19X1, at a cost of $54,000. The trial balances for the two affiliates at December 31, 19X1, are as follows:

	P Company		S Company	
Cash	$ 29,500		$ 8,000	
Accounts receivable	18,000		3,000	
Inventory (1/1)	16,000		4,000	
Investment in S Company	67,500			
Other assets	73,000		62,000	
Accounts payable		$ 22,000		$ 5,000
Other liabilities		6,000		
Capital stock		100,000		50,000
Retained earnings (1/1)		40,000		10,000
Dividends declared	10,000		5,000	
Sales		78,000		40,000
Equity in subsidiary earnings		18,000		
Purchases	42,000		20,000	
Expenses	8,000		3,000	
	$264,000	$264,000	$105,000	$105,000
Inventory (12/31)	$ 10,000		$ 7,000	

The Dividends Declared account is a special classificational refinement that facilitates the analysis in the retained earnings statement division of the consolidated statement working paper. The account has the following properties: it is debited when dividends are declared (rather than Retained Earnings); and at the end of the period, it is closed (along with other nominal accounts) to Retained Earnings. Even though the accounting system of a company does not actually incorporate this refinement, the consolidated working paper can nonetheless be set up as if the account existed. Should one choose not to identify dividends declared separately in the consolidated statement working paper, then all consolidation entries that otherwise would affect this account would be made directly against Retained Earnings.

Investment Elimination Entries.   When the investment is carried on an equity basis and a consolidated income statement, statement of retained earnings, and balance sheet are prepared, it is necessary first to eliminate, or reverse, the effects of the parent company's entries for subsidiary income (or loss) and dividends for the current year. Such an elimination, or reversal, in the consolidated statement working paper removes the measures of this set of intercompany activities during the current year and restores the investment account to that balance which prevailed at the *beginning* of the year (which, in this case, is the date of acquisition). A second eliminating entry is then necessary to eliminate the parent company's investment account (as adjusted by the preceding entry) against its equity in the balances of the stockholders' equity accounts of the subsidiary *as of the beginning of the year.*

During 19X1, the parent company recorded the following two entries under the equity method of accounting for its investment in the subsidiary:

1. To record receipt of dividends from S Company:

Cash (90% × $5,000)	4,500	
Investment in S Company		4,500

2. To recognize equity in S Company's reported earnings:

Investment in S Company	18,000	
Equity in Subsidiary Earnings (90% × $20,000)		18,000

Consequently, the first set of investment elimination entries in the consolidated statement working paper (Illustration 3–2) should reverse the effects of these entries. One modification to a precise reversal of the original entries is, however, necessary. The account, Dividends Declared, is substituted for Cash in the entry recording the receipt of dividends. The reason for this substitution is apparent upon reflection. The Cash account on the balance sheet of the parent company is properly valued at the end of the period—that is, it reflects the value of the parent's cash on hand and in banks. However, the portion of the subsidiary's dividend in its Dividends Declared account that was paid to the parent company represents an inter-

Illustration 3–2

P COMPANY AND SUBSIDIARY S COMPANY
Consolidated Statement Working Paper
For Year Ended December 31, 19X1

	P Company	S Company	Eliminations Dr.	Eliminations Cr.	Minority Interest	Consolidated
Income Statement						
Sales	78,000	40,000				118,000
Equity in subsidiary earnings	18,000		(1b) 18,000			–0–
Inventory (12/31)	10,000	7,000				17,000
Total credits	106,000	47,000				135,000
Inventory (1/1)	16,000	4,000				20,000
Purchases	42,000	20,000				62,000
Expenses	8,000	3,000				11,000
Total debits	66,000	27,000				93,000
	40,000	20,000				42,000
Minority interest in net income—S Company					2,000*	2,000
Net income—carried forward	40,000	20,000	18,000	–0–	2,000	40,000
Retained Earnings Statement						
Retained earnings, 1/1/X1:						
P Company	40,000					40,000
S Company		10,000	(2) 9,000		1,000†	–0–
Net income—brought forward	40,000	20,000	18,000	–0–	2,000	40,000
	80,000	30,000			3,000	80,000
Dividends declared:						
P Company	10,000					10,000
S Company		5,000		(1a) 4,500	500‡	–0–
Retained earnings, 12/31/X1—carried forward	70,000	25,000	27,000	4,500	2,500	70,000
Balance Sheet						
Cash	29,500	8,000				37,500
Accounts receivable	18,000	3,000				21,000
Inventory	10,000	7,000				17,000
Investment in S Company	67,500		(1a) 4,500	(1b) 18,000 (2) 54,000		–0–
Other assets	73,000	62,000				135,000
	198,000	80,000				210,500
Accounts payable	22,000	5,000				27,000
Other liabilities	6,000					6,000
Capital stock:						
P Company	100,000					100,000
S Company		50,000	(2) 45,000		5,000§	–0–
Retained earnings—brought forward	70,000	25,000	27,000	4,500	2,500	70,000
Minority interest in S Co.					7,500	7,500M
	198,000	80,000	76,500	76,500		210,500

(1a, 1b) To reverse the parent company's entries during 19X1 for subsidiary dividends and its interest in subsidiary earnings. (2) To eliminate the January 1, 19X1, investment account balance against 90% of the corresponding stockholders' equity accounts of the subsidiary.

* 10% × $20,000. † 10% × $10,000. ‡ 10% × $5,000. § 10% × $50,000.

company transaction that must be eliminated in the preparation of consolidated statements. With this qualification in mind, the eliminating entries take the following form:

(1a)	Investment in S Company	4,500	
	Dividends Declared—S Company		4,500
(1b)	Equity in Subsidiary Earnings	18,000	
	Investment in S Company		18,000

With the investment account restored to its beginning-of-year balance (and other accounts reflecting the effects of intercompany transactions eliminated), the final investment elimination entry then follows:

(2)	Capital Stock—S Company	45,000	
	Retained Earnings—S Company........................	9,000	
	Investment in S Company		54,000

If the investment cost had *not* been equal to the parent company's equity in subsidiary net assets at the date of acquisition, a differential would of course have been recognized in this second of the two required investment elimination entries. The recognition and related adjustments of differentials in consolidated statement working papers subsequent to the date of acquisition are explained in Chapter 4.

Each division of the consolidated working paper (Illustration 3–2) provides the requisite data for the preparation of one of the series of consolidated statements. While the working paper is subdivided for this purpose, the links that unite the various divisions are also clearly evident. All items on the "net income" line of the income statement division, including elimination debits and credits, are carried forward to the same line description in the retained earnings statement division. Similarly, the totals on the line of the final balance of retained earnings in this division are carried forward to the identical line description in the balance sheet division. These divisions, each representing a formal consolidated statement, articulate with each other. It may be observed that equality of amounts of elimination debits and credits is not preserved in respect to the first two divisions of the working paper; yet total elimination debits and credits for the three divisions are necessarily balanced. It is additionally important to note that consolidated dividends declared are the parent company's dividend declarations. To the extent that subsidiary dividends were intercompany, they were eliminated; remaining amounts of subsidiary dividends are distributed to nonaffiliate minority shareholders. Accordingly, the consolidated dividends declared represent the earnings distribution of the parent company. In this illustration, subsidiary dividends of $5,000 are distributed: $4,500 to the parent and $500 to minority shareholders. The $4,500 payment to P Company is an intercompany transaction and is eliminated in the first of the two investment elimination entries; the $500 payment to nonaffiliate shareholders is extended in the working papers as the minority interest in subsidiary dividends and is therefore deducted.

Observe that the minority interest is given separate column identification in each division of the consolidated working paper. *The amount of the minority interest in subsidiary net income is calculated on the basis of the subsidiary's recorded net income, without regard to eliminated revenue and expense items* This amount is deducted from the combined net incomes of the affiliates, after eliminations, in arriving at consolidated net income. The working paper also discloses how the equity of minority shareholders in retained earnings and capital stock is calculated in the normal progression from one working paper division to another. Note that the *total* minority interest, $7,500, is equal to the minority shareholders' percentage shareholding in the subsidiary (10 percent) multiplied by the total *recorded* shareholders' equity of the subsidiary ($75,000). This relationship will always hold unless there are unrealized intercompany profits to be dealt with, a topic that is covered in Chapters 7, 8, and 9.

Study of the working paper for this illustration will disclose that *the parent company's net income is equal to consolidated net income; also, the parent company's retained earnings are equal to the consolidated retained earnings.* Necessarily, this condition of equivalence will prevail where the investment account is periodically adjusted to reflect the parent's equity in subsidiary net asset changes. Because of these properties, accountants often refer to application of the equity method of accounting as a "one-line consolidation." The investment account incorporates, in summary form, the net asset position of the subsidiary, and the equity in subsidiary earnings account reflects in a single number the parent's share of the subsidiary's revenue and expenses for the period.

The presence of minority shareholders requires special disclosure in the formal consolidated statements. Their equity in subsidiary net income is indicated in the consolidated income statement as a deduction from the combined net incomes, after eliminations, in arriving at consolidated net income. This is consistent with the usual interpretation of consolidated net income as an amount accruing to the majority shareholders. No explicit disclosure of minority interest is required in the consolidated retained earnings statement, and reference has previously been made to the alternative forms of disclosure for minority interests frequently found in consolidated balance sheets.

The formal consolidated statements for this case are shown in Illustration 3–3.

Illustration 3–3

P COMPANY AND SUBSIDIARY S COMPANY
Consolidated Income Statement
For Year Ended December 31, 19X1

Sales		$118,000
Cost of sales:		
Inventory, January 1, 19X1	$20,000	
Purchases	62,000	
Total	$82,000	
Inventory, December 31, 19X1	17,000	65,000
Gross profit		$ 53,000
Expenses		11,000
Combined net income		$ 42,000
Minority interest in subsidiary net income		2,000
Consolidated net income		$ 40,000

P COMPANY AND SUBSIDIARY S COMPANY
Consolidated Statement of Retained Earnings
For Year Ended December 31, 19X1

Retained earnings, January 1, 19X1	$40,000
Consolidated net income	40,000
Total	$80,000
Dividends declared	10,000
Retained earnings, December 31, 19X1	$70,000

P COMPANY AND SUBSIDIARY S COMPANY
Consolidated Balance Sheet
December 31, 19X1

Assets		Equities		
Cash	$ 37,500	Liabilities:		
Accounts receivable	21,000	Accounts payable		$ 27,000
Inventory	17,000	Other liabilities		6,000
Other assets	135,000	Minority interest:		
		Capital stock	$5,000	
		Retained earnings	2,500	7,500
		Shareholders' equity:		
		Capital stock		100,000
		Retained earnings		70,000
Total assets	$210,500	Total equities		$210,500

Consolidated Statement Working Paper—Second Year Subsequent to Acquisition

The consolidated statement working paper for periods subsequent to the first year after acquisition of subsidiary stock is essentially the same, in respect to details of format, eliminations, and extensions, as in the working paper for the year of acquisition. Nonetheless, it is useful to review the mechanics of the investment elimination entries for a second (or later) year to emphasize the specific steps that are followed.

In the previous illustration, only one period of subsidiary operations separated the preparation of the consolidated statements from the date of the acquisition of subsidiary shares. In such a circumstance, the first set of eliminating entries that adjust the investment account to its beginning-of-year balance also restore the account to the original investment cost. The second eliminating entry—to eliminate the investment account (as adjusted by the preceding set of entries) against the parent's equity in the balances of the stockholders' equity accounts of the subsidiary *as of the beginning of the year*—is then identical (in respect to amounts) to the investment elimination entry made at date of acquisition. However, this equivalence of investment elimination amounts persists for but one year under the equity method.[3] In the second (or later) year after acquisition, this eliminating entry will usually be different from what it was in the first (or prior) year, and its elements must be calculated in accordance with the specified procedure: viz, multiply the parent's percentage ownership interest times the balances of each of the stockholders' equity accounts of the subsidiary *as of the beginning of the year*.

Case 2. Preparation of a consolidated statement working paper for the second year after acquisition is illustrated by modifying the data for Case 1 to include the following 19X2 activities:

	P Company	S Company
Net income for 19X2..................	$44,900	$28,000
Dividends declared, 19X2	15,000	10,000

The investment account at December 31, 19X2, accordingly has a balance of $83,700, as reflected below:

Investment in S Company

Investment cost, January 1, 19X1	54,000	Dividends received from S in 19X1	4,500
Equity in S's 19X1 earnings	18,000	Balance, December 31, 19X1	67,500
	72,000		72,000
Balance, December 31, 19X1	67,500	Dividends received from S in 19X2	9,000
Equity in S's 19X2 earnings	25,200	Balance, December 31, 19X2	83,700
	92,700		92,700
Balance, December 31, 19X2	83,700		

---

[3] The equivalence generally continues indefinitely under the cost method, which is illustrated in the Appendix to this chapter.

The investment elimination entries for this example are as follows:

(1) To reverse the effects of parent company entries in 19X2 reflecting its interest in the activities and operations of, and the receipt of dividends from, the subsidiary (see investment account above for 19X2 entries):

(a) Investment in S Company	9,000	
Dividends Declared—S Company		9,000
(b) Equity in Subsidiary Earnings......................	25,200	
Investment in S Company		25,200

For reasons of efficiency in working paper preparation, it is common to combine this first set of investment elimination entries into one compound investment elimination entry, as follows:

Equity in Subsidiary Earnings	25,200	
Dividends Declared—S Company		9,000
Investment in S Company		16,200

(2) To eliminate the investment account (as adjusted by the preceding entry) against the parent's equity in the balances of the stockholders' equity accounts of the subsidiary as of the beginning of 19X2:

Capital Stock—S Company	45,000	
Retained Earnings—S Company........................	22,500	
Investment in S Company		67,500

In calculating the amounts to be eliminated in the second entry, P Company's percentage ownership in S Company (90 percent) is multiplied times the balances of S Company's Capital Stock and Retained Earnings accounts *as of January 1, 19X2* ($50,000 and $25,000, respectively).

The consolidated statement working paper for this case is shown in Illustration 3–4. The reader may again note in this illustration that the balances accumulated in the parent company's accounts for retained earnings, net income for the year, and dividends declared are identical in amount to their consolidated statement equivalents. Further, the total minority inter-

Illustration 3–4

P COMPANY AND SUBSIDIARY S COMPANY
Consolidated Statement Working Paper
For Year Ended December 31, 19X2

	P Company	S Company	Eliminations Dr.	Eliminations Cr.	Minority Interest	Consolidated
Income Statement						
Sales	96,000	63,000				159,000
Equity in subsidiary earnings	25,200		(1) 25,200			–0–
Inventory (12/31)	14,200	9,200				23,400
Total credits	135,400	72,200				182,400
Inventory (1/1)	10,000	7,000				17,000
Purchases	58,000	29,100				87,100
Expenses	22,500	8,100				30,600
Total debits	90,500	44,200				134,700
	44,900	28,000				47,700
Minority interest in net income—S Company					2,800*	2,800
Net income—carried forward	44,900	28,000	25,200	–0–	2,800	44,900
Retained Earnings Statement						
Retained earnings, 1/1/X2:						
P Company	70,000					70,000
S Company		25,000	(2) 22,500		2,500†	–0–
Net income—brought forward	44,900	28,000	25,200	–0–	2,800	44,900
	114,900	53,000			5,300	114,900
Dividends declared:						
P Company	15,000					15,000
S Company		10,000		(1) 9,000	1,000‡	–0–
Retained earnings, 12/31/X2—carried forward	99,900	43,000	47,700	9,000	4,300	99,900
Balance Sheet						
Cash	31,000	12,000				43,000
Accounts receivable	22,000	19,000				41,000
Inventory	14,200	9,200				23,400
Investment in S Company	83,700			(1) 16,200 (2) 67,500		–0–
Other assets	83,000	64,300				147,300
	233,900	104,500				254,700
Accounts payable	30,000	9,000				39,000
Other liabilities	4,000	2,500				6,500
Capital stock:						
P Company	100,000					100,000
S Company		50,000	(2) 45,000		5,000§	–0–
Retained earnings—brought forward	99,900	43,000	47,700	9,000	4,300	99,900
Minority interest in S Co.					9,300	9,300M
	233,900	104,500	92,700	92,700		254,700

(1) To reverse the parent company's entries for subsidiary dividends and its interest in subsidiary earnings.
(2) To eliminate the January 1, 19X2, investment account balance against 90% of the stockholders' equity account balances of the subsidiary.
  * 10% × $28,000.   † 10% × $25,000.   ‡ 10% × $10,000.   § 10% × $50,000.

est ($9,300) is again equal to the minority shareholders' percentage interest in the total shareholders' equity of the subsidiary (10 percent $\times$ $93,000). **Relationship between Investment Account Balance and Net Assets of the Subsidiary.** The equity method of accounting for an investment in the common stock of an affiliate increases the investment account as the affiliate's net assets are increased by operations and decreases it when the affiliate's net assets are decreased by cash dividends. The increases and decreases in the investment account balance are in proportion to the investor company's percentage interest in an affiliate. Since we have assumed in this chapter that the original investment cost was equal to the investor's acquired monetary interest in the affiliate, it follows that the investment account (adjusted in accordance with the equity method) will maintain this proportional relationship at all future points in time. Thus, for our example, the investment account balance of $83,700 on December 31, 19X2, continues to reflect P Company's equity in S Company's recorded net assets (90 percent $\times$ $93,000 = $83,700).

Other Intercompany Transactions

Discussion has heretofore centered on those intercompany transactions involving the purchase of subsidiary stock, reciprocal debtor-creditor relationships among affiliate companies, and the declaration of subsidiary dividends. If there are other intercompany transactions during a period of affiliation, their effects must also be eliminated. One such transaction, which occurs with relative frequency, is the sale of merchandise by one affiliate to another. Since the consolidated income statement should exhibit only those revenues and expenses which result from transactions with nonaffiliates, it is appropriate to eliminate the *total amount* of intercompany sales by a debit to Sales and a credit to Purchases (or Cost of Sales) in the consolidated working paper. Special elimination problems arise if some of the items in the intercompany merchandise shipments are not subsequently resold by the purchasing affiliate during the current period and are accordingly included in its final inventory. The complications created by the profit residue in the final inventory are dealt with in detail in Chapter 7.

Other types of intercompany revenue-expense transactions that must be similarly eliminated in the consolidated working papers include transactions arising from intercorporate financing, or the rendering of services by one affiliate to another. All evidences of these transactions must be removed from the consolidated statements to avoid duplicate measurement. Reciprocal accounts, for which eliminating entries must be made in the consolidated statement working paper, include interest income–interest expense, management fee income–management fee expense, commissions earned–commissions expense, and various others.

Multicompany Affiliations

Our examples to this point have assumed two-party affiliations, a parent company and a single subsidiary. We now will consider the case of a three-party affiliation. It should be noted that an increase in the number of subsidiaries only increases the number of accounts to be dealt with and the eliminations to be made. The principles of consolidated statement preparation developed in the context of two-party affiliations remain unchanged. **Case 3.** The affiliation diagram for this example is as follows:

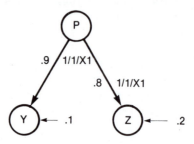

The December 31, 19X1, trial balances for companies, P, Y, and Z are given in Illustration 3–5. The reader should note carefully the additional information included at the foot of the trial balances because this information provides the basis for several adjustments and/or eliminations in the consolidated statement working paper (see Illustration 3–6).

One may observe in Illustration 3–6 that again the parent company's net income and retained earnings are equal in amount to consolidated net income and retained earnings. Further, the investment elimination entries for the two subsidiaries are dealt with separately and are determined for each subsidiary in the same manner previously illustrated for single subsidiary cases. The elimination of intercompany sales is handled in accordance with the discussion in the preceding section, and produces amounts for consolidated sales and purchases that reflect transactions with outside parties. Finally, the "adjustment" is necessary to record on the books of Z Company the transfer of cash from P Company. Unlike eliminating "entries" which are not recorded on the books of any affiliate but merely on the consolidated statement working paper, this adjustment would be recorded on the books of Z Company.

Reconsideration of Basic Definitions

In grappling with the various consolidated statement working paper techniques, one must be careful not to lose touch with the objectives of the process and the underlying definitions that guide our efforts. The objective is to combine the assets, liabilities, revenues, and expenses of the affiliates such that the resulting consolidated financial statements reflect the activi-

Illustration 3–5

	P Company		Y Company		Z Company	
Cash	$ 34,300		$ 8,000		$ 4,000	
Accounts receivable	18,000		3,000		6,000	
Inventory (1/1)	16,000		4,000		3,000	
Investment in Y Company	67,500					
Investment in Z Company	43,200					
Other assets	35,700		62,000		44,000	
Accounts payable		$ 22,000		$ 5,000		$ 4,000
Other liabilities		6,000				1,000
Capital stock		100,000		50,000		40,000
Retained earnings (1/1)		40,000		10,000		5,000
Dividends declared	10,000		5,000		6,000	
Sales		78,000		40,000		30,000
Equity in subsidiary earnings		30,000				
Purchases	42,000		20,000		12,000	
Expenses	9,300		3,000		5,000	
	$276,000	$276,000	$105,000	$105,000	$80,000	$80,000
Inventory (12/31)	$ 10,000		$ 7,000		$ 5,000	

Additional information:
1. P Company acquires 90% of the capital stock of Y Company on January 1, 19X1, for $54,000. On the same date, P Company acquired 80% of the capital stock of Z Company for $36,000.
2. On December 30, 19X1, P Company transferred $1,000 cash to Z Company in partial settlement of a $3,000 obligation, classified by P Company as "Other liabilities." As of December 31, this transfer was not yet recorded by Z Company.
3. The sales of merchandise by Y Company to Z Company during 19X1 were $5,000 (ignore the question of unconfirmed, or unrealized, inventory profit).

ties and financial position of the group as if it were a single (economic) entity. In pursuit of this objective, the definitions of consolidated net income and consolidated retained earnings (see pages 83–84) guide our procedural efforts. It is perhaps useful at this point to reconsider and elaborate upon these basic definitions in the context of the numerical data of Case. 3.

Consolidated Net Income.   Consolidated net income was previously defined as a residual value accruing to the majority shareholders, that is, the shareholders of the parent company. This residual value is produced in the consolidated working paper by combining the revenues, expenses, gains, and losses of the affiliated companies after eliminating intercompany transactions and the parent's recorded equity in subsidiary earnings, and then deducting the amounts of minority interests in the net incomes of the subsidiaries. But consolidated net income can also be determined independent of the consolidated working paper by working only with the net income figures for the affiliates and certain key figures from the eliminating entries. This independent determination can be made using either of two schedular methods, which are labeled the *incremental approach* and the *residual approach*. Since these two methods embody in summary fashion the basic concepts underlying consolidated statement preparation, the authors

Illustration 3–6

P COMPANY AND SUBSIDIARIES
Consolidated Statement Working Paper
For Year Ended December 31, 19X1

	P Company	Y Company	Z Company	Adjustments and Eliminations Dr.	Cr.	Minority Interest Y Company	Z Company	Consolidated
Income Statement								
Sales	78,000	40,000	30,000	(6) 5,000 (1) 18,000 (3) 12,000				143,000
Equity in subsidiary earnings	30,000							–0–
Inventory (12/31)	10,000	7,000	5,000		(6) 5,000			22,000
Total credits	118,000	47,000	35,000					165,000
Inventory (1/1)	16,000	4,000	3,000					23,000
Purchases	42,000	20,000	12,000					69,000
Expenses	9,300	3,000	5,000					17,300
Total debits	67,300	27,000	20,000					109,300
	50,700	20,000	15,000					55,700
Minority interest in net income of—								
Y Company—10% of $20,000						2,000		[2,000]
Z Company—20% of $15,000							3,000	[3,000]
Net income—carried forward	50,700	20,000	15,000	35,000	5,000	2,000	3,000	50,700
Retained Earnings Statement								
Retained earnings, 1/1/X1:								
P Company	40,000							40,000
Y Company		10,000		(2) 9,000		1,000		–0–
Z Company			5,000	(4) 4,000			1,000	–0–
Net income—brought forward	50,700	20,000	15,000	35,000	5,000	2,000	3,000	50,700
Dividends declared:								
P Company	10,000							10,000
Y Company		5,000			(1) 4,500	500		–0–
Z Company			6,000		(3) 4,800		1,200	–0–
Retained earnings, 12/31/X1—carried forward	80,700	25,000	14,000	48,000	14,300	2,500	2,800	80,700

Balance Sheet

	P Company	Y Company	Z Company	Adjustments and Eliminations Dr.	Adjustments and Eliminations Cr.	Minority Interest	Consolidated
Cash	34,300	8,000	4,000	(a) 1,000			47,300
Accounts receivable	18,000	3,000	6,000		(a) 1,000		24,000
Inventory	10,000	7,000	5,000				22,000
Investment in Y Company	67,500				(1) 13,500 (2) 54,000		–0–
Investment in Z Company	43,200				(3) 7,200 (4) 36,000		–0–
Other assets	35,700	62,000	44,000				141,700
	208,700	80,000	59,000				235,000
Accounts payable	22,000	5,000	4,000				31,000
Other liabilities	6,000		1,000	(5) 2,000			5,000
Capital stock:							
P Company	100,000						100,000
Y Company		50,000		(2) 45,000		5,000	–0–
Z Company			40,000	(4) 32,000		8,000	–0–
Retained earnings—brought forward	80,700	25,000	14,000	48,000	14,300	2,500 / 2,800	80,700
Minority interest in Y Company						7,500	7,500M
Minority interest in Z Company						10,800	10,800M
	208,700	80,000	59,000	128,000	128,000		235,000

[deduction]

Explanation of adjustments and eliminations:

(a) Adjustment for unrecorded cash receipt by Z Company. (The obligation from P Company is assumed to be reflected in the accounts receivable of Z Company.)

(1) To reverse the parent company's entries during 19X1 for Y Company dividends and its interest in Y Company earnings.

(2) To eliminate the January 1, 19X1, investment (in Y Company) account balance against 90% of the corresponding stockholders' equity accounts of Y Company.

(3) To reverse the parent company's entries during 19X1 for Z Company dividends and its interest in Z Company earnings.

(4) To eliminate the January 1, 19X1, investment (in Z Company) account balance against 80% of the corresponding stockholders' equity accounts of Z Company.

(5) Elimination of intercompany debt.

(6) Elimination of intercompany sales.

believe special attention should be devoted to the discussion that follows. Additionally, frequent references to these analyses will be found in subsequent chapters.

Incremental Approach to Consolidated Net Income.   Under this approach, consolidated net income is defined as the parent company's net income (loss) from its own operations, increased (decreased) by its equity in subsidiary net income (loss) for the period. In this definition, "net income from its own operations" should be interpreted to include all revenue and expense elements recognized by the parent company during the period *except* income arising from its interest in the subsidiary. Thus, if the current period *reported net income* of a parent company following the equity method of accounting for its investment is available, the parent's net income from its own operations is determined by subtracting the amount of the equity in subsidiary earnings recognized in the current period from the reported net income. If the parent used the cost method of accounting for its investment, the parent's net income from its own operations is determined by subtracting the amount of dividend income from the subsidiary recognized in the current period from the reported net income.

Using the data in Case 3, consolidated net income is determined under this approach as follows:

Parent company's net income from its own operations for 19X1 ($50,700 − $30,000)		$20,700
Increased by—		
Parent company's equity in subsidiaries' net income for 19X1:		
Equity in Y Company's net income (90% × $20,000)	$18,000	
Equity in Z Company's net income (80% × $15,000)	12,000	30,000
Consolidated net income for 19X1		$50,700

As expected, our schedular calculation of consolidated net income yields an amount that is equal to the parent's reported net income (under the equity method of accounting). Indeed, the schedule reveals why this equivalence must always result. The two components of the incremental definition of consolidated net income—(1) the parent's income from its own operations and (2) the parent's equity in subsidiary net income— embody exactly all of the elements of revenue and expense that are recognized under the equity method of accounting. This particular schedular calculation is especially useful when the effects of confirmed and unconfirmed profits from certain types of intercompany transactions are examined in Chapters 7, 8, and 9.

Residual Approach to Consolidated Net Income.   This method employs the same arithmetic processes found in the previously illustrated working papers. Yet attention in this schedule focuses only on summary totals—in particular, the totals of each column of the income statement division of the consolidated statement working paper. The calculation begins with the addition of the *reported* net incomes of the affiliates. From this sum of net incomes is deducted the *net* elimination in the income statement division of the consolidated working paper, that is, the excess of debit eliminations over credit eliminations. The combined net income *remainder* reflects the total equity of all shareholders—both majority and minority. The separation of their interests is accomplished by first calculating the value claim of the minority shareholders. After deducting this value from the total equity, the residual claim of the majority shareholders, or consolidated net income, remains.

Using again the data in Case 3, consolidated net income is determined under this approach as follows:

P Company's net income for 19X1....................................		$50,700
Y Company's net income for 19X1....................................		20,000
Z Company's net income for 19X1...................................		15,000
		$85,700
Less net debit elimination—P Company's recorded interest in subsidiary earnings*		30,000
Total equity..		$55,700
Less minority interest in subsidiary net income:		
Y Company (10% × $20,000).....................................	$2,000	
Z Company (20% × $15,000).....................................	3,000	5,000
Consolidated net income		$50,700

* If the parent used the cost method of accounting for its investment, this net debit elimination would be the parent's recorded dividend income from the subsidiary.

It should be noted that since the elimination of intercompany sales in Case 3 did not result in a *net* debit (or credit) elimination in the income statement division of the consolidated statement working paper, it is not included in this summary calculation of consolidated net income.

Consolidated Retained Earnings. Consolidated retained earnings may be analyzed in a manner similar to that used to analyze consolidated net income. However, when the parent company uses the equity method of accounting, this analysis is generally not a productive venture. Therefore, we merely note again for possible computational convenience that consolidated retained earnings may be simply viewed as consolidated retained earnings at the beginning of the period, increased by consolidated net income, and reduced by the parent company's dividends declared. Applying this definition to the data of Case 3, and recalling that consolidated retained earnings at date of acquisition is equal to the parent company's retained earnings, the December 31, 19X1, consolidated retained earnings balance is calculated as follows:

Consolidated retained earnings, January 1, 19X1..........	$40,000
Consolidated net income for 19X1......................	50,700
	$90,700
P Company dividends declared in 19X1.................	10,000
Consolidated retained earnings, December 31, 19X1.......	$80,700

Appendix A: Illustration of Consolidated Statement Working Paper Techniques when the Investment Account Is Carried under the Cost Method

The consolidated statement techniques described in this and succeeding chapters *are usually based on the assumption that the investment account is carried under the equity method*. However, the following paragraphs illustrate briefly the mechanics of consolidation under the cost method. Recall that regardless which method is used by the parent company to account for its investment in the subsidiary, the consolidated financial statements will be the same in all respects. To emphasize this point, the data used for our two illustrations will reflect the same economic events as are assumed in Cases 1 and 2 in the main body of the chapter.

Consolidated Statement Working Paper—First Year Subsequent to Acquisition

Case A–1. It is assumed, as in Case 1, that P Company acquired 90 percent of the capital stock of S Company on January 1, 19X1, at a cost of $54,000. The trial balances for the two affiliates at December 31, 19X1, are as follows:

	P Company		S Company	
Cash	$ 29,500		$ 8,000	
Accounts receivable.............	18,000		3,000	
Inventory (1/1)	16,000		4,000	
Investment in S Company........	54,000			
Other assets....................	73,000		62,000	
Accounts payable...............		$ 22,000		$ 5,000
Other liabilities.................		6,000		
Capital stock		100,000		50,000
Retained earnings (1/1)...........		40,000		10,000
Dividends declared	10,000		5,000	
Sales		78,000		40,000
Dividend income		4,500		
Purchases......................	42,000		20,000	
Expenses	8,000		3,000	
	$250,500	$250,500	$105,000	$105,000
Inventory (12/31)	$ 10,000		$ 7,000	

The account balances in this trial balance correspond exactly with the balances in Case 1 in the chapter, except for the income that has been recognized under the two different methods and the balance of the investment account.

Under the cost method, the parent company does not give formal accounting recognition to its equity in subsidiary earnings, and the balance of the investment account remains equal to the original cost of the investment. Therefore, the investment elimination entry at the end of the first year of operations is the same as it was at date of acquisition; that is, it continues to relate to subsidiary net worth balances existing at date of acquisition. Thus, for our data, the investment elimination entry at December 31, 19X1, is:

(1) Capital Stock—S Company	45,000	
Retained Earnings—S Company	9,000	
Investment in S Company		54,000

The parent company has recognized dividends declared by the subsidiary during the year as dividend income. Since the intercompany dividends are not properly included in a summation of the two companies' revenues, expenses, gains, and losses arising from transactions *with outside parties* (as if the two companies were a single economic entity), the dividend income of the parent company must be eliminated against the dividends declared by the subsidiary. Thus, the second eliminating entry is:

(2) Dividend Income	4,500	
Dividends Declared—S Company		4,500

The consolidated statement working paper for this case is shown in Illustration 3–7. A comparison of this working paper with the consolidated statement working paper in Illustration 3–2 will confirm the *identity of all amounts in the consolidated column*. Thus as was previously asserted, the choice between the cost and the equity methods of accounting for the investment on the books of the parent company does not affect the results reflected in the consolidated statements. The choice does affect the sources and amounts of income as well as the balance of the investment account on the parent company's books and in the *unconsolidated* financial statements of the parent company; this may be confirmed by comparing the first columns of the two working papers.

Consolidated Statement Working Paper—Second Year Subsequent to Acquisition

Case A–2. The data for Case A–1 are modified to include the following 19X2 activities:

	P Company	S Company
Net income for 19X2...............	$28,700	$28,000
Dividends declared, 19X2	15,000	10,000

Note that P Company's net income again differs from that shown in Case 2 in the chapter because the parent company is recognizing income from S Company's operations on the basis of dividends declared by S Company during 19X2, not income reported by S Company for 19X2.

The eliminating entries for this example are as follows:

(1) To eliminate the investment account against the parent's equity in the balances of the stockholders' equity accounts of the subsidiary *as of the date of acquisition:*

Capital Stock—S Company	45,000	
Retained Earnings—S Company.........................	9,000	
Investment in S Company		54,000

(2) To eliminate intercompany dividend income of the parent against dividends declared by the subsidiary:

Dividend Income...	9,000	
Dividends Declared—S Company		9,000

Note that again the investment elimination entry relates to subsidiary net worth balances existing at date of acquisition. *This relationship will continue to hold in succeeding years as long as the investment account balance remains equal to the original acquisition cost and there are no realignments of the subsidiary's equity components.*[4]

The consolidated statement working paper for this case is shown in Illustration 3–8. Note that the income statement and balance sheet divisions of the consolidated statement working paper for periods subsequent to the first year after acquisition of subsidiary stock are essentially the same

---

[4] Recall from our initial discussion of the cost method that the investment account is changed (reduced) for only two reasons: (1) liquidating dividends paid by the subsidiary and (2) a material and apparently permanent impairment of the value of the investment (usually evidenced by a series of reported losses). The most common realignment of the subsidiary's equity components occurs with the declaration of a stock dividend by the subsidiary.

Illustration 3–7

P COMPANY AND SUBSIDIARY S COMPANY
Consolidated Statement Working Paper
For Year Ended December 31, 19X1

	P Company	S Company	Eliminations Dr.	Eliminations Cr.	Minority Interest	Consolidated
Income Statement						
Sales	78,000	40,000				118,000
Dividend income	4,500		(2) 4,500			–0–
Inventory (12/31)	10,000	7,000				17,000
Total credits	92,500	47,000				135,000
Inventory (1/1)	16,000	4,000				20,000
Purchases	42,000	20,000				62,000
Expenses	8,000	3,000				11,000
Total debits	66,000	27,000				93,000
	26,500	20,000				42,000
Minority interest in net income—S Company					2,000*	2,000
Net income—carried forward	26,500	20,000	4,500	–0–	2,000	40,000
Retained Earnings Statement						
Retained earnings, 1/1/X1:						
P Company	40,000					40,000
S Company		10,000	(1) 9,000		1,000†	–0–
Net income—brought forward	26,500	20,000	4,500	–0–	2,000	40,000
	66,500	30,000			3,000	80,000
Dividends declared:						
P Company	10,000					10,000
S Company		5,000		(2) 4,500	500‡	–0–
Retained earnings, 12/31/X1—carried forward	56,500	25,000	13,500	4,500	2,500	70,000
Balance Sheet						
Cash	29,500	8,000				37,500
Accounts receivable	18,000	3,000				21,000
Inventory	10,000	7,000				17,000
Investment in S Company	54,000			(1) 54,000		–0–
Other assets	73,000	62,000				135,000
	184,500	80,000				210,500
Accounts payable	22,000	5,000				27,000
Other liabilities	6,000					6,000
Capital stock:						
P Company	100,000					100,000
S Company		50,000	(1) 45,000		5,000§	–0–
Retained earnings—brought forward	56,500	25,000	13,500	4,500	2,500	70,000
Minority interest in S Co.					7,500	7,500M
	184,500	80,000	58,500	58,500		210,500

(1) Elimination of investment in subsidiary stock. (2) Elimination of intercompany dividends.
* 10% × $20,000.   † 10% × $10,000.   ‡ 10% × $5,000.   § 10% × $50,000.

Illustration 3–8

P COMPANY AND SUBSIDIARY S COMPANY
Consolidated Statement Working Paper
For Year Ended December 31, 19X2

	P Company	S Company	Eliminations Dr.	Eliminations Cr.	Minority Interest	Consolidated
Income Statement						
Sales	96,000	63,000				159,000
Dividend income	9,000		(2) 9,000			–0–
Inventory (12/31)	14,200	9,200				23,400
Total credits	119,200	72,200				182,400
Inventory (1/1)	10,000	7,000				17,000
Purchases	58,000	29,100				87,100
Expenses	22,500	8,100				30,600
Total debits	90,500	44,200				134,700
	28,700	28,000				47,700
Minority interest in net income—S Company					2,800*	2,800
Net income—carried forward	28,700	28,000	9,000	–0–	2,800	44,900
Retained Earnings Statement						
Retained earnings, 1/1/X2:						
P Company	56,500					56,500
S Company		25,000	(1) 9,000		2,500†	13,500
Net income—brought forward	28,700	28,000	9,000	–0–	2,800	44,900
	85,200	53,000			5,300	114,900
Dividends declared:						
P Company	15,000					15,000
S Company		10,000		(2) 9,000	1,000‡	–0–
Retained earnings, 12/31/X2—carried forward	70,200	43,000	18,000	9,000	4,300	99,900
Balance Sheet						
Cash	31,000	12,000				43,000
Accounts receivable	22,000	19,000				41,000
Inventory	14,200	9,200				23,400
Investment in S Company	54,000			(1) 54,000		–0–
Other assets	83,000	64,300				147,300
	204,200	104,500				254,700
Accounts payable	30,000	9,000				39,000
Other liabilities	4,000	2,500				6,500
Capital stock:						
P Company	100,000					100,000
S Company		50,000	(1) 45,000		5,000§	–0–
Retained earnings—brought forward	70,200	43,000	18,000	9,000	4,300	99,900
Minority interest in S Co.					9,300	9,300M
	204,200	104,500	63,000	63,000		254,700

(1) Elimination of investment in subsidiary stock. (2) Elimination of intercompany dividends.
* 10% × $28,000. † 10% × $25,000. ‡ 10% × $10,000. § 10% × $50,000.

in respect to details of format, eliminations, and extensions, as in the working paper for the year of acquisition. However, one significant difference should be noted in respect to the retained earnings division. The previous illustration clearly indicated that the amount of subsidiary retained earnings at acquisition is partially eliminated with the residual amount extended to the minority interest column. In the consolidated statement working papers of subsequent years, however, it is necessary to recognize the parent company's equity in the *changes* in a subsidiary's retained earnings from the date of acquisition to the beginning of the current year. Under the equity method, this equity is reflected in the retained earnings of the parent company as a consequence of the entries made by the parent to record it in prior years. Under the cost method, recognition of the equity in the "changes" (undistributed earnings from date of acquisition to the beginning of the current year) is accomplished by extending to the Consolidated column of the retained earnings working paper division that part of a subsidiary's retained earnings at the beginning of the year that is neither eliminated as "purchased" retained earnings nor extended to the Minority Interest column. Thus, the amount of retained earnings of S Company on January 1, 19X2, to be extended, $16,000 ($25,000 balance less $9,000 eliminated as "purchased" retained earnings), is allocated $2,500 to minority shareholders and $13,500 to the majority shareholders. The minority interest is 10 percent of the subsidiary's January 1, 19X2, retained earnings balance, that is, 10 percent of $25,000, or $2,500; the majority interest is 90 percent of the *undistributed* subsidiary earnings from the date of acquisition to the *beginning* of the current period, that is, 90 percent of ($25,000 − $10,000), or $13,500.

With these minor modifications in working paper techniques, the resulting balances in the Consolidated column of Illustration 3–8 are again identical to the amounts reflected in the Consolidated column in Illustration 3–4.

Schedular Calculation of Consolidated Net Income

As was pointed out in the main body of the chapter, consolidated net income may be independently determined using either of two schedular methods, labeled the "incremental approach" and the "residual approach." The basic properties of these calculations are the same regardless of whether the parent uses the equity or the cost method of accounting for its investment. The only difference when the parent employs the cost method is that dividend income, rather than equity in subsidiary earnings, is used to determine the parent's net income from its own operations in the incremental calculation and the net debit elimination in the residual calculation. These calculations are displayed in Illustration 3–9 for the data for Case A–2.

Illustration 3–9

SCHEDULAR CALCULATIONS OF 19X2
CONSOLIDATED NET INCOME
(Case A–2 Data)

Incremental approach:

P Company's net income from its own operations for 19X2 ($28,700 − $9,000)	$19,700
Increased by P Company's equity in S Company's net income for 19X2 (90% × $28,000)	25,200
Consolidated net income for 19X2	$44,900

Residual approach:

P Company's net income for 19X2	$28,700
S Company's net income for 19X2	28,000
	$56,700
Less net debit elimination—P Company's recorded dividend income from S Company	9,000
Total equity	$47,700
Less minority interest in S Company's net income for 19X2 (10% × $28,000)	2,800
Consolidated net income for 19X2	$44,900

Schedular Calculation of Consolidated Retained Earnings

The schedular calculation of consolidated retained earnings under the cost method differs from the calculation illustrated for the equity method because consolidated retained earnings at the beginning of the period is usually not included in the available data (except in the year of acquisition). Under the equity method, the balance of the parent company's beginning retained earnings is equal to beginning consolidated retained earnings. Under the cost method, that is usually not the case. However, a form of the incremental approach is available that is closely linked to our explanation of the working paper procedure for years subsequent to acquisition. In particular, we observe that the parent company's retained earnings differs from consolidated retained earnings when the subsidiary has *undistributed earnings since the date of acquisition*. Therefore, we will calculate consolidated retained earnings as the sum of the parent company's retained earnings and the parent company's share of the subsidiary's undistributed earnings since acquisition. This calculation is illustrated below for December 31, 19X2, using the data of Case A–2.

P Company's retained earnings, December 31, 19X2	$70,200
Increased by P Company's equity in S Company's undistributed net income since acquisition 90% × ($43,000 − $10,000)	29,700
Consolidated retained earnings, December 31, 19X2	$99,900

Observe that the subsidiary's undistributed earnings since acquisition is merely the difference between the subsidiary's retained earnings balance at the end of the period ($43,000) and its retained earnings balance at the date of acquisition ($10,000). In the consolidated statement working paper for the year ended December 31, 19X2, the undistributed earnings of S Company at the *beginning* of the year were extended to the Consolidated column because the "carryforward" of consolidated net income for the year from the income statement division of the working paper picked up the parent's share of the subsidiary's current earnings (with current year dividends eliminated). In the schedular calculation, however, our starting point is the parent's *ending* retained earnings balance (which includes the effect of current period dividends by the subsidiary), and thus the undistributed earnings calculation must also be made as of the end of the period.

Appendix B: Accounting for Investments in Joint Ventures

A joint venture is an entity that is owned and operated by a small group of investors termed *venturers*. Each venturer usually plays an active role in the management of the joint venture, such that no one venturer can be said to be in control. That is, control is usually joint in the sense that consent of all venturers is required to decide major operating and financing issues. Joint ventures are utilized as a convenient means of entering foreign markets, e.g., a domestic corporation enters into a joint venture with a foreign corporation, or even with a foreign government. They are also utilized to enter into particularly risky undertakings requiring large capital investment, such as construction and operation of nuclear power plants, real estate development, and oil and gas exploration.

A joint venture may assume any of the following legal forms:

a. A corporate joint venture—in which the venture is organized as a corporation. Rights and rewards of ownership are determined on the basis of shares held.

b. A general partnership—in which the venture is organized as a partnership with each partner assuming unlimited liability. Rights and rewards of ownership are determined by the partnership agreement.

c. A limited partnership—in which the venture is organized as a partnership; but one or more general partners have unlimited liability, and one or more limited partners have limited liability. Rights and rewards of ownership are determined by the partnership agreement. Limited partners usually manage the jointly owned net assets, subject to restrictions placed upon them by general partners.

d. An undivided interest (often termed an *unincorporated joint venture*)—in which ownership of net assets takes neither the form of a corporation nor a partnership. Rights and rewards of ownership are determined by contract among the venturers.

In recent years, the joint venture has been used with increasing frequency. Because of this, the accounting for an investment in a joint venture on the part of a venturer is an important matter. Unfortunately, there is little authoritative guidance on accounting for investments in joint ventures. Extant guidance reflects a disturbing degree of legal form dominating substance. Custom is also reflected.

Corporate Joint Ventures

APB Opinion No. 18, "The Equity Method of Accounting for Investments in Common Stock," paragraph 16, mandates the equity method of accounting for investments in corporate joint ventures (in financial statements issued to shareholders). However, no mention is made of the venturer's ability to exercise significant influence over the operating and financial policies of the venture. Thus, the equity method is appropriate even if the venturer holds a quite small percentage of the shares of the venture. Presumably, this universal application of the equity method is a consequence of the usual case in which the venture is subject to the *joint* control of all venturers (such that *each* venturer thus exercises a significant influence). However, paragraph 3 defines a subsidiary as a corporation that is controlled by another corporation. If one venturer indeed exercises control over the corporate joint venture, the venture is deemed a subsidiary and *not* a corporate joint venture. Thus, the controlling venturer would account for its investment by applying the principles applicable to investments in subsidiaries, i.e., issue consolidated statements if the other criteria for consolidating a subsidiary are met.[5] Similarly, the other venturers would account for their investment using either the cost method or the equity method, depending upon whether they exercise significant influence over the operating and financial policies of the venture.

Partnerships and Undivided Interests

An interpretation of *APB Opinion No. 18* deals with use of the equity method in the case of joint ventures organized as partnerships or undivided interests. However, the interpretation states only that "many of the provisions of *APB Opinion No. 18* would be appropriate in accounting for

---

[5] See Chapter 2 for discussion of the criteria for consolidating a subsidiary.

these unincorporated entities."[6] The interpretation provides examples of these provisions in which a venturer includes in its income the venturer's share of profits or losses of the joint venture and eliminates intercompany profits and losses.[7] Moreover, since income tax effects of partnerships and undivided interests accrue directly to the venturers and are not recorded by the venture, a venturer should accrue income tax effects attributable to the venturer's share of profits or losses.

Particular care must be exercised in determining a venturer's share of profits and losses, and in accruing income tax effects attributable to these profits and losses. For example, a venture agreement may purport to allocate all depreciation expense to one venturer and to allocate all other revenue and expense items equally. However, the agreement may also stipulate that all cash distributions (including those made in liquidation) are to be divided equally.[8] In such an agreement, the purported allocation of depreciation expense has no substance beyond the determination of short-run taxable income. Therefore, all venturers would record equal shares of the venture profit or loss. Differences between these recorded shares of venture profit or loss and each venturer's actual taxable income (arising from the asymmetric allocation of depreciation expense for tax purposes) would be accounted for as timing differences.

Proportionate Consolidation

In some industries, especially the oil and gas industry, accounting for investments in *undivided interests* has gone beyond the "one-line consolidation" approach of the equity method, and has taken the form of a so-called proportionate consolidation (also referred to as a pro rata consolidation). In a proportionate consolidation, a venturer presents in the balance sheet its proportionate share of *each* venture asset and liability. Similarly, the income statement presents the venturer's proportionate share of *each* revenue and expense item. The interpretation sanctions this presentation in cases where it is an established industry tradition.

In application, proportionate consolidation differs from conventional consolidation in two respects. First, it is applied regardless of whether the venturer has control. Second, no minority interest appears. Rather, the

---

[6] *Accounting Interpretation No. 2 of APB Opinion No. 18,* "Investments in Partnerships and Ventures" (New York: AICPA, 1971).

[7] Intercompany profits and losses are discussed in Chapters 7, 8, and 9.

[8] Such provisions enable short-run reductions in taxable income for the venturer allocated the depreciation expense and short-run increases in taxable income for the others. Over the life of the venture, however, the equality of cash distributions assures that all venturers will have equal taxable income (and therefore that the short-run reductions and increases will eventually reverse themselves). It cannot be assumed, however, that the asymmetric allocation of depreciation expense will necessarily be allowed for income tax purposes.

minority interest is simply excluded from every asset, liability, revenue, and expense item.

Balance sheet and income statement data relating to a venturer and a joint venture (in which a 60 percent interest is held) are displayed in the first two columns of Illustration 3–10. In Illustration 3–10, it has been

Illustration 3–10

VENTURER AND JOINT VENTURE
Conventional Consolidation and Proportionate Consolidation

	Venturer	Joint Venture	Conventional Consolidation	Proportionate Consolidation
Income statement:				
Sales......................	$1,000,000	$ 300,000	$1,300,000	$1,180,000
Equity in venture earnings....	60,000			
	$1,060,000	$ 300,000	$1,300,000	$1,180,000
Cost of goods sold	$ 500,000	$ 150,000	$ 650,000	$ 590,000
Other expenses	240,000	50,000	290,000	270,000
Minority interest			40,000	
	$ 740,000	$ 200,000	$ 980,000	$ 860,000
Net income.................	$ 320,000	$ 100,000	$ 320,000	$ 320,000
Balance sheet:				
Cash.......................	$ 420,000	$ 40,000	$ 460,000	$ 444,000
Inventory	600,000		600,000	600,000
Investment in venture	480,000			
Other assets	1,500,000	$1,060,000	$2,560,000	$2,136,000
	$3,000,000	$1,100,000	$3,620,000	$3,180,000
Accounts payable	$2,000,000	$ 300,000	$2,300,000	$2,180,000
Minority interest			320,000	
Capital stock...............	600,000		600,000	600,000
Retained earnings...........	400,000		400,000	400,000
Venturers' equity		800,000		
	$3,000,000	$1,100,000	$3,620,000	$3,180,000

assumed that the venturer uses the equity method for bookkeeping purposes. The second two columns of Illustration 3–10 display conventional and proportionate consolidations. Comparison of the income statement data as portrayed in the conventional and proportionate consolidations reveals equal amounts of net income. In the case of conventional consolidation, all of the venture's revenue and expense items are included, with the attendant recognition of minority interest in the amount of 40 percent of venture net income. In the case of proportionate consolidation, the income statement simply excludes 40 percent of the venture's sales, cost of goods sold, and other expenses. With respect to the balance sheet data, the conventional consolidation includes all of the venture's assets and liabilities, with attendant recognition of minority interest in the amount of 40 percent of the venture's net assets. In contrast, the proportionate consolidation simply excludes 40 percent of the venture's cash, inventory, other assets, and accounts payable.

The rationale underlying proportionate consolidation for undivided interests centers largely on the disclosure of liabilities. The venturers are guarantors, jointly and singly, of the obligations of the venture. The equity method's one-line disclosure of only the venturer's share of venture net assets (in the investment account) is not entirely consistent with this fact. That is, reporting only a net asset suppresses disclosure of obligations for which the venturer has legal responsibility. On the other hand, 100 percent of venture liabilities would be reported in the case of conventional consolidation. For a venturer owning a small interest in the venture, reporting 100 percent of venture liabilities seems overly conservative. Rarely would any one venturer be called upon to pay all venture liabilities. Proportionate consolidation can be thought of as a middle ground between these two extremes in that all venturers disclose their proportionate shares of the venture liabilities of which they are guarantors.

Real Estate Joint Ventures

Interestingly, a committee of the American Institute of CPAs has recommended that accounting for investments in real estate joint ventures be determined by control and not legal form.[9] That is, if any single venturer controls the venture, that venturer should consolidate the investment. Thus, corporate joint ventures, general partnerships, limited partnerships, and undivided interests would all be consolidated by a controlling venturer. Other venturers would use the cost or equity method, depending on their ability to exercise significant influence over the operating and financial policies of the venture. If the venture is subject to joint control, all venturers would use the equity method. However, the scope of the recommendation is limited to real estate ventures, and its relevance beyond this industry is unclear.

Questions

1. Suggest two variables that complicate the preparation of consolidated financial statements when the statements are prepared subsequent to the date of a subsidiary's acquisition by a parent.

---

[9] See *Statement of Position 78–9*, "Accounting for Investments in Real Estate Ventures" (New York: AICPA, 1978).

2. In respect to subsidiary shareholdings, what are the basic differences between the entries recorded by a parent company under the two alternative methods of accounting for the investment?

3. How does the realization criterion underlying the equity method differ from that underlying the cost method?

4. What differences exist in the formal consolidated financial statements when the equity method is used instead of the cost method for consolidated subsidiaries?

5. Is the cost or equity method preferred as a method of accounting for investments in subsidiaries?

6. What statements are generally included in the "family" of consolidated reports?

7. Describe the reasoning underlying the two alternative definitions of consolidated net income.

8. What is the composition of the consolidated retained earnings statement?

9. When using the three-division working paper, do the "debits equal the credits" in *each* of the three sections of the Eliminations columns? If so, why? If not, why not?

10. How is the minority interest in a subsidiary's net income calculated? Is this amount added to or subtracted from the combined net incomes of the affiliates in order to determine "consolidated net income"?

11. For a company using the equity method, describe the relationship between the parent company's net income and the consolidated net income; and between the parent company's retained earnings balance and the consolidated retained earnings balance.

12. How are the elements of the investment elimination entry, eliminating the investment account against the stockholders' equity accounts of the subsidiary, determined under the equity method?

13. For an investment carried under the equity method, what is the relationship between the investment account balance and the net assets of the subsidiary at any point in time?

14. Enumerate five types of intercompany transactions which generate elimination entries in the consolidation process.

15. Define consolidated net income using the incremental approach.

16. Describe the accounting by a venturer for an investment in a joint venture that is jointly controlled and is organized as a corporation, as a partnership, and as an undivided interest. How does your description change if the venturer is in control?

17. Describe the characteristics of a proportionate consolidation. Explain its rationale.

Exercises

Exercise 3–1

Select the best answer for each of the following:

1. What would be the effect on the financial statements if an unconsolidated subsidiary is accounted for by the equity method but consolidated statements are being prepared with other subsidiaries?
    a. All of the unconsolidated subsidiary's accounts will be included individually in the consolidated statements.
    b. The consolidated retained earnings will *not* reflect the earnings of the unconsolidated subsidiary.
    c. The consolidated retained earnings will be the same as if the subsidiary had been included in the consolidation.
    d. Dividend revenue from the unconsolidated subsidiary will be reflected in consolidated net income.
2. How is the portion of consolidated earnings to be assigned to minority interest in consolidated financial statements determined?
    a. The net income of the parent is subtracted from the subsidiary's net income to determine the minority interest.
    b. The subsidiary's net income is extended to the minority interest.
    c. The amount of the subsidiary's earnings is multiplied by the minority's percentage ownership.
    d. The amount of consolidated earnings determined on the consolidated working papers is multiplied by the minority interest percentage at the balance sheet date.
3. Aaron, Inc., owns 80 percent of the outstanding stock of Belle, Inc. Compare the consolidated net earnings of Aaron and Belle *(X)* and Aaron's net earnings if it does *not* consolidate with Belle *(Y)*.
    a. X greater than Y.
    b. X equals Y.
    c. X less than Y.
    d. Cannot be determined.

Exercise 3–2

Select the best answer for each of the following.

1. Parent, Inc., owns a 90 percent interest in Sub, Inc., which is recorded on a cost basis. During the calendar year 19X1, Parent reported net income of $45,000 and Sub reported net income of $20,000. Intercompany interest on bonds was $800. Sub declared and paid a $4,000 dividend during the year. How much is 19X1 *consolidated* net income?
    a. $58,200.
    b. $58,600.
    c. $59,000.
    d. $59,400.

2. On January 1, 19X1, Nair Corporation paid $600,000 for 60,000 shares of Biggs Company's common stock which represents a 25 percent investment in Biggs. Nair has the ability to exercise significant influence over Biggs. Nair received a dividend of $1 per share from Biggs in 19X1. Biggs reported net income of $320,000 for the year ended December 31, 19X1. The balance in Nair's balance sheet account "Investment in Biggs Company" at December 31, 19X1, should be—
    a. $600,000.
    b. $620,000.
    c. $680,000.
    d. $740,000.

(AICPA adapted)

Exercise 3–3

Financial accounting usually emphasizes the economic substance of events even though the legal form may differ and suggest different treatment. For example, under accrual accounting, expenses are recognized when they are incurred (substance) rather than when cash is disbursed (form).

Although the feature of substance over form exists in most generally accepted accounting principles and practices, there are times when form prevails over substance.

Required:

For each of the following topics, discuss the underlying theory in terms of both substance and form, that is, substance over form and possibly form over substance in some cases. Each topic should be discussed independently.
a.   Consolidated financial statements.
b.   Equity method of accounting for investments in common stock.

(AICPA adapted)

Exercise 3–4

On January 1, 19X1, Elizabeth Company acquired an 80 percent interest in Thomas Company at a cost of $72,000. On this date, Thomas Company had capital stock of $50,000 and retained earnings of $40,000.

During 19X1, Thomas Company reported net income of $20,000 and paid cash dividends of $15,000.

Required:
a.   Prepare all entries on the books of Elizabeth Company in 19X1 related to its investment in Thomas Company under (1) the cost method and (2) the equity method.
b.   Assuming Elizabeth Company uses the equity method of accounting for its investment, prepare the investment elimination entries for a consolidated statement working paper on December 31, 19X1.

Exercise 3–5

Little Bit Company acquired a 70 percent interest in Crunch Company on January 1, 19X1, at a cost of $35,000. On this date, Crunch Company had capital stock of $20,000 and retained earnings of $30,000.

During 19X1 and 19X2, Crunch Company reports net income of $20,000 per year and pays cash dividends of $5,000 each year.

Little Bit Company uses the equity method of accounting for its investment in Crunch Company.

Required:
a. Determine the balance of the investment account on December 31, 19X1, and December 31, 19X2.
b. Prepare the investment elimination entries for a consolidated statement working paper on December 31, 19X1, and December 31, 19X2.

Exercise 3–6

On January 1, 19X1, Quittmeyer Company acquired a 90 percent interest in Todd Company at a cost of $90,000. On this date, Todd Company had capital stock of $30,000 and retained earnings of $70,000.

During 19X1, Todd Company reports net income of $40,000 and pays a cash dividend of $10,000. During 19X2, Todd Company reports a net loss of $10,000 and pays a cash dividend of $5,000.

Quittmeyer Company uses the equity method of accounting for its investment in Todd Company.

Required:
a. Prepare the entries on Quittmeyer Company's books in 19X1 and 19X2 related to its investment in Todd Company.
b. Prepare the investment elimination entries for a consolidated statement working paper on December 31, 19X1, and December 31, 19X2.

Exercise 3–7

On January 1, 19X1, Vashik Company acquired a 60 percent interest in CPW Company at a cost of $24,000. On this date, CPW Company had capital stock of $10,000 and retained earnings of $30,000.

During 19X1 and 19X2, CPW Company reports net income of $15,000 each year and pays cash dividends of $10,000 each year.

Vashik Company uses the equity method of accounting for its investment in CPW Company.

Required:
a. Determine the balance of the investment account on December 31, 19X1, and December 31, 19X2.
b. Prepare the investment elimination entries for a consolidated statement working paper on December 31, 19X1, and December 31, 19X2.
c. Calculate the value of the minority interest in CPW Company on December 31, 19X1, and December 31, 19X2.

Exercise 3–8

Snyder Company has an 80 percent interest in Holland Company, purchased in 19X1 at a cost equal to 80 percent of the book value of Holland's recorded net assets.

During 19X5, Snyder Company recorded the following entries:

(1) Investment in Holland Company 16,000
        Equity in Subsidiary Earnings   16,000

(2) Cash.. 4,000
        Investment in Holland Company   4,000

At December 31, 19X5, Holland Company reported capital stock of $50,000 and retained earnings of $100,000 (including 19X5 income and dividends).

Snyder Company uses the equity method of accounting for its investment in Holland Company.

Required:

a. Determine the balance of the investment account on December 31, 19X5.
b. Calculate the value of the minority interest in net income for 19X5 and the total value of the minority interest in Holland Company at December 31, 19X5.
c. Prepare the investment elimination entries for a consolidated statement working paper on December 31, 19X5.

Exercise 3–9

P Company purchased the following investments on January 1, 19X1:

       90% of the capital stock of Y Company, cost $135,000
       80% of the capital stock of Z Company, cost $56,000
       60% of the capital stock of W Company, cost $30,000

Additional data concerning these companies are as follows:

	P Company	Y Company	Z Company	W Company
Capital stock (par value, $1)	$200,000	$100,000	$50,000	$40,000
Retained earnings,				
January 1, 19X1.................	100,000	50,000	20,000	10,000
Net income [loss], 19X1	79,000	40,000	20,000	[5,000]
Cash dividends, 19X1	10,000	5,000	4,000	–0–

P Company carries its investment in subsidiaries on an equity basis; it reported a profit from its own operations in 19X1 of $30,000.

Required:

a. Prepare journal entries for 19X1 on the books of P Company reflecting its transactions with, or interest in, subsidiary companies.
b. Calculate the amount of consolidated net income for 19X1 and the balance of consolidated retained earnings as of December 31, 19X1.
c. Calculate the amount of minority interest in the 19X1 net income [loss] and the December 31, 19X1, retained earnings of subsidiary companies.

Exercise 3–10

The following data relate to companies M, G, and R for the two-year period ending December 31, 19X1:

	M Company	G Company	R Company
Capital stock ($1 par)	$200,000	$100,000	$50,000
Other contributed capital	20,000	3,500	1,000
Retained earnings [deficit], January 1, 19X0	250,000	40,000	[20,000]
Net income (excluding equity in subsidiary profits):			
19X0	90,000	60,000	30,000
19X1	75,000	40,000	40,000
Dividends paid:			
19X0	20,000	4,000	–0–
19X1	20,000	10,000	5,000

In each of the following independent cases, investments in subsidiary stock are carried by the parent on an equity basis. Assume any resulting differential is allocated to land and thus need not be amortized.

Case 1:   M Company purchased 90 percent of the capital stock of G Company on January 1, 19X0, for $130,000.

Case 2:   G Company purchased 60 percent of the capital stock of R Company on January 1, 19X0, for $20,000.

Case 3:   M Company purchased 80 percent of the capital stock of G Company on January 1, 19X1, for $164,000.

Case 4:   M Company purchased 70 percent of the capital stock of R Company on January 1, 19X0, for $20,000 and 60 percent of the capital stock of G Company on January 1, 19X1, for $125,000.

Required:
In each of the above cases:

a.   Calculate the balance of the investment account on December 31, 19X1.

b.   Calculate the amount of consolidated net income for 19X0 and 19X1, and the balance of consolidated retained earnings on December 31, 19X1.

Exercise 3–11

Clark Motor Transit purchased in the open market 75 percent of the capital stock of Sachs and Ward, Inc., on January 1, 19X1, at $14,000 more than 75 percent of its book value. The entire differential is allocable to land. During the following five years, Sachs and Ward, Inc., reported cumulative earnings of $235,000 and paid $45,000 in dividends. On January 1, 19X6, minority shareholders in Sachs and Ward, Inc., have an equity of $57,500 in the net assets of the company.

Required:
If the parent company carries its investment in subsidiary stock on an equity basis—

a.   Determine the January 1, 19X1, cost of the investment, and

b.   Calculate the investment carrying value on December 31, 19X5.

Exercise 3–12

Ashton Corporation has an 80 percent interest in Hubbard Household Equipment Company. During 19X1, Hubbard reported net income of $20,000, and in 19X2, Hubbard reported a loss of $10,000. Ashton had net income from its own operations of $50,000 each year.

Required:
Calculate consolidated net income for 19X1 and 19X2.

Exercise 3–13

P Company purchased a 90 percent interest in S Company on January 1, 19X1. You are given the following information regarding the companies' earnings and dividends:

	P Company	S Company
Retained earnings, December 31, 19X0..........	$100,000	$50,000
Net incomes from own operations:		
19X1.....................................	20,000	15,000
19X2.....................................	30,000	20,000
Dividends declared and paid:		
19X1.....................................	10,000	5,000
19X2.....................................	15,000	5,000

Required:
a. Using the incremental approach, calculate consolidated net income for 19X1 and 19X2.
b. Using the residual approach, calculate consolidated net income for 19X1 and 19X2.
c. Compute consolidated retained earnings as of December 31, 19X1, and December 31, 19X2.

Exercise 3–14

A Company purchased 80 percent of the capital stock of B Company on January 1, 19X0, and 90 percent of the capital stock of C Company on January 1, 19X1.
The following two-year operating summary relates to the affiliated companies:

	A Company	B Company	C Company
Retained earnings, January 1, 19X0	$70,000	$40,000	$35,000
19X0 net income from own operations	40,000	20,000	30,000
19X0 cash dividends............................	–0–	10,000	5,000
19X1 net income from own operations	10,000	15,000	20,000
19X1 cash dividends............................	4,000	6,000	10,000

Required:
a. Using the incremental approach, calculate consolidated net income for 19X0 and 19X1.
b. Using the residual approach, calculate consolidated net income for 19X0 and 19X1.

c. Calculate consolidated retained earnings as of December 31, 19X0, and December 31, 19X1.

Exercise 3–15

P Company acquired a 90 percent interest in the capital stock of Y Company on January 1, 19X1, and an 80 percent interest in the capital stock of Z Company on the same day. You are given the following information regarding the companies' earnings and dividends:

	P Company	Y Company	Z Company
Retained earnings, January 1, 19X1	$60,000	$30,000	$15,000
Net incomes [loss] from own operations:			
19X1......................................	13,200	8,000	[5,000]
19X2......................................	8,400	4,000	7,000
Dividends declared and paid:			
19X1......................................	5,000	2,000	–0–
19X2......................................	–0–	1,000	2,000

Required:
a. Calculate consolidated net income for 19X1 and 19X2.
b. Calculate consolidated retained earnings on December 31, 19X1, and December 31, 19X2.

Exercise 3–16

On January 1, 19X1, Box Corporation made the following investments:

1. Acquired for cash, 80 percent of the outstanding common stock of Valley Corporation at $70 per share. The stockholders' equity of Valley on January 1, 19X1, consisted of the following:

> Common stock, par value $50.............. $50,000
> Retained earnings 20,000

2. Acquired for cash, 70 percent of the outstanding common stock of May Corporation at $40 per share. The stockholders' equity of May on January 1, 19X1, consisted of the following:

> Common stock, par value $20.............. $60,000
> Capital in excess of par value.............. 20,000
> Retained earnings 40,000

The following information on the companies' earnings and dividends for 19X1 is provided:

	Box	Valley	May
Net income [loss] from own operations........	$104,600	$36,000	$[12,000]
Dividends declared and paid	40,000	16,000	9,000

Box Corporation uses the equity method to account for its investments in Valley and May.

Required:

a. What entries should have been made on the books of Box Corporation during 19X1 to record the following?
   (1) Investments in subsidiaries.
   (2) Parent's share of subsidiary income or loss.
   (3) Subsidiary dividends received.

b. Using the "parent company theory," compute the amount of minority interest in each subsidiary's stockholders' equity at December 31, 19X1.

c. Assuming that Box Corporation's retained earnings on January 1, 19X1, amounted to $240,000, what amount should be reported as consolidated retained earnings of Box Corporation and subsidiaries as of December 31, 19X1?

(AICPA adapted)

Problems

Problem 3–17

The Hanna Company purchased 80 percent of the capital stock of the Taylor Corporation on January 1, 19X1, for $48,000, when the latter's capital stock and retained earnings were $50,000 and $10,000, respectively. Trial balances prepared on December 31, 19X1, disclose the following:

	December 31, 19X1	
	Hanna Company	Taylor Corporation
Cash	$ 8,000	$ 5,000
Accounts receivable	21,000	17,000
Inventory (1/1)	15,000	8,000
Investment in Taylor Corporation stock	56,000	
Other assets	57,000	48,000
Dividends declared	10,000	5,000
Purchases	90,000	20,000
Expenses	10,000	7,000
	$267,000	$110,000
Accounts payable	$ 5,000	$ 6,000
Advances from Hanna		4,000
Other liabilities	5,000	
Capital stock	100,000	50,000
Retained earnings	40,000	10,000
Sales	105,000	40,000
Equity in subsidiary earnings	12,000	
	$267,000	$110,000
Inventory (12/31)	$ 20,000	$ 10,000

Required:

a. Prepare a consolidated statement working paper for the year ended December 31, 19X1.

b. Prepare formal consolidated statements.

Problem 3–18

The Parnelli Company purchased 75,000 shares of the capital stock of the Foyt Company on January 1, 19X1, for $90,000. One year later, the following trial balances are prepared:

	Parnelli Company	Foyt Company
Cash...............................	$ 14,000	$ 23,000
Inventory (12/31)...................	45,000	30,000
Investment in Foyt Company	97,500	
Other assets.......................	122,500	80,000
Cost of goods sold	87,000	65,000
Expenses..........................	14,000	16,000
Dividends declared.................	20,000	10,000
	$400,000	$224,000
Accounts payable	$ 9,000	
Dividends payable		$ 10,000
Other liabilities	1,500	3,000
Capital stock (par, $1)	200,000	100,000
Retained earnings..................	64,000	20,000
Sales..............................	118,000	91,000
Equity in subsidiary earnings.........	7,500	
	$400,000	$224,000

Required:

Prepare a consolidated statement working paper for the year ended December 31, 19X1.

Problem 3–19

The Cruse Company purchased 80 percent of the capital stock of Summers, Inc., on January 1, 19X1, for $49,600. On this date, Summers' stockholders' equity consisted of capital stock, $50,000, and retained earnings, $12,000. Two years later, the trial balances of the companies were as follows:

	December 31, 19X2	
	Cruse Company	*Summers, Inc.*
Cash	$ 22,000	$ 12,500
Accounts receivable...............	5,000	17,000
Inventory (1/1)	28,000	11,000
Investment in Summers, Inc.	80,000	
Other assets......................	59,400	80,500
Dividends declared	8,500	5,000
Purchases........................	161,000	83,000
Freight-in	1,000	200
Selling expenses...................	18,000	11,100
Administrative expenses	9,300	5,700
	$392,200	$226,000
Accounts payable..................	$ 18,000	$ 12,000
Other liabilities...................	3,000	16,000
Capital stock	100,000	50,000
Retained earnings	43,000	27,000
Sales	205,000	121,000
Equity in subsidiary earnings	22,400	
Interest income...................	800	
	$392,200	$226,000
Inventory (12/31)	$ 41,000	$ 18,000

The accounts payable of Summers, Inc., include $3,000 payable to Cruse Company.

Required:

Prepare a three-division consolidated statement working paper for the year ended December 31, 19X2.

Problem 3–20

The Weeks Company purchased an 80 percent interest in the Knight Company in 19X1 at a cost equal to the acquired interest in Knight's net assets. On December 31, 19X5, the companies prepare the following trial balances:

	Weeks Company	*Knight Company*
Cash..............................	$ 14,000	$ 23,000
Inventory (12/31)....................	45,000	30,000
Investment in Knight Company	104,000	
Other assets	127,500	80,000
Cost of goods sold	87,000	65,000
Expenses..........................	14,000	16,000
Dividends declared.................	20,000	10,000
	$411,500	$224,000

	Weeks Company	Knight Company
Accounts payable	$ 13,500	$ 3,000
Capital stock.......................	200,000	100,000
Retained earnings...................	64,000	20,000
Sales..............................	118,000	101,000
Equity in subsidiary earnings.........	16,000	
	$411,500	$224,000

Required:

Prepare a three-division consolidated statement working paper for the year ended December 31, 19X5.

Problem 3–21

The Bransford Company purchased an 80 percent interest in the Strandberg Company on January 1, 19X1, at a cost of $256,000, which was equal to the acquired interest in Strandberg's net assets. On December 31, 19X3, the companies prepare the following trial balances:

	Bransford Company	Strandberg Company
Cash	$ 42,000	$ 69,000
Inventory (1/1)	126,000	105,000
Investment in Strandberg Company	312,000	
Other assets..............................	382,500	240,000
Purchases................................	270,000	180,000
Expenses	42,000	48,000
Dividends declared	60,000	30,000
	$1,234,500	$672,000
Accounts payable..........................	$ 40,500	$ 9,000
Capital stock	600,000	300,000
Retained earnings	192,000	60,000
Sales	354,000	303,000
Equity in subsidiary earnings	48,000	
	$1,234,500	$672,000
Inventory (12/31)	$ 135,000	$ 90,000

During 19X3, Strandberg sold merchandise to Bransford in the amount of $53,000. At December 31, 19X3, Strandberg's "Other assets" included a receivable of $6,500 from Bransford (which is included in Bransford's accounts payable).

Required:

Prepare a three-division consolidated statement working paper for the year ended December 31, 19X3.

Problems for Appendices

Problem 3–22(A)

On January 1, 19X1, the Central Company purchased 80 percent of the capital stock of the Western Company for $48,000. On December 31, 19X1, their trial balances are as follows:

	Central Company	Western Company
Cash...	$ 8,000	$ 5,000
Accounts receivable	21,000	17,000
Inventory (1/1)...................................	15,000	8,000
Investment in Western Company capital stock........	48,000	
Other assets	57,000	48,000
Dividends declared...............................	10,000	5,000
Purchases	90,000	20,000
Expenses.......................................	10,000	7,000
	$259,000	$110,000
Accounts payable	$ 5,000	$ 6,000
Other liabilities	5,000	
Advances from Central		4,000
Capital stock....................................	100,000	50,000
Retained earnings...............................	40,000	10,000
Sales..	105,000	40,000
Dividend income.................................	4,000	
	$259,000	$110,000
Inventory (12/31).................................	$ 20,000	$ 10,000

Central Company uses the *cost* method of accounting for its investment in Western Company.

Required:

On December 31, 19X1, prepare consolidated statements supported by a three-division working paper.

Problem 3–23(A)

The Cruse Company purchased 80 percent of the capital stock of Summers, Inc., on January 1, 19X1, for $49,600. On this date, Summers' stockholders' equity consisted of capital stock, $50,000, and retained earnings, $12,000. The Cruse Company uses the *cost* method of accounting for its investment in Summers. Two years later, the trial balances of the companies were as given on the following page.

	December 31, 19X2	
	Cruse Company	Summers, Inc.
Cash	$ 22,000	$ 12,500
Accounts receivable................	5,000	17,000
Inventory (1/1)	28,000	11,000
Investment in Summers, Inc.	49,600	
Other assets.......................	59,400	80,500
Dividends declared	8,500	5,000
Purchases.........................	161,000	83,000
Freight-in.........................	1,000	200
Selling expenses...................	18,000	11,100
Administrative expenses	9,300	5,700
	$361,800	$226,000
Accounts payable..................	$ 18,000	$ 12,000
Other liabilities....................	3,000	16,000
Capital stock	100,000	50,000
Retained earnings	31,000	27,000
Sales	205,000	121,000
Dividend income	4,000	
Interest income....................	800	
	$361,800	$226,000
Inventory (12/31)..................	$ 41,000	$ 18,000

The accounts payable of Summers, Inc., include $3,000 payable to the Cruse Company.

Required:

Prepare a three-division consolidated statement working paper for the year ended December 31, 19X2.

Problem 3–24(A)

The Bransford Company purchased an 80 percent interest in the Strandberg Company on January 1, 19X1, at a cost of $256,000. On this date, Strandberg's stockholders' equity consisted of capital stock, $300,000, and retained earnings, $20,000. The Bransford Company uses the *cost* method of accounting for its investment in Strandberg. On December 31, 19X3, the companies prepare the trial balances given on the following page.

During 19X3, Strandberg sold merchandise to Bransford in the amount of $53,000. At December 31, 19X3, Strandberg's "Other assets" included a receivable of $6,500 from Bransford (which is included in Bransford's accounts payable).

	Bransford Company	Strandberg Company
Cash	$ 42,000	$ 69,000
Inventory (1/1)	126,000	105,000
Investment in Strandberg Company	256,000	
Other assets...............................	382,500	240,000
Purchases..................................	270,000	180,000
Expenses	42,000	48,000
Dividends declared	60,000	30,000
	$1,178,500	$672,000
Accounts payable..........................	$ 40,500	$ 9,000
Capital stock	600,000	300,000
Retained earnings	160,000	60,000
Sales	354,000	303,000
Dividend income	24,000	
	$1,178,500	$672,000
Inventory (12/31)	$ 135,000	$ 90,000

Required:

Prepare a three-division consolidated statement working paper for the year ended December 31, 19X3.

Problem 3–25(A)

On January 1, 19X0, the Belt Company purchased in the open market 90 percent of the capital stock of the Kaplan Company for $135,000 *and* 70 percent of the capital stock of the Baxter Company for $28,000. On this date the account balances of Kaplan and Baxter were as follows:

	Kaplan	Baxter
Capital stock	$100,000	$50,000
Retained earnings [deficit]	50,000	[10,000]

A summary of changes in retained earnings for 19X1 is as follows:

	Belt	Kaplan	Baxter
Retained earnings, January 1	$100,000	$60,000	$20,000
Net income, 19X1	40,000	25,000	10,000
Dividends paid, 19X1	5,000	8,000	4,000

Required:

If the investments in subsidiary stock are carried at *cost—*

a. Prepare on December 31, 19X1, an investment elimination entry for a consolidated statement working paper.

b. Prepare the retained earnings statement section of the three-division consolidated statement working paper for the year ended December 31, 19X1.

Problem 3–26(A)

A summary of the changes in the stockholders' equity of the Dial Company and the Landry Company for the two-year period ending December 31, 19X1, is given as follows:

	Dial Company	Landry Company
Capital stock (no par value), January 1, 19X0:		
Dial Company (20,000 shares)	$120,000	
Landry Company (10,000 shares)		$80,000
Retained earnings, January 1, 19X0	$ 60,000	$40,000
Net income, 19X0	30,00	24,000
	$ 90,000	$64,000
Dividends paid (cash), November 15, 19X0	10,000	8,000
Retained earnings, December 31, 19X0	$ 80,000	$56,000
Net income [loss], 19X1............................	18,000	[4,000]
	$ 98,000	$52,000
Dividends paid (cash), December 15, 19X1............	6,000	10,000
Retained earnings, December 31, 19X1	$ 92,000	$42,000

Dunham, Inc., purchased in the open market the following:

a. 8,000 shares of Landry Company stock on January 1, 19X0, at a cost of $96,000.
b. 18,000 shares of Dial Company stock on January 1, 19X1, at a cost of $180,000.

Dunham uses the *cost* method of accounting for its investment in Landry and Dial. During 19X0 and 19X1, the only source of income for Dunham was subsidiary dividends. On December 31, 19X1, Dunham had retained earnings, exclusive of dividend income, of $50,000. Dunham paid no dividends in 19X0 and 19X1.

Required:
a. Prepare an investment elimination entry for a consolidated statement working paper, December 31, 19X1.
b. Prepare the retained earnings statement section of the three-division consolidated statement working paper for the year ended December 31, 19X1.

Problem 3–27(B)

Beaver, Inc., is general partner in a joint venture organized as a limited partnership. The limited partners are two individuals. The partnership was formed in 19X0. The partnership agreement specifies that revenues and expenses except depreciation expense are to be divided equally among the three partners. Depreciation expense is to be allocated entirely to Beaver. However, all cash distributions, including those made in liquidation, are to be divided equally among the three partners.

The partnership income statement for 19X1 was as follows:

Revenues	$300,000
Depreciation expense	$ 30,000
Other expenses	90,000
Total expenses	$120,000
Net income	$180,000

Beaver's tax rate is 40 percent.

Required:

Prepare all entries on the part of Beaver relating to its partnership investment during 19X1.

Problem 3–28(B)

Jensen Company holds a 55 percent interest in a joint venture organized as an undivided interest. Financial statement data relating to Jensen and the joint venture are as follows:

	Jensen	Joint Venture
Income statement:		
Sales	$200,000	$ 85,000
Equity in venture earnings	13,750	
	$213,750	$ 85,000
Cost of goods sold	$100,000	$ 45,000
Expenses	50,000	15,000
	$150,000	$ 60,000
Net income	$ 63,750	$ 25,000
Balance sheet:		
Cash	$ 50,000	$ 20,000
Receivables	100,000	40,000
Inventory	75,000	50,000
Investment in venture	38,500	
Other assets	35,000	10,000
	$298,500	$120,000
Accounts payable	$ 50,000	$ 20,000
Other liabilities	80,000	30,000
Capital stock	50,000	
Retained earnings	118,500	
Venturers' equity		70,000
	$298,500	$120,000

Required:

Prepare a consolidated balance sheet and income statement for Jensen and its undivided interest using proportionate consolidation.

CHAPTER
4

Consolidated Financial
Reports—Postacquisition
(continued)

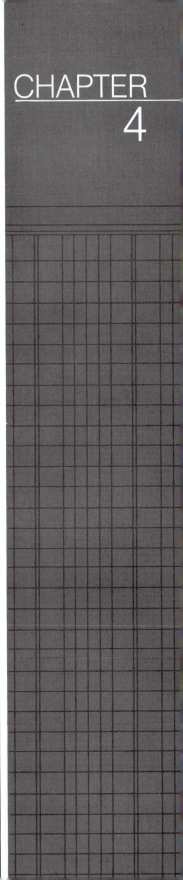

Treatment of Differentials Subsequent to Date of Acquisition

The principles underlying the allocation of the differential to specific assets and liabilities at the date of acquisition were described in Chapter 2. Once allocated, however, there remains the problem of the differential's subsequent disposition.

The basic principle applicable to the allocated differential amounts is to account for them consistent with the accounting for the particular asset (or liability) to which they were assigned. Thus, amounts allocated to accounts whose balances are not normally subject to systematic amortization (e.g., land) will continue to be reported at the same, originally allocated values. Amounts allocated to accounts whose balances are expensed or periodically amortized will be accorded similar treatment in consolidated financial statements.

The reader will recall that an unallocated debit differential is classified as goodwill. This value, like the values of all intangible assets, should be amortized on the basis of the estimated life of the specific asset (in this case, goodwill). It should not be written off in the period of acquisition. Admittedly, it is often difficult to estimate the life of goodwill. But the value of the goodwill will almost inevitably become zero at some future date. In view of this potential dilemma, the Accounting Principles Board set an arbitrary maximum life of 40 years for the amortization of goodwill. Generally, straight-line amortization should be applied. It might be noted that this amortization of goodwill does not create a timing difference for income tax allocation purposes, and thus tax allocation is inappropriate.[1]

An unallocated credit differential (after the specified reallocation to non-current assets) should similarly be amortized systematically to income over the period of time estimated to benefit therefrom, but not to exceed 40 years. No part of this deferred credit should be added directly to stockholders' equity at the date of acquisition.[2]

Application of these principles at the end of an accounting period will generally result in a set of expense adjustments, the total of which is referred to as the *amortization of the differential for the period* (or sometimes simply *differential amortization*).

Since a differential is part of the cost incurred by the parent company, the amortization of this cost is allocated wholly to the majority shareholders. The value of the interest of minority shareholders is calculated, as before, on the basis of accumulations recorded in the subsidiary's equity accounts.

In addition to recognizing the differential amortization in the consoli-

---

[1] *APB, APB Opinion No. 17,* "Intangible Assets" (New York: AICPA, 1970), pars. 23–30.

[2] *APB, APB Opinion No. 16,* "Business Combinations" (New York: AICPA, 1970). pars. 91–92.

dated statement working paper, the parent company must also recognize this expense on its books. *APB Opinion No. 18* states in this regard: "The difference between consolidation and the equity method lies in the details reported in the financial statements. Thus, an investor's net income for the period and its stockholders' equity at the end of the period are the same whether an investment in a subsidiary is accounted for under the equity method or the subsidiary is consolidated."[3] Accordingly, at the same time that the parent records its equity in subsidiary earnings for the period, an additional entry must be made to record the amortization of the differential for the period.

The specific accounting procedures that are employed to reflect the differential amortization are illustrated in two integrated case examples which follow. The first case deals with the period of acquisition, and the second case considers the period subsequent to acquisition. Each example illustrates both the eliminating entries required for the preparation of a consolidated statement working paper and the formal journal entries recorded on the books of the parent company.

Case 1. Amortization of Differential—Period of Acquisition. On January 1, 19X1, P Company purchased an 80 percent interest in S Company for $300,000. On this date, S Company had capital stock of $50,000 and retained earnings of $120,000.

Assume that an examination of S Company's identifiable assets and liabilities revealed that all were recorded at amounts that approximated their fair values except for inventory, plant and equipment, and land. The analysis of these differences is provided as follows:

	Book Value	Fair Value	Excess of Fair Value over Book Value	P Company's 80% Interest in Excess
Inventory	$ 20,000	$ 25,000	$ 5,000	$ 4,000
Plant and equipment (net)	80,000	155,000	75,000	60,000
Land	40,000	65,000	25,000	20,000
	$140,000	$245,000	$105,000	$84,000

The differential generated by this acquisition may be easily determined:

Investment cost	$300,000
P Company's equity in recorded net assets of S Company (80% × $170,000)	136,000
Differential	$164,000

---

[3] *APB, APB Opinion No. 18,* "The Equity Method of Accounting for Investments in Common Stock" (New York: AICPA, 1971), par. 19.

Since the investment cost exceeds the parent's equity in the recorded net assets of the subsidiary, the differential is a debit differential. Based upon the examination of the identifiable assets and liabilities of S Company, $84,000 of the differential will be allocated to the three specific assets. The remaining unallocated debit differential of $80,000 will be classified as goodwill in the consolidated statements.

Each allocated portion of the differential is amortized in accordance with the accounting for the asset to which it is assigned. For purposes of this illustration, we assume that the following determinations were made:

1.   The inventory on hand on January 1, 19X1, was all sold during 19X1.
2.   On January 1, 19X1, the plant and equipment had an expected remaining life of 10 years.
3.   The land is not subject to amortization.

The goodwill requires, of course, an independent assessment of expected useful life. We assume that P Company decided to amortize the goodwill acquired in the combination over the maximum period of 40 years. Based upon these facts, a schedule of differential amortization is presented in Illustration 4–1.

Illustration 4–1

SCHEDULE OF DIFFERENTIAL AMORTIZATION

	Allocated Amount	Annual Amortization		
		Year 1	Years 2–10	Years 11–40
Inventory	$ 4,000	$ 4,000	–0–	–0–
Plant and equipment (net)	60,000	6,000	$6,000	–0–
Land	20,000	–0–	–0–	–0–
Goodwill	80,000	2,000	2,000	$2,000
	$164,000	$12,000	$8,000	$2,000

Assume finally that S Company reported net income of $50,000 for the year ended December 31, 19X1, and paid $12,500 cash dividends during the year.

Parent Company Entries—Year 1. Based upon the information presented in the case and the schedule of differential amortization developed in Illustration 4–1, the parent company would make the following entries during 19X1:

1.   To record receipt of dividends from S Company:

Cash (80% × $12,500)   10,000
    Investment in S Company   10,000

2. To recognize equity in S Company's reported earnings:

Investment in S Company	40,000	
Equity in Subsidiary Earnings (80% × $50,000)		40,000

3. To recognize differential amortization for the period (see Illustration 4–1):

Equity in Subsidiary Earnings	12,000	
Investment in S Company		12,000

Amortization of the differential for the period is charged against the parent company's equity in reported subsidiary earnings because the differential represents the portion of the total investment cost that has not (implicitly) been taken into account in the calculation of subsidiary net income. On the other hand, the remaining portion of the investment cost (i.e., total cost less the differential) corresponds to the parent's equity in the subsidiary's recorded net assets at date of acquisition, and is (implicitly) given recognition in the measurement of subsidiary net income through the subsidiary's normal expense recognition procedures.

Eliminating Entries—Year 1. The investment elimination entries for the consolidated statement working paper at the end of 19X1 are as follows:

(1) To reverse the entries recorded by the parent company during 19X1 (substituting, as before, Dividends Declared for Cash):

(a)	Investment in S Company	10,000	
	Dividends Declared—S Company		10,000
(b)	Equity in Subsidiary Earnings	40,000	
	Investment in S Company		40,000
(c)	Investment in S Company	12,000	
	Equity in Subsidiary Earnings		12,000

(2) To eliminate January 1, 19X1, investment account balance of P Company against the January 1, 19X1, balance of the stockholders' equity accounts of S Company:

Capital Stock—S Company (80% × $50,000)	40,000	
Retained Earnings—S Company (80% × $120,000)	96,000	
Differential	164,000	
Investment in S Company		300,000

Eliminating entries (1a), (1b), and (1c) restore the investment account to its balance at the start of the period. Then this investment account balance is eliminated against the balance in S Company's stockholders' equity accounts at the beginning of the period. As one acquires more proficiency in · making these eliminations, it is, as we have seen, more efficient to compound the three "reversal" entries into a single entry.

As a consequence of these investment elimination entries, the differential as of January 1, 19X1, is set up in the consolidated statement working paper. This differential amount must be allocated as appropriate on January 1, 19X1, and the allocated amounts then amortized for the year. The eliminating entries for these two steps are as follows:

(3)   To allocate the differential as of January 1, 19X1 (see Illustration 4–1):

Inventory (1/1)	4,000	
Plant and Equipment (net)	60,000	
Land	20,000	
Goodwill	80,000	
Differential		164,000

(4)   To amortize the allocated amounts for 19X1 (see Illustration 4–1):

Expenses	8,000	
Plant and Equipment (net)		6,000
Goodwill		2,000

Note that it is not necessary to make a specific amortization entry for the amount of the differential allocated to the January 1 inventory because the beginning inventory is an element of cost of sales in income statement section of the consolidated statement working paper. (Increasing the January 1 inventory without any corresponding increase in the December 31 inventory has the effect of increasing cost of sales by the full $4,000.) In the event that the entire purchased inventory was not sold during 19X1, an additional eliminating entry would be required in order to prevent allocating the full $4,000 to 19X1 operations. If, for example, one fourth of the purchased inventory was still on hand as of December 31, an eliminating entry increasing the December 31 inventory by $1,000 would be required. (Recall that the December 31 inventory appears in both the income statement and balance sheet divisions of the three-division working paper. The December 31 inventory must be increased in both places.) Indeed, assuming that the entire inventory is sold in the year of acquisition is inherently inconsistent with the last-in, first-out method of inventory valuation (absent a decrease in the quantity of inventory). Last-in, first-out inventory valuation, therefore, will often necessitate an additional eliminating entry increasing the December 31 inventory. Additionally, if a more detailed breakdown of expenses is desired, eliminating entry (4) may be modified to identify separately Depreciation Expense ($6,000) and Amortization of Goodwill ($2,000) in lieu of the single charge of $8,000 to Expenses.

Illustration 4–2 displays the consolidated statement working paper for the year ended December 31, 19X1. The balances in the working paper are arbitrarily chosen, except where it is required that they correspond with data previously presented in this example.

Inspection of the working paper in Illustration 4–2 reveals that consolidated net income (and retained earnings) equals the parent company's net income (and retained earnings). Since the differential amortization was consistently applied both in the working paper and on the parent company's books, we would expect this equivalence to continue. Indeed, as previously noted, *APB Opinion No. 18* defines the equity method so as to achieve equivalence.

This question may occur to the reader: Why must the allocation and amortization of the differential be explicitly recognized in the consolidated statement working paper in view of the fact that the parent company has previously recorded the differential and differential amortization for the period on its books? The answer to this question is provided by focusing attention on the different sets of accounts that are included in the parent company and the consolidated financial statements. On the books and in the financial statements of the parent company, the total (unamortized) differential is appropriately included as a component of the investment account, and the differential amortization for the period as an element of the account, Equity in Subsidiary Earnings. However, in the consolidated statements, the specific assets and liabilities that were the source of the differential (because of a difference between their book and fair values at date of acquisition) are individually enumerated. Therefore, the purpose of the differential allocation entry in the working paper is to assign formally or distribute the total (unamortized) differential to the specific assets and liabilities included in the consolidated balance sheet. Similarly, the differential amortization entry in the consolidated statement working paper recognizes and distributes the total amortization for the period to specific expense accounts. Double counting is avoided as a result of the earlier investment elimination entry which reverses the parent company's entries during the current year for subsidiary dividends and its net equity in subsidiary earnings (including the effect of differential amortization). Because the total of the expense assignments is equal to the amount recorded by the parent company in its differential amortization entry, the equivalence pointed out above between consolidated net income (and retained earnings) and the parent company's net income (and retained earnings) is preserved.

Illustration 4–2

P COMPANY AND SUBSIDIARY S COMPANY
Consolidated Statement Working Paper
For Year Ended December 31, 19X1

	P Company	S Company	Eliminations Dr.	Eliminations Cr.	Minority Interest	Consolidated
Income Statement						
Sales	520,000	290,000				810,000
Equity in subsidiary earnings	28,000		(1b) 40,000	(1c) 12,000		–0–
Inventory (12/31)	82,000	30,000				112,000
Total credits	630,000	320,000				922,000
Inventory (1/1)	90,000	20,000	(3) 4,000			114,000
Purchases	250,000	150,000				400,000
Expenses	160,000	100,000	(4) 8,000			268,000
Total debits	500,000	270,000				782,000
	130,000	50,000				140,000
Minority interest in net income—S Company					10,000	10,000
Net income—carried forward	130,000	50,000	52,000	12,000	10,000	130,000
Retained Earnings Statement						
Retained earnings, 1/1/X1:						
P Company	410,000					410,000
S Company		120,000	(2) 96,000		24,000	–0–
Net income—brought forward	130,000	50,000	52,000	12,000	10,000	130,000
	540,000	170,000			34,000	540,000
Dividends declared:						
P Company	40,000					40,000
S Company		12,500		(1a) 10,000	2,500	–0–
Retained earnings, 12/31/X1—carried forward	500,000	157,000	148,000	22,000	31,500	500,000
Balance Sheet						
Cash	50,000	28,000				78,000
Accounts receivable	100,000	60,000				160,000
Inventory	82,000	30,000				112,000
Investment in S Company	318,000		(1a) 10,000 (1c) 12,000	(1b) 40,000 (2) 300,000		–0–
Land	50,000	40,000	(3) 20,000			110,000
Plant and equipment (net)	150,000	72,000	(3) 60,000	(4) 6,000		276,000
Differential			(2) 164,000	(3) 164,000		–0–
Goodwill			(3) 80,000	(4) 2,000		78,000
	750,000	230,000				814,000
Accounts payable	50,000	22,500				72,500
Capital stock:						
P Company	200,000					200,000
S Company		50,000	(2) 40,000		10,000	–0–
Retained earnings—brought forward	500,000	157,500	148,000	22,000	31,500	500,000
Minority interest in S Co.					41,500	41,500M
	750,000	230,000	534,000	534,000		814,000

(1a, 1b, 1c) To reverse the parent company's entries for subsidiary dividends and its interest in subsidiary earnings. (2) To eliminate the January 1, 19X1, investment account balance against 80% of the January 1, 19X1, balances of the stockholders' equity accounts of the subsidiary. (3) To allocate the differential as of January 1, 19X1. (4) To amortize allocated amounts for 19X1.

Refinement of Definitions of Consolidated Net Income.   Recognition of differential amortization necessitates a refinement of the definition of consolidated net income. Under the incremental approach, consolidated net income is redefined as follows: *parent company's net income from its own operations, increased (decreased) by its equity in the subsidiary's reported net income (loss) for the period, and decreased (increased for a credit differential) by the differential amortization for the period.* Applying this revised definition to the data of the example, consolidated net income is determined as follows:

P Company's net income from its own operations for 19X1	
($130,000 − $28,000)	$102,000
Increased by P Company's equity in S Company's reported	
net income for 19X1 (80% × $50,000)	40,000
Decreased by differential amortization for 19X1 ($8,000 + $4,000)........	[12,000]
Consolidated net income for 19X1	$130,000

In a similar manner, the "residual" approach gives recognition to the differential amortization in the adjustment of the sum of the companies' incomes for the "net eliminations" in the income statement section of the consolidated statement working paper. Thus, applying this approach to the data, we obtain the following:

P Company's net income for 19X1................................		$130,000
S Company's net income for 19X1................................		50,000
		$180,000
Less [plus]—net debit [credit] eliminations:		
P Company's recorded interest in S Company's earnings..........	$28,000	
Amortization of differential...................................	12,000	40,000
Total equity		$140,000
Less [plus]—minority interest in S Company's net income		
[loss] (20% × $50,000)..		10,000
Consolidated net income for 19X1................................		$130,000

A comparison of the figures in this schedular calculation with the corresponding column totals in the income statement section of Illustration 4–2 may be informative to the reader.

Case 2.   Amortization of Differential—Period Subsequent to Acquisition.   In the second year after aquisition, assume that S Company reported net income of $40,000 for the year ended December 31, 19X2, and again paid $12,500 cash dividends during the year.

Parent Company Entries—Year 2.   Based upon the assumed income and dividend figures of Case 2 and again referencing Illustration 4–1 for the differential amortization for 19X2, P Company would make the following entries during 19X2:

1. To record receipt of dividends from S Company:

Cash (80% × $12,500) 10,000
    Investment in S Company   10,000

2. To recognize equity in S Company's reported earnings:

Investment in S Company 32,000
    Equity in Subsidiary Earnings (80% × $40,000)   32,000

3. To recognize differential amortization for the period (from Illustration 4–1):

Equity in Subsidiary Earnings 8,000
    Investment in S Company   8,000

Eliminating Entries—Year 2. The investment elimination entries for the consolidated statement working paper at the end of 19X2 are the following:

(1) To reverse the entries recorded by the parent company during 19X2:

(a) Investment in S Company 10,000
    Dividends Declared—S Company   10,000

(b) Equity in Subsidiary Earnings 32,000
    Investment in S Company   32,000

(c) Investment in S Company 8,000
    Equity in Subsidiary Earnings   8,000

(2) To eliminate the January 1, 19X2, investment account balance of P Company against the January 1, 19X2, balances of the stockholders' equity accounts of S Company:

Capital Stock—S Company (80% × $50,000) 40,000
Retained Earnings—S Company (80% × $157,500) 126,000
Differential 152,000
    Investment in S Company   318,000

As a consequence of these investment elimination entries, the *unamortized* differential as of January 1, 19X2, is set up in the consolidated statement working paper. This amount is verified in Illustration 4–3.

The eliminating entries to allocate these unamortized differentials as of January 1, 19X2, and to recognize the differential amortization for 19X2 follow:

(3) To allocate the unamortized differential as of January 1, 19X2 (see Illustration 4–3):

Plant and Equipment (net)...............................	54,000	
Land	20,000	
Goodwill...	78,000	
Differential..		152,000

(4)   To amortize the allocated amounts for 19X2 (see Illustration 4–1):

Expenses...	8,000	
Plant and Equipment (net).........................		6,000
Goodwill..		2,000

Although the differential amortization in elimination entry (4) appears to be the same as it was in 19X1, recall that in 19X1 there was an additional $4,000 amortization of the amount allocated to inventory. Thus, since none of the unamortized differential as of January 1, 19X2, was allocated to inventory, the total differential amortization reflected in the consolidated statement working paper in 19X2 is $8,000, as compared to $12,000 in 19X1.

These elimination entries are reflected in the consolidated statement working paper for the year ended December 31, 19X2, in Illustration 4–4. As before, the balances in the working paper are arbitrarily chosen, except where it is required that they correspond with the data assumed in this example or the figures included in the 19X1 working paper (e.g., December 31, 19X1, inventories are reflected as January 1, 19X2, inventories).

Inspection of the working paper in Illustration 4–4 again reveals that consolidated net income (and retained earnings) equals the parent company's net income (and retained earnings). It is left as an exercise for the reader to make definitional calculations of consolidated net income for 19X2.

Illustration 4–3

SCHEDULE OF UNAMORTIZED DIFFERENTIAL
Allocations as of January 1, 19X2

	Original Amounts Allocated— January 1, 19X1	Amortization for 19X1	Unamortized Amounts— January 1, 19X2
Inventory	$ 4,000	$ 4,000	$ –0–
Plant and equipment (net)...............	60,000	6,000	54,000
Land	20,000	–0–	20,000
Goodwill...............................	80,000	2,000	78,000
	$164,000	$12,000	$152,000

Illustration 4–4

P COMPANY AND SUBSIDIARY S COMPANY
Consolidated Statement Working Paper
For Year Ended December 31, 19X2

	P Company	S Company	Eliminations Dr.	Eliminations Cr.	Minority Interest	Consolidated
Income Statement						
Sales	586,000	250,000				836,000
Equity in subsidiary earnings	24,000		(1b) 32,000	(1c) 8,000		–0–
Inventory (12/31)	110,000	50,000				160,000
Total credits	720,000	300,000				996,000
Inventory (1/1)	82,000	30,000				112,000
Purchases	280,000	120,000				400,000
Expenses	198,000	110,000	(4) 8,000			316,000
Total debits	560,000	260,000				828,000
	160,000	40,000				168,000
Minority interest in net income—S Company					8,000	8,000
Net income—carried forward	160,000	40,000	40,000	8,000	8,000	160,000
Retained Earnings Statement						
Retained earnings, 1/1/X2:						
P Company	500,000					500,000
S Company		157,500	(2) 126,000		31,500	–0–
Net income—brought forward	160,000	40,000	40,000	8,000	8,000	160,000
	660,000	197,500			39,500	660,000
Dividends declared:						
P Company	50,000					50,000
S Company		12,500		(1a) 10,000	2,500	–0–
Retained earnings, 12/31/X2—carried forward	610,000	185,000	166,000	18,000	37,000	610,000
Balance Sheet						
Cash	130,000	36,000				166,000
Accounts receivable	150,000	80,000				230,000
Inventory	110,000	50,000				160,000
Investment in S Company	332,000		(1a) 10,000 (1c) 8,000	(1b) 32,000 (2) 318,000		–0–
Land	50,000	40,000	(3) 20,000			110,000
Plant and equipment (net)	128,000	64,000	(3) 54,000	(4) 6,000		240,000
Differential			(2) 152,000	(3) 152,000		–0–
Goodwill			(3) 78,000	(4) 2,000		76,000
	900,000	270,000				982,000
Accounts payable	90,000	35,000				125,000
Capital stock:						
P Company	200,000					200,000
S Company		50,000	(2) 40,000		10,000	–0–
Retained earnings—brought forward	610,000	185,000	166,000	22,000	18,000	610,000
Minority interest in S Co.					47,000	47,000M
	900,000	270,000	528,000	528,000		982,000

(1a, 1b, 1c) To reverse the parent company's entries for subsidiary dividends and its interest in subsidiary earnings. (2) To eliminate the January 1, 19X2, investment account balance against 80% of the January 1, 19X2, balances of the stockholders' equity accounts of the subsidiary. (3) To allocate the unamortized differential as of January 1, 19X2. (4) To amortize the allocated amounts for 19X2.

Combined Differential Allocation and Amortization Eliminating Entry.
It is instructive, as well as more efficient, to combine the two eliminating
entries for differential allocation and amortization into one compound
eliminating entry. Thus, combining eliminating entries (3) and (4) above,
we obtain the following:

Plant and Equipment (net)	48,000	
Land	20,000	
Goodwill	76,000	
Expenses	8,000	
Differential		152,000

This entry reveals that the differential at the beginning of the year, which is
set up in the consolidated statement working paper by the investment
elimination entry, is subsequently distributed so as to achieve the following two objectives:

1. Recognize *end-of-year* unamortized costs for specific assets and liabilities.
2. Recognize the amortization of costs for the year for specific categories
   of expenses.

Whether the allocation and amortization of the differential is handled by
two entries, as initially illustrated, or one compound entry, both of these
objectives are always achieved.

**Relationship between Investment Account Balance and Net Assets of
Subsidiary.**   In Chapter 3, it was pointed out that the balance of an investment account carried on the equity method reflects at any point in time the
parent company's monetary interest in the recorded net assets of the subsidiary. But this constant relationship holds only when the original cost of
the investment at the date of acquisition is equal to the parent's purchased
interest in the subsidiary's recorded net assets, that is, when there is no
differential. If a differential exists, the investment account balance will
reflect at any point in time the parent's monetary interest in the subsidiary's recorded net assets plus (minus) the unamortized balance of the debit
(credit) differential. Thus, for Case 2, the investment account balance at
December 31, 19X2, can be analyzed as follows:

P Company's monetary interest in S Company's recorded net assets [80% × ($50,000 + $185,000)]	$188,000
Unamortized differential at December 31, 19X2 ($152,000 − $8,000)	144,000
Investment account balance, December 31, 19X2	$332,000

Treatment of Separate Accumulated Depreciation Account.   In most of
our examples, plant and equipment is depicted net of accumulated depreciation. This treatment facilitates the comparison between book and fair
values required for the initial allocation of the differential, and simplifies
the eliminating entries in the consolidated statement working paper. The
analysis remains the same even if a separate accumulated depreciation
account is included in the working paper. However, the eliminating entries
must be modified to reflect the two separate components. For example,
assume that the plant and equipment in our example was disaggregated as
follows:

	Book Value, January 1, 19X1	Fair Value, January 1, 19X1	Difference	P Company's 80% Interest Therein
Plant and equipment (gross)........	$ 240,000	$ 465,000	$ 225,000	$ 180,000
Accumulated depreciation	[160,000]	[310,000]	[150,000]	[120,000]
Plant and equipment (net)..........	$ 80,000	$ 155,000	$ 75,000	$ 60,000

The amount of the differential to be allocated to plant and equipment
remains $60,000 (P Company's proportionate interest in the difference be-
tween fair value and book value), but the eliminating entry at December
31, 19X1, would be modified in the following manner:

Inventory (1/1)	4,000	
Plant and Equipment	180,000	
Land	20,000	
Goodwill..	80,000	
Accumulated Depreciation—Plant and Equipment.........		120,000
Differential...		164,000

The eliminating entry to recognize the amortization of the differential for
19X1 would then be:

Expenses	8,000	
Accumulated Depreciation—Plant and Equipment.........		6,000
Goodwill		2,000

In future periods, the allocation to plant and equipment will remain unchanged, and the effect of prior periods amortization of the differential will
be included in the amount assigned to accumulated depreciation. Thus,

the eliminating entries at December 31, 19X2, would assume the following form:

Plant and Equipment	180,000	
Land	20,000	
Goodwill	78,000	
Accumulated Depreciation—Plant and Equipment		126,000
Differential		152,000
Expenses	8,000	
Accumulated Depreciation—Plant and Equipment		6,000
Goodwill		2,000

Note that there is no substantive change in the values assigned to assets or expenses. Only the form of the entries has been modified to correspond with the assumed change in the working paper accounts associated with plant and equipment.

Realignment of Subsidiary's Shareholders' Equity

Among the more common ways of altering a corporation's capital structure are the declaration of stock dividends, changing the par value of outstanding stock, and appropriations of retained earnings. Such actions by a subsidiary do not affect consolidated net income or retained earnings, but in the year of their occurrence they do require special attention in the consolidated statement working paper.

Stock Dividends.   The parent company, like any investor, records the receipt of dividend shares of stock only by a memorandum entry. The entry made by the issuing company depends upon the size of the stock dividend, but in any case it will decrease retained earnings and increase the subsidiary's paid-in capital. Therefore, in the year a stock dividend is distributed by a subsidiary, an additional eliminating entry must be made in the working paper (prior to making the investment elimination entry) to reverse the parent's share of the amounts recorded by the subsidiary in its stock dividend entry. the investment elimination entry is then made on the basis of the amounts recorded in the subsidiary's stockholders' equity accounts *at the beginning of the year*. (Note that these amounts will *not* be the amounts reflected in the subsidiary's balance sheet and thus in the working paper for capital stock and other contributed capital.) The end result is that the consolidated balance sheet will reflect only stock dividends distributed to nonaffiliates.

For example, assume that an 80 percent owned subsidiary declared a stock dividend during the current year that was recorded by the subsidiary with the following entry:

```
Dividends Declared......................................    100,000
      Capital Stock.........................................           10,000
      Other Contributed Capital..............................          90,000
```

The eliminating entry to reverse the parent's share of this entry would be:

```
Capital Stock..............................................     8,000
Other Contributed Capital..................................    72,000
      Dividends Declared.....................................           80,000
```

The investment elimination entry is then made on the basis of the balances of the subsidiary's stockholders' equity accounts at the *beginning* of the year. The minority interest extensions, however, are based upon the *end-of-year* balances in the subsidiary's stockholders' equity accounts.

In years subsequent to the distribution of the stock dividend, no special modifications of the standard eliminating entries are required.

There is an accounting convention that the sources of cash dividends are the most recently accumulated earnings and the sources of stock dividends are the earliest accumulated earnings. Therefore, more subsidiary stock dividends effectively capitalize a portion of the subsidiary's retained earnings that is either eliminated or allocated to the minority interest. But what happens when the stock dividends are large enough to capitalize earnings accumulated subsequent to acquisition? The parent's share of these earnings is included in consolidated retained earnings. Yet, the capitalized amount is clearly unavailable for dividend distribution by the parent. One position on this circumstance is that the restriction imposed by the capitalization of postacquisition subsidiary earnings warrants classification of this amount as additional paid-in capital in the consolidated balance sheet. However, this position is rejected in current accounting policy with the following argument:

> Occasionally, subsidiary companies capitalize earned surplus [retained earnings] arising since acquisition, by means of a stock dividend or otherwise. This does not require a transfer to capital surplus [additional paid-in capital] on consolidation, inasmuch as the retained earnings in the consolidated financial statements should reflect the accumulated earnings of the consolidated group not distributed to the shareholders of, or capitalized by, the parent company.[4]

_____

[4] AICPA, "Consolidated Financial Statements," *Accounting Research Bulletin No. 51* (New York, 1959), par. 18.

Although the capitalized postacquisition subsidiary earnings need not therefore be transferred to additional paid-in capital in the consolidated balance sheet, the authors believe that disclosure (parenthetically or by footnote) of this permanent limitation on dividend availability should be made in the formal consolidated statements.

Changes in Par Value of Subsidiary Stock.   A subsidiary may change the legal status of its capital stock, either in the amount of the par value, from par value to no par value, or no par value to par value. Such an action has no effect on the investment account of the parent company or on consolidated net income and retained earnings. In the consolidated statement working paper for the year of the change, either the original journal entry can be reversed with an eliminating entry to restore the subsidiary's equity accounts to their beginning of the year balances, or the investment elimination entry may be made against end of the year balances in the contributed capital accounts. The latter alternative is usually simpler if there have been no other transactions during the year affecting the subsidiary's contributed capital.

Appropriation of Retained Earnings.   In the event the subsidiary has an appropriation of retained earnings, this balance should merely be included with the unappropriated retained earnings in the consolidated statement working paper. No special disclosure is necessary in the consolidated statements unless the amount of appropriated retained earnings exceeds the retained earnings existing at date of acquisition, in which case this temporary limitation on dividend availability may be disclosed.

Interim Purchases

Attention has thus far focused on the preparation of consolidated statements where the date of acquisition of subsidiary shares and the beginning of the affiliates' accounting periods are the same. Unfortunately, the accounting convenience provided by this coincidence of dates occurs infrequently. Since a subsidiary's shares are perhaps more often acquired at interim dates, we must consider how the revenue and expenses of the subsidiary from the beginning of the period to the date of acquisition are to be reflected in the consolidated income statement. Current accounting policy prescribes two alternative methods:

> When a subsidiary is purchased during the year, there are alternative ways of dealing with the results of its operations in the consolidated income statement. One method, which usually is preferable, especially where there are several dates of acquisition of blocks of shares, is to include the subsidiary in the consolidation as thought it had been acquired at the beginning of the year, and to deduct at the bottom of the consolidated income statement the preacquisition earnings applicable to each block of stock. This method presents results which are more indicative of the current status of the group,

and facilitates future comparison with subsequent years. Another method of prorating income is to include in the consolidated statement only the subsidiary's revenue and expenses subsequent to the date of acquisition.[5]

Under either method, preacquisition earnings of the subsidiary do not affect consolidated net income. The methods differ only in the amounts of the subsidiary's revenue and expenses that will be included in consolidated revenue and expenses. When the subsidiary's revenues and expenses for the entire year are included in the consolidated income statement, the special deduction for "purchased preacquisition earnings" (which is set up in the investment elimination entry for interim purchases handled this way) compensates for the extra net revenue.

Case 3.   To illustrate the alternative impacts of the two methods on the consolidated income statement, assume that P Company acquired 80 percent of the capital stock of S Company on April 1, 19X1, for $124,000. Assume further that on January 1, 19X1, S Company had outstanding capital stock of $100,000 and retained earnings of $50,000, and that the two companies reported the following operating information for the year ended December 31, 19X1:

	P Company	S Company Total	4/1–12/31 (estimated)	1/1–3/31 (estimated)
Sales.....................	$200,000	$100,000	$75,000	$25,000
Cost of sales.............	$ 90,000	$ 60,000	$45,000	$15,000
Other expenses	50,000	20,000	15,000	5,000
	$140,000	$ 80,000	$60,000	$20,000
Net income...............	$ 60,000	$ 20,000	$15,000	$ 5,000

* Excluding P Company's interest in S Company's earnings.

The consolidated income statements that would be reported under each of the two alternative methods are reflected in Illustration 4–5 and the investment elimination entries are shown in Illustration 4–6.

Whichever method is used, we must estimate the subsidiary's net income from the beginning of the year to the date of acquisition. In the data given for S Company, it is implicitly assumed that income is earned uniformly throughout the year; where there is evidence of pronounced sea-

---

[5] Ibid., par. 11. The problem of dealing with the acquisition of blocks of shares at several different dates is covered in Chapter 10. Additionally, as is explained in Chapter 5 when the combination is accounted for as a pooling of interests, there is but a single way to handle the subsidiary's preacquisition revenues and expenses—they are included in the consolidated income statement *and* there is no deduction for purchased preacquisition earnings.

Illustration 4–5

ALTERNATIVE CONSOLIDATED INCOME STATEMENTS
Statements for Interim Purchase of Case 3

	Method A: Include Revenue and Expenses of Subsidiary for the Entire Year		Method B: Include Only Revenue and Expenses of Subsidiary Subsequent to Date of Acquisition	
Consolidated sales.........................		$300,000		$275,000
Consolidated expenses:				
Cost of sales	$150,000		$135,000	
Other expenses.........................	70,000	220,000	65,000	200,000
		$ 80,000		$ 75,000
Less:				
Minority interest........................	$ 4,000†		$ 3,000‡	
Purchased preacquisition earnings.........	4,000*	8,000	–0–	3,000
Consolidated net income		$ 72,000		$ 72,000

Verification of consolidated net income by definition (incremental approach):

P Company's income from its own operations............	$60,000
Increased by P Company's equity in S Company's *postacquisition* earnings (80% × $15,000)................	12,000
Consolidated net income	$72,000

* 80% × $5,000.
† 20% × $20,000.
‡ 20% × $15,000.

sonality, however, the allocation of revenue and expenses to preacquisition and postacquisition periods should reflect this nonuniformity. Note that the parent's entry to record its equity in subsidiary earnings is unaffected by the choice of the amount of subsidiary revenues and expenses to be included in the consolidated income statement. Whichever method is chosen, the parent records its equity only in the postacquisition earnings of the subsidiary (in Case 3, 80 percent of $15,000).

Under what has been labeled "Method A," the subsidiary's total revenue and expenses for the entire year are included in consolidated revenue and expenses. Therefore, the parent company's acquired interest in the preacquisition earnings of the subsidiary must be recognized as a deduction in the consolidated income statement. In this case, preacquisition earnings were estimated to be $5,000, and the parent's purchased interest was 80 percent thereof, or $4,000. The minority interest in net income is determined by multiplying the minority's fractional interest at the end of the year (20 percent) by the amount of subsidiary net income included in the working paper ($20,000). This calculation of minority interest may be confirmed by considering the different equities of the minority shareholders for the period of time *before* and *after* P Company's acquisition:

January 1 to March 31: 100% of $5,000................. $5,000
April 1 to December 31: 20% of 15,000................. 3,000

$8,000

Subsidiary net income purchased by majority
   shareholders: 80% of $5,000 4,000

Interest in net income accruing to year-end
   minority shareholders............................. $4,000

Under Method B, the subsidiary's revenue and expenses have been included only from the date of acquisition. In effect, this method is implemented *as if the subsidiary closed its books on the date of acquisition.* That is, in the consolidated working paper, S Company's income statement for nine months (April 1–December 31) would be combined with P Company's income statement for the year 19X1 to produce 19X1 consolidated income statement figures. Since no preacquisition earnings are included in the consolidated figures, no adjustment for purchased preacquisition earnings is necessary under this alternative. Minority interest in net income is calculated as before: end-of-year fractional interest (20 percent) multiplied by subsidiary net income included in the working paper (under this method,

Illustration 4–6

ALTERNATIVE INVESTMENT ELIMINATION ENTRIES
Entries for Interim Purchase of Case 3

Method A—Include revenue and expenses of subsidiary for the entire year:

(1)	Equity in Subsidiary Earnings (80% × $15,000)...........	12,000	
	Investment in S Company		12,000
(2)	Capital Stock—S Company	80,000	
	Retained Earnings—S Company (80% × $50,000)	40,000	
	Purchased Preacquisition Earnings (80% × $5,000)	4,000	
	Investment in S Company		124,000

Method B—Include only revenue and expenses of subsidiary subsequent to date of acquisition:

(1)	Equity in Subsidiary Earnings (80% × $15,000)...........	12,000	
	Investment in S Company		12,000
(2)	Capital Stock—S Company	80,000	
	Retained Earnings—S Company (80% × $55,000)	44,000	
	Investment in S Company		124,000

Note: In eliminating entry (1) under both methods, it is assumed that S Company did not declare any dividends *subsequent* to acquisition. If dividends had been declared, the investment account balance would of course be lower and the entry would be modified to incorporate the elimination of the intercompany dividends.

$15,000). Finally, consistent with the "as if closed" approach, the elimination of S Company's retained earnings is based upon the estimated April 1 balance ($50,000 plus $5,000 estimated earnings), not the January 1 balance as in Method A.

In the event the subsidiary had declared cash dividends in the current period *prior* to acquisition, the investment elimination entries under Method A would be modified slightly. However, since the "as if the books were closed" approach of Method B uses the estimated retained earnings balance on the date of acquisition, the effect of the dividend declaration would be included in that estimate.

Case 4. To illustrate the effect of preacquisition dividends, assume S Company's retained earnings balance was $60,000 on January 1, 19X1, and that S Company declared a cash dividend of $10,000 on March 15, 19X1. The net effect of these two assumptions is to leave S Company's book value the same as it was in Case 3, but with modified balances in the shareholders' equity accounts. Drawing upon the rest of the data in Case 3, investment elimination entry (2) for the Method A example in Illustration 5–7 would be changed to the following:

Capital Stock—S Company	80,000	
Retained Earnings—S Company (80% × $60,000)	48,000	
Purchased Preacquisition Earnings (80% × $5,000)	4,000	
Dividends Declared—S Company (80% × $10,000)		8,000
Investment in S Company		124,000

Note that the *net* effect of the retained earnings and dividends declared elements of this entry is the same as the retained earnings elimination in the entry in Illustration 4–6, and all other elements of the two entries are the same. Entry (1) would be unaffected by these assumptions.

In summary, when a subsidiary is acquired during the year, there are two alternative ways of reporting the subsidiary's operating data in the consolidated income statement. One method includes the subsidiary's revenue and expenses for the entire year, with a corresponding deduction for preacquisition earnings purchased by the parent company. This method facilitates comparison of revenue and expense items with their counterparts in subsequent accounting periods (since entire year amounts will appear in subsequent consolidated income statements). The alternative method includes only the subsidiary's revenue and expenses subsequent to the date of acquisition. Consolidated net income will, however, be the same under both methods.[6]

---

[6] When the subsidiary is acquired by a single purchase of stock (rather than several blocks) and the combination is accounted for as a purchase, consideration of the general spirit of *APB Opinion No. 16* would suggest a preference for the alternative of including only the subsidiary's revenue and expenses subsequent to the date of acquisition.

Income Tax Considerations

Consolidated Income Tax Returns.   Technical rules respecting the preparation of consolidated income tax returns are usually complex and are clearly beyond the scope of this text. Yet, a few summary comments seem appropriate.

An election to file either a separate or consolidated tax return is available to member corporations of an "affiliated group." To qualify as an "affiliated group," there must exist a corporate ownership chain in which a major parent corporation owns at least 80 percent of the voting power of all classes of stock of the several affiliates; additionally, at least 80 percent of each class of nonvoting stock of at least one affiliate must also be held by the major parent company. The election to file a consolidated return relates to all domestic affiliates; foreign corporations are not normally includable.

Among the advantages of filing consolidated income tax returns are the following: (1) intercompany dividends are not includable in consolidated taxable income, (2) gains on the sale or exchange of property between members of the affiliated group are usually not recognized, and (3) current year's losses of one affiliate may be offset against the current year's net income of another.

The following disadvantages should also be noted: (1) an election to file a consolidated return applies to all future years unless specified qualifying conditions are met, (2) each affiliate is required to use the same taxable year and to adopt a generally uniform method of accounting, and (3) losses in transactions with affiliate members are not recognized in determining consolidated taxable income.

Provision of Deferred Taxes on Undistributed Earnings of Subsidiaries Not Included in Consolidated Tax Returns.   If a subsidiary is not included in a consolidated tax return (perhaps because it is less than 80 percent owned or it is a foreign subsidiary), the parent company may have to pay income tax on a portion of its recognized interest in the subsidiary's undistributed earnings at some future date. The tax on currently distributed earnings will of course have been paid and recognized by the parent company. The potential tax on the subsidiary's undistributed earnings may be levied upon a future distribution of cash dividends by the subsidiary (usually subject to an 85 percent dividends received deduction), or perhaps on the proceeds of sale upon disposition of all or part of the stock interest.

In view of this potential tax liability of the parent, *APB Opinion No. 23* requires the parent to make a deferred income tax provision on the subsidiary's undistributed earnings *unless* there is strong evidence that the earnings will be permanently invested or that eventual remittance will be in the form of a tax-free liquidation. If either of these conditions exists, a footnote should be added to the consolidated statements indicating the reason why deferred taxes were not provided and the cumulative amount of undistributed earnings on which the parent company has not recognized income taxes. If the conditions are not satisfied, the parent company should debit Income Tax Expense and credit Deferred Tax Liability for the deferred income tax on the subsidiary's undistributed earnings of the current period (taking into account the dividends received deduction or other special income tax provisions that might be applicable). It might be noted that when the equity method is applied to a less than 50 percent-owned investee, *APB Opinion No. 24 requires* tax allocation; no potential "escape" conditions are specified for this type of investment. The deferred tax would be calculated and recorded in the same manner as for a subsidiary.

Case 5. Assume that P Company owns 70 percent of the outstanding common shares of S Company, and that P's equity method income from its investment is $150,000. In addition, assume that this equity method income includes $40,000 in debit differential amortization that is not tax deductible. Lastly, assume that P Company received $60,000 in dividends from S Company, that these dividends are subject to the 85 percent dividend deduction, and that P's applicable income tax rate is 40 percent. The calculation of P Company's deferred taxes on undistributed earnings of S Company appears in Illustration 4–7. Based on this calculation, P Company would record income tax expense of $11,400, taxes currently payable of $3,600, and deferred taxes of $7,800.

When a subsidiary files a separate income tax return (federal or state), the tax paid is a determinant of its net income for the period. Thus, the parent's equity is based upon the subsidiary's reported net income after

Illustration 4–7

CALCULATION OF DEFERRED TAXES ON UNDISTRIBUTED SUBSIDIARY EARNINGS

P Company's equity method earnings	$150,000
Add debit differential amortization	40,000
Earnings which eventually will be received in dividends	$190,000
Dividends received deduction (85%)	161,500
Equity method earnings ultimately subject to taxation	$ 28,500
Tax rate	x .40
P Company's income tax expense due to equity method earnings	$ 11,400
Dividends received from S Company	$ 60,000
Dividends received deduction (85%)	51,000
Taxable income	$ 9,000
Tax rate	x .40
Taxes currently payable	$ 3,600
Income tax expense	$ 11,400
Taxes currently payable	3,600
Deferred taxes	$ 7,800

taxes—as it normally should be. However, when the subsidiary pays income tax in the current period on profits that are considered unrealized on a consolidated basis (unconfirmed intercompany profits), these taxes must be deferred. The procedures applicable to these circumstances are explained in Chapter 8.

In subsequent chapters, we will assume that the affiliates have filed consolidated tax returns and/or deferral of income taxes is inappropriate, unless otherwise indicated.

Combined and Parent Company Financial Statements

In addition to its consolidated statements, a parent company will under certain circumstances include supplemental financial statements in its financial reports to shareholders or regulatory commissions. Two such statements most frequently encountered are combined (or group) financial statements and separate (unconsolidated) parent company statements.

Combined (Group) Financial Statements. Some controlled or related companies are excluded from consolidation because they do not meet all of the requisite tests (see Chapter 2). If there are several of these companies, it is often informative to combine their financial statements into one or more groups. The SEC takes the following position on this matter:

> There may be filed financial statements in which majority-owned subsidiaries not consolidated with the parent are consolidated or combined in one or more groups, and 50 percent or less owned persons the investments in which are accounted for by the equity method are consolidated or combined in one or more groups, pursuant to principles of inclusion or exclusion which will clearly exhibit the financial position and results of operations of the group or groups.[7]

Combined statements are also used to present the financial position and results of operations of two or more companies owned by one individual (the so-called brother-sister corporations) or under common management.

The general principles followed in this combining process are similar to those used in consolidating two or more companies. The accounts of the companies are additively combined, with appropriate elimination of intercompany transactions. However, there usually is no investor/investee relationship between companies included in the group, and thus no investment elimination entry.[8]

Parent Company Statements. Under certain circumstances, a parent company may elect to include its separate financial statements with the consolidated statements in order "to indicate adequately the position of

---

[7] *Regulation S-X, Part 210—Form and Content of Financial Statements,* Article 4-03.

[8] *Accounting Research Bulletin No. 51,* par. 22.

bondholders and other creditors or preferred stockholders of the parent."[9] These statements are encountered more frequently however in filings with the SEC. Most SEC registration and report forms require the filing of separate parent company statements. Since it is generally acknowledged that these statements are not the primary financial statements of a reporting entity, the SEC allows this requirement to be satisfied by including condensed parent company statements in a note to the consolidated statements.[10]

Statement of Changes in Financial Position

In 1963, the Accounting Principles Board issued *Opinion No. 3* encouraging the presentation of a statement of source and application of funds as supplementary information in financial reports. Subsequently, this recommendation was strongly supported by the principal stock exchanges, several regulatory agencies, and the business community at large, resulting in a significant increase in the number of companies presenting the statement. In view of this widespread acceptance, the Board decided in 1971 to require inclusion of this statement in most circumstances:

> The Board concludes that information concerning the financial and investing activities of a business enterprise and the changes in its financial position for a period is essential for financial statement users, particularly owners and creditors, in making economic decisions. When financial statements purporting to present both financial position (balance sheet) and results of operations (statement of income and retained earnings) are issued, a statement summarizing changes in financial position should also be presented as a basic financial statement for each period for which an income statement is presented.[11]

Consistent with its earlier opinion, the Board adopted a broadly based disclosure concept and changed the title of the statement to reflect this concept:

> The Board also concludes that the statement summarizing changes in financial position should be based on a broad concept embracing all changes in financial position and that the title of the statement should reflect this broad concept. The Board therefore recommends that the title be Statement of Changes in Financial Position (referred to below as "the Statement"). The Statement of each reporting entity should disclose all important aspects of its

---

[9] Ibid., par. 23.

[10] Parent company statements are to be included when subsidiary net assets which cannot be distributed to the parent exceed 25 percent of consolidated net assets. The calculation of restricted net assets can be quite complex. See Securities and Exchange Commission, "Codification of Financial Reporting Policies," *Financial Reporting Release No. 1* (Washington, D.C.: U.S. Government Printing Office, 1982), sec. 213.

[11] APB, "Reporting Changes in Financial Position," *APB Opinion No. 19* (New York: AICPA, 1971), par. 7. This statement is also required in SEC filings.

financing and investing activities regardless of whether cash or other elements of working capital are directly affected.[12]

If the financial reports presented by a company are consolidated statements, the statement of changes in financial position must also be on a consolidated basis. The elements of this statement that are unique to the consolidation process are discussed in the following paragraphs.

Typically, the amount of "funds" (cash or working capital) provided by operations is calculated as the reported net income plus nonfund-using expenses minus nonfund-providing credits. These nonfund adjustments include such items as depreciation expense, amortization of intangibles, and equity in unconsolidated affiliates earnings (in excess of dividends received). Since consolidation often establishes goodwill that is subsequently amortized, this adjustment will frequently appear in the "operations" section of the consolidated statement of changes in financial position. Additionally, the income statement deduction for minority interests is not a fund-using item and must be added to consolidated net income to derive "funds provided by operations." The fact that the minority interest deduction in the income statement does not use funds is evidenced by the carry-forward of this item to the retained earnings section of the working paper, and finally to the balance sheet as a long-term equity.

Subsidiary dividend payments to minority shareholders must be disclosed as an application of funds, since the income statement allocation to minority interests is treated as a nonfund-using item. Adequate disclosure in the statement requires that these payments, if material, be shown separately from parent company dividends paid to majority stockholders.

Transactions between affiliates are eliminated in the normal course of preparing a consolidated income statement, statement of retained earnings, and balance sheet. These eliminations are equally applicable to the statement of sources and applications of funds, since interaffiliate transactions do not affect the amount of cash or working capital associated with the consolidated entity.

In the event the parent acquires additional shares of an existing subsidiary, the cost of the acquisition may or may not represent a use of funds. If the shares were purchased directly from the subsidiary corporation, the interaffiliate character of the transaction would eliminate any effect on consolidated funds. If the shares are purchased from outside (minority) interests, the acquisition represents an application of funds.

Case 6.   The consolidated income statement and comparative balance sheets for P Company and its 80 percent owned subsidiary S Company are shown in Illustration 4–8. The following additional data are provided:

1.   The amortization of goodwill recognized in the consolidation amounted to $3,000 for the year 19X1. This amount is included in other operating expenses.

---

[12] Ibid., par. 8.

Illustration 4–8

P COMPANY AND SUBSIDIARY S COMPANY
Consolidated Income Statement
For the Year Ended December 31, 19X1

Sales		$171,000
Expenses:		
Cost of goods sold...........................	$60,000	
Depreciation	15,000	
Other operating expenses	75,000	150,000
Income from operations		$ 21,000
Equity in earnings of unconsolidated affiliates		4,000
Combined net income...........................		$ 25,000
Minority interest in net income		2,000
Consolidated net income		$ 23,000

P COMPANY AND SUBSIDIARY S COMPANY
Consolidated Balance Sheets
December 31, 19X1, and 19X0

	19X1	19X0
Assets		
Cash	$ 24,000	$ 25,000
Receivables	52,000	60,000
Inventory.................................	84,000	49,000
Equipment (net of depreciation)...............	155,000	150,000
Investment in unconsolidated affiliates	27,000	26,000
Goodwill..................................	37,000	40,000
Total assets	$379,000	$350,000
Equities		
Liabilities:		
Accounts payable..........................	$ 65,000	$ 55,000
Bonds payable............................	80,000	100,000
Total liabilities........................	$145,000	$155,000
Minority interest............................	$ 21,000	$ 20,000
Stockholder's equity:		
Common stock	$125,000	$100,000
Retained Earnings	88,000	75,000
Total stockholders' equity	$213,000	$175,000
Total equities...............................	$379,000	$350,000

2. Equipment (net of depreciation) increased by $5,000. This increase was the net result of a $20,000 purchase of equipment and depreciation expense of $15,000.

3. P Company recognized income of $4,000 from its equity in unconsolidated affiliates and received dividend distributions from them of $3,000. Therefore, the investment (on an equity basis) increased by $1,000.

4. Minority interest in net income was $2,000; however, minority interest in the consolidated balance sheet increased by only $1,000. The $1,000

difference represents dividends paid by the subsidiary to minority shareholders. It may be noted that the subsidiary paid dividends of $4,000 to P Company, which amount was appropriately eliminated as an interaffiliate transaction.

5. Long-term debt of S Company of $20,000 was retired during 19X1.
6. P Company common stock was increased by $25,000 during 19X1, which represents a stock issuance to outside parties.
7. Consolidated retained earnings increased by $13,000, although consolidated net income was $23,000. The difference of $10,000 reflects dividends paid to P Company stockholders.

The formal consolidated statement of changes in financial position is presented in Illustration 4–9. This statement is designed (arbitrarily) to analyze changes in terms of working capital.

Illustration 4–9

P COMPANY AND SUBSIDIARY S COMPANY
Consolidated Statement of Changes in Financial Position
For the Year Ended December 31, 19X1

Working capital was provided by:		
Operations:		
Net income	$23,000	
Charges [credits] not affecting working capital:		
Depreciation expense	15,000	
Amortization of goodwill.................................	3,000	
Minority interest in net income	2,000	
Equity in undistributed earnings of unconsolidated affiliates..	[1,000]	$ 42,000
Proceeds from sale of common stock		25,000
		$ 67,000
Working capital was used for:		
Dividends to:		
P Company shareholders....................................		$ 10,000
Minority shareholders.....................................		1,000
Purchase of equipment.......................................		20,000
Retirement of debt...		20,000
		$ 51,000
Increase in working capital		$ 16,000
Changes in working capital:		
Cash		$ [1,000]
Receivables		[8,000]
Inventory..		35,000
Accounts payable..		[10,000]
Increase in working capital		$ 16,000

Appendix: Illustration of Consolidated Statement Working Paper Eliminating Entries for Differential Allocation and Amortization when the Investment Account Is Carried under the Cost Method

Since the investment elimination entry remains unchanged from year to year when the parent company uses the *cost* method to account for its investment, the differential that is set up by this entry will continue to be equal to the total differential at acquisition. Therefore, slightly modified eliminating entries to allocate and amortize the differential are required when the cost method is used, because the entries illustrated in the main body of this chapter are designed to deal with the unamortized differential balance at the beginning of the period (as is set up under working paper techniques for the equity method).

Under the equity method, differential amortization is recorded by the parent company, and the investment account accordingly reduced. However, under the cost method, differential amortization is *not* recorded by the parent company. Therefore, the difference between the balances initially assigned to the differential in the consolidated statement working paper under the two methods is the accumulated amortization of the differential from the date of acquisition to the beginning of the current period. That is, the balance set up for the differential in a "cost-method" working paper will be higher by this amount than the balance set up in an "equity-method" working paper. Since this accumulated amortization for prior periods is an appropriate reduction of consolidated retained earnings at the beginning of the period, it is recorded in the differential allocation eliminating entry as a debit against the beginning retained earnings of the parent company (which extends directly to the consolidated column). Having thus accounted for the "excess" in the differential balance that results when the cost method has been followed, the remainder of the differential allocation entry is the same as it would be in an equity method case. Further, with the same balances being assigned to the specific assets and liabilities under either circumstance, the differential amortization eliminating entry will be identical in both cases.

Applying these observations to the example provided in the main body of the chapter (Cases 1 and 2), we note that *no* differences exist *in the year of acquisition*. The reason for this situation is that the investment elimination entries under the equity method set up the differential at the beginning of the year, and in the first year this coincides with the differential set up under the cost method. Therefore, we will confine our attention to the eliminating entries in the second year (Case 2). For this year, the differential set up under the cost method is $164,000—the total differential at date

Illustration 4–10

P COMPANY AND SUBSIDIARY S COMPANY
Consolidated Statement Working Paper
For Year Ended December 31, 19X2

	P Company	S Company	Eliminations Dr.	Eliminations Cr.	Minority Interest	Consolidated
Income Statement						
Sales	586,000	250,000				836,000
Dividend income	10,000		(2) 10,000			–0–
Inventory (12/31)	110,000	50,000				160,000
Total credits	706,000	300,000				996,000
Inventory (1/1)	82,000	30,000				112,000
Purchases	280,000	120,000				400,000
Expenses	198,000	110,000	(4) 8,000			316,000
Total debits	560,000	260,000				828,000
						168,000
Minority interest in net income—S Company					8,000	8,000
Net income—carried forward	146,000	40,000	18,000	–0–	8,000	160,000
Retained Earnings Statement						
Retained earnings, 1/1/X2:						
P Company	482,000		(3) 12,000			470,000
S Company		157,500	(1) 96,000		31,500	30,000
Net income—brought forward	146,000	40,000	18,000	–0–	8,000	160,000
	628,000	197,500			39,500	660,000
Dividends declared:						
P Company	50,000					50,000
S Company		12,500		(2) 10,000	2,500	–0–
Retained earnings, 12/31/X2—carried forward	578,000	185,000	126,000	10,000	37,000	610,000
Balance Sheet						
Cash	130,000	36,000				166,000
Accounts receivable	150,000	80,000				230,000
Inventory	110,000	50,000				160,000
Investment in S Company	300,000			(1) 300,000		–0–
Land	50,000	40,000	(3) 20,000			110,000
Plant and equipment (net)	128,000	64,000	(3) 54,000	(4) 6,000		240,000
Differential			(1) 164,000	(3) 164,000		–0–
Goodwill			(3) 78,000	(4) 2,000		76,000
	868,000	270,000				982,000
Accounts payable	90,000	35,000				125,000
Capital stock:						
P Company	200,000					200,000
S Company		50,000	(1) 40,000		10,000	–0–
Retained earnings—brought forward	578,000	185,000	126,000	10,000	37,000	610,000
Minority interest in S Company					47,000	47,000M
	868,000	270,000	482,000	482,000		982,000

(1) Elimination of investment in S Company stock. (2) Elimination of intercompany dividends. (3) Allocation of the differential as of date of acquisition to specific assets (unamortized balances as of January 1, 19X2), with the remainder to Retained Earnings—P Company. (4) Amortization of the allocated differential balances for 19X2.

of acquisition. Referring back to the investment elimination entries for 19X2 under the equity method (pages 138–39), we observe a differential of $152,000. The $12,000 difference is the amount of the 19X1 differential amortization (see Illustration 4–3). Therefore, under the cost method, this amount is debited to the retained earnings of P Company in the differential allocation eliminating entry. The amounts allocated to plant and equipment, land, and goodwill are the same as they were under the equity method. The differential allocation eliminating entry for the year ended December 31, 19X2, thus assumes the following form when the cost method has been used:

Retained Earnings—P Company	12,000	
Plant and Equipment (net)	54,000	
Land	20,000	
Goodwill	78,000	
Differential		164,000

As was noted above, since the same amounts are assigned to the specific assets in this entry as were assigned when the equity method was used, the eliminating entry to recognize amortization of these allocated amounts for 19X2 is the same.

Expenses	8,000	
Plant and Equipment (net)		6,000
Goodwill		2,000

These differential allocation and amortization entries are reflected in the consolidated statement working paper for the year ended December 31, 19X2, in Illustration 4–10. The financial statements for the two companies in this working paper reflect the same economic events as the working paper in Illustration 4–4, but P Company's accounts have been restated to reflect its use of the cost method rather than the equity method. Comparison of the Consolidated columns in the two working papers reveals that the same balances are extended for *all* accounts appearing in the consolidated financial statements.

Questions

1. State the basic principle of accounting for differential subsequent to the date of acquisition.

2. How does differential amortization affect the value of the minority interest?

3. Define consolidated net income using the incremental approach, and giving recognition to differential amortization.

4. For an investment carried under the equity method, what is the relationship between the investment account balance and the net assets of the subsidiary at any point in time?

5. If a stock dividend is declared by a subsidiary, what special steps must be taken in the consolidated statement working paper in the year the dividend is declared? In subsequent years?

6. When a subsidiary is purchased during the year, what are the two alternative ways of reflecting its results of operations for the year in the consolidated income statement?

7. Should deferred taxes be provided on the parent's share of undistributed earnings of subsidiaries not included in consolidated tax returns? On the investor's share of undistributed earnings of an investee?

8. When are combined (group) financial statements prepared?

9. What general principles are used in preparing combined (group) financial statements?

10. When are separate parent company financial statements prepared?

11. Enumerate three "nonfund-using expenses or nonfund-providing credits" that may arise as a result of investments in affiliates.

12. How are subsidiary dividend payments disclosed in the consolidated statement of changes in financial position?

Exercises

Exercise 4-1

Select the best answer for each of the following.

1. In a business combination accounted for as a purchase, how should the excess of fair value of net assets acquired over cost be treated?
   a. Amortized as a credit to income over a period *not* to exceed 40 years.
   b. Amortized as a charge to expense over a period *not* to exceed 40 years.
   c. Amortized directly to retained earnings over a period *not* to exceed 40 years.
   d. Allocated as a reduction of noncurrent assets other than long-term investments in marketable securities.

2. On January 1, 19X1, the Robohn Company purchased for cash 40 percent of the 300,000 shares of voting common stock of the Lowell Company for $1,800,000 when 40 percent of the underlying equity in the net assets of Lowell was $1,400,000. Robohn amortizes goodwill over a 40-year period with a full year's amortization taken in the year of the purchase. As a result of this transaction, Robohn has the ability to exercise significant influence over the operating and financial policies of Lowell. Lowell's net income for the year ended December

31, 19X1, was $600,000. During 19X1, Lowell paid $325,000 in dividends to its stockholders. The income reported by Robohn for its investment in Lowell should be—

a. $120,000.
b. $130,000.
c. $230,000.
d. $240,000.

3. On December 1, 19X1, Chest Corporation purchased 200,000 shares representing 45 percent of the outstanding stock of Park Company for cash of $2,500,000. As a result of this purchase, Chest has the ability to exercise significant influence over the operating and financial policies of Park. Forty-five percent of the net income of Park amounted to $20,000 for the month of December and $350,000 for the year ended December 31, 19X1. The appropriate amount of goodwill amortization to be recorded by Chest in 19X1 as a result of its purchase of Park stock would be $10,000. On January 15, 19X2, cash dividends of $0.30 per share were paid to stockholders of record on December 31, 19X1. Chest's long-term investment in Park should be shown in Chest's December 31, 19X1 balance sheet at—

a. $2,450,000.
b. $2,460,000.
c. $2,500,000.
d. $2,510,000.

(AICPA adapted)

Exercise 4–2

On January 1, 19X1, P Company purchased an 80 percent interest in S Company for $120,000. On this date, S Company had capital stock of $25,000 and retained earnings of $50,000.

An examination of S Company's assets and liabilities revealed that book values were equal to fair values for all except plant and equipment (net) which had a book value of $50,000 and a fair value of $75,000. The plant and equipment had an expected remaining life of five years. P Company planned to amortize any goodwill acquired in the combination over 20 years.

During 19X1 and 19X2, P Company reported net income from its own operations of $20,000, and S Company's income was $10,000 per year. S Company did not pay dividends either year.

Required:
a. Prepare the entries that P Company would have made in 19X1 and 19X2 in respect to its investment in S Company.
b. Prepare the eliminating entries for consolidated statement working papers on December 31, 19X1, and December 31, 19X2.
c. Prepare a schedular calculation of consolidated net income for 19X1 and 19X2.

Exercise 4–3

On January 1, 19X1, P Company purchased a 60 percent interest in S Company for $180,000. On this date, S Company had capital stock of $60,000 and retained earnings of $40,000.

An examination of S Company's assets and liabilities revealed that book values were equal to fair values. P Company planned to amortize any goodwill acquired in the combination over the maximum period of 40 years.

During 19X1 and 19X2, P Company's net income from its own operations was $30,000 per year, and S Company's net income amounted to $20,000 per year.

Required:

a. Prepare the entries that P Company would have made in 19X1 and 19X2 in respect to its investment in S Company.

b. Prepare the eliminating entries for consolidated statement working papers on December 31, 19X1, and December 31, 19X2.

c. Prepare a schedular calculation of consolidated net income for 19X1 and 19X2.

Exercise 4–4

On September 1, 19X1, the Horn Company purchased 200,000 shares representing 45 percent of the outstanding stock of Mat Company for cash. As a result of the purchase, Horn has the ability to exercise significant influence over the operating and financial policies of Mat. Goodwill of $500,000 was appropriately recognized by Horn at the date of the purchase.

On December 1, 19X2, Horn purchased 300,000 shares representing 30 percent of the outstanding stock of Simon Company for cash of $2,500,000. The stockholders' equity section of Simon's balance sheet at the date of the acquisition was as follows:

Common stock, par value $2 a share.........	$2,000,000
Additional paid-in capital...................	1,000,000
Retained earnings.........................	4,000,000
	$7,000,000

Furthermore, at the date of acquisition, the fair value of Simon's property, plant, and equipment, net, was $3,800,000, whereas the book value was $3,500,000. For all of the other assets and liabilities of Simon, the fair value and book value was equal. As a result of the transaction, Horn has the ability to exercise significant influence over the operating and financial policies of Simon.

Assume that Horn amortizes goodwill over the maximum period allowed and takes a full year's amortization in the year of purchase.

Required:

Prepare a schedule computing the amount of goodwill and accumulated amortization at December 31, 19X2, and the goodwill amortization for the year ended December 31, 19X2.

(AICPA adapted)

Exercise 4–5

Assume that General Motors acquired all of the outstanding common stock of IBM in an exchange of shares on December 31, 19X1. The combination was accounted for as a purchase, and on this date the fair market value of the shares exchanged was determined to be approximately $37,000,000,000.

The following information was taken from the financial statements of the (assumed) combination participants:

	General Motors	IBM
Recorded net assets, December 31, 19X1	$13,000,000,000	$11,000,000,000
Net income for 19X1	1,250,000,000	2,000,000,000

Assume that all of the differential is allocated to goodwill, and that it will be amortized over the maximum time period.

Required:

a. Assuming that the two companies had earnings from their own operations in 19X2 equal to the 19X1 amounts, and that there were no intercompany transactions during the year, calculate consolidated net income for 19X2.

b. Assuming that the December 31, 19X2, investment elimination entries have already been prepared, prepare the eliminating entries to allocate the differential and to recognize differential amortization for 19X2.

c. If consolidated statements were prepared on January 1, 19X2, what percentage of consolidated net assets was represented by the "purchased" goodwill?

d. Assuming that General Motors had 290 million common shares outstanding in 19X1 and that it issued 610 million additional common shares to acquire IBM, calculate consolidated earnings per share for 19X2. How does this compare to General Motors' earnings per share in 19X1?

Exercise 4–6

On January 1, 19X1, P Company purchased an 80 percent interest in S Company for $140,000. On this date, S Company had capital stock of $25,000 and retained earnings of $50,000.

An examination of S Company's assets and liabilities revealed that book values were equal to fair values for all except plant and equipment (net) which had a book value of $30,000 and a fair value of $75,000. The plant and equipment had an expected remaining life of 10 years. P Company planned to amortize any goodwill acquired in the combination over 40 years.

During 19X1 and 19X2, P Company reported net income from its own operations of $20,000, and S Company's income was $20,000 in 19X1 and $15,000 in 19X2. S Company did not pay dividends either year.

Required:

a. Prepare the entries that P Company would have made in 19X1 and 19X2 in respect to its investment in S Company.

b. Prepare the eliminating entries for consolidated statement working papers on December 31, 19X1, and December 31, 19X2.

c. Prepare a schedular calculation of consolidated net income for 19X1 and 19X2.

Exercise 4–7

On January 1, 19X1, P Company purchased a 60 percent interest in S Company for $220,000. On this date, S Company had capital stock of $60,000 and retained earnings of $40,000.

An examination of S Company's assets and liabilities revealed that book values were equal to fair values. P Company planned to amortize any goodwill acquired in the combination over the maximum period of 40 years.

During 19X1 and 19X2, P Company's net income from its own operations was $30,000 per year, and S Company's net income amounted to $10,000 in 19X1 and $15,000 in 19X2.

Required:
a. Prepare the entries that P Company would have made in 19X1 and 19X2 in respect to its investment in S Company.
b. Prepare the eliminating entries for consolidated statement working papers on December 31, 19X1, and December 31, 19X2.
c. Prepare a schedular calculation of consolidated net income for 19X1 and 19X2.

Exercise 4–8

Jones Company purchased in the open market 80 percent of the capital stock of Irwin, Inc., on January 1, 19X1, at $50,000 more than 80 percent of its book value. The differential was allocated totally to goodwill, with an estimated life of 20 years. During the following five years, Irwin, Inc., reported cumulative earnings of $200,000 and paid $50,000 in dividends. On January 1, 19X6, minority shareholders in Irwin, Inc., had an equity of $70,000 in the net assets of the company.

Required:
If the parent company carries its investment in subsidiary stock on an equity basis—

a. Determine the January 1, 19X1, cost of the investment.
b. Calculate the investment carrying value on December 31, 19X5.

Exercise 4–9

Smith Company purchased in the open market 60 percent of the capital stock of Mori Company on January 1, 19X1, at $100,000 more than 60 percent of its book value. The differential was allocated $40,000 to plant and equipment (net) and $60,000 to goodwill. The plant and equipment had an estimated remaining life of 10 years, and the goodwill was estimated to have a life of 20 years.

On January 1, 19X4, minority shareholders in Mori Company have an equity of $96,000 in the net assets of the company.

Required:
If the parent company carries its investment in subsidiary stock on an equity basis—

a. Determine the net assets of Mori Company on January 1, 19X4.
b. Calculate the investment carrying value on January 1, 19X4.

Exercise 4–10

On January 1, 19X1, P Company purchased an 80 percent interest in S Company for $140,000. On this date, S Company had capital stock of $50,000 and retained earnings of $25,000.

An examination of S Company's assets and liabilities revealed that book values were equal to fair values for all except plant and equipment (net) which had a book value of $100,000 and a fair value of $125,000, and inventory which had a book value of $30,000 and a fair value of $40,000. The plant and equipment had an expected remaining life of five years, and the inventory should all be sold in 19X1. P Company planned to amortize any goodwill acquired in the combination over 20 years.

P Company's income from its own operations was $35,000 in 19X1 and $40,000 in 19X2. S Company's income was $30,000 in 19X1 and $25,000 in 19X2. S Company did not pay any dividends either year.

Required:
a. Prepare the entries that P Company would have made in 19X1 and 19X2 in respect to its investment in S Company.
b. Prepare the eliminating entries for consolidated statement working papers on December 31, 19X1, and December 31, 19X2.
c. Prepare a schedular calculation of consolidated net income for 19X1 and 19X2.

Exercise 4–11

On January 1, 19X1, P Company purchased a 60 percent interest in S Company for $113,000. On this date, S Company had capital stock of $10,000 and retained earnings of $20,000.

An examination of S Company's assets and liabilities revealed that book values were equal to fair values for all except plant and equipment (net) which had a book value of $100,000 and a fair value of $150,000, and inventory which had a book value of $25,000 and a fair value of $30,000. The plant and equipment had an expected remaining life of five years, and the inventory should all be sold in 19X1. P Company planned to amortize any goodwill acquired in the combination over 40 years.

P Company's income from its own operations was $50,000 in 19X1 and $40,000 in 19X2. S Company's income was $35,000 in 19X1 and $30,000 in 19X2. S Company paid cash dividends of $10,000 each year.

Required:
a. Prepare the entries that P Company would have made in 19X1 and 19X2 in respect to its investment in S Company.
b. Prepare the eliminating entries for consolidated statement working papers on December 31, 19X1, and December 31, 19X2.
c. Prepare a schedular calculation of consolidated net income for 19X1 and 19X2.

Exercise 4–12

P Company purchased an 80 percent interest in S Company on January 1, 19X1, for $40,000, when S Company had capital stock of $20,000 and retained earnings of $30,000.

During 19X1, S Company reported net income of $10,000 and paid cash dividends of $5,000. Additionally, S Company paid a 10 percent stock dividend on October 15, 19X1, on which it made the following entry:

Dividends Declared	7,000	
Additional Paid-In Capital		5,000
Capital Stock		2,000

Required:
a. Prepare the entries that P Company would have made in 19X1 in respect to its investment in S Company.
b. Prepare the investment elimination entries for a consolidated statement working paper for the year ended December 31, 19X1.

Exercise 4–13

P Company purchased an 80 percent interest in S Company on March 1, 19X1, for $38,400. On January 1, 19X1, S Company had capital stock of $20,000 and retained earnings of $25,000.

The companies' operating data for 19X1 are as follows:

	P Company*	S Company
Sales	$300,000	$60,000
Cost of sales	$180,000	$30,000
Other expenses	40,000	12,000
	$220,000	$42,000
Net income	$ 80,000	$18,000

    * Excluding P Company's interest in S Company earnings.

It is assumed that S Company's revenue is earned and expenses incurred uniformly throughout the year. Neither company paid any dividends in 19X1.

Required:
a. Prepare a consolidated income statement for 19X1 under each of the two alternative methods of dealing with the subsidiary's operating results for the year.
b. Prepare investment elimination entries for a consolidated statement working paper for the year ended December 31, 19X1, for each of the two alternatives.

Exercise 4–14

P Company purchased a 70 percent interest in S Company on September 1, 19X1, for $70,000. On January 1, 19X1, S Company had capital stock of $50,000 and retained earnings of $30,000.

The companies' operating data for 19X1 are as follows:

	P Company*	S Company
Sales	$140,000	$90,000
Cost of sales	$ 60,000	$45,000
Other expenses	30,000	15,000
	$ 90,000	$60,000
Net income	$ 50,000	$30,000

* Excluding P Company's interest in S Company earnings.

It is assumed that S Company's revenue is earned and expenses incurred uniformly throughout the year. Neither company paid any dividends in 19X1.

Required:

a. Prepare a consolidated income statement for 19X1 under each of the two alternative methods of dealing with the subsidiary's operating results for the year.

b. Prepare investment elimination entries for a consolidated statement working paper for the year ended December 31, 19X1, for each of the two alternatives.

Exercise 4–15

P Company purchased 90 shares of S Company capital stock on May 1, 19X1, in the open market for $16,200. A partial trial balance as of December 31, 19X1, discloses the following balances:

	P Company	S Company
Capital stock ($100 par)	$100,000	$10,000
Retained earnings (1/1)	40,000	5,000
Dividends declared	5,000	2,000
Sales	200,000	40,000
Cost of goods sold	130,000	20,000
Operating expenses	40,000	8,000
Equity in subsidiary earnings	?	

S Company declared a $10 dividend per share on February 1 and July 1.

It is assumed that subsidiary net income is earned uniformly throughout the year.

P Company elects to include S Company's operating results for all of 19X1 in the 19X1 consolidated income statement.

Required:

a. Prepare the entries made by P Company in 19X1 for its investment in S Company.

b. Prepare the investment elimination entries for a consolidated statement working paper for the year ended December 31, 19X1.

c. Prepare the consolidated income statement for the year ended December 31, 19X1.

Exercise 4–16

Allen, Inc., earned $36,000 during 19X1 without significant seasonal fluctuation. The company declared and paid dividends of $3,000 on March 1 and again on August 1. On January 1, 19X1, Allen's stockholders' equity appeared as follows:

Common stock ($10 par)	$300,000
Other contributed capital	50,000
Retained earnings	100,000

On May 1, 19X1, Shores Enterprises purchased a 90 percent interest in Allen, Inc., in the open market at a cost of $503,100. Any differential arising from the combination is to be allocated to goodwill, and amortized over 10 years (including a pro rata allocation to 19X1).

Shores Enterprises reported net income from its own operations in 19X1 of $50,000.

Required:

a. Prepare the entries made by Shores Enterprises in 19X1 for its investment in Allen, Inc.
b. Prepare the eliminating entries for a consolidated statement working paper for the year ended December 31, 19X1, assuming Shores Enterprises elected to include Allen's operating results for all of 19X1 in the 19X1 consolidated income statement.
c. Prepare a schedular calculation of consolidated net income for 19X1, using *(a)* the incremental approach and *(b)* the residual approach.

Exercise 4–17

Amos Company's 19X1 operations included equity method earnings from its investment in 70 percent of the outstanding common shares of Charlotte Chemical Company, computed as follows:

Seventy percent of Charlotte's reported net income	$80,000
Differential amortization.	15,000
Equity method earnings	$65,000

During 19X1, Charlotte declared and distributed a dividend in the amount of $50,000. The dividend received by Amos was subject to the 85 percent dividends received deduction. Amos pays income tax at a 40 percent rate.

Required:

Calculate the income tax expense, deferred taxes, and current tax liability due to Amos Company's investment in Charlotte Chemical Company.

Exercise 4–18

Hawkes Systems, Inc., a chemical processing company, has been operating profitably for many years. On March 1, 19X1, Hawkes purchased 50,000 shares of Diversified Insurance Company stock for $2,000,000. The 50,000 shares represented 25 percent of Diversified's outstanding stock. Both Hawkes and Diversified operate on a fiscal year ending August 31.

For the fiscal year ended August 31, 19X1, Diversified reported net income of $800,000 earned ratably throughout the year. During November 19X0 and February, May, and August 19X1, Diversified paid its regular quarterly cash dividend of $100,000.

Required:

a. Assume that the investment should be classified as a long-term investment in the noncurrent-asset section of Hawkes' balance sheet. The cost of Hawkes' investment equaled its equity in the recorded values of Diversified's net assets; recorded values were not materially different from fair values (individually or collectively). For the fiscal year ended August 31, 19X1, how did the net income reported and dividends paid by Diversified affect the accounts of Hawkes (including Hawkes' income tax accounts)? Indicate each account affected, whether it increased or decreased, and explain the reason for the change in the account balance (such as Cash, Investment in Diversified, etc.). Organize your answer in the following format:

Account Name	Increase or Decrease	Reason for Change in Account Balance

b. Independent of your answer to part *(a)* above, assume Hawkes had purchased 70 percent of Diversified's stock on March 1, 19X1.

   (1) Under certain circumstances Hawkes (the parent) should not accrue income taxes on all or part of its equity in the undistributed earnings of Diversified (its subsidiary). What are these circumstances and what evidence and other considerations must be evaluated to substantiate these circumstances?

   (2) What information should be disclosed in the notes to its financial statements if Hawkes does not accrue income taxes on all or part of its equity in the undistributed earnings of Diversified?

   (3) Would it be appropriate to prepare consolidated financial statements for Hawkes and its subsidiary, Diversified, for the fiscal year ended August 31, 19X1? Explain.

(AICPA adapted)

Exercise 4–19

The consolidated income statement for 19X1 of Clark Corporation and its 80 percent owned subsidiary is as follows:

Sales	$85,000
Cost of goods sold............	30,000
Gross profit..................	$55,000
Operating expenses...........	25,000
Combined income	$30,000
Minority interest..............	1,000
Consolidated net income	$29,000

Required:

a. Is it possible to determine the amount of net income contributed by the parent's own operations? If so, how much was contributed by Clark in 19X1?

b. Assuming that none of the reported expenses represent noncash expenses (e.g., depreciation), what is your best estimate of the net amount of working capital generated by operations during 19X1 and therefore available for use by the consolidated entity?

Exercise 4–20

Using the symbols presented below indicate how each of the following items should be disclosed in the consolidated statement of changes in financial position of the Panozzo Company and its subsidiaries when the format is designed to show changes in *working capital*. There may be more than one answer; if so, indicate all answers.

A   = add in determining funds provided by operations.
S   = subtract in determining funds provided by operations.
OS = other source of working capital.
OU = other use of working capital.
WC = included in schedule of changes in elements of working capital.
N   = not separately disclosed or not included.

1._____ Consolidated net income was $90,000.
2._____ Consolidated accounts receivable decreased $5,000.
3._____ The Panozzo Company declared and paid a 5 percent stock dividend.
4._____ The minority interest in combined earnings totaled $4,000.
5._____ Bonds were issued to an unaffiliated company in exchange for equipment valued at $20,000.
6._____ The Panozzo Company declared and paid a cash dividend of $4,000.
7._____ Long-term debt of the Panozzo Company was converted to common stock.
8._____ Consolidated accounts payable increased $3,000.
9._____ Amortization of a premium on bonds payable to an unaffiliated company totaled $500.
10._____ Equipment, with a book value of zero dollars, was sold to an unaffiliated company for $15,000.

11._____ Equipment costing $8,000 was purchased for cash from an unaffiliated company for cash.
12._____ The Panozzo Company issued 5,000 shares of stock in exchange for 80 percent of the stock of the ABC Company.
13._____ Panozzo's share of the earnings of an unconsolidated subsidiary totaled $4,000. The subsidiary did not pay any cash dividends during the year.
14._____ Consolidated depreciation expense totaled $10,000.
15._____ Panozzo's share of a cash dividend declared and paid by a consolidated subsidiary totaled $4,000.
16._____ The minority interest in a cash dividend declared and paid by a consolidated subsidiary totaled $1,000.
17._____ Amortization of goodwill recognized in the consolidation process totaled $8,000.
18._____ Panozzo's share of the cash dividends of an unconsolidated subsidiary exceeded Panozzo's share of the subsidiary's earnings by $3,000.

Problems

Problem 4–21

The Bunker Company purchased 80 percent of the capital stock of the Hampton Corporation on January 1, 19X1, for $71,200, when the latter's capital stock and retained earnings were $50,000 and $10,000, respectively. Book values were equal to fair values for all assets and liabilities of Hampton Corporation except inventory which had a fair value of $12,000 on January 1, 19X1. Bunker planned to amortize any goodwill over 10 years.

Trial balances prepared on December 31, 19X1, disclose the following:

	Bunker Company	Hampton Corporation
Cash..............................	$ 8,000	$ 5,000
Accounts receivable	21,000	17,000
Inventory (1/1).....................	15,000	8,000
Investment in Hampton	74,000	
Other assets	33,800	48,000
Dividends declared..................	10,000	5,000
Purchases	90,000	20,000
Expenses..........................	10,000	7,000
	$261,800	$110,000
Accounts payable	$ 5,000	$ 10,000
Other liabilities	5,000	
Capital stock.......................	100,000	50,000
Retained earnings...................	40,000	10,000
Sales..............................	105,000	40,000
Equity in subsidiary earnings..........	6,800	
	$261,800	$110,000
Inventory (12/31)....................	$ 20,000	$ 10,000

Required:

a. Prepare the eliminating entries for a consolidated statement working paper for the year ended December 31, 19X1.
b. Prepare a consolidated statement working paper for the year ended December 31, 19X1.

Problem 4–22

P Company purchased 60 percent of the capital stock of S Company on January 1, 19X1, for $46,000 when the latter's capital stock and retained earnings were $30,000 and $10,000, respectively. Book values were equal to fair values for all assets and liabilities of S Company except plant and equipment (net) which had a fair value $20,000 in excess of book value. The plant and equipment had an estimated remaining life of five years, and any goodwill arising from the combination should be amortized over 10 years.

Trial balances for the companies on December 31, 19X2, are shown following:

	P Company	S Company
Cash.	$ 28,800	$ 30,000
Inventory (1/1).	30,000	15,000
Investment in S Company	51,200	
Plant and equipment (net)	80,000	40,000
Dividends declared.	20,000	5,000
Purchases	48,000	23,000
Expenses.	12,000	7,000
	$270,000	$120,000
Accounts payable	$ 24,400	$ 20,000
Capital stock	100,000	30,000
Retained earnings.	50,000	20,000
Sales.	90,000	50,000
Equity in subsidiary earnings	5,600	
	$270,000	$120,000
Inventory (12/31)	$ 20,000	$ 10,000

Required:

a. Prepare the eliminating entries for a consolidated statement working paper for the year ended December 31, 19X2.
b. Prepare a consolidated statement working paper for the year ended December 31, 19X2.

Problem 4–23

On January 1, 19X1, United Distributors purchased 1,200 shares of Texas Wholesalers, Inc., capital stock for $200,000 when its accumulated retained earnings were $50,000. Book values were equal to fair values for all assets and liabilities of the subsidiary except land and building. Information provided by an appraisal survey completed shortly after the investment indicated the following:

	Replacement Cost New	Sound Value
Land	$ 50,000	$ 50,000
Building	280,000	140,000

The original estimate of service life in respect to the building remained unchanged by the appraisal, that is, original estimate, 20 years; remaining life, 10 years.

The December 31, 19X2, trial balances are as follows:

	United Distributors	Texas Wholesalers, Inc.
Inventory (1/1)	$ 50,000	$ 20,000
Land	100,000	40,000
Building	400,000	200,000
Other assets..............................	790,000	135,000
Investment in Texas Wholesalers, Inc.	229,600	
Dividends declared	10,000	5,000
Purchases................................	200,000	70,000
Expenses.................................	50,000	10,000
	$1,829,600	$480,000
Liabilities	$ 296,000	$ 20,000
Accumulated depreciation—building	100,000	120,000
Sales.....................................	300,000	120,000
Equity in subsidiary earnings	20,800	
Capital stock (par, $100)....................	742,000	150,000
Retained earnings..........................	370,800	70,000
	$1,829,600	$480,000
Inventory (12/31)	$ 75,000	$ 10,000

Required:

a. Prepare the eliminating entries for a consolidated statement working paper for the year ended December 31, 19X2.

b. Prepare a consolidated statement working paper for the year ended December 31, 19X2.

Problem 4–24

Hondo Nelson is the sole stockholder of two corporations: Luckenbach Taverns, Inc., and Luckenbach Long Neck Distributors. Financial statements for these companies are presented on page 174.

Statements of Financial Position
December 31, 19X1

	Luckenbach Taverns, Inc.	Luckenbach Long Neck Distributors
Assets		
Cash	$ 10,000	$ 25,000
Receivables	35,000	5,000
Inventory	125,000	100,000
Due from Luckenbach Taverns, Inc.		50,000
Long-lived assets	20,000	150,000
Total assets	$190,000	$330,000
Equities		
Current liabilities	$ 20,000	$ 50,000
Long-term debt...........................	100,000	80,000
Stockholders' equity:		
Capital stock	10,000	10,000
Retained earnings	60,000	190,000
Total equities............................	$190,000	$330,000

Income Statements
For Year Ended December 31, 19X1

	Luckenbach Taverns, Inc.	Luckenbach Long Neck Distributors
Sales	$300,000	$500,000
Cost of sales	$160,000	$200,000
Other expenses...........................	100,000	150,000
Total expenses	$260,000	$350,000
Net income	$ 40,000	$150,000

Mr. Nelson wishes to make an application for a large bank loan in January 19X2, and his accountant suggests that he prepare combined financial statements for his two separate business interests. Mr. Nelson agrees, and the accountant develops the following additional data in his review of the records:

1. During 19X1, Luckenbach Long Neck Distributors made sales of $100,000 to Luckenbach Taverns, Inc. None of these goods remained in the December 31, 19X1, inventory of Luckenbach Taverns, Inc.
2. On December 31, 19X1, Luckenbach Taverns, Inc., owed $50,000 to Luckenbach Long Neck Distributors. This debt was included with a note payable to the bank in "long-term debt." No interest was payable on the debt on December 31, 19X1.

Required:

Prepare a combined statement of financial position on December 31, 19X1, and a combined income statement for 19X1 for Mr. Nelson's two businesses. It is not necessary to prepare a working paper.

Problem 4–25

The consolidated income statement and comparative balance sheets for P Company and its 90 percent owned subsidiary S Company are provided below:

P COMPANY AND SUBSIDIARY S COMPANY
Consolidated Income Statement
For the Year Ended December 31, 19X1

Sales		$150,000
Expenses:		
Cost of goods sold	$50,000	
Depreciation	10,000	
Other operating expenses	60,000	120,000
Income from operations		$ 30,000
Equity in earnings of unconsolidated affiliates		3,000
Combined net income		$ 33,000
Minority interest in net income		1,000
Consolidated net income		$ 32,000

P COMPANY AND SUBSIDIARY S COMPANY
Consolidated Balance Sheets
December 31, 19X1, and 19X0

	19X1	19X0
Assets		
Cash	$ 23,000	$ 12,000
Receivables	50,000	40,000
Inventory	30,000	50,000
Equipment (net of depreciation)	140,000	130,000
Investment in unconsolidated affiliates (equity basis)	7,000	8,000
Goodwill	45,000	50,000
Total assets	$295,000	$290,000
Equities		
Liabilities:		
Accounts payable	$ 25,000	$ 30,000
Bonds payable	50,000	100,000
Total liabilities	$ 75,000	$130,000
Minority interest	$ 8,000	$ 10,000
Stockholders' equity:		
Common stock (no par)	$150,000	$100,000
Retained earnings	62,000	50,000
Total stockholders' equity	$212,000	$150,000
Total equities	$295,000	$290,000

The following additional data are provided:

1. The amortization of goodwill recognized in the consolidation amounted to $5,000 in 19X1. This amount is included in other operating expenses.

2. P Company received $4,000 in dividend distributions from unconsolidated affiliates in 19X1.
3. New equipment in the amount of $20,000 was purchased in 19X1.
4. Dividends of $27,000 were received from S Company during 19X1.
5. P Company issued additional stock during 19X1 to nonaffiliates in the amount of $50,000.

Required:

Prepare a consolidated statement of changes in financial position for 19X1, with changes analyzed in terms of working capital. Make any inferences that are required.

Problem 4–26

The consolidated income statement and comparative balance sheets for P Company and its 60 percent owned subsidiary S Company are provided as shown.

P COMPANY AND SUBSIDIARY S COMPANY
Consolidated Income Statement
For the Year Ended December 31, 19X1

Sales		$100,000
Expenses:		
Cost of goods sold	$40,000	
Depreciation	5,000	
Other operating expenses	15,000	60,000
Income from operations		$ 40,000
Equity in earnings of unconsolidated affiliates		10,000
Combined net income		$ 50,000
Minority interest in net income		4,000
Consolidated net income		$ 46,000

P COMPANY AND SUBSIDIARY S COMPANY
Consolidated Balance Sheets
December 31, 19X1, and 19X0

	19X1	19X0
Assets		
Cash	$ 20,000	$ 10,000
Receivables	35,000	40,000
Inventory	41,000	50,000
Equipment (net of depreciation)	100,000	80,000
Investment in unconsolidated affiliates (equity basis)	106,000	100,000
Goodwill	18,000	20,000
Total assets	$320,000	$300,000

Equities	19X1	19X0
Liabilities:		
Accounts payable....................................	$ 27,000	$ 50,000
Bonds payable.......................................	75,000	50,000
Total liabilities....................................	$102,000	$100,000
Minority interest.......................................	$ 42,000	$ 40,000
Stockholders' equity:		
Common stock (no par)..............................	$100,000	$100,000
Retained earnings	76,000	60,000
Total stockholders' equity	$176,000	$160,000
Total equities...	$320,000	$300,000

The following additional data are provided:

1. The amortization of goodwill recognized in the consolidation amounted to $2,000 in 19X1. This amount is included in other operating expenses.
2. P Company received $4,000 in dividend distributions from unconsolidated affiliates in 19X1.
3. New equipment in the amount of $25,000 was purchased in 19X1.
4. Dividends in the amount of $3,000 were received from S Company in 19X1.
5. S Company issued additional bonds during 19X1 to nonaffiliates in the amount of $25,000.
6. Neither P Company nor S Company engaged in any stock transactions during 19X1.

Required:

Prepare a consolidated statement of changes in financial position for 19X1, with changes analyzed in terms of working capital. Make any inferences that are required.

Problem 4–27

The consolidated income statement and comparative balance sheets for Leisure Time, Inc., and its 80 percent owned subsidiary Travel Coordinators, Inc., are provided below.

LEISURE TIME, INC.
Consolidated Income Statement
For the Year Ended December 31, 19X3
($000)

Sales	$200
Expenses	130
Income from operations...	$ 70
Equity in earnings of unconsolidated affiliates..........................	6
Combined net income	$ 76
Minority interest in net income of Travel Coordinators, Inc..............	5
Consolidated net income...	$ 71

LEISURE TIME, INC.
Consolidated Balance Sheets
December 31, 19X3, and 19X2
($000)

	19X3	19X2
Assets		
Current assets	$182	$200
Equipment (net of depreciation)	190	160
Investment in unconsolidated subsidiaries (equity basis)	204	200
Goodwill	33	40
Total assets...	$609	$600
Equities		
Current liabilities..	$ 50	$100
Long-term debt	250	200
Minority interest	20	20
Stockholders' equity:		
Capital stock (no par)......................................	100	100
Retained earnings	189	180
Total equities	$609	$600

The following additional information is determined:

1. The goodwill in the consolidated balance sheet resulted from Leisure Time, Inc.'s acquisition of Travel Coordinators, Inc., in 19X1.
2. New equipment in the amount of $50,000 was acquired during 19X3; no equipment was retired during the year.
3. Leisure Time, Inc., acquired a 35 percent interest in World-Wide Tours, Inc., during 19X3 at a cost of $8,000; no investments were sold during 19X3.
4. On July 1, 19X3, Travel Coordinators, Inc., reacquired 30 percent of its outstanding shares pro rata from Leisure Time, Inc., and its outside shareholders at a price equal to the book value of the shares on the date of purchase. The acquisition, which cost $10,000 in total, was recorded by Travel Coordinators, Inc., with a debit to Treasury Stock. The proceeds received by Leisure Time, Inc., were credited (properly) to Investment in Travel Coordinators, Inc.
5. No errors or omissions in accounting or consolidation procedures were made.

Required:

Prepare a consolidated statement of changes in financial position for 19X3, with changes analyzed in terms of working capital. Make any inferences that are necessary.

Problems for Appendix

Problem 4–28(A)

P Company purchased 60 percent of the capital stock of S Company on January 1, 19X1, for $46,000 when the latter's capital stock and retained earnings were $30,000 and $10,000, respectively. Book values were equal to fair values for all assets and liabilities of S Company except plant and equipment (net) which had a fair value $20,000 in excess of book value. The plant and equipment had an estimated remaining life of five years, and any goodwill arising from the combination should be amortized over 10 years.

Trial balances for the companies on December 31, 19X2, follow:

	P Company	S Company
Cash............................	$ 28,800	$ 30,000
Inventory (1/1)...................	30,000	15,000
Investment in S Company	46,000	
Plant and equipment (net)	80,000	40,000
Dividends declared...............	20,000	5,000
Purchases	48,000	23,000
Expenses.......................	12,000	7,000
	$264,800	$120,000
Accounts payable.................	$ 24,400	$ 20,000
Capital stock	100,000	30,000
Retained earnings................	47,400	20,000
Sales...........................	90,000	50,000
Dividend income.................	3,000	
	$264,800	$120,000
Inventory (12/31).................	$ 20,000	$ 10,000

P Company uses the *cost* method to account for its investment in S Company.

Required:

a. Prepare the eliminating entries for a consolidated statement working paper for the year ended December 31, 19X2.

b. Prepare a consolidated statement working paper for the year ended December 31, 19X2.

Problem 4–29(A)

On January 1, 19X1, United Distributors purchased 1,200 shares of Texas Whole-salers, Inc., capital stock for $200,000 when its accumulated retained earnings were $50,000. Book values were equal to fair values for all assets and liabilities of the subsidiary except land and building. Information provided by an appraisal survey completed shortly after the investment indicated the following:

	Replacement Cost New	Sound Value
Land	$ 50,000	$ 50,000
Building	280,000	140,000

The original estimate of service life in respect to the building remained unchanged by the appraisal, that is, original estimate, 20 years; remaining life, 10 years.

The December 31, 19X2, trial balances are shown below.

	United Distributors	Texas Wholesalers, Inc.
Inventory (1/1)	$ 50,000	$ 20,000
Land	100,000	40,000
Building	400,000	200,000
Other assets	790,000	135,000
Investment in Texas Wholesalers, Inc.	200,000	
Dividends declared	10,000	5,000
Purchases.	200,000	70,000
Expenses	50,000	10,000
	$1,800,000	$480,000
Liabilities	$ 296,000	$ 20,000
Accumulated depreciation—building	100,000	120,000
Sales	300,000	120,000
Dividend income	4,000	
Capital stock ($100 par)	742,000	150,000
Retained earnings	358,000	70,000
	$1,800,000	$480,000
Inventory (12/31)	$ 75,000	$ 10,000

United Distributors uses the *cost* method to account for its investment in Texas Wholesalers, Inc.

Required:

a. Prepare the eliminating entries for a consolidated statement working paper for the year ended December 31, 19X2.

b. Prepare a consolidated statement working paper for the year ended December 31, 19X2.

CHAPTER 5

Interpretive Problems of
Accounting for Business
Combinations

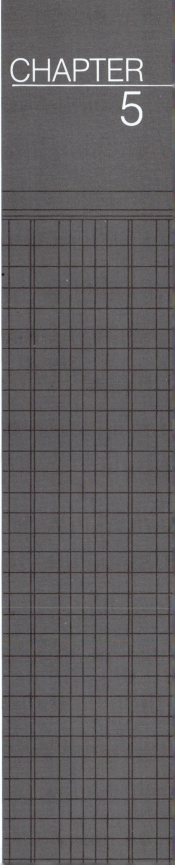

Purchase and Pooling of Interests Accounting

In Chapter 1, the philosophical distinction between a purchase transaction and a pooling of interests transaction was presented. Chapters 2, 3, and 4 were devoted to a discussion of consolidation and separate company financial statements following an acquisition that is to be accounted for as a purchase. In this section, we expand our treatment of business combinations to include pooling of interests accounting for acquisitions. In addition, we will examine the accounting for mergers and consolidations.

Summary of the Criteria for Classifying Business Combinations

Chapter 1 identified 12 required pooling of interests conditions (pages 11–12). If all 12 conditions are met, the combination is classified as a pooling of interests. Collectively, the 12 conditions describe a situation in which a business combination does not involve a purchase/sale transaction. In a pooling of interests, the common stockholders of both combining companies do not give up their ownership interests; they continue as common stockholders of the combined company. The "continuity of ownership interests" characteristic is indicated most directly by the fourth definitional requirement of a pooling. The fourth requirement (see page 11) states that the issuing corporation must issue *only* common stock with rights identical to those of the majority of its outstanding voting common stock, in exchange for substantially all of the voting common stock of the other company. Moreover, this requirement cannot be circumvented by way of treasury stock transactions. Other requirements attempt to ensure that the voting (and other) rights of the newly issued shares are in no way restricted. Still others are intended to ensure that the persons receiving the newly issued shares do not also receive significant amounts of additional compensation that might indicate that they are at least in part selling out.

The requirements for a pooling of interests are very stringent. If *any one* of the 12 conditions is not met, the combination cannot be treated as a pooling; instead, it must be defined as a purchase. In essence, this means that if one or more of the conditions are not satisfied, one stockholder group is interpreted as having sold the assets and liabilities of its company to the other company.

Recall that the legal form of the combination does *not* dictate whether it will be classified as a purchase or a pooling of interests. If the combination is a *consolidation,* where a new corporation replaces all of the constituents, it may be either a purchase or a pooling of interests. And, if the combination is a *merger,* where one of the combining companies remains as the sole, surviving corporation, it may be either a purchase or a pooling of interests. And finally, if the combination is an acquisition, where the combining companies both continue in existence with one as the parent of the other (subsidiary), the combination may be either a purchase or a pooling of interests.

The reader should also understand that most of the accounting issues associated with consolidated financial statements apply equally to pooling of interests and to purchases. In the next subsection, the problem of recognizing and allocating the "differential" is shown to be a problem that applies only to purchase combinations. But subsequent problems such as eliminations of unconfirmed profit on transactions between affiliates, eliminations of parent company investments in the preferred stock of a subsidiary, and changes in the equity of a parent apply to pooling of interests and to purchases.

The remainder of this section includes an examination of (1) the purchase method of accounting, (2) the pooling of interests methods of accounting, and (3) the financial statement consequences produced by the two accounting methods. The importance of these topics is underscored by the FASB's continuing interest and apparent plan to eventually reconsider the whole matter of accounting for business combinations. The Board issued an extensive Discussion Memorandum on this subject in August 1976, but has deferred development of the project pending further progress on its "conceptual framework" project.[1] More recently, the AICPA has issued a number of Issues Papers on the subject.

The Purchase Method of Accounting

The purchase method of accounting for business combinations is simply a specific application of the more general principles of accounting for purchases of all assets. Conventional accounting dictates that purchased assets should be recorded at cost, which is established by the purchase transaction. This rule is complicated in the case of a business combination by the fact that *many* assets and liabilities are acquired rather than one asset or a single class of assets. Therefore, the total cost of the purchase must be allocated among the individual assets received and liabilities assumed. If payment is made in cash, the total cost of the purchased net assets is easily determinable. However, if the payment includes noncash items such as equity securities, the total purchase price (cost) may not be obvious. In such noncash acquisitions, the conventional procedure is to assess the fair market value of the considerations given or the consideration received, whichever is most objectively determinable. This often reduces to assessing fair market value on the basis of the quoted price of the issuing firm's publicly traded shares. A question thus arises regarding on what date the

---

[1] FASB, "Business Combinations and Purchased Intangibles," *Discussion Memorandum*, August, 1976.

price should be obtained. Since an economic motivation for business combinations is production of market value synergy (see Chapter 1), announcement of a forthcoming business combination often triggers a rise in price of the issuing firm's shares. Should the issuing firm's share price be observed before or after announcement? It can be shown that there is no unique answer to this question. A common practice is to use an average of prices observed during a brief period prior to and following announcement.

To provide the basis for a subsequent comparison with the pooling of interest method of accounting, three significant characteristics of the purchase method should be recognized. First, the total cost of acquiring a company typically *is not* equal to the algebraic sum of the fair market values of the company's identifiable assets and liabilities. Appropriate methods of treating such unallocated debit or credit differentials on consolidated statement working papers were discussed in Chapter 4. That discussion obviously applied to cases in which the combination takes the form of an acquisition and a parent-subsidiary relationship results. Where the combination takes the form of a merger or consolidation, the procedures for treating differentials would be expressed in terms of entries made by the surviving corporation. Second, the fair market values of the purchased assets and liabilities, which are recorded on the books of the *combined* entity, frequently differ by substantial amounts from their book values, as previously recorded by the *acquired* company. Third, the retained earnings balance of the acquired company does not carry forward to the combined entity. This is, of course, consistent with conventional practice with respect to recording purchase transactions; the purchase of an income producing asset from a previous user does not result in an increase in the acquiring firm's retained earnings. The previous *earnings* of the asset identify with the selling company and not with the transferred asset. A corollary to this proposition is that balances in the acquired company's revenue and expense accounts at the date of acquisition (i.e., its net income) do not carry forward to the combined company. Thus, they are accounted for in the same manner as are retained earnings of the seller.

As previously indicated, the purchase method entries to record a combination yield equivalent results whatever may be the particular legal form taken by the combination (merger, consolidation, or acquisition). If the sole surviving corporation is one of the combining companies (merger) or is a newly created corporation (consolidation), the entries to record the combining transactions, including the valuation of purchased assets and assumed liabilities at their fair market values, are made on the books of the relevant (new or surviving) corporation. Where a parent-subsidiary relationship is created (acquisition), the investment elimination entries on the consolidated working papers provide the basis for reporting appropriate asset and equity valuations. The reader will recall that the investment elimination entries discussed in Chapters 2, 3, and 4 consistently adhered to the precepts of the purchase method. Preacquisition revenues and expenses (or net income) and retained earnings were either eliminated or were allocated to minority interests; and purchased assets and liabilities were revalued through the allocation of debit or credit differentials, with residual (unallocated) differentials recognized and treated as appropriate under the circumstances.

The Pooling of Interests Method of Accounting

In contrast to purchase combinations, pooling of interests combinations are not best described as purchase/sale transactions. Given the pooling conditions previously described, neither company can be said to *acquire* the other. The history of each combining company can be traced from precombination periods through the act of combining to the continued operations of the combined company. The distinct characteristics and operations of the combining firms are simply commingled in the combined company.

The accounting counterpart of this view involves retaining and aggregating the accounting valuations of the combining companies. Assets and liabilities are carried forward at the valuations reflected in the books of the combining companies; and in most instances, the stockholders' equity accounts of the transferors, excluding common stock retired, are accorded similar treatment. The retained earnings of the new enterprise usually is set equal to the sum of the combining companies' retained earnings. However, it may be less, but never more, than that amount.

In the event that the stated capital (the minimum required contributed capital) of the new entity is greater than the aggregate stated capitals of the combining companies, the retained earnings of the new enterprise may be less than the sum of the amounts recorded on the books of the combining companies. In this instance, the debit difference is first applied to reduce any other contributed capital on the books of the constituents, after which any debit residue is applied in reduction of retained earnings. Where the stated capital of the new enterprise is less than the aggregate stated capitals of its predecessors, the credit difference is reported as an addition to the contributed capital in excess of stated value of the new enterprise.

The following case illustrates accounting values assigned to the stockholders' equity accounts under each of these two pooling of interests conditions.

Case 1.   Consolidation Accounted for as a Pooling of Interests.   The R Corporation is organized on January 1, 19X1, to consolidate companies X and Y; balance sheets of the constituents on this date are as follows:

	X Company	Y Company
Total assets	$310,000	$690,000
Liabilities	$ 10,000	$ 30,000
Capital stock (par, $100).....	200,000	500,000
Other contributed capital.....	40,000	60,000
Retained earnings	60,000	100,000
Total equities...............	$310,000	$690,000

Assumption A.   The R Corporation issues one share of its $50 par value common stock for each $80 of net assets contributed by companies X and Y. The initial entry on the books of R Corporation is as follows:

Assets	1,000,000	
Liabilities..		40,000
Capital Stock (12,000 shares)		600,000
Other Contributed Capital		200,000
Retained Earnings		160,000

Distribution of R Corporation shares:
$300,000/$80 = 3,750 shares to X Company
$660,000/$80 = 8,250 shares to Y Company

In this situation, the $600,000 par value of R Corporation shares is $100,000 less than the outstanding par amount of X Company and Y Company shares. This $100,000 credit difference is added to the Other Contributed Capital balances of X Company and Y Company to determine the $200,000 R Corporation balance. The sum of the retained earnings of companies X and Y is carried forward to the R Corporation without dilution.

Assumption B.   The R Corporation issues one share of its $50 per value common stock for each $60 of net assets contributed by companies X and Y. The initial entry on the books of R Corporation is as follows:

Books of R Corporation

Assets	1,000,000	
Liabilities..		40,000
Capital Stock (16,000 shares)		800,000
Retained Earnings...................................		160,000

Distribution of R Corporation shares:
$300,000/$60 = 5,000 shares to X Company.
$660,000/$60 = 11,000 shares to Y Company.

The stated capital of R Corporation exceeds the aggregate stated capitals of X Company and Y Company; accordingly, the difference of $100,000 is applied to reduce the total amounts of other contributed capital of these companies. The sum of the retained earnings is then carried forward without adjustment. It should be noted that the total stockholders' equity remains the same under both assumptions, as the net assets are recorded at their prior book values.

Case 2.   Merger Accounted for as a Pooling of Interests.   Suppose that the combining companies described in Case 1, X Company and Y Company, agree to combine through a process of merger, whereby X Company will issue 2,400 additional shares of its $100 par, common stock in exchange for the assets and liabilities of Y Company; thereafter, Y Company will distribute the shares to its stockholders in exchange for the outstanding Y Company stock, and Y Company will be terminated. The entry made by X Company to record the combination is as follows:

Books of X Company

Assets	690,000	
Liabilities...		30,000
Capital Stock (2,400 shares)		240,000
Other Contributed Capital		320,000
Retained Earnings...................................		100,000

As a consequence of this entry, X Company's accounts will disclose total assets of $1,000,000; liabilities of $40,000; capital stock of $440,000; other contributed capital of $360,000; and retained earnings of $160,000.

If a pooling of interests takes the acquisition form, the investment account on the parent company's books is debited with the book value of the subsidiary's net assets. The amount of this debit represents an important difference between the pooling of interests method and the purchase method. Under the purchase method, the investment account on the parent company's books is debited with the fair market value of the consideration given, which approximates the fair market value of the net assets received.

On the books of the parent, in recording the issuance of shares under a pooling of interests, it is important to remember that the at-acquisition retained earnings of the subsidiary company are generally carried forward, without deduction, to augment the parent's retained earnings. Accordingly, the parent's retained earnings after recording the combination may be equal to the sum of the precombination retained earnings of both parent and subsidiary affiliates. It will be less than this amount, however, in the event the stated value of the parent's newly issued shares is greater than the sum of the parent's equity in the contributed capital of the subsidiary plus any Other Contributed Capital of the parent that is eliminated in the process of recording the issuance of new shares. Where the stated value of the parent's newly issued shares is less than the corresponding equity in the subsidiary's contributed capital, the credit difference is treated as an increment to Other Contributed Capital.

Case 3.   Acquisition Accounted for as a Pooling of Interests.   The stockholders' equity accounts of A Company and B Company at the date of their combination are as follows:

	A Company	B Company
Common stock (par, $100)	$60,000	$40,000
Other contributed capital...........	6,000	5,000
Retained earnings	44,000	30,000

The stockholders of B Company exchanged 100 percent of their shares for newly issued shares of A Company common stock in the following amounts:

Assumption 1	300 shares
Assumption 2	400 shares
Assumption 3	500 shares
Assumption 4	600 shares

The entry on the books of A Company to record the issuance of shares, for each of the stated assumptions, is presented in Illustration 5–1.

Illustration 5–1

	Assumption							
	1		2		3		4	
	Dr.	Cr.	Dr.	Cr.	Dr.	Cr.	Dr.	Cr.
Investment in B Common Stock...........................	75,000		75,000		75,000		75,000	
Other Contributed Capital	—		—		5,000		6,000	
Common Stock................		30,000		40,000		50,000		60,000
Other Contributed Capital......		15,000		5,000		—		—
Retained Earnings		30,000		30,000		30,000		21,000

The investment elimination entry for a consolidated statement working paper at date of acquisition is the same for all of the assumptions. The entry is:

Common Stock—B Company..................................	40,000	
Other Contributed Capital—B Company.......................	5,000	
Retained Earnings—B Company	30,000	
Investment in B Common Stock...........................		75,000

It should be noted that the investment elimination entry does not include a debit or credit differential. The entries to record the issuance were constructed so that the balance in the Investment in B Common Stock account is exactly equal to the parent's 100 percent equity in the stockholders' equity accounts of the subsidiary. Thus, the pooling of interests method does not involve a revaluation of the assets and liabilities of the affiliates. Based upon this investment elimination entry, the consolidated statement working paper for a pooling of interests is then prepared in the same manner as for a purchase.

Comparative Summary of Purchase and Pooling of Interests Accounting

The criteria used to distinguish between purchase combinations and pooling of interests combinations were discussed in Chapter 1. The purpose of those criteria is to prevent the use of different accounting methods in situations that are essentially similar. Therefore, the purchase and pooling of interests methods *are not alternative* sets of procedures. Nevertheless, an examination of the 12 conditions that lead to the use of the pooling of interests method will disclose that two given combinations may be similar in *many* respects and yet be accounted for by different methods. Consequently, an understanding of the financial statement differences between the two methods is an important factor in the interpretation of the statements. The following discussion, which focuses on these differences, pertains to those situations where combinations are similar in important particulars but are nonetheless sufficiently different to result in the use of different methods.

Consider the difference between the two methods in respect to asset and liability valuation. In the event that an acquired company's net assets have a fair value in excess of book value, the purchase method of accounting results in a debit differential.[2] To the extent this differential is allocated to amortizable assets, future reported expenses will be increased and earnings correspondingly reduced. Further, the unallocated residual amount of differential must also be amortized (see Chapter 4), an expense that is not deductible for income tax purposes. It thereby has a magnified negative influence on future reported earnings. Should the combination be treated as a tax-free reorganization (see Chapter 1), not even the portion that is allocated to specific assets would qualify as a deductible expense. Under these circumstances, a similar business combination, although sufficiently different to require the pooling of interests method, would report smaller asset valuations and higher future earnings. Carrying forward the combined companies' assets at their book values eliminates the future expenses associated with the differential amortization (which is unrecognized). Correspondingly, future net incomes, earnings per share, and rates of return will be larger.

---

[2] In the immediate discussion, it is assumed that the combination takes the form of a parent-subsidiary relationship. But, the same arguments would apply to mergers and consolidations, as is illustrated in Case 4.

If the acquired firm's net assets have a fair market value that is less than book value, the purchase method of accounting results in a credit differential. In accordance with the analysis of differentials presented in Chapter 4, this differential would be allocated to individual assets and liabilities. Thus, conversely to the debit differential illustration, the purchase method would result in smaller reported expenses and larger future net incomes, earnings per share, and rates of return.

Case 4 illustrates the effects of purchase accounting relative to pooling of interests accounting, given a situation in which the fair market value of the acquired company's net assets exceeds their total book value.

Case 4.   On January 1, 19X1, the R Company issued 20,000 common shares in exchange for 100 percent of the S Company's outstanding stock. The balance sheets of R Company and S Company on January 1, 19X1, immediately prior to the combination, are as follows:

	R Company	S Company	Total
Total assets	$2,000,000	$1,000,000	$3,000,000
Liabilities	$ 600,000	$ 300,000	$ 900,000
Common stock ($10 par)	400,000	200,000	600,000
Retained earnings	1,000,000	500,000	1,500,000
Total equities	$2,000,000	$1,000,000	$3,000,000

R Company's common stock was actively traded. Its average price during a brief period surrounding the announcement of the transaction was $120. Because the shares were closely held, S Company's stock had no readily attainable market price. The balance sheet of R Company immediately after the common for common stock exchange will vary depending on which method of accounting is appropriate. In the illustrations of pooling of interests accounting to follow, it is assumed that the combination has met all of the 12 conditions specified in Chapter 1. In the illustrations of purchase accounting, the assumption is made that one of the 12 conditions was not satisfied. For example, at the date of the combination, the combined management expressly stated the intent of selling a significant portion of S Company's assets within two years after the combination and reinvesting the proceeds in a new line of operation.

Illustration 5–2 contains the entries made by R Company and the consolidated working paper elimination entries assuming the transaction is an acquisition classified as both a purchase and a pooling of interests. In addition, the illustration contains the entries made by R Company under both methods assuming the transaction takes the form of a merger with R as the surviving entity. (There are no consolidated working papers since,

Illustration 5–2

	Acquisition				
	R Company Entry		Elimination Entry		
Purchase	Investment in S	2,400,000	Differential	1,700,000	
	Common Stock.	200,000	Common Stock	200,000	
	Other Contributed		Retained Earnings.	500,000	
	Capital	2,200,000	Investment in S . . .		2,400,000
Pooling of interests	Investment in S	700,000	Common Stock	200,000	
	Common Stock.	200,000	Retained Earnings.	500,000	
	Retained Earnings . . .	500,000	Investment in S . . .		700,000

	Merger		
	R Company Entry		Elimination Entry
Purchase	Other Assets (including any goodwill)	2,700,000	Not applicable
	Liabilities	300,000	
	Common Stock.	200,000	
	Other Contributed Capital.	2,200,000	
Pooling of interests	Other Assets	1,000,000	Not applicable
	Liabilities	300,000	
	Common Stock.	200,000	
	Retained Earnings	500,000	

in the case of merger, S Company ceases to exist.) Note that within the purchase and pooling of interests classifications, the only difference between the R Company entries for an acquisition and a merger is that in the case of merger, the assets and liabilities of S Company are recorded individually by R Company. In the case of acquisition, the algebraic sum of these asset and liability values is recorded in R Company's investment account. The consolidated working papers then substitute these individual asset and liability values for the investment account. Thus, the ultimate consolidated balance sheet of R Company and its subsidiary at date of acquisition (and all subsequent financial statements) will be invariant to whether the transaction takes the form of merger or acquisition.

The consolidated working papers under both the purchase and pooling of interests methods of accounting for an acquisition are presented in Illustrations 5–3 and 5–4. Of particular interest is the consolidated stockholders' equity. Under the purchase method, the consolidated stockholders' equity is consistent with a scenario in which R Company purchased net assets at a cost of 2,400,000 and financed the purchase by issuing common shares. In contrast, under the pooling of interests method, the consolidated stockholders' equity is the sum of the precombination stockholders' equities of the constituent companies, as if the two companies had always been operating as one.

Illustration 5–3

R COMPANY AND SUBSIDIARY S COMPANY
Consolidated Statement Working Paper
Combination Accounted for as a Purchase
January 1, 19X1

	R Company	S Company	Eliminations Dr.	Eliminations Cr.	Con- solidated
Other assets	2,000,000	1,000,000			3,000,000
Investment in S	2,400,000			(1) 2,400,000	
Differential			(1) 1,700,000		1,700,000
	4,400,000	1,000,000			4,700,000
Liabilities	600,000	300,000			900,000
Common stock:					
R	600,000				600,000
S		200,000	(1) 200,000		
Other contributed capital	2,200,000				2,200,000
Retained earnings:					
R	1,000,000				1,000,000
S		500,000	(1) 500,000		
	4,400,000	1,000,000	2,400,000	2,400,000	4,700,000

Illustration 5–4

R COMPANY AND SUBSIDIARY S COMPANY
Consolidated Statement Working Paper
Combination Accounted for as a Pooling of Interests
January 1, 19X1

	R Company	S Company	Eliminations Dr.	Eliminations Cr.	Con- solidated
Other assets	2,000,000	1,000,000			3,000,000
Investment in S	700,000			(1) 700,000	
	2,700,000	1,000,000			3,000,000
Liabilities	600,000	300,000			900,000
Common stock:					
R	600,000				600,000
S		200,000	(1) 200,000		
Retained earnings:					
R	1,500,000				1,500,000
S		500,000	(1) 500,000		
	2,700,000	1,000,000	700,000	700,000	3,000,000

Assume that the consolidated net income of R Company and its subsidiary during the years 19X1–X3 was $300,000, $360,000, and $420,000, excluding any deductions for the amortization of a differential. The combination was treated as a "tax-free" reorganization (see Chapter 1). Thus, none of the differential amortizations are tax deductible. Also, assume that the entire differential (arising only under the purchase method) was allocated to assets having remaining estimated useful lives of 17 years. The comparative net incomes and earnings per share under each method are as follows:

	Assuming Pooling of Interests Accounting	Less Differential Amortization	Assuming Purchase Accounting
19X1:			
Net income.................	$300,000	$100,000	$200,000
Earnings per share	$5.00		$3.33
19X2:			
Net income.................	360,000	100,000	260,000
Earnings per share	$6.00		$4.33
19X3:			
Net income.................	420,000	100,000	320,000
Earnings per share	$7.00		$5.33

The essential facts of Case 4 are not atypical. The price paid for S Company, stated in terms of the market value of R Company's common stock, was $2,400,000, while the book value of S Company's stock was $700,000. A market value to book value ratio of 3.4 : 1 is not unusual. Furthermore, the assumed net incomes exhibit realistic relationships to total assets. Thus, the relative effect on the financial statements of the two accounting methods is easily observable.

The assumptions of Case 4 can be adapted to display the relative effect on the financial statements of the two accounting methods when the book value of S Company's net assets exceeds fair market value. For example, it may be assumed that only 5,000 shares of R Company's stock are issued in payment for S Company. The comparative consolidated financial statements in this case are left as an exercise for the reader.

Historical Summaries and Trend Analysis of Combined Business Entities

One method of evaluating the current position and future expectations of a business entity involves a careful examination of the firm's past financial trends and history. To facilitate this type of analysis, published financial reports usually include comparative financial statements for the past two to five years. Additionally, financial summaries (which focus upon such items as sales, earnings, earnings per share, and selected ratios) are frequently provided for as many as the past 10 or 15 years. The preparation and interpretation of these comparative statements and financial summaries are particularly difficult if the period covered by the analysis includes one or more business combinations.

A business combination is usually a critical event in the history of a business entity. Managerial identity, ownership positions, legal structure, the nature of operations and resources as well as their magnitudes, and many other significant aspects of the entity may undergo dramatic change as the result of a combination. Indeed, it can be argued that many business combinations involve such sweeping changes that meaningful comparisons between the combined entity and its precombination constituents are virtually impossible. Nevertheless, there persists a compelling desire for information that may be relevant to future decisions, which has accented the importance of trend analysis extending over periods that include business combinations.

The most basic problem involved in trend analysis of combined business entities relates to the precombination operating periods; the accountant must decide what data of these periods are comparable to the postcombination financial statements. Two alternative approaches to resolving the data selection problem are utilized by accountants. One method is to select the reported precombination financial statements of the *acquiring* firm as the relevant data to compare with the postcombination financial statements of the combined entity. This approach is essentially consistent with the purchase method of accounting. If a combination is interpreted as an acquisition of assets and assumption of liabilities (which is the view implied by purchase accounting), *adjustments* of precombination statements would not appear to be warranted. Thus, historical financial summaries and comparative financial statements prepared in accordance with the purchase method do *not* involve retroactive combining of precombination financial data. The past financial statements of the *acquiring* firm as originally reported are the comparative base.

An alternative approach to historical trend analysis involves restatement of the precombination financial statements to retroactively reflect the combination. This method is a natural counterpart to pooling of interests accounting. Under the pooling perspective, a combined (pooled) entity involves nothing more substantive than the merging of two businesses into a single enterprise. Both continue to exist as one combined entity. Given this perspective, it is consistent to argue for the retroactive combining of precombination financial statements. Such recast statements should be comparable to postcombination statements; therefore, after a pooling of interests combination, any financial reference to precombination periods should be expressed in terms of combined data. For example, where a pooling of interests combination occurs after a balance sheet date but before statements are prepared, the subsequently prepared statements should be prepared on a combined basis.

The decision of whether or not precombination financial data are restated has a significant impact upon the trends displayed by historical comparisons. Case 5 exhibits the differences between the two methods.

Case 5. For several years, G Company and H Company have enjoyed 10 percent growth rates in their sales, earnings, and earnings per share. For 19X1, these firms reported the following data:

	G Company	H Company
Sales	$1,000,000	$750,000
Earnings....................	100,000	75,000
Outstanding shares	100,000	75,000
Earnings per share............	$1.00	$1.00

G Company acquired 100 percent of H Company's stock on January 1, 19X2, in a common for common stock exchange. The exchange ratio was set at .6 to 1. During 19X2, G Company and its subsidiary maintained their historical 10 percent growth rates. Financial data for 19X2 were as follows:

	G Company	H Company	Consolidated
Sales..	$1,100,000	$825,000	$1,925,000
Earnings (excluding parent's equity in subsidiary earnings)	110,000	82,500	192,500
Outstanding shares			145,000*
Earnings per share............................			$1.33

* 100,000 + .6(75,000) = 145,000.

The historical comparisons under both alternative methods are presented in Illustration 5–5. Significantly, the restatement of precombination data results in the 10 percent growth rate being maintained. Thus, if growth rates in sales, earnings, and other operating data are important variables in the decision makers' predictions of future success, restatement would seem appropriate. The large growth rates displayed by comparisons with the unadjusted base are primarily caused by the combinations itself; thus, they are not likely to be maintained over several future periods. Maintaining such growth rates requires increasingly large business combinations. Indeed, the size of the firms to be acquired would have to increase at a geometrical rate.

Illustration 5–5

HISTORICAL COMPARISONS OF FINANCIAL DATA

	19X1 Data		19X2 Data	
	Absolute Amounts	*As a Percentage of 19X0 Amounts**	*Absolute Amounts*	*As a Percentage of 19X1 Amounts*
With retroactive adjustments:				
Sales	$1,750,000	110	$1,925,000	110
Earnings............................	175,000	110	192,500	110
Earnings per share	$1.21	110	$1.33	110
Without retroactive adjustments:				
Sales	$1,000,000	110	$1,925,000	192.5
Earnings............................	100,000	110	192,500	192.5
Earnings per share	$1.00	110	$1.33	133

* The annual growth rate for sales, earnings, and per share was assumed to be 10 percent for years prior to 19X2.

It must be reemphasized that the restatement method is employed only when combinations are accounted for as poolings of interests. The unadjusted method is used if the purchase method is followed.[3] Case 5 was based on the implicit assumption of unique circumstances in which the differences between the purchase and pooling of interests methods did not affect 19X2 combined net income. Consequently, the difference in the reported trends was attributable entirely to the restatement or nonrestatement of the data of precombination periods.

Earnings per Share Analysis

One of the most critical items of information that is drawn from accounting reports is earnings per share. As a summary indicator of current success and future expectations of success, the amount, periodic variation, and growth rate of earnings per share probably have more informational significance than any other data that can be extracted from financial statements. Nonetheless, accountants frequently warn against the dangers of placing an exaggerated emphasis on earnings per share. This summary indicator should always be interpreted in light of all of the other information obtainable from financial statements and other sources. Prudent accountants

---

[3] However, under the purchase method, *APB Opinion No. 16* requires additional, one-time disclosure in the first financial statements issued after the combination. Specifically, the requirement is for footnote disclosure of the current and immediately preceding periods' results of operations based on a pro forma restatement as if the combination had taken place at the beginning of the preceding period. APB, *APB Opinion No. 16* "Business Combinations" [New York: AICPA, 1970], par. 96.)

would acknowledge that proper analysis of all available data is superior to undue reliance on any single item such as earnings per share. Nevertheless, earnings per share continues to be of signal importance to the investing community.

The large number of business combinations in the 1960s was accompanied by an increasing variety of financial methods. Many of these methods have an immediate or potential impact on earnings per share calculations. Even with the employment of more traditional financing methods, the act of combination often causes a sharp discontinuity in the historical trend of earnings per share. As a result, the meaning and reliability of earnings per share calculations must be viewed circumspectly. Understanding these problems and attempts to resolve them is a requisite part of comprehending the broader subject of accounting for business combinations.

In addition to this relationship between earnings per share issues and business combinations, the calculations of earnings per share for consolidated financial statements and for investor companies that use the equity method must be made in accordance with special procedures. Further, unique problems can occur if the securities of one affiliate are convertible into a security of the other affiliate. Thus, earnings per share calculations are an important issue to be understood in the context of learning how to prepare consolidated financial statements.

Case 5 displayed the sharp discontinuities that can occur in historical earnings per share trends when combinations involve traditional common for common stock exchanges. The critical factor that causes this phenomenon is the relative size of the combining firms' price/earnings ratios. Retroactive adjustments (used primarily with pooling of interests accounting) are an attempt to report growth trends that are consistent with internal operations. However, it must be recognized that data once reported are probably never completely overturned in the minds of investors, no matter how forcefully the retroactive adjustments may be emphasized.

Traditional Calculations

Earnings per share is a financial statistic of long standing. Traditionally, it was calculated as a quotient, the numerator of which was net income less preferred dividends declared (including current arrearages) and the denominator of which was the weighted-average number of common shares outstanding. The significance of this calculation as a basic success indicator was implicitly accepted for many years. However, increasing usage of convertible securities, common stock warrants, and stock option plans rendered this traditional calculation misleading and inadequate. As a substitute for this summary statistic, accountants developed two calculations: primary earnings per share and fully diluted earnings per share. Controversy continues as to the importance of these measures as indicants of future business success. Nevertheless, they represent the only evident means of providing the information that was once supplied by the traditional earnings per share calculation.[4]

Primary Earnings per Share

Common Stock Equivalents.   Primary earnings per share is based on a concept of "common stock equivalents" which are added to common stock presently outstanding[5] to determine the denominator in the calculation. In fact, the primary earnings per share statistic is frequently reported in financial statements as "earnings per common share and common equivalent share." The Accounting Principles Board defined the concept of "common stock equivalent" as follows:

> A common stock equivalent is a security which is not, in form, a common stock but which usually contains provisions to enable its holder to become a common stockholder and which, because of its terms and the circumstances under which it was issued, is in substance equivalent to a common stock. The holders of these securities can expect to participate in the application of the value of the common stock resulting principally from the earnings and earnings potential of the issuing corporation. This participation is essentially the same as that of a common stockholder except that the security may carry a specified dividend or interest rate yielding a return different from that received by a common stockholders.[6]

The most prominent types of securities that are, or may be, common stock equivalents are (1) those which are convertible into common stock and (2) common stock options and warrants that allow the holder to purchase common shares at specified prices.

It should be apparent that the definition of common stock equivalents require some more specific operational criteria that may be used to decide whether a specific security should be classified as a common stock equivalent or as a senior security. Without such a definitive standard, the earnings per share calculations of business firms would probably not be based on comparable classifications. With respect to all convertible securities, the Accounting Principles Board stated the following classification criterion:

---

[4] The principal computational and reporting requirements for earnings per share are contained primarily in *APB Opinion No. 15,* which was published in 1968. However, in 1978, the FASB issued *Statement No. 21,* which exempted nonpublic companies from the reporting requirements of *APB Opinion No. 15.* But, if a nonpublic company *chooses* to report earnings per share data, it must follow the *APB Opinion No. 15* requirements.

[5] The amount to be added is the number of common shares that could be issued through conversion or exercise of the common stock equivalents less the number the company could repurchase using the cash proceeds from the exercise of the common stock equivalents.

[6] *APB Opinion No. 15,* "Earnings per Share," par. 25.

a convertible security should be considered as a common stock equivalent at the time of issuance if, based on its market price, it has a cash yield of less than 66⅔% of the then current bank prime interest rate. For any convertible security which has a change in its cash interest rate or cash dividend rate scheduled within the first five years after issuance, the lowest scheduled rate during such five years should be used in determining the cash yield of the security at issuance.[7]

More recently, the Financial Accounting Standards Board altered the criterion by substituting the average Aa corporate bond yield in place of the bank prime interest rate. The bank prime rate is a short-term rate. Substitution of the average Aa corporate bond yield thus makes the classification criterion more internally consistent in that convertible securities are classified by comparing their yield with 66⅔ percent of the average yield of securities of similar maturity. In addition, the effective yield has been substituted for the cash yield. For securities with a fixed maturity date, the effective yield is the discount rate which equates the present value of the interest payments and maturity value with the price at issuance. For securities without a fixed maturity date, e.g., preferred stock, the effective yield is the ratio of the security's stated annual interest or dividend payments to its market price at issuance.[8] The classification criterion is applied only at the time of issue, and the classification status remains unchanged as long as the security remains outstanding.

With respect to common stock options, warrants, and similar obligations, the established criterion is that they be included in the common stock equivalent class at all times. This inclusion is consistent with the fact that such securities generally have no cash yield and therefore derive their value "from their right to obtain common stock at specified prices for an extended period."[9]

Dilutive versus Antidilutive Conversions and Exercises. In respect to the calculation of primary earnings per share, it should be recognized that the assumed conversion or exercise of a common stock equivalent may be either *dilutive* or *antidilutive*; that is, the effect of the assumed conversion maybe either to decrease or to increase the earnings per share figure. However, the underlying purpose of the development of the primary earnings per share statistic was to recognize that some securities (other than common stock) are likely to participate in the value increments of common

---

[7] Ibid., par. 33. If no market price is available at the time of issuance, this test is based on the fair value of the security.

[8] FASB, *Statement of Financial Accounting Standards No. 55*, "Determining whether a Convertible Security Is a Common Stock Equivalent" (Stamford, Conn., 1982) and FASB, "Yield Test for Determining whether a Convertible Security Is a Common Stock Equivalent" (Stamford, Conn., 1985).

[9] *APB Opinion No. 15*, par. 35.

stock that result from growth in earnings. If earnings are not maintained at a level that would eventually make it profitable for security holders to convert or exercise their securities, it can be assumed that such conversions may not take place. As a consequence, the calculation of primary earnings per share is based on the assumed conversion and exercise of common stock equivalents, *only if the effects of the assumed conversions or exercises are dilutive.* Given several different common stock equivalents, there are obviously several different possible earnings per share amounts, depending upon how each common stock equivalent is treated—conversion assumed, or not. The correct treatment of the common stock equivalents is that which results in the lowest earnings per share amount.

Common Stock Warrants. Special consideration must be given to the treatment of common stock warrants (and stock options, etc.) in the calculation of primary earnings per share. So long as the number of common shares that are issuable upon the exercise of warrants is 20 percent or less of the total number of common shares outstanding at the end of the period, the treatment of warrants in this calculation is described as the "treasury stock" method. The cash proceeds from the anticipated exercise of warrants are assumed to be used to repurchase shares of common stock at the average market price during the period. If the exercise price of the warrants is less than the average market price of common stock, more common shares will have been issued than will have been repurchased; thus, the net number of common shares outstanding is increased and the warrants are *dilutive* in effect. However, if the exercise price of the warrants is greater than the average price of common stock, the cash proceeds from the assumed exercise of the warrants would provide for repurchasing more common shares than were issued when the warrants were exercised; thus, the net number of common shares outstanding is decreased and the warrants are *antidilutive.* In the latter situation, the warrants should be disregarded in calculating primary earnings per share, notwithstanding the fact that they are classified as common stock equivalents.

In the event that the number of common shares issuable upon the exercise of warrants (and stock options, etc.) exceeds 20 percent of the number of common shares outstanding at the end of the period, the previously described "treasury stock" method is rejected in the belief that it may not provide an adequate reflection of the potential dilution associated with warrants. The Accounting Principles Board described the alternative method to be utilized, as follows:

> . . . all the options and warrants should be assumed to have been exercised and the aggregate proceeds therefrom to have been applied in two steps:
>
> a. As if the funds were first applied to the repurchase of outstanding common shares at the average market price during the period (treasury stock method) but not to exceed 20% of the outstanding shares; and then

b.   As if the balance of the funds were applied first to reduce any short-term or long-term borrowings and any remaining funds were invested in U.S. government securities or commercial paper, with appropriate recognition of any income tax effect.

The results of steps (a) and (b) of the computation (whether dilutive or antidilutive) should be aggregated and, if the net effect is dilutive, should enter into the earnings per share computation.[10]

To summarize, the denominator in primary earnings per share calculations includes the weighted average of the number of common shares outstanding plus the number of common shares that would have been issued if each dilutive common stock equivalent were converted or exercised. In general, the numerator includes (1) net income, less dividend declarations (including current arrearages) to preferred shares that are classified as senior securities; and (2) the interest charges, less tax effect, on convertible bonds that are classified as dilutive common stock equivalents and on debt that would have been retired with the proceeds from the exercise of dilutive warrants.

Case 6.   Primary Earnings per Share.   Western Calculations, Inc., reported net income for 19X1 of $8,000,000. The firm's common stock is traded actively on the NYSE and had an average market price of $50 during the year; the December 31, 19X1, price was $80. The following securities of Western Calculations were outstanding throughout 19X1:

Long-term debt:
10% bonds, due 19X9 . . . . $ 5,000,000
10.5% 30-year bonds, due 20 years hence, and convertible into
  common stock at the rate of three shares per $100; at issuance,
  the average Aa corporate bond yield was 16.5%; the bonds
  were issued at par   10,000,000

	Outstanding Shares
Stockholders' equity:	
Preferred stock, cumulative as to dividends of $6.00, callable at $100, and convertible into common stock at the rate of two shares for each share of preferred; at issuance, the average Aa corporate bond yield was 13%; issue price, $100	150,000
Preferred stock, cumulative as to dividends of $2.50, callable at $35, and convertible into common stock at the rate of one share for each share of preferred; at issuance, the average Aa corporate bond yield was 14%; issue price, $20	400,000
Common stock	1,500,000
Warrants to purchase common stock:	
100,000 shares at $20.	
200,000 shares at $52.	

Primary earnings per share calculations require a determination of which securities should be classified as common stock equivalents. Apply-

---

[10] Ibid., par. 38.

ing the aforementioned rules, the classification process is summarized in Illustration 5–6.

Based on the analysis of Illustration 5–6, the computation of primary earnings per share is presented in Illustration 5–7.

Illustration 5–6

WESTERN CALCULATIONS, INC.
Classification of Securities
Common Stock Equivalent or Senior

Security	Effective Yield	Average Aa Corporate Bond Yield at Issuance	Common Stock Equivalent/Senior Classification	Criterion
10% bonds.....................			Senior	No common stock characteristics
10.5% bonds	10.5%	16.5%	C/S equivalent	Yield was less than ⅔ of Aa rate
$6.00 preferred stock............	6.0	13%	C/S equivalent	Yield was less than ⅔ of Aa rate
$2.50 preferred stock............	12.5	14.0	Senior	Yield was greater than or equal to ⅔ of Aa rate
Warrants at $20................			C/S equivalent	Always C/S equivalent
Warrants at $52................			C/S equivalent	Always C/S equivalent

Fully Diluted Earnings per Share

Primary earnings per share calculations provide no indication of the potential impact upon common stockholders of possible future conversions or exercises of *senior* securities. To communicate the estimated effect of such contingencies, attention is directed to fully diluted earnings per share. The fully diluted calculation "reflects the dilution of earnings per share that would have occurred if *all* contingent issuances of common stock that would individually reduce earnings per share had taken place at the beginning of the period (or time of issuance of the convertible security, etc., if later)."[11] Fully diluted earnings per share should be reported concurrently with primary earnings per share whenever present contingencies may result in future common stock issuances that would materially dilute primary earnings per share. It should also be reported if conversions taking place during the current period would have materially diluted primary earnings per share had they taken place at the beginning of the period (or date of issuance, if later).

---

[11] Ibid., par. 15. A reduction of less than 3 percent in primary earnings per share is not considered by the Board to be significant enough to warrant the presentation of fully diluted earnings per share.

Illustration 5–7

WESTERN CALCULATIONS, INC.
Primary Earnings per Share

	Shares	Earnings
Reported net income..		$8,000,000
Common shares outstanding	1,500,000	
Dividend requirements on $2.50 preferred stock		
($2.50 × 400,000)		−1,000,000
		$7,000,000
Effect of assumed conversion or exercise of dilutive common stock equivalents:*		
10.5% convertible bonds:		
[3(10,000,000/100)]	300,000	
[.54(.105 × 10,000,000)].................................		567,000
$6.00 convertible preferred stock (2 × 150,000)	300,000	
Warrants for 100,000 at $20 100,000		
(100,000 × 20)/50 .... −40,000	60,000	
Warrants for 200,000 at $52 200,000		
(200,000 × 52)/50 .... −208,000		
	2,160,000	$7,567,000
Primary earnings per share...................................		$3.50

* It should be noted that each of the common stock equivalent securities for which conversion or exercise was assumed had the effect of diluting earnings per share. The warrants for 200,000 common shares at $52 were not included in the calculation since the effect of including them would have been to increase earnings per share. The earnings effect of the 10.5% bond conversion is after taxes (assuming a 46% rate).

The fully diluted calculation closely parallels the calculations for primary earnings per share. The principal difference between the two statistics is that fully diluted calculations include the assumed conversion and exercise of *all* dilutive securities; alternatively, the primary calculations assume the conversion and exercise only of dilutive common stock equivalents. Since the essential purpose of the fully diluted statistic is to show the maximum potential dilution, "the computations of fully diluted earnings per share for each period should exclude those securities whose conversion, exercise or other contingent issuance would have the effect of increasing the earnings per share amount or decreasing the loss per share amount for such period."[12] Regarding the fully diluted calculations, one important modification in the previously described primary earnings per share calculations relates to the assumed exercise of warrants and options. In the primary calculations, it is assumed (under the treasury stock method) that the cash proceeds are used to repurchase common stock at the *average* market price during the period. In fully diluted calculations, "the market price at the

---

[12] Ibid., par. 40.

close of the period reported upon should be used to determine the number of shares which would be assumed to be repurchased . . . if such market price is higher than the average price used in computing primary earnings per share."[13]

Case 7. Fully Diluted Earnings per Share. Case 7 assumes the same data as presented in Case 6. The calculation of fully diluted earnings per share requires the assumed conversion of all dilutive securities including those designated as senior securities in Illustration 5–6. The computation of fully diluted earnings per share is presented in Illustration 5–8.

Illustration 5–8

WESTERN CALCULATIONS, INC.
Fully Diluted Earnings per Share

	Shares	Earnings
Recorded net income		$8,000,000
Common shares outstanding	1,500,000	
Effect of assumed conversion of dilutive common stock equivalents and senior securities:		
10.5% convertible bonds:		
3(10,000,000/100)	300,000	
[.54(.105 × 10,000,000)]		567,000
$6.00 convertible preferred stock (2 × 150,000)	300,000	
$2.50 convertible preferred stock (1 × 400,000)	400,000	
Warrants for 100,000 at $20:		
Shares issued 100,000		
(100,000 × 20)/80 . . . . −25,000	75,000	
Warrants for 200,000 at $52:*		
Shares issued 200,000		
(200,000 × 52)/80 . . . . −130,000	70,000	
	2,645,000	$8,567,000
Fully diluted earnings per share		$3.24

* Note that the warrants for 200,000 common shares at $52 are defined as a common stock equivalent, not as a senior security. Nevertheless, they become dilutive only in the fully diluted earnings per share calculations. This was caused by the increase in the common stock market price from the $50 average price during the year to $80 at the end of the year.

Earnings per Share Calculations Involving Affiliates

Any corporation may have outstanding common stock equivalents or senior securities that involve potential dilution of earnings per share. Additionally, where companies have intercorporate stock investments and the investor corporation uses the equity method or prepares consolidated

---

[13] Ibid., par. 42.

statements, earnings per share calculations for the investor corporation may be affected by the nature of the securities issued by the investee corporation. In other words, if a corporation's net income includes equity method earnings from holding stock of another corporation, the earnings per share calculations for the stockholder corporation must give explicit consideration to potential dilution associated with the investee corporation's earnings. This is also true regarding earnings per share calculations for consolidated financial statements.

To accomplish this objective, primary and fully diluted earnings per share for the investee corporation must first be calculated. Next, in the calculations for the investor corporation, the investor corporation's net income derived from use of the equity method must be recomputed under whatever assumptions have been used in the calculation of the investee corporation's earnings per share. The effect of these assumptions can alter the investee corporation's equity method earnings in at least two ways. First, an assumed conversion of bonds increases the investee corporation's earnings available for common dividends. Second, all assumed conversions of convertible securities and exercises of warrants and options change the number of investee corporation common shares outstanding, and thus can alter the investor corporation's ownership interest.[14] Moreover, in determining the alteration of the investor corporation's ownership interest, it is necessary to consider whether any additional common shares assumed to be issued would be issued to the investor corporation. Ownership interest is a fraction, the numerator of which is common shares held by the investor corporation. The denominator is investee corporation common shares outstanding. If the investor corporation holds any of the convertible securities, options, or warrants that are assumed to have been converted or exercised, the numerator and denominator of ownership interest will increase. The investor corporation's recalculated equity method income can be expressed as shown on the bottom of page 206. The investor corporation's earnings per share is then computed using this recalculated amount of equity method income instead of the actual recorded amount of equity method income.

Case 8.   Western Calculations, Inc., which was analyzed in Cases 6 and 7, is now assumed to be a subsidiary of Northern Computers Corporation. Northern has a simple capital structure with no securities outstanding other than 2,000,000 shares of common stock. The following data are drawn from the records of Northern:

---

[14] Changing the investor corporation's ownership interest can result in second-order effects in the calculation of equity method income. Elimination of intercompany profit as discussed in Chapters 7, 8, and 9 can be affected by a changed ownership interest. Also, increases and decreases in ownership interest can affect amortization of debit differentials, as discussed in Chapter 10.

Investments in Western Calculations, Inc.:
    Common stock, acquired at book value ....   1,200,000 shares
    Warrants to purchase common stock at $20..............   80,000 warrants
    Warrants to purchase common stock at $52..............   40,000 warrants
Net income for 19X1, excluding subsidiary earnings $10,000,000

Equity in subsidiary earnings:		
Subsidiary net income.................................	$8,000,000	
Preferred dividends:		
$2.50 preferred....................................	−1,000,000	
$6.00 preferred....................................	−900,000	
Earnings allocated to common stock	$6,100,000	
Northern equity therein:		
(1,200,000/1,500,000) × $6,100,000		4,880,000
Reported net income (equals consolidated net income)......		$14,880,000

Northern does not have any potential dilution in its capital structure. Nevertheless, it should be emphasized that earnings per share for Northern is *not* determined by dividing Northern's reported net income ($14,880,000) by the number of common shares outstanding (2,000,000). Instead, primary earnings per share is calculated as indicated in Illustration 5–9. Since the $52 warrants were antidilutive in the calculation of primary earnings per share for Western (see Illustration 5–6), they are ignored in the comparable calculation for Western's parent (Illustration 5–9). How-

$$\left[\frac{\text{Investee common shares held by investor} + \begin{array}{c}\text{Additional investee common shares assumed issued to investor through assumed conversion or exercise of dilutive securities}\end{array}}{\text{Investor common shares outstanding} + \begin{array}{c}\text{Additional investee common shares assumed issued through conversion or exercise of dilutive securities}\end{array}}\right] \times \left[\begin{array}{c}\text{Net income available for common dividends, as reported by investee}\end{array} + \begin{array}{c}\text{Increase in net income through assumed conversion of dilutive securities}\end{array}\right]$$

Recalculated investor corporation's ownership interest consistent with assumptions made in calculation of investor corporation's earnings per share

Recalculated investee corporation net income available for common dividends consistent with assumptions made in calculation of investee corporation's earnings per share

Illustration 5-9

NORTHERN COMPUTERS CORPORATION
Primary Earnings per Share Calculation
Parent Company or Consolidated Statements

Number of Western common shares held by Northern	1,200,000
Additional Western common shares assumed to be issued to Northern through exercise of $20 warrants (see Illustration 5–7), 60,000(80,000/100,000)	48,000
Numerator of Northern's ownership interest	1,248,000
Number of Western common shares outstanding	1,500,000
Additional Western common shares assumed to be issued through conversion of 10.5% convertible bonds, $6 convertible preferred stock, and exercise of $20 warrants (see Illustration 5–7)	660,000
Denominator of Northern's ownership interest	2,160,000
Recalculated Northern ownership interest (1,248,000/2,160,000)	57.8%
Recalculated Western income available for common dividends (see Illustration 5–7)	$ 7,567,000
Recalculated Northern ownership interest	× 57.8%
Recalculated Northern equity in Western income	$ 4,373,726
Primary Northern income, excluding equity method income	10,000,000
Recalculated Northern primary income.	$14,373,726
Number of Northern common shares outstanding	2,000,000
Northern primary earnings per share (14,373,726/2,000,000).	$7.19

ever, Northern's ownership of $20 warrants must be incorporated in the calculation since they had a dilutive effect on the subsidiary's earnings per share. In Illustration 5–7, the assumed exercise of these $20 warrants had a net result of 60,000 additional common shares outstanding and the assumed conversions of the 10.5 percent convertible bonds and $6 convertible preferred stock resulted in another 600,000 common shares. Since Northern owns 80 percent of the $20 warrants, Northern would have received 48,000 additional shares (net). Receipt of only 48,000 of 660,000 additional shares issued would drop Northern's ownership interest from 80 percent (1,200,000/1,500,000) to 57.8 percent. In addition, the assumed conversion of the 10.5 percent convertible bonds and $6 convertible preferred stock increased Western's net income from $6,100,000 to $7,567,000. Thus, for purposes of computing Northern's primary earnings per share, Northern's equity in the income of Western is recalculated according to these assumed effects.

Fully diluted earnings per share for Northern Computers Corporation amounts to $7.06, which is not materially less than primary earnings per share. The calculations to confirm this $7.06 amount are left for the reader's exercise.

During the 1960s, some subsidiaries began to issue securities (or warrants) that were convertible (or exercisable) into common stock of the parent. Obviously, the conversion or exercise of these securities would not dilute the subsidiary's earnings per share. Therefore, subsidiary calculations need only reflect the appropriate deductions for current cash payments (e.g., dividends) to holders of such securities.

In calculations for the parent, however, such securities must be classified as common stock equivalents or as senior securities. If their effects are dilutive, the assumed conversion or exercise of these securities must be incorporated in parent calculations. In so doing, consideration must be given to the fact that the subsidiary's earnings per share calculations may have involved deductions for payments to the holders of the securities which are convertible into the parent's stock. Thus, if conversion of those securities is assumed in parent calculations, the subsidiary's deductions for payments to the security holders must be restored to earnings, since no payments to outsiders would have been made if the securities had been converted.[15]

Changing Conversion Rates or Exercise Prices

There are several types of corporate securities and transactions that may cause particular difficulty in earnings per share calculations. For example, a convertible security may stipulate a changing rate of conversion with the passage of time. Similarly, the price to exercise stock warrants may change. The obvious difficulty in such cases is to determine which conversion rate or exercise price should be used in computations of primary and fully diluted earnings per share. With respect to *fully diluted* earnings per share, it is reasonable to utilize the rate or price that will be most favorable to the security holders. Such a rate is consistent with the basic implication of the fully diluted statistic—the implication of portraying the maximum dilution that can occur, given current contingencies. However, conversion rates or exercise prices that are effective only in the distant future probably have little relevance to current security holders. Thus, the Accounting Principles Board concluded that the most attractive rate or price during *only* the 10 years following the latest fiscal period should be used.[16]

Selecting an appropriate conversion rate or exercise price for primary earnings per share calculations is somewhat more arbitrary. As a general

---

[15] In *Accounting Interpretation No. 93 of APB Opinion No. 15,* 100 percent of the restored subsidiary payments is allocated to the parent. This method is followed even when the parent owns less than 100 percent of the subsidiary. There is no obvious rationale for such a treatment. A more logical method would restore the subsidiary's payments to the subsidiary's income in order to determine the parent's equity in subsidiary earnings. (AICPA, *Accounting Interpretation No. 93 of APB Opinion No. 15,* "Securities Issued by Subsidiaries" [New York, 1970].

[16] *APB Opinion No. 15,* par. 58.

rule, it seems appropriate to use the rate or price that is in effect during the period covered by the calculation. The Board provided for the following specific exceptions to this general rule:

> If options, warrants or other common stock equivalents are not immediately exercisable or convertible, the earliest effective exercise price or conversion rate if any during the succeeding five years should be used. If a convertible security having an increasing conversion rate is issued in exchange for another class of security of the issuing company and is convertible back into the same or a similar security, and if a conversion rate equal to or greater than the original rate becomes effective during the period of convertibility, the conversion rate used in the computation should not result in a reduction in the number of common shares (or common share equivalents) existing before the original exchange took place until a greater rate becomes effective.[17]

Contingent Stock Issuances

Contingent stock issuances have been frequently used as part of the financing methods employed in business combinations. They generally involve deferred payments of an indeterminate number of common shares, with the amount to be issued depending on future earnings of the acquired firm. Additionally, the amount to be issued may depend on the market value of the stock at the future date of issuance. Both primary and fully diluted computations of earnings per share may require special refinements when such contingent stock issuances are outstanding.

In an attempt to resolve the difficulties imposed by contingent stock issuances, the Accounting Principles Board recommended specific rules to follow. With respect to primary earnings per share, stock issuances that depend on future earnings levels should be included to the extent that shares will be issued if earnings are maintained at current levels. Further, if the number of shares to be issued depends on the future market price of the stock, the market price at the most recent balance sheet date should be used to estimate the assumed number of shares to be issued.

Fully diluted earnings per share calculations should also reflect (by inclusion in the denominator) contingent stock issuances that relate to future earnings and/or to future stock prices. But they should not be constrained by the primary calculation requirement that limits the issuance to an amount satisfied by the maintenance of current earnings. Thus, fully diluted calculations should assume the highest reasonable dilution level that can occur. Manifestly, the required increase in earnings (to attain the highest dilution level) should also be added to current earnings in the numerator of the statistic. As in the case of primary calculations, the stock price at

---

[17] Ibid., par. 57.

the close of the period being reported should be used if the contingent issuances are dependent on future stock prices.[18]

Restatement of Prior Period's Earnings per Share

Several conditions may justify restating the earnings per share statistics that relate to prior periods. Such restatements would be disclosed in the presentation of comparative statements and in historical financial summaries. Among the events that would lead to restatement of prior periods' earnings per share are the following: (1) if the number of common shares outstanding changes due to stock dividends, stock splits, or reverse stock splits; (2) if prior period adjustments of net income are made; (3) if a business combination has occurred and was accounted for as a pooling of interests; (4) if the prior periods' statistics included contingent stock issuances and at the termination of the contingency agreement the conditions have not been met; and (5) if contingent stock issuances, which were included in the statistics of prior periods and remain contingently effective, are dependent on future earnings and/or stock prices, and the current (end-of-period) price and/or earnings level indicate that the assumptions which were previously used in reporting earnings per share should be modified. However, "previously reported earnings per share data should not be restated to give retroactive effect to shares subsequently issued as a result of attainment of specified increased earnings levels."[19]

Other Problem Areas

The previous discussion of earnings per share analysis clearly displays the variety of problems that have been encountered in recent years. A majority of these problems (and others, some of which are summarized below) have gained significance through the transactions, new financing methods, and internal structures of various combined corporate entities. Frequently, the problem conditions have arisen as a direct result of the combination transactions. Additional characteristics of the problems and recommendations regarding earnings per share analysis are outlined below.

Some of the procedures that have been developed for earnings per share calculations can be interpreted as having definite implications for other parts of the financial statements. For example, if convertible bonds are deemed to be common stock equivalents, should those bonds be classified as liabilities or as a special type of stockholders' equity? Furthermore,

---

[18] Ibid., pars. 62–64.

[19] Ibid., par. 62.

should the interest on those bonds be reported as an expense or as a special distribution of income? Arguments can be advanced in support of both sides of this and other similar issues arising from the earnings per share discussion. The most widely held position is that these specialized earnings per share methods should not affect the traditional methods of measurement and reporting which apply to other parts of the financial statements.[20]

Some corporations have classes of stock outstanding that are not convertible into common stock but which participate in specified ratios with common stock as to dividends. A variety of conditions of this general nature may require an entirely different approach to earnings per share calculations. The alternative approach, referred to as the "two-class method," does not assume conversion of these securities. Instead, it recognizes the distributions made to each class of stock and computes a per share figure for the remaining amount retained. This figure is based on outstanding common shares and common stock equivalents. Finally, the retained earnings per share is added to dividends per common share to determine primary earnings per share.[21]

Segmental Reporting

The various advantages and risks associated with diversified business operations have been discussed in the business community throughout the 20th century. The natural growth of prospering firms has often led to internally generated diversification. Complementing these *internal* processes of widening product lines, expanding geographical sales coverage, and vertical assumption of supplier and seller functions have been periodic surges of diversification by the *external* process of business combination. For example, the merger activity of 1955–70 dramatically enhanced the diversified character of individual business firms.

It should be recognized that the unique accounting problems of reporting the operations of highly diversified businesses are not confined to combined corporate entities. Nevertheless, the processes of combining business enterprises frequently give rise to special accounting problems associated with reporting the results of diversified business activity. An obvious objective of many, perhaps most, of the combinations during the 1960s was diversification. As a consequence, a rounded examination of accounting for combined business entities must include reference to the special problems of accounting for diversified business entities.

---

[20] This position is consistent with the conclusion of the Accounting Principles Board, ibid., par. 39.

[21] Ibid., par. 55.

The Need for Segmental Reports

The basic advantages and limitations associated with consolidated statements were outlined in Chapter 2. Compared with the alternative of presenting only the parent's financial statements, consolidated statements
have uniquely important informational significance. These reports clearly
are a primary source of information for persons concerned with the operations and financial position of the parent's sphere of control. It should be
understood that the interest in, and need for, more detailed reporting on
diversified companies does not negate the need for consolidated reports.
The movement toward more detailed reporting is rather an *expansion* of the
basic consolidated information. Reports that cover significant segments of
a diversified firm should be perceived, therefore, as complementary to the
consolidated statements. In fact, the method of reporting on segments may
involve simply expanding the consolidated statements to include more
detail within these statements.

Taken alone, consolidated financial statements do not provide sufficient
information regarding the various types of business activity undertaken by
the consolidated entity. Revenues, expenses, and assets may be associated
with vastly disparate operations; yet they are aggregated and reported in
total. It should be apparent that decisions concerning widely diversified
firms can often be facilitated by information as to the relative significance to
the firm of distinct subunit operations. R. K. Mautz defined a diversified
company in a manner that emphasized these informational needs.

> A diversified company is . . . a company which either is so managerially
> decentralized, so lacks operational integration, or has such diversified mar-
> kets that it may experience rates of profitability, degrees of risk, and opportu-
> nities for growth which vary within the company to such an extent that an
> investor requires information about these variations in order to make in-
> formed decisions.[22]

As is true for most informational inputs to human decision processes, it
is not possible to specify clearly the precise role played by segmental reports in the decision processes of investors. Nevertheless, the need for
such information on diversified firms has become widely recognized.

Beginning in 1969, segmental information was required in certain reports filed with the SEC. Currently, the primary requirements for reporting
segmental information are contained in *FASB Statement No. 14.* In general,
enterprises are required to disclose segmental information whenever they
issue a complete set of financial statements that present financial position
at the fiscal year-end and results of operations and changes in financial
position for that year in conformity with generally accepted accounting

---

[22] R. K. Mautz, *Financial Reporting by Diversified Companies* (New York: Financial Executives
Research Foundation, 1968), pp. 7–8.

principles.[23] In *Statement No. 21*, the FASB exempted nonpublic enterprises from the segmental reporting requirements. Also, when an enterprise's financial statements are presented in another enterprise's financial report (i.e., the primary reporting enterprise) and certain limiting conditions are satisfied, *FASB Statement No. 24* eliminates the requirements for the financial statements so included (but not for the primary reporting enterprise).[24] Finally, *Statement No. 18* exempted interim financial statements from segmental reporting requirements. However, the SEC has recently proposed that segmental data be reported in interim as well as annual financial statements.

Identifying Significant Segments of a Firm

Selecting the Basis for Segmenting a Firm.   Several alternative ways of segmenting a diversified firm may result in reports that have informational significance to investors. Three important alternatives that have been seriously considered are (1) geographical divisions, (2) product line or industrial divisions, and (3) divisions that conform to the internal structure of managerial control. Of course, other possible bases for segmenting a firm's operations may have significance, particularly in specific industries. For example, a division between government and private operations might provide especially relevant information for firms such as those engaged in air-frame construction.

Arguments can be marshaled in support of each of the three primary alternatives mentioned above. As a general rule, the necessary data can probably be accumulated most accurately and at the smallest additional cost when the basis for division conforms to the internal structure of managerial control. On the other hand, segmentation that meaningfully reflects differences in profitability, degrees of risk, and growth opportunities frequently follows the product lines or industrial categories in which a firm is active. Of course, for many enterprises the industrial classification would conform fairly closely to the above mentioned managerial units of control. A geographical basis of segmentation may be highly informative for some companies, particularly in its ability to accent important distinctions between domestic and foreign operations.

FASB Statement No. 14 calls for information to be presented on each of three items:

a.   The enterprise's operations in different industries.

---

[23] *Statement of Financial Accounting Standards No. 14*, "Financial Reporting for Segments of a Business Enterprise" (1976), par. 3.

[24] *Statement of Financial Accounting Standards No. 24*, "Reporting Segment Information in Financial Statements That Are Presented in Another Enterprise's Financial Report" (1978), par. 5.

b. Its foreign operations and exposure sales.

c. Its major customers.[25]

In respect to item *(b)*, if the export sales of the domestic operations are significant in amount, they should be reported in the aggregate and by appropriate geographical areas. Such sales are considered significant if they amount to 10 percent or more of the company's consolidated sales.[26]

Foreign operations are identified as operations that are located in foreign countries *and* that generate revenue from sales to unaffiliates customers or from intraenterprise sales or simply from transfers between geographical areas. Without specifying the criteria by which foreign operations in different countries should be grouped, *Statement No. 14* indicates that foreign geographical areas may consist of one or more countries, and requires that certain information be presented separately for each significant geographical area and in the aggregate for those geographical areas which are not individually significant. A geographical area is deemed to be significant if its revenues from unaffiliated customers or its identifiable assets are 10 percent or more of the related consolidated amounts.[27]

Given these definitions, *Statement No. 14* requires that for domestic operations and for each foreign geographical area, the following information be reported: (1) sales to unaffiliated customers, (2) intraenterprise sales and transfers between geographical areas, (3) operating profit (loss) or net income or some other measure of profitability between operating profit (loss) and net income, and (4) identifiable assets.[28]

Regarding major customers, the fact and the amount of revenue to each major customer must be reported. The customers need not be individually identified by name, but the industry segment or segments making the sales must be identified. A major customer is one to whom sales equal 10 percent or more of the company's total sales. If several entities are under common control, they are "regarded as a single customer, and the federal government, a state government, a local government . . . , or a foreign government [are each] considered as a single customer."[29]

In addition to the above types of information, *FASB Statement No. 14* calls for a system of segmental reporting based upon an industrial segmentation of the entity. The process of identifying the industrial segments of a firm requires that its products and services be grouped by industry lines.

---

[25] *FASB Statement No. 14,* par. 3.

[26] Ibid., par. 36.

[27] Ibid., pars. 31–34.

[28] Ibid., par. 35.

[29] *Statement of Financial Accounting Standards No. 30,* "Disclosure of Information about Major Customers" (1979), par. 6. Copyright © by the Financial Accounting Standards Board, High Ridge Park, Stamford, Connecticut 06905, U. S. A. Quoted (or excerpted) with permission. Copies of the complete document are available from the FASB.

The definition of an "industry segment" requires that its sales be primarily to unaffiliated customers. In identifying the segments, attention should be given to the nature of the products produced, the nature of the production processes involved, and the markets and marketing methods employed to sell the products. Differences in these factors help to identify different segments.[30]

Determining How Finely a Firm Should Be Segmented.   A problem that relates to the selection of a basis for segmentation is to determine how finely segmented the reports should be. Addressing this question, the FASB stated that an entity should present reports on each industry segment for which one or more of the following tests is satisfied during the year for which financial statements are to be presented:

(A)   Its revenue (including both sales to unaffiliated customers and intersegment sales or transfers) is 10 percent or more of the combined revenue (sales to unaffiliated customers and intersegment sales or transfers) of all of the enterprise's industry segments.

(B)   The absolute amount of its operating profit or operating loss is 10 percent or more of the greater, in absolute amount, of:
  (i)   The combined operating profit of all industry segments that did not incur an operating loss, or
  (ii)   The combined operating loss of all industry segments that did incur an operating loss.

(C)   Its identifiable assets are 10 percent or more of the combined identifiable assets of all industry segments.[31]

In applying the above tests, however, the FASB recognized that abnormal results for a single period may result in a segment meeting one of the 10 percent tests when past periods and future expectations do not support separate reporting of the segment. In such a case, the segment need not be reported. Alternatively, a normally significant segment may happen to fail the tests in a single year, in which case it should be treated as a reportable segment. Also, if a single segment accounts for 90 percent or more of the firm's revenue, operating profit or loss, and identifiable assets, and no other industry segment meets any of the 10 percent tests previously mentioned, reports for that segment need not be presented separate from the consolidated statements for the firm as a whole.[32]

On the other hand, some firms consist of many small segments, most of which may not meet the 10 percent tests listed above. To assure that a substantial portion of a firm's operations be presented in segmental reports, *Statement No. 14* requires that the reports on specific segments should disclose at least 75 percent of the combined revenue from sales to

---

[30] *FASB Statement No. 14*, pars. 10–14, 100.

[31] Ibid., par. 15.

[32] Ibid., pars. 16, 20.

unaffiliated customers. Otherwise, additional industry segments should be identified as reportable segments until the 75 percent test is met.[33]

The SEC apparently concluded that in following the FASB's rules, many firms were not dividing their operations into enough segments. As a consequence, *Accounting Series Release No. 244* was issued. That *Release* discusses the segmentation problem at some length but does not proclaim additional rules for segmentation. Instead, it warns managements to make sure that their segmental disclosures include enough segments to most usefully assist investors in analyzing the registrants' businesses.[34] In essence, the matter of defining segments remains quite subjective, but the SEC stands ready to question and even reject a company's financial statements if they fail to reflect reasonable, informative disclosures according to the FASB's rules.

Intersegmental Transfer Pricing

An important problem that must be resolved for the purposes of segmental reporting is the pricing of intrafirm transfers of goods and services between reporting segments. Some segments may exist entirely for the purpose of providing goods or services to outside customers. Others may be concerned with outside sales *and* intrafirm transfers. To the extent that transfers are made between segments, the reported profits of both the "selling" and "purchasing" segments are directly affected by the prices at which the transfers are recorded.

An ideal basis for setting transfer prices would be the independent market prices for the same goods and services, given a perfectly competitive market. However, good approximations of these conditions rarely exist. One is more likely to discover highly imperfect markets for goods or services that are transferred between segments within an enterprise. Independent market prices for similar goods (given a sensitivity to the quantities being sold) would, however, be a reasonable basis for recording transfer prices whenever such information is available.

As a practical matter, it is perhaps impossible to select a single basis for transfer pricing that would be best in all situations. The FASB *Statement* apparently recognizes this difficulty, and simply concludes that the transfer prices used should be those which are used by the company to price the intersegment sales or transfers.[35]

---

[33] Ibid., pars. 17–18.

[34] Securities and Exchange Commission, "Interpretations, Guidelines and Administrative Determinations of the Commissions's Staff Regarding Classification by Registrants of Their Business into Industry Segments," *Securities Act Release No. 5910, Securities Exchange Act Release 14523* (Washington, D.C., March 3, 1978).

[35] *FASB Statement No. 14,* par. 10.

Allocating Common Costs and Measuring Segmental Profitability

Regardless of the means by which a firm is divided into subunits for reporting purposes, some expenses will be common to two or more of the reporting segments. Typical examples of such expenses would include interest, income taxes, top-management compensation, and general corporate administrative expenses. Depending on the nature of the company's operations, many of the noninventoried expenses may be at times common to more than one subunit.

The allocation of common costs to reporting segments is constrained by two conflicting objectives. On the one hand, the bases of allocation should not be arbitrary. Given this single objective, the accountant would be led to leave many common costs unallocated. Allocations that are patently arbitrary may result in the data being more misleading than informative. On the other hand, one of the primary objectives of segmental reporting is to provide information concerning each segment's contribution to the profitability of the firm. Where common costs remain unallocated, this objective is only partially fulfilled.

The ability to allocate most common costs depends largely upon the organization and operating procedures of each firm. Consequently, *general rules* of allocation are very difficult to prescribe. And, there exist some common expenses (and revenues) for which reasonable allocations between segments are virtually impossible.

In regard to calculating the *operating profit or loss* of each segment, *FASB Statement No. 14* concludes that nine specific items should not be allocated to segments. They are (1) revenue earned at the corporate level and not from the operations of an industry segment; (2) general corporate expenses; (3) interest expense, unless it refers to a segment whose operations are essentially financial in nature; (4) income taxes; (5) equity in income or loss from unconsolidated subsidiaries and other unconsolidated investees; (6) gain or loss on discontinued operations; (7) extraordinary items; (8) minority interest; and (9) the cumulative effect of a change in an accounting principle.[36] On the other hand, the *Statement* does not preclude the possibility of presenting additional measures of segmental profitability (other than operating profit) that would involve allocating some or all of the nine items listed above.

Identifying Segmental Assets

Adequate evaluation of segmental performance requires that the operating profit of each segment be related to the investment of resources in

---

[36] Ibid., par. 10.

Illustration 5–10

INFORMATION ABOUT THE COMPANY'S OPERATIONS IN DIFFERENT INDUSTRIES
Year Ended December 31, 19X1
($000)

	Electronics	Chemicals	Machine Manufacturing	Other Industries	Eliminations	Consolidated
Sales to unaffiliated customers	$1,000	$2,000	$1,500	$ 200		$ 4,700
Intersegment sales	200		500		$[700]	
Total revenue	$1,200	$2,000	$2,000	$ 200	$[700]	$ 4,700
Operating profit	$ 200	$ 250	$ 600	$ 50	–0–	$ 1,100
Equity in net income of Electro Company						100
General corporate expenses						[100]
Interest expense					–0–	[200]
Income from continuing operations before income taxes						$ 900
Identifiable assets on December 31, 19X1	$2,000	$4,000	$6,000	$1,000	–0–	$13,000
Investment in net assets of Electro Company						400
Corporate assets						1,600
Total assets at December 31, 19X1						$15,000

Notes: The Company operates principally in three industries, electronics, chemicals, and machine manufacturing. The electronics operations involve the development and manufacture of microcircuitry. Chemical operations involve the manufacture of a variety of petroleum based chemicals for industrial usage. Machine manufacturing operations involve the development and manufacture of precision measuring and cutting instruments for industrial usage. Intersegment sales are accounted for at market values.

Operating profit is total revenue less operating expenses. In computing operating profit, none of the following items has been added or deducted: general corporate expenses, interest expense, income taxes, equity in income from unconsolidated investee, loss from discontinued operations of the Raychem division (which was part of the Company's operations in the chemical industry), and an extraordinary gain that occurred in the Machine Manufacturing segment of the Company's operations. Operations in the electronics industry had depreciation of $80 and capital expenditures of $100. In the chemical industry they were $100 and $200, respectively, and in machine manufacturing they were $150 and $400, respectively.

The Company has a 40% interest in Electro Company, whose operations are in the United States and are vertically integrated with the Company's operations in electronics.

Identifiable assets by industry are those assets of the Company that are used exclusively in or are reasonably allocable to operations in each industry. Assets employed at the Company's central administrative office are principally cash and marketable securities.

To reconcile industry information to consolidated amounts, $700 of intersegment sales were eliminated. None of the gross profit on these sales remains unrealized at December 31, 19X1, since the transferred goods were used and resold prior to the end of the year.

Source: Adapted from *FASB Statement No. 14,* Appendix F.

segmental operations. However, a complete balance sheet for each segment obviously cannot be prepared. Corporate equities (including liabilities) generally represent undivided interests in the entire net assets of the business, notwithstanding the fact that some may enjoy special rights in the event of insolvency. The measurement of segmental investment is therefore limited to an allocation of assets between the reporting segments.

Some assets are easily identified with a specific segment because they are used exclusively by that segment. Other assets are shared by more than one segment, and a reasonable basis of determining each segment's usage must be identified and used to allocate the assets between the segments.

A few assets such as cash, marketable securities, and other assets that are used at the company's central office should not be allocated to industry segments. Also, the assets identified with a segment should not include investments accounted for by the equity method. This is consistent with the requirement that earnings from equity method investments not be included in the revenues or operating profits of a segment. However, if an unconsolidated subsidiary or other equity method investee is vertically integrated into the operations of a segment, separate disclosure must be made of the enterprise's equity in the net income from the investment and in the net assets of the investee.[37]

An Example of Segmental Reporting

Illustration 5–10 presents an example of segmental reports and related footnotes for a broadly diversified firm. Operations of the firm include activities other than those disclosed as electronics, chemicals, and machine manufacturing. However, none of these other activities satisfied the 10 percent tests of a reportable segment listed by the FASB.

The procedures necessary to prepare such reports depend in large part on the nature of the internal accounting system employed by the firm. Segmental reports may be virtually complete as a consequence of maintaining administrative and budgetary control within the firm. A major factor necessarily is the degree of similarity between reporting segments and the internal structure of control.

Questions

1. Contrast the purchase and pooling of interests methods of accounting with respect to (a) the valuation of net assets, (b) the valuation of individual assets and liabilities, and (c) the amount of retained earnings reported by the combined company.

---

[37] Ibid., pars. 7, 10, 27.

2. In the event a business combination results in a parent-subsidiary relationship between the combining companies, what is the amount recorded in the parent's investment account—
   a. If the purchase method of accounting is employed?
   b. If the pooling of interests method is employed?

3. In postcombination periods the method of presenting financial data that relates to precombination periods is dependent upon how the combination is classified. Explain the difference between the purchase and pooling of interests methods with respect to the presentation of precombination financial information.

4. Define the concept "common stock equivalents" and suggest several reasons for including such items in calculations of primary earnings per share.

5. What is the essential distinction between *primary* earnings per share and *fully diluted* earnings per share?

6. Describe the "treasury stock" method of treating common stock warrants in earnings per share calculations.

7. In respect to the earnings per share calculations of a parent company, what is the potential significance of common stock equivalents and dilutive senior securities issued by a subsidiary?

8. Describe the type of company for which segmental financial reports would appear to have the greatest significance.

9. List three alternative bases for segmenting a diversified firm. Which of the three is preferred?

10. In respect to segmental reports, the allocation of common costs between segments is constrained by two conflicting objectives. What are they?

11. List five situations in which previously reported earnings per share data for past years should be restated in financial presentations referring to prior periods.

12. List four major problems the accountant faces in preparing segmental financial statements for a diversified company.

13. What tests are required by the FASB to determine whether or not an industry segment is significant enough to warrant separate financial disclosure?

14. In deciding upon an appropriate basis for pricing goods and services that are transferred between industry segments, what conclusions were reached by the FASB?

15. Should the income from an investment accounted for by the equity method be included in the operating profit of an industry segment? Under what conditions do equity method investments require separate disclosure in the industrially segmented reports?

Exercises

Exercise 5–1

Statements 1–8 below are made in reference to accounting for business combinations. Select from the phrases *(a)–(d)* the one which is consistent with each statement: *(a)* pooling of interests, *(b)* purchase, *(c)* neither pooling of interests nor purchase, and *(d)* either pooling of interests or purchase.

1. If an acquisition results in a debit differential, the assets of the acquired firm will be valued at less than their book value on the books of the acquired firm.
2. Given credit balances in the retained earnings of the combining companies, consolidated retained earnings are generally greatest under this method.
3. The existence of a credit differential due to an overvalued building on the books of the acquired firm would result in consolidated earnings per share for the next year being least under this method.
4. The combination was finalized nine months after the plan for combination was initiated.
5. The difference between book value and investment cost is recognized under this method.
6. Consolidated retained earnings are always equal to the sum of the retained earnings of the constituents under this method.
7. If investment cost is greater than book value of net assets of the acquired firm, it is possible that goodwill resulting from the combination will appear in the consolidated statements.
8. Several years after the combination, consolidated financial summaries pertaining to precombination periods will depict the historical data of only the acquired firm.

Exercise 5–2

Holtz Company and Frantz, Inc., have agreed to combine their businesses in a single stock for stock transaction, after which Holtz Company will act as the parent and Frantz, Inc., as the subsidiary. According to the agreement, Holtz issued common stock in exchange for 100 percent of Frantz, Inc.'s outstanding shares. Before the stock exchange, which qualified as a pooling of interests, the stockholders' equity accounts of the two companies were as follows:

	Holtz Company	Frantz, Inc.
Common stock ($100 par)	$ 80,000	$80,000
Other contributed capital...........		20,000
Retained earnings	100,000	40,000

Required:

Prepare the entry on the books of Holtz Company to record the issuance of stock for each of the following independent situations. Also show the investment elimination entry at date of combination and calculate consolidated retained earnings in each case.

a. Holtz Company issued 1,200 shares.
b. Holtz Company issued 900 shares.
c. Holtz Company issued 500 shares.

Exercise 5–3

Effective December 31, Alpha proposes to issue additional shares of its common stock in exchange for all of the assets and liabilities of Bravo and Echo, after which the latter two corporations will distribute the Alpha shares to their shareholders in complete liquidation and dissolution. The plan complies with all of the criteria for a pooling of interests. Balance sheets for each of the three companies immediately prior to the merger are given below. The common stock exchange ratios were each negotiated to be 1 : 1.

	Alpha	Bravo	Echo
Assets			
Current assets	$ 2,000,000	$ 500,000	$ 25,000
Fixed assets (net)	10,000,000	4,000,000	200,000
Total assets	$12,000,000	$4,500,000	$225,000
Equities			
Current liabilities	$ 1,000,000	$ 300,000	$ 20,000
Long-term debt	3,000,000	1,000,000	105,000
Common stock ($10 par)	3,000,000	1,000,000	50,000
Retained earnings	5,000,000	2,200,000	50,000
Total equities	$12,000,000	$4,500,000	$225,000

Required:
a. Prepare Alpha's journal entries to record the combination of Alpha, Bravo, and Echo.
b. Assume that the combination fails to meet the criteria for a pooling of interests because Bravo and Echo have not been autonomous entities for two years prior to the combination. The identifiable assets and liabilities of Bravo and Echo are all reflected in the balance sheets (above), and their recorded amounts are equal to their current fair market values. Alpha's common stock is traded actively. An appropriate market price per share is $45. Prepare Alpha's journal entries to record the combination.

(AICPA adapted)

Exercise 5–4

APB Opinion No. 15 discusses the concept of common stock equivalents and prescribes methods to be used for reporting primary earnings per share and fully diluted earnings per share.

Required:

a. Discuss the reasons why securities other than common stock may be considered common stock equivalents for the computation of primary earnings per share.

b. Define the term *senior security* and explain how senior securities that are not convertible enter into the determination of earnings per share data.

c. Explain how convertible securities are determined to be common stock equivalents and how those convertible (senior) securities that are not considered to be common stock equivalents enter into the determination of earnings per share data.

(AICPA adapted)

Exercise 5–5

South Sail Company had the following securities outstanding throughout 19X1:

Common stock, $10 par, average market price during 19X1
   was $60, ending market price was $60 .... 20,000 shares
Warrants to purchase 7,000 common shares at $50 per share.
Bonds payable, 7% issued at par, market price throughout
   19X1 was approximately par $200,000

South Sail Company earned $50,000 net income during 19X1. The effective income tax rate is 46 percent.

Required:

Calculate primary and fully diluted earnings per share for 19X1.

Exercise 5–6

P Company purchased 6,000 of S Company's 10,000 outstanding common share at book value. In addition, S Company has convertible bonds and common stock warrants outstanding, but P Company does not own any of these securities. S Company had net income of $24,000 and primary earnings per share of $2. P Company has net income of $40,000, excluding its equity in S Company's earnings, and has 26,000 common shares outstanding. Also, P Company has outstanding warrants to purchase 5,000 common shares at $10. The average market price of P Company common stock during the year was $50.

Required:

a. Calculate the primary earnings per share of P Company.

b. Now assume that P Company also owns 1,500 of S Company's 1,800 outstanding common stock warrants. Also assume that S Company's calculation of primary earnings per share involved the assumed exercise of the 1,800 warrants for 1,800 common shares and that the cash proceeds from the exercise of warrants was used to repurchase 600 common shares. Calculate P Company's primary earnings per share.

c. Calculate consolidated net income for P Company and its subsidiary.

Exercise 5–7

Jason Company's operations involve four industry segments: A, B, C, and D. During the most recent year, the operating profits or losses of the segments were as follows:

Industry Segment	Operating Profit [Loss]
A.	$[200]
B.	400
C.	50
D.	[400]

Required:

Apply the "operating profit or loss" test required by the FASB to determine which of the four industry segments should be treated as reportable segments.

Exercise 5–8

Western Company's consolidated income statement appears as follows:

WESTERN COMPANY
Statement of Consolidated Income
For the Year Ended July 31, 19X1

Net sales	$38,041,200
Other revenue	407,400
Total revenue	$38,448,600
Cost of products sold	$27,173,300
Selling and administrative expenses	8,687,500
Interest expense	296,900
Total cost and expenses	$36,157,700
Income before income taxes	$ 2,290,900
Provision for income taxes	1,005,200
Net income	$ 1,285,700

Ray Bach, a security analyst, visited the corporate offices of Western Company to obtain more information about the company's operations. In the annual report, Western's president stated that Western was engaged in the pharmaceutical, food processing, toy manufacturing, and metal-working industries. Mr. Bach complained that the income statement was of limited utility in his analysis of the firm's operations. He said analysis of Western's operations required more detailed information showing the profit earned in each of its component industries.

Required:

a. Explain what is meant by the term *conglomerate* company.

b. Discuss the accounting problems involved in measuring net profit by industry segments within a company.

c. With reference to Western Company's statement of consolidated income, identify the specific items where difficulty might be encountered in measuring the profit earned by each of its industry segments and explain the nature of the difficulty.

(AICPA adapted)

Exercise 5–9

For each of the following select the one best answer that either completes the statement or answers the question.

1. Consider a business combination where the purchase method would result in a credit differential that would be allocated to depreciable assets. What would be the future income statement effect of structuring the combination to meet the pooling of interests requirements instead of accounting for it as a purchase?
    a. Smaller net incomes.
    b. Larger reported revenues.
    c. Smaller reported expenses.
    d. Larger net incomes.
2. On November 1, 19X1, Wilkins, Inc., issued shares of its voting common stock in exchange for all of the voting common stock of Dow Company in a business combination appropriately accounted for by the pooling of interests method. Both companies have a December 31 year-end. Net income for each company is as follows:

	Wilkins, Inc.	Dow Company
12 months ended December 31, 19X1.........	$1,300,000	$800,000
2 months ended December 31, 19X1..........	240,000	170,000

Assuming that the net income of Wilkins, Inc., given above does not include its equity in the earnings of Dow Company, the consolidated net income for the year ended December 31, 19X1, should be:
    a. $410,000.
    b. $2,100,000.
    c. $1,470,000.
    d. $1,300,000.
3. On December 31, 19X1, Franklin, Inc., has 2,000,000 shares of authorized $10 par value, voting common stock of which 1,600,000 were issued and outstanding. On December 1, 19X2, Franklin issued 250,000 additional shares of its $10 par value voting common stock in exchange for all 100,000 shares of Burkey Company's outstanding $20 par value voting common stock in a business combination appropriately accounted for by the pooling of interests method. The market value of Franklin, Inc.'s common stock was $30 per share on the date of the business combination. What is the *consolidated common stock* issued and outstanding for Franklin and its subsidiary, Burkey, on December 31, 19X2?

a. $17,000,000.
b. $22,500,000.
c. $18,500,000.
d. $55,500,000.

4. Buffer Corporation issued voting common stock with a stated value of $90,000 and a market value of $180,000 in exchange for *all* of the outstanding common stock of Plate Company. The combination was properly accounted for as a pooling of interests. The stockholders' equity section of Plate Company on the date of the combination was as follows:

Common stock	$ 70,000
Other contributed capital.........	7,000
Retained earnings	50,000
	$127,000

What should be the increase in stockholders' equity of Buffer Corporation on the date of acquisition as a result of this business combination?
a. $37,000.
b. $90,000.
c. $180,000.
d. $127,000.

5. On December 31, 19X1, the Baker Company had 2,000,000 shares of common stock outstanding and 1,000,000 shares of convertible, preferred stock outstanding that were considered common stock equivalents at the time of their issuance. The conversion rate is one common share for one preferred share. During 19X2, Baker declared and paid $2,000,000 cash dividends on the common stock and the $1,000,000 annual cash dividends on the preferred stock. Net income for the year ended December 31, 19X2, was $9,000,000. Assuming an income tax rate of 50 percent, what should be earnings per share for the year ended December 31, 19X2?
a. $1.50.
b. $3.00.
c. $4.00.
d. $4.50.

6. When calculating earnings per share, a company has so many common stock warrants outstanding that the treasury stock method cannot be used. In applying the alternative method, to what extent can the assumed proceeds from the exercise of warrants be used to acquire treasury stock?
a. To the maximum extent possible, given the amount of cash proceeds available.
b. Up to 20 percent of earnings for the period being reporting on.
c. None, until all long-term debt has been, in effect, retired; then, to the maximum extent possible.
d. Up to 20 percent of common stock outstanding before the assumed exercise of warrants.

7. A Company has a simple capital structure consisting of 1,000,000 outstanding common shares. A Company owns 300,000 of B Company's 500,000 outstand-

ing common shares; and B Company has additional common stock equivalents outstanding, none of which is owned by A Company. Net incomes for 19X1 were $500,000 for B Company and $760,000 for A Company, excluding A Company's equity in subsidiary earnings. B Company's primary earnings per share for 19X1 is $0.80. What is A Company's primary earnings per share?

   a. $0.76.
   b. $1.00.
   c. $1.06.
   d. $1.50.

8. Which of the following statements *best* describes the effect of effective yield at issuance of convertible securities on calculating earnings per share (EPS)?

   a. If less than two thirds of the then average Aa corporate bond yield, these securities (if dilutive) are assumed to be converted in calculating fully diluted EPS but *not* primary EPS.

   b. If less than two thirds of the then average Aa corporate bond yield, these securities (if dilutive) are assumed to be converted in calculating primary EPS but *not* fully diluted EPS.

   c. If greater than two thirds of the then average Aa corporate bond yield, these securities (if dilutive) are assumed to be converted in calculating primary EPS and fully diluted EPS.

   d. If greater than two thirds of the then average Aa corporate bond yield, these securities (if dilutive) are assumed to be converted in calculating fully diluted EPS but *not* primary EPS.

9. Regarding the official pronouncements of the FASB and the SEC which contain the rules to be followed in preparing segmental reports, which one of the following statements is true?

   a. *FASB Statement No. 18* expanded the required disclosures of segmental information to include interim financial statements.

   b. *Accounting Series Release No. 244* provided new quantitative rules for determining how finely a firm should be segmented, which replaced the rules originally stated in *FASB Statement No. 14.*

   c. *FASB Statement No. 10* contains the primary rules to be followed in preparing segmental financial reports.

   d. *FASB Statement No. 21* exempted nonpublic enterprises from the segmental reporting requirements contained in *FASB Statement No. 14.*

10. Morgan Company operates in three different industries, each of which is appropriately regarded as a reportable segment. Segment No. 1 contributed 60 percent of Morgan Company's total sales. Sales for Segment No. 1 were $900,000, and traceable costs were $400,000. Total common costs for Morgan were $600,000. Morgan allocates common costs based on the ratio of a segment's sales to total sales, an appropriate method of allocation. What should be the operating profit presented for Segment No. 1 for the year?

   a. $140,000.
   b. $360,000.
   c. $500,000.
   d. $540,000.

(AICPA adapted)

Problems

Problem 5–10

Falcon Company issued additional common shares in exchange for 100 percent of Jones, Inc.'s outstanding stock. The following information pertains to the two firms on the data immediately before the combination occurred:

	Falcon Company	Jones, Inc.
Common stock outstanding, $100 par	$300,000	
Common stock outstanding, $50 par		$100,000
Other contributed capital.....................		40,000
Retained earnings	100,000	60,000

Falcon Company issued 1,200 additional shares (market value of $250 per share) for Jones, Inc., and the combination was accounted for as a pooling of interests.

Required:
a. What differential would be recognized in preparing consolidated statements?
b. What would be consolidated retained earnings on the date of combination?
c. In general journal form, present the entry on the books of Falcon Company to record the stock issuance.
d. In general journal form, present the investment elimination entry for a consolidated balance sheet on the date of combination.
e. Assume now that the combination should be classified as a purchase. Under this assumption, present the entry on the books of Falcon Company to record the stock issuance.
f. Assuming the combination is a purchase, present in general journal form the investment elimination entry for a consolidated balance sheet on the date of combination.

Problem 5–11

On January 1, 19X3, Fox, Inc., issued 100,000 common shares in exchange for all of the outstanding common stock of Weber Company. Fox, Inc., employs the equity method of accounting for its investment in Weber Company; Weber Company has never declared dividends. The combination between Fox, Inc., and Weber Company complied with all of the criteria for a pooling of interests. During 19X3 and 19X4, Weber Company sold merchandise to Fox, Inc., at prices equal to Weber Company's cost. These sales amounted to $50,000 each year. Selected financial data for each of the two companies are as follows:

	19X1	19X2	19X3	19X4
Sales:				
Fox.................................	$400,000	$440,000	$450,000	$500,000
Weber..............................	350,000	400,000	360,000	400,000
Net income:				
Fox (includes subsidiary earnings)........	100,000	150,000	200,000	280,000
Weber..............................	80,000	100,000	80,000	120,000
Earnings per share:				
Fox.................................	$1.00	$1.50	$1.00	$1.40
Weber..............................	0.40	0.50	0.40	0.60

Required:

a. Prepare a four-year financial summary of sales, net income, and earnings per share for Fox, Inc., and its subsidiary, to be included in the 19X4 annual report of Fox, Inc.

b. Assume that the combination did not comply with all of the criteria for a pooling of interests because some of the shares issued by Fox, Inc., to effect the combination were placed in a voting trust which restricted the voting rights of the stockholders. Fox, Inc.'s common stock is actively traded, and its market price has been stable at $40. The book value of Weber Company's common stock was $2,250,000 at the date of the combination. As a result of an analysis of Weber Company's assets and liabilities, the difference between the fair market value of Fox, Inc.'s investment and its equity in Weber Company's recorded net assets was allocated as follows: one half of the difference to fixed assets that have 10 years estimated remaining useful life; and one half of the difference to goodwill, which management decided to amortize over 40 years. Prepare a four-year financial summary similar to that required in *(a)*.

Problem 5–12

In addition to common stock, a company has three different securities outstanding, each of which is a common stock equivalent. The following data show the effects on earnings and common shares outstanding which would result from the assumed conversion of these securities:

	Common Shares Outstanding	Earnings
Common shares outstanding....................................	1,000	
Earnings prior to assumed conversions.........................		$5,000
Impact of assumed conversions of common stock equivalents:		
A...	+1,000	+4,000
B...	+2,000	+3,000
C...	+1,000	+2,000

Required:

Calculate primary earnings per share.

Problem 5–13

Several years ago, Walker Transportation Company purchased 80 percent of Bonanza, Inc.'s outstanding common stock; the total cost of the investment was equal to Walker's equity in Bonanza's recorded net assets. For 19X1, selected financial information for the two companies is presented below. The effective income tax rate is 46 percent.

	Walker	Bonanza
Net income (excluding earnings from subsidiary)	$ 51,000	$ 30,000
Common stock market prices during 19X1:		
Average	90	80
Ending	135	80
Outstanding securities:		
Bonds payable, 6%, due 20 years hence, convertible into common stock at the rate of two shares per $100; bonds issued at par; at the date of issuance, average Aa corporate bond yield was 8%		100,000
Preferred stock, $100 par, 5%, cumulative as to dividends	100,000	
Common stock, $50 par	500,000	300,000
Warrants to purchase common:		
1,000 Bonanza shares at $40		
1,500 Walker shares at $90		

Required:

In respect to the 19X1 consolidated income statement of Walker Transportation Company and its subsidiary, calculate—

a. Primary earnings per share.
b. Fully diluted earnings per share.

Problem 5–14

On January 1, 19X1, Hawkeye, Inc., issued 30-year, convertible bonds which have a total par value of $100,000. The bond indenture requires interest payments during 19X1 equal to 5 percent of par; the rate of interest increases each year for 20 years by .2 percent. Thus, the rate of interest in the 21st year will be 9.0 percent; it will remain at that rate until the bonds mature. The effective yield is 6.8 percent. The rate at which the bonds may be converted into common stock also changes. Conversions cannot be made prior to 19X4, during which year the conversion rate is one share of common stock per $100 of bond par value. Thereafter, the conversion rate increases each year for 10 years at the rate of .1 share per year. Thus, during the 14th year of the bonds' life, the conversion rate will be 2.0 shares of common stock per $100 par value; in subsequent years, the conversion rate remains unchanged.

The bonds were issued at par (assume there are no transfer costs). The effective income tax rate is 46 percent. During 19X1, Hawkeye, Inc., reported net income of $60,000, which included a deduction of $5,000 for interest expense. The company has 10,000 common shares outstanding and no other common stock equivalents or senior securities. The average Aa corporate bond yield on January 1, 19X1, was 8 percent.

Required:

a. Determine whether Hawkeye, Inc.'s bonds payable should be classified as common stock equivalents or senior securities and explain the reasoning underlying your decision.

b. Calculate primary earnings per share for 19X1.

c. Calculate fully diluted earnings per share for 19X1 *or* explain why fully diluted calculations are unnecessary.

Problem 5–15

Toy, Inc., owns 900 shares of Ball Company's outstanding common stock and 360 warrants to purchase Ball Company common stock at $50 per share. The following information pertains to these companies' financial operations and status during 19X1:

	Toy, Inc.	Ball Company
Net income, excluding subsidiary earnings	$20,000	$ 5,000
Common shares outstanding	5,600	1,000
Preferred stock, 7%, cumulative, issued at par ($100), convertible into common at $20 (i.e., 5 shares of common for 1 share of preferred). Average Aa corporate bond yield at issuance was 12%.		
Shares outstanding	800	
Average price of common stock during 19X1	$ 100	$ 300
6%, 30-year bonds, issued at par, convertible into common stock at $200 (a $1,000 bond can be exchanged for 5 common shares). Average Aa corporate bond yield at issuance was 10%. The corporate income tax rate is 46%.		
Bonds outstanding		$200,000

In addition to the above, Ball Company has issued and outstanding 600 warrants to purchase Ball Company common stock at $50 per share. Ball Company also issued warrants to purchase 500 common shares of Toy, Inc., at $20 per share. All of the warrants are outstanding.

Required:

a. Calculate primary earnings per share for Ball Company.

b. Calculate primary earnings per share for Toy, Inc., and its consolidated subsidiary.

c. Calculate consolidated net income.

Problem 5–16

The operations of Cedar Falls Corporation involve eight different industries. Information on these eight industrial segments for the most recent year is as follows:

Industry Segment	Revenue from—		Operating Profit [Loss]	Identifiable Assets
	Unaffiliated Customers	Intersegment Sales		
1	$ 300	$ 100	$ [50]	$ 800
2	800	200	200	1,200
3	5,000	1,000	200	5,000
4	8,000	—	1,100	6,500
5	9,500	—	500	8,500
6	1,200	400	400	1,500
7	1,000	500	[600]	2,000
8	2,000	—	[100]	3,000

An investigation of the operations of recent years suggests that the most recent data are not unusual.

Required:

In anticipation of the need to prepare financial reports on the important segments in which Cedar Falls Corporation operates, and using the criteria required by the FASB, determine which of the eight industry segments should be treated as reportable segments. In other words, for which of the eight should separate financial information be presented?

Problem 5–17

Jamestown Company is a broadly diversified company whose operations involve five major industries: A, B, C, D, and E. Management of Jamestown Company plans to include in the annual report for 19X1 a segmented financial report prepared in accordance with *FASB Statement No. 14.* Financial data relating to segmental operations during 19X1 are presented below:

	A	B	C	D	E
Sales............................	$7,000	$19,000	$150,000	$ 6,000	$12,000
Cost of goods sold.................	$3,000	$12,000	$ 80,000	$ 1,400	$ 7,000
Administrative expenses............	1,000	4,000	24,000	1,000	1,000
Selling expenses	1,000	7,000	29,000	1,600	3,000
Total operating expenses	$5,000	$23,000	$133,000	$ 4,000	$11,000
Operating profit	$2,000	$ [4,000]	$ 17,000	$ 2,000	$ 1,000
Identifiable assets.................	$8,000	$15,000	$ 95,000	$16,000	$35,000

Additional information:

a. Included in the sales of segment E are $4,000 which were sales to segment C. None of items sold to C remain in the December 31, 19X1, assets of C.

b. In addition to the assets identified with industrial segments, the corporate offices have assets of $18,000 on December 31, 19X1.

c. Income taxes amount to 30 percent of net operating profits.

Required:

a. Determine which of the industry segments should be reported separately in segmental reports and state the basis for your decision in each case.

b. Prepare a summarized financial report by segments which is reconciled with summarized consolidated data.

CHAPTER
6

Accounting Research and
Decision Making

Financial Accounting Education and Practice

Financial accounting practice centers largely on the application of rules promulated by such authoritative bodies as the Financial Accounting Standards Board and the Securities and Exchange Commission. Education for financial accounting practice therefore necessarily involves development of some degree of working knowledge of the rules that govern financial reporting. However, the number of such rules is extremely large, and few practitioners hold an exhaustive working knowledge of this body of literature. Rather, the working knowledge is large enough to enable the practitioner to identify the issues present in a wide variety of reporting situations that might arise. These issues are then researched in the authoritative literature. Sometimes this research process reveals unambiguous guidance for the reporting issue at hand. Sometimes it does not. But the practitioner is not afforded the luxury of simply asserting that the issue has no apparent solution. An accounting treatment must be selected. This requires judgment and is therefore difficult.

It is the opinion of the authors that (1) recognizing issues, (2) researching issues in the authoritative literature, and (3) deciding upon accounting treatments are practical skills that are learned through experience. Unfortunately, deferring the development of these skills until one actually begins professional practice can be quite costly. The purpose of this chapter is to enable the student to obtain some early experience in the activities of issue recognition, research, and decision making. It is likely that this experience will be somewhat uncomfortable. The end-of-chapter problem material cannot be solved by reference to similar examples in the text material. Issues must be identified, and research in the authoritative literature must be performed. The student will have to decide when to stop the research process. In many cases, the authoritative literature will have to be interpreted. Some issues will not have solutions that are defensible to the exclusion of alternatives. But, as is the case in accounting practice, a unique solution must be selected in spite of this ambiguity.

Many students will find the placement of this chapter curious—following an introductory treatment of accounting for business combinations. Indeed, it is not obvious precisely when in one's education it is best to embrace the ambiguity which characterizes real-world accounting practice. The important matter is that it be done sometime. The placement of this chapter is largely a function of the end-of-chapter problem material, which contains several items for which an appreciation of the fundamentals of accounting for business combinations is assumed.

The Structure of Accounting Authority

The ability to conduct research in the authoritative literature requires some understanding of what comprises this literature, what bodies have produced it, and by what authority it has been produced. The ultimate source of authority in the United States is, of course, the U.S. Constitution. This document delegates the authority to regulate interstate commerce to Congress. Insofar as interstate commerce relates to trading in securities, Congress has further delegated regulatory authority to the Securities and Exchange Commission through passage of the Securities Exchange Act of 1934. For the most part, accounting rule making by the Securities and Exchange Commission has taken the form of *Accounting Series Releases* and *Staff Accounting Bulletins*. Strictly speaking, an *Accounting Series Release* is interpretable as a rule, and a *Staff Accounting Bulletin* is interpretable as merely an instruction to the staff of the Commission. But as a practical matter, both documents are publicly distributed, and there is little real distinction between the two. Both are considered as comprising authority. However, *Accounting Series Releases* and *Staff Accounting Bulletins* are only applicable to firms whose financial reporting is under the jurisdiction of the Commission.

Recently, the Commission initiated a new release series that takes the place of the *Accounting Series Releases*. Items in this series are titled *Financial Reporting Releases*. *Financial Reporting Release No. 1* is a codification of previous *Accounting Series Releases*. At the time of this writing, it is unclear as to how, other than in name, this new series will be distinct from its predecessor.

The *Financial Reporting Releases* and *Staff Accounting Bulletins* deal largely with matters of accounting principle. Matters of disclosure are the subject of *Regulation S-X* and *S-K*. *Regulation S-X* establishes financial statement disclosure policies. *Regulation S-K* establishes policies regarding disclosures in the nonfinancial statement portions of periodic reports.

Historically, the budget of the Commission has not included large expenditures for accounting rule-making activity. Instead, the Commission has implicitly delegated some of its statutory authority to other entities. Until the early 1970s, the American Institute of CPAs was the recipient of this implied authority. The Institute exercised this authority principally through two committees. Until the early 1960s, the Committee on Accounting Procedure issued a numbered series of accounting rules called *Accounting Research Bulletins*. In the early 1960s, the Institute disbanded this committee and replaced it with another committee, the Accounting Principles Board. During its tenure, the Accounting Principles Board issued a numbered series of *Opinions*. In addition, the Board issued *Interpretations* of these *Opinions* which contained guidance on specific implementation matters.

Like its predecessor committee, the Board was eventually disbanded. The line of authority from the U.S. Constitution to the Board was only implicit at best. That is, no statute specifically granted the Board authority to make binding rules. At base, the Board was only a committee of the Institute, and its clear authority was limited to Institute members. Many individuals who were not Institute members perceived that they were affected by the Board's actions. Consider those corporate managers who might be evaluated on the basis of growth in earnings per share. They might well perceive that a newly promulgated rule that changes reported earnings affects them adversely. Why should such individuals passively allow their personal well-being to be altered by the actions of an organization of which they are not even a member? Indeed, some did not. This was perhaps nowhere more apparent than in events leading up to passage of the Revenue Act of 1971. This piece of legislation provided for a 7 percent "job development" investment tax credit. The Board had anticipated passage of the Act and issued an Exposure Draft of a proposed *Opinion* on accounting for the tax credit. The proposed *Opinion* would require that increases in income due to the tax credit be reported over the life of the related investment (as opposed to immediate income recognition in the year of acquisition). Issuance of the Exposure Draft provoked lobbying activities before the U.S. Senate. These lobbying activities apparently resulted in insertion into the Act a provision that precluded the Board from requiring any particular method of reporting the effect of the tax credit. This action so undermined confidence in the Board's authority that individuals interested in the accounting rule-making process initiated a search for an alternative to the Board.

The search for an alternative led to the establishment of the Financial Accounting Standards Board. Unlike the Accounting Principles Board, the Financial Accounting Standards Board is not a committee of the Institute. Rather, it is a free-standing body whose budget is derived from contributions by a broad constituency of those having an interest in accounting rule making. In addition, *Financial Reporting Release No. 1* (par. 3521) explicitly links the Board with the statutory authority of the Commission. Output of the Board takes the form of *Statements of Financial Accounting Standards* and *Interpretations* of those *Statements*. In addition, the staff of the Board issues *Technical Bulletins* that deal with industry-specific accounting matters and other such matters of limited application. *Technical Bulletins* are exposed to Board members prior to issuance. However, they are not subject to any formal approval by the Board.

Prior to issuance of a *Statement*, the Board takes extraordinary care in soliciting the views of a broad constituency. After announcing the placement of an item on its technical agenda, the Board publishes a *Discussion Memorandum* outlining the issues involved. No position is taken in a *Discussion Memorandum*. The purpose is merely to solicit comment on the issues. A public hearing is then held to provide interested parties a forum for additional commentary. An *Exposure Draft* follows this process. The purpose of an *Exposure Draft* is to announce a tentative position as a basis for yet additional comment. Finally, a *Statement* is issued.

The time lag between placement of an item on the technical agenda and issuance of a *Statement* is often quite long. Many accounting issues arise because of rather sudden alternations of the economic environment in which firms operate, and the operating procedures of the Board are too lengthy to facilitate a timely response to these "emerging problems." For example, in late 1981, Congress passed the Economic Recovery Act of 1981. This legislation created an incentive for a rather complex lease agreement that allowed the transfer of tax benefits of asset ownership from one entity to another. Many firms immediately took advantage of the provisions of the Act. The Board was only able to take the matter of accounting for such lease agreements through the *Exposure Draft* stage as of the end of 1981. Nonetheless, issuance of 1981 financial statements could not be delayed until the Board ultimately promulgated a *Statement*. Interestingly, the tax legislation was subsequently recinded—thus giving rise to an accounting issue which came and went before the Board could act on it.

The inability of the Board to act promptly on "emerging problems" is one reason for the issuance of *Technical Bulletins* (which do not pass through the process leading to issuance of a *Statement*). It also has led to a variety of pronouncements on the part of the American Institute of CPAs. The Institute established an Accounting Standards Executive Committee that has issued *Statements of Position* on accounting matters of concern to the Institute membership. Some of these *Statements of Position* are industry-specific in scope. Others are not. The content of some have subsequently been adopted by the Financial Accounting Standards Board in the form of a *Statement*. The Commission, in its 1978 report to Congress, has stated that it considers *Statements of Position* as constituting "preferable accounting." Because of this sanction, the *Statements of Position* possess authority that extends beyond the membership of the Institute.

It has not been the practice of the Accounting Standards Executive Committee to compete in any sense with the Financial Accounting Standards Board. Rather, its role is more appropriately characterized as one of providing "stop gap" guidance until such time as the Board elects to address an issue. In fact, the Committee has tended to move away from the issuance of *Statements of Position* in favor of writing *Issues Papers* for use by the Board and its staff in developing *Statements* and *Technical Bulletins*. The precise authoritative status of an *Issues Paper* is unclear.

The American Institute of CPAs has also published *Industry Accounting Guides* and *Industry Audit Guides* identifying accounting principles related to specific industries. Like the *Statements of Position*, these *Guides* are said to constitute "preferable accounting" by the Securities and Exchange Commission.

Research Source Materials

The previous section outlined an extensive body of authoritative literature consisting of *Financial Reporting Releases, Staff Accounting Bulletins, Financial*

Reporting Releases, Regulations S-X and *S-K, Accounting Research Bulletins, Accounting Principles Board Opinions* and their *Interpretations, Statement of Financial Accounting Standards* and their *Interpretations, Technical Bulletins, Statements of Position, Issues Papers, Industry Accounting Guides* and *Industry Audit Guides*. Because these pronouncements have been issued by different bodies at different times, they are not totally consistent with one another. (The example in the following section illustrates an inconsistency between an *Interpretation* of *Accounting Principles Board Opinion No. 16* and a *Financial Reporting Release*.) It is, therefore, important to be mindful of the authoritative status of the body that has issued a given pronouncement. It is not possible to develop a complete ranking of the various pronouncements in terms of their authority. For the most part, however, pronouncements by the Securities and Exchange Commission dominate those of the Financial Accounting Standards Board, which in turn dominate those of American Institute of CPAs.

It is somewhat awkward to work with all authoritative pronouncements in their original form. Some have been superceded in whole or in part, and this fact cannot be ascertained by scrutinizing the pronouncement in original form. Fortunately, many pronouncements have been reprinted with superceded provisions deleted. *Financial Reporting Releases* and *Staff Accounting Bulletins* are reprinted by Commerce Clearing House, Inc., in a book titled *SEC Codification of Financial Reporting Policies*. *Accounting Research Bulletins, Accounting Principles Board Opinions* and their *Interpretations, Statements of Financial Standards* and their *Interpretations,* and *Technical Bulletins* are reprinted in an abridged, two volume, form in *Accounting Standards* (current text) by McGraw-Hill Book Company. *Statements of Position* are reprinted in *AICPA Statements of Position of the Accounting Standards Division* by Commerce Clearing House, Inc.

Each of these three works includes a topical index to its contents. Another topical index is the *Index to Accounting and Auditing Technical Pronouncements* published by the American Institute of CPAs. The virtue of this index is its completeness. It includes citations to *Industry Accounting Guides, Industry Audit Guides,* and *Regulations S-X* and *S-K*. These sources are not included in the other topical indexes. However, the *Index to Accounting and Auditing Technical Pronouncements* has a significant weakness. Its references are only to pronouncements or major sections of *Accounting Standards*, and do not include specific paragraph numbers. The other indexes contain references to specific paragraphs. Because of this, it is probably best to research issues by referring initially to the indexes contained in *SEC Codification of Financial Reporting Policies, Accounting Standards,* and *AICPA Statements of Position of the Accounting Standards Division*. Then the *Index to Accounting and Auditing Technical Pronouncements* should be consulted to identify relevant source materials not included in the other three indexes. This approach is taken in the example presented later in this chapter.

The Research Process

Obviously, the research process begins with recognizing the issues involved in a financial reporting situation. This is done on the basis of one's working knowledge of the authoritative accounting literature. Little can be said about how one goes about recognizing issues other than noting the paradox that one must know something about the contents of the literature in order to recognize issues; but the purpose of recognizing issues is to facilitate learning the contents of the literature. The utility of some experience in the conduct of research becomes obvious upon contemplating this circularity.

Identification of issues facilitates development of a list of key words. For example, if one had decided that an issue was whether issuance of parent company warrants in lieu of common shares would rule out accounting for a business combination as a pooling of interests, key words would certainly include *warrants, business combinations,* and *pooling of interests.* Once key words are developed, the various topical indexes are consulted for specific citations listed under these key words.

The obvious next step is to read the cited literature. Sometimes this reading will reveal a clear answer to the issue at hand. Sometimes it will not. When it does not, one must decide whether the situation described in the literature is "close enough" to the issue at hand to support a similar treatment. Deciding how close is "close enough" is difficult. In part, this difficulty is due to the frequent absence from the literature of the rationale underlying specified accounting treatments. For example, section N35.101b of *Accounting Standards* states that *Accounting Principles Board Opinion No. 29* does not apply to exchanges between a corporate joint venture and its owners? Without the rationale for excluding exchanges between a corporate joint venture and its owners, it is difficult to decide whether the exclusion should be extended to exchanges between an unincorporated joint venture and its owners.

In any event, a decision must ultimately be made. Upon making a decision, the research process is documented in some form of memorandum. This memorandum usually is organized into the following sections:

1. A succinct statement of the issues.
2. A narrative of the economic events that gave rise to the transaction for which an accounting treatment must be determined.
3. A review of the relevant authoritative literature.
4. A statement of the decision.

The importance of writing this memorandum in a lucid fashion cannot be overemphasized. It will often be read by individuals who are not intimately familiar with the facts and issues. The reading may occur years after the memorandum is written, and in conjunction with litigation. The memorandum may serve as a guide for future research on a similar issue. It must provide an effective communication.

A Comprehensive Example

We will now "walk through" a real fact situation in order to illustrate the phases of accounting research and decision making. As is often the case, the fact situation is a difficult one: multiple issues are involved, amounts are material, and all answers are not obvious.

The Fact Situation

Dome Petroleum, Ltd., a Canadian Company, tried unsuccessfully to purchase from Conoco, Inc., the latter firm's 52.9 percent interest in Hudson's Bay Oil and Gas Company. Dome then initiated what ultimately evolved into a most bizarre sequence of events. Dome tendered for up to 22,000,000 of Conoco's shares (20 percent of the outstanding shares) at $65. The Conoco shares had been selling at about $50, and the response on the part of Conoco's shareholders was astounding. Almost half of Conoco's shares were offered to Dome. Dome indeed purchased the 22,000,000 shares at $65 and thus owned 20 percent of Conoco. By virtue of owning such a large block of Conoco shares, Dome essentially coerced Conoco into a treasury stock transaction. Dome received what it had wanted all along, the 52.9 percent interest in Hudson's Bay. Conoco received the 22,000,000 of its own shares and cash in the amount of $245,000,000. The treasury shares were then retired. At the time, the carrying value of Conoco's investment in Hudson's Bay was approximately $367,000,000 and Conoco's quarterly income without this transaction was $159,000,000. The transaction was taxable and increased Conoco's current tax payment by $97,000,000.

Meanwhile, Conoco was involved in preliminary negotiations of a business combination with Cities Service Company. Apart from Conoco's treasury stock transaction, the contemplated Conoco/Cities business combination would meet all requirements of a pooling of interests.

The Issues

Several issues arise in the above fact situation. The normal market value of the 22,000,000 Conoco shares received was approximately $1,100,000,000 (22,000,000 × 50). This amount plus the $245,000,000 cash received exceeds the carrying value of the investment in Dome by $978,000,000. Should the treasury stock transaction be recorded at market value with attendant recognition of $978,000,000 in pretax gain? If so, should the gain be classified as extraordinary and reported at its $881,000,000 net of tax amount? Might the gain be classified as discontinued operations?

Of the total market value received of $1,345,000,000 (stock of $1,100,000,000 plus cash of $245,000,000), 18.2 percent was received in the form of cash. As an alternative, then, can the transaction be treated as two separate transactions? In particular, can 18.2 percent of the investment be considered as having been sold for cash of $245,000,000 [with attendant pretax gain recognition of $245,000,000 − .182 (367,000,000) = 178,148,699], and the remaining 81.8 percent of the investment considered swapped for treasury shares without gain recognition. If so, should the tax applicable to the nonrecognized portion of the taxable gain be considered as arising from a permanent difference and therefore reduce current income?

The differences among these alternatives are profound. If the entire gain is to be recognized, the transaction would be recorded with the following entry:

Cash...	245,000,000	
Treasury Stock................................	1,100,000,000	
Income Tax Expense...........................	97,000,000	
Income Tax Payable		97,000,000
Investment in Hudson's Bay		367,000,000
Gain		978,000,000

Given quarterly income without this transaction in the amount of $159,000,000, this treatment results in an increase in quarterly income of 554 percent (881,000,000/159,000,000). Moreover, Conoco's quarterly weighted-average shares outstanding was 103,019,665. Therefore, gain recognition increases earnings per share from $1.54 (159,000,000/103,019,665) to $10.09 (159,000,000 + 881,000,000)/103,019,665).

On the other hand, treating the transactions as two separate transactions gives rise to the following entry (assuming current income is to be reduced by the entire amount of tax applicable to the transaction):

Cash...	245,000,000	
Treasury Stock .818 (367,000,000)	300,148,699*	
Income Tax Expense...........................	97,000,000	
Income Tax Payable		97,000,000
Investment in Hudson's Bay		367,000,000
Gain (245,000,000 − .182 × 367,000,000)........		178,148,699*

* Amounts not rounded.

This treatment results in an increase in quarterly income of 51 percent (81,148,699/159,000,000) and an increase in earnings per share from $1.54 to $2.33.

Finally, there is the matter of the contemplated Conoco/Cities Service business combination. Would the transaction rule out pooling of interests accounting?

Research

Recall that the issues in this fact situation are:

1. Should the entire gain be recognized or can gain recognition be limited to the portion of investment sold for cash?
2. Is any gain to be recognized classifiable as an extraordinary item or discontinued operations?
3. If only a portion of the gain is to be recognized, is the entire amount of tax to be charged to current earnings?
4. Would the transaction rule out a subsequent pooling of interests?

Choice of a starting point is somewhat arbitrary. However, the third issue seems likely to be the most clear-cut. Hence, we shall begin with the question of whether any nonrecognized gain is a permanent difference.

Looking under "Income Tax Expense" in the various indexes, we find reference to permanent differences at I24.521-528 in *Accounting Standards*. No other references appear promising. Reading these paragraphs provides an unambiguous answer. Differences between accounting and taxable income are said to be permanent "if an originating difference is *never* followed by a reverse difference." This appears to be the case with the transaction at hand. The treasury shares acquired have been retired. Under no circumstances will they be reissued in some future period. And even if they were, the difference between cash received and the accounting basis of the shares would not be recorded as a gain. Thus, any difference between the accounting and taxable gain is a permanent difference, and the entire $97,000,000 in tax applicable to the transaction must be recorded currently.

The first issue is much more ambiguous. The index to *Accounting Standards* indicates a definition of "Nonreciprocal Transfers" at N35.102. The other indexes provide no promising references. This paragraph lists distributions of nonmonetary assets to stockholders to acquire outstanding capital stock as an example of nonreciprocal transfers with owners. Similarly, distributions of investments in subsidiaries in a spin-off are listed. It is clear that the Conoco transaction is a nonreciprocal transfer with owners.

Other references to nonreciprocal transfers with owners appear at N35.105 and N35.110. Section N35.105 indicates that a transfer of nonmonetary asset to a shareholder is to be based on fair value and, therefore, gives rise to a gain or loss. Moreover, an example of a distribution of nonmonetary assets to acquire and subsequently retire treasury shares is given. At this point, it would appear that a gain must be recognized.

However, ambiguity is introduced at N35.110. This paragraph appears among a series of "Modifications of the Basic Principle" and states that distributions of nonmonetary assets in a spin-off shall be accounted for on the basis of the recorded values of the assets, i.e., no gain or loss is to be recognized. Moreover, a pro rata distribution of shares of a subsidiary that has been consolidated or accounted for using the equity method is said to be the equivalent of a spin-off.

Section N35.110 is extremely problematic. The Conoco transaction was not a pro rata distribution of its shares of Hudson's Bay Oil and Gas. Rather, the shares were distributed to a single Conoco owner (Dome Petroleum). A literal interpretation of N35.110 thus leads to the disturbing conclusion that whether or not Conoco reports a 554 percent increase in income and earnings per share turns on whether assets are distributed to all shareholders or just one of them. What logic would suggest that whether or not Conoco has indeed realized $881,000,000 in income should depend on a seemingly trivial distinction? The answer to this question is not at all clear because the rationale underlying N35.110 is not documented. Nonetheless, a decision must be made. Should N35.110 be interpreted literally and the entire gain be recognized? Or should one dismiss as trivial the fact that the shares of Hudson's Bay Oil and Gas were distributed to a single Conoco owner, treat the transaction as the equivalent of a spin-off and record the smaller gain? This is indeed a difficult choice, and reasonable individuals might reach different conclusions.

Which treatment would Conoco have favored? One cannot know for sure. However, one suspects that Conoco would have wanted to avoid gain recognition. The period surrounding the transaction was one of intense political controversy regarding whether oil and gas companies were exploiting the so called "energy crisis" and should, therefore, be subjected to a Windfall Profits Tax. Reporting huge increases in profits, particularly those with no corresponding increase in cash flow, would not serve well the interests of an oil and gas company in the political arena. Such political considerations further complicate an already difficult problem.

The results of the actual decision are evidenced by Conoco's second quarter 1981 report. Conoco's reporting was consistent with a literal interpretation of N35.110. The entire gain was included in income.

The second issue relates to gain classification. The index to *Accounting Standards* provides references to definitions of discontinued operations at I13.105 and I13.401. Both references indicate that the discontinued operations classification relates to business segments. Business segments are, in turn, defined at I13.404. This paragraph clearly defines segments as representing a major line of business activity. Thus, the disposal of an oil and gas subsidiary by an oil and gas parent would not be classifiable as a discontinued operation. Definitions of extraordinary items are indicated at I17.106–110. These paragraphs restrict the extraordinary classification to items which are both unusual in nature and infrequent in occurrence. The disposition of an investment in an oil and gas company by an oil and gas company meets neither of the two criteria. Nonetheless, allowing the $881,000,000 gain to enter the determination of income (and earnings per share) from continuing operations is troublesome.

Classifying the gain as ordinary would not likely mislead sophisticated investors and analysts into interpreting the affairs of Conoco as having taken a sudden and very dramatic change for the better. The transaction had received extensive coverage in the financial press and would be described in notes to the financial statements regardless of how the gain might be classified. Thus, the classification issue is not particularly important if sophisticated investors and analysts are taken as the sole audiences of the financial statements. But what of the general news media, legislators, and the like? Would these audiences ever view the complete financial statements? Might they base evaluations on less complete secondary sources such as the "Digest of Earnings" in the *Wall Street Journal?* One cannot be sure. It can therefore be argued that the gain should be classified as extraordinary even though it does not meet the criteria of being unusual in nature and infrequent in occurrence. Indeed, Conoco classified the gain as extraordinary.

The final issue is whether this transaction would rule out pooling of interests accounting for a subsequent Conoco/Cities Service business combination. The index to *Accounting Standards* provides a reference to "Treasury Stock-Business Combinations" at B50.562-568. These paragraphs are an *Interpretation* of *Accounting Principles Board Opinion No. 16.* They remind us that treasury stock acquisitions within two years prior to initiation and between initiation and consumation of a business combination are compatible with the pooling of interests concept only if the acquisitions take place for purposes other than business combinations. And in absence of persuasive evidence to the contrary, it is to be presumed that such acquisitions are undertaken in contemplation of effecting a business combination. In the case of the Conoco treasury stock acquisition, the intent is clear enough. The treasury stock was acquired for a purpose other than effecting a business combination with Cities Service, i.e., for the purpose of terminating the dispute with Dome Petroleum over Hudson's Bay. Presumably, the circumstances surrounding the acquisition would constitute the "persuasive evidence" required by the Interpretation and a Conoco/Cities Service pooling of interests would not be disallowed.

However, the index to *SEC Codification of Financial Reporting Policies* also indicates a reference (under "Business Combinations—Effect of Treasury Stock Transactions") at paragraph 3552. This is a reference to *Financial Reporting Release No. 1.* The *Release* refers to *Accounting Principles Board Opinion No. 16,* and its requirement that allowable treasury stock transactions be consistent with a systematic pattern of acquisitions that is established at least two years before the plan of combination is initiated. The *Release* also states that the absence of reference to the "systematic pattern" requirement in the *Interpretation* has led some accountants to conclude that this requirement has been superceded. It then states that the Commission does not accept this position. Treasury shares acquired during the two years preceding the initiation of a business combination and between its initiation and consumation are to be considered "tainted." The "taint" is said to be removable only through satisfaction of the "systematic pattern" requirement, through reissuance of the treasury shares, or through issuance of an equivalent number of previously unissued shares. The *Release* specifically identifies retirement of treasury shares as an act which does not remove the "taint." Since a *Financial Reporting Release* is of a higher authority than an *Interpretation* of an *Opinion,* one must conclude that the acquisition and subsequent retirement of treasury stock on the part of Conoco would rule out a Conoco/Cities Service pooling of interests.

Indeed, the Conoco/Cities Service business combinations never transpired. But the response on the part of Conoco's shareholders to Dome Petroleum's tender offer drew considerable attention in the financial community. Several companies subsequently tendered offers to buy Conoco. Conoco ultimately merged with Du Pont. Cities Service was acquired by Occidental shortly thereafter.

Problems

Problem 6–1

Hansen Company is considering entering into a business combination with Kimbrell Company. Kimbrell has warrants outstanding that allow the warrant holders to purchase 100,000 shares of common stock at a price of $30 per share. Kimbrell presently has 400,000 common shares outstanding. The contemplated combination would involve issuing Hansen common shares in exchange for all 400,000 Kimbrell outstanding shares. Two alternatives are under consideration relating to the warrants. One involves Hansen's purchasing the warrants for cash. The other involves merely leaving the warrants outstanding.

Required:

Determine whether either of the above alternatives would allow accounting for the Hansen/Kimbrell combination as a pooling of interests.

Problem 6–2

Ace Company has owned a 40 percent interest in Charles Company and has accounted for its investment using the equity method. Ace Company then sells 60 percent of its investment, such that its ownership drops to 14 percent and must switch to the cost method. As of the date of sale, cumulative equity method earnings since acquisition are $1,200,000 and cumulative dividends since acquisition are $400,000. Accordingly, at the date of sale, Ace Company had deferred taxes on its balance sheet of $60,000:

Equity method earnings	$1,200,000
Dividends received	400,000
Excess	$ 800,000
Less dividends received exclusion (85%)	680,000
Amount of excess ultimately taxable	$ 120,000
Tax rate	× .50
Deferred tax balance	$ 60,000

Required:

Determine the disposition of the $60,000 deferred tax balance in the period of sale and/or in subsequent periods.

Problem 6–3

Bell Industries purchased an aircraft by issuing a nonrecourse note. (The note specified that in the event of default, the seller's only recourse is in the form of a return of the aircraft.) The note carries an interest rate of 18 percent, has a term of 10 years, and is the principal amount of $200,000. The note is payable at a minimum rate of $2,000 per month. (Since the normal payments to liquidate a $200,000 obligation are $3,600 per month, making only the minimum payment will necessitate a substantial balloon payment in the tenth year.) The minimum payment is the equivalent of a rental payment of $200 per hour on utilization of 10 hours per month. The actual payment is based on utilization such that utilization in excess of 10 hours per month will increase the required payments and principal will be reduced accordingly. (Utilization is expected to be approximately 15 hours per month, and $200 per hour is a reasonable rental rate.)

Required:

Determine an appropriate method of accounting for this transaction over the life of the note.

Problem 6–4

In 1979, Murphy Company was acquired by Ransom Company in a business combination accounted for as a purchase. Murphy used LIFO inventory valuation. The market value of the inventory at date of acquisition was $40,000,000 larger than Murphy's LIFO basis. There was no minority interest.

Required:

a. In accounting for the excess of purchase price over book value, should the consolidated statements of Ransom allocate the entire $40,000,000 to inventory, or should the valuation be lower due to the fact that $18,000,000 in additional taxes will be paid if the inventory were to be liquidated? (In other words, the current value exceeds the tax basis by $40,000,000. Should the allocation of purchase price take this into account in some way?)

b. Assume the entire $40,000,000 was indeed allocated to inventory. In 1982,

Murphy changed its inventory valuation method to FIFO such that the $18,000,000 in taxes came due immediately. Should the $18,000,000 in taxes be recognized currently, or should the 1979 purchase price be reallocated to reduce inventory and increase goodwill by $18,000,000?

Problem 6–5

Mid-America Savings & Loan holds a portfolio of long-term fixed rate mortgages. It desires to divest itself of the portfolio. However, interest rates have risen substantially and the mortgage loan portfolio's market value has fallen below carrying value. Mid-America enters into transfer agreement with Guarantee Insurance Company. According to the agreement, Mid-America will receive cash in an amount equal to the current market value of the portfolio and its ownership will pass to Guarantee. However, the agreement contains a put option exercisable at maturity. That is, Guarantee can require Mid-America to repurchase the mortgage loans when they mature. The repurchase price is equal to maturity value.

Required:
Determine how Mid-America should account for the transfer agreement.

Problem 6–6

Apple Valley Sales sold to a syndicate of medical doctors a tract of unimproved land. The syndicate planned to build a shopping center on the cite within two years. The cost of Apple Valley of this tract was $11,000,000. The sales price was $15,000,000.

The syndicate financed the purchase as follows:

Cash down payment	$ 3,500,000
Fifteen-year first mortgage from a regionally based insurance company	9,000,000
Ten-year second mortgage loan from Apple Valley Sales.	2,500,000
	$15,000,000

Required:
Determine the appropriate accounting for this transaction (on the part of Apple Valley Sales) at the time of sale.

Problem 6–7

Dorr Company began operations in 1980, and on January 1 of that year acquired an asset costing $150,000. The asset has a 15-year life and is depreciated straight line for accounting purposes and on an accelerated basis for tax purposes. Accounting and taxable income (before taxes) are:

Year	Accounting	Taxable
1980	$ 10,000	$ 1,250
1981	10,000	2,500
1982	10,000	3,750
1983	10,000	5,000
1984	(45,000)	(48,750)
1985	3,000	500
1986	3,000	1,750
1987	3,000	3,000
1988	3,000	4,250
1989	3,000	5,500
1990	3,000	6,750

The loss carryforward due to 1984 operations is not reasonably assured and the tax rate is 50 percent.

Required:

Determine the appropriate recording of tax expense for 1984 through 1990. For simplicity, assume a three-year carryback period and a five-year carryforward period.

Problem 6–8

Mapco, Inc., recently issued $50 million in convertible notes. The notes are convertible into Mapco common stock and pay adjustable interest. The actual interest paid is directly related to the size of common dividends. The redemption price of the notes is below both the issue price and the conversion value.

Required:

Determine an appropriate accounting for the notes.

Problem 6–9

Groff Enterprises seeks to acquire Kinney Corporation. Pooling of interests accounting is sought. The exchange of shares would take place July 15, 1983, and Groff's fiscal year ends December 31, 1983. In addition, Groff plans a public offering of shares as a source of new capital. This offering would take place in November 1983. Dan Collins, the sole stockholder of Kinney will be allowed to include the Groff shares received in the Groff/Kinney combination in this public offering (thus affording Collins the opportunity to sell his Groff shares).

Required:

Determine if the contemplated November 1983 public offering would preclude a Groff/Kinney pooling of interests.

Problem 6–10

Pioneer Savings and Loan, like many thrift institutions, is in a sad financial state. Its loan portfolio, when "marked to market" (valued by discounting its cash inflows at current interest rates) has a value much less than the value of its liabilities. Since it has essentially no other assets besides its loan portfolio, the current market value of its net assets is negative.

Pioneer Savings and Loan was acquired by a stronger financial institution for the grand sum of $1. Because of the negative current value of its net assets, conventional purchase accounting will result in recording over $5,000,000 in goodwill.

Required:

Determine a proper accounting for the acquisition of Pioneer Savings and Loan on the part of its acquirer.

Problem 6–11

The Penn Machinery Group is a company that is primarily involved in equipment sales. In addition, it owns a small fleet of trucks that it has been leasing out on a month to month basis. The largest single stockholder of Penn is Mary Freeman. She is also the chief executive officer. In 1983, Penn negotiated a lease covering its entire rental fleet. The trucks would be leased for three years with a renewal option. The lessee is financially sound.

The year 1983 has not been a good year for Penn. Income for the year is expected to be considerably below prior years. Moreover, due to net operating loss carryforwards, Penn does not expect any 1983 income taxes. Nonetheless, Freeman and other Penn executives are in very high personal tax brackets and are anxious to locate personal tax shelters.

Freeman has proposed selling the rental fleet (at a fair retail price) to a limited partnership. The general partner of this partnership is an independent corporation controlled by Freeman. The limited partners are Freeman and other Penn executives. Instead of Penn leasing the trucks to the lessee, this partnership would be the lessor.

Freeman believes the merits of this arrangement are twofold. First, Penn could report a substantial gain on the sale of the rental fleet. Second, the partners of the limited partnership would realize the tax benefits of asset ownership. It is her assessment that the three-year lease provides approximately a 70 percent payback of the partnership's investment and that, with proper maintenance, the trucks would easily have an economic life well beyond the initial lease term.

Required:

Determine the propriety of Penn's reporting a gain on the sale of its rental fleet.

Problem 6–12

Since 1975, the Chicago Board of trade and other exchanges have introduced trading in interest rate futures contracts. Such a contract is an agreement to purchase (or deliver) debt instruments at a future date, the acquisition (or selling) price of which is fixed at the date one enters into the agreement. As such, these contracts facilitate hedging against adverse effects of future changes in interest rates. For example, a portfolio manager might be concerned about a decline in market value for an investment portfolio of debt securities brought about by a future increase in interest rates. To hedge this risk, the portfolio manager might sell U.S. Treasury bond futures contracts short. If interest rates rise, the decline in value of the investment portfolio will be offset by a gain from the short sale of the U.S. Treasury bonds.

Assume the following data:

Jan. 2   An insurance company purchases $10 million 11⅞ percent U.S. Treasury bonds, due February 1995, for its investment portfolio at 99. In order to protect its liquidity position against rising interest rates, a hedge is entered into against the bonds purchased by selling 100 June U.S. Treasury bond futures contracts (each covering $100,000 face of bonds) short at 98¹⁶/₃₂. (The company agrees to deliver $10 million face to U.S. Treasury bonds in June. The bonds will not actually be purchased on January 2. Instead, the company deposits with a broker a margin requirement of $1,500 cash for each $100,000 futures contract. If the price rises, the company will pay the broker the excess of the June price over 98¹⁶/₃₂, less the margin deposit. If the price falls, the company will receive from the broker the amount by which 98¹¹/₃₂ exceeds the June price. In addition the margin deposit is refunded.

Mar. 31   (the fiscal year-end)   Interest rates have increased, and as a result, the market price of the 11⅞ percent U.S. Treasury bonds, due February 1995, has fallen to 97¹⁶/₃₂ for an unrealized loss in the investment portfolio of $151,500. (The carrying value of the bonds had increased to $1,500 due to discount amortization and the market price has decreased by 1½ percent.) The market price of the June U.S. Treasury bond futures contracts has fallen to 97 for an unrealized gain of $150,000.

Apr. 1   Because liquidity is needed to meet demands of policyholders, the company sells the 11⅞ percent U.S. Treasury bonds, due February 1995. Market prices for both the bond and the futures contract remain unchanged from March 31.

June 1   The market price of U.S. Treasury bonds, due February 1995, has fallen to 96. The company settles its futures contract with the broker.

Required:

Determine the appropriate accounting for all the above events. (Adapted from *Interest Rate Futures Contracts—Accounting and Control Techniques for Insurance Companies* [Chicago: Arthur Andersen & Co.].)

Problem 6–13

Mowen Company is negotiating the acquisition of Meek Company. Mowen desires that the acquisition qualify as a pooling of interests. Approximately 60 days prior to the commencement of negotiations, Richard Stroup increased his holdings of Meek common shares from 20 percent to 30 percent. If the acquisition by Mowen transpires, Stroup will be exposed to potential liability under Section 16(b) of the Securities Exchange Act of 1934. (This section makes it unlawful for "insiders" to earn short-term profits from trading in the stock of a corporation in which they are an "insider." Action can be brought against such parties by either the corporation or its other stockholders. If an action is successful, all short-term profits become payable to the corporation.) Stroup has asked Mowen to provide protection from his potential liability under Section 16(b). Two alternatives are under consideration:

1. Mowen would agree to reimburse Stroup for any judgment that might be levied against him as a result of a successful action brought by another stockholder of Meek. Such a reimbursement would involve a net loss of cash on the part of the combined entity. That is, the judgment paid to Meek would be taxable but the reimbursement paid to Stroup would not be tax deductible. Legal council had advised that the chance of successful action brought by another Meek stockholder is remote. Thus, it is unlikely that any reimbursement will ever have to be paid.

2. Mowen would agree only that its subsidiary (Meek) never will bring action against Stroup under Section 16(b). (This will not, however, rule out the possibility of another Meek stockholder bringing an action.)

Required:

Determine whether either or both of these alternatives would preclude a Mowen/Meek pooling of interests. (Adapted from *Accounting and Auditing Case Studies and Solutions* [New York: Touche Ross & Co., 1981].)

Problem 6–14

Adam Steel computes LIFO inventories using the "dollar value, single-pool base-year double extension" method. Under this method, applicable Treasury Regulations and GAAP allow treating current-year costs of "new items" as if these current costs were actually base-year costs. (Reg. Sec. 1.472-8(e)(2)(iii).)

In 1984, Adam closed its Pittsburg plant which had been making a certain inventory item. Manufacture of this item was transferred to a different plant. Adam maintained that since manufacturing costs were different in the two plants, the inventory item would constitute a "new item" for purposes of LIFO calculations.

The result was dramatic. Treatment as a "new item" produced a substantial increase in ending inventory and increased reported 1983 income from $800,000 to $8,000,000.

Required:

Determine if the treatment of the inventory item as a "new item" is proper. For purposes of reviewing the mechanics of LIFO, see John Taylor, "LIFO: A Different Approach," *Journal of Accountancy* (April 1981), pp. 50–60. Also work through the mechanics of "new item" treatment assuming the following data:

Item	Base-Year Cost	Current Year Cost	Ending Quantity
A	$10	$15	300
B	$20	$25	600
C	$30	$50	700

Assume a beginning inventory (at LIFO cost) of $32,000. Also assume this beginning inventory had a base-year cost of $30,000. Compute the ending LIFO inventory assuming item C is and is not to be treated as a "new item" for which current cost is used in place of base-year cost.

Problem 6–15

Sandmeyer Company is an equipment broker. It enters into the following transaction involving several entities: (1) an electronics manufacturer, (2) a bank, (3) a user, and (4) an owner. Sandmeyer borrows $600,000 from the bank, adds $200,000 of its own money, and purchases an $800,000 piece of "high tech" electronic equipment from the manufacturer. The bank loan will be repaid over five years (the longest loan period the bank would allow).

Sandmeyer sells the equipment to the owner for $800,000, taking $250,000 in cash and the remaining $550,000 in the form of a seven-year note. Sandmeyer then leases the equipment from the owner for seven years. The lease payments exactly coincide in timing and amount with the debt service payments Sandmeyer will receive from the owner. Thus, the only cash effect of the sale and leaseback is the receipt of $250,000.

Sandmeyer then subleases the equipment to the user. The lease term is five years, and the lease payments exactly coincide with the debt service payments Sandmeyer will make to the bank.

The net effect of the transaction is that Sandmeyer has received $250,000 in cash and paid $200,000 in cash. The remaining elements of the transaction are a "wash" in the sense that there are no net cash consequences to Sandmeyer. Sandmeyer will have use of the equipment for two years after the lease between Sandmeyer and the user has expired. Of course, given technological change in the electronics industry, the value of having the services of the equipment five years from now is uncertain.

Required:

Determine an appropriate accounting for this transaction on the part of Sandmeyer in the year the transaction takes place.

Problem 6–16

Protons Company was acquired from J. Edison. Protons manufactures solar energy equipment. Before the acquisition, it was operated by Edison as a sole proprietorship. Edison also operated an ice cream manufacturing business (which was incorporated), and will continue to run (and own) this business in the future.

Required:

Determine if the acquisition of Protons qualifies as a pooling of interests.

UNIT
TWO

Consolidated
Statements: An
Expanded Analysis

CHAPTER
7

Consolidated
Statements—Intercompany
Profit on Asset Transfers

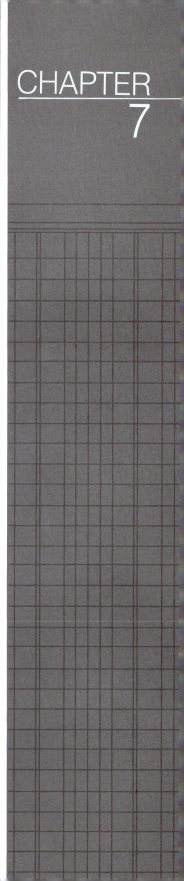

The issue of sales of products and services between affiliates was briefly introduced in Chapter 3. At that time, we noted that there are some special elimination problems when merchandise purchased from an affiliate remains in the ending inventory. Similar problems exist when other types of assets are transferred between affiliates and remain on the balance sheet of the purchasing affiliate at the end of the fiscal year. In Chapters 7 and 8, these issues are examined in detail.

Overview of the Merchandise Transfer Problem

We observed in Chapter 2 that consolidated financial statements are essentially summations of the assets, liabilities, revenues, and expenses of the individual affiliates, *calculated on the basis of transactions with nonaffiliates*. From the perspective of the *economic entity* for which the consolidated statements are prepared, intercompany sales of merchandise are not transactions with nonaffiliates; they are, from this point of view, *intraentity* transactions that should not be included in the amounts reported in the consolidated statements. But the source data for the preparation of consolidated statements are the individual financial statements of the affiliates. Consequently, the existence of intercompany sales has two important implications for the preparation of consolidated statements.

The first implication, which was previously discussed in Chapter 3, is that the total intercompany sales must be eliminated against the total intercompany purchases. The existence of a minority interest in a subsidiary has *no impact* upon the elimination. As a consequence, only transactions with nonaffiliates are reflected in the sales and purchases figures in the consolidated income statement.

The second factor to consider is the time that the intercompany transaction satisfies the profit realization test for the two different accounting entities involved: (1) the selling affiliate as a separate legal entity and (2) the economic entity for which the consolidated financial statements are prepared. Illustration 7–1 depicts the essential elements of the issue. P buys merchandise from S, its 90 percent owned subsidiary. Since the revenue realization test is satisfied from the point of view of S as a separate legal entity, the profit on the sale is properly recognized by S in its individual financial statements. However, the transaction does not satisfy the revenue realization test *from a consolidated viewpoint* until these goods are resold (either in original or modified form) to parties outside of the economic entity (for example, companies X and Y). When the revenue realization test for intercompany transactions has been satisfied through transactions with nonaffiliates, we will say that the intercompany profit has been *confirmed*.

This issue was avoided in Chapter 3 by assuming that the profit realized by the selling affiliate on intercompany sales had also been realized *in the*

Illustration 7–1

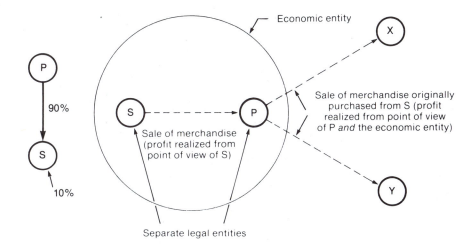

same period by the economic entity by means of sale to nonaffiliates. When realization by the economic entity has not yet taken place at the end of an accounting period in which there was an intercompany sale of merchandise, two overstatements (from a consolidated point of view) result from merely summing the values in the separate financial statements of the affiliates:

1. The profit reported by the selling affiliate on the intercompany sale has not been confirmed by the economic entity and must therefore be eliminated from the current period's operating results in the consolidated working paper.
2. The inventory acquired by the purchasing affiliate in the intercompany sale is valued above its cost to the economic entity because of the unconfirmed intercompany profit included in the transfer price. Consequently, this incremental value must be eliminated from the inventory in the balance sheet division of the consolidated working paper.

Adjustment of these two values and appropriate attention to the possible effect on the measurement of the minority interest in net income constitute the necessary steps that must be taken *in the year of the intercompany sale.*

In the next year, the unconfirmed profit of the prior period is usually confirmed to the economic entity through sale of the merchandise to nonaffiliates. The complete working paper ramifications in the second year are more complex and depend in part upon the method of accounting employed by the parent company. However, the essential point to note at this time is that the confirmed profit is not included in the reported operating results of the affiliate that initially made the intercompany sale. It was reported in the affiliate's operating results in the prior period, but deferred in the consolidated statement working paper. Therefore, by means of a working paper entry this year, the confirmed, but unreported, profit is added to the operating results of the economic entity.

In summary, the individual affiliates' financial statements, which provide the source data for the consolidated statement working paper, may include reported profits that have not yet been confirmed to the economic entity. For example, profits recognized by the individual selling affiliates on intercompany sales in period 1 may not be confirmed to the economic entity until period 2. In this case, the consolidated statement working papers in both periods 1 and 2 must be responsive to the need to reallocate the reported profit in period 1 into the consolidated operating results in period 2. Note, however, that if consolidated statements were prepared for a longer period of time incorporating both periods 1 and 2, the merchandise would have already passed through the purchasing affiliate to outside parties and no unconfirmed profit (on this particular intercompany transaction) would exist. This consequence of extending the time horizon reflects a fundamental property of consolidated income statements. *Although interperiod allocations of affiliates' reported incomes may be necessary, in the long run the total profit reported by the economic entity (before assignment of the minority's share therein) is merely the sum of the reported net incomes (from operations) of the affiliates.*

Before examining in detail the procedures and techniques employed to deal with intercompany inventory profits on the books of the parent and in the consolidated working papers, we first must resolve the following conceptual issues:

1.   How is the intercompany profit measured?
2.   How much of the intercompany profit should be eliminated, and how should the eliminated portion be shared between majority shareholders (the parent company) and minority shareholders?

Determination of Amount of Intercompany Profit

Seller's Gross Profit—The Starting Point.   The first step in dealing with unconfirmed profit on intercompany merchandise transfers is identification of the amount of the profit recognized by the selling affiliate. This amount is usually determined by applying the selling affiliate's applicable *gross profit rate* to the transfer price. It has occasionally been proposed that the *net profit rate* of the selling affiliate is the more appropriate index of the profit recognized by the seller on the intercompany transaction. Use of this rate, however, results in a smaller profit elimination and increases the value assigned to consolidated inventory (held by the purchasing affiliate). The larger inventory value is obtained by (implicitly) capitalizing operating expenses of the seller. Since such expenses are generally inadmissible as inventoriable costs, the gross profit rate is recommended.

Having determined the profit recognized by the seller, we must consider whether any adjustments to this value are appropriate. Three relatively common circumstances that may stimulate the need for such an adjustment are (1) transportation costs on merchandise transfers, (2) inventory market adjustments, and (3) income tax effects.

Transportation Costs on Merchandise Transfers. The transportation costs associated with sales of merchandise from one affiliate to another are valid inventory costs to the consolidated entity. If these transportation costs are paid for by the purchasing affiliate and included in its inventory valuation, no special adjustment is required. However, if the selling affiliate pays for the transportation costs, or if the purchasing affiliate has not capitalized them, the amount of the seller's profit on the intercompany transaction should be reduced by these transportation costs in determining the intercompany profit subject to elimination.

For example, assume that P Company sold merchandise it had produced to its subsidiary, S Company, at a price of $1,000. P Company paid transportation costs of $100 to ship the merchandise to S Company and recorded the expenditure as a selling expense. P Company's gross profit rate on this merchandise is assumed to be 40 percent. These facts are summarized as follows:

Intercompany profit recorded by P Company	$ 400	($1,000 × 40%)
Cost of the merchandise to P Company	600	($1,000 − $400)
Cost of the merchandise recorded by S Company	1,000	(invoice price)
Inventoriable cost to the economic entity	700	($600 + $100)
Amount of adjusted intercompany profit	300	($400 − $100)

Eliminating the adjusted intercompany profit of $300 against the $1,000 inventory cost recorded by S Company results in a $700 value for inventory in the consolidated balance sheet. This effectively capitalizes the transportation costs that were recorded by P Company as a selling expense.

Inventory Market Adjustments. The purchasing affiliate may have applied the "lower-of-cost-or-market" rule to the intercompany merchandise in its ending inventory. If "market" values are currently below the transfer price, the market adjustments recorded by the purchasing affiliate should be considered in determining the amount of the unconfirmed inventory profit. Since the market adjustment has reduced the inventory value below the original transfer price, the amount of this reduction should be used in abatement of the selling affiliate's reported trading profit in determining the unconfirmed profit to be eliminated. If the market adjustment exceeds the trading profit, no elimination for unconfirmed inventory profit is required.

For example, assume that P Company sold merchandise that cost $200 to affiliate S Company at a price of $300. S Company incurred transportation costs of $10 and recorded the merchandise at a cost of $310. At the end of the period, S Company applied the lower-of-cost-or-market rule to reduce the value of this inventory to $280—a $30 reduction. Following the general procedure described above, the adjusted intercompany profit is determined to be $70 ($100 − $30). Elimination of $70 from the inventory carrying value of $280 yields a value of $210, which is the proper inventoriable cost to the economic entity (i.e., $200 cost to P Company plus $10 transportation costs).

Income Tax Effects.   If a consolidated tax return is filed by the affiliates, reported and taxable income are synchronized with respect to profits on intercompany transactions, and there is no income tax effect to be considered. However, if the affiliates file separate income tax returns, income tax will be paid by the selling affiliate on these transactions. Since these profits are to be deferred to a future period in the consolidated financial statements, the related income tax should also be deferred. The net effect of this deferral of income taxes in the consolidated income statement is to defer the intercompany profit "net of taxes." Because the procedures that must be employed to reflect income tax effects tend to distract attention from the basic treatment of intercompany profits in consolidated statements, we will initially assume that the affiliates file consolidated tax returns and thus have no income tax effects. At the end of Chapter 8, a brief explanation of the mechanics of handling income tax effects is provided.

Elimination Principles for Unconfirmed Intercompany Profit

Having established the amount of the intercompany profit subject to elimination, we now turn to the issues of how much of the profit should be eliminated, and how the eliminated amount shall be shared by majority and minority shareholders. Basic accounting policy on these issues was recommended in 1959 in *Accounting Research Bulletin No. 51*, "Consolidated Statements," and still remains part of the authoritative literature:

> The amount of intercompany profit or loss to be eliminated . . . is not affected by the existence of a minority interest. The *complete elimination* of the intercompany profit or loss is consistent with the underlying assumption that consolidated statements represent the financial position and operating results of a single business enterprise. The elimination of the intercompany profit or loss *may* be allocated proportionately between the majority and minority interests.[1]

The policy expressed in this source is thus unequivocal with respect to the amount of the profit to be eliminated—*all, or 100 percent, of the unconfirmed intercompany profit should be eliminated.* However, two alternatives are

---

[1] Committee on Accounting Procedure, *Accounting Research Bulletin No. 51*, "Consolidated Financial Statements" (New York: AICPA, 1959), par. 14. (Emphasis supplied.) Also reproduced in FASB *Accounting Standards—Current Text*, sec. C51.115.

presented for allocating the eliminated profit between majority (parent company) and minority shareholder interests:

1. The eliminated profit may be allocated wholly to the majority shareholders, *or*
2. The eliminated profit may be allocated proportionately between majority and minority shareholders.

Effect of Alternatives on Consolidated Net Income. Further consideration of the basis for the pro rata allocation between majority and minority interests enables us to identify the unique circumstances in which the alternatives produce different results in the consolidated financial statements. The unconfirmed intercompany profit has been recorded on the books of the selling affiliate, and the pro rata allocation between majority and minority shareholders is based upon their interests in this recorded profit. If the parent company is the selling affiliate (commonly referred to as a *downstream sale*), the entire recorded profit accrues to the majority shareholders. Hence, in this circumstance, the two alternatives yield equivalent results—all of the eliminated profit is allocated to the majority shareholders. On the other hand, if the subsidiary is the selling affiliate (referred to as an *upstream sale*), the interests of the majority and minority (if any) shareholders in this unconfirmed intercompany profit are determined by multiplying the amount of the profit by each group's percentage ownership interest in the subsidiary. When the parent owns 100 percent of the subsidiary stock, the majority stockholder interest is equal to the total profit and the two alternatives are again equivalent. However, if the upstream sale is made by a less than 100 percent owned subsidiary, the two alternatives will differ in the amount of the eliminated intercompany profit allocated to the majority shareholders.

These three situations are illustrated below for a $3,000 unconfirmed intercompany profit:

		Selling Affiliate	
	Parent	*100% Owned Subsidiary*	*80% Owned Subsidiary*
Alternative 1 (all of eliminated profit allocated to majority shareholders): Allocation to:			
Majority shareholders	$3,000	$3,000	$3,000
Minority shareholders	–0–*	–0–*	–0–
Alternative 2 (eliminated profit allocated pro rata to majority and minority shareholders): Allocation to:			
Majority shareholders	3,000	3,000	2,400
Minority shareholders	–0–*	–0–*	600

* There are no minority shareholders in the selling affiliate in these situations.

In those situations where the two alternatives allocate the same amount of eliminated intercompany profit to the majority interest, there is of course no differential effect on consolidated net income. However, in the case of unconfirmed profits arising from upstream sales (or sales to another subsidiary) by partially owned subsidiaries, the two alternatives will yield different measures of consolidated net income in the year of the intercompany sale and also in the year (usually the next year) in which the intercompany profit is confirmed by sale of the merchandise to outside parties. To illustrate this effect in the year of sale, we assume that S Company, an 80 percent owned subsidiary of P Company, sold merchandise to P Company in 19X1 at a price of $10,000 and recorded a gross profit on the transaction of $3,000. We further assume that the merchandise remained in P Company's December 31, 19X1, inventory, and that the companies reported the following 19X1 net incomes from their own operations: P Company, $30,000; and S Company, $20,000. Recall that our terminology "net income from own operations" is meant to exclude recorded equity in subsidiary earnings; it is *not* meant to exclude the operating profit recorded by an affiliate on an intercompany sale. Therefore, the $3,000 unconfirmed profit at the end of 19X1 is included in S Company's $20,000 reported net income from its operations. For purposes of this illustration, we modify our residual calculation of consolidated net income by starting with the affiliates' reported net income from their own operations rather than total reported net income. This is an appropriate modification because the recorded equity in subsidiary earnings (the amount of which for cases involving unconfirmed intercompany profits is a topic to be discussed in a subsequent section) is deducted in the "net eliminations" section of the schedule. Additionally, we observe (and demonstrate in a later section) that the total amount of the unconfirmed intercompany profit is a net debit elimination in the income statement division of the consolidated working paper, and recall that the elimination of intercompany sales against intercompany purchases ($10,000 in this illustration) does *not* produce a net debit or credit elimination in the working paper. Based upon these facts and observations, consolidated net income is calculated under the two alternatives in Illustration 7–2.

The $600 difference between the two alternatives is the amount of the minority interest in the $3,000 unconfirmed intercompany profit. If the profit is confirmed in 19X2 (as would normally be the case for merchandise), the minority's share ($600) of the confirmed profit would be recognized in 19X2 under Alternative 2 so that 19X2 consolidated net income would be $600 higher under Alternative 1 than under Alternative 2. Thus, over the two-year period, the difference would be self-reversing. However, the existence of a difference in each of two individual years suggests careful consideration of the question—is one alternative preferable?

Illustration 7–2

**Calculation of Consolidated Net Income under
Alternative Methods of Allocating the
Eliminated Intercompany Profit between
Majority and Minority Shareholders**

	Alternative 1 (All of Eliminated Profit Allocated to Majority Shareholders)	Alternative 2 (Eliminated Profit Allocated Pro Rata to Majority and Minority Shareholders)
P Company income from own operations...............	$30,000	$30,000
S Company income from own operations...............	20,000	20,000
	$50,000	$50,000
Less net debit elimination—unconfirmed intercompany profit in ending inventory of P Company........................	3,000	3,000
Total equity..................................	$47,000	$47,000
Less minority interest in S Company net income:		
Alternative 1 (20% × $20,000)	4,000	
Alternative 2 (20% × $20,000) − (20% × $3,000)................		3,400
Consolidated net income............................	$43,000	$43,600

Evaluation of the Alternatives. At the time *Accounting Research Bulletin No. 51* was adopted (1959), it was customary for most consolidated subsidiaries to have little or no outside shareholder interests. Indeed, at that time, consolidation of subsidiaries with substantial minority interests was even discouraged. Accordingly, the prevalent practice when the policy was established was to eliminate the unconfirmed profit totally against the majority interest. Provision for some very unusual situation may well have been the principal motivation behind the seemingly permissive acceptance of pro rata allocation of the eliminated profit between majority and minority interests. Since 1959, however, the character of parent-subsidiary relationships in business has changed substantially, and it is now common consolidation practice to include affiliates with large minority interests. The two alternatives must, therefore, be judged in a quite different business and accounting context than existed in 1959.

As a point of departure for our analysis, recall that the consolidated financial statements reflect the economic effects of transactions with nonaffiliates. Intercompany sales and purchases are eliminated in total, and when unconfirmed intercompany profits exist at the end of an accounting period, they too are eliminated (from operating results and inventory). Accordingly, it may be argued that from a consolidated point of view, the income statement for the year in which the unconfirmed intercompany profit was recorded by the selling affiliate should reflect results of operations *as if the transaction never occurred.* Following this reasoning, let us assume that the intercompany sale generating the unconfirmed profit in the previous illustration did not take place in 19X1. With this assumption, S Company's net income from its own operations would have been $17,000 ($20,000 − $3,000), and consolidated net income would be calculated as follows:

P Company income from own operations	$30,000
S Company income from own operations	17,000
	$47,000
Less net debit eliminations	–0–
Total equity	$47,000
Less minority interest in S Company net income (20% × $17,000)	3,400
Consolidated net income	$43,600

Compare this amount with the amounts of consolidated net income calculated under the two alternatives in Illustration 7–2. The comparison reveals that this hypothetical "no-sale" situation results in consolidated net income that is equivalent to that produced under the pro rata allocation of the eliminated profit between majority and minority shareholders. Application of Alternative 1, on the other hand, causes consolidated net income to be lower than it would have been if the transaction had not occurred. Since the authors believe that the purpose of the elimination of unconfirmed intercompany profit should be to cancel, not worsen, the consequence of its inclusion in the individual financial statements of the affiliates, we strongly endorse the pro rata allocation of the eliminated profit between majority and minority shareholders as the preferred method. We note also that this method is now frequently applied in practice, and was strongly supported by the AICPA Accounting Standards Executive Committee in a 1981 Issues Paper entitled "Certain Issues That Affect Accounting for Minority Interest in Consolidated Financial Statements." Accordingly, in subsequent discussion and illustrations, *pro rata allocation will be used unless otherwise explicitly noted.*

In concluding this analysis of the amount of intercompany profit to be eliminated, we observed that additional, logically supportable alternatives have been proposed in the accounting literature. Also, the adoption of *APB Opinion No. 18,* "The Equity Method of Accounting for Investments in Common Stock," and *Accounting Interpretation No. 1 of APB Opinion No. 18* has introduced some confusion and possible inconsistencies in the treatment of unconfirmed intercompany profits. These issues are discussed in the Appendix to Chapter 8.

Reported and Confirmed Incomes of Affiliates

The schedular calculations of consolidated net income in the above illustrations using a slightly modified residual approach suggest that unconfirmed intercompany profits must be incorporated into our basic definitions. Under the incremental approach, and *assuming pro rata allocation of eliminated profits,* consolidated net income is now redefined as follows:

Parent company's net income from its own operations that has been confirmed or realized in transactions with nonaffiliates, increased (decreased) by its equity in the subsidiary's net income (loss) that has been confirmed or realized in transactions with nonaffiliates, and decreased (increased for a credit differential) by the differential amortization for the period.

The reader will notice that this rendering is not substantially different from the earlier definition in Chapter 4. It does, however, emphasize the importance of *confirmation or realization of intercompany profit* before it may be included in the calculation of consolidated net income (and thus, by extension, consolidated retained earnings). Because of its generality, it is applicable to all situations involving intercompany profits.

The crucial element in this schedular calculation is the determination of an affiliate's *confirmed income* (from the economic entity's point of view) for the period. Returning to the case of the $3,000 unconfirmed profit at the end of 19X1 as a consequence of the upstream sale by the 80 percent owned subsidiary, S Company's confirmed income for 19X1 is calculated as follows:

S Company's *reported* 19X1 net income from its own operations	$20,000
Less: Unconfirmed intercompany profit included in 19X1 reported net income from own operations	3,000
S Company's *confirmed* 19X1 net income from its own operations	$17,000

It should be observed that *all* of the unconfirmed profit is deducted (or added in the year of confirmation) in arriving at S Company's confirmed net income. Pro rata allocation of the unconfirmed profit between majority and minority shareholders is achieved by using the confirmed income as the basis for calculating P Company's equity in subsidiary earnings (see below) and the minority interest in S Company's 19X1 net income. P Company's confirmed and reported net incomes from its own operations are equal in our illustration ($30,000) because P Company was not the selling affiliate in any intercompany transaction that remains unconfirmed from a consolidated point of view at the end of 19X1. P Company may have engaged in intercompany sales during 19X1, but if so, all these transactions have been confirmed. With these measures of the affiliates' confirmed incomes for 19X1, consolidated net income for 19X1 may be calculated as follows:

P Company's *confirmed* 19X1 net income from its own operations..........	$30,000
Increased by P Company's equity in S Company's *confirmed* 19X1 net income from its own operations (80% × $17,000).................	13,600
Consolidated net income for 19X1.....................................	$43,600

This calculation of consolidated net income corresponds to the amount previously determined by applying the modified residual calculation under the pro rata allocation alternative (see Illustration 7–2). Thus, when a partially owned subsidiary is the selling affiliate, it is clear that this definition is dependent upon the selection of the pro rata allocation alternative.

As we pointed out in our overview of the unconfirmed profit problem, interperiod allocations of affiliates' reported net incomes (from their own operations) may be necessary because of the impact of different underlying accounting entities on the timing of profit realization; however, in the long run, the total profit reported by the economic entity (before assignment of the minority's share therein) is merely the sum of the affiliates' reported net incomes from operations. This observation may be illustrated in terms of an equivalence in the total confirmed and reported net incomes (from operations) over the period of time encompassing both the initiation and the confirmation of the intercompany transaction. Assume that S Company reported net income from its own operations for 19X2 of $15,000, and that the merchandise purchased by P Company from S Company in 19X1 was sold to outside parties in 19X2. We further assume that there were no other unconfirmed profits at the end of 19X2. With these facts, S Company's confirmed and reported net incomes for the two-year period are contrasted below:

	19X1	19X2	Total for 19X1 and 19X2
S Company's *reported* net income from its own operations.........................	$20,000	$15,000	$35,000
Add [subtract]:			
Reported, but unconfirmed, intercompany profits	[3,000]		[3,000]
Confirmed, but unreported, intercompany profits		3,000	3,000
S Company's *confirmed* net income from its own operations.........................	$17,000	$18,000	$35,000

Confirmed net income differs from reported net income in each of the two years because the intercompany profit is recognized at a later date by the economic entity than by S Company. However, the totals (reported and confirmed) for the two-year period are equal. *Therefore, in the long run, reported net incomes (from operations) of the affiliates are the ultimate determinants of consolidated net income.*

Use of the reported profits of the affiliates as the ultimate determinants of consolidated net income is clearly appropriate because the sum of the reported profits of the purchasing and selling affiliate on an intercompany transaction is equal to the profit realized by the economic entity. For example, in our illustration, S Company sold merchandise to P Company for $10,000 and reported a profit of $3,000. This implies that the cost S Company (and the economic entity) incurred to purchase or produce the merchandise was $7,000. In 19X2, assume that P Company sold the merchandise to outside parties for $15,000; with a purchase cost of $10,000, P Company reports a profit of $5,000. From the point of view of the economic entity, the total profit on this sale of merchandise is:

Selling price to outside parties	$15,000
Cost of merchandise to economic entity	7,000
Profit to economic entity	$ 8,000

This $8,000 profit to the economic entity is merely the sum of the reported profits of S Company ($3,000) and P Company ($5,000). Thus, the reported profits of the affiliates properly reflect the economic impact of operations on the net asset position of the economic entity.

The confirmed income of a partially owned subsidiary is also the basis for the calculation of the minority interest in subsidiary net income (assuming the pro rata allocation alternative). Thus, in the long run, measurement of minority interest is also a function of the subsidiary's reported incomes. In this regard, we observe that the reported profit of a subsidiary on an intercompany transaction is dependent upon the transfer price. Since the parent company can obviously influence the amount of this transfer price, one might be inclined to question whether a subsidiary's reported profits on intercompany transactions should be the basic determinant of minority interest (and thus consolidated net income). The reason for the use of this basis is that the agreed-upon selling (transfer) prices determine the actual transfer of resources between the separate legal entities. The minority shareholders' claim is against the net assets of S Company, and the choice of a $10,000 transfer price results in an actual increase of $3,000 in S Company's net assets after the sale to P Company.

We observed above that the definition and calculation of consolidated net income using the incremental approach is dependent upon the method of allocating the eliminated profit between majority and minority shareholders. Our restatement of the definition was based upon the assumption that these profits are allocated pro rata to majority and minority shareholders (as is preferred by the authors). If the alternative method is used (i.e., allocate the eliminated profit wholly to the majority shareholders), the definition of consolidated net income would be changed as follows: *parent company's reported net income from its own operations, increased by its equity in the subsidiary's reported net income from its own operations, decreased by differential amortization for the period, and decreased by reported but unconfirmed intercompany profits or increased by confirmed but unreported intercompany profits.* For simplicity, the possibility of losses or credit differentials have been omitted from the definition; should they exist, they would be handled in the same manner as previously described. Applying this definition to our illustrative data as before, we obtain:

P Company's *reported* 19X1 net income from its own operations $30,000
Increased by P Company's equity in S Company's *reported* 19X1 net
   income from its own operations (80% × $20,000) 16,000
Decreased by reported, but unconfirmed, intercompany profits . . . . [3,000]
Consolidated net income for 19X1 . . . . $43,000

The reader may verify that this amount corresponds to our previous calculation of 19X1 consolidated net income under the assumption that eliminated profits are allocated wholly to the majority shareholders (see Illustration 7–2).

Parent Company Entries for Intercompany Inventory Profits

We have previously observed that the equity method is tantamount to a "one-line consolidation." Accordingly, if intercompany profits exist from a consolidated point of view, the treatment of these profits on the books of the parent company should be consistent with their effect on consolidated net income. *APB Opinion No. 18* offers the following guidance on this matter:

> The difference between consolidation and the equity method lies in the details reported in the financial statements. Thus, an investor's net income for the period and its stockholders' equity at the end of the period are the same whether an investment in a subsidiary is accounted for under the equity method or the subsidiary is consolidated. . . .
>
> Intercompany profits and losses should be eliminated until realized by the investor or investee as if a subsidiary, corporate joint venture or investee company were consolidated.[2]

This statement is explicit on the parent's treatment of intercompany profits—they should be "eliminated" until realized (or confirmed) from a consolidated point of view. There are, however, some classificational is-

_____

[2] *APB, APB Opinion No. 18,* "The Equity Method of Accounting for Investments in Common Stock" (New York: AICPA, 1971), par. 19. Copyright (1971) by the American Institute of CPAs.

sues (not affecting the parent's net income) that are not addressed in this statement; these issues are identified in the following analysis of the parent company's entries. Additionally, one major ambiguity regarding the amount of intercompany profit to be eliminated is discussed in the Appendix to Chapter 8.[3]

As a basis for our discussion, assume that P Company has an 80 percent ownership interest in S Company; that S Company reports 19X1 net income of $100,000; and that at the end of 19X1, there is an unconfirmed inventory profit of $5,000 to be eliminated. Since the entries for the intercompany profit depend upon whether the parent or the subsidiary is the selling affiliate, we consider each possibility as an independent case.

Entries in 19X1—Subsidiary Is Selling Affiliate. The parent company would of course recognize its equity in the *reported* income of the subsidiary in the usual manner:

Investment in S Company......................................	80,000	
Equity in Subsidiary Earnings.............................		80,000

The entry to record the deferral of the unconfirmed intercompany profit depends upon the alternative selected in the consolidated statements for allocating the intercompany profit recorded by the subsidiary between majority and minority shareholders. If the intercompany profit is allocated pro rata to the two shareholder groups, the parent's share of the profit is $4,000 (80 percent × $5,000); if it is allocated wholly to the majority shareholders, the parent's share is $5,000. Assuming the preferred pro rata allocation, the entry for the unconfirmed profit is:

Equity in Subsidiary Earnings (80% × $5,000)	4,000	
Investment in S Company.................................		4,000

The joint effect of these two entries is to recognize the parent's equity in the subsidiary's 19X1 *confirmed* net income of $95,000 ($100,000 − $5,000), that is, 80 percent × $95,000 = $76,000. This entry for the unconfirmed profit seems to be fairly widely accepted in practice, although *Accounting Interpretation No. 1 of APB Opinion No. 18* indicates that it is also permissible to credit inventory instead of the investment account.

Entries in 19X1—Parent Is Selling Affiliate. The parent company would again recognize its equity in the *reported* income of the subsidiary in the usual manner:

Investment in S Company......................................	80,000	
Equity in Subsidiary Earnings.............................		80,000

The majority shareholder interest in the intercompany profit when the parent company is the selling affiliate is the full amount, or $5,000. There-

---

[3] For a more complete discussion of these matters, the reader may consult Thomas E. King and Valdean C. Lembke, "Reporting Investor Income under the Equity Method," *Journal of Accountancy*, September 1976.

fore, in this case, the issue of alternative allocation methods appears not to be a factor.[4] There are, however, several variations in the method of classifying this deferral of unconfirmed profits. One method found in practice is to record the deferral in the same way it is recorded when the subsidiary is the selling affiliate (although the amount is different):

Equity in Subsidiary Earnings (100% × $5,000)   5,000
    Investment in S Company   5,000

The reasoning underlying this particular form of entry is that the intercompany profit is regarded as unrealized as a consequence of P Company's ownership interest in S Company, and that the total economic impact of that ownership affiliation should be reflected in the investment account and the Equity in Subsidiary Earnings account. Others argue, however, that since the reported earnings of the subsidiary do not include this profit, it should not be deferred against the equity in subsidiary earnings; it is the earnings of the parent company that must be adjusted. The following entry defers the intercompany profit directly against the earnings of the parent:

Intercompany Profit Deferred to Future Periods
    (a deduction from gross profit).   5,000
        Deferred Credit for Intercompany Profit   5,000

In a circumstance where this unconfirmed profit is a material portion of the parent's gross profit from its own operations *or* its equity in subsidiary earnings, this (or a similar) entry may be necessary to preclude misinterpretation of the parent's operating results for the period.

Although the consolidated financial statements are not affected by these alternatives, the eliminating entries in the consolidated statement working paper will vary somewhat depending upon the entry made by the parent. *Therefore, in order to avoid unnecessary complications in our explanation of consolidated working paper techniques, we assume that the deferral of intercompany profits is made against equity in subsidiary earnings and the investment account for both upstream and downstream sales.* After the reader has comprehended the basic properties of the working paper techniques, the necessary modifications for alternative parent company entries are relatively easy.

Entries in 19X2—Both Cases.   An intercompany inventory profit that is deferred at the end of one period is assumed to be confirmed during the following period. For our example, the following entry would be made in 19X2 (in addition to recognizing the equity in the subsidiary's reported income for 19X2):

a.   If subsidiary is seller:

Investment in S Company   4,000
    Equity in Subsidiary Earnings   4,000

---

[4] As is discussed in the Appendix to Chapter 8, *Accounting Interpretation No. 1 of APB Opinion No. 18* introduces an apparent inconsistency in the treatment of intercompany profits in the case of downstream sales.

b. If parent is seller:

Investment in S Company	5,000	
Equity in Subsidiary Earnings		5,000

If the intercompany profit were not in fact confirmed in 19X2 through resale to outside parties, its continued existence in the 19X2 ending inventory of the purchasing affiliate would be detected by the accounting system procedures established to identify intercompany profits (i.e., the procedures that first identified the existence of the intercompany profit at the end of 19X1). The entry to again defer this profit, or any portion thereof, would merely reverse the effect of the above entry. Therefore, the assumption we make about confirmation of intercompany profits in the beginning inventory is essentially a procedural, not a substantive, assumption.

Eliminating Intercompany Inventory Profits in the Consolidated Statement Working Paper

We have now discussed the basic principles underlying the set of procedures and techniques employed to deal with intercompany inventory profits in the consolidated statement working paper. These procedures and techniques are explained within the context of a set of integrated two-year numerical examples. Before moving into these examples, we reiterate that *pro rata allocation of intercompany profits, when applicable, is assumed.* Additionally, we suggest two critical variables that the reader should keep clearly in mind while studying the illustrations:

1. Whether the intercompany sale generating the profit was upstream or downstream.
2. Whether the intercompany sale occurred in the current or the prior year.

The first variable, identification of the selling affiliate, is necessary in determining whether there is any minority interest in the recorded intercompany profit. If there is a minority interest in the selling affiliate, a pro rata portion of the profit is allocated to the two shareholder groups. The second variable indicates whether the intercompany profit is in the ending or the beginning inventory of the purchasing affiliate, and consequently whether it should be treated as (1) reported but unconfirmed income or (2) confirmed but unreported income.

In the examples to follow, we assume an unconfirmed intercompany inventory profit originates in 19X1 and is confirmed through sale to outside parties in 19X2. In the first case, the parent is assumed to be the selling company; in the second case, a 90 percent owned subsidiary is the seller. The companies' reported incomes from operations are the same in each case. Therefore, consolidated net income for the two-year period is equal for both cases—although it is different for 19X1 and 19X2 because of the difference in the amount of intercompany profit eliminated. Additionally, to illustrate more clearly the effects of the eliminating entries, accounts reflecting the effects of intercompany transactions are separately labeled. In the absence of this classificational refinement, eliminations are merely made against the single account aggregating transactions with both affiliates and nonaffiliates. Finally, we employ a minimum number of accounts in the consolidated statement working paper to focus attention on the inventory profit eliminations (including the assumption that no differential exists).

Case 1.   Downstream Sale.   It is assumed that P Company acquired its 90 percent ownership interest in S Company on January 1, 19X1, at a cost of $90,000, when S Company had capital stock of $50,000 and retained earnings of $50,000. There was only one intercompany transaction between the affiliates in 19X1. Near the end of 19X1, P Company sold merchandise to S Company for $8,000, on which the recorded gross profit (by the parent) was $3,000. All of this merchandise remains in the inventory of S Company at December 31, 19X1, and thus the entire recorded gross profit of $3,000 is regarded, from a consolidated point of view, as an unconfirmed intercompany inventory profit. During 19X2, there are no intercompany transactions between the affiliates, but the unconfirmed profit of the prior year is confirmed through S Company's sale of the merchandise to outside parties. The companies' *reported net incomes from their own operations* are as follows (*including in 19X1* for P Company the $3,000 gross profit on the intercompany sale):

	19X1	19X2
P Company	$30,000	$30,000
S Company	10,000	10,000

Parent Company Entries for 19X1 and 19X2.   In accordance with the procedures described (and entry format choices made) in the preceding section, P Company makes the following entries in 19X1 to record its equity in S Company's reported earnings and to defer the unconfirmed intercompany profit from the downstream sale:

1.   To record equity in S Company's 19X1 reported income (90 percent × $10,000):

| Investment in S Company .... | 9,000 | |
| Equity in Subsidiary Earnings .... | | 9,000 |

2.   To record *deferral* of parent's interest in intercompany profit (100 percent × $3,000):

| Equity in Subsidiary Earnings .... | 3,000 | |
| Investment in S Company .... | | 3,000 |

P Company's interest in the intercompany profit is 100 percent because the parent was the selling affiliate in the intercompany transaction.

In 19X2, the intercompany profit is confirmed through S Company's sale of the merchandise to outside parties. The parent company entries in 19X2 to record its equity in the subsidiary's reported earnings and the confirmation of the intercompany profit are:

3. To record equity in S Company's 19X2 reported income (90 percent × $10,000):

Investment in S Company	9,000	
Equity in Subsidiary Earnings		9,000

4. To record *confirmation* of parent's interest in intercompany profit (100 percent × $3,000):

Investment in S Company	3,000	
Equity in Subsidiary Earnings		3,000

These entries are reflected in T-account form in Illustration 7–3. Notice the offsetting effect of the two entries for the intercompany profit. In 19X1, when the profit is regarded as unconfirmed, the entry to recognize the deferral reduces the balances of both accounts. However, the 19X2 entry reverses the prior entry; and the December 31, 19X2, balance of Investment in S Company is unaffected by the then-confirmed intercompany profit. The balance in Equity in Subsidiary Earnings is increased by the same amount in 19X2 that it was decreased in 19X1.

Eliminating Entries for 19X1.   The working paper eliminating entries for 19X1 are presented below:

1. To reverse P Company entries during 19X1:

Equity in Subsidiary Earnings	6,000	
Investment in S Company		6,000

2. To eliminate intercompany sales:

Sales	8,000	
Purchases		8,000

3. To eliminate 100 percent of the unconfirmed intercompany profit in the ending inventory of S Company:

Inventory (12/31) (income statement)	3,000	
Inventory (12/31) (balance sheet)		3,000

Illustration 7–3

INVESTMENT-RELATED ACCOUNTS MAINTAINED BY PARENT COMPANY
(For Case 1—Downstream Sale)

Investment in S Company

Investment cost, January 1, 19X1	90,000		(2) Deferral of unconfirmed intercompany profit in S Company's ending inventory	3,000
(1) Equity in S Company's reported 19X1 net income	9,000		Balance, December 31, 19X1	96,000
	99,000			99,000
Balance, December 31, 19X1	96,000			
(3) Equity in S Company's reported 19X2 net income	9,000			
(4) Confirmation of intercompany profit in S Company's beginning inventory	3,000		Balance, December 31, 19X2	108,000
	108,000			108,000
Balance, December 31, 19X2	108,000			

Equity in Subsidiary Earnings

(2) Deferral of unconfirmed intercompany profit in S Company's ending inventory	3,000		(1) Equity in S Company's reported 19X1 net income	9,000
To close to 19X1 income summary	6,000			
	9,000			9,000
To close to 19X2 income summary	12,000		(3) Equity in S Company's reported 19X2 net income	9,000
			(4) Confirmation of intercompany profit in S Company's beginning inventory	3,000
	12,000			12,000

4. To eliminate the investment account balance at the beginning of the year against the beginning-of-year balances in the stockholders' equity accounts of S Company:

Retained Earnings (1/1)—S Company	45,000	
Capital Stock—S Company	45,000	
Investment in S Company		90,000

The consolidated statement working paper for 19X1 is presented in Illustration 7–4. In accordance with our practice, the balances in this and subsequent working papers are arbitrarily chosen, except where it is required that they correspond with data previously presented in the example.

In the working paper [and in eliminating entry (3) above], the total amount of the unconfirmed intercompany profit is eliminated by a debit to the ending inventory as it appears in the income statement division (where it has a credit balance) and a credit to the ending inventory in the balance sheet division. Recall that the *total* amount of the unconfirmed profit is eliminated, whether it is a downstream (as in this case) or upstream sale. It is the allocation of the eliminated profit between the majority and minority shareholders (if any) that depends upon the selling affiliate. Intercompany sales and purchases are eliminated in working paper entry (2) in the same manner as originally illustrated in Chapter 3. As a consequence of these two eliminations, all recorded effects of intercompany activities are deleted, and the consolidated column reflects only transactions with nonaffiliates. Accounts for intercompany purchases and sales are reduced to zero balances, and the ending inventory that S Company acquired from P Company is reduced to P Company's cost.

Recall that it is our practice to identify separately each of the three major components of cost of sales in the income statement division of the working paper: beginning inventory (Dr. balance), purchases (Dr. balance), and ending inventory (Cr. balance). This separate identification displays explicitly the effects of the eliminating entries for intercompany sales and unconfirmed profits. If the three elements have been combined into a single cost of sales figure in the working paper, the credit to Purchases in eliminating entry (2) and the debit to Inventory (12/31) (income statement) in eliminating entry (3) are both made to Cost of Sales.

Eliminating entry (1) to reverse the effects of P Company's entries related to the investment in S Company during 19X1 and eliminating entry (4) to eliminate the investment account against the beginning-of-year balances in the stockholders' equity accounts of S Company are made in the same manner as if there were no intercompany inventory profit. This absence of any effect on these two entries continues throughout our explana-

Illustration 7–4

P COMPANY AND SUBSIDIARY S COMPANY
Consolidated Statement Working Paper
For Year Ended December 31, 19X1
(Downstream Sale)

	P Company	S Company	Eliminations Dr.	Eliminations Cr.	Minority Interest	Consolidated
Income Statement						
Sales:						
To nonaffiliates	92,000	50,000				142,000
Intercompany	8,000	–0–	(2) 8,000			–0–
Equity in subsidiary earnings	6,000	–0–	(1) 6,000			–0–
Inventory (12/31):						
Acquired from nonaffiliates	30,000	2,000				32,000
Acquired from affiliates	–0–	8,000	(3) 3,000			5,000
Total credits	136,000	60,000				179,000
Inventory (1/1):						
Acquired from nonaffiliates	20,000	5,000				25,000
Acquired from affiliates	–0–	–0–				–0–
Purchases:						
From nonaffiliates	70,000	32,000				102,000
Intercompany	–0–	8,000		(2) 8,000		–0–
Expenses	10,000	5,000				15,000
Total debits	100,000	50,000				142,000
						37,000
Minority interest in net income (10% × $10,000)					1,000	1,000
Net income	36,000	10,000	17,000	8,000	1,000	36,000
Retained Earnings Statement						
Retained earnings, 1/1/X1:						
P Company	–0–					–0–
S Company		50,000	(4) 45,000		5,000	–0–
Net income	36,000	10,000	17,000	8,000	1,000	36,000
Retained earnings, 12/31/X1	36,000	60,000	62,000	8,000	6,000	36,000
Balance Sheet						
Other assets	10,000	100,000				110,000
Inventory (12/31):						
Acquired from nonaffiliates	30,000	2,000				32,000
Acquired from affiliates	–0–	8,000		(3) 3,000		5,000
Investment in S Company	96,000			(1) 6,000 (4) 90,000		–0–
	136,000	110,000				147,000
Capital stock:						
P Company	100,000					100,000
S Company		50,000	(4) 45,000		5,000	–0–
Retained earnings	36,000	60,000	62,000	8,000	6,000	36,000
Minority interest in S Company					11,000	11,000M
	136,000	110,000	107,000	107,000		147,000

(1) To reverse P Company entries during 19X1. (2) To eliminate intercompany sales. (3) To eliminate the intercompany profit in S Company's ending inventory. (4) To eliminate the investment account balance at the beginning of the year against the beginning-of-year balances in the stockholders' equity accounts of S Company.

tion of the working paper treatment of intercompany profits in the remainder of this chapter and in Chapter 8.

Since the intercompany profit was generated as a consequence of a downstream sale, all of the eliminated profit is allocated to the majority shareholders. Therefore, minority interest in net income is determined, as before, on the basis of S Company's *reported* net income, and all other minority interest extensions reflect the minority shareholders' 10 percent interest in the reported financial statement values. In our example, the amount assigned to the minority interest in the consolidated balance sheet, $11,000, reflects their 10 percent interest in the subsidiary's recorded net assets of $110,000.

Schedular Calculations of 19X1 Consolidated Net Income. Consolidated net income for 19X1 is determined to be $36,000 in the consolidated statement working paper. This is verified using the incremental approach as follows:

P Company's *confirmed* net income from its own operations for 19X1 ($36,000 − $6,000 − $3,000)...	$27,000
Increased by P Company's equity in S Company's *confirmed* net income for 19X1 (90% × $10,000)........................	9,000
Consolidated net income for 19X1.....................................	$36,000

P Company's confirmed net income from its own operations is determined by subtracting from its reported net income of $36,000 two amounts: (1) the recorded equity in the subsidiary's net income, $6,000, which yields the parent's *reported* net income from its own operations; and (2) the unconfirmed intercompany profit of $3,000, which produces the desired confirmed income measure. No adjustment to the subsidiary's reported net income is required because it includes no unconfirmed profits.

Consolidated net income can also be calculated using the residual approach. Recall that this calculation, in effect, uses the column totals in the income statement division of the working paper; the reader may find it informative to trace each of the figures in the calculation below back to the working paper.

P Company's reported net income for 19X1		$36,000
S Company's reported net income for 19X1		10,000
		$46,000
Less—*net* debit eliminations:		
P Company's recorded equity in S Company's earnings [Elimination (1)]	$6,000	
Deferral of unconfirmed profit in ending inventory [Elimination (3)]	3,000	9,000
Total equity...		$37,000
Minority interest in S Company's net income (10% × $10,000)		1,000
Consolidated net income for 19X1.....................................		$36,000

Finally, observe that consolidated net income (and retained earnings) are equal to the parent company's net income (and retained earnings), as prescribed by *APB Opinion No. 18*.

Relationship between Investment Account Balance and Net Assets of Subsidiary. We observed in Chapter 4 that the proportionality between the balance of the investment account and the recorded net assets of the subsidiary is affected by the unamortized differential balance. In this example, we have assumed that no differential exists. However, recognizing an unconfirmed intercompany profit with an entry to the investment account also affects the proportionality. In particular, when unconfirmed profits exist at the end of an accounting period, the balance of the investment account is equal to the parent's monetary interest in the recorded net assets of the subsidiary, *less* the parent's share of the unconfirmed profit at the end of the year. Thus, for the data of our example, the investment account balance of $96,000 at December 31, 19X1 (see Illustration 7–3), may be analyzed as follows:

P Company's monetary interest in S Company's recorded net assets
(90% × $110,000) $99,000
P Company's share of the unconfirmed intercompany profit at the end
of the year (100% × $3,000) .... [3,000]
Investment account balance, December 31, 19X1 .... $96,000

Eliminating Entries for 19X2. The working paper eliminating entries for 19X2 are presented following:

(1) To reverse P Company entries during 19X2:

Equity in Subsidiary Earnings 12,000
    Investment in S Company 12,000

(2) To recognize confirmation of the intercompany profit in S Company's beginning inventory:

Investment in S Company 3,000
    Inventory (1/1) (income statement)..... 3,000

(3) To eliminate the *adjusted* investment account balance at the beginning of the year against the beginning-of-year balances in the stockholders' equity accounts of S Company:

Retained Earnings (1/1)—S Company	54,000	
Capital Stock—S Company	45,000	
Investment in S Company		99,000

Recall that there were no intercompany transactions during 19X2, and therefore no elimination is required in 19X2 for intercompany sales and purchases. Also, no unconfirmed profit is assumed to exist at the end of the year. The consolidated statement working paper for 19X2 is presented in Illustration 7–5.

Eliminating entry (1) above (and in the working paper) merely reverses, as usual, the net effect of the parent's entries during the year to the investment account. Eliminating entry (2) expunges the intercompany profit from S Company's beginning inventory in the income statement (leaving the $5,000 cost to the economic entity of merchandise sold in 19X2 to nonaffiliates). Confirmation of the profit in 19X2 is achieved via the $3,000 credit in the income statement division of the working paper. The debit portion of this entry restores the investment account balance at the beginning of the year to its proportional relationship with the recorded net assets of S Company at the beginning of the year. Although P Company restored this proportionality in the investment account balance at December 31, 19X2, by means of its 19X2 entry to recognize confirmation of the intercompany profit, the effect of this entry was wiped out with eliminating entry (1)—which restored the actual January 1, 19X2, balance to the investment account in the working paper. The "adjusted" investment account balance at the beginning of the year that results from the combined effects of eliminating entries (1) and (2) is then eliminated in entry (3) against the recorded beginning-of-year balances in the stockholders' equity accounts of S Company. Although this entry is dependent for its validity upon eliminating entry (2), it is nonetheless exactly the same entry that would be made in the absence of intercompany profits (or, as is discussed later, if the parent company elects not to record the intercompany profits in its investment account).

As in 19X1, the existence of an intercompany profit from a downstream sale has no effect on the minority interest calculations or extensions in the consolidated statement working paper. S Company's reported net income and stockholders' equity balances are used, and the final minority interest balance of $12,000 reflects a 10 percent interest in net assets of $120,000. Also, consolidated net income (and retained earnings) are again equal to the parent company's net income (and retained earnings).

Schedular Calculations of 19X2 Consolidated Net Income. Consolidated net income of $42,000 reflected in the working paper is verified using the incremental approach as follows:

P Company's *confirmed* net income from its own operations for 19X2
  ($42,000 − $12,000 + $3,000) $33,000
Increased by P Company's equity in S Company's *confirmed* net
  income for 19X2 (90% × $10,000)   9,000
Consolidated net income for 19X2 . . . . $42,000

Calculation of P Company's confirmed net income from its own operations involves two adjustments: (1) subtraction of the recorded equity in the subsidiary's net income, $12,000, which as in 19X1 yields the parent's *reported* net income from its own operations; and (2) addition of the $3,000 intercompany profit to reflect its confirmation during 19X2. Again, no adjustment to the subsidiary's net income is required because it does not include any unconfirmed profit, nor does it fail to reflect any confirmed profits attributable to S Company.

Calculation of consolidated net income using the residual approach is illustrated below:

P Company's reported net income for 19X2 . . . . $42,000
S Company's reported net income for 19X2   10,000
                                                                                         $52,000
Less [plus]—*net* debit [credit] eliminations:
  P Company's recorded equity in S Company's earnings
    [Elimination (1)] $12,000
  Confirmation of intercompany profit in beginning inventory
    [Elimination (2)] . . . .   [3,000]   9,000
      Total equity $43,000
Minority interest in S Company's net income (10% × $10,000)   1,000
Consolidated net income for 19X2 . . . . $42,000

Again the reader may find it useful to trace these numbers back to the column totals in the income statement division of the consolidated statement working paper (Illustration 7–5).

Relationship between Investment Account Balance and Net Assets of Subsidiary. Although the effects of the intercompany profit arising in 19X1 are still present in 19X2, the entry on the parent company's books in 19X2 to reflect its confirmation erases its impact from the ending balance of the investment account (see Illustration 7–3). Thus, for this example, the investment account balance of $108,000 at December 31, 19X2, has been restored to its proportional relationship with the net assets recorded on the books of S Company (i.e., 90 percent × $120,000).

Case 2.   Upstream Sale.   The data of Case 1 are used for this case, *except* we now assume that S Company, the 90 percent owned subsidiary, is the selling affiliate in the 19X1 intercompany sale that results in a $3,000 unconfirmed inventory profit at December 31, 19X1. The companies' reported net incomes from their own operations remain the same, and thus total consolidated net income for the two years will remain unchanged. How-

Illustration 7–5

P COMPANY AND SUBSIDIARY S COMPANY
Consolidated Statement Working Paper
For Year Ended December 31, 19X2
(Downstream Sale)

	P Com-pany	S Com-pany	Eliminations Dr.	Eliminations Cr.	Minority Interest	Consoli-dated
Income Statement						
Sales:						
To nonaffiliates	100,000	50,000				150,000
Intercompany	–0–	–0–				–0–
Equity in subsidiary earnings	12,000	–0–	(1) 12,000			–0–
Inventory (12/31):						
Acquired from nonaffiliates	20,000	15,000				35,000
Acquired from affiliates	–0–	–0–				–0–
Total credits	132,000	65,000				185,000
Inventory (1/1):						
Acquired from nonaffiliates	30,000	2,000				32,000
Acquired from affiliates	–0–	8,000		(2) 3,000		5,000
Purchases:						
From nonaffiliates	50,000	40,000				90,000
Intercompany	–0–	–0–				–0–
Expenses	10,000	5,000				15,000
Total debits	90,000	55,000				142,000
						43,000
Minority interest in net income (10% × $10,000)					1,000	1,000
Net income	42,000	10,000	12,000	3,000	1,000	42,000
Retained Earnings Statement						
Retained earnings, 1/1/X2:						
P Company	36,000					36,000
S Company		60,000	(3) 54,000		6,000	–0–
Net income	42,000	10,000	12,000	3,000	1,000	42,000
Retained earnings, 12/31/X2	78,000	70,000	66,000	3,000	7,000	78,000
Balance Sheet						
Other assets	50,000	105,000				155,000
Inventory (12/31):						
Acquired from nonaffiliates	20,000	15,000				35,000
Acquired from affiliates	–0–	–0–				–0–
Investment in S Company	108,000		(2) 3,000	(1) 12,000 (3) 99,000		–0–
	178,000	120,000				190,000
Capital stock:						
P Company	100,000					100,000
S Company		50,000	(3) 45,000		5,000	–0–
Retained earnings	78,000	70,000	66,000	3,000	7,000	78,000
Minority interest in S Company					12,000	12,000M
	178,000	120,000	114,000	114,000		190,000

(1) To reverse P Company entries during 19X2. (2) To recognize confirmation of the intercompany profit in S Company's beginning inventory. (3) To eliminate the adjusted investment account balance at the beginning of the year against the beginning-of-year balances in the stockholders' equity accounts of S Company.

ever, 19X1 and 19X2 consolidated net income will change from Case 1 because the intercomany profit is now allocated between the majority and minority shareholders. The reader may observe that this allocation process is reflected in the consolidated statement working paper in two ways:

1. Minority interest in net income in both years is based upon the subsidiary's *confirmed* net income (which is different from reported net income).
2. The eliminating entry in 19X2 to reflect the confirmation of intercompany profit in the beginning inventory requires an allocation between majority and minority shareholders.

Otherwise, the working paper procedures for this upstream case parallel those previously illustrated for the downstream case. Corresponding to the allocation in the consolidated statement working paper, the amount of the intercompany profit recorded by the parent company is less than in the previous case—reflecting its smaller share of the profit. The format of the entries, however, remains unchanged.

Parent Company Entries for 19X1 and 19X2.   The parent company entries in 19X1 to record its equity in S Company's reported earnings and to defer the unconfirmed intercompany profit from the upstream sale are as follows:

1. To record equity in S Company's 19X1 reported income (90 percent × $10,000):

Investment in S Company	9,000	
Equity in Subsidiary Earnings		9,000

2. To record deferral of *parent's interest* in intercompany profit (90 percent × $3,000):

Equity in Subsidiary Earnings	2,700	
Investment in S Company		2,700

Since the intercompany profit was recognized in 19X1 by the subsidiary, it accrues to the benefit of the majority and minority shareholders in proportion to their relative ownership interests in S Company. Thus, the parent company defers only its share of the unconfirmed intercompany profit. The consequence of these two entries is that the parent records its 90 percent interest in S Company's 19X1 confirmed income of $7,000 ($10,000 − $3,000).

In 19X2, the parent company entries to record its equity in the subsidiary's reported 19X2 earnings and the confirmation of the intercompany profit are as follows:

3. To record equity in S Company's 19X2 reported income (90 percent × $10,000):

Investment in S Company	9,000	
Equity in Subsidiary Earnings		9,000

4. To record confirmation of *parent's interest* in intercompany profit (90 percent × $3,000):

Investment in S Company	2,700	
Equity in Subsidiary Earnings		2,700

These entries are again reflected in T-account form in Illustration 7–6. As in the case of the downstream sale in Case 1, the two entries recording the deferral (in 19X1) and the confirmation (in 19X2) of the intercompany profit are offsetting over the two-year period.

Eliminating Entries for 19X1.   The working paper eliminating entries for 19X1 are presented below:

1. To reverse P Company entries for 19X1:

Equity in Subsidiary Earnings	6,300	
Investment in S Company		6,300

2. To eliminate intercompany sales:

Sales..	8,000	
Purchases		8,000

3. To eliminate 100 percent of the unconfirmed intercompany profit in the ending inventory of P Company:

Inventory (12/31) (income statement)	3,000	
Inventory (12/31) (balance sheet)		3,000

4. To eliminate the investment account balance at the beginning of the year against the beginning-of-year balances in the stockholders' equity accounts of S Company.

Retained Earnings (1/1)—S Company	45,000	
Capital Stock—S Company	45,000	
Investment in S Company		90,000

Illustration 7–6

INVESTMENT-RELATED ACCOUNTS
MAINTAINED BY PARENT COMPANY
(For Case 2—Upstream Sale)

Investment in S Company

Investment cost, January 1, 19X1	90,000	(2) Deferral of unconfirmed intercompany profit in P Company's ending inventory	2,700
(1) Equity in S Company's reported 19X1 net income	9,000	Balance, December 31, 19X1	96,300
	99,000		99,000
Balance, December 31, 19X1	96,300		
(3) Equity in S Company's reported 19X2 net income	9,000		
(4) Confirmation of intercompany profit in P Company's beginning inventory	2,700		
	108,000	Balance, December 31, 19X2	108,000
Balance, December 31, 19X2	108,000		108,000

Equity in Subsidiary Earnings

(2) Deferral of unconfirmed intercompany profit in P Company's ending inventory	2,700	(1) Equity in S Company's reported 19X1 net income	9,000
To close to 19X1 income summary	6,300		
	9,000		9,000
To close to 19X2 income summary	11,700	(3) Equity in S Company's reported 19X2 net income	9,000
		(4) Confirmation of intercompany profit in P Company's beginning inventory	2,700
	11,700		11,700

The consolidated statement working paper for 19X1 is presented in Illustration 7–7.

Eliminating entries (2)–(4) above are the same in all respects as they were in Case 1 when the parent was the selling affiliate. Eliminating entry (1) differs in the amount eliminated because the parent company entries for the two cases differ in the amount of unconfirmed profit that is deferred. But eliminating entry (1) merely erases the equity in S Company's earnings recorded by P Company. How then does the working paper combination of the two companies' operating data produce results different from Case 1? The answer to this question lies in the calculation of the minority interest. *All* of the intercompany profit is eliminated from the ending inventory of the purchasing affiliate, whether or not there is an outside shareholder interest in the selling affiliate. This elimination adjusts the inventory to its cost to the economic entity. However, when the selling affiliate is a partially owned subsidiary, a portion of this eliminated intercompany profit is allocated to the minority shareholders *in the income statement* by calculating minority interest in subsidiary net income on the basis of the subsidiary's *confirmed* net income (see Illustration 7–7). Since the confirmed net income of the subsidiary is less than its reported net income in the year in which the recorded profit is deferred, minority interest in net income is smaller (than Case 1) and consolidated net income is larger. This working paper process is consistent with the deferral of unconfirmed intercompany profit on the books of the parent company. All other minority interest calculations are made on the basis of the recorded values in S Company's stockholders' equity accounts. As a consequence of calculating minority interest in net income on the basis of the subsidiary's (lower) confirmed net income, the value assigned to minority interest in the consolidated balance sheet in this case ($10,700) is less than it was in the preceding case ($11,000). This lower value for minority interest is offset by a correspondingly higher value for consolidated retained earnings. The values assigned to the assets in the consolidated balance sheet are the same in both cases.

Relationship between Value of Minority Interest and Net Assets of Subsidiary.   In all previous illustrations, the value of the minority interest in the consolidated balance sheet is the product of the minority shareholders' ownership interest and the recorded net assets of the subsidiary. However, when a portion of an unconfirmed intercompany profit is allocated to the minority shareholders, this relationship is modified. The assertion that the subsidiary's confirmed net income for the year is less than reported net income also implies that the subsidiary's confirmed retained earnings at the end of the year are less than reported retained earnings. Thus, when the subsidiary is the selling affiliate in an intercompany transaction that results in an unconfirmed inventory profit, the minority interest in the consolidated balance sheet is the product of the minority shareholders' ownership interest and the *confirmed* net assets of the subsidiary. The mi-

Illustration 7–7

P COMPANY AND SUBSIDIARY S COMPANY
Consolidated Statement Working Paper
For Year Ended December 31, 19X1
(Upstream Sale)

	P Company	S Company	Eliminations Dr.	Eliminations Cr.	Minority Interest	Consolidated
Income Statement						
Sales:						
To nonaffiliates	100,000	42,000				142,000
Intercompany	–0–	8,000	(2) 8,000			–0–
Equity in subsidiary earnings	6,300	–0–	(1) 6,300			–0–
Inventory (12/31):						
Acquired from nonaffiliates	22,000	10,000				32,000
Acquired from affiliates	8,000	–0–	(3) 3,000			5,000
Total credits	136,300	60,000				179,000
Inventory (1/1):						
Acquired from nonaffiliates	20,000	5,000				25,000
Acquired from affiliates	–0–	–0–				–0–
Purchases:						
From nonaffiliates	62,000	40,000				102,000
Intercompany	8,000	–0–		(2) 8,000		–0–
Expenses	10,000	5,000				15,000
Total debits	100,000	50,000				142,000
						37,000
Minority interest in S Company's *confirmed* 19X1 net income [10% of ($10,000 − $3,000)]					700	700
Net income	36,300	10,000	17,300	8,000	700	36,300
Retained Earnings Statement						
Retained earnings, 1/1/X1:						
P Company	–0–					–0–
S Company		50,000	(4) 45,000		5,000	–0–
Net income	36,300	10,000	17,300	8,000	700	36,300
Retained earnings, 12/31/X1	36,300	60,000	62,300	8,000	5,700	36,300
Balance Sheet						
Other assets	10,000	100,000				110,000
Inventory (12/31):						
Acquired from nonaffiliates	22,000	10,000				32,000
Acquired from affiliates	8,000	–0–		(3) 3,000		5,000
Investment in S Company	96,300			(1) 6,300		–0–
				(4) 90,000		
	136,300	110,000				147,000
Capital stock:						
P Company	100,000					100,000
S Company		50,000	(4) 45,000		5,000	–0–
Retained earnings	36,300	60,000	62,300	8,000	5,700	36,300
Minority interest in S Company					10,700	10,700M
	136,300	110,000	107,300	107,300		147,000

(1) To reverse P Company entries during 19X1. (2) To eliminate intercompany sales. (3) To eliminate the intercompany profit in P Company's ending inventory. (4) To eliminate the investment account balance at the beginning of the year against the beginning-of-year balances in the stockholders' equity accounts of S Company.

nority interest at December 31, 19X1, is calculated for our example as follows:

S Company capital stock....................................		$ 50,000
S Company confirmed 12/31 retained earnings:		
Recorded retained earnings (12/31)	$60,000	
Unconfirmed intercompany profit	[3,000]	57,000
S Company confirmed net assets (12/31)		$107,000
Minority interest therein (10% × $107,000)		$ 10,700

Alternatively, one can view the minority interest at December 31, 19X1, as the interest in recorded net assets ($11,000) less the minority's share of the unconfirmed intercompany profit ($300).

Relationship between Investment Account Balance and Net Assets of Subsidiary.   In the case of the downstream sale, we observed that the proportionality between the investment account balance at the end of the year and the net assets of the subsidiary is affected by the existence of an unconfirmed intercompany profit. The amount of the disturbance, it was pointed out, is the parent's share of the unconfirmed profit at the end of the year. A difference will, therefore, also be present in the case of upstream sales. For the data of our example, the investment account balance of $96,300 at December 31, 19X1 (see Illustration 7–6), may be analyzed as follows:

P Company's monetary interest in S Company's recorded net assets	
(90% × $110,000)	$99,000
P Company's share of the unconfirmed intercompany profit at the end	
of the year (90% × $3,000)...	[2,700]
Investment account balance, December 31, 19X1	$96,300

Schedular Calculations of 19X1 Consolidated Net Income.   Consolidated net income for 19X1 is determined to be $36,300 in the consolidated statement working paper. This is verified using the incremental approach:

P Company's *confirmed* net income from its own operations for 19X1	
($36,300 − $6,300)	$30,000
Increased by P Company's equity in S Company's	
confirmed net income for 19X1 [90% × ($10,000 − $3,000)]	6,300
Consolidated net income for 19X1.....................................	$36,300

Since P Company was not the selling affiliate in an intercompany transaction that resulted in an unconfirmed profit, its confirmed net income from its own operations is determined merely by subtracting the recorded equity in the subsidiary's income, $6,300, from reported net income of $36,300. S Company's confirmed net income for 19X1 is calculated by subtracting the unconfirmed intercompany profit of $3,000 from the reported net income of $10,000; recall that the $3,000 intercompany profit is included in the $10,000 reported profit.

Consolidated net income may also be determined using the residual calculation method:

P Company's reported net income for 19X1		$36,300
S Company's reported net income for 19X1		10,000
		$46,300
Less—*net* debit eliminations:		
P Company's recorded equity in S Company's earnings		
[Elimination (1)]	$6,300	
Deferral of unconfirmed profit in ending inventory		
[Elimination (3)]	3,000	9,300
Total equity...		$37,000
Minority interest in S Company's *confirmed* net income		
[10% × ($10,000 − $3,000)]		700
Consolidated net income for 19X1...................................		$36,300

This calculation summarizes the previously discussed working paper treatment of unconfirmed inventory profits for upstream sales. The full amount of the unconfirmed profit is a net debit elimination in the income statement, but a portion of this eliminated profit is allocated to the minority shareholders in the calculation of minority interest in net income.

Finally, observe that as was the case for the downstream sale, consolidated net income (and retained earnings) are equal to the parent company's net income (and retained earnings).

Eliminating Entries for 19X2.   The working paper eliminating entries for 19X2 are presented below:

(1)   To reverse P Company entries during 19X2:

Equity in Subsidiary Earnings	11,700	
Investment in S Company		11,700

(2)   To recognize confirmation of the intercompany profit in P Company's beginning inventory:

Investment in S Company (90% × $3,000)..................	2,700	
Minority Interest in S Company's 1/1/X2 Unconfirmed		
Retained Earnings (10% × $3,000)	300	
Inventory (1/1) (income statement)....................		3,000

(3)   To eliminate the *adjusted* investment account balance at the beginning

of the year against the beginning-of-year balances in the stockholders' equity accounts of S Company:

Retained Earnings (1/1)—S Company	54,000	
Capital Stock—S Company	45,000	
Investment in S Company		99,000

Again recall that there were no intercompany transactions during 19X2, and therefore no elimination is required in 19X2 for intercompany sales and purchases. Also, no unconfirmed profit is assumed to exist at the end of the year. The consolidated statement working paper for 19X2 is presented in Illustration 7–8.

As noted in our introduction to this upstream case, the eliminating entry that recognizes confirmation of the intercompany profit must be changed in the upstream case to include the minority interest in the intercompany profit. As before, the credit of $3,000 to the beginning inventory in the income statement reduces this component to its cost to the economic entity, and as a consequence reflects confirmation of the intercompany profit in the 19X2 consolidated income statement. The minority's $300 share of this confirmed profit is recognized in the calculation of minority interest in the *confirmed* 19X2 income of S Company, and the remaining $2,700 is thus allocated implicitly to the majority shareholders. The reason for the debit of $300 to Minority Interest in S Company's 1/1/X2 Unconfirmed Retained Earnings is provided by considering three facts. First, the recorded retained earnings of S Company at the beginning of the year *includes* the $3,000 intercompany profit because it was recorded by S Company when the sale was made in 19X1; therefore, from a consolidated point of view, this beginning retained earnings balance includes a $3,000 unconfirmed component. Second, in the consolidated statement working paper, the totals in the income statement division are carried forward into the retained earnings division. Thus, the allocation of the $300 share of the confirmed profit to the minority interest in the income statement division is carried forward into the retained earnings division. Third, as was noted in our discussion of the 19X1 working paper, all minority interest calculations (or extensions) other than minority interest in confirmed income are based upon recorded values in S Company's stockholders' equity accounts. Thus, taking these observations together and referring to Illustration 7–8, the net effect of the $6,000 positive extension and the $300 negative extension to the minority interest in the retained earnings division reflects the minority's share (10 percent) of January 1, 19X2, confirmed retained earnings ($57,000); then recalling that the $1,300 addition to minority interest from the income statement division "carryforward" includes the minority's $300 share of the intercompany profit as confirmed in 19X2, we observe

Illustration 7–8

P COMPANY AND SUBSIDIARY S COMPANY
Consolidated Statement Working Paper
For Year Ended December 31, 19X2
(Upstream Sale)

	P Com-pany	S Com-pany	Eliminations Dr.	Eliminations Cr.	Minority Interest	Consoli-dated
Income Statement						
Sales:						
To nonaffiliates	100,000	50,000				150,000
Intercompany	–0–	–0–				–0–
Equity in subsidiary earnings	11,700	–0–	(1) 11,700			–0–
Inventory (12/31):						
Acquired from nonaffiliates	20,000	15,000				35,000
Acquired from affiliates	–0–	–0–				–0–
Total credits	131,700	65,000				185,000
Inventory (1/1):						
Acquired from nonaffiliates	22,000	10,000				32,000
Acquired from affiliates	8,000	–0–		(2) 3,000		5,000
Purchases:						
From nonaffiliates	50,000	40,000				90,000
Intercompany	–0–	–0–				–0–
Expenses	10,000	5,000				15,000
Total debits	90,000	55,000				142,000
						43,000
Minority interest in S Company's *confirmed* 19X2 net income [10% of ($10,000 + $3,000)]					1,300	1,300
Net income	41,700	10,000	11,700	3,000	1,300	41,700
Retained Earnings Statement						
Retained earnings, 1/1/X2:						
P Company	36,300					36,300
S Company		60,000	(3) 54,000		6,000	–0–
Minority interest in S Company's 1/1/X2 *unconfirmed* retained earnings			(2) 300		[300]	–0–
Net income	41,700	10,000	11,700	3,000	1,300	41,700
Retained earnings, 12/31/X2	78,000	70,000	66,000	3,000	7,000	78,000
Balance Sheet						
Other assets	50,000	105,000				155,000
Inventory (12/31):						
Acquired from nonaffiliates	20,000	15,000				35,000
Acquired from affiliates	–0–	–0–				–0–
Investment in S Company	108,000		(2) 2,700	(1) 11,700		–0–
				(3) 99,000		
	178,000	120,000				190,000
Capital stock:						
P Company	100,000					100,000
S Company		50,000	(3) 45,000		5,000	–0–
Retained earnings	78,000	70,000	66,000	3,000	7,000	78,000
Minority interest in S Company					12,000	12,000M
	178,000	120,000	113,700	113,700		190,000

(1) To reverse P Company entries during 19X2. (2) To recognize confirmation of the intercompany profit in P Company's beginning inventory. (3) To eliminate the *adjusted* investment account balance at the beginning of the year against the beginning-of-year balances in stockholders' equity accounts of S Company.

that the total minority interest in December 31, 19X2, retained earnings includes the minority's share of the intercompany profit. This may be verified by observing that the minority interest ($7,000) in S Company's December 31, 19X2, retained earnings ($70,000) reflects the appropriate 10 percent proportionality relationship. Finally, the $2,700 debit to the investment account restores the balance of this account at the beginning of the year to its proportional relationship with the recorded net assets of S Company at the beginning of the year (in the same manner as in the downstream case). Note that the beginning retained earnings of P Company need no adjustment because P Company's entry on its books at December 31, 19X1, to defer the unconfirmed intercompany profit produces a beginning retained earnings balance that is equal to beginning confirmed retained earnings.

Schedular Calculations of 19X2 Consolidated Net Income.   Consolidated net income for 19X2 (and December 31, 19X2, retained earnings) are again equal to their counterparts in P Company's financial statements. Consolidated net income may be verified using the incremental approach as follows:

P Company's *confirmed* net income from its own operations for 19X2 ($41,700 − $11,700)	$30,000
Increased by P Company's equity in S Company's *confirmed* net income for 19X2 [90% × ($10,000 + $3,000)]	11,700
Consolidated net income for 19X2	$41,700

P Company's confirmed net income from its own operations is calculated as in 19X1. In calculating the 19X2 confirmed net income for S Company, the $3,000 intercompany profit that has been confirmed from a consolidated point of view is added to P Company's 19X2 reported net income of $10,000. The same calculation is of course made in the income statement division of the working paper in determining the minority interest in the subsidiary's confirmed net income.

Using the residual calculation method, we obtain:

P Company's reported net income for 19X2		$41,700
S Company's reported net income for 19X2		10,000
		$51,700
Less [plus]—*net* debit [credit] eliminations:		
P Company's recorded equity in S Company's earnings [Elimination (1)]	$11,700	
Confirmation of intercompany profit in beginning inventory [Elimination (2)]	[3,000]	8,700
Total equity		$43,000
Minority interest in S Company's *confirmed* net income [10% × ($10,000 + $3,000)]		1,300
Consolidated net income for 19X2		$41,700

Relationship between Value of Minority Interest and Net Assets of Subsidiary.   At the end of 19X1, we observed that the value of the minority interest in the consolidated balance sheet was not in its normal proportional relationship to the recorded net assets of the subsidiary because of the intercompany profit on the upstream sale. However, this profit was confirmed in 19X2, and thus at the end of the year, the proportionality is restored. In particular, the minority interest ($12,000) in the balance sheet division of Illustration 7–8 is 10 percent of the net assets of the subsidiary ($120,000).

Relationship between Investment Account Balance and Net Assets of Subsidiary.   In the same manner as in the case of the downstream sale, the investment account balance at December 31, 19X2, of $108,000 (see Illustration 7–6) has again been restored to its 90 percent proportionality relationship with the recorded net assets of the subsidiary ($120,000).

Summary of Consolidated Net Income for Both Cases.   Referencing our working papers for the two cases, we find the following measures of consolidated net income:

	19X1	19X2	Total
Downstream sale (Case 1)	$36,000	$42,000	$78,000
Upstream sale (Case 2).............	36,300	41,700	78,000

The equality of the two-year totals results from the assumption that the affiliates' reported net incomes from their own operations (P Company, $30,000 per year; S Company, $10,000 per year) were the same in each case. Thus, if the accounting period is extended to encompass the two years, no intercompany profits exist (because the products transferred in the intercompany sale have now been sold to outside parties). Hence, consolidated net income for the two-year period is verified by the following simple calculation:

P Company's income from its own operations for 19X1 and 19X2	$60,000
Increased by P Company's equity in S Company's *reported* income for 19X1 and 19X2 (90% × $20,000)...........................	18,000
Consolidated net income for the two years.............................	$78,000

Effect of Allocating All of Eliminated Intercompany Profit against Majority Shareholders.   If the alternative of allocating all of the eliminated intercompany profit against the majority shareholders is selected, all intercompany profit eliminations and calculations are made as has been illustrated for a *downstream sale*. Thus, had this allocation alternative been chosen, the entries on the parent's books and the working paper eliminating entries for Case 2 would have been the same in all respects as they were for Case 1.

Intercompany Profit in Beginning and Ending Inventories.   Our illustrations were designed to isolate the treatment of intercompany inventory profits in either the ending or the beginning inventory. We observed that one eliminating entry is required to defer unconfirmed intercompany profit in the ending inventory, and one eliminating entry is required to recognize the confirmation of this profit in the beginning inventory. These two entries are summarized below (with amounts from the two cases):

	Downstream Sale	Upstream Sale

(1)   To eliminate profit in the *ending* inventory:

Inventory (12/31) (income statement).................	3,000	3,000
Inventory (12/31) (balance sheet).................	3,000	3,000

(2)   To eliminate profit in the *beginning* inventory:

Investment in S Company	3,000	2,700
Minority Interest in S Company's 1/1/X2 Unconfirmed Retained Earnings	–0–	300
Inventory (1/1) (income statement).............	3,000	3,000

Additionally, in the case of upstream sales, minority interest in subsidiary net income is calculated on the basis of the subsidiary's *confirmed* net income. The confirmed net income is calculated by subtracting the total amount of an unconfirmed intercompany profit in the ending inventory from the reported net income of the subsidiary, or by adding the total intercompany profit in the beginning inventory to the reported net income of the subsidiary.

In a situation involving intercompany profits in *both* the beginning and ending inventories, we merely make both eliminating entries in the consolidated statement working paper. Similarly, in the calculation of the subsidiary's confirmed income for the period, its reported income is increased for confirmed intercompany profits applicable to it as the selling affiliate (if any) *and* decreased for unconfirmed intercompany profits applicable to it as the selling affiliate (if any).

Effect of Parent Carrying Investment Account on Cost or Modified Equity Basis. At times, we may encounter a consolidated statement working paper in which the investment account is carried at cost, or some adjusted basis other than the equity method as prescribed in *APB Opinion No. 18*. One variation of the equity method, which we shall label the *modified equity method*, records the equity in reported subsidiary earnings but *does not record* the effects of intercompany profits. For either the modified equity method or the cost method, the eliminating entry illustrated for dealing with intercompany profits in the *beginning* inventory is modified by *changing the debit to the investment account to a debit to the parent's beginning retained earnings*. Since under either of these methods the parent does not book the unconfirmed profit at the end of the preceding year, its retained earnings at the beginning of the year no longer are equal to confirmed retained earnings. The additional debit to minority interest in January 1 unconfirmed retained earnings continues to be necessary for upstream sales. *No changes are required in the eliminating entry to defer an unconfirmed profit in the ending inventory.* The investment elimination entry is then made in the normal manner for an investment account on the cost or equity method, whichever is appropriate, and minority interest in net income continues to be calculated on the basis of the subsidiary's confirmed income for the year.

Questions

1. Describe the general treatment of profits recognized on the sale of merchandise between affiliates.

2. Indicate the profit rate—net or gross—that should be used in determining the amount of unconfirmed intercompany inventory profit to be eliminated, and explain the reasoning for this choice.

3. How are transportation costs incurred in transferring goods between affiliated companies accounted for in determining the amount of the intercompany profit?

4. Assume that two affiliates with intercompany sales of merchandise utilize the "cost or market, whichever is lower" method of pricing their inventories. What would be the effect upon the intercompany profit elimination, given a situation in which period-end market price is lower than the transfer price?

5. In the event that profit exists in inventory purchased from an affiliated company, what elections exist under the provisions of *Accounting Research Bulletin No. 51*, "Consolidated Statements," regarding the elimination of this intercompany profit?

6. Assuming that intercompany inventory profits are eliminated in full (100 percent), what is the impact on consolidated net income of the decision to allocate the eliminated profit pro rata between majority and minority share-

holders rather than wholly against the majority shareholders? What is the impact of this choice upon the inventory acquired from affiliates? What is the impact of this choice upon minority interest in income?

7. Why is it important to distinguish between upstream and downstream sales in the analysis of confirmed or unconfirmed intercompany profits?

8. In what manner is intercompany inventory profit "confirmed" or "realized" from the point of view of the consolidated, or economic, entity?

9. What is the relationship between an affiliate's confirmed and reported incomes (from own operations) in the year of an intercompany sale generating an unconfirmed intercompany profit? In a year in which the previously unconfirmed profit is confirmed? Over the total period of time encompassing sale and subsequent confirmation of the intercompany profit?

10. How is consolidated net income redefined under the incremental approach to give effect to the new variable—intercompany profit?

11. What is the effect of an unconfirmed profit at the end of an accounting period on the proportional relationship between the balance of the investment account (carried under the equity method) and the recorded net assets of a subsidiary? On the proportional relationship between the total minority interest and the recorded net assets of the subsidiary?

Exercises

Exercise 7–1

Item A: X Corporation manufactures at a finished cost of $20 per unit and sells to Y Corporation at $25 per unit. Y Corporation leaves its inventory in the warehouse of X Corporation, withdrawing it only as needed, and pays to X Corporation storage at the rate of 50 cents per unit per month. The units in the inventory of Y Corporation at December 31 were purchased six months previously. Y Corporation resells at $40 FOB shipping point, which is the same price at which X Corporation sells to others.

Item B: X Corporation owns and operates a mine from which item B is extracted. The average cost of mining item B is $5 per ton. The cost of the mine and development thereof is subject to depletion at the rate of $2.50 per ton. The cost of loading on freight cars averages $1 per ton. Y Corporation purchases from X Corporation at cost, FOB the mine, and transports the product to its plant, paying freight of $1.50 per ton. X Corporation sells approximately 75 percent of its mined product to others at a price of $15 per ton, FOB the mine, and Y Corporation sells at a substantial profit after refinement.

Item C: X Corporation buys manufacturing supplies at a price of $50 per unit, less trade discounts of 10/10/20. A portion of the supplies purchased by X Corporation are resold to Y Corporation at a price of $41 FOB Y Corporation's plant. The freight, paid by X Corporation, amounts to 50 cents per unit. Y Corporation does not have access to the market from which X Corporation buys.

Item D: X Corporation manufactures this item at an average cost of $29 per unit and sells its total output to Y Corporation at $35 per unit, FOB X Corporation's plant under terms of a firm contract. The freight amounts to $2 per unit. The amount obtainable from X Corporation is only about 50 percent of the quantity required by Y Corporation. The balance of Y Corporation's requirements are obtained from other sources at a price of $32.50 per unit, FOB Y's plant. Y resells this item at a price that yields $34 per unit after allowing for sales and handling expense.

Item E: X Corporation manufactures at a cost of $6 per unit and sells to Y Corporation and others at $5 per unit, FOB X Corporation's plant. The freight to Y's plant amounts to 75 cents per unit. Y Corporation processes this item and sells it at a profit.

Required:

Assume that there were 10 units of each of the 5 items in the inventory of *each corporation* at the end of their concurrent fiscal years. For each item, determine the appropriate lower-of-cost-or-market inventory valuation:

a. In the separate financial statements of X Corporation and Y Corporation.
b. In the consolidated financial statements, assuming Y Corporation is a 90 percent owned subsidiary of X Corporation.

Provide a brief explanation for your answers.

(AICPA adapted)

Exercise 7–2

P Company has a 90 percent interest in S Company. During 19X1, S Company reported net income of $20,000. Additionally, at the end of the year, S Company's ending inventory includes $15,000 unconfirmed intercompany profit on purchases from P Company.

Required:
a. Prepare the entries that would be made by P Company at the end of 19X1 to record its equity in S Company's income and to defer the unconfirmed profit, using the entry format generally applied throughout the chapter.
b. Prepare the entries that would be made by P Company at the end of 19X1 to record its equity in S Company's income and to defer the unconfirmed profit, assuming the decision was reached to defer the unconfirmed profit directly against the operating results of the parent company.
c. What is the effect of the alternative entries on the parent's *net income* for 19X1? On consolidated net income for 19X1?

Exercise 7–3

P Company has a 90 percent interest in S Company. During 19X1, S Company reported net income of $30,000, and there is an unconfirmed inventory profit of

$4,000 at the end of the year to be eliminated. P Company accounts for its investment in S Company under the equity method.

Required:

In response to the questions below, provide answers for both of the 100 percent intercompany profit elimination alternatives:

a. Assuming that S Company was the seller on the transaction producing the intercompany profit:
    (1) Prepare the entries made by P Company at the end of 19X1 to record its equity in S Company's confirmed profits.
    (2) Prepare the eliminating entry for the consolidated statement working paper at December 31, 19X1, for the unconfirmed profit.
    (3) Calculate minority interest in 19X1 net income.
b. Assuming that P Company was the seller on the transaction producing the intercompany profit:
    (1) Prepare the entries made by P Company at the end of 19X1 to record its equity in S Company's income.
    (2) Prepare the eliminating entry for the consolidated statement working paper at December 31, 19X1, for the unconfirmed profit.
    (3) Calculate minority interest in 19X1 net income.

Exercise 7–4

Kersbergen owns 80 percent of Algoe Ltd.'s common stock. Algoe sells merchandise to Kersbergen at 50 percent over cost. During 19X0 and 19X1, such sales (at transfer or sales prices) amounted to $90,000 and $60,000. At the end of each year Kersbergen had in inventory one half of the amount purchased from Algoe that year. Assume that each firm reported $50,000 net income from their own operations during 19X1 and that Kersbergen allocates intercompany profit pro rata to majority and minority shareholders. Kersbergen uses the equity method to account for its investment in Algoe Ltd.

Required:

Prepare a schedular calculation of consolidated net income for 19X1 using the—

a. Incremental approach.
b. Residual approach.

Exercise 7–5

The Hart Company owns 90 percent of the capital stock of the Lake Company. During 19X1, the Hart Company sold merchandise to the Lake Company for $10,000 and purchased $5,000 of merchandise from the Lake Company. Twenty percent of all intercompany sales remains in the ending inventory of the purchasing affiliate. The beginning inventory of the Hart Company included $500 of merchandise purchased in the previous period from the Lake Company. Each company marks merchandise to sell at 25 percent above cost.

The 19X1 net incomes from their own operations of the Hart Company and the Lake Company were $20,000 and $10,000, respectively. The Hart Company uses the equity method to account for its investment in the Lake Company.

Required:

a. Prepare 19X1 eliminating entries for all eliminations in respect to the intercompany sales. Assume intercompany profits are allocated pro rata to majority and minority shareholders.
b. Calculate the minority interest in subsidiary net income for 19X1.
c. Calculate 19X1 consolidated net income.

Exercise 7–6

P Company owns 80 percent of the capital stock of S Company. For the year ended December 31, 19X1, P Company and S Company reported net incomes from their own operations of $24,000 and $5,000, respectively. The January 1, 19X1, inventory of P Company included a $1,000 profit recorded by S Company on 19X0 sales. During 19X1, P Company and S Company made intercompany sales of $5,000 and $10,000, respectively. Both companies have a gross profit rate (on selling price) of 30 percent. The ending inventory of P Company included $1,000 of these goods, while S Company's ending inventory included $1,500 of goods purchased from P Company.

P Company carries its investment in S Company under the equity method. Intercompany profits are allocated pro rata to majority and minority shareholders.

Required:

a. Prepare eliminating entries in respect to intercompany sales and profits for a consolidated statement working paper for the year ended December 31, 19X1.
b. Calculate minority interest in net income for 19X1.
c. Calculate consolidated net income for 19X1.

Exercise 7–7

P Company purchased in the open market 90 percent of the capital stock of S Company on January 1, 19X1, for $2,200 less than its purchased equity in the book value of S Company stock. The parent uses the equity method. The credit differential was totally assigned to land. On December 31, 19X2, the consolidated balance sheet discloses the value of the minority interest to be $8,608. Other summary information for the years 19X1 and 19X2 is as follows:

	19X1	*19X2*
Consolidated net income	$109,200	$116,900
P Company net income from its own operations.	80,000	60,000

Additionally, an analysis of intercompany sales revealed the existence of the following unconfirmed inventory profits:

	December 31, 19X1	December 31, 19X2
In the inventory of—		
P Company	$2,000	$1,000
S Company	5,000	3,000

Intercompany profits are allocated pro rata to majority and minority shareholders. S Company paid cash dividends of $20,000 in both 19X1 and 19X2.

Required:

a. Compute the cost of the investment in S Company stock at date of acquisition.

b. What is the carrying value of the investment account on December 31, 19X2?

Problems

Problem 7–8

On January 1, 19X1, Moyer Company purchased 90 percent of the capital stock of Bedford, Inc., at a cost of $72,000; on this date, Bedford, Inc., had capital stock of $50,000 and retained earnings of $30,000.

During 19X2, Bedford, Inc., sold merchandise to Moyer Company for $20,000. Of this 19X2 shipment, 30 percent remains in the inventory of Moyer Company on December 31, 19X2. At the beginning of the year (January 1, 19X2), Moyer Company's inventory contained goods purchased from Bedford, Inc., in 19X1 for $3,600. Bedford Inc.'s gross profit rate (on selling price) on these intercompany sales is 50 percent.

In 19X1, Bedford, Inc., reported net income of $25,000 and paid cash dividends of $10,000. On January 1, 19X1, the balance of Moyer's retained earnings was $50,000; during 19X1, Moyer's net income *from its own operations* was $30,000, and it paid cash dividends of $10,000.

Moyer Company uses the equity method to account for its investment in Bedford, Inc. Intercompany profits are allocated *pro rata* between majority and minority shareholders.

The following information is available from the companies' trial balances at December 31, 19X2:

	December 31, 19X2	
	Moyer Company	Bedford, Inc.
Sales.........................	$ 94,000	$43,000
Purchases	50,000	26,000
Expenses.....................	4,000	2,000
Inventory (1/1/X2).............	18,000	8,000
Inventory (12/31/X2)...........	24,000	12,000
Dividends declared............	10,000	5,000
Other assets	123,500	97,000
Capital stock.................	100,000	50,000

Required:

a. Prepare all entries made by Moyer Company in 19X1 and 19X2 associated with its investment in Bedford, Inc.

b. Calculate the balances of the following accounts:
   (1) Equity in subsidiary earnings for 19X1 and 19X2.
   (2) Retained earnings at January 1, 19X2, for Moyer Company and Bedord, Inc.
   (3) Investment in Bedford, Inc., at December 31, 19X2.

c. Using the information presented in the problem and the amounts calculated in (b) above, prepare a consolidated statement working paper for the year ended December 31, 19X2. The eliminating entries should be separately enumerated and keyed to the working paper.

d. Prepare a schedular calculation of consolidated net income for 19X2, using the incremental approach.

Problem 7–9

Use the information of Problem 7–8, *except* now assume that intercompany profits are allocated *wholly* to the majority shareholders. With this change, complete the requirements enumerated in Problem 7–8.

Problem 7–10

Use the information of Problem 7–8, *except* now assume that Moyer Company uses the *modified equity method*, wherein intercompany profits are *not* recorded on the books of the parent company. Dividends received from the subsidiary and the parent's equity in the subsidiary's *reported* net income are recorded in the investment account. In the consolidated financial statements, continue to assume that intercompany profits are allocated pro rata between majority and minority shareholders. With this change, complete the requirements enumerated in Problem 7–8.

Problem 7–11

Use the information of Problem 7–8, *except* now assume that Moyer Company uses the *cost method* to account for its investment in Bedford, Inc. In the consolidated financial statements, continue to assume that intercompany profits are allocated pro rata between majority and minority shareholders. With this change, complete the requirements enumerated in Problem 7–8. [Under requirement (b), calculate the balances of Dividend Income for 19X1 and 19X2 rather than Equity in Subsidiary Earnings.]

Problem 7–12

On June 30, 19X6, Paul Corporation acquired for cash of $19 per share all of the outstanding voting common stock of Sand Corporation. Both companies continued to operate as separate entities, and both companies have calendar fiscal years.

On June 30, 19X6, after closing the nominal accounts, Sand's condensed balance sheet was as follows:

Assets

Cash..	$ 700,000
Accounts receivable, net............................	600,000
Inventories......................................	1,400,000
Property, plant, and equipment, net.................	3,300,000
Other assets.....................................	500,000
Total assets.....................................	$6,500,000

Liabilities and Stockholders' Equity

Accounts payable and other current liabilities..........	$ 700,000
Long-term debt....................................	2,600,000
Other liabilities	200,000
Common stock, par value $1 per share...............	1,000,000
Additional paid-in capital...........................	400,000
Retained earnings..................................	1,600,000
Total liabilities and stockholders' equity..............	$6,500,000

On June 30, 19X6, Sand's assets and liabilities with fair values different from the book values were as follows:

	Fair Value
Property, plant, and equipment, net........	$16,400,000
Other assets.............................	200,000
Long-term debt..........................	2,200,000

The differences between fair values and book values resulted in a charge or credit to depreciation or amortization in the consolidated statements for the year ending December 31, 19X6, as follows:

Property, plant, and equipment, net.......	$500,000 charge
Other assets............................	10,000 credit
Long-term debt.........................	5,000 charge
	$495,000 charge

The amount paid by Paul in excess of the fair value of the net assets of Sand is attributable to expected future earnings of Sand and will be amortized over the maximum allowable period.

On June 30, 19X6, there were no intercompany receivables or payables.

During the six-month period ending December 31, 19X6, Sand acquired merchandise from Paul at an invoice price of $500,000. The cost of the merchandise to Paul was $300,000. At December 31, 19X6, one half of the merchandise was not sold and Sand had not yet paid for any of the merchandise.

The 19X6 net income [loss] for both companies was as follows:

	Paul	Sand
January 1 to June 30	$ 250,000	$ [750,000]
July 1 to December 31.........	1,600,000	1,250,000

The $1,600,000 net income of Paul includes its equity in the *reported* net income of Sand.

On December 31, 19X6, after closing the nominal accounts, the condensed balance sheets for both companies were as follows:

	Paul	Sand
Assets		
Cash...	$ 3,500,000	$ 600,000
Accounts receivable, net	1,400,000	1,500,000
Inventories	1,000,000	2,500,000
Property, plant, and equipment, net	2,000,000	3,100,000
Investment in subsidiary, at equity	20,250,000	—
Other assets	100,000	500,000
Total assets.....................................	$28,250,000	$8,200,000
Liabilities and Stockholders' Equity		
Accounts payable and other current liabilities........	$ 1,500,000	$1,100,000
Long-term debt	4,000,000	2,600,000
Other liabilities	750,000	250,000
Common stock, par value $1 per share..............	10,000,000	1,000,000
Additional paid-in capital	5,000,000	400,000
Retained earnings................................	7,000,000	2,850,000
Total liabilities and stockholders' equity	$28,250,000	$8,200,000

Required:

a. Prepare a consolidated *balance sheet* working paper at December 31, 19X6.
b. Calculate consolidated net income for 19X6.

(AICPA adapted)

Problem 7–13

P Company acquired 80 percent of the stock of S Company on January 1, 19X1, in the open market for a cash payment of $254,400. On that date, the balances of S Company's shareholders' equity accounts were Capital Stock, $100,000, and Retained Earnings, $50,000.

An examination of S Company's assets and liabilities on January 1, 19X1, revealed that book values were equal to fair values for all assets and liabilities except the following:

	Book Value	Fair Value
Inventory.................................	$ 32,000	$ 40,000
Property, plant, and equipment (net)........	260,000	320,000

The inventory on hand on January 1, 19X1 was consumed during 19X1, and the property, plant, and equipment on hand on January 1, 19X1, had an estimated remaining life of 10 years. Any goodwill arising from the combination is to be amortized over the maximum permissible life.

Both companies regularly sell to each other, with a markup of 30 percent on selling price. During 19X5 and 19X6, the intercompany sales and the amounts remaining in the inventories of the purchasing affiliates were:

			Remaining in Ending Inventory of Purchasing Affiliate, 12/31	
	Intercompany Sales			
Selling Affiliate	*19X5*	*19X6*	*19X5*	*19X6*
P Company	$50,000	$60,000	$10,000	$15,000
S Company	30,000	20,000	4,000	2,000

P Company accounts for its investment in S Company using the equity method. You may assume that both companies have properly recorded all transactions and adjustments (including the adjustment of intercompany profits under the equity method of accounting).

The trial balances of the two companies at December 31, 19X6, are provided below:

	P Company	S Company
Property, plant, and equipment (net).......	$ 254,960	$200,000
Inventory (1/1/X6):		
Acquired from nonaffiliates.............	71,000	20,000
Acquired from affiliate	4,000	10,000
Investment in S Company................	250,220	
Purchases:		
From nonaffiliates	400,000	100,000
From affiliate........................	20,000	60,000
Expenses	55,000	10,000
Dividends declared	40,000	15,000
	$1,095,180	$415,000
Other liabilities.........................	$ 110,000	$ 40,000
Capital stock	250,000	100,000
Retained earnings(1/1/X6)	168,000	100,000
Sales:		
To nonaffiliates.......................	495,000	155,000
Intercompany	60,000	20,000
Equity in subsidiary earnings	12,180	
	$1,095,180	$415,000
Inventory (12/31/X6):		
Acquired from nonaffiliates.............	$ 68,000	$ 35,000
Acquired from affiliate	2,000	15,000

Required:

a. Prepare a consolidated statement working paper for the year ended December 31, 19X6. Intercompany profits are to be eliminated using the total (100 percent) method, with pro rata allocation to majority and minority shareholders where appropriate.

b. Prepare a schedular calculation of consolidated net income for 19X6 using the incremental approach.

Problem 7–14

On January 1, 19X1, P Company acquired an 80 percent interest in S Company. The cost of the acquisition, which was for cash in the open market, was $683,600. On the date of acquisition, S Company had capital stock of $300,000 and retained earnings of $100,000. In their evaluation of the fair values of the assets and liabilities of S Company, the management of P Company determined that only one asset, land, had a fair value different from book value. The fair value of the land, which is included in the Property, Plant, and Equipment account, was $72,000 higher than its book value. P Company decides that the amount allocated to Goodwill will be amortized over 15 years.

The affiliates regularly engage in transactions with each other. During 19X5, P Company had sales of $170,000 to S Company, and S Company had sales of $70,000 to P Company. The following information was compiled on intercompany profits in the beginning and ending inventories of the affiliates:

	Intercompany Profit in Inventory	
	January 1, 19X5	December 31, 19X5
Profits recognized by P Company as selling affiliate	$9,000	$13,500
Profits recognized by S Company as selling affiliate	3,600	1,800

P Company accounts for its investment in S Company using the equity method. All transactions and adjustments have been properly recorded. The trial balances of the affiliates at December 31, 19X5, are:

	P Company	S Company
Cash	$ 80,000	$ 15,000
Accounts receivable.	120,000	35,000
Property, plant, and equipment (net) . . .	564,880	550,000
Investment in S Company	750,660	
Inventory (1/1)	225,000	90,000
Purchases.	1,260,000	480,000
Expenses	165,000	30,000
Dividends declared	120,000	45,000
	$3,285,540	$1,245,000
Accounts payable.	$ 140,000	$ 30,000
Other liabilities	190,000	90,000
Common stock	750,000	300,000
Retained earnings	504,000	300,000
Sales	1,665,000	525,000
Equity in subsidiary earnings	36,540	
	$3,285,540	$1,245,000
Inventory (12/31)	$ 210,000	$ 150,000

Required:

a. Prepare a consolidated statement working paper for the year ended December 31, 19X5. Intercompany profits are to be eliminated 100 percent, with pro rata allocation to majority and minority shareholders where appropriate.

b. Prepare a schedular calculation of consolidated net income for 19X5 using the incremental approach.

Problem 7–15

P Company purchased 60 percent of the capital stock of S Company on January 1, 19X1, for $92,000 when the latter's capital stock and retained earnings were $60,000 and $20,000, respectively. Book values were equal to fair values for all assets and liabilities of S Company except plant and equipment (net) that had a fair value $40,000 in excess of book value. The plant and equipment had an estimated remaining life of 5 years, and the goodwill arising from the combination is being amortized over 10 years.

S Company regularly sells merchandise to the parent company. During 19X2, the subsidiary had sales of $30,000 to the parent. The intercompany profit in P Company's beginning inventory was $5,000, and in the December 31, 19X2, inventory it is $1,500.

P Company uses the *modified* equity method to account for its investment in S Company. That is, the parent makes all entries required under the equity method of accounting *except* the entries for intercompany profits.

Trial balances for the companies on December 31, 19X2, are shown following:

	P Company	S Company
Cash	$ 57,600	$ 60,000
Property, plant, and equipment (net)	160,000	80,000
Investment in S Company	102,400	
Inventory (1/1)	60,000	30,000
Purchases	96,000	46,000
Expenses	24,000	14,000
Dividends declared	40,000	10,000
	$540,000	$240,000
Accounts payable	$ 48,800	$ 40,000
Common stock	200,000	60,000
Retained earnings	100,000	40,000
Sales	180,000	100,000
Equity in subsidiary earnings	11,200	
	$540,000	$240,000
Inventory (12/31)	$ 40,000	$ 20,000

Required:

a. Prepare a consolidated statement working paper for the year ended December 31, 19X2. Intercompany profits are to be eliminated 100 percent, with pro rata allocation to majority and minority shareholders where appropriate.

b. Prepare a schedular calculation of consolidated net income for 19X2 using the incremental approach.

CHAPTER
8

Consolidated Statements—
Intercompany Profit on
Asset Transfers (continued)

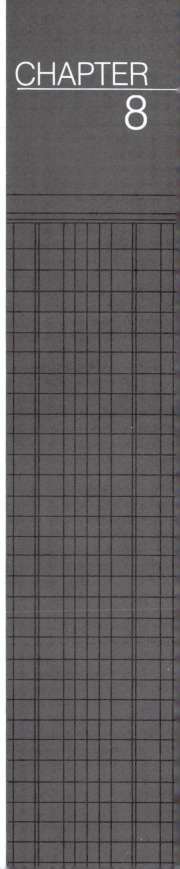

Intercompany Profit—Plant and Equipment

As in the case of intercompany sales of merchandise, the recorded profit on the transfer of plant and equipment between affiliates must be deferred in the consolidated statements until confirmed from a consolidated point of view. Most of the principles underlying this process are the same as explained in Chapter 7 for intercompany sales of merchandise. However, for depreciable assets that are held for use rather than for sale, *confirmation of a portion of the intercompany profit is assumed to occur when depreciation expense is recognized by the purchasing affiliate*. In adopting this criterion, the process of using a depreciable asset is assumed to be comparable to the transaction of resale by the purchasing affiliate in the case of merchandise. Is this in fact a valid assumption? Depreciation expense measures (in principle) the portion of the asset consumed in generating products or services. If these products or services have been sold to nonaffiliates, then it does seem reasonable to conclude that use of the asset confirms a pro rata portion of the intercompany profit through transactions with nonaffiliates. Of course, when the asset is used in manufacturing, the portion that relates to the cost of work in process and finished goods inventories is not actually confirmed until sale of the manufactured product. This is mitigated in the consolidated income statement by a largely offsetting amount in the beginning inventory. Since a precise determination of this amount is often difficult, it is usually ignored.

In the following case, we consider the treatment of an intercompany profit arising from the sale of equipment by a partially owned subsidiary to the parent for the year of sale and the following year. Although confirmation of the total intercompany profit generally extends over a longer period of time, these two years illustrate all of the principles necessary to deal with this class of intercompany profits. Similarly, by choosing an upstream transfer of assets, allocations between majority and minority shareholders are illustrated. For downstream transfers, the entire impact of the intercompany profit that is deferred or confirmed for the period is assigned to the majority shareholders.

Case 1.   Upstream Sale of Plant and Equipment.   We assume that P Company acquired a 60 percent equity in S Company on January 1, 19X1, at a cost of $60,000, when S Company's stockholders' equity accounts were Capital Stock, $75,000, and Retained Earnings, $25,000. There were no intercompany sales of merchandise during 19X1 or 19X2, but on January 2, 19X1, S Company sold equipment carried on its books at a net value of $10,000 (cost, $20,000; accumulated depreciation, $10,000) to P Company for $15,000. The gain of $5,000 is reported separately by S Company as Gain on Sale of Plant and Equipment. The equipment is estimated to have a remaining service life to the purchasing affiliate (P Company) of five years, and straight-line depreciation continues to be appropriate. S Company reported net income of $32,000 for 19X1 and $20,000 for 19X2.

Analysis of Intercompany Profit Confirmation.   The intercompany profit of $5,000 on the sale of the equipment is confirmed through use of the equipment by P Company, the purchasing affiliate. This usage is measured by the depreciation expense recorded by P Company. The following depreciation schedule for the equipment displays the annual confirmation of the intercompany profit:

	P Company's Recorded Depreciation Expense		
	On Cost to the Economic Entity	On Intercompany Profit	Total
19X1	$ 2,000	$1,000	$ 3,000
19X2	2,000	1,000	3,000
19X3	2,000	1,000	3,000
19X4	2,000	1,000	3,000
19X5	2,000	1,000	3,000
	$10,000	$5,000	$15,000

The recorded cost of the equipment to P Company is $15,000, the price paid to S Company in the intercompany transfer of the equipment. Using straight-line depreciation, the depreciation expense recorded by P Company for each of the five years is $3,000. However, from the point of view of the consolidated entity, the unexpired cost of $10,000 is unaffected by the intercompany transfer. Therefore, depreciation expense each year to the consolidated entity is $2,000, and the remaining $1,000 of the depreciation expense recorded by P Company is depreciation on the intercompany profit. This $1,000 increment is eliminated in the consolidated financial statements, and also measures the amount of the intercompany profit that has been confirmed through use in that year (in the same way that elimination of the intercompany profit in the beginning inventory reflected confirmation of the profit).

Parent Company Entries in 19X1 and 19X2.   The parent company's entries in 19X1 to record its equity in the subsidiary's reported net income and to recognize the intercompany profit on the equipment transfer are as follows:

1. To record equity in S Company's 19X1 reported net income (60 percent × $32,000):

        Investment in S Company 19,200
            Equity in Subsidiary Earnings   19,200

2. To record deferral of parent's interest in the intercompany profit (60 percent × $5,000):

        Equity in Subsidiary Earnings 3,000
            Investment in S Company   3,000

3. To record parent's interest in the intercompany profit confirmed during 19X1 (60 percent × $1,000):

Investment in S Company	600	
Equity in Subsidiary Earnings		600

Since the subsidiary was the selling affiliate, the parent's interest in the intercompany profit is based upon the parent's ownership interest in the subsidiary (60 percent). Note that entry (2) defers the parent's share of the intercompany profit as of the date of transfer and entry (3) recognizes the parent's share of the amount confirmed during 19X1. The net effect of the two entries ($2,400) may, of course, be reflected in a single deferral entry—to defer the parent's share of the amount of intercompany profit still unconfirmed at the end of the year [60 percent × ($5,000 − $1,000)].

In 19X2, the parent company's entries to record its equity in the subsidiary's reported 19X2 net income and recognize confirmation of another $1,000 of the intercompany profit on the equipment transfer are as follows:

4. To record equity in S Company's 19X2 reported income (60 percent × $20,000):

Investment in S Company	12,000	
Equity in Subsidiary Earnings		12,000

5. To record parent's interest in the intercompany profit confirmed during 19X2 (60 percent × $1,000):

Investment in S Company	600	
Equity in Subsidiary Earnings		600

The entries for both years are reflected in T-account form in Illustration 8–1. An examination of the investment account reveals the same pattern of deferral and subsequent confirmation of the intercompany profit that exists in the case of intercompany inventory profits, although the total time period over which confirmation takes place is longer. At December 31, 19X2, the investment account still reflects a net deferral of $1,800 ($3,000 − $600 − $600), which is the parent's share of the total unconfirmed profit on this date [60 percent × ($5,000 − $1,000 − $1,000)].

Eliminating Entries for 19X1.   The working paper eliminating entries for 19X1 are presented below:

1. To reverse P Company entries during 19X1:

Equity in Subsidiary Earnings	16,800	
Investment in S Company		16,800

2. To eliminate the intercompany profit on the transfer of equipment and restore the asset and related accumulated depreciation accounts to

Illustration 8–1

INVESTMENT-RELATED ACCOUNTS
MAINTAINED BY PARENT COMPANY
(For Case 1—Intercompany Transfer of Equipment)

Investment in S Company

Investment cost, January 1, 19X1	60,000	(2) Deferral of intercompany profit on transfer of equipment	3,000
(1) Equity in S Company's reported 19X1 net income	19,200	Balance, December 31, 19X1	76,800
(3) Confirmation of intercompany profit on transfer of equipment	600		
	79,800		79,800
Balance, December 31, 19X1	76,800		
(4) Equity in S Company's reported 19X2 net income	12,000		
(5) Confirmation of intercompany profit on transfer of equipment	600	Balance, December 31, 19X2	89,400
	89,400		89,400
Balance, December 31, 19X2	89,400		

Equity in Subsidiary Earnings

(2) Deferral of intercompany profit on transfer of equipment	3,000	(1) Equity in S Company's reported 19X1 net income	19,200
To close to 19X1 income summary	16,800	(3) Confirmation of intercompany profit on transfer of equipment	600
	19,800		19,800
To close to 19X2 income summary	12,600	(4) Equity in S Company's reported 19X2 net income	12,000
		(5) Confirmation of intercompany profit on transfer of equipment	600
	12,600		12,600

Illustration 8–2

RECORDED AND CONSOLIDATED BASIS VALUES
(For Asset Transferred between Affiliates in Case 1)

	January 2, 19X1	December 31, 19X1	December 31, 19X2
Plant and equipment:			
On consolidated basis	$ 20,000	$ 20,000	$ 20,000
Recorded by purchasing affiliate	15,000	15,000	15,000
	$ 5,000	$ 5,000	$ 5,000
Accumulated depreciation:			
On consolidated basis	$[10,000]	$[12,000]	$[14,000]
Recorded by purchasing affiliate	–0–	[3,000]	[6,000]
	$[10,000]	$ [9,000]	$ [8,000]
Unconfirmed intercompany profit	$ 5,000	$ 4,000	$ 3,000

their original cost basis to the consolidated entity as of the beginning of the year (see Illustration 8–2):

Gain on Sale of Plant and Equipment	5,000	
Plant and Equipment	5,000	
Accumulated Depreciation		10,000

3. To eliminate depreciation expense on the intercompany profit:

Accumulated Depreciation	1,000	
Depreciation Expense		1,000

4. To eliminate the investment account balance at the beginning of the year against the beginning-of-year balances in the stockholders' equity accounts of S Company:

Capital Stock—S Company	45,000	
Retained Earnings (1/1)—S Company	15,000	
Investment in S Company		60,000

The consolidated statement working paper for 19X1 is presented in Illustration 8–3.

Illustration 8–3

P COMPANY AND SUBSIDIARY S COMPANY
Consolidated Statement Working Paper
For Year Ended December 31, 19X1

	P Com-pany	S Com-pany	Eliminations Dr.	Eliminations Cr.	Minority Interest	Consoli-dated
Income Statement						
Sales	120,000	80,000				200,000
Equity in subsidiary earnings	16,800		(1) 16,800			–0–
Gain on sale of plant and equipment	–0–	5,000	(2) 5,000			–0–
Inventory (12/31)	30,000	12,000				42,000
Total credits	166,800	97,000				242,000
Inventory (1/1)	40,000	10,000				50,000
Purchases	74,000	50,000				124,000
Other expenses	12,000	5,000				17,000
Depreciation expense	3,000			(3) 1,000		2,000
Total debits	129,000	65,000				193,000
						49,000
Minority interest in S Company's confirmed 19X1 net income [40% × ($32,000 −$5,000 + $1,000)]					11,200	11,200
Net income	37,800	32,000	21,800	1,000	11,200	37,800
Retained Earnings Statement						
Retained earnings, 1/1/X1:						
P Company	40,000					40,000
S Company		25,000	(4) 15,000		10,000	–0–
Net income	37,800	32,000	21,800	1,000	11,200	37,800
Retained earnings, 12/31/X1	77,800	57,000	36,800	1,000	21,200	77,800
Balance Sheet						
Other assets	128,200	141,000				269,200
Inventory	30,000	12,000				42,000
Investment in S Company	76,800			(1) 16,800		–0–
				(4) 60,000		
Plant and equipment (intercompany)	15,000	–0–	(2) 5,000			20,000
	250,000	153,000				331,200
Accumulated depreciation (intercompany)	3,000	–0–	(3) 1,000	(2) 10,000		12,000
Other liabilities	69,200	21,000				90,200
Capital stock:						
P Company	100,000					100,000
S Company		75,000	(4) 45,000		30,000	–0–
Retained earnings	77,800	57,000	36,800	1,000	21,200	77,800
Minority interest in S Company					51,200	51,200M
	250,000	153,000	87,800	87,800		331,200

(1) To reverse P Company entries during 19X1. (2) To eliminate the intercompany profit on the transfer of plant and equipment as of the date of transfer. (3) To eliminate depreciation expense on the intercompany profit. (4) To eliminate the investment account balance at the beginning of the year against the beginning-of-year balances in the stockholders' equity accounts of S Company.

On a consolidated basis, the transferred asset should be reflected in terms of the selling affiliate's original transaction cost and related accumulated depreciation. Illustration 8–2 reveals that the intercompany profit of $5,000 is composed of an understatement of the asset account of $5,000 and an understatement of accumulated depreciation of $10,000. Eliminating entry (2) adjusts these two accounts to their proper consolidated basis at the date of transfer (the combined effect is a $5,000 credit to plant and equipment—*net*) and eliminates the profit on the sale recorded by S Company.

The adjusted asset account continues to be properly stated at the end of the year. However, the accumulated depreciation account must be additionally adjusted for the difference between depreciation recorded by P Company (the purchasing affiliate) for 19X1 and depreciation for the year on the basis of S Company's (the selling affiliate) original transaction cost. As we have previously seen, annual depreciation recorded by P Company (separately identified in the income statement in the working paper) on the basis of a five-year service life, straight-line depreciation, and a $15,000 purchase price amounts to $3,000. The depreciation on the basis of original transaction cost amounts to only $2,000 ($10,000 net book value allocated over the remaining five-year life). The difference of $1,000 recorded by P Company is *depreciation on the intercompany profit*—an overstatement of depreciation expense and accumulated depreciation on a consolidated basis. Eliminating entry (3) adjusts for this overstatement, thereby recognizing as confirmed $1,000 of the intercompany profit.

All of the adjustments in eliminating entries (2) and (3) are based upon the full amount of the intercompany profit, in accordance with the principles of intercompany profit elimination previously discussed. Since the selling affiliate is a 60 percent owned subsidiary, the eliminated profit must be allocated between majority and minority shareholders. Accordingly, minority interest in income is calculated on the basis of S Company's *confirmed* income for 19X1. S Company's confirmed net income for 19X1 of $28,000 is its reported net income ($32,000), less the unconfirmed profit on the intercompany transfer of plant and equipment ($5,000), plus the portion of this intercompany profit confirmed by the recognition of depreciation expense during the year ($1,000). The minority shareholders' interest in this confirmed net income is 40 percent, or $11,200. This amount is entered in the income statement division of the consolidated statement working paper in Illustration 8–3.

The elimination of the investment account balance at the beginning of the year is again made against the *recorded* balances in the stockholders' equity accounts of S Company. As a consequence of these working paper eliminations, consolidated net income (and retained earnings) are again equal to the parent company's net income (and retained earnings).

Eliminating Entries for 19X2.   The eliminating entries for 19X2 are presented below:

1.   To reverse P Company entries during 19X2:

Equity in Subsidiary Earnings............................   12,600
    Investment in S Company   12,600

2.   To eliminate the $4,000 unconfirmed intercompany profit at the beginning of the year (allocated between majority and minority shareholders) and adjust the plant and equipment, and related accumulated depreciation, to their proper consolidated basis balances as of that date (see Illustration 8–2):

Investment in S Company (60% × $4,000)..................   2,400
Minority Interest in S Company's 1/1/X2 Unconfirmed
    Retained Earnings (40% × $4,000)   1,600
Plant and Equipment......................................   5,000
    Accumulated Depreciation............................   9,000

3.   To eliminate depreciation expense on the intercompany profit:

Accumulated Depreciation...............................   1,000
    Depreciation Expense   1,000

4.   To eliminate the "adjusted" investment account balance at the beginning of the year against the beginning-of-year balances in the stockholders' equity accounts of S Company:

Capital Stock—S Company   45,000
Retained Earnings (1/1)—S Company.....................   34,200
    Investment in S Company   79,200

The consolidated statement working paper for 19X2 is presented in Illustration 8–4.

The reasoning underlying the structure of eliminating entry (2) is the same as previously explained for the elimination of intercompany profit in the beginning inventory. The net effect of the $5,000 debit to Plant and

Illustration 8–4

P COMPANY AND SUBSIDIARY S COMPANY
Consolidated Statement Working Paper
For Year Ended December 31, 19X2

	P Company	S Company	Eliminations Dr.	Eliminations Cr.	Minority Interest	Consolidated
Income Statement						
Sales	140,000	85,000				225,000
Equity in subsidiary earnings	12,600		(1) 12,600			–0–
Inventory (12/31)	25,000	15,000				40,000
Total credits	177,600	100,000				265,000
Inventory (1/1)	30,000	12,000				42,000
Purchases	93,000	54,000				147,000
Other expenses	16,500	14,000				30,500
Depreciation expense	3,000			(3) 1,000		2,000
Total debits	142,500	80,000				221,500
						43,500
Minority interest in S Company's confirmed 19X2 net income [40% × ($20,000 + $1,000)]					8,400	8,400
Net income	35,100	20,000	12,600	1,000	8,400	35,100
Retained Earnings Statement						
Retained earnings, 1/1/X2:						
P Company	77,800					77,800
S Company		57,000	(4) 34,200		22,800	–0–
Minority interest in S Company's 1/1/X2 unconfirmed retained earnings			(2) 1,600		[1,600]	–0–
Net income	35,100	20,000	12,600	1,000	8,400	35,100
Retained earnings, 12/31/X2	112,900	77,000	48,400	1,000	29,600	112,900
Balance Sheet						
Other assets	170,600	163,000				333,600
Inventory	25,000	15,000				40,000
Investment in S Company	89,400		(2) 2,400	(1) 12,600		–0–
				(4) 79,200		
Plant and equipment (intercompany)	15,000	–0–	(2) 5,000			20,000
	300,000	178,000				393,600
Accumulated depreciation (intercompany)	6,000	–0–	(3) 1,000	(2) 9,000		14,000
Other liabilities	81,100	26,000				107,100
Capital stock:						
P Company	100,000					100,000
S Company		75,000	(4) 45,000		30,000	–0–
Retained earnings	112,900	77,000	48,400	1,000	29,600	112,900
Minority interest in S Company					59,600	59,600M
	300,000	178,000	101,800	101,800		393,600

[deduction]
(1) To reverse P Company entries during 19X2. (2) To eliminate the unconfirmed profit at the beginning of the year. (3) To eliminate depreciation expense on the intercompany profit. (4) To eliminate the "adjusted" investment account balance at the beginning of the year against the beginning-of-year balances in the stockholders' equity accounts of S Company.

Equipment and the $9,000 credit to Accumulated Depreciation is a reduction of the asset carrying value by $4,000—the amount of unconfirmed intercompany profit at the beginning of the year (see Illustration 8–2). This unconfirmed profit is allocated between the majority and minority shareholders because the subsidiary was the selling affiliate. The $1,600 (40 percent × $4,000) allocated to the minority interest corrects for the overstatement, on a consolidated basis, of S Company's retained earnings on January 1, 19X2; the $2,400 debit to Investment in S Company restores the investment account to its proportional relationship with the recorded net assets of the subsidiary at the beginning of the year, which allows for the normal investment elimination entry against the recorded balances in the stockholders' equity accounts of S Company. Again recall that P Company's beginning retained earnings balance is not overstated because the parent company recorded in 19X1 the effect of the unconfirmed intercompany profit. *If the parent carried its investment account on the cost or modified equity basis,* the parent company's beginning retained earnings would be overstated on a consolidated basis and the $2,400 debit would be made against the parent's retained earnings rather than the investment account. This is, of course, the same adjustment in the eliminating entry that is required for intercompany profit in the beginning inventory when the investment account is on a cost or modified equity basis.

As a consequence of these entries, the December 31, 19X2, balances for Plant and Equipment and Accumulated Depreciation in the Consolidated column are $20,000 and $14,000, respectively. These amounts have previously been determined in Illustration 8–2 to be the correct consolidated basis balances. Additionally, depreciation expense in the consolidated income statement has been reduced to $2,000, the proper amount based upon the $20,000 original cost to S Company. As in 19X1, these eliminations are based upon the total $5,000 intercompany profit, and thus minority interest in net income is calculated on the basis of S Company's *confirmed* net income for 19X2. S Company's confirmed net income for 19X2 of $21,000 is its reported net income ($20,000) plus $1,000 intercompany profit confirmed during 19X2. The minority shareholders' interest in this confirmed net income is 40 percent, or $8,400.

Schedular Calculations of Consolidated Net Income. The amounts determined for consolidated net income for 19X1 and 19X2 in the consolidated statement working papers may be verified by either of the schedular calculations. Both are illustrated. Using the incremental approach, we obtain:

	19X1	19X2
P Company's *confirmed* net income from its own operations:		
19X1: ($37,800 − $16,800)	$21,000	
19X2: ($35,100 − $12,600)		$22,500
Increased by P Company's equity in S Company's *confirmed* net income:		
19X1: [60% × ($32,000 − $5,000 + $1,000)].......................	16,800	
19X2: [60% × ($20,000 + $1,000)]		12,600
Consolidated net income	$37,800	$35,100

The parent company's confirmed net income from its own operations is determined by subtracting the parent's recorded equity in the subsidiary's earnings from its reported income. Since the parent was not the selling affiliate in any transaction generating intercompany profit that was either confirmed or deferred during the two years, no further adjustment is necessary. However, if the parent had been the selling affiliate in such a transaction, the amount of unconfirmed profit would be deducted from, and the amount of confirmed profit added to, the parent's reported income from its own operations (i.e., total reported income less recorded equity in subsidiary earnings). The subsidiary's confirmed income is calculated in the same manner. Notice that allocation of 60 percent of the subsidiary's confirmed income to the majority shareholders in this calculation is complementary to the allocation of 40 percent of the same amount to the minority interest in the income statement division of the consolidated statement working papers.

Using the residual approach, we obtain the following calculations of consolidated net income:

	19X1	19X2
P Company's reported net income	$37,800	$35,100
S Company's reported net income	32,000	20,000
	$69,800	$55,100
Less [plus]—*net* debit [credit] eliminations:		
P Company's recorded equity in S Company's earnings	$16,800	$12,600
Deferral of intercompany profit from sale of equipment..........	5,000	—
Confirmation of intercompany profit in equipment	[1,000]	[1,000]
	$20,800	$11,600
Total equity	$49,000	$43,500
Minority interest in S Company's confirmed net income:		
19X1: [40% × ($32,000 − $5,000 + $1,000)]	11,200	
19X2: [40% × ($20,000 + $1,000)]		8,400
Consolidated net income.......................................	$37,800	$35,100

Each of the figures in these two calculations may be traced back to the income statement divisions of the consolidated statement working papers for the two years. In that sense, the schedular calculation captures the essence of the combining process in the working paper. Beginning with the total of the two affiliates' reported incomes, the parent's recorded equity in subsidiary earnings is deducted by means of an eliminating entry (the entry to reverse the parent's entries for the year); if a subtotal were taken here, we would have the *combined incomes from operations reported* by the affiliates for the period. This "total" is then adjusted to a "consolidated basis" by deducting reported but unconfirmed profits and adding confirmed but unreported profits. The resulting total, labeled total equity, is the affiliates' total *confirmed incomes from operations* for the period. It represents a total equity in the sense that this sum of the affiliates' confirmed incomes is the amount that is allocated between majority and minority shareholder groups. Finally, by deducting the minority interest in the subsidiary's confirmed income for the period, we are left (as a residual) with consolidated net income.

Relationship between Value of Minority Interest and Net Assets of Subsidiary.   We observed in the analysis of upstream sales of merchandise that the proportionality between the minority interest in the consolidated balance sheet and the recorded net assets of the subsidiary is affected by unconfirmed inventory profits. This same effect occurs, as one would expect, in the case of upstream sales of plant and equipment. Furthermore, since the confirmation process generally extends over a longer period of time, the effect persists longer. For our example, it is still present at the end of 19X2 because a portion ($3,000) of the intercompany profit remains unconfirmed. Thus, minority interest in the consolidated balance sheets may be analyzed as follows:

	December 31	
	19X1	*19X2*
Minority interest in S Company's recorded net assets:		
19X1: 40% × $132,000	$52,800	
19X2: 40% × $152,000		$60,800
Less: Minority's share of unconfirmed intercompany profit at year-end:		
19X1: 40% × $4,000	1,600	
19X2: 40% × $3,000		1,200
Minority interest in consolidated balance sheet	$51,200	$59,600

Relationship between Investment Account Balance and Net Assets of Subsidiary.   The proportionality between the balance of the investment account at the end of the period and the recorded net assets of the subsidiary is affected by the existence of unconfirmed intercompany profits, whether arising from downstream or upstream sales. In the case of downstream sales, the entire amount of the intercompany profit unconfirmed at the end of the period is deducted from the investment account. For upstream sales, only the parent's share of the unconfirmed profit is deducted from the investment account; the remainder is allocated to the minority interest as illustrated above. Thus, for our example, the investment account may be reconciled with the recorded net assets of the subsidiary as follows:

	December 31	
	19X1	*19X2*
Parent company's interest in recorded net assets of S Company:		
19X1: 60% × $132,000	$79,200	
19X2: 60% × $152,000		$91,200
Less: Parent company's share of unconfirmed intercompany profit at year-end:		
19X1: 60% × $4,000	2,400	
19X2: 60% × $3,000		1,800
Investment account balance	$76,800	$89,400

Intercompany Profits—Related Topics

Other Asset Transfers

The elimination of the selling company's profit recorded on the intercompany sales of merchandise or plant and equipment applies equally to all forms of asset transfers between affiliates. The basic principles that apply are (1) the acquired asset is adjusted to its original transaction cost to the selling affiliate and (2) the intercompany profit is deferred until the asset is transferred to outside parties (either through sale or use of the asset).

Transfer of Nondepreciable Assets. If the transferred asset is nondepreciable, the unconfirmed intercompany profit is *constant in amount* each year. The profit recorded by the selling affiliate (whether the parent or subsidiary) is eliminated against the asset account. Assuming the profit to be eliminated is $2,000, the eliminating entry in the year of sale is:

Profit on Sale of Long-Lived Assets	2,000	
Long-Lived Assets		2,000

When the sale was made by a partially owned subsidiary, this elimination is allocated between majority and minority shareholders.

Since the asset is nondepreciable, the profit remains unconfirmed for all succeeding periods that it is in the possession of the purchasing affiliate. In these subsequent periods, the $2,000 credit to the asset account remains unchanged. However, the debit(s) depends upon whether the seller was the parent or the subsidiary. For example, if the seller were an 80 percent owned subsidiary, the eliminating entry in all periods subsequent to the period of sale would be:

Investment in Subsidiary (80% × $2,000).......................	1,600	
Minority Interest in 1/1 Unconfirmed Retained		
Earnings (20% × $2,000)	400	
Long-Lived Assets..		2,000

If the parent were the seller, the total $2,000 unconfirmed profit would be debited to the investment account. Whichever entry is appropriate, it is repeated in consolidated statement working papers until disposition of the asset by the purchasing affiliate. Such disposition indicates the point in time at which the transfer profit between affiliates is confirmed from a consolidated point of view. ⸳

Transfer of Services.   Affiliates of a consolidated entity may engage in intercompany sales of services that are capitalized on the books of the purchasing affiliate. For example, the parent may do a management consulting engagement for the subsidiary that is expected to provide benefits for, say, five years. In this case, the profit on the consulting service is initially deferred, and then recognized on a consolidated basis as it is confirmed through the amortization of the intangible asset.

On the other hand, some transfers of services are treated by the purchasing affiliate as period expenses. In these cases, the confirmation of the selling affiliate's profit on the transaction is assumed to occur during the same period as the transfer of services. As a consequence, no elimination entries are required to remove such "profits" from the consolidated statements. The corresponding revenue and expense items must, of course, be eliminated, as for all intercompany transactions.

Transfer Profits before Affiliation

Accountants are not agreed on the treatment to be accorded unrealized, or unconfirmed, profits on assets transferred between companies prior to their affiliation. One position is that the profit element should *not* be eliminated from the relevant asset accounts in consolidated working papers.

The argument in general runs as follows. If a newly acquired subsidiary earns a profit on the transfer of assets to the parent, or to another affiliate, prior to the acquisition of the selling subsidiary's stock by the parent, such profit is one of the factors used to determine the book value of the subsidiary's capital stock at date of acquisition, and is accordingly eliminated in the investment elimination entry; necessarily, this profit should not again emerge as an element of consolidated net income, as the profit appropriately relates to the period in which earned.

A second position supports a deduction of the preaffiliation intercompany profit existing at date of acquisition, with confirmation of such profit deferred to subsequent periods, to be recognized as a consequence of the elimination process. This treatment was cited several years ago as a prevailing practice, based upon a study by the American Institute of Certified Public Accountants.[1] The strength of this position is to be found primarily in its appeal to conservatism with respect to asset valuation, particularly for long-lived assets, and to the fact that intercompany profit should not be solely a function of the affiliation date. When the intercompany profit arises out of transactions during the period of negotiations for an affiliate's capital stock, the argument for elimination gains additional support.

The elimination of the preaffiliation profit defers its recognition until disposition of the relevant assets (merchandise or fixed assets), and results in its subsequent inclusion in consolidated net income and consolidated retained earnings. Presumably the recognition of profit would follow in the next accounting period, in most instances, for items of merchandise, while its recognition in respect to fixed assets would extend over the period of remaining service life of the transferred assets.

If the parent is the selling affiliate in the "intercompany" transaction under consideration, there is no effect on the investment elimination entry at acquisition or in subsequent periods, regardless of the treatment selected. At question is when the profit recognized by the parent company on the transaction should be reported in the consolidated income statement. However, when a newly acquired subsidiary is the selling affiliate, the decision to consider a profit as unconfirmed at acquisition, and thus defer its recognition, also implies that the parent's purchased equity in confirmed subsidiary net assets will be lower than if the profit element were not eliminated. In general, this means that the amount of goodwill arising from the consolidation will be higher. Amortization of the goodwill will therefore offset the confirmed intercompany profit recognized in subsequent periods, although generally in amounts less than the confirmed profit. At the end of the life of the goodwill (or the profit confirmation process, if longer), the net effect on consolidated assets and consolidated retained earnings of deciding to eliminate the "intercompany" profit at

---

[1] Research Department, American Institute of Certified Public Accountants, *Survey of Consolidated Financial Statement Practices* (New York, 1956), p. 21.

acquisition is *zero*. In the interim, however, consolidated net income, consolidated retained earnings, and consolidated assets are affected by this choice.

Deferral of Income Taxes Paid on Intercompany Profits

When the affiliates file *separate* income tax returns, income taxes are paid on intercompany profits in the period the profits are recognized by the selling affiliate. However, the profits, if unconfirmed at the end of the period, are deferred in the consolidated financial statements. Therefore, the applicable income taxes must also be deferred. When this topic was briefly discussed in Chapter 7, it was observed that the *net effect* of the tax deferral in the income statement is to defer the intercompany profit "net of taxes." Prior to *APB Opinion No. 11*, the amount of the unconfirmed intercompany profit was measured "net of taxes," both in the parent (or investor) company's entry to record the unconfirmed profit and in the consolidated statements. *Opinion No. 11*, however, rejected the net of tax presentation in favor of the deferral method.[2] As a consequence, *in the consolidated statements*, the income tax effect is no longer treated as an adjustment to the amount of unconfirmed profit to be eliminated. Rather, the before-tax amount of the intercompany profit is eliminated from the inventory (or fixed asset) and related expense, and the tax deferral (and adjustment of income tax expense) is treated separately. It is still considered appropriate, however, for the parent company to record the equity "pickup" net of taxes.[3]

Case 2. An Intercompany Inventory Profit Example. To illustrate this process, assume that P Company's 80 percent owned subsidiary S Company reported net income of $50,000 in 19X1 and 19X2. Further assume that an intercompany profit of $10,000 remains in P Company's ending 19X1 inventory, and that the merchandise was purchased from S Company in 19X1. Finally, assume that the companies' file separate income tax returns, and that the applicable income tax rate is 40 percent.

Parent Company Entries in 19X1 and 19X2. The parent company makes the following entries in 19X1 to record its equity in subsidiary earnings and to defer the unconfirmed profit:

1. To recognize equity in S Company's reported 19X1 net income (80 percent × $50,000):

Investment in S Company	40,000	
Equity in Subsidiary Earnings		40,000

---

[2] *APB, APB Opinion No. 11*, "Accounting for Income Taxes" (New York: AICPA, 1967), par. 35.

[3] See, for example, *Accounting Interpretation No. 1 of APB Opinion No. 18.*

2. To defer the parent's share of the intercompany profit, $10,000, net of applicable income taxes, $4,000 (80 percent × $6,000):

Equity in Subsidiary Earnings 4,800
      Investment in S Company 4,800

Recall that application of the equity method is in essence a "one-line consolidation." This means that the parent's equity in the subsidiary's net assets is reflected in a single account—the investment account, and its equity in all of the subsidiary's revenues and expenses (including income tax expense) for the period is reflected solely in Equity in Subsidiary Earnings. Accordingly, it is appropriate to combine, or net, the tax effect with the recorded gross profit in the parent company's entry to defer the intercompany profit.

In 19X2, the parent company would make the following entries:

3. To recognize equity in S Company's reported 19X2 net income (80 percent × $50,000):

Investment in S Company 40,000
      Equity in Subsidiary Earnings 40,000

4. To recognize confirmation of the parent's share of the intercompany profit, net of taxes (80 percent × $6,000):

Investment in S Company 4,800
      Equity in Subsidiary Earnings 4,800

Thus, the only effect on the parent company's entries of the deferral of income taxes paid on the intercompany profit is to reduce the amount that is deferred.

Eliminating Entries for 19X1 and 19X2. Although the intercompany profit was handled on the parent company's books "net of taxes," the eliminating entries for the consolidated statement working paper must reflect the income tax effect separately. For 19X1, the following entries are made to defer the unconfirmed intercompany profit and to recognize the related income tax allocation:

(1) To defer the unconfirmed intercompany profit in P Company's ending inventory:

Inventory (12/31)(income statement) 10,000
      Inventory (12/31)(balance sheet) 10,000

(2) To defer the applicable income taxes on the unconfirmed intercompany profit (40 percent × $10,000):

```
Prepaid (Deferred) Income Taxes ......................      4,000
    Income Tax Expense................................                4,000
```

The first eliminating entry is the same entry that is made when there is no income tax effect. It reduces the ending inventory to its cost to the selling affiliate and defers the gross profit recognized on the intercompany transaction. The second entry sets up the prepaid, or deferred, income taxes and reduces the income tax expense recorded by S Company. The net effect *in the income statement* is the deferral of $6,000, which is the intercompany profit, net of taxes; however, this income statement effect occurs through an adjustment of two recorded expenses: cost of sales and income tax expense. As a consequence of these entries, S Company's *confirmed* net income for 19X1 is $44,000 ($50,000 − $10,000 + $4,000), or its reported net income decreased by the unconfirmed intercompany profit, net of taxes.

In 19X2, the profit is assumed to be confirmed. In the year of sale, it was convenient to make two eliminating entries to defer the intercompany profit. In the year of confirmation, it is more convenient to reflect all of the effects of confirmation in a single eliminating entry:

To recognize confirmation of the intercompany profit in the beginning inventory ($10,000) and the related income tax expense thereon ($4,000):

```
Investment in S Company (80% × $6,000) ......................     4,800
Minority Interest in S Company's 1/1/X2 Unconfirmed Retained
    Earnings, Net of Taxes (20% × $6,000)......................     1,200
Income Tax Expense ........................................     4,000
    Inventory (1/1) ........................................              10,000
```

The beginning inventory is reduced to its original cost to the economic entity in the normal manner, thereby reflecting confirmation of the full $10,000 intercompany profit. However, since the income taxes paid on this profit ($4,000) were deferred in 19X1, the related income tax expense must also be recognized. The net effect of these two entries in the income statement division of the working paper is to recognize confirmation of the $6,000 intercompany profit, net of taxes. This $6,000 is then allocated between majority and minority shareholders in the eliminating entry in the normal manner. In addition, S Company's *confirmed* income for 19X2 is $56,000 ($50,000 + $10,000 − $4,000), or its reported income increased by the confirmed intercompany profit, net of taxes. The sum of the confirmed incomes for the two years, $100,000, again equals the sum of S Company's reported incomes for the same two years.

Intercompany Profits on Plant and Equipment.   Recognition of income tax effects on intercompany profits arising from transfers of plant and equipment are handled in a similar manner. A few minor differences in the eliminating entries are, however, required. The unconfirmed intercompany profit at the beginning of the second and succeeding years is adjusted against accounts in the balance sheet (plant and equipment and accumulated depreciation) rather than an account in the income statement (inventory [1/1]). As a consequence, the debit for the related income tax effect is to Prepaid (Deferred) Income Taxes, rather than to Income Tax Expense as in the inventory example. Income tax expense is recognized in conjunction with the adjustment of depreciation expense for the period, with an offsetting credit to prepaid income taxes.

Case 3.   An Intercompany Equipment Profit Example.   To illustrate the eliminating entries in this circumstance, we assume that the intercompany profit on the sale of equipment from S Company (a 60 percent owned subsidiary of P Company) in Case 1 was subject to a 40 percent income tax and that the affiliates filed separate income tax returns. In this modified circumstance, the 19X1 eliminating entries relating to the intercompany profit in Illustration 8–3 would be changed as follows (numbering of original eliminating entries is retained for reference purposes):

(2*a*) To eliminate the intercompany profit on the transfer of equipment and restore the asset and related accumulated depreciation accounts to their original cost basis to the consolidated entity as of the beginning of the year:

Gain on Sale of Plant and Equipment	5,000	
Plant and Equipment	5,000	
Accumulated Depreciation		10,000

(2*b*) To defer the applicable income taxes on the unconfirmed intercompany profit at the beginning of the year (40 percent × $5,000):

Prepaid Income Taxes	2,000	
Income Tax Expense		2,000

(3*a*) To eliminate depreciation expense on the intercompany profit:

Accumulated Depreciation	1,000	
Depreciation Expense		1,000

(3b) To recognize the applicable income tax expense on the confirmed intercompany profit (40 percent × $1,000):

Income Tax Expense	400	
Prepaid Income Taxes		400

The eliminating entries relating to the intercompany profit for 19X2 in Illustration 8–4 would be changed in the following manner:

(2) To eliminate the $4,000 unconfirmed intercompany profit at the beginning of the year, net of taxes of $1,600, against majority and minority shareholders; set up the prepaid taxes on the unconfirmed profit at the beginning of the year; and adjust the plant and equipment, and related accumulated depreciation, to their proper consolidated basis balances as of the same date:

Investment in S Company (60% × $2,400)	1,440	
Minority Interest in S Company's 1/1/X2 Unconfirmed Retained Earnings, Net of Taxes (40% × $2,400)	960	
Prepaid Income Taxes	1,600	
Plant and Equipment	5,000	
Accumulated Depreciation		9,000

(3a) To eliminate depreciation expense on the intercompany profit:

Accumulated Depreciation	1,000	
Depreciation Expense		1,000

(3b) To recognize the applicable income tax expense on the confirmed intercompany profit (40 percent × $1,000):

Income Tax Expense	400	
Prepaid Income Taxes		400

Appendix: Two Additional Intercompany Profit Elimination Methods

Basic accounting policy regarding the amount of intercompany profit to be eliminated was originally promulgated in 1959 in *Accounting Research Bulle-*

tin No. 51, "Consolidated Statements," and still remains part of the authoritative literature. Recall that this policy prescribes elimination of all (100 percent) of the intercompany profit, with the option of either *(a)* assigning all of the eliminated amount to the majority interest or *(b)* allocating the amount pro rata between majority and minority shareholders. These two options differ only in the case of upstream sales by partially owned subsidiaries. However, for cases where differences would result, our analysis suggested that the pro rata allocation is the preferable option.

Two additional intercompany profit elimination methods have received some support in the accounting literature and/or authoritative pronouncements, and they are briefly reviewed below.

Fractional Elimination

In contrast to the two elimination methods summarized above, another position is that only the parent company's equity in the intercompany profit should be regarded as unconfirmed and therefore eliminated. The amount of the elimination is calculated in terms of the parent company's fractional ownership interest in the profit reported by the selling affiliate. Thus, it may be observed that this method differs from the above two methods in terms of the amount eliminated only when a partially owned subsidiary is the selling affiliate. If the parent or a wholly owned subsidiary is the selling affiliate, then by definition the "parent company's fractional interest in the profit reported by the selling affiliate" is 100 percent.

The basic reasoning underlying this elimination method proceeds from the dominant "parent company" orientation of present-day consolidated financial statements. From the point of view of the shareholders of the parent company, the purchase of an asset from a partially owned subsidiary involves an additional cost over the cost of the asset to the subsidiary— the profit accruing to the minority shareholders. And if the asset remains on the books of the parent company at the end of the accounting period, the reasoning continues, the cost assigned to the asset in the consolidated balance sheet should be the cost to the majority shareholders—namely, the cost to the subsidiary plus the portion of the intercompany profit accruing to the minority shareholders in the subsidiary. The value increment added to the asset cost is balanced by a corresponding increase in the value of the minority interest in the consolidated balance sheet.

For example, assume that S Company, an 80 percent owned subsidiary, sells merchandise with a cost of $8,000 to P Company for $12,000, and the merchandise remains in the ending inventory of P Company. Further assume that P Company and S Company report net income from their own operations for the year of $30,000 and $15,000, respectively. Based upon these facts, the parent company would make the following entries (using fractional elimination) at the end of the year:

1. To record equity in S Company's reported net income (80 percent ×
   $15,000):

Investment in S Company	12,000	
Equity in Subsidiary Earnings		12,000

2. To record deferral of parent's share of unconfirmed intercompany
   profit of $4,000 in P Company's ending inventory (80 percent ×
   $4,000):

Equity in Subsidiary Earnings	3,200	
Investment in S Company		3,200

These are, of course, the same entries that P Company would make if it
were eliminating 100 percent of intercompany profits *and* allocating them
pro rata to majority and minority shareholders. However, if the intercompany profits were allocated solely to majority shareholders, the second
entry would reflect a $4,000 deferral.

The eliminating entry under the fractional elimination method to defer
the unconfirmed intercompany profit would be:

To defer parent's share of the unconfirmed intercompany profit of $4,000
in P Company's ending inventory (80 percent × $4,000):

Inventory (12/31)(income statement)	3,200	
Inventory (12/31)(balance sheet)		3,200

This eliminating entry differs in amount from the eliminating entry that
would be made under the total elimination alternatives, wherein all of the
$4,000 would be eliminated.

The minority interest in S Company's net income is calculated on the
basis of the subsidiary's *reported* net income under the fractional elimination method. In this case, the minority interest in net income is $3,000 (20
percent × $15,000). This same amount is assigned to the minority interest
under 100 percent elimination allocated solely to the majority shareholders. However, under 100 percent elimination allocated pro rata to majority
and minority shareholders, the minority interest in net income is based
upon the subsidiary's confirmed net income; for our data, the subsidiary's
confirmed income is $11,000 ($15,000 − $4,000), and the minority interest
therein is $2,200 (20 percent × $11,000).

The following tabulation of amounts that would appear in the consolidated financial statements contrasts the impacts of the three elimination
methods:

		Total (100 Percent) Elimination	
	Fractional Elimination	Allocated Pro Rata to Majority and Minority Shareholders	Allocated Solely to Majority Shareholders
P Company's carrying value for inventory	$12,000	$12,000	$12,000
Less: Amount eliminated....................	3,200	4,000	4,000
Value of inventory in consolidated balance sheet.........................	$ 8,800	$ 8,000	$ 8,000
Minority interest in S Company's net income...........................	$ 3,000	$ 2,200	$ 3,000
Consolidated net income (by residual calculation): Combined incomes from own operations.......................	$45,000	$45,000	$45,000
Less: Amount of intercompany profit eliminated........................	3,200	4,000	4,000
Total equity...........................	$41,800	$41,000	$41,000
Minority interest in net income	3,000	2,200	3,000
Consolidated net income	$38,800	$38,800	$38,000

Thus, fractional elimination yields the same consolidated net income for the period as 100 percent elimination with pro rata allocation (a result suggested by the same entries on the books of the parent company). In further contrast to 100 percent elimination with pro rata allocation, fractional elimination assigns $800 more to inventory (the cost to the parent company shareholders of the minority shareholders' interest in S Company's profit) and $800 more to the value of minority interest. On the other hand, the two 100 percent elimination alternatives assign the same value to inventory (the cost to the selling affiliate) but differ in the amounts assigned to majority and minority shareholders.

The differences between the three elimination methods disappear, of course, in periods following the confirmation of the intercompany profit.

Modified Fractional Elimination

In 1971, the Accounting Principles Board added yet another alternative to the set of "acceptable" methods of dealing with intercompany profits. In *Accounting Interpretation No. 1 of APB Opinion No. 18*, the Board approved, under specified conditions, the following practice:

> [in certain cases], it would be appropriate for the investor to eliminate intercompany profit in relation to the investor's common stock interest in the investee. In these cases, the percentage of intercompany profit to be elimi-

nated *would be the same* regardless of whether the transaction is "downstream" (i.e., a sale by the investor to the investee) or "upstream" (i.e., a sale by the investee to the investor.)[4]

This practice was instituted largely in response to situations where a "joint venture" participant engaged in a large construction project for the joint venture and deferral of all the profit on the project under the equity method would materially affect (distort?) the reported profit of the contractor. However, because of the strong interrelationship between the equity method of accounting and consolidation practices, this interpretation has important implications for the general problem of intercompany profits. Note that if the subsidiary (investee) were the selling affiliate, this new practice would be equivalent, in its income statement impact, to the application of either 100 elimination with pro rata allocation or fractional elimination. However, where the parent (investor) is the seller, all three of the other elimination methods require elimination of the total amount of the intercompany profit. Thus, a new alternative has been spawned by this interpretation. In general, the conditions required for this new alternative to be justified are (1) the exchange price specified in the transaction can be objectively verified as a reasonable value, (2) there is reasonable assurance of realization of the selling price, and (3) there is an effective sharing of the risk of ownership (e.g., the outside ownership interests in the investee must have supplied sufficient capital to bear any possible risk of loss). When these conditions are satisfied (and usually one would expect this only when the investee is not a majority-owned company) and this "modified fractional elimination method" is applied to sales by the parent to an affiliate, the parent's net income would be higher than it would be under the other elimination methods (because a portion of the intercompany profit is considered to be confirmed upon transfers of the asset to the investee).

The treatment of intercompany profits both in consolidation and under the equity method is at the present time subject to a variety of alternative methods. Fractional, or modified fractional, elimination has gained increased acceptance and support during the past decade, and the elimination of 100 percent of intercompany profit totally against the majority shareholders has probably been less frequently elected. This variety is the result of a series of largely uncoordinated developments over a 30-year period. Fortunately, the FASB in early 1982 initiated a project entitled "Accounting for the Reporting Entity, Including Consolidations, the Equity Method, and Related Matters." When completed, this project may bring a greater degree of order and consistency to this and other areas of consolidated financial statements.

---

[4] Ibid. (Emphasis supplied.)

Questions

1. Describe the general treatment of profits recognized on the sale of long-lived tangible assets or services between affiliates.

2. In the event that profit exists in assets purchased from an affiliated company, what elections exist under the provisions of *Accounting Research Bulletin No. 51*, "Consolidated Statements," regarding the elimination of this intercompany profit?

3. Assuming that intercompany profits on sales of property, plant, and equipment or on sales of services are eliminated in full (100 percent), what is the impact on consolidated net income of the decision to allocate the eliminated profit pro rata between majority and minority shareholders rather than wholly against the majority shareholders? What is the impact upon the assets acquired from affiliates of this choice? What is the impact upon minority interest in income of this choice?

4. Why is it important to distinguish between upstream and downstream asset transfers in the analysis of confirmed or unconfirmed intercompany profits?

5. In what manner is the intercompany profit arising from the sale of plant and equipment "confirmed" or "realized" from the point of view of the consolidated, or economic, entity?

6. In what manner is the intercompany profit arising from the sale of nondepreciable assets such as land "confirmed" or "realized" from the point of view of the consolidated, or economic, entity?

7. In what manner is the intercompany profit arising from the sale of services that are capitalized on the books of the purchasing entity "confirmed" or "realized" from the point of view of the consolidated, or economic, entity?

8. What is the relationship between an affiliate's confirmed and reported incomes (from operations) in the year it was the seller of plant and equipment generating an unconfirmed intercompany profit? In a year in which a portion of the previously unconfirmed profit is confirmed? Over the total period of time encompassing sale and subsequent confirmations of the intercompany profit?

9. How is the calculation of consolidated net income using the incremental approach modified by the existence of intercompany profits on the sale of plant and equipment?

10. What is the effect of an unconfirmed profit on the sale of plant and equipment between affiliates on the end-of-period proportional relationship between the balance of the investment account (carried under the equity method) and the recorded net assets of a subsidiary? On the end-of-period proportional relationship between the total minority interest and the recorded net assets of the subsidiary?

11. What are the two alternative treatments of intercompany profits on assets transferred between companies prior to their affiliation?

12. Assuming the affiliates file separate income tax returns, how are income taxes paid by the selling affiliate on intercompany profits treated in the consolidated statements and the equity "pickup"?

13(A). Assuming that fractional elimination of intercompany profits is applied, what is the impact on consolidated net income relative to 100 percent elimination with pro rata allocation to majority and minority shareholders? What is the impact upon the asset acquired from the affiliate? What is the impact upon minority interest in net income?

14(A). What general conditions must be satisfied in order to eliminate (or defer) only the parent's interest in intercompany profits on asset transfers from the parent to an affiliate?

Exercises

Exercise 8–1

Select the best answer for each of the following questions:

1. Eltro Company acquired a 70 percent interest in the Samson Company in 19X2. For the years ended December 31, 19X3, and 19X4, Samson reported net income of $80,000 and $90,000, respectively. During 19X3, Samson sold merchandise to Eltro for $10,000 at a profit of $2,000. The merchandise was later resold by Eltro to outsiders for $15,000 during 19X4. Intercompany profits are allocated pro rata to majority and minority shareholders. For consolidation purposes what is the minority interest's share of Samson's net income for 19X3 and 19X4, respectively?
   a. $23,400 and $27,600.
   b. $24,000 and $27,000.
   c. $24,600 and $26,400.
   d. $26,000 and $25,000.

2. On January 1, 19X5, the Jonas Company sold equipment to its wholly owned subsidiary, Neptune Company, for $1,800,000. The equipment cost Jonas $2,000,000; accumulated depreciation at the time of sale was $500,000. Jonas was depreciating the equipment on the straight-line method over 20 years with *no* salvage value, a procedure that Neptune continued. On the consolidated balance sheet at December 31, 19X5, the cost and accumulated depreciation, respectively, should be—
   a. $1,500,000 and $600,000.
   b. $1,800,000 and $100,000.
   c. $1,800,000 and $500,000.
   d. $2,000,000 and $600,000.

(AICPA adapted)

Exercise 8–2

During its fiscal year ended October 31, 19X1, the S Company, a wholly owned subsidiary of the P Company, sold to the latter, at a profit, materials that it used in constructing a new building for its own use. State (a) how the profit on the sale of these materials should be treated in preparing the consolidated financial statements of the P Company and its subsidiary as of October 31, 19X1, and for the year then ended, respectively; and (b) how it should be treated in preparing financial statements in subsequent years.

(AICPA adapted)

Exercise 8–3

P Company has an 80 percent interest in the capital stock of S Company. On January 1, 19X1, S Company sold equipment, which cost $100,000 ten years ago, to P Company for $80,000. The original estimate of service life was 20 years, and P Company decided that a remaining life of 10 years was reasonable.

During 19X1 and 19X2, the companies' reported incomes from their own operations were P Company, $50,000, and S Company, $40,000. P Company uses the equity method, and intercompany profits are allocated pro rata to majority and minority shareholders.

Required:
a. Prepare eliminating entries related to the asset transfer for a consolidated statement working paper on December 31, 19X1.
b. Prepare eliminating entries related to the asset transfer for a consolidated statement working paper on December 31, 19X2.
c. Prepare a schedular calculation of consolidated net income for 19X1 and 19X2.
d. Calculate minority interest in net income for 19X1 and 19X2.

Exercise 8–4

P Company acquired 80 percent of the capital stock of S Company on January 1, 19X1. On January 1, 19X4, equipment originally costing S Company $60,000 ten years ago was sold to P Company for $70,000. Accumulated depreciation to the date of sale (based upon a 60-year service life) was $10,000. The net incomes of the companies from their own operations were as follows:

	19X4	19X5
P Company	$40,000	$45,000
S Company	38,000	25,000

P Company uses the equity method, and intercompany profits are allocated pro rata to majority and minority shareholders.

Required:
a. Prepare eliminating entries in respect to the equipment transfer for consolidated statement working papers for the years ended December 31, 19X4, and 19X5.
b. Calculate the minority interest in net income for 19X4 and 19X5.
c. Calculate consolidated net income for 19X4 and 19X5.

Exercise 8–5

On January 1, 19X1, Ninemeier Company purchased 90 percent of Black Company's outstanding stock. On January 2, 19X1, Black sold a truck to Ninemeier for $15,000; the truck was carried on Black's books at a cost of $18,000 and accumulated depreciation of $12,000. The truck was expected to have a remaining life of five years, which was consistent with the 15-year life that Black had originally estimated.

The two firms each reported net income from their own operations of $30,000 during 19X1 and 19X2. Ninemeier Company uses the equity method to account for its investment in Black, and intercompany profits are allocated pro rata to majority and minority shareholders.

Required:
a. Prepare the entries that would be made by Ninemeier Company in 19X1 and 19X2 to record its equity in Black's earnings.
b. Prepare the eliminating entries relating to the truck transfer for 19X1 and 19X2 consolidated statement working papers.
c. Prepare a schedular calculation of consolidated net income for 19X1 and 19X2.
d. Calculate minority interest in Black's net income for 19X1 and 19X2.

Exercise 8–6

P Company owns 80 percent of the capital stock of S Company. For the year ended December 31, 19X1, P Company and S Company reported net incomes from their own operations of $24,000 and $5,000, respectively. The January 1, 19X1, inventory of P Company included $1,000 of profit recorded by S Company on 19X0 sales. During 19X1, P Company and S Company made intercompany sales of $5,000 and $10,000, respectively. Both companies have a gross profit rate (on selling price) on intercompany sales of 20 percent. The ending inventory of P Company included $1,000 of goods purchased from S Company, while S Company's ending inventory included $1,500 of goods purchased from P Company.

P Company uses the equity method to account for its investment in S Company, and intercompany profits are allocated pro rata to majority and minority shareholders.

The affiliates file *separate income tax returns,* and thus have to take the income tax deferral into consideration in dealing with intercompany profits. The applicable income tax rate is assumed to be 25 percent.

Required:
a. Prepare the 19X1 entries that would be recorded by P Company in connection with its investment in S Company.
b. Prepare the eliminating entries relating to the intercompany merchandise sales for a 19X1 consolidated statement working paper.
c. Calculate minority interest in S Company's 19X1 net income.
d. Prepare a schedular calculation of consolidated net income for 19X1.

Exercise 8–7

P Company holds 90 percent of the outstanding stock of S Company. On January 1, 19X1, S Company sold equipment to P Company for $25,000 that had a cost of $40,000 and accumulated depreciation of $20,000. The equipment has a remaining life of two years.

P Company uses the equity method to account for its investment in S Company, and intercompany profits are allocated pro rata to majority and minority shareholders. During 19X1 and 19X2, each of the companies reported net income from their own operations of $10,000.

The affiliates file *separate income tax returns,* and thus have to take the income tax deferral into consideration in dealing with intercompany profits. The applicable income tax rate is assumed to be 40 percent.

Required:

a. Prepare the 19X1 and 19X2 entries that would be recorded by P Company in connection with its investment in S Company.
b. Prepare the eliminating entries relating to the intercompany sale of equipment for 19X1 and 19X2 consolidated statement working papers.
c. Calculate minority interest in S Company's 19X1 and 19X2 net income.
d. Prepare a schedular calculation of consolidated net income for 19X1 and 19X2.

Exercises for Appendix

Exercise 8–8(A)

P Company had a 60 percent interest in S Company. During 19X1, both companies reported net incomes from their own operations of $20,000. At the end of 19X1, there were unconfirmed inventory profits on which P Company was the seller of $5,000, and unconfirmed inventory profits on which S Company was the seller of $3,000. Ignore income taxes.

Required:

Prepare a schedular calculation of consolidated net income for 19X1 assuming:

a. One hundred percent elimination, all against the majority shareholders.
b. One hundred percent elimination, allocated pro rata between majority and minority shareholders.
c. Fractional elimination.
d. Modified fractional elimination (assume the general conditions for the applicability of this method are satisfied).

Exercise 8–9(A)

On January 1, 19X1, DFP Company entered into a joint venture with two other companies to manufacture and sell frisbees. The three companies plan to share profits from the joint venture equally.

During 19X1, DFP Company manufactured equipment for the joint venture. The equipment was delivered on December 31, 19X1, at a price of $225,000; DFP Company's manufacturing cost was $150,000. The equipment has an expected useful life of five years.

The joint venture began operations in 19X2 following the receipt of the equipment. It had no income or loss for 19X1, and $60,000 net income in 19X2.

DFP Company reported net income from its own operations (including the sale of the equipment to the joint venture) in 19X1 of $125,000. In 19X2, DFP Company's income from its own operations amounted to $100,000. Ignore income taxes.

Required:

a.   Calculate DFP Company's equity basis net income for 19X1 and 19X2, assuming that 100 percent of the "intercompany profit" is eliminated.

b.   Calculate DFP Company's equity basis net income for 19X1 and 19X2, assuming that "intercompany profits" are eliminated in accordance with the modified fractional method specified in *Accounting Interpretation No. 1 of APB Opinion No. 18.*

Problems

Problem 8–10

The Banner Corporation owns 80 percent of the capital stock of the Ribbon Company. On January 1, 19X1, the Ribbon Company sold fixed assets to the Banner Corporation for $45,000. These assets were purchased 10 years earlier by the Ribbon Company for $50,000. Accumulated depreciation for the ten years to the date of sale (estimated total service life of 25 years) amounted to $20,000.

On December 31, 19X2, the trial balances of the affiliates were as follows:

	Banner Corporation	Ribbon Company
Inventory (1/1)	$ 12,000	$ 10,000
Fixed assets	180,000	64,000
Other assets	115,620	149,700
Investment in Ribbon Company	139,680	
Dividends declared	10,000	8,000
Purchases	80,000	60,000
Expenses	12,000	7,400
	$549,300	$299,100
Liabilities	$ 23,000	$ 8,000
Accumulated depreciation	31,200	24,000
Sales	122,000	89,000
Equity in subsidiary earnings	14,800	
Capital stock	250,000	100,000
Retained earnings	108,300	78,100
	$549,300	$299,100
Inventory (12/31)	$ 13,500	$ 5,900

Banner Corporation uses the equity method to account for its investment in Ribbon Company. Intercompany profits are allocated pro rata between majority and minority shareholders.

Required:

Prepare a consolidated statement working paper for the year ended December 31, 19X2.

Problem 8–11

P Company acquired 90 percent of the stock of S Company on January 1, 19X1, in the open market for a cash payment of $78,500. On that date, the balances of S Company's shareholders' equity accounts were Capital Stock, $50,000, and Retained Earnings, $10,000.

An examination of S Company's assets and liabilities on January 1, 19X1, revealed that book values were equal to fair values for all except inventory, which had a book value of $12,000 and a fair value of $17,000. All of this inventory was sold in 19X1. Any goodwill arising from the combination should be amortized over 20 years.

P Company regularly sells merchandise to S Company, with a markup of 40 percent on selling price. During 19X5, intercompany sales amounted to $20,000, of which $6,000 remained in the ending inventory of S Company. Additionally, S Company's January 1, 19X5, inventory included $3,000 of merchandise purchased in the preceding year from P Company.

On January 2, 19X4, S Company sold a building to P Company for $50,000. On the date of sale, the building was carried on S Company's books (net of accumulated depreciation) at $40,000. The building was estimated to have a remaining life of 10 years on the date of sale.

P Company accounts for its investment in S Company using the equity method. You may assume that both companies have properly recorded all transactions and adjustments (including the adjustment of intercompany profits under the equity method of accounting).

The trial balances of the two companies at December 31, 19X5 are provided below:

	P Company	S Company
Other assets.................	$ 37,800	$110,000
Inventory (1/1/X5)	60,000	10,000
Building (net).................	40,000	
Investment in S Company	99,900	
Purchases.................	90,000	50,000
Expenses.................	70,000	20,000
Dividends declared...............	30,000	5,000
	$427,700	$195,000
Other liabilities	$ 40,000	$ 20,000
Capital stock	100,000	50,000
Retained earnings (1/1/X5)...........	80,000	50,000
Sales.................	200,000	75,000
Equity in subsidiary earnings	7,700	
	$427,700	$195,000
Inventory (12/31/X5)	$ 50,000	$ 15,000

Required:

a. Prepare a consolidated statement working paper for the year ended December 31, 19X5. Intercompany profits are to be eliminated using the total (100 percent) method, with pro rata allocation to majority and minority shareholders where appropriate.

b. Prepare a schedular calculation of consolidated net income for 19X5, using the incremental approach.

Problem 8–12

P Company owns 90 percent of the common stock of S Company. On December 31, 19X4, the trial balances of the affiliates were as follows:

	P Company	S Company
Cash.	$ 26,700	$ 45,000
Accounts receivable	30,000	120,000
Property, plant, and equipment	75,000	
Investment in S Company	149,850	
Inventory (1/1).	90,000	15,000
Purchases	135,000	75,000
Expenses.	105,000	30,000
Dividends declared.	45,000	7,500
	$656,550	$292,500
Accounts payable	$ 60,000	$ 30,000
Accumulated depreciation	15,000	
Common stock	150,000	75,000
Retained earnings.	120,000	75,000
Sales.	300,000	112,500
Equity in subsidiary earnings	11,550	
	$656,550	$292,500
Inventory (12/31).	$ 75,000	$ 22,500

At December 31, 19X3, the unamortized differential amounted to $24,000. This differential was totally assigned to goodwill, and the remaining life was 16 years.

S Company regularly sells to P Company. During 19X4, intercompany sales amounted to $30,000. At the beginning of 19X4, P Company's inventory included intercompany profits of $2,000; at December 31, 19X4, the intercompany profit in P Company's inventory was $4,000.

On January 2, 19X3, S Company sold a warehouse to P Company for $75,000. At that time, the warehouse was carried on S Company's books at a cost of $240,000 and accumulated depreciation of $180,000, and the remaining life of the warehouse was estimated to be 10 years. P Company accepts this estimate of the remaining life and plans to depreciate the asset using the straight-line method.

P Company accounts for its investment in S Company using the equity method. All transactions and adjustments have been properly recorded.

Required:

a. Prepare a consolidated statement working paper for the year ended December 31, 19X4. Intercompany profits are to be eliminated 100 percent, with pro rata allocation to majority and minority shareholders where appropriate.

b. Prepare a schedular calculation of consolidated net income for 19X4 using the incremental approach.

Problem 8–13

P Company holds a 60 percent interest in S Company. The ownership interest was acquired several years ago, and the differential has by now been fully amortized. Normally, the affiliates do not engage in intercompany transactions. However, on January 2, 19X1, S Company sold P Company some equipment it no longer needed for $46,500. On this date, the equipment had a cost of $72,000 and accumulated depreciation of $41,000. The equipment is estimated to have a remaining life of five years, and straight-line depreciation continues to be appropriate.

The trial balances of the affiliates at December 31, 19X1, were as follows:

	P Company	S Company
Other assets..........................	$ 397,420	$437,100
Plant and equipment.................	46,500	
Investment in S Company...........	238,080	
Inventory (1/1)	124,000	31,000
Purchases..........................	229,400	155,000
Expenses	46,500	15,500
Dividends declared	10,000	5,000
	$1,091,900	$643,600
Accumulated depreciation	$ 9,300	
Other liabilities.....................	214,520	65,100
Common stock	310,000	232,500
Retained earnings	134,000	82,500
Sales	372,000	248,000
Equity in subsidiary earnings	52,080	
Gain on sale of equipment...........		15,500
	$1,091,900	$643,600
Inventory (12/31)	$ 93,000	$ 37,200

P Company accounts for its investment in S Company using the equity method. Intercompany profits are eliminated 100 percent, with pro rata allocation to majority and minority shareholders where appropriate. All transactions and adjustments have been properly recorded by the parent company.

Required:

a. Prepare a consolidated statement working paper for the year ended December 31, 19X1.

b. Prepare a schedular calculation of consolidated net income for 19X1 using the incremental approach.

Problem 8–14

The Buckley Company purchased 80 percent of the capital stock of the Carson Company and 70 percent of the capital stock of the Diamond Company on January 1, 19X0.

Intercompany sales of merchandise during 19X1 were as follows:

From	To	Sales	Remaining in Purchaser's 12/31 Inventory
Buckley	Carson	$20,000	$2,000
Carson	Buckley	15,000	1,000
Diamond	Carson	30,000	5,000

Intercompany sales of merchandise during 19X0 include the following:

From	To	Sales	Remaining in Purchaser's 12/31 Inventory
Carson	Buckley	$10,000	$2,000
Diamond	Carson	12,000	3,000

Gross profit rates (based on selling price) for 19X0 and 19X1 were:

Buckley	20%
Carson	25
Diamond	30

During 19X1, the companies reported net income from their own operations as follows:

Buckley..............	$40,000
Carson	30,000
Diamond	20,000

The Buckley Company uses the equity method to account for its investments in Carson and Diamond, and intercompany profits are allocated pro rata to majority and minority shareholders.

The affiliates file *separate income tax returns,* and thus have to take the income tax deferral into consideration in dealing with intercompany profits. The applicable income tax rate is assumed to be 40 percent.

Required:
a. Calculate the intercompany profits, gross and net of taxes, in the beginning and ending 19X1 inventories.
b. Using the incremental approach, prepare a schedular calculation of consolidated net income for 19X1.

  c. Calculate the minority interest in 19X1 net income.
  d. Prepare the eliminating entries related to the intercompany merchandise transactions for a consolidated statement working paper at December 31, 19X1.
  e. Using the residual approach, prepare a schedular calculation of consolidated net income for 19X1.

Problem for Appendix

Problem 8–15(A)

Use the information of Problem 7–8, *except* now assume that Moyer Company uses the *fractional* elimination method for intercompany profits. With this change, complete the requirements enumerated in Problem 7–8. Additionally, as new requirement *(e)*, prepare a comparison of the differences in amounts that would appear in the consolidated financial statements using fractional elimination versus 100 percent elimination with pro rata allocation to majority and minority shareholders.

CHAPTER
9

Consolidated
Statements—
Preference Interests

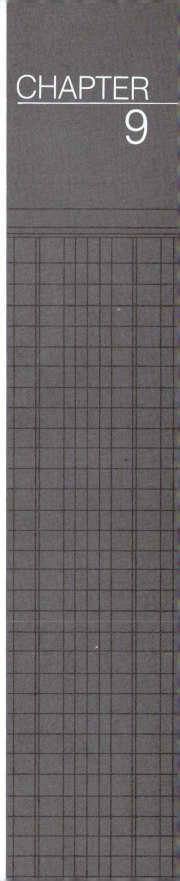

Intercompany Bonds

Whenever a corporation issues bonds and later retires the bonds before they mature, a gain or loss on the retirement of bonds may be recognized. A gain or loss occurs if the retirement price differs from the book value of the bonds on the date of retirement. A similar situation arises when one affiliate in a consolidated entity purchases the outstanding bonds of another affiliate. Consider the diagram below, which portrays aspects of a consolidated entity immediately before an intercompany bond transaction. The parent holds cash, and the subsidiary has outstanding a bond payable. The bond is held by an outside investor.

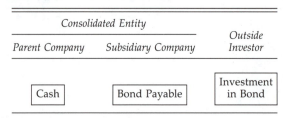

At this point in time, the consolidated entity has an asset (cash) and a liability (bond payable). Now assume the parent purchases the bond payable from the outside investor for cash. Immediately after this transaction, the diagram would be modified as follows:

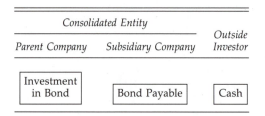

The parent's cash has now moved to the outside investor, and the investor's bond has moved to the parent. The consolidated entity has no liability to the outside investor, only an intercompany receivable and payable. Thus, from the point of view of the consolidated entity, the purchase of an affiliate's bonds by another affiliate constitutes retirement of the bonds. Accordingly, the consolidated statements should reflect this fact. The bond investment should not appear among the assets, the bond payable should not appear among the liabilities, and a gain or loss on bond retirement should appear on the income statement in the period the transaction takes place. The magnitude of this gain or loss is, of course, the difference between the carrying value of the liability and the cash sacrificed to liquidate it. For example, if the liability were carried at $1,000 par less $200 in unamortized discount, retirement of the bonds for $700 cash would give rise to gain in the amount of $100 (since a liability valued at $800 was liquidated by sacrificing an asset valued at only $700). As of the date of the intercompany bond transaction, this amount is necessarily equal to the difference between the carrying values of the intercompany receivable and payable.

Significantly, neither the purchasing affiliate nor the issuing affiliate records the gain or loss as such, although whichever affiliate is the parent will adjust its booking of "equity in subsidiary earnings" so that the parent's recorded net income will equal consolidated net income. Although the bonds are retired from a consolidated point of view, they are not retired from the point of view of either affiliate. The issuing affiliate continues to pay interest and to record the interest expense adjusted for any amortization of premium or discount on bonds payable. Also, the purchasing affiliate records the receipt of interest as Bond Interest Income and then adjusts that income to reflect amortization of any premium or discount on bond investment.

Intercompany Bonds and the Equity Method

Recall that the equity method of accounting is, in essence, a "one-line consolidation." This means that the parent's entries under the equity method are designed to result in net income for the parent that equals consolidated net income. Thus, as mentioned above, a consolidated basis "gain or loss on purchase of affiliate's bonds" must be recorded by the parent under the equity method. A simplified example should emphasize this point.

Case 1. Suppose the P Company bought 100 percent of S Company's outstanding stock on December 31, 19X0, paying book value. S Company has bonds outstanding that were issued at par, $10,000, and that pay *no* cash interest. Neither affiliate had any transactions during 19X1, 19X2, or 19X3, except that P Company purchased the outstanding bonds of S Company on December 31, 19X1, paying $9,700. The bonds mature in two years, on December 31, 19X3.

Entries on the Books of S Company—19X1, 19X2, and 19X3. Consider the entries that would be made on the books of S Company, the issuer of the bonds. Normally, a corporation that issues bonds must record the cash payment of interest each year and also record the amortization of premium or discount on bonds payable. But, S Company issued the bonds at par, and the bonds in this case do not pay any interest. Also, it was assumed that no other transactions occurred. Thus, S Company would not record any entries in 19X1 or 19X2. In 19X3, the only entry on S Company's books would be to record the payment of $10,000 cash upon the maturing of the bonds, as follows:

Bonds Payable. 10,000
    Cash   10,000

Entries on the Books of P Company—19X1.   Now consider the entries that would be made on the books of P Company. The first entry would be to record the purchase of the bonds on December 31, 19X1, and would appear as follows:

Investment in S Company Bonds.	10,000	
Discount on Bond Investment		300
Cash		9,700

Since S Company had no transactions in 19X1, P Company would record its equity in S Company's reported net income as follows:

Investment in S Company Stock	–0–	
Equity in Subsidiary Earnings (100% × $0)		–0–

But, from a consolidated entity point of view, the bonds were retired at a gain of $300, that is, $10,000 − $9,700. Later in the chapter, elimination entries are discussed that result in the reporting of this gain on the consolidated income statement. Since this $300 gain is included in consolidated net income, it must be recognized by P Company under the equity method. To accomplish this, P Company would record the following entry:

Investment in S Company Stock	300	
Equity in Subsidiary Earnings		300

As a consequence of this entry, P Company would report its equity in subsidiary earnings to be $0 + $300 = $300. Given that P Company had no other transactions, its net income would be $300, which equals consolidated net income.

Entries on the Books of P Company—19X2.   Since P Company's investment in bonds does not generate any cash receipts from interest, the normal entry to record the receipt of cash would not be necessary. However, the bonds have only two more years until maturity, and the discount on bond investment must be amortized over two years. Assuming straight-line amortization of interest,[1] the entry to record the amortization would be as follows:

Discount on Bond Investment	150	
Bond Interest Income		150

Recall that from a consolidated entity point of view, the entire $300 discount on bond investment was a "gain on purchase of affiliate's bonds,"

---

[1] In order to simplify the discussion and to focus attention upon the consolidation process and the development of appropriate elimination entries, the examples of this chapter assume that amortization of premium or discount on bonds payable and on bond investments are calculated by the straight-line method. However, the reader should remember that *APB Opinion No. 21* requires that premium or discount on bonds payable and on bond investments be amortized according to the "interest" method, whereby a constant interest rate (the effective rate) is applied to the beginning-of-year carrying value to determine the total interest expense or income for the period. The cash transfer of interest is then subtracted from the expense or income to determine the current year's amortization of premium or discount. Other methods such as straight-line amortization may be used only if the results do not materially differ from those obtained under the interest method.

and it was reported on the consolidated income statement for 19X1. Also, since the equity method is a one-line consolidation, P Company recorded the entire $300 gain last year as part of its "equity in subsidiary earnings." Therefore, P Company's 19X2 entry to amortize the discount amounts to a double counting of $150 gain on the books of P Company. To avoid this double counting, and to continue with the requirement that P Company's net income must equal consolidated net income, the equity method entries in 19X2 are designed to offset the amortization entry. The equity method entries are as follows:

To record P Company's equity in S Company's reported net income:

Investment in S Company Stock	–0–	
Equity in Subsidiary Earnings (100% × $0)		–0–

To offset the amortization of discount on bond investment:

Equity in Subsidiary Earnings	150	
Investment in S Company Stock		150

Entries on the Books of P Company—19X3.

P Company's entries in 19X3 would parallel those made in 19X2. The discount on bond investment would be amortized as follows:

Discount on Bond Investment	150	
Bond Interest Income		150

Entries under the equity method would be as follows:

Investment in S Company Stock	–0–	
Equity in Subsidiary Earnings (100% × $0)		–0–

Equity in Subsidiary Earnings	150	
Investment in S Company Stock		150

Finally, P Company would record the receipt of cash from S Company upon the maturing of the bonds, as follows:

Cash	10,000	
Investment in S Company Bonds		10,000

To summarize the effects of these entries on the books of P Company, consider first the impact on net income in each year and in total. These effects are shown in the following table:

	Net Income Effect of Discount Amortization	Net Income Effect of Equity Method Entries	Combined Net Income Effect
19X1	–0–	$+300	$+300
19X2	$+150	–150	–0–
19X3	+150	–150	–0–
Total	$+300	–0–	$+300

Note also the effects of these entries on the Investment in S Company Stock account. Initially, the equity method entry on December 31, 19X1, had the effect of increasing the Investment in S Company Stock balance by $300. This $300 increase in the equity in S Company's net assets resulted from effectively retiring $10,000 of S Company's debt at a price of $9,700. The equity method entries in 19X2 and 19X3 reduced the balance in the Investment in S Company Stock account by $150 each year, so that the effect of the intercompany bonds was eventually eliminated from that account. However, a $150 decrease in Discount on Bond Investment was also recorded each of the two years. The net effect of these two sets of entries was to recognize a change in the *form* of the $300 asset from Investment in S Company Stock to Investment in S Company Bonds. When the bonds were redeemed at maturity, the *form* of the asset again changed to cash.

Entries and Eliminations at Date of Purchase

The facts of Case 1 were obviously simplified; the bonds paid no cash interest, they were issued at par, and neither affiliate had any transactions other than those relating to the bonds. Nevertheless, from the discussion of Case 1, it is apparent that intercompany bondholdings require special elimination entries when preparing consolidated statements.

Consider the eliminations that would be required if one affiliate purchased another affiliate's bonds on the last day of the accounting period and consolidated statements were to be prepared. To remove the intercompany indebtedness, it is conventional to eliminate the *par* value of the bond investment and the *par* value of the bond liability, as follows:

Bonds Payable... (par)		
Investment in Bonds..	(par)	

At the date of the bond acquisition, the above elimination would leave any premium or discount on bonds payable *and* premium or discount on bond investment as amounts yet to be eliminated. Most frequently, the intercompany bonds would have been issued at some previous date to outside parties; the current acquisition of the bonds by the purchasing affiliate would therefore be made from outside parties. As a consequence, the current amount of premium or discount on bonds payable may be substantially different from the amount of discount or premium on bond investment. The algebraic sum of these items determines the consolidated basis gain or loss on the purchase of intercompany bonds. This is, of course, equivalent to the previous statement that the gain or loss is calculated as the difference between the carrying value of the bond liability and the acquisition cost of the bond investment. Elimination entries that remove these premium or discount balances also accomplish the recognition of the gain or loss on the consolidated income statement.

Case 2.   Y Company issued $5,000 (par) bonds payable several years ago at a premium. After several years of amortization, at the current date, the premium on bonds payable account has a remaining balance of $250. At the current date, X Company (Y Company's parent) has acquired these bonds in the open market at a price of $5,140, recording the purchase as follows:

Investment in Y Company Bonds	5,000	
Premium on Bond Investment	140	
Cash		5,140

The consolidated basis gain on the purchase of these intercompany bonds is calculated as $110 ($5,250 carrying value less $5,140 purchase price). The elimination entries for consolidated working papers at the date of purchase are as follows:

Bonds Payable	5,000	
Investment in Y Company Bonds		5,000
Premium on Bonds Payable	250	
Loss [Gain] on Purchase of Affiliate's Bonds		250
Loss [Gain] on Purchase of Affiliate's Bonds	140	
Premium on Bond Investment		140

Analysis of Gain or Loss

Upon recognition of a gain or loss on the purchase of intercompany bonds, it then becomes necessary to determine an appropriate allocation of the gain or loss between the purchasing and issuing affiliates in order to measure their confirmed incomes. Should one or both of the affiliates have minority stockholders, the allocation of gain or loss will affect the calculations of minority interest in combined net income and thus the determination of consolidated net income.

It may be argued that the total gain or loss should be allocated to the company that issued the bonds. The purchasing company would thus be perceived as simply an *agent* for the issuing affiliate; given this interpretation, the act of purchasing is deemed to be on behalf of the issuing firm which is the principal to the transaction. On the other hand, it can be argued that the gain or loss should be allocated entirely to the purchasing affiliate. In this instance, emphasis is placed on the purchase transaction, which is regarded as the critical event giving rise to the gain or loss. This event being undertaken by the purchasing affiliate, it follows that the gain or loss should be attributed to the purchaser.

However, neither of these alternatives is consistent with the basic principle underlying the measurement of affiliates' confirmed incomes. In calculating the confirmed income of an affiliate, we merely defer (for unconfirmed profits on asset transfers) or accelerate (for gain or loss on constructive retirement of bonds) amounts that the affiliate has reported or will report as income (or expense) in its individual financial statements. Referring back to the Case 2 data, neither X nor Y will report $110 "income" over the life of the bonds. Therefore, the total (net) gain cannot be allocated to only one of the affiliates; both must share in the allocation.

A consistent method of allocating the gain or loss between affiliates is produced by measuring each affiliate's gain or loss relative to the par value of the bonds (that is, as if the bonds had been retired at their par value). Thus, the gain or loss of the issuing affiliate is determined by comparing the carrying value of the bond liability (at the date the bonds are acquired by the purchasing affiliate) with the par value. Similarly, the gain or loss of the purchasing affiliate is determined by comparing its purchase price with par value. In other words, at the date of purchase, any premium on intercompany bonds payable represents gain to the issuing company; similarly, a discount on intercompany bonds payable would represent loss to the issuing company. A premium on bond investment represents a loss to the purchasing company; a discount on bond investment represents a gain. The algebraic sum of gains or losses of both affiliates constitutes the total consolidated basis gain or loss. In our example, Y Company would be allocated a $250 gain and X Company would be allocated a $140 loss, which sum to a net gain of $110.

To understand this preferred allocation, consider the nature of the accounts Premium on Bond Investment and Premium on Bonds Payable. Premium on Bond Investment represents an amount that will eventually be transformed (through amortization) into debits to Interest Income on future separate company income statements of X Company. Premium on Bonds Payable represents an amount that will eventually be transformed (through amortization) into credits to Interest Expense on future separate company income statements of Y Company. That is, X Company's future income will be reduced by $140, and Y Company's future income will be increased by $250.

X Company		Y Company	
Premium on Bond Investment	Transformed into debits in future separate company income statements	**Premium on Bonds Payable**	Transformed into credits in future separate company income statements
$140		$250	

The algebraic sum of the effects of future amortization is the \$110 gain on the intercompany bond transaction. Thus, the recording of the gain in consolidation merely constitutes an acceleration of a $250 - \$140 = \$110$ net credit from future separate company statements to the current consolidated statements. It is illogical for the *time* in which elements of income appear on financial statements to affect their allocation between majority and minority shareholders. Under the preferred method, \$140 is allocated to X Company and \$250 to Y; and the allocation of gain or loss between majority and minority shareholders is not affected by the mere movement of elements of income from the future to the present. In this sense, the preferred allocation is consistent with the treatment explained in Chapters 7 and 8 for measuring an affiliate's confirmed income when there are intercompany profits on asset transfers.

Of course, the above analysis assumes an allocation of intercompany profits pro rata between majority and minority shareholders. Should one wish to allocate such "consolidated basis" gains or losses wholly to the majority shareholders, calculation of the individual affiliates' confirmed income is unnecessary. The entire gain or loss (\$110 gain in our example) is allocated to the majority shareholders, regardless of its source.

Entries and Eliminations after Date of Purchase

After the date of purchase, the issuing and purchasing affiliates will necessarily record cash transfers of interest. At consolidation points, such accumulations of intercompany interest expense and revenue should be eliminated against each other. Additionally, it may be necessary to eliminate reciprocal accounts of interest receivable and interest payable. The par value of bonds payable and bond investment must also be eliminated, as previously discussed.

As each period passes, the issuing affiliate records amortization of any premium or discount on bonds payable. But, in the consolidated statements, the full amount of the premium or discount existing on the date of purchase was recognized as gain or loss. Thus, the subsequent amortizations of premium or discount would constitute *double* counting of the gain or loss, unless they are eliminated. The current amortization of premium or discount, which shows up as an adjustment to Bond Interest Expense, therefore must be eliminated in preparing the consolidated working paper each year. Any unamortized premium or discount on bonds payable that remains at the end of the period must also be eliminated. If the bonds were purchased before the end of a period, the amortization of premium or discount as well as any remaining premium or discount balance are eliminated against the gain or loss account. In subsequent periods, when the issuing affiliate is a subsidiary with a minority interest outstanding, the minority interest's equity in the eliminated amortization plus remaining premium or discount is eliminated against an account called Minority Interest in Confirmed but Unrecorded (1/1) Retained Earnings. The parent's interest in the amortization plus the remaining premium or discount was booked by the parent under the equity method as an adjustment to the carrying value of the Investment in Subsidiary Stock account. Hence, the parent's interest is eliminated against the Investment in Subsidiary Stock account.

The entries and eliminations relating to a purchasing affiliate are generally parallel to those for the issuing affiliate. As each period passes, the purchasing affiliate records amortization of any premium or discount on bond investment. Nevertheless, the full amount of premium or discount on bond investment that resulted from the bond purchase was previously recognized as loss or gain in the consolidated statements. Once again, the subsequent amortizations of premium or discount would constitute double counting of the loss or gain, unless they are eliminated. Where the purchasing affiliate is the parent, the equity method entries also recognize the loss or gain on the books of the parent, adjusting the Investment in Subsidiary Stock account for the parent's equity in the loss or gain. Furthermore, in subsequent periods, the equity method entries offset the amortizations of premium or discount on bond investment with corresponding adjustments to the Investment in Subsidiary Stock account. Thus, when the current amortization plus the remaining unamortized premium or discount are eliminated, the elimination should be against the Investment in Subsidiary Stock account.

The following case is used to illustrate the entries booked by the affiliates and the eliminations necessary to prepare consolidated statements. Observe that the facts of Case 3 involve an expansion of those presented in Case 2.

Case 3.   Subsidiary Company's Bonds Completely Acquired by Parent.   On January 1, 1978, Y Company issued $5,000 (par), 9 percent bonds, due January 1, 1988. Interest is payable semiannually on July 1 and January 1. The cash proceeds from the issue were $6,250, and the $1,250 premium is being amortized at the rate of $125 per year. On January 1, 1985, at which date Y Company had common stock of $100,000 and both companies had zero retained earnings, X Company purchased 80 percent of Y Company's outstanding stock for $80,000. On December 31, 1985, X Company purchased the Y Company bonds at a cost of $5,140 plus $225 accrued interest for six months.

Before the eliminations to prepare consolidated statements can be understood, the entries booked by each of the affiliates must be absolutely clear in the reader's mind. Consider first the entries made on the books of Y Company.

Entries on the Books and the Issuing (Subsidiary) Affiliate.   When Y Company first issued the bonds on January 1, 1978, it recorded the issuance as follows:

Cash	6,250	
Bonds Payable		5,000
Premium on Bonds Payable		1,250

During the period 1978 through 1984, Y Company recorded cash payments of interest each year that amounted to 9 percent × $5,000 = $450. In addition, it amortized $125 of premium on bonds payable each year. The sequence of entries each year, beginning with the July 1 payment of interest, were exactly like the following entries for 1985 (and January 1, 1986):

On July 1, 1985:

| Interest Expense | 225 | |
| Cash | | 225 |

On December 31, 1985:

| Interest Expense | 225 | |
| Accrued Interest Payable | | 225 |

| Premium on Bonds Payable | 125 | |
| Interest Expense ($1,250/10 years = $125) | | 125 |

On January 1, 1985:

| Accrued Interest Payable | 225 | |
| Cash | | 225 |

Even though Y Company's bonds were purchased by an affiliate on December 31, 1985, Y Company would still consider the bonds to be outstanding and would continue making entries such as the above until the bonds matured on January 1, 1988. At that time the repayment of the bonds would be recorded with an additional entry, as follows:

On January 1, 1988:

| Bonds Payable | 5,000 | |
| Cash | | 5,000 |

Entries on the Books of the Purchasing (Parent) Affiliate—1985. Entries on the books of X Company reflect the normal recordings of a bondholder and also the equity method entries resulting from its parent-subsidiary relationship with Y Company. The equity method entries obviously must be based on Y Company's reported net incomes, which are as follows:

	1985	1986
Y Company's net income, excluding the effects of interest	$20,000	$10,000
Cash payments of interest (9% × $5,000 = $450)	−450	−450
Amortization of premium on bonds payable	+125	+125
Reported net incomes	$19,675	$ 9,675

Based on these facts, the entries made on the books of X Company during 1985 are as follows:

On January 1, 1985 (to record the purchase of Y Company stock):

Investment in Y Company Stock 80,000
    Cash   80,000

On December 31, 1985 (to record the purchase of Y Company bonds):

Investment in Y Company Bonds   5,000
Premium on Bond Investment   140
Accrued Interest Receivable.   225
    Cash   5,365

On December 31, 1985 (to record its equity in Y Company's reported net income), X Company made the following entry:

Investment in Y Company Stock (80% × $19,675). 15,740
    Equity in Subsidiary Earnings.   15,740

On a consolidated basis, the bonds were retired on December 31, 1985, and the existing premium on bonds payable is "gain" attributed to the issuing, subsidiary company. The remaining balance in the Premium on Bonds Payable account is $250 on December 31, 1985; that is, $1,250 − (8 × $125) = $250. Under the equity method, X Company must record its equity in the consolidated basis gain attributed to Y Company, as follows:

Investment in Y Company Stock (80% × $250)   200
    Equity in Subsidiary Earnings.   200

In addition, under the equity method, X Company must record the consolidated basis gain or loss attributed to itself as the purchaser of the bonds. Since the bonds were purchased at a premium of $140, that is the amount of the loss, and X Company's equity therein is, of course, 100 percent. The entry is:

Equity in Subsidiary Earnings.   140
    Investment in Y Company Stock   140

To summarize the results of the previously discussed entries by Y Company and by X Company, and also to disclose additional information about the net income of X Company resulting from its own operations, the relevant account balances of the two companies are presented on the following page:

	December 31, 1985	
Accounts	X Company Dr. [Cr.]	Y Company Dr. [Cr.]
Bonds payable, 9%		$ [5,000]
Premium on bonds payable		[250]
Accrued interest payable...........................		[225]
Interest expense....................................		325
Other income accounts, excluding the effects of interest and excluding equity in subsidiary earnings.............................	$[30,000]	[20,000]
Investment in Y Company bonds	5,000	
Premium on bond investment	140	
Accrued interest receivable........................	225	
Investment in Y Company stock ($80,000 + $15,740 + $200 − $140)................	95,800	
Equity in subsidiary earnings ($15,740 + $200 − $140).........................	[15,800]	

Bond Elimination Schedule.   A schedule of eliminations in respect to the intercompany bonds is presented in Illustration 9–1. The bond elimination schedule presents a complete summarization of the bond elimination entries that must be made on successive consolidation dates starting with the date of bond acquisition and terminating on the day before the bonds mature. However, at this point, concentrate on the December 31, 1985, columns of the schedule.

The top half of Illustration 9–1 summarizes each affiliate's account balances related to bonds, the eliminations that must be made in the consolidation process, and the resultant amounts that appear on consolidated financial statements. The bottom half of the schedule presents (in general journal form) the elimination entries that are entered on consolidated working papers to accomplish the results disclosed in the top half of the schedule.

It is evident that the consolidated basis gain (or loss) on the purchase of intercompany bonds should be recognized in the year of acquisition. In Illustration 9–1, this gain of $110 is entered on the consolidated income statement for 1985. The $325 interest expense ($450 cash transfer less $125 amortization of premium on bonds payable) for 1985 is extended to the Consolidated Amounts column because the bonds were held throughout 1985 by outside parties. Since X Company paid those outside parties the last six months' interest ($225) as a part of its purchase price, Accrued Interest Receivable and Accrued Interest Payable are reciprocal accounts between the affiliates and must be eliminated.

A partial consolidated working paper for 1985 is presented in Illustration 9–2. The reader is encouraged to review the initial facts of Case 3 presented

Illustration 9–1

BOND ELIMINATION SCHEDULE—Dr. [Cr.]

	December 31, 1985			December 31, 1986			December 31, 1987		
	Recorded Amounts	Eliminated Amounts	Consolidated Amounts	Recorded Amounts	Eliminated Amounts	Consolidated Amounts	Recorded Amounts	Eliminated Amounts	Consolidated Amounts
Accounts on the books of X Company:									
Investment in Y Company bonds	$ 5,000	$[5,000]	-0-	$ 5,000	$[5,000]	-0-	$ 5,000	$[5,000]	-0-
Premium on bond investment	140	[140]	-0-	70	[70]	-0-	-0-	-0-	-0-
Bond interest income	-0-	-0-	-0-	[380]	380	-0-	[380]	380	-0-
Accrued interest receivable	225	[225]	-0-	225	[225]	-0-	225	[225]	-0-
Accounts on the books of Y Company:									
Bonds payable	[5,000]	5,000	-0-	[5,000]	5,000	-0-	[5,000]	5,000	-0-
Premium on bonds payable	[250]	250	-0-	[125]	125	-0-	-0-	-0-	-0-
Bond interest expense	325	-0-	$ 325	325	[325]	-0-	325	[325]	-0-
Accrued interest payable	[225]	225	-0-	[225]	225	-0-	[225]	225	-0-
Account created by elimination entries:									
Loss [gain] on purchase of bonds	-0-	[110]	[110]	-0-	-0-	-0-	-0-	-0-	-0-

Below are elimination entries to accomplish the above:

	December 31, 1985		December 31, 1986		December 31, 1987	
	Debit	Credit	Debit	Credit	Debit	Credit
Bonds Payable	5,000		5,000		5,000	
Investment in Y Company Bonds		5,000		5,000		5,000
Accrued Interest Payable	255		225		225	
Accrued Interest Receivable		225		225		225
Bond Interest Income			450		450	
Bond Interest Expense				450		450
Loss [Gain] on Purchase of Bonds	140					
Premium on Bond Investment		140				
Premium on Bonds Payable	250					
Loss [Gain] on Purchase of Bonds		250				
Investment in Y Company Stock			140		70	
Premium on Bond Investment				70		
Bond Interest Income				70		70
Premium on Bonds Payable			125			
Bond Interest Expense			125		125	
Investment in Y Company Stock				200		100
Minority Interest in Confirmed but						
Unrecorded (1/1) Retained Earnings				50		25

Illustration 9–2

X COMPANY AND SUBSIDIARY Y COMPANY
Partial Consolidated Statement Working Paper
For Year Ended December 31, 1985

	X Company	Y Company	Eliminations Dr.	Eliminations Cr.	Minority Interest	Consolidated
Income Statement						
Net income, before interest and equity in subsidiary earnings	30,000	20,000				50,000
Equity in subsidiary earnings	15,800		(5) 15,800			–0–
[.8($19,675 + $250) − $140]						
Interest expense		[325]				[325]
Gain on purchase of affiliate's bonds			(3) 140	(4) 250		110
Net income	45,800	19,675				49,785
Minority interest						
.2($19,675 + $250)					3,985	[3,985]
Net income—carried foreward	45,800	19,675	15,940	250	3,985	45,800
Retained Earnings Statement						
Retained earnings, 1/1/85:						
X Company	–0–					
Y Company		–0–	(6) –0–			
Net income—brought forward	45,800	19,675	15,940	250	3,985	45,800
Retained earnings, 12/31/85— carried forward	45,800	19,675	15,940	250	3,985	45,800
Balance Sheet						
Debits:						
Investment in Y Company stock	95,800			(5) 15,800		–0–
				(6) 80,000		
Investment in Y Company bonds	5,000			(1) 5,000		–0–
Premium on bond investment	140			(3) 140		–0–
Accrued interest receivable	225			(2) 225		–0–
Credits:						
Bonds payable		5,000	(1) 5,000			–0–
Premium on bonds payable		250	(4) 250			–0–
Accrued interest payable		225	(2) 225			–0–
Common Stock—Y Company		100,000	(6) 80,000		20,000	–0–

[deduction]

on page 354 and to review the entries booked by each affiliate, and then to confirm the correctness of the balances in the first two columns of Illustration 9–2. Next, observe the elimination entries in Illustration 9–2. The entries numbered (1) through (4) are the same as those shown in the December 31, 1985, columns of Illustration 9–1. The elimination entries numbered (5) and (6) are the standard investment elimination entries. Entry (5) reverses the effects of the equity method bookings in 1985, as follows:

Equity in Subsidiary Earnings..................................15,800
　　Investment in Y Company Stock ....　　　15,800

And entry (6) eliminates the parent's remaining investment account balance against the parent's equity in the subsidiary's reported stockholders' equity accounts at acquisition, as follows:

Common Stock—Y Company....................................80,000
Retained Earnings—Y Company ....–0–
　　Investment in Y Company Stock ....　　　80,000

Entries on the Books of the Purchasing (Parent) Affiliate—1986.
During 1986, X Company received cash interest from Y Company and recorded the receipts as follows:

On January 1, 1986:

Cash 225
　　Accrued Interest Receivable................................　　225

By the year-end, X Company had earned another half-year's accrued interest, which was recorded as follows:

On December 31, 1986:

Accrued Interest Receivable.................................... 225
　　Interest Income...　　225

X Company also needed to record the annual amortization of premium on bond investment. Since the original premium was $140, and the bonds had two years to maturity, the first year's amortization was recorded as follows:

On December 31, 1986:

Interest Income... 70
　　Premium on Bond Investment ....　　70

Finally, X Company needed to record its equity in subsidiary earnings for 1986. Y Company's reported net income for 1986 was $9,675 (see page 355), and X Company's 80 percent equity therein is $9,675 × 80 percent = $7,740. The entry to record X Company's equity in Y Company's *reported* net income is:

On December 31, 1986:

Investment in Y Company Stock 7,740
　　Equity in Subsidiary Earnings..............................　　7,740

Recall that under the equity method, the 1985 net income of X Company included its equity in the net gain on purchase of affiliate's bonds. That was $140 loss attributed to X Company as the purchaser of the bonds and 80 percent of the $250 gain attributed to Y Company as the issuer of the bonds. But, in 1986, X Company also recorded amortization of premium on bond investment in the amount of $70. To prevent double counting of this item on X Company's books, the equity method entries for 1986 must include the following:

On December 31, 1986:

Investment in Y Company Stock	70	
Equity in Subsidiary Earnings		70

Also, Y Company's reported net income in 1986 included amortization of premium on bonds payable in the amount of $125, and X Company recorded 80 percent of this amount in the process of booking its equity in the reported net income of Y Company. Double counting of this item on X Company's books is prevented by the following entry:

Equity in Subsidiary Earnings	100	
Investment in Y Company Stock		100

Bond Elimination Schedule—Subsequent Years.   Return your attention to the bond elimination schedule in Illustration 9–1 on page 358. In years subsequent to the year of purchase, consolidated net income should not include any of the premium amortizations recorded by the affiliates. Since the total amount of those premiums was included in the gain reported in 1985, the inclusion of future premium amortizations would constitute double counting of the gain on the consolidated income statement. Accordingly, the amounts of amortization subsequently recorded by each affiliate should be eliminated to avoid duplicate measurement.

In the December 31, 1986, columns of the bond elimination schedule, the last elimination entry refers to Y Company's $125 amortization of Premium on Bonds Payable plus the $125 remaining, unamortized balance in the Premium on Bonds Payable account. The $250 sum of these two amounts represents the initial gain attributed to Y Company as the issuer of the bonds. This gain was included on the consolidated income statement in 1985. Thus, the 1986 (and 1987) amortization of the gain must be eliminated to avoid double counting on the consolidated income statement. Further, since the Bonds Payable account is eliminated, the remaining, unamortized Premium on Bonds Payable at the end of 1986 must also be eliminated.

Since the $250 gain was attributed to Y Company, the minority interest has an equity of 20 percent × $250 = $50 in the gain. Note that the elimination entry allocates $50 to the minority interest. On the consolidated working paper, the minority interest will also be allocated 20 percent of Y Company's *reported* January 1, 1986, retained earnings. The sum of these two allocations to the minority interest provides a total allocation that equals 20 percent of Y Company's *confirmed* retained earnings on January 1, 1986.

Observe that the final elimination entry in the December 31, 1986, columns of the bond elimination schedule allocates the remaining $200 to the Investment in Y Company Stock account; in other words, this amount is allocated to the parent. At the end of 1985, X Company recorded this $200 gain by debiting the Investment in Y Company Stock account and crediting Equity in Subsidiary Earnings (see this entry on page 356). The December 31, 1986, credit elimination of $200 reverses the previous year's booking by X Company. In other words, when the parent booked the $200 gain in 1985, it was in effect adjusting its Investment in Y Company Stock account balance *from* 80 percent of Y Company's *recorded* stockholders' equity to 80 percent of Y Company's *confirmed* stockholders' equity. The 1986 elimination entry returns the investment account balance back to 80 percent of Y Company's *reported* stockholders' equity. Thereafter, the investment elimination entry offsets 80 percent of the *reported* Y Company stockholders' equity accounts against the remaining investment account balance.

Now review the next to last elimination entry in the December 31, 1986, columns of the bond elimination schedule, Illustration 9–1, page 358. That entry refers to X Company's $70 amortization of premium on bond investment plus the $70 remaining balance in the Premium on Bond Investment account. The $140 sum of these two eliminations represents the initial loss attributed to X Company as the purchaser of the intercompany bonds. In the 1985 consolidated income statement, this $140 was reported as loss (or reduced gain) on purchase of affiliate's bonds. Since the $140 was reported as "gain" in 1985, it should *not* be reported again in 1986 and 1987 in the form of reduced interest income (by $70 each year). Instead, it should be eliminated. And since the Investment in Y Company Bonds is eliminated, the remaining Premium on Bond Investment should also be eliminated.

Not only was this $140 loss (reduced gain) reported in 1985 on the consolidated income statement, it was also entered on X Company's books as a reduction in Equity in Subsidiary Earnings with a corresponding credit to Investment in Y Company Stock (see entry on page 356). The elimination entry reverses this X Company booking by allocating (returning) the $140 to Investment in Y Company Stock.

The eliminations disclosed in the December 31, 1987, columns of the bond elimination schedule parallel those shown for 1986. And the explanations of those entries would essentially repeat the explanations offered for the 1986 elimination entries.

Consolidated Working Paper—1986   A partial consolidated working paper for 1986 is presented in Illustration 9–3. Observe that the eliminations first shown in the December 31, 1986, columns of the bond elimination schedule (Illustration 9–1, page 358) are entered in the consolidated working paper and identified as elimination entries (1) through (5). Elimination

Illustration 9–3

X COMPANY AND SUBSIDIARY Y COMPANY
Partial Consolidated Statement Working Paper
For Year Ended December 31, 1986

	X Company	Y Company	Eliminations Dr.		Eliminations Cr.		Minority Interest	Consolidated
Income Statement								
Net income, before interest and equity in subsidiary earnings	25,000	10,000						35,000
Equity in subsidiary earnings	7,710		(6)	7,710				–0–
.8($9,675 − $125) + $70								
Interest income	380		(3)	450	(4)	70		–0–
Interest expense		[325]	(5)	125	(3)	450		–0–
Net income	33,090	9,675						35,000
Minority interest .2($9,675 − $125)							1,910	[1,910]
Net income—carried forward	33,090	9,675		8,285		520	1,910	33,090
Retained Earnings Statement								
Retained earnings, 1/1/86:								
X Company	45,800							45,800
Y Company		19,675	(7)	15,740			*3,935	–0–
Minority interest in confirmed but unrecorded (1/1) retained earnings					(5)	50	50	
Net income—brought forward	33,090	9,675		8,285		520	1,910	33,090
Retained earnings, 12/31/86— carried forward	78,890	29,350		24,025		570	5,895	78,890
Balance Sheet								
Debits:								
Investment in Y Company stock	103,510		(4)	140	(5)	200		–0–
					(6)	7,710		
					(7)	95,740		
Investment in Y Company bonds	5,000				(1)	5,000		–0–
Premium on bond investment	70				(4)	70		–0–
Accrued interest receivable	225				(2)	225		–0–
Credits:								
Bonds payable		5,000	(1)	5,000				–0–
Premium on bonds payable		125	(5)	125				–0–
Accrued interest payable		225	(2)	225				–0–
Common stock—Y Company		100,000	(7)	80,000			20,000	–0–

[deduction]
* .2($19,675).

(6) in the consolidated working paper reverses X Company's 1986 recording of its equity in subsidiary earnings, as follows:

Equity in Subsidiary Earnings.................................... 7,710
  Investment in Y Company Stock   7,710

Elimination (7) in the consolidated working paper for 1986 is as follows:

Common Stock—Y Company	80,000	
Retained Earnings, January 1, 1986, Y Company	15,740	
Investment in Y Company Stock		95,740

The $80,000 elimination of common stock is 80 percent of the $100,000 common stock outstanding. The $15,740 elimination of retained earnings is 80 percent of Y Company's *reported* retained earnings on January 1, 1986, that is, .8 × $19,675 = $15,740. The $95,740 elimination of the investment in Y Company stock is the remaining balance in the investment account after eliminating the 1986 equity in subsidiary earnings ($7,710), the $140 loss associated with X Company as purchaser of the bonds, and the $200 equity of X Company in Y Company's gain on purchase of affiliate's bonds, that is ($103,510 + $140 − $200 − $7,710) = $95,740.

Note in the consolidated working paper that the minority interest is allocated 20 percent × $19,675 = $3,935 of the January 1 reported Y Company retained earnings. To this is added the $50 minority interest's equity in the confirmed but unrecorded January 1 retained earnings, so that the total allocation of January 1 retained earnings to the minority interest is $3,935 + $50 = $3,985, which is 20 percent of Y Company's *confirmed* January 1 retained earnings.

The similarity between the eliminations for intercompany bond holdings and the eliminations of intercompany profit on depreciable asset transfers should now be apparent. In the case of asset transfers, an unconfirmed profit is recorded by the selling affiliate; it is deferred in the consolidated statements and is given recognition only in future periods as confirmation is accomplished through depreciation. In the case of intercompany bonds, the gain or loss is regarded as confirmed at the date of acquisition and is so recognized in the consolidated statements. The affiliates, however, record their respective elements of the gain or loss over future periods in the form of premium or discount amortizations; accordingly, *double* recognition is avoided by eliminating, in the consolidated working papers, the effects produced by these subsequent amortizations. Consequently, the result of the elimination process is to *defer* recognition of profit (or loss) on asset transfers and to *accelerate* its recognition in respect to intercompany-held bonds. In both instances, there is an evident underlying philosophy of reporting profits or losses only at the time they are confirmed by transactions with nonaffiliate parties. Obviously, this philosophy is just as applicable to the eliminations of intercompany inventory profit as it is to intercompany depreciable asset transfers and bond holdings.

Case 4.   Parent Company's Bonds Partially Acquired by Subsidiary Affiliate.

The following data relate to A Company and its 80 percent owned subsidiary, B Company:

| | January 1, 1985, Balances ||
Accounts	A Company Dr. [Cr.]	B Company Dr. [Cr.]
Bonds payable, 8%	$[20,000]	
Premium on bonds payable.................	[600]	
Investment in A Company bonds		$5,000
Discount on bond investment		[90]

B Company purchased $5,000 of A Company's bonds on January 1, 1985, for $4,910. The bonds were originally issued several years ago and mature on January 1, 1988. Interest is payable semiannually on July 1 and January 1.

The bond elimination schedule for A Company and B Company is presented in Illustration 9–4. At the date the bonds were acquired, their carrying value on the books of A Company was $5,150. Since the acquisition cost was $4,910, the purchase of the affiliate's bonds resulted in a total gain of $240, which was allocated $150 to the issuer (A Company) and $90 to the purchaser (B Company). Since the date of acquisition was January 1, 1985, the $240 gain is reported on the consolidated income statement for the year ended December 31, 1985. During 1985, the affiliates recorded amortizations of premium on bonds payable ($50) and discount on bond investment ($30), which, in effect, amount to part of the $240 gain. Nevertheless, these adjustments to interest income and interest expense are eliminated so that the full $240 will be disclosed as gain rather than partially as adjustments to interest income and expense.

Two significant differences between Case 4 and Case 3 can be observed by comparing Illustration 9–4 with Illustration 9–1. First, Case 3 involved a purchase of the entire amount of bonds that the affiliate had issued. By comparison, in Case 4, only $5,000 of the outstanding bonds ($20,000) was purchased. Thus, the account balances associated with the $15,000 of bonds that remain outstanding must be extended to the Consolidated Amounts column; only the amounts pertaining to the intercompany bonds are eliminated. Second, in Case 3, the parent purchased the subsidiary's bonds, whereas in Case 4, the subsidiary purchased the parent's bonds. A comparison of the two bond elimination schedules indicates that the elimination procedures are the same regardless of which affiliate is the issuer and which is the purchaser.

To continue Case 4 so as to illustrate the consequences of this situation

Illustration 9–4

BOND ELIMINATION SCHEDULE—Dr. [Cr.]

	December 31, 1985			December 31, 1986			December 31, 1987		
	Recorded Amounts	Eliminated Amounts	Consolidated Amounts	Recorded Amounts	Eliminated Amounts	Consolidated Amounts	Recorded Amounts	Eliminated Amounts	Consolidated Amounts
Accounts on the books of A Company:									
Bonds payable	$[20,000]	$ 5,000	$[15,000]	$[20,000]	$ 5,000	$[15,000]	$[20,000]	$ 5,000	$[15,000]
Premium on bonds payable	[400]	100	[300]	[200]	50	[150]	-0-	-0-	-0-
Bond interest expense	1,400	[350]	1,050	1,400	[350]	1,050	1,400	[350]	1,050
Accrued interest payable	[800]	200	[600]	[800]	200	[600]	[800]	200	[600]
Accounts on the books of B Company:									
Investment in A Company bonds	5,000	[5,000]	-0-	5,000	[5,000]	-0-	5,000	[5,000]	-0-
Discount on bond investment	[60]	60	-0-	[30]	30	-0-	-0-	-0-	-0-
Bond interest income	[430]	430	-0-	[430]	430	-0-	[430]	430	-0-
Accrued interest receivable	200	[200]	-0-	200	[200]	-0-	200	[200]	-0-
Account created by elimination entries:									
Loss [gain] on purchase of affiliate's bonds	-0-	[240]	[240]	-0-	-0-	-0-	-0-	-0-	-0-

Below are elimination entries to accomplish the above:

	December 31, 1985		December 31, 1986		December 31, 1987	
	Debit	Credit	Debit	Credit	Debit	Credit
Bonds Payable	5,000		5,000		5,000	
Investment in A Company bonds		5,000		5,000		5,000
Accrued Interest Payable	200		200		200	
Accrued Interest Receivable		200		200		200
Bond Interest Income	400		400		400	
Bond Interest Expense		400		400		400
Premium on Bonds Payable	100		50		—	
Gain on Purchase of Affiliate's Bonds	50		50		50	
Investment in B Company Stock		150		100		50
Discount on Bond Investment	60		30		—	
Bond Interest Income	30		30		30	
Gain on Purchase of Affiliate's Bonds		90		48		24
Investment in B Company Stock		—		—		—
Minority Interest in Confirmed but Unrecorded (1/1) Retained Earnings				12		6

upon the consolidated statement working papers, assume the following net incomes of A Company and B Company. The indicated net income amounts exclude the effects of interest and A Company's net incomes exclude its equity in subsidiary earnings.

	1985	1986
A Company	$40,000	$30,000
B Company	15,000	20,000

Partial consolidated statement working papers for 1985 and 1986 are presented in Illustration 9–5 and Illustration 9–6.

Illustration 9–5

A COMPANY AND SUBSIDIARY B COMPANY
Partial Consolidated Statement Working Paper
For Year Ended December 31, 1985

	A Company	B Company	Eliminations Dr.		Eliminations Cr.		Minority Interest	Consolidated
Income Statement								
Net income, before interest and parent's equity in subsidiary earnings	40,000	15,000						55,000
Equity in subsidiary earnings	*12,492		(6)	12,492				–0–
Interest income		430	(3)	400				–0–
			(5)	30				
Interest expense	[1,400]		(4)	50	(3)	400		[1,050]
Gain on purchase of affiliate's bonds					(4)	150		
					(5)	90		240
Net income	51,092	15,430						54,190
Minority interest [20% of (15,430 + 90 − 30)]							3,098	[3,098]
Net income—carried forward	51,092	15,430		12,972		640	3,098	51,092
Balance Sheet								
Debits:								
Investment in B Company stock	xx				(x)	xx		–0–
					(6)	12,492		
Investment in A Company bonds		5,000			(1)	5,000		–0–
Accrued interest receivable		200			(2)	200		–0–
Credits:								
Bonds payable	20,000		(1)	5,000				15,000
Premium on bonds payable	400		(4)	100				300
Accrued interest payable	800		(2)	200				600
Discount on bond investment		60	(5)	60				–0–

(x) Partial investment elimination under the equity method.
* [80%(15,430 + 90 − 30) + 150 − 50].
[deduction]

Illustration 9–6

A COMPANY AND SUBSIDIARY B COMPANY
Partial Consolidated Statement Working Paper
For Year Ended December 31, 1986

	A Company	B Company	Eliminations Dr.		Eliminations Cr.		Minority Interest	Consolidated
Income Statement								
Net income, before interest and parent's equity in subsidiary earnings	30,000	20,000						50,000
Equity in subsidiary earnings [80% (20,430 − 30) − 50]	16,270		(6)	16,270				−0−
Interest income		430	(3)	400				−0−
			(5)	30				
Interest expense	[1,400]		(4)	50	(3)	400		[1,050]
Net income	44,870	20,430						48,950
Minority interest [20% of (20,430 − 30)]							4,080	[4,080]
Net income—carried forward	44,870	20,430		16,750		400	4,080	44,870
Retained Earnings Statement								
Retained earnings, 1/1/86:								
A Company	51,092							51,092
B Company		15,430	(x)	12,344			*3,086	−0−
Minority interest in confirmed but unrecorded (1/1) retained earnings					(5)	†12	12	
Net income—brought forward	44,870	20,430		16,750		400	4,080	44,870
Retained earnings, 12/31/86—carried forward	95,962	35,860		29,094		412	7,178	95,962
Balance Sheet								
Debits:								
Investment in B Company stock	xx				(4)	100		−0−
					(5)	48		
					(6)	16,270		
					(x)	xx		
Investment in A Company bonds		5,000			(1)	5,000		−0−
Accrued interest receivable		200			(2)	200		−0−
Credits:								
Bonds payable	20,000		(1)	5,000				15,000
Premium on bonds payable	200		(4)	50				150
Accrued interest payable	800		(2)	200				600
Discount on bond investment		30	(5)	30				−0−

[deduction]
* [20% of (15,430)].
† [20% of (90 − 30)].
(x) Partial investment elimination entry under the equity method.

Interim Purchases of Intercompany Bonds

Cases 3 and 4 involved purchases of intercompany bonds on the first day of the accounting period. If the purchases are made at some interim date between interest payment dates, *no* conceptual differences are introduced. Proper recognition of the amortizations of discounts or premiums during the remaining months of the first interest period must, of course, be given. But the procedures for doing so parallel completely those which were illustrated in Case 3 and Case 4.

Preferred Stock

Many corporations issue preferred stock as well as common stock. If a subsidiary has both common and preferred stock outstanding, several unique difficulties may arise in the preparation of consolidated statements. The parent may, of course, acquire all, some, or none of the subsidiary's preferred stock. Whether or not the parent holds some of the subsidiary's outstanding preferred stock, the consolidated financial statements must take into account the fact that part of the subsidiary's net income and perhaps retained earnings must be allocated to preferred stock with the residual amount accruing to common stockholders. If the parent holds some of the preferred stock, the parent's investment must be eliminated against the preferred stockholders' equity accounts. To calculate the appropriate amounts to be eliminated as part of the preferred stock investment elimination, and also the amounts to be eliminated as part of the common stock investment elimination, the subsidiary's retained earnings balance at the date of acquisition must first be allocated between the two classes of stock. After the date of acquisition, the postacquisition subsidiary earnings must be allocated between preferred and common shares so that the calculations of majority and minority interests therein will correctly reflect the rights of each security.

Allocation of Earnings

The general process of allocating a subsidiary's net income or retained earnings is depicted in Illustration 9–7. Obviously, the allocation of net income between preferred and common stock depends on the characteristics of the preferred stock. If the preferred stock is cumulative, the allocation of a subsidiary's retained earnings also is affected by the fact of the preferred stock's being in arrears or not being in arrears. Once the net income or retained earnings has been allocated between preferred stock and common stock, each portion can be further divided between that which accrues to the parent company and that which accrues to minority interests.

Illustration 9–7

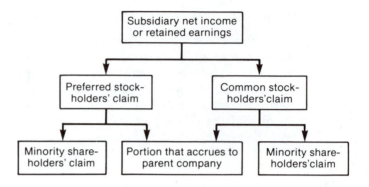

The parent's total equity in a subsidiary's net income or retained earnings derives (1) from net income or retained earnings that accrues to common shares owned by the parent, and (2) if the parent also owns some of the subsidiary's preferred shares, from net income or retained earnings that accrues to preferred shares owned by the parent. Similarly, the minority interest's equity in subsidiary net income or retained earnings may derive from both common shares and/or preferred shares of the subsidiary that are owned by the minority interest.

Since the various features of preferred stock are discussed in detail in *Intermediate Accounting* of this series, the present discussion only summarizes the effects of various preferred stock characteristics on the allocation of earnings between preferred and common shares.

1.   Where the preferred stock is nonparticipating and noncumulative, the accumulated subsidiary retained earnings relate totally to the common shares. The allocation of a subsidiary's net income in the income statement of the working paper depends on whether or not the subsidiary declared dividends. To the extent dividends were declared to the nonparticipating, noncumulative, preferred stock, net income should be allocated to the preferred shares with the remainder going to common shares. Thus, if no dividends were declared, all of the net income would be allocated to common shares.

2.   In the event that the preferred stock is nonparticipating but cumulative, only that portion of retained earnings that is equal to any arrearage in dividends on preferred stock is allocated to preferred shares; the remainder relates to common shares. In calculating the allocation of subsidiary net income between majority and minority interests, the current year's preference dividend to preferred shares must be allocated to the preferred shares whether it was declared or went into arrears. In either case, the preferred shares receive credit for an amount of income equal to the preferred dividend. Even if the total amount of net income earned by the subsidiary was insufficient to pay the preferred dividend, an amount equal to the prefer-

red dividend is allocated to preferred stock, with the residual amount of "loss" going to the common shares. Case 5 illustrates the preparation of consolidated statements in which the subsidiary's preferred stock is cumulative and nonparticipating.

3. Where preferred stock is fully participating, the allocation of retained earnings and net income can be more complex. To understand the reasons for the allocation process, recall the normal procedures for calculating dividend payments to fully participating, preferred stock and to common stock. When paying dividends in a typical year with *no* arrearages, *first*, the preferred stock receives its preference rate, for example, 8 percent. *Second*, the common stock receives the same rate, for example, 8 percent. And *third*, the preferred stock and common stock share ratably in the remaining dividends declared; that is, remaining dividends are allocated on the basis of the total par amount of preferred stock outstanding relative to the total par amount of common stock outstanding.

Regarding the *second* step, this privilege of common stock, to receive an amount equal to the preference rate before the participation feature of the preferred stock comes into play, generally applies only to current dividends, *not* to arrearages. In other words, if current income is actually paid out currently, the common stock will receive the benefit of the second step. But, if the income in excess of the preferred stock's preference is not paid out currently, then whenever it is paid out, it will be shared ratably by the two classes of stock.

To clarify the above discussion, suppose a company has $100,000 of 8 percent, fully participating, cumulative preferred stock outstanding, and $200,000 of common stock outstanding. Net income is $36,000 each year for two years. If the entire net income is paid currently in dividends, the allocation between preferred stock and common stock would be as follows:

	Year 1		Year 2	
	Preferred	Common	Preferred	Common
First, preferred gets 8%:				
(8% × $100,000)......................	$ 8,000		$ 8,000	
Second, common gets 8%:				
(8% × $200,000)		$16,000		$16,000
Third, remainder allocated ratably:				
(100/300) ($36,000 − $24,000)	4,000		4,000	
(200/300) ($36,000 − $24,000).............		8,000		8,000
Totals	$12,000	$24,000	$12,000	$24,000

But, suppose that in Year 1, the dividend declaration is only $8,000. Then, in Year 2, the total remaining net income for the two years is declared in dividends, that is, $28,000 + $36,000 = $64,000. In this situation, the allocation would be as follows:

	Year 1		Year 2	
	Preferred	Common	Preferred	Common
First, preferred gets 8%:				
(8% × $100,000)	$8,000		$ 8,000	
Second, common gets 8%:				
(8% × $200,000)				$16,000
Third, remainder allocated ratably:				
(100/300) ($64,000 − $24,000)...............			13,333	
(200/300) ($64,000 − $24,000)...............				26,667
Totals.............................	$8,000	–0–	$21,333	$42,667

Comparing the two previous situations, when the income was paid out currently, the preferred received $12,000 + $12,000 = $24,000; the common received $24,000 + $24,000 = $48,000. But, when the income was not paid out currently, the preferred received $8,000 + $21,333 = $29,333; and the common received $0 + $42,667 = $42,667. In the second situation, when Year 1 dividends were limited to $8,000, the common *permanently lost* the benefit of receiving the "second step" distribution of 8 percent, or $16,000. Instead, when the retained Year 1 net income was finally paid out in dividends, that $16,000 was shared ratably by preferred and common shares; the common shares received only (200/300) ($16,000) or $10,667, which is $16,000 − $10,667 = $5,333 less than the common shares would have received if the $16,000 had been paid out in Year 1.

Obviously, when preferred stock is participating, the allocation of net income depends on the level of current dividend declarations. Although the allocation procedures must depend on the extent of the participation feature, the general rules for fully participating, preferred stock are described below.

When allocating retained earnings, if the fully participating preferred stock is cumulative and in arrears, the amount of the arrearage goes to preferred stock and the residual retained earnings balance is allocated ratably between preferred and common shares. If the fully participating preferred stock is not in arrears or is not cumulative, the total amount of subsidiary retained earnings is allocated ratably to preferred and common shares.

When allocating net income with fully participating, preferred stock, *first*, the preferred is allocated its preference rate if the dividend was actually paid; and if the dividend was not paid, the preferred is allocated the preference rate only if the preferred is cumulative. *Second*, the common shares are allocated an amount equal to the preferred dividend rate, but only to the extent that this amount was actually declared in dividends to the common. *Third*, any remaining net income is allocated ratably between preferred and common shares.

4.   Preferred stock that is convertible into common stock is generally treated in accordance with its other preference characteristics (as outlined above) until such time as the conversion takes place. The act of conversion frequently changes the equity of the parent in the subsidiary, which topic is examined in Chapter 10.

Treatment in Consolidated Statements— Nonparticipating, Cumulative, Preferred Stock

Case 5.   On December 31, 19X1, X Company purchased 90 percent of the common stock of Y Company for $126,000 and 30 percent of its cumulative, nonparticipating, 8 percent preferred stock for $14,000. The preferred stock was not in arrears at the date of acquisition. Account balances for the two companies are as follows:

	December 31, 19X1 Dr. [Cr.]	
	X Company	Y Company
Investment in Y Company preferred stock	$ 14,000	
Investment in Y Company common stock	126,000	
Other assets....................................	160,000	$ 190,000
Common stock (par, $100)	[200,000]	[100,000]
Preferred stock (par, $100)		[50,000]
Retained earnings...............................	[100,000]	[40,000]

Preferred Stock Differentials and Eliminations Entries.   Observe from the facts in Case 5 that the $14,000 cost of preferred stock is $1,000 less than its book value. Thus, the preferred stock investment could be eliminated on consolidated statement working papers, as follows:

```
Preferred Stock—Y Company (30% × $50,000) ................... 15,000
    Investment in Y Company Preferred Stock ...................         14,000
    Differential on Preferred Stock ..............................          1,000
```

If such a differential applied to common stock, it would be allocated toward the revaluation of Y Company's assets and liabilities. However, unless the preferred stock were participating, changes in asset values would not normally impact on the market values of the preferred stock. Conversely, if the market price of preferred stock changes after it is issued, which gives rise to a differential, the existence of that differential should not be viewed as evidence of changes in asset or liability values. Instead, a preferred stock differential normally relates to changes in interest rates since the stock was originally issued. Thus, in the present case, the $1,000 does not imply that the net assets of Y Company require revaluation.

From the perspective of the consolidated entity, the purchase of preferred stock is comparable to the retirement of preferred stock by a single corporation; as a consequence, similar procedures should be employed. If the differential is a debit, it should be subtracted from Other Contributed Capital of the parent or, if none is available, it should be subtracted from the retained earnings balance of the parent. And if the preferred stock differential is a credit, it should be added to Other Contributed Capital.

Since the present case involves a credit differential, a second elimination entry is necessary as follows:

Differential on Preferred Stock	1,000	
Other Contributed Capital		1,000

A more efficient means of eliminating the preferred stock would involve a single, combined entry, as follows:

Preferred Stock—Y Company	15,000	
Investment in Y Company Preferred Stock		14,000
Other Contributed Capital		1,000

This combined form of elimination entry is used in the remaining illustrations in this chapter.

The consolidated balance sheet working paper for December 31, 19X1, is presented in Illustration 9–8. Observe in that illustration that the preferred shareholders have *no* equity in the retained earnings of Y Company.

Since the preferred stock is nonparticipating and is not in arrears, the equity of preferred shareholders is limited to the par value of the stock. If an arrearage had existed, an amount of retained earnings equal to the arrearage would have been allocated to preferred stock and the elimination entry for the parent's equity in preferred stock would have included a debit to retained earnings equal to 30 percent of the amount allocated to cover the arrearage.

Continuing the example of Case 5, assume that the 19X2 net incomes of the two companies, excluding X Company's equity in subsidiary earnings and excluding X Company's income from owning Y Company preferred

Illustration 9–8

X COMPANY AND SUBSIDIARY Y COMPANY
Consolidated Balance Sheet Working Paper
December 31, 19X1

| | X Company | Y Company | Eliminations | | Consolidated |
			Dr.	Cr.	
Investment in Y Common stock:					
Preferred stock	14,000			(2) 14,000	–0–
Common stock	126,000			(1) 126,000	–0–
Other assets	160,000	190,000			350,000
	300,000	190,000			350,000
Preferred stock		50,000	(2) 15,000		35,000 M
Common stock:					
X Company	200,000				200,000
Y Company		100,000	(1) 90,000		10,000 M
Retained earnings:					
X Company	100,000				100,000
Y Company		40,000	(1) 36,000		4,000 M
Other contributed capital				(2) 1,000	1,000
	300,000	190,000	141,000	141,000	350,000

stock, are X Company, $20,000; and Y Company, $1,000. Y Company paid cash dividends of $4,000.

Investments in a Subsidiary's Preferred Stock and the Equity Method.
Note that Y Company's 19X2 net income of $1,000 is not as large as is the preferred dividend requirement of 8% × $50,000 = $4,000. Nevertheless, the preferred stock must be allocated its preferred dividend with the residual profit or loss allocated to common stock. Even if the preferred dividend were not paid and went into arrears, the allocation of net income between preferred and common must provide for the dividend. *APB Opinion No. 18* states:

> When an investee has outstanding cumulative preferred stock, an investor should compute its share of earnings (losses) after deducting the investee's preferred dividends, whether or not such dividends are declared.[2]

In the present case, the preferred dividends were paid. But whether they were or not, the allocation of subsidiary earnings would be determined as follows:

---

[2] APB, *APB Opinion No. 18,* "The Equity Method of Accounting for Investments in Common Stock" (New York: AICPA, 1971), par. 19(k).

	Allocated to X Company	Allocated to Minority Interest	Y Company Net Income
Preferred stock allocation	(30%) $ 1,200	(70%) $2,800	$ 4,000
Residual loss to common stock	(90%) [2,700]	(10%) [300]	[3,000]
Totals	$[1,500]	$2,500	$ 1,000

X Company would record the receipt of the cash dividend to preferred shares, as follows:

Cash (30% × $4,000)... 1,200
    Equity in Subsidiary Earnings from Preferred
      Stock (or Preferred Dividend Income)...................... 1,200

And the end-of-year entry to record the equity in subsidiary earnings that resulted from owning common stock is:

Equity in Subsidiary Earnings from Common Stock................ 2,700
    Investment in Y Company Common Stock.................... 2,700

The consolidated working paper for 19X2 is presented in Illustration 9–9. Note that the first elimination entry offsets the parent's recorded income from holding Y Company's preferred stock against the dividends declared by Y Company. In elimination entry (2), the parent's recorded equity in subsidiary income from common stock is offset against the Investment in Y Company Common Stock account. Elimination (3) is the investment elimination entry for preferred stock, and elimination (4) is the final investment elimination entry for common stock.

The minority interest's equity in January 1, 19X2, retained earnings is 10 percent × $40,000 = $4,000, which is the equity of minority common stockholders. Since dividends are not in arrears, the preferred shareholders have no equity in retained earnings.

Observe in Illustration 9–9 that the reported net income of X Company ($18,500) is equal to consolidated net income. Since X Company recorded the equity in subsidiary earnings which derived from preferred stock and the equity in subsidiary earnings which derived from common stock, its books reflect the "one-line consolidation" objective of the equity method.

However, recall that Y Company paid the preferred dividend ($4,000) during 19X2. An interesting question arises when consideration is given to situations where preferred dividends fall into arrears.

Normally, preferred stock is accounted for according to the cost method, whereby income is recorded only upon the declaration of dividends to the preferred stockholders. Suppose the cost method were used by X Company during 19X2 and also suppose that Y Company failed to pay the $4,000 dividend to preferred stockholders. In that event, X Company

Illustration 9–9

X COMPANY AND SUBSIDIARY Y COMPANY
Consolidated Statement Working Paper
For Year Ended December 31, 19X2

	X Company	Y Company	Eliminations Dr.	Eliminations Cr.	Minority Interest	Consolidated
Income Statement						
Net income, before equity in subsidiary earnings	20,000	1,000				21,000
Equity in subsidiary earnings:						
From preferred stock .3($4,000)	1,200		(1) 1,200			–0–
From common stock .9($1,000 − 4,000)	[2,700]			(2) 2,700		–0–
	18,500	1,000				21,000
Minority interest:						
Preferred stock [.7(4,000)]					2,800	[2,800]
Common stock [.1(1,000 − 4,000)]					[300]	300
Net income—carried forward	18,500	1,000	1,200	2,700	2,500	18,500
Retained Earnings Statement						
Retained earnings, 1/1/X2:						
X Company	100,000					100,000
Y Company		40,000	(4) 36,000		4,000	–0–
Net income—brought forward	18,500	1,000	1,200	2,700	2,500	18,500
	118,500	41,000			6,500	118,500
Dividends declared (preferred)		4,000		(1) 1,200	2,800	
Retained earnings, 12/31/X2— carried forward	118,500	37,000	37,200	3,900	3,700	118,500
Balance Sheet						
Investment in Y Company:						
Common stock	123,300		(2) 2,700	(4) 126,000		–0–
Preferred stock	14,000			(3) 14,000		–0–
Other assets	181,200	187,000				368,200
	318,500	187,000				368,200
Preferred stock		50,000	(3) 15,000		35,000	–0–
Common stock:						
X Company	200,000					200,000
Y Company		100,000	(4) 90,000		10,000	–0–
Retained earnings—brought forward	118,500	37,000	37,200	3,900	3,700	118,500
Other contributed capital				(3) 1,000		1,000
Minority interest					48,700	48,700 M
	318,500	187,000	144,900	144,900		368,200

[deduction]

would not record the 30 percent × $4,000 = $1,200 income from owning preferred stock. Consequently, X Company's reported net income would be $18,500 − $1,200 = $17,300.

But, in the consolidated income statement, the net income would be $18,500. After the parent's and the subsidiary's incomes from their own operations were added in the consolidated income statement (giving a combined net income of $21,000 in Illustration 9–9), the only deductions would be the allocations to minority interests for their preferred stock holdings (70 percent × $4,000) and common stock holdings (10 percent × [$1,000]). Even though the preferred dividends were not paid, the current arrearage must be allocated to preferred stock for the purpose of calculating the minority interest's equity; otherwise the equity of common stockholders would be overstated. That is, it would fail to reflect the future obligation to pay the arrearage before any of the income could be paid to common stockholders. Thus, the consolidated income statement would appear exactly as it does in the final column of Illustration 9–9.

To summarize, if the parent uses the cost method to account for its investment in a subsidiary's cumulative, preferred stock, and if the preferred dividends are not paid and go into arrears, the parent's net income will not equal consolidated net income.

Another possibility is for the parent to record its equity in the preferred dividend, even though it is not paid, by debiting the Investment in Y Company Preferred Stock account and crediting Equity in Subsidiary Earnings from Preferred Stock. Then, when the dividend is eventually paid, the receipt would be treated as a liquidating dividend, that is, it would be credited to Investment in Y Company Preferred Stock. In effect, this would constitute equity method accounting for preferred stock.

The arguments in support of this equity method alternative appear significant, notwithstanding the absence of any authoritative position on the issue. If the investor (parent) has a significant financial influence over the investee, enough that the equity method is warranted for common stock, then surely that influence would apply with equal force to the matter of deciding when dividends will be paid to preferred stock. Also, as previously mentioned, *APB Opinion No. 18* requires that the current dividend to cumulative preferred stock be subtracted before calculating the equity of common stockholders in net income, even though the dividend is in arrears. It seems consistent to add the dividend in arrears to income earned by preferred stock owned by the stockholder, if it is to be so allocated when determining the income accruing to common stock.

Definitional Calculation of Consolidated Net Income

Consolidated net income in Case 5 may be stated definitionally as follows:

	19X2
X Company's net income (excluding equity in subsidiary earnings and dividend income).	$20,000
X Company's equity in Y Company's net income:	
30% of Y Company's net income allocated to preferred stock: 30% × ($4,000)	1,200
90% of Y Company's net income allocated to common stock: 90% × ($1,000 − $4,000)	[2,700]
Consolidated net income	$18,500

Questions

1. To what extent does the purchase by one affiliate of the bonds of another affiliate parallel the acquisition and retirement by one company of all (or part) of its own outstanding bonds payable?

2. Explain the nature of the "gain or loss" on the acquisition of intercompany bonds. How is this amount determined? To what extent should it be allocated between the participating affiliates?

3. Indicate what the arguments are for assigning the total gain or loss on the purchase of intercompany bonds to the issuing company. To the purchasing company.

4. In respect to intercompany bonds, the recorded amortizations of premiums and discounts on the books of the relevant affiliates are eliminated in consolidated statement working papers to avoid "double recognition." Explain this concept of double recognition and indicate why an elimination is necessary.

5. In regard to the elimination of profit on interaffiliate sales of depreciable assets, the effect of the elimination entries is to defer the profit recorded by the selling affiliate and formally recognize it over the remaining life of the relevant assets. Compare this profit *deferral* with the accounting consequence produced by elimination entries for interaffiliate bond holdings.

6. What complexity is introduced in the elimination process if an affiliate's bonds are purchased between interest dates?

7. Describe in general terms the earnings allocation problem associated with the elimination process as a result of the subsidiary's having both common and preferred stock outstanding.

8. Assume that a subsidiary has both common and preferred stock outstanding and the preferred stock is noncumulative and nonparticipating. On what

basis should the retained earnings of the subsidiary be allocated between preferred and common shares for the purpose of preparing the investment elimination entry? How would your answer differ if the preferred stock were cumulative, in arrears, and fully participating?

9. Suppose a subsidiary has outstanding $100,000 of 9 percent, nonparticipating, cumulative, preferred stock that is owned entirely by minority interests. Since 1975, the parent has owned 100 percent of the subsidiary's common stock. On December 31, 1985, the preferred stock is three years in arrears. On the consolidated income statement for 1985, the minority interest deduction should be either $9,000 or $27,000. Which is correct? Explain why.

10. Refer to Question 9. Suppose the retained earnings balance of the subsidiary on December 31, 1985, is $20,000. What amount should be reported on the consolidated balance sheet as minority interest in retained earnings?

11. Refer to Question 9. Suppose the subsidiary earns net income of $30,000 and pays dividends of $40,000 during 1986. What is the minority interest deduction on the consolidated income statement for 1986?

Exercises

Exercise 9–1

Each of the following independent situations pertain to a parent (P) which owns 80 percent of a subsidiary company (S). In each case, you are to determine the consolidated basis "gain or loss on purchase of affiliate's bonds," the amount of gain or loss that is attributed to the issuer of the bonds, and the amount of gain or loss attributed to the purchaser of the bonds.

Case A: P Company issued at par $50,000 of 20-year, 8 percent bonds payable. Four years later, S Company purchased 50 percent of these bonds at a cost equal to par.

Case B: P Company issued $50,000 of 20-year, 8 percent bonds payable at 106 percent of par. S Company purchased 40 percent of the bonds directly from P Company.

Case C: P Company issued $50,000 of 20-year, 8 percent bonds payable at 84 percent of par. Five years later, S Company purchased 100 percent of these bonds at a cost of $48,000.

Case D: S Company issued $80,000 of 10-year, 9 percent bonds payable at 95 percent of par. After four years, P Company purchased 75 percent of these bonds at a cost of $61,000.

Case E: S Company issued $80,000 of 12-year, 9 percent bonds payable at 105 percent of par. After seven years, P Company purchased 60 percent of these bonds at a cost of $49,000.

Exercise 9–2

On December 31, 1985, Racket Corporation acquired 90 percent of Net Corporation's outstanding stock at a cost of $90,000 cash. On the same date, Net Corporation purchased 100 percent of Racket Corporation's outstanding bonds at a cost of $9,000 plus accrued interest receivable of $450. Interest on the bonds is paid January 1 and July 1, and both companies amortize premiums or discounts using the straight-line method. The following data relate to these two companies immediately after the purchases took place:

	December 31, 1985	
	Racket Corporation Dr. [Cr.]	Net Corporation Dr. [Cr.]
9% bonds payable, due December 31, 1989	$[10,000]	
Discount on bonds payable........................	500	
Accrued interest payable	450	
Investment in Net Corporation stock	90,000	
Investment in Racket Corporation bonds		$ 10,000
Accrued interest receivable		450
Discount on bond investment		[1,000]
Common stock....................................		[70,000]
Retained earnings		[30,000]
Annual net income for 1986 (excluding the effects of interest)		[15,000]

Required:

a. Prepare the journal entry on the books of Net Corporation to record its purchase of Racket Corporation bonds on December 31, 1985, and the entries during 1986 to account for the investment in bonds.

b. Prepare the journal entry on the books of Racket Corporation to record its equity in subsidiary earnings for 1985. (Note that Racket Corporation's equity in subsidiary earnings for 1985 is limited to its equity in the gain or loss on purchase of affiliate's bonds.) Also, prepare the journal entries on the books of Racket Corporation during 1986 which relate to its bonds payable and its investment in Net Corporation.

Exercise 9–3

Refer to the facts provided in Exercise 9–2.

Required:

Present in journal form all of the elimination entries for consolidated statement working papers on—

a. December 31, 1985.
b. December 31, 1986.

Exercise 9–4

On January 1, 19X0, Raines Company issued $200,000 of 8 percent, 10-year bonds at 105 percent of par. Interest is payable July 1 and January 1. On January 1, 19X8, Rapco Company, which is a 90 percent subsidiary of Raines Company, acquired $100,000 of these bonds, paying 102 percent of par. Assume that both companies use straight-line amortization of premiums and discounts.

When Raines Company purchased its 90 percent interest in Rapco Company stock, the price paid was equal to the stock's book value. During 19X8, the net incomes of the two companies, not including interest expense deductions or interest income additions and not including equity in subsidiary earnings, were as follows: Raines, $40,000; and Rapco, $20,000. Neither company paid dividends during 19X8.

Required:

a. Present the journal entries recorded by Rapco Company during 19X8 to account for its investment in Raines Company bonds.
b. Present the journal entries recorded by Raines Company during 19X8 to account for its bonds payable and to account for its equity in Rapco Company.

Exercise 9–5

Refer to the facts provided in Exercise 9–4. Raines Company purchased its 90 percent interest in Rapco Company's outstanding stock on January 1, 19X8, at which time Rapco had common stock of $60,000 and retained earnings of $40,000. Raines paid $90,000 for the stock.

Required:

Using the information given in Exercise 9–4 as well as that provided above, present in journal form all of the elimination entries for consolidated statement working papers on December 31, 19X8.

Exercise 9–6

On July 1, 1984, Kinkel Company purchased $200,000 of Brennon Company's 8 percent bonds in the open market at 111½ and accrued interest. These bonds are part of an original issue of $1,000,000 bonds sold on January 1, 1976, at 105 percent of par. Interest is paid annually on January 1. The bonds mature on January 1, 1996. Periodic straight-line amortization has been recorded by each company on December 31.

Required:

If Kinkel Company owns a 90 percent interest in the capital stock of Brennon Company, present in journal form the elimination entries relating to the intercompany bonds on consolidated statement working papers for the year ended December 31, 1985. Do not show the eliminations related to Kinkel Company's "equity in subsidiary earnings."

Exercise 9–7

Parent Company owns 70 percent of Subsidiary Company's outstanding stock. On January 1, 19X1, Parent Company paid $21,000 to buy all of Subsidiary Company's outstanding 11 percent bonds, which have a par value of $20,000, and which pay interest semiannually on July 1 and January 1. Subsidiary Company's accounts on January 1, 19X1, showed an unamortized premium on bonds payable of $800. The bonds mature on January 1, 19X5, and both companies are assumed to amortize premiums and discounts on a straight-line basis. Subsidiary Company reported net income for 19X2 of $40,000, excluding the effects of interest expense.

Required:
a. Calculate the amount of the gain or loss on purchase affiliate's bonds and indicate the amounts that should be attributed to each affiliate.
b. Calculate the minority interest's equity in 19X2 net income.
c. Prepare the entries on Parent Company's books to record its equity in subsidiary earnings for 19X2.
d. In general journal form, present the elimination entries related to the bonds on consolidated working papers for 19X2.

Exercise 9–8

On December 31, 1985, A Company acquired 80 percent of B Company's common stock for $200,000 and 60 percent of B Company's 8 percent, preferred stock for $50,000. Account balances for the companies are as follows:

	A Company	B Company
Preferred stock, $100 par		$ 80,000
Common stock, $50 par	$400,000	100,000
Other contributed capital		15,000
Retained earnings.	200,000	20,000

Required:
Prepare elimination entries to be used in consolidated working papers on December 31, 1985, under each of the following conditions:

a. The preferred stock is cumulative, nonparticipating, and is *not* in arrears.
b. The preferred stock is noncumulative and fully participating.
c. The preferred stock is cumulative, fully participating, and one year in arrears.
d. The preferred stock is cumulative, nonparticipating, and two years in arrears.

Exercise 9–9

Bolts, Inc., acquired 90 percent of Washer, Inc.'s common stock and 60 percent of its 9 percent, preferred stock on December 31, 19X1, at which date the companies had the following stockholders' equity account balances:

	Bolts, Inc.	Washer, Inc.
Preferred stock, $100 par		$100,000
Common stock, $50 par	$300,000	150,000
Other contributed capital	10,000	30,000
Retained earnings	90,000	40,000

Required:

Prepare elimination entries for the consolidated balance sheet working paper as of December 31, 19X1, under each of the following circumstances:

a. The preferred stock is cumulative and nonparticipating, and dividends are not in arrears. Bolts, Inc., paid $100,000 for the preferred stock and $250,000 for the common stock.

b. The preferred stock is cumulative, nonparticipating, and two years in arrears. Bolts, Inc., paid $70,000 for the preferred stock and $250,000 for the common stock.

c. The preferred stock is cumulative, fully participating, and dividends are not in arrears. Bolts, Inc., paid $75,000 for the preferred stock and $200,000 for the common stock.

Exercise 9–10

Franks Company has $100,000 of 9 percent, preferred stock outstanding and $200,000 of common stock outstanding. Calculate *(a)* the amount of Franks Company's net income that should be included in the consolidated net income with its parent (Moore Company), and *(b)* the amount of the minority interest's equity in net income, under each of the following, independent situations.

Case A: Moore Company owns 40 percent of the preferred stock and 80 percent of the common stock. The preferred stock is cumulative, nonparticipating, and not in arrears. Net income of Franks Company is $50,000.

Case B: Moore owns 70 percent of the preferred stock and 80 percent of the common stock. The preferred is cumulative, nonparticipating, and not in arrears. Net income of Franks Company is $3,000.

Case C: Moore owns none of the preferred stock and 90 percent of the common stock. The preferred stock is cumulative, nonparticipating, and two years in arrears. Net income of Franks Company is $5,000.

Case D: Moore owns 30 percent of the preferred stock and 90 percent of the common stock. The preferred stock is cumulative, fully participating, and not in arrears. Net income of Franks Company is $30,000, of which $27,000 was declared and paid as dividends.

Problems

Problem 9–11

On January 1, 1985, the White Company owns 90 percent of the capital stock of Kaplan Company and 70 percent of the capital stock of the Jensen Company. On

January 1, 1979, the Kaplan Company issued $200,000 of 7 percent, 10-year bonds to nonaffiliates at 96. On January 1, 1985, the Jensen Company acquired $60,000 of these bonds at 103. Interest payable January 1 and July 1.

The following data relate to the period January 1, 1985, through December 31, 1986:

	White Company	Kaplan Company	Jensen Company
Retained earnings (1/1/85)	$415,000	$283,000	$196,000
Net income (exclusive of interest and equity in subsidiary earnings):			
1985......................................	100,000	50,000	60,000
1986......................................	85,000	45,000	38,000

Required:

a. Prepare eliminating entries in respect to intercompany bonds for inclusion on consolidated statement working papers for years ended December 31, 1985, 1986, 1987, and 1988. Do not prepare the elimination entries relating to White Company's "equity in subsidiary earnings."

b. Calculate consolidated net income for 1985 and 1986.

Problem 9–12

The South Company has a controlling interest in the North Corporation, having acquired 80 percent of its capital stock in 19X0. On January 1, 19X6, the North Corporation had outstanding a $300,000 issue of 8 percent bonds payable, interest payable on January 1 and July 1. The unamortized discount on these bonds as of January 1, 19X6, amounted to $9,000. The bonds are due January 1, 19X9.

On May 1, 19X6, the South Company acquired $75,000 of these bonds at 101.6 plus accrued interest. The 19X6 net incomes of the affiliates, exclusive of interest and excluding South Company's equity in North Corporation's earnings, follows:

South Company $80,000
North Corporation 60,000

Required:

a. Prepare the eliminating entries in respect to intercompany bonds for 19X6 through 19X8.

b. Prepare a consolidated income statement working paper for the year ended December 31, 19X6.

Problem 9–13

On December 31, 19X0, Allen Company purchased in the open market, $1,000,000 par value of Dahl Company's bonds. The bonds mature December 31, 19X5, pay interest at the rate of 10 percent annually on December 31, and had originally sold several years earlier to earn an annual rate of return of 9 percent. The purchase price on December 31, 19X0, was the amount that will enable Allen to earn an annual rate of return of 12 percent. Allen accounts for its investment in the bonds using the effective interest method of amortization. Similarly, Dahl accounts for the bonds payable using the effective interest method of amortization.

Allen owns 90 percent of the outstanding common shares of Dahl. Allen's income from its own operations was $150,000 annually during the period 19X0 through 19X5. Dahl's income during the same period was $120,000 annually. Allen accounts for its investment in Dahl common stock using the equity method (pro rata allocation of intercompany profits and losses).

Required:
a. Compute the carrying value of the bonds payable as it would appear on Dahl's balance sheet as of December 31, 19X0.
b. Compute the price Allen paid for the bonds on December 31, 19X0.
c. Compute the consolidated basis gain or loss that would be reported on the 19X0 consolidated financial statements.
d. Compute consolidated net income and the minority interest in net income for the years 19X0 through 19X5.
e. Prepare the consolidated worksheet elimination entries relating to the intercompany bond investment for 19X0 and 19X1.

Problem 9–14

On January 1, 19X1, X Company acquired 800 shares of Y Company's common stock for $17,000 and 180 shares of its 9 percent cumulative, nonparticipating preferred stock for $16,000. On this date, dividends were not in arrears, and the stockholders' equity accounts of Y Company were:

Common stock ($10 par value)	$10,000
Preferred stock ($100 par value)	20,000
Retained earnings............................	12,000

During 19X1, Y Company reported earnings of $10,000 and paid $7,000 in dividends. X Company earned $10,000, exclusive of its equity in subsidiary earnings from preferred stock and common stock.

Required:
a. Prepare the journal entries on X Company's books to record its equity in subsidiary earnings for 19X1 from preferred stock and from common stock. Assume that any differential on common stock is allocated to land. Also record X Company's receipt of dividends.
b. Calculate the minority interest in subsidiary net income for 19X1.
c. Present in journal form the elimination entries for December 31, 19X1, consolidated statement working papers.
d. Suppose that in 19X2, Y Company failed to pay any dividends. Describe the alternative accounting treatments available to X Company in respect to its investment in preferred stock. What effects will X Company's decision have on its unconsolidated financial statements in comparison with its consolidated financial statements?
e. Return your attention to 19X1. If the preferred stock had been cumulative and fully participating, calculate the consolidated net income for 19X1 and the minority interest in the subsidiary's net income.

Problem 9–15

| | Balances, December 31, 1985 | | | |
| | P Company | | S Company | |
	Debit	Credit	Debit	Credit
Cash..........................	$ 23,000		$ 30,000	
Accounts receivable	94,000		60,000	
Inventory (1/1/85)—cost.........	105,000		51,000	
Investment in stock of S	166,000			
Investment in bonds of S	51,800			
Other assets	445,000		210,000	
Current liabilities...............		$ 163,000		$ 17,100
Bonds payable—5%				200,000
Deferred bond premium				5,400
Sales.........................		630,000		340,000
Purchases	485,000		300,000	
Operating expenses	92,000		70,000	
Other expenses	22,000		15,500	
Interest		3,800		
Dividends paid	20,000		10,000	
Retained earnings (1/1/85)........		107,000		84,000
Common stock.................		600,000		100,000
	$1,503,800	$1,503,800	$746,500	$746,500

Additional information:

a. The investment in stock of S Company represents a 90 percent interest which was acquired January 1, 1985, for $175,000. At the same time $50,000 face amount of bonds of S were acquired for $52,000. These bonds had been issued on January 1, 1975, at 106 and are due January 1, 1995. S Company has recorded the amortization of the bond premium applicable to 1985 as an adjustment of interest expense. The stock and the bonds were purchased in the open market. Any difference between the stock purchase cost and book value is related to land owned by S Company.

b. Included in the Purchases account of S Company is a total of $180,000 of goods bought from P Company at 120 percent of cost to P Company. The closing inventory of S Company is estimated to include the same proportion of these purchases as of other purchases.

c. Inventories at December 31, 1985, at cost to each company, were:

> P Company $80,000
> S Company.......... 45,000

d. Although P Company uses the equity method, it has not yet recorded its equity in subsidiary earnings.

Required:

Prepare the income statement section of the three division working paper for the year ended December 31, 1985.

(AICPA adapted)

Problem 9–16

Four years ago, The American Company acquired 50 percent of the preferred stock of the Banner Corporation for $55,000 and 90 percent of that corporation's common stock for $195,000. At acquisition date, the Banner Corporation had retained earnings of $60,000, and dividends on the 5 percent, cumulative preferred stock were not in arrears. The investments were incorrectly recorded by The American Company at the book value shown by the Banner Corporation at date of acquisition. However, the excess of book values over the cost of common stock was known to relate to overvalued land on the books of Banner Corporation. Management has now decided that the Investment in Banner Corporation Preferred Stock account should have been maintained in accordance with the cost method.

Consolidated statements are now being prepared as of December 31, 1985, for The American Company and its subsidiary. The financial position of the individual companies was as follows on that date:

THE AMERICAN COMPANY

Assets		Equities	
Miscellaneous assets	$116,000	Liabilities	$ 50,000
Investments:		Preferred stock (4%)	100,000
Banner preferred	50,000	Common stock	100,000
Banner common	234,000	Retained earnings	150,000
Total assets	$400,000	Total equities	$400,000

BANNER CORPORATION

Assets		Equities	
Miscellaneous assets	$400,000	Liabilities	$ 60,000
		Preferred stock (5%)*	100,000
		Common stock	200,000
		Retained earnings	40,000
Total assets	$400,000	Total equities	$400,000

* Preferred stock dividends are three years in arrears. No dividends have been paid on common since acquisition by The American Company. Profit in 1982 was $8,000, but losses during the past three years have totaled $23,000.

Required:

a. Present in journal form the elimination entries on December 31, 1985.

b. Prepare a consolidated balance sheet working paper as of December 31, 1985.

(AICPA adapted)

Problem 9–17 (Comprehensive Review Problem)

Mass Company purchased Able Company on January 1, 19X1, by paying $690,000 cash in exchange for 90 percent of Able's outstanding common stock. At the date of acquisition, Able had the following stockholders' equity account balances:

Preferred stock, 9%, cumulative, nonparticipating, $20 par, 10,000 shares outstanding, no dividend arrearage	$200,000
Common stock, $10 par, 50,000 shares outstanding	500,000
Retained earnings	80,000

An analysis of Able Company's asset and liability accounts on January 1, 19X1, revealed the following differences between book values and market values: land costing $150,000 had a market value of $170,000; and buildings with a book value of $208,000 had a market value of $260,000, 13 years remaining useful life, and no estimated salvage value. Mass Company decided that any goodwill arising from the acquisition should be amortized over 40 years.

On January 2, 19X1, Able Company sold to Mass Company equipment having a cost of $40,000 and a book value of $20,000. Mass paid Able $30,000. The estimated remaining life of the equipment at the date of transfer was eight years, and straight-line depreciation based on an assumption of no salvage value is being used by Mass to depreciate the equipment.

On July 1, 19X1, Mass purchased $40,000 of Able Company's 8 percent bonds on the open market at 111½ plus accrued interest. These bonds are part of an original $200,000 issue of 20-year bonds that were sold 8½ years before Mass Company's purchase of the bonds. The original sales price was 110. Interest is paid annually on January 1. Periodic amortization (straight line) has been recorded by each company on December 31.

On January 2, 19X2, Mass acquired 2,000 shares of Able Company's preferred stock on the open market at a cost of $37,500. Dividends were not in arrears at the time of purchase.

Able sold merchandise to Mass Company for $17,000 in 19X1 and for $40,000 in 19X2. Able marked this merchandise to sell at 20 percent above its cost. Thirty percent of the 19X2 sales remains in the inventory of Mass Company on December 31, 19X2. On January 1, 19X2, Mass Company's inventory contained goods purchased from Able in 19X1 for $7,200 (also billed to Mass Company at a markup of 20 percent on Able's cost).

On December 31, 19X2, Mass Company owed Able $4,000 on open account. This stemmed from the merchandise purchases in 19X2.

Able Company's reported net income and dividend declarations during 19X1 and 19X2 were:

Year	Reported Net Income	Dividends	
		To Preferred	To Common
19X1.............	$58,000	$18,000	–0–
19X2.............	50,000	18,000	–0–

Required:
a. In general journal form, present elimination entries for a consolidated balance sheet working paper on January 1, 19X1. Show calculations to support the allocation of differential and the amounts to be amortized in future years.
b. Prepare journal entries to record Mass Company's purchase of Able Company bonds, the accrual and receipt of interest, and the amortization of premium or discount on bond investment during 19X1 and 19X2.
c. Prepare journal entries to record Mass Company's receipt of dividends and equity in subsidiary earnings for (1) 19X1 and (2) 19X2. Show any supporting calculations that are used to determine the various elements in Mass Company's equity in subsidiary earnings.
d. In general journal form, present elimination entries for a three-part, consolidated working paper (1) on December 31, 19X1, and (2) on December 31, 19X2.
e. Calculate the minority interest in (1) 19X1 net income and (2) 19X2 net income.

Consolidated Statements—
Changes in Parent
Company's Equity

A parent company's monetary equity in the recorded net assets of a subsidiary increases over time as the subsidiary increases its net assets through operations, and decreases each time the subsidiary declares a cash dividend. The entries to record these changes under the equity method were initially illustrated in Chapter 3 and have been repeated many times. In addition to these now familiar sources, changes in a parent company's equity in the net assets of an affiliate also occur as a result of transactions that increase or decrease the parent's proportionate ownership interest. Transactions of this type include the following:

1. Parent company purchases of additional shares of the subsidiary from the public.
2. Parent company sales to the public of all or a portion of the shares of the subsidiary that it owns.
3. Subsidiary sales or purchases of its own capital stock.

Such changes must be appropriately accounted for both under the equity method of accounting for an investment (including investment in less than 50 percent-owned companies) and in the consolidation process.[1] This chapter explains the basic principles and techniques that are applicable to this class of transactions.

Incremental Purchases of Subsidiary Stock from the Public

A parent company may acquire a controlling interest in a subsidiary company with a single purchase of its shares, or a series of purchases may be required to gain control. On those occasions when blocks of stock are acquired at different dates, the cost of each block should be related to the corresponding book value of the subsidiary shares on the same date. Although the preparation of consolidated statements necessarily must be deferred until majority ownership of subsidiary shares exists, it remains important to analyze the cost of each block separately and in terms of the relevant acquisition book value.

Current accounting policy supports this individual block analysis:

> When one company purchases two or more blocks of stock of another company at various dates and eventually obtains control of the other company, the date of acquisition (for the purpose of preparing consolidated statements) depends on the circumstances. If two or more purchases are made over a

---

[1] APB, *APB Opinion No. 18*, "The Equity Method of Accounting for Investments in Common Stock" (New York: AICPA, 1971), par. 19.

period of time, the earned surplus [retained earnings] of the subsidiary at acquisition should generally be determined on a step-by-step basis.[2]

However, the policy continues:

> if small purchases are made over a period of time and then a purchase is made which results in control, the date of the latest purchase, *as a matter of convenience,* may be considered as the date of acquisition.[3]

The latter treatment excludes from consolidated retained earnings the subsidiary's undistributed profits that accrued to the partial holdings prior to the establishment of control. This potential exclusion of subsidiary earnings can be defended only in terms of materiality or convenience.

Case 1.   Block Purchases in the Open Market.   P Company acquired shares of S Company's stock according to the following schedule:

Date	Number of Shares	Cost
January 1, 19X1................	200	$30,000
January 1, 19X2................	100	17,500
January 1, 19X3................	100	20,000

On January 1, 19X1, S Company had $50,000 of capital stock (par, $100) outstanding and retained earnings of $20,000. Annual profits for 19X1, 19X2, and 19X3 are assumed to be $10,000 in each year.

Assuming the individual block purchases are eliminated on a step-by-step basis, as is preferred, the purchased equity in the net assets of the subsidiary and the related differential for each block are as follows:

	First Block (40%)	Second Block (20%)	Third Block (20%)
Investment cost	$30,000	$17,500	$20,000
Purchased equity in subsidiary net assets............	28,000[1]	16,000[2]	18,000[3]
Differential	$ 2,000	$ 1,500	$ 2,000

[1] 40% of $70,000.
[2] 20% of $80,000.
[3] 20% of $90,000.

---

[2] Committee on Accounting Procedure, *Accounting Research Bulletin No. 51,* "Consolidated Financial Statements" (New York: AICPA, 1959), par. 10. This same position is also endorsed for the application of the equity method in *APB Opinion No. 18,* par. 19m.

[3] Ibid. (Emphasis supplied.)

Of course, the investment account will be increased over the three-year period to reflect the parent's equity in the subsidiary's reported earnings. Assuming for the sake of simplicity that the differentials are allocated to nonamortizable assets, the balance of the investment account at the end of 19X3 may be analyzed as follows:

	Acquisition Cost	Equity in Subsidiary Earnings	Carrying Value, December 31, 19X3
First block	$30,000	$12,000[1]	$42,000
Second block.............	17,500	4,000[2]	21,500
Third block	20,000	2,000[3]	22,000
Total	$67,500	$18,000	$85,500

[1] 40% of $30,000.
[2] 20% of $20,000.
[3] 20% of $10,000.

It is normal for the parent company to combine the several blocks of subsidiary shares in a single investment account. Consequently, it is sufficient to make one summary elimination for the total investment. At December 31, 19X3, the investment elimination entries would be:

(1)	Equity in Subsidiary Earnings (80% × $10,000)	8,000	
	Investment in S Company		8,000
(2)	Capital Stock (80% × $50,000)............................	40,000	
	Retained Earnings [80% × ($20,000 + $20,000)]	32,000	
	Differential...	5,500	
	Investment in S Company ($85,500 − $8,000)...........		77,500

Observe that the value of the differential in the investment elimination entry is the sum of the differentials identified in the analysis of the individual blocks. This results from the assumption that the differentials were all allocated to nonamortizable assets.

The series of purchases enumerated in this case do not seem to conform to the situation for which accounting policy permits an exception to the step-by-step analysis. If this option were selected, however, the blocks would be analyzed as follows:

	First Block (60%) 1/1/X1 and 1/1/X2 Purchases	Second Block (20%) 1/1/X3 Purchase
Investment cost	$47,500[1]	$20,000
Purchased equity in subsidiary		
net assets.	48,000[2]	18,000[3]
Differential	$ [500]	$ 2,000

[1] $30,000 + $17,500.
[2] 60% of $80,000.
[3] 20% of $90,000.

The first block in this analysis is not accumulated until control is established with the January 1, 19X2, purchase. At that time, the costs of the January 1, 19X1, and January 1, 19X2, purchases are combined, and the purchased equity is based upon the balances in the subsidiary's stockholders' equity accounts on January 1, 19X2. The second block in the analysis is equivalent in all respects to the third block in the previous analysis. As a consequence of waiting until control is achieved to make the first elimination, the total (net) differential is $1,500. In contrast, in the previous analysis, the total differential was $5,500. The $4,000 (credit) difference is the equity of the January 1, 19X1, purchase (40 percent) in the subsidiary's 19X1 net income ($10,000). When the differentials are assigned to non-amortizable assets, the difference persists in the consolidated statements. However, when the differentials are allocated to amortizable assets, the $4,000 difference would disappear at the end of the amortization period.

Whichever method is selected (and the step-by-step approach seems clearly preferable in this hypothetical situation), consolidated financial statements would of course not be prepared until control is established. In these statements, minority interests are calculated in the normal manner, that is, multiplication of the end-of-period minority interest percentage times the relevant subsidiary values (net income, beginning retained earnings, etc.).

Case 2. Block Purchases and Amortizable Differentials. If the differentials are assigned to amortizable assets (and liabilities), as would normally be the case, the process of differential allocation must be applied to each block using fair values on the date of acquisition. The principles underlying this process, however, remain unchanged. Furthermore, the allocation and amortization schedules for the separate blocks may be combined into a single schedule for purposes of the eliminating entry in the consolidated statement working paper.

For example, assume that an analysis of S Company's assets and liabilities in Case 1 (using the step-by-step approach) determined that fair value differed from book value only for plant and equipment (net), and the amounts of the differentials from the three blocks allocable to this asset are calculated in the following manner:

		Plant and Equipment (net)		
	Book Value	Fair Value	Excess	P Company's Interest in Excess
Block 1 (1/1/X1)—40%	$28,250	$29,500	$1,250	$ 500 (40% × $1,250)
Block 2 (1/1/X2)—20%	32,000	34,500	2,500	500 (20% × $2,500)
Block 3 (1/1/X3)—20%	40,000	47,500	7,500	1,500 (20% × $7,500)

Using these values, and recalling that the remaining amount of the differential not allocated to specific identifiable assets and liabilities is assigned to goodwill, the differential allocation and amortization schedule, by blocks and in summary, is developed in Illustration 10–1. It is assumed that the estimated remaining life for the plant and equipment is 5 years at each date of purchase and that goodwill is amortized over a 10-year period

Illustration 10–1

DIFFERENTIAL ALLOCATION AND AMORTIZATION SCHEDULE
(Case 2)

	Differential	Differential Amortization*			
		19X1	19X2	19X3	19X4
Block 1 (1/1/X1):					
Plant and equipment	$ 500	$100	$100	$100	$100
Goodwill	1,500	150	150	150	150
Total	$2,000	$250	$250	$250	$250
Block 2 (1/1/X2):					
Plant and equipment	$ 500	—	$100	$100	$100
Goodwill	1,000	—	100	100	100
Total	$1,500		$200	$200	$200
Block 3 (1/1/X3):					
Plant and equipment	$1,500	—	—	$300	$300
Goodwill	500	—	—	50	50
Total	$2,000			$350	$350
Combined blocks:					
Plant and equipment	$2,500	100	200	$500	$500
Goodwill	3,000	150	250	300	300
Total	$5,500	$250	$450	$800	$800

* Assumed lives:
1. Plant and equipment has a remaining life of five years at the date of each purchase.
2. Goodwill is amortized over a 10-year life from the date of each acquisition.

following its acquisition. Additionally, the differential amortization schedule is only extended through 19X4, as this is sufficient for our purposes; extending it further is, of course, a simple matter.

The investment account balance at December 31, 19X3, is determined under this modified Case 1 circumstance as follows:

Total cost		$67,500
Add equity in S Company's reported net income:		
19X1: 40% × $10,000	$4,000	
19X2: 60% × $10,000	6,000	
19X3: 80% × $10,000	8,000	18,000
Less: Differential amortization:		
19X1...	$ 250	
19X2...	450	
19X3...	800	[1,500]
Investment account balance, December 31, 19X3		$84,000

Additionally, the unamortized balances of the amounts allocated to plant and equipment and goodwill at December 31, 19X3, may be calculated:

Plant and equipment:		
Total amount allocated		$2,500
Less: Amortization ($100 + $200 + $500)		[800]
Balance, December 31, 19X3		$1,700
Goodwill:		
Total amount allocated		$3,000
Less: Amortization ($150 + $250 + $300)		[700]
Balance, December 31, 19X3		$2,300

These calculations enable us to prepare the eliminating entries for a consolidated statement working paper at December 31, 19X3:

(1)	Equity in Subsidiary Earnings ($8,000 − $800)	7,200	
	Investment in S Company		7,200
(2)	Capital Stock (80% × $50,000).............................	40,000	
	Retained Earnings (80% × $40,000)	32,000	
	Differential.......................................	4,800	
	Investment in S Company ($84,000 − $7,200)............		76,800
(3)	Plant and Equipment (net)................................	1,700	
	Goodwill..	2,300	
	Depreciation Expense	500	
	Amortization of Goodwill...............................	300	
	Differential.......................................		4,800

The only differences in these eliminating entries from those of Case 1 are introduced by the allocation and amortization of the differential; and in this respect, we are able to use the summary allocation and amortization schedule in the same manner that a single-purchase schedule was used in Chapter 4. Thus, block purchases in the open market introduce complexity in the supporting calculations, but the basic principles that are applied to each separate purchase are unchanged.

Sales of Subsidiary Stock to the Public

Sales of subsidiary shares to the public are accounted for by the parent company essentially as are other disposals of its corporate assets. The investment account is adjusted to the date of sale for the parent company's equity in subsidiary earnings and differential amortization to that time, and this adjusted carrying value is matched against the proceeds of sale to determine the trading gain or loss.[4]

When the parent sells only a portion of its investment in the subsidiary, the carrying value of the shares sold may be determined in several different ways. For federal income tax purposes, either specific identification or the first-in, first-out rule must be used, and these methods are also generally acceptable for financial reporting. However, the strongest conceptual case can be made, in the opinion of the authors, for use of the *average carrying value* of all shares held. All of the shares are interchangeable and of equal economic value. Thus, it seems more reasonable to measure the "adjusted cost" of the shares that were sold using an overall average, rather than allowing selection of particular stock certificates or an artificial flow assumption determine the amount of profit to be reported. When the average carrying value method is used to determine the gain for financial reporting purposes, the difference between this gain and the taxable gain is a timing difference that requires income tax allocation.

Case 3.   Partial (Interim) Sale of Holdings of Subsidiary Stock.   Using the data of Case 1 in this example, it is assumed that on March 31, 19X4, P Company sold 100 shares of S Company's stock (representing 20 percent of the outstanding shares) to nonaffiliate interests for $25,000. During 19X4, S Company reported net income of $10,000, earned uniformly throughout the year. P Company uses the average carrying value of the shares to determine the gain or loss on the sale. We continue to assume the allocated differential is not subject to amortization. Income tax allocation is ignored.

Parent Company Entries.   We previously determined that (with non-amortizable differentials) the carrying value of the investment on December 31, 19X3, is $85,500. The investment account would be further adjusted to the date of sale as follows:

Investment in S Company...	2,000	
Equity in Subsidiary Earnings [80% × (3/12 × $10,000)]		2,000

---

[4] See *APB Opinion No. 18*, par. 19f.

After this entry, the average carrying value of the 400 shares of stock held by P Company is $218.75 per share ($87,500 ÷ 400 = $218.75). The entry to record the sale would therefore be:

Cash	25,000	
Investment in S Company (100 × $218.75)		21,875
Gain on Sale of Stock		3,125

Following the sale, P Company holds 300 shares of S Company's outstanding stock, or a 60 percent equity interest. Accordingly, at the end of 19X4, P Company would record its interest in S Company's income for the last nine months of the year as follows:

Investment in S Company	4,500	
Equity in Subsidiary Earnings [60% × (9/12 × $10,000)]		4,500

The changes in the investment account balance are summarized following:

Balance, December 31, 19X3	$ 85,500
Equity in subsidiary earnings, 1/1–3/31 (80% × $2,500)	2,000
Sale of 100 shares (100 × $218.75)	[21,875]
Balance, March 31, 19X4 (300 × $218.75)	$ 65,625
Equity in subsidiary earnings, 4/1–12/31 (60% × $7,500)	4,500
Balance, December 31, 19X4	$ 70,125

Eliminating Entries. In the preparation of a consolidated statement working paper for a year in which a portion of the parent's investment is sold, we are confronted with different percentage ownership interests held by majority and minority shareholders before and after the date of sale. Which should be used in the calculations of amounts for the eliminating entries? A similar situation arose in Chapter 4 in our discussion of interim purchases of subsidiary stock, and the answer to the question was *end-of-period percentage ownership interests*. An obvious reason for this choice is provided by considering again the nature of minority interest *in the consolidated balance sheet*. Ignoring the transient effects of unconfirmed intercompany profits, the value of the minority interest reflects the minority shareholders' proportionate interest in the recorded net assets of the subsidiary *on that date*. Since the accumulation of the minority interest in the three-division consolidated statement working paper is a function of the percentage interest used in eliminations and extensions, it is clear that the end-of-period percentage interests must be employed. A complication arising from this choice is its effect on the allocation of income in the consolidated income statement. Recall that the basic process operating in the income statement division of the working paper is (1) a combining of the confirmed incomes of the affiliates (labeled total equity in our residual calculations), and then (2) subtracting the income allocable to the minority shareholders. If the percentage ownership interests of the two shareholder groups remain constant over the period, this process allocates shares of income that are equal to amounts *earned* on the shareholdings. However, if the percentage ownership interests change during the period, the working paper process will allocate end-of-period *claims* against the net assets generated by operations during the period—*whether earned or purchased*. In the case of interim purchases (under the option of including subsidiary revenue and expenses for the entire period), the lack of distinction between earned and purchased claims was corrected by including an income statement charge (debit) for "purchased preacquisition earnings." A similar adjustment is required when the parent sells a portion of its equity interest. Note that in the case of a sale, there is no alternative to reporting all of the subsidiary's revenue and expenses for the period. If the parent held a controlling interest in the subsidiary for the entire period (and a *retained* controlling interest is a precondition for preparation of consolidated financial statements), all of the subsidiary's revenue and expenses for the period were revenue and expenses of the economic entity, and thus they must be disclosed in the consolidated income statement.

Although there are different procedures that may be employed to deal with this problem in the case of a sale, the most straightforward way is to eliminate (or reverse) Equity in Subsidiary Earnings *on the shares retained by the parent company at the end of the period*. After this elimination, the Equity in Subsidiary Earnings will have a residual balance reflecting the recorded equity in subsidiary earnings from the beginning of the year to the date of sale on the shares that were sold. Extension of this value to the Consolidated column implicitly adjusts minority interest expense to the amount of combined income *earned* by outside (minority) interests during the period. In our example, the parent company held a 60 percent interest in the subsidiary at the end of the period. Using end-of-period percentage ownership interests and recalling that the subsidiary reported net income of $10,000 for the period, the eliminating entry would be;

(1)   Equity in Subsidiary Earnings (60% × $10,000)   6,000
            Investment in S Company   6,000

Since the balance in Equity in Subsidiary Earnings is $6,500 (see parent company entries above), this leaves $500 to be extended to the Consolidated column.

The validity of this adjustment may be confirmed by analyzing the earned and allocated shares of the subsidiary's $10,000 net income for the period. Consider first the portions of the subsidiary's net income *earned* by the two shareholder groups:

Majority shareholders:
1/1–3/31:
    On "sold" shares (20% × $2,500) . . . . $ 500
    On "retained" shares (60% × $2,500) . . . .   1,500 $ 2,000
  4/1–12/31 (60% × $7,500)   4,500
                                     $ 6,500

Minority shareholders:
  1/1–3/31 (20% × $2,500) . . . . $ 500
  4/1–12/31 (40% × $7,500)   3,000   3,500
                                     $10,000

In the income statement division of the consolidated statement working paper, the extension of the $500 equity in subsidiary earnings on the sold shares to the Consolidated column results in the following allocation of incomes:

Reported net income of the subsidiary (all confirmed, and thus
  allocable to either majority or minority shareholders) $10,000
Less amount allocated to minority:
  Minority interest in subsidiary's net income based upon
    end-of-period ownership interest (40% × $10,000) . . . . $4,000 (Dr.)
  Equity in subsidiary earnings extended to
    Consolidated column . . . .   500 (Cr.)   3,500
Residual allocated to majority shareholders . . . . $ 6,500

Thus, with the $500 credit in the Consolidated column from the equity on sold shares offsetting a portion of the $4,000 minority interest expense based upon the minority's *end-of-period* percentage ownership interest, the allocations in the consolidated income statement to the two classes of shareholders are equivalent to the previously calculated earned incomes. Based upon the reasoning of this analysis, it seems appropriate to disclose the equity on sold shares as an offset to minority interest expense, rather than as a separate item, in the consolidated income statement. Note, however, that this offset is only in the income statement (or the Consolidated column in the income statement division of the working paper). The full $4,000 recorded in the *Minority Interest column* as a consequence of using end-of-period interests represents a valid *claim* by the minority shareholders against the recorded net assets of the subsidiary. The fact that $3,500 was earned and $500 purchased from majority shareholders is not a relevant consideration in respect to the final balance sheet value for the minority interest.

The investment elimination entry is also based upon *end-of-period* ownership interests:

(2) Capital Stock—S Company (60% × $50,000)................	30,000	
Retained Earnings—S Company (60% × $50,000)...........	30,000	
Differential (300/400 × $5,500)	4,125	
Investment in S Company ($70,125 − $6,000)...........		64,125

In this eliminating entry, it should be noted that the differential is the proportionate part of the total differential that is attributable to the retained shares. The portion of the total differential associated with the sold shares (on an *average* basis) has been matched (together with these shares' average equity in the subsidiary's net assets) against the sales proceeds in determining the trading gain on the sale. This is appropriate, as the differential is part of the parent company's total carrying value of the shares.

These data are presented in a partial consolidated statement working paper in Illustration 10–2, in which it is further assumed that P Company's 19X4 net income (exclusive of the gain on the sale of stock and the equity in subsidiary earnings) was $25,000, and its January 1, 19X4, retained earnings amounted to $80,000. Note that the minority interest in S Company's net income and beginning retained earnings is calculated using the 40 percent ownership interest held by the minority shareholders *at the end of the period.* As a consequence, the minority interest in December 31, 19X4,

Illustration 10–2

P COMPANY AND SUBSIDIARY S COMPANY
Partial Consolidated Statement Working Paper
For Year Ended December 31, 19X4

	P Company	S Company	Eliminations Dr.	Eliminations Cr.	Minority Interest	Consolidated
Income Statement						
Net income (excluding gain on sale of stock and equity in subsidiary earnings)	25,000	10,000				35,000
Gain on sale of stock	3,125					3,125
Equity in subsidiary earnings	6,500		(1) 6,000			500
	34,625	10,000				38,625
Minority interest in S Company net income—40% of $10,000					4,000	4,000
Net income	34,625	10,000	6,000	–0–	4,000	34,625
Retained Earnings Statement						
Retained earnings, 1/1/X4:						
P Company	80,000					80,000
S Company		50,000	(2) 30,000		20,000	–0–
Net income	34,625	10,000	6,000	–0–	4,000	34,625
Retained earnings, 12/31/X4	114,625	60,000	36,000	–0–	24,000	114,625

retained earnings ($24,000) reflects a 40 percent interest in the recorded balance ($60,000). Applying the same procedure to the subsidiary's capital stock will yield a total value for the minority interest that is 40 percent of the subsidiary's recorded net assets—an amount that equals the claim that this shareholder group holds.

Schedular Calculation of Consolidated Net Income.   The working paper produces consolidated net income for 19X4 of $34,625. This amount is confirmed by incremental calculation:

P Company's income from its own operations:		
Reported income (exclusive of trading gain and equity in		
subsidiary earnings)	$25,000	
Trading gain on sale of subsidiary stock	3,125	$28,125
Increased by—		
80% of three months' 19X4 subsidiary net income		
(80% × $2,500)	2,000	
60% of nine months' 19X4 subsidiary net income		
(60% × $7,500)	4,500	6,500
Consolidated net income for 19X4................................		$34,625

This schedular calculation indicates that no substantive changes in the basic definition of consolidated net income have occurred. The trading gain on the sale of the subsidiary's stock is a valid component of the parent's confirmed income for the period (whether from operations or not is a moot point). Additionally, the $500 equity on the sold shares does not enter the calculation in any special way. Rather, it is a component of the parent's equity in the subsidiary's confirmed income for the portion of the year in which 80 percent of the subsidiary's stock was held by the parent.

Effects of Differential Amortization.   When the parent's investment account includes a differential that is subject to amortization, adjustment of the investment account to the date of sale includes recognition of differential amortization in addition to the parent's equity in subsidiary net income. Then, the *unamortized* differential at the date of sale would be allocated between the sold and the retained shares. Amortization for the remainder of the year after the sale is based upon the portion of the unamortized differential allocated to the retained shares.

The eliminating entries are similarly modified. The "reversal" entry is based upon the equity in subsidiary earnings, net of differential amortization, on the retained shares. The differential set up in the investment elimination entry is the unamortized differential applicable to the retained shares at the beginning of the year. Differential amortization is then recognized in the consolidated statement working paper on this unamortized differential balance (as allocated to specific assets). The differential amortization on the portion of the beginning-of-year differential applicable to the sold shares is included with the uneliminated equity in subsidiary earnings (as originally recorded by the parent). As a matter of convenience, we usually extend this "net" value to the Consolidated column. If classifica-tional precision were desired, the amortization of the differential on the sold shares should be separately allocated to the appropriate expense cate-gories, and the gross equity in subsidiary earnings on the sold shares offset against minority interest expense.

Case 4. Partial Interim Sale with Differential Amortization. To illus-trate the effects of an amortizable differential on the calculations, we aug-ment our analysis of the sale in Case 3 with the analysis of the differential in Case 2. Since the shares sold were not identified with any particular block, the summary differential allocation and amortization schedule in Illustration 10–1 provides the basic data for this example. This summary may be condensed for our present purposes as follows:

	Total Differential	Differential Amortization 19X1–X3	Unamortized Differential 1/1/X4	Differential Amortization 19X4	Unamortized Differential 12/31/X4
Plant and equipment........	$2,500	$ 800	$1,700	$500	$1,200
Goodwill..................	3,000	700	2,300	300	2,000
	$5,500	$1,500	$4,000	$800	$3,200

Recall also that as a consequence of incorporating differential amortization in Case 2, the balance of the investment account on January 1, 19X4, is $84,000 (in contrast to the $85,500 in Case 3). This balance is composed of the following two components:

Equity in S Company's net assets
  [80% × ($50,000 + $50,000)] $80,000
Unamortized differential 4,000
                                                                   $84,000

Because the carrying value of the shares on January 1, 19X4, in this case is different from the carrying value on the same date in Case 3, the trading gain or loss on the sale of the stock will also be different.

Parent Company Entries. Three entries, or sets of entries, are made to the investment account in 19X4 (the year of sale):

1. Adjustment of the investment account to the date of sale (March 31, 19X4, in our example) by recognizing:
   a. Equity in S Company's net income for the first three months of 19X4 on *all* of the shares.
   b. Differential amortization for the first three months of 19X4 on *all* of the shares.
2. Write-off of the portion of the adjusted investment account balance that is applicable to the "sold" shares.

3. Adjustment of the investment account to the end of the year by recognizing:

   a. Equity in S Company's net income for the last nine months of 19X4 on the *retained* shares.

   b. Differential amortization for the last nine months of 19X4 on the *retained* shares.

The only change in these entries from the previous case is the recognition of differential amortization.

Recall that the parent company is using the average carrying value of the shares as the basis for determining the trading gain or loss on the sale of stock. This implies that the equity in net assets *and* the unamortized differential are allocated proportionately to the "sold" and "retained" shares. Since the parent company started the year with 400 shares, the 100 sold shares are allocated one fourth of these two components of the investment account balance, and the remaining three fourths of the balance is allocated to the retained shares. These proportionate allocations provide the starting point for the analysis of changes in the investment account in Illustration 10–3, and are similarly reflected in the division of the equity in subsidiary earnings and differential amortization between the two classes of shares. Based upon the values calculated in Illustration 10–3, the parent company's entries for 19X4 are summarized below:

1. To adjust investment account to date of sale:

   a. Equity in S Company's net income for first three months of 19X4 [80 percent × (3/12 × $10,000)]:

Investment in S Company............................	2,000	
Equity in Subsidiary Earnings		2,000

   b. Differential amortization for first three months of 19X4 (3/12 × $800):

Equity in Subsidiary Earnings	200	
Investment in S Company........................		200

2. To record sale of 100 shares for $25,000:

Cash	25,000	
Investment in S Company (1/4 × $85,800)		21,450
Gain on Sale of Stock		3,550

3. To adjust investment account to end of year:

   a. Equity on retained shares in S Company's net income for last nine months of 19X4 [60 percent × (9/12 × $10,000)]:

Investment in S Company...........................	4,500	
Equity in Subsidiary Earnings		4,500

Illustration 10–3

ANALYSIS OF INVESTMENT ACCOUNT—SOLD AND RETAINED SHARES
(Case 4)

	Sold Shares (100 Shares)		Retained Shares (300 Shares)		Investment Account		
	Equity in S Company's Net Assets	Unamortized Differential	Equity in S Company's Net Assets	Unamortized Differential	Equity in S Company's Net Assets	Unamortized Differential	Total
Balance, 1/1/X4	$ 20,000	$1,000	$60,000	$3,000	$ 80,000	$4,000	$ 84,000
(1) Adjustment of investment account to date of sale (3/31/X4):							
(a) Equity in S Company's net income [400/500 × (3/12 × $10,000)]	500		1,500		2,000		2,000
(b) Amortization of differential (3/12 × $800)		[50]		[150]		[200]	[200]
Adjusted balance, 3/31/X4	$ 20,500	$ 950	$61,500	$2,850	$ 82,000	$3,800	$ 85,800
(2) Written off in sale	[20,500]	[950]	–0–	–0–	[20,500]	[950]	[21,450]
Balance after sale, 3/31/X4	–0–	–0–	$61,500	$2,850	$ 61,500	$2,850	$ 64,350
(3) Adjustment of investment account to end of year:							
(a) Equity in S Company's net income [300/500 × (9/12 × $10,000)]	–0–		4,500		4,500		4,500
(b) Amortization of differential [300/400 × (9/12 × $800)]	–0–	–0–		[450]		[450]	[450]
Balance, 12/31/X4	–0–	–0–	$66,000	$2,400	$ 66,000	$2,400	$ 68,400

b. Differential amortization on retained shares for last nine months of
19X4 [3/4 × (9/12 × $800)]:

Equity in Subsidiary Earnings 450
    Investment in S Company....................... 450

Note in entry (2) that the adjusted balance of the investment account is
obtained by combining the two entries in (1) with the beginning balance of
$84,000. Also, in respect to differential amortization, the $800 applicable to
the total 400 shares for 19X4 is allocated $200 to the sold shares and $600 to
the retained shares. The recognized differential amortization of $200 for the
first three months includes $50 (3/12 × $200) on the sold shares and $150
(3/12 × $600) on the retained shares. Since the March 31, 19X4, unamor-
tized differential applicable to the sold shares is written off when they are
sold, the differential amortization for the last nine months of 19X4 is based
only on the amount applicable to the retained shares (9/12 × $600).

Eliminating Entries.   The eliminating entries for a consolidated statement
working paper at December 31, 19X4, are based upon the same principles
and reasoning developed in Case 3, modified only to incorporate differential allocation and amortization on the retained shares.

(1) To reverse recorded equity in subsidiary earnings, net of differential
amortization, on the *retained* shares (from Illustration 10–3, $6,000 −
$600):

Equity in Subsidiary Earnings 5,400
    Investment in S Company 5,400

(2) To eliminate the investment account against the beginning-of-year
balances in S Company's stockholders' equity accounts, based upon P
Company's end-of-year ownership interest:

Capital Stock (60% × $50,000)........................... 30,000
Retained Earnings (60% × $50,000) 30,000
Differential (300/400 × $4,000)........................... 3,000
    Investment in S Company ($68,400 − $5,400) 63,000

The investment account balance at the end of the year is readily available in Illustration 10–3. Additionally, observe that the differential set
up by this entry is the unamortized balance at the beginning of the
year applicable to the retained shares. This is consistent with the
result obtained in Case 3.

(3)   To recognize amortization of the differential applicable to the retained shares and set up end-of-year asset balances:

Plant and Equipment—Net (3/4 × $1,200)	900	
Goodwill (3/4 × $2,000)	1,500	
Depreciation expense (3/4 × $500)	375	
Amortization of Goodwill (3/4 × $300)	225	
Differential		3,000

The partial consolidated statement working paper (employing the same assumptions as Case 3) reflecting these eliminating entries is displayed in Illustration 10–4.

The amount of equity in subsidiary earnings (net of differential amortization) extended to the Consolidated column in the working paper is $450. This amount is the difference between the $500 equity in subsidiary net income and the $50 differential amortization for the first three months of 19X4 on the sold shares. The reasoning underlying the extension of the $500 has been previously explained. Classifying the $50 differential amortization with this amount, rather than including proportionate parts in De-

Illustration 10–4

P COMPANY AND SUBSIDIARY S COMPANY
Partial Consolidated Statement Working Paper
For Year Ended December 31, 19X4

	P Company	S Company	Eliminations Dr.	Eliminations Cr.	Minority Interest	Consolidated
Income Statement						
Net income (excluding gain on sale of stock and equity in subsidiary earnings)	25,000	10,000	(3) 600			34,400
Gain on sale of stock	3,550					3,550
Equity in subsidiary earnings (net of differential amortization)	5,850		(1) 5,400			450
	34,400	10,000				38,400
Minority interest in S Company net income— 40% × $10,000					4,000	4,000
Net income	34,400	10,000	6,000	–0–	4,000	34,400
Retained Earnings Statement						
Retained earnings, 1/1/X4:						
P Company	80,000					80,000
S Company		50,000	(2) 30,000		20,000	–0–
Net income	34,400	10,000	6,000	–0–	4,000	34,400
Retained earnings, 12/31/X4	114,400	60,000	36,000	–0–	24,000	114,400

preciation Expense and Amortization of Goodwill, is a debatable issue among accountants. Since the income earned on the sold shares is reflected in the $500 extension, the authors believe that is marginally preferable to combine the applicable differential amortization with it.

Schedular Calculation of Consolidated Net Income. Consolidated net income for 19X4 of $34,400 in the partial consolidated statement working paper is confirmed by schedular calculation (using the incremental approach), as follows:

P Company's income from its own operations:		
Reported income (exclusive of trading gain		
and equity in subsidiary earnings)...............	$25,000	
Trading gain on sale of subsidiary stock............	3,550	$28,550
Increased by:		
80% of three months' 19X4 subsidiary		
net income (80% × $2,500).......................	$ 2,000	
60% of nine months' 19X4 subsidiary		
net income (60% × $7,500)......................	4,500	6,500
Decreased by differential amortization:		
1/1–3/31	$ 200	
4/1–12/31	450	[650]
Consolidated net income for 19X4		$34,400

This calculation adds the recognition of differential amortization to the elements previously included in Case 3.

Subsidiary Stock Transactions

In the previous two sections of this chapter, we have examined parent company transactions with third parties in which a parent company's percentage ownership interest and its monetary equity in a subsidiary's net assets increased or decreased. The same effects may occur when a subsidiary issues additional shares of stock or repurchases treasury shares on a nonratable basis between majority and minority shareholders. The impact of these stock transactions by a subsidiary upon the parent company's accounting for its investment and the consolidated financial statements is largely a product of two variables:

1. The change in the parent's *percentage ownership interest* in the subsidiary produced by the transaction.
2. The change in the parent's *dollar equity in the subsidiary's net assets* produced by the transaction.

The relevance of each of these two key variables is considered in turn.

Change in Parent's Percentage Ownership Interest. When a subsidiary issues additional stock or repurchases treasury shares on a nonratable basis between majority and minority shareholders, the parent company's percentage ownership interest in the subsidiary increases or decreases. The same effect could have been achieved through the parent's purchase or sale of subsidiary shares in the open market. Indeed, the transaction may be restructured so that both the parent and the subsidiary have the same economic effects as they have in the nonratable stock transaction by the subsidiary. An example of such a restructuring is provided in the Appendix to this chapter. The parent company has the option of selecting either of these methods of changing its ownership percentage. Therefore, since the two alternatives are fundamentally equivalent in terms of economic substance, the authors take the position that the accounting impacts of subsidiary transactions of a capital nature should be consistent with the accounting for purchases or sales in the open market analyzed in the two preceding sections of the chapter. In essence, we argue for the primacy of economic substance over form.

Having established this fundamental perspective on subsidiary transactions of a capital nature, the key element that must be initially calculated is the *direction* of the change in the parent's percentage ownership interest. When the transaction *increases* the parent's percentage ownership interest, it is viewed as analogous to a purchase from third parties; if the parent's ownership percentage *decreases*, it is treated as analogous to a sale to third parties.

Accounting for the transaction by the parent company and in the consolidated statements is based upon the principles applicable to open-market purchases and sales. In the case of a purchase of additional shares of the subsidiary in the open market, the purchased equity in the subsidiary's net assets is compared with the cost of the investment, and any difference is added to (or subtracted from) the unamortized differential on previous stockholdings. In the same fashion, the net change in the parent's dollar equity in a subsidiary's net assets produced by a subsidiary stock transaction that *increases* the parent's percentage ownership interest is compared with the parent's cost or proceeds, if any, and the difference is treated as an adjustment of the previously existing unamortized differential.

When the parent sells a portion of its stockholdings in a subsidiary in the open market, the proceeds of sale are matched against the dollar equity in subsidiary net assets *and* the unamortized differential applicable to those shares, and the difference is recognized as a gain or loss on the sale. Based upon the perspective we have adopted, similar treatment is accorded subsidiary transactions of a capital nature which result in *decreases* in the parent's percentage ownership interest. Some accountants believe, however, that change in equity "gains" properly relate to contributed capital. Their argument rests on the assumption that it is improper to allow an affiliate's trading in its own stock to be the source of a "profit" element in the calculation of consolidated net income and retained earnings. Accordingly, they support crediting these "gains" to consolidated paid-in capital. However, there is, we believe, a basic fallacy in this position. Under the prevailing philosophy of a majority interest orientation in the consolidated statements, consolidated paid-in capital should reflect transactions between the parent company and *its shareholders*. Any transactions of this type are not the source of profit in the consolidated income statement. However, subsidiary transactions in its own stock are a different matter. As previously discussed, subsidiary stock transactions that result in a decrease in the parent's ownership percentage are equivalent, in substance, to sales of the subsidiary stock in the open market by the parent company—a transaction that most agree generates gains and losses. Accordingly, we conclude that the argument against recognition of gains on subsidiary stock transactions that decrease the parent's percentage ownership interest is based upon an unwarranted focus of attention on the form of the transaction (the purchase or sale of the subsidiary's stock) rather than its substance. Prior to 1980, the "paid-in capital" treatment was generally supported (or required) in practice. However, in June 1980, the AICPA Accounting Standards Executive Committee released an Issues Paper supporting the "gain or loss" treatment ("Accounting in Consolidation for Issuances of a Subsidiary's Stock"). Further, in May 1983, the SEC issued *Staff Accounting Bulletin 51*, which generally endorsed the AICPA position as authoritative guidance on this matter until the FASB completes its current project on consolidated statements.

When a subsidiary's stock transaction leaves the parent company's percentage ownership interest *unchanged,* this implies that the parent purchased or sold its pro rata share of the subsidiary stock issue or treasury stock purchase. In this case, the change in the parent's dollar equity in the subsidiary's net assets will be equal to the parent's cost or proceeds, and the investment account is merely increased or decreased by the amount of the parent's cash disbursement or receipt.

The type of accounting (purchase or sale) is indicated by the *direction* of the change in the parent's ownership percentage. The *amount* of this change is used in the calculation of the values assigned to affected accounts. The calculational procedures are explained in subsequent illustrations and discussion.

Change in Parent's Dollar Equity in Subsidiary Net Assets.   The second key variable is the amount of the change in the parent's dollar equity in the subsidiary's net assets produced by the transaction. As was noted above, the amount of the adjustment to the unamortized differential (for transactions equivalent to a purchase) and the amount of gain or loss on the sale (for transactions equivalent to open-market sales) depend upon the change in the parent's equity in net assets.

Since a subsidiary's stock transactions affect the balances in the shareholders' equity accounts of the subsidiary, and usually the parent's percentage ownership interest as well, a special analytical procedure is required to measure the change in the parent's equity in net assets. First, the parent's equity in the subsidiary net assets is calculated immediately *before* and immediately *after* the subsidiary's stock transaction. Then, the change in the parent company's equity in the net assets is determined by taking the difference between these two amounts. By isolating the effect of this single transaction, it follows that the computed change in the parent's dollar equity is properly identifiable with the subsidiary's stock transaction.

Knowledge of the relationship between the exchange price of the shares issued or repurchased and the book value (to the subsidiary) of the subsidiary's outstanding shares at the time of the transaction enables us to make some general observations about the change in the parent's equity in the subsidiary's net assets. If a subsidiary issues new shares, or reacquires outstanding shares, at an exchange price that is equal to the book value of the subsidiary's outstanding shares, the change in the parent company's dollar equity will be equal to the cost the parent incurs or the proceeds it receives. If the parent is not a party to the transaction, its equity in the subsidiary's net assets will not change. However, when the exchange price is more or less than the current book value of the shares, the change in the parent's equity in net assets will usually not equal the consideration given or received, if any. The specific amount and direction of the change depends upon the exchange price, the book value, and the number of shares purchased or sold by the parent (which determines its consideration given or received, and the change in its percentage ownership interest). In the case of a subsidiary stock transaction accounted for as a *purchase*, knowledge that the change in equity will equal the consideration given or received, if any, by the parent is sufficient to conclude that there will be no adjustment of the existing unamortized differential. However, for transactions accounted for as a *sale*, the gain or loss depends upon both the change in the parent's equity in net assets and the unamortized differential applicable to the percentage interest that is "sold." Therefore, in this type of circumstance, knowing that the change in equity will equal the consideration given or received permits only the more limited conclusion that the gain or loss will equal the unamortized differential applicable to the "sold" interest.

In the illustrations to follow, we assume for simplicity of exposition that the subsidiary stock transactions take place at the beginning of the year. The principles that are illustrated, together with the principles previously described for interim purchases and sales, apply to interim subsidiary stock transactions. Additionally, two types of subsidiary stock transactions are separately discussed: (1) issuance of new subsidiary shares and (2) repurchase of treasury shares. While these two classes of stock transactions have some unique properties that are best considered independently, it is important to keep in mind that the type of transaction is not one of the two critical variables. The change in the parent's percentage ownership interest and the change in the parent's dollar equity in the subsidiary's net assets are the central elements in our analysis, and they may increase, decrease, or remain unchanged (depending upon the particular factual context) in either of these types of stock transactions.

Issuance of New Subsidiary Shares

For the cases to follow, we assume that on January 1, 19X1, S Company had outstanding capital stock (par, $100) of $100,000, and retained earnings of $150,000. On this date, P Company held 800 of S Company's shares (an 80 percent ownership interest), and the Investment in S Company account had a balance of $260,000. Since P Company's equity in the net assets of S Company is $200,000 (80 percent × $250,000), the investment account includes an unamortized differential of $60,000. The book value of S Company's outstanding shares is $250 per share ($250,000/1,000).

Case 5. New Shares Totally Subscribed by the Parent (Increase in Parent's Ownership Percentage). Assume that on January 1, 19X1, S Company issued an additional 200 shares of stock at a price of $340 per share, all of which were purchased by P Company.

As a consequence of this transaction, the subsidiary's net assets increased by $68,000 ($340 × 200), and the parent's proportionate ownership interest increased from 80 percent (800/1,000) to 83.3 percent (1,000/1,200). The change in the parent's dollar interest is determined by calculating the parent's equity in the subsidiary's net assets immediately before and immediately after the capital transaction.

	S Company's Net Assets		P Company's Equity in S Company's Net Assets		Increase [Decrease] in P Company's Equity
	Before Transaction	After Transaction	Before Transaction (80%)	After Transaction (10/12)	
Capital stock..........	$100,000	$120,000	$ 80,000	$100,000	$20,000
Retained earnings	150,000	150,000	120,000	125,000	5,000
Other contributed capital..............	–0–	48,000	–0–	40,000	40,000
	$250,000	$318,000	$200,000	$265,000	$65,000

Since the parent company's proportionate ownership interest *increased*, the transaction is viewed as a *purchase*. Accordingly, the $3,000 difference between the parent's cost ($68,000) and the increase in its equity in the subsidiary's net assets ($65,000) is treated as an addition to the unamortized differential. This $3,000 would be allocated to specific assets of the subsidiary based upon their current fair values and the parent's proportionate increase in ownership interest (in this case, 3.3 percent), and amortized over their remaining lives.

If a consolidated statement working paper were prepared immediately after this transaction, the following investment elimination entry would be made:

```
Capital Stock (10/12 × $120,000) ...........................   100,000
Retained Earnings (10/12 × $150,000)........................   125,000
Other Contributed Capital (10/12 × $48,000) ................    40,000
Differential...............................................    63,000
    Investment in S Company (260,000 + $68,000)............            328,000
```

The $63,000 differential established in this entry is the sum of the previously existing unamortized differential of $60,000 and the $3,000 incurred in the purchase of 200 additional shares from the subsidiary.

In this example, the exchange price ($340) for the sale of new shares was more than the book value of the existing shares ($250). If the exchange price had been equal to the book value, no additional differential would have resulted; if the exchange price had been less than the book value, a negative (credit) differential on this transaction would have resulted. These relationships are illustrated below for exchange prices of (a) $250 and (b) $190 (ignoring the components of S Company's stockholders' equity):

	S Company's Net Assets		P Company's Equity in S Company's Net Assets		Increase [Decrease] in P Company's Equity	Investment Cost	Differential Dr. [Cr.]
	Before Transaction	After Transaction	Before Transaction (80%)	After Transaction (10/12)			
a. Exchange price ($250) equal to book value.......	$250,000	$300,000	$200,000	$250,000	$50,000	$50,000	–0–
b. Exchange price ($190) less than book value......	250,000	288,000	200,000	240,000	40,000	38,000	$[2,000]

If an investment elimination entry for a consolidated statement working paper were prepared for these two alternative situations, the differential set up for alternative (a) would be $60,000, the preexisting unamortized differential, and for alternative (b), $58,000 ($60,000 − $2,000).

Case 6. New Shares Totally Subscribed by Third Parties (Decrease in Parent's Ownership Percentage). Assume now that on January 1, 19X1, S Company issued the 200 additional shares to third parties (instead of P Company) at the same price of $340 per share (more than book value).

This transaction again increases the net assets of S Company by $68,000, but P Company's proportionate ownership interest *decreases* from 80 percent (800/1,000) to 66.67 percent (800/1,200). The change in P Company's dollar interest in S Company as a consequence of this transaction is calculated in the same manner as before (again ignoring the components of S Company's stockholders' equity):

> P Company's equity in S Company's net assets:
> After transaction [8/12 × ($250,000 + $68,000)] $212,000
> Before transaction (8/10 × $250,000) 200,000
> Increase [decrease] in equity . . . . $ 12,000

Thus, the issue of subsidiary shares to third parties at more than book value results in an increase in the parent company's monetary equity in the subsidiary's net assets in the amount of $12,000. Because the parent's percentage *ownership interest declined,* this transaction is treated as a *sale.* To compute the gain or loss, the parent's increase in equity in the subsidiary's net assets must be adjusted for the portion of the preexisting unamortized differential that relates to the "sold" ownership interest. This amount is calculated by a pro rata allocation of the differential to the retained and "sold" ownership interests as follows:

	Percentage Ownership Interest	Pro Rata Allocation	Unamortized Differential
After subsidiary stock transaction:			
Retained	66.7	5/6	$50,000
"Sold"	13.3	1/6	10,000
Before subsidiary stock transaction.	80.0	1.0	$60,000

Thus, the net gain (loss) is computed:

> Increase in equity in S Company's net assets $12,000
> Portion of preexisting differential allocated to "sold" interest 10,000
> Net gain [loss] on transaction . . . . $ 2,000

This gain is *recorded by the parent company* with the following entry:

> Investment in S Company 2,000
> Gain on Subsidiary Stock Transaction. 2,000

Note that this entry is a composite of two adjustments to the investment account: (1) an increase of $12,000 to reflect the parent's increased equity in the subsidiary's net assets and (2) a decrease of $10,000 to the previously recorded unamortized differential. For purposes of the parent's subsequent differential amortization entries, and in the consolidation process, the $10,000 decrease in the previously recorded unamortized differential of $60,000 would generally be allocated pro ratably to the specific assets to which the $60,000 had been assigned. For example, if the $60,000 unamortized differential before the subsidiary's stock transaction had been allocated $15,000 to plant and equipment and $45,000 to goodwill, then after the transaction the remaining $50,000 would be allocated as follows:

	Unamortized Differential before Transaction	Differential Allocated to "Sold" Interest	Unamortized Differential after Transaction
Plant and equipment	$15,000	$ [2,500]	$12,500
Goodwill	45,000	[7,500]	37,500
	$60,000	$[10,000]	$50,000

If a consolidated statement working paper were prepared immediately after the subsidiary sale of stock, the following investment elimination entry would be made:

Capital Stock (8/12 × $120,000)	80,000	
Retained Earnings (8/12 × $150,000).	100,000	
Other Contributed Capital (8/12 × $48,000)	32,000	
Differential.	50,000	
Investment in S Company ($260,000 + $2,000).		262,000

The differential set up by this eliminating entry is the value identified with the retained ownership interest. The $2,000 "gain on subsidiary stock transaction" recorded by the parent company would be extended to the Consolidated column in the income statement division of the working paper (for the year in which the transaction took place). The question of whether or not deferred income taxes are to be concurrently recognized should be resolved in accordance with the principles of *APB Opinion No. 23.*

In this example, the sale of subsidiary shares was made at a price in excess of the book value of the shares. In general, if the exchange price exceeds book value, the parent's equity in the subsidiary's net assets will increase. If the exchange price is less than book value, the parent's equity will decrease. Since the sale of 200 shares decreases the parent's percentage ownership interest the same amount regardless of the exchange price, the portion of the differential to be allocated to the "sale transaction" (from the parent company's point of view) remains the same. Thus the adjusted gain or loss will always result in a loss unless the exchange price is at least greater than book value. The effects of two alternative exchange prices, *(a)* $250 and *(b)* $190, for the sale of the 200 shares are illustrated below:

	(a) Exchange Price ($250) Equal to Book Value	*(b)* Exchange Price ($190) Less than Book Value
P Company's equity in S Company's net assets:		
After transaction......................................	$200,000*	$192,000†
Before transaction (8/10 × $250,000)....................	200,000	200,000
Increase [decrease] in parent's equity....................	–0–	$ [8,000]
Differential allocated to "sold" interest...................	$ 10,000	10,000
Net gain [loss] on transaction	$ [10,000]	$ [18,000]

* 800/1200 × ($250,000 + $50,000).
† 800/1200 × ($250,000 + $38,000).

New Shares Nonratably Subscribed by Majority and Minority Shareholders.   Cases 5 and 6 illustrate two special instances of a nonratable issue of the new shares—the parent either purchased all of the new shares or none of them. Many other possibilities exist. In all such cases, however, the same principles apply. If the parent company subscribes to more than its preexisting ownership percentage, the transaction is treated like a purchase; the difference between the parent's cost and its change in equity is added to (or subtracted from) the unamortized differential. If the parent subscribes to less than its ownership percentage, the transaction is treated like a sale; the difference between the parent's cost and its change in equity, adjusted for the portion of the differential allocable to the ownership percentage that is "sold," is reported as a gain or loss.

New Shares Ratably Subscribed by Majority and Minority Shareholders.   If the new issue of subsidiary shares is ratably subscribed by the majority and minority shareholders (i.e., the parent purchases the same percentage of these shares as its proportionate ownership interest), the parent company's ownership percentage remains unchanged. Additionally, regardless of the relationship between the exchange price for the new shares and the book value of the old shares, the change in the parent company's equity will equal its cost, and thus there is no "excess" or "difference" to be analyzed.

Interim Subsidiary Stock Issue.   If the new issue of subsidiary shares takes place during the year, the principles described above for the treatment of a change in the parent's equity apply in the same manner. Additionally, we must draw upon the previously described principles for interim purchases or sales.

For example if the parent increased its percentage ownership interest through an interim purchase of all of the new shares (as in Case 5), the analysis of the change in its dollar equity would incorporate the subsidiary's estimated earnings from the beginning of the year to the date of the stock transaction (as illustrated in Chapter 4). Assuming a preexisting controlling interest, the interim purchase alternative of presenting operating data for the subsidiary for the entire year would normally be appropriate. Therefore, the investment elimination entry for the year the transaction occurs would include a component for "purchased preacquisition earnings." The amount of this component would be calculated by multiplying the parent's *increase in ownership percentage* by the subsidiary's estimated earnings to the date of the transaction. Otherwise, the transaction would be analyzed in the same manner as in Case 5.

Similarly, if the parent's ownership interest were decreased because third parties purchased all of the new stock issue (as in Case 6), the analysis would again include the subsidiary's estimated earnings to the date of the stock transaction. Additionally, as in the example of interim sales presented earlier in this chapter, the reversal of the parent's entries to record its equity in subsidiary earnings would be based upon the retained ownership percentage, and the Consolidated column would include an extension for "equity in subsidiary earnings, net of applicable differential amortization" for the sold interest. The gain or loss on the sold interest would be calculated as in Case 6, where the unamortized differential allocation would now be calculated on the basis of the value as of the date of the stock transaction.

In both types of situations, the parent would record its equity in subsidiary earnings prior to the new stock issue based upon its ownership percentage during that time, and its equity for the remainder of the year based upon the adjusted ownership percentage. Differential amortization would also be recorded for the two time periods based upon the beginning-of-year differential value and the adjusted differential value, respectively.

Subsidiary Repurchase of Treasury Shares

Case 7. Treasury Shares Repurchased Exclusively from Minority Shareholders (Increase in Parent's Ownership Percentage).   Continuing with our basic data for P Company and its 80 percent-owned subsidiary S Company, and disregarding the previous two cases dealing with the issuance of new shares, assume that on January 1, 19X1, S Company repurchased all of the 200 shares held by minority shareholders at a price of $300 per share.

As a consequence of this transaction, S Company's net assets decreased by $60,000 ($300 × 200), and P Company's proportionate ownership interest increased from 80 percent to 100 percent. The change in P Company's monetary interest in S Company resulting from this treasury stock transaction by the subsidiary is calculated by means of the same analytical procedure that we employed for new stock issues by the subsidiary:

P Company's equity in S Company's net assets:
    After transaction [100% × ($250,000 − $60,000)] $190,000
    Before transaction (80% × $250,000)   200,000
Increase [decrease] in equity . . . . $[10,000]

Thus, the subsidiary's repurchase of its outstanding shares from minority shareholders at more than book value results in a decrease in the parent company's monetary equity in the subsidiary's net assets in the amount of $10,000. Because the parent's percentage ownership interest *increased*, this change in equity is treated as an adjustment of the unamortized differential.[5] With no change in the balance of the investment account, a decrease in the parent's equity in net assets implies that the previously recorded unamortized differential will be increased by the same amount. In this example, the unamortized differential increases from $60,000 to $70,000. No entry is made on the books of the parent company. However, the adjustment must be taken into account in the parent's subsequent differential amortization entries (with the $10,000 allocated on the basis of current fair values for subsidiary assets and an "acquired" ownership percentage from this transaction of 20 percent). Additionally, the adjusted differential will be picked up in the investment elimination entry.

Assuming that S Company recorded the acquisition of its shares in a Treasury Stock account, the investment elimination entries for a consolidated statement working paper prepared immediately after this transaction are the following:

(1) Capital Stock (200 × $100)   20,000
     Retained Earnings.   40,000
       Treasury Stock (200 × $300).   60,000

(2) Capital Stock [100% × ($100,000 − $20,000)].   80,000
     Retained Earnings [100% × ($150,000 − $40,000)]   110,000
     Differential ($60,000 + $10,000).   70,000
       Investment in S Company   260,000

---

[5] Even if the original combination were treated as a pooling of interests, the acquisition of an additional interest from the minority shareholders at a subsequent date would be accounted for as a purchase (see *APB Opinion No. 16*, pars. 5 and 43, and *Accounting Interpretation No. 26 of APB Opinion No. 16*).

The exchange price in this example was more than the book value of the subsidiary's shares. If the exchange price had been less than book value, the parent's equity in the net assets of the subsidiary would have increased, resulting in a negative (credit) differential adjustment.

Case 8.   Treasury Shares Repurchased Exclusively from Parent Company (Decrease in Parent's Ownership Percentage).   Assume now that on January 1, 19X1, S Company repurchased 200 of its outstanding shares from P Company (instead of the minority shareholders) at a price of $300 per share.

This transaction again decreases S Company's net assets by $60,000, and P Company's proportionate ownership interest decreases from 80 percent (800/1,000) to 75 percent (600/800). The change in P Company's monetary interest in S Company's net assets is:

P Company's equity in S Company's net assets:
After transaction [75% × ($250,000 − $60,000)]	$142,500
Before transaction (80% × $250,000)	200,000
Increase [decrease] in equity	$ [57,500]

Because the parent's percentage ownership interest declined, P Company will recognize a gain (loss) in an amount equal to the excess of the sales proceeds over the sum of (1) the decrease in its equity in S Company's net assets and (2) the proportionate part of the unamortized differential applicable to the "sold" interest.

In this example, a 5 percent interest was sold and 75 percent retained. Thus, P Company will record the following entry for the transaction:

Cash (200 × $300)	60,000	
Loss on Sale of Stock to Subsidiary...........................	1,250	
Investment in S Company [$57,500 + (5/80 × $60,000)]		61,250

Assuming again that S Company recorded the acquisition of its shares in a Treasury Stock account, the investment elimination entries for a consolidated statement working paper prepared immediately after this transaction are:

(1)	Capital Stock (200 × $100)	20,000	
	Retained Earnings......................................	40,000	
	Treasury Stock......................................		60,000
(2)	Capital Stock [75% × ($100,000 − $20,000)]...............	60,000	
	Retained Earnings [75% × ($150,000 − $40,000)]	82,500	
	Differential (75/80 × $60,000).........................	56,250	
	Investment in S Company ($260,000 − $61,250)		198,750

If the exchange price had been less than book value, the decrease in the parent company's equity would have exceeded the proceeds of sale, and thus the loss on the sale transaction would have been greater.

Other types of nonratable repurchases of treasury stock by the subsidiary, ratable repurchases, and interim treasury stock transactions by the subsidiary are treated in a manner analogous to that described in the previous section on new stock issues. Accordingly, those discussions are not repeated.

Effect on Fundamental Definition of Consolidated Net Income

In the case of subsidiary transactions of a capital nature that *decrease* the parent company's percentage ownership interest, the parent company recognizes a gain or loss on its books. This gain or loss is considered confirmed from a consolidated point of view, and is extended to the Consolidated column of the working paper. Accordingly, this element of the parent company's reported net income is treated in the same manner as a sale of a portion of the investment to third parties in the schedular calculation of consolidated net income.

Subsidiary transactions of a capital nature that *increase* the parent company's percentage ownership interest have no income effect. Accordingly, the only effect of these transactions on the schedular calculation of consolidated net income is the need to calculate the parent's share of the subsidiary's reported net income before and after the transaction on the basis of the two different ownership percentages.

Unconfirmed Profit on Asset Transfers

Special consideration must be given to intercompany profits when there is a change (either an increase or decrease) in the parent company's percentage interest in the selling affiliate. In respect to asset transfers between affiliates, it is important that the process of profit confirmation be identified with specific time periods. The amount of cumulative confirmed profits at the start of the current year necessarily relates to that period between the originating intercompany transaction and this date; the amount of profit confirmation during the current year must identify with the relevant fractional parts of the year *before* and *after* the change in the parent company's percentage equity in the selling subsidiary. Once these broad time intervals have been associated with the relevant confirmed profit elements, two methods of analysis are available to the accountant.

One method, which is preferred by the authors, is to calculate the amount of the investment elimination elements and the change in the parent's monetary equity on the basis of the *confirmed* net income and retained earnings of the subsidiary at the date of change in the parent company's equity percentage. Since an economic entity is preexistent to this transaction, it is plausible that the purchased or sold net assets should be based upon subsidiary earnings which are then confirmed on a consolidated basis. Calculations of consolidated net income and retained earnings of subsequent periods would allocate confirmed profits of these periods on the basis of equity interests then existing. The definitional calculation of consolidated net income, therefore, would continue to accumulate incremental interests of confirmed subsidiary net income based upon the parent's percentage interests during the fractional periods for which the different equity interests prevail. For purposes of consolidated working paper preparation, intercompany profits are eliminated and minority interests calculated on the basis of equity percentages existing at the *end* of the accounting period. Additionally, the reversal of equity in subsidiary earnings is based upon the recorded equity on the retained shares, which is equal to the confirmed income applicable to those shares when the equity method is used. However, when the parent has used the modified equity method (not recording deferral and confirmation of intercompany profits), the parent's equity in unconfirmed profits originating in prior periods is recorded in the beginning retained earnings of the parent based upon the percentage ownership interest then prevailing. To the extent that these profits have been confirmed during the current period *prior* to the change in the percentage equity, the amount of this confirmed profit allocable to the sold shares must be taken out of the parent's beginning retained earnings and added to the equity in subsidiary earnings that is extended to the Consolidated column. For example, in the case of intercompany profits in the beginning inventory that are confirmed prior to the change in the percentage ownership, this is accomplished by debiting the parent's beginning retained earnings for its share of the unconfirmed profit at the beginning of the year based upon the parent's equity percentage at that time and crediting equity in subsidiary earnings for the interest of the sold shares in the profit confirmed prior to sale; the debit to minority interest in beginning unconfirmed retained earnings is still based upon the minority's ending equity percentage, and of course the credit to the beginning inventory (or cost of sales) is for the full amount of the intercompany profit. To the extent that the unconfirmed profit at the beginning of the year has not been confirmed prior to the change in percentage interest, the parent using the modified equity method must adjust its retained earnings for the equity of the sold shares in this unconfirmed profit, because this equity, when confirmed, will accrue to the minority shareholders. The adjustment is recorded on the parent's books with a debit to Retained Earnings and a credit to the investment account.

A second basic elimination method calculates the amount of investment elimination elements and the change in the parent's monetary equity on the basis of *reported* net income and retained earnings. Because the net assets of the subsidiary used in the calculation of the change in the parent's equity are increased by this assumption, the method results in a smaller "gain on sale of interest" or a smaller differential, depending upon whether the parent's percentage interest is decreased or increased. Whether the investment account should be adjusted to reflect the parent company's new percentage interest in the unconfirmed profits is an unsettled issue. Whichever choice is made on this matter, allocation of confirmed profits in the future should be on a consistent basis.

Since specific identification of items of inventory containing intercompany profit is often difficult to determine accurately, accountants may be justified in applying the rule of first-in, first-out with respect to the flow of inventory costs. If there is evidence to indicate that the refinement introduced by the intraperiod calculation is not materially different from an application of year-end percentages, the latter rates may be used without unusual distortion of consolidated net income.

The above commentary is equally applicable to the analysis of profit confirmation in respect to the gain (or loss) on the acquisition of intercompany bonds.

Appendix: Restructuring the Form of the Subsidiary Stock Transaction in Case 6

If a subsidiary company purchases or sells its own capital stock on a *nonratable* basis between the parent company and the minority shareholders, the parent's percentage ownership interest will change. The same effect on the parent's ownership interest could be achieved simply by the parent purchasing or selling subsidiary shares in the open market. If the infusion of new capital into the subsidiary were also desired, the transaction may still be restructured to involve an open-market purchase or sale of subsidiary shares, and yet all parties continue to have the same economic effects as they did in the nonratable purchase or sale by the subsidiary of its own capital stock. Any of these alternative transaction forms may be selected by the parent company. Therefore, since the alternatives are fundamentally equivalent in terms of economic substance, we have argued that the accounting impacts of subsidiary transactions of a capital nature should be consistent with the accounting for purchases or sales of the subsidiary's stock in the open market by the parent.

In this Appendix, we illustrate two alternative transaction forms for the example presented in Case 6. First, we will alter the transaction such that the same effect on the parent's ownership interest is achieved without the subsidiary issuing capital stock. Any requirements for funds on the part of the subsidiary could be handled by advances from the parent company. In our second illustration, the transaction is structured in a manner that produces exactly the same economic effects on all parties as in the original facts of the case.

We have chosen Case 6 to illustrate the restructuring options available to the parent because the situation in this case involves a decrease in the parent's percentage ownership interest as a consequence of a subsidiary stock transaction. We argue that such a change is equivalent to a sale of an asset by the parent company, but others have argued that any "gains" on this type of transaction should be credited to paid-in capital. This elaboration of the case may be helpful to the reader in evaluating the relative merits of the two positions. Similar restructuring options are, of course, available for all types of subsidiary transactions in its own capital stock.

Case 6 in Brief

On January 1, 19X1, P Company owned 80 percent of S Company's 1,000 shares of outstanding capital stock. S Company has net assets of $250,000, and the balance of the Investment in S Company account is $260,000. These facts imply that the unamortized differential is $60,000 (assuming no unconfirmed profits).

It is assumed in Case 6 that S Company issues 200 additional shares of its capital stock to third parties at a price of $340 per share. The transaction increases S Company's net assets to $318,000, and decreases P Company's proportionate ownership interest in S Company from 80 percent (800/1,000) to 66.67 percent (800/1,200).

P Company's gain on the sale of this portion of its ownership interest, effected through the issuance of shares by the subsidiary, is calculated as follows:

P Company's equity in S Company's net assets:

After transaction (8/12 × $318,000)	$212,000
Before transaction (8/10 × $250,000)	200,000
Increase in equity	$ 12,000
Portion of preexisting differential allocated to "sold" interest (13.3/80 × $60,000)	10,000
Net gain on transaction	$ 2,000

This gain is recorded by the parent company with the following entry:

Investment in S Company	2,000	
Gain on Subsidiary Stock Transaction		2,000

Thus, after the transaction has been recorded, the investment account has a balance of $262,000, composed of the following elements:

Equity in subsidiary net assets
(8/12 × \$318,000) \$212,000
Unamortized differential (applicable
to retained interest) 50,000
\$262,000

First Alternative Transaction Form

The reduction of P Company's ownership interest in S Company from 80 percent to 66.67 percent could have been accomplished through an open-market sale by P Company of 133 shares of S Company. With an initial stockholding of 800 shares, this would leave P Company with 667 of the 1,000 outstanding shares of S Company. At the assumed market price of \$340 per share, such a transaction would be recorded by P Company as follows:

Cash (133 × \$340) 45,220
    Investment in S Company (133/800 × \$260,000) 43,225
    Gain on Sale of Subsidiary Stock 1,995

Although there is a slight rounding variation, the gain on this transaction is the same as the \$2,000 gain recognized in Case 6—the value received in excess of the carrying value for a 13.33 percent interest in S Company.

Whether the parent company elects to dispose of this ownership interest through an open-market sale of shares of the subsidiary or by having the subsidiary issue additional shares of stock to third parties, the accounting for the value received for the interest is consistent. There is, however, a difference in the amount of funds provided by outside parties to the economic entity. In Case 6 as originally formulated, the subsidiary received \$68,000 from third parties for the 200 new shares; in this restructuring, the parent receives \$45,220 from third parties for the 133 shares of S Company that it sold in the open market. If funds are needed by the subsidiary, the parent company can set up an advance to the subsidiary. The difference in the total amount of funds provided to the economic entity by outside parties is not, we believe, a substantive economic difference justifying different accounting for the "gain." Further, if desired, the transaction can be restructured as a two-stage transaction in which all economic effects are identical.

Second Alternative Transaction Form

To achieve exactly the same effects as are produced by Case 6, the transaction is here restructured as a two-stage transaction. First, the subsidiary issues the 200 new shares of stock at \$340 per share *pro rata* to the parent company and third parties. This means that the parent company purchases 160 shares (80 percent × 200) of the new stock issue, and third parties purchase 40 shares. Second, the parent company immediately sells 160 shares from its portfolio of shares of S Company in the open market at the same $340 price. The two transactions are depicted graphically in Illustration 10–5. Note that the final result is the sale of 200 new shares of S

Illustration 10–5

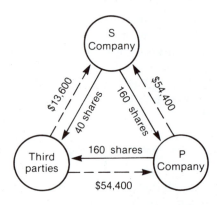

Company stock to third parties at $340 per share, with the total proceeds of $68,000 going to S Company. There is no change in the cash position of P Company. These are precisely the effects of Case 6.

P Company is a party to both transactions, and thus has a journal entry for each of them. In the case of the pro rata issuance of stock, P Company makes the following entry:

Investment in S Company (160 × $340)....................	54,400	
Cash		54,400

Since the new issue of stock was pro rata, there is no adjustment to the preexisting unamortized differential of $60,000. This is confirmed below:

P Company's equity in S Company's net assets:	
After transaction (80% × $318,000)	$254,400
Before transaction (80% × $250,000)	200,000
Increase in equity.......................................	$ 54,400
Cost of additional shares	54,400
Differential from transaction	–0–

The sale of the 160 shares of S Company stock in the open market is then recorded by P Company as follows:

Cash (160 × $340)	54,400	
Investment in S Company [160/960 × ($260,000 + $54,400)]		52,400
Gain on sale of subsidiary stock.........................		2,000

Under this alternative, we again recognize the same profit on the disposal of the 13.33 percent ownership interest in S Company. Additionally, all of the economic and accounting effects are identical to those of Case 6.

Questions

1. Enumerate three types of transactions that change a parent's ownership interest in a subsidiary.

2. When a parent gains control of a subsidiary by acquiring several blocks of stock at different dates, there are two alternative methods of determining the investment elimination of the subsidiary's retained earnings. What is the nature of these alternatives? Which is preferred?

3. How does a parent company account for its sales of subsidiary stock to the public?

4. When the parent company sells a portion of its subsidiary stock to the public, how is the carrying value of the stock determined?

5. Why is it necessary to distinguish between blocks of a subsidiary's stock purchased in the open market and stock acquired directly from the subsidiary?

6. How are subsidiary transactions of a capital nature similar to the parent's purchases or sales of the subsidiary's stock in the open market?

7. In general, how are subsidiary transactions of a capital nature accounted for?

8. Explain the theoretical disagreement over "gains" resulting from a decrease in a parent company's proportionate ownership interest due to a subsidiary's stock transaction.

9. Describe the analytical procedure used to identify the change in the parent's equity from a subsidiary stock transaction.

10. Describe the two alternative methods of calculating the investment elimination elements and the change in the parent's monetary equity at the date of a change in the parent company's equity percentage when unconfirmed intercompany profits exist as a result of prior transactions between the affiliates.

Exercises

Exercise 10–1

On January 1, 19X1, S Company had outstanding capital stock (par, $10) of $10,000 and retained earnings of $90,000. P Company made the following purchases of S Company stock in the open market:

February 1, 19X1—600 shares, cost $70,000
October 1, 19X1—200 shares, cost $27,000

During 19X1, S Company reported net income (earned uniformly over the year) of $30,000, and P Company reported net income from its own operations, exclusive of the equity in subsidiary earnings, of $40,000. Assume all differentials are assigned to nonamortizable assets.

Required:
a. Prepare the entry that would be made by the parent company at December 31 to recognize its equity in subsidiary earnings.
b. Prepare the investment elimination entries for a three-division consolidated statement working paper at December 31, 19X1. (Assume P Company includes all of S Company's 19X1 operating data in the consolidated income statement.)
c. Prepare schedular calculations of consolidated net income for 19X1 using (1) the incremental approach and (2) the residual approach.

Exercise 10–2

On January 1, 19X1, S Company had outstanding capital stock (par, $10) of $20,000 and retained earnings of $80,000. P Company held 1,200 of the S Company shares, and the Investment in S Company account had a balance of $90,000. On this date, P Company purchased an additional 600 shares of S Company stock in the open market at a cost of $50,000.

The unamortized differential prior to the acquisition of the new block of shares was allocated $11,000 to plant and equipment (net) and the remainder to goodwill. An appraisal of the subsidiary's assets and liabilities on January 1, 19X1, indicated that the fair value of the plant and equipment (net) was $200,000 and its book value was $170,000; for all other assets and liabilities, book values equaled fair values. The estimated remaining lives of the plant and equipment and the goodwill were 5 years and 20 years, respectively.

During 19X1, S Company reported net income of $30,000.

Required:
a. Calculate the amounts of the total differential from both blocks to be allocated to plant and equipment and goodwill on January 1, 19X1, after the purchase of S Company stock.
b. Prepare the entries that would be made by P Company on December 31, 19X1, to record its equity in subsidiary earnings and differential amortization.
c. Prepare the investment elimination and differential amortization entries for a three-division consolidated statement working paper on December 31, 19X1.

Exercise 10–3

On January 1, 19X1, S Company had outstanding capital stock (par, $10) of $10,000 and retained earnings of $30,000. P Company held 800 of the S Company shares, and the Investment in S Company account had a balance of $48,000.

On January 1, 19X1, P Company sold 100 of its 800 S Company shares to third parties at a price of $50 per share. P Company uses the average carrying value of the shares to determine the gain or loss on the sale.

The unamortized differential on January 1, 19X1, was allocated wholly to plant and equipment (net), with an estimated remaining life of five years. S Company reported net income of $15,000 for 19X1, and P Company's 19X1 net income, exclusive of its equity in S Company's earnings and the gain or loss on the sale of subsidiary stock, was $25,000.

Required:
a. Prepare the entries that would be made by P Company during 19X1.
b. Reconcile the balance of the investment account at December 31, 19X1, with the sum of the parent's equity in subsidiary net assets and the unamortized differential.
c. Prepare the investment elimination and differential amortization entries for a three-division consolidated statement working paper on December 31, 19X1.
d. Prepare schedular calculations of consolidated net income for 19X1 using (1) the incremental approach and (2) the residual approach.

Exercise 10–4

On January 1, 19X1, S Company had outstanding capital stock (par, $10) of $20,000 and retained earnings of $80,000. P Company held 1,800 of the S Company shares, and the Investment in S Company account had a balance of $105,000. On this date, S Company issued an additional 1,000 shares of stock at a price of $80 per share, all of which were purchased by third parties.

Required:
a. Determine the gain or loss that P Company realized on this transaction.
b. Prepare any journal entries that would be made by P Company.
c. Assuming a consolidated statement working paper were prepared immediately after this transaction, prepare the investment elimination entry.
d. Assuming that the unamortized differential before this transaction was allocated wholly to goodwill and that its remaining life was estimated to be 20 years, prepare the entry that P Company would make at December 31, 19X1, to record differential amortization.

Exercise 10–5

On January 1, 19X1, S Company had outstanding capital stock (par, $10) of $20,000 and retained earnings of $80,000. P Company held 1,800 of the S Company shares, and the Investment in S Company account had a balance of $105,000. On this date, S Company issued an additional 1,000 shares of stock at a price of $40 per share, all of which were purchased by third parties.

Required:
a. Determine the gain or loss that P Company realized on this transaction.
b. Prepare any journal entries that would be made by P Company.
c. Assuming a consolidated statement working paper were prepared immediately after this transaction, prepare the investment elimination entry.

d. Assuming that the unamortized differential before this transaction was allocated wholly to goodwill and that its remaining life was estimated to be 20 years, prepare the entry that P Company would make at December 31, 19X1, to record differential amortization.

Exercise 10–6

On January 1, 19X1, S Company had outstanding capital stock (par, $10) of $20,000 and retained earnings of $80,000. P Company held 1,800 of the S Company shares, and the Investment in S Company account had a balance of $130,000. On this date, S Company issued an additional 2,000 shares of stock at a price of $80 per share, all of which were purchased by P Company.

Required:
a. Determine the change in P Company's equity and the differential adjustment as a result of the subsidiary stock transaction.
b. Prepare any journal entries that would be made by P Company.
c. Assuming a consolidated statement working paper were prepared immediately after this transaction, prepare the investment elimination entry.
d. Assume that $15,000 of the unamortized differential before the subsidiary stock transaction was allocated to plant and equipment (net) and the remainder to goodwill. Additionally, on this date, the fair value of the plant and equipment (net) was $400,000 and its book value was $360,000; for all other assets, book values equaled fair values. Calculate the amounts of the total adjusted differential allocated to plant and equipment (net) and goodwill after the subsidiary stock transaction.
e. Assuming that on January 1, 19X1, the estimated remaining lives of the plant and equipment and the goodwill were 5 years and 20 years, respectively, prepare the entry that P Company would make at December 31, 19X1, to record differential amortization.

Exercise 10–7

On January 1, 19X1, S Company had outstanding capital stock (par, $10) of $20,000 and retained earnings of $80,000. P Company held 1,800 of the S Company shares, and the Investment in S Company account had a balance of $130,000. On this date, S Company issued an additional 2,000 shares of stock at a price of $40 per share, all of which were purchased by P Company.

Required:
a. Determine the change in P Company's equity and the differential adjustment as a result of the subsidiary stock transaction.
b. Prepare any journal entries that would be made by P Company.
c. Assuming a consolidated statement working paper were prepared immediately after this transaction, prepare the investment elimination entry.
d. Assume that $15,000 of the unamortized differential before the subsidiary stock transaction was allocated to plant and equipment (net) and the remainder to goodwill. Additionally, on this date, the fair value of the plant and equipment

(net) was $400,000 and its book value was $360,000; for all other assets, book values equaled fair values. Calculate the amounts of the total adjusted differential allocated to plant and equipment (net) and goodwill after the subsidiary stock transaction.

e. Assuming that on January 1, 19X1, the estimated remaining lives of the plant and equipment and the goodwill were five years and 20 years, respectively, prepare the entry that P Company would make at December 31, 19X1, to record differential amortization.

Exercise 10–8

On January 1, 19X1, S Company had outstanding capital stock (par, $10) of $20,000 and retained earnings of $80,000. P Company held 1,800 of the S Company shares, and the Investment in S Company account had a balance of $110,000. On this date, S Company repurchased all 200 of its shares held by minority shareholders at a price of $100 per share.

Required:

a. Determine the change in P Company's equity and the differential adjustment as a result of the subsidiary's repurchase of its shares.
b. Prepare any journal entries that would be made by P Company.
c. Assuming a consolidated statement working paper were prepared immediately after this transaction, prepare the investment elimination entry (S Company recorded the repurchased shares at cost in a Treasury Stock account).
d. Assume that $14,000 of the unamortized differential before the subsidiary stock transaction was allocated to plant and equipment (net) and the remainder to goodwill. Additionally, on this date, the fair value of the plant and equipment (net) was $100,000 and its book value was $60,000; for all other assets, book values equaled fair values. Calculate the amounts of the total adjusted differential allocated to plant and equipment (net) and goodwill after the subsidiary stock transaction.
e. Assuming that on January 1, 19X1, the estimated remaining lives of the plant and equipment and the goodwill were 4 years and 10 years, respectively, prepare the entry that P Company would make at December 31, 19X1, to record differential amortization.

Exercise 10–9

On January 1, 19X1, S Company had outstanding capital stock (par, $10) of $20,000 and retained earnings of $80,000. P Company held 1,800 of the S Company shares, and the Investment in S Company account had a balance of $110,000. On this date, S Company repurchased 400 of its shares from P Company at a price of $40 per share.

Required:

a. Determine the gain or loss that P Company realized on this transaction.
b. Prepare any journal entries that would be made by P Company.
c. Assuming a consolidated statement working paper were prepared immediately

after this transaction, prepare the investment elimination entries (S Company recorded the repurchased shares at cost in a Treasury Stock account).

d. Assume that $14,000 of the unamortized differential before the subsidiary stock transaction was allocated to plant and equipment (net) and the remainder to goodwill. Calculate the amounts of the total adjusted differential allocated to plant and equipment (net) and goodwill after the subsidiary stock transaction.

e. Assuming that on January 1, 19X1, the estimated remaining lives of the plant and equipment and the goodwill were 5 years and 10 years, respectively, prepare the entry that P Company would make at December 31, 19X1, to record differential amortization.

Exercise 10–10

On January 1, 19X1, S Company had outstanding capital stock (par, $10) of $10,000 and retained earnings of $40,000. P Company held 700 of the S Company shares, and the Investment in S Company account had a balance of $38,500. On this date, S Company repurchased 400 shares of its outstanding stock at a price of $60 per share. Three hundred shares were purchased from P Company, and the remaining 100 shares were purchased from minority shareholders.

Required:
a. Determine the gain or loss that P Company realized on this transaction.
b. Prepare any journal entries that would be made by P Company.
c. Assuming a consolidated statement working paper were prepared immediately after this transaction, prepare the investment elimination entries (S Company recorded the repurchased shares at cost in a Treasury Stock account).

Exercise 10–11

On January 1, 19X1, S Company had outstanding capital stock (par, $10) of $10,000 and retained earnings of $40,000. P Company held 700 of the S Company shares, and the Investment in S Company account had a balance of $38,500. On this date, S Company repurchased 400 shares of its outstanding stock at a price of $60 per share. Two hundred shares were repurchased from P Company, and the remaining 200 shares were purchased from minority shareholders.

Required:
a. Determine the change in P Company's equity and the differential adjustment as a result of the subsidiary's treasury stock transaction.
b. Prepare any journal entries that would be made by P Company.
c. Assuming a consolidated statement working paper were prepared immediately after this transaction, prepare the investment elimination entries (S Company recorded the repurchased shares at cost in a Treasury Stock account).

Exercise 10–12

On January 1, 19X1, S Company had outstanding capital stock (par, $100) of $100,000 and retained earnings of $150,000. P Company held 800 of the S Company shares, and the Investment in S Company account had a balance of $260,000. On this date, S Company issued an additional 200 shares of stock at a price of $340 per share. P Company purchased 100 shares of the stock, and the remaining 100 shares were purchased by third parties.

Required:

a. Determine the gain or loss that P Company realized on this transaction.
b. Prepare any journal entries that would be made by P Company.
c. Assuming a consolidated statement working paper were prepared immediately after this transaction, prepare the investment elimination entry.
d. Assuming that the unamortized differential before this transaction was allocated $12,000 to plant and equipment and the remainder to goodwill, determine the amounts of the adjusted differential that would be allocated to these assets.

Exercise 10–13

On January 1, 19X1, S Company had capital stock (par, $100) of $100,000 and retained earnings of $100,000. P Company held 600 of S Company's 1,000 outstanding shares, and the Investment in S Company account had a balance of $140,000. On this date, S Company issued an additional 1,000 shares at a price of $250 per share. P Company purchased 800 shares, and the remaining 200 shares were purchased by third parties.

Required:

a. Determine the change in P Company's equity and the differential adjustment as a result of the subsidiary stock transaction.
b. Prepare any journal entries that would be made by P Company.
c. Assuming a consolidated statement working paper were prepared immediately after this transaction, prepare the investment elimination entry.

Exercise 10–14

On January 1, 19X1, S Company had outstanding capital stock (par, $100) of $100,000 and retained earnings of $150,000. P Company held 800 of the S Company shares, and the Investment in S Company account had a balance of $260,000. On this date, S Company issued an additional 200 shares of stock. P Company purchased its ratable share of this new issue, or 160 shares; the remaining 40 shares were purchased by third parties.

Required:

a. Confirm that the increase in the parent company's equity is equal to its cost regardless of the relationship between the exchange price of the new shares and the book value of the old shares by calculating the parent's increase in equity and its cost for each of the following alternative exchange prices:
    (1) $250 per share (equal to book value per share).
    (2) $340 per share (greater than book value per share).
    (3) $190 per share (less than book value per share).
b. Prepare the investment elimination entry for a consolidated statement working

paper prepared immediately after the new issue of subsidiary shares for each of the three alternative exchange prices.

Exercise 10–15

On January 1, 19X1, S Company had outstanding capital stock (par, $100) of $100,000 and retained earnings of $150,000. P Company held 800 of the S Company shares, and the Investment in S Company account had a balance of $260,000. On this date, S Company issued an additional 200 shares of stock at a price of $190 per share. P Company purchased 100 shares of the stock, and the remaining 100 shares were purchased by third parties.

Required:
a. Determine the gain or loss that P Company realized on this transaction.
b. Prepare any journal entries that would be made by P Company.
c. Assuming a consolidated statement working paper were prepared immediately after this transaction, prepare the investment elimination entry.
d. Assuming that the unamortized differential before this transaction was allocated $12,000 to plant and equipment and the remainder to goodwill, determine the amounts of the adjusted differential that would be allocated to these assets.

Exercise 10–16

On January 1, 19X1, S Company had capital stock (par, $100) of $100,000 and retained earnings of $100,000. P Company held 600 of S Company's 1,000 outstanding shares, and the Investment in S Company account had a balance of $140,000. On this date, S Company issued an additional 1,000 shares at a price of $150 per share. P Company purchased 800 shares, and the remaining 200 shares were purchased by third parties.

Required:
a. Determine the change in P Company's equity and the differential adjustment as a result of the subsidiary stock transaction.
b. Prepare any journal entries that would be made by P Company.
c. Assuming a consolidated statement working paper was prepared immediately after this transaction, prepare the investment elimination entry.

Exercise 10–17

On January 1, 19X1, S Company had outstanding capital stock (par, $10) of $20,000 and retained earnings of $80,000. P Company held 1,800 of the S Company shares, and the Investment in S Company account had a balance of $110,000. On this date, S Company repurchased 500 of its outstanding shares of stock. P Company sold its ratable share, or 450 shares, and the remaining 50 shares were repurchased from the minority shareholders.

Required:

a. Confirm that the decrease in the parent company's equity is equal to its proceeds regardless of the relationship between the exchange price of the repurchased shares and their book value by calculating the parent's decrease in equity and its proceeds for each of the following alternative exchange prices:
   (1) $50 per share (equal to book value per share).
   (2) $60 per share (greater than book value per share).
   (3) $40 per share (less than book value per share).
b. Prepare the investment elimination entries for a consolidated statement working paper prepared immediately after the subsidiary's repurchase of treasury shares for each of the three alternative exchange prices. (Assume the subsidiary recorded the reacquired shares at cost in a Treasury Stock account.)

Problems

Problem 10–18

On January 1, 19X1, S Company had outstanding capital stock (par, $10) of $10,000 and retained earnings of $30,000. P Company made the following purchases of S Company stock in the open market:

> January 1, 19X1—50 shares, cost $2,500
> July 1, 19X1—100 shares, cost $5,500
> October 1, 19X1—750 shares, cost $45,000

During 19X1, S Company reported net income (earned uniformly over the year) of $20,000 and P Company reported net income from its own operations, exclusive of the equity in subsidiary earnings, of $50,000. Assume all differentials are assigned to nonamortizable assets.

Required:

a. Assuming the individual block purchases are eliminated on a step-by-step-basis:
   (1) Prepare the entry that would be made by the parent company at December 31 to recognize its equity in subsidiary earnings.
   (2) Prepare the investment elimination entries for a three-division consolidated statement working paper at December 31, 19X1. (Assume that P Company elects to include the results of S Company's operations for all of 19X1 in the 19X1 consolidated income statement.)
   (3) Prepare schedular calculations of consolidated net income for 19X1 using (a) the incremental approach and (b) the residual approach.
b. Assuming that the last purchase is treated as the date of acquisition, repeat the three requirements in (a) above.

Problem 10–19

On January 1, 19X1, S Company had outstanding capital stock (par, $5) of $10,000 and retained earnings of $50,000. P Company held 1,800 of the S Company shares, and the Investment in S Company account had a balance of $84,000.

On September 30, 19X1, P Company sold 600 of the S Company shares it held to third parties at a price of $25 per share. P Company uses the average carrying value of the shares to determine the gain or loss on the sale.

The differential is allocated wholly to Land, and thus is not subject to amortization. During 19X1, S Company reported net income (earned uniformly over the year) of $20,000 and P Company's net income, exclusive of its equity in S Company's earnings and the gain or loss on the sale of subsidiary stock, was $50,000.

Required:

a. Prepare the entries that would be made by P Company during 19X1.
b. Reconcile the balance of the investment account at December 31, 19X1, with the sum of the parent's equity in subsidiary net assets and the differential.
c. Prepare the investment elimination entries for a three-division consolidated statement working paper on December 31, 19X1.
d. Prepare schedular calculations of consolidated net income for 19X1 using (1) the incremental approach and (2) the residual approach.

Problem 10–20

On January 1, 19X1, S Company had outstanding capital stock (par, $10) of $20,000 and retained earnings of $80,000. P Company held 1,800 of the S Company shares, and the Investment in S Company account had a balance of $117,000.

On July 1, 19X1, P Company sold 200 of its S Company shares to third parties at a price of $80 per share. P Company uses the average carrying value of the shares to determine the gain or loss on the sale.

The unamortized differential on January 1, 19X1, was allocated wholly to goodwill, with an estimated remaining life of 10 years. During 19X1, S Company reported net income of $10,000 (earned uniformly throughout the year), and P Company reported net income, exclusive of its equity in S Company's earnings and the gain or loss on the sale of subsidiary stock, of $20,000.

Required:

a. Prepare the entries that would be made by P Company during 19X1.
b. Reconcile the balance of the investment account at December 31, 19X1, with the sum of the parent's equity in subsidiary net assets and the unamortized differential.
c. Prepare the investment elimination and differential amortization entries for a three-division consolidated statement working paper on December 31, 19X1.
d. Prepare schedular calculations of consolidated net income for 19X1 using (1) the incremental approach and (2) the residual approach.

Problem 10–21

On January 1, 19X1, S Company had outstanding capital stock (par, $5) of $10,000 and retained earnings of $50,000. P Company held 1,800 of the S Company shares, and the Investment in S Company account had a balance of $84,000.

On July 1, 19X1, S Company issued an additional 1,000 shares to third parties at a price of $70 per share.

The differential as of January 1, 19X1, is allocated wholly to goodwill, which has an estimated life of 10 years. During 19X1, S Company reported net income (earned uniformly over the year) of $20,000, and P Company's net income, exclusive of its equity in S Company's earnings and the gain or loss on the subsidiary stock transaction, was $50,000.

Required:

a. Determine the gain or loss that P Company realized on the subsidiary's stock transaction.
b. Prepare all investment-related journal entries that would be made by P Company in 19X1.
c. Reconcile the balance of the investment account at December 31, 19X1, with the sum of the parent's equity in subsidiary net assets and the unamortized differential.
d. Prepare the eliminating entries for a three-division consolidated statement working paper on December 31, 19X1.
e. Assuming that P Company's retained earnings on January 1, 19X1, amounted to $100,000, and that neither company paid any dividends, prepare a partial consolidated statement working paper (income statement and retained earnings statement divisions) for the year.
f. Prepare a schedular calculation of consolidated net income for 19X1 using the incremental approach.

Problem 10–22

On January 1, 19X1, S Company had outstanding capital stock (par, $10) of $20,000 and retained earnings of $80,000. P Company held 1,800 of the S Company shares, and the Investment in S Company account had a balance of $130,000.

On July 1, 19X1, S Company issued an additional 2,000 shares of stock at a price of $100 per share, all of which were purchased by P Company.

The differential as of January 1, 19X1, is allocated wholly to goodwill, which has an estimated life of 10 years. At July 1, 19X1, the book values of S Company's assets and liabilities were equal to their fair values. P Company decides to amortize any goodwill arising from the July 1 purchase of shares over the remaining life of the existing goodwill. During 19X1, S Company reported net income (earned uniformly over the year) of $40,000, and P Company's net income, exclusive of its equity in S Company's earnings, was $60,000.

Required:

a. Determine the change in P Company's equity and the differential adjustment as a result of the subsidiary stock transaction.
b. Prepare all investment-related journal entries that would be made by P Company in 19X1.
c. Reconcile the balance of the investment account at December 31, 19X1, with the sum of the parent's equity in subsidiary net assets and the unamortized differential.
d. Prepare the eliminating entries for a three-division consolidated statement working paper on December 31, 19X1. (Assume P Company includes all of S Company's 19X1 operating data in the consolidated income statement.)

e. Assuming that P Company's retained earnings on January 1, 19X1, amounted to $150,000, and that neither company paid any dividends, prepare a partial consolidated statement working paper (income statement and retained earnings statement divisions) for the year.

f. Prepare a schedular calculation of consolidated net income for 19X1 using the incremental approach.

Problem 10–23

P Company purchased 800 shares of S Company stock on January 1, 19X1, for $120,000, when S Company had capital stock ($100 par) of $100,000 and retained earnings of $50,000. P Company purchased an additional 100 shares on July 1, 19X2, for $17,700. On July 1, 19X3, S Company issued 200 new shares to minority shareholders for $40,000.

Intercompany profit on asset transfers by S Company to P Company existed as follows:

1. Unconfirmed inventory profit of $2,000 reported in 19X1, confirmed in the last six months of 19X2.
2. Unconfirmed inventory profit of $1,000 reported in the first six months of 19X2, confirmed in the first six months of 19X3.
3. Unconfirmed profit of $10,000 on the transfer of plant and equipment on July 2, 19X2, and this asset has an expected life of 10 years.

P Company had an annual net income of $100,000 (exclusive of its equity in S Company's earnings and the gain or loss on the subsidiary stock transaction), and S Company earned $20,000 uniformly over each year.

Assume calculations of changes in equity are based upon confirmed profits. Differentials, if any, are to be allocated to nonamortizable assets.

Required:

a. Prepare schedular calculations of consolidated net income for 19X2 using both the incremental and the residual approaches.

b. Prepare schedular calculations of consolidated net income for 19X3 using both the incremental and the residual approaches.

Problem 10–24

Presented below are the trial balances of P Company and its subsidiary S Company at December 31, 19X3:

	P Company	S Company
Cash	$ 486,000	$ 249,600
Accounts receivable	235,000	185,000
Inventories (12/31)	475,000	355,000
Machinery and equipment (net)	2,231,000	530,000
Investment in S Company bonds	58,000	
Investment in S Company stock	954,000	
Unamortized discount on bonds payable		2,400
Cost of sales	2,982,000	1,015,000
Operating expenses	400,000	377,200
Interest expense		7,800
Dividends declared	170,000	100,000
	$7,991,000	$2,822,000
Accounts payable	$ 384,000	$ 62,000
Bonds payable		120,000
Common stock	1,200,000	250,000
Other contributed capital		50,000
Retained earnings (1/1)	2,100,000	640,000
Sales	4,000,000	1,700,000
Equity in subsidiary earnings	232,000	
Dividend income	75,000	
	$7,991,000	$2,822,000

Additional information:
1. On January 3, 19X1, P Company acquired from John Simmons, the sole stockholder of S Company, for $440,000 cash, both a patent valued at $40,000 and 80 percent of the outstanding stock of S Company. The net book value of S Company's stock on the date of acquisition was $500,000, and the book values of the individual assets and liabilities were equal to their fair values. P Company charged the entire $440,000 to the Investment in S Company Stock account. The patent, for which no amortization has been charged, had a remaining legal life of four years as of January 3, 19X1.
2. On July 1, 19X3, P Company reduced its investment in S Company to 75 percent of S Company's outstanding common stock by selling shares for $70,000 to an unaffiliated company at a profit of $16,000. P Company recorded the proceeds as a credit to its investment account.
3. For the six months ended June 30, 19X3, S Company had net income of $140,000. P Company recorded 80 percent of this amount on its books of account prior to the time of sale.
4. During 19X2, S Company sold merchandise to P Company for $130,000, which was at a markup of 30 percent over S Company's cost. On January 1, 19X3, $52,000 of this merchandise remained in P Company's inventory. This mer-

chandise was subsequently sold by P Company in February 19X3 at a profit of $8,000.

5. In November 19X3, P Company sold merchandise to S Company for the first time. P Company's cost for this merchandise was $80,000, and the sale was made at 120 percent of cost. S Company's inventory at December 31, 19X3, contained merchandise that was purchased from P Company at a cost to S Company of $24,000.

6. On December 31, 19X3, there was a $45,000 payment in transit from S Company to P Company. Accounts receivable and accounts payable include intercompany receivables and payables.

7. In December 19X3, S Company declared and paid cash dividends of $100,000 to its stockholders.

8. On December 31, 19X3, P Company purchased for $58,000, 50 percent of the outstanding bonds of S Company. The bonds mature on December 31, 19X7, and were originally issued at a discount. On December 31, 19X3, the balance in S Company's account, "Unamortized Discount on Bonds Payable," was $2,400. It is the intention of the management of P Company to hold these bonds until their maturity.

Required:

a. Prepare a three-division consolidated statement working paper for the year ended December 31, 19X3. Intercompany profits are to be 100 percent eliminated, and allocated pro rata to majority and minority shareholders.

b. Prepare a schedular calculation of consolidated net income for 19X3, using the incremental approach.

(AICPA adapted)

Problem 10–25

P Company acquired control of S Company on June 30, 19X1, by purchasing for $394,800 cash in the open market 2,800 shares of S Company common stock. On that date, S Company had 4,000 issued shares of $100 par value common stock, 500 shares of which were held as treasury stock and carried at par.

On January 1, 19X3, P Company acquired at a cost of $35,000, 200 additional shares from a minority stockholder. On December 31, 19X3, by agreement with the minority stockholders, P Company acquired the 500 shares held in the treasury of S Company at a cost of $90,000.

The following analysis of S Company's Other Contributed Capital and Retained Earnings is provided:

	Other Contributed Capital	Retained Earnings
Credits		
June 30, 19X1...............................	$ 74,300	$ 43,745
Earnings, 6/30 to 12/31/X1		35,306
Earnings, 19X2.............................		65,754
Earnings, 19X3.............................		51,025
Premium on sale of treasury stock.............	40,000	
	$114,300	$195,830
Debits		
Dividends paid, 12/1/X1		$ 35,000
Dividends paid, 12/5/X2		35,000
Dividends paid, 12/15/X3		40,000
	–0–	$110,000
Balance, 12/31/X3	$114,300	$ 85,830

At the date of each acquisition of S Company shares, the book and fair values of S Company's assets and liabilities were equal. Any goodwill arising from the acquisitions should be amortized over a 10-year period from the date of each acquisition.

The following information has been excerpted from the companies' trial balances at December 31, 19X3:

	P Company	S Company
Other assets...	$300,000	$680,130
Investment in S Company	?	
Accounts payable	100,000	80,000
Capital stock	200,000	400,000
Other contributed capital	300,000	114,300
Retained earnings—P Company:		
From own operations, *excluding* any effects of investment in S Company	129,514	
From investment in S Company......................	?	
Retained earnings—S Company........................		85,830

Required:

a. Assuming that P Company uses the equity method to account for its investment in S Company, calculate the correct balances at December 31, 19X3, for—
   (1) Investment in S Company.
   (2) Retained earnings—P Company.

b. Using the balances calculated in (a) above, prepare a consolidated balance sheet working paper at December 31, 19X3.
   (Note: Round all calculations to the nearest dollar.)

(AICPA adapted)

Problem 10–26

The December 31, 19X3, trial balances of Pulsar Corporation and its subsidiary, Shaker Corporation, are presented below:

	Pulsar	Shaker
Cash..................................	$ 167,250	$101,000
Accounts receivable	178,450	72,000
Notes receivable	87,500	28,000
Dividends receivable	36,000	
Inventories.........................	122,000	68,000
Property, plant, and equipment (net) ...	370,000	188,000
Investment in Shaker.................	240,800	
	$1,202,000	$457,000
Accounts payable	222,000	76,000
Notes payable	79,000	89,000
Dividends payable		40,000
Common stock ($10 par value)	400,000	100,000
Retained earnings....................	501,000	152,000
	$1,202,000	$457,000

Pulsar initially acquired 60 percent of the outstanding common stock of Shaker in 19X1. In this purchase, there was no differential. As of December 31, 19X3, the percentage of Shaker's common stock owned by Pulsar is 90 percent. An analysis of the Investment in Shaker account is provided below:

Date	Description	Amount
12/31/X1	Acquired 6,000 shares	$ 70,800
12/31/X2	60% of 19X2 net income of $78,000	46,800
9/1/X3	Acquired 3,000 shares	92,000
12/31/X3	Subsidiary income for 19X3	67,200*
12/31/X3	90% of dividends declared	(36,000)
		$240,800

* Subsidiary income for 19X3:
  60% × $96,000........... $57,600
  30% × (4/12 × $96,000)... 9,600
  $67,200

Assume that Shaker's net income is earned ratably during the year. Any differential is to be allocated to goodwill and amortized over 60 months.

On December 15, 19X3, Shaker declared a cash dividend of $4 per share of common stock, payable to shareholders on January 7, 19X4.

During 19X3, Pulsar sold merchandise to Shaker. Pulsar's cost for this merchandise was $68,000, and the sale was made at 125 percent of cost. Shaker's inventory at December 31, 19X3, included merchandise purchased from Pulsar at a cost to Shaker of $35,000.

In December 19X2, Shaker sold merchandise to Pulsar for $67,000, which was at a markup of 35 percent over Shaker's cost. On January 1, 19X3, $54,000 of this merchandise remained in Pulsar's inventory. This merchandise was subsequently sold by Pulsar at a profit of $11,000 during the first six months of 19X3.

On October 1, 19X3, Shaker sold for $42,000, excess equipment to Pulsar. Data relating to this equipment is as follows:

Book value on Shaker's books	$36,000
Method of depreciation	Straight-line
Estimated remaining life on 10/1/X3	10 years

Near the end of 19X3, Shaker reduced the balance of its intercompany account payable to Pulsar to zero by transferring $8,000 to Pulsar. This payment was still in transit on December 31, 19X3.

Required:

Prepare a consolidated balance sheet working paper at December 31, 19X3 for Pulsar Corporation and its subsidiary Shaker Corporation. Supporting computations should be in good form. Intercompany profits should be eliminated using the 100 percent, pro rata method.

(AICPA adapted)

CHAPTER
11

Consolidated Statements—
Special Ownership
Configurations

Multilevel Affiliations

Affiliation diagrams have heretofore usually been of the following basic form:

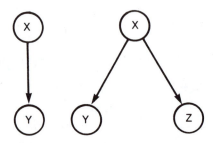

Affiliation diagrams for a parent company and three or more subsidiaries may be depicted by merely extending the second level of the diagram horizontally as necessary. In each of these cases, control is *directly* exercised by the parent company over all members of the affiliation. Yet, on occasions, the intercorporate stock arrangements may indicate one subsidiary's control over other subsidiaries; in this instance, the parent's control over second-level subsidiaries is, at least in part, *indirect* in nature. In such cases, the associations are best described as multilevel affiliations.

In a multilevel affiliation, at least one company other than the parent company will be an "investor company," and each "investor company" will carry its investment in affiliates on an equity basis. Accordingly, the calculation of amounts for the investment elimination entries, minority interests, equities in affiliates' earnings, and so forth, will be based upon the results of applying equity method accounting. Otherwise, parent company entries are made and consolidated statement working paper techniques applied as described in previous chapters.

The following two cases illustrate affiliations that are multilevel in form. The account balances that relate to each of these examples are as follows:

| | January 1, 19X1 | | |
	P Company	Y Company	Z Company
Capital stock................	$200,000	$100,000	$50,000
Retained earnings	80,000	20,000	10,000

It is assumed that each company reported income, exclusive of any equity in affiliates' earnings, of $10,000 each year. Additionally, for reasons of simplicity, it is assumed that no dividends were declared, and that all differentials relate to nonamortizable assets.

Case 1.   Y Company purchased 80 percent of the capital stock of Z Company on January 1, 19X1, for $50,000. One year later, P Company purchased 90 percent of the capital stock of Y Company for $125,000. As a consequence of these transactions, the affiliation diagram for this multi-level affiliation is as follows:

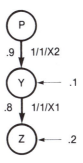

Since both P Company and Y Company hold stock investments in affiliates, each will record an equity in an affiliate's earnings and each will be subject to an investment elimination entry in the consolidated statement working paper. The purchased equity in the net assets of the affiliate and the related differential for each of these two investments are analyzed following:

	P Company in Y Company (1/1/X2)	Y Company in Z Company (1/1/X1)
Investment cost..............................	$125,000	$50,000
Purchased equity in affiliate's net assets:		
Capital stock................................	$ 90,000	$40,000
Retained earnings	34,200*	8,000
	$124,200	$48,000
Differential	$ 800	$ 2,000

* 90% × $38,000.

Y Company's purchased equity in Z Company's net assets is based upon the amounts for capital stock and retained earnings at January 1, 19X1. However, since P Company purchased the shares of Y Company one year later, Y Company's retained earnings must be modified for its 19X1 operations. During 19X1, Y Company's income, *on an equity method basis,* is $18,000 [$10,000 + (80 percent × $10,000)], and thus its retained earnings balance on January 1, 19X2, when acquired by P Company, is $38,000.

At the end of 19X2, the companies each record their equities in affiliates' 19X2 earnings (if any) in accordance with *APB Opinion No. 18*. In order to properly pick up the full equity at each level, the calculations of these equity interests *begin at the lowest level of the affiliation structure and work*

Illustration 11–1

P COMPANY AND SUBSIDIARY COMPANIES
Partial Consolidated Statement Working Paper
For Year Ended December 31, 19X2

	P Company	Y Company	Z Company	Eliminations Dr.	Eliminations Cr.	Minority Interests Y Company	Minority Interests Z Company	Consolidated
Income Statement								
Net income (excluding equity in affiliates' earnings)	10,000	10,000	10,000					30,000
Equity in affiliates' earnings	16,200	8,000		(1) 24,200				–0–
Minority interests						1,800	2,000	[3,800]
Net income	26,200	18,000	10,000	24,200	–0–	1,800	2,000	26,200
Retained Earnings Statement								
Retained earnings, 1/1/X2:								
P Company	90,000							90,000
Y Company		38,000		(3) 34,200		3,800		–0–
Z Company			20,000	(2) 16,000			4,000	–0–
Net income	26,200	18,000	10,000	24,200		1,800	2,000	26,200
Retained earnings, 12/31/X2	116,200	56,000	30,000	74,400	–0–	5,600	6,000	116,200
Balance Sheet								
Investment in Y Company	141,200				(1) 16,200 (3) 125,000			–0–
Investment in Z Company		66,000			(1) 8,000 (2) 58,000			–0–
Differential—P Company in Y Company				(3) 800				800
Differential—Y Company in Z Company				(2) 2,000				2,000
Capital stock:								
P Company	200,000							200,000
Y Company		100,000		(3) 90,000		10,000		–0–
Z Company			50,000	(2) 40,000			10,000	–0–
Retained earnings	116,200	56,000	30,000	74,400		5,600	6,000	116,200
Minority interest—Y Company						15,600		15,600M
Minority interest—Z Company					–0–	15,600	16,000	16,000M

[deduction]
Explanation of eliminations:
(1) To reverse 19X2 entries by investor companies recognizing their equities in affiliates' earnings. (2) Investment elimination entry for Y Company's investment in Z Company. (3) Investment elimination entry for P Company's investment in Y Company.

upward. Thus, in our example, we begin with Z Company. Z Company holds no ownership interest in affiliates, and as a result its equity-based net income is equal to its income from operations ($10,000). Moving up one level to Company Y, its equity in Z Company's 19X2 equity-based net income amounts to $8,000 (80 percent × $10,000). Adding this equity in affiliates' earnings to income from operations of $10,000 yields 19X2 equity-based net income for Company Y of $18,000. Finally, moving to the top level of the affiliation structure, P Company's equity in Y Company's 19X2 equity-based net income is $16,200 (90 percent × $18,000), which when combined with P Company's income from operations of $10,000 produces equity-based net income for 19X2 for P Company of $26,200.

A partial consolidated statement working paper for this affiliation for the year ended December 31, 19X2, is presented in Illustration 11–1. Note that minority interests are based simply on the subsidiaries' recorded incomes and net assets, which in the case of Y Company reflects its equity interest in Z Company.

Consolidated net income for 19X2 may be confirmed by definition (incremental approach) as follows:

P Company's income from its own operations	$10,000
Increased by its equity in Y Company's reported (equity basis) income: 90% × $18,000	16,200
Consolidated net income for 19X2	$26,200

Case 2. On January 1, 19X1, P Company purchased 80 percent of the capital stock of Y Company for $100,000 and 70 percent of the capital stock of Z Company for $43,000. One year later, Y Company purchased 20 percent of the capital stock of Z Company for $15,000.

The affiliation diagram and the analysis of the purchased equities in the net assets of affiliates are presented following:

Affiliation Diagram

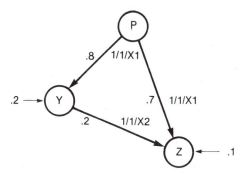

	P Company in Y Company (1/1/X1)	P Company in Z Company (1/1/X1)	Y Company in Z Company (1/1/X2)
Investment cost	$100,000	$43,000	$15,000
Purchased equity in affiliate's net assets:			
Capital stock	$ 80,000	$35,000	$10,000
Retained earnings	16,000	7,000	4,000*
	$ 96,000	$42,000	$14,000
Differential	$ 4,000	$ 1,000	$ 1,000

* 20% × $20,000.

In Case 1, Y Company was, technically, both a "parent" and a subsidiary, and P Company's control over Z Company was indirect through Y Company. In this example, however, P Company exercises direct control over both subsidiaries, and only obtains additional indirect control over Z Company through Y Company's 20 percent equity in Z Company.

Y Company should again carry its investment in Z Company on the equity basis because "significant influence" is clearly exerted over the financial and operating policies of Z Company. Even if a second-level "investor company" holds less than a 20 percent interest in another affiliate in a multilevel affiliation, the equity method is justified under *APB Opinion No. 18* when significant influence and/or control is exerted through a combination of direct and indirect shareholdings. Note that if the acquisitions had been reversed in time, that is, if Y Company had first acquired its interest in Z Company and then P Company acquired controlling interests in the two companies, the acquisition of Z Company would be in essence a step-by-step acquisition that would require a retroactive adjustment of Y Company's investment account if it were not previously carried on an equity basis. In the event a second-level "investor company" does not carry its investment on the equity basis, a working paper adjustment would be required to convert it to an equity basis prior to the preparation of eliminating entries.

A partial consolidated statement working paper for this affiliation for the year ended December 31, 19X2, is presented in Illustration 11–2. As in the previous example, the investment accounts are carried under the equity method, and minority interest calculations are based upon the subsidiaries' recorded incomes and net assets.

Consolidated net income for 19X2 may again be confirmed by definition (incremental approach) as follows:

P Company's income from its own operations.........		$10,000
Increased by its equity in affiliates' reported (equity basis) incomes:		
Y Company: 80% × $12,000	$9,600	
Z Company: 70% × $10,000	7,000	16,600
Consolidated net income for 19X2...................		$26,600

Effects of Differential Amortization

In the previous two illustrations, we assumed that all differentials were allocated to nonamortizable assets. If these differentials were allocated to amortizable assets, as they normally would be, differential amortization would have to be taken into account in calculating consolidated net income and the minority interests in subsidiaries with investments in other affiliates. The parent company's differential amortization would be allocated wholly to the majority shareholders, as in previous chapters, and thus poses no new problems. Differential amortization by a subsidiary with an investment in another affiliate must be allocated between the parent company and the subsidiary's minority shareholders. Since differential amortization would be recorded by the subsidiary in calculating its equity basis net income, the parent company would automatically recognize its proper share of this expense when it records its equity in the subsidiary on the basis of the subsidiary's equity basis net income. Furthermore, in the preparation of the consolidated statement working paper, the subsidiary's differential amortization is appropriately taken into account in the calculation of minority interests when the subsidiary's equity basis net income is used. Thus, the procedures illustrated above are appropriate for cases involving amortizable as well as nonamortizable differentials as long as the subsidiary has properly calculated its equity basis net income. Of course, on the consolidated statement working paper, the differentials must be allocated to specific assets (and liabilities), and appropriate amortizations recognized thereon.

Chain Control (Indirect) Less than 50 Percent

On occasion, intercorporate stock ownership arrangements may indicate a chain of interests, the product of which does not represent control of the lower-level subsidiary, where control is defined in terms of the 50

Illustration 11–2

P COMPANY AND SUBSIDIARY S COMPANY
Partial Consolidated Statement Working Paper
For Year Ended December 31, 19X2

	P Company	Y Company	Z Company	Eliminations Dr.	Eliminations Cr.	Minority Interests Y Company	Minority Interests Z Company	Consolidated
Income Statement								
Net income (excluding equity in affiliates' earnings)	10,000	10,000	10,000					30,000
Equity in affiliates' earnings	16,600	2,000		(1) 18,600				–0–
Minority interest						2,400	1,000	[3,400]
Net income	26,600	12,000	10,000	18,600	–0–	2,400	1,000	26,600
Retained Earnings Statement								
Retained earnings, 1/1/X2:								
P Company	105,000*							105,000
Y Company		30,000		(2) 24,000		6,000		–0–
Z Company			20,000	(3) 14,000 (4) 4,000			2,000	–0–
Net income	26,600	12,000	10,000	18,600	–0–	2,400	1,000	26,600
Retained earnings, 12/31/X2	131,600	42,000	30,000	60,600	–0–	8,400	3,000	131,600

Balance Sheet

	P Company	Y Company	Z Company	Eliminations (Dr)	Eliminations (Cr)	Minority Interest—Y	Minority Interest—Z	Consolidated
Investment in Y Company	117,600†				(1) 9,600 / (2) 108,000			–0–
Investment in Z Company	57,000‡				(1) 7,000 / (3) 50,000			–0–
Investment in Z Company		17,000§			(1) 2,000 / (4) 15,000			–0–
Differential—P Company in Y Company				(2) 4,000				4,000
Differential—P Company in Z Company				(3) 1,000				1,000
Differential—Y Company in Z Company				(4) 1,000				1,000
Capital stock:								
P Company	200,000							200,000
Y Company		100,000		(2) 80,000		20,000		–0–
Z Company			50,000	(3) 35,000 / (4) 10,000			5,000	–0–
Retained earnings	131,600	42,000	30,000	60,600		8,400	3,000	131,600
Minority interest—Y Company						28,400		28,400M
Minority interest—Z Company							8,000	8,000M
				28,400	–0–			

[deduction]
* $80,000 + [$10,000 + (80% × $10,000) + (70% × $10,000)].
† $100,000 + [(80% × $10,000) + (80% × $12,000)].
‡ $43,000 + [(70% × $10,000) + (70% × $10,000)].
§ $15,000 + (20% × $10,000).
Explanation of eliminations:
(1) To reverse 19X2 entries by investor companies recognizing their equities in affiliates' earnings.
(2) Investment elimination entry for P Company's investment in Y Company.
(3) Investment elimination entry for P Company's investment in Z Company.
(4) Investment elimination entry for Y Company's investment in Z Company.

percent stock ownership minimum. The following diagram is an example of such an affiliation:

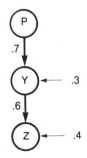

In this instance, the preparation of consolidated statements is still warranted, notwithstanding the 42 percent indirect interest of P Company in Z Company. Clearly the question of control relates to *direct* share ownership. In the illustration depicted above, control is confirmed by the percentages of stock owned independently by P Company and Y Company. While the product of equities in the chain are factors in the determination of consolidated net income and consolidated retained earnings, it is not a determinant in establishing a minimal condition for preparation of consolidated financial statements.

Intercompany Profit in Multilevel Affiliations

Previous discussion of the elimination of the intercompany profit on asset transfers has focused on affiliations in which the subsidiary is one level removed from the parent company. The calculation of consolidated net income is not fundamentally altered by the intercompany profit element existing at the second level of a multilevel affiliation. Assuming 100 percent elimination with pro rata allocation to majority and minority shareholders, the equity in an affiliate's net income is calculated using the affiliate's *confirmed* equity basis net income for the period. Similarly, in the consolidated statement working paper, the minority interest in net income is based upon the subsidiary's confirmed equity basis net income. This procedure allocates the intercompany profit on the basis of the direct and/or indirect ownership interest in the selling affiliate.[1]

---

[1] When the 100 percent elimination is allocated wholly to the majority shareholders regardless of the selling affiliate, the calculations of consolidated net income and minority interests in net income are based upon the subsidiaries' equity basis net incomes, *unadjusted* for intercompany profits, with the entire amount of the intercompany profit allocated to the parent. This procedure results, of course, in a different measure of consolidated net income. If the fractional elimination method were used, minority interest in net income is based upon the subsidiary's equity basis net income, unadjusted for intercompany profits, *and* the amount of the profit eliminated is determined using the parent's ownership interest (direct and/or indirect) in the selling affiliate.

Consider the following data and affiliation diagram in respect to companies P, Y, and Z:

Affiliation Diagram

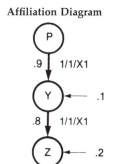

19X2 Net Incomes, Excluding
Equities in Affiliates' Earnings

P Company $20,000
Y Company 10,000
Z Company 5,000

The net income of Z Company is assumed to contain an element of unconfirmed intercompany profit in the amount of $2,000, and Y Company's 19X1 net income included $1,000 intercompany profit that was confirmed in 19X2.

Assuming 100 percent elimination of intercompany profits with pro rata allocation to majority and minority shareholders, consolidated net income for 19X2 may be determined using the incremental approach and working from the lowest level upward as follows:

$$Z \text{ Company's confirmed net income} = \$5,000 - \$2,000$$
$$= \$3,000$$

$$\begin{aligned}Y \text{ Company's confirmed} \\ \text{equity basis net income} &= \$10,000 + \$1,000 + (80\% \times \$3,000) \\ &= \$13,400\end{aligned}$$

$$\begin{aligned}\text{Consolidated net income (or} \\ P \text{ Company's confirmed} \\ \text{equity basis net income)} &= \$20,000 + (90\% \times \$13,400) \\ &= \$32,060\end{aligned}$$

The consolidated statement working paper development of this measure of consolidated net income is reflected, in summary form, in the following residual calculation:

Reported net incomes:

P Company (equity basis)...	$32,060
Y Company (equity basis)	13,400
Z Company	5,000
	$50,460

Deduct [add]—net debit [credit] eliminations in the income statement division:

Equity in affiliates' earnings ($3,400 + $12,060)	$15,460
Intercompany profits:	
Confirmed in 19X2..	[1,000]
Unconfirmed in 19X2..	2,000
	$16,460
Total equity (to be allocated to majority and minority interests)	$34,000
Minority interests:	
Y Company:	
10% of [$10,000 + $1,000 + (80% × $3,000)].............................	$ 1,340
Z Company:	
20% of ($5,000 − $2,000)..	600
	$ 1,940
Consolidated net income for 19X2	$32,060

The effect of the allocation of the intercompany profits may be seen from a different perspective by calculating P Company's interest in the equity basis net income of Y Company, unadjusted for intercompany profits, and then deducting directly therefrom the parent's interest in the confirmed and unconfirmed intercompany profits. This approach is displayed below:

Y Company's equity basis income, unadjusted for intercompany profits:	
$10,000 + (80% × $5,000)...	$14,000
P Company's equity basis income, unadjusted for intercompany profits:	
$20,000 + (90% × $14,000)..	$32,600
Add [deduct] P Company's interest, direct and/or indirect, in confirmed	
[unconfirmed] intercompany profits:	
Direct interest in Y Company's $1,000 confirmed profit (90% × $1,000)	900
Indirect interest in Z Company's $2,000 unconfirmed profit	
(90% × 80% × $2,000)..	[1,440]
Consolidated net income	$32,060

This calculational format reveals that the majority shareholders are allocated $900 of the confirmed intercompany profit and $1,440 of the unconfirmed intercompany profit; the remainder is allocated to the minority shareholders. The calculation also provides the basis for comparing pro rata allocation with the alternative of assigning all of the intercompany profits to the majority shareholders. Under this alternative elimination method, consolidated net income would be:

P Company's equity basis income, unadjusted for intercompany profits.........	$32,600
Add [deduct] the full amount of confirmed [unconfirmed] intercompany profits:	
Confirmed profit...	1,000
Unconfirmed profit	[2,000]
Consolidated net income	$31,600

The difference in the two amounts of consolidated net income is, of course, reflected in the amounts assigned to the minority interests in Companies Y and Z.

Bilateral Stockholdings—Traditional Allocation Method

In all of our previous examples, attention was focused on unilateral ownership by one or more companies of corporate shares of other affiliated companies. On occasions one may encounter a bilateral stockholding, wherein two or more of the affiliated companies are related through the reciprocal ownership of corporate stock. In the discussion to follow, we consider the problems associated with bilateral stockholdings. First, the traditional method of allocating the affiliates' income between majority and minority shareholders is explained. Thereafter, an alternative method—the treasury stock method—is briefly outlined.

Bilateral Stockholdings Not Involving Parent Company

Case 3. Consider the following affiliation diagram:

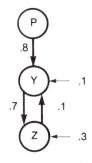

If the net incomes of companies P, Y, and Z *from their own operations* are $50,000, $20,000, and $10,000, respectively, one method of apportioning the total of their net incomes of $80,000 between majority and minority shareholders is by successive iteration, a variate on the trial and error method. A second method is algebraic simplification. Whichever the

method chosen, the first step is to determine the net income of each reciprocally related member of the affiliation *on an equity basis*. The equity basis
net income is the net income of an affiliate reckoned in terms of its interdependency with other affiliates. In other words, the equity basis net income
of a company equals the net income earned on its own operations plus its
equity (accruing from its ownership of stock) in the equity basis net incomes of other affiliates. The second step is to allocate the equity basis net
incomes of the several affiliates to the majority and minority interests.

Successive Iteration. Where the involvements of intercompany stockholdings are not especially complex and where the number of mutually
related companies is not unusually large, the successive iteration method
may be easily applied. Illustration 11–3 indicates that the successive itera-

Illustration 11–3

	Y Company			Z Company		
	Net Income from Own Operations	70% of Net Income of Z Company	Equity Basis Net Income	Net Income from Own Operations	10% of Net Income from Y Company	Equity Basis Net Income
1.............	$20,000	$7,000.00	$27,000.00	$10,000	$2,700.00	$12,700.00
2.............	20,000	8,890.00	28,890.00	10,000	2,889.00	12,889.00
3.............	20,000	9,022.30	29,022.30	10,000	2,902.23	12,902.23
4.............	20,000	9,031.56	29,031.56	10,000	2,903.16	12,903.16
5.............	20,000	9,032.21	29,032.21	10,000	2,903.22	12,903.22
6.............	20,000	9,032.25	29,032.25	10,000	2,903.23	12,903.23
7.............	20,000	9,032.26	29,032.26	10,000	2,903.23	12,903.23
8.............	20,000	9,032.26	29,032.26	10,000	2,903.23	12,903.23

tion method proceeds with a progression of successive estimates. At each
step, the equity pickup uses the estimate of the affiliate's equity basis net
income from the preceding step. The sequence of steps in the calculation
continues, as illustrated, until solution values stabilize. In this illustration,
no change in the amount of equity basis net incomes for Y Company and Z
Company results after step 7. Since there is no bilateral affiliation involving
the parent company, P Company is not included in the iterative process in
Illustration 11–3. In general, only those subsidiary affiliates whose equity
basis net incomes include an interest, direct or indirect, in bilaterally related affiliates must be included in this type of calculation.

Allocation of net incomes of the affiliate companies *to outside shareholder
interests* (majority and minority shareholders) is accomplished in the following manner:

P Company's net income from its own operations........	$50,000.00	
80% of Y Company's equity basis net income		
(80% of $29,032.26)...............................	23,225.81	
Consolidated net income.............................		$73,225.81
Minority interest in Y Company:		
10% of Y Company's equity basis net income		
(10% of $29,032.26)...............................		2,903.22
Minority interest in Z Company:		
30% of Z Company's equity basis net income		
(30% of $12,903.23)...............................		3,870.97
Total net incomes of affiliate companies		
from their own operations		$80,000.00

Although the aggregated equity basis net incomes exceed the aggregated net incomes of the bilateral affiliates *from their own operations*, it should be observed that the allocation process results in the calculation of majority and minority interests equal in amount to the total operating incomes of the three affiliates. This condition must exist, regardless of the type or complexity of the interdependency relationships. Note that Z Company's equity basis net income does not enter the calculation of consolidated net income; it is utilized only to determine the equity of Z Company's minority interest. This is appropriate since Y Company's equity basis net income includes Y's equity in Z's net income. P Company's equity in Z's net income is, therefore, included in consolidated net income as a part of the calculation that includes P's equity in Y's equity basis net income (80 percent of $29,032.26).

Although the equity basis net incomes determined in the first step are used only as an "intermediate calculation," they are subject to interpretation. One way of viewing these calculations is to assume that each mutually related company paid dividends in the amount of their income from their own operations; then they paid another dividend equal to the amount received from their investments in affiliates; and so forth. When this process stabilizes, in the same manner as it did in the successive iteration calculation, the equity basis net incomes would be equal to the total amount of dividends paid by each affiliate.[2] Since each company in the bilateral relationship would also receive dividends in an amount equal to their equity in the affiliate's earnings, the net cash outflow for each company would equal its net income from operations. Additionally, the dividends paid to majority and minority shareholders would be equal to the interests calculated in our allocation of equity basis net incomes. The same result is achieved, more simply, if each company merely pays a dividend equal to its equity basis net income. Thus, the equity basis net incomes

---

[2] This interpretation was suggested by Roman Weil, "Reciprocal or Mutual Holdings: Allocating Earnings and Selecting the Accounting Method," *The Accounting Review*, October 1973, p. 753.

uniquely determine the amount that can be distributed in the form of dividends and still maintain the net assets of the firms at their beginning-of-year levels. Since this result precisely reflects the basic capital mainte-nance criterion used by accountants in determining net income (i.e., net income is measured by the excess of net assets at the end of the period over beginning-of-period net assets), it provides strong theoretical support for the validity of the traditional allocation method.

In view of the above properties, it seems reasonable to conclude that the "equity basis net incomes" reflect appropriate equity method accounting for investments in mutually related companies.[3] As is discussed later in connection with the entries to be made by the affiliates, however, this conclusion reveals certain possible inconsistencies in *APB Opinion No. 18*. **Algebraic Solution.** The same interdependency structure may be more formally expressed as a system of linear equations. Where such a system is relatively simple with only two or three affiliates, algebraic simplification is perhaps the most easily applied solution form. Assume the following nota-tion:

Y = net income of Y Company on an equity basis
Z = net income of Z Company on an equity basis

The problem may now be formulated and solved as follows:

$$Y = \$20,000 + .7Z$$
$$Z = \$10,000 + .1Y$$

$$Y = \$20,000 + .7(\$10,000 + .1Y)$$
$$Y = \$20,000 + \$7,000 + .07Y$$
$$.93Y = \$27,000$$
$$Y = \$29,032.26$$

$$Z = \$10,000 + .1(\$29,032.26)$$
$$Z = \$10,000 + \$2,903.23$$
$$Z = \$12,903.23$$

As noted previously, P Company is not in the interdependency structure and thus is excluded from the system of equations. Given the above equity basis net incomes of Y Company and Z Company, the allocation of the total net incomes of the affiliates is made in the same amounts as in the illustra-tion of the successive iteration method.

Bilateral Stockholdings Involving Parent Company

The previous illustration in Case 3 dealt with mutually related subsidi-ary affiliates. The calculation of equity basis net incomes is not essentially

---

[3] Ibid., p. 754.

different when the parent is also bilaterally related to one or more affiliates. However, since the outside shareholder interest in the parent company is less than 100 percent (because one or more of the affiliates owns stock in the parent), the parent's equity basis net income must be allocated to the outside shareholders in the same way that the subsidiaries' equity basis net incomes were allocated to the minority shareholders in the previous illustration.

Case 4. Consider now the following affiliation diagram:

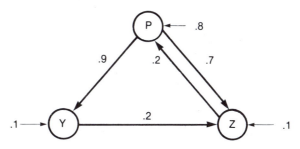

Companies P, Y, and Z are again assumed to have net incomes from their own operations of $50,000, $20,000, and $10,000.

The equity basis net incomes of the affiliates are calculated algebraically as follows:

P = net income of P Company on an equity basis
Y = net income of Y Company on an equity basis
Z = net income of Z Company on an equity basis

$$P = \$50,000 + .9Y + .7Z$$
$$Y = \$20,000 + .2Z$$
$$Z = \$10,000 + .2P$$

$$P = \$50,000 + .9(\$20,000 + .2Z) + .7Z$$
$$P = \$50,000 + \$18,000 + .18Z + .7Z$$
$$P = \$68,000 + .88Z$$

$$P - \$68,000 + .88(\$10,000 + .2P)$$
$$P = \$68,000 + \$8,800 + .176P$$
$$.824P - \$76,800$$
$$P = \$93,203.88$$

$$Z = \$10,000 + .2(\$93,203.88)$$
$$Z = \$10,000 + \$18,640.78$$
$$Z = \$28,640.78$$

$$Y = \$20,000 + .2(\$28,640.78)$$
$$Y = \$20,000 + \$5,728.16$$
$$Y = \$25,728.16$$

The equity basis net incomes of the three affiliates are allocated to majority and minority shareholder interests as follows:

Consolidated net income:
    80% of P Company's equity basis net income (80% of $93,203.88)..... $74,563.10
Minority interest in Y Company:
    10% of Y Company's equity basis net income (10% of $25,728.16) 2,572.82
Minority interest in Z Company:
    10% of Z Company's equity basis net income (10% of $28,640.78) 2,864.08
        Total net incomes of affiliates from their own operations $80,000.00

In consolidated net income determination, only the nonaffiliate shareholders of the parent company constitute the majority interest. In this case, 20 percent of P Company's stock is held by Z Company; accordingly, the outside interest in P Company of 80 percent is the equity multiplier in calculating consolidated net income.

Intercompany Profit on Asset Transfers

For eliminations of intercompany profit on the transfer of assets between affiliates, the same elimination procedures control in respect to reciprocally related companies as for unilateral or multilevel affiliations.
Case 5.   Bilateral Stockholdings Not Involving Parent.   The following affiliation diagram is assumed:

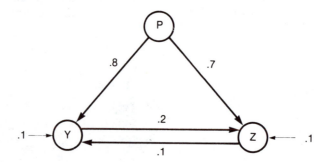

Inventory profit currently recorded by Z Company, which is unconfirmed from a consolidated standpoint, is $9,800.
    Assume the following notation:

P_E = interest of P Company in the unconfirmed inventory profit on an equity basis
Y_E = interest of Y Company in the unconfirmed inventory profit on an equity basis
Z_E = interest of Z Company in the unconfirmed inventory profit on an equity basis

The various interests in the unconfirmed inventory profit are reflected as follows:

$$P_E = .8Y_E + .7Z_E$$
$$Y_E = .2Z_E$$
$$Z_E = \$9,800 + .1Y_E$$

By substitution and simplification, solution values are determined to be:

$$P_E = \$8,600$$
$$Y_E = \$2,000$$
$$Z_E = \$10,000$$

In the consolidated working paper, the eliminating entry in respect to intercompany inventory profit is as follows:

Inventory (income statement division)	9,800	
Inventory (balance sheet division)		9,800

Assuming pro rata allocation, minority shareholders must absorb a ratable amount of the eliminated inventory profit, calculated as follows:

Minority in Y Company (10% of $2,000)	$ 200
Minority in Z Company (10% of $10,000)	1,000
	$1,200

Thus the total elimination of $9,800 is allocated:

To the majority shareholders	$8,600
To the minority shareholders	1,200
	$9,800

Each affiliate's confirmed equity basis net income may be determined by subtracting these interests in the unconfirmed inventory profit from their equity basis net incomes calculated as before. These interests also provide the basis for fractional elimination of intercompany profits, should that method be preferred.

If we are only interested in the amounts assigned to majority and minority interests under 100 percent elimination with pro rata allocation, confirmed equity basis net incomes may be calculated directly in one algebraic solution by incorporating the unconfirmed profit(s) with the affiliates' net incomes from their own operations. For example, given net incomes from their own operations of $50,000, $20,000, and $10,000 for companies P, Y, and Z, respectively, and the $9,800 unconfirmed inventory profit reported by Z, the equation system for the mutually related subsidiaries would take the following form:

$$Y = \$20,000 + .2Z$$
$$Z = \$200 + .1Y$$

Z Company's net income in the second equation is reduced to $200 by deducting the $9,800 of unconfirmed inventory profit from the recorded net income of $10,000. By substitution and simplification, solution values are determined to be:

$$Y = \$20,448.98$$
$$Z = \$2,244.90$$

Allocation of the net incomes of the affiliate companies is then made as follows:

P Company's net income from its own operations.............	$50,000.00
80% of Y Company's equity basis net income	
(80% of $20,448.98)....................................	16,359.18
70% of Z Company's equity basis net income	
(70% of $2,244.90)....................................	1,571.43
Consolidated net income.................................	$67,930.61
Minority interest in Y Company:	
10% of Y Company's equity basis net income	
(10% of $20,448.98)....................................	2,044.90
Minority interest in Z Company:	
10% of Z Company's equity basis net income	
(10% of $2,244.90)....................................	224.49
Total confirmed net incomes of affiliates..............	$70,200,000

This method implicitly deducts the majority and minority interests in the unconfirmed inventory profit, as calculated above, from the allocated shares of total net income.

Case 6. Bilateral Stockholdings Involving Parent.   The following is an illustration of an affiliation involving intercompany profit in which the parent is bilaterally related to one subsidiary:

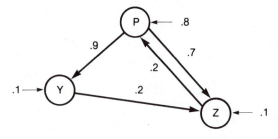

Inventory profit currently recognized by Z Company, although unconfirmed from a consolidated standpoint, is assumed to be $8,240.

Notation:

P_E = interest of P Company in the unconfirmed inventory profit on an equity basis

Y_E = interest of Y Company in the unconfirmed inventory profit on an equity basis

Z_E = interest of Z Company in the unconfirmed inventory profit on an equity basis

The interests in the unconfirmed inventory profit are:

$$P_E = .9Y_E + .7Z_E$$
$$Y_E = .2Z_E$$
$$Z_E = \$8,240 + .2P_E$$

By substitution and simplification, solution values are determined to be:

$$P_E = \$8,800$$
$$Y_E = \$2,000$$
$$Z_E = \$10,000$$

Since consolidated net income is but 80 percent of the parent company's equity basis net income (recall that only the parent company's shares held by nonaffiliate interests are determinants of consolidated net income), the effect of the above unconfirmed profit elimination is a reduction of consolidated net income by $7,040 (80 percent of $8,800).

The eliminating entry for consolidated working papers is:

Inventory (income statement division).........................	8,240	
Inventory (balance sheet division).........................		8,240

The amounts of minority interests in the unconfirmed profit on a consolidated basis are calculated as follows:

Minority interest in Y Company (10% of $2,000)...........	$ 200
Minority interest in Z Company (10% of $10,000).........	1,000
	$1,200

Thus, the total elimination of $8,240 is allocated:

To the majority shareholders	$7,040
To the minority shareholders	1,200
	$8,240

Effects of Differential Amortization

Our illustrations of allocating income between majority and minority shareholders in a bilateral stockholding have ignored the existence of differential amortization. Normally, affiliates with an investment in another affiliate will have a differential that must be allocated and amortized, and thus differential amortization must be incorporated into our calculations.

In the case of multilevel affiliations, it was pointed out that use of a subsidiary's equity basis income will result in a proper allocation of the differential amortization between majority and minority shareholders. In bilateral affiliations, the same effect can be achieved by deducting each affiliate's differential amortization for the period from its income from operations, and then calculating the affiliates' equity basis incomes. Alternatively, the proper allocations of the affiliates' differential amortizations may be separately calculated in the same manner as was illustrated for unconfirmed intercompany profits. Note that if the parent company is bilaterally related to one or more of the subsidiaries, a portion of the parent company's differential amortization will be allocated to the minority shareholders; in all previous circumstances, the parent company's differential amortization was borne wholly by the majority shareholders.

Purchase of Shares in a Mutually Related Subsidiary

Reference has been repeatedly made to the necessity of eliminating the parent company's purchased equity in the accumulated retained earnings of a subsidiary at date of acquisition, assuming the purchase method of accounting for the acquisition is employed. In the event the subsidiary is a preexisting member of a reciprocally related corporate affiliation, it is important that the equity basis retained earnings of the subsidiary on this date be used as a basis for determining the amount of the retained earnings elimination. Similarly, where the parent is a controlling shareholder in a subsidiary prior to the latter's purchase of the parent's stock, it is also important that the parent's equity basis retained earnings be used in calculating the amount of the retained earnings elimination; necessarily, this amount is the at-acquisition equity basis retained earnings of the parent.

Recording Equity in Affiliates' Earnings

The parent company in an affiliation involving bilateral stockholdings should carry its investment under the equity method, just like any other parent company.[4] There is a problem, however, in determining the proper

[4] It is possible to construct hypothetical mutual stockholdings for which determination of the "parent" company is a moot point—for example, A Company owns 60 percent of B Company and B Company owns 60 percent of A Company. Although such stockholdings would seldom be encountered in practice, the situation tantalized us briefly in 1982 when Bendix Corporation and Martin Marietta were engaged in their classic "takeover battle."

carrying value for the investment when the parent company is bilaterally related to one or more of its subsidiaries. In particular, should the parent company record (1) its "equity basis" net income as calculated in the examples above, or (2) the majority interest in its "equity basis" net income, that is, consolidated net income? Although we have previously observed that the equity basis net income value seems to reflect the basic equity method concept, recall that *APB Opinion No. 18* states the following application principle: "The difference between consolidation and the equity method lies in the details reported in the financial statements. Thus, an investor's *net income for the period and its stockholders' equity at the end of the period* are the same whether an investment in a subsidiary is accounted for under the equity method or the subsidiary is consolidated. . . ."[5] In view of this stated principle, the appropriate value to be recorded for a parent company under existing accounting authority would appear to be the majority interest in the parent's equity basis net income.[6]

Recording the majority interest in the parent's equity basis net income will achieve equality between the parent company's net income and consolidated net income, as prescribed in *APB Opinion No. 18*. However, achieving the prescribed equality between the parent company's stockholders' equity and consolidated stockholders' equity is a problem that appears insoluble when the parent company and a subsidiary are bilaterally related. In consolidation, the subsidiary's investment in the parent company will be eliminated against the parent's stockholders' equity accounts. But there is no apparent way of achieving this elimination on the parent company's books that has any economic justification. Thus, in general, the parent company's stockholders' equity will be greater than consolidated stockholders' equity.[7]

In our consideration of multilevel affiliations earlier in this chapter, it was asserted that subsidiaries with an investment in another affiliate should carry the investment under the equity method. Use of this method provides relevant information to the subsidiary's minority shareholders, facilitates the consolidation process, and seems generally consistent with the "significant influence" criterion of *APB Opinion No. 18*. It is debatable, however, whether these same arguments can be used to justify the equity method for subsidiaries involved in a mutual stockholding. Particularly is

---

[5] APB, "The Equity Method of Accounting for Investments in Common Stock," *APB Opinion No. 18* (New York: AICPA, 1971), par. 19. (Emphasis supplied.)

[6] Whether this conclusion is equally valid for mutually related companies not in a parent-subsidiary relationship is less clear. An interesting situation of this type involved two of Hong Kong's largest companies—Hongkong Land and Jardine Matheson. Each company held approximately a 40 percent equity in the other company, and their adoption in 1981 of the equity method of accounting generated a great deal of comment in the financial press. See Financial Times *World Accounting Report* (New York: FT Publications Inc.), October 1981 and November 1981.

[7] Apparently when *Opinion No. 18* was prepared, the Accounting Principles Board did not consider the special case of mutual stockholdings.

this true when the reciprocal stockholdings exist between a subsidiary and the parent company. Accordingly, no general rule is appropriate for the method of accounting for a subsidiary's investment in an affiliate where mutual stockholdings are involved. Rather, each case must be evaluated on its individual merits.

Investment Elimination Entry

In the preparation of a consolidated statement working paper, all entries on the books of "investor" companies to recognize equities in affiliates' earnings for the period must be reversed, and the investment accounts must be eliminated against the related stockholders' equity accounts. Since one or more of the subsidiaries may not carry their investments on an equity basis, no general rules can be established for the investment elimination entries. In any particular circumstance, one may use the calculated minority (or majority) interest in the subsidiary's (or parent's) equity basis income and the minority (or majority) interest in January 1 retained earnings from the prior year's consolidated statement working paper for the appropriate extensions to the Minority Interest (or Consolidated) column, and the remainder of the subsidiary's (or parent's) January 1 retained earnings is eliminated against the appropriate investment account. In the year of acquisition, of course, the elimination of the retained earnings at acquisition is based upon the supplementary calculation of purchased retained earnings. The eliminations against stockholders' equity accounts other than retained earnings will generally be analogous to eliminations for unilateral ownership configurations.

Matrix Applications for Complex Affiliations

The benefits to be derived from a matrix formulation of "complex" intercorporate stockholdings are significant and are illustrated in the paragraphs which follow.

Assume the following affiliation diagram and supporting data for the year 19X1 are given:

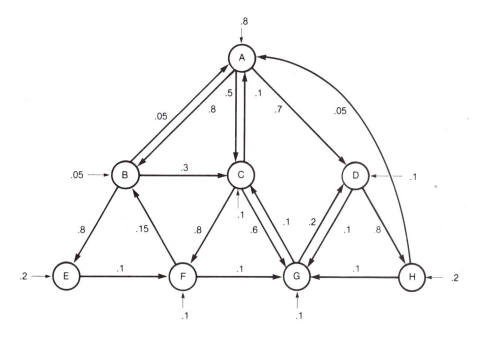

The affiliates' net incomes from their own operations are:

A Company	$ 40,000
B Company	30,000
C Company	30,000
D Company	40,000
E Company	10,000
F Company	20,000
G Company	10,000
H Company	20,000
	$200,000

As illustrated previously, the equity basis net incomes of the individual companies may be defined in algebraic form. Letting $A, B, \ldots, H$ denote net incomes of the respective companies on an equity basis, there results:

$$A - \$40,000 + .80B + .50C + .70D$$
$$B = \$30,000 + .80E + .30C + .05A$$
$$C = \$30,000 + .80F + .60G + .10A$$
$$D = \$40,000 + .80H + .10G$$
$$E = \$10,000 + .10F$$
$$F = \$20,000 + .15B + .10G$$
$$G = \$10,000 + .10C + .20D$$
$$H = \$20,000 + .05A + .10G$$

These equations may be arranged in a form exhibiting the underlying matrix structure as follows:

$$
\begin{aligned}
+ \quad A - .80B - .50C - .70D & = \$40{,}000 \\
- .05A + \quad B - .30C \qquad\qquad - .80E & = \$30{,}000 \\
- .10A \qquad\quad + \quad C \qquad\qquad\qquad\qquad - .80F - .60G & = \$30{,}000 \\
+ \quad D \qquad\qquad\qquad\qquad\quad - .10G - .80H & = \$40{,}000 \\
+ \quad E - .10F & = \$10{,}000 \\
- .15B \qquad\qquad\qquad\qquad\quad + \quad F - .10G & = \$20{,}000 \\
- .10C - .20D \qquad\qquad\qquad\qquad + \quad G & = \$10{,}000 \\
- .05A \qquad\qquad\qquad\qquad\qquad\qquad\qquad - .10G + \quad H & = \$20{,}000
\end{aligned}
$$

Based upon this equation system, the problem may be easily expressed in matrix form:

$$
\begin{bmatrix}
1 & -.80 & -.50 & -.70 & 0 & 0 & 0 & 0 \\
-.05 & 1 & -.30 & 0 & -.80 & 0 & 0 & 0 \\
-.10 & 0 & 1 & 0 & 0 & -.80 & -.60 & 0 \\
0 & 0 & 0 & 1 & 0 & 0 & -.10 & -.80 \\
0 & 0 & 0 & 0 & 1 & -.10 & 0 & 0 \\
0 & -.15 & 0 & 0 & 0 & 1 & -.10 & 0 \\
0 & 0 & -.10 & -.20 & 0 & 0 & 1 & 0 \\
-.05 & 0 & 0 & 0 & 0 & 0 & -.10 & 1
\end{bmatrix}
\begin{bmatrix} A \\ B \\ C \\ D \\ E \\ F \\ G \\ H \end{bmatrix}
=
\begin{bmatrix}
\$40{,}000 \\ \$30{,}000 \\ \$30{,}000 \\ \$40{,}000 \\ \$10{,}000 \\ \$20{,}000 \\ \$10{,}000 \\ \$20{,}000
\end{bmatrix}
$$

There now remains the arithmetical problem of calculating the inverse of this 8×8 coefficient matrix. After this inverse is computed, the matrix formulation assumes the form shown in Illustration 11–4.

By the simple process of matrix multiplication, the values for the equity basis net incomes of the eight companies are easily determined:

$$
\begin{bmatrix} A \\ B \\ C \\ D \\ E \\ F \\ G \\ H \end{bmatrix}
=
\begin{bmatrix}
\$203{,}322 \\ \$80{,}741 \\ \$99{,}114 \\ \$70{,}245 \\ \$13{,}550 \\ \$35{,}507 \\ \$33{,}961 \\ \$33{,}562
\end{bmatrix}
$$

Illustration 11–4

$$
\begin{bmatrix} A \\ B \\ C \\ D \\ E \\ F \\ G \\ H \end{bmatrix}
=
\begin{bmatrix}
1.19654 & 1.09201 & 1.01394 & 1.01372 & .87361 & .89852 & .88069 & .81097 \\
.10622 & 1.15050 & .43101 & .13985 & .92040 & .43685 & .32746 & .11188 \\
.14971 & .27266 & 1.24678 & .28506 & .21813 & 1.01924 & .90131 & .22805 \\
.05244 & .05040 & .06535 & 1.08473 & .04032 & .05631 & .24009 & .86778 \\
.00185 & .01763 & .00784 & .00455 & 1.01410 & .10768 & .01629 & .00364 \\
.01848 & .17631 & .07843 & .04552 & .14105 & 1.07685 & .16293 & .03642 \\
.02546 & .03735 & .13775 & .24545 & .02988 & .11319 & 1.13815 & .19636 \\
.06237 & .05834 & .06447 & .07523 & .04667 & .05624 & .15785 & 1.06018
\end{bmatrix}
\begin{bmatrix}
\$40{,}000 \\ \$30{,}000 \\ \$30{,}000 \\ \$40{,}000 \\ \$10{,}000 \\ \$20{,}000 \\ \$10{,}000 \\ \$20{,}000
\end{bmatrix}
$$

Consolidated net income for 19X1 and the minority interests in subsidiary net incomes are now calculated as before:

Allocation of net incomes:

Consolidated net income (.80 × $203,322).............		$162,658
Minority interests:		
B Company (.05 × $80,741)........................	$4,037	
C Company (.10 × $99,114).......................	9,911	
D Company (.10 × $70,245)	7,025	
E Company (.20 × $13,550).......................	2,710	
F Company (.10 × $35,507).......................	3,551	
G Company (.10 × $33,961)	3,396	
H Company (.20 × $33,562)	6,712	37,342
Total net incomes of affiliates		$200,000

The increased number of affiliates and the additional involvements of the incorporate stockholdings obviously introduce a number of complications in the arithmetic calculations of the equity basis net incomes. However, once these values are determined, the allocation of net incomes is only slightly more tedious than less complex affiliation structures.

A problem such as this may be solved using the iterative (trial and error) method. However, the practical value of the matrix method derives from the *permanence* of the inverse of the coefficient matrix. If there are no changes in the intercorporate shareholdings, the equity basis net incomes are easily determined each period (month, quarter, etc.) with one matrix multiplication. This characteristic of the matrix representation greatly alleviates the arithmetic complexities, as a single calculation of the inverse of the coefficient matrix provides a continuing basis for the relatively simple calculation of the affiliates' equity basis net incomes in subsequent periods. Multiplication of these values by the appropriate majority or minority shareholder interests then gives the desired solutions.[8]

Bilateral Stockholdings—Treasury Stock Method

Some accountants take the position that the purchase of a parent company's stock by a subsidiary affiliate is not essentially unlike the parent's acquisition of "treasury shares." Where such stockholdings are thus accorded the status of treasury shares, it is appropriate to deduct the cost of these shares from the amounts of contributed capital and retained earnings of the parent company in the preparation of consolidated financial statements. It should be noted that the traditional allocation method, explained above, also removes the parent company's shares held by affiliates from the consolidated balance sheet through the elimination of the affiliate's investment account against the stockholders' equity accounts of the par-

---

[8] Weil, "Reciprocal or Mutual Holdings," has shown that the second step of multiplying by the external shareholder interests may also be incorporated in the matrix solution, thus reducing the calculation to a single matrix multiplication.

ent. Thus, both methods are in conformity with current accounting policy, which states: "Shares of the parent held by a subsidiary should not be treated as outstanding stock in the consolidated balance sheet."[9]

The methods do differ, however, in their conception of the nature of the transaction and their allocation of equities in net income and net assets between majority and minority interests. The treasury stock method presumes that the subsidiary is acting on behalf of the parent, and thus the investment in the parent company's shares should be accounted for in the same manner as if the parent had reacquired the shares. In order to achieve total equivalence, minority interest calculations (in net income and retained earnings) must exclude dividends received by the subsidiary from its investment in the parent. Although this practice is advocated by some accountants, the authors believe that it is unwarranted. Each time the parent declares a cash dividend, the majority shareholders incur an explicit cost for this use of subsidiary assets. The amount of the cost equals the minority's share of the dividend received by the subsidiary. Accordingly, it seems appropriate to calculate minority interest in net income on the basis of the subsidiary's recorded net income (including the dividend income from the parent). As a consequence of this procedure, the minority interest in the consolidated balance sheet will remain equal to the minority shareholders' percentage ownership interest multiplied by the net assets of the subsidiary. The traditional allocation method, on the other hand, recognizes this cost on an "accrual basis" by allocating a portion of the parent's current income to the shares held by the subsidiary. This method yields measures of majority and minority interests which reflect current equities in the net assets (excluding the bilateral stockholdings) of the two companies, rather than basing them, in part at least, on the dividend policies of the parent company.[10]

If consolidated statements are prepared on the date reciprocal ownership of shares is established, the traditional allocation and treasury stock methods produce similar results (varying only in the amount of the differential in this transaction). Also, if the *total* amount of the subsidiaries' outstanding shares are held either by the parent or other subsidiaries, the effects produced on consolidated statements are again essentially the same. However, where neither condition prevails, the allocated amounts from applying the two methods will often continue to diverge, in some instances materially, depending upon the dividend policy of the parent company.

---

[9] Committee on Accounting Procedure, *Accounting Research Bulletin No. 51*, "Consolidated Financial Statements" (New York: AICPA, 1959), par. 13. Also reproduced in FASB *Accounting Standards—Current Text*, sec. C51.114.

[10] A survey of accounting practice suggested that normally the treasury stock method is applied in practice when a subsidiary holds shares of the parent company. Accountants International Study Group, *Consolidated Financial Statements: Current Recommended Practices In Canada, the United Kingdom, and the United States*, 1973, par. 67.

In the following example, consolidated balance sheets are prepared both on the date of bilateral affiliation and on a subsequent date.

Case 7. On January 1, 19X1, P Company purchased 80 percent of the capital stock (par, $100) of Y Company concurrent with the latter's purchase of 20 percent of the capital stock (par, $100) of P Company. The balance sheets of each company after the investment transactions are illustrated in the following table:

	P Company	Y Company
Assets		
Investments in corporate stock:		
P Company		$ 50,000
Y Company	$120,000	
Other assets	170,000	95,000
Total assets	$290,000	$145,000
Equities		
Liabilities	$ 10,000	$ 5,000
Capital stock	200,000	100,000
Retained earnings	80,000	40,000
Total equities	$290,000	$145,000

A consolidated balance sheet on this date using the treasury stock method follows.

P COMPANY AND SUBSIDIARY
Consolidated Balance Sheet
(Treasury Stock Method)
January 1, 19X1

Assets

Other assets		$265,000
Cost of investment in excess of corresponding book value of subsidiary stock		8,000
Total assets		$273,000

Equities

Liabilities		$ 15,000
Minority interest:		
Capital stock, Y Company	$ 20,000	
Retained earnings, Y Company	8,000	28,000
Owner's equity:		
Capital stock, P Company:		
Issued	$200,000	
Held by Y Company	40,000	
Held by nonaffiliates		160,000
Retained earnings:		
P Company retained earnings	$ 80,000	
Less: Premium on treasury stock purchased	(10,000)	70,000
Total equities		$273,000

The reader will note that the traditional allocation solution, incorporating the investment elimination of Y Company in P Company (see page 475), would add to the consolidated balance sheet a $6,000 credit differential (contra to the $8,000 debit differential) and reduce consolidated retained earnings to $64,000 (P's retained earnings of $80,000, less the $16,000 investment elimination of Y Company in P Company).

Case 8.   In this example, the data of Case 7 are repeated, adjusted for 19X1 earnings. It is assumed that the net income of each affiliate from its own operations for 19X1 is $30,000, with a corresponding increase in the amount of "other assets," and no dividends are paid by either company. Differential amortization is ignored.

A consolidated balance sheet on December 31, 19X1, follows (treasury stock method).

P COMPANY AND SUBSIDIARY
Consolidated Balance Sheet
(Treasury Stock Method)
December 31, 19X1

Assets

Other assets...		$325,000
Cost of investment in excess of corresponding book value of subsidiary stock.............................		8,000
Total assets...		$333,000

Equities

Liabilities...		$ 15,000
Minority interest:		
Capital stock, Y Company	$ 20,000	
Retained earnings, Y Company........................	14,000	34,000
Owner's equity:		
Capital stock, P Company:		
Issued	$200,000	
Held by Y Company	40,000	
Held by nonaffiliates		160,000
Retained earnings:		
P Company retained earnings.........................	*$134,000	
Less: Premium on treasury stock purchased	(10,000)	124,000
Total equities...		$333,000

* $110,000 + 80% of $30,000 = $134,000.

Use of the traditional allocation method would yield different allocations of retained earnings between majority and minority shareholders. At acquisition, the following investment eliminations would be made:

	Dr. [Cr.]	
	P Company in Y Company	Y Company in P Company
Capital stock	$ 80,000	$ 40,000
Retained earnings............	32,000	16,000
Differential	8,000	[6,000]
Investment	$[120,000]	$ [50,000]

The conventional solution provides for the elimination of the "investment" of Y Company in P Company, in addition to the principal investment elimination of P Company in Y Company. The interdependency structure with respect to the allocation of the affiliates' net incomes may be represented as follows:

P = net income of P Company on an equity basis
Y = net income of Y Company on an equity basis

$$P = \$30,000 + .8Y$$
$$Y = \$30,000 + .2P$$

By substitution and simplification, solution values are:

$$P = \$64,285.71; \quad 80\% \text{ whereof} = \$51,428.57$$
$$Y = \$42,857.14; \quad 20\% \text{ whereof} = \$8,571.43$$

It follows that the allocation at December 31, 19X1, of $132,000 of retained earnings of companies P and Y (the combined retained earnings, $180,000, less the sum of the retained earnings eliminations, $48,000) is as follows:

Consolidated retained earnings ($64,000 + $51,428.57)..........	$115,428.57
Minority interest ($8,000 + $8,571.43)........................	16,571.43
Total...	$132,000.00

In the previously illustrated treasury stock treatment, the following allocation was made:

Consolidated retained earnings (net of premium on treasury stock purchased)...............................	$124,000
Minority interest [20% × ($40,000 + $30,000)]	14,000
Total...	$138,000

The difference of $6,000 ($138,000 − $132,000) is attributable to the aforementioned alternative of either eliminating 20 percent of the retained earnings of the parent company ($16,000), or charging the premium on the treasury stock ($10,000) against consolidated retained earnings. However, the important difference exhibited in the postacquisition consolidated balance sheets is the disparity in the relative shares of the remaining retained earnings; this difference is a function of the different allocation ratios inherent in each method.

The allocation differences are magnified as the nonaffiliate shareholder interests in the mutually related affiliates increase; additionally, these differences continue to increase in succeeding consolidated financial statements.[11]

Questions

1. Define *multilevel affiliation* and illustrate by example (diagram) such an affiliation.

2. In a multilevel affiliation, what method of accounting is used for a subsidiary's 30 percent investment in another affiliate? A 10 percent investment?

3. How is differential amortization recorded by a subsidiary with an investment in another affiliate allocated between majority and minority shareholders?

4. When intercompany profit exists at the second level of a multilevel affiliation, how is the minority interest in net income calculated if the elimination is allocated pro rata between majority and minority shareholders? If the elimination is allocated wholly against the majority shareholders?

5. A Company is the owner of 55 percent of the outstanding stock of B Company, while B Company holds 60 percent of the shares of C Company. Are consolidated statements justified? What is the criterion to apply in making such a decision?

6. Define *bilateral stockholding* and illustrate by example (diagram) such an affiliation.

7. What is meant by "equity basis net incomes" of reciprocally related members of an affiliation?

8. Briefly describe the successive iteration method in the context of a consolidation process involving reciprocal stockholdings.

9. Given a situation in which the affiliates of a consolidated entity have reciprocal stockholdings, explain why the sum of the equity basis net incomes exceeds the sum of the affiliates' net incomes from their own operations, notwithstanding the fact that the ultimate determination of majority and minority

---

[11] A technique incorporating the treasury stock method for calculating consolidated net income and the traditional allocation method for calculating, as supplementary information, minority interest is proposed in Enrico Petri and Roland Minch, "The Treasury Stock Method and Conventional Method in Reciprocal Stockholdings—An Amalgamation," *The Accounting Review,* April 1974. Its validity, like the validity of the two methods individually, depends upon one's conception of the nature of a transaction wherein the subsidiary acquires the parent's stock.

interests are equal in total to the summed net incomes from the affiliates' own operations.

10. Explain any additional complications in the calculation of consolidated net income that result from a situation in which the bilateral stockholdings involve the parent.

11. How is the elimination of intercompany profits on the transfer of assets complicated by the existence of reciprocal stockholdings?

12. How is differential amortization allocated between majority and minority shareholders in a bilateral stockholding?

13. When the parent company is bilaterally related to one or more of its subsidiaries, what amount is recorded by the parent company to recognize its equity in affiliates?

14. What do you see as the principal advantage of the matrix method over the other calculation methods in determining the equity basis net incomes of reciprocally related affiliates?

15. How does the determination of minority interests differ as between the treasury stock method and the traditional allocation method?

Exercises

Exercise 11–1

On January 1, 19X1, P Company acquired a 90 percent interest in R Company, R Company acquired an 80 percent interest in S Company, and S Company acquired a 70 percent interest in T Company. Each of the companies earned $5,000 from their own operations during 19X1, except P Company which as a holding company had no income from operations.

No dividends were paid by any of the affiliates during 19X1. Ignore differentials.

Required:
Prepare a schedular calculation of consolidated net income for 19X1 using the incremental approach.

Exercise 11–2

Bravo Company purchased 70 percent of Charlie Company's outstanding stock on January 1, 19X1. Alpha Company purchased 80 percent of Bravo Company's outstanding stock on January 1, 19X2. Each of the three companies earned $10,000 from their own operations during 19X1 and 19X2. Each of the three companies declared annual dividends of $6,000 during 19X1 and 19X2. Each of the three firms had retained earnings of $50,000 on January 1, 19X1.

Assume differentials are allocated to nonamortizable assets.

Required:
a. What is Alpha Company's purchased equity in Bravo Company's retained earnings on January 1, 19X2?

b. Prepare the entries made on the books of Alpha Company and Bravo Company during 19X2 to account for their interests in affiliates.
c. Prepare a schedular calculation of consolidated net income for 19X2 using the incremental approach.
d. Calculate consolidated retained earnings at December 31, 19X2.

Exercise 11–3

On January 1, 19X1, P Company acquired a 90 percent interest in Y Company and Y Company acquired a 70 percent interest in Z Company. In these investment transactions, P Company had a debit differential of $25,000 and Y Company had a debit differential of $15,000. Both differentials were allocated wholly to goodwill, which is to be amortized over a 10-year period.

During 19X1, the companies reported the following incomes from their own operations:

P Company	$30,000
Y Company	20,000
Z Company	10,000

Required:
a. Prepare the entries made on the books of P Company and Y Company at the end of 19X1 to record their equities in affiliates' earnings and differential amortization.
b. Prepare a schedular calculation of consolidated net income for 19X1 using the incremental approach.

Exercise 11–4

On January 1, 19X1, P Company purchased 80 percent of the outstanding stock of Y Company and 70 percent of the outstanding stock of Z Company. On the same date, Y Company acquired 20 percent of Z Company's stock.

During 19X1, the companies reported the following incomes from their own operations:

P Company	$40,000
Y Company	30,000
Z Company	20,000

The net income of Z Company for 19X1 contains an element of unconfirmed inter-company profit in the amount of $5,000. Intercompany profits are allocated pro rata to majority and minority shareholders.

Required:
a. Prepare a schedular calculation of consolidated net income for 19X1 using the incremental approach.
b. Prepare a residual calculation of consolidated net income for 19X1.

Exercise 11–5

On January 1, 19X1, Seydel, Inc., purchased 90 percent of White Corporation's outstanding stock and concurrently White Corporation purchased 80 percent of Hanson Company's outstanding stock. On January 2, 19X1, Hanson sold a truck to Seydel for $15,000. The truck had a book value to Hanson of $10,000 and was expected to be useful for another five years.

The three firms each reported net income from their own operations of $10,000 during 19X1. Intercompany profit eliminations are allocated pro rata to majority and minority shareholders.

Required:
a. Prepare the eliminating entries relating to the truck sale that would be necessary for a consolidated statement working paper for the year ended December 31, 19X1.
b. Prepare a schedular calculation of consolidated net income for 19X1.
c. Calculate minority interests in net income for 19X1.

Exercise 11–6

A Company owns 80 percent of the capital stock of B Company, 70 percent of the capital stock of C Company, 60 percent of the capital stock of D Company, and 70 percent of the capital stock of E Company. Additionally, B Company owns 20 percent of the capital stock of C Company, D Company owns 30 percent of the capital stock of E Company, C Company owns 10 percent of the capital stock of B Company, and E Company owns 20 percent of the capital stock of D Company.

Net incomes from operations in 19X1 were:

Company A.	$ 54,000
Company B	30,000
Company C	26,400
Company D	40,000
Company E	39,000
	$189,400

Required:
Using the traditional allocation method, compute consolidated net income for 19X1, and the minority interests in subsidiary net income. (Solution hint: Draw the affiliation diagram.)

Exercise 11–7

The financial facts shown below pertain to corporations R and S that had mutual holdings of capital stock during and at the end of the fiscal year ended December 31, 19X1.

	Corporation	
	R	S
Of the issued capital stock:		
R owns	10%	50%
S owns	20%	10%
Net assets (exclusive of investment accounts), December 31, 19X1...	$540,000	$590,000

There has been no change in the mutual holdings during the year.

Required:
Compute the dollar equity of outside shareholders in the total net assets of R and S, respectively.

(AICPA adapted)

Exercise 11–8

P Company owns 80 percent of the capital stock of S Company, and S Company owns 10 percent of the capital stock of P Company. During 19X1, the companies' net incomes from their own operations were:

P Company	$20,000
S Company	15,000

Purchase differentials have been amortized in prior years. No dividends were paid by P Company in 19X1.

Required:
a. Using the traditional allocation method, compute consolidated net income for 19X1 and the minority interest in S Company's net income.
b. Using the treasury stock method, compute consolidated net income for 19X1 and the minority interest in S Company's net income.

Exercise 11–9

A company owns 90 percent of the capital stock of B Company, 80 percent of the capital stock of C Company, and 80 percent of the capital stock of D Company. Additionally, C Company owns 80 percent of the capital stock of E Company and E Company holds 5 percent of the outstanding stock of C Company.

Net incomes for the year 19X1 from the companies' own operations were:

A Company	$50,000
B Company	30,000
C Company	32,000
D Company	30,000
E Company	20,000

Required:
Using the traditional allocation method, compute consolidated net income for 19X1 and the minority interests in subsidiary net income. (Hint: Draw the affiliation diagram.)

Problems

Problem 11–10

On January 1, 19X1, B Company purchased an 80 percent interest in C Company. A Company purchased a 90 percent interest in B Company on January 1, 19X3. Both A and B utilize the equity method in accounting for their interests in subsidiaries.

Relevant data for 19X3 is as follows:

	A Company	B Company	C Company
Common stock, January 1, 19X3	$200,000	$100,000	$50,000
Retained earnings, January 1, 19X3..............	100,000	26,000	18,000
Investment in C Company, January 1, 19X3.......		56,400	
Investment in B Company, January 1, 19X3.......	120,000		
Net income for 19X3, excluding equity			
in affiliates' income	20,000	10,000	10,000
Dividends paid in 19X3	10,000	5,000	6,000

Assume both differentials are allocated to Land.

Required:
a. Prepare the investment elimination entries for a consolidated balance sheet on January 1, 19X3.
b. Prepare a *partial* consolidated statement working paper for 19X3.
c. Prepare a schedular calculation of consolidated net income for 19X3 using the incremental approach.

Problem 11–11

On January 1, 19X1, P Company acquired an 80 percent interest in Y Company at a cost of $78,000, and Y Company acquired a 90 percent interest in Z Company at a cost of $56,000. The stockholders' equity accounts of the affiliates on this date were:

	P Company	Y Company	Z Company
Capital stock	$50,000	$40,000	$20,000
Retained earnings.............	30,000	20,000	20,000

The differentials are to be allocated wholly to goodwill and are to be amortized over a 10-year period.

Each of the three companies earned $10,000 from their own operations during 19X1 and 19X2. No dividends were paid by any of the affiliates.

Required:
a. Prepare the entries made on the books of P Company and Y Company at the end of 19X2 to record their equities in affiliates' earnings for 19X2 and differential amortization for 19X2.
b. Prepare a *partial* consolidated statement working paper for the year ended December 31, 19X2. (Hint: Make the income statement division eliminations for

differential amortization against "net income, excluding equity in affiliates' earnings.")

c. Prepare a schedular calculation of consolidated net income for 19X2 using the incremental approach.

Problem 11–12

Y Company purchased 80 percent of Z Company's outstanding stock on January 1, 19X1, for $32,000, and on January 1, 19X2, P Company purchased 80 percent of Y Company's stock for $57,600. Each of the three companies earned $20,000 from their own operations during 19X1 and 19X2, and each had capital stock and retained earnings of $10,000 and $30,000, respectively, on January 1, 19X1.

The net income of Z Company for 19X1 contains an element of unconfirmed inventory profit of $5,000, and Z Company's net income for 19X2 contains unconfirmed inventory profits at the end of that year of $2,000. Assume intercompany profits are allocated pro rata between majority and minority interests.

No dividends were paid by the affiliates during 19X1 or 19X2. Differentials, if any, are assumed to be allocated to nonamortizable assets.

Required:

a. Prepare a schedular calculation of consolidated net income for 19X2:
    (1) Using the incremental approach.
    (2) Using the residual approach.
b. Calculate the balances at December 31, 19X2, of the two investment accounts.
c. Prepare a *partial* consolidated statement working paper for the year ended December 31, 19X2. (Hint: Make the income statement division eliminations for intercompany profits in beginning and ending inventory against "net income, excluding equity in affiliates' earnings.")

Problem 11–13

For the year 19X1, companies X, Y, and Z have net incomes from their own operations of $30,000, $20,000, and $9,500, respectively.

Required:

Using the traditional allocation method, compute consolidated net income and the minority interest in subsidiary net income for the year 19X1 in each of the following independent cases:

Case 1: X Company has an 80 percent interest in Y Company, and Y Company has a 10 percent interest in X Company.

Case 2: X Company owns 80 percent of the stock of Y Company, Y Company owns 80 percent of the stock of Z Company, and Z Company has a 10 percent interest in Y Company.

Case 3: X Company has a 90 percent interest in Y Company, Y Company has a 60 percent interest in Z Company, and Z Company has a 10 percent interest in X Company.

Problem 11-14

On January 1, 19X0, the Gregory Company purchased 80 percent of the capital stock of the Morris Company and 60 percent of the capital stock of the Adams Company. On January 1, 19X1, the Morris Company purchased 30 percent of the capital stock of the Adams Company. Also on January 1, 19X1, the Adams Company purchased 20 percent of the capital stock of the Gregory Company.

During 19X1, the net incomes from operations were:

Gregory Company.............	$42,800
Morris Company	40,000
Adams Company.............	10,000

Required:

a. Calculate consolidated net income for 19X1.

b. Calculate the interests of the majority and minority shareholders in intercompany profit, assuming that unconfirmed inventory profit is included in the selling affiliates' 19X1 incomes as follows:

Morris Company	$3,000
Adams Company...............	2,000

c. Still assuming the existence of the unconfirmed inventory profits, calculate consolidated net income for 19X1 and the minority interests in net income when the eliminated intercompany profit is allocated:
(1) Pro rata to majority and minority shareholders.
(2) Wholly to majority shareholders.

Problem 11-15

A diagram depicting the intercompany stock ownership of companies X, Y, and Z on January 1, 19X1, follows:

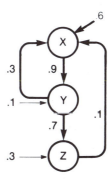

Net incomes from operations for 19X1 were:

X Company	$71,000
Y Company	37,600
Z Company	35,400

Y Company's net income includes $3,000 of unconfirmed profit in the ending inventory of X Company; the originating sale was made during 19X1.

Required:

Prepare the eliminating entry for unconfirmed inventory profit and calculate majority and minority interests in 19X1 net income assuming:

a. Pro rata allocation of the unconfirmed profit.
b. Allocation of the unconfirmed profit wholly to the majority shareholders.

Problem 11–16

On January 1, 19X1, P Company acquires 90 percent of the capital stock of S Company for $37,000 and S Company acquires 20 percent of the capital stock of P Company for $20,000. The stockholders' equity accounts of the companies on this date were:

	P Company	S Company
Capital stock...................	$20,000	$10,000
Retained earnings	50,000	20,000

The differentials are to be allocated wholly to goodwill and are to be amortized over a 10-year period.

Both companies earned $10,000 from their own operations during 19X1, and neither paid any dividends.

Required:

a. Using the traditional allocation method, calculate consolidated net income for 19X1 and minority interest in S Company's net income.
b. Using the treasury stock method, calculate consolidated net income for 19X1 and minority interest in S Company's net income.
c. Calculate the values that would be shown for minority interest and stockholders' equity in the December 31, 19X1, consolidated balance sheet under each of the two methods.

Consolidated Statements—Miscellaneous; Branch Accounting

The Entity Theory

The preparation of consolidated financial statements has heretofore emphasized the unique importance of the controlling shareholders—that is, those individuals (excluding affiliates) owning voting shares of the parent company. This parent company concept is essentially a *proprietary theory* approach—similar in concept to most of the accounting conventions for single enterprises. Notwithstanding this emphasis, special effort has been made to disclose the value of the rights of minority claimants. The separateness of this shareholder interest group is indicated by its classification between the liabilities and stockholders' equity divisions in the consolidated balance sheet.

Theorists have sometimes taken the position, however, that the various owner and creditor claimants have an undivided and indistinguishable interest in the total resources of an enterprise. An extension of this concept to the preparation of consolidated financial statements was made in 1944 by Maurice Moonitz in a monograph, *The Entity Theory of Consolidated Statements*. This monograph gives expression, in perhaps its most refined form, to the relevance of the entity concept to the reports of corporate affiliations. In respect to equity interests, the entity theory, literally interpreted, denies the primacy of the controlling shareholder group; rather, this interest is fused with those of minority shareholders and is accorded no preferential accounting treatment, either in measurement or classification.

Prevailing practices of consolidated statement preparation cannot be neatly summarized as being wholly consistent with either the parent company or entity concepts.[1] These theories do not provide contradictory arguments for all aspects of consolidated statement preparation. Nevertheless, the entity theory has definite implications regarding several computations and forms of presentation in consolidated statements. Specific areas influenced by the principal thrust of the entity theory argument include the calculation of the differential at acquisition, the amount of the unconfirmed (or unrealized) profit elimination on asset transfers among affiliates, the elimination of unamortized discounts or premiums on intercompany bondholdings, and the calculations and disclosure of the equity of minority shareholders and consolidated net income. Presumably the basic conceptual issues raised by these and other theories[2] of consolidated statements will be addressed in the current FASB project, "Accounting for the Reporting Entity, Including Consolidations, the Equity Method, and Related Matters."

---

[1] A recent study suggested that the parent company concept is generally applied in practice, although there is some diversity in applying it. Accountants International Study Group, *Consolidated Financial Statements: Current Recommended Practices in Canada, the United Kingdom, and the United States*, 1973, pars. 23–27.

[2] See George C. Baxter and James C. Spinney, "A Closer Look at Consolidated Financial Statement Theory," *CA Magazine*, January 1975.

Debit and Credit Differentials

If less than 100 percent of a subsidiary company's stock is purchased by a parent company, the difference between the acquisition cost and the corresponding purchased equity in the subsidiary's net assets is generally recognized as a debit or credit differential, which is then allocated to specific assets and liabilities. The entity theorist would formally recognize the *total* differential implicit in the purchase cost, not merely the excess amount attributable to the majority interest payment. For example, if 90 percent of a subsidiary's capital stock is acquired at a cost of $8,100 more than the equity in the corresponding book value of the subsidiary's shares, a differential would be recognized under the entity concept in the amount of $9,000 ($8,100 ÷ 90 percent), appropriate credit therein being given to minority shareholders for $900. Thus, the $8,100 reflects the "excess cost" of a 90 percent interest in the undervalued or unrecorded assets—tangible or intangible, and the $9,000 indicates the total difference between the fair value and the book value of these net assets.

Intercompany Profit

Reference has been made previously to the necessity of eliminating unconfirmed intercompany profit on sales of merchandise or other assets between corporate affiliates. The previous discussion of this matter recognized several alternative procedures. The entity theorist would argue for a total elimination of the intercompany profit element, proportionally applied to majority and minority shareholders. This view harmonizes with the concept of an integrated proprietary equity. Allocation of the intercompany profit wholly to the majority shareholders, or application of the fractional elimination method, accords a special status to the majority shareholders which is inconsistent with the perspective of the entity theory.

The same reasoning leads to support for pro rata allocation of the gain or loss on the constructive retirement of bonds. The basis for the allocation is, of course, the amount of the unamortized discounts or premiums on the intercompany-held bonds that are recorded on each of the affiliate's books.

Minority Shareholder Interests and Consolidated Net Income

The acceptance of the entity notion for consolidated statements carries with it the obligation to regard all shareholders as equal per share claimants to the combined resources of the affiliated companies. The presentation of shareholders' interests should be made in such manner as to clearly indicate the values attributable to controlling and noncontrolling interests, *but without reference to legal preference or implications as to hierarchical status.*

Clearly, according to this view, an identification of minority interests as liabilities in consolidated statements is inappropriate; it may also be argued that the compromise consolidated balance sheet position between the liabilities and the controlling stockholders' equity divisions violates the spirit of the entity theory.

Additionally, the measurement of consolidated net income is necessarily independent of assignments of interests therein to the shareholder groups. Thus, consolidated net income must be redefined under the entity theory as the confirmed profits of the parent company from its own operations, plus the confirmed profits of the subsidiary company, less the amortization of the total differential implicit in the purchase cost. In contrast to the conventional calculation technique, this revised definition focuses upon the income aggregates after eliminations but before deduction of "minority interest." The consolidated net income is then allocated between the two shareholder groups in the normal manner. Calculation of consolidated retained earnings, and relative interests therein, proceeds in a similar fashion.

Illustrative Problem—Entity Theory

P Company purchased 90 percent of the capital stock of S Company on January 1, 19X1, for $64,800. Trial balances of the affiliates on December 31, 19X1, are as follows:

	P Company	S Company
Investment in S Company	$ 88,020	
Inventory (1/1)	30,000	$ 20,000
Other assets	127,200	89,000
Purchases	90,000	70,000
Expenses	10,000	8,000
	$345,220	$187,000
Liabilities	$ 2,000	$ 7,000
Capital stock	100,000	50,000
Retained earnings	60,000	20,000
Sales	160,000	110,000
Equity in subsidiary earnings	23,220	
	$345,220	$187,000
Inventory (12/31)	$ 20,000	$ 15,000

Sales of merchandise by S Company to P Company during 19X1 amounted to $40,000; the cost of these goods to S Company was $32,000; $5,000 of this merchandise remained in the inventory of P Company on December 31, 19X1. The differential is allocated wholly to goodwill, and amortized over a 10-year period.

The differential for this example is calculated as follows:

Investment cost	$64,800
Purchased equity in S Company net assets:	
Capital stock (90% × $50,000).	$45,000
Retained earnings (90% × $20,000)	18,000
	$63,000
Excess of P Company's cost over purchased equity	
in recorded net assets of S Company	$ 1,800

Under the parent company concept, a differential of $1,800 would be recognized in the consolidated statement working paper, and allocated to specific assets and liabilities based upon the parent's share of the difference between fair value and book value. Under the entity concept, however, the $1,800 is regarded as a measure of 90 percent (the purchased interest) of the *total* differential between the fair value and the book value of S Company. Accordingly, the total differential of $2,000 ($1,800 ÷ 90 percent)[3] would be recognized in the consolidated statement working paper, with $200 credit therein being given to the minority shareholders for their interest in this unrecorded value (10 percent × $2,000).

The investment elimination entry at acquisition under the entity concept would be:

Capital Stock.	45,000	
Retained Earnings	18,000	
Differential.	2,000	
Minority Interest in Differential		200
Investment in S Company.		64,800

Allocation and amortization of the $2,000 differential on the consolidated statement working paper is consistent with the procedure outlined in Chapter 4, except that under the entity concept, amortization must be allocated between the majority and minority shareholders. Note that the majority shareholders' interest in the values assigned to assets (and the subsequent amortization thereof) is the same as it is under the parent company concept—90 percent of $2,000, or $1,800. Thus, as was observed above, the entity concept results in the recognition of additional values allocable to the minority shareholders, without changing the values attributed to majority shareholders.

---

[3] Viewed from a different perspective, the parent's investment cost of $64,800 for a 90 percent ownership interest implies a total fair value for S Company's net assets of $72,000 ($64,800 ÷ 90 percent). Since the total book value of S Company's net assets is $70,000, this calculation yields a total differential of $2,000. The two calculational approaches are equivalent.

Illustration 12–1

P COMPANY AND SUBSIDIARY S COMPANY
Consolidated Statement Working Paper (Entity Concept)
For Year Ended December 31, 19X1

	P Company	S Company	Eliminations Dr.	Eliminations Cr.	Consolidated	Assignable to Minority	Assignable to Majority
Income Statement							
Sales	160,000	110,000	(5) 40,000		230,000		
Equity in subsidiary earnings	23,220		(1) 23,220		–0–		
Inventory (12/31)	20,000	15,000	(6) 1,000*		34,000		
Total credits	203,220	125,000			264,000		
Inventory (1/1)	30,000	20,000			50,000		
Purchases	90,000	70,000		(5) 40,000	120,000		
Expenses	10,000	8,000	(4) 200		18,200		
Total debits	130,000	98,000			188,200		
Net income	73,220	27,000	64,420	40,000	75,800		
Assignable to minority shareholders						2,580†	
Assignable to majority shareholders							73,220‡
Net income	73,220	27,000	64,420	40,000	75,800	2,580	73,220
Retained Earnings Statement							
Retained earnings, 1/1/X1:							
P Company	60,000				60,000		60,000
S Company		20,000	(2) 18,000		2,000	2,000	
Net income	73,220	27,000	64,420	40,000	75,800	2,580	73,220
Retained earnings, 12/31/X1	133,220	47,000	82,420	40,000	137,800	4,580	133,220
Balance Sheet							
Other assets	127,200	89,000			216,200		
Inventory	20,000	15,000		(6) 1,000	34,000		
Investment in S Company	88,020			(1) 23,220 (2) 64,800	–0–		
Differential			(2) 2,000	(3) 2,000	–0–		
Goodwill			(3) 2,000	(4) 200	1,800		
	235,220	104,000			252,000		
Liabilities	2,000	7,000			9,000		
Minority interest in differential				(2) 200	200	200	
Capital stock:							
P Company	100,000				100,000		100,000
S Company		50,000	(2) 45,000		5,000	5,000	
Retained earnings	133,220	47,000	82,420	40,000	137,800	4,580	133,220
	235,220	104,000	131,420	131,420	252,000	9,780	233,220

* Gross profit percentage: $8,000/$40,000 = 20\%. Unconfirmed inventory profits: 20\% of $5,000 = $1,000.

† 10\% ($27,000 − $1,000) − 10\% ($200) = $2,580.

‡ $50,000 + 90\% ($27,000 − $1,000) − 90\% ($200) = $73,220.

Illustration 12–2

P COMPANY AND SUBSIDIARY S COMPANY
Consolidated Income Statement (Entity Concept)
For Year Ended December 31, 19X1

Sales			$230,000
Cost of sales:			
Inventory, January 1, 19X1		$ 50,000	
Purchases		120,000	
		$170,000	
Inventory, December 31, 19X1		34,000	136,000
Operating margin			$ 94,000
Expenses			18,200
Consolidated net income			$ 75,800
Assignable to minority shareholders			$ 2,580
Assignable to majority shareholders			73,220

P COMPANY AND SUBSIDIARY S COMPANY
Consolidated Balance Sheet (Entity Concept)
December 31, 19X1

Assets		*Equities*	
Inventory	$ 34,000	Liabilities	$ 9,000
Other assets	216,200	Stockholders' equity:	
Goodwill	1,800	Majority shareholders	233,220
		Minority shareholders	9,780
Total assets	$252,000	Total equities	$252,000

On the books of the parent company, differential amortization is based upon the parent's interest in the total differential, or $1,800. Elimination of unconfirmed intercompany profits is also still based upon the parent's interest therein. Hence, parent company accounting for its investment is unaffected by the choice of the entity or parent company concept for the consolidated statements.

The consolidated statement working paper for this example is presented in Illustration 12–1. The modification in format reflects the different orientation of the entity concept. Formal financial statements are presented in Illustration 12–2. Observe that the amounts assigned to majority shareholders interests in these statements are equivalent to the amounts that would be identified as consolidated net income and consolidated stockholders' equity under the parent company concept.

The Trial Balance Working Paper

The three-division form of consolidated statement working paper has been consistently used throughout the previous chapters. Consistency of usage has obvious advantages for instructional purposes. There are, however, a

Illustration 12–3

P COMPANY AND SUBSIDIARY S COMPANY
Trial Balance Consolidated Statement Working Paper
For Year Ended December 31, 19X1

Debits	P Company	S Company	Eliminations Dr.	Eliminations Cr.	Income Statement	Retained Earnings Statement	Minority Interest	Balance Sheet
Cash	29,500	8,000						37,500
Accounts receivable	18,000	3,000						21,000
Merchandise inventory (1/1/X1)	16,000	4,000			20,000			–0–
Investment in S Company	74,500			(1) 13,500 (2) 61,000				
Other assets	66,000	62,000						128,000
Dividends declared	10,000	5,000		(1) 4,500		10,000	500	
Purchases	42,000	20,000			62,000			
Expenses	8,000	3,000			11,000			
Differential			(2) 7,000					7,000
	264,000	105,000						
Merchandise inventory (12/31/X1)	10,000	7,000						17,000
Income statement debits—S Company —deducted contra		27,000						
Total debits—deducted contra					93,000	10,000	500	210,500

Credits

Account							
Accounts payable	22,000	5,000				5,000	27,000
Other liabilities	6,000						6,000
Capital stock:							
P Company	100,000						100,000
S Company		50,000	(2) 45,000			40,000	5,000
Retained earnings, 1/1/X1:							
P Company	40,000	10,000					
S Company		40,000	(2) 9,000			40,000	1,000
Sales	78,000			118,000			
Equity in subsidiary earnings	18,000		(1) 18,000				
	264,000	105,000					
Merchandise inventory (12/31/X1)	10,000	7,000		17,000			
Total credits				135,000 [93,000]	40,000 [10,000]	6,000 [500]	
Total debits				42,000			
Combined net income							
Income statement credits—S Company		47,000					
Income statement debits—S Company		27,000					
Net income—S Company		20,000		[2,000]	40,000	2,000	
Minority interest—10% whereof		2,000					
Consolidated net income				40,000	70,000		
Consolidated retained earnings							70,000
Minority interest in S Company						7,500	7,500M
			79,000	79,000			210,500

[deduction]

wide variety of working paper forms that can be used in the preparation of consolidated statements. Regardless of the particular form used, the fundamental principles of consolidated statement preparation remain the same. Specific forms may have special advantages in differing situations, but the resultant consolidated statements are not dependent on the form selected.

Our usual working paper procedure is to initially organize the basic financial information of the affiliates into the three statement divisions, and then to extend the combined account balances, net of eliminations, to a single Consolidated column. An alternative working paper format begins simply with the trial balances of the affiliates, and provides vertical columns for the individual financial statements, arranged in sequence, to which the combined account balances, net of eliminations, are extended. This type of working paper is usually referred to as a trial balance working paper.

To illustrate this working paper format, assume that P Company acquired 90 percent of the capital stock of S Company on January 1, 19X1, at a cost of $61,000. The December 31, 19X1, trial balances of companies P and S are as follows:

	P Company		S Company	
Cash	$ 29,500		$ 8,000	
Accounts receivable	18,000		3,000	
Merchandise (1/1/X1)	16,000		4,000	
Investment in S Company	74,500			
Other assets	66,000		62,000	
Accounts payable		$ 22,000		$ 5,000
Other liabilities		6,000		
Capital stock		100,000		50,000
Retained earnings (1/1/X1)		40,000		10,000
Dividends declared	10,000		5,000	
Sales		78,000		40,000
Equity in subsidiary earnings		18,000		
Purchases	42,000		20,000	
Expenses	8,000		3,000	
	$264,000	$264,000	$105,000	$105,000
Merchandise (12/31/X1)	$ 10,000		$ 7,000	

Based on the data provided above, a trial balance working paper is presented in Illustration 12–3. (Allocation of the differential is ignored.)

In a modified form of this trial balance working paper, sometimes encountered on the *Uniform Certified Public Accountant Examination*, one column labeled Consolidated Balances replaces the last four columns in Illustration 12–3. Using this format, a separate "row" must be provided to accumulate the minority interest additions and deductions; otherwise, the working paper operations are similar to those illustrated.

Consolidated Statements—A Review

Consolidated financial statements are the summary reports of an affiliation of companies, prepared without regard to the separate legal status of member affiliates. Among the criteria for determining the propriety of including the accounts of a subsidiary in consolidated statements are the parent company's ownership of more than 50 percent of its voting shares, the present exercise and anticipated continuity of effective managerial and financial control by the parent company, a general homogeneity of assets and operations of the affiliates, and a general coincidence of accounting periods. Consolidated statements purport to reflect the results of transactions of the affiliated companies with nonaffiliate interests; accordingly, to the extent that there are intercompany transactions among the affiliates, their effects must be excluded from the accounts of the consolidated statements. Among the more important types of such eliminations are the following:

1. *Investment elimination.* Of first importance in the sequence of eliminations is the elimination of the investment account of the parent company against the parent's equity in the corresponding book value of the subsidiary's capital stock. Essentially, this elimination results in a substitution of the subsidiary's net assets for the parent company's investment account. The substitution is made in terms of total subsidiary net assets, and the minority shareholders' equity therein is given appropriate recognition in the financial statements. In the event that there exist several classes of subsidiary stock, an appropriate allocation of the subsidiary's total stockholders' equity is made between the different classes. If the subsidiary's shares are purchased in blocks at different dates, the book value appertaining to each block is analyzed separately at the relevant acquisition date. Although control may be deferred until a subsequent purchase, the elimination in respect to the first purchase should relate to the at-acquisition book value of subsidiary stock. Where shares are purchased directly from a subsidiary affiliate, it is important to determine the changes produced in the accounts of the subsidiary as a result of the new issue. This provides the basis for comparing the parent's equity in the stockholders' equity accounts of the subsidiary immediately before the new issue with the equity immediately after the issuance. The variation in dollar equity is identified as the increase (decrease) attributable to the new issue. The accounting treatment of this change is governed by the direction of the change in the parent's percentage ownership interest. If it increases, the transaction is handled like a purchase; if it decreases, the transaction is regarded as a sale.

2. *Asset-liability eliminations.* All assets that arise out of intercompany transactions for which there exist offsetting liabilities on the books of an affiliate must be eliminated. The amount of the elimination is 100 percent,

notwithstanding the parent company's less-than-100-percent share owner-ship in the relevant affiliate.

3. *Revenue-expense eliminations.* Revenues and expenses produced by intercompany transactions must also be totally eliminated. As in the case of asset-liability eliminations, the amount of the elimination is not a function of the parent company's equity in the participating affiliates.

4. *Intercompany profit eliminations.* To the extent that profit recognized from asset transfers between affiliates has not been confirmed, or realized, to the economic entity by means of sale to outside parties, it must be eliminated in the consolidated statement working paper. Under current accounting policy, the total amount of the unconfirmed profit is eliminated from the inflated asset value, and the profit deferral may be either charged wholly against the majority shareholders or allocated pro rata to majority and minority shareholders. The authors believe the strongest case can be made for pro rata allocation. In subsequent periods, when the intercom-pany profit is confirmed, an eliminating entry recognizes the confirmed profit in the consolidated statements. Because of the "one-line consolida-tion" property of the equity method of accounting, the parent company must also defer, and subsequently recognize, the intercompany profit by means of an entry on its books. The amount recorded by the parent com-pany is equal to the amount assigned to the majority shareholders in the consolidated statement working paper.

It is important to remember that the choice of allocation alternatives affects the reported interests of minority shareholders. Pro rata allocation implies that minority interests are calculated on the basis of a subsidiary's *confirmed* net income or retained earnings. Allocation of the unconfirmed profit wholly to the majority shareholders means that minority interests are based upon a subsidiary's reported net income and retained earnings.

5. *Intercompany bond eliminations.* As in the case of other intercom-pany transactions, it is important to eliminate the effects of intercompany-held bonds. No special difficulty is encountered where the carrying value of the bond investment and the book value of the bond liability are both equal to the par value of the bonds. However, where this equivalence does not exist, due to unamortized issuance discount or premium and/or pur-chase discount or premium, there exists a consolidated basis "gain or loss" on the acquisition (constructive retirement) of these bonds. The alterna-tives regarding allocation of this intercompany gain or loss between major-ity and minority shareholders are the same as for intercompany profits on asset transfers.

Branch Accounting

Major business expansion projects generally entail significant organiza-tional changes. Such expansions often occur through mergers or acquisitions. On other occasions, expansion may be accomplished by the creation of new sales—and perhaps production—outlets to exploit heretofore undeveloped geographic areas or to more intensively cultivate existing markets. In the latter instance, agencies or branch offices are often the optimal organizational forms.

Agencies and Branches

While both the agency and the branch office are vehicles for enlarging sales volume, they exhibit a number of significant operational differences. An agency usually carries sample or display merchandise and accepts orders for delivery by the home office only. The credit status of prospective buyers is appraised by the home office; and customers' remittances are normally made to the home office. On the other hand, a branch normally carries a full complement of merchandise, makes the usual warranties respecting quality, makes collections of accounts receivable, and functions in many respects as an autonomous and formally structured business unit.

While these characteristics are descriptive in general terms of the typical agency and branch, it is not unusual to find compromise forms of business subdivisions. On occasions, the agency may carry a full line of merchandise, make collections of accounts receivable, or otherwise accept responsibilities normally reserved to the branch. Similarly, a branch may sometimes be denied some of the autonomy of operation previously noted.

The extent of branch self-management is a function of corporate policy in regard to decentralized operating and administrative control. While different branches within the same company may be accorded different degrees of administrative authority, the status of each branch as an operating subdivision will usually be established by general standards which extend company-wide.

The data accumulation process for the operations of agencies does not introduce any new accounting problems, as an agency is essentially little more than an extension of existing sales territories. Consequently, the discussion that follows will be confined to accounting for branches. As will become readily apparent, most of the special aspects of branch accounting are analogous to concepts and procedures previously discussed in our coverage of consolidated financial statements.

Branch Accounts

Branch accounting is essentially an application of the controlling account principle in which the subsidiary records are those of a reasonably independent operating unit. In respect to transactions with the branch, it is conventional for the home office to adopt an account terminology that clearly identifies and describes branch operations. The accounts are selected on the basis of expected frequency of use, their relevance to branch operations, and their contribution to overall accounting control. The general ledger controlling account is variously referred to as Branch Current, Branch Account, or Investment in Branch.

Equivalence of debit and credit balances is preserved in the branch ledger by the use of a Home Office Current account, which is reciprocal to the Branch Current account. The Home Office Current account has a number of properties that traditionally characterize a proprietorship account, particularly in respect to the branch closing process; branch profits and losses are periodically closed thereinto. However, viewed more precisely, the account has no special identity, and its balance is perhaps best described as merely the algebraic sum of all other account balances in the branch ledger.

The Branch Current account is normally charged with the cost of assets or services contributed to the branch by the home office and is credited with remittances from the branch. Periodically, the account is adjusted to give effect to branch net income or loss. Where there are numerous branches, the use of separate current accounts for each branch is often desirable. Although there is no evident consensus as to the specific accounts most appropriate for inclusion in the branch records, it is usual to find only those accounts most closely allied with branch operations, such as those which relate to sales, accounts receivable, inventories, expenses incurred by the branch, and so forth. It is not uncommon to find the accounts for the branch fixed assets in the home office records; yet, depreciation expense in respect thereto may be recorded by the branch making use of the property. In some instances, other expenses incurred by the home office that are in support of branch operations may also be allocated to the benefiting branch. Notice of such expense assignment should be given the relevant branch for purposes of entry in the branch records. Such an identification of expenses with specific branches makes it possible to measure more accurately the operating efficiency of each branch as an independent entity. Those expenses incurred by the home office for the benefit of several branches that do not accommodate to convenient allocation, however, are best reflected in aggregates in combined financial statements of the branches and the home office. If expenses applicable to one or more branches are not formally assigned to, and recorded by, the branches, they are usually charged against the branch net income or loss recorded by the home office in its closing process.

Illustrative Entries

The following transactions relate to the establishment of a branch and its first month's operations:

1. Cash is transferred to the branch, $1,000.
2. Merchandise costing $5,000 is shipped to the branch. Billing of home office shipments to the branch is at cost.

3. Expenses are incurred and paid by the branch, $200.
4. Additional merchandise, costing $2,500, is acquired by the branch from outside wholesalers.
5. Branch credit sales are $8,000.
6. Branch collections on account amount to $4,700.
7. Cash remitted by the branch to the home office is $1,000.
8. Closing entries are prepared by the branch; a monthly operating summary is submitted to the home office. The month-end branch inventory is $1,800.

Journal entries for these transactions are recorded on the books of the home office and the branch in Illustration 12–4. Additional entries by the home office are necessary to close the revenue and expense accounts from its own operations. It should be noted that the Shipments to Branch account (on the home office books) is a contra account to Purchases or Cost of Goods Manufactured on the books of the home office; consequently, it necessarily *always* reflects the *cost* of goods shipped and is closed at the end of the accounting period. Contrariwise, the Shipments from Home Office account (on the branch books) is equivalent to a Purchases account and accordingly reflects the intracompany billing price; it also is closed at the end of the accounting period. These reciprocal accounts are used for the purpose of maintaining accounting control of intracompany merchandise shipments.

At completion of a period of branch operations, it is customary for the branch to render operating and position statements to the home office, supported in most instances by transaction details in respect to branch inventories and the Home Office Current account. The latter information may be especially useful for foreign branches or where there are numerous cash remittances to and from the home office. Once these data are compiled, it is frequently desirable to prepare combined financial statements of the home office and branch.

Combined Financial Statements

While the separate statements of the branch and home office disclose useful information in respect to the operations of each division, they do not adequately convey important analytical data about the composite business unit. To merely include in the home office operating statement a single figure for branch net income or loss is not fully informative. Summary disclosures concerning total sales, cost of sales, and operating expenses of the business unit as a whole are often more meaningful than data revealed in the separate statements of the affiliate divisions; indeed, they are required in company-wide policy decisions.

Combined statements of the home office and branch are needed to reflect the effects of transactions of the total business entity with outside interests. Accordingly, the effects of transactions between the home office

Illustration 12–4

JOURNAL ENTRIES FOR
BRANCH'S FIRST MONTH OF OPERATIONS

Home Office Books

		Dr.	Cr.
(1)	Branch Current	1,000	
	Cash		1,000
(2)	Branch Current	5,000	
	Shipments to Branch		5,000
(7)	Cash	1,000	
	Branch Current		1,000
(8)	Branch Current	2,100	
	Branch Net Income		2,100

Branch Books

		Dr.	Cr.
(1)	Cash	1,000	
	Home Office Current		1,000
(2)	Shipments from Home Office	5,000	
	Home Office Current		5,000
(3)	Expenses	200	
	Cash		200
(4)	Purchases	2,500	
	Accounts Payable		2,500
(5)	Accounts Receivable	8,000	
	Sales		8,000
(6)	Cash	4,700	
	Accounts Receivable		4,700
(7)	Home Office Current	1,000	
	Cash		1,000
(8)	Sales	8,000	
	Merchandise Inventory	1,800	
	Purchases		2,500
	Shipments from Home Office ...		5,000
	Expenses		200
	Income Summary		2,100
	Income Summary	2,100	
	Home Office Current		2,100

and branches (or between branches) must be eliminated to avoid overstatement or duplicate measurement in the accounts. Combined statements make use of the *principle of substitution*—the branch's asset, liability, and operating accounts are substituted for the Branch Current account. This is accomplished in a combined statement working paper by *eliminating* the Branch Current account against the Home Office Current account. To the extent that there are evidences in other accounts of intracompany transactions, their effects must also be eliminated. For example, balances found in the reciprocal Shipments to Branch–Shipments from Home Office accounts, and Remittances to Home Office–Remittances from Branch accounts (the latter accounts reflecting periodic cash transfers) must also be eliminated, as they represent only the internal movements of company resources. *The eliminating entries are working paper entries only;* accordingly, they are not entered on the books of either the home office or the branch.

One familiar form of combined statement working paper is given in Illustration 12–5. As a basis for this illustration, the trial balance information for the home office and branch of X Company on December 31, 19X1, is provided following:

	Home Office	Branch
Cash	$ 40,000	$15,000
Accounts receivable	22,000	20,000
Merchandise (1/1)	15,000	
Branch current	17,000	
Other assets	14,000	
Purchases	65,000	9,000
Shipments from home office		12,000
Expenses	7,000	4,000
	$180,000	$60,000
Liabilities	$ 8,000	$12,000
Capital stock	50,000	
Retained earnings	10,000	
Home office current		17,000
Sales	100,000	31,000
Shipments to branch	12,000	
	$180,000	$60,000
Merchandise (12/31)	$ 10,000	$ 4,000

The working paper (Illustration 12–5) is divided into three divisions to accommodate the preparation of the income statement, the retained earnings statement, and the balance sheet. The balances in the reciprocal accounts are eliminated as noted. The reader will observe that the working paper in Illustration 12–5 refers to retained earnings balances in respect to both the home office and the branch. As noted earlier, the branch does not ordinarily accumulate branch profits and losses in a retained earnings ac-

Illustration 12–5

X COMPANY
Combined Statement Working Paper
For Year Ended December 31, 19X1

	Home Office	Branch	Eliminations Dr.	Eliminations Cr.	Combined
Income Statement					
Sales	100,000	31,000			131,000
Merchandise (12/31)	10,000	4,000			14,000
Shipments to branch	12,000		(2) 12,000		–0–
Total credits	122,000	35,000			145,000
Merchandise (1/1)	15,000				15,000
Purchases	65,000	9,000			74,000
Shipments from home office		12,000		(2) 12,000	–0–
Expenses	7,000	4,000			11,000
Total debits	87,000	25,000			100,000
Net income	35,000	10,000	12,000	12,000	45,000
Retained Earnings Statement					
Retained earnings, 1/1/X1	10,000	–0–			10,000
Net income	35,000	10,000	12,000	12,000	45,000
Retained earnings, 12/31/X1	45,000	10,000	12,000	12,000	55,000
Balance Sheet					
Cash	40,000	15,000			55,000
Accounts receivable	22,000	20,000			42,000
Merchandise (12/31)	10,000	4,000			14,000
Branch current	17,000			(1) 17,000	–0–
Other assets	14,000				14,000
	103,000	39,000			125,000
Liabilities	8,000	12,000			20,000
Capital stock	50,000				50,000
Retained earnings	45,000	*10,000	12,000	12,000	55,000
Home office current		17,000	(1) 17,000		–0–
	103,000	39,000	29,000	29,000	125,000

* Increment to Home Office Current due to periodic branch net income.

count; rather, it records such profits and losses as adjustments in the Home Office Current account, and the beginning balance of "retained earnings" of the branch will always necessarily be zero. Accordingly, variation in the balances of the Home Office Current account as found in the combined statement working paper and as reported in the branch's period-end balance sheet may be explained in terms of the branch's periodic profit or loss. However, the working paper format does indicate the total retained earnings for the composite entity at the end of the period, that is, the accumulated earnings of the home office increased or decreased by the branch net profit or loss for the period.

The formal combined statements are easily prepared using the data found in the Combined column of the working paper. The combined statements for X Company are presented in Illustration 12–6.

Illustration 12–6

X COMPANY
Income Statement
For Year Ended December 31, 19X1

Sales		$131,000
Cost of sales:		
Merchandise, January 1, 19X1	$15,000	
Purchases	74,000	
	$89,000	
Merchandise, December 31, 19X1	14,000	75,000
Gross margin		$ 56,000
Expenses		11,000
Net income		$ 45,000

X COMPANY
Retained Earnings Statement
For Year Ended December 31, 19X1

Retained earnings, January 1, 19X1	$10,000
Net income, 19X1	45,000
Retained earnings, December 31, 19X1	$55,000

X COMPANY
Balance Sheet
December 31, 19X1

Assets		Equities	
Cash	$ 55,000	Liabilities	$ 20,000
Accounts receivable	42,000	Capital stock	50,000
Merchandise	14,000	Retained earnings	55,000
Other assets	14,000		
Total assets	$125,000	Total equities	$125,000

Branch Billing in Excess of Cost

When the home office ships merchandise to the branch, it may elect to bill the branch at a value in excess of cost—either at retail price or at a selected percentage markup on cost. Under either of these conditions, the branch manager frequently is not given complete information concerning the cost of branch shipments. Therefore, net profit as reckoned by the branch will necessarily require adjustment by the home office to the extent of realized intracompany profit; only the intracompany profit in the unsold branch merchandise is deferred. Consider the following transactions that illustrate the accounting consequences of this type of billing:

Illustration 12–7

JOURNAL ENTRIES FOR
INTRACOMPANY INVENTORY SHIPMENTS
WITH TRANSFER PRICES IN EXCESS OF COST

Home Office Books

(1)	Branch Current	5,000	
	Shipments to Branch (at cost)		4,000
	Intracompany Inventory Profit		1,000
(3)	Branch Current	500	
	Branch Net Income		500
	Intracompany Inventory Profit	500	
	Branch Net Income		500

Branch Books

(1)	Shipments from Home Office (at billing price) ..	5,000	
	Home Office Current		5,000
(2)	Accounts Receivable	3,000	
	Sales		3,000
(3)	Merchandise Inventory	2,500	
	Sales	3,000	
	Shipments from Home Office		5,000
	Income Summary		500

1. Merchandise costing the home office $4,000 is billed to the branch at $5,000. The branch is not informed of the merchandise cost.
2. One half of the above shipment is sold by the branch for $3,000.
3. The branch closes its books and reports its net income to the home office.

The journal entries for these transactions, or events, are recorded on the books of the home office and branch in Illustration 12–7.

The net income calculation of the branch is based upon the transfer price of the merchandise. The home office, possessed of complete information in respect to intracompany billing, is able to make appropriate adjustment for the intracompany inventory profit. That amount of the profit on the original shipment subsequently *confirmed* by branch sales is appropriately transferred in the home office closing process to branch net income. The amount of profit identified with unsold branch merchandise is reserved as a credit in the Intracompany Inventory Profit account until the relevant units are sold. The balance in the Intracompany Inventory Profit account should be reported as a deduction from the balance in the Branch Current account in the balance sheet of the home office. In combined statements prepared before closing, the Intracompany Inventory Profit account is eliminated as a part of the Shipments to Branch–Shipments from Home Office elimination and accordingly does not appear as an extended value in the combined statement working paper. Additionally, the unconfirmed profit in the ending inventory of the branch is eliminated. To the extent that the accountant may favor disclosing the amount of inventory profit, it may be retained in the combined balance sheet as a deduction from the profit-inflated inventory, reducing the latter to cost.

Illustrative Problem

The following illustrative problem introduces a combined statement working paper involving residual intracompany inventory profit. The trial balances of the home office and branch on December 31, 19X1, are as follows:

	Home Office	Branch
Cash	$ 40,000	$ 15,000
Accounts receivable.................	22,000	20,000
Merchandise (1/1)	15,000	12,000
Branch current	53,000	
Other assets........................	14,000	50,000
Purchases...........................	65,000	9,000
Shipments from home office..........		36,000
Expenses	7,000	4,000
	$216,000	$146,000
Liabilities	$ 18,000	$ 12,000
Capital stock	50,000	
Retained earnings	10,000	
Home office current.................		53,000
Sales	100,000	81,000
Shipments to branch.................	30,000	
Intracompany inventory profit	8,000	
	$216,000	$146,000
Merchandise (12/31)	$ 10,000	$ 4,800

The home office bills all shipments to the branch at 20 percent above cost. The branch's beginning and ending inventories consist exclusively of merchandise purchased from the home office.

The combined statement working paper for this problem is shown in Illustration 12–8. It may be observed that the beginning inventory of the branch, $12,000, is profit inflated to the extent of $2,000. This amount must be eliminated from both the Merchandise, January 1 and Intracompany Inventory Profit accounts. Similarly, Shipments from Home Office, $36,000, contains a profit factor of $6,000, which reconciles the contra shipment accounts. It is important that the reciprocal shipment accounts be eliminated, together with the residual $6,000 of intracompany inventory profit. Finally, there remains an elimination in respect to the profit element in the final inventory of the branch. The branch inventory, $4,800, contains $800 of intracompany profit. It is sufficient to make this elimination by merely reducing the inventory value as it appears in the income statement division and also as it appears in the balance sheet division of the combined statement working paper.

The home office may elect to bill the branch at retail price. Such a billing often serves to improve merchandise control in respect to branch operations. Where the billing is made at an established sales price, necessarily the difference between the value of goods available for sale and the value of goods sold is the retail value of unsold merchandise. Comparison of this amount with a physical inventory permits easy detection of inventory discrepancies. By the simple expedient of applying the relevant gross profit

Illustration 12–8

X COMPANY
Combined Statement Working Paper
For Year Ended December 31, 19X1

	Home Office	Branch	Eliminations Dr.	Eliminations Cr.	Combined
Income Statement					
Sales	100,000	81,000			181,000
Merchandise (12/31)	10,000	4,800	(4) 800		14,000
Shipments to branch	30,000		(3) 30,000		–0–
Total credits	140,000	85,800			195,000
Merchandise (1/1)	15,000	12,000		(2) 2,000	25,000
Purchases	65,000	9,000			74,000
Shipments from home office		36,000		(3) 36,000	–0–
Expenses	7,000	4,000			11,000
Total debits	87,000	61,000			110,000
Net income	53,000	24,800	30,800	38,000	85,000
Retained Earnings Statement					
Retained earnings, 1/1/X1	10,000	–0–			10,000
Net income	53,000	24,800	30,800	38,000	85,000
Retained earnings, 12/31/X1	63,000	24,800	30,800	38,000	95,000
Balance Sheet					
Cash	40,000	15,000			55,000
Accounts receivable	22,000	20,000			42,000
Merchandise (12/31)	10,000	4,800		(4) 800	14,000
Branch current	53,000			(1) 53,000	–0–
Other assets	14,000	50,000			64,000
	139,000	89,800			175,000
Liabilities	18,000	12,000			30,000
Capital stock	50,000				50,000
Retained earnings	63,000	*24,800	30,800	38,000	95,000
Home office current		53,000	(1) 53,000		–0–
Intracompany inventory profit	8,000		(2) 2,000		–0–
			(3) 6,000		
	139,000	89,800	91,800	91,800	175,000

* Increment to Home Office Current due to periodic branch net income.

rate, the inventory at retail may be translated to cost. The use of this method obviously results in the calculation of a branch net loss in an amount equal to the branch's operating expenses. Combined statements are prepared in the same manner as illustrated previously for billings in excess of cost.

The transfer price for intracompany shipments of merchandise may be based upon competitive quotations from outside suppliers. In this circumstance, the branch income statement would provide a fairly reliable index of the branch's operating efficiency. Where the billing is at retail price, the branch's operating statement can hardly be more than a statistical summary of revenues and expenses. In this instance, an index of the branch management's efficiency must necessarily relate to the minimization of operating expenses, or more precisely, maximization of sales volume and minimization of the ratio of operating expenses to sales.

Reconciling Adjustments

All intracompany reciprocal account balances must be eliminated in the preparation of a combined financial statement for the branch and home office. Sometimes these accounts will *not* carry equivalent balances on specified statement dates. It is accordingly necessary to determine the reason(s) for the discrepancies, and to make adjustments to establish reciprocity prior to making the eliminating entries. Three common sources of difference between the Branch Current account and the Home Office Current account are:

1. End-of-period billings by the home office for the branch's share of expenses recorded on the books of the home office that have not been recorded by the branch.
2. Cash remittances in transit between the branch and the home office (or vice versa) that have not been recorded in the same accounting period by the recipient entity.
3. Merchandise shipments in transit between the home office and the branch (or vice versa) that have not been recorded in the same accounting period by the recipient entity.

Identification of these and other sources of discrepancy between the Branch Current and Home Office Current accounts is accomplished by reviewing records of end-of-period transactions as recorded on both sets of books, and on occasions by reconciling recorded figures. For example, if all of the branch's acquisitions of merchandise are shipments from the home office, the total merchandise accounted for by the branch (as reflected by the sum of its cost of sales and ending inventory) should equal the value of merchandise made available to it during the period (as reflected by the sum of its beginning inventory and the value of shipments from the home office). These reconciling adjustments may be entered on the combined statement working paper in the same manner as the eliminating entries; they are, however, usually identified by a different system of indexing.

Transshipments of Merchandise

Economic conditions may sometimes make it necessary for one branch to ship merchandise previously received from the home office to another branch. In such a circumstance, it is important that each branch record the transaction so as to give appropriate recognition to the effect produced *on the home office books*. For example, the receiving branch should debit the accounts of the assets received and credit the Home Office Current account; contrariwise, the shipping branch should reduce by appropriate entries both its Home Office Current account and the accounts for the assets transferred. It is unusual for branches to carry current accounts with other branches; rather, interbranch transactions are ordinarily analyzed in terms of accountability to the home office.

Freight on assets transferred by the home office to a branch is properly included as an element of asset cost to the receiving branch. However, where assets are transshipped from one branch to another, it is appropriate to include in the cost of the asset only that amount of freight that would have been paid had the shipment been directed originally from the home office to the ultimate branch recipient. Payments in excess of this amount are normally charged to expense by the home office, the assumption being that the home office is at least nominally responsible for the excess charge resulting from indirect routing.

Freight on branch transshipments is illustrated below. It is assumed that merchandise costing the home office $1,000 is shipped to Branch A. Freight on this shipment, $80, is paid by the home office. Subsequently, these goods are transshipped to Branch B, with the payment of additional freight of $40 by Branch A. It is determined that direct routing from the home office to Branch B would have resulted in an aggregate freight cost of $100. Entries for these transactions are as follows:

Home Office

Branch A Current..	1,080	
Shipments to Branch A......................................		1,000
Cash		80
Shipments to Branch A...	1,000	
Shipments to Branch B......................................		1,000
Branch B Current..	1,100	
Excess Freight on Branch Transshipment.........................	20	
Branch A Current..		1,120

Branch A

Shipments from Home Office....................................	1,000	
Freight-In...	80	
Home Office Current		1,080
Home Office Current	1,120	
Shipments from Home Office...............................		1,000
Freight-In..		80
Cash		40

Branch B

Shipments from Home Office....................................	1,000	
Freight-In...	100	
Home Office Current		1,100

Other Accounting Systems

On occasions, the home office may elect to centralize the accounting for all branch operations within the structure of home office records. This may result in the creation of a separate set of accounts to identify the details of branch operations, or these operations may be subsumed in the same system of accounts as are used in nonbranch transactions. In either circumstance, the documentary evidences of all branch transactions must be regularly submitted to the home office for entry. Such a system is not essentially unlike that used for agencies.

On other occasions, the accounting system may take the form of a complete record-keeping by *both* branch and home office in respect to all branch transactions. Necessarily this duplication has disadvantages. Yet, the more complete dissemination of accounting information may, in fact, promote greater operating efficiencies in the administrative decentralization than the added cost of maintaining duplicate records would appear to indicate.

Questions

1. Describe briefly the parent company and entity concepts of consolidated financial statements.

2. What effect(s) does the adoption of the entity concept of consolidated financial statements have on entries made by the parent company to record its equity in earnings of affiliates and differential amortization?

3. Which concept of consolidated financial statements is generally used in practice?

4. Describe the calculations of debit and credit differentials where the entity theory of consolidated statements is accepted.

5. What is the entity theorist's position regarding the amount of elimination of intercompany profits on asset transfers?

6. What is the relationship between the amounts of consolidated net income and stockholders' equity assignable to majority shareholders under the entity concept and the amounts of consolidated net income and stockholders' equity reported under the parent company concept?

7. What is the relationship between and the function of the Branch Current and Home Office Current accounts?

8. What is meant by the "principle of substitution" as applied to branch accounting?

9. If the home office elects to bill the branch for merchandise at a price in excess of cost, why would it be preferable to use a price above cost but less than retail?

10. What are "reconciling adjustments" in branch accounting?

Exercises

Exercise 12–1

P Company owns 80 percent of S Company. During 19X1, both companies had incomes from their own operations of $25,000.

Required:
a. Under the parent company concept, calculate consolidated net income for 19X1.
b. Under the entity concept, calculate consolidated net income and the amounts assignable to majority and minority shareholders for 19X1.

Exercise 12–2

P Company purchased 80 percent of the capital stock of S Company on January 1, 19X1, for $52,000, when the book value of S Company's net assets was $50,000. The differential is to be allocated wholly to goodwill, which is to be amortized over 10 years. P Company uses the *entity* concept in the preparation of consolidated financial statements. During 19X1, both companies had incomes from their own operations of $20,000.

Required:
a. Calculate the total differential implicit in the purchase price.
b. Prepare P Company's entries at December 31, 19X1, to record its equity in S Company's 19X1 earnings and differential amortization for the year.
c. Calculate the amount of goodwill amortization that would be reported in the 19X1 consolidated income statement.
d. Calculate consolidated net income and the amounts assignable to majority and minority shareholders for 19X1.

Exercise 12–3

P Company owns 70 percent of S Company. During 19X1, both companies had incomes from their own operations of $10,000. P Company's income includes $2,000 of unconfirmed intercompany profit, and S Company's income includes $3,000 of unconfirmed intercompany profit.

P Company uses the *entity* concept in the preparation of consolidated financial statements. At the date of acquisition, the total differential was determined to be $40,000. This differential was allocated to goodwill, and is being amortized over 10 years (including 19X1).

Required:
a. Prepare P Company's entries at December 31, 19X1, to record its equity in S Company's 19X1 earnings and differential amortization for the year.
b. Calculate consolidated net income and the amounts assignable to majority and minority shareholders for 19X1.

Exercise 12–4

P Company purchased 80 percent of the capital stock of S Company on January 1, 19X1, for $70,000, when S Company had capital stock of $10,000 and retained earnings of $40,000. An appraisal of S Company's assets and liabilities on this date indicated that plant and equipment (net) had a fair value of $100,000 and a book value of $80,000, and that the book values of all other assets and liabilities were equal to fair values. Assume the plant and equipment has a remaining life of 5 years, and goodwill is to be amortized over 10 years.

P Company's retained earnings on January 1, 19X1, were $60,000. During 19X1, the companies had incomes from their own operations as follows: P Company—$30,000; and S Company—$10,000. P Company uses the *entity* concept in the preparation of consolidated financial statements.

Required:
a. Calculate the total differential implicit in the purchase price.
b. Determine the allocation of the *total* differential to specific assets and the annual amortization for the next 10 years.
c. Prepare the entries on P Company's books at December 31, 19X1, to record its equity in S Company's 19X1 earnings and differential amortization for the year.
d. Prepare the investment elimination and differential allocation and amortization entries for a three-division consolidated statement working paper at December 31, 19X1.
e. Calculate 19X1 consolidated net income and December 31, 19X1, consolidated retained earnings, and indicate the amounts assignable to majority and minority shareholders.

Exercise 12–5

On January 1, 19X1, A Company acquired 80 percent of the capital stock of B Company and 90 percent of the capital stock of C Company.

The following operating summary relates to the affiliation for the year ended December 31, 19X4:

	Companies		
	A	B	C
Income from operations	$65,000	$40,000	$26,000
Recognized intercompany inventory profit, unconfirmed on—			
January 1		6,000	
December 31	4,000	1,000	2,000

A Company acquired on January 1, 19X4, machinery and equipment from B Company on which the latter recorded a profit of $10,000. On January 1, 19X4, it was estimated that the equipment had a remaining service life of 10 years.

C Company acquired on January 1, 19X4, $20,000 of 7 percent bonds of A Company for $23,000. The bonds with 20 years' maturity were issued by A Company 10 years before the intercompany purchase, at 90.

Required:
Using the parent company concept, calculate consolidated net income for 19X4.

Exercise 12–6

Edwards Company opened a Dallas branch in January 19X7. During 19X7, Edwards recorded merchandise transfers to the branch and merchandise returns from the branch with the following entries:

Branch Current...	156,000	
Sales		156,000
Sales Returns...	3,900	
Branch Current.......................................		3,900

Transfers to and from the branch were recorded by Edwards at 130 percent of Edwards' cost.

The Dallas branch reported to the home office a net loss of $12,000 for 19X7. In addition, the branch reported a closing inventory of $65,000, all of which was acquired from the home office.

Required:

Assume that the home office books have not been closed for 19X7. Prepare the journal entries on the books of the home office that are necessary at the end of 19X7 to (1) correct the accounts of the home office and (2) recognize the results of branch activities during 19X7.

Exercise 12–7

On July 1, the Demaris Company, central distributor for Arlo Metal Castings, Inc., organized a southwest sales outlet in El Paso. Following are the home office–branch transactions for the month of July:

July 1 The Demaris Company transferred $2,500 to its El Paso branch.

      2 Merchandise costing the home office $3 per unit was shipped to the branch at an invoice price of $5 per unit. One thousand units were shipped on July 2; a second order was to be filled by local suppliers.

      2 Shipping costs on the above were paid:

By the home office..........	$150
By the branch	50

      5 Additional merchandise was acquired by the El Paso branch from regional distributors, 500 units at $3.10.

      7 Display equipment was purchased by the home office, cost $3,600, and delivered to the El Paso branch. Fixed asset accounts are kept by the home office.

    10 Branch sales for the period July 3–10: on account, 800 units at $5.

    18 Branch collections on account, $3,200.

    25 Branch sales for the period July 11–24: on account, 500 units at $5.

    29 Cash remittance by branch to home office, $1,000.

    30 Monthly summary of branch cash expenses:

Advertising	$ 40
Sales commissions	650
Miscellaneous	10

July 31   Depreciation recorded by the Demaris Company for July included $150 that related to the display equipment used by the El Paso branch. Insurance on this equipment was amortized by the home office in the amount of $25.

31   Inventories of merchandise at El Paso on July 31 included:

> From the home office . . . . 150 units @ $5.00
> From local suppliers . . . .   50 units @ $3.10

Required:

Journalize the above transactions on the books of the Demaris Company and the El Paso branch office and prepare closing entries for July month-end statements.

Problems

Problem 12–8

The Tucker Company acquired an 80 percent interest in the capital stock of the Taylor Corporation on January 1, 19X1, for $90,000. On December 31, 19X1, the trial balances of the affiliated companies are as follows:

	Tucker Company	Taylor Corporation
Cash.	$ 40,000	$ 32,000
Receivables.	20,000	16,000
Merchandise (1/1).	12,000	8,000
Investment in Taylor Corporation common stock.	114,000	
Long-lived assets.	93,000	41,000
Other assets	17,000	35,000
Dividends declared.		10,000
Purchases	50,000	43,000
Expenses.	18,000	15,000
	364,000	$200,000
Payables	$ 12,000	$ 10,000
Capital stock:		
Tucker Company.	100,000	
Taylor Corporation.		60,000
Retained earnings:		
Tucker Company.	120,000	
Taylor Corporation		40,000
Sales.	100,000	90,000
Equity in subsidiary earnings.	32,000	
	364,000	$200,000
Merchandise (12/31).	$ 10,000	$ 16,000

Assume the differential is allocated to "Other assets," and is *not* subject to amortization.

· *Required:*

Using the entity theory, prepare:

a. A consolidated statement working paper for the year ended December 31, 19X1.

b. A consolidated balance sheet as of December 31, 19X1, and a consolidated income statement for the year then ended.

Problem 12–9

On January 1, 19X1, the Irwin Corporation acquired 90 percent of the capital stock of the Prentice Company for $84,000 and 80 percent of the capital stock of Simons, Inc., for $70,000. Accumulated retained earnings of the Prentice Company and Simons, Inc., at acquisition were $40,000 and $20,000, respectively.

Trial balances of the affiliate companies on December 31, 19X2 are as follows:

	Irwin Corporation	Prentice Company	Simons, Inc.
Cash	$ 19,000	$ 23,000	$ 7,000
Receivables	41,000	27,000	12,000
Merchandise (1/1)	11,000	8,000	7,000
Investment in Prentice Company	119,100		
Investment in Simons, Inc.	86,000		
Other assets	8,000	74,000	86,000
Dividends declared		6,000	4,000
Purchases	57,000	64,000	33,000
Expenses	10,600	5,000	10,000
	$351,700	$207,000	$159,000
Payables	$ 18,000	$ 5,000	$ 12,000
Capital stock	100,000	50,000	60,000
Retained earnings	119,000	70,000	35,000
Sales	94,000	82,000	52,000
Equity in subsidiary earnings	20,700		
	$351,700	$207,000	$159,000
Merchandise (12/31)	$ 6,000	$ 10,000	$ 8,000

During 19X2, Simons, Inc., made sales to the Irwin Corporation in the amount of $12,000. In respect to these sales, $4,000 remain in the December 31 inventory of Irwin. Simons, Inc., regularly marks up goods 25 percent on selling price on sales to both affiliates and nonaffiliates.

Assume the differentials are allocated to "Other assets" and are *not* subject to amortization.

Required:

Using the entity theory, prepare a consolidated statement working paper for the year ended December 31, 19X2.

Problem 12–10

The Cruse Company purchased 80 percent of the capital stock of Summers, Inc., on January 1, 19X1, for $49,600. One year thereafter, trial balances of the respective companies were as follows:

	December 31, 19X1	
	Cruse Company	Summers, Inc.
Cash	$ 23,400	$ 12,500
Notes receivable.....................	5,000	2,000
Merchandise (1/1)	28,000	11,000
Investment in Summers, Inc.	68,000	
Other assets.........................	58,000	80,500
Dividends declared	8,500	5,000
Purchases...........................	161,000	83,000
Freight-in...........................	1,000	200
Selling expenses.....................	18,000	11,100
Administrative expenses	9,300	5,700
	$380,200	$211,000
Accounts payable.....................	$ 18,000	$ 12,000
Other liabilities.....................	3,000	16,000
Capital stock	100,000	50,000
Retained earnings	31,000	12,000
Sales	205,000	121,000
Equity in subsidiary earnings	22,400	
Interest income......................	800	
	$380,200	$211,000
Merchandise (12/31)	$ 41,000	$ 18,000

"Other liabilities" of Summers, Inc., include a $3,000 noninterest-bearing note payable to the Cruse Company.

Required:

Prepare a *trial balance* consolidated statement working paper for the year ended December 31, 19X1.

Problem 12–11

The individual and consolidated statements of companies X and Y for the year ending December 31, 19X2, are as shown on the following page:

	X Company	Y Company	Consolidated
Cash and receivables	$ 35,000	$108,000	$ 97,400
Inventories	40,000	90,000	122,000
Plant (net)	460,000	140,000	600,000
Goodwill			50,000
Investment in Y	276,900		
X bonds owned		103,000	
	$811,900	$441,000	$869,400
Current payables	$ 70,000	$ 23,000	$ 53,000
Dividends payable	10,000	8,000	12,400
Mortgage bonds	200,000	50,000	150,000
Capital stock	300,000	200,000	300,000
Retained earnings	231,900	160,000	231,900
Minority interest			122,100
	$811,900	$441,000	$869,400
Sales	$600,000	$400,000	$760,000
Cost of sales	360,000	280,000	403,000
Gross profit	$240,000	$120,000	$357,000
Operating expenses	130,000	54,000	184,000
Operating profit	$110,000	$ 66,000	$173,000
Interest income	1,800	5,000	1,800
Equity in subsidiary earnings	14,325	–0–	–0–
Total	$126,125	$ 71,000	$174,800
Interest expense	$ 10,000	$ 3,000	$ 8,000
Provision for income taxes	56,000	34,000	90,000
Nonrecurring loss			3,000
Amortization of goodwill			6,250
Minority interest			7,425
Net income	$ 60,125	$ 34,000	$ 60,125
Dividends	20,000	16,000	20,000
Transfer to retained earnings	$ 40,125	$ 18,000	$ 40,125

X Company purchased its 70 percent interest in Y Company on January 1, 19X1. X Company sells its product in part to Y Company for further processing, and in part to other firms. The inventories of Y Company included an intercompany markup at both the beginning and end of the year. Cash transfers are made between the companies according to working capital needs.

Early in 19X2, Y Company purchased $100,000 face value of the bonds of X Company as a temporary investment. These are carried on Y's books at cost.

Eliminations of intercompany profits are allocated pro rata between majority and minority shareholders.

Required:

On the basis of the information you can develop from an analysis of the individual and consolidated statements, answer the nine questions below.

Show clearly all computations necessary to support your answers.

1. Does X Company carry its *Investment in Y* on the cost or equity basis? State the reason for your conclusion.

2. The Goodwill is based upon a revaluation of the *total* (entity concept) of Y Company's net assets on the basis of the price paid by X Company for its interest in Y Company on January 1, 19X1, and it is being amortized over 10 years. What was the balance of Goodwill on the date of acquisition?

3. What is the nature of *Nonrecurring Loss* on the consolidated income statement? Show the consolidating elimination entry from which it originated.

4. Show the amounts of intercompany debts, excluding the bonds, and show which company is the debtor and which is the creditor in each instance.

5. Prepare a schedule reconciling the sum of the *Cost of Sales* of X and Y individually with the *Consolidated Cost of Sales*. Show clearly the intercompany markup in the beginning and ending inventories of Y Company and how you determined the amounts.

6. Prepare a schedule reconciling the balance of *Minority Interest* in the December 31, 19X2, consolidated balance sheet with Y Company's net assets and other appropriate values.

7. Prepare a schedule reconciling the balance of the *Investment in Y* at December 31, 19X2, with Y Company's net assets and other appropriate values.

8. Prepare a schedular calculation, using the incremental approach, of consolidated net income for 19X2. (Hint: Although X Company used the entity concept in valuing Y Company's assets at acquisition, the parent company concept is used to determine consolidated net income.)

9. Confirm the calculation of minority interest in net income for 19X2.

(AICPA adapted)

Problem 12–12

On April 1, 19X4, Reid, Inc., purchased 100 percent of the common stock of Arrow Manufacturing Company for $5,850,000 and 20 percent of its preferred stock for $150,000. At the date of purchase the book and fair values of Arrow's assets and liabilities were as follows:

	Book Value	Fair Value
Assets		
Cash	$ 200,000	$ 200,000
Notes receivable	85,000	85,000
Accounts receivable, net	980,000	980,000
Inventories	828,000	700,000
Land	1,560,000	2,100,000
Machinery and equipment	7,850,000	10,600,000
Accumulated depreciation	[3,250,000]	[4,000,000]
Other assets	140,000	50,000
Total assets	$ 8,393,000	$10,715,000

	Book Value	Fair Value
Equities		
Notes payable...	$ 115,000	$ 115,000
Accounts payable......................................	400,000	400,000
Subordinated debentures—7%............................	5,000,000	5,000,000
Preferred stock; noncumulative, nonparticipating, par value $5 per share; authorized, issued and outstanding 150,000 shares	750,000	—
Common stock; par value $10 per share; authorized, issued, and outstanding 100,000 shares..................	1,000,000	—
Additional paid-in capital (common stock)	122,000	—
Retained earnings	1,006,000	—
Total equities...	$ 8,393,000	

Additional information:
1. By the year-end, December 31, 19X4, the following transactions had occurred:
   (i) The balance of Arrow's net accounts receivable at April 1, 19X4, had been collected.
   (ii) The inventory on hand at April 1, 19X4, had been charged to cost of sales. Arrow used a perpetual inventory system in accounting for inventories.
2. Prior to 19X4, Reid had purchased at face value $1,500,000 of Arrow's 7 percent subordinated debentures. These debentures mature on October 31, 19X8, with interest payable annually on October 31.
3. As of April 1, 19X4, the machinery and equipment had an estimated remaining life of six years. Arrow uses the straight-line method of depreciation. Arrow's depreciation expense calculation for the nine months ended December 31, 19X4, was based upon the old depreciation rates.
4. The other assets consist entirely of long-term investments made by Arrow and do *not* include any investment in Reid.
5. During the last nine months of 19X4, the following intercompany transactions occurred between Reid and Arrow.

	Reid to Arrow	Arrow to Reid
Net sales................................	$158,000	$230,000
Included in purchaser's inventory at December 31, 19X4	36,000	12,000
Balance unpaid at December 31, 19X4	16,800	22,000

Reid sells merchandise to Arrow at cost. Arrow sells merchandise to Reid at regular selling price including a normal gross profit margin of 35 percent. There were *no* intercompany sales between the two companies prior to April 1, 19X4.
6. Accrued interest on intercompany debt is recorded by both companies in their respective accounts receivable and accounts payable accounts.
7. The Investment in Arrow Manufacturing Company account includes Reid's investment in Arrow's debentures and its investment in the common and preferred stock of Arrow.
8. Reid's policy is to amortize goodwill over a 20-year period.

The trial balances of the companies at December 31, 19X4, were as follows:

	Reid	Arrow
Cash	$ 822,000	$ 530,000
Notes receivable		85,000
Accounts receivable (net)	2,758,000	1,368,400
Inventories	3,204,000	1,182,000
Land	4,000,000	1,560,000
Machinery and equipment	15,875,000	7,850,000
Buildings	1,286,000	
Investment in Arrow Manufacturing Company	7,500,000	
Other assets	263,000	140,000
Cost of sales	10,600,000	3,160,000
Selling, general, and administrative expenses	3,448,500	1,063,900
Depreciation expense—machinery and equipment	976,000	588,750
Depreciation expense—buildings	127,000	
Interest expense	806,000	269,400
	$51,665,500	$17,797,450
Accumulated depreciation—machinery and equipment	$ 6,301,000	$ 3,838,750
Accumulated depreciation—buildings	372,000	
Notes payable		115,000
Accounts payable	1,364,000	204,000
Long-term debt	10,000,000	
Subordinated debentures—7%		5,000,000
Preferred stock		750,000
Common stock	2,400,000	1,000,000
Additional paid-in capital	240,000	122,000
Retained earnings	12,683,500	1,006,000
Sales	18,200,000	5,760,000
Interest revenue	105,000	1,700
	$51,665,500	$17,797,450

Reid's revenue and expense figures are for the 12-month period, while Arrow's are for the last 9 months of 19X4. Both companies made all the adjusting entries required for separate financial statements unless stated to the contrary.

Required:

Prepare a working paper to combine the trial balances of the two affiliates into a consolidated trial balance at December 31, 19X4. Use the following column headings:

Trial Balances		Adjustments and Eliminations		Consolidated Trial Balance
Reid, Inc.	Arrow Manufacturing Company	Dr.	Cr.	

Round all computations to the nearest dollar. Show supporting computations in good form.

(AICPA adapted)

Problem 12–13

During 19X1, Thomas Company acquired a controlling interest in Frankfort Consultants, Inc. Trial balances of the companies at December 31, 19X1, are presented below:

	Thomas Company	Frankfort Consultants, Inc.
Cash...	$ 100,000	$ 80,000
Notes receivable	100,000	
Accounts receivable (net)	200,000	100,000
Accrued interest receivable......................	2,000	
Inventories	924,000	125,000
Investment in Frankfort Consultants, Inc.	475,000	
Property, plant, and equipment (net)	750,000	350,000
Deferred charges...............................	25,000	
Patents.......................................		50,000
Cost of sales...................................	1,350,000	525,000
Administrative and selling expenses	251,000	173,000
Interest expense		2,000
	$4,177,000	$1,405,000
Accounts payable	$ 425,000	$ 80,000
Notes payable		75,000
Dividend payable		5,000
Capital stock..................................	300,000	100,000
Retained earnings..............................	1,650,000	395,000
Sales and services..............................	1,800,000	750,000
Interest income	2,000	
	$4,177,000	$1,405,000

The following information is available regarding the transactions and accounts of the companies:

1. An analysis of the Investment in Frankfort Consultants, Inc.:

Date	Description	Amount	Interest Acquired
January 1, 19X1	Investment	$325,000	70%
September 30, 19X1	Investment	105,000	20
		$430,000	90%
December 31, 19X1	90% of Frankfort Consultants, Inc., income for 19X1	45,000	
		$475,000	

The net income of Frankfort Consultants, Inc., for the nine months ended September 30, 19X1, was $25,000.

2. An analysis of the companies' retained earnings accounts:

	Thomas Company	Frankfort Consultants, Inc.
Balance, January 1, 19X1	$1,605,000	$400,000
December 31, 19X1:		
Cash dividend declared (payable		
January 15, 19X2)		[5,000]
90% of Frankfort Consultants, Inc.		
net income for 19X1	45,000	
Balance, December 31, 19X1	$1,650,000	$395,000

3. On the dates of both acquisitions of stock of Frankfort Consultants, Inc., the fair and book values of Frankfort's assets and liabilities were equal. The values for the assets of Frankfort on these two dates were:

	January 1, 19X1	September 30, 19X1
Inventories	$110,000	$ 60,000
Property, plant, and equipment (net)	400,000	362,500
Patents	100,000	62,500

On January 1, 19X1, the estimated remaining useful lives of the property, plant, and equipment and the patents were eight years and two years, respectively. No additions were made to either of these accounts during 19X1. All of the inventory on hand on both dates was sold during 19X1. Any goodwill arising from the acquisitions is to be amortized over the maximum possible life.

4. On September 30, 19X1, Thomas Company loaned its subsidiary $100,000 on an 8 percent note. Interest and principal are payable in quarterly installments beginning December 31, 19X1. This note is the only note receivable that Thomas Company holds.

5. Frankfort's sales are principally engineering services billed at cost plus 50 percent. During November and December of 19X1, $40,000 was billed to Thomas Company of which $16,500 was treated as a deferred charge at December 31, 19X1.

6. During the year, parent company sales to the subsidiary aggregated $60,000, of which $16,000 remained in the inventory of Frankfort Consultants, Inc., at December 31, 19X1.

7. In the last quarter of 19X1, the subsidiary constructed certain tools at a cost of $15,000 that were sold to Thomas Company for $25,000. The parent depreciates such tools using the straight-line method over a five-year life. One-half year's depreciation is provided in the year of acquisition.

Required:

a. Prepare a consolidated statement working paper for the year ended December 31, 19X1. (Assume intercompany profits are to be allocated pro rata to majority and minority shareholders.)

b. Using the incremental approach, prepare a schedular calculation of consolidated net income for 19X1.

(AICPA adapted)

Problem 12–14

Peoria Company acquired all of the outstanding $10 par voting common stock of Seagate, Inc., on December 31, 19X4, in exchange for 90,000 shares of its $10 par voting common stock in a business combination that meets all of the conditions for a pooling of interests. On the acquisition date, Peoria's common stock had a closing market price of $26 per share on a national stock exchange. Both corporations continued to operate as separate businesses maintaining separate accounting records with years ending December 31.

On December 31, 19X4, after the nominal accounts were closed and immediately after acquisition, the condensed balance sheets for both corporations were as follows:

	Peoria	Seagate
Cash...	$ 750,000	$ 300,000
Accounts receivable, net	1,950,000	750,000
Inventories	2,100,000	950,000
Land...	500,000	200,000
Depreciable assets, net	4,160,000	1,800,000
Investment in Seagate	2,205,000	
Long-term investments and other assets...............	785,000	350,000
	$12,450,000	$4,350,000
Accounts payable and other current liabilities...........	$ 1,750,000	$ 945,000
Long-term debt	1,500,000	1,200,000
Common stock ($10 par value)	3,000,000	900,000
Additional paid-in capital	1,370,000	175,000
Retained earnings...................................	4,830,000	1,130,000
	$12,450,000	$4,350,000

Peoria recorded its investment in Seagate at the underlying equity in the net assets of Seagate of $2,205,000. On December 31, 19X4, Seagate's assets and liabilities had fair values equal to the book balances with the exception of land, which had a fair value of $400,000. Peoria's accounting policy is to amortize excess cost over fair market value of net assets acquired over a 40-year period.

Seagate's long-term debt consisted of 9%, 10-year bonds, issued at face value on June 30, 19X0, and due on June 30, 19X10. Interest is paid semiannually on June 30 and December 31. Peoria had purchased Seagate's bonds at face value of $250,000. There was no change in Peoria's ownership of Seagate's bonds through December 31, 19X4.

During the three-month period ended December 31, 19X4, Peoria purchased merchandise from Seagate at an aggregate invoice price of $600,000. Peoria had not paid for the merchandise as of December 31, 19X4. The amount of profit realized by Seagate on these transactions was $120,000. At December 31, 19X4, one half of the merchandise remained in Peoria's inventory. There were no intercompany merchandise transactions prior to October 1, 19X4.

The 19X4 net income amounts per the separate books of Peoria and Seagate were $2,100,000 and $1,125,000, respectively.

The balances in retained earnings at December 31, 19X3, were $1,600,000 and $275,000 for Peoria and Seagate, respectively. On December 15, 19X4, Seagate paid a cash dividend of $3 per share on its common stock.

Required:

a. Determine consolidated net income for 19X4 for Peoria Company and its subsidiary.
b. Prepare a consolidated statement of retained earnings for the year ended December 31, 19X4.
c. Prepare a consolidated balance sheet working paper at December 31, 19X4. Show supporting computations in good form.

(AICPA adapted)

Problem 12–15

The Cincinnati home office of The Geis Company regularly acquires merchandise at a cost of $4 a unit, which is subsequently marked to sell at $6 a unit by both the home office and its Athens branch. During 19X7, the home office purchased 4,000 units, sold 3,000 units, and shipped 500 units to the branch. During 19X8, the home office purchased an additional 4,500 units, sold 3,200 units, and made a second shipment of 1,000 units to the Athens branch.

Branch sales of units acquired from the home office were 400 units in 19X7 and 900 units in 19X8.

Required:

a. Journalize all transactions on the books of The Geis Company and its Athens branch (including closing entries) for the years 19X7 and 19X8 *if* the home office bills merchandise shipped to the branch at $4 a unit.
b. Same conditions as in *(a)* except that the home office bills merchandise shipped to the branch at $5 a unit.

Problem 12–16

Using the data of Problem 12–15, prepare working papers for a *combined* income statement for The Geis Company and its Athens branch for the years 19X7 and 19X8 if—

a. The home office bills merchandise shipped to the branch at $4 a unit.
b. The home office bills merchandise shipped to the branch at $5 a unit.

Problem 12–17

The Longley Company of Indianapolis regularly distributes its products through branch retail outlets. Shipments to its Muncie branch, which was established at the beginning of the year, are billed as follows: Case A, at cost; Case B, 25 percent above cost; and Case C, retail price at date of shipment.

During the year, the Muncie branch received merchandise from the home office, cost, $60,000. Additionally, the branch recorded credit sales of $81,000; made collections on account, $64,000; paid expenses, $14,000; and remitted cash to the Indianapolis home office, $61,200. The December 31 final inventory of the branch was Case A, $6,000; Case B, $7,500; and Case C, $9,000.

The trial balance of the Indianapolis home office on December 31 was as follows:

	Case A	Case B	Case C
Cash.........................	$ 39,000	$ 39,000	$ 39,000
Accounts receivable..........	45,000	45,000	45,000
Branch current...............	[1,200]	13,800	28,800
Purchases....................	150,000	150,000	150,000
Expenses.....................	17,200	17,200	17,200
	$250,000	$265,000	$280,000
Accounts payable.............	$ 20,000	$ 20,000	$ 20,000
Shipments to branch..........	60,000	60,000	60,000
Intracompany inventory profit	–0–	15,000	30,000
Capital stock................	40,000	40,000	40,000
Sales........................	130,000	130,000	130,000
	$250,000	$265,000	$280,000
Merchandise (12/31)..........	$ 8,000	$ 8,000	$ 8,000

Required:

a. Journalize the transactions of the branch for the year, as recorded by the Indianapolis home office and the Muncie branch.
b. Prepare closing entries for the branch and home office.
c. Prepare a combined statement working paper (Case C only).

Problem 12–18

Sales distribution of the Electronic Transistor Company is principally conducted by its home office and one centrally located branch. Units of merchandise shipped to the branch are uniformly priced at 120 percent of cost. The trial balances of the home office and branch at December 31, 19X1, are as follows:

	December 31, 19X1	
	Home Office	Branch
Cash.........................	$ 125,200	$ 17,600
Marketable securities........	229,000	
Accounts receivable (net)....	172,700	84,300
Inventory (1/1)..............	341,000	133,200
Branch current...............	122,300	
Fixed assets (net)...........	1,172,600	
Purchases....................	2,450,000	
Expenses.....................	381,000	78,100
Shipments from home office...		811,200
	$4,993,800	$1,124,400
Accounts payable.............	$ 397,000	$ 12,400
Accrued expenses.............	14,100	1,700
Capital stock................	1,000,000	
Retained earnings............	172,300	
Home office current..........		72,300
Sales........................	2,547,000	1,038,000
Shipments to branch..........	701,000	
Intracompany inventory profit	162,400	
	$4,993,800	$1,124,400
Inventory (12/31)............	$ 284,000	$ 120,000

An examination of duplicate deposit tickets on January 3, 19X2, discloses that the branch made a $20,000 deposit to the credit of the home office on December 31, 19X1.

Required:

a. Prepare a working paper for a combined statement for the home office and branch for the year ended December 31, 19X1.

b. Journalize adjusting and closing entries for the branch and home office.

Problem 12–19

You are the accountant for the Johnson Export Company. The trial balance at December 31, 19X3, follows:

	Home Office	Branch
Cash	$ 15,000	$ 2,000
Accounts receivable..................	20,000	17,000
Inventory (12/31/X3)	30,000	8,000
Fixed assets—net....................	150,000	
Branch office current................	44,000	
Cost of sales	220,000	93,000
Expenses	70,000	41,000
	$549,000	$161,000
Accounts payable....................	$ 23,000	
Mortgage payable....................	50,000	
Capital stock	100,000	
Retained earnings (1/1/X3)...........	26,000	
Sales	350,000	$150,000
Accrued expenses		2,000
Home office current.................		9,000
	$549,000	$161,000

The following additional information is also brought to your attention:

1. The branch receives all of its merchandise from the home office. The home office bills goods to the branch at 125 percent of cost. During 19X3, the branch was billed for $105,000 on shipments from the home office.

2. The home office credits Sales for the invoice price of goods shipped to the branch.

3. On January 1, 19X3, the inventory of the home office was $25,000. The branch books showed a $6,000 inventory.

4. The home office billed the branch for $12,000 on December 31, 19X3, representing the branch's share of expenses paid at the home office. The branch has not recorded this billing.

5. All cash collections made by the branch are deposited in a local bank to the account of the home office. Deposits of this nature included the following:

Amount	Date Deposited by Branch	Date Recorded by Home Office
$5,000	December 28, 19X3	December 31, 19X3
3,000	December 30, 19X3	January 2, 19X4
7,000	December 31, 19X3	January 3, 19X4
2,000	January 2, 19X4	January 5, 19X4

6. Expenses incurred locally by the branch are paid from an imprest bank account that is reimbursed periodically by the home office. Just prior to the end of the year the home office forwarded a reimbursement check in the amount of $3,000 that was not received by the branch office until January 19X4.
7. It is not necessary to make provisions for federal income tax.

Required:
a. Prepare a working paper for a combined statement for the home office and branch for the year ended December 31, 19X3.
b. Prepare a reconciliation of the Branch Office Current and Home Office Current accounts showing the correct book balance.

(AICPA adapted)

Problem 12–20

The Koufax Sporting Goods Company of Los Angeles decided on July 1 to establish sales branches in Chicago and New York as a means of expanding and improving its services to customers in these areas. Transactions with these branches for the month of July are as follows:

July 1 The home office transferred $75,000 cash to the Chicago branch and $100,000 to the New York branch to be used as working funds.
2 Merchandise costing $310,000 was shipped to the New York branch and was billed at 140 percent of cost. Freight charges, paid by the home office, amounted to $1,400.
3 Merchandise costing $225,000 was shipped to the Chicago branch and was billed at a 25 percent markup on the invoice price. Freight charges of $888 were paid by the Chicago branch.
10 Fixed assets costing $400,000 were purchased for the use of the Chicago branch, and $500,000 were purchased for the New York branch. General ledger control over fixed assets is maintained by the home office.
15 Timely reporting is facilitated by the use of electronic data processing equipment; as a consequence, the first semimonthly summary of operating data was received on July 15 and disclosed the following:

	Branches	
	Chicago	*New York*
Credit sales	$42,000	$57,000
Collections on account	34,000	41,000
Expenses.	8,000	12,000
Payments on account.	6,400	9,700

July 17 Merchandise previously shipped to Chicago was transshipped to New York. These goods, on which freight charges amounted to $147, had been billed to Chicago at $20,000. Additional freight paid by the New York Branch for the transshipment amounted to $68. Had the shipment been initially directed to New York, transportation costs would have totaled $175.

20 The home office shipped additional merchandise to branches as follows: Chicago, $150,000 cost; and New York, $200,000 cost. The terms of branch billing remain unchanged. Freight charges, paid by the home office, were $700 on the Chicago shipment and $1,150 on the New York shipment.

31 The semimonthly operating summary is as follows:

	Branches	
	Chicago	New York
Credit sales	$122,100	$150,800
Collections on account	97,700	128,100
Expenses	19,000	27,000
Payments on account	19,600	26,300

31 Cash remittances to the home office were:

New York branch	$125,000
Chicago branch	100,000

Required:

a. Prepare journal entries for July for each branch and the home office. (In the home office books, use separate accounts in respect to the transactions of each branch.)

b. Prepare closing entries, given the following additional information:

(1) Inventories, July 31:

New York branch	$560,000
Chicago branch	360,000

Inventories are determined by physical count; freight charges on merchandise shipments are not allocated to inventory.

(2) Depreciation on fixed assets is regularly recorded by the home office. Depreciation expense for the month of July is:

Property at New York branch	$500
Property at Chicago branch	400

CHAPTER
13

Accounting for International
Operations

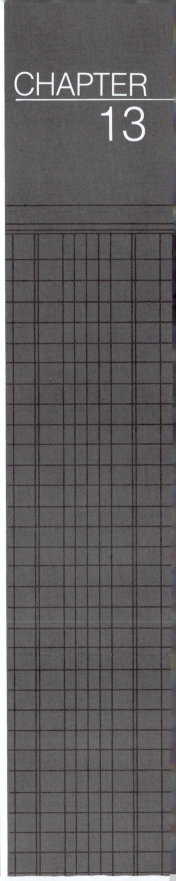

International operations of one type or another are an important part of many companies' total activities. In some cases, these operations consist solely of trading activity (imports or exports) with suppliers or customers that are domiciled in other countries. In other circumstances, the international activities may include foreign branches, investees, or subsidiaries engaged in production and/or sales. Both types of international involvement introduce new accounting issues. A brief overview of the major accounting problems follows.

The first class of problems stems from foreign currency transactions. When companies located in different countries engage in transactions, one of the companies will normally have a receivable or payable that involves "foreign" currency. The initial accounting problem is the assignment of a value to this receivable or payable. Subsequently, the value of the foreign currency will usually fluctuate, and appropriate accounting recognition of this event is another new problem. These and related issues are discussed in this chapter.

The other main class of problems arises when financial statements that are expressed in one currency must be translated into another currency. This problem commonly occurs with foreign subsidiaries. The currency of the parent company's country of residence will normally be identified as the unit of account for aggregating financial information about the firm's total worldwide operations. Yet, the basic financial records of the foreign subsidiary are typically maintained in the local (foreign) currency of the particular country within which the subsidiary is located. Thus, a major task in accounting for the firm's foreign operations is converting or restating the subsidiary's financial statements into the parent's chosen reporting currency so that they may be consolidated with those of the parent and any other subsidiaries. The process by which this is accomplished is discussed in Chapter 14.

A central accounting objective in both situations is the measurement and disclosure of changes in the values assigned to assets and liabilities as a consequence of fluctuations in the value of the foreign currency relative to the domestic currency. This type of change in value is referred to by accountants as an *exchange gain or loss,* and it occurs in the general ways shown in Illustration 13–1.

The principal source of accounting authority for issues related to both foreign currency transactions and foreign currency financial statements is *Statement of Financial Accounting Standards No. 52,* "Foreign Currency Translation" (FASB, 1981). Before examining these accounting issues in more detail, we first briefly review the basic characteristics and terminology applicable to currency exchange rates.

Illustration 13–1

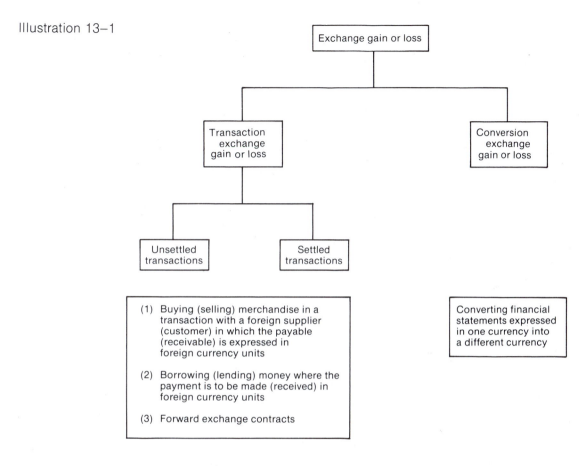

Currency Exchange Rates

From the perspective of any given country, foreign currencies may be viewed as commodities that have specifiable *prices* in terms of the domestic currency. These prices, or rates of exchange, express the relative values of the two currencies. Historically, these rates purported to equate the gold content of the different currencies. However, this is no longer a significant relationship. Presently, two principal types of exchange rates are important: (1) *free* rates, which reflect the fluctuating market prices of the currency as an economic good (a function of supply and demand); and (2) *official* rates, which are established by governments. A given country may have several official rates, each of which pertains to a designated type of economic and financial activity and each of which reflects governmental policies in respect to desired economic development. For example, one rate may apply to the conversion of a country's currency for the purpose of importing new capital goods into the country, and a less favorable rate for conversion of its currency in order to make a dividend payment to owners domiciled in another country. The existence of a multiple rate structure requires the choice of a rate for financial accounting purposes by individuals doing business with, or holding ownership interests in, companies located in such a country. The particular choices specified by current accounting policy are covered in connection with the discussion of foreign currency transactions and foreign currency financial statements.

Since the currency exchange rate between two countries is a ratio of relative values, it may be stated in terms of either country's currency. If one unit of foreign currency is expressed in terms of its domestic monetary equivalent, the exchange rate is said to be quoted *directly*. On the other hand, if one unit of domestic currency is set equal to its equivalent in foreign units, the quotation is said to be *indirect*. One quotation is the reciprocal of the other. In the United States at the present time, foreign exchange rates are quoted both ways. For example, the following quotations as of January 4, 1985, were made available through the financial press:

Country (Currency)	(Direct Quotation) U.S. Dollar Equivalent of One Foreign Unit	(Indirect Quotation) Units of Foreign Currency Equivalent to One U.S. Dollar
Britain (pound)......................	$1.1535	0.8669 pounds
Japan (yen)	0.003950	253.15 yen
Switzerland (franc)	0.3799	2.6320 francs

If the exchanged currencies are to be delivered immediately, the exchange rate is referred to as the *spot rate.* In addition to immediate delivery, a market also exists for future delivery of exchanged currencies (for example, in 30, 90, or 180 days). *Future, or forward, rates* express the rate of exchange that is presently agreed upon for delivery of foreign currency units at a specified future date. The futures market allows a company to hedge against fluctuations in the spot exchange rate.

At present, certain conversions of financial statement values from one currency to another use exchange rates in effect at different points in time. For these accounting purposes, a *current exchange rate* is a rate prevailing at the balance sheet date of the converted financial statements, and a *historical exchange rate* is a rate that existed at the time a particular transaction or event took place.

Foreign Currency Transactions

In transactions between enterprises that are located in two different countries with different currencies, one of the parties to the transaction must accept its obligation (or receive its payment) in terms of a "foreign" currency. Measurement of such receivables or payables *denominated*[1] in units of foreign currency is a fundamental task in accounting for foreign currency transactions. Changes in the values of these accounts receivable or payable between the date of billing and the date of payment as a consequence of fluctuations in exchange rates are called *exchange gains or losses.* Appropriate disclosure of these gains or losses is a second major accounting issue.

For example, if a domestic importer who purchases merchandise abroad is billed *in a foreign currency,* the invoice amount may be measured in domestic currency merely by multiplying it by the current rate of exchange (free or official) at the billing date. To extinguish the created debt, however, the domestic importer must at some time between the billing date and the due date acquire foreign currency. In the event that exchange rates have fluctuated in the period between the date of purchase and the subsequent acquisition of foreign currency, gain or loss clearly results and identifies with the domestic importer. Had the billing been expressed in domestic monetary units, the exchange risk would have been with the foreign exporter. Indeed, when the transaction is billed in domestic currency units, it does not matter whether the other party is a domestic or foreign company. A transaction is a *foreign currency transaction* only when it is denominated in a "foreign" currency.

One other matter of terminology is important to clarify at this point. We have heretofore referred to "domestic" currency and "foreign" currency to distinguish between the currency a firm normally deals with and uses for accounting and financial reporting purposes, and some other currency that may have been specified in a foreign currency transaction. A more generic term is used in the authoritative literature to make this distinction. A firm's *functional currency* is defined to be the "currency of the primary economic environment in which the entity operates; normally, that is the currency of the environment in which an entity primarily generates and expends cash" (*FASB Statement No. 52,* par. 5). Thus, we are assuming above that the domestic currency for our domestic importer is in fact its functional currency. And a foreign currency is any currency other than a firm's functional currency. We will continue to use the terms domestic and foreign currency where it seems natural. More will be said about the concept of functional currency in Chapter 14, as it is an important variable in the conversion of foreign currency financial statements.

---

[1] An asset or liability is *denominated* in a particular currency if its value is fixed in terms of that currency. Thus, in general, the familiar accounting distinction between monetary and nonmonetary assets and liabilities also distinguishes assets and liabilities that are denominated in some particular currency and those that are not. Note that *any* asset or liability may be *measured* in any number of different currencies; indeed, such measurement is the function of accounting. For example, a firm's cash balance in a U.S. bank is denominated in U.S. dollars, but measures of its value at any point in time may be expressed in many different currencies. Similarly, a nonmonetary asset such as land, which is not denominated in any currency, may also be measured in different currencies.

To guard against the hazards of loss from exchange rate fluctuations, our domestic importer, concurrent with the purchase of merchandise that is invoiced in units of foreign currency, may elect to purchase units of this foreign currency for future delivery. Billing and settlement are thereby made in terms of the same rate of exchange. A similar precaution may be taken in respect to a domestic exporter, who may elect to sell foreign currency for future delivery when the settlement of the account receivable is to be made in foreign monetary units.

Illustrative Import/Export Transactions

Case 1.   In order to illustrate the accounting for import-export operations, consider the following transactions for the Leader Corporation (alternative billing terms will be considered separately):

1.   The Leader Corporation (domiciled in the United States) sold merchandise to the East Indies Company of London when the rate of exchange between dollars and pounds was $1.50. The billing is expressed in dollars/pounds as follows: (*a*) $15,000 and (*b*) 10,000 pounds.

2.   The Leader Corporation purchased merchandise from the Alps Company, which is based in Switzerland, when the rate of exchange between the dollar and the Swiss franc was $0.50. The billing is expressed in dollars/francs as follows: (*a*) $25,000 and (*b*) 50,000 francs.

3.   Payment of the East Indies Company account with the Leader Corporation was received when the exchange rate was $1.52.

4.   Remittance was made to the Alps Company by the Leader Corporation when the exchange rate was $0.51.

Ignoring the effects of commissions and other service charges, the entries on the books of the Leader Corporation for these transactions are shown in Illustration 13–2.

These entries illustrate two important features of accounting for foreign currency transactions. First, on the date of sale or purchase, the transaction is measured and recorded *in dollars* on the books of the Leader Corporation (a U.S. corporation using dollars as its functional currency) at the same value under the two alternative billing assumptions. If the billing is in units of foreign currency, the dollar measure is obtained by multiplying the units of foreign currency by the prevailing spot exchange rate. In either case, the dollar amount recorded presumably reflects the value (in dollars) of the merchandise purchased or sold. Second, the billing terms place the risk of foreign currency exchange rate fluctuations on one company or the other. If the billing is in domestic currency units, Leader Corporation is not exposed to any risk from exchange rate fluctuations. Regardless of the exchange rate prevailing on the date the transaction is settled, the number of dollars received or paid is fixed by the sales or purchase contract and is equal to the amount recorded on the date of sale or purchase. Therefore, no ex-

Illustration 13-2

		(a) Where Billing Is in Domestic Currency (Dollars)		(b) Where Billing Is in Foreign Currency (Pounds Sterling or Swiss Francs)	
(1)	Accounts Receivable	15,000		15,000	
	Sales		15,000		15,000
(2)	Purchases..................................	25,000		25,000	
	Accounts Payable.......................		25,000		25,000
(3)	Cash	15,000		15,200	
	Exchange Gain				200
	Accounts Receivable		15,000		15,000
(4)	Accounts Payable..........................	25,000		25,000	
	Exchange Loss			500	
	Cash		25,000		25,500

Note: Dollar values assigned to receivables, payables, and other accounts *denominated in foreign currency units* are shaded here and throughout this chapter.

change gain or loss can occur. This situation is illustrated in column (a) for transactions (3) and (4). On the other hand, if the billing is in foreign currency units, Leader Corporation assumes the risk of foreign currency fluctuations. For example, in the sale to the East Indies Company, billing alternative (b) specifies a contract price of 10,000 pounds sterling. On the date this transaction is settled, East Indies Company fully discharges its obligation by remitting 10,000 pounds, regardless of the exchange rate on that date. In transaction (3b), it is assumed that the Leader Corporation immediately converted these foreign currency units into U.S. dollars at the prevailing exchange rate (10,000 pounds × $1.52 = $15,200). The exchange gain of $200 results from the collection of $15,200 in full settlement of an account valued on Leader's books at $15,000. Transaction (4b) illustrates the incurrence of an exchange loss as a consequence of remitting 50,000 Swiss francs, which cost Leader Corporation $25,500 on that date (50,000 × $0.51), in settlement of a liability carried on Leader's books at $25,000.

The risk of exchange gains or losses can be *hedged* by buying or selling foreign currency for future delivery on the same date that a company purchases or sells merchandise with payment terms denominated in foreign currency units.

Case 2. The use of a forward exchange contract in the futures market to hedge an operating transaction is illustrated in the context of Leader Corporation's transaction with the Alps Company. Assume now that the following transactions took place:

1. The Leader Corporation purchased merchandise from the Alps Company for 50,000 Swiss francs when the exchange rate between dollars

Illustration 13–3

	Merchandise Purchase Transaction		Hedging Transaction	
(1) Purchases....................................	25,000			
Accounts Payable (Alps Company)		25,000		
Swiss Francs Due from Exchange Broker (50,000 francs @ $0.50)			25,000	
Dollars Payable to Exchange Broker				25,000
(2) Foreign Currency (50,000 francs @ $0.51)			25,500	
Exchange Gain or Loss				500
Swiss Francs Due from Exchange Broker				25,000
Dollars Payable to Exchange Broker			25,000	
Cash				25,000
Accounts Payable (Alps Company)	25,000			
Exchange Gain or Loss	500			
Foreign Currency		25,500		

and Swiss francs was $0.50. Concurrent with the purchase of merchandise, the Leader Corporation also purchased 50,000 Swiss francs for future delivery (on a date coinciding with the due date of the obligation to Alps Company) at $0.50.

2.   On the due date of the obligation to Alps Company, the Leader Corporation took delivery of the 50,000 Swiss francs on the futures contract and remitted these to Alps Company in full settlement of its account. On this date, the exchange rate between dollars and Swiss francs was $0.51.

Again ignoring the effects of commissions and other service charges, the entries on the books of Leader Corporation for these transactions are as shown in Illustration 13–3.

The entries related to the hedging transaction[2], are displayed separately

---

[2] Since the forward exchange contract is an executory contract until that future date when the two currencies are exchanged, strict adherence to conventional accounting principles would not call for an accounting entry on the date the contract is signed. Accounting principles do require recognition of exchange gains or losses on the contract at the settlement date and at intervening financial statement dates. Thus, *FASB Statement 52* discusses valuation of forward contracts only in terms of measurement of exchange gains or losses, viz., multiplication of a particular foreign currency exposure by the change in a *specified* exchange rate. For pedagogical reasons, however, we believe that it is informative to recognize the values implicitly being assigned to both the currency receivable and the currency payable in the form of a journal entry, and thus we follow that practice in this chapter. The gains and losses recognized by this procedure are, of course, consistent with *Statement 52*. By "netting" the separate receivable and payable accounts recorded in these entries, one obtains the balance sheet element that would be recognized if only gains or losses were recorded.

to distinguish the effects of currency exchange rate fluctuations on the forward exchange contract from the same effects on the account payable to the supplier (Alps Company). Because the spot and forward exchange rates were assumed equal (although there is usually a small difference, as is discussed later), the exchange gain on the forward contract exactly offsets the exchange loss on the account payable denominated in Swiss francs. This is precisely the desired effect when a forward exchange contract is purchased to hedge an open account payable (or receivable). The hedge eliminates the risk of future currency rate fluctuations on the payable denominated in units of foreign currency through the purchase of the required number of Swiss francs for delivery on the date the account is to be settled. Thus, on the settlement date, the Leader Corporation receives the 50,000 Swiss francs from the exchange broker at the previously agreed price in dollars ($25,000), and these Swiss francs are remitted to Alps Company. Whatever the exchange rate on the settlement date, it has no economic impact (favorable or unfavorable) on the Leader Corporation.

For accounting purposes, each of the contracts is separately recorded because each carries different rights and obligations. Although some of the underlying rights and obligations are denominated in dollars and some in Swiss francs, all are measured in dollars when recorded on Leader Corporation's books. Thus, in the merchandise purchase transaction, the account payable to Alps Company is measured in dollars by applying the current exchange rate to the obligation in Swiss francs; the value assigned to Purchases is based on this same calculation. In the purchase of Swiss francs for future delivery, the Leader Corporation acquired a receivable denominated in foreign currency (50,000 Swiss francs) and gave a promise to pay in dollars ($25,000). On the date of settlement, the Leader Corporation executes its futures contract by paying the exchange broker $25,000 and receiving foreign currency (50,000 Swiss francs). The foreign currency is measured in dollars by using the exchange rate on this date ($0.51). As a result of this valuation, an exchange gain of $500 is recognized. Note that if Leader Corporation had been speculating in foreign currency, rather than hedging its merchandise purchase transaction, the $500 gain would properly be reported as income of the period. However, since the Swiss francs are remitted to Alps Company in settlement of the account payable, a concurrent and offsetting exchange loss is recognized. Accounts payable is carried on Leader Corporation's books at $25,000, and therefore it is debited for this amount when the account is settled. The foreign currency sent to Alps in settlement of the account is valued at $25,500, and therefore it must be credited for this amount. The difference is the $500 exchange loss.

In a similar fashion, the receivable from the East Indies Company in Case 1(b), where the billing is assumed to be in pounds sterling, could have been hedged by *selling* pounds sterling for future delivery. If this had been done, the $200 exchange gain realized as a consequence of holding a receivable denominated in pounds during a period of time when the pound increased in value relative to the dollar would have been eliminated. Viewed retrospectively, such a result does not seem desirable. Unfortunately, one cannot usually predict which way the exchange rates will move. The *purpose of a hedge* is to eliminate exposure to foreign currency fluctuations (whether favorable or unfavorable), thus allowing the company to earn its anticipated operating profit on the transaction with the foreign customer.

Exchange Gains and Losses

Two alternative views of exchange gains and losses arising from sales and purchase transactions have been expressed in the accounting literature and considered by accounting standard-setting boards. In brief, these two positions are as follows:

1. *One-transaction perspective.* Under this view, exchange gains or losses resulting from trade receivables or payables should be offset against the amount recorded in Sales or Purchases in the original transaction. The cost or revenue recognized under this procedure is equal to the consideration in dollars required to discharge the indebtedness at the time of final settlement. The recommended treatment is a consequence of viewing a purchase or sale and the subsequent payment or collection as both components of a *single transaction.*

2. *Two-transaction perspective.* Proponents of this view argue that the decision to assume the risk on the open receivable or payable is separable from the sale or purchase transaction, and thus any exchange gains or losses should be disclosed separately in the income statement as "financial" items. The billing denominated in foreign currency units is assumed to reflect a freely negotiated, dollar-equivalent exchange price based on rates of exchange prevailing at the date of purchase or sale. Therefore, the entry to initially record the purchase or sale is assumed to correctly measure the operating cost or revenue. If the company elects not to settle immediately and not to hedge the open receivable or payable, the resulting exchange gain or loss reflects a financial decision to speculate in exchange rate fluctuations; accordingly, any gain or loss resulting from this decision should be recognized and disclosed in the income statement as a financial item.

The two-transaction perspective was given authoritative support with the adoption of *FASB Statement No. 8* in October 1975. *FASB Statement No. 52* continues the requirement for separate recognition and disclosure of exchange gains and losses.

In the illustrative entries in Cases 1 and 2, all transactions were assumed to have been settled within the same accounting period. If there were an intervening balance sheet date, receivables or payables denominated in a foreign currency must be revalued using the current exchange (spot) rate. Exchange gains and losses resulting from the revaluation are accounted for in the same manner as exchange gains and losses from completed transactions.

Thus, to recap present accounting policy related to import/export transactions denominated in a foreign currency:

1. At the transaction date, each asset, liability, revenue, or expense should be measured using the current spot rate.
2. At any balance sheet date, recorded receivables or payables denominated in a foreign currency that remain unsettled should be adjusted to reflect the current spot rate.
3. Exchange gains or losses resulting from settlement or valuation of an open account are normally recognized in the current income statement as a separate item.[3]

Forward Exchange Contracts—An Elaboration

In Case 2, a forward exchange contract was combined with a single merchandise purchase transaction to illustrate the *hedging* opportunity available to an importer. Forward contracts are used by firms to manage a variety of types of exposure to foreign currency exchange rate risks, as well as to speculate in exchange rate fluctuations. These contracts are, by definition, foreign currency transactions, as they specify the exchange of two currencies at some future date. At most one of these currencies can be a firm's functional currency, and thus the contract creates a receivable or a payable denominated in a "foreign" currency. We now elaborate on the accounting issues and policies associated with forward contracts.

Measurement and reporting principles applicable to forward exchange contracts depend on the reason for the contract. For accounting purposes, there are two main types of forward exchange contracts: (1) hedges and (2) speculation. Further, under current accounting policy, there are several different types of hedges that are identified for some form of special accounting treatment. These accounting categories are summarized below:

A. Hedges
    1. Hedge of a foreign currency commitment.
    2. Hedge of a net investment (ownership interest) in a foreign entity.

---

[3] There are two exceptions to this general rule (*FASB Statement 52*, par. 20). If exchange gains or losses result from foreign currency transactions that are (1) designated, effective economic hedges of a *net investment* (or ownership interest) in a foreign entity or (2) intercompany transactions of a long-term nature between companies that are consolidating their financial results or using the equity method to report them, they are not included in income of the current period. Instead, the exchange gains or losses are reported as part of shareholders' equity in a manner consistent with the accounting for translation of foreign currency financial statements. This topic is covered in Chapter 14.

3.   Other hedges of a foreign currency exposure (including receivables and payables from import/export transactions).

B. Speculation

Characteristics of Accounting Categories.   The first category, *hedges of foreign currency commitments,* recognizes that exposure to the risk of exchange rate fluctuations may occur *prior to the date an accounting transaction occurs.* For example, a U.S. company may sign a contract to manufacture and deliver goods to a foreign customer for a fixed price denominated in units of foreign currency. This *commitment* does not provide the basis for an accounting entry until the goods are delivered. However, from the point of view of the U.S. firm, the commitment exposes them to the same risk of foreign currency fluctuations as would an open, recorded account receivable. Therefore, if the company does not want to carry this risk, it may enter into a forward exchange contract. Such a contract is classified, for accounting purposes, as the hedge of a foreign currency commitment, and any exchange gains or losses on the contract are given special accounting recognition until the sale of the goods is recorded.

The second category of hedges includes forward contracts that are *designated, effective hedges of a net investment in a foreign entity* (e.g., a foreign subsidiary). Since the investment, or ownership interest, is an asset, the only form of forward contract that would qualify as an effective economic hedge of the exposure would be the sale of the functional currency of the foreign entity for future delivery. One could also hedge the investment by incurring debt denominated in the foreign entity's functional currency; this possibility was noted earlier as one of the exceptions to the general accounting rule for exchange gains and losses realized on receivables and payables. If the forward contract (or other payable) indeed hedges the investment, then the accounting for exchange gains or losses on the hedging transaction should be consistent with the recognition of the offsetting exchange gains or losses on the net investment. In order to achieve this objective, special accounting rules are required for this type of hedge.

The final category of hedges includes *all other forward contracts that cover some type of foreign currency exposure.* The most common type of hedge falling into this category is the forward contract designed to eliminate the exposure created by trade receivables or payables denominated in a foreign currency. On occasions, a forward contract that is initially in another category will change into this hedging category. For example, a forward contract obtained to hedge the foreign currency commitment described above might be continued in effect after the date the goods were delivered. If so, the contract would after that date provide a hedge against the recorded account receivable and would be classified in this general hedging category. Although the nature of the foreign currency risk remains substantially the same, the different classification produces some differences in accounting, as explained below.

Finally, if the purpose of the forward contract is to speculate in exchange rate fluctuations in anticipation of realizing a gain, the contract is classified as a *speculative* forward exchange contract. Although all of the categories are specified in terms of the *intent or motivation* for entering into the contract, the three types of hedging contracts also require the independent existence of additional criteria (a foreign currency commitment or an exposed net asset or liability position). Therefore, one would normally expect forward exchange contracts to be classified as speculative when the contracts do not meet the criteria of any of the hedging categories.

Spot and Forward Exchange Rates. In most cases, forward exchange rates differ slightly from the current spot rate. For example, consider the following quotations as of January 4, 1985, for the West German mark and the Canadian dollar:

	(Direct Quotations) U.S. Dollar Equivalent of	
	One West German Mark	One Canadian Dollar
Spot rate	$0.3157	$0.7572
Forward rates:		
30-day forward	0.3164	0.7563
90-day forward	0.3181	0.7551
180-day forward	0.3212	0.7538

When the forward price is higher (as in the case of the West German mark), the difference is referred to as a *premium*; when it is lower (as for the Canadian dollar), it is called a *discount*. While there are many factors that contribute to the existence and amount of a discount or premium at any point in time, in general discounts and premiums tend to reflect the interest rate differentials between the two currencies in the Euromarket for currencies.[4] Since the current spot rate and the relevant forward rate are both used in accounting for forward contracts classified as hedges, the premium or discount also becomes part of the accounting for these contracts.

---

[4] The Euromarket for currencies is an international market for currencies that is free of regulations. The market consists of deposits and loans of freely convertible currencies, with interest rates reflecting the supply and demand for the currencies. The market for dollars is referred to as the Eurodollar market. Whenever the discount or premium in the futures market fails to reflect the interest rate differentials in the Euromarket, there is an opportunity for arbitrage transactions, which restore the equivalence.

Accounting Procedures for Forward Exchange Contracts.   In the following summary of accounting procedures for forward contracts, we assume that the functional currency of the firm entering into the forward contract is the dollar and further that the dollar is one of the two currencies specified in the contract.

We observed in our earlier illustration that the amount of *dollars* receivable from or payable to the exchange broker is determined by the applicable forward rate on the date the contract is signed. Thereafter, this receivable or payable is not revalued, as it is denominated in the functional currency. The receivable or payable associated with the foreign currency component of the contract is, however, subject to periodic revaluation as exchange rates fluctuate. Note also that a discount or premium will be recognized for accounting purposes only if the current spot rate is used to measure this foreign currency receivable or payable on the date the contract is initially recorded.

In the case of *speculative contracts,* management takes a forward contract position that will be profitable if the forward rates move in the direction they have predicted. Consistent with this focus on the forward rates, the foreign currency component of speculative contracts is valued for accounting purposes using the current forward rate applicable to the contract. Accordingly, when the contract is initially recorded, both the receivable and the payable are valued using the same exchange rate, and there is no discount or premium recognized for accounting purposes. At future balance sheet dates, the applicable forward rate is the current rate for forward exchange contracts with a delivery period equal to the remaining life of the contract being valued. For example, if a forward contract calling for delivery of foreign currency units in 60 days is purchased on December 1, its remaining life on December 31 is 30 days. Therefore, the forward rate for 30-day contracts is used to value the foreign currency component of the contract on December 31. Exchange gains or losses that result from changes in the values assigned to speculative contracts are recognized in the income statement of the period in which they occur.

When a forward contract is acquired to *hedge an identifiable foreign currency commitment,*[5] the dollar cost or revenue associated with the underlying transaction is fixed in terms of the current exchange rate. Any gain (loss) in value on the foreign currency component of the forward contract will be offset by a corresponding loss (gain) in value on the receivable or payable that will be recorded on the transaction date. The current spot

---

[5] *FASB Statement No. 52,* par. 21, establishes the following two conditions for this type of hedge: (1) ''The foreign currency transaction [including but not limited to forward contracts] is designated as, and is effective as, a hedge of a foreign currency commitment,'' and (2) ''The foreign currency commitment is firm.''

exchange rate is used to value the foreign currency component of the forward contract, and exchange gains and losses that result from revaluations over the commitment period are **deferred** until the underlying transaction is recorded. The deferred exchange gain or loss is then offset directly against the revenue or cost recognized when the transaction is recorded. The discount or premium on forward contracts that hedge commitments is initially recorded as Deferred Discount (Premium) on Forward Contracts, and may be subsequently handled in either of two ways:

1. Amortize to income over the life of the contract (corresponding to its interest rate differential characteristics); or
2. Include the portion applicable to the commitment period with the deferred exchange gain or loss to be offset against the revenue or cost recorded at the date of the transaction (resulting in a measure of revenue or cost, net of this cost of hedging).

The foreign currency component of forward contacts that *hedge a net investment in a foreign entity* are valued using the current spot rate. Exchange gains and losses on these contracts are not recognized as income but rather are included as a separate component of shareholders' equity. As will be seen in Chapter 14, this disposition is consistent with the treatment of the "exchange gains and losses" that result from translating the financial statement of the foreign entity into dollars. In this way, the exchange gains or losses on the forward contract properly offset the gains or losses on the exposure being hedged. Amortization of the discount or premium on this type of forward contract may be either recognized in the current income statement or included with the exchange gains and losses in the separate component of shareholders' equity.

Finally, the foreign currency component of all *other hedging contracts* is also valued using the current spot rate. This matches the value assigned to the foreign currency hedge with the value assigned to the asset or liability exposure. Exchange gains and losses that result from revaluations of the forward contract (due to changes in the spot rate) are recognized as income or loss of the period in which they occur. Recall that an exposed asset or liability position will also be valued at the current spot rate and any exchange gains or losses included in the income statement. Thus, the net impact in the income statement will only reflect the unhedged portion of the foreign currency exposure. The discount or premium on these hedges must be amortized to income over the life of the forward contract.

These accounting procedures for forward exchange contracts are summarized in Illustration 13–4.

Case 3. Hedging a Foreign Currency Commitment.

Assume that on July 15, 19X1, a U.S. firm contracts to manufacture and deliver merchandise to a

Illustration 13–4

ACCOUNTING PROCEDURES FOR
FORWARD EXCHANGE CONTRACTS

Type	Exchange Rate Used to Value Foreign Currency Units Receivable or Payable	Treatment of Exchange Gain or Loss	Treatment of Amortization of Discount or Premium
1. Hedge of identifiable foreign currency commitment.............	Current spot rate	Deferred to date transaction is recorded and then offset against the dollar measure of cost or revenue	May treat the same as the exchange gain or loss or include in the current income statement
2. Hedge of a net investment in a foreign entity..........	Current spot rate	Include as a separate component of shareholders' equity	May treat the same as the exchange gain or loss or include in the current income statement
3. Other hedges of foreign currency exposures.........	Current spot rate	Include in the current income statement	Include in the current income statement
4. Speculative contracts.......	Current forward rate (for a time period equal to the remaining life of the contract)	Include in the current income statement	Not separately measured

customer in West Germany on December 15, 19X1, at a price of 300,000 marks. On July 15, the spot rate for marks is $0.50, and the firm's expected cost of sales is $100,000. Thus, the contract provides a gross margin of $50,000 based on current exchange rates. However, the U.S. firm does not have a binding claim against the customer until the merchandise is delivered, and we further assume that the terms of the contract allow 30 days for payment. Accordingly, payment will probably not be received until January 14, 19X2. During this six-month period of time, the U.S. firm is exposed to the risk of fluctuations in the exchange rate for the mark. The firm decides to cover this risk by entering into a forward exchange contract to deliver 300,000 marks in six months at the current forward rate of $0.51. Recall that this forward rate fixes the number of dollars ($153,000) that the firm will receive from the exchange broker in return for the 300,000 marks. The obligation to deliver the 300,000 marks represents a hedge of a foreign currency commitment (for the first five months of the contract) and thus is valued at the current spot rate of $0.50. The difference of $0.01 in the two rates is the premium on the forward contract, aggregating $3,000 (300,000 × $0.01) on this contract. The following future spot rates are assumed: September 30, 19X1—$0.55; and December 15, 19X1–$0.58.

The accounting entries for the commitment and the related hedge are presented in Illustration 13–5 from the date the commitment is incurred through the transaction date. We have incorporated the *additional assumption* that the firm elects to defer the amortization of the premium on the forward contract and offset it against the sales revenue recognized at the transaction date.

Illustration 13–5

	Commitment and Sale Transaction	Forward Exchange Contract
(1) At July 15, 19X1 (commitment date):		
Dollars Receivable from Exchange Broker (300,000 × $0.51).................		153,000
Deferred Premium on Forward Contract (300,000 × $0.01).............		3,000
Marks Payable to Exchange Broker (300,000 × $0.50)...............		150,000
(2) At September 30, 19X1 (for quarterly financial statements):		
Deferred Exchange Gain or Loss		15,000
Marks Payable to Exchange Broker...............................		15,000
[(300,000 × $0.55) − $150,000]		
(3) At December 15, 19X1 (transaction date):		
Deferred Exchange Gain or Loss		9,000
Marks Payable to Exchange Broker...............................		9,000
[(300,000 × $0.58) − $165,000]		
Accounts Receivable	174,000	
Sales	174,000	
(300,000 × $0.58)		
Sales		24,000
Deferred Exchange Gain or Loss		24,000
($15,000 + $9,000)		
Deferred Premium on Forward Contract		2,500
Sales		2,500
(5/6 × $3,000)		

As a consequence of these accounting entries, the net credit to Sales is $152,500 ($174,000 − $24,000 + $2,500). Note that without the adjustment arising from the premium on the forward contract, the net credit to Sales would be $150,000—the spot rate, dollar equivalent of the sales price on July 15, 19X1, when the commitment was incurred. Additionally, the following receivables and payables exist on December 15, 19X1:

	12/15/X1 Dollar Measure
Claims denominated in marks:	
Accounts receivable	$174,000
Marks payable to exchange broker	174,000
Claims denominated in dollars:	
Dollars receivable from exchange	
broker.................................	153,000

The two claims denominated in marks have the same dollar measure because they both represent a claim for 300,000 marks. Furthermore, the obligation to the exchange broker is expected to be satisfied with the marks that will be received from the customer.

Case 4. Hedge of an Exposed Asset Position.   Continuing the illustration we began in Case 3, from December 15, 19X1, until January 14, 19X2, the forward exchange contract hedges the receivable denominated in marks. Thus, it falls into the category of *other hedging contracts.* Note that the dollar measures assigned to the two claims denominated in marks continue to be appropriate, as they are based upon the spot rate. Further, the balance of the Deferred Premium on Forward Contract of $500 must now be amortized to income over the remaining 30-day life of the contract. For this illustration, we assume the following spot rates: December 31, 19X1—$0.56; and January 14, 19X2—$0.62. The entries that are made with these facts are shown in Illustration 13–6.

In 19X1, the exchange loss of $6,000 on the open accounts receivable resulting from the decline in the current spot rate to $0.56 is exactly offset by the exchange gain on the forward contract. Therefore, the net income effect in 19X1 is the $250 other income from amortization of the premium on the forward contract. On January 14, 19X2, the current spot rate has risen to $0.62, and the collection of the 300,000 marks from the customer yields an exchange gain of $18,000—the difference between the current value of the foreign currency received ($186,000) and the carrying value of the accounts receivable ($168,000). This exchange gain is exactly offset by the exchange loss on the forward contract, and again the only net income effect is provided by the amortization of the premium on the forward contract.

Illustration 13–6

	Exposed Asset Position	Forward Exchange Contract
(1) At December 31, 19X1 (for annual financial statements):		
Marks Payable to Exchange Broker		6,000
Exchange Gain or Loss		6,000
[(300,000 × $0.56 − $174,000]		
Exchange Gain or Loss	6,000	
Accounts Receivable	6,000	
[(300,000 × $0.56) − $174,000]		
Deferred Premium on Forward Contract		250
Other Income		250
[1/2 × $500]		
(2) At January 14, 19X2 (maturity of forward contract and collection of accounts receivable):		
Foreign Currency (300,000 × $0.62).	186,000	
Exchange Gain or Loss	18,000	
Accounts Receivable	168,000	
Marks Payable to Exchange Broker		168,000
Exchange Gain or Loss		18,000
Foreign Currency		186,000
Cash	153,000	
Dollars Receivable from		
Exchange Broker.		153,000
Deferred Premium on Forward Contract		250
Other Income		250

Although in this simple case it seems unnecessary to value and record the offsetting exchange gains and losses on the receivable and the forward contract, the two contracts have different legal and economic rights and obligations. Furthermore, in practice, it may often be difficult to relate specific hedging transactions with specific open accounts. Of course, in order to classify and account for a particular forward contract as a hedge rather than a speculative contract, one must be able to identify on an aggregate basis that the contract properly relates to a foreign currency exposure.

Accounting for the hedge of a *net investment in a foreign entity* would follow the same pattern as illustrated for this receivable. Since both types of exposure result from assets denominated in a foreign currency, the characteristics of forward contracts hedging either of them would be the same. Measurement of exchange gains and losses and amortization of the discount or premium on the forward contract would also be the same. The major difference in accounting is the way these items are reported. For hedges of a net investment, exchange gains and losses would be included as a separate component of shareholders' equity rather than in the income statement. Also, for these hedges the firm has the option to include discount or premium amortization with the exchange gains or losses in shareholders' equity.

Case 5. Speculation in Foreign Currency Exchange Price Fluctuations.   Management of a U.S. firm believes that the exchange rate for the Canadian dollar will increase in the near future, and so they decide to purchase Canadian dollars for future delivery. In particular, assume that on December 1, 19X1, the firm purchased 100,000 Canadian dollars for delivery in 90 days. On this date, the spot rate for the Canadian dollar is $0.75, and the 90-day futures rate is $0.74. Assuming further that on December 31, 19X1, the forward rate for a 60-day delivery (the remaining time on the forward contract) is $0.76 and that on March 1, 19X2, the spot rate is $0.72, the firm would make the following entries for this speculative forward contract:

1. At December 1, 19X1 (purchase of contract):

Canadian Dollars Receivable from
    Exchange Broker (100,000 × $0.74)......................... 74,000
        U.S. Dollars Payable to Exchange Broker   74,000

2. At December 31, 19X1 (for financial statement purposes):

Canadian Dollars Receivable from
    Exchange Broker 2,000
        Exchange Gain or Loss   2,000
    [(100,000 × $0.76) − $74,000]

3. At March 1, 19X2 (maturity of forward contract):

U.S. Dollars Payable to Exchange Broker 74,000
    Cash (U.S. Dollars).....................................   74,000

Foreign Currency—Canadian Dollars
    (100,000 × $0.72)...................................... 72,000
Exchange Gain or Loss 4,000
    Canadian Dollars Receivable from
        Exchange Broker   76,000

As was indicated previously, a forward contract entered into for speculative purposes is valued at the current forward rate for the remaining life of the contract. Thus, on December 31, 19X1, the forward rate for a 60-day delivery was used because the contract matures on March 1, 19X2. This valuation results in an exchange gain of $2,000 (because the Canadian dollar has strengthened relative to the U.S. dollar in the interim), and this gain is recognized in the 19X1 income statement. Final settlement on March 1, 19X2, produces an exchange loss of $4,000 because the Canadian dollar weakened relative to the U.S. dollar in this period; this loss is recognized in the 19X2 income statement. Overall, the firm incurred an exchange loss of $2,000, as can be verified by comparing the $74,000 paid to the exchange broker with the $72,000 value of the 100,000 Canadian dollars received. Note that the spot rate for Canadian dollars is used only to value the currency received upon the maturity of the forward contract; otherwise, forward rates are used for valuation purposes. If the forward contract had been sold before maturity, the spot rates would not have been used for any valuation purpose.

In this example, a speculative forward contract was individually identified. In principle, the same accounting treatment would seem to apply to the amounts of any hedging contracts in excess of the related foreign currency exposure. While *FASB Statement 52* does incorporate the substance of this observation, there are two qualifications we should note. First, and most importantly, the measurement of "excess" amounts over the related exposure includes recognition of tax effects. For example, if a forward contract exceeds the related foreign currency commitment in order to provide a hedge on an after-tax basis, the excess portion of the hedge that covers the tax effect is also deferred and recognized as an offset in the period in which the tax effects are recognized.[6] Recognition of after-tax effects is also included in the discussion of hedges of net investments in a foreign entity.[7] Second, the language of *Statement 52* is somewhat ambiguous with respect to how the exchange gain or loss on the after-tax excess is to be measured. Specifically, it is not clear whether forward rates are to be used to measure exchange gains or losses only on *contracts* that are classified as speculative, or for any *amounts* that are determined to be speculative. Because exchange gains or losses are produced by *changes* in rates over the period, use of either the spot or the forward rates will probably yield substantially the same results.

Multiple Exchange Rates

If transactions are denominated in a foreign currency that has multiple exchange rates, the following rates should be used:

1. At the transaction date, the transaction should be measured and recorded at the rate at which that particular type of transaction could be then settled.

---

[6] *FASB Statement No. 52*, par. 21.
[7] *FASB Statement No. 52*, par. 129.

2. At a subsequent balance sheet date, receivables and payables denominated in a foreign currency should be translated at the rate at which they then could be settled.

Normally, the applicable rate will remain unchanged between the transaction date and the settlement date.

Questions

1. Define currency exchange rates.
2. Distinguish between free and official rates of exchange.
3. Distinguish between quoting an exchange rate for a given currency "directly" and "indirectly."
4. Distinguish between spot and forward rates of exchange.
5. Distinguish between current and historical rates of exchange.
6. Explain the concept of functional currency.
7. Explain what is meant by accountants when they refer to a "foreign currency transaction."
8. When do exchange gains or losses occur in import/export transactions?
9. How should exchange gains or losses arising from import/export transactions be reported?
10. Describe briefly what is meant by a hedging transaction.
11. Summarize current accounting policy related to import/export transactions denominated in a foreign currency.
12. Enumerate the four major accounting categories of forward contracts.
13. Summarize current accounting policy for forward contracts.
14. When multiple exchange rates exist, what rate should be used in translating foreign currency transactions?

Exercises

Exercise 13–1

Bill Branch is planning a trip through several foreign countries. He plans to purchase and evaluate a variety of products sold in each country that he is considering for the inventory of his import shop. In anticipation of the trip, Branch purchases $500 worth of each country's currency. He received the following amounts:

Country	Currency	Amount Received
Belgium	Franc	29,175
Denmark	Krone	5,810
France..........	Franc	4,700
Italy............	Lira	970,000

Required:

State the exchange rate between U.S. dollars and each foreign currency purchased by Branch. Express each rate:

a. Directly.
b. Indirectly.

Exercise 13–2

Journalize the following transactions of the Black and White Company (a New York corporation) arising from its foreign import/export operations:

June 1 Purchased merchandise from an Edinburgh, Scotland, manufacturer at an invoice cost of 1,000 pounds. On this date, the exchange rate for pounds is $1.20.

5 Purchased merchandise from a Glasgow, Scotland, manufacturer. The billing is rendered for $2,000. The exchange rate for pounds is $1.21.

7 Sold merchandise to a Toronto wholesaler. Billing price is 4,000 Canadian dollars, and the exchange rate for Canadian dollars is $0.80.

15 Paid 500 pounds on account to the Edinburgh manufacturer. The exchange rate is $1.15.

20 Paid the amount due the Glasgow manufacturer. The exchange rate is $1.18.

25 Returned merchandise to the Edinburgh manufacturer and received credit for 100 pounds. The exchange rate is $1.15.

28 Received full payment on account from the Toronto wholesaler. The exchange rate is $0.76.

30 Remitted final payment to the Edinburgh manufacturer. The exchange rate is $1.16.

Exercise 13–3

Prepare the journal entries to record the following transactions on the books of the Schwab Corporation.

a. The Schwab Corporation purchased merchandise from the Z Company of Portugal for 200,000 escudos when the exchange rate for escudos was $0.005. Concurrently, the Schwab Corporation purchased 100,000 escudos for future delivery at $0.005.

b. The Schwab Corporation paid the Z company for transaction (a) when the exchange rate for the escudo was $0.0045. The futures purchased in (a) were received from the exchange broker.

c. The Schwab Corporation sold merchandise to the D company of Finland for 10,000 markkas when the exchange rate for the markka was $0.16. Concurrently, the Schwab Corporation sold 5,000 markkas for future delivery at $0.16.

d. The Schwab Corporation received payment from the D company for transaction (*c*) when the exchange rate for the markka was $0.15. The futures sold in (*c*) were delivered to the exchange broker.

Exercise 13–4

The X Corporation, a U.S. company whose functional currency is the dollar, engaged in the following international transactions during December, 19X1 (all purchase and sales invoices are denominated in the foreign currency):

1. The X Corporation sold merchandise to the Y Company of Italy for 2,000,000 lire when the exchange rate for the lira was $0.00052. Concurrently, the X Corporation sold 1,000,000 lire for future delivery at $0.00052.

2. The X Corporation received payment from the Y Company in respect to transaction (1) when the exchange rate for the lira was $0.0006. The lire sold in (1) were delivered to the exchange broker.

3. The X Corporation purchased merchandise from the A Company of Great Britain for 5,000 pounds when the exchange rate for the pound was $1.20. Concurrently, the X Corporation purchased 5,000 pounds for future delivery at $1.20.

4. The X Corporation received the pounds purchased in (3) from the exchange broker. X Corporation then paid A company for the merchandise purchased in transaction (3) using these pounds. On this date, the exchange rate for the pound was $1.25.

5. The X Corporation sold merchandise to the B Company of Mexico for 100,000 pesos when the exchange rate for the peso was $0.0045.

6. The X Corporation purchased merchandise from the C Company of Mexico for 200,000 pesos when the exchange rate for the peso was $0.0045.

Required:

a. Prepare the journal entries to record the above transactions on the books of the X Corporation.

b. If the debts created by the last two transactions remain unpaid on December 31, 19X1, discuss their valuation if the exchange rate is $0.005. Would your answer be different if the X Corporation had purchased, or sold, foreign exchange (pesos) for future delivery?

Exercise 13–5

McCaskill, Inc., decides to speculate in the forward contract market. On May 1, 19X1, McCaskill purchases 2,000,000 Japanese yen for delivery in 90 days. On this date, the spot rate for the yen was $0.00395, and the 90-day forward rate was $0.003976.

McCaskill's fiscal year ends on June 30, and any necessary accounting adjustments related to this forward contract must therefore be recorded. On June 30,

19X1, the spot rate for the yen was $0.00417 and the forward rates were: 30-day, $0.00429; and 90-day, $0.00454.

Required:

Prepare the necessary journal entries to record these events on McCaskill's books on May 1 and June 30.

Exercise 13–6

Select the best answer for each of the following questions.

1. Corvus, Inc., a U.S. corporation, ordered a machine from Walker Company of New Zealand on July 15, 19X4, for 100,000 New Zealand (N.Z.) dollars when the spot rate for N.Z. dollars was $0.4955. Walker shipped the machine on September 1, 19X4, and billed Corvus for 100,000 N.Z. dollars. The spot rate was $0.4875 on this date. On October 25, 19X4, when the spot rate was $0.4855, Corvus bought 100,000 N.Z. dollars and paid the invoice. In Corvus' income statement for the year ended December 31, 19X4, how much should be reported as foreign exchange gain?

   a. $0.
   b. $200.
   c. $800.
   d. $1,000.

2. On Oct. 1, 19X1, Rock Company loaned $120,000 to a foreign supplier, evidenced by an interest bearing note due on October 1, 19X2. The note is denominated in the currency of the borrower and was equivalent to 840,000 local currency units (LCU) on the loan date. The note principal was appropriately included at $140,000 in the receivables section of Rock's December 31, 19X1, balance sheet. The note principal was repaid to Rock on the October 1, 19X2, due date when the exchange rate was 8 LCU to $1. In its income statement for the year ended December 31, 19X2, what amount should Rock include as a foreign currency transaction gain or loss?

   a. $0.
   b. $15,000 loss.
   c. $15,000 gain.
   d. $35,000 loss.

3. Jones, Inc., a U.S. corporation, bought machine parts from Klaus Co. of West Germany on March 1, 19X1 for 30,000 marks, when the spot rate for marks was $0.4895. Jones' year-end was March 31, 19X1, when the spot rate for marks was $0.4845. Jones bought 30,000 marks and paid the invoice on April 20, 19X1, when the spot rate was $0.4945. How much should be shown in Jones' income statements as foreign exchange gain or loss for the years ended March 31, 19X1 and 19X2?

	19X1	19X2
a.	$0	$0
b.	$0	$150 loss
c.	$150 loss	$0
d.	$150 gain	$300 loss

4. On November 30, 19X0, Pabst Publishing Company, located in Wisconsin, executed a contract with John Coors, an author from Canada, providing for payment of 10% royalties on Canadian sales of Coors' book. Payment is to be made in Canadian dollars each January 10 for the previous year's sales. Canadian sales of the book for the year ended December 31, 19X1 totaled 50,000 Canadian dollars. Pabst paid Coors his 19X1 royalties on January 10, 19X2. Pabst's 19X1 financial statements were issued on February 1, 19X2. Spot rates for Canadian dollars were as follows:

November 30, 19X0—$0.87.
January 1, 19X1—$0.88.
December 31, 19X1—$0.89.
January 10, 19X2—$0.90.

How much should Pabst accrue for royalties payable at December 31, 19X1?
a. $4,350.
b. $4,425.
c. $4,450.
d. $4,500.

(AICPA adapted)

Exercise 13–7

The Financial Accounting Standards Board discusses certain terminology essential to accounting for foreign currency transactions in its *Statement No. 52*. Included in the discussion is a definition of and distinction between the terms "measure" and "denominate."

Required:
Define the terms "measure" and "denominate," and give a brief example that demonstrates the distinction between accounts measured in a particular currency and accounts denominated in a particular currency.

(AICPA adapted)

Exercise 13–8

A U.S. parent company, with the U.S. dollar as its functional currency, had two types of intercompany accounts with its subsidiary in France during 19X5.

(1) Advance to the subsidiary of 1,000,000 francs to provide working capital. This advance is evidenced by a demand note, denominated in francs. The note has been outstanding without change for the three years since the French affiliate was acquired, and the chief financial officer indicates that the parent does not plan to call for payment in the forseeable future.
(2) Trade receivables (denominated in francs) arising from regular sales to the affiliate. Although individual invoices are paid in the normal 30-day credit period, there has been an average balance of 500,000 francs outstanding during the past several years, and the balance on the aggregate invoices outstanding at any time has not fallen below 400,000 francs since the two companies affiliated. At December 31, 19X5, the total receivable is 600,000 francs. The chief financial officer expects the aggregate receivables to exceed 500,000

francs for the forseeable future. During 19X5, the parent company recorded a net exchange gain on the intercompany trade receivables of $18,000.

At January 1, 19X5, the spot rate for francs was $0.10, and at December 31, 19X5, it was $0.12.

Required:

Explain how the parent company would account for the exchange gains realized during 19X5 on these intercompany accounts. (Hint: You may wish to consult *FASB Statement 52* and any other relevant authoritative materials that are available for additional guidance.)

Exercise 13–9

During 19X6, Bell International Banks, Inc., incurred exchange losses of $300,000 on a series of forward exchange contracts in which Bell purchased pounds sterling for future delivery in exchange for U.S. dollars (Bell's functional currency). These forward contracts were intended to hedge the rental contract for its London office that Bell signed at the beginning of the year committing the firm to a fixed price denominated in pounds sterling. In view of this designated purpose, the controller of Bell has taken the position that these losses should be included with the rent expense in the 19X6 consolidated financial statements.

Required:

Discuss the propriety of the controller's position. Include in your answer any additional facts that would have to be determined. (Hint: You may wish to consult *FASB Statement 52* and any other relevant authoritative materials that are available for additional guidance.)

Exercise 13–10

On August 15, 19X1, Jones Corporation (a U.S. company) signed a contract with an Italian customer to construct and deliver machinery on or before February 15, 19X2. The price specified in the contract was 150,000 Swiss francs, and the spot rate for the Swiss franc on this date was $0.42.

The price of the Swiss franc fell over the next two weeks. In order to partially hedge this foreign currency commitment, on September 1, 19X1, Jones entered into a forward contract to deliver 100,000 Swiss francs in 180 days in exchange for U.S. dollars. On this date, the spot rate for Swiss francs was $0.40, and the 180-day forward rate was $0.41.

On December 11, 19X1, after the Swiss franc had strengthened to $0.50, Jones reached an agreement with the exchange broker to close the contract for $9,000—the difference between the current value of the Swiss francs ($50,000) and the broker's U.S. dollar obligation to Jones ($41,000). Jones paid the $9,000, and the contract was cancelled.

Required:

a. Prepare entries to record the 19X1 events described above for Jones Corporation.
b. Describe how the exchange loss and the premium on the forward contract

would be reported in Jones' 19X1 financial statements. (Hint: You may wish to consult *FASB Statement 52* and any other relevant authoritative materials that are available for additional guidance.)

Problems

Problem 13–11

On October 1, 19X1, Advanced Electronics, Inc., secured an order from a company located in France for a new computer, to be delivered on April 1, 19X2. The sales price, which is payable in francs, is 200,000 francs. The 180-day delivery schedule allows for custom manufacture, delivery, and installation. Payment is due on delivery.

The spot rate for francs on October 1, 19X1, is $0.13. In order to protect itself against foreign currency fluctuations, Advanced Electronics, Inc., sold 200,000 francs for delivery in 180 days at a price of $0.12 in the forward market.

The following additional exchange rates prevailed:

(a)   December 31, 19X1:
    (1)   Spot rate—$0.11
    (2)   Forward rate for 90-day delivery—$0.10.
(b)   April 1, 19X2:
    Spot rate—$0.09.

Assume that the forward contract qualifies as a hedge of an identifiable foreign currency commitment and that Advanced Electronics elects to offset any discount or premium on the forward contract against the recorded value for sales.

Required:
a.   Prepare the entries that would be made by Advanced Electronics, Inc., for these transactions on—
    (1)   October 1, 19X1.
    (2)   December 31, 19X1 (when the firm's annual report is prepared).
    (3)   April 1, 19X2.

b.   Indicate the classification and valuation of accounts that would be reported in Advanced Electronics' balance sheet on December 31, 19X1.

Problem 13–12

On December 1, 19X3, Micro Systems, Inc. (a U.S. company), placed an order with a company located in the Netherlands for laboratory equipment, to be delivered in 60 days. The purchase price, which is payable in guilders, is 300,000 guilders. Payment is due on delivery.

The spot rate for guilders on December 1, 19X3, is $0.20. On this same date, Micro Systems elected to hedge the foreign currency commitment by purchasing 300,000 guilders for delivery in 60 days at a price of $0.21 in the forward market.

The following additional exchange rates prevailed:

(a)   December 31, 19X3:
  (1)   Spot rate—$0.22.
  (2)   Forward rate for 30-day delivery—$0.228.
(b)   January 30, 19X4:
  Spot rate—$0.17.

Assume that the forward contract qualifies as a hedge of an identifiable foreign currency commitment and that Micro Systems elects to amortize any discount or premium on the forward contract against income.

Required:
a.   Prepare the entries that would be made by Micro Systems for these transactions on—

  (1)   December 1, 19X3.
  (2)   December 31, 19X3 (when the firm's annual report is prepared.)
  (3)   January 30, 19X4.

b.   Indicate the classification and valuation of accounts that would be reported in Micro Systems' financial statements on December 31, 19X3.

Problem 13–13

Daley International, a Chicago-based firm, enters into a 90-day forward contract on December 1, 19X1, to deliver 500,000 units of foreign currency (FC) at a price of $1.75. Management decided to sell these units of foreign currency for future delivery for two reasons: (1) to hedge an exposed net asset position of FC 300,000 from its import/export operations and (2) to speculate in exchange price fluctuations to the extent of the remainder of the contract. The spot rate on this date is FC 1= $1.77. On March 1, 19X2, the terms of the forward contract are executed.

The following exchange rates prevailed:

(a)   December 31, 19X1:
  (1)   Spot rate—$1.82.
  (2)   Forward rate for—
      (i)   60-day delivery—$1.80.
      (ii)   90-day delivery—$1.79.
(b)   March 1, 19X2:
  (1)   Spot rate—$1.85.
  (2)   Forward rate for—
      (i)   60-day delivery—$1.835.
      (ii). 90-day delivery—$1.83.

Required:
a.   Prepare the entries that would be made by Daley International for this forward contract on—

  (1)   December 1, 19X1.
  (2)   December 31, 19X1 (when the firm's annual report is prepared).
  (3)   March 1, 19X2.

    b. Indicate the classification and valuation of accounts related to this forward contract transaction that would be reported in Daley International's 19X1 financial statements.

    c. Prepare a reconciliation of the total gain or loss ultimately realized on the maturity of this forward contract with the expense or income recognized in the 19X1 and 19X2 income statements.

CHAPTER
14

Accounting for International
Operations (continued)

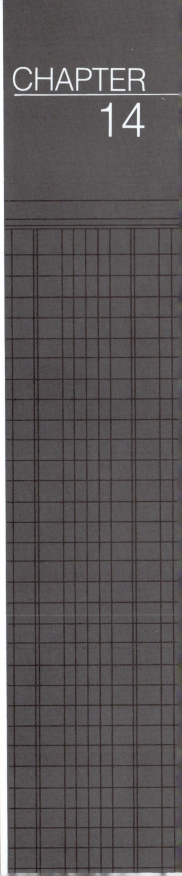

The second major topic in accounting for international operations is the translation or restatement of foreign currency financial statements into domestic currency. Obviously, this conversion process is an essential first step in recording a domestic firm's equity in the earnings of a foreign subsidiary or investee, or in preparing combined or consolidated financial statements for a domestic firm with one or more foreign branches or subsidiaries. As in the preceding chapter, we continue to assume that the principal accounting entity is a U.S. corporation with the U.S. dollar as its functional currency.

Under *FASB Statement No. 52*, there are two primary objectives for the translation of a foreign firm's financial statements from its *functional currency* into the *reporting currency* of the parent (or investor) company:

1. Provide information that is generally compatible with the expected economic effects of a rate change on an enterprise's cash flows and equity.
2. Reflect in consolidated statements the financial results and relationships of the individual consolidated entities as measured in their *functional currencies* in conformity with U.S. generally accepted accounting principles [GAAP].[1]

The relationship of these *Statement No. 52* objectives to previous objectives is discussed in the next section. One element that remained unchanged, however, is the requirement that the financial statements be prepared in conformity with U.S. GAAP. If the foreign currency statements were initially prepared using accounting principles different from those that are generally acceptable in the United States, translation procedures will not remedy this deficiency. In such cases, the foreign currency statements must first be adjusted to conform to U.S. accounting principles and then translated and incorporated (through combination, consolidation, or equity method) into the financial statement of a U.S. firm.

Evolution of Translation Principles

A number of different methods of translating the assets and liabilities in foreign currency financial statements have been applied in accounting practice at one time or another. The first method to achieve general acceptance (*Accounting Research Bulletin No. 4*, "Foreign Operations and Foreign Exchange," 1939) was the *current-noncurrent* method. Under this method,

---

[1] *FASB Statement No. 52*, par. 4. Note that *Statement No. 52* does *not* cover translation of foreign currency financial statements for purposes other than consolidation, combination, or application of the equity method (par. 2).

current assets and liabilities were translated at the current exchange rate, and all other assets and liabilities were translated at the historical exchange rate in effect on the date they were recorded. Additionally, translation losses were recognized in income, but translation gains were deferred. This method was subject to criticism on several grounds, including the arbitrariness of the current-noncurrent accounting classification and the resulting dissimilar treatment given to inventory and other real assets and to short-term and long-term debt. Because of its conceptual weaknesses, the current-noncurrent method was gradually superseded in practice (without *formal* authoritative support) by the *monetary-nonmonetary* method. Under this method, all monetary assets and liabilities were translated at the current exchange rate, and nonmonetary assets and liabilities were translated at the applicable historical exchange rates. Treatment of translation gains and losses varied as would be expected with an evolving practice standard. In 1972 a research study was released by the AICPA in which yet another method was proposed—the *temporal* method.[2] Under the temporal method, assets and liabilities are translated in a manner that retains the accounting principles that have been applied to them. For example, if an asset is measured at original transaction cost, a historical translation rate would be used; if it were valued at replacement cost, a current translation rate would be appropriate. As long as original transaction costs are used to value nonmonetary assets and liabilities, as they generally are today, the temporal method produces results essentially equivalent to the monetary-nonmonetary method. However, if accounting principles were to be modified, the methods would yield different results.

In one of its first major releases, the FASB in 1975 adopted the temporal method for translation of foreign currency financial statements. As viewed by the Board, this method achieved the following translation objectives:

> For the purpose of preparing an enterprise's financial statements, the objective of translation is to measure and express (a) in dollars and (b) in conformity with U.S. generally accepted accounting principles the assets, liabilities, revenue, or expenses that are measured or denominated in foreign currency. Remeasuring in dollars the assets, liabilities, revenue, or expenses measured or denominated in foreign currency should not affect either the measurement bases for assets and liabilities or the timing of revenue and expense recognition otherwise required by generally accepted accounting principles. That is, translation should change the *unit of measure* without changing accounting principles.[3]

---

[2] Leonard Lorensen, "Reporting Foreign Operations of U.S. Companies in U.S. Dollars," *Accounting Research Study No. 12* (New York: AICPA, 1972).

[3] FASB, *Statement of Financial Accounting Standards No. 8*, "Accounting for the Translation of Foreign Currency Transactions and Foreign Currency Financial Statements" (Stamford, Conn.: 1975).

Even though accounting principles may be maintained, changing the unit of measurement generates translation "gains and losses" from exchange rate fluctuations in the same manner as the *remeasurement* of foreign currency receivables and payables did in Chapter 13. Under any translation method, these "gains and losses" are generated *only on those assets and liabilities that are translated at the current rate.* Thus, *Statement 8* (the temporal method) generally produced gains or losses on a firm's net monetary asset or liability exposure, and these gains or losses were recognized in the current income statement.

In the period immediately following the adoption of *Statement 8,* the U.S. dollar was generally weakening against most major currencies. As a consequence, companies were reporting large exchange *losses* on foreign investments because of the fairly common net monetary liability exposure. To many managers in these firms, the reported results seemed inconsistent with "economic reality." Their view resulted from a different perspective on the foreign investments and the foreign currency risks—one that incorporated a foreign entity's nonmonetary assets together with the net monetary liability position. When the *overall* investment in a foreign entity is viewed this way, the foreign currency exposure changes from a net monetary liability to a *net asset.* Seen this way, the U.S. investor is benefiting from the exchange rate changes when the foreign currency gains in value relative to the dollar.

A method that includes this broader view of the foreign currency exposure is the *current rate method.* Under this method, all assets and liabilities are translated at the rate of exchange prevailing at the translation date. As a consequence, its proponents argue, the translated values reflect the dollar equivalents of the values (however measured) in the foreign currency financial statements, and further the accounting results are consistent with economic effects. The principal objection to this method is the contention that it yields translated values that depart from historical-cost-based accounting for assets and liabilities carried at cost (although the translated values are in general not equal to the current-dollar equivalents of the market values of the assets and liabilities). Since the purpose of translation is usually to provide a basis for incorporating these assets and liabilities, and/or results of operations, in the financial statements of a U.S. firm, opponents of the method argue that such a departure is unjustified under present historical-cost-based GAAP.

The dissatisfaction with *Statement 8* was sufficiently widespread, however, that the FASB agreed to reconsider accounting policy for foreign currency translation. The result of a comprehensive and controversial review was the issuance in 1981 of *Statement 52.* Under the provisions of this standard, the *current rate method* was selected as the most appropriate means of achieving the objectives for the translation of a foreign entity's financial statements from its functional currency into the parent's (or investor's) reporting currency. Note that these objectives represent a change from a "single unit of measure" concept to multiple units of measure where foreign affiliates' functional currencies differ from the parent's reporting currency. This change was due to the Board's determination (with three Board members dissenting) that only by maintaining the functional currency relationships was it possible to meaningfully aggregate the separate financial statements. For this reason, the new foreign currency conversion process is often referred to as a functional currency approach.

If a foreign entity's functional currency is not the same as the local currency in which its books and records are maintained, the *temporal method* must be applied to *remeasure* the financial statements into the functional currency. The objective of this remeasurement process is to generate the same financial statement values that would have resulted if the books had been kept in the functional currency. After the financial statements have been remeasured from the recordkeeping currency into the foreign entity's functional currency, they can then be *translated* into the parent's reporting currency using the current rate method. However, if a foreign entity's functional currency differs from its local currency, it is usually because its functional currency is the parent company's reporting currency. In these cases, no further currency conversions are required after remeasurement into the functional currency.

Gains or losses on the conversion of foreign currency financial statements are reported in different ways, depending upon the nature of the conversion. The gains or losses resulting from remeasurement (using the temporal method) into the foreign entity's functional currency are recognized in income in the same manner as the remeasurement of receivables or payables denominated in a foreign currency (Chapter 13). Indeed, in *Statement 52* terms both processes are equivalent. Both are *remeasurements* of balances that are denominated in a foreign currency into a firm's functional currency. As such, changes in values (as measured in the functional currency) reflect changes in expected cash flows, and thus they are reported in income. On the other hand, the Board concluded that gains or losses resulting from the *translation* of a foreign currency financial statement (using the current rate method) are not related to the foreign entity's functional cash flows from operations and are only indirectly related to the parent (or investor) company's reporting currency cash flows. The indirect effect is on the amount of the net investment that could be realized on sale or liquidation. Accordingly, these gains or losses are *not* included in income of the current period. Instead, they are reported as a separate component of shareholders' equity. If the investment in the foreign entity is sold or partially liquidated, the cumulative translation gain or loss applicable to the sold interest is removed from shareholders' equity and included with the gain or loss on the sale.

A schematic presentation of these *Statement 52* rules for the translation of foreign currency financial statements is depicted in Illustration 14–1.

Illustration 14–1

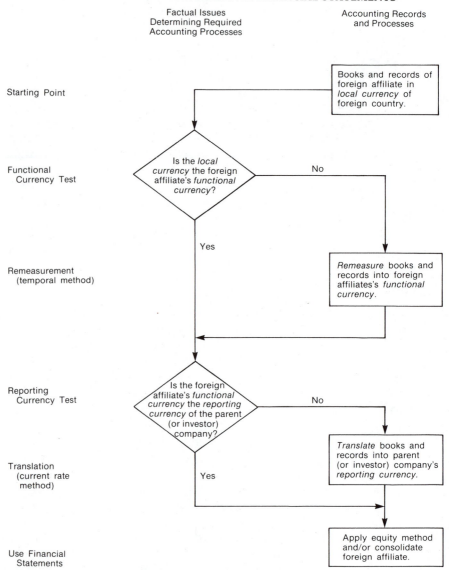

TRANSLATING FOREIGN CURRENCY FINANCIAL STATEMENTS

Factual Issues
Determining Required
Accounting Processes

Accounting Records
and Processes

Starting Point

Books and records of
foreign affiliate in
local currency of
foreign country.

Functional
Currency Test

Is the *local
currency* the foreign
affiliate's *functional
currency*?

No

Remeasurement
(temporal method)

Yes

Remeasure books and
records into foreign
affiliates's *functional
currency*.

Reporting
Currency Test

Is the foreign
affiliate's *functional
currency* the *reporting
currency* of the parent
(or investor)
company?

No

Translation
(current rate
method)

Yes

Translate books and
records into parent
(or investor) company's
reporting currency.

Use Financial
Statements

Apply equity method
and/or consolidate
foreign affiliate.

The Functional Currency Concept

The FASB's definition of a firm's *functional currency* was briefly introduced in Chapter 13. In the most general terms, it is the "currency of the primary economic environment in which the firm operates; normally, that is the currency of the environment in which an entity primarily generates and expends cash" (*FASB Statement No. 52*, par. 5). Determination of the functional currency in some cases may be easy; in other circumstances, it may be more ambiguous. *Statement 52* includes some additional guidelines to assist in making this determination.

First, the Board observes that the foreign operations of a multinational enterprise may fall into one of two extreme types. The first class includes those foreign operations that are "primarily a direct and integral component or extension of the parent company's operations" (*FASB Statement No. 52*, par. 81). For the subsidiary of a U.S. parent, this means that managerial attention is focussed on the *dollar* implications of all financing, investment, and operating activities, whether or not transaction(s) are actually denominated in dollars. In this case, the functional currency of the subsidiary is the dollar—the parent's currency. At the other end of the spectrum, a subsidiary may be highly autonomous, with operations that are self-contained within a particular foreign economic environment. The activities are regularly assessed not in terms of their effects on dollar flows, but rather in terms of the foreign currency of the country in which the subsidiary is domiciled. Although the net foreign currency inflows may be distributed to the parent in the form of dividends, often they are reinvested in the foreign operation. In this case, the subsidiary's functional currency is its local (foreign) currency.

Many cases in practice may fall somewhere between these two relatively well-defined classes. In these cases, the FASB has suggested (*FASB Statement No. 52,* Appendix A) some additional factors that management should consider in arriving at a decision concerning the functional currency of foreign affiliates. Although a foreign affiliate's functional currency might be any currency, these criteria focus on a simple choice between the parent's reporting currency and the foreign affiliate's local (foreign) currency. The criteria in general terms are as follows:

1. *Cash flow indicators.* Do the cash flows impact the parent company's dollar cash flows on a regular basis?
2. *Sales price indicators.* Are the foreign affiliate's prices responsive to short-term fluctuations in exchange rates?
3. *Sales market indicators.* Are the affiliate's products sold in its local market for a price denominated in the local currency or in the parent's environment?
4. *Expense indicators.* Are costs primarily incurred in local markets, or from the parent company's country?
5. *Financing indicators.* Are debts denominated in, and serviced by, foreign currency or the parent's currency?
6. *Intercompany transactions and arrangements indicators.* Are the operations and management of the foreign affiliate relatively autonomous, or are there many intercompany transactions and control arrangements?

These indicators must be considered collectively by management in reaching its conclusion about the functional currency of the foreign affiliate. In making this judgment, they should consider which functional currency would best meet the objectives of translation under *Statement No. 52*. Once the functional currency (or currencies) has been determined for a foreign affiliate, it should not be changed unless the underlying economic relationships and circumstances change significantly.

If a foreign affiliate has more than one distinct and separable operation conducted in different economic environments, each distinct operation may be regarded as an entity with a unique functional currency. For example, a single foreign subsidiary domiciled in France may have relatively autonomous operations in France and Spain. In this case, each of the two separate operations would be considered an entity with its own functional currency.

Highly Inflationary Economies

A foreign affiliate may be domiciled in a country whose currency has been subject to a great deal of inflation. In these circumstances, the financial statement values assigned to long-lived assets may lack economic significance when they are translated at the current exchange rate. The Board considered several possible remedies for this potential problem and finally decided that the financial statements of foreign affiliates operating in *highly inflationary* economies must be *remeasured as if the affiliate's functional currency were the parent's reporting currency*. In other words, a highly inflationary currency cannot serve as an entity's functional currency. Guidelines were provided for determining whether or not an economy is "highly inflationary." In its most definitive guideline, the Board stated that if the *cumulative* inflation for the past three years has been *approximately* 100 percent or more, then an economy should be classified as "highly inflationary." This rather specific definition was, however, tempered by the Board's further statement that it should be applied with judgment (par. 109). One specific additional factor mentioned in *Statement 52* is the trend of inflation, as contrasted to the absolute rate for the three-year period.

Initial Investment in Foreign Affiliate

The procedures for translation of foreign currency financial statements specified in *FASB Statement No. 52* are applicable only when the statements are to be incorporated into those of a parent (or investor) company through consolidation and/or application of the equity method. In view of this fact, the logical place to begin our explanation of these accounting processes is the initial investment in the foreign entity. For reasons of clarity of exposition, we will focus on a 100 percent acquisition of a foreign subsidiary. The basic principles presented are, however, applicable to all levels of investment that are accounted for under the equity method.

On the date of acquisition, *all* balance sheet accounts of the subsidiary are translated into dollars using the current exchange rate. This principle holds whether the newly acquired subsidiary's functional currency is its local currency, the parent's reporting currency, or some other currency. At subsequent financial statement conversion dates, this date-of-acquisition exchange rate is the relevant exchange rate for any of these assets, liabilities, or shareholders' equity accounts that are to be remeasured or translated using *historical* rates.

For a combination accounted for as a purchase, the differential (in dollars) is easily determined by comparing the dollar cost with the dollar value of the translated net assets of the subsidiary. This differential measured in dollars may then be allocated to specific assets and liabilities based on the dollar differences between fair and book values. These procedures are completely consistent with our treatment of differentials in prior chapters, and they permit the preparation of a consolidated balance sheet incorporating the foreign affiliate on the date of acquisition. However, subsequent accounting for the differential draws on the translation principles of the current rate method or the temporal method, depending on the determination of the subsidiary's functional currency. Accordingly, explanation of the accounting for the differential subsequent to acquisition is deferred until the two translation methods are covered.

Case 1. Acquisition of a Foreign Subsidiary.   Monroe Co. (a Wisconsin firm) purchased 100 percent of the outstanding capital stock of Bordeaux Co. (a French corporation) on January 1, 19X1, for $150,000. The book and fair values of Bordeaux Co.'s assets and liabilities on January 1, 19X1, were as follows:

	In French Francs	
	Book Value	Fair Value
Cash and receivables	200,000	200,000
Plant and equipment (net)..........	1,000,000	1,600,000
	1,200,000	1,800,000
Current payables	100,000	100,000
Long-term debt	700,000	700,000
	800,000	800,000
Net assets	400,000	1,000,000
Composed of:		
Capital stock....................	100,000	
Retained earnings	300,000	
	400,000	

The exchange rate for francs on January 1, 19X1, was $0.125.

Bordeaux Co.'s foreign currency balance sheet must be translated into dollars in order to make the necessary date-of-acquisition calculations that are routinely involved with new subsidiaries, as well as to allow preparation of a consolidated balance sheet. This translation is accomplished by converting each account balance at the current exchange rate of $0.125, as depicted below:

	In French Francs	Exchange Rate	In U.S. $
Cash and receivables.................	200,000	$0.125	25,000
Plant and equipment (net)............	1,000,000	0.125	125,000
	1,200,000		150,000
Current payables	100,000	0.125	12,500
Long-term debt.....................	700,000	0.125	87,500
Capital stock	100,000	0.125	12,500
Retained earnings	300,000	0.125	37,500
	1,200,000		150,000

The differential is easily calculated, in both U.S. dollars and French francs, as follows:

	In U.S. $	In French Francs
Investment cost	150,000	1,200,000*
Purchased equity in book value of subsidiary's net assets..............	50,000†	400,000
Differential	100,000	800,000

* $150,000 / $0.125.
† [100% × (400,000 × $0.125)].

This example is continued for the first year of the subsidiary's operations in conjunction with the explanation of the two foreign currency conversion methods that must be used under *Statement 52*—the current rate method and the temporal method. It is then used to illustrate the appropriate accounting for the differential.

Accounting Procedures for the Translation Process (Current Rate Method)

The current rate method is used to *translate* foreign currency financial statements measured in a foreign affiliate's functional currency into the parent's reporting currency. The objective of the method is to restate the financial statements into dollars in a way that will reflect the same economic results and relationships that exist in the functional currency statements.

The rules for implementation of the current rate method are reasonably simple. All assets and liabilities are translated at the current exchange rate on the balance sheet date. Revenues and expenses (and gains and losses) are translated using the exchange rate that was in effect on the date that they were recognized. Since it is normally impractical to make the conversions on a transaction-by-transaction basis, it is permissible to use an appropriately weighted average exchange rate for the period to translate *all* of the income statement elements.[4]

The dollar values assigned to the foreign affiliate's assets and liabilities in the translation process determine the *total* dollar value of the shareholder's equity. In the financial statements, however, this amount must be allocated between paid-in capital, cumulative translation gains or losses, and retained earnings. In order to capture "changes" that occur over time in either the cumulative translation adjustment account or retained earnings, the paid-in capital accounts are translated using the relevant *historical exchange rates*. In the absence of any additional stock transactions, the single relevant historical rate is the exchange rate that prevailed on the date the parent made the investment. The beginning-of-period retained earnings and the beginning-of-period cumulative translation adjustment are entered into the dollar-based trial balance *at the dollar values determined for each at the end of the preceding period*. Any direct charges or credits to retained earnings during the period (such as dividend payments) are translated at the exchange rate in effect on the date the transaction took place.

Applying these procedures to a foreign currency trial balance produces a trial balance in dollars that usually is not "in balance." The difference in the totals for the debits and credits measures the *translation gain or loss* for the current year resulting from exchange rate fluctuations. If the debits exceed the credits, the difference reflects a translation gain; if the credits exceed the debits, the difference is a translation loss. The translation gain or loss determined in this manner is entered into the trial balance (in dollars), and the necessary equality of debits and credits is restored.

This procedure is illustrated in Case 2, which continues the example introduced in Case 1.

Case 2. Translation of Foreign Subsidiary's Financial Statements.   In this continuation of Case 1, we assume that the determination has been made by the management of Monroe Co. that *Bordeaux Co.'s functional currency is the French franc*. Accordingly, Bordeaux Co.'s financial state-

---

[4] The reader will recall that the same approximation technique is used for certain revenue and expense measurements under both constant dollar and current cost accounting. It also is used for selected revenue and expense remeasurements under the temporal method of foreign currency conversion.

ments in French francs will be *translated into dollars using the current rate method*. We assume also that Monroe Co. uses the equity method to account for its investment in Bordeaux.

Bordeaux Co.'s trial balance at December 31, 19X1 is presented below:

	Francs
Cash and receivables............	1,150,000
Plant and equipment (net).......	750,000
Depreciation expense............	250,000
Other expenses.................	350,000
	2,500,000
Current payables	200,000
Long-term debt.................	700,000
Sales..........................	1,200,000
Capital stock	100,000
Retained earnings, 1/1..........	300,000
	2,500,000

The exchange rate on January 1, 19X1, the date of investment, was $0.125. We now assume that at December 31, 19X1, the exchange rate is $0.10 and that the average for 19X1 was $0.11. Additionally, it is assumed that: (1) all monetary assets and liabilities are denominated in French francs; (2) no plant and equipment was acquired or retired during 19X1; and (3) sales were made, and expenses incurred, uniformly over the period.

Based on these data, the working paper for translating Bordeaux Co.'s foreign currency financial statements into dollars is displayed in Illustration 14–2.

Since this is the first year of affiliation, there is no cumulative translation adjustment at the beginning of the period. We enter this as a "zero" in the working paper to emphasize the procedure that is followed in future periods, viz., entering the beginning-of-period dollar measure for both retained earnings and cumulative translation adjustment. Note that the code indicated for the translation of retained earnings also reflects the general rule to be applied to beginning retained earnings. In fact, the dollar value was actually established on January 1 (the date of acquisition). In all subsequent periods, however, the value used in the working paper will be that indicated by our code. As previously noted, the translation gain or loss for the year is determined by comparing the total debits and credits in the dollar-based trial balance and entering the amount necessary to restore equality.

Equity Method Entries.   Monroe Co. would make the following two entries at December 31, 19X1, to record its equity (in this case, 100 percent) in Bordeaux Co.'s 19X1 earnings (in dollars) of $66,000 *and* in the 19X1

Illustration 14–2

BORDEAUX CO.
Foreign Currency Translation Working Paper
For Year Ended December 31, 19X1
(Current Rate Method)

	Trial Balance 12/31/X1 (in francs)	Exchange Rate Code	Exchange Rate Rate	Trial Balance 12/31/X1 (in dollars)	Income Statement (in dollars)	Balance Sheet (in dollars)
Cash and receivables	1,150,000	C	0.100	115,000		115,000
Plant and equipment (net)	750,000	C	0.100	75,000		75,000
Depreciation expense	250,000	A	0.110	27,500	27,500	
Other expenses	350,000	A	0.110	38,500	38,500	
Translation loss for 19X1				16,000		
Net profit from operations					66,000	
	2,500,000			272,000	132,000	190,000
Current payables	200,000	C	0.100	20,000		20,000
Long-term debt	700,000	C	0.100	70,000		70,000
Sales	1,200,000	A	0.110	132,000	132,000	
Capital stock	100,000	H	0.125	12,500		12,500
Retained earnings (1/1)	300,000	P	—	37,500		37,500
Cumulative foreign exchange translation adjustments (1/1)		P	—	–0–		–0–
Net profit from operations						66,000
Translation loss for 19X1						(16,000)
	2,500,000			272,000	132,000	190,000

Code:
C = Current rate of exchange at December 31, 19X1.
A = Average rate of exchange for 19X1.
H = Historical rate of exchange.
P = Dollar balance, end of preceding period.

translation loss of $16,000 occurring because of exchange rate fluctuations:

(1) Investment in Bordeaux Co.   66,000
         Equity in Subsidiary Earnings   66,000

(2) Cumulative Foreign Exchange
         Translation Adjustments   16,000
         Investment in Bordeaux Co.   16,000

The equity in subsidiary earnings is included in Monroe Co.'s income for the current period in the normal manner. However, the translation loss recognized in 19X1 under the current rate method is charged directly to the special shareholders' equity account which has been designated to accumulate these translation adjustments.

Analysis of Translation Loss.   Applying the current rate method procedures in the foreign currency translation working paper produced, as a
balancing figure, a $16,000 translation loss for the current period. It is
instructive to calculate this loss directly, based on the foreign currency
exposure defined by the current rate method, for the additional perspective it provides on the nature and source of translation gains and losses
under the method.

Assets and liabilities that are translated at historical rates are unaffected
by exchange rate changes because they are always assigned the dollar
value established on the date they were acquired or incurred. *Therefore,
regardless of the method used, the sources of exchange gains and losses in the
translation process are assets and liabilities that are translated using the current
exchange rate.* Since all assets and liabilities are translated at the current rate
under the current rate method, the foreign currency exposure risk is identified with the *aggregate net assets of the foreign affiliate.* That is to say, translation gains or losses for the period result from the effects of changes in the
exchange rate on the subsidiary's net asset position at the time of the
change. Decreases in the exchange rate cause the dollar value of the subsidiary's net assets to decline and thus produce exchange losses. Exchange
gains result when the rates increase.

Using the subsidiary's beginning net asset position and assuming that
the change in net assets occurred uniformly over the year, the translation
loss determined indirectly in the working paper is calculated directly as
follows:

Translation loss on beginning net assets	
[400,000 × ($0.125 − $0.10)]	$10,000
Translation loss on the increase in net assets	
during 19X1*	
[600,000 × ($0.11 − $0.10)]	6,000
	$16,000

> * The 600,000 increase in net assets, measured in French francs, is
> the difference between Bordeaux Co.'s 12/31/X1 net asset position of
> 1,000,000 francs and the 1/1/X1 net asset position of 400,000 francs.

Assuming that the beginning net asset position was held for the entire
year, the loss due to the decrease in the exchange rate from $0.125 at the
beginning of the year to $0.10 at the end of the year is $10,000—the net
assets at the beginning of the year measured in French francs (400,000
francs) multiplied by the decrease in the rate. Assuming the increase in the
subsidiary's net assets occurred uniformly over the period (an assumption
that was incorporated in the working paper when *all* revenue and expense
accounts were translated at the average rate), these net assets of 600,000
francs were acquired, *on average,* when the exchange rate was $0.11—the

19X1 average rate. Therefore, the translation loss on this increase of 600,000 francs in net assets is calculated using the decrease from $0.11 to $0.10, resulting in a loss of $6,000. The sum of these two losses is the $16,000 loss reflected in the working paper.

Accounting Procedures for the Remeasurement Process (Temporal Method)

The temporal method is used to *remeasure* an affiliate's foreign currency financial statements into its *functional currency*. The objective of this remeasurement process is to generate the same financial statement values that would have resulted if the books had been kept in the functional currency. If the affiliate's functional currency is not the parent's reporting currency, the remeasured statements should then be translated into the reporting currency using the current rate method.

We have previously observed that, under the temporal method, assets and liabilities are to be remeasured in a manner that is consistent with the accounting principles that have been applied to them. Normally, this principle results in the translation of *monetary assets and liabilities using the current exchange rate and nonmonetary assets and liabilities at the relevant historical rate*. The relevant historical rate is the more recent of two exchange rates: (1) the rate that prevailed on the date the asset (or liability) was acquired (or incurred) or (2) the rate prevailing on the date the parent (or investor) company acquired the ownership interest in the foreign affiliate.

Any revenue or expense that can be identified directly with an asset or liability translated at a historical rate shall also be translated using this same rate. Common examples are cost of sales and depreciation expense. All other revenue and expenses are translated using an appropriately weighted average exchange rate for the period (in the same manner as under the current rate method). The result of these procedures should be remeasured values which approximate the amounts that would have obtained had the original transactions been measured in the functional currency on the dates they were recognized.

The shareholders' equity accounts are converted into dollars in the same manner as under the current rate method. Paid-in capital accounts are converted at historical rates, and the beginning-of-period retained earnings is restated at the dollar value determined at the end of the preceding period. The exchange gain or loss resulting from this remeasurement process is *included in the affiliate's income statement (in dollars) for the current period* and thereby becomes part of retained earnings (in dollars). Hence, there is no account under the temporal method that is similar to the cumulative translation adjustment account maintained under the current rate method.

When these procedures are applied in a foreign currency translation working paper, the exchange gain or loss from remeasurement is determined in the same manner as under the current rate method. It is the difference between the total dollar value of the debits and the credits in the trial balance which has been remeasured into dollars. This is illustrated in Case 3, which continues Case 1 under the alternative assumption that Bordeaux Co.'s functional currency is the dollar rather than the French franc.

Case 3. Remeasurement of Foreign Subsidiary's Financial Statements.   In Case 2, it was assumed that the management of Monroe Co. determined that Bordeaux Co.'s functional currency was the French franc. This determination meant that the current rate method was used to translate Bordeaux Co.'s 19X1 financial statements. In this example, we make the alternative assumption that *management has determined Bordeaux Co.'s functional currency to be the dollar.* Accordingly, Bordeaux Co.'s 19X1 financial statements in French francs must be remeasured into dollars using the temporal method. Since the dollar is Monroe Co.'s reporting currency, no further translation is required.

The working paper for remeasuring Bordeaux's Co.'s foreign currency financial statements into dollars is shown in Illustration 14–3. Recall from Case 2 that the exchange rate at the beginning of 19X1 was $0.125, the average for 19X1 was $0.11, and the ending rate was $0.10. Also, the following assumptions continue from Case 2: (1) all monetary assets and liabilities are denominated in French francs; (2) no plant and equipment was acquired or retired during 19X1; and (3) sales were made and expenses incurred uniformly over 19X1.

Since the nonmonetary assets (plant and equipment) were acquired and the capital stock issued before January 1, 19X1, the relevant historical rate for the remeasurement of these accounts is the rate prevailing on January 1, 19X1—the date that Monroe Co. purchased Bordeaux Co. Additionally, the dollar value of retained earnings was fixed on this date of combination; hence, it is the same value that is used under the current rate method. In subsequent periods, the beginning dollar value of retained earnings will *not* be the same for the two methods because of the differences in the conversion rules and the income recognition principles. Finally, note that depreciation expense is remeasured using the historical rate applicable to plant and equipment. Even though in this and the preceding case all expenses are assumed to be incurred uniformly over the period, the measurement of depreciation expense is identified directly with an asset that is remeasured into dollars using a historical rate. Hence, in accordance with the previously stated principles for the temporal method, depreciation expense is remeasured using the same historical rate.

Bordeaux Co.'s 19X1 net income, in dollars, is composed of income from operations of $62,250 and the exchange gain from remeasurement of

Illustration 14–3

BORDEAUX CO.
Foreign Currency Translation Working Paper
For Year Ended December 31, 19X1
(Temporal Method)

	Trial Balance (in francs)	Code	Rate	Trial Balance 12/31/X1 (in dollars)	Income Statement (in dollars)	Balance Sheet (in dollars)
Cash and receivables.................	1,150,000	C	0.100	115,000		115,000
Plant and equipment (net).............	750,000	H	0.125	93,750		93,750
Depreciation expense	250,000	H	0.125	31,250	31,250	
Other expenses.....................	350,000	A	0.110	38,500	38,500	
Net profit (including remeasurement gain)					68,750	
	2,500,000			278,500	138,500	208,750
Current payables	200,000	C	0.100	20,000		20,000
Long-term debt.....................	700,000	C	0.100	70,000		70,000
Sales	1,200,000	A	0.110	132,000	132,000	
Capital stock ..`.....................	100,000	H	0.125	12,500		12,500
Retained earnings (1/1)..............	300,000	P	—	37,500		37,500
Remeasurement exchange gain for 19X1				6,500	6,500	
Net profit (including remeasurement gain)						68,750
	2,500,000			278,500	138,500	208,750

Code:
C = Current rate of exchange at December 31, 19X1.
A = Average rate of exchange for 19X1.
H = Historical rate of exchange.
P = Dollar balance, end of preceding period.

$6,500. Obviously income from operations, as measured in French francs, is the same in both Case 2 and Case 3. However, income from operations, *as measured in dollars,* differs from that produced under the current rate method because of the use of the historical rate to remeasure depreciation expense.

Equity Method Entries.   Since the remeasurement exchange gain for 19X1 of $6,500 is a determinant of the affiliate's 19X1 net income (in dollars), Monroe Co. makes only one entry in this case:

Investment in Bordeaux Co.................................... 68,750
        Equity in Subsidiary Earnings............................   68,750

In the single entry, Monroe Co. recognizes its equity (100 percent) in both the exchange gain resulting from the remeasurement of Bordeaux Co.'s financial statements into dollars and the dollar measure of Bordeaux Co.'s 19X1 income from operations.

Analysis of Remeasurement Exchange Gain.   When the current rate method was applied (Case 2) to Bordeaux Co.'s 19X1 foreign currency financial statements, a $16,000 translation *loss* was determined for 19X1. However, when the temporal method was applied to the same data in Illustration 14–3, a $6,500 remeasurement exchange *gain* for 19X1 resulted. Although different labels are attached to the two measures in accordance with *Statement 52* terminology, both result from the effect of exchange rate fluctuations on assets and liabilities converted using current exchange rates.

Under the temporal method, only monetary assets and liabilities are translated using current exchange rates. Accordingly, the firm's net monetary asset or liability position defines its foreign currency exposure under this method. Because this exposure is different from the exposure defined under the current rate method, the measure of the exchange gain or loss is different.

In our example, the exposed net asset (liability) position, in francs, was composed of the following accounts:

	In Francs	
	12/31/X1	1/1/X1
Assets translated at current rate:		
Cash and receivables	1,150,000	200,000
Liabilities translated at current rate:		
Current payables	200,000	100,000
Long-term debt	700,000	700,000
	900,000	800,000
Exposed net asset (liability) position.........	250,000	(600,000)

The exposed net liability position of 600,000 francs at the beginning of the year was converted into an exposed net asset position of 250,000 francs at the end of the year. This change of 850,000 francs resulted from an inflow of net monetary assets from sales (1,200,000) and the outflow of net monetary assets reflected in other expenses (350,000).

Since the exchange rate between francs and dollars fell during 19X1 (i.e., the dollar strengthened relative to the franc), an exchange *gain* resulted from being in an exposed *liability* position. However, this was offset, in part, as monetary assets were accumulated over the period. Assuming that the change occurred uniformly over the period, the remeasurement gain for 19X1 is calculated directly as follows:

Exchange *gain* on beginning exposed net monetary liability position [600,000 × ($0.125 − $0.10)]...	$15,000
Exchange *loss* on net monetary asset inflow over the year [850,000 × ($0.11 − $0.10)]..	8,500
Remeasurement exchange gain for 19X1	$ 6,500

The gain on the beginning net monetary liability position is not completely offset by the loss on the net monetary asset inflow, even though this inflow is larger than the beginning position, because the inflow was assumed to occur, on average, when the exchange rate was $0.11.

Comparative 19X1 financial statements for Bordeaux Co., in dollars, resulting from application of the current rate method and the temporal method are reflected in Illustration 14–4.

Illustration 14–4

BORDEAUX CO.
Comparative 19X1 Financial Statements
(in dollars)

	Current Rate Method				Temporal Method			
	12/31/X1		1/1/X1		12/31/X1		1/1/X1	
Cash and receivables		115,000		25,000		115,000		25,000
Plant and equipment (net)		75,000		125,000		93,750		125,000
		190,000		150,000		208,750		150,000
Current payables................	20,000		12,500		20,000		12,500	
Long-term debt	70,000	90,000	87,500	100,000	70,000	90,000	87,500	100,000
Capital stock....................	12,500		12,500		12,500		12,500	
Retained earnings	103,500		37,500		106,250		37,500	
Cumulative translation adjustment	(16,000)	100,000	–0–	50,000	–0–	118,750	–0–	50,000
		190,000		150,000		208,750		150,000
Sales...........................			132,000				132,000	
Expenses, gains, and losses:								
Depreciation expense..........		27,500				31,250		
Other expenses		38,500				38,500		
Exchange loss (gain)..........		–0–	66,000			(6,500)	63,250	
			66,000				68,750	

Accounting for Differentials

As was previously observed, a differential may be measured and allocated on the date of acquisition of a new foreign subsidiary by translating the book and fair values of the subsidiary's net assets on that date using the current exchange rate. This information permits the parent company to prepare a consolidated balance sheet on the acquisition date. However, accounting for the differential of a foreign affiliate subsequent to acquisition involves some special techniques.

Paragraph 101 of *Statement 52* identifies the allocated amounts, including any goodwill, with the foreign affiliate, and requires that they be translated from the affiliate's local currency into the parent's reporting currency in accordance with all provisions of this standard. Hence, if the foreign affiliate's functional currency is its local currency, the differential allocations are translated using the current rate method. Application of this method to the differential allocation and amortization schedule (in foreign currency units) will produce translated dollar values *and* a *translation adjustment on the unamortized differential.* This translation adjustment will occur each time the affiliate's financial statements are translated into dollars. On the other hand, if the affiliate's functional currency is the parent's reporting currency, then the temporal method is used to translate the differential. For amounts allocated to assets or liabilities translated at historical rates, the values in dollars are fixed at acquisition, and thus the differential allocation and amortization schedule is also *fixed in dollars.* No further translations would be needed. For amounts allocated to assets or liabilities that are translated using current rates (e.g., long-term debt), it would seem appropriate to account for these allocations in the same way as under the current rate method. We should note, however, that some accountants interpret the sketchy language of paragraph 101 to imply that the allocated amounts are denominated in the *functional currency of the foreign affiliate.*[5] If this view is what is intended by the FASB, then the differential would be *completely* fixed in the parent's reporting currency whenever the reporting currency is the functional currency of the foreign affiliate.

Case 4.   Accounting for the differential subsequent to acquisition is illustrated using the data presented in Case 1 for Monroe's acquisition of Bordeaux. We additionally assume that Bordeaux Co.'s functional currency was as determined in Case 2—the French franc. Thus, the current rate method is used to translate Bordeaux Co.'s foreign currency financial statements, *and* the allocated differential amounts (in French francs) are also translated using the current exchange rate. As a practical matter, one can regard the translation of the affiliate's financial statements and the translation of the allocated differential amounts as two separate tasks. They are integrated in the books of the parent company by appropriate equity method entries and in the consolidated financial statements through the eliminating entries for differential allocation and amortization.

In Case 1, the differential was determined in both francs and dollars as shown below:

	$	Francs
Investment cost	150,000	1,200,000
Purchased equity in book value of subsidiary's net assets	50,000	400,000
Differential	100,000	800,000

---

[5] See, for example, Deloitte, Haskins & Sells, *Foreign Currency Translation—Issues and Answers,* January 1982, p. 10.

Additionally, the only account in Bordeaux Co.'s January 1, 19X1, balance sheet which had a fair value different from book value was plant and equipment (net), with a difference of 600,000 francs. We will assume that the plant and equipment is depreciated over four years and that any goodwill arising from the combination is to be amortized over 10 years. With these facts, the differential allocation and amortization schedule in Illustration 14–5 can be prepared.

Illustration 14–5

DIFFERENTIAL ALLOCATION AND AMORTIZATION SCHEDULE
(Current Rate Method)

	1/1/X1 Allocation			19X1 Amortization			12/31/X1		
	Francs	Rate	Dollars	Francs	Rate	Dollars	Francs	Rate	Dollars
Plant and equipment (net)	600,000	0.125	75,000	150,000	0.11	16,500	450,000	0.10	45,000
Goodwill......................	200,000	0.125	25,000	20,000	0.11	2,200	180,000	0.10	18,000
	800,000		100,000	170,000		18,700	630,000		63,000

Calculation of Translation Loss on Differential:

1/1/X1 balance...........................	$100,000
Less: 19X1 amortization	18,700
12/31/X1 balance before translation loss.....	81,300
12/31/X1 balance calculated on end-of-year unamortized differential allocations.......	63,000
Translation loss for 19X1 on differential.....	$ 18,300

The differential, as measured in francs, exhibits a normal pattern in the differential allocation and amortization schedule in Illustration 14–5. The beginning balance of 800,000 francs is reduced by amortization of 170,000 francs, yielding an ending balance of 630,000 francs. However, because of fluctuations in the exchange rate, the differential measured in dollars does *not* reflect this simple relationship between beginning and ending balances. In addition to the effect of the amortization for the period, the ending balance of the differential in dollars is decreased when the exchange rate falls and increased when the exchange rate rises. In Illustration 14–5, the dollar values for 19X1 amortization and the 12/31/X1 ending balance are both determined by *translating the corresponding values in francs.* Using these separately translated values, the 19X1 translation loss may then be inferred, as shown in Illustration 14–5. The loss of $18,300 can be confirmed by direct calculation as follows:

Translation loss on beginning differential amount	
[800,000 × ($0.125 − $0.10)]	$20,000
Adjustment to beginning balance for 19X1 amortization	
[170,000 × ($0.11 − $0.10)]	(1,700)
Translation loss for 19X1.	$18,300

The adjustment for 19X1 amortization recognizes the fact that Monroe did not have a foreign currency exposure for the entire year on the beginning balance of the differential. As with other calculations, it is assumed that the amortization was incurred uniformly over the year, thus justifying use of the average 19X1 exchange rate.

Equity Method Entries. Monroe Co. would make the following entries in 19X1 to record amortization of the differential *and* the translation loss incurred on the differential:

(1) Equity in Subsidiary Earnings   18,700
         Investment in Bordeaux Co.   18,700
     [Amortization of the differential]

(2) Cumulative Foreign Exchange
     Translation Adjustments   18,300
         Investment in Bordeaux Co.   18,300
     [Translation loss on differential]

The dollar measure of the amortization of the differential is included in Monroe Co.'s 19X1 income. The translation loss on the differential is accumulated in the same shareholders' equity account that was used in Case 2 for the translation loss on the net assets recorded on Bordeaux Co.'s books.

The entries to the Investment in Bordeaux Co. account from Case 2 (translation of Bordeaux Co.'s financial statements) and Case 4 (accounting for the differential) are summarized below:

Initial investment, 1/1/X1	$150,000
Equity in Bordeaux Co.'s 19X1 income	
from operations.	66,000
Translation loss—translation of Bordeaux Co.'s	
19X1 financial statements	(16,000)
Amortization of differential for 19X1	(18,700)
Translation loss—translation of differential	(18,300)
Balance of investment account, 12/31/X1	$163,000

Using the relationship between the investment account and the recorded net assets of a subsidiary, we can confirm this recorded balance as follows:

Equity in Bordeaux Co.'s 12/31/X1 net assets of
   1,000,000 francs [100% × (1,000,000 × $0.10)] ... $100,000
Unamortized differential (Illustration 14–5)........   63,000
Computed investment account balance, 12/31/X1 .. $163,000

Case 5. If Bordeaux Co.'s *functional currency is determined to be the dollar,* as in Case 3, the allocation and amortization schedule can be prepared, *in dollars,* on January 1, 19X1. The differential amortization would then be recorded each year in the normal manner. There would not be, however, any translation gains or losses, because the amounts assigned to plant & equipment and to goodwill are expressed in dollars—not in a foreign currency. The differential allocation and amortization schedule for this circumstance is shown in Illustration 14–6.

Illustration 14–6

DIFFERENTIAL ALLOCATION AND AMORTIZATION SCHEDULE
(in dollars)
(Temporal Method)

		Amortization/Year	
	Allocation	*19X1–X4*	*19X5–X10*
Plant and equipment (net).........	$ 75,000	$18,750	$ —
Goodwill.......................	25,000	2,500	2,500
	$100,000	$21,250	$2,500

With the differential fixed in dollars, there is *no* translation loss related to the differential. Hence, the only entry made by Monroe Co. under the equity method is the entry to record differential amortization for 19X1:

Equity in Subsidiary Earnings................................   21,250
   Investment in Bordeaux Co.   21,250
   [Amortization of differential]

The entries to the investment account from this case and Case 3 (remeasurement of Bordeaux Co.'s financial statements under the assumption that its functional currency is the dollar) are summarized below:

Initial investment, 1/1/X1.................... $150,000
Equity in Bordeaux Co.'s 19X1 income
   (including remeasurement gain)............   68,750
Amortization of differential for 19X1..........   (21,250)
Balance of investment account, 12/31/X1 ...... $197,500

The relationship between this balance, the unamortized differential, and the net assets of the subsidiary is more involved than in the preceding case.

The dollar value of the equity in the subsidiary's 12/31/X1 net assets of 1,000,000 francs cannot be translated using only the current exchange rate. Rather, the monetary assets and liabilities of the subsidiary are translated at the current exchange rate, and the nonmonetary assets and liabilities are translated using the appropriate historical rate(s). With this modification, these elements can be reconciled as follows:

Equity in net assets of Bordeaux Co.:		
Net monetary assets (250,000 francs @ $0.10)	$25,000	
Nonmonetary assets (750,000 francs @ $0.125)	93,750	$118,750
Unamortized differential ($100,000 − $21,250)		78,750
Computed investment account balance, 12/31/X1		$197,500

Consolidating a Foreign Subsidiary

After the foreign currency financial statements of a foreign subsidiary have been translated or remeasured into dollars, these statements may be consolidated with the financial statements of the parent company in a manner very similar to the consolidation of a domestic subsidiary. There are some modifications to the eliminating entries when the current rate method has been used because of the "deferred" exchange gains and losses from the translation of the foreign currency statements and the differential. These are illustrated for the Monroe/Bordeaux affiliation in Case 6.

Case 6. Consolidation of Bordeaux Co.'s financial statements with those of Monroe Co. is illustrated in this case under the assumption that Bordeaux Co.'s functional currency is the French franc. The data and supporting analyses for this form of the affiliation are included in Cases 2 and 4. In order to simplify the consolidation, we assume that Monroe Co.'s only asset is its investment in Bordeaux Co. and that it has no liabilities. We further assume that at January 1, 19X1, Monroe's retained earnings were zero. With these assumptions, the eliminating entries for the consolidated statement working paper for the year ended December 31, 19X1 (Illustration 14–7) are as follows:

(1) To reverse entries made by Monroe during 19X1 related to its investment in Bordeaux:

Equity in Subsidiary Earnings	47,300	
Cumulative Translation Adjustments.....................		34,300
Investment in Bordeaux Co.............................		13,000

(2) To eliminate the investment account against the beginning-of-year shareholders' equity:

Capital stock—Bordeaux....................................	12,500	
Retained Earnings, 1/1—Bordeaux.........................	37,500	
Differential..	100,000	
Investment in Bordeaux Co..............................		150,000

(3)   To allocate and amortize the differential, including recognition of the translation loss thereon:

Depreciation Expense.......................................	16,500	
Other Expenses..	2,200	
Plant and Equipment (net).................................	45,000	
Goodwill..	18,000	
Cumulative Translation Adjustments........................	18,300	
Differential..		100,000

Illustration 14–7

MONROE CO. AND SUBSIDIARY BORDEAUX CO.
Consolidated Statement Working Paper
For Year Ended December 31, 19X1

	Monroe Co.	Bordeaux Co.	Eliminations Dr.	Eliminations Cr.	Consolidated
Income Statement					
Sales.....................................		132,000			132,000
Equity in subsidiary earnings................	47,300	(1)	47,300		–0–
Total credits..........................	47,300	132,000			132,000
Depreciation expense		27,500 (3)	16,500		44,000
Other expenses.............................		38,500 (3)	2,200		40,700
Total debits		66,000			84,700
Net income	47,300	66,000	66,000	–0–	47,300
Retained Earnings Statement					
Retained earnings, 1/1:					
Monroe Co..............................	–0–				–0–
Bordeaux Co.		37,500 (2)	37,500		–0–
Net income—brought forward..............	47,300	66,000	66,000	–0–	47,300
Retained earnings, 12/31.................	47,300	103,500	103,500	–0–	47,300
Balance Sheet					
Cash and receivables.......................		115,000			115,000
Plant and equipment (net)...................		75,000 (3)	45,000		120,000
Investment in Bordeaux Co.	163,000		(1)	13,000	–0–
			(2)	150,000	
Differential................................		(2)	100,000 (3)	100,000	–0–
Goodwill....................................		(3)	18,000		18,000
	163,000	190,000			253,000
Current payables		20,000			20,000
Long-term debt............................		70,000			70,000
Common stock:					
Monroe Co..............................	150,000				150,000
Bordeaux Co.		12,500 (2)	12,500		–0–
Retained earnings	47,300	103,500	103,500	–0–	47,300
Cumulative translation adjustments	(34,300)	(16,000) (3)	18,300 (1)	34,300	(34,300)
	163,000	190,000	297,300	297,300	253,000

Similar eliminations would be made in succeeding years. One modification should, however, be noted. In addition to eliminating beginning-of-year shareholders' equity, the investment elimination entry must be expanded to also eliminate the beginning-of-year cumulative translation adjustment included in the the subsidiary's dollar-based financial statements.

Consolidated Statement of Changes in Financial Position

In preparing a consolidated statement of changes in financial position that includes one or more foreign affiliates, the increases or decreases in account balances caused by funds-generating or funds-using activities must be separated from changes due to fluctuations in the exchange rate. This is particularly critical when the functional currency is the local currency of the affiliate, and the current rate is used to translate all assets and liabilities.

Little guidance is provided in *Statement 52* on how exchange rate effects are to be incorporated in this financial statement. In paragraph 100, the FASB notes that the flexibility permitted in the preparation of the statement of changes in financial position is not changed by this foreign currency translation standard. The Board further reaffirms existing policy dealing with inclusions in the statement: ". . . Opinion 19 does require disclosure of all important changes in financial position regardless of whether cash or working capital is directly affected and that requirement is not changed in any way by this Statement." This provision might be interpreted to require enumeration of the translation gains or losses on each of the asset and liability accounts of the foreign affiliate(s). These changes are, of course, offset by the change in the shareholders' equity account for all assets and liabilities other than the resource whose change is being explained (for example, cash or working capital). Thus, the most compact statement results from including only the translation gain or loss on cash or working capital.

Case 7.   The effects of foreign currency translation on a statement of changes in financial position are illustrated in this case with Bordeaux Co.'s 19X1 financial statement data in dollars produced by translation under the current rate method. With appropriate attention to intercompany items, the statement prepared for Bordeaux Co. can be easily incorporated into Monroe's consolidated statement of changes in financial position.[6] Since the translation gains and losses were Bordeaux Co.'s only source or use of funds other than operations in 19X1, the impact of this new variable is highlighted.

---

[6] A worksheet methodology for incorporating multiple foreign subsidiaries in a consolidated statement of changes in financial position is described in Frank R. Rayburn and G. Michael Crooch, "Currency Translation and the Funds Statement: A New Approach," *Journal of Accountancy,* October 1983.

The 19X1 foreign currency financial statements for Bordeaux Co. are translated into dollars under the current rate method in Illustration 14–2. This process produced a translation loss of $16,000 on Bordeaux Co.'s composite net assets. This aggregate loss must be broken down into the component gains and losses on the individual asset and liability accounts in order to fully explain changes in these accounts in the statement of changes in financial position. The calculation of the individual gains and losses is shown in Illustration 14–8.

Illustration 14–8

CALCULATION OF TRANSLATION GAINS AND LOSSES ON BORDEAUX CO.'S INDIVIDUAL ACCOUNTS

	Cash and Receivables			Current Payables		
	Francs	Exchange Rate	Dollars	Francs	Exchange Rate	Dollars
Beginning balance	200,000	0.125	25,000	100,000	0.125	12,500
Net increase (decrease) for 19X1...........	950,000	0.110	104,500	100,000	0.110	11,000
			129,500			23,500
Ending balance	1,150,000	0.100	115,000	200,000	0.100	20,000
Translation loss (gain)....................			14,500			(3,500)

	Plant and Equipment (Net)			Long-Term Debt		
	Francs	Exchange Rate	Dollars	Francs	Exchange Rate	Dollars
Beginning balance	1,000,000	0.125	125,000	700,000	0.125	87,500
Net increase (decrease) for 19X1...........	(250,000)	0.110	(27,500)	–0–	0.110	–0–
			97,500			87,500
Ending balance	750,000	0.100	75,000	700,000	0.100	70,000
Translation loss (gain)....................			22,500			(17,500)

Recap of translation losses (gains):
Cash and receivables..............	14,500
Current payables	(3,500)
Working capital.................	11,000
Plant and equipment (net).........	22,500
Long-term debt...................	(17,500)
Translation loss for 19X1.........	16,000

In Illustration 14–9, we observe that Bordeaux Co.'s working capital increased $82,500 during 19X1. This increase is explained in its statement of changes in financial position for the year. Two alternative levels of disclosure are exhibited in this illustration. In the compact presentation (Alternative I), the 19X1 translation loss on working capital is included as an explanatory factor. All other translation gains or losses do not directly

Illustration 14–9

BORDEAUX CO.
Translated Statement of Changes in
Financial Position
For Year Ended December 31, 19X1

Alternative I: Disclose only translation loss on working capital			Alternative II: Comprehensive disclosure of translation gains and losses		
Working capital provided:			Working capital provided:		
Operations:			Operations:		
Net income....................	66,000		Net income....................	66,000	
Depreciation expense..........	27,500	93,500	Depreciation expense..........	27,500	93,500
			Reduction in plant and		
Working capital applied:			equipment due to		
Effect of foreign exchange			foreign exchange		
translation on working			translation.....................		22,500
capital		11,000			116,000
Increase in working capital					
during 19X1		82,500	Working capital applied:		
			Reduction in long-term		
			debt and shareholders'		
			equity due to foreign		
			exchange translation:		
			Long-term debt	17,500	
			Cumulative translation		
			adjustment	16,000	33,500
			Increase in working capital		
			during 19X1		82,500

Schedule of Working Capital Changes for 19X1:

	12/31/X1	1/1/X1	Increase (Decrease)
Cash and receivables	115,000	25,000	90,000
Current payables	20,000	12,500	7,500
Working capital	95,000	12,500	82,500

affect working capital and thus are excluded from the statement. On the other hand, if one views each gain or loss as significant financial events, they can be included in the statement as illustrated in Alternative II. Note that in this format the translation loss on the working capital is the only translation gain or loss that is excluded from the statement. However, the *net* effect of the elements included is precisely the $11,000 loss included under Alternative I. Thus, the alternatives are substantively equivalent, but differ in the amount and type of information they provide.

Remeasuring Inventory Valued Using Lower of Cost or Market

Normally inventories are *remeasured* under the temporal method using historical rates. That is, the beginning inventory would be converted using the beginning-of-period historical rate, purchases at the average rate, and ending inventory at the rate prevailing when it was acquired. However, if the inventory is to be valued using the "lower of cost or market" rule, the comparison between cost and market must be made *in the functional currency*. This means (under the remeasurement process) that both cost and market as measured in the local currency must be remeasured into the functional currency, and the lower of the two functional currency values selected as the remeasured value for the inventory (*Statement 52*, par. 49).

Case 8.   A foreign subsidiary whose functional currency is the dollar has inventory at December 31, 19X1, that was purchased for 1,000 local currency units when the exchange rate between a unit of its local currency (LC) and the dollar was LC 1 = $5. The following two independent situations are considered:

	Situation 1	Situation 2
Market (replacement cost).........	LC 1,100	LC 900
Exchange rate—12/31/X1..........	LC 1 = $4	LC 1 = $6

The cost and market values, in dollars, are calculated below:

	Situation 1	Situation 2
Cost (1,000 × $5)	$5,000	$5,000
Market:		
(1) 1,100 × $4...............	4,400	
(2) 900 × $6..................		5,400
Lower of cost or market		
(in dollars):		
(1) Market	4,400	
(2) Cost.....................		5,000

Thus, in situation 1, market (1,100) is higher than cost (1,000) in local currency units, but when the comparison is made in dollars, market ($4,400) is lower than cost ($5,000). Since the appropriate comparison is in dollars (the functional currency), the inventory is remeasured at $4,400, and the inventory write-down recognized in the income statement (in dollars). Situation 2 illustrates the converse case. In dollars, market ($5,400) is higher than cost ($5,000), and inventory is therefore translated at cost, even though in units of local currency, cost (1,000) is higher than market (900). These differences occur because of the amount and direction of changes in the exchange rate from the date of acquisition of the inventory.

In the example, market was assumed to be equal to current replacement cost. However, in accordance with current accounting policy on the lower of cost or market rule, market must not exceed net realizable value or be less than net realizable value reduced by an allowance for a normal profit margin. The ceiling and floor on market are obtained in local currency units and then translated into the functional currency. Determination of market is then based on applying the standard tests to the three values measured in the functional currency.

Foreign Branches

Branch operations are normally closely integrated with the operations of other organizational units of a firm. Hence, in most cases the functional currency of a foreign branch would be the reporting currency of the home office, and the temporal method would be used to convert the branch's foreign currency financial statements. Those branch accounts that have reciprocal balances among the home office accounts are translated simply by restating them to the balance of the contra account on the home office books. This procedure produces the same result as if each transaction recorded in the reciprocal accounts were translated using the exchange rate prevailing on the date of the transaction.

Relevant Exchange Rates

When multiple exchange rates exist, the rate to be used in translating or remeasuring foreign currency financial statements is normally the rate that is applicable to conversion of the foreign currency for purposes of dividend remittances. This rate was selected by the Board because potential cash flows from a foreign affiliate can only be converted into the reporting currency at this rate.

Use of the dividend remittance rate for translating foreign currency statements may, on occasion, cause a difference between intercompany receivables and payables. If an intercompany account is subject to settlement at a special exchange rate, translation of the foreign affiliate's receivable or payable using the dividend remittance rate may produce a difference in the two balances. Until the account is settled, the *difference* is treated as a receivable or payable in the consolidated financial statements.

Intercompany profits are measured using the exchange rate prevailing on the date of the intercompany transaction. Subsequent changes in exchange rates do not affect the amount of this profit.

Financial Statement Disclosures

Statement 52 requires the following disclosures relating to foreign currency transactions and translations:

1. The aggregate transaction gain or loss included in determining net income for the period shall be disclosed in the financial statements or notes thereto. . . .

2. An analysis of the changes during the period in the separate component of equity for cumulative translation adjustments shall be provided in a separate financial statement, in notes to the financial statements, or as part of a statement of changes in equity. At a minimum, the analysis shall disclose:

    a. Beginning and ending amount of cumulative translation adjustments.

    b. The aggregate adjustment for the period resulting from translation adjustments . . . and gains and losses from certain hedges and intercompany balances. . .

    c. The amount of income taxes for the period allocated to translation adjustments. . .

    d. The amounts transferred from cumulative translation adjustments and included in determining net income for the period as a result of the sale or complete or substantially complete liquidation of an investment in a foreign entity. . .[7]

An example of this type of disclosure from Johnson & Johnson's 1982 financial statements is displayed in Illustration 14–10.

Illustration 14–10

ILLUSTRATIVE FOREIGN CURRENCY DISCLOSURE
JOHNSON & JOHNSON 1982 FINANCIAL STATEMENTS

Note 4. Foreign Currency Translation

In 1981, the Company adopted *FAS No. 52*, Foreign Currency Translation, which replaced *FAS No. 8*. The financial statements for 1980 have not been restated for the change as the effect of *FAS No. 52* in that year was immaterial. Under *FAS No. 8*, net earnings would have been reduced by $58.6 million or $.32 per share in 1981. Net currency transaction gains and losses included in net earnings were a gain of $4.6 million in 1982 and losses of $.7 million and $.1 million in 1981 and 1980.

Under *FAS No. 52*, balance sheet currency effects are recorded in a separate component of stockholders' equity. This equity account includes the results of translating all balance sheet assets and liabilities at current exchange rates except for those located in highly inflationary economies, principally Argentina, Brazil, Colombia, and Mexico.

An analysis of the changes during 1982 and 1981 in the separate component of stockholders' equity for cumulative currency translation adjustments follows:

	Dollars in Millions	
	1982	*1981*
Beginning of year	$ (85.7)	(5.0)
Translation adjustments	(76.8)	(78.6)
Income taxes allocated to translation adjustments	(1.0)	(2.1)
End of year	$(163.5)	(85.7)

Translation adjustments relate primarily to inventories and property, plant and equipment and do not exist in terms of functional currency cash flows. *FAS No. 52* provides that these translation adjustments should not be reported as part of operating results since realization is remote unless such international businesses were sold or liquidated.

---

[7] *Statement No. 52*, pars. 30–31.

Reporting on Foreign Affiliates

Foreign affiliates should be consolidated and/or accounted for using the equity method only if the parent company is able to exercise control (or significant influence) over them. In determining the presence of effective parental control, the same criteria should apply for both foreign and domestic affiliates. Yet the accountant should be especially alert to the limitations of consolidated financial statements which include foreign subsidiaries. The following provision from an early ARB was referenced by the FASB in *Statement 52:*

> In view of the uncertain values and availability of the assets and net income of foreign subsidiaries subject to controls and exchange restrictions and the consequent unrealistic statements of income that may result from the translation of many foreign currencies into dollars, careful consideration should be given to the fundamental question of whether it is proper to consolidate the statements of foreign subsidiaries with the statements of United States companies. Whether consolidation of foreign subsidiaries is decided upon or not, adequate disclosure of foreign operations should be made."[8]

Current accounting policy indicates at least four methods of disclosing in financial statements information respecting foreign subsidiaries:

(a) To exclude foreign subsidiaries from consolidation and to furnish (1) statements in which only domestic subsidiaries are consolidated and (2) as to foreign subsidiaries, a summary in suitable form of their assets and liabilities, their income and losses for the year, and the parent company's equity therein. The total amount of investments in foreign subsidiaries should be shown separately, and the basis on which the amount was arrived at should be stated. If these investments include any surplus [retained earnings] of foreign subsidiaries and such surplus had previously been included in consolidated surplus, the amount should be separately shown or earmarked in stating the consolidated surplus in the statements here suggested. The exclusion of foreign subsidiaries from consolidation does not make it acceptable practice to include intercompany profits which would be eliminated if such subsidiaries were consolidated.

(b) To consolidate domestic and foreign subsidiaries and to furnish in addition the summary described in (a) (2) above.

(c) To furnish (1) complete consolidated statements and also (2) consolidated statements for domestic companies only.

(d) To consolidate domestic and foreign subsidiaries and to furnish in addition parent company statements showing the investment in and income

---

[8] *Accounting Research Bulletin 43*, Chapter 12, par. 8. Also reproduced in FASB *Accounting Standards—Current Text*, sec. C51.105.

from foreign subsidiaries separately from those of domestic subsidiaries.[9]

Although information on foreign subsidiaries may be presented in several ways, increasingly they are included in the consolidated statements.

Questions

1. What are the objectives of the current rate method for translating foreign currency financial statements?

2. What are the objectives of the temporal method for remeasuring foreign currency financial statements?

3. How are assets and liabilities in foreign currency financial statements translated under the current rate method?

4. How are revenue and expense items in foreign currency financial statements translated under the current rate method?

5. How are the translation gains or losses arising from the translation of foreign currency financial statements under the current rate method reported under current accounting policy?

6. How are assets and liabilities in foreign currency financial statements remeasured under the temporal method?

7. How are revenue and expense items in foreign currency financial statements remeasured under the temporal method?

8. How are the exchange gains or losses arising from the remeasurement of foreign currency financial statements under the temporal method reported under current accounting policy?

9. Explain the process one uses to determine the appropriate methods for converting an affiliate's foreign currency financial statements into the desired reporting currency.

10. Explain the concept of functional currency.

11. What is a "highly inflationary economy"? What is the significance of this concept for foreign currency translation?

12. How are the assets and liabilities of a newly acquired foreign subsidiary translated on the date of acquisition? What is the significance of these rates in later periods?

13. How are the shareholders' equity accounts of a foreign subsidiary translated into the parent's reporting currency? How are they remeasured into the parent's reporting currency?

---

[9] *Accounting Research Bulletin 43,* Chapter 12, par. 9. Also reproduced in FASB *Accounting Standards—Current Text,* sec. C51.106.

14. How is the cumulative translation adjustment recognized in the translation of foreign currency financial statements under the current rate method?

15. How is the differential accounted for under the current rate method? How is it accounted for under the temporal method?

16. What entries are recorded by a parent company under the equity method for a foreign subsidiary whose financial statements are translated into the parent's reporting currency using the current rate method?

17. What entries are recorded by a parent company under the equity method for a foreign subsidiary whose financial statements are remeasured into the parent's reporting currency?

18. Explain the process for applying the "lower of cost or market" rule to inventory when the temporal method is used to remeasure the inventory into the parent's reporting currency.

19. When multiple exchange rates exist, what rate should be used in translating foreign currency financial statements?

20. What exchange rate should be used in eliminating intercompany profits?

Exercises

Exercise 14–1

Indicate whether the following accounts on the books of a foreign affiliate would be remeasured (temporal method) into the parent's reporting currency at the current or the historical rate:

1. Patents.
2. Accrued wages payable.
3. Marketable equity securities carried at cost.
4. Deferred income.
5. Inventory carried at cost.
6. Allowance for doubtful accounts.
7. Inventory carried at net realizable value.
8. Property, plant, and equipment.
9. Accumulated depreciation.
10. Advances to unconsolidated subsidiaries.

Exercise 14–2

Dhia Products Company was incorporated in the state of Virginia in 19X0 to do business as a manufacturer of medical supplies and equipment. Since incorporating, Dhia has doubled in size about every three years and is now considered one of the leading medical supply companies in the country.

During January 19X4, Dhia established a subsidiary, Ban, Ltd., in the emerging nation of Shatha. Dhia owns 90 percent of the outstanding capital stock of Ban; the remaining 10 percent of Ban's outstanding capital stock is held by Shatha citizens, as required by Shatha constitutional law. The investment in Ban, accounted for by Dhia by the equity method, represents about 18 percent of the total assets of Dhia at December 31, 19X7, the close of the accounting period for both companies. The management of Dhia has determined that Ban's functional currency is the dollar.

Required:

a. What criteria should Dhia Products Company use in determining whether it would be appropriate to prepare consolidated financial statements with Ban, Ltd., for the year ended December 31, 19X7? Explain your answer.

b. Independent of your answer to (a), assume it has been appropriate for Dhia and Ban to prepare consolidated financial statements for each year 19X4 through 19X7. But before consolidated financial statements can be prepared, the individual account balances in Ban's December 31, 19X7, adjusted trial balance must be translated into the appropriate number of United States dollars. For each of the 10 accounts listed below, taken from Ban's adjusted trial balance, specify what exchange rate (for example, average exchange rate for 19X7, current exchange rate at December 31, 19X7, etc.) should be used to translate the account balances into dollars and explain why that rate is appropriate. Number your answers to correspond with each account listed below.

1. Cash in Shatha National Bank.
2. Trade accounts receivable (all from 19X7 revenues).
3. Supplies inventory (all purchased during the last quarter of 19X7).
4. Land (purchased in 19X4).
5. Short-term note payable to Shatha National Bank.
6. Capital stock (no par or stated value and all issued in January 19X4).
7. Retained earnings, January 1, 19X7.
8. Sales revenue.
9. Depreciation expense (on buildings).
10. Salaries expense.

(AICPA adapted)

Exercise 14–3

Select the best answers for the following questions under each of the two alternative assumptions: (a) translation using the current rate method is appropriate, and (b) remeasurement using the temporal method is appropriate.

1. Certain balance sheet accounts of a foreign subsidiary of the Brown Company at December 31, 19X7 have been translated into United States dollars as follows:

| | Translated at | |
	Current Rates	Historical Rates
Marketable equity securities carried at cost......	$100,000	$110,000
Marketable equity securities carried at current market price	120,000	125,000
Inventories carried at cost.........	130,000	132,000
Inventories carried at net realizable value	80,000	84,000
	$430,000	$451,000

What amount should be shown in Brown's balance sheet at December 31, 19X7, as a result of the above information?

a. $430,000.
b. $436,000.
c. $442,000.
d. $451,000.

2. When translating an amount for fixed assets shown on the statement of financial position of a foreign subsidiary, the appropriate rate of translation is the—
   a. Current exchange rate.
   b. Average exchange rate for the current year.
   c. Historical exchange rate.
   d. Average exchange rate over the life of each fixed asset.

3. The year-end balance of accounts receivable on the books of a foreign subsidiary should be translated by the parent company for consolidation purposes at the—
   a. Historical rate.
   b. Current rate.
   c. Negotiated rate.
   d. Spot rate.

4. If a parent company bills all sales to a foreign subsidiary in terms of dollars and is to be repaid in the same number of dollars, the purchases account on the subsidiary's trial balance will be converted to U.S. dollars by using—
   a. The average exchange rate for the period.
   b. The exchange rate at the beginning of the period.
   c. The exchange rate at the end of the period.
   d. The amount showing in the parent's accounts for sales to the subsidiary.

5. United Company purchased with U.S. dollars all the outstanding common stock of Wilson Company, a Canadian corporation. At the date of purchase, a portion of the investment account was appropriately allocated to goodwill. One year later, after an exchange rate decrease (U.S. dollars have become more valuable), the goodwill should be shown in the consolidated balance sheet at what amount?
   a. An increased amount, less amortization.
   b. The same amount, less amortization.
   c. A lesser amount, less amortization.

    d. An increased or lesser amount depending on management policy, less amortization.

                                      (AICPA adapted)

Exercise 14–4

Select the best answers for the following questions under each of the two alternative assumptions: *(a)* translation using the current rate method is appropriate, and *(b)* remeasurement using the temporal method is appropriate.

1. Ben Company has a receivable from a foreign customer which is payable in the local currency of the foreign customer. On December 31, 19X6, this receivable was appropriately included in the accounts receivable section of Ben's balance sheet at $450,000. When the receivable was collected on January 4, 19X7, Ben converted the local currency of the foreign customer into $440,000. Ben also owns a foreign subsidiary in which exchange gains of $45,000 resulted as a consequence of translation in 19X7. What amount, if any, should be included as an exchange gain or loss in Ben's 19X7 consolidated income statement?

    a. $0.
    b. $10,000 exchange loss.
    c. $35,000 exchange gain.
    d. $45,000 exchange gain.

2. On January 1, 19X8, the James Company formed a foreign subsidiary. On February 15, 19X8, James' subsidiary purchased 100,000 local current units (LCU) of inventory. Twenty-five thousand LCU of the original inventory purchased on February 15, 19X8, made up the entire inventory on December 31, 19X8. The exchange rates were 2.2 LCU to $1 from January 1, 19X8, to June 30, 19X8, and 2 LCU to $1 from July 1, 19X8, to December 31, 19X8. The December 31, 19X8, inventory balance for James' foreign subsidiary should be translated into United States dollars of—

    a. $10,500.
    b. $11,364.
    c. $11,905.
    d. $12,500.

3. The Seed Company owns a foreign subsidiary with 2,400,000 local currency units (LCU) of property, plant, and equipment before accumulated depreciation at December 31, 19X8. Of this amount, 1,500,000 LCU were acquired in 19X6 when the rate of exchange was 1.5 LCU to $1, and 900,000 LCU were acquired in 19X7 when the rate of exchange was 1.6 LCU to $1. The rate of exchange in effect at December 31, 19X8, was 1.9 LCU to $1. The weighted average of exchange rates that were in effect during 19X8 was 1.8 LCU to $1. Assuming that the property, plant, and equipment are depreciated using the straight-line method over a 10-year period with no salvage value, how much depreciation expense relating to the foreign subsidiary's property, plant, and equipment should be charged in Seed's consolidated income statement for 19X8.

    a. $126,316.
    b. $133,333.

     c. $150,000.
     d. $156,250.

(AICPA adapted)

Exercise 14–5

Select the best answers for the following questions.

1. The balance in Davong Corporation's foreign exchange loss account from 19X1 transactions with foreign suppliers was $6,500 at December 31, 19X1, *before* any necessary year-end adjustment(s) relating to the following:

    (i)   Davong had a $10,000 translation loss resulting from the translation of the accounts of its wholly owned foreign subsidiary from its functional currency into dollars for the year ended December 31, 19X1.

    (ii)   Davong had an account payable to an unrelated foreign supplier payable in the local currency of the foreign supplier on January 12, 19X2. The U.S. dollar equivalent of the payable was $50,000 on the November 13, 19X1, invoice date, and it was $53,000 on December 31, 19X1.

    In Davong's 19X1 consolidated income statement, what amount should be included as foreign exchange loss?

    a. $19,500.
    b. $16,500.
    c. $9,500.
    d. $6,500.

2. A subsidiary's functional currency is the local currency, which has not experienced significant inflation. The appropriate exchange rate for translating the depreciation on plant assets in the income statement of the foreign subsidiary is the

    a.   Exit exchange rate.
    b.   Historical exchange rate.
    c.   Weighted average exchange rate over the economic life of each plant asset.
    d.   Weighted average exchange rate for the current year.

3. Losses resulting from the process of translating a foreign entity's financial statements from the functional currency, which is experiencing a 3 percent inflation rate, to U.S. dollars should be included as a(an)

    a.   Deferred charge.
    b.   Separate component of stockholders' equity.
    c.   Component of income from continuing operations.
    d.   Extraordinary item.

4. Tate Corporation had a $20,000 translation loss adjustment resulting from the translation of the accounts of its wholly owned foreign subsidiary from its functional currency into dollars for the year ended December 31, 19X5. Tate also had a receivable at the beginning of the year from a foreign customer, which was payable in the local currency of the foreign customer. On December 31, 19X4, this receivable for 100,000 local currency units (LCU) was appropriately included in Tate's balance sheet at $55,000. When the receivable was collected on February 10, 19X5, the exchange rate was 2 LCU to $1. In Tate's

19X5 consolidated income statement, what amount should be included as foreign exchange loss?

a. $0.

b. $5,000.

c. $20,000.

d. $25,000.

5. On January 1, 19X2, Norton Company established a wholly owned foreign subsidiary. The subsidiary purchased merchandise at a cost of 720,000 local currency units (LCU) on February 15, 19X2. The purchase price was equivalent to $180,000 on this date. The subsidiary's inventory at December 31, 19X2, consisted solely of merchandise purchased on February 15, 19X2, and amounted to 240,000 LCU. The exchange rate was 6 LCU to $1 on December 31, 19X2, and the average rate of exchange was 5 LCU to $1 for 19X2. Assume that the LCU is the functional currency of the subsidiary. In Norton's December 31, 19X2, consolidated balance sheet, the subsidiary's inventory balance of 240,000 LCU should be translated into U.S. dollars at

a. $40,000.

b. $48,000.

c. $60,000.

d. $84,000.

(AICPA adapted)

Exercise 14–6

FASB Statement 52 indicates that determination of a functional currency is a judgmental matter involving a number of guidelines. However, once management has selected a functional currency, this decision shall be consistently applied unless "significant changes in economic facts and circumstances indicate clearly that the functional currency has changed."

Explain the accounting implications if the functional currency changes (a) from a foreign currency to the reporting currency and (b) from the reporting currency to a foreign currency. (Hint: After considering these questions, you may wish to consult *FASB Statement 52.*)

Exercise 14–7

Inventory on hand at December 31, 19X1, has a cost of 10,000 local currency units (LCU). The inventory was acquired when the exchange rate was LCU 1 = $0.70. The lower of cost or market rule is used to value the inventory. For each of the following independent cases, calculate the dollar value that would be assigned to the inventory when it is remeasured into dollars under the *temporal method*.

	Case 1	Case 2	Case 3	Case 4
Replacement cost	LCU 11,000	LCU 11,000	LCU 9,000	LCU 9,000
Net realizable value	14,000	16,000	10,000	10,000
Net realizable value, less an allowance for normal profit margin	10,000	12,000	7,000	7,000
Exchange rate, 12/31/X1	$0.60	$0.50	$0.80	$0.75

Exercise 14–8

A U.S. company purchased a 100 percent interest in a subsidiary in Great Britain on January 1, 19X1, at a cost of 1,000,000 pounds sterling. The exchange rate on this date was $1.20. The functional currency of the newly acquired subsidiary was determined to be pounds sterling. For simplicity, we assume there was no differential.

In order to hedge against a continuing decline in the value of the pound relative to the U.S. dollar, the parent on January 1, 19X1, borrowed 1,500,000 pounds from a London bank. The pounds sterling denominated loan is designated a hedge, on an after-tax basis, of the net investment in the British subsidiary.

At December 31, 19X1, the exchange rate for the pound is $1.10, and the weighted average for 19X1 was $1.14. The subsidiary reported 19X1 net income of 200,000 pounds sterling. The parent does not record deferred taxes on the subsidiary's net income in accordance with *APB Opinion 23.*

The loan remained outstanding during all of 19X1. Therefore, the exchange gain or loss on the loan creates a timing difference for income tax allocation purposes. The U.S. parent's marginal income tax rate is 40 percent.

Required:

Prepare the entries that the U.S. parent would make on its books at December 31, 19X1, to record its equity in the subsidiary's 19X1 operations (including the translation gain or loss) and to adjust the balance of the loan payable for exchange rate fluctuations. Assume no prior entries have been made to the loan payable and ignore interest. Explain the reasons for your treatment of the exchange gains or losses. (Hint: It may be useful to review paragraphs 20–21, and the related paragraphs in the Basis for Conclusions, in *FASB Statement No. 52.*)

Problems

Problem 14–9

P Co. purchased all of the outstanding stock of its new foreign subsidiary, S Co., on January 1, 19X1, for $40,000. The exchange rate on that date between the dollar and S Co.'s local currency units (LCU) was LCU 1 = $0.40. S Co. had recorded net assets on that date of 70,000 LCU. The fair value of S Co.'s property, plant, and equipment (life of 5 years) was 10,000 LCU's greater than book value; the remainder of the differential was allocated to goodwill (life of 20 years). It is determined that S Co.'s functional currency is its local currency.

On December 31, 19X1, the exchange rate is LCU 1 = $0.45. The weighted average exchange rate for 19X1 was LCU 1 = $0.42.

Required:

a. Prepare a differential allocation and amortization schedule for 19X1 in both dollars and LCUs.
b. Prepare the entries that would be recorded by P Co. in 19X1 under the equity method with respect to the differential.

Problem 14–10

Mission Company is a foreign subsidiary of a U.S. parent. Mission's trial balances at the beginning and end of 19X1, in local currency units (LCU), are shown below:

	12/31/X1	1/1/X1
Cash.........................	300,000	300,000
Plant and equipment (net)	2,400,000	2,000,000
Depreciation expense............	200,000	
Other expenses	500,000	
	3,400,000	2,300,000
Current payables...............	50,000	150,000
Long-term debt	1,000,000	1,000,000
Capital stock..................	500,000	500,000
Retained earnings, 1/1/X1	650,000	650,000
Sales.........................	1,200,000	
	3,400,000	2,300,000

The following additional information is provided:

(1) Mission's functional currency is its local currency.
(2) The exchange rates between the dollar and the LCU for 19X1 were:
    January 1, 19X1—$0.30.
    Average for 19X1—$0.36.
    December 31, 19X1—$0.40.
    The exchange rate was $0.25 on the date that Mission was acquired by its U.S. parent, and there has been no change in Mission's capital structure since then. On December 31, 19X0, Mission's retained earnings had a credit balance of $175,000, and the cumulative translation adjustment had a credit balance of $45,000.
(3) There were no retirements of plant and equipment during 19X1.

Required:
a. Prepare a foreign currency translation working paper for Mission Co. for the year ended December 31, 19X1.
b. Prepare a statement of changes in financial position, *in dollars,* for Mission Co. for the year ended December 31, 19X1, with changes analyzed in terms of working capital. Disclose translation gains or losses on individual accounts in the statement. Make any additional inferences that are necessary.

Problem 14–11

This problem (and the following four problems) continue the data presented in the chapter for Monroe Co. and its French subsidiary, Bordeaux Co., to the year 19X2. *In solving these problems, you may on occasions need to refer to the text for 19X1 data.*

Bordeaux Co.'s trial balance at December 31, 19X2 follows:

	Francs
Cash and receivables............	1,600,000
Plant and equipment (net).......	1,300,000
Depreciation expense...........	300,000
Other expenses................	500,000
	3,700,000
Current payables	300,000
Long-term debt.................	900,000
Sales.........................	1,500,000
Capital stock	100,000
Retained earnings, 1/1...........	900,000
	3,700,000

The exchange rate between the dollar and the franc at December 31, 19X2, is $0.12, and the weighted average 19X2 rate was $0.105.

Assume for this problem that Bordeaux Co.'s *functional currency is the French franc.*

Required:

a. Prepare a foreign currency translation working paper for Bordeaux Co. for the year ended December 31, 19X2.

b. Prepare the entries that would be recorded by Monroe Co. in 19X2 under the equity method with respect to the conversion of Bordeaux Co.'s financial statements into dollars.

Problem 14–12

Use the information of Problem 14–11, *except* now assume that *Bordeaux Co.'s functional currency is the dollar.* For simplicity, assume that the newly acquired plant and equipment was purchased at the average rate for 19X2 and that Bordeaux Co. does *not* depreciate new equipment purchases in the year of acquisition. With these new assumptions, complete the requirements enumerated in Problem 14–11.

Problem 14–13

Using the information of Problem 14–11, *(a)* prepare the differential allocation and amortization schedule for 19X2, in francs and dollars, and *(b)* prepare the entries that would be recorded by Monroe Co. in 19X2 under the equity method with respect to the differential.

Problem 14–14

Using the information of Problem 14–11, prepare a statement of changes in financial position for Bordeaux Co. for the year ended December 31, 19X2, with changes analyzed in terms of working capital. Assume that the acquisition of new plant and equipment and the issuance of new debt occurred at the weighted average exchange rate for 19X2. Disclose the effect of translation gains and losses only in terms of the direct effect on working capital. Make any other inferences that are necessary.

Problem 14–15

Monroe Co.'s trial balance at December 31, 19X2 follows:

Investment in Bordeaux Co.	$259,200	
Capital stock		$150,000
Retained earnings, 1/1		47,300
Cumulative foreign exchange translation adjustments		6,250
Equity in subsidiary earnings		55,650
		$259,200

This trial balance is based on the determination that Bordeaux Co.'s functional currency is the French franc. The accounts reflect all required equity method entries for 19X2, including those related to translation effects. Note that we continue to assume that Monroe Co.'s only asset is its investment in Bordeaux Co. and that it has no liabilities.

Required:

Using the information in Problems 14–11 and 14–13, prepare a consolidated statement working paper for Monroe Co. and its subsidiary Bordeaux Co. for the year ended December 31, 19X2.

Problem 14–16

May Corporation, a Seattle firm, holds an 80 percent ownership interest in Seneque Co., a South African corporation. This interest was acquired when Seneque Co. was chartered. It has been determined that the dollar is the functional currency of Seneque Co.

Seneque Co.'s trial balance at December 31, 19X7, is presented below:

	Rands
Cash	60,000
Accounts receivable	100,000
Airplanes (net)	500,000
Depreciation expense	80,000
Other expenses	160,000
	900,000
Allowance for doubtful accounts	10,000
Notes payable	200,000
Capital stock	100,000
Retained earnings (1/1)	290,000
Revenue	300,000
	900,000

The capital stock was issued seven years ago when the company was formed to provide charter air service; at that time, the exchange rate was $0.80. The current fleet of airplanes was acquired three years ago when the exchange rate was $0.90; the notes were given to a local bank at the same time. Revenue and other expenses were realized uniformly over 19X7. The spot rates for rands in 19X7 were:

January 1	$0.57
Average for 19X7	0.53
December 31	0.50

Retained earnings in the December 31, 19X6, balance sheet (in dollars) of Seneque Co. amounted to $333,700.

Required:

a. Prepare a foreign currency translation working paper for Seneque Co. for the year ended December 31, 19X7.

b. Prepare the entries that would be recorded by May Corporation in 19X7 under the equity method with respect to the conversion of Seneque Co.'s financial statements into dollars.

Problem 14–17

Use the information of Problem 14–16, *except* now assume that (1) Seneque Co.'s *functional currency is the rand*, (2) the December 31, 19X6, retained earnings (in dollars) was $200,000, and (3) the December 31, 19X6, cumulative foreign exchange translation adjustments (in dollars) had a *debit* balance of $57,700. With these changes, complete the requirements enumerated in Problem 14–16.

Problem 14–18

Faison Importers, Inc., a Virginia firm, holds a 70 percent interest in Mommessin Corporation, a French company. The ownership interest was acquired when Mommessin Corporation was initially incorporated. It has been determined that the dollar is the functional currency of Mommessin Corporation.

The trial balance of Mommessin Corporation at December 31, 19X1, is as follows:

	Francs
Cash	40,000
Accounts receivable	20,000
Inventory	60,000
Plant and equipment (net)	100,000
Cost of sales	110,000
Depreciation expense	20,000
Expenses	50,000
	400,000
Notes payable	60,000
Capital stock	100,000
Retained earnings (1/1)	60,000
Sales	180,000
	400,000

The capital stock was issued and plant and equipment acquired four years ago when the exchange rate for the French franc was $0.30. Revenue and expenses were realized uniformly over 19X1, and the average exchange rate for 19X1 was $0.22. Retained earnings in the December 31, 19X0, balance sheet (in dollars) of Mommessin Corporation amounted to $15,200. The spot rate for the French franc at January 1, 19X1, was $0.23, and at December 31, 19X1, it was $0.20.

Inventory of 70,000 francs at the beginning of the year was acquired during the last quarter of 19X0 when the exchange rate was $0.23. Purchases of 100,000 francs were made uniformly over 19X1. The ending inventory was acquired during the fourth quarter of 19X1 when the average exchange rate was $0.21.

Required:
a. Prepare a foreign currency translation working paper for Mommessin Corporation for the year ended December 31, 19X1.
b. Prepare the entries that would be recorded by Faison Importers, Inc., in 19X1 under the equity method with respect to the conversion of Mommessin Corporation's financial statements into dollars.

Problem 14–19

Use the information of Problem 14–18, *except* now assume that (1) Mommessin Corporation's *functional currency is the franc*, (2) the December 31, 19X0, retained earnings (in dollars) was $25,000, and (3) the December 31, 19X0, cumulative foreign exchange translation adjustments (in dollars) had a *debit* balance of $18,200. With these changes, complete the requirements enumerated in Problem 14–18.

Problem 14–20

Carter Company, an Atlanta-based firm, purchased 100 percent of the outstanding capital stock of Fritz Corporation, a West German firm, on January 1, 19X2, for $380,000. The book and fair values of Fritz Corporation's assets and liabilities on this date are as follows (in marks):

	Marks	
	Book Value	*Fair Value*
Cash............................	100,000	100,000
Accounts receivable..............	150,000	150,000
Inventory	250,000	300,000
Plant and equipment (net).........	400,000	600,000
	900,000	1,150,000
Bank notes and bonds payable	300,000	300,000
Net assets.......................	600,000	850,000
Composed of:		
Capital stock	100,000	
Retained earnings..............	500,000	
	600,000	

The inventory is sold uniformly over 19X2 with none left at the end of the year. The plant and equipment has a remaining life of 10 years, and any goodwill arising from the acquisition should be amortized over 20 years.

The exchange rate between the dollar and the mark was $0.40 on January 1, 19X2, $0.35 on December 31, 19X2, and the weighted average for 19X2 was $0.38.

Required:

a. Assuming that Fritz Corporation's functional currency is the dollar, prepare a differential allocation and amortization schedule that covers the life of the differential. Also, prepare the entry or entries that would be recorded by Carter Company in 19X2 under the equity method with respect to the differential.

b. Assuming that Fritz Corporation's functional currency is the mark, prepare a differential allocation and amortization schedule for 19X2 in both dollars and marks. Also, prepare the entry or entries that would be recorded by Carter Company in 19X2 under the equity method with respect to the differential.

Problem 14–21

The adjusted trial balances of the Dallas Company and its Dutch branch on December 31, 19X7, were as follows:

	Home Office (Dollars)		Branch (Guilders)	
Cash	$ 27,800		18,300	
Accounts receivable.......................	32,000		30,000	
Allowance for doubtful accounts		$ 400		300
Merchandise inventory (1/1)	24,000		9,000	
Plant and equipment......................	140,000		68,000	
Accumulated depreciation..................		25,000		12,000
Accounts payable.........................		20,000		7,000
Shipments from home office................			30,000	
Shipments to branch.......................		7,000		
Branch current	17,360			
Home office current.......................				76,000
Sales		100,000		78,000
Purchases................................	76,360		10,000	
Expenses	12,000		8,000	
Capital stock		150,000		
Retained earnings		27,120		
	$329,520	$329,520	173,300	173,300
Merchandise inventory (12/31)	$18,000		10,000	

The plant and equipment carried on the books of the branch were acquired in Dutch markets in 19X1 when the exchange rate was $0.26.

The branch inventory on January 1 included 7,000 guilders of merchandise received from the home office, which was billed at the home office cost of $1,470; the remainder was acquired from local suppliers in Holland when the exchange rate was $0.23. All shipments to the branch during 19X7 were billed at cost.

The December 31 branch inventory consisted of 5,500 guilders of merchandise acquired by current shipment from the home office; the home office cost of this merchandise is $1,250. All other merchandise was purchased locally *throughout the year*. Annual adjustments for depreciation (5 percent annual rate) and doubtful accounts (1 percent of receivable balance) have been made.

Exchange rates are as follows:

January 1, 19X7............	$0.23
December 31, 19X7.........	0.20
Average for 19X7	0.24

Branch operations are fully integrated with home office operations. As a consequence, it has been determined that the functional currency of the branch is the dollar.

Required:

a.   Prepare a foreign currency translation working paper to convert the branch trial balance to dollars.

b.   Journalize closing entries for the home office.

Accounting for Partnerships

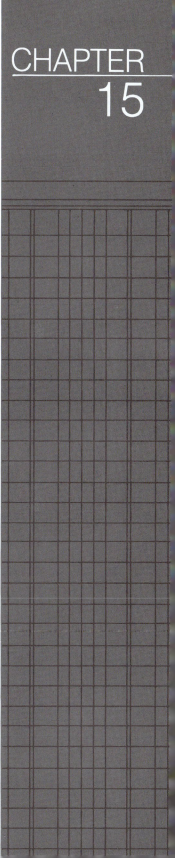

CHAPTER
15

Formation and Operation
of Partnerships

The partnership is a form of business affiliation involving two or more individuals associated in a joint profit-making endeavor. A number of problems peculiar to this type of organizational structure require unique accounting procedures for reporting on partnership operations and for disclosing the economic and legal equities of various interested parties in partnership assets. These accounting techniques will be the focus of attention in the following three chapters.

Nature of a Partnership

Although the common law originally provided the legal framework within which partnership operations were generally conducted, most states have now adopted the Uniform Partnership Act, or some variant thereof, as the controlling statutory authority. Emphasis will hereafter be directed toward relevant provisions of this Act which is reproduced in an Appendix to this chapter.

Aggregative versus Entity Concept

Section 6 of the Uniform Partnership Act defines a partnership as "an association of two or more persons to carry on as co-owners a business for profit."[1] This definition suggests an aggregative, or proprietary, concept of the partnership as the underlying legal philosophy. A partnership is perceived as being nothing more than an aggregation of the rights and responsibilities of the individual partners. Such a notion was fundamental to the structure of the common law and has been extended in the Uniform Partnership Act in the provision that the individual partners are jointly liable for all debts and obligations of the partnership (Section 15). Yet, the dominant theme of the Act nonetheless appears to rest upon a concept of the partnership as a legal entity, separate and distinct from the individual partners. This point of view is implicit in numerous provisions, among which are the following:

1. In the event of liquidation, partnership creditors have priority in respect to the assets of the partnership, and creditors of the individual partners are given priority in respect to the partners' personal assets (Section 40).
2. Title to partnership assets may be vested in the name of the partnership (Section 8).
3. A clear distinction is drawn between the partners' rights to partnership assets and their interests in the partnership (Sections 25 and 26).

---

[1] Section 2 defines the terms *person* and *business* as they are used in the definition of a partnership; Section 6 provides criteria for the legal determination of the *existence* of a partnership.

4. A continuity of partnership organization may exist under circumstances which formerly, under the common law, would have caused a dissolution of the partnership (see, for example, Section 23, continuation of the partnership beyond a fixed term, and Section 27, assignment of a partner's interest in the partnership).

Notwithstanding this evolving legal conception of the partnership organization, many current accounting practices continue to emphasize the aggregative aspects of the partnership. This is no doubt due in large measure to an inheritance of the proprietary emphasis from both accounting and law, and it derives additional support from current provisions of the Internal Revenue Code. The following two examples illustrate the basic proprietary emphasis of the Code:

1. When individual partners contribute assets to the partnership, the existing tax bases transfer to the partnership, regardless of market values existing at the time of the contribution.
2. The income tax is levied on the individual partners' shares of periodic net income of the partnership and is reported in their separate returns; it is not assessed on the net income of the partnership.

The existence of such tax legislation partially explains the continuing infusion of the aggregative notion in partnership accounting. It does not, however, provide strong theoretical justification for the practice.

Specific examples of the aggregative and entity concepts of the partnership will be referred to subsequently in this chapter.

Partnership Agreement

Before a particular organizational form is selected for a business activity, the interested parties should carefully analyze the advantages and disadvantages of alternative types of organizations—the corporation, general partnership, limited partnership, and so forth. If a general partnership is regarded as the best choice, the partners should proceed to agree on basic provisions within which they will operate—from initial formation, through operating routines and realignment of ownership interests, to eventual dissolution of the partnership. Appropriate attention to the details of these provisions at the time the partnership is initially formed will minimize or eliminate the subsequent emergence of possible inequities and legal uncertainties regarding the relationship between partners and their relations with outside parties.

The partnership agreement may be either a written or an oral contract. However, a formal, written agreement between the partners, often called the articles of partnership, or copartnership, is the best method of delineating the individual partners' rights and responsibilities. The importance of this agreement cannot be overemphasized. Although the Uniform Partnership Act imposes certain obligations upon the partnership that may not be avoided or overcome, such as joint liability for all partnership debts, most of the provisions of this act control *only* in the absence of an express agreement to the contrary between the partners. Indeed, judicial remedy is often based upon the court's interpretation of what the partners *intended*, when in fact the partners may not have anticipated a particular problem currently in dispute. Consequently, partners would be wise to seek the counsel of both an accountant and an attorney in formulating a comprehensive, *written* agreement indicating their intentions in various areas of partners' responsibilities and interests which if omitted or ambiguously drafted may subsequently cause dispute and possibly litigation.

Important provisions in the articles of partnership, including the purpose of the partnership, management rights and authority, and causes of dissolution, should reflect clearly the partners' intentions in terms of prevailing legal doctrine. There are also a number of legally unregulated areas of mutual interest to the several partners that have significant accounting (and equity) implications. The accountant may offer valuable counsel in these areas. Among the more important accounting-related issues that should be resolved in the agreement are the following:

1. The assets that the partners initially are to contribute to the partnership and the monetary value to be ascribed thereto should be itemized.
2. A clear distinction should be drawn between the individual partners' initial interests in partnership capital and their interests in subsequent profits or losses. If the initial interest in capital is not consistent with a summation of the agreed-upon values for the contributed assets, the agreement should be specific in regard to the treatment of this difference. For example, if the partners insist upon an equal dollar interest in capital even though the valuations of their contributed assets are not equal, two different accounting solutions are possible: (*a*) either a bonus, or capital transfer, may be effected between the partners in order to equalize their capital credits; or (*b*) intangible assets, which may derive from unusual managerial ability or widespread customer appeal and which apparently are implicit in such an agreement, may be recognized in the accounts. Although the judgment of the partners should not be the principal criterion for recognizing intangible assets in the partnership books, an explicit indication in the partnership agreement of the purported existence of such intangibles does provide an initial argument for account recognition.
3. The basis for dividing partnership profits should be expressly stated. In the absence of a contrary agreement, Section 18 of the Uniform Partnership Act provides that the partners shall share equally in profits. If it is desired that individual partners be rewarded for their separate capital contributions and/or services to the partnership before

any residual profits are allocated according to a profit-sharing ratio, the basis or monetary value for each factor should be specified.

4. If contributed capital is to be a basis for allocating partnership profits, the agreement should normally be responsive to the following questions:

    a. Is the allocation to be based on initial capital contributions, or capital as adjusted by subsequent contributions, profits, and/or withdrawals?

    b. If the allocation is computed upon adjusted capital, is it to be based upon beginning, average, or ending capital balances for the year?

    c. In the event average or ending capital balances are used, what treatment should be accorded current withdrawals? In particular, if it is desired to distinguish between capital withdrawals and withdrawals in anticipation of the current period's profits, the basis for the distinction should be expressly stated. Moreover, where the distinction is made, the accounting treatment of amounts available for withdrawal but permitted to remain in the business must be established.

5. Section 18 of the Act further provides that losses are to be shared in the profit-sharing ratio. Thus, if it is desired to protect a partner, whose principal contribution is service, from incurring a disproportionate share of possible losses, special loss-sharing ratios should be indicated.

6. The bases for calculating the monetary equity of a withdrawing partner, either through retirement or death, should be outlined. A withdrawal may involve consideration of such factors as the possible revaluation of tangible assets and the recognition of implicit intangible asset values.

7. If net income and the partners' drawing accounts are to be closed to the capital accounts at the end of the accounting period, thereby increasing or decreasing the total contributed capital, this closing sequence should be indicated. Such a provision may be important in the event the partnership is dissolved and assets are distributed to the retiring partners.

Although this list of significant provisions is necessarily incomplete, it does indicate the *type* of accounting considerations that are important in a careful formulation of the partnership agreement.

Partnership Formation

Recording the Initial Contributions

The initial formation of a partnership presents relatively few difficult accounting problems. In the event that there exists a predecessor business, an election must be made as to whether its records are to be preserved; if not, new books must be opened. In the former case, only those entries necessary to record the contributions of partners not previously affiliated with the predecessor are required; in the latter case, all contributions must be entered in the new records. Based upon the provisions of the partnership agreement, the opening journal entries for the new partnership record the assets contributed and the liabilities assumed. The partners' respective dollar interests in the initial capital of the organization are entered as credits to their individual capital accounts. The following two cases illustrate typical accounting entries to open the books of a new partnership.

Case 1.   The partnership agreement of X and Y lists the following assets that are to constitute the resources of the new XY Partnership:

	Contributed by	
	X	Y
Cash	$10,000	$20,000
Merchandise		10,000
Building		30,000
Furniture and equipment	5,000	

The building is subject to a mortgage loan of $25,000, which is to be assumed by the partnership. The values represent the partners' best estimates of fair market values.

The journal entry to open the books of the partnership is as follows:

Cash	30,000	
Inventory	10,000	
Building	30,000	
Furniture and Equipment	5,000	
Mortgage Payable		25,000
X, Capital		15,000
Y, Capital		35,000

In this case, the partners' capital credits are based upon the fair market value of the net assets contributed by each partner.

Case 2.   Assume that in the previous illustration, the partnership agreement provided that the partners initially should have an equal interest in partnership capital (or partnership net assets).

Two accounting solutions are possible. If the partners wish to record only the tangible assets identified in the partnership agreement, the capital accounts are equalized by transferring capital equity from Y to X so that each partner receives a capital credit of $25,000 (one half of $50,000 net assets).

```
Cash .....................................................30,000
Inventory ................................................10,000
Building .................................................30,000
Furniture and Equipment...................................  5,000
    Mortgage Payable.......................................              25,000
    X, Capital.............................................              25,000
    Y, Capital.............................................              25,000
```

Accountants characterize this type of entry as one in which Y pays a "bonus" of $10,000 to X, in the form of the increased monetary equity in the recorded net assets of the firm. Why would Y agree to pay this "bonus"? Presumably Y believes that X brings some intangible economic value to the partnership in addition to the assets enumerated in the partnership agreement. Whether this additional value will be realized is uncertain at this time. Accordingly, the "bonus" method of equalizing the capital credits reflects a traditional accounting "wait and see" attitude toward alleged intangible assets.

Alternatively, we might regard the different values of contributed net assets as sufficiently strong evidence to justify recognition of an intangible asset contributed by X to the partnership. In the absence of any other information, this asset is presumed to be goodwill. Assigning a value of $20,000 to the goodwill acknowledges equal contributions of net assets by both X and Y. The entry under this alternative is:

```
Cash .....................................................30,000
Inventory ................................................10,000
Building .................................................30,000
Furniture and Equipment...................................  5,000
Goodwill (or some other intangible asset) ................20,000
    Mortgage Payable.......................................              25,000
    X, Capital.............................................              35,000
    Y, Capital.............................................              35,000
```

The net assets of the partnership under this alternative, often referred to as the "goodwill method," are $70,000, including $50,000 of net tangible assets and $20,000 of goodwill. More will be said about the bonus and goodwill methods in Chapter 16.

If the partners' future interests in partnership profits and losses are also to be equal, the choice of either method (bonus or goodwill) will produce no inequity in the relative monetary interest of the two partners, as they will share equally in the subsequent gain or loss, of whatever amount, on the realization of the intangible asset. However, recording the goodwill in the partnership books may have a significant effect on the balance sheet of the partnership. If the amount of such goodwill is material, adequate disclosure of the nature of this asset should be included in a partnership balance sheet prepared for the use of third parties.

The above examples refer to the source of new partnership assets in terms of the contributing partners. On occasions, one or more of the new partners may contribute the assets and liabilities of an existing business to the new partnership. In such a circumstance, it is important that the assets be appraised at the time the new partnership is formed. Existing book values of the contributed assets may be grossly inadequate as a measure of the relative capital investments of the partners in the new venture.

Income Tax Considerations

Although the problems in income tax accounting are not a principal concern of this text, certain *fundamental* income tax concepts are briefly considered within the context of partnership formation. Basically the Internal Revenue Code adopts the aggregative theory and treats the partnership as a conduit through which net income of the firm is allocated to the partners *as if* they had individually earned it. With this partnership conception, two value bases are particularly relevant to initial formation of the firm:

1.   The tax "basis" of the *assets* contributed to the partnership.
2.   The tax "basis" of the partners' dollar *interest* in the partnership.

No taxable gain or loss is assumed to result from the contribution of property to a partnership by an individual partner. Rather, the partnership adopts the same *asset* basis, or unamortized cost, for income tax purposes as applied to the individual partner in respect to the calculation of his personal tax liability. It is unlikely that this value will be equivalent to the fair market value of the asset at the date of contribution. Although the market valuation of contributed assets is an important determinant in computing the dollar interest of the partners in the capital of the new firm, the tax-basis valuation will necessarily modify the relative interests of the partners for income tax purposes.

The tax "basis" of a partner's *interest* in the firm is defined as *the sum of the bases of the individual assets he contributes to the firm, increased by any liabilities of other partners that he assumes, and decreased by his personal liabilities, if any, that are assumed by other partners.* Thus, the sum of the bases of the contributed assets is equal to the sum of the bases of the partners' separate interests in the partnership. It should be noted that partnership liabilities are excluded from this basic equation, as they are implicitly included in the bases of the partners' separate interests.

The following case illustrates these provisions.

Case 3. Using the data of Case 1 and assuming that the basis of the building to Y is $20,000, that other assets have a tax basis equal to their present market values, and that X agrees to accept joint liability for the mortgage on the building, the income tax implications of the initial formation may be reflected in the following schedule:

	Tax Bases of the Assets to the Partnership	Tax Bases of the Partners' Interests in the Partnership
Cash.................................	$30,000	
Merchandise.........................	10,000	
Building.............................	20,000	
Furniture and equipment	5,000	
Partner X's interest....................		$27,500
Partner Y's interest....................		37,500
Totals.........................	$65,000	$65,000

Note that the sum of the asset bases, $65,000, equals the sum of the bases of the partners' interests. The computation of the interests of X and Y is made as follows:

	X	Y
Bases of assets contributed:		
Cash..	$10,000	$ 20,000
Inventory.....................................		10,000
Building......................................		20,000
Furniture and equipment	5,000	
	$15,000	$ 50,000
Add: Liabilities assumed by X (½ of $25,000 mortgage)	12,500	
Deduct: Personal liability transferred to X...........		[12,500]
	$27,500	$ 37,500

The implications of the tax bases associated with the partnership formation are to reduce, *for tax purposes*, the depreciable cost of partnership assets by $10,000 and to alter the relative monetary interests of the individual partners. The ultimate effect of these changes will be reflected in the periodic determination of taxable net income for the partnership to be allocated to the individual partners, and in the computation of taxable gain or loss in the event one or both partners elect to dispose of their interests in the firm.

Partnership Operations

Accounting for the operations of a partnership is not essentially unlike accounting for other profit-oriented businesses. The primary operational objective of the accounting process continues to be the determination of periodic net income. To this end, a partnership is perceived as a separate and distinct accounting entity. Net income is calculated in the traditional manner, that is, by relating periodic revenues and expenses, with only the accounting treatment of salary payments to the partners and interest on capital investments subject to theoretical dispute.

The special problems of accounting for partnership operations are classified for discussion purposes as follows:

1. Establishing the nature and determining the amount of the relative interests of the partners in the firm.
2. Determining the proper allocation of partnership net income between the partners.
3. Preparing financial statements for the partnership: the balance sheet, income statement, and statement of partners' capital.

Nature and Amount of Relative Interests

The partners' interests in, and obligations to, the partnership may be dichotomized initially into (1) debtor-creditor relationships and (2) capital equities and/or deficiencies. In many cases, these divisions are essentially arbitrary in nature, but in light of generally accepted accounting practices, they may materially influence the financial statements of the partnership.
Debtor-Creditor Relationships.   If in addition to contributions to the capital of the firm, a partner advances money to the partnership in the form of a loan, with provision that it be repaid within a specified period of time, appropriate recognition of the separateness of the accounting entity and the nature of the transaction requires that such an advance be recorded as a partnership liability. Similarly, advances to individual partners, which are to be repaid subsequently to the partnership, are properly classified as partnership receivables. Interest expense and/or income generated by these explicitly conceived contractual obligations are normally included (subtracted or added) in the periodic computation of partnership net income. This treatment is consistent with the classification of the originating transaction as a business loan and with the acceptance of the separate entity status of the partnership.
Capital Equities and/or Deficiencies.   The total capital equity of the partnership is, of course, equal to the difference between partnership assets and liabilities. It is necessary, however, that the amount of each partner's capital credit in the firm be independently calculated and recorded. Normally, two accounts are maintained for each partner: (1) a drawing, or personal, account; and (2) a capital account. The drawing account is debited with the partner's withdrawals of cash or other assets during the period, and is credited with his equity in partnership net income. The capital account, as previously mentioned, initially reflects the dollar investment of each partner at the date of formation of the partnership. Subsequently, additional investments or withdrawals that are believed to be relatively

permanent in character are entered in the account. If the partners should so elect, the balance of the drawing account may be periodically transferred to the capital account. As will be discussed later, it is possible that a more informative statement of financial position may result from segregating capital transactions from those that summarize profits. Where the transactions are thus separated, the closing of the drawing accounts to capital accounts may prove undesirable.

Conventionally, interest credits on capital equities are not accounted for as partnership expenses. Interest credits on partners' loans, however, are deducted as a determinant of partnership net income. Thus, the objectivity of net income determination is at least partially compromised if the partners, at their discretion, can control whether additional equity shall be provided by partners' loans or accumulated profits. However, in this connection, a subtlety often overlooked relates to the implicit interest on "excessive" capital contributions. In the absence of a contrary agreement, Section 18(c) of the Uniform Partnership Act provides that a partner, who in aid of the partnership makes any payment or advance beyond the amount of capital that he agreed to contribute, shall be paid interest from the date of the payment or advance. An extension of this argument implies that from a legal point of view, profit accumulations of the partnership *may* be the basis of interest payments to individual partners. In point of fact, little substantive difference exists between accumulated profits and loans to the partnership. It would appear that the accounting problem is eliminated only where there is a complete acceptance of the proprietary theory, wherein no expense or income may be generated in transactions with the owners, *or* by a complete acceptance of the entity theory, wherein the expense of total capital (creditors' and owners') is recognized.

Allocating Net Income to Partners

Some of the fundamental problems underlying the allocation of partnership net income were discussed earlier in terms of eliminating unnecessary ambiguity from the partnership agreement. Note that the allocation of net income to the partners involves recording the respective shares in the equity accounts of the partners. It does not involve distributions of cash or other assets from the partnership to the individual partners. The problem of agreeing on periodic withdrawals of assets by the partners is a separate matter, and partners may agree that some portion of each partner's allocated net income will be reinvested in the business and not withdrawn.

The three most commonly used bases for allocating partnership net income are:

1. Specified ratios.
2. Relative capital investments of the partners.
3. Service contributions of the partners.

Frequently, some weighted combination of these several bases is used to reward the partners.

Specified Ratios.   As noted before, the Uniform Partnership Act provides that in the absence of an explicit contrary agreement, profits are to be allocated equally (equal ratios) among the partners. If the partners prefer some other uniform basis of allocation, negotiated ratios may be specified in the partnership agreement.

Case 4.   Assume that X and Y agree to divide profits from their partnership operations in a ratio of 3 : 1, that is, 75 percent to X and 25 percent to Y. If net income for the year is $60,000, the following journal entry indicates the allocation of profits:

Income Summary.. 60,000		
X, Drawing (¾ × $60,000)....................................	45,000	
Y, Drawing (¼ × $60,000)....................................	15,000	

In the absence of this specific profit-sharing agreement, each partner would have received $30,000. In both cases, the allocation of profits is uniform. Each partner receives a predetermined percentage of profits, without regard to the magnitude of such profits.

Relative Capital Investments.   Because capital is an income-producing factor, it may be important to consider the partners' respective capital investments in allocating partnership net income. If partners are to be rewarded, in part at least, in proportion to the relative magnitudes of their investments of capital, it is imperative that there be an unequivocal statement in the partnership agreement concerning the computation of these capital balances. As indicated earlier, if average or ending capital balances are to be used, the treatment of withdrawals, or amounts available for withdrawal, may pose a problem.

The following data will be used in Cases 5 and 6 to illustrate alternative approaches to the allocation of net income when it is based upon the partners' relative capital investments.

X, Capital

2/1	10,000		1/1 Balance	50,000
			4/1	10,000
			8/1	20,000
			11/1	20,000

X, Drawing

1/1–12/1 ($1,000/month, per agreement)	12,000		

Y, Capital

4/1	5,000		1/1 Balance	25,000
7/1	10,000		9/1	15,000

Y, Drawing			
1/1–12/1 ($1,000/month, per agreement)	12,000		

Income Summary			
		12/31	50,000

It is assumed that withdrawals *in excess of* the $1,000 monthly allowance are to be accounted for as permanent reductions in capital; accordingly, they are entered as debits to the partners' capital accounts.

Case 5.   Interest on Beginning Capital Balances.   In this example, it is assumed that each partner is to receive a 6 percent return (interest) on capital investment, calculated in terms of the capital balances at the beginning of the year, with the remaining profit (or loss) to be distributed in a ratio of 4:6 to X and Y, respectively. Computation of the allocated partnership net income is as follows:

	X	Y	Total
Interest:			
6% × $50,000	$ 3,000		$ 3,000
6% × $25,000		$ 1,500	1,500
Remainder (in residual profit-sharing ratio):			
4/10 × $45,500................................	18,200		18,200
6/10 × $45,500................................		27,300	27,300
	$21,200	$28,800	$50,000

Case 6.   Interest on Average Capital Balances.   In this example, each partner is assumed to receive a 6 percent return (interest) on his *average* capital investment, utilizing the basis previously described for determining capital withdrawals. Since each partner withdrew the total amount allowable each month, no problem arises concerning amounts available for withdrawal but not actually withdrawn. After interest allowances, the residual profit element is again to be allocated in the ratio 4:6.

The first step in determining profit allocations is to calculate the average capital balance for each partner. This may be accomplished by weighting each new capital balance by the number of months (or other appropriate time interval) that the balance remains unchanged; by adding each of these products and dividing by the sum of weights, an average balance is determined. Calculation for the data in this example is made as follows:

	Capital Balance	Weighting Factor— Number of Months	Weighted Product
X's capital balance:			
January 1–February 1	$50,000	1	$ 50,000
February 1–April 1	40,000	2	80,000
April 1–August 1	50,000	4	200,000
August 1–November 1	70,000	3	210,000
November 1–December 31	90,000	2	180,000
		12	$720,000
Average capital balance ($720,000 ÷ 12)			$ 60,000
Y's capital balance:			
January 1–April 1	$25,000	3	$ 75,000
April 1–July 1	20,000	3	60,000
July 1–September 1	10,000	2	20,000
September 1–December 31	25,000	4	100,000
		12	$255,000
Average capital balance ($255,000 ÷ 12)			$ 21,250

Following the calculation of average capital balances, the several profit elements are allocated as follows:

	X	Y	Total
Interest:			
6% × $60,000	$ 3,600		$ 3,600
6% × $21,250		$ 1,275	1,275
Remainder (in residual profit-sharing ratio):			
4/10 × $45,125	18,050		18,050
6/10 × $45,125		27,075	27,075
	$21,650	$28,350	$50,000

The ending capital balances of the partners may also be used as a basis for interest allowances in net profit distribution. Or, alternatively, the total net profit for the accounting period may be allocated on the basis of relative capital investments. However, it is perhaps more usual for partnership agreements to specify that only a *reasonable* return should accrue from the investment of capital and that additional excess earnings of the partnership should be divided in some specified ratio to compensate the partners for the disproportionate contributions they make to the operation of the business. Furthermore, in determining the base to be used in computing the return on investments, the beginning or average capital balances are frequently preferred—the beginning balance because of the simplicity of calculation, or the average capital balance because it provides a more refined measurement of the actual capital available to the firm *during* the accounting period.

Services Rendered.   In order to reward the individual partners for their different service contributions to the operation of the partnership, salary allowances are often provided as an additional basis for allocating partnership net income. This basis, as in the case of interest allowances on capital investments, is frequently used in combination with negotiated ratios or other allocation bases. Where the partners contribute a disproportionate amount of time and talent to partnership activities, inclusion of a provision for salaries in the allocation basis may contribute to a more equitable distribution of the net income of the business.

Case 7.   Using the data of Case 6, with the additional provision that salaries of $6,000 and $12,000 are to be awarded to X and Y, respectively, the net profit is allocated as follows:

	X	Y	Total
Salary allowances.........	$6,000	$12,000	$18,000
Interest credits	3,600	1,275	4,875
Remainder:			
4/10 × $27,125..........	10,850		10,850
6/10 × $27,125..........		16,275	16,275
	$20,450	$29,550	$50,000

Normally, salary allowances to partners are accounted for as an *allocation* of net income rather than as a *determinant* of net income. This practice has no effect upon the ultimate capital accumulations of the various partners. However, it results in an amount of partnership net income that is in excess of that calculated for a corporation wherein salaries to officer-shareholders are subtracted as expenses even though the officer-shareholders may have a status comparable to that of partners in a partnership.

If the salary of an officer-stockholder of a closely held corporation is treated as an expense when it meets the test of reasonableness, why is not the salary of a partner similarly a factor in net income determination if it satisfies the same criterion? Oddly enough, the entity theory is adopted in accounting for one type of transaction between the partners and the firm (debtor-creditor relationships), while the proprietary theory is reflected in another type of transaction (salaries to partners) between the same parties. While little theoretical support can be marshalled for the traditional accounting distinction between corporate officers (expenses) and salaries of partners (allocations of income), it persists in current accounting practice. Because of this inconsistency, net income comparisons between partnerships and corporations often are not meaningful unless adjustments are made for salaries to partners.

Order of Distribution.   If the net income is insufficient to cover the prescribed allocations for salaries and/or interest on capital balances, two alternatives are available. First, the partners may elect that the allocation for salaries and interest on investment be made and that the earnings deficiency produced by these allocations be allocated in the residual profit- and loss-sharing ratio, or loss-sharing ratio if separate ratios exist. Second, a sequence of allocations may be specified, with the provision that at each stage available net income is to be allocated to the fullest extent possible. This necessarily requires that the relative ratio of the partners' earned salaries or interest on investment be used to allocate that amount of net income remaining after prior allocations, if any, that is insufficient to make a total allocation for a profit-sharing factor. Consider the following data:

	X	Y	Total
Earned salaries	$10,000	$5,000	$15,000
Earned interest	4,000	6,000	10,000

If X and Y agreed that available earnings are to be allocated first for salaries, then for interest on capital investment, and finally in the residual profit-sharing ratio, this second method yields the following types of allocations of earnings when there are insufficient profits to make total allocations for both salaries and interest:

	X	Y	Total
Case I (net income, $9,000):			
Salaries:			
X (10/15 × $9,000)	$ 6,000		$ 6,000
Y (5/15 × $9,000)		$3,000	3,000
	$ 6,000	$3,000	$ 9,000
Case II (net income, $20,000):			
Salaries	$10,000	$5,000	$15,000
Interest:			
X (4/10 × $5,000)	2,000		2,000
Y (6/10 × $5,000)		3,000	3,000
	$12,000	$8,000	$20,000

The net income would be allocated differently if the first method were employed, that is, salaries and interest would be first allocated, after which the resulting deficiency would be allocated.

   This situation reflects yet another instance requiring adequate forward planning in the formulation of the partnership agreement. In the absence of such an agreement, or where the agreement is silent as to the order of earnings allocation, the first method discussed is generally followed. It may be observed that this method implicitly treats the salaries and interest on capital investments as a partnership expense, and thus makes but one actual allocation of net (residual) income, viz, partnership net income after partners' salaries and interest on their investments.

Correction of Prior Years' Net Income. Accounting policy for prior period adjustments has undergone revision on numerous occasions. Presently, the FASB's definition of prior period adjustments is so narrow that they are practically precluded in all but a very few situations.[2] However, one must keep in mind that the pronouncements of the FASB are guided by objectives that might not apply in many partnership situations. Recently, the FASB enunciated its objectives for financial reporting. The first stated objective is that "financial reporting should provide information that is useful to present and potential investors and creditors and other users in making rational investment, credit, and similar decisions."[3] To the extent a general objective such as this implicitly guided previous pronouncements, they may be inappropriate for certain partnership accounting applications. More specifically, the objectives that underlie decisions on prior period adjustments are likely to be quite different than the one quoted above.

In partnership accounting, corrections of prior years' net income may have direct economic implications in terms of how the economic consequences of partnership operations are allocated between the partners. Regardless of the potential impact, if any, on future investment and credit decisions, partners are likely to be most interested in using accounting procedures that provide an equitable allocation of net incomes between the partners.

In some cases, the decision whether to treat an item as a prior period adjustment or as a part of current net income would have no impact on the allocation of net income between partners. This would be so if the identity of the partners is currently the same as in the year to which the adjustments or corrections relate and the profit- and loss-sharing ratios remain unchanged, with no special constraints on allocations of salaries and/or interest.

If these rather restrictive conditions are not fully satisfied, however, the accountant must examine more carefully a proposed correction or adjustment of prior years' net income. In determining whether specific items should be treated as prior period adjustments, the principles to be generally followed have been enunciated by the APB in *Opinion No. 9* and *Opinion No. 20* and by the FASB in *Statement No. 16*. But, where the income allocation between partners is directly affected by the prior period adjust-

---

[2] *FASB Statement No. 16*, pars. 10–14. For a more complete discussion of prior period adjustment criteria, see Glenn A. Welsch, Charles T. Zlatkovich, and Walter T. Harrison, *Intermediate Accounting*, 6th ed. (Homewood, Ill.: Richard D. Irwin, 1982).

[3] *FASB, Statement of Financial Accounting Concepts No. 1*, "Objectives of Financial Reporting by Business Enterprises" (Stamford, Conn., 1978), par. 34.

ment decisions, the agreed-upon will of the partners should dominate over the pronouncements of the APB, FASB, or other rule-making bodies. For example, partners may feel that a material bad debt that was not adequately allowed for during the period of sale should be treated as a prior period adjustment, notwithstanding the APB and FASB conclusions to the contrary.

The accountant may often be called upon to provide consultation as to the appropriate treatment of items that are potentially prior period adjustments. Although the APB and FASB pronouncements may be relied upon as an expression of norms, consideration should be given to three basic alternatives:

1. The amount of the adjustment is minor. In this circumstance, the adjustment may be absorbed in the current period's net income without material effect on the partners' capital balances.
2. The adjustment is material in amount but is not easily identified with a specific period or periods. An example of such an adjustment may be a correction of the allowance for uncollectible accounts. In this case, the gain or loss resulting from over- or underallowances in prior periods may be absorbed in the current period, or an arbitrary allocation to prior periods may be made, depending upon the decision of the partners.
3. The adjustment is material in amount and is identifiable with specific accounting periods. This condition may exist where clerical or bookkeeping errors are discovered. In this type of circumstance, equity would seem to call for a recomputation of the allocations of adjusted net incomes for the affected periods.

Of course, corrections or prior periods' net incomes may not be the only, nor the most significant, adjustments that affect an equitable allocation of partnership net income. The existence of material, extraordinary or nonrecurring gains or losses raises the question as to the specific period or periods to which they properly relate. Where this problem exists, the traditional realization criterion should be applied until further refinements in accounting methodology permit a more accurate determination of periodic net income.

Financial Statement Presentation

Income Statement. As previously indicated, accounting practice conventionally regards interest on partners' loans as a partnership expense, while it excludes partners' salaries and interest on capital as factors in profit determination. The exclusions are normally cited in an appendage to the income statement, which contains the allocation of the net income elements. The following income statement follows the traditional format:

XY PARTNERSHIP
Income Statement
For Year Ended December 31, 19X1

Sales		$100,000
Cost of goods sold......................		60,000
Gross profit............................		$ 40,000
Operating expenses:		
Interest on partners' loans..............	$ 1,000	
Other expenses........................	19,000	20,000
Net income		$ 20,000

Allocated as follows:

	X	Y	Total
Partners' salaries	$ 8,000	$4,000	$12,000
Interest on capital	–0–	2,000	2,000
Remainder equally.............	3,000	3,000	6,000
	$11,000	$9,000	$20,000

If the position is taken that partners' salaries are "reasonable compensation for services rendered," consistent reporting would require disclosure of the $12,000 as an operating expense, with a corresponding reduction of net income to $8,000.

Statement of Partners' Capital.   Just as changes in corporate retained earnings are reported separately in a statement of retained earnings, so are the changes in the partners' equity reported separately in a statement of partners' capital. This statement typically assumes the following form:

XY PARTNERSHIP
Statement of Partner's Capital
For Year Ended December 31, 19X1

	X	Y	Total
Capital, January 1	$10,000	$20,000	$30,000
Net income for the year.........	11,000	9,000	20,000
	$21,000	$29,000	$50,000
Withdrawals	12,000	10,000	22,000
Capital, December 31	$ 9,000	$19,000	$28,000

Balance Sheet.   The usual partnership balance sheet reflects the proprietary concept in its equity section, as the capital accounts of the partners are separately disclosed. Following is an abbreviated example of this format:

XY PARTNERSHIP
Balance Sheet
December 31, 19X1

Assets		*Equities*		
Cash	$ 6,000	Current liabilities		$30,000
Accounts receivable	12,000	Loans payable		25,000
Inventory	20,000	Capital:		
Fixed assets (net)	40,000	X	$ 9,000	
Other assets	5,000	Y	19,000	28,000
Total assets	$83,000	Total equities		$83,000

Possibly, a more meaningful disclosure may result if the equity section were divided into capital and accumulated profits divisions. In addition to the fact that Section 40 of the Uniform Partnership Act makes such a distinction, albeit a vague one, between partners' capital and accumulated partnership profits, potentially useful information respecting the financial management of the business is provided if this distinction is maintained in the balance sheet. Also, for credit purposes, the balances of the individual partners' accounts are relatively unimportant, as the partners remain jointly liable for partnership obligations, settlement to be made from their personal assets should this be necessary. Additionally, the information relating to the individual partners' equities in the business is reported in detail in the statement of partners' capital.

Questions

1. What is the essential nature of a partnership? What distinguishes it from other forms of business organization?

2. Enumerate five important provisions that should be explicitly considered in the partnership agreement.

3. The partnership agreement of the ABC partnership provides that "profits and losses shall be shared in the ratio of the partners' capital balances." Can you foresee any problems with the language of this profit-sharing arrangement? Should such an agreement be in writing to have full legal effect on the parties?

4. How is the tax "basis" of a partner's interest in the partnership defined? Is this concept different from the tax basis of the assets a partner contributes?

5. What are three commonly used bases for allocating partnership net income to the partners?

6. What is the justification for salary allowances in a partnership agreement? Why is interest on capital balances frequently included in a partnership agreement as a basis for profit distribution?

7. "The pronouncements of the APB and FASB may not always serve as appropriate guidelines for partnership accounting." Explain the basis for this statement.

8. If by agreement the partners wish to begin with equal interests in the partnership net assets yet do not contribute assets of equal value, what methods might be used to record the formation of the partnership?

9. What alternatives exist for correction of prior years' net income when (a) the amount of the adjustment is minor, (b) the adjustment is material in amount but is not easily identifiable with a specific period or periods, or (c) the adjustment is material in amount and is identifiable with specific accounting periods?

10. What advantages may derive from reporting partners' capital accounts on the balance sheet *divided between contributed capital and accumulated profits?* Does present practice more closely approximate the proprietary or entity concept of the partnership?

11. Explain why salaries to partners are typically accounted for as allocations of income rather than as expenses.

12. What advantage would result from reporting the salaries and interest paid on partners' capital balances as *expenses* on the income statement rather than recognizing them as earnings distributions?

Exercises

Exercise 15–1

Partnership contracts usually specify a profit and loss ratio. They may also provide for such additional profit- and loss-sharing features as salaries, bonuses, and interest allowances on invested capital.

Required:

a. What is the objective of profit- and loss-sharing arrangements? Why may there be a need for features in addition to a simple profit and loss ratio? Discuss.

b. Discuss the arguments for recording salary and bonus allowances to partners as charges to operations.

c. What are the arguments against treating partnership salary and bonus allowances as expenses? Discuss.

d. In addition to its other profit- and loss-sharing features, a partnership agreement may state that "interest is to be allowed on invested capital." List the additional provisions that should be included in the partnership agreement so that "interest to be allowed on invested capital" can be computed.

(AICPA adapted)

Exercise 15–2

For each of the following, select the one best answer that either completes the sentence or answers the question.

1. Which of the following statements concerning partnerships is true?

    a. A dominant theme in the Uniform Partnership Act is that a partnership is a legal entity, separate and distinct from the individual partners.

    b. Individual partners are jointly liable for the debts and obligations of a partnership.

    c. Income tax is levied on the individual partners' shares of the net income of a partnership and is reported in their personal tax returns.

    d. In the event of liquidation, partnership creditors generally have priority in respect to the assets of the partnership and separate creditors in respect to the personal assets of the partners.

    e. All of the above are true.

2. For income tax purposes, the tax basis of a partner's interest in a partnership is generally equal to—

    a. The fair market values of the assets at date of contribution.

    b. The unamortized cost of the assets to the partner.

    c. The sum of the fair market values of the assets the partner contributes to the firm, increased by any liabilities of other partners which he assumes, and decreased by any of his personal liabilities that are assumed by other partners.

    d. The sum of the bases of the individual assets the partner contributes to the firm, decreased by his share of partnership liabilities.

    e. The sum of the bases of the assets the partner contributes, increased by any liabilities of other partners that he assumes, and decreased by any of his personal liabilities that are assumed by other partners.

3. Which of the following statements about partnership accounts is true?

    a. Two accounts are generally maintained for each partner, a drawing account and a capital account.

    b. The drawing account is credited with the partner's withdrawals of cash or other assets during the period.

    c. The drawing account is credited with the partner's equity in the final allocation of net income.

    d. Answers a and c are correct but b is false.

    e. Answers a, b, and c are all correct.

4. Partners A and B agree that B is to receive a $10,000 salary from their partnership and remaining profits are to be divided in a 3:2 ratio. If net income for the year is $75,000, how will the allocation of profits be made?

    a. $32,500 to A and $42,500 to B.

    b. $39,000 to A and $36,000 to B.

    c. $26,000 to A and $49,000 to B.

    d. $45,000 to A and $30,000 to B.

    e. $37,500 to A and $37,500 to B.

5. In the absence of a partnership agreement, income is usually allocated to partners according to the following:

    a. Salaries, and the remainder by capital ratio.

    b. Interest on capital, salaries, and the remainder by capital ratio.

    c. By capital ratio.

    d. Salaries, interest on capital, and the remainder by capital ratio.

    e. Equal amounts of income to each partner.

Exercise 15–3

The partnership of Julie and Tim was formed on February 28, 19X1. At that date, the following assets were contributed:

	Julie	Tim
Cash	$35,000	$ 15,000
Merchandise		45,000
Building		100,000
Furniture and equipment	25,000	

The building is subject to a mortgage loan of $30,000 that is to be assumed by the partnership. The partnership agreement provides that Julie and Tim share profits or losses equally.

Required:
a. What are the capital balances of the partners on February 28, 19X1?
b. If the partnership agreement states that the initial capital balances of the partners should be equal and no recognition should be given to any intangible assets contributed, what are the partners' capital balances on February 28, 19X1?
c. Given the facts stated in requirement (b) except that any contributed goodwill should be recognized in the accounts, what are the partners' capital balances on February 28, 19X1? How much goodwill should be recognized?

(AICPA adapted)

Exercise 15–4

Smith and Jones are partners in the Smith Travel Agency. Their capital account balances on January 1, 19X1, are $40,000 and $20,000, respectively. They agree that partnership profits are to be distributed as follows:

	Smith	Jones
Salary	$3,000	$9,000
Interest on beginning capital balances	5%	5%
Bonus	25% of net income *after* salaries and bonus *but before* interest has been deducted	None
Residual profit or losses	70%	30%

Required:
Calculate the distribution of 19X1 partnership profits (identifying the profit elements separately) if the partnership net income before salaries, interest, and bonus is $60,000.

Exercise 15–5

Brad and Jeff joined in a partnership on January 1, 19X1. The partners share equally in profits, losses, and capital. Jeff contributed land valued at $10,000 that had a tax basis of $8,000. He also contributed a building valued at $130,000 that had a tax basis of $70,000. The partnership assumes a mortgage loan against the building and land in the amount of $40,000. Brad contributed $50,000 cash, and equipment valued at $50,000 that had a tax basis of $20,000. There was no goodwill contributed.

Required:

a. Prepare a general journal entry to record the formation of the partnership and the contributions of the partners.

b. Prepare a schedule showing the tax bases of the partnership's assets and the bases of the partners' interests in the partnership.

Exercise 15–6

Walker, Wayne, and Monroe are partners sharing profits and losses as follows:

Salaries:	
Walker	$ 9,000
Wayne..	6,000
Monroe..	4,000
Interest (6%) on the following average capital balances:	
Walker, capital	50,000
Wayne, capital	25,000
Monroe, capital...	40,000

Residual profits or losses are divided equally.

Required:

If the partnership net income for 19X1 is reported to be $13,000, indicate the distribution to each partner. Identify the profit and loss elements separately.

Exercise 15–7

Rogers and Horn share profits 3 : 4 after annual salary allowances of $17,000 and $18,000, respectively; however, if partnership net income is insufficient to make these distributions in full amount, net income shall be divided equally between the partners. In 19X1, the following errors were discovered:

1. Depreciation for 19X0 was understated by $4,200.
2. Inventory on December 31, 19X0, was overvalued by $22,800.

The partnership net income for 19X0 was reported to be $49,000.

Required:

Indicate the correcting entry or entries necessary upon discovery of these errors.

Exercise 15–8

A, B, and C are partners and share profits and losses as follows: Salaries of $20,000 to A; $15,000 to B; and none to C. If net income exceeds salaries, then a bonus is allocated to A. The bonus is 5 percent of net income after deducting salaries and the bonus. Residual profits or residual losses are allocated 10 percent to A, 20 percent to B, and 70 percent to C.

Required:

a. If net income before salaries and bonus is $70,000, how should it be allocated among the partners?

b. Suppose that after the allocation of requirement *(a)* was recorded and the books were closed, the partners discovered an error and that correction of the error would reduce net income from $70,000 to $30,000. The error involved understated depreciation expense. Present the journal entry to correct the accounts, and show any supporting calculations.

Exercise 15–9

Joe Conn developed an interesting idea for marketing sailboats in Death Valley. He interested Rob White in joining him in a partnership. Following is the information you have collected relative to their original contributions.

Rob contributed $30,000 cash, a tract of land, and delivery equipment. Joe contributed $60,000 cash. After giving special consideration to the tax bases of the assets contributed, the relative usefulness of the assets to the partnership versus the problems of finding buyers for the assets and contributing cash, and other such factors, the partners agreed that Joe's contribution was equal to 40 percent of the partnership's tangible assets, measured in terms of the fair value of the assets *to the partnership.* However, since the marketing idea originated with Joe, it was agreed that he should receive credit for 50 percent of the recorded capital. Recent sales of land similar to that contributed by Rob suggest a market value of $40,000. Likewise, recent sales of delivery equipment similar to that contributed by Rob suggest $40,000 as the market value of the equipment. These sales, of course, were not entirely representative of the particular assets contributed by Rob and therefore may be a better indicator of their *relative* values than their absolute values. In reflecting on their venture, the partners agree that it is a rather risky affair in respect to anticipated profits. Hopefully, however, they will be able to build good customer relations over the long run and establish a permanent business with an attractive long-run rate of return.

Required:

a. Journalize the partners' contributions under the most appropriate method, given the circumstances.

b. Journalize their contributions under another method, probably less appropriate.

c. State why you think method *(a)* is better than *(b)* in this situation.

Problems

Problem 15–10

Rankin and Bend organized the RB partnership on January 1, 19X1. The following entries were made in their capital accounts during 19X1:

	Debit	Credit	Balance
Rankin, capital:			
January 1		$20,000	$20,000
April 1................		5,000	25,000
October 1		5,000	30,000
Bend, capital:			
January 1		40,000	40,000
March 1	$10,000		30,000
September 1...........	10,000		20,000
November 1...........		10,000	30,000

Required:

If the partnership net income, computed without regard to salaries or interest, is $20,000 for 19X1, indicate its division between the partners under the following independent profit-sharing conditions:

a. Interest at 8 percent is allowed on average capital investments, and the remainder is divided equally.
b. A salary of $9,000 is to be credited to Bend; 8 percent interest is allowed each partner on his ending capital balance; residual profits or losses are divided 60 percent to Rankin and 40 percent to Bend.
c. Salaries are allowed Rankin and Bend in amounts of $8,300 and $9,500, respectively, and residual profits or residual losses are divided in the ratio of average capital balances.
d. A bonus of 20 percent of partnership net income is credited to Rankin, a salary of $5,000 is allowed to Bend, and residual profits or residual losses are shared equally. (The bonus and salary are regarded as "expenses" for purposes of calculating the amount of the bonus.)

Problem 15–11

Board and Huff organize the B & H partnership on January 1, 19X1, with capital contributions of $40,000 and $60,000, respectively. It is agreed that each will be allowed a salary credit of $4,000 annually plus an additional 5 percent credit for interest on the beginning-of-year capital balances. Residual profits are to be divided equally.

	Profits Before Interest and Salaries	Cash Withdrawals Board	Cash Withdrawals Huff
Year			
19X1..............	$20,000	$3,000	$10,500
19X2..............	17,325	4,500	6,250

Required:

a. Prepare a statement of partners' capital accounts for the two years ended December 31, 19X2.
b. Prepare closing entries as of December 31, 19X2.

Problem 15–12

A, B, and C have been partners throughout the year 19X1. The average balances for the year and their balances at the end of the year before closing the nominal accounts are as follows:

	Average Balances	Balances December 31, 19X1
A	Cr. $80,000	Cr. $60,000
B	Cr. 5,000	Dr. 4,000
C	Cr. 15,000	Cr. 19,000

The profit for 19X1 is $64,000 before charging partners' drawing allowances (salaries) and before interest on average balances at the agreed rate of 4 percent per annum. A is entitled to a drawing account credit of $10,000, B of $8,000, and C of $7,000 per annum. The balance of the profit is to be distributed at the rate of 60 percent to A, 30 percent to B, and 10 percent to C.

It is intended to distribute amounts of cash to the partners so that after credits and distributions as indicated in the preceding paragraph, the balances in the partners' accounts will be proportionate to their profit-sharing ratio. None of the partners is to pay in any money, but it is desired to distribute the lowest possible amount of cash.

Required:

Prepare a schedule of the partners' capital accounts, showing balances at the end of 19X1 before closing, the allocations of the net profit for 19X1, the cash distributed, and the closing balances.

(AICPA adapted)

Problem 15–13

The Don-Dave-Doug partnership was formed in 19X0. Don contributed a major portion of the capital, and Dave and Doug provided important management skills and experience. The partnership agreement specifies that the accounting records shall be maintained on the accrual basis and that the net income shall be distributed to the partners as follows:

1. Each partner shall receive 5 percent interest on the balance in his capital account at the beginning of the year.
2. Dave and Doug shall each receive a commission of 10 percent of net income determined under *cash basis* accounting after deducting the normal allowance for depreciation and the interest on capital. For this purpose, all merchandise purchased is to be regarded as an expense.
3. The net income remaining after deducting the interest on capital and commissions due to Dave and Doug shall be distributed equally, except that the total portion of net income to Don must not be less than 50 percent of the net income determined under the firm's accrual accounting system.

There were no changes in the partners' capital accounts during 19X1. The partnership comparative balance sheet follows.

DON-DAVE-DOUG PARTNERSHIP
Comparative Balance Sheet

	December 31, 19X0		December 31, 19X1	
Assets				
Cash		$ 7,000		$ 11,120
Accounts receivable—customers	$ 5,000		$ 6,000	
Allowance for doubtful accounts	200	4,800	120	5,880
Inventory		26,000		29,000
U.S. government bonds (at cost)				8,000
Fixed assets (at cost)	$120,000		$220,000	
Accumulated depreciation	40,300	79,700	46,300	173,700
Prepaid expenses		600		800
Total assets		$118,100		$228,500
Liabilities and Capital				
Accounts payable—trade..................		$ 6,200		$ 8,000
Accrued wages		5,500		5,000
Accrued taxes		500		500
Deferred income..........................		5,900		
Bonds payable............................				90,000
Net income, 19X1.........................				25,000
Partners' capitals:				
Don......................................	$ 80,000		$ 80,000	
Dave	15,000		15,000	
Doug....................................	5,000	100,000	5,000	100,000
Total liabilities and capital		$118,100		$228,500

Required:
Given the balance sheets above, prepare—

a. A schedule, supported by computational detail, showing the adjustments necessary to convert the net income for 19X1 from an accrual basis to a cash basis.
b. A statement, supported by computational detail, indicating the distribution of 19X1 net income to the partners.

(AICPA adapted)

Problem 15–14

Brown and Sharp, architectural designers and interior decorators, combined May 1, 19X1, agreeing to share profits: Brown, 80 percent; and Sharp, 20 percent. Brown contributed furniture and fixtures, $3,000, and cash, $2,000; Sharp contributed cash, $500.

They plan to submit monthly bills and make the following arrangements with their clients:

1. The salaries of draftsmen and shoppers, who are paid on an hourly basis, shall be billed to clients at an hourly rate for time spent on each job, plus 125 percent for overhead and profit and plus 4½ percent for payroll taxes.
2. Partners' time on jobs shall be billed at $10 an hour.
3. A 10 percent service fee shall be charged on purchases of furniture, drapes, and so forth, installed on the jobs. (Brown and Sharp will pay the vendors and charge their clients for these purchases but would like to have their operating statements reflect only revenue from services.)
4. There will be no service fee on taxis, telephone, and other expenses identifiable to jobs and charged to clients.

Voucher register totals for May are given below:

Credits

Vouchers payable	$3,469
Taxes withheld—federal income	93
Taxes withheld—FICA	27
Income from charges to jobs for partners' time	790
Total	$4,379

Debits

Purchases and expenses chargeable to clients	$1,615
Partners' drawings (Brown, $100; Sharp, $125)	225
General expenses	784
Jobs in process:	
Draftsmen's salaries	940
Partner's time	790
Petty cash fund	25
Total	$4,379

The first debit column in the voucher register is analyzed as follows:

Purchases subject to 10% fee:		
Client M, Job 51	$1,210	
Client H, Job 52	320	$1,530
Expenses chargeable to clients:		
Client M 51	$ 23	
Client M 54	7	
Client H 52	19	
Client L 53	36	85
		$1,615

The client has not yet authorized them to do Job M 54. The partners are confident, however, that the job will be authorized and the above expenses, as well as charges for time spent by Brown and a draftsman on preliminary designs, will be billed and collected.

The payroll analysis is summarized below. Partners' time on jobs, charged to the jobs at $5 an hour, is summarized in the payroll analysis for convenience in posting costs to job sheets, although the partners are not paid for direct time on jobs.

	Secretary	Draftsmen	Brown	Sharp
Job:				
M 51......................		$ 312	$120	$150
H 52......................		276	60	115
L 53		304	65	160
M 54......................		48	120	
		$ 940	$365	$425
General expenses:				
General office	$160	40		
Idle time..................		60		
Total payroll...........	$160	$1,040		

Journal entries recorded depreciation on furniture and fixtures of $25 and the employer's share of federal and state taxes of $54.

There were no cash receipts other than the original investment. The cash disbursements book shows the following totals:

Debit:	Vouchers payable.............	$2,373
Credit:	Cash	2,358
Credit:	Discount on purchases	15

Required:

a. Compute billings to clients for May.

b. Prepare a work sheet showing the balance sheet, profit and loss general ledger accounts, and the profit allocation at May 31, 19X1. Show how you arrive at these balances by entering all May transactions on the work sheet. Use the accounts indicated in the voucher register.

(AICPA adapted)

Problem 15–15

You are engaged to assist the B & M Footcover Company, a partnership, that was organized on January 2, 19X1, and has operated one year unsuccessfully. Barnes, who owns Boot Distributors Company, contributed $12,000 in inventory for a 50 percent interest in B & M Footcover Company. On the same date, January 2, 19X1, Monroe, who owns Dress Shoe Distributors Company, contributed $2,000 cash and $10,000 in inventory for a 50 percent interest. All profits and losses are shared equally.

While examining the records of B & M Footcover Company, you determine the following facts:

1. An incompetent part-time bookkeeper had discarded all cash register tapes and invoices for expenses and purchases. He also served as bookkeeper for the Dress Shoe Distributors Company.

2. The partners state that the only existing payables are to themselves and are as follows:

Boot Distributors Company	$ 7,500
Dress Shoe Distributors Company	4,500
	$12,000

3. You prepare the following summary of cash transactions from bank statements and canceled checks:

Cash balance, January 2, 19X1		$ 2,000
Receipts:		
Sales	$48,000	
Inventory liquidation...........................	6,000	54,000
		$56,000
Disbursements:		
Purchases.....................................	$26,000	
Operating expenses.............................	15,000	
Leasehold improvements (five-year lease)..........	6,000	
Liquidating expenses...........................	4,000	51,000
Cash balance, December 31, 19X1		$ 5,000

4. On December 31, 19X1, each partner was paid $2,500 in partial settlement of the $12,000 liability.
5. The partners indicate that the dollar amounts of regular sales of boots and dress shoe were approximately equal, and that the dollar amounts of liquidation sale of boots and dress shoes were also approximately equal. There was a uniform markup of 20 percent on cost of boots and 50 percent on cost of dress shoes. All sales were for cash. The ending inventory of merchandise was liquidated on December 31, 19X1, for 50 percent of the retail sales price.
6. The partners believe that some dress shoes may have been returned to Dress Shoe Distributors Company; there is no record of such returns, however, on the books of either company.

Required:
a. Estimate the unrecorded amount of dress shoes returned to Dress Shoe Distributors Company, if any.
b. Prepare an income statement for the partnership for 19X1.
c. Prepare a statement of changes in partners' capital accounts in 19X1.

(AICPA adapted)

Problem 15–16

Burns/Walker Company is a partnership that has not maintained adequate accounting records because it has been unable to employ a competent bookkeeper. The company sells hardware items to the retail trade and also wholesales to builders and contractors. As the company's CPA, you have been asked to prepare the company's financial statements as of June 30, 19X1.

Your working papers provide the following postclosing trial balance at December 31, 19X0:

BURNS/WALKER COMPANY
Postclosing Trial Balance
December 31, 19X0

Cash	$10,000	
Accounts receivable....................................	9,050	
Allowance for bad debts		$ 600
Merchandise inventory.................................	35,000	
Prepaid insurance	150	
Automobiles	8,200	
Allowance for depreciation—automobiles		4,250
Furniture and fixtures.................................	1,600	
Allowance for depreciation—furniture and fixtures		650
Accounts payable......................................		14,650
Bank loan payable		8,000
Accrued expenses		200
Burns, capital		17,500
Walker, capital		18,150
	$64,000	$64,000

You are able to collect the following information at June 30, 19X1.

a. Your analysis of cash transactions, derived from the company's bank statements and checkbook stubs, is as follows:

Deposits:	
Cash receipts from customers ($30,000 of this amount	
represents collections on receivables including	
redeposited protested checks totaling $600)	$48,700
Bank loan, 1/2/X1 (4/2/X1, 10% discounted).....................	7,800
Bank loan, 4/1/X1 (7/30/X1, 10% discounted)....................	8,700
Sale of old automobile	45
Total deposits	$65,245
Disbursements:	
Payments to merchandise creditors............................	$31,000
Payments to Internal Revenue Service on Walker's 19X1	
declaration of estimated income tax	3,000
General expenses..	7,000
Bank loan, 1/2/X1...	8,000
Bank loan, 4/2/X1...	8,000
Payment for new automobile	2,400
Protested checks..	700
Burns, withdrawals	5,000
Walker, withdrawals...	2,500
Total disbursements	$67,600

b. The protested checks include customers' checks totaling $600 that were rede-
posited and a $100 check from an employee that is still on hand.

c. Accounts receivable from customers for merchandise sales amount to $15,050 and include accounts totaling $800 that have been placed with an attorney for collection. Correspondence with the client's attorney reveals that one of the accounts for $175 is uncollectible. Experience indicates that 1 percent of credit sales will prove uncollectible.

d. On April 1, a used automobile was purchased. The list price of the automobile was $2,900, and $500 was allowed for the trade-in of an old automobile, even though the dealer stated that its condition was so poor that he did not want it. The client sold the old automobile, which cost $1,600 and was fully depreciated at December 31, 19X0, to an auto wrecker for $45. The old automobile was in use up to the date of its sale.

e. Depreciation is recorded by the straight-line method and is computed on acquisitions to the nearest full month. The estimated life for furniture and fixtures is 10 years and for automobiles is three years. (Salvage value is to be ignored in computing depreciation. No asset other than the car in item [d] was fully depreciated prior to June 30, 19X1.)

f. Other data as of June 30, 19X1, include the following:

Merchandise inventory	$32,000
Prepaid insurance	80
Accrued expenses	176

g. Accounts payable to merchandise vendors total $9,750. There is on hand a $800 credit memorandum from a merchandise vendor for returned merchandise; the company will apply the credit to July merchandise purchases. Neither the credit memorandum nor the return of the merchandise had been recorded on the books.

h. Profits and losses are divided equally between the partners.

Required:

Prepare a work sheet that provides on the accrual basis information regarding transactions for the six months ended June 30, 19X1, the results of the partnership operations for the period, and the financial position of the partnership at June 30, 19X1.

(AICPA adapted)

Problem 15–17

The Allen, Hamp, & Lamb Partnership engaged you to adjust its accounting records and convert them uniformly to the accrual basis in anticipation of admitting Dow as a new partner. Some accounts are on the accrual basis, and others are on the cash basis. The partnership's books were closed at December 31, 19X1, by the bookkeeper who prepared the general ledger trial balance that appears below:

ALLEN, HAMP & LAMB PARTNERSHIP
General Ledger Trial Balance
December 31, 19X1

Cash	$ 18,000	
Accounts receivable.........................	50,000	
Inventory	26,000	
Land	9,000	
Buildings	50,000	
Allowance for depreciation—buildings.........		$ 19,000
Equipment.................................	56,000	
Allowance for depreciation—equipment		6,000
Goodwill...................................	5,000	
Accounts payable............................		55,000
Allowance for future inventory losses		4,000
Allen, capital...............................		40,000
Hamp, capital		60,000
Lamb, capital...............................		30,000
	$214,000	$214,000

Your inquiries disclosed the following:

a. The partnership was organized on January 1, 19X0, with no provision in the partnership agreement for the distribution of partnership profits and losses. During 19X0, profits were distributed equally among the partners. The partnership agreement was amended effective January 1, 19X1, to provide for the following profit and loss ratio: Allen, 50 percent; Hamp, 25 percent; and Lamb, 25 percent. The amended partnership agreement also stated that the accounting records were to be maintained on the accrual basis and that any adjustments necessary for 19X0 should be allocated according to the 19X0 distribution of profits.

b. The following amounts were not recorded as prepayments or accruals:

	December 31	
	19X1	*19X0*
Prepaid insurance	$ 700	$ 800
Advances from customers	1,550	1,100
Accrued interest expense...........		450

The advances from customers were recorded as sales in the year the cash was received.

c. In 19X1, the partnership recorded a provision of $4,000 for anticipated declines in inventory prices. You convinced the partners that the provision was unnecessary and should be removed from the books.

d. The partnership charged equipment purchased for $8,000 on January 3, 19X1, to expense. This equipment has an estimated life of 10 years and an estimated salvage value of $1,000. The partnership depreciates its capitalized equipment under the income tax declining balance method at twice the straight-line depreciation rate.

e. The partners agreed to establish an allowance for doubtful accounts at 2 percent of current accounts receivable and 5 percent of past-due accounts. At December 31, 19X0, the partnership had $39,000 of accounts receivable, of which only $4,000 was past due. At December 31, 19X1, 12 percent of accounts receivable was past due, of which $4,000 represented sales made in 19X0 and was generally considered collectible. The partnership had written off uncollectible accounts in the year the accounts became worthless as follows:

	Account Written Off in—	
	19X1	*19X0*
19X1 accounts	$800	
19X0 accounts	700	$250

Required:

Prepare a work sheet showing the adjustments and the adjusted trial balance for the partnership on the accrual basis at December 31, 19X1. All adjustments affecting income should be made directly to partners' capital accounts. Number your adjusting entries. Supporting computations should be in good form.

(AICPA adapted)

Appendix: The Uniform Partnership Act

Part I: Preliminary Provisions

§1. Name of Act

This act may be cited as Uniform Partnership Act.

§2. Definition of Terms

In this act, "Court" includes every court and judge having jurisdiction in the case.

"Business" includes every trade, occupation, or profession.

"Person" includes individuals, partnerships, corporations, and other associations.

"Bankrupt" includes bankrupt under the Federal Bankruptcy Act or insolvent under any state insolvent act.

"Conveyance" includes every assignment, lease, mortgage, or encumbrance.

"Real property" includes land and any interest or estate in land.

§3. Interpretation of Knowledge and Notice

(1)   A person has "knowledge" of a fact within the meaning of this act not only when he has actual knowledge thereof, but also when he has knowledge of such other facts as in the circumstances shows bad faith.

(2)   A person has "notice" of a fact within the meaning of this act when the person who claims the benefit of the notice:

(a)   States the fact to such person, or

(b)   Delivers through the mail, or by other means of communication, a written statement of the fact to such person or to a proper person at his place of business or residence.

§4. Rules of Construction

(1)   The rule that statutes in derogation of the common law are to be strictly construed shall have no application to this act.

(2)   The law of estoppel shall apply under this act.

(3)   The law of agency shall apply under this act.

(4)   This act shall be so interpreted and construed as to effect its general purpose to make uniform the law of those states which enact it.

(5)   This act shall not be construed so as to impair the obligations of any contract existing when the act goes into effect, nor to affect any action or proceedings begun or right accrued before this act takes effect.

§5. Rules for Cases Not Provided for in This Act

In any case not provided for in this act the rules of law and equity, including the law merchant, shall govern.

Part II: Nature of Partnership

§6. Partnership Defined

(1)   A partnership is an association of two or more persons to carry on as co-owners a business for profit.

(2)   But any association formed under any other statute of this state, or any statute adopted by authority, other than the authority of this state, is not a partnership under this act, unless such association would have been a partnership in this state prior to the adoption of this act; but this act shall

apply to limited partnerships except in so far as the statutes relating to such partnerships are inconsistent herewith.

§7.   Rules for Determining the Existence of a Partnership

In determining whether a partnership exists, these rules shall apply:

(1)   Except as provided by section 16 persons who are not partners as to each other are not partners as to third persons.

(2)   Joint tenancy, tenancy in common, tenancy by the entireties, joint property, common property, or part ownership does not of itself establish a partnership, whether such co-owners do or do not share any profits made by the use of the property.

(3)   The sharing of gross returns does not of itself establish a partnership, whether or not the persons sharing them have a joint or common right or interest in any property from which the returns are derived.

(4)   The receipt by a person of a share of the profits of a business is prima facie evidence that he is a partner in the business, but no such inference shall be drawn if such profits were received in payment:

(a)   As a debt by installments or otherwise,

(b)   As wages of an employee or rent to a landlord,

(c)   As an annuity to a widow or representative of a deceased partner,

(d)   As interest on a loan, though the amount of payment vary with the profits of the business,

(e)   As the consideration for the sale of a good-will of a business or other property by installments or otherwise.

§8.   Partnership Property

(1)   All property originally brought into the partnership stock or subsequently acquired by purchase or otherwise, on account of the partnership, is partnership property.

(2)   Unless the contrary intention appears, property acquired with partnership funds is partnership property.

(3)   Any estate in real property may be acquired in the partnership name. Title so acquired can be conveyed only in the partnership name.

(4)   A conveyance to a partnership in the partnership name, though without words of inheritance, passes the entire estate of the grantor unless a contrary intent appears.

Part III: Relations of Partners to Persons Dealing with the Partnership

§9.   Partner Agent of Partnership as to Partnership Business

(1)   Every partner is an agent of the partnership for the purpose of its business, and the act of every partner, including the execution in the partnership name of any instrument, for apparently carrying on in the usual way the business of the partnership of which he is a member binds the partnership, unless the partner so acting has in fact no authority to act for the partnership in the particular matter, and the person with whom he is dealing has knowledge of the fact that he has no such authority.

(2)   An act of a partner which is not apparently for the carrying on of the business of the partnership in the usual way does not bind the partnership unless authorized by the other partners.

(3)   Unless authorized by the other partners or unless they have abandoned the business, one or more but less than all the partners have no authority to:

(a)   Assign the partnership property in trust for creditors or on the assignee's promise to pay the debts of the partnership,

(b)   Dispose of the good-will of the business,

(c)   Do any other act which would make it impossible to carry on the ordinary business of a partnership,

(d)   Confess a judgment,

(e)   Submit a partnership claim or liability to arbitration or reference.

(4)   No act of a partner in contravention of a restriction on authority shall bind the partnership to persons having knowledge of the restriction.

§10.   Conveyance of Real Property of the Partnership

(1)   Where title to real property is in the partnership name, any partner may convey title to such property by a conveyance executed in the partnership name; but the partnership may recover such property unless the partner's act binds the partnership under the provisions of paragraph (1) of section 9, or unless such property has been conveyed by the grantee or a person claiming through such grantee to a holder for value without knowledge that the partner, in making the conveyance, has exceeded his authority.

(2)   Where title to real property is in the name of the partnership, a conveyance executed by a partner, in his own name, passes the equitable interest of the partnership, provided the act is one within the authority of the partner under the provisions of paragraph (1) of section 9.

(3) Where title to real property is in the name of one or more but not all the partners, and the record does not disclose the right of the partnership, the partners in whose name the title stands may convey title to such property, but the partnership may recover such property if the partners' act does not bind the partnership under the provisions of paragraph (1) of section 9, unless the purchaser or his assignee, is a holder for value, without knowledge.

(4) Where the title to real property is in the name of one or more or all the partners, or in a third person in trust for the partnership, a conveyance executed by a partner in the partnership name, or in his own name, passes the equitable interest of the partnership, provided the act is one within the authority of the partner under the provisions of paragraph (1) of section 9.

(5) Where the title to real property is in the names of all the partners a conveyance executed by all the partners passes all their rights in such property.

§11. Partnership Bound by Admission of Partner

An admission or representation made by any partner concerning partnership affairs within the scope of his authority as conferred by this act is evidence against the partnership.

§12. Partnership Charged with Knowledge of or Notice to Partner

Notice to any partner of any matter relating to partnership affairs, and the knowledge of the partner acting in the particular matter, acquired while a partner or then present to his mind, and the knowledge of any other partner who reasonably could and should have communicated it to the acting partner, operate as notice to or knowledge of the partnership, except in the case of a fraud on the partnership committed by or with the consent of that partner.

§13. Partnership Bound by Partner's Wrongful Act

Where, by any wrongful act or omission of any partner acting in the ordinary course of the business of the partnership or with the authority of his co partners, loss or injury is caused to any person, not being a partner in the partnership, or any penalty is incurred, the partnership is liable therefor to the same extent as the partner so acting or omitting to act.

§14. Partnership Bound by Partner's Breach of Trust

The partnership is bound to make good the loss:

(a) Where one partner acting within the scope of his apparent authority receives money or property of a third person and misapplies it; and

(b)   Where the partnership in the course of its business receives money or property of a third person and the money or property so received is misapplied by any partner while it is in the custody of the partnership.

§15.   Nature of Partner's Liability

All partners are liable

(a)   Jointly and severally for everything chargeable to the partnership under sections 13 and 14.

(b)   Jointly for all other debts and obligations of the partnership; but any partner may enter into a separate obligation to perform a partnership contract.

§16.   Partner by Estoppel

(1)   When a person, by words spoken or written or by conduct, represents himself, or consents to another representing him to any one, as a partner in an existing partnership or with one or more persons not actual partners, he is liable to any such person to whom such representation has been made, who has, on the faith of such representation, given credit to the actual or apparent partnership, and if he has made such representation or consented to its being made in a public manner he is liable to such person, whether the representation has or has not been made or communicated to such person so giving credit by or with the knowledge of the apparent partner making the representation or consenting to its being made.

(a)   When a partnership liability results, he is liable as though he were an actual member of the partnership.

(b)   When no partnership liability results, he is liable jointly with the other persons, if any, so consenting to the contract or representation as to incur liability, otherwise separately.

(2)   When a person has been thus represented to be a partner in an existing partnership, or with one or more persons not actual partners, he is an agent of the persons consenting to such representation to bind them to the same extent and in the same manner as though he were a partner in fact, with respect to persons who rely upon the representation. Where all the members of the existing partnership consent to the representation, a partnership act or obligation results; but in all other cases it is the joint act or obligation of the person acting and the persons consenting to the representation.

§17.   Liability of Incoming Partner

A person admitted as a partner into an existing partnership is liable for all the obligations of the partnership arising before his admission as though he had been a partner when such obligations were incurred, except that this liability shall be satisfied only out of partnership property.

Part IV: Relations of Partners to One Another

§18. Rules Determining Rights and Duties of Partners

The rights and duties of the partners in relation to the partnership shall be determined, subject to any agreement between them, by the following rules:

(a) Each partner shall be repaid his contributions, whether by way of capital or advances to the partnership property and share equally in the profits and surplus remaining after all liabilities, including those to partners, are satisfied; and must contribute towards the losses, whether of capital or otherwise, sustained by the partnership according to his share in the profits.

(b) The partnership must indemnify every partner in respect of payments made and personal liabilities reasonably incurred by him in the ordinary and proper conduct of its business, or for the preservation of its business or property.

(c) A partner, who in aid of the partnership makes any payment or advance beyond the amount of capital which he agreed to contribute, shall be paid interest from the date of the payment or advance.

(d) A partner shall receive interest on the capital contributed by him only from the date when repayment should be made.

(e) All partners have equal rights in the management and conduct of the partnership business.

(f) No partner is entitled to remuneration for acting in the partnership business, except that a surviving partner is entitled to reasonable compensation for his services in winding up the partnership affairs.

(g) No person can become a member of a partnership without the consent of all the partners.

(h) Any difference arising as to ordinary matters connected with the partnership business may be decided by a majority of the partners; but no act in contravention of any agreement between the partners may be done rightfully without the consent of all the partners.

§19. Partnership Books

The partnership books shall be kept, subject to any agreement between the partners, at the principal place of business of the partnership, and every partner shall at all times have access to and may inspect and copy any of them.

§20. Duty of Partners to Render Information

Partners shall render on demand true and full information of all things affecting the partnership to any partner or the legal representative of any deceased partner or partner under legal disability.

§21. Partner Accountable as a Fiduciary

(1) Every partner must account to the partnership for any benefit, and hold as trustee for it any profits derived by him without the consent of the other partners from any transaction connected with the formation, conduct, or liquidation of the partnership or from any use by him of its property.

(2) This section applies also to the representatives of a deceased partner engaged in the liquidation of the affairs of the partnership as the personal representatives of the last surviving partner.

§22. Right to an Account

Any partner shall have the right to a formal account as to partnership affairs:

(a) If he is wrongfully excluded from the partnership business or possession of its property by his co-partners,

(b) If the right exists under the terms of any agreement,

(c) As provided by section 21,

(d) Whenever other circumstances render it just and reasonable.

§23. Continuation of Partnership beyond Fixed Term

(1) When a partnership for a fixed term or particular undertaking is continued after the termination of such term or particular undertaking without any express agreement, the rights and duties of the partners remain the same as they were at such termination, so far as is consistent with a partnership at will.

(2) A continuation of the business by the partners or such of them as habitually acted therein during the term, without any settlement or liquidation of the partnership affairs, is prima facie evidence of a continuation of the partnership.

Part V: Property Rights of a Partner

§24. Extent of Property Rights of a Partner

The property rights of a partner are (1) his rights in specific partnership property, (2) his interest in the partnership, and (3) his right to participate in the management.

§25. Nature of a Partner's Right in Specific Partnership Property

(1) A partner is co-owner with his partners of specific partnership property holding as a tenant in partnership.

(2)   The incidents of this tenancy are such that:

(a)   A partner, subject to the provisions of this act and to any agreement between the partners, has an equal right with his partners to possess specific partnership property for partnership purposes; but he has no right to possess such property for any other purpose without the consent of his partners.

(b)   A partner's right in specific partnership property is not assignable except in connection with the assignment of rights of all the partners in the same property.

(c)   A partner's right in specific partnership property is not subject to attachment or execution, except on a claim against the partnership. When partnership property is attached for a partnership debt the partners, or any of them, or the representatives of a deceased partner, cannot claim any right under the homestead or exemption laws.

(d)   On the death of a partner his right in specific partnership property vests in the surviving partner or partners, except where the deceased was the last surviving partner, when his right in such property vests in his legal representative. Such surviving partner or partners, or the legal representative of the last surviving partner, has no right to possess the partnership property for any but a partnership purpose.

(e)   A partner's right in specific partnership property is not subject to dower, courtesy, or allowances to widows, heirs, or next of kin.

§26.   Nature of Partner's Interest in the Partnership

A partner's interest in the partnership is his share of the profits and surplus, and the same is personal property.

§27.   Assignment of Partner's Interest

(1)   A conveyance by a partner of his interest in the partnership does not of itself dissolve the partnership, nor, as against the other partners in the absence of agreement, entitle the assignee, during the continuance of the partnership, to interfere in the management or administration of the partnership business or affairs, or to require any information or account of partnership transactions, or to inspect the partnership books; but it merely entitles the assignee to receive in accordance with his contract the profits to which the assigning partner would otherwise be entitled,

(2)   In case of a dissolution of the partnership, the assignee is entitled to receive his assignor's interest and may require an account from the date only of the last account agreed to by all the partners.

§28.   Partner's Interest Subject to Charging Order

(1)   On due application to a competent court by any judgment creditor of a partner, the court which entered the judgment, order, or decree, or any

other court, may charge the interest of the debtor partner with payment of the unsatisfied amount of such judgment debt with interest thereon; and may then or later appoint a receiver of his share of the profits, and of any other money due or to fall due to him in respect of the partnership, and make all other orders, directions, accounts and inquiries which the debtor partner might have made, or which the circumstances of the case may require.

(2)   The interest charged may be redeemed at any time before foreclosure, or in case of a sale being directed by the court may be purchased without thereby causing a dissolution:

(a)   With separate property, by any one or more of the partners, or

(b)   With partnership property, by any one or more of the partners with the consent of all the partners whose interests are not so charged or sold.

(3)   Nothing in this act shall be held to deprive a partner of his right, if any, under the exemption laws, as regards his interest in the partnership.

Part VI: Dissolution and Winding Up

§29.   Dissolution Defined

The dissolution of a partnership is the change in the relation of the partners caused by any partner ceasing to be associated in the carrying on as distinguished from the winding up of the business.

§30.   Partnership Not Terminated by Dissolution

On dissolution the partnership is not terminated, but continues until the winding up of partnership affairs is completed.

§31.   Causes of Dissolution

Dissolution is caused:

(1)   Without violation of the agreement between the partners,

(a)   By the termination of the definite term or particular undertaking specified in the agreement,

(b)   By the express will of any partner when no definite term or particular undertaking is specified,

(c)   By the express will of all the partners who have not assigned their interests or suffered them to be charged for their separate debts, either before or after the termination of any specified term or particular undertaking,

(d)   By the expulsion of any partner from the business bona fide in accordance with such a power conferred by the agreement between the partners;

(2)   In contravention of the agreement between the partners, where the circumstances do not permit a dissolution under any other provision of this section, by the express will of any partner at any time;

(3)   By any event which makes it unlawful for the business of the partnership to be carried on or for the members to carry it on in partnership;

(4)   By the death of any partner;

(5)   By the bankruptcy of any partner or the partnership;

(6)   By decree of court under section 32.

§32.   Dissolution by Decree of Court

(1)   On application by or for a partner the court shall decree a dissolution whenever:

(a)   A partner has been declared a lunatic in any judicial proceeding or is shown to be of unsound mind,

(b)   A partner becomes in any other way incapable of performing his part of the partnership contract,

(c)   A partner has been guilty of such conduct as tends to affect prejudicially the carrying on of the business.

(d)   A partner wilfully or persistently commits a breach of the partnership agreement, or otherwise so conducts himself in matters relating to the partnership business that it is not reasonably practicable to carry on the business in partnership with him,

(e)   The business of the partnership can only be carried on at a loss,

(f)   Other circumstances render a dissolution equitable.

(2)   On the application of the purchaser of a partner's interest under sections 28 or 29:

(a)   After the termination of the specified term or particular undertaking.

(b)   At any time if the partnership was a partnership at will when the interest was assigned or when the charging order was issued.

§33.   General Effect of Dissolution on Authority of Partner

Except so far as may be necessary to wind up partnership affairs or to complete transactions begun but not then finished, dissolution terminates all authority of any partner to act for the partnership,

(1)   With respect to the partners,

(a)   When the dissolution is not by the act, bankruptcy or death of a partner; or

(b)   When the dissolution is by such act, bankruptcy or death of a partner, in cases where section 34 so requires.

(2)   With respect to persons not partners, as declared in section 35.

§34. Right of Partner to Contribution from Co-partners after Dissolution

Where the dissolution is caused by the act, death or bankruptcy of a partner, each partner is liable to his co-partners for his share of any liability created by any partner acting for the partnership as if the partnership had not been dissolved unless

(a) The dissolution being by act of any partner, the partner acting for the partnership had knowledge of the dissolution, or

(b) The dissolution being by the death or bankruptcy of a partner, the partner acting for the partnership had knowledge or notice of the death or bankruptcy.

§35. Power of Partner to Bind Partnership to Third Persons after Dissolution

(1) After dissolution a partner can bind the partnership except as provided in paragraph (3)

(a) By any act appropriate for winding up partnership affairs or completing transactions unfinished at dissolution;

(b) By any transaction which would bind the partnership if dissolution had not taken place, provided the other party to the transaction

(I) Had extended credit to the partnership prior to dissolution and had no knowledge or notice of the dissolution; or

(II) Though he had not so extended credit, had nevertheless known of the partnership prior to dissolution, and having no knowledge or notice of dissolution, the fact of dissolution had not been advertised in a newspaper of general circulation in the place (or in each place if more than one) at which the partnership business was regularly carried on.

(2) The liability of a partner under paragraph (1b) shall be satisfied out of partnership assets alone when such partner had been prior to dissolution

(a) Unknown as a partner to the person with whom the contract is made; and

(b) So far unknown and inactive in partnership affairs that the business reputation of the partnership could not be said to have been in any degree due to his connection with it.

(3) The partnership is in no case bound by any act of a partner after dissolution

(a) Where the partnership is dissolved because it is unlawful to carry on the business, unless the act is appropriate for winding up partnership affairs; or

(b) Where the partner has become bankrupt; or

(c) Where the partner has no authority to wind up partnership affairs; except by a transaction with one who

(I)   Had extended credit to the partnership prior to dissolution and had no knowledge or notice of his want of authority; or

(II)   Had not extended credit to the partnership prior to dissolution, and, having no knowledge or notice of his want of authority, the fact of his want of authority has not been advertised in the manner provided for advertising the fact of dissolution in paragraph (1bII).

(4)   Nothing in this section shall affect the liability under section 16 of any person who after dissolution represents himself or consents to another representing him as a partner in a partnership engaged in carrying on business.

§36.   Effect of Dissolution on Partner's Existing Liability

(1)   The dissolution of the partnership does not of itself discharge the existing liability of any partner.

(2)   A partner is discharged from any existing liability upon dissolution of the partnership by an agreement to that effect between himself, the partnership creditor and the person or partnership continuing the business; and such agreement may be inferred from the course of dealing between the creditor having knowledge of the dissolution and the person or partnership continuing the business.

(3)   Where a person agrees to assume the existing obligations of a dissolved partnership, the partners whose obligations have been assumed shall be discharged from any liability to any creditor of the partnership who, knowing of the agreement, consents to a material alteration in the nature or time of payment of such obligations.

(4)   The individual property of a deceased partner shall be liable for all obligations of the partnership incurred while he was a partner but subject to the prior payment of his separate debts.

§37.   Right to Wind Up

Unless otherwise agreed the partners who have not wrongfully dissolved the partnership or the legal representative of the last surviving partner, not bankrupt, has the right to wind up the partnership affairs; provided, however, that any partner, his legal representative or his assignee, upon cause shown, may obtain winding up by the court.

§38.   Rights of Partners to Application of Partnership Property

(1)   When dissolution is caused in any way, except in contravention of the partnership agreement, each partner, as against his co-partners and all persons claiming through them in respect of their interests in the partner-

ship, unless otherwise agreed, may have the partnership property applied to discharge its liabilities, and the surplus applied to pay in cash the net amount owing to the respective partners. But if dissolution is caused by expulsion of a partner, bona fide under the partnership agreement and if the expelled partner is discharged from all partnership liabilities, either by payment or agreement under section 36(2), he shall receive in cash only the net amount due him from the partnership.

(2)   When dissolution is caused in contravention of the partnership agreement the rights of the partners shall be as follows:

(a)   Each partner who has not caused dissolution wrongfully shall have,

I.   All the rights specified in paragraph (1) of this section, and

II.   The right, as against each partner who has caused the dissolution wrongfully, to damages for breach of the agreement.

(b)   The partners who have not caused the dissolution wrongfully, if they all desire to continue the business in the same name, either by themselves or jointly with others, may do so, during the agreed term for the partnership and for that purpose may possess the partnership property, provided they secure the payment by bond approved by the court, or pay to any partner who has caused the dissolution wrongfully, the value of his interest in the partnership at the dissolution, less any damages recoverable under clause (2aII) of this section, and in like manner indemnify him against all present or future partnership liabilities.

(c)   A partner who has caused the dissolution wrongfully shall have:

I.   If the business is not continued under the provisions of paragraph (2b) all the rights of a partner under paragraph (1), subject to clause (2aII), of this section,

II.   If the business is continued under paragraph (2b) of this section the right as against his co-partners and all claiming through them in respect of their interests in the partnership, to have the value of his interest in the partnership, less any damages caused to his co-partners by the dissolution, ascertained and paid to him in cash, or the payment secured by bond approved by the court, and to be released from all existing liabilities of the partnership; but in ascertaining the value of the partner's interest the value of the good-will of the business shall not be considered.

§39.   Rights Where Partnership Is Dissolved for Fraud or Misrepresentation

Where a partnership contract is rescinded on the ground of the fraud or misrepresentation of one of the parties thereto, the party entitled to rescind is, without prejudice to any other right, entitled,

(a)   To a lien on, or a right of retention of, the surplus of the partnership property after satisfying the partnership liabilities to third persons for any sum of money paid by him for the purchase of an interest in the partnership and for any capital or advances contributed by him; and

(b) To stand, after all liabilities to third persons have been satisfied, in the place of the creditors of the partnership for any payments made by him in respect of the partnership liabilities; and

(c) To be indemnified by the person guilty of the fraud or making the representation against all debts and liabilities of the partnership.

§40. Rules for Distribution

In settling accounts between the partners after dissolution, the following rules shall be observed, subject to any agreement to the contrary:

(a) The assets of the partnership are:

I. The partnership property,

II. The contributions of the partners necessary for the payment of all the liabilities specified in clause (b) of this paragraph.

(b) The liabilities of the partnership shall rank in order of payment, as follows:

I. Those owing to creditors other than partners,

II. Those owing to partners other than for capital and profits,

III. Those owing to partners in respect of capital,

IV. Those owing to partners in respect of profits.

(c) The assets shall be applied in order of their declaration in clause (a) of this paragraph to the satisfaction of the liabilities.

(d) The partners shall contribute, as provided by section 18 (a) the amount necessary to satisfy the liabilities; but if any, but not all, of the partners are insolvent, or, not being subject to process, refuse to contribute, the other partners shall contribute their share of the liabilities, and, in the relative proportions in which they share the profits, the additional amount necessary to pay the liabilities.

(e) An assignee for the benefit of creditors or any person appointed by the court shall have the right to enforce the contributions specified in clause (d) of this paragraph.

(f) Any partner or his legal representative shall have the right to enforce the contributions specified in clause (d) of this paragraph, to the extent of the amount which he has paid in excess of his share of the liability.

(g) The individual property of a deceased partner shall be liable for the contributions specified in clause (d) of this paragraph.

(h) When partnership property and the individual properties of the partners are in possession of a court for distribution, partnership creditors shall have priority on partnership property and separate creditors on individual property, saving the rights of lien or secured creditors as heretofore.

(i) Where a partner has become bankrupt or his estate is insolvent the claims against his separate property shall rank in the following order:

I.   Those owing to separate creditors,

II.   Those owing to partnership creditors,

III.   Those owing to partners by way of contribution.

§41.   Liability of Persons Continuing the Business in Certain Cases

(1)   When any new partner is admitted into an existing partnership, or when any partner retires and assigns (or the representative of the deceased partner assigns) his rights in partnership property to two or more of the partners, or to one or more of the partners and one or more third persons, if the business is continued without liquidation of the partnership affairs, creditors of the first or dissolved partnership are also creditors of the partnership so continuing the business.

(2)   When all but one partner retire and assign (or the representative of a deceased partner assigns) their rights in partnership property to the remaining partner, who continues the business without liquidation of partnership affairs, either alone or with others, creditors of the dissolved partnership are also creditors of the person or partnership so continuing the business.

(3)   When any partner retires or dies and the business of the dissolved partnership is continued as set forth in paragraphs (1) and (2) of this section, with the consent of the retired partners or the representative of the deceased partner, but without any assignment of his right in partnership property, rights of creditors of the dissolved partnership and of the creditors of the person or partnership continuing the business shall be as if such assignment had been made.

(4)   When all the partners or their representatives assign their rights in partnership property to one or more third persons who promise to pay the debts and who continue the business of the dissolved partnership, creditors of the dissolved partnership are also creditors of the person or partnership continuing the business.

(5)   When any partner wrongfully causes a dissolution and the remaining partners continue the business under the provisions of section 38(2b), either alone or with others, and without liquidation of the partnership affairs, creditors of the dissolved partnership are also creditors of the person or partnership continuing the business.

(6)   When a partner is expelled and the remaining partners continue the business either alone or with others, without liquidation of the partnership affairs, creditors of the dissolved partnership are also creditors of the person or partnership continuing the business.

(7)   The liability of a third person becoming a partner in the partnership continuing the business, under this section, to the creditors of the dissolved partnership shall be satisfied out of partnership property only.

(8)   When the business of a partnership after dissolution is continued under any conditions set forth in this section the creditors of the dissolved partnership, as against the separate creditors of the retiring or deceased partner or the representative of the deceased partner, have a prior right to any claim of the retired partner or the representative of the deceased partner against the person or partnership continuing the business, on account of the retired or deceased partner's interest in the dissolved partnership or on account of any consideration promised for such interest or for his right in partnership property.

(9)   Nothing in this section shall be held to modify any right of creditors to set aside any assignment on the ground of fraud.

(10)   The use by the person or partnership continuing the business of the partnership name, or the name of a deceased partner as part thereof, shall not of itself make the individual property of the deceased partner liable for any debts contracted by such person or partnership.

§42.   Rights of Retiring or Estate of Deceased Partner When the Business Is Continued

When any partner retires or dies, and the business is continued under any of the conditions set forth in section 41(1, 2, 3, 5, 6), or section 38(2b) without any settlement of accounts as between him or his estate and the person or partnership continuing the business, unless otherwise agreed, he or his legal representative as against such persons or partnership may have the value of his interest at the date of dissolution ascertained, and shall receive as an ordinary creditor an amount equal to the value of his interest in the dissolved partnership with interest, or, at his option or at the option of his legal representative, in lieu of interest, the profits attributable to the use of his right in the property of the dissolved partnership; provided that the creditors of the dissolved partnership as against the separate creditors, or the representative of the retired or deceased partner, shall have priority on any claim arising under this section, as provided by section 41(8) of this act.

§43.   Accrual of Actions

The right to an account of his interest shall accrue to any partner, or his legal representative, as against the winding up partners or the surviving partners or the person or partnership continuing the business, at the date of dissolution, in the absence of any agreement to the contrary.

Part VII: Miscellaneous Provisions

§44.   When Act Takes Effect

This act shall take effect on the ....
day of .... one thousand nine hundred and ....

§45.   Legislation Repealed

All acts or parts of acts inconsistent with this act are hereby repealed.

CHAPTER
16

Realignment of
Ownership Structure

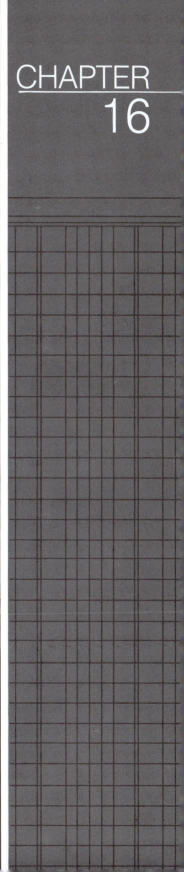

Introduction

Basic Legal Provisions

Under common law, any change in the ownership structure of a partnership resulted in its dissolution, although concurrently a new partnership was often formed. In many instances, the legal dissolution was not a reflection of an overt intention to interrupt the continuity of partnership operations. However, the existence of this common-law provision, together with numerous concepts concerning the nature of partnership dissolution, often created problems that disrupted and sometimes terminated the operations of the business. Problems often created by this legal dissolution include, among others, the determination of equitable settlements to the partners and the computation of their taxable net income. Provisions of the Uniform Partnership Act partially ameliorate the dangers of an unexpected dissolution by stating more precisely the nature of a dissolution, and also by reducing the number of conditions under which the partnership may be dissolved.

Section 29 of the Act defines *dissolution* of a partnership as "the change in the relation of the partners caused by any partner ceasing to be associated in the carrying on as distinguished from the winding up of the business." The following partial enumeration from Sections 31 and 32 indicates the various types of conditions that constitute a legal dissolution of a partnership:

1. By completion of a definite term of existence (or a particular undertaking) specified in the partnership agreement.
2. By the express will of any partner when no definite term of existence is specified in the agreement.
3. By the death of a partner.
4. By decree of a court for various reasons.
5. By the bankruptcy of any partner or the partnership.

It should be noted, however, that conveyance of an interest in the partnership does not of itself constitute a dissolution (Section 27), and although the admission or retirement of a partner by implication dissolves the partnership, according to Section 41 (1), this provision has little *functional* significance if the partnership is immediately reestablished without actually terminating its operations. Furthermore, various states have adapted for their own purposes certain provisions of the Uniform Partnership Act such that the partners are permitted to include in the articles of copartnership further restrictions on dissolution. For example, the Texas Uniform Partnership Act allows a provision to be included in the partnership agreement prescribing that the death of a partner is not a cause of dissolution. In view of this trend toward greater permanency in the partnership structure, the *legal* problems associated with ownership realignment need not be emphasized in the following discussion.

Types of Realignment

In order to facilitate a systematic review of the accounting problems involved in changes in the ownership structure, three general classes of realignment will be considered:

1. Admission of a new partner.
2. Retirement of a partner.
3. Death of a partner.

These classes are obviously not mutually exclusive. For example, a new partner may be admitted to an existing partnership by purchasing the interest of a retiring partner. Nonetheless, the above classes do provide a framework for analyzing most of the basic accounting problems associated with the realignment of ownership interests.

Admission of a New Partner

There are two principal bases upon which a new partner may be admitted to an existing partnership. Either the new partner may invest cash or other assets in the business so that the net assets of the partnership are increased by his contribution, or he may purchase an interest directly from one or more of the existing partners. In the latter case, the consideration merely passes between the partners, acting as individuals, and partnership net assets are usually not altered. The firm's potential need for additional resources is often an important determining factor as to the method elected to admit a new partner. For example, a deficiency in current working capital may be the compelling initial motivation for the admission of a new partner. Once the partners have selected a basis for admitting a new partner, his capital credit must be duly recorded, as well as any necessary adjustments to the capital accounts of the existing partners and/or the assets of the partnership.

Prior to the admission of a new partner, a careful analysis is generally required of the partnership's asset (and liability) values as well as of the asset values to be contributed by the new partner. In this analysis, three types of assets should be considered:

1. Existing assets, tangible and intangible, presently recorded in the books of the partnership should be appraised and their current market values established. Although the accountant may elect not to record appraisal increments, these values should nonetheless be considered

in analyzing the basis of the admission "price" to be paid by the new partner.

2. Unrecorded partnership assets, particularly intangible assets, may be inferred from a comparison of the price paid by the new partner for an interest in the partnership and the preexistent capital after adjustment for appraisal increments. Unrecorded assets may include identifiable items and also goodwill attributable to the existing partners.

3. The assets to be contributed by the new partner must be valued. In addition, a comparison of the admission price with the new partner's equity in identifiable assets may suggest that goodwill is being contributed by the new partner.

After this analysis has been completed, the appropriate capital account balance for each partner can be derived from the asset and liability values to be recorded.

Admission with Payment to the Partnership

The entries to record the admission of a new partner vary depending upon the results of the analysis described in the previous paragraph. A sequence of three cases will be used to illustrate alternative entries to record the admission of a new partner under varying fact conditions. In each case, the new partner contributes assets to the partnership in payment for being admitted as a partner.

Case 1.   Assume that X and Y are partners with capital balances of $7,000 and $3,000, respectively. The profit- and loss-sharing ratio is 60:40. Z invests tangible assets valued at $15,000 for a 50 percent interest in the capital of the partnership. Concurrently, an appraisal of existing partnership net assets reveals a current market valuation of $15,000.

An analysis of these data indicates that Z is investing $15,000 for a one-half interest in partnership net assets, which after the investment by Z have a total fair market value of $30,000. The data thus imply that unrecorded assets do not exist. However, the accountant must elect whether or not to record the appraisal increment for existing partnership assets. The alternative entries to record the admission of Z are as follows:

1. *Appraisal increment recorded:*

Assets	5,000	
X, Capital		3,000
Y, Capital		2,000
Assets	15,000	
Z, Capital		15,000

2. *Appraisal increment not recorded:*

Assets	15,000	
X, Capital (60% × $2,500)		1,500
Y, Capital (40% × $2,500)		1,000
Z, Capital		12,500

In the first entry, the existing assets are restated to reflect the results of the appraisal. The increment in the value of existing assets is precisely the amount necessary to explain the $30,000 total value of the partnership that is inferred from Z's purchase of a 50 percent interest for $15,000.

Recorded assets prior to Z's admission.............	$10,000
Value increment per appraisal....................	5,000
Assets contributed by Z	15,000
Total asset value after Z's admission.........	$30,000

Since the $30,000 value of identifiable assets fully explains the inferred total value of the partnership, the potential existence of goodwill is denied. Corresponding to the revaluation of assets, the capital accounts of the old partners are credited by an amount equal to the increment in asset values. The increment is allocated between the partners on the basis of their profit-sharing percentages. Note that under this alternative, Z's capital account is credited for the full $15,000 amount of his investment. One argument in favor of this method is that the capital credit in the full amount of the contribution has psychological appeal to the new partner.

In the second alternative, Z is merely given a 50 percent interest in the *recorded values* of the net assets (without appraisal increment adjustments) of the new partnership, and X and Y are awarded capital credits as consideration for Z's newly acquired, implicit interest in the difference between fair and book values of the partnership assets. In effect, X and Y transfer to Z $2,500 of their preexisting interests in these unrecorded values ($5,000 appraisal increment) when Z is given a 50 percent interest in partnership assets, and they are correspondingly rewarded in their capital accounts.

Hereafter, it will be assumed that the *recorded* assets of the firm are properly valued, or that an adjustment for current market values has previously been recorded in the old partners' capital accounts. Further analysis of each situation, however, may disclose the existence of *unrecorded* goodwill. Whether or not such goodwill should be recorded raises the same questions as did the discussion in Chapter 15 of recording the partners' original contributions to the partnership. Accordingly, the bonus and goodwill methods are also alternative accounting solutions to the admission of a new partner to the partnership.

Case 2.   X and Y are partners with capital balances of $40,000 and $10,000, respectively. Profits and losses are shared in the ratio of 80:20. Z invests tangible assets valued at $30,000 for a 25 percent interest in the capital of the new partnership.

Observe that Z has acquired a $20,000 (25 percent × $80,000) interest in the tangible net assets of the firm, inclusive of Z's contribution, at a cost of $30,000. Since it is assumed that all tangible assets are properly valued, Z is apparently paying $10,000 for a one-fourth interest in *unrecorded* intangible assets of the partnership. Conventionally, this type of intangible asset is described as partnership "goodwill." The amount of the goodwill can be determined by applying the following standard procedure:

1. Let C equal the total new capital of the firm, including the as yet undetermined goodwill, and solve the following two equations:
   a. (Fractional interest in capital retained by the old partners) $\times$ C = Total recorded capital balances of old partners.
   b. (Fractional interest in capital obtained by the new partner) $\times$ C = Investment of the new partner.
2. Determine the amount of implied goodwill by subtracting the total recorded net assets of the *new* firm (including the tangible assets contributed by the new partner) from the larger amount computed for C in (1) above. If *(a)* is larger, we infer that the new partner is contributing goodwill in addition to the assets identified in his investment; if *(b)* is larger, we conclude that the partnership possessed goodwill.

This procedure may be applied to the data of Case 2 in the following manner:

1. Computation of alternative capital balances:

   a. $.75(C) = \$50,000$
   $C = \$66,667$
   b. $.25(C) = \$30,000$
   $C = \$120,000$

2. Computation of goodwill:

$$\text{Goodwill} = \$120,000 - \$80,000$$
$$= \$40,000$$

To understand why the procedure works, consider the following. If the new partner's cost is larger than his interest in recorded assets (as in Case 2), he is paying for something (unrecorded goodwill) in addition to the recorded assets. Since the new partner is paying for it, by inference, the old partners already have generated the unrecorded goodwill. Hence, if goodwill is to be recorded, the old partners' capital accounts should be credited with their earned equity in the goodwill. Prior to making such adjustments, the old partners' capital accounts cannot be relied upon to calculate the total capital of the firm, including goodwill. Thus, equation *(a)* does not provide a reliable measure of the firm's total capital. But, since the new partner's cost reflects the value of his interest in the firm's total capital including goodwill generated by the old partners, equation *(b)* can be used to infer total capital.

The $40,000 valuation for goodwill may also be explained in different terms by reconsidering the details of the investment transaction. It was noted that Z paid $10,000 more than his acquired capital interest in the net tangible assets of the new firm. It is now evident that this $10,000 was a payment for a one-fourth interest in the unrecorded goodwill of $40,000.

The two alternative methods for recording the entry of the new partner into the partnership are:

1. *Bonus method:*

Assets 30,000		
X, Capital (⅘ × $10,000)	8,000	
Y, Capital (⅕ × $10,000)	2,000	
Z, Capital (¼ × $80,000)	20,000	

2. *Goodwill method:*

Goodwill. 40,000		
X, Capital (⅘ × $40,000)	32,000	
Y, Capital (⅕ × $40,000)	8,000	
Assets 30,000		
Z, Capital	30,000	

Regardless of which method is used, note that the resultant capital balances are in the agreed upon percentage relationship; that is, Z has a 25 percent interest while partners X and Y share a 75 percent interest.

	X	Y	Z	Total
Balances prior to Z's entry.	$40,000	$10,000	—	$ 50,000
1. Bonus method adjustments	8,000	2,000	$20,000	30,000
Resulting totals	$48,000	$12,000	$20,000	$ 80,000
Percentage of total	60%	15%	25%	100%
Balances prior to Z's entry.	$40,000	$10,000	—	$ 50,000
2. Goodwill method adjustments	32,000	8,000	$30,000	70,000
Resulting totals	$72,000	$18,000	$30,000	$120,000
Percentage of total	60%	15%	25%	100%

The equivalence of the two methods with respect to the relative equities of the partners is subject to certain constraints to be investigated at a later point.

These two methods are, in substance, identical with the alternative methods used in Case 1. In Case 2, however, the recorded tangible assets are assumed to be correctly valued. Thus, the accountant's decision relates to the propriety of recording implicit goodwill rather than of recording appraisal increments (or decrements). Generally, the evidence supporting the existence and amount of "goodwill" is less persuasive than that provided by an appraisal that indicates the market replacement values of tangible assets. Nevertheless, the desirability of giving the new partner credit for the full amount of the cost may outweigh the undesirability of recording a subjective valuation for goodwill.

Case 3. X and Y are partners with capital balances of $50,000 and $30,000, respectively. Except for possible goodwill, all assets are assumed to be recorded at their current values. Profits and losses are shared in the ratio of 70:30. Z invests tangible assets valued at $15,000 for a 20 percent interest in the capital of the new partnership.

In this instance, Z acquires an interest of $19,000 (⅕ × $95,000) in the net tangible assets of the firm at a cost of $15,000. By implication Z has contributed an additional, undeclared asset to the partnership for which he receives additional capital credit. The standard procedure may again be applied to estimate the amount of the implicit goodwill:

1. Computation of alternative capital balances:

    a. .80(C) = $80,000
               C = $100,000
    b. .20(C) = $15,000
               C = $75,000

2. Computation of goodwill:

$$\text{Goodwill} = \$100,000 - \$95,000 = \$5,000$$

Note that equation (a) is used to infer the total capital of the firm. Since the new partner is contributing goodwill in addition to tangible assets valued at $15,000, the $15,000 alone does not represent 20 percent of the firm's total capital; thus, equation (b) cannot be used. But, the summed capital accounts of the old partners should equal 80 percent of the firm's total capital, and equation (a) is appropriate.

In other words, the existing partners have acquired an 80 percent interest in the implicit goodwill contributed by Z when it accrues to the benefit of the partnership. For this interest, they have given to Z a $4,000 interest in partnership assets in excess of the tangible assets he contributed to the firm ($19,000 − $15,000). Therefore, the amount of the goodwill, as measured by the price imposed upon Z for his interest in net tangible assets, is $5,000 ($4,000 ÷ .80).

Either the goodwill or the bonus method may again be used to record this transaction:

1. *Bonus method:*

```
Assets ........................................ 15,000
X, Capital (70% × $4,000)......................  2,800
Y, Capital (30% × $4,000)......................  1,200
    Z, Capital (20% × $95,000)..........................  19,000
```

2. *Goodwill method:*

```
Assets ........................................ 15,000
Goodwill....................................... 5,000
    Z, Capital ...........................................  20,000
```

Recall that the agreed-upon terms for Z's entry were that Z was to receive a 20 percent interest in capital. Both methods are consistent with that agreement. Under the bonus method, the total recorded capital of the firm is $95,000 ($50,000 + $30,000 + $15,000), and Z's capital account is 20 percent of $95,000, or $19,000. Under the goodwill method, the firm's total recorded capital is $100,000 ($50,000 + $30,000 + $15,000 + $5,000), and Z's capital account is 20 percent of $100,000, or $20,000.

In the previous three cases, it may be observed that *the profit and loss ratios were used when allocating goodwill among the partners or when a bonus was allocated between the partners.* For example, if a bonus was given to the new partner, each of the old partners was charged for a portion of the bonus in accordance with his profit- and loss-sharing percentage. Similarly, when a bonus was given to the old partners, it was allocated between them on the basis of their profit and loss ratio.

Goodwill can be perceived as being the present value of future net income in excess of normal. If goodwill is not recognized, the future net income will be allocated in accordance with the profit-sharing ratio as the net income is realized. The decision to presently book the present value of that income does not alter the fact that it is income to the partners. Thus, it should be shared in accordance with the profit and loss ratio. In a similar manner, a bonus to the old partners increases their capital accounts in apparent reflection of their operating effectiveness. And, from the perspective of the old partners, the bonus has exactly the same impact as would additional partnership net income; thus, it is also shared in accordance with the profit and loss ratio. If the old partners are charged for a bonus that is given to the new partner, the bonus may be viewed as a cost that is incurred and charged to the old partners. From this perspective, it should be treated like an expense that is chargeable to the old partners.

We also observe that the recipient(s) of the bonus under the bonus method is the contributor(s) of the goodwill to the new partnership. In Case 2, X and Y contributed the goodwill (through the old partnership) and received the bonuses; in Case 3, Z contributed the goodwill and received the bonus. This relationship may be a useful check for the reader in properly identifying the contributor of the goodwill.

A Comparison of the Bonus and Goodwill Methods

Accounting problems of recording asset revaluations and/or implicit goodwill have been considered relative to the alternative *bonus* method of recording a new partner's admission with payment to the partnership. However, an understanding of the implications of selecting one method or the other requires further analysis of the conditions under which the two methods are ultimately equivalent in terms of their effects on the relative equities of the individual partners.

Assume that goodwill is recorded and subsequently proves to have been overstated. A condition of equivalence would require that after the write-down adjustment to eliminate the recorded goodwill (loss realization), the individual partners' capital accounts should be equivalent to those balances that would have resulted had the bonus method been originally used. Alternatively, if the bonus method is initially employed and subsequently a determinable amount of goodwill is confirmed by an objective transaction of the partnership, a similar requirement of equality is imposed to establish equivalence.

The conditions necessary to achieve equivalence of these alternative methods will be introduced by means of an example. Using the data of Case 3, the effect of recording the admission of Z with goodwill recognized, and subsequently writing off the total amount of this intangible, is contrasted with the capital balances obtained by initially applying the bonus method (see Illustration 16–1). Interim transactions are ignored in order to isolate the equity effects of the two methods. Three different profit and loss ratios are assumed:

	Profit and Loss Ratios		
	X	Y	Z
Situation 1	56%	24%	20%
Situation 2	49	21	30
Situation 3	60	20	20

Illustration 16–1 isolates in Situation 1 the two conditions necessary for the equivalence of the bonus and goodwill methods:

1. The percentage interest in profits and losses of the new partner must be the same as his initial fractional interest in the partnership capital.
2. The new (or adjusted) percentage interests in profits and losses of the old partners must be in the same relative proportion as their old percentage interests.

In Situation 1, Z has a 20 percent interest in profits and losses, which is equal to his initial fractional interest in partnership capital, and the new percentage interests in profits and losses of X and Y are in the same relative proportion as their prior percentage interests—80 percent of 70 percent for X, and 80 percent of 30 percent for Y, or $70:30 = 56:24$. In Situation 2, the new percentage interests in profits and losses of the old partners are in the same relative proportion, but the interest of Z in profits and losses exceeds his initial fractional interest in capital; consequently, an advantage accrues to X and Y equivalent in amount to the disadvantage to Z. In Situation 3, the new percentage interests of X and Y are in a different proportion than

Illustration 16–1

	X	Y	Z	Total
Bonus method:				
Capital balances	$47,200	$28,800	$19,000	$ 95,000
Goodwill method:				
Situation 1:				
Initial capital balances.................	$50,000	$30,000	$20,000	$100,000
Write-off of goodwill.................	[2,800]	[1,200]	[1,000]	[5,000]
Ending capital balances	$47,200	$28,800	$19,000	$ 95,000
Difference between methods				
after write-off	–0–	–0–	–0–	–0–
Situation 2:				
Initial capital balances.................	$50,000	$30,000	$20,000	$100,000
Write-off of goodwill.................	[2,450]	[1,050]	[1,500]	[5,000]
Ending capital balances	$47,550	$28,950	$18,500	$ 95,000
Difference between methods				
after write-off	$ 350	$ 150	$ [500]	–0–
Situation 3:				
Initial capital balances.................	$50,000	$30,000	$20,000	$100,000
Write-off of goodwill.................	[3,000]	[1,000]	[1,000]	[5,000]
Ending capital balances	$47,000	$29,000	$19,000	$ 95,000
Difference between methods				
after write-off	$ [200]	$ 200	–0–	–0–

existed prior to the admission of Z, that is, $70:30 \neq 60:20$; this condition results in an advantage to Y and a disadvantage to X.

Admission with Payment to the Existing Partner(s)

A second basic method of acquiring an interest in a partnership is to purchase a capital equity directly from one or more of the old partners, without an increase in partnership assets. In this section, two cases will be distinguished:

1. Purchase of a portion of one partner's interest.
2. Purchase of a partial interest uniformly from all of the existing partners.

In both instances, the ownership structure is numerically enlarged by the conveyance of an interest in the existing partnership to a new member. The purchase of one partner's total interest in a partnership, thereby replacing the old partner with a new partner, will be discussed in a subsequent section that deals with the retirement of partners.

If an existing partner sells a portion of his interest in capital and profits to another individual, the only entry *required* on the books of the partnership is one that establishes the new partner's capital credit by a transfer of the amount of the purchased interest from the capital account of the selling partner. For example, if X and Y are partners, with capital balances of $60,000 and $40,000, respectively, and Y sells one fourth of his interest to Z for $12,000, the only entry required on the partnership books is:

Y, Capital (¼ × $40,000) 10,000
    Z, Capital.   10,000

The cash consideration that passes between the old and new partner is established independently by Y and Z and need not be reflected in the above entry on the partnership books. From the point of view of the partnership entity, Y has merely transferred a personal asset to a new partner, viz, one fourth of his *recorded* interest in partnership capital; only this fact need be recognized in the partnership accounts.

If in the preceding illustration Z had purchased a one-fourth interest in the partnership by means of a direct purchase from *both* X and Y for $30,000 (a ratable transfer of one fourth of the monetary interest of each in the partnership), the accounting entry to record the capital transfer is essentially the same. Each partner conveys to Z one fourth of his interest in the *recorded* capital of the firm.

X, Capital (¼ × $60,000) 15,000
Y, Capital (¼ × $40,000) 10,000
    Z, Capital.   25,000

Again, the cash price for the purchased interests is not a compelling factor affecting the partnership accounts, as the sale represents an *independent* transaction between the existing partners and the incoming partner. The transaction may be compared to the sale of shares of corporate stock in the open market subsequent to their original issuance; the total stockholders' equity of the corporate entity remains unaffected by the sale. Only the identity and the relative interests of the various owners are changed.

Two problems intrude upon this relatively simple accounting framework for recording the purchase of a partnership interest directly from one or more partners. First, an argument can be made that the cash price established in the sale of an interest should be used as an independent index of the current value of the partnership net assets. If this premise is accepted and if the recorded net assets of the partnership are assumed to reflect current market values, the purchase price may be used to estimate the amount of goodwill possessed by the preexistent partnership. Returning to the previous example in which Z purchased a one-fourth ratable interest from X and Y for $30,000, there is an indication that the total value of the partnership net assets may be $120,000 (one fourth of the total value = $30,000). Since the recorded partners' equity presently is only $100,000, implicit goodwill of $20,000 may be inferred from this purchase. If the goodwill were recorded, and assuming X and Y share profits and losses equally, the entries to record the admission of Z are:

Goodwill..	20,000	
X, Capital..		10,000
Y, Capital..		10,000
X, Capital (¼ × $70,000)	17,500	
Y, Capital (¼ × $50,000)	12,500	
Z, Capital...		30,000

In an analogous manner, goodwill identified with the new partner may be computed. The advantages and disadvantages of recording the implicit goodwill in either case, and the requisite conditions for the equivalence of this and the preceding method, are the same as those discussed earlier in this chapter.

A second problem arising from the purchase of an interest from more than one existing partner concerns the distribution settlement of cash to the selling partners. This is ultimately a matter of negotiation between the new partner and each of the old partners or between the old partners. Frequently, however, the accountant is consulted and asked to suggest a basis for distributing the cash contributed by the new partner. Using the above data, the following tabulation is the conventional approach:

	X	Y	Total
Capital balances, as recorded	$60,000	$40,000	$100,000
Implicit goodwill—allocated in profit and loss ratio	10,000	10,000	20,000
Adjusted capital balances...............................	$70,000	$50,000	$120,000
Retained capital—three fourths of adjusted balances	52,500	37,500	90,000
Capital transferred to Z—basis for allocation of cash	$17,500	$12,500	$ 30,000

An analysis of this schedule of cash distribution raises several questions concerning its general validity. Since the sale was assumed to be independent of the partnership entity, one may take the position that it is inappropriate to utilize present partners' capital balances and provisions of the partnership agreement (i.e., the profit and loss ratios of X and Y) as a basis for determining the cash allocations. In this case, the capital balances are not in the profit- and loss-sharing ratios; consequently, X and Y are surrendering an interest in recorded partnership capital according to one ratio, 60 : 40, and they are forsaking an interest in future profits in another ratio, 50 : 50. The above schedule indicates the accepted method of recording, on the partnership books, the existence of implicit goodwill, and the resulting transfers of capital from X and Y to Z. The schedule, however, may not represent the most appropriate allocation of the $30,000 between the amount paid for an interest in present partnership capital and the amount paid for an interest in future profits and losses. Clearly, the ultimate decision in respect to cash distributions remains with the old partners.

One may also appropriately question the basic premise underlying the conventional computation of implicit goodwill. It is tacitly assumed that the capital balances of the old partners and the purchase price of the new partner may serve as a basis for inferring the existence of unrecorded goodwill. However, as noted above, the new partner is, in fact, buying an interest in both present capital *and* future profits; accordingly, it is questionable whether only one of these components should be used in computing the amount of goodwill. For example, the price paid for a partnership interest that is in excess of identifiable net assets acquired may be a payment for the excess earning capacity of the business (goodwill); or, it may represent the purchase of a greater interest in profits than in capital. If the latter interpretation prevails, the existence and amount of goodwill is an indeterminate element and should be recorded only when supporting evidence is compelling.

Legal Status of a New Partner

Section 27 of the Uniform Partnership Act confers upon any partner the right to convey by assignment to a third party his interest in the partnership—which is, as previously noted, personal property. This assignment does not, however, give the assignee authority to participate in the management of the business. Rather, it entitles him merely to receive the profits and in the case of dissolution to receive an interest in net assets that would normally accrue to the assignor.

However, if the existing partners agree to admit by assignment a new partner to the ownership structure, as is implicitly done when a prospective partner invests assets in the business, the new partner assumes the same rights and obligations as the old partners. This assumption is modified somewhat in Section 17 of the Act, in which it is provided that the new partner is personally liable for only those liabilities created subsequent to his admission to the firm. Thus, if dissolution should occur shortly after the admission of a new partner, it is necessary to distinguish between "old" and "new" liabilities of the partnership. The reader will note that the accounting treatment previously discussed for the "purchase of an interest" implicitly assumes that the assignee is admitted to the partnership with the status of a new partner, that is, no special equity status is identified.

Tax Basis of a New Partner

The tax basis of a new partner admitted by investing assets in the business is determined in the same manner as was outlined in the preceding chapter, viz, his basis is the sum of the bases of the contributed assets plus the amount of any partnership liabilities assumed by the new partner, and less the amount of any personal liabilities of the new partner that is assumed by the existing partners.

Case 4.   Assume the following data for the XY Partnership:

	Tax Basis	Book Value
Assets	$50,000	$60,000
Liabilities	18,000	18,000
Capital (interest) of partners:		
X............................	30,000	25,000
Y............................	20,000	17,000

Z is admitted to a one-fourth interest in the capital, profits, and losses of XY Partnership by investing $14,000 cash (one fourth of the net assets of the new firm), and he assumes a one-fourth responsibility for present partnership obligations.

Assuming X and Y have equal interests in profits and losses, the tax bases of the contributed assets and relevant capital adjustments are given as follows:

	Tax Bases			
	Assets	X	Y	Z
Prior to Z's entry	$ 50,000	$ 30,000	$ 20,000	—
Adjustments to reflect Z's entry...........	+14,000	−2,250	−2,250	$+18,500
Adjusted balances	$ 64,000	$ 27,750	$ 17,750	$ 18,500

The basis of Z's interest can be proved:

Basis of assets contributed	$14,000
Partnership liabilities assumed (¼ × $18,000)..........	4,500
	$18,500

Although Z acquired a one-fourth interest in future profits and losses of the partnership, he also assumed responsibility for one fourth of the existing partnership liabilities. This is recognized in the reduction of X's and Y's tax bases by $2,250 each, the amount of partnership liabilities transferred to Z. Importantly, the sum of the asset tax bases, $64,000 ($50,000 + $14,000), is equal to the sum of the bases of the partners' capital interests in the firm, $64,000 ($27,750 + $17,750 + $18,500).

When a new partner purchases an interest *directly* from one or more of the existing partners, Section 742 of the Internal Revenue Code states that the basis of the new partner's interest in the firm is determined in a manner similar to Case 4. In essence, his basis is the price paid to acquire the interest, adjusted for liabilities that he assumes and/or liabilities that the other partners assume. Obviously, the tax basis of the new partner's interest can be different from the tax basis of the old partners' interests. This difference is subject to alternative tax treatments, and partners should obtain expert tax counsel when making decisions on this matter.

Retirement or Death of a Partner

Retirement of a Partner

If one of the partners desires to withdraw from the partnership and he is not in violation of the agreement between the partners (Section 31),[1] two sections of the Uniform Partnership Act are relevant. As noted previously, Section 27 permits a partner to convey his interest in the partnership either to the existing partners or to a third party. If sold to a third party, the assignee is admitted to the partnership and is accorded the status of partner *only* with the consent of the continuing partners. If they should disapprove, the assignee is entitled to receive the profits that would have accrued to the assignor. But he is not otherwise entitled to management privileges.

If there is no express agreement as to the settlement of accounts with a retiring partner, Section 42 provides that the retiring partner is entitled to have the value of his equity at the date of retirement ascertained, and to receive, as an ordinary creditor, an amount equal to this value plus an interest credit on this amount. However, at his option, he may retain a passive interest in the firm and receive, in lieu of interest, the "profits attributable to the use of his right in the property of the dissolved partnership." Determining the value of a retiring partner's equity is often a basic issue in the settlement arrangement. The accounting problems of reclassifying the retiring partner's capital equity as a liability and the treatment of any assigned value increment in excess of recorded capital will be considered in the following discussion.

Sale of an Interest to a New Partner

The sale of a retiring partner's interest to a new partner introduces no special problems other than those relating to a conveyance of an interest. The admission of the new partner is recorded merely by transferring the recorded capital interest of the retiring partner to the new partner; how-

---

[1] If the withdrawal and the resulting partnership dissolution is in contravention of the articles of copartnership, the retiring partner is liable for damages suffered by the innocent partners (Section 38).

ever, the conditions of admission may indicate the presence of partnership goodwill. If goodwill is to be formally recognized in the accounts, the recorded amount is normally the *total* amount of goodwill attaching to the partnership entity, not merely the amount that relates to the retiring partner. However, in the event goodwill previously existed in the partnership books and is reduced as a consequence of the retirement of a partner, that is, the goodwill attaches primarily to the retiring partner as a separate individual, the purchase transaction may indicate the amount of "lost" goodwill.

Sale of an Interest to Continuing Partners

If the continuing partners acquire the interest of a retiring partner, whether negotiating jointly or separately *outside* the partnership or jointly *within* and *through* the partnership entity, the essence of the accounting problem remains substantially unchanged. If the purchase is completed independently of the partnership, the transaction is analogous to the sale of an interest to a third party. And if the retiring partner sells his interest to the partnership entity, the substance of the transaction is unchanged but the partnership assumes the obligation to make payment to the retiring partner—essentially a liquidating distribution. As before, partnership goodwill may be inferred if the purchase price (or the computed amount of a liquidating settlement) exceeds the recorded capital of the retiring partner. In this case, however, the evaluation of goodwill is subject to greater question, as the parties to the transaction are not mutually independent. The accountant, therefore, should be especially circumspect in recording partnership goodwill in this instance. The following case illustrates the sale to the partnership of a retiring partner's interest.

Case 5.   Z elects to retire from XYZ Partnership, and the remaining partners agree to purchase his interest through the partnership. The partners share profits and losses equally. On this date, the balance sheet of the partnership is as follows:

XYZ PARTNERSHIP
Balance Sheet
Date of Proposed Retirement

Assets		*Equities*	
Assets......................	$110,000	Liabilities.....................	$ 10,000
		X, capital.....................	30,000
		Y, capital.....................	30,000
		Z, capital.....................	40,000
Total assets..................	$110,000	Total equities	$110,000

An examination of the values of existing assets and an estimate of prospective earnings for future years indicate that Z's interest is worth considerably more than his recorded capital credit. It is determined that the current market value of the partnership assets is $140,000. After negotiation with Z and in consideration of the demonstrated excess earnings potential of the partnership, it is agreed that Z shall receive $60,000 for his capital interest, payment to be made in four annual installments, with interest of 9 percent accruing annually on the unpaid balance.

As a consequence of Z's retirement, the partnership is legally dissolved. The first accounting objective, therefore, is to determine and record the status of the retiring partner and to establish a proper basis of accounting for the partnership as a continuing entity. From this point of view, it is appropriate to adjust the assets to their current market values. Accordingly, the entry to record the value adjustments is as follows (assuming profits and losses are shared equally):

Assets	30,000	
X, Capital		10,000
Y, Capital		10,000
Z, Capital		10,000

The entry to adjust the equity of the retiring partner in the continuing partnership may be made in either of two ways. Using a method similar to the bonus method previously discussed, the entry may take the following form:

Method 1:

Z, Capital	50,000	
X, Capital	5,000	
Y, Capital	5,000	
Notes Payable to Z		60,000

Since Z received $10,000 more than his recorded capital interest after adjustments were made for asset revaluations, there is evidence that the partnership has unrecorded goodwill. Should the partners elect to recognize a value for goodwill, the conventional approach has been to record it in the following manner:

Method 2:

Z, Capital	50,000	
Goodwill	10,000	
Notes Payable to Z		60,000

The entry is based upon the long-established accounting precept that only *purchased* goodwill should be expressed quantitatively in the accounts. However, the reader will recognize that this precept, even if valid or useful, is inappropriate when applied in this instance. There has been no purchase of goodwill. The goodwill, if it exists, is an asset of the partnership, a measurement of which has been established independently of the settlement with the retiring partner. Clearly, the partnership did not acquire its own goodwill, nor did it transfer a portion of it to the retiring partner. If the goodwill identifies and remains with Z, no payment would be made therefor, as its value to the partnership would necessarily dissipate with the withdrawal of the retiring partner. Rather, the transaction merely offers evidence, however cogent, as to the existence and amount of partnership goodwill. If the accountant is persuaded that the $10,000 excess payment does, in fact, represent a valid measure of a one-third interest in the unrecorded goodwill—giving due attention to the imponderables of such a calculation—then either the total amount of goodwill ($30,000) should be recorded, or none should be recorded with the bonus method used to record the retirement. It appears inconsistent to recognize the existence of intangibles and then to record but a fraction of their value. If the total amount of goodwill is to be recorded, the following entries should be made:

Method 2 (as modified):

Goodwill	30,000	
X, Capital		10,000
Y, Capital		10,000
Z, Capital		10,000
Z, Capital	60,000	
Notes Payable to Z		60,000

These two methods may be analyzed as before for equivalence in respect to their effects on the partners' equities.

Death of a Partner

The death of a partner dissolves a partnership under provisions of the Uniform Partnership Act (Section 31). However, modifications of the Act adopted by a number of states permit the partners to prevent dissolution by including a contrary provision in the partnership agreement.

It is important that the partnership agreement specify the procedures to be followed upon the death of a partner whether or not legal dissolution is a consequence of the death. Whether the surviving partners acting separately or the partnership as an entity purchases the interest of the deceased partner, a determination of the value of this equity at the date of death is an important first consideration. Where the partnership continues as an operating entity under the control of the surviving partners, the agreement may provide that payments for this interest be based upon recorded partnership values, or that a revaluation of assets be made and the adjusted capital interests be based thereon.[2] Where the agreement is silent in respect to

---

[2] Again, the problem of determining the amount of goodwill to be recognized may arise. The argument for recording only the "purchased" goodwill is subject to the same limitation as in the case of a retiring partner.

payments made for a deceased partner's interest, the amount of settlement is the result of negotiations between the estate of the deceased partner and the surviving partners. The estate is accorded the same status under Section 42 as a retiring partner, viz, the option to receive either interest on an unliquidated capital balance, or profits attributable to the use of this equity.

Once the capital interest of the deceased partner is determined, the remaining partners must agree upon an acceptable means of settlement. Life insurance coverage in respect to individual partners is one commonly employed method of meeting this contingency. Two types of life insurance are often used: (1) cross-insurance and (2) entity insurance. If cross-insurance is utilized, the lives of individual partners are insured by the other partners independently of the partnership. Where this type of coverage exists, the partnership does not incur an expense. If entity insurance is used, the partnership insures the lives of each of the partners, and although nondeductible for income tax purposes, the premium payments represent proper expense charges in determining partnership net income.

If insurance is not available, the partners must decide whether to make a liquidating payment in cash or to make distributions of assets in kind. If the partnership is to be terminated, it is probable that distribution will be made in specific assets. However, if it is anticipated that partnership operations will continue, a method of installment cash payments, with interest, is a common method of discharging the obligation to the estate of the deceased partner.

Legal Status of a Retiring or Deceased Partner

The fact of partnership dissolution does not of itself result in the discharge of individual partners from unpaid partnership debts. However, Section 36 provides that "a partner is discharged from any existing liability upon dissolution of the partnership by an agreement to that effect between himself, the partnership creditors and the person or partnership continuing the business." Assuming proper notice is given past and prospective creditors, the retiring or deceased partner is, at most, liable for only those obligations existing at the date of dissolution.

Questions

1. What circumstances or conditions cause a legal dissolution of a partnership?

2. Discuss two alternative explanations and related accounting treatments of the following situation. A new partner is admitted to a partnership on the basis of contributing additional assets. Further, the new partner's agreed-upon interest in the previously recorded equity of the partnership plus the tangible assets he contributed is smaller than the value of the assets he contributed.

3. What is the usual accounting procedure for calculating the value of unrecorded intangibles ("goodwill") implied in the transaction to admit a new partner who contributes additional assets to the partnership?

4. What two conditions are necessary for the bonus method and goodwill method to have equivalent effects on the relative balances in the capital accounts?

5. Partners A and B have equal capital balances and share profits and losses in a 70:30 ratio. Upon admission of C to the partnership, goodwill is recognized and allocated to the capital accounts of A and B. Should the goodwill be allocated on a 50:50 basis or a 70:30 basis? Why?

6. Partners A and B have equal capital balances and share profits and losses in a 70:30 ratio. Upon admission of C to the partnership, C's capital account is credited with a bonus. In charging the bonus to the capital accounts of A and B, on what basis should it be allocated? Why?

7. If a partner sells part of his interest in the partnership to another individual, is the purchase price reflected on the books of the partnership? Why, or why not?

8. What special problems may arise when a new partner acquires a partnership interest directly from one or more partners?

9. Suppose an existing partnership plans to admit a new partner whose profit- and loss-sharing percentage will be different from his percentage interest in partnership capital. In this instance, explain why the conventional approach to calculating goodwill to be recorded with the new partner's admission might not be appropriate.

10. If goodwill is to be recognized at the time of a partner's retirement, should the partnership recognize the entire amount of goodwill or merely that portion of the intangible associated with the retiring partner? Explain.

11. In the event of a partner's death, is there concurrent dissolution of the partnership or may the enterprise continue in existence?

12. What is the general method for determining the tax basis of a new partner's interest in a partnership?

13. Enumerate several important factors that the accountant should consider in evaluating the appropriateness of recognizing implied goodwill upon the retirement and/or withdrawal of a partner from a partnership.

Exercises

Exercise 16–1

Johnson and Danos are partners sharing profits and losses 70:30, respectively. Their capital account balances are Johnson, $42,000; and Danos, $28,000. Journalize the admission of Uecker to the partnership under the following independent conditions:

a. Uecker invests $30,000 for a one-fourth interest in partnership capital. Goodwill implicit in the investment is to be recorded.
b. Uecker invests $10,000 for a one-fifth interest in partnership capital. Total capital after the admission of Uecker is to be $80,000.
c. Uecker purchases one third of the interests of the existing partners, paying $18,000 to each partner. Goodwill implied by the purchase price is to be recorded.

Exercise 16–2

DeShazo and Wilkins share profits equally and have equal investments in their partnership. The partnership's net assets are carried on the books at $28,000. Kratz is admitted to the partnership with a one-third interest in profits and net assets. Kratz pays $10,000 cash into the partnership for his interest.

Prepare journal entries to show three possible methods of recording on the partnership books the admission of Kratz. State the conditions under which each method would be appropriate.

(AICPA adapted)

Exercise 16–3

Select the answer in each of the following that best completes the sentence or answers the question.

a. Which of the following conditions constitutes a legal dissolution of a partnership?
   (1) Completion of a definite term of existence specified in the partnership agreement.
   (2) Death of a partner.
   (3) Bankruptcy of any partner.
   (4) Admission or retirement of a partner.
   (5) All of the above.
b. When admitting a new partner into an existing partnership, any allocation of goodwill to the old partners is based upon—
   (1) Their profit and loss ratio.
   (2) An equal distribution among the partners.
   (3) The carrying values of the assets each partner has contributed to the partnership.
   (4) The fair market values of the assets each partner has contributed to the partnership.
   (5) The relative capital balances of the partners.
c. A and B are partners with capital balances of $40,000 and $15,000, respectively. Profits and losses are shared in the ratio of 80 : 20. C invests in the partnership assets valued at $60,000 for a 50 percent interest in capital and profits and losses. Under the bonus method, how will the various capital accounts be affected?
   (1) C's, credited $60,000; A's, debited $4,000; B's, debited $1,000.
   (2) C's, credited $57,500; A's, credited $2,000; B's, credited $500.

   (3) C's, credited $57,500; A's, debited $500; B's, debited $2,000.
   (4) C's, credited $60,000; A's, debited $2,500; B's, debited $2,500.
   (5) None of the above.
d. John and Sam are partners with capital balances of $20,000 and $10,000, respectively. Profits and losses are shared in the ratio of 60:40. Pat invests in the partnership tangible assets valued at $5,000 for a 20 percent interest in capital, profits, and losses. Assuming that the recorded assets of the firm are properly valued, the amount of goodwill is—
   (1) $7,500.
   (2) $5,000.
   (3) $2,500.
   (4) $2,000.
   (5) $1,500.
e. Necessary conditions for the bonus and goodwill methods to be equivalent are—
   (1) The percentage interest in profits and losses of the new partner must be the same as his initial fractional interest in the partnership capital.
   (2) The new (or adjusted) percentage interests in profits and losses of the old partners must be in the same relative proportion as their old percentage interests.
   (3) The percentage interests in profits and losses of the old partners must be in proportion to their capital balances.
   (4) (1) and (2) are both necessary.
   (5) (1) and (3) are both necessary.

Exercise 16–4

Journalize the admission of Banks to the partnership of Walton and Rose in each of the following independent cases. The capital balances of Walton and Rose are $10,000 and $10,000; they share profits and losses equally.

a. Banks is admitted to a one-third interest in capital, profits, and losses with a contribution of $10,000.
b. Banks is admitted to a one-fourth interest in capital, profits, and losses with a contribution of $12,000. Total capital of the new partnership is to be $32,000.
c. Banks is admitted to a one-fifth interest in capital, profits, and losses upon contributing $3,000. Total capital of the new partnership is to be $25,000.
d. Banks is admitted to a one-fifth interest in capital, profits, and losses by the purchase of one fifth of the interests of Walton and Rose for $5,500, paying the money directly to the old partners. Total capital of the new partnership is to be $20,000.
e. Same conditions as in (d), except that the new partnership capital is to be $27,500.
f. Banks is admitted to a one-third interest in capital, profits, and losses upon contributing $7,000, after which each partner is to have an equal capital equity in the new partnership.
g. Banks is admitted to a one-fifth interest in capital, profits, and losses upon contributing $7,000. Total capital of the new partnership is to be $35,000.

Exercise 16–5

X and Y, who share profits and losses in the ratio of 60:40, agree to admit Z to the partnership. Z is to pay each of the old partners cash for one third of each's interest, and thus will own a one-third interest in profits, losses, and capital. The identifiable net assets of the partnership are recorded at their fair values, and X and Y each have capital balances of $30,000. The partners wish to decide how Z's total cash payment of $25,000 should be distributed between X and Y.

Required:
a. Show the traditionally suggested allocation of cash between X and Y.
b. Explain why the traditional allocation of cash (calculated in response to requirement [a]) may not be fair to X.
c. Show the journal entry to record Z's entry to the partnership assuming that goodwill is not to be recognized.

Exercise 16–6

Two long-time partners, Pop and Pam, finally decided that their partnership did not have enough push to compete in the modern world. As a consequence, they are considering the admission of Pow to the partnership. Prior to Pow's entry, the capital interests of Pop and Pam are $24,000 and $36,000, respectively. They share profits and losses in a 30:70 ratio. Several alternative plans for admitting Pow are being considered, each of which is described below:

1. Pow contributes $18,000 cash to the partnership in exchange for a 25 percent interest in capital, profits, and losses.
2. Pow pays $10,000 to the partners in exchange for a 25 percent interest in capital, profits, and losses. Thus, 25 percent of each partner's interest is transferred to Pow. Pop and Pam agree to distribute the $10,000 between them such that Pop receives $4,000 and Pam receives $6,000.
3. Pow contributes $18,000 to the partnership in exchange for a 20 percent interest in profits, losses, and capital.

Required:
For each of the three alternatives: *(a)* present the journal entries to reflect the goodwill method of recording the events, and *(b)* present the journal entries to reflect the bonus method of recording the events.

Exercise 16–7

Tim retired from the Fastball Partnership on January 1, 19X1. In accordance with the provisions of the partnership agreement, Tim was paid $80,000 from the partnership assets in satisfaction of his one-third interest. This amount was based on a formula that was specified in the original partnership agreement. It was determined by such factors as number of years of service to the partnership, capital contributed, and recent years' sales and earnings performance of the partnership. Tim's capital balance on January 1, 19X1, was $60,000. Bud and Helen, the other partners, each have one-third interests and $60,000 capital balances. Assume that the tangible assets of the partnership are correctly valued.

Required:

a. Journalize Tim's retirement under each of three alternative methods.
b. Discuss the relative merits of each method, noting the conditions under which each may draw the greatest support. As a part of your answer, state which method appears least appropriate under the circumstances.

Problems

Problem 16–8

Chaney and White are partners in the Celtie Company and have capital balances of $67,000 and $48,000, respectively, on December 31, 19X1. Profits and losses are shared 60 : 40. Moore is admitted to the partnership on January 2, 19X2, by investing $45,000 for a one-fourth interest in capital and profits.

Required:

a. Prepare journal entries to record the admission of Moore under both the bonus and goodwill methods.
b. Assuming the goodwill method is used to record the admission of Moore *and* that subsequently the goodwill is written off, compare the effect of this treatment on the partners' capitals with that of the bonus method under the following three independent conditions (ignore the effects of other changes in capital):

	Percentage Interest in Profits		
	Chaney	White	Moore
Case 1	45%	30%	25%
Case 2	40	37	23
Case 3	48	30	22

Problem 16–9

Frantz, Herring, and May are partners. Their profit-sharing ratio and capital balances on December 31, 19X1, are as follows:

Partners	Profit-Sharing Ratio	Capital Balance
Frantz	60%	$97,000
Herring	30	65,000
May	10	38,000

Casey is admitted to the partnership on January 1, 19X2, by investing $40,000 for a 20 percent interest in capital and profits.

Required:

a. Prepare journal entries for each of three alternative methods of recording the admission of the new partner.

b. Assume that Casey purchased a 20·percent interest in the partnership ratably from the existing partners by paying $42,000 cash directly to the partners. Prepare journal entries for each of two alternative methods of recording the admission of Casey.

Problem 16–10

A, B, and C decide to practice accounting together as of January 1, 19X1. They enter into an agreement under which they share profits and losses in the proportion of 50 percent, 25 percent, and 25 percent, respectively, and agree to contribute $50,000 in cash in these same proportions to provide working capital. They decide to keep their books on a cash basis.

On January 1, 19X2, B died and the remaining partners agreed to admit D, giving him a 20 percent share in the profits with a minimum guarantee of $10,000 per year whether operations are profitable or not. A and C have percentages of 40 and 40, respectively. This partnership is of one year's duration, and at the end of this period C decides to retire but permits the use of his name in future partnerships subject to the payment to him of $5,000 per annum to be treated as an expense of the partnership.

As of January 1, 19X3, a partnership is formed in which C's name is utilized in accordance with his proposal and to which E is admitted. The partners' interests in this partnership are as follows: A, 40 percent; D, 30 percent; and E, 30 percent.

Since there were no substantial accruals at the end of the year, disbursements for expenses made during any one period were treated as expenses of the then current partnership. These disbursements were $70,000 in 19X1, $90,000 in 19X2, and $90,000 in 19X3.

Receipts of fees were as follows:

	Earned by Partnership		
	No. 1	*No. 2*	*No. 3*
19X1..........	$ 80,000		
19X2..........	160,000	$40,000	
19X3..........		50,000	$60,000

Each new partnership agreement provided for the newly created partnership to purchase from the old partnership the $50,000 capital originally paid in by A, B, and C. The agreements also provided that the partners should bear the cost of acquisition of this amount in the proportion which they shared profits (and losses). However, it was agreed that an incoming partner, or one acquiring an increased percentage, need not make his contribution in cash immediately but could have the same charged to his drawing account. All such partners availed themselves of this privilege. Partners selling all or a part of their interests in capital are credited through their drawing accounts and immediately withdraw the amount of such credit. In addition to drawings made under this agreement, the partners or their heirs made cash drawings as follows:

	A	B	C	D	E
19X1...........	$10,500	$27,750	$13,750		
19X2...........	40,000	6,000	5,000	$7,000	
19X3...........	10,000	8,750	11,250	1,000	$5,000

Required:

Prepare schedules or statements showing the details of transactions in the partners' drawing accounts and capital accounts for each of the years involved. These accounts should be in such form that the balance at the end of each year that was available for withdrawal by each partner is shown in that partner's drawing account. The capital accounts are to reflect only the $50,000 original investment.

(AICPA adapted)

Problem 16–11

Randy and Roy have been operating a business for several years as partners, during which time they have divided profits equally. They need additional capital to expand their business and have agreed to admit Dan to the partnership as of January 1, 19X7, with a one-third interest in profits and in the capital. Dan is to pay cash into the business as additional capital in an amount equal to one half of the combined capital of the present two partners, redetermined as follows:

The average partnership profits, after partners' salaries, for the past two years are to be capitalized at the rate of 10 percent per annum, which will redetermine the aggregate capital of the two present partners. Before such capitalization of profits, the accounts are to be adjusted for errors and omissions.

The business has not followed a strict accrual basis of accounting. As a result, the following items have been omitted from the books:

Item	Balance 12/31/X4	Balance 12/31/X5	Balance 12/31/X6
Accrued expenses	$3,201	$2,472	$3,829
Prepaid expenses..........	1,010	812	872
Accrued income...........	—	250	130

In addition, no provision has been made for loss on uncollectible accounts. It is agreed that a provision of $4,500 is needed as of December 31, 19X6, of which $600 is for 19X5 accounts. Charge-offs have been made to expense in 19X4 of 19X3 and prior accounts—$1,200; in 19X5 of 19X4 accounts—$3,100, and of 19X5 accounts—$400; in 19X6 of 19X5 accounts—$2,100, and of 19X6 accounts—$525.

The inventory at December 31, 19X6, contains some obsolete goods carried at cost of $4,400. A 20 percent write-down is to be made to reduce these items to their present value.

In 19X5 and 19X6, salaries of $3,000 for each partner were taken out of the business and charged to expense before determining profits. It has been agreed that the salaries should have been $2,000 each.

The following financial data are available:

Balance Sheet
December 31, 19X6

Assets		Equities	
Cash	$23,100	Accounts payable	$ 43,200
Accounts receivable	42,500	Notes payable.................	25,000
Notes receivable..............	6,000	Accumulated depreciation—	
		fixtures.....................	5,300
Merchandise..................	64,000	Randy, capital	38,100
Store fixtures	12,400	Roy, capital...................	36,400
Total assets	$148,000	Total equities	$148,000

	19X4	19X5	19X6
Profit per books	$ 8,364	$ 8,419	$10,497
Randy, capital.............	20,000	24,000	38,100
Roy, capital	25,000	33,000	36,400

Required:

Show the computation of the amount that Dan will pay into the partnership, and prepare a balance sheet as it would appear after adjustment for errors and omissions and after redetermination of capital accounts and receipt of Dan's capital contribution as of January 1, 19X7.

(AICPA adapted)

Problem 16–12

You have been engaged to prepare financial statements for the partnership of Alexander, Randolph, and Ware as of June 30, 19X1. The partnership was formed originally by Alexander and Barnes on July 1, 19X0. At that date Barnes contributed $400,000 cash. Alexander contributed land, building, and equipment with market values of $110,000, $520,000, and $185,000, respectively. The land and building were subject to a mortgage securing an 8 percent note (interest rate of similar notes at July 1, 19X0). The note is due in quarterly payments of $5,000 plus interest on January 1, April 1, July 1, and October 1 of each year. Alexander made the July 1, 19X0, principal and interest payment personally. The partnership then assumed the obligation for the remaining $300,000 balance.

The partnership agreement provided that Alexander had contributed a certain intangible benefit to the partnership due to his many years of business activity in the area to be serviced by the new partnership. The assigned value of this intangible asset plus the net tangible assets he contributed gave Alexander a 60 percent initial capital interest in the partnership. Alexander was designated to receive an annual salary of $24,000 plus an annual bonus of 4 percent of net income after deducting his salary but before deducting interest on partners' capital investments (see below). Both the salary and the bonus are operating expenses of the partnership. Each partner is to receive a 6 percent return on his average capital investment, such interest to be an expense of the partnership. All residual profits or losses are to be shared equally.

On October 1, 19X0, Barnes sold his partnership interest and rights as of July 1, 19X0, to Ware for $370,000. Alexander agreed to accept Ware as a partner if he would contribute sufficient cash to meet the October 1, 19X0, payment on the mortgage. Ware made the payment from personal funds.

On January 1, 19X1, Alexander and Ware admitted a new partner, Randolph, who invested $150,000 cash for a 10 percent capital interest based on the initial investments at July 1, 19X0, of Alexander and Barnes. At January 1, 19X1, the book value of the partnership's assets and liabilities approximated their market values. Randolph contributed no intangible benefit to the partnership. Similar to the other partners, Randolph is to receive a 6 percent return on his average capital investment. His investment also entitled him to 20 percent of the partnership's profits or losses as defined above. However, for the year ended June 30, 19X1, Randolph would receive one half of his pro rata share of the profits or losses.

The accounting records show that on February 1, 19X1, Other Miscellaneous Expenses had been charged $3,600 in payment of hospital expenses incurred by Alexander's eight-year-old daughter.

All salary payments to Alexander have been charged to his drawing account. On June 1, 19X1, Ware made a $33,000 withdrawal. These are the only transactions recorded in the partners' drawing accounts. Since Ware's withdrawal is not an expense of the partnership, it is understood to be a reduction in his capital investment. The trial balance as of June 30, 19X1, is as follows:

	Dr. [Cr.]
Current assets	$ 307,100
Fixed assets, net	1,285,800
Current liabilities	[157,000]
8% mortgage note payable	[290,000]
Alexander, capital	[515,000]
Randolph, capital	[150,000]
Ware, capital	[400,000]
Alexander, drawing	24,000
Randolph, drawing	—
Ware, drawing	33,000
Sales	[872,600]
Cost of sales	695,000
Administrative expenses	16,900
Other miscellaneous expenses	11,100
Interest expense	11,700

Required:

Prepare a working paper to adjust the net income [loss] and partners' capital accounts for the year ended June 30, 19X1, and to close the net income [loss] to the partners' capital accounts at June 30, 19X1. Amortization of goodwill, if any, is to be over a 10-year period. Using the following column headings and begin with balances per books as shown.

Description	Net Income [Loss] Cr. [Dr.]	Partners' Capital			Other Accounts	
		Alexander Cr. [Dr.]	Randolph Cr. [Dr.]	Ware Cr. [Dr.]	Amount Dr. [Cr.]	Name
Book balances at June 30, 19X1	$137,900	$515,000	$150,000	$400,000		

(AICPA adapted)

Problem 16–13

The partnership agreement of Fry, Hill, Barnes, Smith, and Nash contained a buy and sell agreement, among numerous other provisions, which would become operative in case of the death of any partner. Some provisions contained in the buy and sell agreement were as follows:

ARTICLE V. *Buy and Sell Agreement*

1.   Purposes of the Buy and Sell Agreement.

(a)   The partners mutually desire that the business shall be continued by the survivors without interruption or liquidation upon the death of one of the partners.

(b)   The partners also mutually desire that the deceased partner's estate shall receive the full value of the deceased partner's interest in the partnership and that the estate shall share in the earnings of the partnership until the deceased partner's interest shall be fully purchased by the surviving partners.

2.   Purchase and Sale of Deceased Partner's Interest.

(a)   Upon the death of the partner first to die, the partnership shall continue to operate without dissolution.

(b)   Upon the decedent's death, the survivors shall purchase and the executor or administrator of the deceased partner's estate shall sell to the surviving partners the deceased partner's interest in the partnership for the price and upon the terms and conditions hereinafter set forth.

(c)   The deceased partner's estate shall retain the deceased partner's interest until the amount specified in the next paragraph shall be paid in full by the surviving partners.

(d)   The parties agree that the purchase price for the partnership interest shall be an amount equal to the deceased partner's capital account at the date of death. Said amount shall be paid to the legal representative of decedent as follows:

(i)   The first installment of 25 percent of said capital account shall be paid within 60 days from the date of death of the partner or within 30 days from the date on which the personal representative of decedent becomes qualified by law, whichever date is later, and

(ii)   The balance shall be due in four equal installments which shall be due and payable annually on the anniversary date of said death.

3.   Deceased Partner's Estate's Share of the Earnings.

(a)   The partners mutually desire that the deceased partner's estate shall be guaranteed a share in the earnings of the partnership over the period said

estate retains an interest in the partnership. Said estate shall not be deemed to have an interest in the partnership after the final installment for the deceased partner's capital account is paid even though a portion of the guaranteed payments specified below may be unpaid and may be due and owing.

(b) The deceased partner's estate's guaranteed share of the earnings of the partnership shall be determined from two items and shall be paid at different times as follows:

(i) First, interest shall be paid on the unpaid balance of the deceased partner's capital account at the same date the installment on the purchase price is paid. The amount to be paid shall be an amount equal to accrued interest at the rate of 6 percent per annum on the unpaid balance of the purchase price for the deceased partner's capital account.

(ii) Second, the parties agree that the balance of the guaranteed payment from the partnership earnings shall be an amount equal to 30 percent of the deceased partner's share of the aggregate gross receipts of the partnership for the full 36 months preceding the month of the partner's death. Said amount shall be payable in 48 equal monthly installments without interest, and the first payment shall be made within 60 days following the death of the partner or within 30 days from the date on which the personal representative of deceased becomes qualified, whichever date is later; provided, however, that the payments so made under this provision during any 12-month period shall not exceed the highest annual salary on a calendar-year basis received by the partner for the three calendar years immediately preceding the date of his death. In the event that said payment would exceed said salary, then an amount per month shall be paid which does not so exceed said highest monthly salary, and the term over which payments shall be paid to the beneficiary shall be lengthened out beyond the said 48 months in order to complete said payments.

Fry and Nash were both killed simultaneously in an automobile accident on January 10, 19X3. The surviving partners notified the executors of both estates that the first payment due under the buy and sell agreement would be paid on March 10, 19X3, and that subsequent payments would be paid on the 10th day of each month as due.

The following information was determined from the partnership's records:

Partner	Profit- and Loss- Sharing Ratio	Capital Account on January 10, 19X3	Annual Salaries to Partners by Years		
			19X0	19X1	19X2
Fry	25	$26,000	$16,500	$16,500	$16,800
Hill	25	21,970	15,000	15,750	16,500
Barnes	20	4,780	12,000	13,000	14,000
Smith	15	5,860	9,600	10,800	12,000
Nash..............	15	6,700	8,400	9,600	11,800

The partnership's gross receipts for the three prior years were:

19X0............	$296,470
19X1............	325,310
19X2............	398,220

Required:

Prepare a schedule of the amounts to be paid to the Fry Estate and to the Nash Estate in March 19X3, December 19X3, and January 19X4. The schedule should identify the amounts attributable to earnings and to interest in the guaranteed payments and to capital. Supporting computations should be in good form.

(AICPA adapted)

Problem 16–14

The trial balance of AB, a partnership, on January 1, 19X1, is shown below. Profits and losses were to be shared equally by A and B.

	Debit	Credit
Cash	$ 68,000	
Accounts receivable...	50,000	
Notes receivable...	40,000	
Merchandise inventories	35,000	
Land	85,000	
Buildings and equipment—less allowance for depreciation	28,000	
Investments—at cost..	35,000	
Prepaid insurance	6,000	
Office supplies	3,000	
Bank loans...		$ 45,000
Accounts payable..		48,000
Accrued taxes		2,500
First-mortgage, 7% long-term notes		55,500
Capital accounts:		
A		104,000
B		95,000
	$350,000	$350,000

As of December 31, 19X1, C purchased for $100,000 in cash from partners A and B a one-third interest in the partnership; each partner agreed to transfer one third of his individual capital account to C. Prior to C's admission, it was decided that a valuation reserve of $7,000 should be provided with respect to the investments; that an allowance for bad debts should be established in the amount of $8,000; and that the valuation of buildings and equipment should be reduced to $23,000. Profit sharing by C commenced on January 1, 19X2.

As of December 31, 19X2, D was admitted to a one-fourth interest in partnership profits and contributed the following assets from a business previously operated by him as a sole proprietor:

Cash	$60,000
Inventory.................	70,000
Investments..............	10,000

The following liabilities incurred by D in his previous business were assumed by the new partnership:

Accounts payable..........	$20,000
Bank loans................	24,000

As an inducement to merge his enterprise with the ABC partnership, D was allowed goodwill of $14,000. Profits were to be shared equally by A, B, C, and D in the new firm, commencing January 1, 19X3.

Additional data to be used in the solution of this problem are as follows:

	Year Ended December 31	
	19X1	*19X2*
Profit of the firm	$18,000	$27,000
Drawings:		
A	13,000	10,000
B....................	7,000	6,000
C	—	14,000

For the purposes of simplicity, it is assumed that profits for each year were realized in cash and that the balance sheet of the firm on January 1, 19X1, did not change during the two-year period, except as indicated in the terms of this problem.

Required:

a. Prepare an interim work sheet for the two-year period from January 1, 19X1, through December 31, 19X2. Goodwill is not to be recorded upon C's entry, and only the $14,000 granted to D is to be recorded upon his entry to the partnership.

b. Prepare journal entries to record the admission of C and D, assuming goodwill is implicitly determined and recorded in each instance. In the case of D's entry, record all of the implicit goodwill and disregard the $14,000 limit mentioned previously in the problem.

(AICPA adapted)

Problem 16–15

Wonderland is a family partnership engaged in the wholesale trade. It closes its books at December 31. During the year, all transactions are recorded on a cash receipts and disbursement basis. However, at the end of the fiscal year, adjustment is made to what was termed the "inventory account" for all items necessary to reflect operations and financial position on an accrual basis.

Partner E died on October 31, 19X1. His will left equal shares in his estate to partners A and C and an outsider, F. For purposes of this problem, assume no probate period and that E's estate was distributed immediately. All remaining partners, together with F, agreed that the business of Wonderland would continue as a partnership of A, B, C, D, and F, with beginning interest on November 1,

19X1, as computed on a proper accrual basis to October 31, and after distribution of E's interest on that date.

Depreciation of fixed assets may be ignored.

Balances as shown by the books of the firm were as follows:

	January 1, 19X1	October 31, 19X1
Cash	$ 42,000	$ 55,000
Inventory account	195,000	195,000
Fixed assets.................	60,000	59,000
Accruals....................	29,000	16,000
Notes payable...............	100,000	60,000
Partners' equities............	168,000	168,000
Sales	—	2,000,000
Purchases...................	—	1,725,000
Operating expenses..........	—	210,000

In addition to the above, the following information concerning the inventory account was available:

At January 1, 19X1: accounts receivable, $80,000; merchandise, $200,000; freight claims (on incoming merchandise), $2,000; prepaid operating expenses, $10,000; accounts payable, $90,000; and allowances due customers, $7,000. At October 31, 19X1: accounts receivable, $83,300; merchandise, $221,000; freight claims (on incoming merchandise), $1,500; prepaid operating expenses, $6,000; accounts payable, $85,000; and allowances due customers, $8,000.

Partners' equities and profit- and loss-sharing ratio are as follows:

	Equities	Profit and Loss Ratio
A...........	$ 10,500	6.25%
B...........	52,500	31.25
C...........	77,000	37.50
D...........	7,000	12.50
E...........	21,000	12.50
	$168,000	100.00%

Required:

a. Prepare an income statement for the period January 1 to October 31, 19X1.

b. Prepare a statement of financial position on November 1, 19X1.

(AICPA adapted)

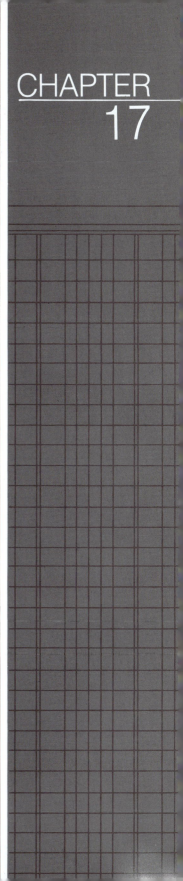

CHAPTER
17

Partnership Liquidation

Introduction

The Liquidation Process

The nature of partnership dissolution, viz, "the change in the relation of the partners caused by any partner ceasing to be associated in the carrying on as distinguished from the winding up of the business" (Section 29), was discussed in the previous chapter. In that chapter, attention was focused on the continuity of partnership operations. Emphasis will now be placed upon the accounting problems and procedures involved in the winding up (liquidation) of partnership affairs—that interval of time between legal *dissolution* and effective *termination* of partnership operations.

Accounting Problems in Partnership Liquidation

The basic objectives of the partnership during the liquidation process are to convert the firm's assets to cash with minimum loss in value (*realization* of assets), to discharge valid partnership liabilities, and to distribute cash and any unrealized assets to the individual partners in an equitable manner. The primary objective underlying the accounting function during the liquidation process is to provide information adequate for an equitable disbursement of the partnership assets to creditors and partners, in compliance with the law. The accounting focus is therefore shifted from the measurement of periodic income to the determination of realization gains and losses, the allocation of these gains and losses among the partners, the payment of partnership creditors, and the planning and recording of asset distributions to partners. Careful attention must be given to relevant provisions of the state partnership act, the partnership agreement, and in some instances, state and federal insolvency (bankruptcy) statutes. It is especially important that the accounting process be guided primarily by legal rights and obligations.

Basic Dichotomy—Partnership Solvency and Insolvency

Since the liquidation of solvent and insolvent partnerships introduces essentially different problems, each condition will be separately considered. For purposes of the following discussion, a partnership is regarded as insolvent when its recorded assets are not sufficient to discharge existing partnership liabilities, that is, an entity approach to the condition of insolvency. From a purely legal point of view, however, partnership insolvency is defined in terms of the underlying aggregative concept: "The now settled view is that a partnership is insolvent only when the surplus of *individual* assets [of the partners] over *non-partnership debts* is insufficient, together with partnership assets to pay partnership obligations."[1] This more restrictive definition of partnership insolvency will be illustrated as a special condition of entity insolvency, viz, that circumstance where the separate net assets of individual partners are inadequate to discharge the partnership obligations not paid with partnership assets.

In the process of liquidating a partnership that is solvent by the entity definition, there are two alternative ways of proceeding with the liquidation. First, under the "simple liquidation" process, all of the partnership assets are realized or converted *before* any distributions are made to the partners. In this case, the accounting treatment is relatively simple. Since the amount of the total liquidation gain or loss is known before asset distributions to partners, the accountant needs only to indicate a distribution of assets that complies with the order or priority established by existing statutes.

Second, under the "installment payments" approach to liquidation, the partners elect to receive liquidating payments in a series of installments *prior* to the time at which partnership assets are completely realized or converted. In this case, the accountant must develop a plan of settlement that will produce the same ultimate distribution as if payments had been deferred until all of the noncash assets were converted.

Following an examination of simple liquidations, the accounting problems associated with installment payments will be analyzed. Separate consideration will be given to situations in which there exists one insolvent partner, so long as all are not insolvent. In the final section of this chapter, the accounting problems associated with insolvent partnerships will be analyzed. The rights of both partnership creditors and individual creditors will be examined with reference to provisions of the Uniform Partnership Act, the Federal Bankruptcy Act, and selected decisions of the common law.

Simple Liquidation

Basic Distributive Rights

In a simple liquidation, all of the partnership assets are converted into cash before any distribution is made to creditors or to individual partners. The distribution of assets is made in the order of priority established in the Uniform Partnership Act where that Act is operative. Section 40 (B) of the Act provides:

---

[1] Reed Rowley, *Rowley on Partnership* (New York: The Bobbs-Merrill Co., Inc. 1960), vol. II, p. 85. (Emphasis supplied).

The liabilities of the partnership shall rank in order of payment, as follows:
(I)   Those owing to creditors other than partners,
(II) Those owing to partners other than for capital and profits,
(III) Those owing to partners in respect of capital,
(IV) Those owing to partners in respect of profits.

Since the conversion of all noncash assets precedes the distribution of cash to the partners, the total amount of gain or loss on realization is known at the time of distribution. Unless a specific *liquidation* gain and loss ratio is indicated in the partnership agreement, the gain or loss should be allocated to the partners in the current profit and loss residual ratio; salary and interest factors are disregarded. This basis for distribution appears equitable, as realization gains or losses frequently reflect, in large part, adjustments of prior years' reported profits, which were distributed on this basis. Additionally, gains or losses that can be attributed to the *fact* of liquidation are in essence components of the overall profitability of the business, and thus should relate to individual partners in the same ratio as normal periodic earnings and losses of the partnership.

Where current profits are transferred in the closing entry sequence to the partners' capital accounts, priorities (III) and (IV) of Section 40 (B) coalesce. In any event, the distinction between capital and profits is of no practical consequence, unless a "deficit" in the profits account is not absorbed by, or offset against, capital balances before distribution of cash to individual partners. Since an "equitable" settlement is the controlling consideration in most partnership law, the existence of a nonabsorbed deficit condition seems unlikely, unless expressly anticipated and provided for in the partnership agreement. Consequently, elements (III) and (IV) will hereafter be considered as one priority status.

The basic rights of creditors and partners in a simple liquidation are illustrated in the paragraphs that follow.

Case 1.   The balance sheet of the WaTex Company at the date of dissolution is as follows:

Assets		Equities	
Cash	$10,000	Liabilities	$12,000
Noncash assets	80,000	Capital:	
		Able	31,000
		Holmes	20,000
		Thomas	27,000
Total assets	$90,000	Total equities	$90,000

During liquidation, $50,000 is realized from the conversion of the noncash assets. The partners share profits and losses in the ratio 5:3:2.

Given these data, a *partnership liquidation schedule* may be prepared as in Illustration 17–1. *The schedule of partnership liquidation is the primary historical statement that reflects partnership transactions during the period of liquidation.*

Illustration 17-1

WATEX COMPANY
Schedule of Partnership Liquidation
Dr. [Cr.]

	Assets		Priority Claims	Claimants		
				Residual Equities		
	Cash	Noncash		Able	Holmes	Thomas
Profit and loss ratio				50%	30%	20%
Preliquidation balances	$ 10,000	$ 80,000	$[12,000]	$[31,000]	$[20,000]	$[27,000]
Realization of assets and allocation of loss	50,000	[80,000]		15,000	9,000	6,000
Predistribution balances	$ 60,000	–0–	$[12,000]	$[16,000]	$[11,000]	$[21,000]
Cash distribution:						
Priority claims	[12,000]		12,000			
Partners' residual equities.............	[48,000]			16,000	11,000	21,000
Termination of partnership..............	–0–	–0–	–0–	–0–	–0–	–0–

The schedule indicates the condition of the partnership at the date of dissolution (preliquidation balances), gains and losses sustained in the conversion of noncash assets, the allocation of gains and losses to the partners in their profit and loss ratio, and the distribution of cash in the order of payment specified in Section 40 (B). The same schedular format may be expanded to include other significant events during the liquidation process.

Partners' Debit Balances

In the previous illustration, each of the partners had a sufficiently large credit balance in his capital account to absorb his proportionate share of the realization loss. However, such a favorable circumstance does not always exist. Frequently, an individual partner's share of the realization loss will exceed his capital credit, producing a *debit balance* in his capital account. This capital deficiency creates a valid claim of the partnership against the partner. Section 18 (A) specifies that "each partner . . . must contribute toward the losses, whether of capital or otherwise, sustained by the partnership according to his share in the profits." Additionally, Section 40 (D) provides that "the partners shall contribute, as provided by Section 18 (A), the amount necessary to satisfy the liabilities; but if any, but not all, of the partners are insolvent, or, not being subject to process, refuse to contribute, the other partners shall contribute their share of the liabilities, and, in the relative proportions in which they share the profits, the additional amount necessary to pay the liabilities."

Since Section 40 relates to the sequence of distribution of partnership assets in settlement of partnership liabilities, it is important that the term *liability* in this particular usage be fully understood. This section of the Act contemplates that liabilities may be generated either by accumulated losses from operations, realization losses, or the *loss* incurred when a partner with a debit balance in his capital account fails to contribute personal assets sufficient in amount to remove this deficit. In fact, Section 40 (A) defines the assets of a partnership to include contributions due from the partners for this cause.[2] Consequently, a partner's failure to contribute to the extent of his capital deficiency is equivalent to a realization loss for the remaining partners. Thus, if an amount equal to a debit balance is not collected from the delinquent partner, it is allocated in total to the remaining partners as if it were a realization loss; the allocation is made in the ratio of the remaining partners' original shares of profits and losses. For example, assume X, Y, and Z share profits and losses in the ratio 5 : 3 : 2. If Y should fail to contribute to the partnership the amount of a debit balance in his capital account, X and Z will share this loss (a capital deficiency) in the ratio 5 : 2, that is, 5/7 to X and 2/7 to Z. If X should fail to contribute for a preexistent capital deficiency, Y and Z would share this loss in the ratio 3 : 2, that is 3/5 to Y and 2/5 to Z.

The effects of partners' debit balances on the liquidation process and their treatment in the partnership liquidation schedule are illustrated in the following case.

Case 2.   The balance sheet of Super Serv Company immediately prior to the liquidation of the partnership is given below:

Assets		*Equities*	
Cash	$ 5,000	Liabilities	$15,000
Noncash assets	45,000	Capital:	
		Johnson	9,000
		Granof	6,000
		Deakin	20,000
Total assets	$50,000	Total equities	$50,000

The partners share profits and losses in the ratio 4 : 4 : 2. It is assumed that Johnson and Deakin have personal resources sufficient in amount to "make good" capital debit balances that may be created during the liquidation process. Granof has no available personal assets. The noncash assets of the partnership are sold for $15,000.

A partnership liquidation schedule based upon these data is shown in Illustration 17–2.

---

[2] The discerning reader will note that this provision is consistent with the legal definition of partnership insolvency, whereby insolvency is impossible unless the claims against the individual partners are uncollectible due to a condition of personal insolvency.

Illustration 17–2

SUPER SERV COMPANY
Schedule of Partnership Liquidation
Dr. [Cr.]

	Assets		Priority Claims	Claimants		
				Residual Equities		
	Cash	Noncash		Johnson	Granof	Deakin
Profit and loss ratio				40%	40%	20%
Preliquidation balances	$ 5,000	$ 45,000	$[15,000]	$[9,000]	$[6,000]	$[20,000]
Realization of assets and allocation						
of loss	15,000	[45,000]		12,000	12,000	6,000
Balances.	$ 20,000	–0–	$[15,000]	$ 3,000	$ 6,000	$[14,000]
Absorption of Granof's balance (4:2)				4,000	[6,000]	2,000
Balances.	$ 20,000	–0–	$[15,000]	$ 7,000	–0–	$[12,000]
Contribution by Johnson.	7,000			[7,000]		
Predistribution balances	$ 27,000	–0–	$[15,000]	–0–	–0–	$[12,000]
Cash distribution:						
Priority claims	[15,000]		15,000			
Partners' residual equities.	[12,000]					12,000
Termination of partnership.	–0–	–0–	–0–	–0–	–0–	–0–

In this instance, Granof's uncollectible debit balance generates an additional "realization loss" to be absorbed by Johnson and Deakin in their relative profit and loss ratio, whereas Johnson contributes personal assets to restore the debit balance in his capital account to zero. It should be noted that even if Johnson had failed to contribute personal assets, the partnership would have remained solvent, since cash was otherwise available to discharge liabilities to partnership creditors.

Partners' Loans

In the distribution of partnership assets, the Uniform Partnership Act ranks payments to partners in respect to loans ahead of payments on their capital accounts. However, this priority has functional significance *only* if it is contemplated that payments are to be made to partners with capital deficiencies. And, as a matter of fact, repayment of a partner's loan is not generally made where the partner has a capital deficiency. If in liquidation a partner's capital account has a debit balance, the partner is required by Section 18 of the Act to contribute an amount equal to his debit balance. Of course, the partnership may be unable to collect this amount from the delinquent partner. Under these circumstances, if partnership assets are first distributed to the partner in repayment of his loan, the assets may be permanently lost. In effect, the distribution in repayment of a (deficient) partner's loan increases the partnership losses to be allocated to the remaining (solvent) partners, assuming the deficient partner does not satisfy his obligation. To prevent this sequence of events, the rule of *setoff* has been generally accepted by the courts as a means of achieving an equitable settlement. Accordingly, debit balances are offset against partners' loans to the fullest extent possible, *before* any cash distribution is made.[3]

Application of the rule of setoff is illustrated in the following case.

Case 3. The preliquidation balances of the assets and equities of the Austin Appliance Partnership are given below:

Assets		*Equities*		
Cash	$ 20,000	Liabilities		$ 40,000
Noncash assets	80,000	Partners' loans:		
		Bruns	$ 4,000	
		Jensen	5,000	
		Miles	7,000	16,000
		Partners' capital:		
		Bruns	$10,000	
		Jensen	12,000	
		Miles	16,000	
		Schiff	6,000	44,000
Total assets	$100,000	Total equities		$100,000

The partners share profits and losses in the ratio 3:3:2:2. Bruns, Jensen, and Miles are committed to making contributions for any debit balances that may be created by loss absorption and are assumed to have sufficient personal assets for this purpose; Schiff has only $2,000 of available personal assets. The noncash assets are sold during liquidation for $30,000.

A partnership liquidation schedule for this case in given in Illustration 17–3.

This case illustrates the offset principle as it relates to the loans of two partners (Bruns and Jensen), a partial contribution by Schiff in reduction of a capital deficiency, the absorption of the capital debit residue of Schiff by the remaining partners (Bruns, Jensen, and Miles), and a full contribution by a partner (Bruns) in respect to an existing debit balance. The occurrence of two separate offsets of Jensen's loan against a debit balance in his capital account was merely a consequence of the schedular sequence. If the complete liquidation relationship between Schiff and the partnership (partial contribution and absorption of residue debit balance) had been first established, only one setoff—$3,750 in amount—would have been required in respect to Jensen. Of course, the total effect would remain unchanged.

---

[3] This general provision may be challenged by the individual creditors of an insolvent partner. In the event of such a challenge, the accountant should advise the withholding of cash in an amount equal to the loan balance pending a final determination of priorities.

Illustration 17–3

AUSTIN APPLIANCE PARTNERSHIP
Schedule of Partnership Liquidation
Dr. [Cr.]

	Assets			Claimants / Residual Equities						
	Cash	Noncash	Priority Claims	Bruns Loan	Bruns Capital	Jensen Loan	Jensen Capital	Miles Loan	Miles Capital	Schiff Capital
Profit and loss ratio					30%		30%		20%	20%
Preliquidation balances	$20,000	$80,000	$[40,000]	$[4,000]	$[10,000]	$[5,000]	$[12,000]	$[7,000]	$[16,000]	$[6,000]
Realization of assets and allocation of loss	30,000	[80,000]			15,000		15,000		10,000	10,000
Balances	$50,000	–0–	$[40,000]	$[4,000]	$5,000	$[5,000]	$3,000	$[7,000]	$[6,000]	$4,000
Offset of loans against debit balances:										
Bruns				4,000	[4,000]					
Jensen						3,000	[3,000]			
Balances	$50,000	–0–	$[40,000]	–0–	$1,000	$[2,000]	–0–	$[7,000]	$[6,000]	$4,000
Contribution by Schiff	2,000									[2,000]
Balances	$52,000	–0–	$[40,000]	–0–	$1,000	$[2,000]	–0–	$[7,000]	$[6,000]	$2,000
Absorption of Schiff's debit balance (3:3:2)					750		750		500	[2,000]
Balances	$52,000	–0–	$[40,000]	–0–	$1,750	$[2,000]	$750	$[7,000]	$[5,500]	–0–
Additional offset against Jensen's loan balance						750	[750]			
Balances	$52,000	–0–	$[40,000]	–0–	$1,750	$[1,250]	–0–	$[7,000]	$[5,500]	–0–
Contribution by Bruns for debit balance	1,750				[1,750]					
Predistribution balances	$53,750	–0–	$[40,000]	–0–	–0–	$[1,250]	–0–	$[7,000]	$[5,500]	–0–
Cash distribution:										
Priority claims	[40,000]		40,000							
Partners' loans	[8,250]					1,250		7,000		
Partner's residual equity	[5,500]								5,500	
Termination of partnership	–0–	–0–	–0–	–0–	–0–	–0–	–0–	–0–	–0–	–0–

Liquidation Expenses

In each of the previous cases, the reference to "realization of assets and allocation of loss" indicated the *net* proceeds realized on the disposition of noncash assets. Such a description is appropriate when an item of expense is directly related to the sale of an asset, for example, commissions on sales. If, however, expenses are incurred during the liquidation process and they are not directly associated with specific assets but rather are identifiable only with the liquidation process or period, it may be preferable to separately disclose such expenses in the liquidation schedule. Whatever the treatment, no substantive change will result in the distribution of partnership assets. The "residual" profit and loss ratio properly relates to the allocation of expenses as well as to gains and losses from realization of assets. If one of the partners assumes sole responsibility for managing or directing the liquidation activities and is accorded a specific fee for such service, this cost should be clearly disclosed as a separate liquidation expense, with a corresponding increase in the relevant partner's capital account. Such an assignment discloses more completely the effect of the expense on the liquidation process. It also precludes a premature distribution of cash to this managing partner. Such a distribution might be subject to legal challenge should a debit balance ultimately exist in his capital account.

Installment (Periodic) Payments

Basic Accounting Problem

Under conditions of simple liquidation, the total gain or loss on the realization of assets, including the effects of liquidation expenses, is known before distribution of cash is made to individual partners. However, if the liquidation period extends over a prolonged period of time, it may be appropriate to make partial distributions of cash periodically to the partners *before* all of the assets have been realized. In this regard, the accountant often assumes a fiduciary status with respect to the claims of both partnership creditors and the individual partners against the available cash of the partnership. Therefore, he must be particularly circumspect in determining the amount of each installment payment in order to avoid an overdistribution to one or more of the partners. The fiduciary may be held liable for losses that proceed from excessive distributions. Thus, a distribution procedure is needed that will enable the accountant to compute periodic payments that may be made safely without undue risk of personal liability.

In the traditional approach to this problem, each time cash is to be distributed the accountant estimates the *largest potential loss* that may be incurred in future realizations of noncash assets. Since the equities of the partners are based upon the book values of the partnership assets, the total recorded value of the noncash assets approximates the maximum potential loss to the partnership.[4] If the accountant *assumes* the actual incurrence of the maximum potential loss, he may easily compute its hypothetical effect on the individual partners' capital balances. Any debit balance in a partner's capital account that results from this loss allocation process represents still another *potential* loss to the other partners in that it may not be satisfied by contributions of the deficient partner. Accordingly, it should be allocated to the remaining partners—in effect, it is a reallocation of a portion of the maximum potential loss to the partnership. This sequence of hypothetical loss absorptions will result in one or more partners' capital accounts having credit balances which, in total, are equal to the cash available for distribution to partners. Initially, this amount is the total cash less claims of outside creditors. After obligations to creditors are discharged, the residual amount of cash on hand may be distributed in amounts equal to these adjusted credit balances. Then, if the noncash assets in fact prove worthless and if all debit balances are absorbed in sequence, a zero balance will necessarily exist in each of the partners' capital accounts. Since cash distributions are not made to any partner who conceivably could end up with a debit balance under the worst possible asset realization circumstance, the cash payments calculated in this manner are usually referred to as *safe payments.*

Periodic Computation of Safe Payments to Partners

The procedure outlined above, expressed in the form of a *partnership liquidation schedule* and supported by a *calculation of safe installment payments,* is illustrated in Case 4 which follows.

Case 4.   On January 1, 19X1, Dahl, Hersey, and Katz agree to dissolve their partnership. Their preliquidation capital balances and percentage interests in profits and losses are the following:

Partner	Capital	Ratio
Dahl.................	$25,000	50%
Hersey...............	45,000	30
Katz	15,000	20

The partnership has cash of $5,000 and noncash assets of $85,000; liabilities to outside creditors amount to $5,000. The partners elect to make periodic distributions of all accumulated cash at the end of each month during the liquidation process. The following data relate to the realization of assets:

---

[4] See page 711 for a more precise statement of the maximum potential loss.

	Book Values	Net Proceeds
January.............	$25,000	$20,000
February	40,000	20,000
March.............	10,000	5,000
April..............	10,000	2,000

The partnership liquidation schedule and the supporting calculation of safe installment payments are shown in Illustrations 17–4 and 17–5. Several important conclusions can be drawn from an analysis of the illustrations in this case:

1. The total cash payments to each partner are equivalent to the amount of a single payment computed under a simple liquidation procedure. This is illustrated as follows:

Simple Liquidation Method

	Dahl	Hersey	Katz
Preliquidation balances....................	$25,000	$45,000	$15,000
Realization loss ($85,000 − $47,000)	19,000	11,400	7,600
Partners' claims	$ 6,000	$33,600	$ 7,400

Installment Payments Method
(from Illustration 17–4)

	Dahl	Hersey	Katz
January......................	–0–	$20,000	–0–
February.....................	$2,500	11,500	$6,000
March	2,500	1,500	1,000
April	1,000	600	400
Total payments..........	$6,000	$33,600	$7,400

2. The ratio of the partners' capital balances at the end of February exhibits a significant relationship: *the ratio of capital balances is equal to the profit and loss ratio.* When this condition exists, all subsequent installment distributions are based upon the profit and loss ratio (see March and April installment payments in Illustration 17–4). Future losses, should they occur, are allocated on this basis, and thus the availability of cash for distribution to partners indicates that the total equity of the partners exceeds the total potential loss. The computation of safe payments is, in fact, an iterative process that systematically causes the ratio of partners' equities to converge to the profit and loss ratio as rapidly as can be accomplished by controlling cash distributions to partners. Therefore, after one payment is

Illustration 17–4

DAHL, HERSEY, AND KATZ PARTNERSHIP
Schedule of Partnership Liquidation
Dr. [Cr.]

	Assets		Priority Claims	Claimants — Residual Equities		
	Cash	Noncash		Dahl	Hersey	Katz
				50%	30%	20%
Profit and loss						
Preliquidation balances	$ 5,000	$ 85,000	$[15,000]	$[25,000]	$[45,000]	$[15,000]
Realization of assets and allocation of loss	20,000	[25,000]		2,500	1,500	1,000
Balances	$ 25,000	$ 60,000	$[15,000]	$[22,500]	$[43,500]	$[14,000]
Payment of liabilities	[5,000]		5,000			
Balances	$ 20,000	$ 60,000	–0–	$[22,500]	$[43,500]	$[14,000]
January installment payment:						
(see supporting schedule—Illustration 17–5)	[20,000]				20,000	
Balances	–0–	$ 60,000	–0–	$[22,500]	$[23,500]	$[14,000]
Realization of assets and allocation of loss	$ 20,000	[40,000]		10,000	6,000	4,000
Balances	$ 20,000	$ 20,000	–0–	$[12,500]	$[17,500]	$[10,000]
February installment payment						
(see supporting schedule—Illustration 17–5)	[20,000]			2,500	11,500	6,000
Balances	–0–	$ 20,000	–0–	$[10,000]	$ [6,000]	$ [4,000]
Realization of assets and allocation of loss	$ 5,000	[10,000]		2,500	1,500	1,000
Balances	$ 5,000	$ 10,000	–0–	$ [7,500]	$ [4,500]	$ [3,000]
March installment payment						
(see supporting schedule—Illustration 17–5)	[5,000]			2,500	1,500	1,000
Balances	–0–	$ 10,000	–0–	$ [5,000]	$ [3,000]	$ [2,000]
Realization of assets and allocation of loss	$ 2,000	[10,000]		4,000	2,400	1,600
Balances	$ 2,000	–0–	–0–	$ [1,000]	$ [600]	$ [400]
Final payment to partners	[2,000]			1,000	600	400
Termination of partnership	–0–	–0–	–0–	–0–	–0–	–0–

Illustration 17–5

DAHL, HERSEY, AND KATZ PARTNERSHIP
Calculation of Safe Installment Payments
Dr. [Cr.]

	Residual Equities		
	Dahl	*Hersey*	*Katz*
Profit and loss ratio	50%	30%	20%
Computation of January installment:			
Predistribution balances	$[22,500]	$[43,500]	$[14,000]
Potential loss—noncash assets—$60,000	30,000	18,000	12,000
Balances	$ 7,500	$[25,500]	$ [2,000]
Potential loss—Dahl's debit balance	[7,500]	4,500	3,000
Balances	–0–	$[21,000]	$ 1,000
Potential loss—Katz's debit balance................		1,000	[1,000]
Safe payments to partners	–0–	$[20,000]	–0–
Computation of February installment:			
Predistribution balances	$[12,500]	$[17,500]	$[10,000]
Potential loss—noncash assets—$20,000	10,000	6,000	4,000
Safe payments to partners	$ [2,500]	$[11,500]	$ [6,000]
Computation of March installment:			
Predistribution balances	$ [7,500]	$ [4,500]	$ [3,000]
Potential loss—noncash assets—$10,000	5,000	3,000	2,000
Safe payments to partners	$ [2,500]	$ [1,500]	$ [1,000]

allocated among two or more partners, subsequent distributions to these partners will be in the same ratio as their relative profit and loss ratio. Additionally, after a payment has been made to all partners, the ratio of the partners' equities will be equal to the profit and loss ratio. This fact is confirmed by data of Case 4 with the February installment payment. In this case, a supporting calculation to determine safe payments to partners is unnecessary *after* the February distribution.

3.   The order of payments in the schedule of partnership liquidation is consistent with the order of priority established in the Uniform Partnership Act. Distributions are first made to creditors; subsequent payments, as cash becomes available, are to partners.

Partners' Loans

It has been noted previously that in partnership liquidation a partner's loan balance should be offset against a debit balance in his capital account. Accordingly, liquidating payments are based upon each partner's *total* equity (or net equity in the event of a capital deficit) in the partnership. This principle is equally valid in the case of installment payments made to partners during the period of liquidation. The total equity of each partner (the sum of both loan and capital balances) should be entered in the calculation of safe installment payments. Entering the total equity implicitly recognizes the relevance of setoff in the event a partner's capital balance is completely absorbed in the process of allocating potential losses. In the schedule of partnership liquidation, however, indicated payments to each partner are traditionally reported as first in abatement of loans and second in reduction of capital balances.

The addition of this variable, partners' loans, to a liquidation process involving installment distributions is illustrated in the following case.

Case 5. The partners of the Jackson Company agree to dissolve their partnership on March 31, 19X1. Their preliquidation capital and loan account balances and the profit and loss ratio are as follows:

Partner	Capital	Loan	Ratio
W..............	$16,000	$4,000	50%
X..............	29,000	2,000	20
Y..............	23,000		20
Z..............	9,000	1,000	10

The partnership has a cash balance of $10,000 and noncash assets of $80,000; obligations to outside creditors amount to $6,000. Available cash is to be distributed at the end of each month during the period of liquidation. Assets are realized as follows:

	Book Values	Net Proceeds
April............	$54,000	$30,000
May.............	24,000	18,000
June	2,000	–0–

The partnership liquidation schedule is given in Illustration 17–6, and the supporting calculation of safe installment payments is displayed in Illustration 17–7.

Case 5 accents several concepts previously discussed:

1. Although the total equity (capital and loan balance) of each partner is used in the calculation of safe installment payments, any cash distribution to a partner is assumed to apply first against the partner's loan account, with any remaining payment made against his capital balance.

2. Since installment payments were made to X, Y, and Z in April, the ratio of their *total equities* at the end of April should be equal to their

Illustration 17–6

JACKSON COMPANY
Schedule of Partnership Liquidation
Dr. [Cr.]

	Assets		Priority Claims	Claimants — Residual Equities						
				W		X		Y	Z	
	Cash	Noncash		Loan	Capital	Loan	Capital	Capital	Loan	Capital
Profit and loss ratio...........					50%		20%	20%		10%
Preliquidation balances..........	$ 10,000	$ 80,000	$[6,000]	$[4,000]	$[16,000]	$[2,000]	$[29,000]	$[23,000]	$[1,000]	$[9,000]
Realization of assets and allocation of loss........	30,000	[54,000]			12,000		4,800	4,800		2,400
Balances.................	$ 40,000	$ 26,000	$[6,000]	$[4,000]	$ [4,000]	$[2,000]	$[24,200]	$[18,200]	$[1,000]	$[6,600]
Payment to creditors...........	[6,000]		6,000							
Balances.................	$ 34,000	$ 26,000	–0–	$[4,000]	$ [4,000]	$[2,000]	$[24,200]	$[18,200]	$[1,000]	$[6,600]
April installment payment (see supporting schedule—Illustration 17–7).........	[34,000]					2,000	17,000	11,000	1,000	3,000
Balances.................	–0–	$ 26,000	–0–	$[4,000]	$ [4,000]	–0–	$ [7,200]	$ [7,200]	–0–	$[3,600]
Realization of assets and allocation of loss........	$ 18,000	[24,000]			3,000		1,200	1,200		600
Balances.................	$ 18,000	$ 2,000	–0–	$[4,000]	$ [1,000]	–0–	$ [6,000]	$ [6,000]	–0–	$[3,000]
May installment payment (see supporting schedule—Illustration 17–7).........	[18,000]			4,000			5,600	5,600		2,800
Balances.................	–0–	$ 2,000	–0–	–0–	$ [1,000]	–0–	$ [400]	$ [400]	–0–	$ [200]
Realization of assets and allocation of loss........	–0–	[2,000]			1,000		400	400		200
Termination of partnership......	–0–	–0–	–0–	–0–	–0–	–0–	–0–	–0–	–0–	–0–

Illustration 17–7

JACKSON COMPANY
Calculation of Safe Installment Payments
Dr. [Cr.]

	Residual Equities (Capital and Loan Balances)			
	W	X	Y	Z
Profit and loss ratio......................	50%	20%	20%	10%
Computation of April installment:				
Predistribution balances..................	$[8,000]	$[26,200]	$[18,200]	$[7,600]
Potential loss—noncash assets—$26,000.......................	13,000	5,200	5,200	2,600
Balances..............................	$ 5,000	$[21,000]	$[13,000]	$[5,000]
Potential loss—W's debit balance	[5,000]	2,000	2,000	1,000
Safe payments to partners...............	–0–	$[19,000]	$[11,000]	$[4,000]
Computation of May installment:				
Predistribution balances..................	$[5,000]	$ [6,000]	$ [6,000]	$[3,000]
Potential loss—noncash assets—$2,000.......................	1,000	400	400	200
Safe payments to partners...............	$[4,000]	$ [5,600]	$ [5,600]	$[2,800]

relative profit and loss ratio. This equality is confirmed by the schedule of partnership liquidation (7200 : 7200 : 3600 = 20 : 20 : 10). The schedule additionally indicates that subsequent distributions to these partners are made in their relative profit and loss ratio (e.g., in May, 5600 : 5600 : 2800 = 20 : 20 : 10). Since an installment payment is made to W in May, all of the partners' equities at May 31 are in their respective profit and loss ratio; subsequent distributions, if any, would be made on the basis of this ratio.

Liquidation Expenses and Unrecorded Liabilities

The total potential loss of a partnership has heretofore been assumed to be equal to the book value of noncash assets. This assumption is true *only* if the assets are determined to be completely worthless, *and* if *additional* expenses are not incurred in the process of liquidation, *and* if all partnership liabilities have been properly recorded. However, if liquidation expenses, including disposal costs for noncash assets, should exceed the proceeds from asset realization, the actual loss suffered will be greater than the assumed loss. Additionally, unrecorded liabilities to outside creditors may be discovered during the period of liquidation; necessarily, these claims will rank ahead of the residual claims of partners. Therefore, in order to avoid personal liability, the accountant should explicitly recognize these items in the liquidation schedule where the amounts are predictable with reasonable accuracy. In the calculation of safe installment payments, provision may be made for estimated future liquidation expenses and unrecorded liabilities by treating them as additions to the potential loss as previously determined. This adjustment has the effect of reserving cash in an amount equal to the total of anticipated liquidation expenses and unrecorded liabilities.

Cash Predistribution Plan

The previous discussion has shown how the accountant, acting as fiduciary or as advisor to the fiduciary, can move through the period of partnership liquidation, paying creditors and making periodic payments to partners that are reasonably "safe." In other words, those partners who receive cash payments are not apt to find their capital accounts reduced to debit balances from subsequent partnership losses. These safe payments are made possible by the information provided in the calculations of safe installment payments.

However, at the beginning of the liquidation process, it may be desirable to develop an overall plan for making future cash payments. For example, creditors or partners may ask the fiduciary to estimate when cash is likely to be distributed to them. To answer such an inquiry, the fiduciary must first project the timing and amounts of cash receipts from the realization of assets. No doubt this will vary greatly depending upon the particular circumstances of the partnership in question. The type of assets involved, the condition and location of the assets, the quantities of assets, and the markets available for selling the assets are some of the factors that must be considered. Because the problems of making such cash projections vary so much with the particular situation, and because they are not unique to partnership accounting, they are not considered further.

But, projecting cash receipts from the liquidation of assets is only the first step in responding to inquiries about future cash payments. The second step is to prepare a plan for the future distribution of cash, whenever it becomes available. This plan is called the *cash predistribution plan*. It is designed to show the sequence and amounts of payments that will be made to creditors and partners if, and when, cash becomes available during the liquidation period.

The following sequence of operations is used in establishing the predetermined order and amount of distribution payments:

1. Using each partner's residual equity (combined capital and loan balances) and percentage interest in profits and losses, compute the partners' *loss-absorption potentials*. The amount of this potential for each partner is the amount of possible loss the partnership may incur before the partner is obliged to contribute new assets to the partnership, i.e., his residual equity divided by his percentage interest in profits and losses.

For example, if Baker and Moore have equities (including loans) of $48,000 and $40,000, respectively, and share profits and losses in the ratio 6:4, a table of loss-absorption potentials may take the following form:

BAKER-MOORE PARTNERSHIP
Loss-Absorption Potentials

Partner	Equities	Profit and Loss Ratio	Loss-Absorption Potentials	Order of Equity Absorption
Baker............	$48,000	60%	$ 80,000 = ($48,000 ÷ .60)	1
Moore...........	40,000	40	100,000 = ($40,000 ÷ .40)	2

A loss of $80,000 would totally absorb Baker's equity in the partnership (including any possible offset of a loan balance should one exist), whereas a loss of $100,000 would be required before Moore's total equity would be absorbed.

2.   After calculating the loss-absorption potential of each partner, prepare a schedule that assumes potential losses in sequence such that the amount of each assumed loss is sufficient to absorb the equity of exactly one partner, beginning with the partner having the smallest loss-absorption potential. The order of this equity absorption is indicated in the table of loss-absorption potentials, i.e., in the order of ascending amounts of loss-absorption potentials.

If the Baker-Moore Partnership has cash of $7,000, noncash assets of $93,000, and liabilities of $12,000, such a schedule would assume the following form:

BAKER-MOORE PARTNERSHIP
Schedule of Loss Absorption
Dr. [Cr.]

	Assumed Losses	Baker	Moore
Profit and loss ratio		60%	40%
Preliquidation balances.............................		$[48,000]	$[40,000]
Potential loss to absorb Baker's equity	$[80,000]	48,000	32,000
Balances		$ –0–	$ [8,000]
Potential loss to absorb Moore's remaining equity......	[8,000]		8,000
Balance			$ –0–

In this simple case, the total potential loss is attributed to the degree of realization of noncash assets. Therefore, as noted before, the book value of noncash assets is generally assumed to establish a maximum possible loss. This case illustrates the important principle that after one partner's equity has been totally eliminated, additional losses are absorbed by the remaining partners in their relative profit and loss ratio. Given the assumption that debit balances will *not* be restored to zero by contributions, no benefit is to be derived by allocating subsequent assumed losses to all partners; doing so would simply require a reallocation of the debit balances created in the first allocation. In this example, Moore is the only remaining partner with an equity; consequently, he must absorb 100 percent of all additional losses, and a loss of $8,000 would thus completely absorb his $8,000 equity. In the schedule, the sequence progresses until all partners' equities have been reduced to zero, unless the cash on hand exceeds the claims of outside creditors; in this event, the schedule should be continued until a balance remains in but one partner's capital account.

3. Using the above schedule, which indicates the effect of loss absorption on the several equities, construct a predistribution plan indicating in sequence the distribution of cash as it is made available to the partnership. This is accomplished by reverse movement through the loss-absorption schedule, as the continued availability of cash systematically negates the assumption of potential losses. The resulting cash predistribution plan is given below:

BAKER-MOORE PARTNERSHIP
Cash Predistribution Plan

		Distributions		
		Priority Claims	Baker	Moore
Preliquidation cash balance..............	$ 7,000	100%		
Subsequent collections (on realization of noncash assets):				
First.................................	$ 5,000	100%		
Next	8,000			100%
Next	80,000		60%	40%
Noncash assets....................	$93,000			
Any additional cash collected.............			60%	40%

It should be observed that any available cash in excess of the $93,000 book value of noncash assets implies a net realization gain, which must be credited to the partners in accordance with the partners' profit- and loss-sharing ratio. The percentages in the schedule may be easily converted to dollar amounts and also included in the cash predistribution plan; however, this translation would not indicate explicitly the proper distribution if only a portion of the indicated cash were made available.

The cash predistribution plan will serve as a guide for cash payments throughout the liquidation period, *if it is interpreted carefully and if certain events do not occur*. First, the process of liquidating a business invariably involves incurring some expenses. These liquidation expenses *are not* estimated and included among the priority claims shown in the cash predistribution plan. Hence, the plan should be interpreted as specifying cash payments to be made from cash balances and receipts, *net* of liquidation expense payments to nonpartners. Thus, the total amount to be paid for priority claims before partners receive any cash necessarily will exceed the amount listed in the cash predistribution plan.

Second, unrecorded liabilities to outside creditors may be discovered during the liquidation period; if so, the amount of priority claims disclosed in the cash predistribution plan must be augmented by the amount of these newly discovered liabilities. Finally, if for some reason one of the partners should contribute additional assets to the partnership, the loss-absorption potential of that partner will be enlarged by the contribution. Hence, the original cash predistribution plan will be invalidated and a new plan must be prepared.

INSOLVENT PARTNERSHIP

Basic Rights

In an earlier discussion, partnership insolvency was said to exist where recorded partnership assets are insufficient to discharge partnership liabilities. As noted, this definition emphasizes the financial condition of the partnership, viewed as a separate and distinct entity. It thereby ignores the existence and potential value of the partnership claim against the individual partners for debit balances in their capital accounts; at least one such debit balance must exist if partnership liabilities exceed partnership assets. In the discussion to follow, it is initially assumed that the partnership creditors first exhaust partnership assets in discharging partnership liabilities, and thereafter make claims against the partners jointly for any remaining unpaid balances of partnership debts. Two conditions are possible:

1.   One or more of the individual partners possesses separate net assets sufficient to meet the claims of the partnership creditors (i.e., legally, the partnership is not insolvent).
2.   The partners individually do not have sufficient assets to discharge all existing partnership debts (i.e., the partnership is legally insolvent, and considering the claims of partnership creditors, all of the partners are individually insolvent). In this case, the order of distributing the partners' individually owned assets depends upon the relative rights of partnership and individual creditors.

To determine the basic rights of creditors, it is important first to marshal the assets of both the partnership and the several partners. This legal doctrine, *marshaling of assets,* prescribes that partnership assets and individual assets constitute separate pools of resources against which partnership creditors and individual creditors, respectively, have initial and separate recourse. If the partnership is insolvent, partnership assets are completely exhausted in the *partial* settlement of partnership debts. If the partnership is solvent, creditors of individual partners have a claim against the remaining partnership assets to the extent of the partner's residual interest therein. Once individual creditors have satisfied their claims against individual assets, the partnership creditors may recover from the partners' separately owned assets to the extent of their unsatisfied claims, *regardless of the equity status of the partner in the firm* (debit or credit balance). A special point of interest in this allocation process is the definition of individual and partnership assets and liabilities. A difficult and legally unresolved problem relates to a debit balance existing in an insolvent partner's capital account (whether or not the *other* partners are insolvent). Section 40 (i) of the Uniform Partnership Act is explicit on this point:

> Where a partner has become bankrupt or his estate is insolvent the claims against his separate property shall rank in the following order:
> (I)   Those owing to separate creditors,
> (II) Those owing to partnership creditors,
> (III) Those owing to partners by way of contribution.

Under this Act, the obligation to the partnership, and the remaining partners, for a debit balance does not constitute a *separate* or *individual* liability of the insolvent partner. The language of the Federal Bankruptcy Act, which emphasizes the marshaling principle, would also appear to support this position. There exists, however, a possible legal *interpretation* of the "contribution obligation" as constituting an individual liability of the partner. In this regard, the following observations made at the time the Uniform Partnership Act was formulated are relevant:

> It is to be hoped that eventually in all our courts of insolvency the liability of the partner to contribute to the payment of partnership liabilities, correctly described by the Act as a partnership asset, will be treated as on a parity with his other liabilities for purpose of distribution of his insolvent estate.[5]

> This [Section 40 (i)] however introduces several changes into the law as it is established by the weight of authority. A partner who has paid the partnership debts can at present [prior to passage of the Act] prove for contribution against the insolvent partner's estate and share *pari passu* with his other separate creditors.[6]

---

[5] Judson A. Crane, "The Uniform Partnership Act—A Criticism," *Harvard Law Review*, June 1915, pp. 784–85.

[6] Ibid., p. 786.

A contrary opinion is expressed in the following terms:

> It is submitted that the partner, by paying the partnership debts, should be held to have stepped into the right of the partnership creditors against the assets of the insolvent partner. He should not obtain, however, in respect to that estate a better position than the person whose claim he has paid. Indeed, if he were allowed to do so, the rule giving priority to separate creditors on the separate estate would be to that extent nullified.[7]

The first opinion (Crane) appears to support the position that a partner's debit balance in his capital account, particularly if it represents an obligation to a solvent partner who has personally discharged the total claims of partnership creditors, constitutes a separate liability of the insolvent partner. The counterargument, however, focuses on the apparent *equity* of the provision in the Uniform Partnership Act. It may be concluded, therefore, that in those states which have not adopted the Uniform Partnership Act, or in federal bankruptcy cases, it is possible that the individual partner's estate may be prorated among his separate creditors and his obligation to the partnership.[8]

The basic rights of creditors, following the marshaling of assets principle, may then be summarized as follows:

1. Partnership creditors should seek the discharge of partnership debts by first exhausting partnership assets (exclusive of contributions of partners) to the extent of their claims.
2. A partner's individual creditors should first seek recourse against his separate assets to the extent of their claims. Under the Uniform Partnership Act, amounts due to the partnership by way of contribution do not constitute individual liabilities; under common law, or in federal bankruptcy cases, the contribution requirement *may* be construed as an individual liability sharing *pari passu* with other individual liabilities.
3. To the extent of their unsatisfied claims, partnership creditors may prove against the residual assets of an individual partner after his separate creditors have been satisfied, regardless of the amount of his residual interest in the partnership.
4. To the extent of their unsatisfied claims, a partner's individual creditors may prove against the *recorded* interest of the individual partner in the residual assets of a solvent partnership.

---

[7] William Draper Lewis, "The Uniform Partnership Act," *Harvard Law Review*, January 1916, pp. 307–8.

[8] Even other interpretations have been made. In *Robinson* v. *Security Co.*, Ann Cas 1915C, 1170, it was held that a judgment should be rendered "dividing the distributable assets belonging to the estate of each partner ratably among the separate creditors of such partners together with the partnership creditors." Marshaling of assets was not applied even *in form* in this case.

5. If a partner pays more than his share of partnership liabilities, he has a claim, as measured by the resulting credit balance in his account, against those partners with debit balances (representing their unrequited share of partnership losses).

Accounting Analysis of the Insolvent Partnership

Determination of amounts to be allocated to the various creditor and equity interests will be illustrated under each of the two conditions of insolvency: (1) an insolvent partnership with at least one solvent partner, and (2) an insolvent partnership with all partners insolvent.

Case 6. At Least One Solvent Partner.   The trial balance of the ABC Partnership, after realization of assets but before distribution of cash to either creditors or partners, is as follows:

	Debit	Credit
Cash	$20,000	
Liabilities		$30,000
A, capital		10,000
B, capital	5,000	
C, capital	15,000	
	$40,000	$40,000

A, B, and C share profits and losses in the ratio 2:4:4. The separate financial status of each individual partner, excluding his interest in, or obligation to, the partnership, is as follows:

	Assets (Realizable Value)	Liabilities
A	$ 5,000	$20,000
B.............	6,000	4,000
C	30,000	10,000

Given these data, it is apparent that both A and B are insolvent. A's individual liabilities exceed his individual assets and his interest in the firm (even assuming his partnership interest is recoverable at book value), and B's obligations to individual creditors ($4,000) and to the partnership ($5,000) exceed his individual assets. It is assumed further that partnership creditors obtain a judgment against C and that he makes full payment of the partnership obligations to its outside creditors, using his separate assets as necessary. Schedules of partnership liquidation and distribution of separate assets of the individual partners under the provisions of the Uniform Partnership Act are given in Illustrations 17–8 and 17–9.

Illustration 17-8

ABC PARTNERSHIP
Schedule of Partnership Liquidation
Dr. [Cr.]

			Claimants		
				Residual Equities	
	Cash	Priority Claims	A	B	C
Profit and loss ratio..............................			20%	40%	40%
Balances...	$ 20,000	$[30,000]	$[10,000]	$ 5,000	$ 15,000
Payment of liabilities	[20,000]	20,000			
Balances...	–0–	$[10,000]	$[10,000]	$ 5,000	$ 15,000
Establish status of each partner's personal solvency. Record payment of partnership liabilities by C from his separate assets.............		10,000			[10,000]
Balances...	–0–	–0–	$[10,000]	$ 5,000	$ 5,000
Contribution by B................................	$ 2,000			[2,000]	
Balances...	$ 2,000	–0–	$[10,000]	$ 3,000	$ 5,000
Allocation of B's debit balance.....................			1,000	[3,000]	2,000
Balances...	$ 2,000	–0–	$ [9,000]	–0–	$ 7,000
Contribution by C................................	7,000				[7,000]
Balances...	$ 9,000	–0–	$ [9,000]	–0–	–0–
Distribution of cash..............................	[9,000]		9,000		
Termination of partnership........................	–0–	–0–	–0–	–0–	–0–

Illustration 17-9

A, B, AND C
Schedule of Distribution of Separate Assets

	A	B	C
Separate assets	$ 5,000	$ 6,000	$ 30,000
Separate liabilities (Rank I)..........................	[20,000]	[4,000]	[10,000]
Separate capital [deficit]	$[15,000]	$ 2,000	$ 20,000
Payment of partnership debts (Rank II)			[10,000]
Separate capital [deficit]	$[15,000]	$ 2,000	$ 10,000
Payment of debt to partnership (Rank III)		[2,000]	[7,000]
Separate capital [deficit]	$[15,000]	–0–	$ 3,000
Distribution of cash by partnership	9,000		
Separate capital [deficit]	$ [6,000]	–0–	$ 3,000
Obligations of B to A and C through the partnership....	1,000	$[3,000]	2,000
Separate capital [deficit]	$ [5,000]	$[3,000]	$ 5,000

If the Uniform Partnership Act is not controlling in this case *and* if the partners' obligations to the firm are adjudged individual liabilities sharing *pari passu* with other individual obligations, the schedule will be modified only by the amount of B's contribution to the firm (since A, the second insolvent partner, does not have an obligation to contribute to the partnership). The amount of B's contribution is calculated as follows:

| | | B | |
	Liabilities	Ratio of Assets to Liabilities	Asset Settlement
To partnership.............	$5,000	⅔	$3,334
Separate creditors	4,000	⅔	2,666
	$9,000		$6,000

Under these conditions, A, the only partner with a credit balance, will receive $445 more than under the provisions of the Uniform Partnership Act, C will contribute $889 less to the partnership, and B's personal creditors will receive $1,334 less.

Case 7.   All Partners Insolvent.   Assume the same facts as in Case 6, except that C has separate assets of $10,000 rather than $30,000. In this circumstance, the partnership is legally insolvent, as it will be shown that there are insufficient partnership assets and net assets of individual partners to make a full settlement with partnership creditors.

Under the provisions of the Uniform Partnership Act, the partnership creditors will receive the $20,000 of partnership cash and the $2,000 excess assets of B (those not required to discharge separate debts), leaving a deficiency in payments to partnership creditors of $8,000. The $22,000 distribution to these creditors will necessarily be made according to priorities established by law.[9]

If the partners' obligations to the partnership are considered separate (individual) liabilities and are accorded the same status as other separate liabilities, the distribution of separate property is calculated as follows:

| | | B | |
	Liabilities	Ratio of Assets to Liabilities	Asset Settlement
To partnership.............	$5,000	⅔	$3,334
Separate creditors	4,000	⅔	2,666
	$9,000		$6,000

---

[9] These priorities are discussed in Chapter 18.

	Liabilities	C Ratio of Assets to Liabilities	Asset Settlement
To partnership	$15,000	⅖	$ 6,000
Separate creditors.........	10,000	⅖	4,000
	$25,000		$10,000

The allocation of B's separate assets remains unchanged in this case, as there is no adjustment of B's financial status. Consequently, where the partners' obligations to contribute to the firm for debit balances are confirmed legally and given an equal status with their separate liabilities, the partnership creditors will receive an additional $7,334 ($1,334 + $6,000) from the partnership, $1,334 being contributed by B and $6,000 being contributed by C. It should be noted, however, that this calculational technique ignores the subtlety introduced by the inherent variability of the obligation to the partnership when two or more partners are involved, that is, the undischarged balance must be absorbed by the remaining partners, which accordingly alters the relative ratio of liabilities to separate creditors and to the partnership.

Comprehensive Illustration

Case 8 illustrates the preparation of a cash predistribution plan, a partnership liquidation schedule, and the related supporting calculations and schedules, given a more complex situation in which four partners decide to liquidate their partnership and one of the four partners is insolvent.

Case 8.   The partners of Slippery Walk Company agree to dissolve their partnership on July 1, 19X1, since the operations of the company have met with financial difficulties. The preliquidation capital and loan account balances and profit and loss ratio are as follows:

Dr. [Cr.]

Partner	Capital	Loan	Ratio
James	$[36,000]	$[14,000]	20%
McDonald	[28,000]	4,000 *	20
Pearson	[12,000]	[4,000]	50
Quigley	[30,000]		10

* Loan to McDonald from Slippery Walk Company.

The partners and creditors have agreed that Quigley should oversee the liquidation of the partnership's assets and distribution of cash to creditors

Illustration 17–10

SLIPPERY WALK COMPANY
Supporting Schedules for Cash Predistribution Plan

A. Schedule of Loss-Absorption Potentials

Partner	Equities	Profit and Loss Ratio	Loss-Absorption Potentials	Order of Equity Absorption
James.....................	$50,000	20%	$250,000 = ($50,000/.20)	3
McDonald	24,000	20	120,000 = ($24,000/.20)	2
Pearson..................	16,000	50	32,000 = ($16,000/.50)	1
Quigley.................	30,000	10	300,000 = ($30,000/.10)	4

B. Schedule of Loss Absorption, Dr. [Cr.]

	Assumed Losses	James	McDonald	Pearson	Quigley
Profit and loss ratio..........		20%	20%	50%	10%
Preliquidation equities		$[50,000]	$[24,000]	$[16,000]	$[30,000]
Potential loss to absorb Pearson's equity...........	$[32,000]	6,400	6,400	16,000	3,200
Balances		$[43,600]	$[17,600]	–0–	$[26,800]
Potential loss to absorb McDonald's equity ($17,600/.40)..............	[44,000]	17,600	17,600		8,800
Balances		$[26,000]	–0–		$[18,000]
Potential loss to absorb James' equity ($26,000/(2/3)).	[39,000]	26,000			13,000
Balances		–0–			$ [5,000]
Potential loss to absorb Quigley's remaining equity .	[5,000]				5,000
Balance					–0–

and partners. Quigley forecasts that it will take approximately three months to complete the liquidation. The partners request that available cash be distributed at the end of each month, and they inquire of Quigley as to when they should expect to participate in the cash distribution. As a consequence, Quigley wishes to develop a cash predistribution plan. In anticipation of doing so, the calculations leading to the distribution of cash payments to partners are prepared as shown in Illustration 17–10.

The assets and liabilities of Slippery Walk Company on July 1, 19X1, are cash, $6,000; noncash assets, $244,000; and liabilities, $130,000. Using the calculations shown in Illustration 17–10 and the information about liabilities, the cash predistribution plan is as follows:

SLIPPERY WALK COMPANY
Cash Predistribution Plan

	Priority Claims	Distributions			
		James	McDonald	Pearson	Quigley
Cash distributions:					
First $130,000......................	100%				
Next 5,000					100%
Next 39,000		66⅔%			33⅓
Next 44,000		40	40%		20
All additional payments		20	20	50%	10

Quigley anticipates that the realization of noncash assets will follow the pattern below:

July 19X1	$144,000 net cash proceeds
August 19X1	20,000 net cash proceeds
September 19X1	20,000 net cash proceeds

Based upon this information and the cash predistribution plan, Quigley is able to answer the partners' and creditors' inquiries as to when they might anticipate receiving cash. Quigley's forecast is based on his plan to retain $10,000 cash at the end of July and $4,000 at the end of August as a reserve for future unrecorded liabilities. By the end of September, Quigley expects that all liquidation expenses and unrecorded liabilities will be known so that a final cash distribution can be made. His forecast is summarized below:

Forecasted Schedule of Payments

Payee	July 31 Payments	August 31 Payments	September 30 Payments
Creditors.......................	$130,000		
James..........................	3,333	$17,333	$11,733
McDonald......................			6,400
Pearson........................			
Quigley........................	6,667	8,667	5,867
Total expected payments	$140,000	$26,000	$24,000
Cash to be held in reserve	$ 10,000	$ 4,000	–0–

Quigley's forecast is based upon his subjective estimates of when and how much cash will be generated from the liquidation of assets. Actual events may differ substantially from his expectations.

Contrary to the cash predistribution plan and Quigley's forecast of payments, which are *ex ante* statements of what is expected to happen in the future, the schedule of partnership liquidation is a historical document that reports the actual transactions which occur during the liquidation period. The schedule of partnership liquidation for Slippery Walk Company is based upon the following events that took place during the three-month liquidation of the company.

| | Liquidation of Noncash Assets | | |
	Discovery of Unrecorded Liabilities	*Cash Proceeds Net of Liquidation Expenses*	*Book Values of Liquidated Assets*
During July	–0–	$136,000	$180,000
During August.	$8,000	22,000	18,000
During September	–0–	20,000	46,000

Cash disbursements at the end of each month amounted to all available cash balances except for a $10,000 cash reserve at the end of July and a $4,000 cash reserve at the end of August. During the month of August, Pearson contributed $5,000 to the partnership to partially compensate for his capital deficiency. He was unable to make any further contributions.

The schedule of partnership liquidation is presented in Illustration 17–11.

The actual sequence of cash distributions, as presented in Illustration 17–11, is precisely consistent with the cash predistribution plan except for the $8,000 payment for liabilities which were discovered in August, after the cash predistribution plan was prepared. Nevertheless, Pearson's $5,000 contribution of cash to the partnership (in August) potentially could have altered the sequence of payments from that which was indicated by the cash predistribution plan. That plan was constructed on the assumption that none of the partners would be able to make additional investments to cover capital deficiencies. Pearson's $5,000 contribution obviously strengthened his capital position relative to the other partners. Thus, his stronger position would warrant his participation in cash distributions somewhat sooner than was indicated by the cash predistribution plan. However, since the total amount of available cash was not large enough to provide any cash return to Pearson, the actual distribution of cash did in fact conform to the predistribution plan.

The cash predistribution plan is prepared prior to the liquidation period and must be based upon conservative assumptions with respect to future events. Because future events may turn out to be inconsistent with those assumptions and as a precautionary confirmation of the decisions to dis-

Illustration 17–11

SLIPPERY WALK COMPANY
Schedule of Partnership Liquidation
Dr. [Cr.]

| | Assets | | | | | Claimants / Residual Equities | | | | |
	Cash	Noncash	Priority Claims	James Loan	James Capital	McDonald Loan	McDonald Capital	Pearson Loan	Pearson Capital	Quigley Capital
Profit and loss ratio					20%		20%		50%	10%
Preliquidation balance	$ 6,000	$ 244,000	$[130,000]	$[14,000]	$[36,000]	$ 4,000	$[28,000]	$[4,000]	$[12,000]	$[30,000]
Realization of assets and allocation of loss—July	136,000	[180,000]			8,800		8,800		22,000	4,400
Balances	$ 142,000	$ 64,000	$[130,000]	$[14,000]	$[27,200]	$ 4,000	$[19,200]	$[4,000]	$ 10,000	$[25,600]
Payment of creditors	[130,000]		130,000							
July 31 installment payment	[2,000]									2,000
Balances on July 31	$ 10,000	$ 64,000	$ –0–	$[14,000]	$[27,200]	$ 4,000	$[19,200]	$[4,000]	$ 10,000	$[23,600]
Realization of assets and allocation of gain—August	22,000	[18,000]			[800]		[800]		[2,000]	[400]
Recognition of unrecorded liabilities			$ [8,000]		1,600		1,600		4,000	800
Contribution by Pearson	5,000								[5,000]	
Balances	$ 37,000	$ 46,000	$ [8,000]	$[14,000]	$[26,400]	$ 4,000	$[18,400]	$[4,000]	$ 7,000	$[23,200]
Payment of creditors	[8,000]		8,000							
August 31 installment	[25,000]			14,000	667					10,333
Balances on August 31	$ 4,000	$ 46,000	$ –0–	$ –0–	$[25,733]	$ 4,000	$[18,400]	$[4,000]	$ 7,000	$[12,867]
Realization of assets and allocation of loss—September	20,000	[46,000]			5,200		5,200		13,000	2,600
Offset of loans against capital accounts						[4,000]	4,000	4,000	[4,000]	
Balances	$ 24,000	–0–	–0–	–0–	$[20,533]	–0–	$ [9,200]	–0–	$ 16,000	$[10,267]
Allocation of Pearson's capital deficiency					6,400		6,400		[16,000]	3,200
Balances	$ 24,000	–0–	–0–	–0–	$[14,133]	–0–	$ [2,800]	–0–	–0–	$ [7,067]
September 30 installment	[24,000]				14,133		2,800			7,067
Termination of partnership	–0–	–0–	–0–	–0–	–0–	–0–	–0–	–0–	–0–	–0–

Illustration 17–12

SLIPPERY WALK COMPANY
Schedule of Safe Installment Payments
Dr. [Cr.]

	Partners' Equities			
	James	*McDonald*	*Pearson*	*Quigley*
Profit and loss ratio	20%	20%	50%	10%
Computation of July 31 payment:				
Predistribution balances	$[41,200]	$[15,200]	$ 6,000	$[25,600]
Potential loss, $80,000*	32,000	32,000	[6,000]	16,000
Balances	$ [9,200]	$ 16,800	–0–	$ [9,600]
Potential loss, $16,800	11,200	[16,800]		5,600
Balances	$ 2,000	–0–		$ [4,000]
Potential loss, $2,000	[2,000]			2,000
Safe payment to partner	–0–			$ [2,000]
Computation of August 31 payment:				
Predistribution balances	$[40,400]	$[14,400]	$ 3,000	$[23,200]
Potential loss, $53,000†	21,200	21,200	[3,000]	10,600
Balances	$[19,200]	$ 6,800	–0–	$[12,600]
Potential loss, $6,800	4,533	[6,800]		2,267
Safe payments to partners	$[14,667]	–0–		$[10,333]

Computation of September 30 payment:
Predistribution balances constitute safe payments to partners since no potential losses exist.

* $64,000 noncash assets + $10,000 reserve for unrecorded liabilities + $6,000 capital deficiency of Pearson = $80,000.

† $46,000 noncash assets + $4,000 reserve for unrecorded liabilities + $3,000 capital deficiency of Pearson = $53,000.

tribute cash, it is wise to prepare a calculation of safe installment payments in support of each cash distribution. Illustration 17–12 presents this calculation for Slippery Walk Company.

Questions

1. What are the principal activities of a partnership during the liquidation process?

2. What is the order of priority for the distribution of assets under Section 40 (B) of the Uniform Partnership Act?

3. If after liquidation of the partnership assets, a partner has a debit balance in his capital account, what procedure would be followed if the partner is solvent (i.e., he holds personal assets sufficient to cover the capital deficiency)? What if the partner is insolvent?

4. Explain the rule of "setoff."

5. If one partner is assigned the role of managing the liquidation process and is to be compensated for this service by the partnership, how should the compensation be recorded in the records of the partnership?

6. If installment (periodic) payments are to be made during the course of liquidation, what factors might the accountant be concerned with in determining the amounts of cash or other assets to be distributed?

7. Describe the role and usefulness of a schedule of safe (installment) payments.

8. How are loans from partners accounted for in the schedule of partnership liquidation and in the schedule of safe (installment) payments?

9. What hypothetical losses and/or hypothetical cash transfers are recorded in a schedule of partnership liquidation?

10. What is a cash predistribution plan? What are loss-absorption potentials?

11. To what extent does a cash predistribution plan reflect the actual gains or losses resulting from the liquidation of assets?

12. How should expected liquidation expenses and/or unrecorded liabilities be treated in proceeding with the process of liquidation by installments?

13. What events would cause the safe distribution of cash to differ in sequence from that indicated by a cash predistribution plan?

14. Briefly explain the marshaling of assets principle.

Exercises

Exercise 17–1

Ball, Ludick, and Thatcher are partners in the BLT Company and have capital balances on January 1, 19X1, of $70,000, $35,000, and $52,000, respectively. After electing to liquidate the business, the partners convert the noncash assets of $117,000 into $92,000 cash. All the liabilities, totaling $15,000, are paid; and the remaining cash is distributed among the partners. They share profits and losses: Ball, 60 percent; Ludick, 30 percent; and Thatcher, 10 percent.

Required:
Prepare a partnership liquidation schedule showing how cash is distributed.

Exercise 17–2

For each of the following, select the one best answer that either completes the sentence or answers the question:

a. In terms of the legal definition of insolvency, a partnership is insolvent only when—
  (1) The partnership assets are insufficient to pay partnership obligations.
  (2) The surplus of individual partners' assets over nonpartnership debts is insufficient, together with partnership assets, to pay partnership obligations.

(3)   The partners' individual assets together with partnership assets are insufficient to pay partnership obligations.

(4)   The partnership is declared bankrupt by court decree.

(5)   None of the above.

b.   In terms of the entity definition of insolvency, a partnership is insolvent only when—

(1)   Its recorded assets are insufficient to pay existing partnership liabilities.

(2)   The surplus of the individual partners' assets over nonpartnership debts is insufficient, together with partnership assets, to pay partnership liabilities.

(3)   The partners' individual assets together with partnership assets are insufficient to pay partnership liabilities.

(4)   The partnership is declared bankrupt by court decree.

(5)   None of the above.

c.   If a partnership has only noncash assets, all liabilities have been properly recorded, and no additional liquidation expenses are incurred, the maximum potential loss of the partnership upon liquidation is:

(1)   The fair market value of the assets.

(2)   The book value of the assets.

(3)   The fair value of the assets less any proceeds that can be expected from selling the assets.

(4)   The book value of the assets less recorded liabilities.

(5)   None of the above.

d.   If Simpson and Coolidge have equities of $75,000 and $60,000, respectively, and share profits and losses in the ratio of 6:4, their respective loss-absorption potentials are:

(1) $105,000 and $125,000.

(2) $125,000 and $150,000.

(3) $450,000 and $240,000.

(4) $75,000 and $60,000.

(5) $81,000 and $54,000.

e.   XYZ Partnership is in the process of liquidation. The profit and loss ratio is 5:3:2 for X, Y, and Z, respectively. Preliquidation balances are Cash (Dr.), $10,000; Noncash Assets (Dr.), $25,000; Priority Claims (Cr.), $12,000; X, Capital (Cr.), $10,000; Y, Capital (Cr.), $7,800; and Z, Capital (Cr.), $5,200. The noncash assets are sold for $5,000, net of liquidation expenses. Cash distribution to partners at the conclusion of the liquidation process will be:

(1)   X, $0; Y, $1,800; and Z, $1,200.

(2)   X, $833; Y, $666; and Z, $1,500.

(3)   X, $5,000; Y, $3,000; and Z, $2,000.

(4)   X, $1,000; Y, $1,000; and Z, $1,000.

(5)   X, $0; Y, $0; and Z, $0.

Exercise 17–3

The James, Allen, and Burk Partnership has not been successful; hence, the partners have sadly concluded that operations must be terminated and their partnership liquidated. Profits and losses are shared as follows: James, 45 percent;

Allen, 35 percent; and Burk, 20 percent. As the accountant placed in charge of this partnership, you have responsibility for the liquidation and distribution of assets. When you assume your responsibilities, the partnership balance sheet is as follows:

Assets		Equities	
Cash	$18,000	Liabilities	$12,000
Other assets	54,000	Loan from James	18,000
		James, capital	6,000
		Allen, capital	30,000
		Burk, capital	6,000
Total assets	$72,000	Total equities	$72,000

During the first two months of your duties, the following events occur:

1. Assets having a book value of $40,000 are sold for $12,000 cash.
2. Previously unrecorded liabilities of $1,000 are recognized.
3. Before distributing available cash balances to creditors and partners, you conclude that a cash reserve of $1,000 should be set aside for future potential expenses.
4. Remaining cash balances are distributed to creditors and partners.

Required:
Prepare a schedule of partnership liquidation that covers all of the events described above.

Exercise 17–4

The balance sheet of the Oslo Company just prior to liquidation is as follows:

Assets		Equities	
Assets	$258,000	Accounts payable	$ 18,000
		Bates, loan	12,000
		Bates, capital	28,000
		Hunt, capital	80,000
		Riley, capital	120,000

Bates, Hunt, and Riley share profits and losses in the ratio of 1:4:5, respectively.

Required:
Construct a systematic plan showing how cash should be distributed to the various equities as it becomes available during the liquidation process.

Exercise 17–5

The XYZ Partnership is being dissolved. All liabilities have been liquidated. The balance of assets on hand are being realized by a comparatively slow conversion schedule. The following are details of partners' accounts:

Partners	Capital Account (Original Investment)	Current Account (Undistributed Earnings Net of Drawings)	Loans to Partnership	Profit and Loss Ratio
X	$20,000	$1,500 credit	$15,000	40%
Y	25,000	2,000 debit		40
Z	10,000	1,000 credit	5,000	20

Required:

Prepare a predistribution plan showing how cash payments should be made to the partners as assets are realized.

(AICPA adapted)

Exercise 17–6

A, B, C, and D agree to dissolve their partnership. Their preliquidation capital and loan account balances are as follows:

	Capital	Loan
A	$28,000	$7,000
B.............	41,000	2,000
C	18,000	
D	12,000	2,000

They share profits and losses 40:30:20:10. Unpaid liabilities at date of dissolution amount to $10,000; noncash assets total $105,000.

During the first month of liquidation, assets having a book value of $55,000 were sold for $31,000. During the second month, assets recorded at $32,000 were sold for $28,000. During the third month, the remaining unsold assets were determined to be worthless.

Required:

Prepare a schedule of liquidation indicating the cash distribution that is made at the end of each month of the liquidation period.

Exercise 17–7

Partners A, B, and C who share profits and losses 50:30:20 elect to liquidate the partnership business. Their preliquidation capital balances are A, $30,000; B, $30,000; and C, $10,000. Partnership unpaid liabilities amount to $6,500.

Required:

Prepare a schedule indicating the distribution of cash as it becomes available in the realization process.

Exercise 17–8

Awn, Barket, and Thompkins share profits and losses from their partnership in the ratio of 20 percent, 35 percent, and 45 percent, respectively. Capital and loan balances related to each partner are as follows:

	Loan to Partner from Partnership	Loan to Partnership from Partner	Capital
Awn		$20,000	$40,000
Barket...................	$7,000		28,000
Thompkins		10,000	35,000

Assets of the partnership include cash of $9,000, inventory of $32,000, receivables of $26,000, and plant and equipment of $77,000. Partnership liabilities amount to $18,000.

Required:

Prepare a plan showing how cash would be distributed in sequential payments if the business were liquidated.

Problems

Problem 17–9

On August 25, 19X1, Norton, Olson, and Parker entered into a partnership agreement to acquire a speculative second mortgage on undeveloped real estate. They invested $55,500, $32,000, and $12,500, respectively. They agreed on a profit and loss ratio of $4:2:1$, respectively.

On September 1, 19X1, they purchased for $100,000 a mortgage note with an unpaid balance of $120,000. The amount paid included interest accrued from June 30, 19X1. The note principal matures at the rate of $2,000 each quarter. Interest at the annual rate of 8 percent computed on the unpaid balance is also due quarterly.

Regular interest and principal payments were received on September 30 and December 31, 19X1. A working capital imprest fund of $150 was established, and collection expenses of $70 were paid in December.

In addition to the regular September payment on September 30, the mortgagor made a lump-sum principal reduction payment of $10,000 plus a penalty of 2 percent for prepayment.

Because of the speculative nature of the note, the partners agree to defer recognition of the discount until their cost has been fully recovered.

Required:

a. Assuming that no cash distributions were made to the partners, prepare a schedule computing the cash balance available for distribution to the partners on December 31, 19X1.

b. After payment of collection expenses the partners expect to have cash in the total amount of $170,000 available for distribution to themselves for interest and return of principal. They plan to distribute the cash as soon as possible so that they can individually reinvest the cash.

   Prepare a schedule as of September 1 showing how the total cash of $170,000 should be distributed to the individual partners by installments as it becomes available.

(AICPA adapted)

Problem 17–10

Ray, Mona, and Matt, partners in the Quality Photography Company, prepare to liquidate their business. On December 31, 19X1, the partnership account balances are as follows:

Cash	$ 5,430	Trade payables	$13,910
Other assets	61,870	Loans from partners:	
		Ray	8,000
		Mona	4,000
		Matt	9,000
		Capital balances:	
		Ray	18,100
		Mona	3,090
		Matt	11,200
	$67,300		$67,300

Ray, Mona, and Matt share profits and losses 50:30:20.

It is agreed that cash made available during liquidation shall be distributed to the partners at the end of each month. However, an amount sufficient to provide for anticipated future expenses and unrecorded liabilities is to be withheld.

A summary of transactions for the three-month liquidation period is as follows:

	Liquidation of Noncash Assets		Liquidation Expenses	Newly Discovered Unrecorded Partnership Liability	Estimated Future Expenses and Unrecorded Liabilities
	Book Value	Cash Realized			
January	$24,700	$18,180	$860	–0–	$3,000
February	33,170	26,810	800	$2,000*	3,350
March	4,000	3,200	200	–0–	–0–

* The partnership bookkeeper failed to record the real property tax liability in December 19X1.

Required:

Prepare a partnership liquidation schedule indicating amounts of periodic cash distributions.

Problem 17–11

The partners of the Lomax Company agreed to dissolve their partnership on March 31, 19X1. Their preliquidation capital and loan account balances and the profit and loss ratio were the following:

Partner	Capital	Loan	Ratio
W	$16,000	$4,000	40%
X	29,000	7,000	30
Y	8,000		20
Z	9,000	1,000	10

The partnership had a cash balance of $10,000 and noncash assets of $70,000; obligations to outside creditors amounted to $6,000. Available cash was to be distributed at the end of each month during the period of liquidation. Assets were realized as follows:

	Book Values	Net Proceeds
April............	$54,000	$26,000
May.............	14,000	14,000
June	2,000	–0–

Required:

a. On the basis of information available on March 31, prepare a plan for the distribution of cash.

b. Prepare a schedule showing how the April and May disbursements of cash were distributed.

Problem 17–12

A, B, and C formed the ABC Company, a partnership, with A contributing $12,000 of capital, B contributing $8,000, and C contributing $6,000. In their partnership agreement, A, B, and C provided that the partnership was to exist for 20 years, but the partners made no provision as to the proportions in which profits and losses were to be shared. During the course of operating the partnership, A made a loan of $1,000 to the partnership that has not been repaid, and the partnership also owes outside creditors additional amounts that exceed the value of partnership assets by $3,000.

Required:

a. Under the Uniform Partnership Act, in absence of a specific agreement between the parties, how is the compensation and profit for each partner determined during the course of operating the partnership?

b. Under the Uniform Partnership Act—
   (1) If A wishes to terminate the partnership but B and C do not, does A have the right to withdraw from the partnership? *Explain.*
   (2) If A, B, and C agree to terminate the partnership, how will losses be divided?

c. Discuss—
   (1) The rule of "marshaling of assets."
   (2) The distinction between the "dissolution" of the partnership and the "winding up" of partnership affairs.

d. If D becomes a partner in ABC Company and replaces A, what is D's liability with respect to obligations arising before his admission to the partnership?

(AICPA adapted)

Problem 17–13

Newman, Jones, and Huber are partners in the Newman Wholesale Company and share profits and losses 50:30:20. Their capital balances on January 1, 19X1, are:

Newman................ $ 5,000 debit
Jones ....   39,000 credit
Huber ....   24,000 debit

The partnership liabilities are $15,000. On liquidation, the noncash assets of $18,000 are converted into $4,000 cash. The nonbusiness (personal) assets and liabilities of each partner are the following:

Partner	Assets	Liabilities
Newman	$13,000	$14,000
Jones..............	17,000	6,400
Huber.............	21,000	3,200

Required:

Prepare a partnership liquidation schedule according to the provisions of—

a. Bankruptcy law.
b. Uniform Partnership Act.

Problem 17–14

Mettlen, Cundiff, Jentz, and Nelson decide to dissolve their partnership. Accordingly, they plan a program of piecemeal conversion of assets in order to minimize liquidation losses. Partners share profits and losses as follows: Mettlen, 40 percent; Cundiff, 35 percent; Jentz, 15 percent; and Nelson, 10 percent. The period of liquidation begins on June 1, 19X1, when the trial balance of the partnership is as follows:

	Debit	Credit
Cash	$ 200	
Receivables	25,900	
Inventory (6/1/X1).............	42,600	
Equipment (net)	19,800	
Accounts payable............		$ 3,000
Mettlen, loan.................		6,000
Cundiff, loan.................		10,000
Mettlen, capital..............		20,000
Cundiff, capital..............		21,500
Jentz, capital		18,000
Nelson, capital		10,000
	$88,500	$88,500

Required:

a. Prepare a schedule as of June 1, 19X1, showing how cash will be distributed among partners as it becomes available.
b. On July 31, 19X1, cash of $12,700 is available for payment to creditors and partners. How should it be distributed?
c. Assume that the partnership elects to continue operations rather than suffer liquidation. Subsequent to this decision, the partnership earns profits of

$23,625. How should the profits be distributed if, in addition to the aforementioned profit-sharing arrangement, it was provided that Nelson receive a bonus of 5 percent of the net income from operations, such bonus to be treated as a partnership expense?

(AICPA adapted)

Problem 17–15

The United Service Company, a partnership, prepared the following trial balance after realization of noncash assets but before distribution of cash to creditors or partners:

	Debit	Credit
Cash	$10,000	
Liabilities		$40,000
Ficken, capital	20,000	
Powell, capital		30,000
Carlson, capital	40,000	
	$70,000	$70,000

The individual financial status of each partner, excluding his relationship to the partnership is:

	Assets	Liabilities
Ficken	$40,000	$ 30,000
Powell	50,000	100,000
Carlson	80,000	30,000

Required:

a. Prepare a schedule of partnership liquidation and a schedule indicating the partners' personal financial status under the provisions of the Uniform Partnership Act.

b. Calculate the amounts the partnership and the creditors of the separate partners would receive if the partners' obligations to the firm were adjudged individual liabilities.

Problem 17–16

Mathis, Overton, and Downey are partners sharing profits in the ratio of 4 : 3 : 2, respectively. The partnership and two of the partners are currently unable to make full payment of their obligations to creditors. The balance sheet of the partnership and an enumeration of the assets and liabilities of the separate partners are as follows:

MOD PARTNERSHIP
Balance Sheet

Assets		Equities		
Cash	$ 500	Accounts payable		$37,000
Other assets	60,500	Capital:		
		Mathis	$10,000	
		Overton	6,000	
		Downey	8,000	24,000
Total assets	$61,000	Total equities		$61,000

Assets and Liabilities of Partners M, O, and D
Excluding Partnership Interests

Partner	Cash and Cash Value of Personal Assets	Liabilities
Mathis................	$31,000	$20,000
Overton	9,450	11,900
Downey	4,000	5,000

Required:

a. Assuming that "other assets" are converted into $33,500 cash, prepare a partnership liquidation schedule *and* a complementary schedule indicating the distribution of partners' personal assets according to the provisions of the Uniform Partnership Act.

b. Calculate the minimum amount that must be realized from the sale of noncash partnership assets in order that the personal creditors of Overton will receive full settlement of their claims.

(AICPA adapted)

Fiduciary and
Institutional Accounting

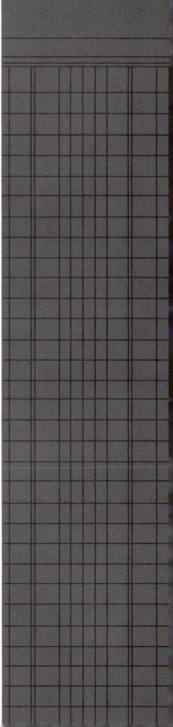

Corporate Liquidation and Reorganization

Accounting problems relating to the expansion of corporate businesses through mergers and acquisitions have been considered earlier. Additionally, based on the *continuity assumption* with respect to corporate affiliation, there was presented an extended analysis of the preparation of consolidated financial statements. Notwithstanding accountants' general support of this assumption in most instances, one must remain sensitive to the fact that on occasions circumstances may call for business contraction, or disinvestment. Where economic misfortune or financial distress is sufficiently severe, it becomes necessary to acknowledge the inevitability of business failure.

U.S. business failures reached a postwar high point of 17,705 in 1961. Following an irregular history thereafter, there was evidenced a noticeable upturn in business casualties beginning in 1979, reaching a level of 16,794 in 1981, with a preliminary estimate of 25,346 in 1982.[1] These data affirm that the presumption of continuity of corporate life in some instances is manifestly refutable.

Given the economic reality of business failure, it may be useful to examine following some of the accounting problems which relate to corporate liquidation and reorganization.

Liquidation

A corporation's existence may be terminated either by *voluntary* or *involuntary* petition. Voluntary dissolution may be initiated by the incorporators in the event that the corporation has not commenced business or issued shares of stock; subsequently, a corporation may be voluntarily dissolved with consent of the shareholders. Involuntary dissolution may be initiated by the corporate shareholders (or directors), by the state, or by creditors.

In respect to action taken by the state, the Business Corporation Act of Texas, for example, provides that a corporation may be involuntarily dissolved as a consequence of any of the following:

(1) The corporation or its incorporators have failed to comply with a condition precedent to incorporation; or

(2) The original articles of incorporation or any amendments thereof were procured through fraud; or

(3) The corporation has continued to transact business beyond the scope of the purpose or purposes of the corporation as expressed in its articles of incorporation; or

(4) A misrepresentation has been made of any material matter in any application, report, affidavit, or other document submitted by such corporation pursuant to this Act.

---

[1] *The 1981 Dun & Bradstreet Business Failure Record* (New York: Dun & Bradstreet, Inc., 1983), p. 2.

(5)   The corporation has failed to file any report within the time required by law, or has failed to pay any fees, franchise taxes or penalties prescribed by law when the same have become due and payable;

(6)   The corporation has failed to maintain a registered agent in this state as required by law; or

(7)   When a corporation is convicted of a felony or when a high managerial agent is convicted of a felony in the conduct of the affairs of the corporation, the Attorney General may file an action to involuntarily dissolve the corporation in a district court of the county in which the registered office of the corporation is situated. . . . The court may dissolve the corporation involuntarily if it is established that:

(a)   The corporation, or a high managerial agent acting in behalf of the corporation, has engaged in a persistent course of felonious conduct; and

(b)   To prevent future felonious conduct of the same character, the public interest requires such dissolution [Texas Business Corporation Act, Art. 7.01, as amended 1977].

A debtor's financial distress may be produced by, or result in, a condition of *insolvency*. It is important to distinguish between insolvency in the equity sense and its bankruptcy meaning. *Equity insolvency* exists when a debtor is unable to pay his debts as they mature. *Bankruptcy insolvency* is interpreted by the relevant bankruptcy statutes as a condition where the aggregate of a debtor's property at fair valuation is less than the amount of his existing liabilities [Section 101 (26)].[2] It is apparent that insolvency in the bankruptcy sense may exist without a condition of equity insolvency, for example, where there has been a value shrinkage in noncurrent assets without a parallel reduction in the amount of long-term debt. It is perhaps more usual to find the converse, that is, an insolvent debtor in the equity sense who is solvent by the bankruptcy definition.

Early in the history of the United States, the Congress was given constitutional authority to enact uniform bankruptcy laws. The first act was passed in 1800. Other laws were enacted in 1841 and 1867, after the repeal of predecessor statutes. A fourth National Bankruptcy Act was enacted in 1898. This Act, although frequently amended, remained operative until superceded by the Bankruptcy Reform Act of 1978. This legislation became effective in October 1979 with respect to bankruptcy proceedings initiated thereafter. This law, hereinafter referred to as the BRA, contains the substantive provisions of liquidation proceedings (Chapter 7) as well as financial rehabilitation (Chapter 11) for those seeking relief under Title 1.

It is important that state *insolvency* legislation and jurisdiction be clearly distinguished from federal *bankruptcy* legislation and jurisdiction. Insolvency laws are the enactments of the several states relating to the equitable distribution of the resources of a distressed debtor, while the Bankruptcy

---

[2] Citations to national bankruptcy statutes in this chapter will refer to Title 1 of the Bankruptcy Reform Act of 1978 unless otherwise noted. Indicated sections are from this Act.

Reform Act is the controlling federal statute in such proceedings. The federal law is accorded superior constitutional status, and the insolvency laws of the several states must necessarily be consistent therewith. The state statutes remain operative to the extent they do not controvert the federal Act.

Bankruptcy Reform Act of 1978

A business enterprise confronted with the possibility of financial failure may undertake reorganization or dissolution voluntarily or involuntarily under the aegis of federal or state law. However, an insolvent debtor's action taken under state laws resulting in voluntary or involuntary receivership automatically provides a basis for legal action under the Bankruptcy Reform Act.

One of the purposes of the BRA is to provide for an orderly and equitable distribution of a distressed debtor's property among his creditors; once the bankruptcy proceedings are terminated, the debtor is discharged of most of his unpaid debts (some are not dischargeable), after which he may initiate steps for financial rehabilitation and renew business operations.

Who May Be a Debtor.   Any person, except a railroad, a domestic financial institution (insurance company, bank, building and loan association, credit union, etc.), and a foreign financial institution may be a debtor under provisions of this Act [Section 109(b)].

A *voluntary* case may be initiated by the filing with the bankruptcy court of a petition by an entity that qualifies as a debtor as so defined.

In regard to *involuntary* dissolution, a case may be initiated by the filing with a bankruptcy court a petition by:

(1)   three or more entities, each of which is either a holder of a claim against such person[3] that is not contingent as to liability or an indenture trustee representing such a holder, if such claims aggregate at least $5,000 more than the value of any lien on property of the debtor securing such claims held by the holders of such claims;

(2)   if there are fewer than 12 such holders, excluding any employee or insider of such person, by one or more of such holders that hold in the aggregate at least $5,000 of such claims [Section 303(b)].

Courts of Bankruptcy.   In Title 2 of the BRA, it is provided that:

(1)   There shall be in each judicial district, as an adjunct to the district court for such district, a bankruptcy court which shall be a court of record known as the United States Bankruptcy Court for the district.

(2)   Each bankruptcy court shall consist of the bankruptcy judge or judges for the district in regular active service. Justices or judges desig-

---

[3] The expression *person* includes an individual, partnership, or corporation.

nated and assigned shall be competent to sit as judges of the bankruptcy court [Section 151].[4]

It is usual after the commencement of an involuntary case that the court at the request of parties in interest appoint an interim trustee to take possession of the property of the estate of the debtor and to operate any business associated therewith. Subsequently, a permanent trustee is usually selected by a creditor committee.

The duties of the trustee shall be to:

(1)   collect and reduce to money the property of the estate for which such trustee serves, and close up such estate as expeditiously as is compatible with the best interests of parties in interest;

(2)   be accountable for all property received;

(3)   investigate the financial affairs of the debtor;

(4)   if a purpose would be served, examine proofs of claims and object to the allowance of any claim that is improper;

(5)   if advisable, oppose the discharge of the debtor;

(6)   unless the court orders otherwise, furnish such information concerning the estate and the estate's administration as is requested by a party in interest;

(7)   if the business of the debtor is authorized to be operated, file with the court and with any governmental unit charged with responsibility for collection or determination of any tax arising out of such operation, periodic reports and summaries of the operation of such business, including a statement of receipts and disbursements, and such other information as the court requires; and

(8)   make a final report and file a final account of the administration of the estate with the court [Section 704].

Liquidation Sequence.   The progress of dissolution in respect to a distressed debtor consists essentially of (1) the marshaling and protection of the debtor's property, (2) conversion of the noncash assets, (3) equitable distribution of the proceeds from conversion to those creditors having provable claims and in the order of their priority, and (4) formal discharge of the debtor.

The trustee accepts custodial responsibility for the debtor's property for the purpose of preserving and protecting the interests of the several creditors. Legal title to such property vests in the trustee when it is surrendered to his custody.

---

[4] On June 28, 1982, the Supreme Court declared unconstitutional certain provisions of the BRA relating to the authority of bankruptcy judges. These and other provisions having to do with jurisdictional questions remain the subject of pending congressional amending legislation.

Concurrent with the filing of a petition, the debtor must provide certain relevant information to the court and/or trustee. He has a duty to:

(1)   file a list of creditors, and unless the court orders otherwise, a schedule of assets and liabilities, and a statement of the debtor's financial affairs;

(2)   if a trustee is serving in the case, cooperate with the trustee as necessary to enable the trustee to perform the trustee's duties under this title;

(3)   if a trustee is serving in the case, surrender to the trustee all property of the estate and any recorded information, including books, documents, records, and papers, relating to property of the estate [Section 521].

A creditor having a claim against a debtor's estate must timely file a *proof of claim* or interest. If a creditor does not file such a claim, the debtor may elect to file it. A claim or interest, is deemed allowed, unless a party in interest objects. After notice and hearing, the court shall determine the magnitude of the claim and shall allow it for the determined amount [Sections 501, 502].

Liabilities Having Priority.   Certain classes of a distressed debtor's obligations must be fully satisfied before settlement is made with other creditors. A priority status attaches to the following partial enumeration of debts and expenses, and distribution is made in the indicated order:

(1)   Administrative expenses, fees and charges assessed against the estate;

(2)   Unsecured claims for wages, salaries or commissions earned within 90 days before the date of the filing of the petition (but only to the extent of $2,000 for each such individual);

(3)   Allowed unsecured claims for contributions to employee benefit plans arising from services rendered within 180 days of the filing of the petition (but only to the extent of $2,000 per employee);

(4)   Allowed unsecured claims of individuals arising from deposits for purchase, lease, or rental of property or services, limited to $900 for each such individual;

(5)   Allowed unsecured claims of governmental units in respect to taxes [Section 507].

Setoff.   In respect to mutual debts or credits between the estate of a debtor and his creditors, one obligation may be set off against the other, with only the balance to be allowed or paid [Section 553].

Discharge of Debtor.   Following the conversion of a debtor's assets and an equitable distribution of the proceeds among his several creditors, the debtor is released from all of his debts provable in bankruptcy. A discharge in the bankruptcy provides an effective release in respect to these debts unless:

(1)   The debtor is not an individual;

(2)   The debtor, with intent to hinder, delay, or defraud a creditor or an officer of the estate charged with custody of property under this title, has transferred, removed, destroyed, mutilated, or concealed, or has permitted to be transferred, removed, destroyed, mutilated, or concealed:

(a)   the property of the debtor, within one year before the date of the filing of the petition; or

(b)   property of the estate, after the date of the filing of the petition;

(3)   The debtor has concealed, destroyed, mutilated, falsified, or failed to keep or preserve any recorded information, including books, documents, records, and papers, from which the debtor's financial condition or business transactions might be ascertained, unless such act or failure to act was justified under all of the circumstances of the case;

(4)   The debtor knowingly and fraudulently, in or in connection with the case:

(a)   made a false oath or account;

(b)   presented or used a false claim;

(c)   gave, offered, received, or attempted to obtain money, property, or advantage, or a promise of money, property, or advantage, for acting or forbearing to act; or

(d)   withheld from an officer of the estate entitled to possession under this title, any recorded information, including books, documents, records, and papers, relating to the debtor's property or financial affairs;

(5)   The debtor has failed to explain satisfactorily, before determination of denial of discharge under this paragraph, any loss of assets or deficiency of assets to meet the debtor's liabilities;

(6)   The debtor has refused, in the case:

(a)   to obey any lawful order of the court, other than an order to respond to a material question or to testify;

(b)   on the ground of privilege against self-incrimination, to respond to a material question approved by the court or to testify, after the debtor has been granted immunity with respect to the matter concerning which such privilege was invoked; or

(c)   on a ground other than the properly invoked privilege against self-incrimination, to respond to a material question approved by the court or to testify [Section 727].

Assignment for Benefit of Creditors

Liquidation proceedings normally are carried out through formal bankruptcy *or* an informal assignment for the benefit of creditors. The latter proceeding is merely an arrangement whereby the corporate property is transferred to designated assignees (the assignees frequently are also creditors). The assignee compares to a trustee in bankruptcy proceedings. He takes possession of the debtor's assets, converts the noncash assets, makes distributions to creditors with due regard to the priority of their claims, and renders a final accounting upon a closing of the estate. Assignment may be preferred to bankruptcy proceedings in that the debtor has the authority to designate the liquidator (assignee), often enjoys reduced legal expenses, and has fewer constraints as to time in respect to conversion and ultimate distribution. Unlike bankruptcy proceedings, there is no formal discharge of the distressed debtor in an assignment for the benefit of creditors.

Many states have enacted statutes that provide for assignments. An assignment for the benefit of creditors constitutes an act of bankruptcy, however; and the assignee is compelled to surrender custody of the debtor's property should a petition in bankruptcy be filed.

The Statement of Affairs

Previous reference has been made to the importance of filing schedules of assets, liabilities, and exempt property by the debtor. Failure to file such reports may result in the debtor's loss of discharge or his suffering of other penalties. Among the reports of special importance is the *statement of affairs.* This statement, which details the realization proceeds expected from the conversion of the debtor's assets juxtaposed against the claims of secured and unsecured creditors, may be especially useful in aiding the debtor in determining the extent of his financial deficiency.[5]

The statement of affairs exhibits some of the properties of the familiar corporate balance sheet; yet, there are significant differences. Most importantly, the underlying assumption of business continuity is rejected in favor of a liquidation emphasis; manifestly, this has implications for the valuation of corporate assets. In general, expected realizable values are substituted for unamortized costs. In order to assign these values to individual assets, however, the "liquidation concept" must be more definitively formulated. For example, anticipated liquidation within 30 days often produces a different estimate of realizable value than a liquidation period of six months. Thus, if the ultimate liquidation period is indefinite, adequate disclosure may be better served by preparing more than one statement under different time assumptions. The classificational format of the balance sheet is essentially an ordered enumeration of assets in relative liquidity sequence, with liabilities grouped in two broad time-oriented classes. In the statement of affairs, however, the assets are classified according to their availability to creditors, viz, those pledged with fully secured creditors, those pledged with partially secured creditors, and those

---

[5] This statement is essentially the accountant's configuration and should not be confused with the statement required by the BRA which is fundamentally a questionnaire, consisting of 21 questions related to the debtor's property and conduct.

which are free or unencumbered. Similarly, liabilities are classed in terms of their legal preferences, viz, priority claims, obligations that are fully secured, obligations that are partially secured, and unsecured claims. It is evident that the statement of affairs is primarily oriented toward the legal status of claims against the enterprise rather than the cost of future service potentials. As an obvious corollary of this new emphasis, stockholders' equity accounts lose their significance in the statement of affairs. In fact, they are only included in a supporting statement, primarily as an explanation of the current insolvency condition.

Illustrative Problem.   Preliminary to the preparation of a statement of affairs, a conventional balance sheet should be prepared, supported by additional supplementary data, including estimates of realization proceeds from noncash assets. Other relevant information should also be accumulated in respect to pledged assets and liabilities that are expected to emerge during the course of the liquidation proceedings.

The balance sheet of the Deskins Company on March 31, 19X0, is as follows:

THE DESKINS COMPANY
Balance Sheet
March 31, 19X0

Assets

Cash.	$ 1,850
Accounts receivable	21,200
Notes receivable	15,000
Merchandise	41,000
Arco common stock (60 shares at cost)	5,800
Land	6,500
Building (net of depreciation)	92,000
Machinery and equipment (net of depreciation).	43,000
Total assets.	$226,350

Equities

Bank loan—First State Bank.	$ 10,000
Notes payable	70,000
Accounts payable	90,625
Accrued wages	3,775
Accrued interest:	
Bank loan	375
Notes payable	600
Capital stock	150,000
Retained earnings [deficit]	[99,025]
Total equities	$226,350

Based upon an estimated interval of time for liquidation, the land is appraised at $7,800 and the building is estimated to have a current market value of $85,000. The machinery and equipment are valueless except as salvage, $8,000. Merchandise has a current salable value of $20,000. On

March 31, the Arco common stock is quoted on the security exchange at 110. Receivables are estimated to be collectible according to the following schedule:

Notes receivable...............	100%
Accounts receivable:	
$10,000	100%
10,000	70%
1,200	Uncollectible

The First State Bank loan is secured by the Arco common stock, and the notes payable are secured by a first mortgage on the land and building.

The statement of affairs of the Deskins Company is shown in Illustration 18–1.

A *deficiency account* (Illustration 18–2) frequently is appended to the statement of affairs and provides supporting detail in respect to estimated gains and losses on realization, the algebraic sum of which, when added to the total stockholders' equity reflected in the balance sheet, explains the impairment of capital—the estimated deficiency to unsecured creditors.

Statement Annotations

Assets Pledged with Fully Secured Creditors.   In this category are listed those assets having a fair valuation equal to, or in excess of, the debts for which they have been pledged as collateral.

Assets Pledged with Partially Secured Creditors.   Under this heading are listed those assets having a fair valuation less than the amount of the debts for which they have been pledged to secure.

Free (or Uncommitted) Assets.   These assets are unencumbered and are not otherwise identified with a specific liability. This includes that portion of assets pledged with fully secured creditors in excess of the amount of the related liability.

Liabilities Having Priority.   These are debts that, by statute—Section 507—must be liquidated before uncommitted assets are available for the payment of unsecured debts.

Fully Secured Liabilities.   There are liabilities that are protected by the pledge of specific assets that are expected to realize at least as much as the amount of the related obligations.

Partially Secured Liabilities.   These liabilities represent obligations of the debtor for which specific assets have been pledged, the estimated value of which is less than the related obligation. The amount of these liabilities not covered by secured assets reverts to the status of unsecured claims.

Unsecured Liabilities.   These debts have no designated legal priority, and no specific property is available as collateral to ensure their payment.

Illustration 18–1

THE DESKINS COMPANY
Statement of Affairs
March 31, 19X0

Book Value					Realizable Value
	Assets				
	Assets pledged with fully secured creditors:				
$ 6,500	Land	$ 7,800			
92,000	Building	85,000	$92,800		
	Notes payable	$70,000			
	Accrued interest	600	70,600	$22,200	
	Assets pledged with partially secured creditors:				
5,800	Arco common stock...............................		$6,600		
	Bank loan—First State Bank	$10,000			
	Accrued interest	375	10,375		
	Free assets:				
1,850	Cash..			1,850	
15,000	Notes receivable			15,000	
21,200	Accounts receivable			17,000	
41,000	Merchandise			20,000	
43,000	Machinery and equipment.........................			8,000	
	Realizable value of uncommitted assets			$84,050	
	Liabilities having priority			3,775	
	Net free assets.................................			$80,275	
	Estimated deficiency to unsecured creditors			14,125	
$226,350				$94,400	

Book Value				Unsecured
	Equities			
	Liabilities having priority:			
$ 3,775	Accrued wages	$ 3,775		
	Fully secured creditors:			
70,000	Notes payable	$70,000		
600	Accrued interest	600		
	Partially secured creditors:			
	Bank loan—First State Bank:			
10,000	Principal	$10,000		
375	Accrued interest	375		
		$10,375		
	Arco common stock.............................	6,600	$ 3,775	
	Unsecured creditors:			
90,625	Accounts payable		90,625	
	Stockholders' equity:			
150,000	Capital stock			
[99,025]	Retained earnings [deficit]			
$226,350			$94,400	

Illustration 18–2

THE DESKINS COMPANY
Deficiency Account
March 31, 19x0

Estimated losses:		Estimated gains:	
Accounts receivable	$ 4,200	Land	$ 1,300
Merchandise	21,000	Arco common stock.........	800
Machinery and equipment	35,000	Capital stock	150,000
Building	7,000	Retained earnings [deficit].....	[99,025]
		Estimated deficiency to	
		unsecured creditors	14,125
	$67,200		$ 67,200

Stockholders' Equity. The balances of capital stock and retained earnings are entered only in the Book Value column in the statement of affairs. However, they are included in the deficiency account, indicating thereby the extent to which estimated gains and losses on realization can be absorbed by the existing stockholders' equity.

Special Problems

Reserves. Accountants are encouraged to limit use of the word *reserve* and to adopt more descriptive and more meaningful terminology. Notwithstanding the fact of poor terminological identification, these items must nonetheless be properly classified in the statement of affairs. When the term is used to describe a valuation account, the balance should be deducted from the related asset, with the "net" value of the asset extended to the Book Value column in the statement of affairs. In the case of liability "reserves," credit balances should be classified in a manner consistent with the priority and security provisions cited earlier. Indeed, such items in the liability category frequently have a priority status, such as "Reserve for Federal Income Taxes." Appropriations of retained earnings, or "surplus reserves," are elements of the stockholders' equity and should be so reported.

Contingent Liabilities. Since contingent liabilities, as such, have no place in the statement of affairs, their probable status by the end of the liquidation period must be ascertained and correctly described. For example, notes receivable that have been discounted, for which there is little likelihood of dishonor, should be omitted from the statement of affairs. In respect to those notes for which dishonor is likely, however, the face amount of the notes should be reported as a liability on the credit side of the statement and extended to the Unsecured column.

Other "contingent" liabilities should be similarly reported in the statement of affairs as unsecured claims to the extent there is a reasonable probability that such an obligation will, in fact, exist within the period during which a claim may be filed.

Accrued Interest. Accrued interest receivable or payable should be added to the obligation to which it relates. In the event a note receivable is pledged to secure a debt, the interest accrued thereon is usually considered as additional security and is reported as a complement of the note. Similarly, accrued interest on notes payable should be associated with the related notes.

Prepaid Insurance. The appropriate treatment in the statement of affairs of unexpired premiums on insurance depends upon the circumstances of each case. Although there may be a determinable cash surrender value of an insurance policy, it is not available except upon cancellation of the policy; further, the cash surrender value may expire before the expected date at which liquidation will be completed. Accordingly, unless such cancellation is expected, it is usual to report unexpired premiums only in terms of book value, without an anticipation of any realizable value.

Discount on Capital Stock. In the event capital stock is sold at a discount, creditors often have a claim against the shareholders in the amount of any unpaid discount. If it is probable that the discount is recoverable from existing shareholders, that is, if it has a cash realizable value, then it is appropriate to report this value as an unencumbered asset, but only to the extent of the creditors' deficiency. However, because there may exist reasonable doubt as to the accuracy of other realizable values, it may be expedient to evaluate the discount at its total collectible amount—whether or not necessary to cover a creditor deficiency.

Extended Usefulness of the Statement of Affairs

The statement of affairs presently occupies a relatively unimportant position in the catalog of accounting reports. Its status is at least partially related to the essentially ex post facto nature of the statement. It may, in fact, be categorized as a financial autopsy, as it reflects the undesirable financial circumstance which then exists, with an analysis of the individual value losses generating the impairment of capital.

It is not inconceivable, however, that the concepts embodied in the statement of affairs might be usefully employed in the forward planning of management. For example, in preparing financial statements for short-term credit purposes, the concept of value is often more significant than that of unexpired costs. Rather than modify or provide interpretive elaboration of the conventional balance sheet to reflect such value adjustments, such as lower of cost or market in respect to inventories—an essentially inconsistent position when related to the going-concern assumption—the accountant might profitably extend the use of the statement of affairs. With an accepted emphasis on realizable asset values and the legal status of debts, this statement may be a valuable tool for financial analysis and interpretation. By recognizing the need for unique financial statements for various special purposes, balance sheet concepts may be more easily integrated with the income determination objective without undesirable exceptions.

Reorganization

As an alternative to liquidation, a distressed debtor may attempt to rehabilitate a financially floundering business through reorganization. Usually, the value of business resources to a going concern is greater than the realization proceeds that derive from forced liquidation. A debtor contemplating some form of continuity of corporate life, instead of immediate dissolution, has recourse to both judicial and nonjudicial remedies. Among the latter are arrangements entered into by the creditors to extend the settlement period, composition agreements, voluntary assignments for the benefit of creditors, and creditor management committees. Judicial remedies usually involve formal reorganization under Chapter 11 of the Bankruptcy Reform Act. Proceedings under this chapter are referred to as rehabilitative actions, whereas the forms of relief discussed earlier are called straight bankruptcies.

Nonjudicial Remedies

Extending the Settlement Period.   Where the debtor's distress is clearly temporary in nature, it may be expedient—and advantageous—for his creditors to merely extend the period for the payment of outstanding obligations. This arrangement allows the debtor to continue management of the business, wherein he may be expected to convert such assets, without pain of forced liquidation, as will produce realization proceeds sufficient to liquidate existing debts. Such an agreement is often effective where the scale of business is small and there are relatively few creditors.

Composition Settlement.   A settlement by composition refers to an arrangement, contractually entered into by the debtor and his creditors *and* between the several creditors, in which the creditors agree to accept less than original contract amounts in full payment of their claims. These settlements, which originate with the debtor, provide for ratable distribution of the debtor's assets in full discharge of his obligations. Usually, in circumstances where composition settlements are employed, the debtor is insolvent within the bankruptcy meaning of this expression.

If there is a small number of dissenting creditors, a composition may nonetheless be executed if the assenting creditors allow full, or some preferred, payment of the obligations of the dissenting group. Throughout the proceedings, the debtor must remain completely candid in respect to disclosing his total assets; he must demonstrate no unauthorized preference for any creditor. The means of payment are usually cash and/or notes. Such an arrangement frequently is favored by the creditors in that it often prevents costly delays in final debt retirement.

Voluntary Assignment for the Benefit of Creditors. An insolvent debtor may elect to convey his property by assignment to a trustee or assignee for the benefit of his creditors. The purpose of such assignment is to enable the debtor's representative to convert the property, as may be necessary, and to distribute the proceeds ratably among the creditors. If contractually agreed to by the several creditors, the assignment may result in the debtor's discharge from his debts. Should there remain any undistributed assets, they are returned by the trustee to the debtor. A voluntary assignment for the creditors' benefit constitutes an act of bankruptcy.

Creditor Management Committee. The creditor management committee is a form of debtor-creditor alliance that provides for creditor committee management of the debtor's business for the purposes of rehabilitation, reorganization, or eventual liquidation. The control of the business rests with the committee, which may elect to contribute new capital if it appears financially and operationally feasible. Frequently, it is necessary to make use of an extension of the settlement period as a vehicle of financial revival. Properties are normally returned to the debtor when obligations have been discharged or otherwise provided for.

Judicial Remedies

Should the debtor prefer to employ legal remedies instead of the nonjudicial alternatives outlined above, he will in most instances elect to initiate reorganization proceedings under the debtor relief provisions of the Bankruptcy Reform Act.

A petition for reorganization under Chapter 11 of the BRA is filed with the Bankruptcy Court. As soon as practicable thereafter, the court shall appoint a committee of creditors holding unsecured claims, which committee normally will consist of the creditors holding the seven largest claims against the debtor. On the request of a party in interest, the court may also order the appointment of additional committees of creditors or of equity security holders [Section 1102].

A committee appointed under this authority may:

(1) consult with the trustee or debtor in possession concerning the administration of the case;

(2) investigate the acts, conduct, assets, liabilities, and financial condition of the debtor, the operation of the debtor's business and the desirability of the continuance of such business, and any other matter relevant to the case or to the formulation of a plan;

(3)   participate in the formulation of a plan, advise those represented by such committee of such committee's recommendations as to any plan formulated, and collect and file with the court acceptances of a plan;

(4)   request the appointment of a trustee or examiner, if a trustee or examiner, as the case may be, has not previously been appointed; and

(5)   perform such other services as are in the interest of those represented [Section 1103].

In respect to reorganizations initiated by the debtor, the court may either continue the "debtor in possession" to conduct the affairs of the business or may appoint a trustee.[6] In the event a trustee is appointed, he shall (among other duties):

(1)   be accountable for all property received;

(2)   examine proofs of claims and object to the allowance of any claim that is improper;

(3)   furnish such information concerning the estate and the estate's administration as is requested by a party in interest;

(4)   file a list of creditors, a schedule of assets and liabilities, and a statement of the debtor's financial affairs with the court;

(5)   prepare and file a reorganization plan; and

(6)   once the court confirms a plan of reorganization, file such additional reports considered necessary by the court [Section 1106].

The filed plan of reorganization must in all respects be fair and equitable, preserving the priorities of various parties at interest. The plan must also provide adequate means for its own execution, such as:

(1)   retention by the debtor of all or any part of the property of the estate;

(2)   transfer of all or any part of the property of the estate to one or more entities, whether organized before or after the confirmation of such plan;

(3)   merger or consolidation of the debtor with one or more persons;

(4)   sale of all or any part of the property of the estate, either subject to or free of any lien, or the distribution of all or any part of the property of the estate among those having an interest in such property of the estate; and

(5)   issuance of securities of the debtor, or of any entity referred to in (2) or (3) above, for cash, for property, for existing securities, or in exchange for claims or interests, or for any other appropriate purpose [Section 1123].

After a plan has been filed, it must be accepted by creditors of the debtor, which in most instances calls for approval of two thirds in amount

---

[6] A trustee must be appointed if the debtor's fixed, liquidated and unsecured debts (other than debts for goods, services or taxes) exceed $5,000,000.

and one half in number of the allowed claims of each class of creditors. The court must likewise approve of the fairness of the plan's conditions, that it does not discriminate against any class or group of creditors, and that the plan accords with all provisions of Chapter 11 of the BRA.

Trustee's Accounts

In the event that a fiduciary assumes responsibility for the management of a distressed business, the appropriate scope of the system of accounts to be maintained must be established. Where a trustee is appointed by the court, legal title to the assets of the debtor is usually conveyed to the trustee, who is then accountable to the court of his appointment, to the creditors, and to other interested parties. The trustee may elect to open new books of account, or he may continue the old books. The books of the distressed debtor are occasionally continued primarily for reasons of simplicity in record-keeping. Frequently, however, it may be desirable to open new books to facilitate distinguishing between those obligations of the debtor that existed prior to the appointment of the trustee and those created after his appointment.

In the event that a separate set of accounts is maintained by the trustee, it is important to determine specifically which of the debtor's assets are to be conveyed to the trustee. His accountability necessarily relates only to those assets designated by the order of this appointment. The debts preexistent to the trusteeship usually remain in the debtor's books, although their liquidation frequently is the responsibility of the trustee. For this reason, the trustee should clearly identify "new" and "old" debts; similarly, a distinction should be made between the "old" assets and those newly acquired during trusteeship. This is particularly important in respect to receivables. Receivable balances existing previous to the appointment of a trustee are the responsibility of the fiduciary only in respect to collection; accountability in respect to balances created subsequent to the trustee's appointment extends both to the prudence of granting credit and also to the effectiveness in account collection. Procedural details in accounting for a trusteeship arrangement are described in the illustrative example to follow.

Illustrative Problem.   The account balances of the Insolvo Company on March 31, 19X0, are as follows:

Cash	$ 600
Accounts receivable	4,000
Notes receivable	5,800
Merchandise	18,000
Long-lived assets	24,000
Other assets	2,600
	$55,000

Illustration 18–3

Trustee's Books			Corporation's Books		
(1) Cash...................................	600		**(1)** Charles Louis, Trustee.............	52,600	
Accounts Receivable (old).............	4,000		Allowance for Doubtful Accounts....	400	
Notes Receivable....................	5,800		Accumulated Depreciation..........	2,000	
Merchandise, April 1.................	18,000		Cash............................		600
Long-lived Assets...................	24,000		Accounts Receivable.............		4,000
Other Assets.......................	2,600		Notes Receivable................		5,800
Allowance for Doubtful Accounts (old)...		400	Merchandise......................		18,000
Accumulated Depreciation..........		2,000	Long-lived Assets.................		24,000
Insolvo Company—in Trusteeship......		52,600	Other Assets.....................		2,600
(2) Purchases.........................	40,000		**(2)** No entry.		
Accounts Payable (new).............		40,000			
(3) Cash...................................	4,000		**(3)** No entry.		
Accounts Receivable (new)...........	69,000				
Sales..............................		73,000			
(4) Cash...................................	57,900		**(4)** No entry.		
Notes Receivable....................		4,800			
Accounts Receivable (old).............		2,100			
Accounts Receivable (new).............		51,000			
(5) Accounts Payable (new).............	34,000		**(5)** Accounts Payable.................	16,000	
Insolvo Company—in Trusteeship....	16,000		Charles Louis, Trustee...........		16,000
Operating Expenses.................	2,500				
Trustee's Expenses.................	1,000				
Cash............................		53,500			

(6) Depreciation Expense 1,200
    Bad Debts Expense 2,550
      Accumulated Depreciation 1,200
      Allowance for Doubtful Accounts (old) .. 950
      Allowance for Doubtful Accounts (new) .. 1,600

    Bad Debts Expense 1,000
    Allowance for Doubtful Accounts (old) .. 400
      Notes Receivable 1,000
      Accounts Receivable (old) 400

(7) Sales 73,000
    Merchandise, August 31 16,000
      Merchandise, April 1 18,000
      Purchases 40,000
      Operating Expenses 2,500
      Trustee's Expenses 1,000
      Bad Debts Expense 3,550
      Depreciation Expense 1,200
      Income Summary 22,750

    Income Summary 22,750
      Insolvo Company—in Trusteeship 22,750

(6) No entry.

(7) Charles Louis, Trustee 22,750
      Income Summary 22,750

    Income Summary 22,750
      Retained Earnings 22,750

Allowance for doubtful accounts	$	400
Accumulated depreciation		2,000
Accounts payable		21,000
Capital stock		40,000
Retained earnings [deficit]		[8,400]
		$55,000

A petition for reorganization under Chapter 11 was filed by the Insolvo Company, and Charles Louis was duly appointed trustee to assume management responsibility on April 1. For the period April 1 through August 31, the following transactions were completed:

1. All corporate assets were transferred to the trustee; existing debts of the Insolvo Company were continued in the corporate books of account; new accounts were opened by the trustee in respect to the transferred assets.
2. Credit purchases of merchandise were $40,000.
3. Credit sales amounted to $69,000; cash sales were $4,000.
4. Collections of cash were made on:

Notes receivable	$	4,800
Accounts receivable (old)		2,100
Accounts receivable (new)		51,000

5. Payments were made by the trustee as follows:

Accounts payable (old)	$16,000
Accounts payable (new)	34,000
Operating expenses	2,500
Trustee's expenses	1,000

6. Adjustments recorded on August 31 by the trustee were:

Depreciation (5 months)	$1,200
Estimated doubtful accounts:	
Accounts receivable (old)	950
Accounts receivable (new)	1,600
Accounts written off:	
Accounts receivable (old)	400
Notes receivable	1,000

7. Closing entries were made by both the trustee and the Insolvo Company on August 31; unsold merchandise on this date was $16,000.

Entries for these transactions are journalized in Illustration 18–3.

A working paper that combines the accounts of the corporation and the trustee (before giving effect to closing entries) for the purpose of preparing

Illustration 18–4

THE INSOLVO COMPANY—IN TRUSTEESHIP
Combined Account Working Paper
For Five Months Ended August 31, 19X0

	Trustee's Accounts	Insolvo Accounts	Eliminations Dr.	Eliminations Cr.	Income Statement	Balance Sheet
Cash	9,000					9,000
Accounts receivable (old)	1,500					1,500
Accounts receivable (new)	18,000					18,000
Merchandise (4/1)	18,000				18,000	
Long-lived assets	24,000					24,000
Other assets	2,600					2,600
Purchases	40,000				40,000	
Operating expenses	2,500				2,500	
Trustee's expenses	1,000				1,000	
Depreciation expense	1,200				1,200	
Bad debts expense	3,550				3,550	
Charles Louis, trustee		36,600		(1) 36,600		
	121,350	36,600				
Merchandise (8/31)	16,000					16,000
Net income					22,750	
					89,000	71,100
Allowance for doubtful accounts (old)	950					950
Allowance for doubtful accounts (new)	1,600					1,600
Accumulated depreciation	3,200					3,200
Accounts payable (old)		5,000				5,000
Accounts payable (new)	6,000					6,000
Capital stock		40,000				40,000
Retained earnings [deficit]		[8,400]				[8,400]
Sales	73,000				73,000	
Insolvo Company—in trusteeship	36,600		(1) 36,600			
	121,350	36,600				
Merchandise (8/31)	16,000				16,000	
Net income						22,750
			36,600	36,600	89,000	71,100

conventional financial statements is shown in Illustration 18–4. The formal statements may be easily extracted therefrom.

In the event that the trusteeship is terminated on August 31, a return of the corporate management to Insolvo officials by Charles Louis would be recorded by an entry in the books of the trustee as follows:

The Insolvo Company—in Trusteeship 59,350
Allowance for Doubtful Accounts (old)   950
Allowance for Doubtful Accounts (new) 1,600
Accumulated Depreciation. 3,200
Accounts Payable (new). 6,000
   Cash   9,000
   Accounts Receivable (old)   1,500
   Accounts Receivable (new) 18,000
   Merchandise 16,000
   Long-lived Assets. 24,000
   Other Assets   2,600

The contra entry in the Insolvo Company books is:

Cash 9,000
Accounts Receivable 19,500
Merchandise 16,000
Long-lived Assets. 24,000
Other Assets 2,600
   Allowance for Doubtful Accounts   2,550
   Accumulated Depreciation.   3,200
   Accounts Payable.   6,000
   Charles Louis, Trustee 59,350

Realization and Liquidation Account

Conventional financial statements often reflect only an ancillary objective of a fiduciary; it may be more important to summarize periodically the liquidation and distribution activities of the fiduciary. A special report that accommodates this objective is the *realization and liquidation account*. The reference to *account* in the title of the report accents the traditional format of the statement. Other arrangements of the account information are to be found, although only the conventional or orthodox form is presented here.

The realization and liquidation account is essentially a statement of accountability, reflecting the activities of the fiduciary in converting the debtor's noncash assets and proceeding with the orderly distribution of the proceeds in settlement of the debtor's several liabilities. To this report is normally appended the fiduciary's Cash account. The orthodox report form consists essentially of three principal divisions. These basic segments are outlined as follows:

Assets			
Assets to be realized	xxx	Assets realized (conversion proceeds)	xxx
Assets acquired (or discovered)	xxx	Assets not realized	xxx

Liabilities			
Liabilities liquidated	xxx	Liabilities to be liquidated	xxx
Liabilities not liquidated	xxx	Liabilities incurred	xxx

Revenues and Expenses; Gains and Losses			
Supplementary charges	xxx	Supplementary credits	xxx

A summation of the debits in the three statement categories juxtaposed against the summation of credits will disclose an imbalance, which may be described as the net gain or loss for the liquidation period.

Using the data for the trusteeship previously discussed, the conventional realization and liquidation account takes the form shown in Illustration 18–5. The trustee's Cash account is given following:

Cash			
(1) Balance, March 31	600	(5) Accounts payable (old)	16,000
(3) Sales	4,000	(5) Accounts payable (new)	34,000
(4) Accounts receivable (old)	2,100	(5) Operating expenses	2,500
(4) Accounts receivable (new)	51,000	(5) Trustee's expenses	1,000
(4) Notes receivable	4,800	Balance, August 31	9,000
	62,500		62,500
Balance, August 31	9,000		

The Insolvo Company's stockholders' equity accounts are:

Capital Stock			
		(1) Balance, March 31	40,000

Retained Earnings			
(1) Balance, March 31	8,400	Net income (April 1 to August 31)	22,750

The use of the numeric codes to identify contra elements in the realization and liquidation account indicates that the statement may be easily prepared by entering the transactions of the fiduciary directly into the relevant statement categories. This connective notation would not, however, appear in the formal report.

Statement Annotations

Assets to Be Realized. Included in this category are the *carrying values* of all assets of the debtor at the date of the fiduciary's appointment (or at the beginning of the current period if the statement is not a cumulative record of fiduciary activities).

Assets Acquired. These are additional assets that are acquired (or discovered) during the period of fiduciary accountability.

Assets Realized. This description reflects the extent of conversion of noncash assets, with the *realization proceeds* therefrom the appropriate value measure.

Illustration 18–5

THE INSOLVO COMPANY
CHARLES LOUIS TRUSTEE
Realization and Liquidation Account
April 1, 19X0, to August 31, 19X0

Assets to be realized:				**Liabilities to be liquidated:**	
(1) Accounts receivable (old)	4,000			(1) Accounts payable (old)	21,000
Less: Allowance for doubtful accounts (old)	400	3,600		**Liabilities incurred:**	
(1) Notes receivable		5,800		(2) Accounts payable (new)	40,000
(1) Merchandise		18,000		**Supplementary credits:**	
(1) Long-lived assets	24,000			(2) Sales	73,000
Less: Accumulated depreciation	2,000	22,000		**Assets realized:**	
(1) Other assets		2,600		(4) Accounts receivable (old)	2,100
Assets acquired:				(4) Accounts receivable (new)	51,000
(3) Accounts receivable (new)		69,000		(4) Notes receivable	4,800
Supplementary charges:				**Assets not realized:**	
(2) Purchases		40,000		Accounts receivable (old)	1,500
(5) Operating expenses		2,500		Less: Allowance for doubtful accounts (old)	950
(5) Trustee's expenses		1,000		Accounts receivable (new)	18,000
Liabilities liquidated:				Less: Allowance for doubtful accounts (new)	1,600
(5) Accounts payable (old)		16,000		Merchandise	16,000
(5) Accounts payable (new)		34,000		Long-lived assets	24,000
Liabilities not liquidated:				Less: Accumulated depreciation	3,200
Accounts payable (old)		5,000		Other assets	2,600
Accounts payable (new)		6,000			
Net income		22,750			
		248,250			248,250

(On the credit side, amounts carried to the outer column: Accounts not realized — Accounts receivable (old), 550; Accounts receivable (new), 16,400; Long-lived assets, 20,800.)

Assets Not Realized. This summarizes the assets on hand at the date of the preparation of the statement, usually valued at the same amount indicated in the original accountability (assets to be realized or assets acquired).

Liabilities to Be Liquidated. These obligations of the debtor are those existing at the date of appointment of the fiduciary (or the beginning of the current period if the statement is not a cumulative record of fiduciary activities).

Liabilities Incurred. These liabilities are the additional obligations assumed by the fiduciary during the period of his accountability.

Liabilities Liquidated. These are the debt cancellations during the period, identified by creditor class.

Liabilities Not Liquidated. These are the unpaid claims existing at the end of the period to which the statement refers.

Supplementary Charges. For the most part, these are the expenses incurred during the period of trusteeship, although they do not include asset expirations or specific losses on the conversion of noncash assets.

Supplementary Credits. These credits include revenues earned during the period, other than amortization of deferred income items; specific gains on the conversion of noncash assets are not included.

Special Problems

The reader will observe that the net income (or loss) for the period is the algebraic sum of the debit and credit balances in the above 10 categories. Additionally, it is important to note that because asset credits are expressed in terms of realization proceeds, net income (or loss) is partially explained in terms of the changes in asset categories as well as by the supplementary charges and credits for the period.

Sales and Purchases. The fiduciary may record merchandise purchased as either "assets acquired" or as "supplementary charges." Similarly, sales may be recorded as either "assets realized" or as "supplementary credits." If operating transactions are relatively numerous, the supplementary charge-credit categories are preferred.

Cash Discounts. The fiduciary may choose between one of two alternative methods in recording cash discounts in respect to receivables and payables. For accounts payable, the amount of the obligation net of discounts and allowances may be debited to "liabilities liquidated" when payment is made. Although the discount and allowance variance between "liabilities to be liquidated" and "liabilities liquidated" is not specifically identified by this treatment, the variance nonetheless enters the calculation of realization gain or loss, as there will be no remaining balance in "liabilities not liquidated."

If the fiduciary should elect to debit "liabilities liquidated" with the invoice billing (gross) when payment is made, then a contra credit equal to the amount of discounts and allowances will appear as a "supplementary credit." This purchase discount and allowance credit is again a factor in the calculation of realization gain or loss, although in this instance it is separately identified.

A parallel accounting treatment may be applied to receivable balances and related sales discounts and allowances.

Depreciation and Uncollectibles.   Depreciation expense and estimated bad debts usually are not separately identified in the realization and liquidation account. They are reflected, however, in the estimated period-end balances in the accumulated depreciation and allowance for uncollectibles accounts, which are reported contra in "assets not realized." The expenses are thus factors in the calculation of net income or loss for the period.

Accruals.   Where the amounts of accrued income items in the "assets to be realized" category are subsequently realized at larger amounts, two alternative accounting treatments are available. The accountant may credit "assets realized" with the amount accrued at the start of the period, crediting the additional amount collected to "supplementary credits." Or, the increase in the amount of the accrual since the start of the period may be entered as accrued interest in "assets acquired," with a contra credit to "supplementary credits." The subsequent collection may then be recorded by a credit to "assets realized." Comparable treatment may be accorded accrued expenses.

Favorable or Unfavorable Settlement of Liabilities.   In the event that the creditors agree to accept less than face value for their obligations, the settlement discount should be preferably reported as a "supplementary credit," with the total amount of the canceled obligation reported as "liabilities liquidated." In the event a premium payment is required in order to liquidate an overdue indebtedness, accounting treatment would parallel that for a discount settlement; accordingly, the amount of the premium should be entered as a "supplementary charge."

In measuring gain or loss on the favorable settlement of liabilities, recognition must also be given to the reasonableness of the interest rate on the new debt. *FASB Interpretation No. 2*, "Imputing Interest on Debt Arrangements Made under the Federal Bankruptcy Act," states in this regard:[7]

> *APB Opinion No. 21* applies to notes issued by a debtor in a reorganization, arrangement, or under other provisions of the Federal Bankruptcy Act. A note issued under such circumstances in exchange (in whole or in part) for an existing note or notes shall be considered a "note exchanged for property" for purposes of applying *APB Opinion No. 21*. In addition, an existing note shall be considered as originating in a reorganization, arrangement, or under other provisions of the Federal Bankruptcy Act and therefore as being a new

---

[7] While this interest imputation refers to the 1898 Act (as amended), presumably the interpretation would likewise apply to the 1978 BRA. *FASB Interpretation No. 2* essentially confirmed the application of *Opinion No. 21* in re the 1898 Act.

note if its original terms are modified, altered, or otherwise changed as a part of the agreement with creditors. Accordingly, interest shall be imputed by applying *APB Opinion No. 21* if the new note does not specify interest or specifies an interest rate which is unreasonable in the particular circumstances.

Questions

1. Who may initiate a petition for the *voluntary* dissolution of a corporation? The *involuntary* dissolution of a corporation?

2. Distinguish between *bankruptcy insolvency* and *equity insolvency*.

3. What is the liquidation sequence once a debtor has been judicially determined a bankrupt?

4. Certain classes of a distressed debtor's liabilities must be fully satisfied before other creditors can receive a settlement. What are they?

5. What is a statement of affairs? What distinguishes this statement from the conventional balance sheet?

6. How should contingent liabilities be reported in the statement of affairs?

7. Can you project an extension in the usefulness of a statement of affairs for financially prospering enterprises—the going concerns?

8. What is meant by the expression "debtor in possession"?

9. What unique classification and descriptive distinctions should be made in the set of accounts that are prepared to record the actions of the trustee in a reorganization?

10. What purpose is served by the preparation of the realization and liquidation account? In outline, cite the several categories found in the realization and liquidation account.

Exercises

Exercise 18–1

An accountant is often confronted with problems relating to bankruptcy proceedings. The following items relate to pertinent points of law with which the accountant should be familiar. Determine whether each legal conclusion is true or false according to bankruptcy law. For items which are false, explain why they are false.

a. Insolvency in the bankruptcy sense is a financial status in which the aggregate fair value of the assets of an entity is not sufficient to pay outstanding liabilities.

b. A preference in bankruptcy prefers one creditor over the others.

c. The Bankruptcy Reform Act specifically grants the exclusive original jurisdiction over bankruptcy proceedings to one of 12 Bankruptcy Courts.
d. The filing of a voluntary petition in bankruptcy does not automatically operate as an adjudication or determination that the petitioner is bankrupt.
e. The Bankruptcy Reform Act considers a partnership as an entity separate from the partners.
f. Federal, state, and local taxes are discharged by bankruptcy.
g. Insolvency in the bankruptcy sense is the same as insolvency in the equity sense.
h. A trustee in a bankruptcy proceeding is usually elected by the creditors.
i. A priority in a bankruptcy proceeding is given for administration costs including accountants' and attorneys' fees.

(AICPA adapted)

Exercise 18–2

Each of the following relates to points of bankruptcy law. Select the one BEST answer for each of the following items:

1. The highest priority for payment in full before general creditors' claims in a bankruptcy proceeding is assigned—
    a. Wages, in a limited amount, if earned within three months preceding bankruptcy.
    b. Wages owed to an insolvent employee.
    c. Administration costs of bankruptcy.
    d. Unpaid federal income taxes.
2. Under Chapter 11 of the Bankruptcy Reform Act, a plan to be accepted and confirmed by the court—
    a. Must be accepted by all creditors.
    b. May be approved by a majority of creditors by number.
    c. May be approved by one third of the creditors by number if their claims equal two thirds of provable claims.
    d. Requires approval of a majority as to number of creditors and two thirds as to amount of claims of creditors where claims have been proved and allowed.
3. Which of the following statements *best* describes a composition agreement unanimously agreed to by all creditors?
    a. It provides for the appointment of a fiduciary to take over and operate the debtor's business.
    b. It is subject to approval by a federal district court judge.
    c. It provides for a discharge of the debts included in the composition agreement upon performance by the debtor.
    d. It binds only those creditors who do *not* subsequently withdraw from the agreement prior to its consummation.
4. Dexter had assets of $80,000 and liabilities of $100,000, all unsecured. He owed $25,000 to each of the following: Petrie, Dey, Mabley, and Norris. Petrie, Dey, and Mabley agreed with each other and with Dexter to accept 70 cents on the dollar in immediate satisfaction of their debts. Under these circumstances—

a. The agreement is void for lack of consideration.

b. The agreement would *not* constitute an action justifying commencement of an involuntary case.

c. Norris would be bound by the agreement.

d. The agreement described is an assignment for the benefit of the creditors.

5. Ted Dolson has filed a voluntary petition in bankruptcy. His assets are listed as $4,200, and his liabilities, $18,750. His creditors include (1) three employees who have *not* been paid wages for six weeks at $100 per week per employee, (2) the U.S. government for $6,900 in back income and social security taxes, (3) his former wife for back alimony payments of $3,000, and (4) suppliers for goods purchased on open account for $7,050. In this situation—

a. All the debts in question are dischargeable in bankruptcy.

b. Claims must be filed within three months of the filing of the petition in bankruptcy.

c. The wage earners have the first priority after administration costs.

d. The U.S. government claim will take precedence over the security interests of secured creditors.

(AICPA adapted)

Exercise 18–3

For several years Martin supplied raw materials to Western, Inc., who processed the goods into a finished product for sale to retail customers.

Martin supplied goods to Western on credit terms, and to secure his claim for unpaid goods, Martin obtained and properly perfected a "floating lien" on all of the goods sold to Western.

Six months ago, Martin heard that Western, Inc., was in financial difficulty and stopped selling goods to the firm. Martin was not paid by Western for several shipments of goods and heard that recently Western made a general assignment for the benefit of its creditors. Also Martin heard that a group of Western's creditors may attempt to place Western into bankruptcy.

Required:

a. Under what circumstances may Western's creditors proceed to have Western adjudicated an involuntary bankrupt?

b. Assume that Western's creditors may proceed to have it adjudicated an involuntary bankrupt. What action would they have to take in order to commence a bankruptcy proceeding?

c. Will the number of creditors required to commence an involuntary bankruptcy proceeding vary depending upon the number of Western's creditors? Explain.

d. How will Martin be treated in the bankruptcy proceedings if Western is adjudicated a bankrupt? Explain.

(AICPA adapted)

Exercise 18–4

Indicate whether the following legal conclusions are true or false, according to general principles of bankruptcy law.

a. In order for a person to be adjudged a distressed debtor under the Bankruptcy Reform Act—
    (1) He must owe debts totaling more than $2,000.
    (2) There must be at least three creditors.
    (3) A petition in bankruptcy must be filed by a majority of creditors.
    (4) The creditor must agree to the commencement of bankruptcy proceedings.
    (5) A petition in bankruptcy must be filed.
b. Bankruptcy proceedings may be instituted against any person or corporation, including—
    (6) A married woman.
    (7) A domestic insurance corporation.
    (8) A banking corporation.
    (9) A building and loan corporation.
    (10) A partnership.
c. Classes of claims that have priority under the provisions of the Bankruptcy Reform Act include:
    (11) Expenses of bankruptcy administration.
    (12) Wages earned within one year before the date of bankruptcy.
    (13) Debts of less than $50.
    (14) Taxes.
    (15) Claims of creditors that are outstanding for more than three years.
d. Debts discharged by completion of bankruptcy proceedings and discharge of the debtor include:
    (16) Contract obligations that are not due until three years following the filing of the petition.
    (17) Trade accounts payable.
    (18) Taxes.
    (19) Fines or penalties to governmental units.
    (20) A debt arising from the commission of a willful injury.

(AICPA adapted)

Exercise 18–5

In the course of examining the financial statements of Superior Systems, Inc., the financial vice president discloses that the corporation has a serious collection problem with one of its customers, Vizar Components, Inc. Vizar is approximately $10,000 in arrears; its checks have been returned for insufficient funds. Other creditors have similar claims against Vizar.

You have also learned that the principal creditors, including Superior, have held a meeting to consider possible alternative courses of action. During the meeting, an examination of the financial statements of Vizar revealed that it was in a difficult current position, but that it had sufficient assets to meet liabilities in the event of a bankruptcy proceeding. The meeting also revealed that Vizar's problems had built up over the past two years due to poor management. The company appears to have significant potential to return to profitability if properly managed.

What are the viable alternatives to a bankruptcy proceeding? Explain.

(AICPA adapted)

Exercise 18–6

During the examination of the financial statements of Delta Corporation, you note that as of September 30, 19X0:

1. Current liabilities exceed current assets.
2. Total assets substantially exceed total liabilities.
3. Cash position is poor, and current payables are considerably in arrears.
4. Trade and secured creditors are pressing for payment, and several lawsuits have been commenced against Delta.

Further investigation reveals the following:

1. On August 31, 19X0, Delta made a $1,000 payment to Oliveros on a $20,000 mortgage indebtedness over one year in arrears. The fair market value of the mortgaged property is $35,000.
2. On September 20, 19X0, a trade creditor, Miller, obtained a judgment against Delta which under applicable law constitutes a lien on Delta's real property.
3. On September 22, 19X0, Delta paid a substantial amount to Helms, a supplier, on an account over one year old.
4. On September 27, 19X0, Delta executed and delivered a financing statement to Honea, a vendor, from whom Delta had purchased some new machinery six months earlier. Honea duly filed and perfected the financing statement.

Required:

a. As of September 30, 19X0, could the creditors of Delta file an involuntary petition in bankruptcy against Delta if a sufficient number of them having a sufficient amount of claims decide to do so? Explain.

b. Independent of your answer to requirement (a), assume the same facts set out above except that Delta's total liabilities exceed total assets and that on October 2, 19X0, Delta filed a voluntary petition in bankruptcy, and a trustee has been appointed.
   (1) What are the rights, if any, of the trustee against each of the creditors involved in the four transactions stated in the problem? Explain.
   (2) What are the general requirements for creditors to be entitled to vote on and participate in a bankruptcy proceeding? Explain for each of the four creditors involved whether he meets these requirements. Why?

(AICPA adapted)

Exercise 18–7

Cassens, Inc., experienced economic misfortune in respect to credit deficiencies during 19X0 following which its balance sheet disclosed the following on December 31:

Assets		Equities	
Cash	$ 1,506	Trade accounts payable	$265,000
Accounts receivable	96,183	Capital stock	100,000
Merchandise	176,021	Retained earnings	40,000
Long-lived assets—net	131,290		
Total assets	$405,000	Total equities	$405,000

Following the appointment of R. M. Guy, trustee, who was authorized to operate the business, the properties disclosed above were transferred to him; Guy insisted that accounts receivable and merchandise be written down to $76,300 and $145,055, respectively.

During the first six months of 19X1, the trustee collected old receivable balances, suffering additional loss of $5,035. During this period, credit sales were made for $185,000, of which $132,400 were collected. Trade accounts payable of $160,000 were paid by the trustee as well as trusteeship expenses of $36,100. Properties, and related obligations, were returned to the Cassens management on July 1, after depreciation on long-lived assets was allowed to the extent of $6,563. The cost of unsold merchandise on July 1 was $18,460.

Required:

a. Prepare entries for both the trustee and Cassens, Inc., to record the transactions described above.

b. Submit to the management a balance sheet of Cassens, Inc., following the restoration of original custody.

Exercise 18–8

Channel Service, Inc., has convened a meeting of its creditors to effectuate a composition settlement. Prepare a *statement of affairs* for the forthcoming meeting. The company's balance sheet discloses:

Assets		Equities	
Cash	$ 317	Accrued wages	$ 1,575
Accounts receivable	14,329	Accounts payable	41,585
Supplies	1,479	Mortgage on trucks	19,300
Trucks	28,770	Capital stock	5,000
		Less deficit	[22,565]
Total assets	$44,895	Total equities	$ 44,895

Current value estimates for assets are:

Supplies	$ 610
Trucks	22,500
Accounts receivable	12,500

Problems

Problem 18–9

I. M. Train, toy manufacturer, on October 31, 19X0, prepared the following enumeration of resources and creditor claims:

Resources:
  Petty cash, $250, including expense vouchers for $119.
  Cash, $2,615.
  Accounts receivable, $3,680, of which $3,380, are believed to be collectible.

Toy materials and supplies, $12,000; estimated market value, $8,400.
Toys in process, $8,100; estimated market value, $2,000.
Building, $20,000; estimated market value, $9,000.
Display equipment, $11,800; estimated market value, $8,200.

Claims:
Accounts payable:

Gem Supply Company	$ 2,800
Ornamental Trinkets, Inc.	6,300
R. M. Brown	15,000
A. K. Moyer...	1,700

Notes payable:
American State Bank, $20,000. The display equipment is pledged as collateral.
Texas Finance Company, $15,000. Unsecured notes receivable, $10,000 and warehouse receipts for finished goods are pledged as collateral. The finished goods (manufactured toys) have a book value of $8,000 and an estimated current value of $7,500. The notes receivable are estimated to be fully collectible.
Accrued wages, $1,750.

Required:

a. Prepare a statement of affairs as of October 31, 19X0.
b. Prepare a schedule of payments to creditors on this date, indicating whether the amount of the settlement is a full or partial liquidation.

Problem 18–10

A receiver was appointed on September 30, 19X0, for Green, Inc. On this date, the following balance sheet accounts are available:

Assets

Petty cash..............................			$ 120
Cash in bank..........................			2,400
Accounts receivable....................	$32,000		
Notes receivable.......................	20,000	$52,000	
Allowance for bad debts...............		340	51,660
Accrued interest, notes receivable........			600
Merchandise			29,200
Prepaid insurance			240
Prepaid advertising			190
Building	$80,000		
Accumulated depreciation	21,000		59,000
Furniture and fixtures..................	$ 7,200		
Accumulated depreciation	1,600		5,600
Organization costs.....................			1,740
Goodwill..............................			4,000
Total assets			$154,750

Equities

Accrued wages........................	$ 2,800	
Accrued property taxes.................	1,810	
Accounts payable......................	79,800	
Notes payable........................	15,000	
Accrued interest payable	150	$ 99,560
Contributed capital:		
Common stock	$70,000	
Premium...........................	2,000	
	$72,000	
Retained earnings:		
Deficit.............................	16,810	55,190
Total equities..........................		$154,750

It is estimated that conversion of assets will realize cash in the following amounts:

Notes receivable (with accrued interest).........	$19,100
Accounts receivable..........................	25,000
Merchandise	19,000
Building	25,000
Furniture and fixtures.......................	2,000

Notes payable of $10,000 are secured by merchandise, the book value of which is $20,000. Notes payable of $5,000 are secured by the furniture and equipment. Interest expense is allocable ratably to all outstanding notes payable.

Required:
a. Prepare a statement of affairs as of September 30.
b. Prepare a supporting deficiency account or report on this date.

Problem 18–11

The Machine Manufacturing Company has been forced into bankruptcy as of April 30, 19X0. The following list of account balances was prepared by the company bookkeeper as of April 30, 19X0:

Cash......................................	$ 2,700
Accounts receivable	39,350
Notes receivable	18,500
Inventories:	
Raw materials	19,600
Work in process	35,100
Finished machines	12,000
Supplies	6,450
Tools	14,700
Prepaid expenses	950
Plant and property:	
Land	20,000
Buildings................................	75,000
Machinery	80,900
	$325,250

Note payable to the First Bank	$ 15,000
Notes payable to suppliers...................	51,250
Accounts payable	52,000
Accrued salaries and wages.................	8,850
Accrued property taxes.....................	2,900
Employees' taxes withheld..................	1,150
Accrued wage taxes........................	600
Accrued interest on bonds..................	1,800
First-mortgage bonds payable...............	90,000
Accumulated depreciation—buildings.........	33,750
Accumulated depreciation—machinery	32,100
Common stock ($100 par value)	75,000
Deficit	[39,150]
	$325,250

Additional information:

1. Of the total accounts receivable, $10,300 are believed to be good. The other accounts are doubtful, but it seems probable that 20 percent finally can be collected.

2. A total of $15,000 of the notes receivable have been pledged to secure the note payable to the First Bank. All except $2,500 of these appear to be good. Interest of $800 is accrued on the $12,500 of good notes pledged and $300 is accrued on the $15,000 payable to the bank. The remaining notes are not considered collectible.

3. The finished machines are expected to be sold for one third above their costs, but expenses in disposing of them will equal 20 percent of their sales price. Work in process can be completed at an additional cost of $15,400, of which $3,700 would be material used from the raw material inventory. The work in process, when completed, will probably sell for $40,000, and costs of sale will be 20 percent of sales price. The raw material not used will realize $8,000. Most of the value of tools consists of special items. After completion ·of work in process, the tools should sell for $3,000. The supply inventory which will not be needed to complete work should sell for $1,000.

4. Land and buildings are mortgaged as security for bonds. They have an appraised value of $95,000. The company recently purchased $20,000 of machinery on a conditional sales contract. It still owes $12,000 principal on this contract which is included in the notes payable. These machines, having a current used value of $10,000, are repossessed. The Machine Manufacturing Company remains liable for the unpaid obligation. Depreciation taken on these machines amounts to $1,800. The remaining machinery is believed to be salable at $10,000, but costs of selling it may be $1,000.

Required:

a. Prepare a statement showing the estimated deficiency to unsecured creditors, indicating clearly the causes of the deficiency. You need not consider any expenses of liquidation that are not stated in the information given.

b. Compute the percentage of probable payments to unsecured creditors.

(AICPA adapted)

Problem 18–12

The financial condition of the Rawley Manufacturing Corporation was very unstable, although it had unimpaired contributed capital in the amount of $60,000 and accumulated earnings of $8,522. This condition was attributable to a deficiency of quick assets: cash, $265; and trade receivables, $4,062. Its current obligations to trade creditors amounted to $25,289. Other assets were raw materials, $16,000; work in process, $34,400; finished goods, $5,700; and machinery and dies, $33,384. In order to continue operations, it was necessary to obtain sufficient cash to meet current payrolls and to pay miscellaneous expenses.

At a meeting of the principal creditors, it was decided to advance $6,000 to the Rawley Manufacturing Corporation to enable it to meet obligations presently due; additionally, it was decided to permit continuance of operations until the present in-process stock could be completed and sold. These operations were to be conducted by a trustee chosen by the creditors.

Transactions completed during the trusteeship were cash disbursements for labor, $16,625; for expenses, $4,530; and for additional dies, $750; raw materials purchased on account, $6,300; sales on account, $72,300; loss on collection of old accounts, $380; expenses incurred, on account, $15,000. Unliquidated account balances at the termination of the trusteeship period were as follows: accounts receivable (new), $3,382; accounts payable (new), $89; raw materials, $2,000; finished goods, $30,000; and machinery and dies, $34,134.

Required:

Prepare in orthodox form a statement of realization and liquidation with supporting schedules. Ignore the effects of depreciation in the determination of operating profit.

Problem 18–13

The Noel Corporation is in financial difficulty because of a deficiency in sales volume. Its stockholders and principal creditors want an estimate of the financial results of the liquidation of the assets and liabilities and the dissolution of the corporation. The corporation's trial balance follows:

NOEL CORPORATION
Postclosing Trial Balance
December 31, 19X2

	Debit	Credit
Cash	$ 1,000	
Accounts receivable	20,500	
Allowance for bad debts		$ 350
Inventories	40,000	
Supplies inventory	3,000	
Downhill Railroad 5% bonds	5,000	
Accrued bond interest receivable	750	
Advertising	6,000	
Land	4,000	
Building	30,000	
Accumulated depreciation—building		5,000
Machinery and equipment	46,000	
Accumulated depreciation—machinery and equipment		8,000
Accounts payable		26,000
Notes payable—bank		25,000
Notes payable—officers		20,000
Payroll taxes payable		800
Wages payable		1,500
Mortgage payable		42,000
Mortgage interest payable		500
Capital stock		50,000
Retained earnings	29,100	
Reserve for product guarantees		6,200
	$185,350	$185,350

The following information has been collected in anticipation of a meeting of the stockholders and principal creditors to be held on January 2, 19X3.

1. Cash includes a $300 protested check from a customer. The customer stated that he would have funds to honor the check in about two weeks.
2. Accounts receivable include accounts totaling $10,000 that are fully collectible and have been assigned to the bank in connection with the notes payable. Included in the unassigned receivables is an uncollectible account of $150. The Allowance for Bad Debts account of $350 now on the books will adequately provide for other doubtful accounts.
3. Purchase orders totaling $9,000 are on hand for the corporation's products. Inventory with a book value of $6,000 can be processed at an additional cost of $400 to fill these orders. The balance of the inventory, which includes obsolete materials with a book value of $1,200, can be sold for $10,500.
4. In transit at December 31 but not recorded on the books was a shipment of defective merchandise being returned by a customer. Mr. Noel, president of the corporation, had authorized the return and the refund of the purchase price of $250 after the merchandise had been inspected. Other than this return Mr. Noel knows of no other defective merchandise that would bear upon the appropriated Reserve for Product Guarantees account. The merchandise being returned has no salvage value.

5. The Supplies Inventory is comprised of advertising literature, brochures, and other sales aids. These could not be replaced for less than $3,700.
6. The Downhill Railroad bonds are recorded at face value. They were purchased six years earlier for $600, and the adjustment to face value was credited to Retained Earnings. At December 31, 19X2, the bonds were quoted at 18.
7. The Advertising account represents the future benefits of a 19X2 advertising campaign. Ten percent of certain advertising expenditures were placed in the account. Mr. Noel stated that this was too conservative and that 20 percent would result in a more realistic measure of the market that was created.
8. The land and building are in a downtown area. A firm offer of $50,000 has been received for the land that would be used as a parking lot; the building would be razed at a cost of $12,000 to the buyer. Another offer of $40,000 was received for the real estate that the bidder stated would be used for manufacturing that would probably employ some Noel employees.
9. The highest of the offers received from used machinery dealers was $18,000 for all of the machinery and equipment.
10. One creditor, whose account for $1,000 is included in the accounts payable, confirmed in writing that he would accept 90 cents on the dollar if the corporation paid him by January 10.
11. Wages payable include year-end adjustments of $325 payable to certain factory employees for their overtime during the busy season.
12. The mortgage payable is secured by the land and building. The last two monthly principal payments of $200 each were not made.
13. Estimated liquidation expenses amount to $3,200.
14. For income tax purposes the corporation has the following net operating loss carry-overs (the tax rate is 50 percent):

19X0.................	$10,000
19X1.................	12,000
19X2.................	8,000

Required:

a. Prepare a statement of affairs. Assets should be classified according to their availability for secured and unsecured creditors, and liabilities should be classified according to their legal priority and secured status. The statement should have the following column headings:

For Assets:
  Book Value
  Assets
  Appraised Value
  Estimated Amount Available
  Loss or Gain on Realization

For Liabilities and Capital:
  Book Value
  Liabilities and Capital
  Amount Unsecured

b. Prepare a schedule indicating the estimated settlement per dollar of unsecured liabilities.

(AICPA adapted)

Problem 18–14

The Boutique Company was unable to meet its obligations. As a result, John Nunn was appointed trustee on February 5, 19X0. The following accounts were taken from the books as of that date:

Cash	$ 560
Accounts receivable	6,210
Merchandise	16,536
Prepayment of expenses	704
Fixtures	12,942
	$36,952

Accounts payable	$16,100
Notes payable	3,500
Accrued wages, taxes, etc.	1,200
Accrued rent	600
Accumulated depreciation	3,803
Capital stock	10,000
Retained earnings	1,749
	$36,952

In the period from February 5, to April 30, 19X0, the trustee's actions resulted in the following:

1. An audit of the accounts receivable disclosed that there were an additional $237 of accounts receivable that had not been brought on the books.
2. Merchandise costing $7,500 wsa sold for cash.
3. A portion of the fixtures, which cost $5,376 and had accumulated depreciation of $942, was sold.
4. Accounts receivable totaling $1,882 were collected. Other accounts amounting to $741 have been determined to be worthless.
5. Claims have been approved and paid for $1,010 of the wages and taxes that were accrued at February 5. Wage claims for $125 that were unrecorded on February 5 have also been approved and paid. Other claims have not yet been paid.
6. Expenses for wages and supplies used in liquidating the business to April 30 amounted to $1,300. Fees for the trustee need not be considered.
7. Rent under leases has continued to accrue in the amount of $900. Interest of $70 has accrued on notes payable.
8. Cash receipts and cash disbursements show the following:

Cash receipts:	
Collection of accounts	$1,882
Sales of merchandise	8,300
Sale of fixtures	1,000
Cash disbursements:	
Accrued wages and taxes	1,135
Expenses of the trusteeship	1,300

Required:

Prepare a formal statement of realization and liquidation and related gain and loss account for the period ended April 30, 19X0.

(AICPA adapted)

Problem 18–15

JONES, INC.
Balance Sheet, as of March 31, 19X5
(Prepared by the Company's Bookkeeper)

Assets

Current assets:

Cash		$ 2,000	
Notes receivable	$ 4,640		
Less: Notes receivable discounted	4,640		
Accounts receivable		4,000	
U.S. Treasury bonds		10,000	
Inventories:			
Finished goods	$15,000		
Work in process	4,500		
Raw materials	6,000	25,500	
Total current assets			$ 41,500

Other assets:

Subscriptions to capital stock			12,500
Investments			2,300
Property and equipment:			
Real estate		$ 45,000	
Factory equipment		24,000	
		$ 69,000	
Less: Accumulated depreciation		20,000	49,000
Total assets			$105,300

Liabilities

Current liabilities:

Notes payable:			
To Manufacturers' Trust Co.	$10,000		
To Alex Smith	25,000	$ 35,000	
Accounts payable		24,000	
Accrued liabilities:			
Salaries and wages	$ 992		
Property taxes	460	1,452	
Total current liabilities			$ 60,452

Long-term liabilities:

First mortgage on real estate		$ 15,000	
Second mortgage on real estate		20,000	35,000
Total liabilities			$ 95,452

Capital

Capital stock—authorized, subscribed, and issued, 500 shares, par $100 per share		$ 50,000	
Less: Deficit		[40,152]	9,848
Total liabilities and capital			$105,300

An analysis of the company's accounts disclosed the following:

1. Jones, Inc., started business with authorized capital of $50,000, represented by shares of $100 par value each. Of the 500 authorized shares, 375 were fully paid at par and 125 were subscribed at par, payment to be made on call.
2. The Manufacturers' Trust Company holds $10,000 of U.S. Treasury bonds as security for its $10,000 loan; it also holds the first mortgage of $15,000 on the company's real estate, interest on which is paid through March 31, 19X5.
3. The real estate includes land, which cost $5,000, and a building erected thereon at a cost of $40,000. Of the accumulated depreciation, $5,000 is applicable to the building and $15,000 to the factory equipment. The realizable value of the real estate is estimated to be $30,000.
4. The note payable to Alex Smith is secured by a chattel mortgage on factory equipment and the inventories. Interest on the note has been paid through March 31, 19X5.
5. Alex Smith holds the second mortgage on the real estate.
6. The notes receivable, $4,640, which were discounted, though not yet due, are deemed uncollectible.
7. Of the $4,000 of accounts receivable, $2,000 are considered good; of the remaining $2,000 it is expected that one half will be uncollectible.
8. Inventories are valued at cost; finished goods are expected to yield 110 percent of cost. Goods in process cost $4,500 and have a realizable value, if scrapped, of $900. It is estimated, however, that the work in process can be completed into finished goods by the use of $1,200 of raw material and an expenditure of $1,400 for labor and other costs. The raw material deteriorates rapidly, and is estimated to realize only 25 percent of cost.
9. The factory equipment, which cost $24,000 on April 1, 19X0, is considered to have a realizable value of $5,000 at March 31, 19X5.
10. The subscription to the capital stock for 125 shares at par, is due from Wyman Jones, president of the company, and is fully collectible.
11. Investments include 15 shares (a 1 percent interest) of the common stock of the Bourbon Company, acquired at a cost of $1,500, but with a market value of $3,390 at March 31, 19X5; and 20 shares of treasury stock for which the company paid $800.
12. No expenses of liquidation nor accruals not specifically mentioned need be considered.

The committee has called for payment of the capital stock subscription and has decided to have the goods in process converted into finished goods, which are expected to realize 110 percent of cost. Completion of goods in process can be done so quickly that no further expenses than those mentioned above will be incurred.

Required:

a. Prepare a statement of affairs on March 31, 19X5.
b. Prepare a supporting deficiency account detailing estimated gains and losses.
c. Calculate amounts and settlement percentages for each class of creditors.

(AICPA adapted)

Problem 18–16

The Neversink Corporation advises you that it is facing bankruptcy proceedings. As the company's CPA you are aware of its condition.

The balance sheet of the Neversink Corporation at June 30, 19X0, and supplementary data are presented below:

Assets

Cash..	$ 2,000
Accounts receivable, less allowance for bad debts	70,000
Inventory, raw material...............................	40,000
Inventory, finished goods.............................	60,000
Marketable securities	20,000
Land...	13,000
Buildings, less accumulated depreciation	90,000
Machinery, less accumulated depreciation	120,000
Goodwill	20,000
Prepaid expenses	5,000
Total assets.......................................	$440,000

Liabilities and Capital

Accounts payable	$ 80,000
Notes payable	135,000
Accrued wages	15,000
Mortgages payable	130,000
Common stock......................................	100,000
Retained earnings [deficit]	[20,000]
Total liabilities and capital	$440,000

Supplementary data:
1. Cash includes a $500 travel advance that has been expended.
2. Accounts receivable of $40,000 have been pledged in support of bank loans of $30,000. Credit balances of $5,000 are netted in the accounts receivable total.
3. Marketable securities consisted of government bonds costing $10,000 and 500 shares of Bartlett Company stock. The market value of the bonds is $10,000, and the stock is quoted at $18 per share. The bonds have accrued interest due of $200. The securities are collateral for a $20,000 bank loan.
4. Appraised value of raw materials is $30,000, and finished goods is $50,000. For an additional cost of $10,000, the raw materials would realize $70,000 as finished goods.
5. The appraised value of fixed assets is land, $25,000; buildings, $110,000; and machinery, $75,000.
6. Prepaid expenses will be exhausted during the liquidation period.
7. Accounts payable include $15,000 of withheld payroll taxes and $6,000 of obligations to creditors who have been assured by the president they would be paid. There are unrecorded employer's payroll taxes in the amount of $500.
8. Wages payable are not subject to any limitations under bankruptcy laws.
9. Mortgages payable consist of $100,000 on land and buildings and a $30,000 chattel mortgage on machinery. Total unrecorded accrued interest on these mortgages amounted to $2,400.

10. Estimated legal fees and expenses in connection with the liquidation are $10,000.
11. Probable judgment on a pending damage suit is $50,000.
12. You have not rendered an invoice for $5,000 for last year's audit, and you estimate a $1,000 fee for liquidation stock.

Required:

a. Prepare a statement of affairs.
b. Compute the estimated settlement per dollar of unsecured liabilities.

(AICPA adapted)

Accounting for Estates and Trusts

Administration by a Fiduciary

Introduction

A *fiduciary* is a person to whom is entrusted the property of another for safekeeping, management, and/or distribution, and who is accountable therefore to various interested parties. Either an individual or a corporation may serve in this capacity. The importance of the fiduciary relationship, which is essentially a custodial or stewardship arrangement, has been indicated previously in references to trustees for financially distressed businesses. The fiduciary occupies an equally important role in respect to the administration of estates and trusts.

Upon the death of an individual, the *decedent,* it is necessary that a personal representative of the deceased assume custody and control of his estate. In the event that the decedent has executed a valid will in which is indicated his choice of a representative, his wishes will normally control. In such a circumstance, the decedent is said to have died *testate,* he is referred to as the *testator,* and when confirmed by court appointment, his representative is known as the *executor.* Should the decedent fail to execute a valid will, he is said to have died *intestate,* and his representative selected by the court is known as an *administrator.* If there exists a will, the last expressions of the decedent contained therein usually will govern the distribution of his estate; if no will exists, or if the will is determined to be invalid, the various state *laws of descent and distribution* will control the disposition of the decedent's estate. The laws of descent control the disposition of real property; the laws of distribution regulate the disposition of personal property.

The administration of estates normally comes within the purview of courts referred to as *probate, surrogate, orphan's,* or *county* courts. Before a will can become an effective instrument of fiduciary authority, it must be *admitted to probate.* To probate a will is to prove its validity, that is, to prove that it was executed by a competent decedent without duress or other improper influence, and that it represents the last expressions of the decedent concerning the disposition of his property. Witnesses to the signing of the will may be called upon to testify as to these and other matters and to the genuineness of the various signatures. Once the will is admitted to probate, the court may then proceed to the appointment of an executor. If the person named in the will is able and willing to serve, he is usually confirmed by the court and is issued *letters testamentary,* which are the evidence of his formal authority to assume the role of fiduciary. If an administrator is appointed, he is similarly issued *letters of administration* empowering him to act as fiduciary.

Role of the Fiduciary in Estate Administration

While one is not bound to accept appointment as a fiduciary, once it has been accepted there is a commitment to faithfully discharge the obligations of that trust. The fiduciary must first seek out and take possession of the property of the deceased; he is then charged with exercising reasonable prudence in respect to the care and management of the property. Consequently, he is required to keep estate resources invested to the extent that investments may profitably be made; to liquidate all just debts of the decedent, including estate and inheritance taxes; and to distribute the decedent's property according to the provisions of the will or in the manner prescribed by law.

Real property of the testator usually passes directly by *devise* to *devisees* identified in the will, legal title vesting in the latter at the date of the decedent's death. However, since the fiduciary is frequently called upon to include both real and personal property in various reports required by governmental agencies, including those submitted for federal estate and state inheritance tax purposes, it may be desirable to include real property in the inventory of the decedent's assets. While the fiduciary has no accountability with respect thereto, he may petition the court to allow the sale of such property in order to meet the obligations of the decedent when personal property is clearly inadequate for this purpose.

Inventory of Assets

The fiduciary is required to submit a complete inventory of the properties of the decedent to the court of his appointment. This inventory should contain a full and complete description of all assets that are entrusted to the care and management of the fiduciary. Some of the assets may have no apparent value; yet, for reasons of completeness in the enumeration, such items should be detailed, with an indication of no value. Among the assets often included in an estate inventory are bank balances, valuables in locked depositories, corporate and government securities, advances to legatees, accrued interest, dividends receivable, accounts and other receivables, judgments payable to the estate, and interests in jointly owned property. The proceeds from a life insurance policy for which the estate is the indicated beneficiary are properly included as an estate asset; in the event that other beneficiaries are specified, payment is made directly to those named, and the relevant insurance contracts are excluded from the estate inventory. Where the estate includes a partnership interest, this property right must be disclosed and evaluated. Liquidation of the partnership may be necessary unless continuity is provided for and assured by the decedent's will or the partnership agreement. If liquidation is not required, valuation problems are likely to arise unless a means of arriving at a value of the partnership interest is specified in the partnership agreement or in a buy-sell agreement.

The assignment of value to estate assets is the primary responsibility of the fiduciary, although he may be aided by court-appointed appraisers. For example, the Texas Probate Code (as amended, 1977) provides:

Within ninety days after his qualification, unless a longer time shall be granted by the court, the representative shall file with the clerk of court a verified, full and detailed inventory, in one written instrument, of all the property of such estate which has come to his possession or knowledge, which inventory shall include:

(a)   all real property of the estate situated in the State of Texas;
(b)   all personal property of the estate wherever situated.

The representative shall set out in the inventory his appraisement of the fair market value of each item thereof as of the date of death in the case of grant of letters testamentary or of administration or as of the date of grant of letters of guardianship, as the case may be; provided that if the court shall appoint an appraiser or appraisers of the estate; the representative shall determine the fair market value of each item of the inventory with the assistance of such appraiser or appraisers and shall set out in the inventory such appraisement. The inventory shall specify what portion of the property, if any, is separate property and what portion, if any, is community property. If any property is owned in common with others, the interest owned by the estate shall be shown, together with the names and relationship, if known, of co-owners. Such inventory, when approved by the court and duly filed with the clerk of court, shall constitute for all purposes the inventory and appraisement of the estate referred to in this Code. The court for good cause shown may require the filing of the inventory and appraisement at a time prior to ninety days after the qualification of the representative [Section 250].

The statutes of the various states often provide that in addition to real property, specific items of personalty pass directly to the distributees. These may include specified household items, clothing of the decedent, and other personal effects that are considered of special value to the surviving spouse and/or minor children. Legal title to all personal property not so exempted vests in the fiduciary. Only those items of personalty for which the fiduciary assumes legal responsibility are included in the inventory of assets.

When assets are discovered subsequent to the filing of the inventory, it is appropriate that the fiduciary file a supplemental report, enumerating these additions. The sum of the original and supplemental listings comprises the *corpus*, or the *principal*, of the estate at date of the decedent's death.

Claims against the Estate

The fiduciary is obliged in most states to give public notice to those having claims against the estate of the decedent requesting them to make a presentment of these claims within a specified period of time. Presentment may be made either to the fiduciary or to the court. The fiduciary must necessarily determine the validity of the claims, rejecting those considered to be invalid; in this connection, he is required to exhaust all appropriate legal defenses, including the statute of limitations and the statute of frauds. The length of time allowed for creditors to file a claim against the estate varies among the several states; a period frequently prescribed is one year from the date of the publication of the first notice. In many states this period has been shortened to six months or less.

Once the validity of claims has been confirmed, the fiduciary must establish the *sequence of paying* the various obligations and proceed with their settlement. In the event the estate is solvent, the order of settlement may not be especially important. However, for insolvent estates, the statutes provide the priority sequence which the fiduciary must follow if he is to avoid personal liability for improper distribution. The following order of payment is fairly typical:

1. Funeral and administration expenses.
2. Debts that are secured by a lien on the decedent's property.
3. Taxes, including estate and inheritance taxes.
4. Judgments in force that are a lien against property of the decedent at time of death.
5. Provable debts against the estate.
6. Wages due domestics or other employees.
7. Sustenance payments to the widow for a specified period of time.

The Texas Probate Code (as amended, 1977) provides for the following priorities in respect to the claims against the estates of decedents:

> Class 1. Funeral expenses and expenses of last sickness for a reasonable amount to be approved by the court, not to exceed one thousand dollars, any excess to be classified and paid as other unsecured claims.
> Class 2. Expenses of administration and expenses incurred in the preservation, safe-keeping, and management of the estate.
> Class 3. Claims secured by mortgage or other liens so far as the same can be paid out of the proceeds of the property subject to such mortgage or other lien, and when more than one mortgage or lien shall exist upon the same property, the oldest shall be first paid; but no preference shall be given to such mortgage or lien.
> Class 4. All other claims legally exhibited within six months after the original grant of letters testamentary or of administration.
> Class 5. All claims legally exhibited after the lapse of six months from the original grant of letters testamentary or of administration. [Section 322].

Where the decedent's estate is small, the involvements of estate administration may be reduced somewhat. The Model Small Estates Act provides for the following simplified procedure:

> *Summary Administration of Small Estates.* If it shall appear at the time of the appointment of a personal representative or at any time subsequent thereto by an allegation in the petition for the appointment of the personal representative, by a separate affidavit or otherwise, that the value of the entire estate,

less liens and encumbrances, does not exceed [$10,000], the court in its discretion may authorize a summary administration of the estate in any one or more of the following respects:

(1) By ordering that notice be given to creditors to present their claims within [three (3) months] after the first publication of such notice or be barred as in other cases;

(2) By dispensing with notice by publication in any or all subsequent portions of such proceeding and ordering that notice be given by posting or mailing in lieu of publication;

(3) By appointing but one appraiser for valuing the assets of the estate;

(4) By dispensing entirely with the appointment of an appraiser, if the value of the estate is readily determinable, and by authorizing the personal representative alone to appraise the estate;

(5) By exercising its discretion in fixing the amount of the bond of the personal representative, or dispensing with such bond, but in the absence of special circumstances, the bond shall be fixed in the amount of the value of any part of the estate which the court can determine from examination that the personal representative could easily convert during the period of administration plus the value of the gross annual income of the estate;

(6) By conferring upon the personal representative full power to sell, lease for periods not exceeding one year, mortgage, assign, transfer or convey any property of the estate upon such terms and conditions and for such considerations as he may determine, without any other order or confirmation of the court; or

(7) By ordering final distribution of the estate at any time after the expiration of such [three (3) months'] period after the first publication of notice to creditors.

In any such case creditors not presenting their claims within the time stated in the notice to creditors shall be barred as in other cases. No error in the statement of the value of the estate or the subsequent discovery of additional assets shall affect the validity of any order directing the summary administration of the estate or any order or proceeding in connection with the administration of the estate. Any person dealing with a personal representative upon whom powers have been conferred as herein prescribed shall be entitled to rely fully upon the powers so conferred upon him, but such personal representative in exercising any such powers shall be held accountable to the estate and shall make a final report and account of his administration to be settled by the court as in other cases [Model Small Estates Act, Section 11, 9C, (Pocket Part) U.L.A., 1967 edition].[1]

Bequests of Personal Property

A testator's bequest of personal property is referred to as a *legacy;* the recipient is called a *legatee.* Legacies are classified as specific, demonstrative, general, and residual.

---

[1] Uniform Laws and Model Acts are promulgated by the National Conference of Commissioners on Uniform State Laws. Such laws may be adopted by the various state legislatures verbatim, in modified form, or not at all.

1. A *specific* legacy is a bequest of personal property that is specifically identified in the will; it normally consists of such items as clothing, ornaments, furniture, securities, and other personal effects.
2. A *demonstrative* legacy is a testamentary bequest payable out of a designated fund or specified asset accumulation. Gifts of cash payable out of a designated bank account and the bequest of a quantity of grain from a specified granary are examples of demonstrative legacies.
3. A *general* legacy, unlike a demonstrative legacy, is a bequest of money or other property without special designation as to source.
4. A *residual* legacy is the terminal distribution of personal property after all debts have been paid and all other legacies distributed or otherwise provided for. A residual legatee receives the residue of the estate.

Legacies are distributed in the order of the above enumeration; in the event there is insufficient property to satisfy all legacies, they will be abated or scaled down in the reverse of this order. A legacy may not always be paid, even though there exists a solvent estate; in such an instance, the default is termed a "failure" of a legacy. Failure may exist where the legatee has died previous to the testator's death, the property has undergone deterioration or has suffered destruction, or there exist provisions in the will which controvert public policy.

The statutes of many states provide for bequests by *advancement* where the decedent dies intestate. Should the decedent during his lifetime make a gift of property to individuals (usually children or lineal descendents) who would otherwise be entitled to inherit a part of the estate of the donor upon his death, the bequest may be regarded as an advancement in anticipation of the advancee's intestate share. However, all gratuitous *inter vivos* transfers before death are regarded as absolute gifts, not advancements, unless contrary intent can be demonstrated.

Role of the Fiduciary in Trust Administration

Provision may be made by a testate decedent that property comprising his estate, or a part thereof, shall be placed in trust. A *trust* is an arrangement whereby title to property is transferred to a *trustee,* either an individual or corporation, who holds or manages the property for the benefit of others. While there are various types of trusts, two classes predominate— living trusts and testamentary trusts. *Living trusts,* or *trusts inter vivos,* are created and become operative during the lifetime of the creator. A *testamentary trust* is created by provision in the will of a testator. In the event the trustee is also specified in the will, he becomes a *testamentary trustee.*

A trust is created or established by a *donor, trustor,* or *founder;* those expected to derive benefit therefrom are *beneficiaries.* The trust agreement may provide that the principal of the trust shall eventually be distributed to one beneficiary while income is to be currently awarded another. However, the principal and income beneficiary may be the same person; for example, the income only of a trust may be distributed to a beneficiary until he attains his majority, after which the principal is conveyed to him. The income beneficiary is called a *cestui que trust*. If he receives income for life, he is referred to as a *life tenant*. The recipient of the principal of the trust is termed a *remainderman*. If the beneficiary has the ability to designate who will receive the income or the principal at some later date, he is referred to as having a *power of appointment*.

A trustee normally has only such authority as is conveyed to him by the trust instrument. This authority usually includes:

1. The incurrence of those costs and expenses necessary to the preservation of the trust principal.
2. The sale, exchange or improvements in respect to existing realty.
3. The settlement, totally or by compromise, of claims against the trust estate.
4. The making of new investments and disposition of existing investments.
5. The distribution of property to distributees as provided in the trust agreement.
6. The making of advances to beneficiaries.
7. The payment to or expending of income for the benefit of minors.

A testamentary trustee does not accept an accountability as a fiduciary until trust property is conveyed to him. Legal title to real property customarily vests in the trustee upon the decedent's death; title to personal property, however, passes to the trustee with the transfer of property. The trustee is charged with exercising that degree of care in respect to trust property as he would exercise as a reasonably prudent business executive acting in his own self-interest. The creator of a trust may, by provision in the trust instrument, reserve unto himself the right to relieve the trustee from duties and liabilities otherwise imposed upon him; similarly, by express provision in the trust instrument, the creator of the trust may add to or impose new duties, restrictions, privileges, and powers upon the trustee. The trustee may also be relieved of his duties by a court of competent jurisdiction. The Uniform Trusts Act specifically provides that such a court may, for cause shown and upon notice to the beneficiaries, relieve a trustee from any or all of the duties and restrictions that would otherwise be imposed upon him [Uniform Trusts Act, Section 19, 9C, U.L.A., 1967 edition].

The trustee should weigh carefully the desirability of investing uncommitted cash accumulations in income-producing assets, subject to existing statutory constraints. Where there is reasonable doubt as to the propriety of a proposed course of action in respect to investments, the trustee should seek the opinion of legal counsel; he is usually allowed a reasonable period of time in which to make such investments without penalty for uninvested funds. He is under a special duty to keep separate the trust assets from his own property, unless a contrary provision exists in the trust instrument. In the event of loss that may arise from commingling of trust and other properties, courts have held the trustee guilty of a breach of trust.

Estate Planning

Estate planning may be described as the arranging of one's financial affairs in a manner that maximizes the amount of wealth that may be preserved within some group, typically a family unit. It focuses importantly upon minimizing income, estate, gift, and generation skipping transfer taxes.[2] Nontax objectives, such as maintaining control of a business, are also important, but because personal goals often differ from one individual to another, this discussion will be confined to tax considerations. The estate planning process encompasses projecting the combined effect of the income tax and transfer (estate, gift, and generation skipping) tax results to the family unit. One should not elect automatically a technique, such as a gift, that minimizes estate tax costs but rather should weigh the estate tax savings against the loss of beneficial income tax treatment otherwise available.

In many instances one makes lifetime gifts as part of his comprehensive estate plan. He additionally plans for the transfer of assets at death in a manner that is designed to maximize the wealth of the family by carefully considering the provisions of his will. As previously noted, if he should die without a will, the relevant state law will determine to whom property is to be distributed. Often if a person dies intestate, the estate tax cost is higher than if the person had died with a will that took advantage of various opportunities for tax savings.

Lifetime gifts offer substantial opportunities for saving transfer taxes, especially if the donor transfers appreciating property. The transfer tax value of the property is "frozen" at its date-of-gift value. Consequently, postgift appreciation escapes transfer taxation. In addition, an annual exclusion is available for gift tax purposes, there is no counterpart to this in the estate tax rules.

---

[2] Estate and gift taxes have been in effect for several decades. The generation skipping transfer tax was added to the statute by the Tax Reform Act of 1976. Congress' purpose in initiating this tax was to impose a transfer tax on dispositive arrangements that resulted in the levying of a gift or estate tax only once in several generations. The typical type arrangement at which the generation skipping transfer tax was aimed was one in which a person created a trust and named his child and then his grandchild to receive the income for life, and upon the grandchild's death the assets to pass to the great-grandchild.

The annual exclusion exempts from gift taxation the first $10,000 in value that the donor gives to each donee each year. The exclusion is available with respect to an unlimited number of donees. Because it is an annual exclusion, it starts anew each year. In addition, amounts that a donor pays directly for medical care and tuition for others are not treated as gifts. Thus, each year a grandparent might give each of four grandchildren shares of stock worth $10,000 and pay each grandchild's medical bills and private school or college tuition and not make any taxable transfers. In addition, an unlimited amount of property can be given to one's spouse tax-free.

Gift-splitting provisions enable married donors to treat gifts made by one spouse as if they are made equally by both spouses. Thus, in effect, a donor can double the per-donee annual exclusion. The gift-splitting provisions are especially beneficial if one of the spouses possesses a disproportionate amount of the wealth. Still another advantage of lifetime gifts is that they shift the income from the gifted property to another taxpayer, generally a person in a lower income tax bracket. Moreover, any gift taxes paid reduce the amount in the estate tax base unless the donor dies within three years of having made the gift.

Because the computation of the gift tax is cumulative in its effect, the donor's marginal rate is a function of all of the taxable gifts made during his lifetime. The current period's gift tax is calculated by determining the tax on all (both previous and current) taxable gifts and reducing this amount by the tax on previous taxable gifts. Donors making gifts in excess of the excludable amount will not necessarily have to pay gift tax on their transfers. A credit is available to apply against the gift tax otherwise owed. The amount of the credit, $96,300 for 1984, rises gradually until it peaks at $192,800 in 1987 and later years.

The Tax Reform Act of 1976 (TRA) provided for unification of estate and gift taxes to remove some of the bias in favor of lifetime transfers. As a result of the 1976 law, the tax rates are currently the same for both gift and estate tax purposes. In addition, the TRA further unified the two transfer taxes by incrementing the death tax base by amounts of taxable gifts made after 1976. The addition is at date-of-gift values. Any gift tax paid on such gifts is deducted in calculating the estate tax balance payable. Addition of the taxable gifts to the tax base at death, however, does force the estate into a higher marginal tax bracket. Notwithstanding the move toward unification, lifetime gifts still help to minimize transfer taxes, as previously noted.

In determining the estate tax liability the first step involves the valuation of all properties owned by the decedent at death and certain other properties, such as insurance on his own life that the decedent may have given away within three years of death. Valuation is at date-of-death or alternate-valuation-date values. The alternate valuation date is usually six months after date of death. Deductions are available for debts, funeral expenses, administrative expenses (for example, attorneys fees and court costs), and bequests to charitable organizations. Also, all amounts bequested to the surviving spouse are deducted. The residual net figure, called the taxable estate, is incremented under the unification principle by all taxable gifts made after 1976. However, as noted earlier, the taxable gifts are included in the tax base at date-of-gift values, which usually are lower than values at death. Once the estate tax is computed, it is reduced by a credit of one of the following amounts:

Year of Death	Amount of Credit
1984	$ 96,300
1985	121,800
1986	155,800
1987 and later	192,800*

*The unified credit has been phased in gradually from $6,000 for gifts made in the first half of 1977 and $30,000 for gifts made in the second half of 1977 and for estates of persons dying in 1977.

A credit of $192,800 effectively negates (or cancels) the tax on tax bases of $600,000 or lower. Accordingly, for persons dying in 1987 and later, no estate tax will be owed unless the estate, net of all deductions, exceeds $600,000. Moreover, because there is no ceiling on the amount deductible for bequests to one's spouse, the death of the first spouse can be completely free of estate tax notwithstanding the size of the estate. In order to avoid "wasting" the credit it will be attractive for persons with large estates to leave all but $600,000 to their spouses if they die in 1987 or later.

The timing of the transfer of the property—during lifetime or at death—has implications to the recipient when he disposes of the property. His gain or loss on sale is the difference between the sales price of the property and its basis. The technique for computing basis varies depending upon whether the seller received the property as a gift or by inheritance. For gift property that has appreciated before being given away, the donee's basis is the donor's basis plus the pro rata portion of the gift taxes attributable to the appreciation.[3]

If a person inherits property from a decedent, his basis in the property is its date-of-death or alternate-valuation-date value.[4] Thus, any pre-death appreciation totally escapes income taxation. These rules for inherited property are referred to as step-up in basis rules.

---

[3] If the gift was made prior to 1977, in general, the entire gift taxes paid are added to the donor's basis. For property which has declined in value when given away, the rules are more complex and beyond the depth of this text.

[4] If the executor elects to value the decedent's property at alternate-valuation-date values, the heir's basis is the value on the alternate valuation date, which is six months after date of death.

The basis rules have planning implications. If an elderly prospective donor anticipates that the recipient will sell the property, it may be advantageous to have the property taxed in the estate in order for the recipient to get a higher basis.

The basis rules for inherited and gifted property are illustrated in the examples following.

Example 1: T died in 1983. His sole asset, stock that he purchased for $10,000 in 1934, passed to V in accordance with T's will. The stock was valued at $98,000 on T's estate tax return. Under the step-up in basis rules, V's basis is $98,000.

Example 2: T purchased stock in 1934 for $10,000. In 1983, when the stock was worth $98,000, T gave it to V. T paid no gift tax. V's basis is $10,000, the same as T's basis.

Dual Bases of Accountability

Principal (Corpus) and Income Distinguished

It is especially important that the fiduciary carefully identify those elements that comprise the principal of an estate or trust and those that make up its income. A testator's direction that the principal and income from an estate shall be distributed to different beneficiaries accents the importance of this distinction. The distinction between principal and income can also be important in the computation of income taxes. The principal-income distinction is difficult to make, and often subtle, because of the diverse provisions of state statutes and the special characteristics of the elements themselves. The decedent may expressly indicate, either in the will or in the trust indenture, the criteria to be used in making the identification; where no such provision exists, the courts must necessarily look to the statutes for distinguishing characteristics. It is important that accounting records be established and maintained by the fiduciary in such manner as to preserve this distinction.

The Revised Uniform Principal and Income Act provides that in the absence of any contrary terms in the trust instrument, principal and income shall be defined as follows:[5]

> (a) Income is the return in money or property derived from the use of principal, including return received as
>> (1) rent of real or personal property, including sums received for cancellation or renewal of a lease;
>> (2) interest on money lent, including sums received as consideration for the privilege of prepayment of principal except as provided in section 7 on bond premium and bond discount;

---

[5] This statute has been adopted in 21 states.

(3)   income earned during administration of a decedent's estate as provided in section 5;

(4)   corporate distributions as provided in section 6;

(5)   accrued increment on bonds or other obligations issued at discount as provided in section 7;

(6)   receipts from business and farming operations as provided in section 8;

(7)   receipts from disposition of natural resources as provided in sections 9 and 10;

(8)   receipts from other principal subject to depletion as provided in section 11;

(9)   receipts from disposition of underproductive property as provided in section 12.

(b)   Principal is the property which has been set aside by the owner or the person legally empowered so that it is held in trust eventually to be delivered to a remainderman while the return or use of the principal is in the meantime taken or received by or held for accumulation for an income beneficiary. Principal includes

(1)   consideration received by the trustee on the sale or other transfer of principal or on repayment of a loan or as a refund or replacement or change in the form of principal;

(2)   proceeds of property taken on eminent domain proceedings;

(3)   proceeds of insurance upon property forming part of the principal except proceeds of insurance upon a separate interest of an income beneficiary:

(4)   stock dividends, receipts on liquidation of a corporation, and other corporate distributions as provided in section 6;

(5)   receipts from the disposition of corporate securities as provided in section 7;

(6)   royalties and other receipts from disposition of natural resources as provided in sections 9 and 10;

(7)   receipts from other principal subject to depletion as provided in section 11;

(8)   any profit resulting from any change in the form of principal except as provided in section 12 on underproductive property;

(9)   receipts from disposition of underproductive property as provided in section 12;

(10)   any allowances for depreciation established under sections 8 and 13(a) (2).

(c)   After determining income and principal in accordance with the terms of the trust instrument or of this Act, the trustee shall charge to income or principal expenses and other charges as provided in section 13 [Revised Uniform Principal and Income Act, Section 3, 7A, U.L.A., 1978 edition].

In respect to charges against and credits to income and principal, the Revised Uniform Principal and Income Act contains the following general provisions:

(a)   Unless the will otherwise provides and subject to subsection (b), all expenses incurred in connection with the settlement of a decedent's estate, including debts, funeral expenses, estate taxes, interest and penalties concerning taxes, family allowances, fees of attorneys and personal representatives, and court costs shall be charge against the principal of the estate.

(b)   Unless the will otherwise provides, income from the assets of a decedent's estate after the death of the testator and before distribution, including income from property used to discharge liabilities, shall be determined in accordance with the rules applicable to a trustee under this Act and distributed as follows:

(1)   to specific legatees and devisees, the income from the property bequeathed or devised to them respectively, less taxes, ordinary repairs, and other expenses of management and operation of the property, and an appropriate portion of the interest accrued since the death of the testator and of taxes imposed on income (excluding taxes on capital gains) which accrue during the period of administration;

(2)   to all other legatees and devisees, except legatees of pecuniary bequests not in trust, the balance of the income, less the balance of taxes, ordinary repairs, and other expenses of management and operation of all property from which the estate is entitled to income, interest accrued since the death of the testator, and taxes imposed on income (excluding taxes on capital gains) which accrue during the period of administration, in proportion to their respective interests in the undistributed assets of the estate computed at times of distribution on the basis of inventory value.

(c)   Income received by a trustee under subsection (b) shall be treated as income of the trust [Revised Uniform Principal and Income Act, Section 5; 7A, U.L.A., 1978 edition].

There are a number of circumstances for which the above generalizations are not completely descriptive. They are discussed in the following section.

Special Problems

Accrued Items.   Accruals of income at the date of the decedent's death are normally regarded as components of estate principal; such accruals often consist of interest on receivable or investment balances. Interest on these assets earned during tenancy is regarded as income of the estate. In respect to savings accounts and time deposits, accrued interest is regarded as either principal or income depending upon when the interest credit is made available to the depositor. Accrued interest payable normally follows the same classification rules with respect to income or principal as does interest receivable, that is, interest accrued to the date of the testator's death is a debt of the estate and accordingly chargeable to principal when disbursed; interest paid or incurred subsequently is ordinarily chargeable to income.

In most states, rents receivable at the date of the decedent's death are includable in the principal of the estate; the amount of rent earned during tenancy is regarded as income. Similarly, rent expense payable at date of death is a charge against the estate principal, while accruals thereafter are charges against income.

It is assumed that taxes on real property of the testator customarily do not accrue. The tax expense rather is regarded as relating to the period when the tax becomes a lien on the assessed property. Where the lien becomes effective before the decedent's death, the tax expense is chargeable to the principal of the estate; where the lien becomes effective subsequent to the decedent's death, the expense is a charge against income. As indicated earlier, estate taxes are levied against and payable out of the principal assets of the estate. Income taxes, however, must be identified with the elements making up the taxable base. The amount of income tax that relates to gains or losses on the conversion of principal assets is chargeable to principal; the amount levied on normal operating net income during the administration of the estate is chargeable against income. Income taxes for a fractional period prior to the decedent's death are payable out of the principal of the estate.

Dividends Received. Corporate dividends are not generally accounted for on an accrual basis. Ordinary cash dividends declared prior to the decedent's death are a part of the principal of the estate; declarations subsequent to death usually represent income of the estate. In some states, the significant identifying date is the date of record. In respect to dividends that are declared and received during tenancy, the statutes of the several states are not wholly agreed as to the most appropriate accounting classification. Some follow the Massachusetts rule, which generally provides that all cash dividends, whatever their magnitude and from whatever source, are to be regarded as income accruing to the income beneficiary; stock dividends, however, are regarded as additions to principal. In application of this rule, the *form* of the dividend controls. Other states follow the Pennsylvania rule that emphasizes the *source* of the declaration. If it is determined that the dividend is payable out of earnings accumulated prior to the creation of the trust estate, all dividends—whether in cash or shares of stock—are regarded as belonging to principal. However, if it is established that only those earnings accumulated subsequent to the formation of the trust estate are declared as dividends, the receipt (including the market value of stock dividends) is accorded the status of income. The distinction is frequently implemented in terms of whether the dividend is ordinary or extraordinary. Where dividends relate partially to earnings accumulated prior to the creation of the trust estate and partially subsequent thereto, the fiduciary may apportion the receipt as between income and principal. In this allocation, reliance is usually placed on the relative book values of the corporate stock at the date of the decedent's death and at the date of the dividend payment. If the book value after the dividend payment is less than the book value at date of the decedent's death, an amount equivalent to the reduction in value shall be credited to principal with the residual amount of the receipt regarded as income. Stock dividends are accorded parallel treatment, although the allocation is made in terms of shares of stock.

Stock rights that are a part of the decedent's estate at death, or that are acquired subsequently in respect to corporate securities belonging to the deceased at date of death, are elements of principal; accordingly, proceeds from the sale of such rights, reflecting conversion gains and losses, are also regarded as principal.

In respect to corporate distributions, the underlying emphasis of the Massachusetts rule is clearly reflected in the Revised Uniform Principal and Income Act:

> (a)   Corporate distributions of shares of the distributing corporation, including distributions in the form of a stock split or stock dividend, are principal. A right to subscribe to shares or other securities issued by the distributing corporation accruing to stockholders on account of their stock ownership and the proceeds of any sale of the right are principal.
>
> (b)   Except to the extent that the corporation indicates that some part of a corporate distribution is a settlement of preferred or guaranteed dividends accrued since the trustee became a stockholder or is in lieu of an ordinary cash dividend, a corporate distribution is principal if the distribution is pursuant to
>
> (1)   a call of shares;
>
> (2)   a merger, consolidation, reorganization, or other plan by which assets of the corporation are acquired by another corporation; or
>
> (3)   a total or partial liquidation of the corporation, including any distribution which the corporation indicates is a distribution in total or partial liquidation or any distribution of assets, other than cash, pursuant to a court decree or final administrative order by a government agency ordering distribution of the particular assets.
>
> (c)   Distributions made from ordinary income by a regulated investment company or by a trust qualifying and electing to be taxed under federal law as a real estate investment trust are income. All other distributions made by the company or trust, including distributions from capital gains, depreciation, or depletion, whether in the form of cash or an option to take new stock or cash or an option to purchase additional shares, are principal.
>
> (d)   Except as provided in subsections (a), (b), and (c), all corporate distributions are income, including cash dividends, distributions of or rights to subscribe to shares or securities or obligations of corporations other than the distributing corporation, and the proceeds of the rights or property distributions. Except as provided in subsections (b) and (c), if the distributing corporation gives a shareholder an option to receive a distribution either in cash or in its own shares, the distribution chosen is income.
>
> (e)   The trustee may rely upon any statement of the distributing corporation as to any fact relevant under any provision of this Act concerning the source or character of dividends or distributions of corporate assets [Revised Uniform Principal and Income Act, Section 6, 7A, U.L.A., 1978 edition].

These provisions, particularly subsection (e), extend the "form" test of the Massachusetts rule to include a "source" test in certain instances. However, this latter criterion logically does not include ordinary stock dividends, as in the Pennsylvania rule.

In most states, the courts have held that dividends payable from sources other than earnings relate to principal. Script and property dividends are accorded treatment equivalent to cash dividends. Liquidating dividends are accounted for by the fiduciary as in a commercial enterprise, that is, they are regarded as a return of capital and are accordingly classified as adjustments of principal.

Partnership Earnings.   It is normally assumed that partnership profits do not accrue. Partnership net income is determined as a consequence of, and concurrent with, a formal closing of the partnership books. Where the partnership books are closed upon the death of a partner, the calculated share of profits assigned to the deceased partner for the fractional period previous to the date of death is normally regarded as principal of his estate. In the event the partners, pursuant to provisions of the partnership agreement, elect not to close the partnership books until a date subsequent to the testator's death, there is no evident consensus among accountants as to the disposition of partnership earnings for the interval between the last closing date prior to the decedents' death and the subsequent closing date. Should the partnership agreement provide for interest on partners' capitals, such interest prior to the decedent's death is includable in principal; that which accrues during the subsequent period is income.

Depreciation and Maintenance.   Depreciation (or value exhaustion) may or may not be chargeable against the income of an estate or trust during a period of tenancy. This question depends upon the testator's intentions, as indicated in the will or trust instrument, in respect to preserving the principal of the estate intact. In the absence of any indication of the testator's intent, state law controls.

Expenditures for repairs, and other maintenance outlays, the effect of which is to materially improve or enhance the value of estate or trust properties follow traditional rules of capitalization, that is, they are normally chargeable to principal. However, those expenditures the benefits of which merely preserve the normal operating efficiency of the depreciable assets are regarded as income charges. Where the benefits relate partially to principal and partially to income, an apportionment of the expenditure should be made, based upon estimates of measurable benefit.

In the event that trust estate properties consist of wasting assets, that is, mineral deposits, timber, and so forth, the wishes of the testator or state law will also control in respect to charges for depletion.[6] If there is persua-

---

[6] For example, the Revised Uniform Principal and Income Act provides that with respect to receipts for royalties for mineral interests, 27.5 percent of gross receipts (but not to exceed 50 percent of net receipts before deducting depletion) is to be added to principal as a depletion allowance [Revised Uniform Principal and Income Act, Section 9, 7A, U.L.A., 1978 edition].

sive evidence that the testator intended to preserve for the remainderman the undiminished value of the original property, the fiduciary should withhold for the remainderman income in an amount equal to the value exhaustion for depletion. However, if the evidence indicates that income, without reduction in amount for depletion, should accrue to the benefit of the income beneficiary, the principal should be reduced accordingly by the amount of cumulative depletion allowances.

Discount/Premium on Bond Investments.   Corporate bonds held by the decedent are usually evaluated in terms of prices established by exchange quotations or over-the-counter trading at the date of the decedent's death. To the extent that premiums or discounts are reflected in these quotations, a question exists as to subsequent amortization by the fiduciary. A position often taken is that no provision should be made for the amortization of premium or the accumulation of discount. According to this view, principal is not regarded as having been affected so long as the estate consists of the specific assets inventoried, and the periodic interest receipts are classified as estate income. Consequently, the act of disposing of the bonds becomes the critical point for recognizing the increase or impairment in the value of estate corpus.

In respect to bonds *acquired by the fiduciary during tenancy*, however, premiums are customarily amortized while discounts are not amortized. This convention in respect to amortization is manifestly inconsistent with the treatment of premiums or discounts on bond investments included in the original estate inventory. Of course, the wishes of the testator will prevail should they indicate otherwise. In recording amortization, it is important to recognize that brokerage expenses and transfer fees are elements of investment cost. As in the case of securities existing at date of death, gains and losses on the conversion of subsequently acquired investments are regarded as principal.

Expenses.   Those expenses that are clearly identifiable with the conservation, management, and distribution of the principal of the trust-estate are appropriate charges against principal; however, income of the trust-estate must bear the charges for expenses that pertain to the earning of income during a period of tenancy. The Revised Uniform Principal and Income Act enumerates various expense items to be charged either against income or against principal.

(a)   The following charges should be made against income:

(1)   ordinary expenses incurred in connection with the administration, management, or preservation of the trust property, including regularly recurring taxes assessed against any portion of the principal, water rates, premiums on insurance taken upon the interests of the income beneficiary, remainderman, or trustee, interest paid by the trustee, and ordinary repairs;

(2)   a reasonable allowance for depreciation on property subject to depreciation under generally accepted accounting principles, but no allowance shall be made for depreciation of that portion of any real property used by a beneficiary as a residence or for depreciation of any property held by the trustee on the effective date of this Act for which the trustee is not then making an allowance for depreciation;

(3)   one-half of court costs, attorney's fees, and other fees on periodic judicial accounting, unless the court directs otherwise;

(4)   court costs, attorney's fees, and other fees on other accountings or judicial proceedings if the matter primarily concerns the income interest, unless the court directs otherwise;

(5)   one-half of the trustee's regular compensation, whether based on a percentage of principal or income, and all expenses reasonably incurred for current management of principal and application of income;

(6)   any tax levied upon receipts defined as income under this Act or the trust instrument and payable by the trustee.

(b)   If charges against income are of unusual amount, the trustee may by means of reserves or other reasonable means charge them over a reasonable period of time and withhold from distribution sufficient sums to regularize distributions.

(c)   The following charges shall be made against principal:

(1)   trustee's compensation not chargeable to income under subsections (a) (4) and (a) (5), special compensation of trustees, expenses reasonably incurred in connection with principal, court costs and attorney's fees primarily concerning matters of principal, and trustee's compensation computed on principal as an acceptance, distribution, or termination fee;

(2)   charges not provided for in subsection (a), including the cost of investing and reinvesting principal, the payments on principal of an indebtedness (including a mortgage amortized by periodic payments of principal), expenses for preparation of property for rental or sale, and, unless the court directs otherwise, expenses incurred in maintaining or defending any action to construe the trust or protect it or the property or assure the title of any trust property;

(3)   extraordinary repairs or expenses incurred in making a capital improvement to principal, including special assessments, but, a trustee may establish an allowance for depreciation out of income to the extent permitted by subsection (a) (2) and by section 8;

(4)   any tax levied upon profit, gain, or other receipts allocated to principal notwithstanding denomination of the tax as an income tax by the taxing authority;

(5)   if an estate or inheritance tax is levied in respect of a trust in which both an income beneficiary and a remainderman have an interest, any amount apportioned to the trust, including interest and penalties, even though the income beneficiary also has rights in the principal.

(d)   Regularly recurring charges payable from income shall be apportioned to the same extent and in the same manner that income is apportioned under section 4 [Revised Uniform Principal and Income Act, Section 13, 7A, U.L.A., 1978 edition].

Fiduciary Accounts and Reports

Fiduciary accounting accents the importance of delegated authority. The accounts of the fiduciary should clearly disclose the measure of his accountability and the extent to which it has been discharged. This emphasis on accountability compels a change in the fundamental accounting equation, which is modified as follows:

$$\text{Estate (trust) assets} = \text{Accountability}$$

It is evident that this accountability is stated in terms of total assets, without deducting the amount of existing claims against the estate or trust. A fiduciary is responsible for all of the assets entrusted to him; payment of existing claims is one way that a fiduciary discharges that responsibility.

The accounts and reports of the fiduciary should be kept in such form and detail as to sharply focus upon the *dual* responsibility of the fiduciary—in respect to income *and* in respect to principal. While the statutes of the various states provide important criteria for making this distinction, in many instances they do not prescribe the exact form and content of the fiduciary's accounts and reports.

Accounting Procedures and Entry Sequence for an Estate

Once the inventory of the decedent's assets has been filed, books of the estate should be opened in which are debited the accounts for assets enumerated in the inventory with a contra credit to Estate Principal, or Estate Corpus. Separate, or hyphenated, accounts should be provided for cash that is includable in the principal of the estate and cash which accumulates during tenancy and otherwise qualifies as estate income. The valuations assigned the various noncash assets are those indicated in the inventory. The Estate Principal, or Estate Corpus, account is credited with the gross amount of the inventory and represents the *initial* accountability of the fiduciary. In the event that other assets are discovered subsequent to the filing of the inventory, accounts should be opened for such assets with appropriate credits to Assets Subsequently Discovered. This account is a suspended credit to Estate Principal, to which it is closed at the end of the fiduciary accounting period.

Liabilities of the decedent are not recorded by the fiduciary until paid. Upon payment, an account—Debts of the Decedent Paid—is debited for the liquidation settlement. This transaction represents a reduction in the accountability of the fiduciary; accordingly, Debts of the Decedent Paid is essentially a suspended debit to Estate Principal. In respect to both assets and liabilities, the amount of account detail (and the necessity for subsidiary records) will be governed by the magnitude and diversity of assets in, and the number of claimants against, estate properties.

Gains or losses on the conversion of principal assets increase or decrease the accountability of the fiduciary in respect to the principal of the estate. Gain on Realization should be credited for conversion gains, and Loss on Realization should be debited for conversion losses; both accounts are closed to Estate Principal at the end of the accounting period. The increased (decreased) accountability of the fiduciary as a consequence of his profitable (unprofitable) employment of estate assets is not an attempt to measure net income; rather, it reflects a dominant stewardship orientation, the historical prototype of which is found in the master-slave relationship of Roman times. In this era, the slave was charged with funds entrusted to him by his master and with the increase attributable to fortunate investments; subsequently, he was discharged of his accountability to the extent of his repayment of resources advanced or accumulated or by other disposition as directed by the master. Most economic theories of income and asset valuation manifestly are not relevant to this type of fiduciary relationship. Correspondingly, the objectives of income determination and of stewardship reporting are essentially contradictory and are not accommodated by a single theoretical framework.

In addition to paying the debts of the decedent, the accountability of the fiduciary is further decreased by disbursements for funeral and administration expenses. A single Funeral and Administration Expenses account may be used for these outlays, or it may be desirable to identify the various expenses separately. Where a single account is used, its inclusions usually consist of expenses of last illness, funeral expenses, payments to the executor or trustee for administrative services to conserve the estate principal, accountant's, attorney's, and appraiser's fees, and court costs. The fiduciary's accountability in respect to principal is also decreased by the payment of estate taxes and the distribution of legacies. If a legacy involves the distribution of specific assets, the valuation assigned the distributed assets is the carrying value (accountability basis) of each asset, regardless of its current market value. This procedure is consistent with a stewardship, or accountability, objective. Where there are relatively few legatees, a single account—Legacies—may be sufficient; however, if the number of legatees is large, it may be desirable to use a separate account for each legatee. Where state inheritance taxes are to be charged against the legatee's accounts, or where it is necessary to reduce the legacies, it is especially important that separate accounts be maintained.

In respect to the fiduciary's accountability as to income, it is conventional to open an Income account to which are credited the various items of income for the estate. One account may be used for this purpose, or where there are numerous sources of income, several accounts that are descriptive as to source may be appropriate. Similarly, expenses incurred that are chargeable to such income should be debited to an Expenses-Income account or to several expense accounts detailing the nature of the expense. It is important that account designations clearly indicate an identification with either income or principal, where the conventional terminology does not convey the fact of this association. Distributions to income beneficiaries are usually charged to a Distribution to Income Beneficiary account, with the name of the indicated donee often appended.

Illustrative Problem

The following is a simplified case illustration of estate-trust accounting. Louis Martin died on June 1, 19X0. His will, admitted to probate on June 10, 19X0, provided that Paul Martin, Sr., son of the decedent, be appointed executor. The will also provided that specific legacies of $2,500 cash be awarded to Paul Jr. and Charles, grandsons of the decedent; $12,000 and the decedent's personal automobile to Paul Sr.; personal effects and estate income to the widow, Pamela; and the remainder of the estate property, after payment of debts and expenses and distribution of legacies, to be placed in trust. The income from the trust is to be paid to the widow during her lifetime, with the principal to be distributed equally to Paul Jr. and Charles upon the widow's death.

Paul Martin, Sr., filed the following inventory with the probate court on June 25:

Cash in bank	$ 28,000
Personal effects	750
Life insurance policies payable to the estate	30,000
1,000 shares of Edens Company $50 par value common stock—at market	49,000
500 shares of Cincy, Inc., 6%, $30 par value preferred stock—at market	15,000
20 Burnett Corporation 5%, 30-year $1,000 bonds (interest payable March 1 and September 1)	19,600
Automobile	2,600
Dividend receivable (declared May 15, payable July 15, Edens Company common)	1,500
Interest receivable (Burnett Corporation bonds)	250
	$146,700

On the same date, the fiduciary opened accounts for the estate of Louis Martin and recorded the inventory as follows:

June 25	Cash—Principal	28,000	
	Personal Effects	750	
	Life Insurance	30,000	
	Edens Company Common Stock	49,000	
	Cincy, Inc., Preferred Stock	15,000	
	Burnett Corporation Bonds	19,600	
	Automobile	2,600	
	Dividend Receivable	1,500	
	Interest Receivable	250	
	Estate Principal		146,700

Transactions and entries of the fiduciary in the period following were:

June 28   Public notice was given that creditors of the estate of the decedent should make a presentment of their claims.

July 15   Paid funeral expenses, $1,400.

Funeral and Administration Expenses	1,400	
Cash—Principal		1,400

July 16   Collected dividends on Edens stock.

Cash—Principal	1,500	
Dividend Receivable		1,500

July 20   Undeposited cash $1,200, was discovered among the decedent's personal belongings.

Cash—Principal	1,200	
Assets Subsequently Discovered		1,200

July 31   Received payment on insurance policies.

Cash—Principal	30,000	
Life Insurance		30,000

Aug. 15   Sold 100 shares of Cincy, Inc., stock for $4,000.

Cash—Principal	4,000	
Cincy, Inc., Preferred Stock		3,000
Gain on Realization		1,000

Sept. 1   Collected interest on Burnett Corporation bonds.

Cash—Principal	250	
Cash—Income	250	
Interest Receivable		250
Income		250

Sept. 15   Paid debts of the decedent, $2,950.

Debts of the Decedent Paid	2,950	
Cash—Principal		2,950

Oct.   1   Paid cash legacies provided for in the will.

Legacy—Paul Martin, Sr.	12,000	
Legacy—Paul Martin, Jr.	2,500	
Legacy—Charles Martin	2,500	
Cash—Principal		17,000

Oct.   3   Delivered automobile (current market value, $1,800) to Paul Martin, Sr.

Legacy—Paul Martin, Sr.	2,600	
Automobile		2,600

Oct.   3   Delivered decedent's personal effects to widow.

Legacy—Pamela Martin	750	
Personal Effects		750

Oct. 10   Collected cash dividend of $1,000 on Edens Company common stock.

Cash—Income	1,000	
Income		1,000

Oct. 15   Paid attorney's fees, $1,000, and other administrative expenses, $2,500. Of the latter, $200 relate to income.

Funeral and Administration Expenses	3,300	
Expenses—Income...	200	
Cash—Principal		3,300
Cash—Income		200

Oct. 30   Three percent semiannual dividend declared on Cincy, Inc., preferred stock.

Dividend Receivable	360	
Income		360

Nov. 1   Income of the estate in the amount of $500 is distributed to the widow.

Distribution to Income Beneficiary—Pamela Martin	500	
Cash—Income		500

Nov. 5   Two hundred shares of Edens Company common stock were sold for $9,000.

Cash—Principal	9,000	
Loss on Realization	800	
Edens Company Common Stock		9,800

Dec. 1 $250 interest accrued on Burnett Corporation bonds to December 1.

Interest Receivable..	250	
Income		250

Dec. 1   The executor rendered an accountability report to the probate court.

Charge and Discharge Statement

A report detailing the particulars of estate administration should be prepared and submitted periodically to the court of appropriate jurisdiction. Such a report is the *charge and discharge* statement. It may be regarded as an interim or a final statement of the fiduciary's accountability, depending upon the period of time normal to the completion of the settlement of the estate. The general form of the statement is normally prescribed by the statutes of the various states; however, there is no apparent consensus as to a single most desirable form. The two-division statement to be illustrated in the following pages is generally descriptive of many of the reports presently in use.

The *charge and discharge* statement is a classified enumeration of the estate resources for which the fiduciary is accountable, and a description of the manner in which he has discharged his accountability during the period of his administration. His responsibilities for principal and income are separately reported. In respect to *principal*, the report indicates those asset categories for which the fiduciary *charges* himself or has accepted a custodial responsibility. They include:

1. Assets enumerated in the inventory.
2. Assets subsequently discovered.
3. Gains recognized on the conversion or other disposition of principal assets.

There follows the discharge of the fiduciary's accountability, that is, the offered justification for which the fiduciary *credits* himself. These credits include:

1. Payment of funeral and administration expenses.
2. Debts of the decedent paid.
3. Estate and inheritance taxes paid.
4. Payment or distribution of legacies.
5. Losses realized on conversion or other disposition of principal assets.

To the extent that there remains an undistributed asset accumulation, as would exist in respect to an interim report, or in a final report preceding the transfer of assets to a testamentary trust, these accounts should be enumerated with assigned valuations.

In respect to income, the fiduciary *charges* himself for income earned since the date of the decedent's death. Items of income, if significant, should be identified as to source. Dispositions of income for which the fiduciary customarily *credits* himself include:

1. Expenses that are chargeable to such income.
2. Payments or other distributions to income beneficiaries.

Some accountants prefer to prepare separate reports for income and principal; their contents would necessarily be the same as the categories described above for a two-division statement.

Using the data of the estate of Louis Martin, a charge and discharge statement as of December 1 would assume the form shown in Illustration 19–1. This statement is a summary report and where necessary should be supported by schedules providing informative details with respect to each of the major categories. If subsequent reports are necessary, they are prepared on a cumulative basis and will continue to disclose fully the fiduciary's activities during the period of his accountability.

Illustration 19–1

ESTATE OF LOUIS MARTIN
PAUL MARTIN, SR., EXECUTOR
Charge and Discharge Statement
June 1, 19X0 to December 1, 19X0

As to Principal

I charge myself with:

Assets per inventory.............................		$146,700
Assets subsequently discovered..................		1,200
Gain on realization		1,000
Total		$148,900

I credit myself with:

Funeral and administration expenses	$ 4,700	
Debts of decedent paid..........................	2,950	
Legacies paid or distributed:		
Paul Martin, Sr.	14,600	
Paul Martin, Jr..............................	2,500	
Charles Martin	2,500	
Pamela Martin...............................	750	
Loss on realization............................	800	28,800
Balance as to principal		$120,100

Which includes:

Cash		$ 49,300
Edens Company common stock..................		39,200
Cincy, Inc., preferred stock.....................		12,000
Burnett Corporation bonds		19,600
Total		$120,100

As to Income

I charge myself with:

Income collected or accrued		$ 1,860

I credit myself with:

Expenses chargeable to income	$ 200	
Distribution to income beneficiary...............	500	700
Balance as to income.............................		$ 1,160

Which includes:

Cash		$ 550
Dividend receivable............................		360
Interest receivable		250
Total		$ 1,160

Closing Entries

When activities of estate administration are concluded, a final report is rendered, after which the fiduciary closes the accounts of the estate. In respect to principal, this involves closing to Estate Principal those relevant accounts created during the administration representing increases or decreases in the fiduciary's accountability. Accordingly, Assets Subsequently

Discovered, Gains and Losses on Realization, Debts of the Decedent Paid, Legacies Paid or Distributed, and Funeral and Administration Expenses are closed to Estate Principal. Similarly, the accounts that are chargeable to income should be closed thereunto. They include Expenses—Income and Distributions to Income Beneficiary. Unless assets remain for some ultimate disposition, these entries should reduce all accounts to zero balances.

Properties Transferred to Trustee

In the illustration begun earlier in this chapter, provision was made for the transfer of estate properties to a trustee *after* the fiduciary's payment of debts of the decedent and expenses of administration and the payment and/or delivery of legacies. If it is assumed that the transfer of properties is made concurrent with the rendering of the charge and discharge statement on December 1, 19X0, the following entries are required to close the books of the estate and to open the trust accounts:

Executor's Books

Dec. 1	Assets Subsequently Discovered	1,200	
	Gain on Realization	1,000	
	Estate Principal		2,200
1	Estate Principal	28,800	
	Debts of the Decedent Paid		2,950
	Funeral and Administration Expenses		4,700
	Legacy—Paul Martin, Sr.		14,600
	Legacy—Paul Martin, Jr.		2,500
	Legacy—Charles Martin		2,500
	Legacy—Pamela Martin		750
	Loss on Realization		800
1	Income	700	
	Expenses—Income		200
	Distribution to Income Beneficiary		500
1	Estate Principal	120,100	
	Income	1,160	
	V. L. Ree, Trustee		121,260
1	V. L. Ree, Trustee	120,100	
	Cash—Principal		49,300
	Edens Company Common Stock		39,200
	Cincy, Inc., Preferred Stock		12,000
	Burnett Corporation Bonds		19,600
1	V. L. Ree, Trustee	1,160	
	Cash—Income		550
	Dividend Receivable		360
	Interest Receivable		250

Trustee's Books

1	Cash—Principal...................................... 49,300	
	Edens Company Common Stock....................... 39,200	
	Cincy, Inc., Preferred Stock 12,000	
	Burnett Corporation Bonds........................... 19,600	
	Trust Principal	120,100
1	Cash—Income 550	
	Dividend Receivable 360	
	Interest Receivable 250	
	Income...	1,160

The trustee normally accepts fiduciary responsibility concurrent with the transfer of trust property to him. All accrued income prior to the creation of a living trust is includable as trust principal; income earned thereafter is distributable to income beneficiaries. In respect to testamentary trusts, however, the trust usually becomes effective at date of death and income earned thereafter is trust income, notwithstanding a delay in the transfer of trust properties to the trustee.

The trustee's accounting essentially parallels that of the executor. The Trust Principal and Income accounts are the summary accounts of the trustee, indicating his separate accountability as to both principal and income.

The trustee should render periodic reports of his stewardship to the court recounting the activities of his trust administration. As in the case of estates, the content of such statements depends upon the statutory provisions of the relevant state. The Uniform Trustees Accounting Act suggests that interim reports contain:

(a) the period which the account covers;

(b) the names and addresses of the living beneficiaries known to the trustee, with a statement as to those known to be minors or under legally declared disability; and a description of any possible unborn or unascertained beneficiaries; and the name of the surety or sureties on the trustee's bond with the amount of such bond;

(c) in a separate schedule the trust principal on hand at the beginning of the accounting period and the then status of its investment; the investments received from the settlor and still held; additions to trust principal during the accounting period with the dates and sources of acquisition; investments collected, sold or charged off during the accounting period, with the consequent loss or gain and whether credited to principal or income; investments made during the accounting period, with the date, source and cost of each; deductions from principal during the accounting period, with the date and purpose of each; and trust principal on hand at the end of the accounting period, how invested, and the estimated market value of each investment;

(d) in a separate schedule the trust income on hand at the beginning of the accounting period, and in what form held; trust income received during the accounting period, when, and from what source; trust income paid out during the accounting period, when, to whom, and for what purpose; trust income on hand at the end of the accounting period, and how invested;

(e)   that neither any seller of, nor buyer from, the trustee of trust property during the accounting period was at the time of such sale or purchase (1) in the case of a corporate trustee, an affiliate, or any officer, employee, or nominee of the trustee or of an affiliate; or was (2) in the case of a noncorporate trustee a relative, partner, employer, employee, or business associate; but none of the provisions of this subsection shall apply to purchases and sales made by brokers for the trustee or to stock exchanges;

(f)   a statement of unpaid claims with the reason for failure to pay them, including a statement as to whether any estate or inheritance taxes have become due with regard to the trust property, and if due, whether paid;

(g)   a brief summary of the account;

(h)   such other facts as the court may by rule or court order require. Within thirty days after the end of each yearly period thereafter during the life of the trust the testamentary trustee then in office shall file with the same court an intermediate account under oath showing corresponding facts regarding the current accounting period [Uniform Trustees Accounting Act, Section 3, 9C, U.L.A., 1967 edition].

As to the final accounting, the Act provides:

Within [   ] days after the termination of every testamentary trust the trustee, and in the case of the transfer of the trusteeship due to the death, resignation, removal, dissolution, merger or consolidation of a sole trustee, the successor in interest of the old trustee, shall file with the [probate court of the country where the will was admitted to probate] a final account under oath, showing for the period since the filing of the last account the facts required by Section 3 regarding intermediate accountings and in case of termination of the trust the distribution of the trust property which the accountant proposes to make [Uniform Trustees Accounting Act, Section 4, 9C, U.L.A., 1967 edition].

Questions

1.   Briefly describe the responsibilities of a fiduciary (executor, administrator) in the administration of an estate.

2.   What types of assets are frequently excluded from the fiduciary's inventory of assets?

3.   What is a typical *sequence of payment* for the various estate obligations?

4.   The fiduciary must distinguish in his records between the principal (corpus) and the income of an estate or trust. Why?

5.   As a general rule, how are accruals of income and expense identified with the principal and with the income of an estate?

6. Should depreciation be charged against the principal or income of an estate?

7. What is the fundamental equation for fiduciary accounting? For what reason is this expression stated in terms of claims against the estate or trust?

8. Once an inventory of the decedent's assets has been filed, what accounts should be opened by the executor (administrator) in which to record the transactions for the estate?

9. What is the *charge and discharge statement?* What information does it provide?

10. In respect to an intestate decedent, what is meant by the expression "bequest by advancement"?

Exercises

Exercise 19–1

Read the introductory facts below and then denote whether each of the sentences below is true or false according to the general principles of trust law, such as the Revised Uniform Principal and Income Act. If an answer is false, explain why it is false.

Accountant Smathers is trustee of a testamentary trust established by Parker's will. The corpus of the trust consists of "blue-chip" securities and a large office building subject to a mortgage. The will provides that trust income is to be paid to Parker's wife during her lifetime, that the trust will terminate on her death, and that the corpus is then to be distributed to the Brookdale School for Boys.

a. If Smathers receives a cash dividend on one of the trust securities, he may not use it to purchase additional securities for the trust corpus without compensating Parker's wife.

b. If Smathers receives a 5 percent stock dividend, he should distribute it to Mrs. Parker.

c. The cost of insurance on the office building should be deducted by Smathers from the income paid to Mrs. Parker.

d. Monthly principal payments to amortize the mortgage are deducted from Mrs. Parker's income.

e. Proceeds from fire insurance on the office building would be a part of the corpus.

(AICPA adapted)

Exercise 19–2

Refer to the facts and the instructions of Exercise 19–1 to answer the following true-false questions:

a. The cost of exercising stock warrants is chargeable to trust income.

b. The Brookdale School is the remainderman of the trust created under Parker's will.

    c. The beneficiaries of the trust have an equitable interest in the trust income and corpus.

    d. The beneficiaries of the trust would have standing in court to proceed against the trustee for waste of the corpus.

    e. If Mrs. Parker and the Brookdale School agree to terminate the trust and divide the corpus, Smathers would have to comply with their wishes.

(AICPA adapted)

Exercise 19–3

Each of the following relates to accounting for estates or trusts. Select the best answer in each expression:

1. To *probate* a will is to:
   a. Examine its provisions in respect to conformance with relevant model uniform laws if they are operative in the state.
   b. Review its fairness with respect to natural children and other lineal descendents.
   c. Prove its validity as to genuineness of the decedent's signature, his last expression of preferences, and his mental capacity at date of execution.
2. The executor, in respect to solvent estates, must accord *highest* priority to the following if he is to avoid personal liability for improper distribution:
   a. Wages due domestics or other employees.
   b. Provable debts against the estate.
   c. Taxes, including estate and inheritance taxes.
   d. Funeral and administrative expenses.
3. The legacy given first rank in order of distribution is:
   a. Demonstrative legacy.
   b. Specific legacy.
   c. Residual legacy.
   d. General legacy.
4. The recipient of the principal of a trust is termed a:
   a. Life tenant.
   b. *Cestui que trust.*
   c. Remainderman.
   d. Donee.
5. Income taxes payable by the executor of an estate during the period of his fiduciary responsibility:
   a. Are chargeable against income of the estate.
   b. Must be identified with the elements making up the taxable base, that is, charges apportioned between income and principal.
   c. Are chargeable against the principal of the estate.

Exercise 19–4

Lloyd Carlisle died on January 18, 19X0. His will was admitted to probate on February 5, and Arthur Waddell was appointed executor of the estate. The following transactions relate to the executorial period, February 6 through July 1, 19X0:

a. Waddell filed the following inventory of Carlisle's assets with the court:

Cash on deposit, Second National Bank . . . . $ 5,690
Undeposited currency.   220
Common stock, Stuchell Corporation:
    1,000 shares (par, $10) @ $27   27,000
6%, 20-year Harley Company debentures:
    10 bonds @ $200   2,000
Automobile   4,300
Household furnishings.   1,950
Life insurance, payable to the estate.   10,000
Dividends receivable, Stuchell stock:
    Dividend declared January 15, 19X0   800
Interest receivable:
    Harley Company bonds (January 1 and July 1)
        January 1 to January 18   6

b. Funeral expenses of $934 were paid by Waddell.
c. Six $1,200 Arnheim, Inc., bonds, 5 percent November 1 and May 1, were discovered upon search of the decedent's personal belongings.
d. The life insurance policy was collected.
e. Notice was published for the presentment of claims against the estate, after which debts of the decedent amounting to $1,450, were validated and paid.
f. The dividend on Stuchell stock was collected.
g. All of the common stock of the Stuchell Corporation was sold for cash, $24,600.
h. Executorial fees were paid Waddell in the amount of $2,100.
i. The May 1 interest collection was made on Arnheim, Inc., bonds.
j. The automobile was sold for $3,100 cash.
k. According to the conditions of the will, a cash legacy was paid to Mary Carlisle, the widow, in amount of $10,000.
l. The July 1 interest collection was made on Harley Company debentures.
m. All income earned to July 1 was distributed to the widow; all other assets remaining in the estate were distributed equally to Tom and Larry Carlisle, sons of the decedent.

Required:
a. Journalize the above transactions on the books of Arthur Waddell, executor.
b. Make closing entries on July 1 to close the executor's books.

Exercise 19–5

Albert Sims, attorney-at-law, died on July 1, 19X0. His partner, Henry Creek, was appointed executor of his estate and filed with the probate court on July 18 the following inventory of assets of the deceased:

Deposit balance, First State Bank	$ 4,800
4% RX bonds, interest payable April 1 and October 1 (par, $40,000)	32,200
Accrued interest on RX bonds	400
6% cumulative Cleburne, Inc., preferred stock, 200 shares (par, $35,000)	19,300
100 shares of Bancroft-Benson no-par common stock	4,200
Value of properties established by court-appointed appraisers:	
Office building of the law partnership (separately owned by Simon)	46,000
Automobile	2,200
	$109,100

An additional 200 shares of Bancroft-Benson were discovered by the executor on September 1.

The office building was sold on September 14 to Bruegman and Sons, realtors, for $41,000; the 300 shares of Bancroft-Benson were sold on September 21 for $13,100. On October 1, interest was collected on the RX bonds.

During the three months ended October 1, 19X0, the executor made the following payments:

Funeral expenses	$ 2,500
Administrative expenses	1,900
Debts of the decedent	15,500

The will of the deceased provides that legacies and income be distributed as follows:

To widow, Mary.
Cash, $17,000
Cleburne stock
Income of estate

To son, Arnold:
Cash, $10,000
Automobile

To son, Charles:
Cash, $10,000
RX bonds
The residue

Required:

a. Prepare the executor's journal entries for estate transactions for the quarter ended October 1, 19X0.

b. Journalize the distribution of income and the distribution of legacies on October 2, making closing entries for the estate.

Exercise 19–6

Ken Zimmer was named executor of the estate of Vern Mann, who died on March 13, 19X0. On December 31, 19X0, the executor prepared the following trial balance:

ESTATE OF VERN MANN
Trial Balance
December 31, 19X0

	Debit	Credit
Investments:		
Stocks	$18,500	
Bonds	42,000	
Accrued interest receivable	75	
Cash—principal	10,850	
Cash—income	2,125	
Household effects	2,375	
Loss on realization	650	
Gain on realization		$ 1,200
Assets subsequently discovered		5,520
Debts of decedent paid	5,600	
Funeral expenses	950	
Administration expenses	2,570	
Estate corpus		79,275
Income		3,575
Expenses—income	380	
Distribution to income beneficiary	995	
Legacy—Lucy Mann	2,500	
	$89,570	$89,570

Required:
Prepare a charge and discharge statement for the estate of Vern Mann.

Exercise 19–7

Alex Dunn, Jr., died on January 15, 19X0; his records disclose the following estate:

Cash in bank	$ 3,750
6% note receivable, including $50 accrued interest	5,050
Stocks	50,000
Dividends declared on stocks	600
6% mortgage receivable, including $100 accrued interest	20,100
Real estate—apartment house	35,000
Household effects	8,250
Dividend receivable from Alex Dunn, Sr., trust fund	250,000
Total	$372,750

Twenty-five years earlier, the late Alex Dunn, Sr., created a trust fund, with his son, Alex Dunn, Jr., as life tenant, and his grandson as remainderman. The assets in the fund consist solely of the outstanding capital stock of Dunn, Inc., namely,

2,000 shares of $100 par each. At the creation of the trust, the book—as well as the market—value of these shares was $400,000 and at January 1, 19X0, was $500,000. On January 2, 19X0, Dunn, Inc., declared a 125 percent cash dividend payable February 2, 19X0, to shareholders of record January 12, 19X0.

The executor's transactions from January 15, to 31, 19X0, were as follows:

Cash receipts:

Jan. 20	Dividends		$ 1,500.00
	25	6% notes receivable	5,000.00
		Interest accrued on note	58.33
		Stocks sold, inventoried at $22,500	20,000.00
		6% mortgage sold	20,100.00
		Interest accrued on mortgage	133.33
	28	Sale of assets not inventoried	250.00
	29	Real estate sold	30,000.00
			$77,041.66

Cash disbursements:

Jan. 20	Funeral expenses		$ 750.00
	23	Decedent's debts	8,000.00
	25	Decedent's bequests	10,000.00
	31	Distribution of income to widow	500.00
			$19,250.00

Required:

Prepare a charge and discharge statement for the executor for the period from January 15 to January 31, 19X0.

(AICPA adapted)

Problems

Problem 19–8

Cal Chase, partner in Chase-Dacey Farm Implements, died on March 31, 19X0. Nat Dacey was named executor of his partner's estate which consisted of the following:

Cash	$ 25,100
Livestock	48,000
Ranch land and improvements including farm buildings, fencing, etc.—at appraised valuation	31,600
4% Gantry Company debentures, interest January 1 and July 1 (par, $60,000)	52,000
Interest receivable—Gantry Company debentures	600
150 shares Collegaire common stock (par, $30,000)	26,000
One-half interest in Chase-Dacey partnership—at appraised valuation	84,000
	$267,300

Legacies are to be distributed as follows:

1. Livestock and ranch properties to the widow, Shirley, together with the deceased's partnership interest in Chase-Dacey Farm Implements.
2. $30,000 par value of Gantry Company debentures to son, Richard.
3. Collegaire common stock to Fabens Military Academy.
4. Residual estate, after payments of funeral and administrative expenses, debts of decedent and other specific bequests, to the widow. Income of the estate, excluding partnership net income, is to be distributed as collected to the son, Richard. The interest of the deceased in partnership net income was 50 percent and is bequeathed to the widow.

Transactions of the executor were:

Apr. 2 Filed the March 31 inventory of the deceased.
15 Paid funeral and administrative expenses, $6,200.
30 Sold $30,000 par value of Gantry Company debentures for $23,500 and accrued interest.
30 Distributed estate income.
May 1 Paid debts of decedent, $9,400.
10 Paid federal estate and state inheritance taxes, $28,700.
20 Dividends declared on Collegaire stock on April 14 were received, $600.
21 Distributed estate income.
July 1 Collected interest on Gantry Company debentures.
1 Partnership profits for the second quarter of 19X0 are reported to be $7,000.
1 Distributed estate income, legacies, and residual estate properties as provided in the will.

Required:
a. Prepare entries on the books of the executor through July 1, 19X0.
b. Journalize entries to close the books of the estate.

Problem 19–9

L. K. Daniel was appointed executor of the estate of Lucile Martin who died February 6, 19X0, leaving the following assets:

Cash in the Last National Bank	$ 9,200
Investments in corporate stocks	69,500
Jewelry	21,250
Building	51,000
Life insurance payable to the estate	10,000

The above valuations for buildings, investments, and jewelry reflect market conditions on February 6.

Following probate of the will and upon review of other family commitments, it is determined that Lucile Martin, a widow at the time of her death, had advanced to her two surviving sons and one daughter the following amounts prior to death: Charles, $16,500; Stephen, $14,350; and Ellen, $7,650.

Payments made by Daniel during the executorial period were:

Attorneys' fees	$1,950
Inheritance taxes	7,550
Debts of the decedent	1,200
Funeral expenses	1,450

The will of the deceased provided that any one of the surviving children should have an option to receive as a legacy the widow's jewelry at a valuation of $25,000; Ellen exercised this option. The securities were sold for $72,000, and the building was purchased by a local realtor for $55,000. The life insurance was collected on May 15.

The residue of the estate was to be divided equally among the three children, given that the advances and bequests made previous to and during the executorial period be regarded as a portion of such distributive shares.

Final distributions were made and the estate was closed on June 1.

Required:

Prepare a charge and discharge statement for L. K. Daniel on June 1, detailing by supporting schedule the composition of the legacy to each child.

Problem 19–10

Arthur Taine died in an accident on May 31, 19X0. His will provided that all just debts and expenses be paid and that his property be disposed of as follows:

Personal residence—devised to Bertha Taine, widow.

U.S. Treasury bonds and Puritan Company stock—to be placed in trust. All income to go to Bertha Taine during her lifetime, with right of appointment upon her death.

Seneca Company mortgage notes—bequeathed to Elaine Taine Langer, daughter.

Cash—a bequest of $10,000 to David Taine, son.

Remainder of estate—to be divided equally between the two children, Elaine Taine Langer and David Taine.

The will further provided that during the administration period Bertha Taine was to be paid $300 a month out of estate income, calculated and reported on a cash basis. David Taine was named as executor and trustee.

An inventory of the decedent's property was prepared. The fair market value of all items as of the date of death was determined. The preliminary inventory, before the computation of any appropriate income accruals on inventory items, follows:

Personal residence property	$ 45,000
Jewelry—diamond ring	9,600
York Life Insurance Company—term life insurance policy on life of Arthur Taine:	
Beneficiary—Bertha Taine, widow.	120,000
Granite Trust Company—3% savings bank account, Arthur Taine, in trust for Philip Langer (grandchild), interest credited January 1 and July 1; balance May 31, 19X0.	400
Fidelity National Bank—checking account; balance May 31, 19X0.	143,000
$100,000 U.S. Treasury bonds, 3%, interest payable March 1 and September 1...	100,000

800 shares Puritan Company common stock................................	64,000
700 shares Meta Mfg. Company common stock............................	70,000
$9,700 Seneca Company first-mortgage notes, 6%, 1982, interest payable May 31 and November 30...	9,900

The executor opened an estate bank account to which he transferred the decedent's checking account balance. Other deposits, through July 1, 19X1, were as follows:

Interest collected on bonds:	
$100,000 U.S. Treasury:	
September 1, 19X0..	$ 1,500
March 1, 19X1...	1,500
Dividends received on stock:	
800 shares Puritan Company:	
June 15, 19X0, declared May 7, 19X0, payable to holders of record as of May 27, 19X0...	800
September 15, 19X0...	800
December 15, 19X0	1,200
March 15, 19X1..	800
June 15, 19X1	800
Net proceeds of June 19, 19X0, sale of 700 shares of Meta Mfg. Company........	68,810

Payments were made from the estate's checking account through July 1, 19X1, for the following:

Funeral expenses	$ 2,000
Assessments for additional pre-19X0 federal and state income taxes ($1,700) plus interest ($110) to May 31, 19X0..	1,810
19X0 income taxes of Arthur Taine for the period January 1, 19X0, through May 31, 19X0, in excess of amounts paid by the decedent on declarations of estimated tax	9,100
Federal and state fiduciary income taxes, fiscal years ending June 30, 19X0 ($75), and June 30, 19X1 ($1,400)..	1,475
Federal and state estate taxes	58,000
Monthly payments to Bertha Taine: 13 payments of $300	3,900
Attorney's and accountant's fees...	25,000

The executor waived his commission. However, he desired to receive his father's diamond ring in lieu of the $10,000 specific legacy. All parties agreed to this in writing, and the court's approval was secured. All other specific legacies were delivered by July 15, 19X0.

Required:

Prepare a charge and discharge statement as to principal and income, and its supporting schedules, to accompany the attorney's formal court accounting on behalf of the executor of the estate of Arthur Taine for the period from May 31, 19X0, through July 1, 19X1. The following supporting schedules should be included:

1. Original Capital of Estate.
2. Gain on Disposal of Estate Assets.
3. Loss on Disposal of Estate Assets.

4. Funeral, Administration, and Other Expenses.
5. Debts of Decedent Paid.
6. Legacies Paid or Delivered.
7. Assets (Corpus) on Hand, July 1, 19X1.
8. Proposed Plan of Distribution of Estate Assets.
9. Income Collected.
10. Distribution of Income.

(AICPA adapted)

Problem 19–11

Using the data of Problem 18–12, prepare a charge and discharge statement for the trustee for the interim period of operations and partial liquidation of the Rawley Manufacturing Corporation.

Problem 19–12

The estate of Gaylon Miles, deceased, consisted of the following assets that were appraised as required by the county court following admission of the will to probate and appointment of Newton Burns as executor:

	Appraised Value	Disposition under the Will
Miles building	$87,000	To his daughter, Mary.
6% mortgage, interest payable June 1 and December 1...............	35,000	To the widow, Margaret Miles, for life, and then to his two sons, Jeff and Andrew, equally.
Vacant real estate:		
Lot 1......................	20,000	Cash to Jeff, Andrew, and Mary,
Lot 2......................	18,000	$10,000 each, and the balance of the estate to the widow.
Home.......................	29,000	
Household effects	1,500	
Cash........................	12,500	

At the time of death (June 30, 19X0), the accrued interest amounted to $175. Debts amounting to $2,400, funeral expenses of $1,450, and the probate expenses amounting to $900 were paid in cash. In September 19X0, Lot 1 was sold for $22,000, and by the consent of all parties Jeff took Lot 2 in discharge of the bequest to him and paid the estate $9,000 in cash.

The widow died on May 1, 19X1, at which date the accrued interest amounted to $875. The widow left her entire estate to Mary.

The interest on the mortgage was promptly collected on December 1, 19X0, and June 1, 19X1. All legacies were paid.

Required:

Prepare a charge and discharge statement for Newton Burns in respect to the estate of Gaylon Miles upon closing of the estate on July 15, 19X1.

Problem 19–13

The will of E. M. Dodd, who died on December 31, 19X0, provided cash bequests of $40,000 to Mrs. Dodd and $15,000 each to two children, the residuary estate to be divided equally among the three beneficiaries. Mrs. Dodd was appointed executrix and trustee without fees or other emoluments.

By court order Mrs. Dodd was to receive a family allowance of $4,000 a month, commencing January 1, 19X1, payable from income or from any cash principal available if the income should be inadequate. The estate never had enough cash available to pay the full allowance nor could any part of the cash bequests be paid. Accordingly a considerable liability to Mrs. Dodd had accumulated toward the end of 19X6 for the unpaid portion of the family allowance, as shown by the following trial balance of the estate ledger at December 31 of that year:

	Debit	Credit
Cash	$ 200	
Securities	20,000	
Building A	200,000	
Accumulated depreciation		$ 36,000
Building B	160,000	
Accumulated depreciation		38,400
Mortgage—building B		32,000
Revolving fund—building A	1,800	
Revolving fund—building B	2,400	
Mrs. E. M. Dodd—family allowance		288,000
Mrs. E. M. Dodd—paid on account	178,000	
Estate corpus		168,000
	$562,400	$562,400

The balance in the estate corpus account was made up as follows:

Appraisal of assets	$365,000
Deduct—funeral expenses, etc.	15,000
	$350,000
Add—income:	
Dividends received	6,000
Rentals, after deducting expenses and mortgage interest to date	100,000
	$456,000
Deduct—family allowance	288,000
Balance	$168,000

For want of cash the beneficiaries decided to settle all liabilities by transfer of property, and they requested their attorney to petition the court for approval of the following agreement to take effect as of December 31, 19X6.

The building B and its revolving fund are to be conveyed to Mrs. Dodd subject to the mortgage. In turn she agrees to waive all her claims against the estate for expenditures not refunded to her, including one of $5,000 for estate income taxes paid by her and not collected from the estate, and in addition to pay attorney's fees of $6,000 for the estate. Furthermore, all beneficiaries agree to have the family allowance discontinued after December 31, 19X6, and also to waive their claims to the cash bequests.

The court gave its approval to the agreement and ordered an intermediary accounting by the trustee as of December 31, 19X6.

Required:
Based upon the above information, prepare:

a. Columnar work sheet showing the trial balance before and after adjustment.
b. Statement of Mrs. Dodd's account.
c. Trustee's intermediary accounting in the form of a charge and discharge statement.

(AICPA adapted)

Problem 19–14

James Roe died on December 31, 19X0, and left an estate that was to be divided equally among his four children, all legally of age:

> Mary Roe Powell   Edward Roe
> Albert Roe   Ethel Roe

All funeral expenses, doctor's bills, and other liabilities, including all death duties and estate taxes, were to be paid by the Cohasset Trust Company from a fund that had been provided by the deceased during his lifetime and was on deposit with the trust company. Any balance remaining in this fund, after all payments had been made, was to be retained by the trust company in payment for its services. The trust company agreed to accept that balance in full settlement.

Two trusts will ultimately be set up—one for Mary and the other for Ethel. The eldest son, Albert, was appointed sole executor and trustee of the estate and of the trusts to be created. The principal of each trust was to remain intact during the beneficiary's lifetime, but each beneficiary had the right of appointment (by this right each daughter could direct to whom the principal of her trust should be paid at her death). The two sons, Albert and Edward, were each to receive their one-quarter share without any restrictions. The net income from the estate was to be distributed semiannually.

The inventory of the estate consisted of:

Cash in bank	$ 100,000
$400,000, 3⅜% municipal bonds at market value	400,000
20,000 shares of no-par value stock of Roe Manufacturing Company, appraised at	5,400,000
1,000 shares Cohasset Trust Company stock of $100 par, market value $300 per share	300,000
Waterfront property at Cohasset Bay, appraised at	800,000
	$7,000,000

The heirs decided to leave the estate undivided for the present under the trusteeship of Albert Roe who, with his brother Edward and his brother-in-law John Powell, continued the management of the Roe Manufacturing Company.

The coupons of the municipal bonds were payable on June 30 and December 31. The Roe Manufacturing Company continued to pay each month a dividend of 50 cents per share and the Cohasset Trust Company paid a dividend of $12.50 per share, both on June 1 and December 1. No income was received from the Cohasset Bay property.

On July 1, 19X1, Ethel Roe was killed in an automobile accident. By the terms of her will, appointing Albert Roe executor, she left $500,000 in specific bequests, the balance of her estate to be equally divided among her brothers and sister. The estate of Ethel Roe consisted solely of her interest in the estate of her father, with the exception of cash in bank which was just enough to pay burial costs, death duties, and all other liabilities.

The executor of the estate of James Roe, with the consent of the court and of the other heirs, decided to advance to the estate of Ethel Roe the $500,000 required to pay the specific bequests and to charge the amount against her share in the estate of James Roe. It was likewise decided to grant the requests of Albert Roe for an advance of $200,000 and of Edward Roe for an advance of $100,000 against their shares in the latter estate. Both agreed to interest charges on these advances from July 1, 19X1, at a reasonable rate that would also be fair to the Mary Roe Powell trust, but no interest would be charged on the $500,000 advanced to the estate of Ethel Roe.

In order to provide the necessary cash funds on August 1, 19X1, the $400,000 municipal bonds and the 1,000 shares of Cohasset Trust Company stock were sold, respectively for $420,000 and $320,000 net after broker's commissions, taxes, and other selling expenses, and on that date the above advances were made.

No change in the executorship and trusteeship of Albert Roe was to take place on account of Ethel Roe's death, but with the consent of the court and of the heirs, her remaining interest in her father's estate was to be divided as of the date of her death in accordance with the terms of her will.

The trustee paid the following expenses in 19X1:

Incidental expenses for the year applicable in equal amounts to the six months
  before and after the death of Ethel Roe .... $ 1,290
Taxes on real estate, payable in June and December 18,000

Trustee's commissions at the legal rates for "receiving and paying out" as follows:

5% on the first	$ 2,000
2½% on the next	20,000
1½% on the next	28,000
2% on the balance.	

One half of these rates is for receiving and one half for paying. The same rates apply to principal and to income cash. These commissions are paid June 30 and December 31.

Required:

a. Prepare a columnar work sheet to which the transactions in the six months before and after division of the Ethel Roe estate are posted so as to produce the balance sheets of the estate of James Roe immediately after the division of the estate of Ethel Roe on July 1, 19X1, and on December 31, 19X1. Show the calculation of the rate of interest charged to Albert and Edward Roe and give the reason why the use of that rate should be considered fair to the Mary Roe Powell trust.

b. Prepare the trustee's intermediary accounting as at December 31, 19X1, in the form of a charge and discharge statement, showing the payments to each beneficiary.

(AICPA adapted)

CHAPTER
20

Accounting for State and
Local Governmental Units

The economic impact of state and local governments is overwhelming. Annual expenditures of these governmental units exceed one sixth of the nation's estimated gross national product. The *1982 Census of Governments*[1] reported the existence of over 80,000 state and local governmental units, comprised of states, counties, cities, towns, and numerous school and special districts. Special districts, as defined by the Census Bureau, are limited-purpose governmental units (other than school districts) existing as separate entities with substantial fiscal and administrative independence from general-purpose local governments. In excess of 47,000 of the governmental units have issued debt securities to the general public with an outstanding value of over $400 billion. Due to the significant economic impact of the governmental sector of our economy, there have been long-standing efforts on the part of governmental management, public interest groups, and the accounting profession to establish uniform reporting standards for these nonbusiness entities.

In recent years, the AICPA and FASB have focused on the development of accounting principles for nonbusiness organizations in addition to developing reporting rules for profit-oriented business enterprises. Nonbusiness organizations include governmental units and other nonprofit organizations, such as charitable foundations, colleges and universities, voluntary health and welfare organizations, some hospitals, professional societies, and civic organizations. This chapter focuses on the accounting principles applicable to state and local governmental units. The following chapter deals with accounting for other nonbusiness organizations.

Historical Perspective of Authoritative Pronouncements

Prior to 1979, the primary source of governmental accounting principles was *Governmental Accounting, Auditing, and Financial Reporting (GAAFR)*, published in 1968 by the National Committee on Governmental Accounting. This document was recognized as authoritative generally accepted accounting principles by the AICPA in its 1974 audit guide, "Audits of State and Local Governmental Units."

In 1974, the Municipal Finance Officers Association established the National Council on Governmental Accounting (NCGA), which consisted of 21 members who served four-year terms on a part-time, voluntary basis. In 1979, the NCGA issued *Statement 1*, "Governmental Accounting and Financial Reporting Principles," which restated and superseded *GAAFR*.

---

[1] *1982 Census of Governments (Final), Governmental Organization*, Vol. 1, (Washington, D.C.: U.S. Department of Commerce, Bureau of the Census, August 1983).

Statement 1 contains 12 principles of accounting for state and local governmental units and remains the primary authoritative pronouncement on governmental accounting. The AICPA, in its *Statement of Position 80-2* (June 30, 1980), stated that financial statements presented in accordance with the NCGA's *Statement 1* are considered to be in conformity with generally accepted accounting principles.

During 1980, the FASB issued *Statement of Financial Accounting Concepts No. 4 (SFAC No. 4)*, "Objectives of Financial Reporting by Nonbusiness Organizations." The statement lists seven objectives of financial reporting by nonbusiness organizations. These objectives are presented in the following chapter on accounting for nongovernmental nonprofit entities. *SFAC No. 4* (par. 3) states:

> On the basis of its study to date, the Board is aware of no persuasive evidence that the objectives in this Statement are inappropriate for general purpose external financial reports of governmental units. Nonetheless, the appropriate structure for setting financial accounting and reporting standards for state and local governmental units continues to be discussed. Pending resolution of that issue, the Board has deferred a final decision on whether the objectives set forth in this Statement should apply to general purpose external financial reporting by state and local governmental units.[2]

During 1984, the Governmental Accounting Standards Board (GASB) was formed by the Financial Accounting Foundation, which also funds and appoints members of the FASB. The GASB will establish and promulgate governmental accounting standards in the same fashion as the FASB establishes reporting standards for profit-oriented enterprises, providing for broad public participation in all stages of the standard-setting process.

Shortly after its formation, the GASB issued *Statement No. 1*, "Authoritative Status of NCGA Pronouncements and AICPA Industry Audit Guide," which provides that all NCGA pronouncements in effect as of June 1984 remain in effect until amended or superseded by a subsequent GASB pronouncement. The seven statements issued by the NCGA, together with their effective dates, are listed below:

Statement 1	"Governmental Accounting and Financial Reporting Principles" (effective for fiscal years ending after June 30, 1980).
Statement 2	"Grant, Entitlement, and Shared Revenue Accounting and Reporting by State and Local Governments" (effective for fiscal years ending after June 30, 1980).
Statement 3	"Defining the Governmental Reporting Entity" (effective for fiscal years ending after December 31, 1982).

---

[2] FASB, *Statement of Financial Accounting Concepts No. 4*, "Objectives of Financial Reporting by Nonbusiness Organizations" (Stamford, Conn., 1980), par. 3.

Statement 4	"Accounting and Financial Reporting Principles for Claims and Judgments and Compensated Absences" (effective for fiscal years beginning after December 31, 1982).
Statement 5	"Accounting and Financial Reporting Principles for Lease Agreements of State and Local Governments" (effective for fiscal years beginning after June 30, 1983).
Statement 6	"Pension Accounting and Financial Reporting: Public Employee Retirement Systems and State and Local Government Employees" (effective for fiscal years beginning after June 15, 1982).
Statement 7	"Financial Reporting for Component Units within the Governmental Reporting Entity" (effective for fiscal years ending after June 30, 1984).

Statement 1 promulgated 12 principles of governmental accounting, which, together with *Statement 2*, are the subject of the remainder of this chapter. *Statements 3* through *7* are beyond the scope of this text. The interested reader will find a more detailed discussion of these additional principles in texts devoted exclusively to the subject of governmental accounting. The following section of this chapter lists the 12 principles from *Statement 1* in summary form, including an outline of the types of funds and account groups that should be utilized as separate accounting entities for various governmental functions. The remaining sections of the chapter present discussions and examples related to these 12 principles.

Summary Statement of Principles of Governmental Accounting

The reader should be familiar with the 12 principles of governmental accounting prior to working through the illustrations and problems that follow. These 12 principles, as given in *Statement 1* in summary form, are presented below.

Accounting and Reporting Capabilities

1.   A governmental accounting system must make it possible both: (a) to present fairly and with full disclosure the financial position and results of financial operations of the funds and account groups of the governmental unit in conformity with generally accepted accounting principles; and (b) to determine and demonstrate compliance with finance-related legal and contractual provisions.

Fund Accounting Systems

2.   Governmental accounting systems should be organized and operated on a fund basis. A fund is defined as a fiscal and accounting entity with a self-balancing

set of accounts recording cash and other financial resources, together with all related liabilities and residual equities or balances, and changes therein, which are segregated for the purpose of carrying on specific activities or attaining certain objectives in accordance with special regulations, restrictions, or limitations.

Types of Funds

3. The following types of funds should be used by state and local governments:

Governmental Funds

(1) *The General Fund*—to account for all financial resources except those required to be accounted for in another fund.

(2) *Special Revenue Funds*—to account for the proceeds of specific revenue sources (other than special assessments, expendable trusts, or for major capital projects) that are legally restricted to expenditure for specified purposes.

(3) *Capital Projects Funds*—to account for financial resources to be used for the acquisition or construction of major capital facilities (other than those financed by proprietary funds, Special Assessment Funds, and Trust Funds).

(4) *Debt Service Funds*—to account for the accumulation of resources for, and the payment of, general long-term debt principal and interest.

(5) *Special Assessment Funds*—to account for the financing of public improvements or services deemed to benefit the properties against which special assessments are levied.

Proprietary Funds

(6) *Enterprise Funds*—to account for operations (a) that are financed and operated in a manner similar to private business enterprises—where the intent of the governing body is that the costs (expenses, including depreciation) of providing goods or services to the general public on a continuing basis be financed or recovered primarily through user charges; or (b) where the governing body has decided that periodic determination of revenues earned, expenses incurred, and/or net income is appropriate for capital maintenance, public policy, management control, accountability, or other purposes.

(7) *Internal Service Funds*—to account for the financing of goods or services provided by one department or agency to other departments or agencies of the governmental unit, or to other governmental units, on a cost-reimbursement basis.

Fiduciary Funds

(8) *Trust and Agency Funds*—to account for assets held by a governmental unit in a trustee capacity or as an agent for individuals, private organizations, other governmental units, and/or other funds. These include (a) Expendable Trust Funds, (b) Nonexpendable Trust Funds, (c) Pension Trust Funds, and (d) Agency Funds.

Number of Funds

4. Governmental units should establish and maintain those funds required by law and sound financial administration. Only the minimum number of funds consistent with legal and operating requirements should be established, however, since unnecessary funds result in inflexibility, undue complexity, and inefficient financial administration.

Accounting for Fixed Assets and Long-Term Liabilities

5.   A clear distinction should be made between (a) fund fixed assets and general fixed assets and (b) fund long-term liabilities and general long-term debt.

a.   Fixed assets related to specific proprietary funds or Trust Funds should be accounted for through those funds. All other fixed assets of a governmental unit should be accounted for through the General Fixed Assets Account Group.

b.   Long-term liabilities of proprietary funds, Special Assessment Funds, and Trust Funds should be accounted for through those funds. All other unmatured general long-term liabilities of the governmental unit should be accounted for through the General Long-Term Debt Account Group.

Valuation of Fixed Assets

6.   Fixed assets should be accounted for at cost or, if the cost is not practicably determinable, at estimated cost. Donated fixed assets should be recorded at their estimated fair value at the time received.

Depreciation of Fixed Assets

7.   a.   Depreciation of general fixed assets should not be recorded in the accounts of governmental funds. Depreciation of general fixed assets may be recorded in cost accounting systems or calculated for cost finding analyses; and accumulated depreciation may be recorded in the General Fixed Assets Account Group.

b.   Depreciation of fixed assets accounted for in a proprietary fund should be recorded in the accounts of that fund. Depreciation is also recognized in those Trust Funds where expenses, net income, and/or capital maintenance are measured.

Accrual Basis in Governmental Accounting

8.   The modified accrual or accrual basis of accounting, as appropriate, should be utilized in measuring financial position and operating results.

a.   *Governmental fund* revenues and expenditures should be recognized on the modified accrual basis. Revenues should be recognized in the accounting period in which they become available and measurable. Expenditures should be recognized in the accounting period in which the fund liability is incurred, if measurable, except for unmatured interest on general long-term debt and on special assessment indebtedness secured by interest-bearing special assessment levies, which should be recognized when due.

b.   *Proprietary fund* revenues and expenses should be recognized on the accrual basis. Revenues should be recognized in the accounting period in which they are earned and become measurable; expenses should be recognized in the period incurred, if measurable.

c.   *Fiduciary fund* revenues and expenses or expenditures (as appropriate) should be recognized on the basis consistent with the fund's accounting measurement objective. Nonexpendable Trust and Pension Trust Funds should be accounted for on the accrual basis; Expendable Trust Funds should be accounted for on the modified accrual basis. Agency Fund assets and liabilities should be accounted for on the modified accrual basis.

d. *Transfers* should be recognized in the accounting period in which the interfund receivable and payable arise.

Budgeting, Budgetary Control, and Budgetary Reporting

9. a. An annual budget(s) should be adopted by every governmental unit.
   b. The accounting system should provide the basis for appropriate budgetary control.
   c. Budgetary comparisons should be included in the appropriate financial statements and schedules for governmental funds for which an annual budget has been adopted.

Transfer Revenue, Expenditure, and Expense Account Classification

10. a. Interfund transfers and proceeds of general long-term debt issues should be classified separately from fund revenues and expenditures or expenses.
    b. Governmental fund revenues should be classified by fund and source. Expenditures should be classified by fund, function (or program), organization unit, activity, character, and principal classes of objects.
    c. Proprietary fund revenues and expenses should be classified in essentially the same manner as those of similar business organizations, functions, or activities.

Common Terminology and Classification

11. A common terminology and classification should be used consistently throughout the budget, the accounts, and the financial reports of each fund.

Interim and Annual Financial Reports

12. a. Appropriate interim financial statements and reports of financial position, operating results, and other pertinent information should be prepared to facilitate management control of financial operations, legislative oversight, and, where necessary or desired, for external reporting purposes.
    b. A comprehensive annual financial report covering all funds and account groups of the governmental unit—including appropriate combined, combining, and individual fund statements; notes to the financial statements; schedules; narrative explanations; and statistical tables—should be prepared and published.
    c. General purpose financial statements may be issued separately from the comprehensive annual financial report. Such statements should include the basic financial statements and notes to the financial statements that are essential to fair presentation of financial position and operating results (and changes in financial position of proprietary funds and similar Trust Funds).[3]

---

[3] National Council on Governmental Accounting, *Governmental Accounting and Financial Reporting Principles*, Municipal Finance Officers Association of the United States and Canada (Chicago, 1979), pp. 2–4.

Basic Concepts of Governmental Accounting for the General Fund

Several fundamental propositions that relate to governmental accounting for the general fund will be discussed before attention is directed to more specific accounting relationships. Following a discussion of the notions of fund accounting, the reader is introduced briefly to the related concept of budgetary accounting and the modified accrual basis of accounting as it relates to governmental transactions.

The Nature of Funds

Accounting is the process by which transactions of an *entity* are recorded, classified, summarized, and reported to users. Partnerships, corporations, and corporate affiliations are typical examples of profit-oriented entities to which the accounting process is applied. In governmental accounting, the primary accounting unit is referred to as a *fund.* Just as the corporate entity takes on an identity separate from its legal owners, a *fund* of a governmental unit is treated as a separate entity for accounting purposes. The governmental accounting process summarizes, classifies, records, and reports the transactions of these individual funds as if they stand alone, separate from the constituents that provide the resources to the governmental unit. Therefore, the governmental accounting process is a means by which the accomplishments and service efforts of the *fund* are recorded. A separate fund should be utilized to record the transactions of a *specific activity* with specific underlying objectives. The specific activity and objectives are usually conditioned by special regulations, restrictions, and/ or limitations, since the fund is a *fiscal entity* authorized by law to raise revenues and make expenditures. The set of accounts for each fund is self-balancing, including assets—debits to the fund; liabilities—credits to the fund; resource inflows—credits to the fund; resource outflows—debits to the fund; and residual equities—a residual credit balance would indicate the existence of available resources not yet spent, and a residual debit balance would indicate a shortfall where expenditures exceed available resources for the accounting period. The principal emphasis of fund theory is that it focuses on a specified area of operations, a center of interest, which does not depend upon legal or other forms of personality.

Expendable and Nonexpendable Funds

An *expendable* fund is an aggregation of resources that are totally available for expenditure in achieving the objectives of the fund. Revenues for such a fund may be obtained from taxes, fees, special assessments, proceeds from bond issues, or interfund and intergovernmental transfers. Fund *expenditures* include disbursements for services, supplies, *and equipment*. Since existing fixed assets represent prior expenditures of a fund, they are excluded from an enumeration of resources of an expendable fund.

A nonexpendable fund requires that the principal or capital balance of the fund be preserved intact. A revolving fund which is expected to generate revenues sufficient in amount to cover operating expenses of the fund, without dilution of capital, is an example of a nonexpendable fund. Additionally, a trust fund which permits the expenditure of income only is a nonexpendable fund. The expendable fund will be emphasized in this chapter with only brief mention of nonexpendable funds.

Allotments and Apportionments

Allotments (state and local) and apportionments (federal) are *methods of allocating* appropriations over the budget period. They represent a partial release of a unit's appropriation for a given subinterval of time by the legislative or administrative body, and operate as a form of expenditure control. This type of control is designed to prevent overexpenditure in the early part of the budget period; the hope is to eliminate the need for deficiency appropriations that might otherwise develop at the end of the period. Where the number of administrative levels within a governmental entity is large (as, for example, in the federal government), both of these terms may be used to describe the allocation process at different levels of the organization.

Account Groups for General Fixed Assets and General Long-Term Debt

Account groups for general fixed assets and general long-term debt are also established as separate self-balancing accounting entities in a governmental accounting system. They differ from funds in that they do not represent fiscal entities with specific objectives and purposes. Rather, they merely summarize, in money terms, the total *general* fixed assets and *general* long-term debt of the government. Each of these account groups is explained in more detail later. However, before commencing our coverage of the various funds, it is important to note that the account groups compile information only on fixed assets and long-term debt that are not assignable to specific funds. Fixed assets related to specific Proprietary or Trust Funds are included in the accounts of those funds. Hence, only acquisitions of fixed assets by Governmental Funds (which are recorded in those funds as expenditures in the period they are acquired) are included in the General Fixed Assets Group. Similarly, long-term debt issued and to be repaid by Proprietary, Trust, and Special Assessment Funds, even when backed by the full faith and credit of the governmental entity, are included in the accounts of those specific funds. All other long-term debt is included in the General Long-Term Debt Group.

Budgetary Accounting

Authority for the operation of a fund related to a specific activity or set of objectives is formally given when the legislature or city council adopts the budget. The budget is utilized for both planning and control purposes. Initially, the governmental budget is an estimate of anticipated expenditures during a given period or for a specified purpose, with proposed methods of financing the budget objectives—that is, a planning budget. Once approved by the governing body, however, the estimated expenditures are translated into expenditure authorizations—either by legislation or approval at a higher administrative level. Thus, the budget becomes a relatively inflexible control device which operationally prohibits unfavorable variances from budgetary estimates by mandating legal ceilings on the amount of prospective expenditures.

Unlike the accounting for profit-oriented business enterprises, in governmental accounting the authorized budget is often formally recognized in special *budgetary accounts*. These budgetary accounts constitute a formal record of the financial plan, as compared with *proprietary accounts* which record the actual transactions. Control is achieved by keeping track of the comparative balances in related budgetary and proprietary accounts. If the debit balance in the budgetary account Estimated Revenues exceeds the related credit balance in the proprietary account Revenues, this may signal a potential shortfall (deficit) unless anticipated expenditures are reduced to compensate for the difference. Likewise, an excess of actual expenditures over budgeted appropriations can be avoided by comparing the balance in the budgetary Appropriations account (authorized total expenditures) with the related balance in the proprietary Expenditures accounts (actual resource outflows) and Encumbrances (contracted future outflows). Indeed, subsequent analysis will show how corresponding budgetary and proprietary accounts are closed in one entry, thereby leaving a permanent record of the difference between budgeted and actual data. It should be obvious, however, that budgetary accounting aids in controlling only the amount of the total expenditures for each program; without further analyses and additional controls, this technique fails to measure the type of efficiency indicated by a comparison of "standard costs" of program accomplishments with actual costs.

In addition to recording the budget into budgetary accounts, proper budgetary control requires the use of an encumbrance system in which a record of further commitments is established as soon as orders are placed or contracts are issued. Once the anticipated expenditure has been established, the account Encumbrances is debited and the account Reserve for Encumbrances is credited in anticipation of the expenditure. When the actual liability is determined, the entry for the encumbrance is reversed, and the actual expenditure and liability are recorded. Appropriations for salaries and wages, bond interest, and other recurring expenditures often are not encumbered but are recorded concurrent with the liquidating payment. The encumbrance approach is illustrated in a later section of this chapter.

Modified Accrual Basis

The modified accrual basis of accounting that is used for accounting for governmental funds is characterized, to a large extent, by imposition of restrictive criteria on the recognition of revenue prior to receipt of cash. Two criteria must be satisfied: (1) the revenue must be measurable, and (2) the revenue must be available, that is, collectible within or soon after the current period so that it is available for payment of obligations incurred during the same period. The recognition of expenses or expenditures under the modified accrual method is similar to the straight accrual basis. One prominent exception, unmatured interest on general long-term debt and on special assessment indebtedness secured by interest-bearing special assessment levies, should be recognized when due. In addition, most short-term prepaid expenses (e.g., prepaid insurance) need not be allocated between periods, and purchases of inventory usually may be recognized either as expenditures of a governmental fund when purchased (purchases method) or when consumed (consumption method).

A clear distinction must be maintained between revenues, expenditures, and *transfers in* and *out* of funds. If a cash receipt (disbursement) would be considered a revenue (expenditure) to the governmental entity as a whole, it is credited (debited) in the fund's accounts to Revenue (Expenditures); otherwise, it is usually recorded as an operating transfer. Two exceptions to this general rule are *quasi-external transactions* and *reimbursements*. Quasi-external transactions are transactions between funds that would be regarded as sources of revenue, expenditures, or expenses if the two funds were not part of the same governmental unit (e.g., billings from an Internal Service Fund or payments in lieu of taxes by an Enterprise Fund). Reimbursements are interfund transfers that essentially levy the economic impact of resource flows on the fund to which they are properly assignable, and thus are recorded as Expenditures (or Expenses) by the fund making the payment and as an offset to previously recorded Expenditures (or Expenses) by the fund receiving the transfer.

Residual equity transfers are resource inflows to a fund due to the elimination of another fund with a credit in the fund balance immediately prior to the transfer. As such, residual equity transfers are not recognized as revenue in the fund receiving the transfer. Alternatively, the amount would be reported as an "other change in the fund balance" on the Statement of Revenues, Expenditures, and Changes in Fund Balance with an entry that debits assets for those transferred, and credits the Unreserved Fund Balance (or other appropriate account(s) if restrictions are placed on the use of these resources).

Recognition of Grants, Entitlements, and Shared Revenue from Other Governments

Statement 2, issued by the NCGA and effective for fiscal years ending after June 30, 1980, discusses the principles of revenue recognition related to grants, entitlements, and shared revenue from other governmental units. A *grant* is defined as a contribution or gift of cash or other assets from another government to be used or expended for a specified purpose, activity, or facility. *Capital grants* are restricted by the grantor for the acquisition and/or construction of fixed (capital) assets. All other grants are *operating grants*.

An *entitlement* is the amount of payment to which a state or local government is entitled as determined by the federal government (e.g., the Director of the Office of Revenue Sharing) pursuant to an allocation formula contained in applicable statutes. A *shared revenue* is a revenue levied by one government but shared on a predetermined basis, often in proportion to the amount collected at the local level, with another government or class of government.

The use of special revenue funds to account for these sources of revenue is *not required* unless legally mandated. The basis of accounting for these types of resource inflows to a governmental unit is determined by the fund type in which the transactions are recorded. Transactions of this nature which are accounted for in governmental funds other than proprietary funds (Enterprise and Internal Service Funds) and certain nonexpendable fiduciary funds (Nonexpendable Trust and Pension Trust Funds) should be recorded on the *modified* accrual basis. Otherwise, the accrual basis is to be applied.

Grants, entitlements, or shared revenues recorded in governmental funds (General, Special Revenue, Capital Projects, Debt Service, and Special Assessment Funds) should be recognized as revenue in the accounting period when they become susceptible to accrual under the modified accrual basis (amount is measurable and available). If the use of the grant, entitlement, or shared revenue is generally unrestricted (except that failure to comply with prescribed regulations would cause a forfeiture of the resources), such resources should be recorded as revenue at the time of receipt or earlier if the modified accrual criteria are met. If the act of making a prescribed expenditure is the prime factor for determining eligibility for the resource, revenue should be recognized when the expenditure is made. Similarly, if cost sharing or matching requirements exist, revenue recognition depends upon compliance with these requirements. Under these circumstances, if the resource is received prior to the satisfaction of the legal restriction, it should be recorded as *deferred revenue*. Once the legal restriction is satisfied (e.g., the expenditure is made), the amount would be cleared out of deferred revenue and recognized as *revenue*.

Grants, entitlements, or shared revenues received for proprietary fund operating purposes, or which may be utilized for either operations or capital expenditures at the discretion of the recipient government, should be recognized as "nonoperating" revenues in the accounting period in which they are earned and become measurable (accrual basis). Such resources restricted for the acquisition or construction of capital assets should be recorded as contributed equity.

Grants, entitlements, or shared revenues recorded in Trust Funds should be recognized as revenue on a basis consistent with the fund's measurement objective (governmental or proprietary). Revenue is not recognized in Agency Funds. Such resources initially recorded in Agency Funds are subsequently recognized as asset(s) and revenues in the fund(s) financed according to the applicable revenue recognition criteria.[4]

Illustrations of Accounting for the General Fund

The General Fund is used to account for all revenues, and the activities financed by these revenues, which are not reflected in a special fund. In terms of scope, most of the current operations of the governmental unit are financed by the General Fund. Accordingly, a variety of sources provide revenue for, and a wide range of activities are financed by, this omnibus fund.

The principal revenue sources of the General Fund of a municipality include such items as property taxes, licenses, fines, penalties, and other fees. Conventional expenditure classifications include the functions provided by the fire, police, and sanitation departments, and administrative or clerical activities. Some capital outlays also are directly financed by the General Fund. An additional classification (referred to as *object* classification) indicating the purpose of the outlay, for example, wages, supplies, and so forth, will often support these primary (functional) expenditure summaries.

Recording the Budget

In accounting for the General Fund, the budget which has been approved by the appropriate governing body should be formally journalized into the accounts of the fund. Such an entry would take the following form:

---

[4] *Statement 2*, "Grant, Entitlement, and Shared Revenue Accounting and Reporting by State and Local Governments," National Council on Governmental Accounting.

Estimated Revenues 200,000		
Appropriations...		198,000
Fund Balance...		2,000

In this particular instance, authority was granted to spend a maximum of $198,000 in conducting the operations of the General Fund. It was also estimated that $200,000 would be collected in revenue from sources such as property taxes, license fees, etc. Note that Estimated Revenues is debited, and Appropriations (budgeted maximum expenditures) is credited in the above entry. These *budgetary accounts* are recorded in a fashion that is contrary to the recording of the related *proprietary accounts*—Revenues and Expenditures—for control purposes. By entering the budgetary accounts with the debits and credits reversed from the usual way of recording actual revenues (credits) and expenses (debits), the expected residual equity for the entire accounting period is journalized at the beginning of the period. Recording the budget is an attempt to control the actual expenditure level so that a deficit in the fund may be avoided. As actual revenues are collected or accrued and actual expenditures and encumbrances are made, revenues will be credited and expenditures debited as always. At any time throughout the accounting period, the actual revenues can be compared with the estimated revenues to determine if the budget is on target. Also, as of any point in time during the period, the total actual expenditures and encumbrances can be compared with the legal ceiling on expenditures, called appropriations, to ensure that current expenditures do not exceed the legal limit. The $2,000 credit to the Fund Balance is in anticipation of a surplus for the accounting period resulting from Estimated Revenues exceeding Appropriations. Although the closing entry process will be illustrated in detail in a later section of the chapter, it is shown below that, if actual revenues and expenditures were equal to the estimated amounts in the budget, the closing process would not change the $2,000 surplus in the Fund Balance account. The closing entries in this instance would be:

Revenues 200,000		
Estimated Revenues		200,000
Appropriations... 198,000		
Expenditures...		198,000

Since the *Fund Balance* account is not affected by this closing entry, the amount which was originally set up when the budget was recorded— $2,000 credit—remains unchanged in the ledger, indicating that the expected surplus was actually realized. Note that the budgetary accounts are closed out in addition to the actual revenue and expenditure accounts. If Appropriations had exceeded the actual Expenditures made during the period by $2,000, the closing entry above would be changed to include a credit to Expenditures of $196,000 and a credit to the Fund Balance of $2,000. The total surplus in the Fund Balance account at the end of the period would be $4,000. On the other hand, if estimated revenues had exceeded actual revenues by $2,000, the closing entry would include a debit to Revenues of $198,000 and a debit to the Fund Balance of $2,000. The remaining balance in the residual Fund Balance account would be zero, indicating that the anticipated surplus was not achieved because the actual revenues were less than the budgeted amount. In this case the actual revenues equaled the actual expenditures, leaving no surplus or deficit in the Fund Balance.

Recording Actual Transactions

The accounts Revenues, Encumbrances (recall that this account is debited for amounts representing orders or contracts related to future expenditures), and Expenditures are summary accounts in the general ledger of the Fund. Subsidiary ledgers are also maintained for these summary categories so that planned and actual revenues and expenditures can be classified according to function. The accumulation of detailed operating expenditures by functions is particularly important, since comparison of these totals (past and future expenditures) with the amounts appropriated discloses the degree of compliance with budgetary restrictions.

Perhaps the single most important objective of fund accounting is *expenditure control*. In order to assure compliance with the formal budget, both the appropriated amounts and the related actual expenditures are recorded in subsidiary ledgers by function (i.e., fire, police, sanitation, etc.). The accounting system should be structured so that overexpenditure within any functional category is avoided. Prior to the approval of any new expenditure within a given functional category, the cumulative actual expenditures for this function covering the current fiscal period should be compared with the related appropriated amount. Once the cumulative actual expenditures equal the amount appropriated for the operation of the governmental function, additional expenditures would be illegal unless authority for additional expenditures is given.

If an expenditure does not represent a claim against an individual, an organizational entity, or some other fund, it is recorded merely as an Expenditure. Accordingly, the purchase of a fixed asset with General Fund resources is accounted for not unlike a current "expense."

Many of the earned revenues of a General Fund are recorded when received in cash. Property taxes—often a principal source of General Fund revenue—will, however, frequently satisfy the criteria for accrual. If the property taxes are levied and are collectible during the current period, an entry of the following form is made:

Taxes Receivable.	150,000	
Allowances for Uncollectible Accounts		10,000
Revenues		140,000

At the time any portion of the tax levy becomes delinquent, it is transferred to Taxes Receivable—Delinquent, and the related allowance account is reclassified accordingly. If the receivable balance is ultimately collected, the allowance is closed to the Fund Balance account. Property taxes that are levied but not available until a subsequent period, and taxes that are collected in advance, should be credited to Deferred Revenues rather than Revenues; the deferred revenues are then recognized as revenue in the period they become available or to which they apply. Additional sources of revenue that often satisfy the criteria for accrual include grants from other governments and amounts due from routine services that are regularly billed.

This proprietary account for revenues actually earned is usually supported by detailed source data in the same subsidiary ledger that is used for estimated revenues. Thus, both estimated and actual revenues, classified by sources, are juxtaposed in the same subsidiary revenues ledger.

Recording Encumbrances

Typical entries to record an encumbrance of $11,000 and to record the subsequent reversal and related expenditure of $10,500 (here for an amount less than that anticipated) are as follows:

Encumbrances...	11,000	
Reserve for Encumbrances............................		11,000
Expenditures..	10,500	
Vouchers (Accounts) Payable		10,500
Reserve for Encumbrances...............................	11,000	
Encumbrances..		11,000

Note that the original entry setting up the encumbrance is reversed when the actual expenditure is made. A sequence of events that would lead to these entries would include (a) the placing of an order or entering of a contract to purchase goods or services with an estimated price of $11,000, and (b) the receipt of an invoice for payment which discloses the actual liability at $10,500.

The accounts Encumbrances and Reserve for Encumbrances are offsetting memorandum accounts in the general ledger. Both accounts represent the amount that should be deducted from the Appropriations account in order to determine the estimated expendable balance of appropriations. For this reason, the account Reserve for Encumbrances can be thought of as an "appropriations control" account. As orders are placed and encumbrances are recorded, the unencumbered and unexpended balance of appropriations can be derived by reducing the total appropriations for the current fiscal period by the sum of the cumulative expenditures recorded for the period *and* the outstanding balance in Reserve for Encumbrances.

Closing the Budgetary and Proprietary Accounts

At the end of the fiscal period, the budgetary and operating accounts are closed, and residual balances are transferred to the Fund Balance account. Given a circumstance where estimated revenues exceed actual revenues and where appropriations exceed expenditures and encumbrances, the following closing entries are illustrative:

(a)	Revenues..	199,000	
	Fund Balance	1,000	
	Estimated Revenues		200,000
(b)	Appropriations.......................................	198,000	
	Expenditures......................................		180,000
	Fund Balance		18,000
(c)	Reserve for Encumbrances	15,000	
	Encumbrances		15,000
(d)	Fund Balance	15,000	
	Fund Balance Reserved for Encumbrances		15,000

The first two closing entries (a) and (b), with each corresponding set of budgetary and proprietary accounts being closed in a separate entry, result in separate debits and/or credits to the Fund Balance, each of which indicates the difference between budgeted and actual data. Together with the initial budgeted surplus of $2,000, these closing entries result in a $19,000 credit (surplus) balance in the Fund Balance account. The remaining two entries result in (c) the removal of the memorandum accounts Encumbrances and Reserve for Encumbrances from the general ledger balances at year-end, and (d) the reservation of a portion of the fund balance for specific appropriation in the following year to cover orders placed in the preceding year. Alternatively, this amount could be disclosed in the notes to financial statements. The Fund Balance Reserved for Encumbrances represents the amount of the year-end total fund balance that must be appropriated next year to authorize completion of transactions in process at the end of the current year. The remaining unreserved fund balance would be available for new appropriations originating in the next year.

Prior to the issuance of *Statement 1*, the AICPA *Industry Audit Guide*, "Audits of State and Local Governmental Units," which was published in 1974, allowed the use of the so-called encumbrances method of accounting. Under this method, encumbrances outstanding at year-end were treated as expenditures in annual financial statements. Under *Statement 1*, encumbrances outstanding at year-end *may not be reported as expenditures* in annual financial statements.

Upon recording these closing entries in the general ledger, the actual "surplus" from the operations of the current period which is available for next period's appropriations is $4,000 (based on estimated future expenditures toward current orders totaling $15,000), as derived below:

Actual Revenues.	$199,000
Actual Expenditures	180,000
Net.	19,000
Encumbrances (estimated future expenditures)	15,000
Surplus from Current Operations	$ 4,000

At the beginning of the following year, the memorandum accounts would be reopened with the following entries:

(a) Fund Balance Reserved for Encumbrances.   15,000
   Fund Balance   15,000

(b) Encumbrances   15,000
   Reserve for Encumbrances   15,000

Entry *(a)* closes out the account Fund Balance Reserved for Encumbrances to zero, and increases the unreserved fund balance by a like amount. Entry *(b)* reopens the memorandum accounts related to encumbrances as if the orders had been placed and the encumbrances recorded in the current year. As invoices are received for the actual expenditures, the memorandum accounts are reversed as usual, and actual expenditures are recorded. The expenditures are reported in the current year's financial statements even though the orders were placed in the preceding year.

Other Reserves

Other segregations of fund assets for specific purposes may also be indicated by establishing other *reserves*. For example, assume that a $50,000 advance is made to an internal printing shop operated as an Internal Service Fund, and this is recorded by debiting Advances to Internal Service Funds and crediting Cash. These resources are not available for current expenditures, and thus a reserve may be established with the following entry:

Fund Balance.   50,000
   Reserve for Advances to Internal Service Funds   50,000

Another commonly encountered reserve is the Reserve for Inventory. If the purchase of inventory was originally debited to an inventory account (the consumption method), the entry to establish the reserve would have the same form as the above entry. Additionally, the inventory account would be credited and expenditures would be debited with the amount of the inventory used up during the current period. However, if the acquisition of inventory is debited to Expenditures (the purchases method), the entry to recognize the inventory and set up the reserve would involve a debit to Inventory and a credit to Reserve for Inventory for the amount of inventory not yet used up. Of course, either method of initially recording inventory purchases leads to the same ultimate reserve balances at the end of the period. The unreserved fund balance would differ under the two alternative methods by the difference in the amounts recognized as expenditures.

In addition to reserves, governmental units often designate a portion of the Fund Balance for certain purposes. For example, $25,000 of the Fund Balance may be designated for possible equipment replacements with the following entry:

Fund Balance...	25,000	
Fund Balance Designated for Equipment Replacements.......		25,000

Unlike reserves, the designated portions of the fund balances do not represent prior uses of resources. Instead, they reflect management's anticipation of possible future uses—including uses in subsequent periods if the funding authority may be legally carried forward. In this sense, they are analogous to appropriations of retained earnings in normal commercial accounting.

As a consequence of reserves and designations, the total fund equity at any point in time may be initially split between the reserved and unreserved fund balance. The unreserved fund balance is then divided between designated and undesignated fund balance. The undesignated fund balance reflects the resources available for current expenditures. If assets that have been reserved for a particular use are withdrawn from that use (through, for example, repayment of an advance), or if certain designations are deemed by management to be unnecessary, the original entry establishing the reserve or the designated fund balance is reversed.

Financial Statements for the General Fund

The catalog of financial statements for the General Fund usually includes (1) a balance sheet; (2) a statement of revenues, expenditures, and changes in fund balance; (3) a statement of revenues, expenditures, and changes in fund balance—budget versus actual; and (4) a statement of changes in financial position. The balance sheet is relatively conventional. However, because expenditures for long-lived assets are recorded in the Expenditures account, rather than capitalized, the assets of the General Fund usually consist of relatively liquid assets—cash, receivables, and possibly inventory and advances to other funds. The liabilities will consist primarily of short-term obligations because long-term debt is separately disclosed in the statement of long-term debt. And, as mentioned above, the fund equity consists of reserved, designated, and undesignated fund balances. The statements of revenues and expenditures—both actual, and budget versus actual—have traditionally included encumbrances. However, *Statement 1* recommends that, where legally feasible, these statements exclude encumbrances and report only revenues and expenditures for the period. The comparison of budget versus actual is also recommended for Special Revenue Funds and on occasions is presented for other governmental funds. With this possible difference between types of governmental funds, this enumeration of financial statements for the General Fund is generally applicable to all governmental funds.

Comprehensive Illustrative Entries for General Fund

The January 1, 19X1, trial balance of the municipality of Cityville is given below:

MUNICIPALITY OF CITYVILLE
Trial Balance
January 1, 19X1

	Debit	Credit
Cash	150,000	
Accounts receivable.................................	29,000	
Material and supplies	38,000	
Due from federal government.........................	260,000	
Taxes receivable—delinquent	75,000	
Allowance for uncollectible taxes—delinquent...........		10,000
Vouchers payable....................................		185,000
Unreserved fund balance.............................		254,000
Fund balance reserved for material and supplies........		38,000
Fund balance reserved for encumbrances		65,000
Totals	552,000	552,000

Entries to record typical transactions of the General Fund during 19X1, together with related descriptions, are given below, followed by closing entries and the General Fund Financial Statements at year end.

Prior to recording transactions occurring during 19X1, entries would be recorded to reopen the Encumbrances and Reserve for Encumbrances memorandum accounts, as follows:

(a) Fund Balance Reserved for Encumbrances   65,000
      Unreserved Fund Balance   65,000

To clear out the Fund Balance Reserved for Encumbrances and record the amount as a portion of the Unreserved Fund Balance for the current accounting period.

(b) Encumbrances—Prior Year   65,000
      Reserve for Encumbrances—Prior Year   65,000

To reopen the memorandum accounts related to encumbrances outstanding at the end of the preceding accounting period.

Transactions during 19X1, followed by the entries to record each transaction, are given next.

(1) The city council approved the budget for 19X1, which included $2,200,000 in estimated revenues and $2,150,000 in total appropriations.

Estimated Revenues..................................... 2,200,000
    Appropriations   2,150,000
    Unreserved Fund Balance............................   50,000

(2) Transfers of funds from the city electric utility were authorized in the adopted budget amounting to $165,000.

| Due from Enterprise Fund | 165,000 | |
| Transfers In | | 165,000 |

(3) Transfers to the Debt Service Fund and Special Assessment Fund were authorized in the budget amounting to $300,000 and $200,000, respectively.

Transfers Out	500,000	
Due to Debt Service Fund		300,000
Due to Special Assessment Fund		200,000

(4) Property tax statements were issued to property owners. The tax levy was 7 percent of total property valuations of $21,428,571. Estimated uncollectible taxes are recorded based on 2 percent of the total tax levy. Since the revenue is measurable and available during 19X1, the modified accrual basis of accounting results in the following entry:

Taxes Receivable	1,500,000	
Allowance for Uncollectible Taxes		30,000
Revenues-Taxes		1,470,000

(5) Purchase orders for goods and services were issued totaling $1,200,000.

| Encumbrances | 1,200,000 | |
| Reserve for Encumbrances | | 1,200,000 |

(6) Invoices for goods and services previously ordered were received totaling $1,160,000. This amount included $75,000 for orders placed in the preceding year, which had been estimated at $65,000 and $1,085,000 for orders placed in the current year, which had been estimated at $1,070,000.

| Reserve for Encumbrances—Prior Year | 65,000 | |
| Encumbrances—Prior Year | | 65,000 |

| Reserve for Encumbrances | 1,070,000 | |
| Encumbrances | | 1,070,000 |

(Reverses previously recorded encumbrances.)

| Expenditures | 1,160,000 | |
| Vouchers payable | | 1,160,000 |

(Records actuals invoice amounts as expenditures.)

(7) Orders were placed for additional material and supplies inventory amounting to $20,000.

| Encumbrances | 20,000 | |
| Reserve for Encumbrances | | 20,000 |

(8) Routine services were provided and billed to outside parties amounting to $75,000.

| Accounts Receivable | 75,000 | |
| Revenues-Services | | 75,000 |

(9)   Cash was collected from property tax levies, amounting to $1,475,000 and from other accounts receivable amounting to $45,000. The amount collected from tax levies included $65,000 related to levies in the prior year.

Cash...	1,520,000	
Taxes Receivable..................................		1,410,000
Taxes Receivable—Delinquent.......................		65,000
Accounts Receivable...............................		45,000

(10) The City Council authorized the write-off of the remaining Taxes Receivable which were levied in the prior year. The 1-1-X1 trial balance included $75,000 in *Taxes Receivable,* and $65,000 was collected this year.

Allowance for Uncollectible Taxes—Delinquent............	10,000	
Taxes Receivable—Delinquent.......................		10,000

(11) License fees, permit fees, and other service charges were collected amounting to $235,000. Since these fees are not measurable in advance, the modified accrual method does not apply.

Cash...	235,000	
Revenues-Licenses, Fees, Permits and Other Service Charges.............................		235,000

(12) The inventory and related invoice was received for the previous order, amounting to $22,000. Cityville uses the purchase method to account for inventory acquisitions.

Expenditures	22,000	
Vouchers Payable		22,000
Reserve for Encumbrances	20,000	
Encumbrances		20,000

(13) Wages and salaries are accrued amounting to $200,000. These accruals are not originally recorded as encumbrances because they are paid shortly after they are incurred.

Expenditures	200,000	
Vouchers Payable		200,000

(14) The transfer from the Enterprise Fund was received.

Cash...	165,000	
Due from Enterprise Fund		165,000

(15) Outstanding vouchers payable are paid amounting to $1,500,000.

Vouchers Payable	1,500,000	
Cash..		1,500,000

(16) The transfers out to the Debt Service Fund and the Special Assessment Fund were paid.

Due to Debt Service Fund..............................	300,000	
Due to Special Assessment Fund	200,000	
Cash..		500,000

(17) Taxes Receivable not yet collected became delinquent during the year.

Taxes Receivable—Delinquent	90,000	
Allowance for Uncollectible Taxes	30,000	
Taxes Receivable		90,000
Allowance for Uncollectible Taxes—Delinquent		30,000

(18) The grant due from the federal government was received in cash.

Cash	260,000	
Due from Federal Government		260,000

(19) Material and Supplies inventory on hand at the end of the year amounted to $32,000.

Fund Balance Reserved for Materials and Supplies	6,000	
Material and Supplies		6,000

Once these entries are posted to the respective accounts, the following pre-closing trial balance is derived.

MUNICIPALITY OF CITYVILLE
Pre-Closing Trial Balance
December 31, 19X1

	Debit	Credit
Cash	330,000	
Accounts receivable	59,000	
Material and supplies	32,000	
Taxes receivable—delinquent	90,000	
Expenditures	1,382,000	
Encumbrances	130,000	
Transfers out	500,000	
Estimated revenues	2,200,000	
Allowance for uncollectible taxes—delinquent		30,000
Vouchers payable		67,000
Revenues-taxes		1,470,000
Revenues-services		75,000
Revenues-licenses, fees, permits and other service charges		235,000
Transfers in		165,000
Appropriations		2,150,000
Unreserved fund balance		369,000
Reserve for material and supplies		32,000
Reserve for encumbrances		130,000
	4,723,000	4,723,000

The closing process is then performed to clear all nominal accounts (revenues, expenditures and budgetary accounts, transfers in and out, and the encumbrances memorandum accounts) to zero balances and to reclassify the Reserve for Encumbrances as a reserved portion of the fund balance.

Illustration 20–1

MUNICIPALITY OF CITYVILLE
General Fund Balance Sheet
December 31, 19X1

Assets

Cash		$330,000
Accounts receivable		59,000
Material and supplies		32,000
Taxes receivable—delinquent	90,000	
Allowance for uncollectible taxes—delinquent	(30,000)	60,000
Total assets		$481,000

Liabilities and Fund Balance

Vouchers payable	$ 67,000
Fund balance reserved for material and supplies	32,000
Fund balance reserved for encumbrances	130,000
Unreserved fund balance	252,000
Total liabilities and fund balance	$481,000

MUNICIPALITY OF CITYVILLE
General Fund Statement of Revenues,
Expenditures, and Changes in Fund Balance
For the Fiscal Year Ended December 31, 19X1

Revenues:	
Taxes	$1,470,000
Services	75,000
Licenses, fees, permits, and other service charges	235,000
Total revenues	1,780,000
Expenditures (although not indicated here, expenditures should be subcategorized by governmental function. See Illustration 20–3 at the end of the chapter for an example of functional subcategories.)	1,382,000
Excess revenues over expenditures	398,000
Other financing sources (uses):	
Operating transfers in	165,000
Operating transfers out	(500,000)
Total other financing sources (uses)	(335,000)
Excess of revenues and other sources over expenditures and other uses	63,000
Other changes in the unreserved fund balance:	
Increase in fund balance reserved for encumbrances	(65,000)
Unreserved fund balance—January 1, 19X1	254,000
Unreserved fund balance—December 31, 19X1	$ 252,000

(20)   Closing Entries for 19X1.

Revenues—Taxes	1,470,000	
Revenues—Services	75,000	
Revenues—Licenses, fees, permits and other		
service charges	235,000	
Transfers In	165,000	
Unreserved Fund Balance	255,000	
Estimated Revenues		2,200,000

To close actual revenues and transfers in against
budgeted revenues.

Appropriations	2,150,000	
Expenditures		1,382,000
Transfers Out		500,000
Unreserved Fund Balance		268,000

To close actual expenditures, and transfers out against
appropriations.

Reserve for Encumbrances	130,000	
Encumbrances		130,000

To reverse the balances in the encumbrances
memorandum accounts.

Unreserved Fund Balance	130,000	
Fund Balance Reserved for Encumbrances		130,000

To record the Fund Balance Reserved for Encumbrances,
which represents a portion of the fund balance that must
be appropriated in the following year to pay for orders
placed in the preceding year.

After these closing entries are recorded, the General Fund Financial
Statements, presented in Illustration 20–1, would be drawn from the pre-
and post-closing trial balances.

Other required financial statements for Cityville would include a Statement of Revenue, Expenditures, and Changes in Fund Balance—Budget
and Actual and a Statement of Changes in Financial Position.

Accounting for Other Governmental Funds and Account Groups

The accounting procedures related to other governmental funds are similar
to those just described for the General Fund. The following sections illustrate typical transactions related to other funds and account groups.

Special Revenue Funds

Special Revenue Funds are established to account for special sources of
revenue which are to be used to finance specified activities (excluding
special assessments, major capital projects, and expendable trusts). They
are usually provided for by statute or charter. Typical activities include the
operations of public parks and schools which are administered by special
boards or commissions. The number of Special Revenue Funds utilized

should be kept to a minimum, however, since the usual activities of these funds often may be satisfactorily financed and managed through the General Fund, thereby eliminating unnecessary confusion in the financial reports and minimizing rigidities in the financial structure which hinder planning.

Once created, however, each Special Revenue Fund should be accounted for as a separate entity. Resources are restricted to the activities anticipated by the creating authority and should not be diverted to other uses. The operation of a Special Revenue Fund is usually controlled by the general budget of the governmental unit, and budgetary accounts are recommended. The accounting sequence for such a fund and the periodic financial statements are essentially the same as those prepared for the General Fund.

Illustrative Entries.   The following entries are among the more common entries of a Special Revenue Fund. Assume that a city finances a research library by levying a special property tax. In addition, $10,000 is provided annually from the General Fund to supplement operational expenses. An entry to record the budget would be as follows:

Estimated Revenues	80,000	
Appropriations		77,000
Fund Balance		3,000

If taxes levied amount to $80,000, and none are deemed to be uncollectible, the entry would be:

Taxes Receivable	80,000	
Revenues		80,000

The entry to record the amount receivable from the General Fund is:

Due from General Fund	10,000	
Operating Transfers In (from General Fund)		10,000

This entry maintains the distinction between revenues of the fund and operating transfers received from another fund.

When the library staff orders books estimated to cost $26,000, the entry is as follows:

Encumbrances	26,000	
Reserve for Encumbrances		26,000

Because of unexpected price changes, the books actually cost $27,500. The following entry is made to record receipt of the books:

Expenditures	27,500	
Vouchers Payable		27,500

Reserve for Encumbrances	26,000	
Encumbrances		26,000

Recall that more than one Special Revenue Fund may be established within a single governmental unit. The entries within each self-contained set of accounts are similar in form to those illustrated above for the research library. In addition, the closing entries for all Special Revenue Funds would be comparable to those illustrated for the General Fund, since budgetary accounts are usually employed in both types of funds.

Capital Projects Funds

Capital Projects Funds are established to account for the *receipt* and *expenditure* of all resources used for the acquisition of *major*, long-term capital additions, excluding those acquisitions accounted for in Special Assessment, Proprietary, and Trust Funds. It provides a formal accounting mechanism that assists administrators in ensuring that revenues dedicated to capital acquisition projects are used solely for that purpose, and to report thereon. Each Capital Projects Fund typically exists only for the duration of the specific project or series of related projects. Budgetary accounts usually are not employed in a Capital Projects Fund, but accounting for encumbrances is recommended.

Since the purpose of the fund is to account for the acquisition and disposition of resources, the fund usually contains accounts only for relatively liquid assets and the liabilities to be liquidated by those assets. *Neither the capital assets acquired nor any long-term debt incurred to finance the acquisition are accounted for in the Capital Projects Fund.* Rather, they are recorded in the General Fixed Assets and General Long-Term Debt Groups of accounts.

A Capital Projects Fund has three fairly common sources of financial resources: (1) transfers from other funds—usually the General Fund; (2) grants from other governmental units; and (3) the proceeds of bond issues. In the past, receipts from all three sources were classified as revenue of the Capital Projects Fund. However, the reporting of these receipts (or accruals thereof) under *Statement 1* calls for separate classification of each. Transfers from other funds would be recorded in a Transfers In account. Grants from other governmental units would be recorded as Intergovernmental Revenue. The proceeds of bond issues are reported as such in the statement of revenues, expenditures, and changes in fund balances, and thus should be recorded as Proceeds of General Obligation Bond Issue. Frequently, applicable statutory authority prohibits the issuance of bonds at a discount. Thus, the interest rate on the bonds will be adjusted to produce a small premium. If the total proceeds of the bond issue are available for the capital acquisition, the total proceeds will be credited to Proceeds of General Obligation Bond Issue. However, as is often the case, if only the par value of the bonds is available for the purchase or construction of the capital project, the par value of the bonds is credited to Proceeds of General Obligation Bond Issue, and the premium is credited to Premium on Bond Issue. This premium reflects an obligation on the part of the Capital Projects Fund to transfer this amount of resources to the fund responsible for making interest and principal payments on the bond issue—usually the Debt Service Fund.

Illustrative Entries.   The construction of a new city hall is used to provide examples of the more common entries in a Capital Projects Fund. Assume that $4,000,000 is authorized to construct the building, and that $500,000 is to be provided by the General Fund, $1,500,000 from a general obligation bond issue, and $2,000,000 from an agency of the federal government. Further, assume that the cash is received from the General Fund and the federal governmental agency (if not, the receivables would usually be accrued) and the proceeds of the bond issue are $1,600,000. The compound entry to record these transactions is:

Cash	4,100,000	
Transfers In (from General Fund)		500,000
Intergovernmental Revenues		2,000,000
Proceeds of General Obligation Bond Issue		1,500,000
Premium on Bonds		100,000

Since only $4,000,000 was authorized, the premium on the bond issue is transferred to the Debt Service Fund. This is recorded as follows:

Premium on Bonds	100,000	
Cash		100,000

The construction project is initiated by engaging an architect. The estimated fee is $120,000. Assuming encumbrance accounting is used (although budgetary accounts are not used), the commitment would be recorded:

Encumbrances	120,000	
Reserve for Encumbrances		120,000

The architect completes his work and submits a bill for $127,500. This liability is recorded in the following manner:

Reserve for Encumbrances	120,000	
Encumbrances		120,000
Expenditures	127,500	
Vouchers Payable		127,500

When the architect is paid, the following entry is made:

Vouchers Payable	127,500	
Cash		127,500

Entries like these illustrated for the architect would be made for all other expenditures on the project. Assuming that the project is completed with total expenditures of $3,800,000 and that all of the activity took place during the current fiscal year, the following closing entry would be made:

Transfers In	500,000	
Intergovernmental Revenues	2,000,000	
Proceeds of General Obligation Bond Issue	1,500,000	
Expenditures		3,800,000
Fund Balance		200,000

When all liabilities have been discharged and the project is completed, the unexpended cash of $200,000 is transferred to the Debt Service Fund, and this Capital Projects Fund is terminated:

Fund Balance	200,000	
Cash...		200,000

The new city hall is recorded in the General Fixed Asset Group of accounts at its cost of $3,800,000, and the general obligation bonds are recorded in the General Long-Term Debt Group of accounts at their par value of $1,500,000.

Debt Service Funds

If long-term debt is to be repaid from the resources of Special Assessment Funds or is issued to support the activities of Enterprise Funds, those designated funds generally account for the servicing of the debt. Regarding other long-term, governmental debt, Debt Service Funds are established to account for payments of interest, principal, and other related charges.

Budgetary accounts are often employed to record estimated interfund transfers and earnings necessary to service the debt. In this case, the Appropriations account is credited for the debt-servicing payments that must be made during the period. Earnings and transfers to the fund are credited to Revenues or Transfers In, and cash payments for interest, debt retirements, and fiscal agent service costs are debited to Expenditures. In the case of term bonds, the Debt Service Fund accumulates investments until the maturity date of the bonds, at which time its aggregate resources should be at least equal in amount to the maturity value of the bonds. The bonds are not recorded as liabilities of the Debt Service Fund until they mature, at which time the bond liability is credited and Expenditures is debited.

Illustrative Entries. The following entries are among the more common entries of a Debt Service Fund. Assume that on January 1, 6 percent bonds payable with a face value of $100,000 will mature. Interest at 6 percent will fall due on January 1 and July 1 with respect to the $1,000,000 of bonds maturing in later years.

The entry to record the budget is:

Estimated Revenues and Transfers	166,000	
Appropriations		166,000

The following entry records a transfer from the General Fund to service the debt:

Cash	166,000	
Transfers In (from General Fund)		166,000

On January 1 the entries below are made to record the entry for the liability and the subsequent payment:

Expenditures	136,000	
Bonds Payable		100,000
Interest Payable		36,000

Bonds Payable	100,000	
Interest Payable	36,000	
Cash		136,000

The July 1 $30,000 liability and payment are recorded in a like manner. At year end the closing entry is:

Transfers In	166,000	
Appropriations	166,000	
Expenditures		166,000
Estimated Revenues and Transfers		166,000

Note that the "accrued" interest on the $1,000,000 of bonds outstanding at the end of the year is *not* recorded. As was previously pointed out, this is one of the major differences between the modified accrual method and the accrual method in respect to expenditures. The liability for interest is not recorded *until it becomes due*.

Special Assessment Funds

Special Assessment Funds are used primarily to finance permanent improvements or services, such as sidewalks or road construction, which are to be paid for wholly, or in part, from special tax levies against the benefited properties. Improvements or services of this type are to be distinguished from those which benefit the entire community and are paid for from general revenues or through the issuance of general obligation bonds. For each special assessment project, a new fund is created. If the improvements are initially to be financed by bond issues (pending receipt of assessments), the bond proceeds are accounted for by this fund, as well as the assessments ultimately collected, which are then used to pay the bond interest and principal. The improvements resulting from authorization of this special tax assessment are not, however, recorded in the Special Assessment Funds. The costs incurred in the construction or purchase of the improvements are debited to Expenditures, and this account is closed to Fund Balance each fiscal year. The cost of the improvements is included in the general fixed asset group of accounts.

Budgetary accounts are usually not employed in Special Assessment Funds, but encumbrance accounting may be used.

Illustrative Entries. As a basis for illustrating some common entries in Special Assessment Funds, assume that a city council authorizes construction of sidewalks in a new subdivision. The property owners benefiting from these improvements are to be assessed for the cost, with payment to be made over five years; interest at 8 percent is charged on the unpaid balance. The fund is to issue bonds to finance the project until the assessments are collected. In order to provide initial working capital, the General Fund is to advance $25,000 to the Special Assessment Fund.

The $25,000 is received from the General Fund and recorded as follows:

Cash...	25,000	
Due to General Fund..................................		25,000

A contract is signed with a local construction company to make the improvements at a cost of $200,000.

Encumbrances..	200,000	
Reserve for Encumbrances............................		200,000

An 8 percent bond issue with face value of $200,000 is sold by the Special Assessment Fund at par. The bonds are to be redeemed through the special assessments levied on the property owners, but the full faith and credit of the governmental unit is also pledged to make the bonds more attractive to investors. The sale of bonds is recorded as follows:

Cash...	200,000	
Bonds Payable..		200,000

Note again that the long-term liability is recorded in the Special Assessment Fund because debt service is to be provided by this fund. Since the governmental unit is contingently liable for payment of the bonds, this fact should be disclosed in the notes to the financial statements of the city.

The special assessment is levied on the property owners in the amount of $200,000. This is recorded:

Assessments Receivable................................	200,000	
Revenue...		200,000

Normally, the Assessments Receivable would be broken down into current and deferred portions.

The contractor completes the improvements, and no adjustments to the contract price are required. The liability is recorded:

Reserve for Encumbrances	200,000	
Encumbrances		200,000
Expenditures	200,000	
Vouchers Payable		200,000

On the last day of the fiscal year, interest in the amount of $8,000 comes due on the bonds payable and the assessments receivable:

Expenditures	8,000	
Interest Payable		8,000
Interest Receivable	8,000	
Revenue		8,000

The closing entry for this first year of the Special Assessment Fund is as follows:

Revenue	208,000	
Expenditures		208,000

Enterprise Funds

Enterprise Funds exist primarily to finance services rendered to the public. They are typically self-supporting and include such activities as electric, gas, or water utilities, air terminal service, and public housing. The accounting for such funds follows the basic pattern of accounting for a commercial business enterprise. Revenues and *expenses* are measured on an accrual basis, and accounts for Contributed Capital and Retained Earnings are substituted for Fund Balance. Budgets are frequently prepared, and expenditures are not controlled by means of restrictive appropriations.

Fixed assets acquired and used by Enterprise Funds should be capitalized and carried in the enumeration of fund assets; their costs should be systematically allocated (charged to depreciation expense) over their estimated lives.

Financial statements of Enterprise Funds are analogous to those prepared for private enterprises. In the case of an Enterprise Fund balance sheet, fixed assets are often listed first in the enumeration of assets, and bonds payable ranked first in the order of fund liabilities. This variant from the conventional balance sheet classification sequence is adopted to accent the dominant long-term character of the funds.

Illustrative Entries.   The following entries concerning the operation of a bus service by a city are among the more common entries of an Enterprise Fund.

A summary entry recording the bus service revenue for the year would be as follows:

Cash.. 2,200,000
    Bus Service Revenue 2,200,000

The following entry records the purchase of buses on credit:

Buses in Service...................................... 230,000
    Vouchers Payable 230,000

Depreciation and other operating expenses are recorded in the same manner as for commercial organizations. At year-end the nominal accounts are closed to retained earnings.

If one fourth of the net income for the year is required to be transferred to the General Fund as of March 1 of the succeeding year and net income is $120,000, the following entry would be made:

Retained Earnings..................................... 30,000
    Due to General Fund 30,000

Internal Service Funds

Internal Service Funds (sometimes referred to as Revolving Funds, Working Capital Funds, or Intragovernmental Service Funds), are established to finance activities of a manufacturing or service nature—for example, shops and garages, central purchases, and stores departments. These functional unit subdivisions provide services primarily for the benefit of other departments of the governmental unit and are to be distinguished from activities financed primarily from the sale of products or services to the public; the latter are typically accounted for by Enterprise Funds.

An Internal Service Fund may be initially established and financed by advances from the General Fund, by the sale of bonds, or by resources contributed by two or more funds. This initial contribution may be reported as Capital, or Contributions from the X Fund. The fund operates, and is accounted for, in much the same manner as a commercial business enterprise (and an Enterprise Fund), except that its objective is to earn sufficient revenues to absorb operating costs rather than to maximize profits.

Cost accounting records aid in establishing prices for services performed by Internal Service Funds for other departments. Necessarily, the total expenditures of such a fund are limited to the amounts which various departments are authorized to spend for its services. Consequently, it is unnecessary for a legislative body to restrict its expenditures through appropriations. A formal plan or legal budget is not required, and budgetary accounts to indicate compliance with statutory provisions are unnecessary.

Fixed assets which are acquired by an Internal Service Fund are recorded as assets of the fund, as depreciation thereon must be provided for and included in the pricing base if the fund is to be kept intact.

The financial statements required for adequate reporting of an Internal Service Fund include a balance sheet and a statement of operations. The forms of these statements essentially parallel those of conventional statements for a commercial enterprise engaged in a similar activity.

Illustrative Entries.   The following entries are among the more common entries of an Internal Service Fund. Assume that a city decides to acquire and to issue all supplies centrally. The following entry illustrates the receipt of $80,000 cash and $12,600 of supplies from the General Fund:

Cash	80,000	
Inventory of Supplies	12,600	
Contribution from General Fund		92,600

Part of the cash is used to purchase a warehouse costing $50,000 (with $10,000 of this amount allocated to land) and a delivery truck costing $12,000. The purchase is recorded as follows:

Land	10,000	
Building	40,000	
Delivery Truck	12,000	
Cash		62,000

The following entries journalize the issuance of supplies costing $6,000 to the General Fund (at a markup of 25 percent on cost) and the later collection of the amount due:

Cost of Supplies Issued	6,000	
Inventory of Supplies		6,000
Due from General Fund	7,500	
Billings to Departments		7,500
Cash	7,500	
Due from General Fund		7,500

The following entry records the purchase of supplies costing $14,500 on credit:

Inventory of Supplies	14,500	
Vouchers Payable		14,500

Depreciation is recorded on the buildings and the truck as follows:

Warehousing Expenses	5,000	
Delivery Expenses	3,000	
Accumulated Depreciation—Buildings		5,000
Accumulated Depreciation—Delivery Equipment		3,000

At year-end all revenue and expense accounts are closed, and the excess of billings over costs is recorded as a credit to Retained Earnings.

Trust and Agency Funds

Trust and Agency Funds are created to account for money and property received and held by a governmental unit as trustee, or agent, for individuals or other government units. Separate accounts should be established and maintained for the transactions and balances of each Trust or Agency Fund. With the exception of Pension Funds, budgetary accounts are not required in accounting for this type of fund. Agency Funds are used primarily to account for money collected for some other entity. The accounting procedures significantly parallel those found in nongovernmental fiduciary accounting. Where the corpus of a Trust Fund is nonexpendable, a distinction between principal and income should be carefully preserved.

Illustrative Entries—Trust Funds.   The following entries are among the common entries of a nonexpendable Trust Fund in which no principal may be expended.

The receipt of a $500,000 cash gift from a wealthy citizen would be recorded:

Cash	500,000	
Endowment Principal Fund Balance		500,000

The entry to record the investment of the cash would be as follows:

Investments	500,000	
Cash		500,000

Earnings of the Trust Fund are to be expended on native trees and shrubs to be planted on city-owned land. Earnings of the fund are recorded:

Cash	30,000	
Interest Revenue		30,000
Interest Revenue	30,000	
Due to Endowment Earnings Fund		30,000

The entry to record the transfer to the Endowment Earnings Fund is:

Due to Endowment Earnings Fund	30,000	
Cash		30,000

All of the above entries are recorded in the Endowment Principal Fund. The remaining entries illustrated are recorded in the Endowment Earnings Fund.

Due from Endowment Principal Fund	30,000	
Revenues		30,000
Cash	30,000	
Due from Endowment Principal Fund		30,000
Expenditures	29,750	
Cash		29,750

The excess of revenues over expenditures is closed to the fund balance.
Illustrative Entries—Agency Funds. The following entries appear frequently in an Agency Fund. Assume that the city collects some property taxes on behalf of a separate school district. The following entry would be made to record the amount to be collected and remitted to the school district:

Taxes Receivable for Other Funds and Units..................	480,000	
Due to Other Taxing Units.............................		480,000

The collection and subsequent remittance of the school district taxes are recorded by the following entries:

Cash..	480,000	
Taxes Receivable for Other Funds and Units..............		480,000
Due to Other Taxing Units.................................	480,000	
Cash..		480,000

General Fixed Assets—A Self-Balancing Group of Accounts

The accounts for Enterprise Funds, Internal Service Funds, and Trust Funds include fixed assets which are the property of these funds. Other fixed assets of the governmental unit, however, are grouped in a general category—General Fixed Assets. These assets are frequently acquired using the proceeds of general obligation bonds, that is, they are financed from Capital Projects Funds; they may also be purchased out of general revenues, financed from special assessments, or acquired by gift. Since they are not properly regarded as assets of the acquiring fund, the cost is recorded as an Expenditure. Accordingly, this class of fixed assets is carried in a separate, self-balancing set of accounts.

Fixed assets should be valued at original cost, or, if acquired by gift, at appraised valuation at date of receipt; the contra credit(s) is made to one or more investment accounts. The investment accounts are designed to disclose the sources of the resources used to acquire the fixed assets, for example, General Fund revenues, general obligation bonds, federal grants, and so forth. Since general fixed assets are assumed to be nonproductive of taxes or other general revenues, depreciation is not usually recorded in the general accounting records. This failure to record cost expiration is a significant point of departure from profit-oriented enterprise accounting, wherein depreciation is an important factor in net income determination. Any disposition of fixed assets is recorded by reversing the entry of acquisition.

The balance sheet of the General Fixed Asset Group should disclose both the amount of fixed assets, classified by type, and the corresponding investment accounts indicating the source of the asset acquisitions. In addition, a statement of the changes in general fixed assets for the period, classified by source, function, and activity may be useful.

Illustrative Entries.   The following entries are typical of the entries made in the General Fixed Assets Group of accounts.

The city hall completed during the period (discussed on pages 854–55) would be recorded as follows:

Buildings..	3,800,000	
Investment in General Fixed Assets—Capital		
Projects Fund—General Fund Revenues.............		300,000
Investment in General Fixed Assets—Capital		
Projects Fund—Federal Grant......................		2,000,000
Investment in General Fixed Assets—Capital		
Projects Fund—Bond Issue		1,500,000

The sidewalks financed by special assessments on the property owners (discussed on pages 857–58) are recorded:

Improvements Other than Buildings	200,000	
Investment in General Fixed Assets—Special		
Assessments Fund—Property Owners Assessments ..		200,000

Additionally, we assume that land (for use in any manner desired) was received as a gift from a citizen, with a fair market value of $55,000, and an old building owned by the city with a cost of $745,000 (originally purchased with General Fund revenues) was sold for $100,000. The following entries would be made for these events:

Land...	55,000	
Investment in General Fixed Assets—Donations		55,000
Investment in General Fixed Assets—General		
Fund Revenues	745,000	
Buildings...		745,000

Note in the last entry that the amount of the proceeds of sale are not relevant to the entry in the General Fixed Assets Group of accounts. The original cost of the building is removed from these accounts, regardless of the proceeds. The proceeds would usually be recognized as revenue in the General Fund.

General Long-Term Debt—A Self-Balancing Group of Accounts

This collection of accounts is neither used to account for the proceeds from the sale of bonds, nor for the payment of principal and interest thereon. Rather, it is merely used to record the *unmatured principal* of outstanding general long-term debt (not recorded in Special Assessments, Proprietary, or Trust funds) of the governmental unit at a specific point in time. There is, however, a relationship between this group of accounts and other funds. At the time bonds are issued (the proceeds of which are

Illustration 20–2

NAME OF GOVERNMENTAL UNIT
Combined Balance Sheet—All Fund Types and Account Groups
December 31, 19X2

	Governmental Fund Types					Proprietary Fund Types		Fiduciary Fund Type	Account Groups		Totals (Memorandum Only)	
	General	Special Revenue	Debt Service	Capital Projects	Special Assessment	Enterprise	Internal Service	Trust and Agency	General Fixed Assets	General Long-Term Debt	December 31, 19X2	December 31, 19X1
Assets												
Cash	$258,500	$101,385	$43,834	$431,600	$232,185	$257,036	$29,700	$216,701	—	—	$1,570,941	$1,258,909
Cash with fiscal agent			102,000						—	—	102,000	—
Investments, at cost or amortized cost	65,000	37,200	160,990					1,239,260	—	—	1,502,450	1,974,354
Receivables (net of allowances for uncollectibles):												
Taxes	58,300	2,500	3,829					580,000	—	—	644,629	255,400
Accounts	8,300	3,300		100		29,130			—	—	40,830	32,600
Special assessments					646,035				—	—	646,035	462,035
Notes						2,350			—	—	2,350	1,250
Loans								35,000	—	—	35,000	40,000
Accrued interest	50	25	1,557		350	650		2,666	—	—	5,298	3,340
Due from other funds	2,000					2,000	12,000	11,189	—	—	27,189	17,499
Due from other governments	30,000	75,260		640,000					—	—	745,260	101,400
Advances to Internal Service Funds	65,000								—	—	65,000	75,000
Inventory of supplies, at cost	7,200	5,190				23,030	40,000		—	—	75,420	70,900
Prepaid expenses						1,200			—	—	1,200	900
Restricted assets:												
Cash						113,559			—	—	113,559	272,968
Investments, at cost or amortized cost						176,800			—	—	176,800	143,800
Land						211,100	20,000		$1,259,500	—	1,490,600	1,456,100
Buildings						447,700	60,000		2,855,500	—	3,363,200	2,836,700
Accumulated depreciation						[90,718]	[4,500]		—	—	[95,218]	[83,500]
Improvements other than buildings						3,887,901	15,000		1,036,750	—	4,939,651	3,922,200
Accumulated depreciation						[348,944]	[3,000]		—	—	[351,944]	[283,750]
Machinery and equipment						1,841,145	25,000		452,500	—	2,318,645	1,924,100
Accumulated depreciation						[201,138]	[9,400]		—	—	[210,538]	[141,900]
Construction in progress						22,713			1,722,250	—	1,744,963	1,359,606
Amount available in Debt Service Funds									—	$ 210,210	210,210	284,813
Amount to be provided for retirement of general long-term debt									—	1,889,790	1,889,790	1,075,187
Total assets	$494,350	$224,860	$312,210	$1,071,700	$878,570	$6,375,514	$184,800	$2,084,816	$7,326,500	$2,100,000	$21,053,320	$17,059,911

Liabilities and Fund Equity

Liabilities:

Vouchers payable	$118,261	$33,850	—	—	$29,000	$20,600	$131,071	$15,000	$3,350	—	—	$351,132	$223,412
Contracts payable	57,600	18,300	—	—	69,000	50,000	8,347	—	—	—	—	203,247	1,326,511
Judgments payable	—	2,000	—	—	22,600	11,200	—	—	—	—	—	35,800	32,400
Accrued liabilities	—	—	—	—	—	10,700	16,870	—	4,700	—	—	32,270	27,417
Payable from restricted assets:													
Constructional contracts	—	—	—	—	—	—	17,760	—	—	—	—	17,760	—
Fiscal agent	—	—	—	—	—	—	139	—	—	—	—	139	—
Accrued interest	—	—	—	—	—	—	32,305	—	—	—	—	32,305	67,150
Revenue bonds	—	—	—	—	—	—	48,000	—	—	—	—	48,000	52,000
Deposits	—	—	—	—	—	—	63,000	—	—	—	—	63,000	55,000
Due to other taxing units	—	—	—	—	—	—	—	—	680,800	—	—	680,800	200,000
Due to other funds	24,189	2,000	—	—	1,000	—	—	—	—	—	—	27,189	17,499
Due to student groups	—	—	—	—	—	—	—	—	1,850	—	—	1,850	1,600
Deferred revenue	15,000	—	—	—	—	—	—	—	—	—	—	15,000	3,000
Advance from General Fund	—	—	—	—	—	—	—	65,000	—	—	—	65,000	75,000
Matured bonds payable	—	—	—	100,000	—	—	—	—	—	—	—	100,000	—
Matured interest payable	—	—	—	2,000	—	—	—	—	—	—	—	2,000	—
General obligation bonds payable	—	—	—	—	—	—	700,000	—	—	—	2,100,000	2,800,000	2,110,000
Revenue bonds payable	—	—	—	—	—	—	1,798,000	—	—	—	—	1,798,000	1,846,000
Special assessment bonds payable	—	—	—	—	—	555,000	—	—	—	—	—	555,000	420,000
Total liabilities	$215,050	$56,150	—	$102,000	$121,600	$647,500	$2,815,492	$80,000	$690,700	—	$2,100,000	$6,828,492	$6,456,989
Fund equity:													
Contributed capital	—	—	—	—	—	—	$1,392,666	$95,000	—	—	—	$1,487,666	$815,000
Investment in general fixed assets	—	—	—	—	—	—	—	—	—	$7,326,500	—	7,326,500	5,299,600
Retained earnings:													
Reserved for revenue bond retirement	—	—	—	—	—	—	129,155	—	—	—	—	129,155	96,975
Unreserved	—	—	—	—	—	—	2,038,201	9,800	—	—	—	2,048,001	1,998,119
Fund balances:													
Reserved for encumbrances	$38,000	$46,500	—	—	$941,500	$185,000	—	—	—	—	—	1,211,000	410,050
Reserved for inventory of supplies	7,200	5,190	—	—	—	—	—	—	—	—	—	12,390	10,890
Reserved for advance to Internal Service Funds	65,000	—	—	—	—	—	—	—	—	—	—	65,000	75,000
Reserved for loans	—	—	—	—	—	—	—	—	50,050	—	—	50,050	45,100
Reserved for endowments	—	—	—	—	—	—	—	—	134,000	—	—	134,000	94,000
Reserved for employees' retirement system	—	—	—	—	—	—	—	—	1,426,201	—	—	1,426,201	1,276,150
Unreserved:													
Designated for debt service	—	—	—	210,210	—	46,070	—	—	—	—	—	256,280	325,888
Designated for subsequent years' expenditures	50,000	—	—	—	—	—	—	—	—	—	—	50,000	50,000
Undesignated	119,100	117,020	—	—	8,600	—	—	—	[216,135]	—	—	28,585	106,150
Total fund equity	$279,300	$168,710	—	$210,210	$950,100	$231,070	$3,560,022	$104,800	$1,394,116	$7,326,500	—	$14,224,828	$10,602,922
Total liabilities and fund equity	$494,350	$224,860	—	$312,210	$1,071,700	$878,570	$6,375,514	$184,800	$2,084,816	$7,326,500	$2,100,000	$21,053,320	$17,059,911

The notes to the financial statements are an integral part of this statement.

Source: *Statement 1: Governmental Accounting and Financial Reporting Principles* (Chicago: Municipal Finance Officers Association of the United States and Canada, 1979), pp. 30–31.

Illustration 20–3

NAME OF GOVERNMENTAL UNIT
Combined Statement of Revenues, Expenditures, and Changes in Fund Balances—
All Governmental Fund Types and Expendable Trust Funds
For the Fiscal Year Ended December 31, 19X2

	Governmental Fund Types					Fiduciary Fund Type	Totals (Memorandum Only) Year Ended	
	General	Special Revenue	Debt Service	Capital Projects	Special Assessment	Expendable Trust	December 31, 19X2	December 31, 19X1
Revenues:								
Taxes	$ 881,300	$ 189,300	$ 79,177	—	—	—	$1,149,777	$1,137,900
Special assessments levied	—	—	—	—	$240,000	—	240,000	250,400
Licenses and permits	103,000	—	—	—	—	—	103,000	96,500
Intergovernmental revenues	186,500	831,100	41,500	$1,250,000	—	—	2,309,100	1,258,800
Charges for services	91,000	79,100	—	—	—	—	170,100	160,400
Fines and forfeits	33,200	—	—	—	—	—	33,200	26,300
Miscellaneous revenues	19,500	71,625	7,140	3,750	29,095	$ 200	131,310	111,500
Total revenues	$1,314,500	$1,171,125	$127,817	$1,253,750	$269,095	$ 200	$4,136,487	$3,041,800
Expenditures:								
Current:								
General government	$ 121,805	—	—	—	—	—	$ 121,805	$ 134,200
Public safety	258,395	$ 480,000	—	—	—	—	738,395	671,300
Highways and streets	85,400	417,000	—	—	—	—	502,400	408,700
Sanitation	56,250	—	—	—	—	—	56,250	44,100
Health	44,500	—	—	—	—	—	44,500	36,600
Welfare	46,800	—	—	—	—	—	46,800	41,400
Culture and recreation	40,900	256,450	—	—	—	—	297,350	286,400
Education	509,150	—	—	—	—	$ 2,420	511,570	512,000
Capital outlay	—	—	—	$1,625,500	$313,100	—	1,938,600	803,000

Debt service:								
Principal retirement	—	—	$ 60,000	—	—	—	60,000	52,100
Interest and fiscal charges	—	—	$ 40,420	—	28,000	—	68,420	50,000
Total expenditures	$1,163,200	$1,153,450	$100,420	$1,625,500	$341,100	$ 2,420	$4,386,090	$3,039,800
Excess of revenues over [under] expenditures	$ 151,300	$ 17,675	$ 27,397	$ [371,750]	$ [72,005]	$ [2,220]	$ [249,603]	$ 2,000
Other financing sources (uses):								
Proceeds of general obligation bonds	—	—	—	$ 900,000	—	—	$ 900,000	—
Operating transfers in	—	—	—	64,500	$ 10,000	$ 2,530	77,030	$ 89,120
Operating transfers out	[74,500]	—	—	—	—	—	[74,500]	[87,000]
Total other financing sources (uses)	$ [74,500]	—	—	$ 964,500	$ 10,000	$ 2,530	$ 902,530	$ 2,120
Excess of revenues and other sources over [under] expenditures and other uses	$ 76,800	$ 17,675	$ 27,397	$ 592,750	$ [62,005]	$ 310	$ 652,927	$ 4,120
Fund balances—January 1	202,500	151,035	182,813	357,350	293,075	26,555	1,213,328	1,209,208
Fund balances—December 31	$ 279,300	$ 168,710	$210,210	$ 950,100	$231,070	$26,865	$1,866,255	$1,213,328

The notes to the financial statements are an integral part of this statement.

Source: *Statement 1: Governmental Accounting and Financial Reporting Principles* (Chicago: Municipal Finance Officers Association of the United States and Canada, 1979), p. 33.

generally accounted for through a Capital Projects Fund), a credit entry is made in the General Long-Term Debt Group of accounts to record the liability created by the issue. The offsetting debit is to an account entitled Amount to Be Provided for Payment of Principal. Annual increases in the balance of Debt Service Funds should be reflected in this group of accounts to the extent that these investment amounts are specifically designated for payment of the principal. To the extent that the Debt Service Fund accumulation relates to bond principal, Amount in Debt Service Fund is debited and Amount to Be Provided for Payment of Principal is credited. As liquidating payments are applied in reduction of bond principal out of the Debt Service Fund resources, the originating entry to record the liability is reversed to the extent of debt abatement and the appropriate contra account is credited.

For reporting purposes, a statement of general long-term debt should be prepared indicating the amount of bonds payable in future years and the amount presently available and to be provided for their retirement.

Illustrative Entries.   The following entries are among the more common entries of the General Long-Term Debt Group of accounts.

The following entry is made to record the issuance of $1,500,000 of bonds, the proceeds of which were used to construct a new city hall, as described on page 854.

Amount to Be Provided for Payment of		
Term Bonds	1,500,000	
Term Bonds Payable.		1,500,000

On page 856 an entry illustrated the transfer from the General Fund to the Debt Service Fund of $166,000 to be used to pay interest and to retire $100,000 of serial bonds. This transaction calls for the following entry in the General Long-Term Debt Group of accounts:

Amount Available in Debt Service Fund for		
Payment of Regular Serial Bonds	100,000	
Amount to Be Provided for Payment of		
Regular Serial Bonds		100,000

The above results in a reduction in the amount "to be provided." The redemption of the bonds results in the journalizing of:

Regular Serial Bonds Payable.	100,000	
Amount Available in Debt Service Fund		
for Payment of Regular Serial Bonds		100,000

Annual Financial Reports of State and Local Governments

Principle 12 of *Statement 1* recommends a comprehensive annual financial statement covering all funds and account groups of the governmental unit. The financial report should include combined and combining fund statements, as well as individual fund statements and notes to these financial statements. *Combined* statements include the financial statements of various fund types in one single statement—usually in a columnar format. Although memorandum totals are also presented, these totals do *not* reflect "consolidated" values, as interfund transactions and debts are not eliminated. The combined statements are intended to provide an overview of the governmental unit's financial position and operating results. Examples of a combined balance sheet and a combined statement of revenues, expenditures, and changes in fund balances are presented in Illustrations 20–2 and 20–3. *Combining* statements are at a lower level of aggregation, and present in columnar form the financial statements of each fund of a particular fund type. Thus, if a governmental unit has three special revenue funds, a combining balance sheet for all special revenue funds would present the assets, liabilities, and fund balances of each of the three funds, and the "totals column" of this statement would agree with the figures included for Special Revenue Funds in the combined balance sheet. *Individual* fund financial statements are prepared when it is desirable to present more detail than is available in the combining statements, or when the governmental unit only has one fund of a particular type (and thus would not prepare a combining statement).

Questions

1. What is a "fund" in a governmental accounting context?

2. Distinguish between *expendable* and *nonexpendable* funds.

3. What are the primary objectives of a governmental budget for an expendable fund?

4. Distinguish between *budgetary* and *proprietary* accounts.

5. What is the purpose of a system of encumbrances? How does it differ from a system of obligations?

6. Describe the nature and purpose of an appropriation.

7. Describe the two basic objectives of governmental accounting.

8. Describe the funds that are recommended by *Statement 1* as generally necessary in accounting for state and local governments.

9. What is the purpose of the two account groups used in accounting for state and local governments?

10. Explain the basis for recognition of revenue under the modified accrual basis of accounting.

11. Explain how operating transfers in and out of funds are different from revenues and expenditures of the funds.

12. Distinguish between *combined, combining,* and *individual* financial statements.

Exercises

Exercise 20–1

Select the best answer for the following.

1. The operations of a public library receiving the majority of its support from property taxes levied for that purpose should be accounted for in—
   a. The General Fund.
   b. A Special Revenue Fund.
   c. An Enterprise Fund.
   d. An Internal Service Fund.
   e. None of the above.
2. The liability for general obligation bonds issued for the benefit of a municipal electric company and serviced by its earnings should be recorded in—
   a. An Enterprise Fund.
   b. The General Fund.
   c. An Enterprise Fund and the General Long-Term Debt Group.
   d. An Enterprise Fund and disclosed in the notes to the financial statements.
   e. None of the above.
3. The proceeds of a federal grant made to assist in financing the future construction of an adult training center should be recorded in—
   a. The General Fund.
   b. A Special Revenue Fund.
   c. A Capital Projects Fund.
   d. A Special Assessment Fund.
   e. None of the above.
4. The receipts from a special tax levy to retire and pay interest on general obligation bonds issued to finance the construction of a new city hall should be recorded in a—
   a. Debt Service Fund.
   b. Capital Projects Fund.
   c. Revolving Interest Fund.
   d. Special Revenue Fund.
   e. None of the above.
5. The operations of a municipal swimming pool receiving the majority of its support from charges to users should be accounted for in—
   a. A Special Revenue Fund.
   b. The General Fund.
   c. An Internal Service Fund.
   d. An Enterprise Fund.
   e. None of the above.
6. The fixed assets of a central purchasing and stores department organized to serve all municipal departments should be recorded in—
   a. An Enterprise Fund and the General Fixed Assets Group.
   b. An Enterprise Fund.
   c. The General Fixed Assets Group.
   d. The General Fund.
   e. None of the above.

7. The monthly remittance to an insurance company of the lump sum of hospital-surgical insurance premiums collected as payroll deductions from employees should be recorded in—
   a. The General Fund.
   b. An Agency Fund.
   c. A Special Revenue Fund.
   d. An Internal Service Fund.
   e. None of the above.

8. Several years ago a city provided for the establishment of a sinking fund to retire an issue of general obligation bonds. This year the city made a $50,000 contribution to the sinking fund from general revenues and realized $15,000 in revenue from securities in the sinking fund. The bonds due this year were retired. These transactions require accounting recognition in—
   a. The General Fund.
   b. A Debt Service Fund and the General Long-Term Debt Group of accounts.
   c. A Debt Service Fund, the General Fund, and the General Long-Term Debt Group of accounts.
   d. A Capital Projects Fund, a Debt Service Fund, the General Fund, and the General Long-Term Debt Group of accounts.
   e. None of the above.

(AICPA adapted)

Exercise 20–2

Select the best answer for each of the following.

1. A city realized large capital gains and losses on securities in its Library Endowment Fund. In the absence of specific instructions from the donor or state statutory requirements, the general rule of law holds that these amounts should be charged or credited to—
   a. General Fund income.
   b. General Fund principal.
   c. Trust Fund income.
   d. Trust Fund principal.
   e. None of the above.

2. The activities of a central motor pool which provides and services vehicles for the use of municipal employees on official business should be accounted for in—
   a. An Agency Fund.
   b. The General Fund.
   c. An Internal Service Fund.
   d. A Special Revenue Fund.
   e. None of the above.

3. A transaction in which a municipal electric utility paid $150,000 out of its earnings for new equipment requires accounting recognition in—
   a. An Enterprise Fund.
   b. The General Fund.
   c. The General Fund and the General Fixed Assets Group of accounts.
   d. An Enterprise Fund and the General Fixed Assets Group of accounts.
   e. None of the above.

4. In order to provide for the retirement of general obligation bonds, a city invests a portion of its general revenue receipts in marketable securities. This investment activity should be accounted for in—
   a. A Trust Fund.
   b. The Enterprise Fund.
   c. A Special Assessment Fund.
   d. A Special Revenue Fund.
   e. None of the above.

5. The activities of a municipal employee retirement plan which is financed by equal employer and employee contributions should be accounted for in—
   a. An Agency Fund.
   b. An Internal Fund.
   c. A Special Assessment Fund.
   d. A Trust Fund.
   e. None of the above.

6. A city collects property taxes for the benefit of the local sanitary, park, and school districts and periodically remits collections to these units. This activity should be accounted for in—
   a. An Agency Fund.
   b. The General Fund.
   c. An Internal Service Fund.
   d. A Special Assessment Fund.
   e. None of the above.

7. A transaction in which a municipal electric utility issues bonds (to be repaid from its own operations) require accounting recognition in—
   a. The General Fund.
   b. A Debt Service Fund.
   c. Enterprise and Debt Service Funds.
   d. An Enterprise Fund, a Debt Service Fund, and the General Long-Term Debt Group of accounts.
   e. None of the above.

8. A transaction in which a municipality issued general obligation serial bonds to finance the construction of a fire station requires accounting recognition in the—
   a. General Fund.
   b. Capital Projects and General Funds.
   c. Capital Projects Fund and the General Long-Term Debt Group of accounts.
   d. General Fund and the General Long-Term Debt Group of accounts.
   e. None of the above.

9. Expenditures of $200,000 were made during the year on the fire station in item 8. This transaction requires accounting recognition in the—
   a. General Fund.
   b. Capital Projects Fund and the General Fixed Assets Group of accounts.
   c. Capital Projects Fund and the General Long-Term Debt Group of accounts.
   d. General Fund and the General Fixed Assets Group of accounts.
   e. None of the above.

(AICPA adapted)

Exercise 20–3

The statements below are based on the information from the following journal entries. Select the best answer for each statement.

The following related entries were recorded in sequence in the General Fund of a municipality:

1.	Encumbrances...	12,000	
	Reserve for Encumbrances............................		12,000
2.	Reserve for Encumbrances................................	12,000	
	Encumbrances...		12,000
3.	Expenditures..	12,350	
	Vouchers Payable.....................................		12,350

1. The sequence of entries indicates that—
   a. An adverse event was foreseen and a reserve of $12,000 was created; later the reserve was canceled, and a liability for the item was acknowledged.
   b. An order was placed for goods or services estimated to cost $12,000; the actual cost was $12,350 for which a liability was acknowledged upon receipt.
   c. Encumbrances were anticipated but later failed to materialize and were reversed. A liability of $12,350 was incurred.
   d. The first entry was erroneous and was reversed; a liability of $12,350 was acknowledged.
2. Entries similar to those for the General Fund may also appear on the books of the municipality's—
   a. General Fixed Assets Group.
   b. General Long-Term Debt Group.
   c. Trust Fund.
   d. Special Revenue Fund.
3. Assuming appropriate governmental accounting principles were followed, the entries—
   a. Occurred in the same fiscal period.
   b. Did *not* occur in the same fiscal period.
   c. Could have occurred in the same fiscal period, but it is impossible to be sure of this.
   d. Reflect the equivalent of a "prior period adjustment" had the entity concerned been one operated for profit.
4. Immediately after entry number 1 was recorded, the municipality had a balanced General Fund budget for all transactions. What would be the effect of recording entries two and three?
   a. *Not* change the balanced condition of the budget.
   b. Cause the municipality to show a surplus.
   c. Cause the municipality to show a deficit.
   d. *Not* affect the current budget but would affect the budget of the following fiscal period.

(AICPA adapted)

Exercise 20–4

The following items pertain to state and local governmental units. Select the best answer for each.

1. What type of account is used to earmark the fund balance to liquidate the contingent obligations of goods ordered but *not* yet received?
    a. Appropriations
    b. Encumbrances.
    c. Obligations.
    d. Reserve for Encumbrances.
2. Premiums received on general obligation bonds are generally transferred to what fund or group of accounts?
    a. Debt Service.
    b. General Long-Term Debt.
    c. General.
    d. Special Revenue.
3. Self-supporting activities that are provided to the public on a user charge basis are accounted for in what fund?
    a. Agency.
    b. Enterprise.
    c. Internal Service.
    d. Special Revenue.
4. A city should record depreciation as an expense in its—
    a. General Fund and Enterprise Fund.
    b. Internal Service Fund and General Fixed Assets Group of accounts.
    c. Enterprise Fund and Internal Service Fund.
    d. Enterprise Fund and Capital Projects Fund.

(AICPA adapted)

Exercise 20–5

The following items pertain to state and local governmental units. Select the best answer for each.

1. Authority granted by a legislative body to make expenditures and to incur obligations during a fiscal year is the definition of an—
    a. Appropriation.
    b. Authorization.
    c. Encumbrance.
    d. Expenditure.
2. An account for expenditures does *not* appear in which fund?
    a. Capital Projects.
    b. Enterprise.
    c. Special Assessment.
    d. Special Revenue.
3. Part of the general obligation bond proceeds from a new issuance was used to pay for the cost of a new city hall as soon as construction was completed. The remainder of the proceeds was transferred to repay the debt. Entries are needed to record these transactions in the—

a. General Fund and General Long-Term Debt Group of Accounts.

b. General Fund, General Long-Term Debt Group of accounts, and Debt Service Fund.

c. Trust Fund, Debt Service Fund, and General Fixed Assets Group of accounts.

d. General Long-Term Debt Group of accounts, Debt Service Fund, General Fixed Assets Group of accounts, and Capital Projects Fund.

4. Cash secured from property tax revenue was transferred for the eventual payment of principal and interest on general obligation bonds. The bonds had been issued when land had been acquired several years ago for a city park. Upon the transfer, an entry would *not* be made in which of the following?

a. Debt Service Fund.

b. General Fixed Assets Group of accounts.

c. General Long-Term Debt Group of accounts.

d. General Fund.

5. Equipment in general governmental service that had been constructed 10 years before by a Capital Projects Fund was sold. The receipts were accounted for as unrestricted revenue. Entries are necessary in the—

a. General Fund and Capital Projects Fund.

b. General Fund and General Fixed Assets Group of accounts.

c. General Fund, Capital Projects Fund, and Enterprise Fund.

d. General Fund, Capital Projects Fund, and General Fixed Assets Group of accounts.

(AICPA adapted)

Exercise 20–6

The following statements refer to transactions of Brockton City. Select the best answer for each of the following items.

1. In preparing the General Fund budget of Brockton City for the forthcoming fiscal year the city council appropriated a sum greater than expected revenues. This action of the council will result in—

a. A cash overdraft during that fiscal year.

b. An increase in encumbrances by the end of that fiscal year.

c. A decrease in the fund balance.

d. A necessity for compensatory offsetting action in the Debt Service Fund.

2. Brockton City's water utility, which is an enterprise fund, submits a bill for $9,000 to the General Fund for water service supplied to city departments and agencies. Submission of this bill would result in—

a. Creation of balances which will be eliminated on the city's combined balance sheet.

b. Recognition of revenue by the Water Utility Fund and of an expenditure by the General Fund.

c. Recognition of an encumbrance by both the Water Utility Fund and the General Fund.

d. Creation of a balance which will be eliminated on the city's combined statement of changes in fund balances.

3. Brockton City's water utility, which is an Enterprise Fund, transferred land and a building to the general city administration for public use at *no* charge to the city. The land was carried on the water utility books at $4,000, and the building at a cost of $30,000 on which $23,000 depreciation had been recorded. In the year of the transfer what would be the effect of the transaction?
    a. Reduce retained earnings of the water utility by $11,000 and increase the fund balance of the General Fund by $11,000.
    b. Reduce retained earnings of the water utility by $11,000 and increase the total assets in the General Fixed Assets Group by $11,000.
    c. Reduce retained earnings of the water utility by $11,000 and increase the total assets in the General Fixed Assets Group by $34,000.
    d. Have *no* effect on a combined balance sheet for the city.

4. Brockton City has approved a special assessment in accordance with applicable laws. Total assessments of $500,000, including 10 percent for the city's share of the cost, have been levied. The levy will be collected from property owners in 10 equal annual installments commencing with the current year. Recognition of the approval and levy will result in entries of
    a. $500,000 in the Special Assessment Fund and $50,000 in the General Fund.
    b. $450,000 in the Special Assessment Fund and $50,000 in the General Fund.
    c. $50,000 in the Special Assessment Fund and $50,000 in the General Fund.
    d. $50,000 in the Special Assessment Fund and *no* entry in the General Fund.

5. What would be the effect on the General Fund balance in the current fiscal year of recording a $15,000 purchase for a new fire truck out of General Fund resources, for which a $14,600 encumbrance had been recorded in the General Fund in the previous fiscal year?
    a. Reduce the General Fund balance $15,000.
    b. Reduce the General Fund balance $14,600.
    c. Reduce the General Fund balance $400.
    d. Have *no* effect on the General Fund balance.

6. Brockton City's Debt Service Fund (for term bonds) recorded required additions and required earnings for the current fiscal year of $15,000 and $7,000, respectively. The actual revenues and interest earnings were $16,000 and $6,500, respectively. What are the necessary entries to record the year's actual additions and earnings in the Debt Service Fund and in the General Long-Term Debt Group, respectively?
    a. $22,500 and $22,000.
    b. $22,000 and $22,000.
    c. $22,500 and $22,500.
    d. $22,500 and *no* entry.

7. Brockton City serves as collecting agency for the local independent school district and for a local water district. For this purpose, Brockton has created a single Agency Fund and charges the other entities a fee of 1 percent of the gross amounts collected. (The service fee is treated as General Fund revenue.) During the latest fiscal year, a gross amount of $268,000 was collected for the independent school district and $80,000 for the water district. As a consequence of the foregoing, Brockton's General Fund should—
    a. Recognize receipts of $348,000.
    b. Recognize receipts of $344,520.

  c. Record revenue of $3,480.

  d. Record encumbrances of $344,520.

8. When Brockton City realized $1,020,000 from the sale of a $1,000,000 bond issue, the entry in its Capital Project Fund was

Cash..	1,020,000	
Proceeds of General Obligation Bonds		1,000,000
Premium on Bonds.....................................		20,000

 Recording the transaction in this manner indicates that—

  a. The $20,000 *cannot* be used for the designated purpose of the fund but must be transferred to another fund.

  b. The full $1,020,000 can be used by the Capital Project Fund to accomplish its purpose.

  c. The nominal rate of interest on the bonds is below the market rate for bonds of such term and risk.

  d. A safety factor is being set aside to cover possible contract defaults on the construction.

9. What will be the balance sheet effect of recording $50,000 of depreciation in the accounts of a utility, an Enterprise Fund, owned by Brockton City?

  a. Reduce total assets of the Utility Fund and the General Fixed Assets Group by $50,000.

  b. Reduce total assets of the utility fund by $50,000 but have *no* effect on the General Fixed Assets Group.

  c. Reduce total assets of the General Fixed Assets Group by $50,000 but have *no* effect on assets of the Utility Fund.

  d. Have *no* effect on total assets of either the Utility Fund or the General Fixed Assets Group.

(AICPA adapted)

Exercise 20–7

 William Bates is executive vice president of Mavis Industries, Inc., a publicly held industrial corporation. Bates has just been elected to the city council of Gotham City. Prior to assuming office as a city councilman, he asks you, as his CPA, to explain the major differences that exist in accounting and financial reporting for a large city when compared to a large industrial corporation.

Required:

a. Describe the major differences that exist in the purpose of accounting and financial reporting and in the types of financial reports of a large city when compared to a large industrial corporation.

b. Why are inventories often ignored in accounting for local governmental units? Explain.

c. Under what circumstances should depreciation be recognized in accounting for local governmental units? Explain.

(AICPA adapted)

Exercise 20–8

a. Reference is frequently made in governmental accounting to "budgetary" and "proprietary" accounts. Define these expressions as they relate to the governmental entity. Do budgetary accounts have a parallel in commercial enterprise accounting? Does the budget occupy the same role in both accounting systems?

b. The concept of a "fund" is inherent in governmental accounting systems. Discuss the nature of this concept, and distinguish the unique characteristics of the various equities which are implicit therein.

Exercise 20–9

The accounting system of the City of Hemp is organized and operated on a fund basis. Among the types of funds used are a General Fund, a Special Revenue Fund, and an Enterprise Fund.

Required:

a. Explain the basic differences in revenue recognition between the accrual basis of accounting and the modified accrual basis of accounting as it relates to governmental accounting.

b. What basis of accounting should be used for each of the following funds. Explain.
    1. General Fund.
    2. Special Revenue Fund.
    3. Enterprise Fund.

c. How should fixed assets and long-term liabilities related to the General Fund and to the Enterprise Fund be accounted for?

d. How should the balance sheets of the General Fund, the Special Revenue Fund, and the Enterprise Fund be handled when preparing the comprehensive annual financial report? Explain.

(AICPA adapted)

Exercise 20–10

Select the best answer for each of the following.

1. A building was donated to Palm City during 19X1. It's original cost to the donor was $100,000. Accumulated depreciation at the date of the gift amounted to $60,000. Fair market value at the date of the gift was $300,000. In the general fixed assets account group, at what amount should Palm record this donated fixed asset?
    a. $300,000.
    b. $100,000.
    c. $40,000.
    d. $0.

Questions 2 through 4 are based on the following data relating to Lily Township:

Printing and binding equipment used for servicing all of Lily's departments and agencies, on a cost-reimbursement basis.............	$100,000
Equipment used for supplying water to Lily's residents	900,000
Receivables for completed sidewalks to be paid for in installments by affected property owners..	950,000

Cash received from federal government, dedicated to highway
maintenance, which must be accounted for in a separate fund 995,000

2. How much should be accounted for in a Special Revenue Fund or funds?
   a. $995,000.
   b. $1,050,000.
   c. $1,095,000.
   d. $2,045,000.
3. How much could be accounted for in an Internal Service Fund?
   a. $100,000.
   b. $900,000.
   c. $950,000.
   d. $995,000.
4. How much could be accounted for in an Enterprise Fund?
   a. $100,000.
   b. $900,000.
   c. $950,000.
   d. $995,000.

Questions 5 through 7 are based on the following data:

The City Council of Vein City adopted its budget for the year ending July
31, 1985, comprising estimated revenues of $30,000,000 and appropriations of
$29,000,000. Vein formally integrates its budget into the accounting records.

5. What entry should be made for budgeted revenues?
   a. Memorandum entry only.
   b. Debit Estimated Revenues Receivable Control, $30,000,000.
   c. Debit Estimated Revenues Control, $30,000,000.
   d. Credit Estimated Revenues Control, $30,000,000.
6. What entry should be made for budgeted appropriations?
   a. Memorandum entry only.
   b. Credit Estimated Expenditures Payable Control, $29,000,000.
   c. Credit Appropriations Control, $29,000,000.
   d. Debit Estimated Expenditures Control, $29,000,000.
7. What entry should be made for the budgeted excess of revenues over appropriations?
   a. Memorandum entry only.
   b. Credit Budgetary Fund Balance, $1,000,000.
   c. Debit Estimated Excess Revenues Control, $1,000,000.
   d. Debit Excess Revenues Receivable Control, $1,000,000.
8. The following items were among Pain Township's general fund expenditures
   during the year ended July 31, 19X1:

   Minicomputer for tax collector's office $44,000
   Equipment for Township Hall 80,000

   How much should be classified as fixed assets in Pain's general fund balance
   sheet at July 31, 19X1?
   a. $124,000.
   b. $80,000.
   c. $44,000.
   d. $0.

9. Aerial Village issued the following bonds during the year ended June 30, 19X1:

For installation of street lights, to be assessed against properties
 benefited $300,000
For construction of public swimming pool; bonds to be paid from
 pledged fees collected from pool users......................... 400,000

How much should be accounted for through debt service funds for payments of principal over the life of the bonds?

a. $0.
b. $300,000.
c. $400,000.
d. $700,000.

Questions 10 and 11 are based on the following data:

Alby Township's fiscal year ends on June 30. Alby uses encumbrance accounting. On April 5, 19X1, an approved $1,000 purchase order was issued for supplies. Alby received these supplies on May 2, 19X1, and the $1,000 invoice was approved for payment.

10. What journal entry should Alby make on April 5, 19X1, to record the approved purchase order?

		Debit	Credit
a.	Memorandum entry only	—	—
b.	Encumbrances Control	1,000	
	Fund Balance Reserved for Encumbrances.................		1,000
c.	Supplies	1,000	
	Vouchers Payable		1,000
d.	Encumbrances Control	1,000	
	Appropriations Control...................................		1,000

11. What journal entry or entries should Alby make on May 2, 19X1, upon receipt of the supplies and approval of the invoice?

		Debit	Credit
a.	Appropriations Control.....................................	1,000	
	Encumbrances Control		1,000
	Supplies	1,000	
	Vouchers Payable		1,000
b.	Supplies	1,000	
	Vouchers Payable		1,000
c.	Fund Balance Reserved for Encumbrances.....................	1,000	
	Encumbrances		1,000
	Expenditures Control....................................	1,000	
	Vouchers Payable		1,000
d.	Encumbrances Control	1,000	
	Appropriations Control.................................		1,000
	Fund Balance..	1,000	
	Vouchers Payable		1,000

(AICPA adapted)

Exercise 20–11

Select the best answer for each of the following.

1. Which of the following accounts of a governmental unit is (are) closed out at the end of the fiscal year?

	Estimated Revenues	Fund Balance
a.	No	No
b.	No	Yes
c.	Yes	Yes
d.	Yes	No

2. Which of the following accounts of a governmental unit is credit when a purchase order is approved?
    a.   Reserve for Encumbrances.
    b.   Encumbrances.
    c.   Vouchers Payable.
    d.   Appropriations.

3. Repairs that have been made for a governmental unit, and for which a bill has been received, should be recorded in the general fund as a debit to an
    a.   Expenditure.
    b.   Encumbrance.
    c.   Expense.
    d.   Appropriation.

4. A debt service fund of a municipality is an example of which of the following types of fund?
    a.   Fiduciary.
    b.   Governmental.
    c.   Proprietary.
    d.   Internal Service.

5. Revenues of a special revenue fund of a governmental unit should be recognized in the period in which the
    a.   Revenues become available and measurable.
    b.   Revenues become available for appropriation.
    c.   Revenues are billable.
    d.   Cash is received.

6. Which of the following funds of a governmental unit would use the general long-term debt account group to account for unmatured general long-term liabilities?
    a.   Special Assessment.
    b.   Capital Projects.
    c.   Trust.
    d.   Internal Service.

7. Which of the following funds of a governmental unit uses the same basis of accounting as an enterprise fund?
    a.   Special Revenue.
    b.   Internal Service.
    c.   Expendable Trust.
    d.   Capital Projects.

8. Which of the following funds of a governmental unit could use the general fixed assets account group to account for fixed assets?
    a. Internal Service.
    b. Enterprise.
    c. Trust.
    d. Special Assessment.

9. A state governmental unit should use which basis of accounting for each of the following types of funds?

	Governmental	Proprietary
a.	Cash	Modified accrual
b.	Modified accrual	Modified accrual
c.	Modified accrual	Accrual
d.	Accrual	Accrual

(AICPA adapted)

Problems

Problem 20–12

The following account balances were included in the January 1, 19X2, trial balance of the General Fund of the city of Tallwood:

Fund balance reserved for encumbrances	$20,000
Unreserved fund balance.............................	42,000

During the 19X2 fiscal year, the General Fund engaged in the following transactions:

a. The budget for the 19X2 fiscal year was adopted, with estimated revenues of $300,000 and appropriations of $293,000.
b. The general tax levy for the year was $250,000; estimated uncollectible accounts amount to $10,000.
c. Wages and salaries in the amount of $90,000 were approved for payment. (These expenditures were processed without prior encumbrance.)
d. Supplies ordered in 19X1 were received at a cost of $21,000. This closes all purchase orders from the prior year.
e. Negotiations for the purchase of a building were completed, the construction cost of which was estimated to be $150,000. The city decided to account for this building purchase through the General Fund, rather than setting up a Capital Projects Fund.
f. Payment was made for the approved vouchers in (c) and (d) above.
g. Revenue from licenses and fees in the amount of $55,000 was collected.
h. Collections of current taxes in the amount of $200,000 were received.
i. The purchase of the building in (e) above was approved for payment, the settlement price being $140,000.
j. $10,000 was received from the sale of fixed assets no longer needed.

k. An invoice of $20,000 was received for gas and electricity from the city's utility (an Enterprise Fund).

l. Orders were placed for supplies in the amount of $60,000.

Required:

a. Prepare journal entries to record these 19X2 transactions of the General Fund and indicate what other funds, if any, are affected.

b. Prepare closing entries for the General Fund.

c. Prepare an analysis of Fund Balance for 19X2.

Problem 20–13

The Sleepy Haven Township's adjusted trial balance for the General Fund at the close of its fiscal year ending June 30, 19X2, is shown following:

SLEEPY HAVEN TOWNSHIP
General Fund Trial Balance
June 30, 19X2

	Debit	*Credit*
Cash	$ 1,100	
Taxes receivable—current (Note 1)	8,200	
Allowance for uncollectible taxes—current		$ 150
Taxes receivable—delinquent	2,500	
Allowance for uncollectible taxes—delinquent.....................		1,650
Miscellaneous accounts receivable (Note 1).......................	4,000	
Allowance for uncollectible accounts.............................		400
Due from Internal Service Fund.................................	5,000	
Expenditures (Note 2)...	75,500	
Encumbrances..	3,700	
Revenues (Note 3)..		6,000
Due to Enterprise Fund		1,000
Vouchers payable...		2,000
Fund balance reserved for encumbrances—prior year		4,400
Reserve for encumbrances.....................................		3,700
Miscellaneous revenue (Note 4).................................		700
Appropriations...		72,000
Unreserved fund balance.......................................		8,000
	$100,000	$100,000

Note 1: The current tax roll and miscellaneous accounts receivable, recorded on the accrual basis as sources of revenue, amounted to $50,000 and $20,000, respectively. These items have been recorded on the books subject to a 2% provision for uncollectible accounts.

Note 2: Includes $4,250 paid during the fiscal year in settlement of all purchase orders outstanding at the beginning of the fiscal year.

Note 3: Represents the difference between the budgeted (estimated) revenues of $70,000 and the actual revenues realized during the fiscal year.

Note 4: Represents the proceeds from sale of equipment damaged by fire.

Required:

a. Prepare in columnar form an Analysis of Changes in Fund Balance for the year ending June 30, 19X2, with column headings: "Estimated," "Actual," and "Excess or Deficiency of Actual Compared with Estimated."

b. Prepare a General Fund balance sheet at June 30, 19X2.

(AICPA adapted)

Problem 20–14

The following balances relate to the General Fund of the city of Valhalla on July 1, 19X8:

Cash	$28,500	Vouchers payable...............	$12,000
Taxes receivable—		Fund balance reserved for	
delinquent	31,200	encumbrances...............	14,000
Allowance for uncollectible taxes		Fund balance reserved for	
receivable—delinquent........	[2,800]	materials and supplies	5,300
Materials and supplies	5,300	Unreserved fund balance........	30,900
	$62,200		$62,200

During the fiscal year ended June 30, 19X9, the following transactions were completed:

a. The annual budget was adopted by the city council; it provided for estimated revenues of $325,000 and appropriations of $330,000.

b. The current year's tax bill was levied in the amount of $300,000, of which $14,000 of receivable balances were estimated to be uncollectible.

c. Vouchers were approved in respect to all encumbrances of July 1, 19X8. Orders for new equipment were placed in the amount of $28,000.

d. Receivables for delinquent taxes were collected, $23,000, with interest and penalties of $460.

e. Cash of $10,000 was advanced to the General Fund by the Debt Service Fund.

f. The equipment ordered in (c) was vouchered for $30,000.

g. Vouchers were approved for wages and salaries, $225,000.

h. Vouchers were approved for the purchase of materials and supplies, $65,000.

i. Collections of $274,000 were made in respect to current year tax assessments; unpaid receivable balances were transferred to the Taxes Receivable—Delinquent account.

j. Additional collections for the issuance of licenses and permits amounted to $33,000.

k. Vouchers were paid, $330,000.

l. Orders were placed for additional materials and supplies in the amount of $20,000.

m. The materials and supplies account and the related reserve account were adjusted to reflect supplies on hand on June 30, 19X9, of $12,000.

Required:

a. Prepare journal entries for the General Fund for the transactions enumerated above.

b. Journalize closing entries for the General Fund for the fiscal year ended June 30, 19X9.

c. Prepare a balance sheet for the General Fund as of June 30, 19X9.

Problem 20–15

The Town of Sargentville uses budgetary accounts and maintains accounts for each of the following types of funds and account groups:

Symbol	Fund
A	Capital Projects Fund
B	General Long-Term Debt
C	General Fund
D	Property Accounts (General Fixed Assets)
E	Debt Service Fund
F	Special Assessment Fund
G	Special Revenue Fund
H	Trust and Agency Fund
S	Enterprise Fund
T	Internal Service Fund

The chart of accounts of the *General Fund* follows:

Symbol	Account
1	Appropriations
2	Cash
3	Due from Other Funds
4	Due to Other Funds
5	Encumbrances
6	Expenditures
7	Reserve for Encumbrances
8	Revenues
9	Revenues (estimated)
10	Vouchers Payable
11	Fund Balance
12	19X7 Taxes Receivable

The following transactions were among those occurring during 19X7:

a. The 19X7 budget was approved. It provided for $520,000 of General Fund revenue and $205,000 of school fund revenue.

b. The budgeted appropriations for the General Fund amounted to $516,000.

c. An advance of $10,000 was made from the General Fund to a fund for the operation of a central printing service used by all departments of the municipal government. (This had not been budgeted and is not expected to be repaid).

d. Taxes for General Fund revenues were levied, totaling $490,000.

e. Contractors were paid $200,000 for the construction of an office building. The payment was from proceeds of a general bond issue of 19X6.

f. Bonds of a general issue, previously authorized, were sold at par for $60,000 cash.

g. Orders were placed for supplies to be used by the health department—estimated cost, $7,500.

h. Vouchers approved for payment of salaries of town officers in the amount of $11,200. (No encumbrances are recorded for wages and salaries.)

i. The supplies ordered in (g) were received, and vouchers were approved for the invoice price of $7,480.

j. Fire equipment was purchased for $12,500, and the voucher approved.

k. A payment of $5,000 was made by the General Fund to a fund for eventual redemption of general obligation bonds.

l. Of the taxes levied in (d), $210,000 were collected.

m. Taxes amounting to $1,240, written off as uncollectible in 19X4, were collected.

n. $1,000 of the advance made in *(c)* was returned because it was not needed.

o. Supplies for general administrative use were requisitioned from the store's fund. A charge of $1,220 is made for the supplies.

p. The General Fund advanced $30,000 cash to provide temporary working capital for a fund out of which payment will be made for a new sewerage installation. Eventual financing will be by means of assessments on property holders on the basis of benefits received.

q. Equipment from the highway department was sold for $7,000 cash.

r. The town received a cash bequest of $75,000 for the establishment of a Scholarship Fund.

s. Previously approved and entered vouchers for payment of police department salaries of $6,200 and for the transfer of $500 to the Police Pension Fund were paid.

t. Receipts from licenses and fees amounted to $16,000.

Required:

Prepare a table indicating for each transaction, by means of the appropriate numerals, the account debited and the account credited in the General Fund. If a transaction requires an entry in any fund(s) other than the General Fund, indicate the fund(s) affected by the appropriate notation.

(AICPA adapted)

Problem 20–16

The following transactions represent practical situations frequently encountered in accounting for municipal governments. Each transaction is independent of the others.

1. The city council of Bernardville adopted a budget for the general operations of the government during the new fiscal year. Revenues were estimated at $695,000. Legal authorizations for budgeted expenditures were $650,000.

2. Taxes of $160,000 were levied for the Special Revenue Fund of Millstown. One percent was estimated to be uncollectible.

3. *a.* On July 25, 19X1, office supplies estimated to cost $2,390 were ordered for the city manager's office of Bullersville. Bullersville, which operates on the calendar year, does not maintain an inventory of such supplies.

   b. The supplies ordered July 25 were received on August 9, 19X1, accompanied by an invoice for $2,500.

4. On October 10, 19X1, the General Fund of Washingtonville repaid to the Utility Fund a loan of $1,000 plus $40 interest. The loan had been made earlier in the fiscal year.

5. A prominent citizen died and left 10 acres of undeveloped land to Harper City for a future school site. The donor's cost of the land was $55,000. The fair value of the land was $85,000.

6. *a.* On March 6, 19X1, Dahlstrom City issued 6 percent special assessment bonds payable March 6, 19X7, at face value of $90,000. Interest is payable annually. Dahlstrom City, which operates on the calendar year, will use the proceeds to finance a curbing project.

   b. On October 29, 19X1, the full $84,000 cost of the completed curbing project was accrued. Also, appropriate closing entries were made with regard to the project.

7. *a.* Conrad Thamm, a citizen of Basking Knoll, donated common stock valued at $22,000 to the city under a trust agreement. Under the terms of the agreement, the principal amount is to be kept intact; use of revenue from the stock is restricted to financing academic college scholarships for needy students.

   b. On December 14, 19X1, dividends of $1,100 were received on the stock donated by Mr. Thamm.

8. *a.* On February 23, 19X1, the town of Lincoln, which operates on the calendar year, issued 6 percent general obligation bonds with a face value of $300,000 payable February 23, 19X6, to finance the construction of an addition to the city hall. Total proceeds were $308,000. The excess over par that was received was transferred to the fund responsible for payments of principal and interest.

   b. On December 31, 19X1, the addition to the city hall was officially approved, the full cost of $297,000 was paid to the contractor, and appropriate closing entries were made with regard to the project. (Assume that no entries have been made with regard to the project since February 23, 19X1.)

Required:

For each transaction, prepare the necessary journal entries for *all* of the funds and groups of accounts involved. *No explanation of the journal entries is required.* Use the following headings for your working paper.

Trans- action Number	Journal Entries	Dr.	Cr.	Fund or Group of Accounts

In the far right column, indicate in which fund or group of accounts each entry is to be made, using the coding below:

Funds:
General	G
Special Revenue	SR
Capital Projects	CP
Debt Service	DS
Special Assessments	SA
Enterprise	E
Internal Service	IS
Trust and Agency	TA

Groups of accounts:
General Fixed Assets	GFA
General Long-Term Debt	LTD

(AICPA adapted)

Problem 20–17

The City of Bel Air entered into the following transactions during the year 19X1:

a. A bond issue was authorized by vote to provide funds for the construction of a new municipal building which it was estimated would cost $500,000. The bonds were to be paid in 10 equal installments from a Debt Service Fund, payments being due March 1 of each year. Any balance of the Capital Projects Fund is to be transferred directly to the Debt Service Fund.

b. An advance of $40,000 was received from the General Fund to underwrite a deposit on a land contract of $60,000. The deposit was made.

c. Bonds of $450,000 were sold for cash at 102. It was decided not to sell all of the bonds because the cost of the land was less than was expected. All of the proceeds of the bond issue were available to the capital projects fund.

d. Contracts amounting to $380,000 were let to Michela and Company, the lowest bidder, for the construction of the municipal building.

e. The temporary advance from the General Fund was repaid and the balance on the land contract was paid.

f. Based on the architect's certificate, a check for $320,000 for the work completed to date was issued.

g. Due to changes in the plans the contract with Michela and Company was revised to $440,000; the remainder of the bonds were sold at 101.

h. Before the end of the year the building had been completed and a check for $115,000 was issued to the contractor in final payment for the work.

i. Closing entries were made, and the balance in the fund was transferred to the Debt Service Fund.

Required:

a. Record the above transactions in Capital Projects Fund T-accounts. Designate the entries in the T-accounts by the letters which identify the data.

b. Prepare applicable fund balance sheets as of December 31, 19X1, considering only the proceeds and expenditures from Capital Projects Fund transactions.

(AICPA adapted)

Problem 20–18

The Cobleskill city council passed a resolution requiring a yearly cash budget by fund for the city beginning with its fiscal year ending September 30, 19X7. The city's financial director has prepared a list of expected cash receipts and disbursements, but he is having difficulty subdividing them by fund. The list follows:

Cash receipts:

Taxes:

General property	$ 685,000
School	421,000
Franchise	223,000
	$1,329,000

Licenses and permits:

Business licenses	$ 41,000
Automobile-inspection permits	24,000
Building permits	18,000
	$ 83,000

Cash receipts: (continued)

Intergovernmental revenue:

Sales tax	$1,012,000
Federal grants	128,000
State motor vehicle tax	83,500
State gasoline tax	52,000
State alcoholic beverage licenses	16,000
	$1,291,500

Charges for services:

Sanitation fees	$ 121,000
Sewer connection fees	71,000
Library revenues	13,000
Park revenues	2,500
	$ 207,500

Bond issues:

Civic center	$ 347,000
General obligation	200,000
Sewer	153,000
Library	120,000
	$ 820,000

Other:

Proceeds from the sale of investments	$ 312,000
Sewer assessments	50,000
Rental revenue	48,000
Interest revenue	15,000
	$ 425,000
	$4,156,000

Cash disbursements:

General government	$ 671,000
Public safety	516,000
Schools	458,000
Sanitation	131,000
Library	28,000
Rental property	17,500
Parks	17,000
	$1,838,500

Debt service:

General obligation bonds	618,000
Street construction bonds	327,000
School bonds	119,000
Sewage disposal plant bonds	37,200
	$1,101,200

Investments	$ 358,000
State portion of sales tax	$ 860,200

Capital expenditures:

Sewer construction (assessed area)	$ 114,100
Civic center construction	73,000
Library construction	36,000
	$ 223,100
	$4,381,000

The financial director provides you with the following additional information:

1. A bond issue was authorized in 19X6 for the construction of a civic center. The debt is to be paid from future civic center revenues and general property taxes.
2. A bond issue was authorized in 19X6 for additions to the library. The debt is to be paid from general property taxes.
3. General obligation bonds are paid from general property taxes collected by the General Fund.
4. Ten percent of the total annual school taxes represents an individually voted tax for payment of bonds the proceeds of which were used for school construction.
5. In 19X4, a wealthy citizen donated rental property to the city. Net income from the property is to be used to assist in operating the library. The net cash increase attributable to the property is transferred to the library on September 30 of each year.
6. All sales taxes are collected by the city; the state receives 85 percent of these taxes. The state's portion is remitted at the end of each month.
7. Payment of the street construction bonds is to be made from assessments previously collected from the respective property owners. The proceeds from the assessments were invested, and the principal of $312,000 will earn $15,000 interest during the coming year.
8. In 19X6, a special assessment in the amount of $203,000 was made on certain property owners for sewer construction. During fiscal 19X7, $50,000 of this assessment is expected to be collected. The remainder of the sewer cost is to be paid from a $153,000 bond issue to be sold in fiscal 19X7. Future special assessment collections will be used to pay principal and interest on the bonds.
9. All sewer and sanitation services are provided by a separate Enterprise Fund.
10. The federal grand is for fiscal 19X7 school operations.
11. The proceeds remaining at the end of the year from the sale of civic center and library bonds are to be invested.

Required:

Prepare a budget of cash receipts and disbursements by fund for the year ending September 30, 19X7. All interfund transfers of cash are to be included.

(AICPA adapted)

Problem 20–19

You were engaged to examine the financial statements of the Mayfair School District for the year ended June 30, 19X1, and were furnished the General Fund trial balance given below.

Your examination disclosed the following information:

1. The recorded estimate of losses for the current year taxes receivable was considered to be sufficient.
2. The local government unit gave the school district 20 acres of land to be used for a new grade school and a community playground. The unrecorded estimated value of the land donated was $50,000. In addition a state grant of

$300,000 was received, and the full amount was used in payment of contracts pertaining to the construction of the grade school. Purchases of classroom and playground equipment costing $22,000 were paid from general funds.

MAYFAIR SCHOOL DISTRICT
General Fund Trial Balance
June 30, 19X1

	Debit	Credit
Cash..	$ 47,250	
Taxes receivable—current year	31,800	
Estimated losses—current year taxes........................		$ 1,800
Temporary investments.....................................	11,300	
Inventory of supplies......................................	11,450	
Buildings..	1,300,000	
Estimated revenues	1,007,000	
Appropriations—operating expenses.........................		850,000
Appropriations—other expenditures		150,000
State grant revenue		300,000
Bonds payable		1,000,000
Vouchers payable		10,200
Due to Internal Service Fund...............................		950
Operating expenses:		
Administration..	24,950	
Instruction	601,800	
Other...	221,450	
Transfer to Debt Service Fund (principal and interest)	130,000	
Capital outlays (equipment).................................	22,000	
Revenues from tax levy, licenses, and fines...................		1,008,200
General Fund balance		87,850
	$3,409,000	$3,409,000

3. Five years ago, a 4 percent, 10-year, sinking fund bond issue in the amount of $1,000,000 for constructing school buildings was made and is outstanding. Interest on the issue is payable at maturity. Budgetary requirements of an annual contribution of $130,000 ($90,000 principal and $40,000 interest) and accumulated earnings to date aggregating $15,000 were accounted for in separate Debt Service Fund accounts.

4. Outstanding purchase orders for operating expenses not recorded in the accounts at year-end were as follows:

Administration	$1,000
Instruction	1,200
Other....................	600
Total	$2,800

No purchase orders were outstanding on July 1, 19X0.

5. The school district operated a central machine shop. Billings amounting to $950 were recorded in the accounts of the General Fund but not in the Internal Service Fund.

Required:
a. Prepare the formal adjusting and closing entries for the General Fund.
b. The foregoing information disclosed by your examination was recorded only in the General Fund. Prepare the formal adjusting journal entries for the (1)

General Fixed Asset Group, (2) General Long-Term Debt, and (3) Internal Service Fund, to correct the failure to record the relevant transactions of 19X1 and previous years.

c. Prepare a balance sheet at June 30, 19X1, and a statement of revenues, expenditures, and encumbrances for the fiscal year ended June 30, 19X1, for the General Fund.

(AICPA adapted)

Problem 20–20

The city of Happy Hollow has engaged you to examine its financial statements for the year ended December 31, 19X1. The city was incorporated as a municipality and began operations on January 1, 19X1. You find that a budget was approved by the city council and was recorded, but that all transactions have been recorded on the cash basis. The bookkeeper has provided an Operating Fund trial balance. Additional information is given below:

1. Examination of the appropriation-expenditure ledger revealed the following information:

	Budgeted	Actual
Personal services	$ 45,000	$38,500
Supplies	19,000	11,000
Equipment...............	38,000	23,000
Totals	$102,000	$72,500

2. Supplies and equipment in the amounts of $4,000 and $10,000, respectively, had been received, but the vouchers had not been paid at December 31.
3. At December 31, outstanding purchase orders for supplies and equipment not yet received were $1,200 and $3,800, respectively.
4. The inventory of supplies on December 31 was $1,700 by physical count. The decision was made to record the inventory of supplies. A city ordinance requires that expenditures are to be based on purchases, not on the basis of usage.
5. Examination of the revenue subsidiary ledger revealed the following information:

	Budgeted	Actual
Property taxes...........	$102,600	$ 96,000
Licenses	7,400	7,900
Fines	4,100	4,500
Totals	$114,100	$108,400

It was estimated that 5 percent of the property taxes would not be collected. Accordingly, property taxes were levied in an amount so that collections would yield the budgeted amount of $102,600.

6. On November 1, 19X1, Happy Hollow issued 8 percent General Obligation Term Bonds with $200,000 face value for a premium of $3,000. Interest is payable each May 1 and November 1 until the maturity in 10 years. The city

CITY OF HAPPY HOLLOW
Worksheet to Correct Trial Balance
December 31, 19X1

	Operating Fund Trial Balance	Adjustments		General Fund	Debt Service Fund	Capital Projects Fund	General Fixed Assets	General Long-Term Debt
		Debit	Credit					
Debits								
Cash	$238,900							
Expenditures	72,500							
Estimated revenues	114,100							
Equipment								
Encumbrances								
Inventory of supplies								
Taxes receivable—current								
Amount to be provided for the payment of term bonds								
Amount available in Debt Service Fund—term bonds								
	$425,500							
Credits								
Appropriations	102,000							
Revenues	108,400							
Bonds payable	200,000							
Premium on bonds payable	3,000							
Fund balance	12,100							
Proceeds of bond issue								
Vouchers payable								
Investment in general fixed assets—General Fund revenue								
Reserve for encumbrances								
Reserve for inventory of supplies								
Estimated uncollectible current taxes								
	$425,500							

council ordered that the cash from the bond premium be set aside and restricted for the eventual retirement of the debt principal. The bonds were issued to finance the construction of a city hall, but no contracts had been let as of December 31.

Required:

a. Complete the worksheet showing adjustments and distributions to the proper funds or groups of accounts in conformity with generally accepted accounting principles applicable to governmental entities. (Formal adjusting entries are not required.)

b. Identify the financial statements that should be prepared for the General Fund. (You are not required to prepare these statements.)

c. Draft formal closing entries for the General Fund.

(AICPA adapted)

Problem 20–21

The city of Eau Claire provides electric energy for its citizens through an operating department. All transactions of the electric department are recorded in a self-sustaining fund supported by revenue from the sales of energy. Plant expansion is financed by the issuance of bonds which are repaid out of revenues.

All cash of the electric department is held by the city treasurer. Receipts from customers and others are deposited in the treasurer's account. Disbursements are made by drawing warrants on the treasurer.

The following is the post-closing trial balance of the department as of June 30, 19X4:

Cash on deposit with city treasurer	$ 2,250,000	
Due from customers.	2,120,000	
Other current assets	130,000	
Construction in progress	500,000	
Land.	5,000,000	
Electric plant	*50,000,000	
Accumulated depreciation—electric plant.		$10,000,000
Accounts payable and accrued liabilities		3,270,000
5% electric revenue bonds		20,000,000
Accumulated earnings		26,730,000
	$60,000,000	$60,000,000

* The plant is being depreciated on the basis of a 50-year composite life.

During the year ended June 30, 19X5, the department had the following transactions:

1. Sales of electric energy—$10,700,000.
2. Purchases of fuel and operating supplies (on account)—$2,950,000.
3. Construction of miscellaneous system improvements financed from operations (on account)—$750,000.
4. Fuel consumed—$2,790,000.

5. Miscellaneous plant additions and improvements placed in service—$1,000,000 (depreciate ½ year).
6. Wages and salaries paid—$4,280,000.
7. Sale on December 31, 19X4, of 20-year, 5 percent electric revenue bonds, with interest payable semiannually—$5,000,000. '
8. Expenditures out of bond proceeds for construction of Steam Plant Unit No. 1 and control house—$2,800,000.
9. Operating materials and supplies consumed—$150,000.
10. Payments received from customers—$10,500,000.
11. Expenditures out of bond proceeds for construction of Steam Plant Unit No. 2—$2,200,000.
12. Warrants drawn on city treasurer in settlement of accounts payable—$3,045,000.
13. Warrants drawn on city treasurer for interest—$1,125,000. Interest on the bonds issued 12/31/X4 during the construction period is capitalized as part of the cost of the steam plant.
14. Steam plant is placed in service, June 30, 19X5.

Required:

A *worksheet* for the Revenue Fund of the electric department showing:

a. The balance sheet amounts at June 30, 19X4.
b. The transactions for the year.
c. The balance sheet amounts at June 30, 19X5.
d. The sources and applications of working capital during the year.

(AICPA adapted)

Problem 20–22

The following information pertains to the operations of the General Fund of the X County. Functions of this county government include operating the county jail and caring for the county courts.

Funds to finance the operations are provided from a levy of county taxes against the various towns of the county, from the state distribution of unincorporated business taxes, from board of jail prisoners assessed against the towns and against the state, and from interest on savings accounts.

The balances in the accounts of the fund on January 1, 19X1, were as follows:

Cash in savings accounts	$ 60,650
Cash in checking accounts	41,380
Cash on hand (undeposited prisoners' board receipts)	320
Inventory of jail supplies	3,070
Due from towns and state for board of prisoners	3,550
General Fund balance	108,970

The budget for the year 19X1 as adopted by the county commissioners provided for the following items of revenue and expenditure:

(1)	Town and county taxes	$20,000
(2)	Jail operating costs	55,500

(3)	Court operating costs........................	7,500
(4)	Unincorporated business tax	18,000
(5)	Board of prisoners (revenue)	5,000
(6)	Commissioners' salaries and expenses.........	8,000
(7)	Interest on savings	1,000
(8)	Miscellaneous expenses......................	1,000

General Fund balance was appropriated in sufficient amount to balance the budget. At December 31, 19X1, the jail supply inventory amounted to $5,120, cash of $380 was on hand, and $1,325 of prisoners' board bills were unpaid. The following items represent all of the transactions which occurred during the year, with all current bills vouchered and paid by December 31, 19X1:

Item (1) was transacted exactly as budgeted.	
Item (2) cash expenditures amounted to	$55,230
Item (3) amounted to	7,110
Item (4) amounted to	18,070
Item (5) billings amounted to	4,550
Item (6) amounted to	6,670
Item (7) amounted to	1,050
Item (8) amounted to	2,310

During the year, $25,000 was transferred from the savings accounts to the checking accounts.

Required:

From the above information, prepare a worksheet providing columns to show:

a. The transactions for the year.
b. Variances between budgeted and actual revenues and expenditures for the year.
c. Balance sheet of the General Fund, December 31, 19X1.

(AICPA adapted)

Problem 20–23

The general fund trial balance of the city of Soulna at December 31, 19X0, was as follows:

	Debit	*Credit*
Cash	$ 62,000	
Taxes receivable—delinquent	46,000	
Estimated uncollectible taxes—delinquent..........		$ 8,000
Stores inventory—program operations.............	18,000	
Vouchers payable................................		28,000
Fund balance reserved for stores inventory.........		18,000
Fund balance reserved for encumbrances		12,000
Unreserved fund balance.........................		60,000
	$126,000	$126,000

Collectible delinquent taxes are expected to be collected within 60 days after the end of the year. Any taxes remaining uncollected at that time are authorized to be written off by the city Board of Commissioners. Soulna uses the "purchases" method to account for stores inventory. The following data pertain to 19X1 general fund operations:

1. *Budget adopted:*

Revenues and other financing sources:	
Taxes..	$220,000
Fines, forfeits, and penalties......................	80,000
Miscellaneous revenues	100,000
Share of bond issue proceeds....................	200,000
	$600,000
Expenditures and other financing uses:	
Program operations.............................	$300,000
General administration..........................	120,000
Stores—program operations	60,000
Capital outlay..................................	80,000
Periodic transfer to special assessment fund........	20,000
	$580,000

2. Taxes were assessed at an amount that would result in revenues of $220,800, after deduction of 4 percent of the tax levy as uncollectible.

3. Orders placed but not received:

Program operations...........	$176,000
General administration........	80,000
Capital outlay	60,000
	$316,000

4. The city Board of Commissioners designated $20,000 of the unreserved undesignated fund balance for possible future appropriation for capital outlay.

5. Cash collections and transfer:

Delinquent taxes..........................	$ 38,000
Current taxes.............................	226,000
Refund of overpayment of invoice for purchase of equipment (equipment purchased during current year)	4,000
Fines, forfeits, and penalties..............	88,000
Miscellaneous revenues	90,000
Share of bond issue proceeds..............	200,000
Transfer of residual equity of a discontinued fund	18,000
	$664,000

(Note: The city Board of Commissioners authorized the write-down of the Estimated Uncollectible Taxes balance to 4 percent of the outstanding balance in Taxes Receivable. Since this write-down is to be made in the same accounting period as the initial estimate was recorded, the adjustment should be restored to revenue.)

6. Cancelled encumbrances:

	Estimated	Actual
Program operations	$156,000	$166,000
General administration	84,000	80,000
Capital outlay	62,000	62,000
	$302,000	$308,000

7. Additional vouchers:

Program operations.......................	$188,000
General administration....................	38,000
Capital outlay	18,000
Transfer to Special Assessment Fund	20,000
	$264,000

8. Alfred, a taxpayer, overpaid his 19X1 taxes by $2,000. He applied for a $2,000 credit against his 19X2 taxes. The city Board of Commissioners granted his request.
9. Vouchers paid amounted to $580,000.
10. Stores inventory on December 31, 19X1, amounted to $12,000.
11. The remaining uncollected taxes receivable assessed for 19X1 and the related allowance account are to be reclassified as delinquent.

Required:
a. Prepare journal entries to record the effects of the foregoing transactions.
b. Prepare a pre-closing trial balance as of December 31, 19X1.
c. Prepare all closing entries. Any outstanding encumbrances should be reclassified as Reserved Fund balance.
d. Prepare a General Fund balance sheet and a statement of revenues, expenditures, and changes in fund balance as of December 31, 19X1, and for the year ended December 31, 19X1, respectively.

(AICPA adapted)

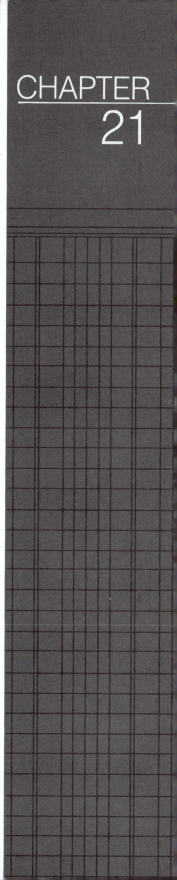

CHAPTER
21

Accounting for Other
Nonbusiness Organizations

This chapter deals with accounting for nonbusiness organizations other than state and local governmental units. The fund accounting procedures discussed in the previous chapter for governmental units provide a sound basis for understanding the principles applicable to accounting for other nonbusiness organizations. However, the procedures to be applied by nongovernment nonprofit organizations, and the inherent terminology, are different. The term *nonbusiness organization* will be used throughout this chapter in reference to nongovernment nonprofit entities which fall into one of the four categories given below:

1. Colleges and Universities.
2. Hospitals.
3. Voluntary Health and Welfare Organizations.
4. Other Nonprofit Organizations.

The first two categories are well-known. Voluntary Health and Welfare Organizations are nonprofit entities, such as mental health associations, family planning organizations, The United Way, etc., that are supported largely by public contributions and operate on a not-for-profit basis. Other nonprofit organizations include private and community foundations, performing arts organizations, cemetery organizations, civic organizations, professional associations, private elementary and secondary schools, and other truly nonprofit organizations not included in the other three categories. A characteristic common to all nonbusiness organizations is that, unlike profit-oriented enterprises, they are operated for the benefit of outside parties, rather than for the sole benefit of proprietors or investors. Therefore, the concept of profit, or net income, is not meaningful. Instead, management is concerned with the efficient and rational allocation of resources which are provided by outside contributors.

Authoritative Pronouncements

During the early 1970s, the AICPA issued three *Industry Audit Guides* which have become authoritative references of accounting procedures applicable to nonbusiness organizations. Unlike FASB Statements and Accounting Principles Board Opinions, these audit guides are not "accounting standards." They are, however, considered substantial sources of authoritative support for accounting procedures applicable to nonbusiness organizations. In addition to the audit guides, the AICPA issued a *Statement of Position* (*SOP*) in 1978 that represents an authoritative source of accounting principles and reporting standards applicable to other nonprofit organizations not covered by the audit guides. These authoritative documents are listed below, under the respective category to which they apply:

1. Colleges and Universities—*Audits of Colleges and Universities,* 2d ed. (AICPA, 1975).
2. Hospitals—*Hospital Audit Guide,* 4th ed. (AICPA, 1982).
3. Voluntary Health and Welfare Organizations—*Audits of Voluntary Health and Welfare Organizations* (AICPA, 1974).
4. Other Nonprofit Organizations—*Statement of Position 78-10,* "Accounting Principles and Reporting Practices for Certain Nonprofit Organizations," (AICPA, 1979).

Several AICPA *SOP*s have been issued as amendments to the audit guides in an effort to establish consistency among them. In 1979, the FASB announced, in *Statement of Financial Accounting Standards No. 32,* its intent to study these audit guides and *SOP*s with the objective of rethinking the issues and releasing new standards related to nonbusiness organizations.

During 1980, the FASB issued *Statement of Financial Accounting Concepts No. 4 (SFAC No. 4),* "Objectives of Financial Reporting by Nonbusiness Organizations." *SFAC No. 4* represents the FASB's attempt to define a conceptual framework of financial accounting by nonbusiness organizations. The *Statement* sets forth seven objectives of financial reporting by nonbusiness organizations, which are given below in summary form:

—Financial reporting by nonbusiness organizations should provide information that is useful to present and potential resource providers and other users in making rational decisions about the allocation of resources to those organizations.

—Financial reporting should provide information to help present and potential resource providers and other users in assessing the services that a nonbusiness organization provides and its ability to continue to provide those services.

—Financial reporting should provide information that is useful to present and potential resource providers and other users in assessing how managers of a nonbusiness organization have discharged their stewardship responsibilities and about other aspects of their performance.

—Financial reporting should provide information about the economic resources, obligations, and net resources of an organization, and the effects of transactions, events, and circumstances that change resources and interests in those resources.

—Financial reporting should provide information about the performance of an organization during a period. Periodic measurement of the changes in the amount and nature of the net resources of a nonbusiness organization and information about the service efforts and accomplishments of an organization together represent the information most useful in assessing its performance.

—Financial reporting should provide information about how an organization obtains and spends cash or other liquid resources, about its borrowing and repayment of borrowing, and about other factors that may affect an organization's liquidity.

—Financial reporting should include explanations and interpretations to help users understand financial information provided.[1]

These objectives suggest that the financial reports of nonbusiness entities should focus on resource flows; that is, the resource inflows and outflows of the organization. In particular, the reports should indicate how managers have discharged their stewardship responsibilities, and how the organization obtains and expends its resources. Note that the objectives emphasize *service efforts* and *accomplishments* rather than *potential future cash flows,* which was the focus of objectives published by the FASB related to business enterprises.

To date, no statements have been issued by the FASB detailing specific accounting principles applicable to nonbusiness organizations. As progress is made through the remainder of this chapter, the reader will encounter several inconsistencies among the AICPA Audit Guides applicable to the various forms of nonbusiness organizations. Perhaps these inconsistencies will be alleviated via the adoption of future FASB Standards related to nonbusiness organizations.

Distinguishing Characteristics of Nonbusiness Organizations

In some respects, nonbusiness organizations resemble profit-oriented business enterprises, but in many ways they are different. According to *SFAC No. 4,* the "distinguishing characteristics" of nonbusiness organizations include:

> (a) receipts of significant amounts of resources from resource providers who do not expect to receive either repayment or economic benefits proportionate to resources provided, (b) operating purposes that are primarily other than to provide goods or services at a profit or profit equivalent, and (c) absence of defined ownership interests that can be sold, transferred, or redeemed, or that convey entitlement to a share of a residual distribution of resources in the event of liquidation of the organization.[2]

These distinguishing features result in transactions not encountered by profit-oriented enterprises, including the receipt of contributions and grants, and the absence of transactions with owners. As a result, the fund accounting approach introduced in the previous chapter on governmental accounting is also appropriate when accounting for other nonbusiness organizations.

---

[1] FASB, *Statement of Financial Accounting Concepts No. 4,* "Objectives of Financial Reporting by Nonbusiness Organizations" (Stamford Conn., 1980), pp. xiii–xiv.

[2] Ibid., p. x.

Funds Used by Nonbusiness Organizations

As with governmental units, the accounting *entity* for nonbusiness organizations is the fund. For some organizations, one current unrestricted fund is sufficient to account for all functions, operations, and resource allocations. An *unrestricted fund* is utilized to account for resource flows which require authorization by the board of directors, but are not restricted to specific uses by donor request. On the other hand, a current *restricted fund* would be used to account for resources that can only be applied to specific uses as specified by the donor. These funds are analogous to the General Fund and the Special Revenue Fund used by governmental units. Other funds which are used by nonbusiness organizations include:

Plant Fund (called Land, Building, and Equipment Fund for Voluntary Health and Welfare Organizations)—used to account for the acquisition of major capital assets and related long-term debt.

Loan Fund—used to account for loans provided to students and staff of colleges and universities, hospitals, etc.

Endowment Fund—comparable to a nonexpendable trust fund of a governmental unit. The income earned on fund resources is usually expendable, whereas the principal is maintained either for a specified period of time or in perpetuity.

Agency Fund—used to account for assets held in a custodial relationship.

Annuity and Life Income Fund—used to account for resources from which payments are made to designated recipients for a specific period (annuity fund) or for the duration of the recipient's lifetime (life income fund).

Accounting for the Unrestricted Fund

As mentioned previously, the unrestricted fund of a nonbusiness organization resembles the general fund of a governmental unit. The unrestricted fund would include financial resources for use in carrying out the operations of the organization in an effort to accomplish its objectives.

Accounting for Revenues

The accrual basis of accounting, as it applies to profit-oriented enterprises, also generally applies to nonbusiness organizations. Therefore, revenues are recorded when earned and classified by source. Primary sources of revenue to hospitals include patient service revenue, other operating revenue, and nonoperating revenue. For colleges and universities, revenue is provided by tuition and fees, appropriations and grants from governmental units (including the federal government), and private gifts from donors. Voluntary health and welfare organizations and other nonprofit organizations receive resources principally from contributions or from membership fees and earnings on investments.

Contributions from governmental units, other nonbusiness organizations, and individuals are categorized either as *support*, which is available for current operations, or *capital additions* which are limited in use. Capital additions were defined in the AICPAs *SOP 78-10*, as follows:

> Capital additions include nonexpendable gifts, grants, and bequests restricted by donors to endowment, plant, or loan funds either permanently or for extended periods of time. Capital additions also include legally restricted investment income and gains or losses on investments held in such funds that must be added to the principal. Capital additions do not include donor-restricted gifts for program or supporting services.[3]

Hospitals and colleges and universities accrue revenue at full amounts, even though a portion of the billed amount is to be waived. To illustrate, assume that Cityville Hospital is to record the following patient revenue for January, 19X1:

Gross patient service revenue...	$40,000
Charity allowances...	1,000
Amount to be received from WeCare, Inc., for services to indigent patients	500
Contractual adjustment allowed to Medicare	2,000
6% of gross patient service revenue is estimated as uncollectible	

Charity allowances are provided to indigent patients who cannot totally afford the care they receive. Also, hospitals often enter contracts with institutions such as the U.S. government (Medicare and Medicaid programs), state medical care programs, Blue Cross, and other private medical insurance carriers to provide adjustments to (reductions in) full billing rates. These Charity Allowances and Contractual Adjustments, along with Provisions for Uncollectible Accounts, are contrarevenue accounts which are deducted from Patient Service Revenue in the hospital's statement of activity. The entries for Cityville Hospital for January, 19X1 are:

Accounts Receivable	40,000	
Patient Service Revenue...................................		40,000
To record gross patient revenue for the month of January, 19X1.		

---

[3] AICPA, *Statement of Position 78-10*, "Accounting Principles and Reporting Practices for Certain Nonprofit Organizations" (New York, 1978), p. 19.

Accounts Receivable	500	
Charity Allowances	500	
Contractual Adjustments	2,000	
Provision for Uncollectible Accounts	2,400	
Allowances for Uncollectible Accounts		5,400

To record the allowances for uncollectible accounts estimated
for January, 19X1, including charity allowances, contractual
adjustments, and an offset to be received from WeCare, Inc.,
for care to indigent patients.

Of course, the Allowances for Uncollectible Accounts is a contra asset
account which is deducted from accounts receivable on the fund balance
sheet. An uncollectible account would be written off in the customary
fashion by debiting the allowance account and crediting Accounts Receivable.

Donated Materials and Services

In addition to earned fees and contributions, donated materials or services represent additional sources of revenue to nonbusiness organizations. Donated material would be recorded at its current fair value as
illustrated in the following journal entry to the current unrestricted fund of
Thrift Store, Inc.:

Inventory	500	
Other Donated Operating Support		500

To record the current fair value of donated clothing to
Thrift Store, Inc.

Donated services would be recorded in the unrestricted fund as salary
expense if the services are performed in an employee-employer capacity.
The donation should be measured using the salary rate currently in effect
for similar services. For example, assume an individual donates services as
a salesperson for Thrift Store, Inc., for one 40-hour week, and the usual
hourly rate for salespersons is $4 per hour. The entry to record the dona-
tion is:

Salary Expense	160	
Other Donated Operating Support		160

To record the donation of services as a salesperson for the
first week in January, 19X1.

The value assigned to donated services must be reduced by the value of
any amenities provided to the donor, such as the meals commonly provided by hospitals to volunteer nurses' aides. *SOP 78-10* established the
following criteria which must be met for donated services to qualify as
recordable (the donated service must satisfy every criteria):

> *a.* The services performed are significant and form an integral part of the
> efforts of the organization as it is presently constituted; the services

would be performed by salaried personnel if donated or contributed services were not available for the organization to accomplish its purpose; and the organization would continue this program or activity.

b. The organization controls the employment and duties of the service donors. The organization is able to influence their activities in a way comparable to the control it would exercise over employees with similar responsibilities. This includes control over time, location, nature, and performance of donated or contributed services.

c. The organization has a clearly measurable basis for the amount to be recorded.

d. The services of the reporting organization are not principally intended for the benefit of its members. Accordingly, donated and contributed services would not normally be recorded by organizations such as religious communities, professional and trade associations, labor unions, political parties, fraternal organizations, and social and country clubs.[4]

Typical donated services that do not qualify for recording include (a) participation of volunteers in philanthropic activities, (b) supplementary efforts of volunteer workers that are provided directly to beneficiaries of the organization, and (c) periodic services of volunteers in concentrated fund-raising drives.

In addition to these criteria applicable to other nonprofit organizations, colleges and universities operated by religious groups should report the value of services donated by members of the religious group.

Pledges

Pledges of future contributions are often made by donors to nonbusiness organizations. Even though pledges represent commitments made by donors, they are usually unenforceable contracts. Unrestricted pledges should be recorded as Pledges Receivable and Support Revenue by nonbusiness organizations, with the following possible exception given in "Audits of Colleges and Universities":

> Pledges of gifts, including uncollected subscriptions, subscription notes, and estate notes, should be disclosed in the notes unless they are reported in the financial statements. The notes to the financial statements should disclose the gross amounts by time periods over which the pledges are to be collected and related restrictions, if any, as to use.
>
> If the pledges are reported in the financial statements, they should be accounted for at their estimated net realizable value in the same manner as gifts received (except as to asset classification, for which pledges would be reported as a receivable), and credited to unrestricted revenues, deferred income, current restricted funds, plant funds, etc., as appropriate. The esti-

---

[4] Ibid, pp. 23–24.

mated net realizable value comprehends the present value of long-term pledges and reductions for any allowance for uncollectible pledges.[5]

Of course, when pledges are recorded, an appropriate estimation of uncollectible amounts should also be recognized in the accounts. To illustrate, assume that $18,000 of pledges are made to Thrift Store, Inc., from their fund raising drive for 19X1, and 10 percent of the pledges are estimated as uncollectible. The following entry would be recorded in the unrestricted fund:

Pledges Receivable	18,000	
Provision for Uncollectible Pledges	1,800	
Donated Support		18,000
Allowance for Uncollectible Pledges		1,800

Again, the account Provision for Uncollectible Pledges is a contrarevenue account which is deducted from Donated Support in the 19X1 statement of activity. The Allowance for Uncollectible Pledges is a contra asset applied to reduce Pledges Receivable to its estimated net realizable value.

Designated Funds

The board of directors of a nonbusiness organization has the authority to designate a portion of the unrestricted fund balance for specific uses, similar to appropriations of retained earnings by profit-oriented enterprises. These designations by the board of directors should not be confused with the *restricted fund*, which is the entity used to account for donated funds which are restricted to specific uses *by donor request*. To illustrate the accounting for designations, assume the Board of Directors of Thrift Store, Inc., earmarks $15,000 of the unrestricted fund balance for acquisition of a delivery truck to be used for picking up and transporting donated materials. The required entry to the unrestricted fund is:

Undesignated Fund Balance	15,000	
Designated Fund Balance		15,000
To record designation of a portion of the unrestricted fund balance for purchase of a delivery truck.		

The designated fund balance would be reported in the balance sheet of the unrestricted fund as a portion of the total fund balance.

Mandatory and Nonmandatory Transfers

Nonbusiness organizations frequently transfer resources between funds. The *Industry Audit Guide*, "Audits of Colleges and Universities," defines mandatory and nonmandatory transfers, as follows:

---

[5] AICPA, *Industry Audit Guide*, "Audits of Colleges and Universities" (New York, 1973), p. 8.

Mandatory Transfers. This category should include transfers from the Current Funds group to other fund groups arising out of (1) binding legal agreements related to the financing of educational plant, such as amounts for debt retirement, interest, and required provisions for renewals and replacements of plant not financed from other sources and (2) grant agreements with agencies of the federal government, donors, and other organizations to match gifts and grants to loan and other funds. Mandatory transfers may be required to be made from unrestricted or restricted current funds.

Nonmandatory Transfers. This category should include those transfers from the Current Funds group to other fund groups made at the discretion of the governing board to serve a variety of objectives, such as additions to loan funds, additions to quasi-endowment funds, general or specific plant additions, voluntary renewals and replacements of plant, and repayments on debt principal. It also may include the retransfer of resources back to current funds.[6]

The account Transfers to Other Funds is debited, and Cash is credited when resources are transferred out of a fund. The fund receiving the resources would debit Cash and credit Transfers from Other Funds. Both mandatory and nonmandatory transfers are reportedly separately in the statement of activity and in the statement of changes in fund balances.

Expenses and Expenditures

Expenses of a nonbusiness organization are recognized when incurred, under the accrual basis (e.g., when materials and services are received). Typical expenses include wages and salaries, supplies, maintenance and repairs, research and development, etc. According to the AICPA *Industry Audit Guides* and *SOP 78-10*, depreciation expense should be recognized in the statement of activity by all nonbusiness organizations with the exception of colleges and universities. "Audits of Colleges and Universities" states:

> Depreciation allowance, however, may be reported in the balance sheet and the provision for depreciation reported in the statement of changes in the balance of the investment-in-plant fund subsection of the plant funds group.[7]

In addition, *SOP 78-10* identifies as nondepreciable those assets that are *not exhaustible,* such as historical treasures, landmarks, cathedrals, and structures used as houses of worship.[8]

Assets and Liabilities

Most of the assets and liabilities of a nonbusiness organization are similar to corresponding items on the balance sheets of profit-oriented enterprises. Colleges and universities and voluntary health and welfare organi-

---

[6] Ibid., p. 104.

[7] Ibid., p. 10.

[8] SOP 78-10, p. 36.

zations account for plant assets in a separate Plant Fund. Alternatively, hospitals are required to account for plant assets in the unrestricted fund, as stated in the following excerpt from the "Hospital Audit Guide":

> Property, plant, and equipment and related liabilities should be accounted for as part of unrestricted funds, since segregation in a separate fund would imply the existence of restrictions on asset use.[9]

See Illustrations 20–3 through 20–6 at the end of this chapter for sample financial statements of various nonbusiness organizations. A thorough study of these sample financial statements will reveal the inconsistencies among the AICPA *Industry Audit Guides*, and will aid the reader in understanding the accounting principles applicable to the related nonbusiness organization.

Accounting for Restricted Fund

Like the unrestricted fund, the resources of a restricted fund are generally available for current use. However, the assets of a *restricted fund* are expendable only as authorized by the donor. Restricted funds of hospitals can include (1) funds for specific operating purposes, (2) funds for additions to property, plant, and equipment, and endowment funds, per the AICPAs "Hospital Audit Guide."[10] Alternatively, restricted funds of colleges and universities and voluntary health and welfare organizations are limited to specific operating uses by their respective audit guides.

Resources contained in restricted funds are obtained from (1) restricted donations and grants from individuals or governmental units, (2) revenue from restricted fund investments, (3) gains on sales of investments in the restricted funds, and (4) restricted income from endowment funds.

The accounting treatments for recognizing restricted fund resource flows are outlined in Illustration 21–1 for the various types of nonbusiness organizations.

Revenue or support is not recognized in the restricted fund by colleges and universities, voluntary health and welfare organizations, and other nonprofit organizations until the related expenditure (or expense) takes place and is recorded. This achieves a "matching" of the timing of revenue and expense (expenditure) recognition in a manner similar to the application of the "matching concept" by profit-oriented enterprises.

Hospitals do not recognize revenues or expenses (expenditures) in the restricted fund. To the contrary, the restricted fund is simply used as a means of segregating restricted assets prior to their use. When the "restricted" expenditures are made, the Restricted Fund Balance is reduced as

---

[9] AICPA, *Industry Audit Guide*, "Hospital Audit Guide" (New York, 1972), p. 4.

[10] Ibid., p. 9. "Audits of Colleges and Universities," p. 16, and "Audits of Voluntary Health and Welfare Organizations," p. 2.

Illustration 21–1

ACCOUNTING TREATMENT OF RESTRICTED FUND RESOURCE FLOWS

Type of Nonbusiness Organization	Resource Inflows (Donations, etc.)	Resource Outflows (Expenditures, etc.)
Hospitals	DEBIT—Asset (i.e., Cash) CREDIT—Restricted Fund Balance	CREDIT—Asset (i.e., Cash) DEBIT—Restricted Fund Balance
Colleges and Universities......	Same as Hospitals	DEBIT—Expenditures CREDIT—Asset *and* DEBIT—Restricted Fund Balance CREDIT—Revenue or Support
Voluntary Health and Welfare Organizations	DEBIT—Asset CREDIT—Deferred Revenue or Deferred Support (Liability)	DEBIT—Expense CREDIT—Asset *and* DEBIT—Deferred Revenue or Deferred Support CREDIT—Revenue or Support
Other Nonprofit Organizations	Same as Voluntary Health and Welfare Organizations	

is the Asset account, and a corresponding entry is made in the Unrestricted Fund to record the expense (expenditure) and recognize the revenue or support.

To illustrate these varying procedures, assume that on January 1, 19X1, John Doe donated $100,000 to a nonbusiness organization, and earmarked the funds for a specified use. Assume $50,000 of these resources were applied to the specified use on April 30, 19X1. The 19X1 entries required in the restricted and unrestricted funds of the various nonbusiness organizations are illustrated below.

John Doe

For Hospitals	*Restricted Fund*		
Jan. 1	Cash	100,000	
	Restricted Fund Balance..................		100,000
	To record donation, by John Doe, of resources earmarked for a specified use.		
April 30	Restricted Fund Balance.....................	50,000	
	Cash (or Payable to Unrestricted Fund)		50,000
	To record the use of restricted fund assets for their specified purpose.		

For Hospitals

John Doe
Unrestricted Fund

April 30	Expenditures...............................	50,000	
	Support from Restricted Fund		50,000
	To recognize the expenditure of resources from the John Doe Restricted Fund for their specified purpose, and to recognize the related revenue.		

If the specified purpose was for the acquisition of a plant asset, the entries in the unrestricted fund on April 30th would include:

Cash	50,000	
Unrestricted Fund Balance		50,000
To record receipt of cash from the John Doe Restricted Fund to be used for the specified purpose of acquiring a plant asset.		
Plant Asset	50,000	
Cash		50,000
To record acquisition of plant asset.		

Unlike all other nonbusiness organizations, the operating statement of a hospital's restricted fund does not explicitly reveal the matching of revenue and expense recognition for restricted expenditures. In the judgement of the authors, this is not conceptually correct. Since restricted resources are to be used only for specified purposes, it is desirable to rely on the accounting procedures to serve as a control to ensure that the resources are not applied to purposes other than those specified by the donor. This control would be achieved if expenses or expenditures of restricted assets are recorded solely in the restricted fund.

For Colleges
and
Universities

John Doe
Restricted Fund

Jan. 1	Cash	100,000	
	Restricted Fund Balance..................		100,000
	To record donation, by John Doe, of resources earmarked for specified uses.		
April 30	Expenditures...............................	50,000	
	Cash		50,000
	To record the use of restricted assets for their specified purpose.		
	Restricted Fund Balance.....................	50,000	
	Support from Restricted Fund		50,000
	To recognize a portion of John Doe's contribution as support matched with the related expenditure recorded in the contemporaneous entry given above.		

*For Voluntary
Health and
Welfare
Organizations
and Other
Nonprofit
Organizations*

*John Doe
Restricted Fund*

Jan. 1   Cash 100,000
            Deferred Support from
                Restricted Fund 100,000
            To record donation, by John Doe, of
            resources earmarked for specific uses.

April 30   Expenses 50,000
                Cash 50,000
            To record the use of restricted fund assets for
            their specified purpose.

            Deferred Support from
                Restricted Fund 50,000
                    Support from Restricted Fund 50,000
            To recognize a portion of John Doe's
            contribution as support matched with the
            related expense recorded in the
            contemporaneous entry given above.

Contributions that are intended by donors to be used for operations of a future period, but are not limited to specific types of uses, and prepayments of service fees or other revenues are to be reported as *deferred support* or *unearned revenue* in the liabilities section of the unrestricted fund balance sheet.

Accounting for Plant Fund

As with the accounting procedures for the restricted fund, the various *Industry Audit Guides* require accounting procedures for the acquisition of plant assets which are inconsistent across the various classes of nonbusiness organizations. Hospitals account for most of the transactions related to plant assets in the unrestricted fund. The "Hospital Audit Guide"[11] states that a plant replacement and expansion fund is a subdivision of the restricted fund category of a hospital, and generally includes cash, investments, and receivables earmarked by donors for expenditures for plant assets.

For the other classes of nonbusiness organizations, a plant fund is typically used to account for (1) the accumulation of resources for the acquisition of plant assets, (2) the actual acquisition or disposal of plant assets, (3) liabilities related to such acquisitions, and (4) depreciation of the plant

---

[11] "Hospital Audit Guide," pp. 9 and 41.

assets. In addition, colleges and universities use the plant fund to account for the servicing of liabilities included in the plant fund, and *do not* record or report depreciation expense on plant assets.

The *Industry Audit Guide*, "Audits of Colleges and Universities," describes the accounting for plant funds as follows:

> The plant funds group consists of (1) funds to be used for the acquisition of physical properties for institutional purposes but unexpended at the date of reporting; (2) funds set aside for the renewal and replacement of institutional properties; (3) funds set aside for debt service charges and for the retirement of indebtedness on institutional properties; and (4) funds expended for and thus invested in institutional properties.
>
> Some institutions combine the assets and liabilities of the four subfund groups for reporting purposes; however, separate fund balances should be maintained. Resources restricted by donors or outside agencies for additions to plant should be recorded directly in the particular fund subgroup, generally unexpended plant funds.[12]

In contrast, the *Industry Audit Guide*, "Audits of Voluntary Health and Welfare Organizations," describes the plant fund accounting as follows:

> *Land, building and equipment fund* (often referred to as plant fund) is often used to accumulate the net investment in fixed assets and to account for the unexpended resources contributed specifically for the purpose of acquiring or replacing land, buildings, or equipment for use in the operations of the organization. Mortgages or other liabilities relating to these assets are also included in this fund. When additions to land, buildings, or equipment used in carrying out the organization's program and supporting services are acquired with unrestricted fund resources, the amount expended for such assets should be transferred from the unrestricted fund to the plant fund and should be accounted for as a direct addition to the plant fund balance. Gains or losses on the sale of fixed assets should be reflected as income items in the plant fund accounts. The proceeds from the sale of fixed assets that are not legally required to be reinvested in fixed assets should be transferred to the unrestricted fund; such transfers should be reflected as direct reductions and additions to the respective fund balances.[13]

To illustrate the various plant fund accounting procedures applicable to nonbusiness organizations, excluding hospitals, assume the following:

1. During early 19X1, cash is moved to the plant fund to acquire plant assets as described below:

Donations (January through March)	$ 50,000
Designations from the unrestricted fund balance (February 15 board meeting)	25,000
Liabilities (incurred January 1 for acquisition of land)	30,000
Total resources	$105,000

---

[12] "Audits of Colleges and Universities," p. 44.

[13] "Audits of Voluntary Health and Welfare Organizations," pp. 2–3.

2. Land was acquired on June 30, 19X1, as a building site for $35,000. $5,000 of the total acquisition price was used from the unrestricted unexpended fund balance, and the remainder was financed by the liability incurred on January 1, 19X1.
3. Depreciation expense on other plant assets totaled $75,000 for 19X1.
4. Principal and interest payments on the January 1, 19X1, liability are $10,000 and $3,000, respectively, and are paid on December 31, 19X1.

The entries related to these transactions are given in the side-by-side presentation in Illustration 21–2 for both classes of organizations and separated by funds.

Illustration 21–2

ACCOUNTING FOR PLANT FUND FOR 19X1

Date	Description and Accounts	Colleges and Universities Debit	Colleges and Universities Credit	Voluntary Health and Welfare Organizations Debit	Voluntary Health and Welfare Organizations Credit
		Unrestricted Fund			
February 15	To record the board designation:				
	Nonmandatory Transfer to Plant Fund	25,000			
	Transfer to Plant Fund..............			25,000	
	Cash.........................		25,000		25,000
		(Subgroup) Unexpended Plant Fund		*Land, Building, and Equipment Fund*	
January 1	To record liability incurred to acquire land:				
	Cash............................	30,000		30,000	
	Liabilities.....................		30,000		30,000
January– March	To record donations received for acquisition of plant assets:				
	Cash............................	50,000		50,000	
	Restricted Unexpended Fund Balance		50,000		
	Deferred Support				50,000
February 15	To record transfer from unrestricted fund due to board designation:				
	Cash............................	25,000		25,000	
	Unrestricted Unexpended Fund Balance		25,000		
	Transfer from Unrestricted Fund.......................				25,000

Illustration 21–2 *(concluded)*

ACCOUNTING FOR PLANT FUND FOR 19X1

Date	Description and Accounts	Colleges and Universities		Voluntary Health and Welfare Organizations	
		Debit	Credit	Debit	Credit
		(Subgroup) Unexpended Plant Fund		*Land, Building, and Equipment Fund*	
June 30	To record acquisition of land:				
	Land............................	35,000		35,000	
	Cash.........................		35,000		35,000
	To record transfer of land to investment in properties subgroup:				
	Liabilities.........................	30,000		No entry	
	Unrestricted Unexpended Fund Balance...................	5,000			
	Land.........................		35,000		
		(Subgroup) Investment in Properties		*Land, Building, and Equipment Fund*	
	To record land in the investment in properties subgroup of the Plant Fund:				
	Land............................	35,000		No Entry	
	Liability......................		30,000		
	Investment in Properties........		5,000		
During 19X1	To record depreciation expense:				
	Depreciation expense..............	No Entry		75,000	
	Accumulated Depreciation......				75,000
December 31	To record reduction of principal portion of liabilities and resultant increase in Investment in Properties:				
	Liability.........................	10,000		No Entry	
	Investment in Properties........		10,000		
		(Subgroup) Debt Retirement Fund			
	To record payment of interest and principal on liability:				
	Interest Expense...................	*		3,000	
	Liability.........................			10,000	
	Unexpended Fund Balance..........	13,000			
	Cash.........................		13,000		13,000

* Interest expense is not recognized in the Plant Fund of colleges and universities.

Accounting for Loan Fund

Loan funds are often established by nonbusiness organizations to provide loans to students and the staff of colleges and universities, hospital staff, and individuals who benefit from the operations of other nonprofit organizations (e.g., loans to minority accounting students provided by a state society of CPAs). The loans are usually *revolving* in nature, which implies that repayments are utilized to finance new loans. Loans Receivable is debited and Cash is credited when loans are paid out of the fund. The entry to set up the allowance for uncollectible loans would include a direct debit to the Fund Balance (in lieu of a contra revenue account) with an accompanying credit to the contra receivable Allowance for Uncollectible Loans account. Interest paid on the loans would be credited directly to the Fund Balance, generally when the cash is received.

Accounting for Endowment Fund

An endowment fund of a nonbusiness organization would be established to account for resources that are set aside for a period of time with the restriction that the principal remain intact. The earnings of the fund assets may be expended, or required to be accumulated with the principal until a later date. Therefore, endowment funds are similar in nature to the Nonexpendable Trust Fund of a governmental unit. A *pure endowment fund* would contain donated resources to be held in perpetuity. On the other hand, the principal of a *term endowment fund* would become expendable after a period of time specified by the donor.

Except for colleges and universities, endowments that have been designated by the board of directors out of unrestricted fund assets must be accounted for in the unrestricted fund. Transfers out of the unrestricted fund of a college or university for endowment purposes must be accounted for as a nonmandatory transfer from the current unrestricted fund, and set up in a separate Quasi-Endowment Fund.

The income earned by an endowment fund is either (*a*) transferred to the unrestricted fund where it would be recognized as nonoperating revenue, or (*b*) transferred to a restricted fund if the donor has requested it be used for specific purposes. Gains and losses on investments would be recorded as increases or decreases to the principal included in the endowment fund balance, unless otherwise specified by the donor.

Accounting for Pooled Investments

When funds of a nonbusiness organization have cash available in excess of that needed to support current operations, it is customarily invested in securities and other property. Investments can be reported at cost *or* market by nonbusiness organizations, as long as the method is consistently applied. Investments from different funds are often pooled to provide greater efficiency, investing effectiveness, and flexibility. Once pooled, these resources loose their separate fund identities. Investment income and changes in equity related to pooled investments, including realized gains and losses, are allocated on a pro rata basis to the separate funds participating in the investment pool, using the market value of the equity as of the date of the most recent equity change.

To illustrate, assume that on January 1, 19X1, the following investments were pooled:

From	Cost	Market Value at January 1, 19X1	Prorated Equity Percentage
Unrestricted Fund.............	$ 20,000	$ 25,000	12.5%
John Doe Restricted Fund......	38,000	35,000	17.5
Plant Fund	60,000	75,000	37.5
Endowment Fund.............	67,000	65,000	32.5
Totals.................	$185,000	$200,000	100.0%

The above prorated equity percentages, based on the market values of the investments at the date they were contributed to the pool, would be applied to the investment income earned by the pool in order to determine the income to be allocated to each of the given funds. If the investment pool earned $10,000 during the first six months of 19X1, the funds would be allocated the following amounts:

To	Amount Allocated
Unrestricted Fund............	$ 1,250 (12.5%)
John Doe Restricted Fund.....	1,750 (17.5%)
Plant Fund	3,750 (37.5%)
Endowment Fund............	3,250 (32.5%)
Total.................	$10,000

Each fund's cash account would be debited for these respective amounts, and the appropriate account would be credited, dependent on the type of fund and nonbusiness organization (i.e., Investment Revenue would be credited in the unrestricted fund and Deferred Support would be credited in the restricted fund of a voluntary health and welfare organization).

Realized gains and losses would be allocated to the respective funds using these prorated equity percentages, and the new equity percentages would not change. If additional investments are contributed to the pool by a fund, revised prorated equity percentages would be established using the market value of the new contribution, and the market value of the entire pool exclusive of the new contribution, as of the date of the new contribution. For example, assume that the John Doe Restricted Fund contributed additional investments to the pool on August 1, 19X1, with a fair market value on that date of $75,000. The market value of the investment pool, exclusive of the new contribution, was $300,000 on August 1. The new prorated equity percentages after the new contribution would be computed as shown below:

Funds in Pool		Adjusted Equity in Investment Pool	Prorated Equity Percentages
Unrestricted Fund (300,000 × .125)		$ 37,500	10%
John Doe Restricted Fund:			
Past equity (300,000 × .175)	$52,500		
Additional contribution (use fair value). . . .	75,000	127,500	34%
Plant Fund (300,000 × .375)		112,500	30%
Endowment Fund (300,000 × .325)		97,500	26%
Fair Value of Pool on August 1		$375,000	100%

The total fair value of the entire investment pool, exclusive of the new addition, is prorated to the separate funds using the old prorated equity percentages. The new addition is added at its current fair value. The resulting prorated equity percentages are then derived in the usual manner. These new prorated equity percentages would remain in effect until the composition of the equity in the pool changes again. Of course, the allocation of realized gains and losses would not change the percentages, even though the total equity in the pool changes. Additions to and withdrawals from the investment pool by any fund will necessarily change the prorated equity percentages.

On August 1, 19X1, the carrying values of the Investments accounts within each fund would be adjusted to reflect the new equities given above, and related gains or losses would also be recognized.

Accounting for Agency Fund

Agency funds are used to account for assets held by a nonbusiness organization in a custodial relationship with outside parties. These assets would be included in the financial statements of the nonbusiness organization, with the agency *fund balance* being reported as a liability. The assets can be disbursed only at the discretion of their owners, the outside parties.

Accounting for Annuity and Life Income Fund

An *annuity fund* would be used to account for resources that have been donated to a nonbusiness organization for the specific purpose of providing a designated beneficiary with periodic fixed payments of cash or other assets. A *life income fund* would be used if payments are to be made for the remainder of the beneficiary's life from the income earned by the fund assets. The amounts paid out of an annuity fund are fixed, whereas the income paid out of a life income fund will vary. At the end of the annuity period, or as of the date of death of the beneficiary, the fund assets would be transferred to other funds as specified by the donor, or to the unrestricted fund in the absence of any specific donor request.

To illustrate, assume that on January 1, 19X1, $50,000 cash is donated to a nonbusiness organization to establish the John Doe Annuity Fund. The donor specified that John Doe is to be paid $5,000 at the end of each of the next 10 years. Any unexpended assets after the 10th year are to be used at the discretion of the organization. The organization expects that the fund assets will earn an average of 10 percent per year. Entries to record the establishment of, and periodic changes in, the annuity fund for 19X1 are given below:

JOHN DOE ANNUITY FUND

Jan. 1	Cash	50,000	
	Annuity Payable		30,723
	Fund Balance		19,277
	To record the establishment of the John Doe Annuity Fund.		

Note that the Annuity Payable account is initially recorded at the estimated present value of the future payments, using the 10 percent discount rate. The remaining credit to the Fund Balance account reflects the estimated present value of the residual equity in the fund. If the expected interest rate of 10 percent is actually realized, then at the end of 10 years, the Annuity Payable account will contain a zero balance, and the Cash and Fund Balance accounts will contain the original $19,277 plus interest compounded annually at 10 percent.

Assuming the cash was contributed to an investment pool on January 1, 19X1, the following additional entry would be recorded in the annuity fund:

Investments	50,000	
Cash		50,000
To record the contribution of $50,000 cash to the investment pool.		

Now assume that on December 31, 19X1, the income and realized gains allocated to the annuity fund from the investment pool totaled $4,900 and $600, respectively. The required annuity payment is to be transferred to the annuity fund from the investment pool each December 31, and paid out to the annuitant. Any additional income (loss) and realized gains (losses) allocated from the investment pool is to be added to (deducted from) the annuity fund's equity in the investment pool. The entries made in the annuity fund on December 31 are given below:

Cash	5,000	
Investments	500	
Annuity Payable		5,500

To record the allocation of income and realized gains, and the
transfer of cash from the investment pool to the annuity fund.

Notice that the entire income plus the realized gain allocated from the investment pool is credited to the Annuity Payable account. This is because the balance in the account at any point in time reflects the *estimated* present value of future cash flows. In some years, the realized rate of return might exceed 10 percent, and in other years it might be lower. Any remaining balance in the Annuity Payable account after the last required annuity payment will be transferred to the Fund Balance, and then the unexpended Fund Balance will be transferred to the unrestricted fund.

The entry to record the payment to the annuitant would be:

Annuity Payable	5,000	
Cash		5,000

To record payment to annuitant on December 31.

Financial Statements of Nonbusiness Organizations

Annual reports for nonbusiness organizations should include the following financial statements:

1. Statement of activity.
2. Balance sheet.
3. Statement of changes in fund balances (may be appended to the statement of activity).

Typically, the various funds used by the organization will be reported in a *combined financial statement,* which would disclose separate fund amounts, as well as total combined amounts. The "Hospital Audit Guide" and *SOP 78-10* recommend a *statement of changes in financial position* for hospitals and other nonprofit organizations, and "Audits of Voluntary Health and Welfare Organizations" requires a *statement of functional expenses* in support of the total program and supporting services expenses for the period.

Sample sets of financial statements for each category of nonbusiness organization are presented in the remaining Illustrations 21–3 through 21–6 in this chapter. These samples should be closely scrutinized by the reader. The differences in many of the procedures required by the various audit guides are readily apparent when the samples are compared. Also, the samples reveal "systems of accounts" which would be used to record and classify revenue, expense, and expenditure transactions for each type of organization.

Illustration 21–3

SAMPLE FINANCIAL STATEMENTS FOR COLLEGES AND UNIVERSITIES

EXHIBIT A

SAMPLE EDUCATIONAL INSTITUTION
Balance Sheet
June 30, 19—
with comparative figures at June 30, 19—

Assets

	Current Year	Prior Year
Current funds:		
Unrestricted:		
Cash	$ 210,000	110,000
Investments	450,000	360,000
Accounts receivable, less allowance of $18,000 both years	228,000	175,000
Inventories, at lower of cost (first-in, first-out basis) or market	90,000	80,000
Prepaid expenses and deferred charges	28,000	20,000
Total unrestricted	1,006,000	745,000
Restricted:		
Cash	145,000	101,000
Investments	175,000	165,000
Accounts receivable, less allowance of $8,000 both years	68,000	160,000
Unbilled charges	72,000	—
Total restricted	460,000	426,000
Total current funds	1,466,000	1,171,000
Loan funds:		
Cash	30,000	20,000
Investments	100,000	100,000
Loans to students, faculty, and staff, less allowance of $10,000 current year—$9,000 prior year	550,000	382,000
Due from unrestricted current funds	3,000	—
Total loan funds	683,000	502,000
Endowment and similar funds:		
Cash	100,000	101,000
Investments	13,900,000	11,800,000
Total endowment and similar funds	14,000,000	11,901,000

Liabilities and Fund Balances

	Current Year	Prior Year
Current funds:		
Unrestricted:		
Accounts payable	$ 125,000	100,000
Accrued liabilities	20,000	15,000
Students' deposits	30,000	35,000
Due to other funds	158,000	120,000
Deferred revenue	30,000	20,000
Fund balance	643,000	455,000
Total unrestricted	1,006,000	745,000
Restricted:		
Accounts payable	14,000	5,000
Fund balances	446,000	421,000
Total restricted	460,000	426,000
Total current funds	1,466,000	1,171,000
Loan funds:		
Fund balances:		
U.S. Government grants refundable	50,000	33,000
University funds:		
Restricted	483,000	369,000
Unrestricted	150,000	100,000
Total loan funds	683,000	502,000
Endowment and similar funds:		
Fund balances:		
Endowment	7,800,000	6,740,000
Term endowment	3,840,000	3,420,000
Quasi-endowment-unrestricted	2,360,000	1,741,000
Total endowment and similar funds	14,000,000	11,901,000

Illustration 21–3 (continued)

SAMPLE EDUCATIONAL INSTITUTION
Balance Sheet
June 30, 19—
with comparative figures at June 30, 19—

EXHIBIT A

Assets

Assets	Current Year	Prior Year
Annuity and life income funds:		
Annuity funds:		
Cash	55,000	45,000
Investments	3,260,000	3,010,000
Total annuity funds	3,315,000	3,055,000
Life income funds:		
Cash	15,000	15,000
Investments	2,045,000	1,740,000
Total life income funds	2,060,000	1,755,000
Total annuity and life income funds	$5,375,000	4,810,000
Plant funds:		
Unexpended:		
Cash	$ 275,000	410,000
Investments	1,285,000	1,590,000
Due from unrestricted current funds	150,000	120,000
Total unexpended	1,710,000	2,120,000
Renewal and replacement:		
Cash	5,000	4,000
Investments	150,000	286,000
Deposits with trustees	100,000	90,000
Due from unrestricted current funds	5,000	—
Total renewal and replacement	260,000	380,000
Retirement of indebtedness:		
Cash	50,000	40,000
Deposits with trustees	250,000	253,000
Total retirement of indebtedness	300,000	293,000

Liabilities and Fund Balances

Liabilities and Fund Balances	Current Year	Prior Year
Annuity and life income funds:		
Annuity funds:		
Annuities payable	2,150,000	2,300,000
Fund balances	1,165,000	755,000
Total annuity funds	3,315,000	3,055,000
Life income funds:		
Income payable	5,000	5,000
Fund balances	2,055,000	1,750,000
Total life income funds	2,060,000	1,755,000
Total annuity and life income funds	$5,375,000	4,810,000
Plant funds:		
Unexpended:		
Accounts payable	$ 10,000	—
Notes payable	100,000	—
Bonds payable	400,000	—
Fund balances:		
Restricted	1,000,000	1,860,000
Unrestricted	200,000	260,000
Total unexpended	1,710,000	2,120,000
Renewal and replacement:		
Fund balances:		
Restricted	25,000	180,000
Unrestricted	235,000	200,000
Total renewal and replacement	260,000	380,000
Retirement of indebtedness:		
Fund balances:		
Restricted	185,000	125,000
Unrestricted	115,000	168,000
Total retirement of indebtedness	300,000	293,000

Investment in plant:			Investment in plant:		
Land	500,000		Notes payable	790,000	810,000
Land improvements	1,000,000		Bonds payable	2,200,000	2,400,000
Buildings	25,000,000		Mortgages payable	400,000	200,000
Equipment	15,000,000		Net investment in plant	38,210,000	36,540,000
Library books	100,000				
Total investment in plant	41,600,000		Total investment in plant	41,600,000	39,950,000
Total plant funds	43,870,000		Total plant funds	43,870,000	42,743,000
	500,000				
	1,110,000				
	24,060,000				
	14,200,000				
	80,000				
	39,950,000				
	42,743,000				
Agency funds:			Agency funds:		
Cash	50,000	70,000	Deposits held in custody for others	110,000	90,000
Investments	60,000	20,000			
Total agency funds	$ 110,000	90,000	Total agency funds	$ 110,000	90,000

See accompanying Summary of Significant Accounting Policies and Notes to Financial Statements

Illustration 21–3 (continued)

SAMPLE EDUCATIONAL INSTITUTION
Statement of Changes in Fund Balances
Year Ended June 30, 19—

	Current Funds		Loan Funds	Endowment and Similar Funds	Annuity and Life Income Funds	Plant Funds			
	Unrestricted	Restricted				Unexpended	Renewal and Replacement	Retirement of Indebtedness	Investment in Plant
Revenues and other additions:									
Educational and general revenues	$5,300,000								
Auxiliary enterprises revenues	2,200,000								
Expired term endowment revenues	40,000								
Expired term endowment—restricted						50,000			
Gifts and bequests—restricted		370,000	100,000	1,500,000	800,000	115,000		65,000	15,000
Grants and contracts—restricted		500,000							
Governmental appropriations—restricted						50,000			
Investment income—restricted		224,000	12,000	10,000		5,000	5,000	5,000	
Realized gains on investments—unrestricted				109,000					
Realized gains on investments—restricted			4,000	50,000		10,000	5,000	5,000	
Interest on loans receivable			7,000						
U.S. Government advances			18,000						
Expended for plant facilities (including $100,000 charged to current funds expenditures)									1,550,000
Retirement of indebtedness									220,000
Accrued interest on sale of bonds								3,000	
Matured annuity and life income funds restricted to endowment				10,000					
Total revenues and other additions	7,540,000	1,094,000	141,000	1,679,000	800,000	230,000	10,000	78,000	1,785,000

Expenditures and other deductions:									
Educational and general expenditures	4,400,000	1,014,000							
Auxiliary enterprises expenditures	1,830,000								
Indirect costs recovered		35,000							
Refunded to grantors		20,000	10,000						
Loan cancellations and write-offs			1,000						
Administrative and collection costs			1,000					1,000	
Adjustment of actuarial liability for annuities payable					75,000				
Expended for plant facilities (including noncapitalized expenditures of $50,000)						1,200,000	300,000		
Retirement of indebtedness								220,000	
Interest on indebtedness								190,000	
Disposal of plant facilities									115,000
Expired term endowments ($40,000 unrestricted, $50,000 restricted to plant)				90,000					
Matured annuity and life income funds restricted to endowment					10,000				
Total expenditures and other deductions	6,230,000	1,069,000	12,000	90,000	85,000	1,200,000	300,000	411,000	115,000
Transfers among funds—additions/(deductions):									
Mandatory:									
Principal and interest	(340,000)							340,000	
Renewals and replacements	(170,000)						170,000		
Loan fund matching grant	(2,000)		2,000						
Unrestricted gifts allocated	(650,000)		50,000	550,000		50,000			
Portion of unrestricted quasi-endowment funds investment gains appropriated	40,000			(40,000)					
Total transfers	(1,122,000)		52,000	510,000		50,000	170,000	340,000	
Net increase/(decrease) for the year	188,000	25,000	181,000	2,099,000	715,000	(920,000)	(120,000)	7,000	1,670,000
Fund balance at beginning of year	455,000	421,000	502,000	11,901,000	2,505,000	2,120,000	380,000	293,000	36,540,000
Fund balance at end of year	$ 643,000	446,000	683,000	14,000,000	3,220,000	1,200,000	260,000	300,000	38,210,000

See accompanying Summary of Significant Accounting Policies and Notes to Financial Statements

Illustration 21–3 *(continued)*

	SAMPLE EDUCATIONAL INSTITUTION		EXHIBIT C

SAMPLE EDUCATIONAL INSTITUTION   **EXHIBIT C**
Statement of Current Funds Revenues, Expenditures, and Other Changes
Year Ended June 30, 19—
With Comparative Figures for 19—

	Current Year			Prior Year Total
	Unrestricted	*Restricted*	*Total*	*Total*
Revenues:				
Educational and general:				
Student tuition and fees	$2,600,000		2,600,000	2,300,000
Governmental appropriations	1,300,000		1,300,000	1,300,000
Governmental grants and contracts	35,000	425,000	460,000	595,000
Gifts and private grants	850,000	380,000	1,230,000	1,190,000
Endowment income	325,000	209,000	534,000	500,000
Sales and services of educational departments	90,000		90,000	95,000
Organized activities related to educational departments	100,000		100,000	100,000
Other sources (if any)				
Total educational and general	5,300,000	1,014,000	6,314,000	6,080,000
Auxiliary enterprises	2,200,000		2,200,000	2,100,000
Expired term endowment	40,000		40,000	
Total revenues	7,540,000	1,014,000	8,554,000	8,180,000
Expenditures and mandatory transfers:				
Educational and general:				
Instruction and departmental research	2,820,000	300,000	3,120,000	2,950,000
Organized activities related to educational departments	140,000	189,000	329,000	350,000
Sponsored research		400,000	400,000	500,000
Other separately budgeted research	100,000		100,000	150,000
Other sponsored programs		25,000	25,000	50,000
Extension and public service	130,000		130,000	125,000
Libraries	250,000		250,000	225,000
Student services	200,000		200,000	195,000
Operation and maintenance of plant	220,000		220,000	200,000
General administration	200,000		200,000	195,000
General institutional expense	250,000		250,000	250,000
Student aid	90,000	100,000	190,000	180,000
Educational and general expenditures	4,400,000	1,014,000	5,414,000	5,370,000
Mandatory transfers for:				
Principal and interest	90,000		90,000	50,000
Renewals and replacements	100,000		100,000	80,000
Loan fund matching grant	2,000		2,000	
Total educational and general	4,592,000	1,014,000	5,606,000	5,500,000

Illustration 21–3 *(concluded)*

SAMPLE EDUCATIONAL INSTITUTION EXHIBIT C
Statement of Current Funds Revenues, Expenditures, and Other Changes
Year Ended June 30, 19—
With Comparative Figures for 19—

	Current Year			Prior Year Total
	Unrestricted	*Restricted*	*Total*	*Total*
Auxiliary enterprises:				
Expenditures	1,830,000		1,830,000	1,730,000
Mandatory transfers for:				
Principal and interest	250,000		250,000	250,000
Renewals and replacements	70,000		70,000	70,000
Total auxiliary enterprises	2,150,000		2,150,000	2,050,000
Total expenditures and mandatory transfers	6,742,000	1,014,000	7,756,000	7,550,000
Other transfers and additions/(deductions):				
Excess of restricted receipts over transfers to revenues		45,000	45,000	40,000
Refunded to grantors		(20,000)	(20,000)	
Unrestricted gifts allocated to other funds	(650,000)		(650,000)	(510,000)
Portion of quasi-endowment gains appropriated	40,000		40,000	
Net increase in fund balances	$ 188,000	25,000	213,000	160,000

See accompanying Summary of Significant Accounting Policies and Notes to Financial Statements

Source: AICPA, *Industry Audit Guide,* "Audits of Colleges and Universities" (New York, 1973), pp. 60–67.

Illustration 21–4

SAMPLE FINANCIAL STATEMENTS FOR HOSPITALS

EXHIBIT A

SAMPLE HOSPITAL
Balance Sheet
December 31, 19—
With Comparative Figures for 19—

Unrestricted Funds

Assets	Current Year	Prior Year
Current:		
Cash	$ 133,000	$ 33,000
Receivables (Note 3)	1,382,000	1,269,000
Less estimated uncollectibles and allowances	(160,000)	(105,000)
	1,222,000	1,164,000
Due from restricted funds	215,000	—
Inventories (if material, state basis)	176,000	183,000
Prepaid expenses	68,000	73,000
Total current assets	1,814,000	1,453,000
Other:		
Cash (Note 2)	143,000	40,000
Investments (Notes 1 and 2)	1,427,000	1,740,000
Property, plant, and equipment (Notes 4 and 5)	11,028,000	10,375,000
Less accumulated depreciation	(3,885,000)	(3,600,000)
Net property, plant, and equipment	7,143,000	6,775,000
Total (Note 2)	$10,527,000	$10,008,000

Liabilities and Fund Balances	Current Year	Prior Year
Current:		
Notes payable to banks	$ 227,000	$ 300,000
Current installments of long-term debt (Note 5)	90,000	90,000
Accounts payable	450,000	463,000
Accrued expenses	150,000	147,000
Advances from third-party payors	300,000	200,000
Deferred revenue	10,000	10,000
Total current liabilities	1,227,000	1,210,000
Deferred revenue—third-party reimbursement (Note 4)	200,000	90,000
Long-term debt (Note 5):		
Housing bonds	500,000	520,000
Mortgage note	1,200,000	1,270,000
Total long-term debt	1,700,000	1,790,000
Fund balance*	7,400,000	6,918,000
Total	$10,527,000	$10,008,000

Restricted Funds

Assets

Specific purpose funds:		
Cash	$ 1,260	$ 1,000
Investment (Note 1)	200,000	70,000
Grants receivable	90,000	—
Total specific purpose funds	$ 291,260	$ 71,000
Plant replacement and expansion funds:		
Cash	$ 10,000	$ 450,000
Investments (Note 1)	800,000	290,000
Pledges receivable, net of estimated uncollectibles	20,000	360,000
Total plant replacement and expansion funds	$ 830,000	$ 1,100,000
Endowment funds:		
Cash	$ 50,000	$ 33,000
Investments (Note 1)	6,100,000	3,942,000
Total endowment funds	$ 6,150,000	$ 3,975,000

Liabilities and Fund Balances

Specific purpose funds:		
Due to unrestricted funds	$ 215,000	$ —
Fund balances:		
Research grants	15,000	30,000
Other	61,260	41,000
	76,260	71,000
Total specific purpose funds	$ 291,260	$ 71,000
Plant replacement and expansion funds:		
Fund balances:		
Restricted by third-party payors	$ 380,000	$ 150,000
Other	450,000	950,000
Total plant replacement and expansion funds	$ 830,000	$ 1,100,000
Endowment funds:		
Fund balances:		
Permanent endowment	$ 4,850,000	$ 2,675,000
Term endowment	1,300,000	1,300,000
Total endowment funds	$ 6,150,000	$ 3,975,000

See accompanying Notes to Financial Statements.

* Composition of the fund balance may be shown here, on the Statement of Changes in Fund Balance (such as illustrated in Exhibit D), or in a footnote.

Illustration 21–4 *(continued)*

SAMPLE HOSPITAL		EXHIBIT B
Statement of Revenues and Expenses		
Year Ended December 31, 19—		
With Comparative Figures for 19—		

	Current Year	*Prior Year*
Patient service revenue	$8,500,000	$8,000,000
Allowances and uncollectible accounts (after deduction of related gifts, grants, subsidies, and other income—$55,000 and $40,000) (Notes 3 and 4)	(1,777,000)	(1,700,000)
Net patient service revenue	6,723,000	6,300,000
Other operating revenue (including $100,000 and $80,000 from specific purpose funds)	184,000	173,000
Total operating revenue	6,907,000	6,473,000
Operating expenses:		
Nursing services	2,200,000	2,000,000
Other professional services	1,900,000	1,700,000
General services	2,100,000	2,000,000
Fiscal services	375,000	360,000
Administrative services (including interest expense of $50,000 and $40,000)	400,000	375,000
Provision for depreciation	300,000	250,000
Total operating expenses	7,275,000	6,685,000
Loss from operations	(368,000)	(212,000)
Nonoperating revenue:		
Unrestricted gifts and bequests	228,000	205,000
Unrestricted income from endowment funds	170,000	80,000
Income and gains from board-designated funds	54,000	41,000
Total nonoperating revenue	452,000	326,000
Excess of revenues over expenses	$ 84,000	$ 114,000

See accompanying Notes to Financial Statements.

Illustration 21–4 *(continued)*

	SAMPLE HOSPITAL **Statement of Changes in Fund Balances** **Year Ended December 31, 19—** **With Comparative Figures for 19—**	EXHIBIT C

	Current Year	*Prior Year*
Unrestricted Funds		
Balance at beginning of year	$6,918,000	$6,242,000
Excess of revenues over expenses	84,000	114,000
Transferred from plant replacement and expansion funds to finance property, plant, and equipment expenditures	628,000	762,000
Transferred to plant replacement and expansion funds to reflect third-party payor revenue restricted to property, plant, and equipment replacement	(230,000)	(200,000)
Balance at end of year	$7,400,000*	$6,918,000
Restricted Funds		
Specific purpose funds:		
Balance at beginning of year	$ 71,000	$ 50,000
Restricted gifts and bequests	35,000	20,000
Research grants	35,000	45,000
Income from investments	35,260	39,000
Gain on sale of investments	8,000	—
Transferred to:		
Other operating revenue	(100,000)	(80,000)
Allowances and uncollectible accounts	(8,000)	(3,000)
Balance at end of year	$ 76,260	$ 71,000
Plant replacement and expansion funds:		
Balance at beginning of year	$1,100,000	$1,494,000
Restricted gifts and bequests	113,000	150,000
Income from investments	15,000	18,000
Transferred to unrestricted funds (described above)	(628,000)	(762,000)
Transferred from unrestricted funds (described above)	230,000	200,000
Balance at end of year	$ 830,000	$1,100,000
Endowment funds:		
Balance at beginning of year	$3,975,000	$2,875,000
Restricted gifts and bequests	2,000,000	1,000,000
Net gain on sale of investments	175,000	100,000
Balance at end of year	$6,150,000	$3,975,000

See accompanying Notes to Financial Statements.
* Composition of the balance may be shown here, on the balance sheet, or in a footnote.

Illustration 21–4 *(continued)*

SAMPLE HOSPITAL   EXHIBIT D
Statement of Revenues and Expenses and
Changes in Unrestricted Fund Balance
(Alternative Presentation)
Year Ended December 31, 19—
With Comparative Figures for 19—

| | *Current Year* | | | | *Prior Year* |
	Operations	*Other*	*Plant*	*Total*	*Total*
Patient service revenue	$8,500,000	—	—	$8,500,000	$8,000,000
Allowances and uncollectible accounts (after deduction of related gifts, grants, subsidies, and other income—$55,000 and $40,000) (Notes 3 and 4)	(1,777,000)	—	—	(1,777,000)	(1,700,000)
Net patient service revenue	6,723,000	—	—	6,723,000	6,300,000
Other operating revenue (including $100,000 and $80,000 from specific purpose funds)	184,000	—	—	184,000	173,000
Total operating revenue	6,907,000	—	—	6,907,000	6,473,000
Operating expenses:					
Nursing services	2,200,000			2,200,000	
Other professional services	1,900,000			1,900,000	
General services	2,100,000			2,100,000	
Fiscal services	375,000			375,000	
Administrative services (including interest expense of $50,000 and $40,000)	400,000			400,000	
Provision for depreciation	300,000			300,000	
Total operating expenses	7,275,000			7,275,000	
Loss from operations	(368,000)	—	—	(368,000)	(212,000)
Nonoperating revenue:					
Unrestricted gifts and bequests	—	$ 228,000	—	228,000	205,000
Unrestricted income from endowment funds	—	170,000	—	170,000	80,000
Income and gains from board-designated funds	—	24,000	$ 30,000	54,000	41,000
Excess of revenues over expenses	(368,000)	422,000	30,000	84,000	114,000
Fund balance at beginning of year	153,000	1,780,000	4,985,000	6,918,000	6,242,000
Transferred from restricted funds	—	—	628,000	628,000	762,000
Transferred to restricted funds	(230,000)	—	—	(230,000)	(200,000)
Intra-fund transfers	832,000	(632,000)	(200,000)	–0–	–0–
Fund balance at end of year	$ 387,000	$1,570,000	$5,443,000	$7,400,000	$6,918,000

See accompanying Notes to Financial Statements.
Note: If the alternative format above is presented, the total column must be included to present fairly the information contained therein.

Illustration 21–4 *(concluded)*

SAMPLE HOSPITAL EXHIBIT E
Statement of Changes in Financial Position of
Unrestricted Fund
With Comparative Figures for 19—
Year Ended December 31, 19—

	Current Year	Prior Year
Funds provided:		
Loss from operations	$ (368,000)	$ (212,000)
Deduct (add) items included in operations not requiring (providing) funds:		
Provision for depreciation	300,000	250,000
Increase in deferred third-party reimbursement	110,000	90,000
Revenue restricted to property, plant, and equipment replacement transferred to plant replacement and expansion fund	(230,000)	(200,000)
Funds required for operations	(188,000)	(72,000)
Nonoperating revenue	452,000	326,000
Funds derived from operations and nonoperating revenues	264,000	254,000
Decrease in board-designated funds	210,000	—
Property, plant, and equipment expenditures financed by plant replacement and expansion funds	628,000	762,000
Decrease in working capital	—	46,000
	$1,102,000	$1,062,000

	Current Year	Prior Year
Funds applied:		
Additions to property, plant, and equipment	$ 668,000	$ 762,000
Reduction of long-term debt	90,000	90,000
Increase in board-designated funds	—	210,000
Increase in working capital	344,000	—
	$1,102,000	$1,062,000
Changes in working capital:		
Increase (decrease) in current assets:		
Cash	$ 100,000	$ (50,000)
Receivables	58,000	75,000
Due from restricted funds	215,000	(100,000)
Inventories	(7,000)	16,000
Prepaid expenses	(5,000)	1,000
	361,000	(58,000)
Increase (decrease) in current liabilities:		
Note payable to banks	(73,000)	50,000
Accounts payable	(13,000)	10,000
Accrued expenses	3,000	2,000
Advances from third-party payors	100,000	40,000
Deferred revenue	—	2,000
	17,000	104,000
Increase (decrease) in working capital	$ 344,000	$ (46,000)

See accompanying Notes to Financial Statements.

Source: AICPA, *Industry Audit Guide,* "Hospital Audit Guide" (New York, 1972), pp. 40–47.

Illustration 21–5

SAMPLE FINANCIAL STATEMENTS FOR
VOLUNTARY HEALTH AND WELFARE ORGANIZATIONS

EXHIBIT A

VOLUNTARY HEALTH AND WELFARE SERVICE
Statement of Support, Revenue, and Expenses
and Changes in Fund Balances
Year Ended December 31, 19X2
with Comparative Totals for 19X1

	19X2				Total All Funds	
	Current Funds		Land, Build- ing and Equip- ment Fund	Endowment Fund		
	Unrestricted	Restricted			19X2	19X1
Public support and revenue:						
Public support:						
Contributions (net of estimated uncollectible pledges of $195,000 in 19X2 and $150,000 in 19X1)	$3,764,000	$162,000	$ —	$ 2,000	$3,928,000	$3,976,000
Contributions to building fund	—	—	72,000	—	72,000	150,000
Special events (net of direct costs of $181,000 in 19X2 and $163,000 in 19X1)	104,000	—	—	104,000	92,000
Legacies and bequests	92,000	—	—	4,000	96,000	129,000
Received from federated and nonfederated campaigns (which incurred related fund-raising expenses of $38,000 in 19X2 and $29,000 in 19X1)	275,000	—	—	—	275,000	308,000
Total public support	4,235,000	162,000	72,000	6,000	4,475,000	4,655,000
Revenue:						
Membership dues	17,000	—	—	—	17,000	12,000
Investment income	98,000	10,000	—	—	108,000	94,000
Realized gain on investment transactions	200,000	—	—	25,000	225,000	275,000
Miscellaneous	42,000	—	—	—	42,000	47,000
Total revenue	357,000	10,000	—	25,000	392,000	428,000
Total support and revenue	4,592,000	172,000	72,000	31,000	4,867,000	$5,083,000

Expenses:						
Program services:						
Research	1,257,000	155,000	2,000	—	$1,414,000	$1,365,000
Public health education	539,000	—	5,000	—	544,000	485,000
Professional education and training	612,000	—	6,000	—	618,000	516,000
Community services	568,000	—	10,000	—	578,000	486,000
Total program services	2,976,000	155,000	23,000	—	3,154,000	2,852,000
Supporting services:						
Management and general	567,000	—	7,000	—	574,000	638,000
Fund raising	642,000	—	12,000	—	654,000	546,000
Total supporting services	1,209,000	—	19,000	—	1,228,000	1,184,000
Total expenses	4,185,000	155,000	42,000	—	$4,382,000	$4,036,000
Excess (deficiency) of public support and revenue over expenses	407,000	17,000	30,000	31,000		
Other changes in fund balances:						
Property and equipment acquisitions from unrestricted funds	(17,000)	—	17,000	—		
Transfer of realized endowment fund appreciation	—	—	—	(100,000)		
Returned to donor	100,000	(8,000)	—	—		
Fund balances, beginning of year	5,361,000	123,000	$696,000	2,017,000		
Fund balances, end of year	$5,851,000	$132,000	$696,000	$1,948,000		

(See accompanying notes to financial statements)

Illustration 21–5 (continued)

VOLUNTARY HEALTH AND WELFARE SERVICE
Statement of Functional Expenses
Year Ended December 31, 19X2
with Comparative Totals for 19X1

19X2

| | Program Services | | | | | Supporting Services | | | Total Expenses | |
	Research	Public Health Education	Professional Education and Training	Community Services	Total	Management and General	Fund Raising	Total	19X2	19X1
Salaries	$ 45,000	$291,000	$251,000	$269,000	$ 856,000	$331,000	$368,000	$ 699,000	$1,555,000	$1,433,000
Employee health and retirement benefits	4,000	14,000	14,000	14,000	46,000	22,000	15,000	37,000	83,000	75,000
Payroll taxes, etc.	2,000	16,000	13,000	14,000	45,000	18,000	18,000	36,000	81,000	75,000
Total salaries and related expenses	51,000	321,000	278,000	297,000	947,000	371,000	401,000	772,000	1,719,000	1,583,000
Professional fees and contract service payments	1,000	10,000	3,000	8,000	22,000	26,000	8,000	34,000	56,000	53,000
Supplies	2,000	13,000	13,000	13,000	41,000	18,000	17,000	35,000	76,000	71,000
Telephone and telegraph	2,000	13,000	10,000	11,000	36,000	15,000	23,000	38,000	74,000	68,000
Postage and shipping	2,000	17,000	13,000	9,000	41,000	13,000	30,000	43,000	84,000	80,000
Occupancy	5,000	26,000	22,000	25,000	78,000	30,000	27,000	57,000	135,000	126,000
Rental of equipment	1,000	24,000	14,000	4,000	43,000	3,000	16,000	19,000	62,000	58,000
Local transportation	3,000	22,000	20,000	22,000	67,000	23,000	30,000	53,000	120,000	113,000
Conferences, conventions, meetings	8,000	19,000	71,000	20,000	118,000	38,000	13,000	51,000	169,000	156,000
Printing and publications	4,000	56,000	43,000	11,000	114,000	14,000	64,000	78,000	192,000	184,000
Awards and grants	1,332,000	14,000	119,000	144,000	1,609,000	—	—	—	1,609,000	1,448,000
Miscellaneous	1,000	4,000	6,000	4,000	15,000	16,000	21,000	37,000	52,000	64,000
Total expenses before depreciation	1,412,000	539,000	612,000	568,000	3,131,000	567,000	650,000	1,217,000	4,348,000	4,004,000
Depreciation of buildings and equipment	2,000	5,000	6,000	10,000	23,000	7,000	4,000	11,000	34,000	32,000
Total expenses	$1,414,000	$544,000	$618,000	$578,000	$3,154,000	$574,000	$654,000	$1,228,000	$4,382,000	$4,036,000

(See accompanying notes to financial statements)

Illustration 21–5 (continued)

VOLUNTARY HEALTH AND WELFARE SERVICE
Balance Sheets
December 31, 19X2 and 19X1

EXHIBIT C

CURRENT FUNDS

Unrestricted

Assets	19X2	19X1	Liabilities and Fund Balances	19X2	19X1
Cash	$2,207,000	$2,530,000	Accounts payable	$ 148,000	$ 139,000
Investments (Note 2):			Research grants payable	596,000	616,000
For Long-term purposes	2,727,000	2,245,000	Contributions designated for future		
Other	1,075,000	950,000	periods	245,000	219,000
			Total liabilities and deferred revenues	989,000	974,000
Pledges receivable less allowance for uncollectibles of $105,000 and $92,000	475,000	363,000	Fund balances:		
			Designated by the governing board for:		
Inventories of educational materials, at cost	70,000	61,000	Long-term investments	2,800,000	2,300,000
			Purchases of new equipment	100,000	—
Accrued interest, other receivables and prepaid expenses	286,000	186,000	Research purposes (Note 3)	1,152,000	1,748,000
			Undesignated, available for general activities (Note 4)	1,799,000	1,313,000
			Total fund balance	5,851,000	5,361,000
Total	$6,840,000	$6,335,000	Total	$6,840,000	$6,335,000

Restricted

Assets	19X2	19X1	Liabilities and Fund Balances	19X2	19X1
Cash	$ 3,000	$ 5,000	Fund balances:		
Investments (Note 2)	71,000	72,000	Professional education	$ 84,000	$ —
Grants receivable	58,000	46,000	Research grants	48,000	123,000
Total	$ 132,000	$ 123,000	Total	$ 132,000	$ 123,000

Illustration 21–5 (concluded)

EXHIBIT C

VOLUNTARY HEALTH AND WELFARE SERVICE
Balance Sheets
December 31, 19X2 and 19X1

Assets	19X2	19X1	Liabilities and Fund Balances	19X2	19X1
			LAND, BUILDING AND EQUIPMENT FUND		
Cash	$ 3,000	$ 2,000	Mortgage payable, 8% due 19XX	$ 32,000	$ 36,000
Investments (Note 2)	177,000	145,000	Fund balances:		
Pledge receivable less allowance for uncollectibles of $7,500 and $5,000	32,000	25,000	Expended	484,000	477,000
			Unexpended—restricted	212,000	172,000
Land, buildings and equipment, at cost less accumulated depreciation of $296,000 and $262,000 (Note 5)	516,000	513,000	Total fund balance	696,000	649,000
Total	$ 728,000	$ 685,000	Total	$ 728,000	$ 685,000
			ENDOWMENT FUNDS		
Cash	$ 4,000	$ 10,000	Fund balance	$1,948,000	$2,017,000
Investments (Note 2)	1,944,000	2,007,000			
Total	$1,948,000	$2,017,000	Total	$1,948,000	$2,017,000

(See accompanying notes to financial statements)

Source: AICPA, Industry Audit Guide, "Audits of Voluntary Health and Welfare Organizations" (New York, 1974), pp. 42–47.

Illustration 21–6

SAMPLE FINANCIAL STATEMENTS FOR OTHER NONPROFIT ORGANIZATIONS

SAMPLE INDEPENDENT SCHOOL
Balance Sheet
June 30, 19X1

EXHIBIT A

	Operating Funds	Plant Funds	Endowment Funds	Total All Funds
Assets				
Cash	$ 87,000	$ 15,000	$ 19,000	$ 121,000
Accounts receivable, less allowance for doubtful receivables of $3,000	34,000	—	—	34,000
Pledges receivable, less allowance for doubtful pledges of $10,000	—	75,000	—	75,000
Inventories, at lower of cost (FIFO) or market	7,000	—	—	7,000
Investments (Note 2)	355,000	10,000	100,000	465,000
Land, buildings, equipment, and library books, at cost less accumulated depreciation of $980,000 (Note 3)	—	2,282,000	—	2,282,000
Other assets	17,000	—	—	17,000
Total assets	$500,000	$2,382,000	$119,000	$3,001,000
Liabilities and Fund Balances				
Accounts payable and accrued expenses	$ 13,000	—	—	$ 13,000
Deferred amounts (Note 6)				
Unrestricted	86,000	—	—	86,000
Restricted	27,000	$ 100,000	—	127,000
Long-term debt (Note 4)	—	131,000	—	131,000
Total liabilities	126,000	231,000	—	357,000
Fund balances				
Unrestricted				
Designated by the governing board for long-term investment	355,000	—	—	355,000
Undesignated	19,000	—	—	19,000
	374,000	—	—	374,000
Restricted—nonexpendable	—	—	$119,000	119,000
Net investment in plant	—	2,151,000	—	2,151,000
Total fund balances	374,000	2,151,000	119,000	2,644,000
Total liabilities and fund balances	$500,000	$2,382,000	$119,000	$3,001,000

Illustration 21–6 (*continued*)

	Operating Funds					
	Unre-stricted	Re-stricted	Total	Plant Funds	Endowment Funds	Total All Funds
Support and revenue						
Tuition and fees	$ 910,000	—	$ 910,000	—	—	$ 910,000
Contributions	104,000	$80,500	184,500	—	—	184,500
Endowment and other investment income	23,000	1,500	24,500	—	—	24,500
Net loss on investment transactions	(8,000)	—	(8,000)	—	—	(8,000)
Auxiliary activities	25,000	—	25,000	—	—	25,000
Summer school and other programs	86,000	—	86,000	—	—	86,000
Other sources	26,000	—	26,000	—	—	26,000
Total support and revenue	1,166,000	82,000	1,248,000	—	—	1,248,000
Expenses						
Program services						
Instruction and student activities	798,000	43,000	841,000	$ 69,000	—	910,000
Auxiliary activities	24,000	—	24,000	—	—	24,000
Summer school and other programs	91,000	—	91,000	7,000	—	98,000
Financial aid	—	37,000	37,000	3,000	—	40,000
Total program services	913,000	80,000	993,000	79,000	—	1,072,000
Supporting services						
General administration	147,000	2,000	149,000	13,000	—	162,000
Fund raising	12,000	—	12,000	1,000	—	13,000
Total supporting services	159,000	2,000	161,000	14,000	—	175,000
Total expenses	1,072,000	82,000	1,154,000	93,000	—	1,247,000
Excess (deficiency) of support and revenue over expenses before capital additions	94,000	—	94,000	(93,000)	—	1,000

SAMPLE INDEPENDENT SCHOOL
Statement of Support and Revenue, Expenses,
Capital Additions, and Changes in Fund Balances
Year Ended June 30, 19X1

EXHIBIT B

Illustration 21–6 (*continued*)

SAMPLE INDEPENDENT SCHOOL EXHIBIT B
Statement of Support and Revenue, Expenses,
Capital Additions, and Changes in Fund Balances
Year Ended June 30, 19X1

| | Operating Funds | | | | | |
	Unre- stricted	Re- stricted	Total	Plant Funds	Endowment Funds	Total All Funds
Capital additions						
Contributions and bequests	—	—	—	80,000	$ 30,000	110,000
Investment income	—	—	—	5,000	—	5,000
Net gain on investment transactions	—	—	—	1,000	2,000	3,000
Total capital additions	—	—	—	86,000	32,000	118,000
Excess (deficiency) of support and revenue over expenses after capital additions	94,000	—	94,000	(7,000)	32,000	119,000
Fund balances at beginning of year	387,000	—	387,000	2,047,000	91,000	2,525,000
Transfers						
Equipment acquisitions and principal debt service payments	(111,000)	—	(111,000)	111,000	—	—
Realized gains on endowment funds utilized	4,000	—	4,000	—	(4,000)	—
Fund balances at end of year	$ 374,000	—	$ 374,000	$2,151,000	$119,000	$2,644,000

Illustration 21–6 *(concluded)*

SAMPLE INDEPENDENT SCHOOL   EXHIBIT C
Statement of Changes in Financial Position
Year Ended June 30, 19X1

	Operating Funds	Plant Funds	Endowment Funds	Total All Funds
Resources provided				
Excess (deficiency) of support and revenue over expenses before capital additions	$ 94,000	$ (93,000)	—	$ 1,000
Capital additions				
Contributions and bequests	—	80,000	$ 30,000	110,000
Investment income	—	5,000	—	5,000
Net gain on investments	—	1,000	2,000	3,000
Excess (deficiency) of support and revenue over expenses after capital additions	94,000	(7,000)	32,000	119,000
Items not using (providing) resources				
Provision for depreciation	—	93,000	—	93,000
Net (gain) loss on investment transactions	8,000	(1,000)	(2,000)	5,000
Decrease in inventories	2,000	—	—	2,000
Increase in deferred amounts	3,000	75,000	—	78,000
Proceeds from sale of investments	160,000	2,000	47,000	209,000
Total resources provided	267,000	162,000	77,000	506,000
Resources used				
Purchases of equipment	—	145,000	—	145,000
Reduction of long-term debt	—	52,000	—	52,000
Purchases of investments	210,000	6,000	136,000	352,000
Increase in other assets	1,000	—	—	1,000
Increase in accounts and pledges receivable	3,000	60,000	—	63,000
Decrease in accounts payable and accrued expenses	3,000	—	—	3,000
Total resources used	217,000	263,000	136,000	616,000
Transfers				
Equipment acquisitions and principal debt service payments	(111,000)	111,000	—	—
Realized gains on endowment funds utilized	4,000	—	(4,000)	—
Total transfers	(107,000)	111,000	(4,000)	—
Increase (decrease) in cash	$ (57,000)	$ 10,000	$ (63,000)	$(110,000)

Source: *AICPA, Audit and Accounting Guide,* "Audits of Certain Nonprofit Organizations" (New York, 1981), pp. 101–4.

Questions

1. What characteristics distinguish nonprofit organizations from profit-oriented enterprises?

2. Are board-designated funds of a nonprofit organization included in the unrestricted fund or the restricted fund category? Explain.

3. Differentiate between revenue, support, and capital additions of nonprofit organizations.

4. Define the following terms applicable to nonprofit organizations:
   a. Unrestricted Fund.
   b. Restricted Fund.
   c. Agency Fund.
   d. Term Endowment Fund.
   e. Pledge.

5. Nonprofit organizations distinguish between restricted and unrestricted funds. Why is this distinction important?

6. How should a nonprofit organization record a donated service in its accounting records?

7. How should a nonprofit organization record donated material in its accounting records?

8. How are net patient service revenues of hospitals measured? Explain each component of net patient service revenues.

9. Do voluntary health and welfare organizations recognize support and revenue from pledges when the pledges are received or when cash is received? Explain.

10. How should the revenues from pooled investments be allocated to each participating fund?

11. Universities and hospitals often reduce their standard service charge to students or patients. How are these reductions reflected in the operating statements of these organization?

12. How does an Annuity Fund differ from Life Income Fund?

13. What subgroups are included in the plant funds grouping of colleges and universities? Describe the transactions accounted for within each subgroup.

14. What basic financial statements should be included in the financial reports of a nonprofit organization?

Exercises

Exercise 21–1

Select the best answer for each of the following.
Questions 1 through 3 are based on the following data:

Under Abbey Hospital's established rate structure, the hospital would have earned patient service revenue of $6,000,000 for the year ended December 31, 1983. However, Abbey did not expect to collect this amount because of charity allowances of $1,000,000 and discounts of $500,000 to third-party payers. In May 1983, Abbey purchased bandages from Lee Supply Co. at a cost of $1,000. However, Lee notified Abbey that the invoice was being canceled and that the bandages were being donated to Abbey. At December 31, 1983, Abbey had board-designated assets consisting of cash $40,000, and investments $700,000.

1. For the year ended December 31, 1983, how much should Abbey record as patient service revenue?
   a. $6,000,000.
   b. $5,500,000.
   c. $5,000,000.
   d. $4,500,000.

2. For the year ended December 31, 1983, Abbey should record the donation of bandages as
   a. A $1,000 reduction in operating expenses.
   b. Nonoperating revenue of $1,000.
   c. Other operating revenue of $1,000.
   d. A memorandum entry only.

3. How much of Abbey's board-designated assets should be included in the unrestricted fund grouping?
   a. $0.
   b. $40,000.
   c. $700,000.
   d. $740,000.

4. On May 1, 1984, Lila Lee established a $50,000 endowment fund, the income from which is to be paid to Waller Hospital for general operating purposes. Waller does not control the fund's principal. Anders National Bank was appointed by Lee as trustee of this fund. What Journal entry is required on Waller's book?

		Debit	Credit
a.	Memorandum entry only...........		
b.	Nonexpendable endowment fund...	$50,000	
	Endowment Fund Balance......		$50,000
c.	Cash	50,000	
	Endowment Fund Balance......		50,000
d.	Cash	50,000	
	Nonexpendable Endowment Fund......................		50,000

5. Glenmore Hospital's property, plant, and equipment (net of depreciation) consists of the following:

Land	$ 500,000
Buildings.................	10,000,000
Movable equipment........	2,000,000

What amount should be included in the restricted fund grouping?

   a. $0.

   b. $2,000,000.

   c. $10,500,000.

   d. $12,500,000.

6. Depreciation should be recognized in the financial statements of

   a.   Proprietary (for-profit) hospitals only.

   b.   Both proprietary (for-profit) and not-for-profit hospitals.

   c.   Both proprietary (for-profit) and not-for-profit hospitals, only when they are affiliated with a college or university.

   d.   All hospitals, as a memorandum entry not affecting the statement of revenues and expenses.

7. On July 1, 1982, Lilydale Hospital's board of trustees designated $200,000 for expansion of out-patient facilities. The $200,000 is expected to be expended in the fiscal year ending June 30, 1985. In Lilydale's balance sheet at June 30, 1983, this cash should be classified as a:

   a.   Restricted current asset.

   b.   Restricted noncurrent asset.

   c.   Unrestricted current asset.

   d.   Unrestricted noncurrent asset.

8. An unrestricted pledge from an annual contributor to a voluntary not-for-profit hospital made in December 1982 and paid in cash in March 1983 would generally be credited to:

   a.   Nonoperating Revenue in 1982.

   b.   Nonoperating Revenue in 1983.

   c.   Operating Revenue in 1982.

   d.   Operating Revenue in 1983.

(AICPA adapted)

Exercise 21–2

Select the best answer for each of the following.

1. Donated medicines which normally would be purchased by a hospital should be recorded at fair market value and credited directly to:

   a.   Other Operating Revenue.

   b.   Other Nonoperating Revenue.

   c.   Fund Balance.

   d.   Deferred Revenue.

2. A gift to a voluntary not-for-profit hospital that is not restricted by the donor should be credited directly to:

   a.   Fund Balance.

   b.   Deferred Revenue.

   c.   Other Operating Revenue.

   d.   Nonoperating Revenue.

3. During the year ended December 31, 1983, Melford Hospital received the following donations stated at their respective fair values:

Employee services from members of a religious group.................... $100,000
Medical supplies from an association of physicians (These supplies were
  restricted for indigent care and were used for such purpose in 1983)..... $30,000

How much revenue (both operating and nonoperating) from donations should Melford report in its 1983 statement of revenues and expenses?

a. $0.
b. $30,000.
c. $100,000.
d. $130,000.

Questions 4 through 7 refer to the accounts of a large non-profit hospital which properly maintains four funds: operating, special purpose, endowment, and plant.

4. How should charity service, contractual adjustments, and bad debts be classified in the statement of revenues and expenses for the hospital?
   a. All three should be treated as expenses.
   b. All three should be treated as deductions from patient service revenues.
   c. Charity service and contractual adjustments should be treated as a revenue deduction, while bad debts should be treated as an expense.
   d. Charity service and bad debts should be treated as expenses, while contractual adjustments should be treated as a revenue deduction.

5. Depreciation on some hospital fixed assets, referred to as "minor equipment," is not accounted for in the conventional manner. How is depreciation with respect to these assets accounted for?
   a. Ignore on the basis of immateriality.
   b. Handled in essentially the same manner as if assets were assigned to the activities of a city and were accounted for in its general fund.
   c. Determined periodically by inventorying minor equipment and writing the assets down to their value at the inventory date.
   d. Recognized only when minor equipment is replaced.

6. To assure the availability of money for improvements, replacement, and expansion of plant, it would be most desirable for the hospital to
   a. Use accelerated depreciation to provide adequate funds for eventual replacement.
   b. Use the retirement or replacement system of depreciation to provide adequate funds.
   c. Sell assets at earliest opportunity.
   d. Transfer cash from the operating fund to the plant fund in amounts at least equal to the periodic depreciation charges.

7. The endowment fund consists of several small endowments, each for a special purpose. The hospital treasurer has determined that it would be legally possible and more efficient to "pool" the assets and allocate the resultant revenue. The soundest basis on which to allocate revenue after assets are "pooled" and comply with the special purposes of each endowment would be to:
   a. Determine market values of securities or other assets included in each endowment at the time of transfer to the pool and credit revenue to each endowment on that pro rata basis.

   b. Determine book values of each endowment at the time of transfer to the pool and credit revenue to each endowment on that pro rata basis.

   c. Apportion future revenue according to the moving-average ratio in which the various endowments have earned revenue in the past.

   d. Ask the trustee who administers the pooled assets to make the determination since (s)he is in a position to know which assets are making the greatest contribution.

(AICPA adapted)

Exercise 21–3

Select the best answer for each of the following.

1. For the spring semester of 1984, Lane University assessed its students $3,400,000, (net of refunds), covering tuition and fees for educational and general purpose. However, only $3,000,000 was expected to be realized because scholarships totaling $300,000 were granted to students, and tuition remissions of $100,000 were allowed to faculty members' children attending Lane. How much should Lane include in educational and general current funds revenues from student tuition and fees?

   a. $3,400,000.
   b. $3,300,000.
   c. $3,100,000.
   d. $3,000,000.

2. The following funds were among those on Kery University's books at April 30, 1984:

Funds to be used for acquisition of additional properties for university purpose (unexpended at 4/30/84)	$3,000,000
Funds set aside for debt service charges and for retirement of indebtedness on university properties ..	$5,000,000

How much of the above-mentioned funds should be included in the plant funds?

   a. $0.
   b. $3,000,000.
   c. $5,000,000.
   d. $8,000,000.

3. Which of the following should be used in accounting for not-for-profit colleges and universities?

   a. Fund accounting and accrual accounting.
   b. Fund accounting and not accrual accounting.
   c. Accrual accounting and not fund accounting.
   d. Neither accrual accounting nor fund accounting.

4. Which of following receipts is properly recorded in a restricted current fund in the books of a university?

   a. Tuition.
   b. Student laboratory fees.
   c. Housing fees.
   d. Research grants.

5. During the years ended June 30, 1982, and 1983, Sonata University conducted a cancer research project financed by a $2,000,000 gift from an alumnus. This entire amount was pledged by the donor on July 10, 1981, although he paid only $500,000 at that date. The gift was restricted to the financing of this research project. During the two-year research period, Sonata's related gift receipts and research expenditures were

	Year Ended June 30,	
	1982	1983
Gift receipts	$1,200,000	$ 800,000
Cancer research expenditures	900,000	1,100,000

How much gift revenue should Sonata report in the restricted column of its statement of current funds revenues, expenditures, and other charges for year ended June 30, 1983?

a. $0.
b. $800,000.
c. $1,100,000.
d. $2,000,000.

6. For the fall semester of 1983, Cranbrook College assessed its students $2,300,000 for tuition and fees. The net amount realized was only $2,100,000 because of following revenue reductions:

Refund occasioned by class cancellations and student withdrawals	$ 50,000
Tuition remissions granted to faculty members' families	10,000
Scholarships and fellowships	140,000

How much should Cranbrook report for the period for unrestricted current funds revenues from tuition and fees?

a. $2,100,000.
b. $2,150,000.
c. $2,250,000.
d. $2,300,000.

7. Which of the following is/are utilized for current expenditures by a not-for-profit university?

	Unrestricted Current Funds	Restricted Current Funds
a.	No	No
b.	No	Yes
c.	Yes	No
d.	Yes	Yes

8. In the loan fund of a college or university, each of the following types of loans would be found except:

a. Student.
b. Staff.
c. Building.
d. Faculty.

9. On January 2, 1983, John Reynolds established a $500,000 trust, the income from which is to be paid to Mansfield University for general operating purposes. The Wyndham National Bank was appointed by Reynolds as trustee of the fund. What journal entry is required on Mansfield's books?

> *a.*   Memorandum entry only.
>
> *b.*   Cash $500,000
>   Endowment Fund Balance........... $500,000
>
> *c.*   Nonexpendable Endowment Fund $500,000
>   Endowment Fund Balance........... $500,000
>
> *d.*   Expendable Funds..................... $500,000
>   Endowment Fund Balance........... $500,000
>
> (AICPA adapted)

Exercise 21–4

Select the best answer for each of the following.
Questions 1 and 2 are based on the following data:

Community Service Center is a voluntary welfare organization funded by contributions from the general public. During 1983, unrestricted pledges of $900,000 were received, half of which were payable in 1983, with the other half payable in 1984. It was estimated that 10 percent of these pledges would be uncollectible. In addition, Selma Zorn, a social worker on Community's permanent staff, earning $20,000 annually for a normal workload of 2,000 hours, contributed an additional 800 hours of her time to Community, at no charge.

1. How much should Community report as net contribution revenue for 1983 with respect to the pledges?
    a. $0.
    b. $405,000.
    c. $810,000.
    d. $900,000.
2. How much should Community record in 1983 for contributed service expense?
    a. $8,000.
    b. $4,000.
    c. $800.
    d. $0.
3. Cura Foundation, a voluntary health and welfare organization supported by contributions from the general public, included the following costs in its statement of functional expenses for the year ended December 31, 1983:

> Fund-raising $500,000
> Administrative (including data processing)........   300,000
> Research......................................   100,000

Cura's functional expenses for 1983 program services included:
    a. $900,000.
    b. $500,000.
    c. $300,000.
    d. $100,000.

4. A reason for a voluntary health and welfare organization to adopt fund accounting is that
   a. Restrictions have been placed on certain of its assets by donors.
   b. It provides more than one type of program service.
   c. Fixed assets are significant.
   d. Donated services are significant.
5. Which of the following funds of a voluntary health and welfare organization does not have a counterpart fund in governmental accounting?
   a. Current—unrestricted.
   b. Land, building, and equipment.
   c. Custodian.
   d. Endowment.
6. A voluntary health and welfare organization received a pledge in 1982 from a donor specifying that the amount pledged be used in 1984. The donor paid the pledge in cash in 1983. The pledge should be accounted for as:
   a. A deferred credit in the balance sheet at the end of 1982, and as support in 1983.
   b. A deferred credit in the balance sheet at the end of 1982 and 1983, and as support in 1984.
   c. Support in 1982.
   d. Support in 1983, and no deferred credit in the balance sheet at the end of 1982.

(AICPA adapted)

Exercise 21–5

On January 1, 19X2, three funds of Community Service Center, a voluntary welfare organization, pooled their individual investments as follows:

	Cost	Current Fair Value
Unrestricted Fund	$150,000	$170,000
Restricted Fund	190,000	148,750
Endowment Fund	90,000	106,250
Totals	$430,000	$425,000

During the year ended December 31, 19X2, the Community Service Center investment pool received dividends and interest totaling $51,000 and reinvested realized gains of $12,750.

Required:

Prepare journal entries on December 31, 19X2, for each of the three funds to reflect the results of the investment's operations during 19X2.

Exercise 21–6

Under its established rate structure, National Hospital, a nonprofit organization, would have earned patient service revenues of $7,500,000 for the year ended December 31, 19X1. However, National did not expect to collect this amount because of charity allowances of $1,000,000, provision for doubtful accounts of $225,000, and discounts of $500,000 to third-party payors.

Required:

Prepare the necessary journal entries on December 31, 19X1, to record the foregoing in National Hospital's accounting records.

Exercise 21–7

During 19X6, volunteer nurses' aides donated their services to Local Hospital at no cost. If regular employees had provided the service rendered by the volunteers, their salaries would have totaled $8,500. While working for the hospital, the volunteers received complimentary meals from the hospital cafeteria, which normally would have cost $700. The volunteer nurses' aides services met the specifications for donated services in *Statement of Position 78-10,* "Accounting Principles and Reporting Practices for Certain Nonprofit Organizations.

Required:

Prepare the journal entry necessary in the Local Hospital Unrestricted Fund to record the services donated to Local Hospital during 19X6.

Exercise 21–8

For the spring semester of 19X6, Franklin University assessed its students $3,520,000 for tuition and fees. The net amount realized was only $3,020,000 because the following reductions:

Refund occasioned by class cancellation and student withdraw	$80,000
Tuition remissions granted to faculty members' families.........................	$120,000
Scholarships and Fellowships	$300,000

Required:

How much should Franklin University report for the period for unrestricted current funds revenues from tuition and fees?

Problems

Problem 21–9

Among the transactions of the Unrestricted Fund of Public Hospital, a nonprofit organization, for the year 19X6, were the following:

1. Gross patient service revenue of $720,000 was billed to patients. Provision was made for indigent patient charity allowances of $35,000, of which amount $23,000 was receivable from Goodwill Welfare, Inc; contractual adjustments were allowed to Medicare totaling $36,000, and doubtful accounts were estimated at $30,000.

2. Received and expended $15,000 from Mark Wilson Restricted Fund for new equipment, as authorized by the donor.
3. Donated services approximating $72,000 at going salary rates were received from volunteer nurse's aides. Meals costing $1,800 were served to the volunteer nurses at no charges by Public Hospital cafeteria.
4. New pledges, due in one year, totaling $120,000 were received from various donors. Collections on pledges amounted to $80,000, and the provision for doubtful pledges for 19X6 was $12,000.

Required:

a. Prepare the journal entries for the above 19X6 transactions of the Public Hospital Unrestricted Fund.
b. Prepare journal entries required for other funds of Public Hospital as indicated by the transactions of the Unrestricted Fund.

Problem 21–10

The following events were recorded on the books of Goodwill Hospital for the year ended December 31, 19X6.

1. Revenues from patient services totaled $20,000,000. The allowances for uncollectibles was established at $4,200,000. Of the $20,000,000 revenues, $8,000,000 was recognized under cost reimbursement agreements. This revenue is subject to audit and retroactive adjustment by third-party payors (estimated adjustments are included in the allowance account).
2. Patient service revenue is accounted for at established rates on an accrual basis.
3. Other operating revenue totaled $200,000, of which $120,000 was from specific purpose funds.
4. Goodwill received $280,000 in unrestricted gifts and bequests. They are recorded at fair market value when received.
5. Endowment funds earned $120,000 in unrestricted income.
6. Board designated funds earned $120,000 in income.
7. Goodwill's operating expenses for the year amounted to $17,250,000. This included $625,000 in straight-line depreciation.

Required:

Prepare a statement of revenues and expenses for goodwill for the year ended December 31, 19X6.

(AICPA adapted)

Problem 21–11

The four funds of National Welfare Foundation, a nonprofit organization, formed an investment pool on January 1, 19X7. On that date, costs and current fair values of the investment pool were as follows:

	Cost	Current Fair Value
Unrestricted Fund.........	$35,000	$ 46,000
Restricted Fund	25,000	25,300
Plant Fund	50,000	57,500
Endowment Fund	80,000	101,200
Totals	$180,000	$230,000

During the year ended December 31, 19X7, the investment pool reinvested realized gains totaling $20,000 and received dividends and interest totaling $18,000, which was distributed to the participating funds. On January 1, 19X8, the Heitman Life Income Fund entered the National Welfare Center investment pool with investments having a cost of $50,000 and a current fair value of $70,000. Immediately prior to this addition to the pool, the current fair value of the investment pool was $280,000. During the year ended December 31, 19X8, the investment pool reinvested realized gains totaling $30,000 and received dividends and interest totaling $40,000 which was distributed to participating funds.

Required:
a. Compute the following:
   1. Original equity percentages, January 1, 19X7.
   2. Revised equity percentages, January 2, 19X8.
b. Prepare journal entries on December 31, 19X7, for each of the four participating funds to reflect the results of the investment pool's operation during 19X7.
c. Prepare journal entries on December 31, 19X8, for each of the five participating funds to reflect the results of the investment pool's operation during 19X8.

Problem 21–12

The December 31, 19X7, balance sheet for American Blood Donors Association is presented below.

AMERICAN BLOOD DONORS ASSOCIATION
Balance Sheet
December 31, 19X7

Assets

Cash...............................	$ 470,000
Accounts receivable	160,000
Allowance for doubtful accounts........	(30,000)
Pledges receivable....................	930,000
Allowance for doubtful pledges	(130,000)
Inventories	400,000
Investments	19,300,000
Land................................	1,300,000
Building and improvement.............	46,500,000
Equipment	2,700,000
Accumulated depreciation	(13,500,000)
Other assets	200,000
Total assets..........................	$ 58,300,000

Liabilities

Accounts payable	$	700,000
Accrued expenses		130,000
Deferred revenue-unrestricted		100,000
Deferred support-restricted		6,000,000
Deferred capital addition		1,600,000
Long-term debt		7,350,000
Total liabilities		$ 15,880,000

Fund Balances

Plant	$	29,000,000
Endowment		3,850,000
Restricted		1,300,000
Unrestricted		8,270,000
Total fund balances		42,420,000
Total liabilities and fund balances		$ 58,300,000

Additional information concerning the balance sheet is as follows:

1. Except for $70,000 of cash, the Endowment Fund is made up of investments only. There are no liabilities.
2. The Plant Fund has no current liabilities and includes some investments and $15,000 in cash.
3. In addition to investments, the Current Restricted Fund consists of the pledges receivable, $35,000 of accounts payable, and cash of $155,000.

Required:

Prepare a corrected balance sheet for the American Blood Donors Association at December 31, 19X7, using the following columnar format.

Account Titles	Current Unrestricted $	Current Restricted $	Plant $	Endowment $	Total $

(AICPA adapted)

Problem 21–13

The following transactions of Citizen College occurred during 19X7. The funds involved are: the Endowment Fund, the Annuity Fund, the Plant Fund—Unexpended, the Plant Fund—Investment in Plant, the Loan Fund, the Unrestricted Current Fund, and the Restricted Current Fund.

January 1

1. A gift of $10,000 was received from Sam Waller. The principal was to be held intact and the income used for any purpose designated by the governing board.
2. Byron Scofield donated $20,000. The principal was to be held intact and the income used for scholarships for worthy students.
3. Dan Persons donated $30,000, of which the principal was to remain intact while the interest was to be used for student loans. All income is to be reloaned; all losses from loans are to be charged against income.

4. A gift of $205,000 was received from Mike Bedwell. Semiannual payments of $10,000 are to be made to the donor during his lifetime. The fund is then to be used to purchase or construct a students' residence. Mr. Bedwell has a life expectancy of five years, and investments are expected to earn 8 percent annually.

5. Julie Johnson donated 1,000 shares of BIM stock, which had a market value of $150 per share on that date. All income received from the shares is to be held intact, and the shares cannot be held over five years. Once the board sells the shares, all the proceeds are to be used to build a student hospital.

6. The assets of the Waller and Scofield funds were consolidated into a pooled investment account by the governing board (in proportion to the principal accounts). Electric Power Bonds worth $30,000 were purchased. The 12 percent interest was payable on January 1 and July 1.

7. The Persons Fund cash is used to purchase Great Company 10 percent bonds at par for $30,000. January 1 and July 1 are the interest dates.

8. $200,000 of 8 percent U.S. Treasury notes were purchased at par with cash from the Bedwell Fund. The interest dates are January 1 and July 1.

July 1

9. The interest has been received on all bonds and notes and has been transferred to the proper funds. Dividends of $4,000 are received from BIM stock.

10. The stipulated payment is made to Mr. Bedwell from the Endowment Fund.

11. Electric Power Company bonds bought for $20,000 are sold at 102. The gain is added to the principal.

12. A $300 student loan was made from the Persons Fund.

October 1

13. A notice of Mike Bedwell's death is received. There is no liability to his estate.

14. The Scofield Scholarship Fund awards a $200 scholarship.

15. $200,000 par U.S. Treasury notes are sold for $206,000.

December 1

16. Interest on bonds is received.

17. $100 of principal and $5 of interest were repaid on student loan.

18. A building was purchased for $250,000 using the funds available from the Bedwell gift. The residence hall will have a 20-year mortgage payable to account for the balance.

Required:

Using the following format, record the journal entries necessary for each event. Ignore closing entries.

Event   Fund   Journal Entry

(AICPA adapted)

Problem 21–14

The current funds balance sheet of Big State University at the end of its fiscal year ended June 30, 19X6 is as follows:

BIG STATE UNIVERSITY
Current Funds Balance Sheet
June 30, 19X6

Assets

Current funds:
Unrestricted:

Cash	$210,000
Account receivable (less allowance for doubtful accounts, $9,000)................	341,000
State appropriations receivable..............	75,000
Total unrestricted......................	626,000

Restricted:

Cash	7,000
Investments...............................	60,000
Total restricted	67,000
Total assets	$693,000

Liabilities and Fund Balance

Current funds:
Unrestricted:

Accounts payable..........................	$ 45,000
Deferred revenues	66,000
Fund balance..............................	515,000
Total unrestricted......................	626,000

Restricted:

Fund balance..............................	67,000
Total restricted	67,000
Total liabilities and fund balance	$693,000

The following transactions occurred during the fiscal year ended June 30, 19X6:

1. On July 7, 19X6, a gift of $100,000 was received from an alumnus. The alumnus requested that one half of the gift be used for the acquisition of books for the university library and that the remainder be used for the establishment of a scholarship. The alumnus further requested that the revenue generated by the scholarship fund be used annually to award a scholarship to a qualified disadvantaged student, with the principal remaining intact. On July 20, 19X6, the board of trustees resolved that the cash of the newly established scholarship (endowment) fund would be invested in bank certificates of deposit. On July 21, 19X6, the certificates of deposit were acquired.

2. Revenue from student tuition and fees applicable to the year ended June 30, 19X7, amounted to $1,900,000. Of this amount, $66,000 was collected in the prior year, and $1,686,000 was collected during the year ended June 30, 19X7. In addition, on June 30, 19X7, the university had received cash of $158,000, representing tuition and fees for the session beginning July 1, 19X7.

3. During the year ended June 30, 19X7, the university had collected $349,000 of the outstanding accounts receivable at the beginning of year. The balance was determined to be uncollectible and was written off against the allowance account. On June 30, 19X7, the allowance account was increased by $3,000.

4. During the year, interest charges of $6,000 were earned and collected on late student fee payments.

5. During the year the state appropriation was received. An additional unrestricted appropriation of $50,000 was made by the state, but had not been paid to the university as of June 30, 19X7.

6. Unrestricted cash gifts totaling $25,000 were received from alumni of the university.

7. During the year, restricted fund investments of $21,000 were sold for $26,000. Investment earnings amounting to $1,900 were received (credit Fund Balance).

8. During the year, unrestricted operating expenses of $1,777,000 were recorded. On June 30, 19X7, $59,000 of these expenses remained unpaid.

9. Restricted cash of $13,000 was spent for authorized purposes during the year. An equal amount was transferred from the fund balance to revenue of the restricted fund.

10. The accounts payable on June 30, 19X6, were paid during the year.

11. During the year, $7,000 interest was earned and received on the certificate of deposit acquired in accordance with the board of trustees resolution (in item 1).

Required:

a. Prepare journal entries to record, in summary form, the transactions for the year ended June 30, 19X7.

The following format should be used:

		Current Funds					
		Unrestricted		*Restricted*		*Endowment Fund*	
Transaction	*Account*	*Dr*	*Cr*	*Dr*	*Cr*	*Dr*	*Cr*

b. Prepare a statement of changes in fund balances for the year ended July 30, 19X7.

c. Prepare a statement of current funds revenues, expenditures, and other changes for the year ended June 30, 19X7.

(AICPA adapted)

Problem 21–15

In 1950 a group of civic-minded citizens in Cityville organized a nonprofit sports club for local youth, and called it Cityville Sports Committee. Each of the committee's 100 members contributed $1,000 towards the club's capital, and in turn received a participation certificate. In addition, each participant agreed to pay dues of $200 a year for the club's operations. All dues have been collected in full by the end of each fiscal year ending March 31. Members who have discontinued their participation have been replaced by an equal number of new members through transfer of the participation certificates from the former members to the new ones. Following is the club's trial balance at April 1, 1982:

	Debit	*Credit*
Cash	$ 9,000	
Investments (at market,		
equal to cost).....................	58,000	
Inventories.........................	5,000	
Land	10,000	
Building	164,000	
Accumulated depreciation,		
building		$130,000
Furniture and equipment.............	54,000	
Accumulated depreciation,		
furniture and equipment		46,000
Accounts payable....................		12,000
Participation certificates		
(100 at $1,000 each)		100,000
Cumulative excess of revenue		
over expenses.....................		12,000
	$300,000	$300,000

Transactions for the year ended March 31, 1983, were as follows:

1. Collections from participants for dues was $20,000.
2. Snack bar and soda fountain sales were $28,000.
3. Interest and dividends received totaled $6,000.
4. Additions to voucher register were:
   House expenses—$17,000.
   Snack bar and soda fountain—$26,000
   General and administrative—$11,000
5. Vouchers paid totaled $55,000.
6. Assessments for capital improvements not yet incurred (assessed March 20, 1983; none collected by March 31, 1983; deemed 100 percent collectible during year ending March 31, 1984) = $10,000.
7. Unrestricted bequest received was $5,000.

Adjustment data:
1. Investments are valued at market, which amounted to $65,000 at March 31, 1983. There were no investment transactions during the year.
2. Depreciation for the year:
   Building—$4,000
   Furniture and equipment—$8,000
3. Allocation of depreciation:
   House expenses—$9,000
   Snack bar and soda fountain—$2,000
   General and administrative—$1,000
4. Actual physical inventory at March 31, 1983, was $1,000, and pertains to the snack bar and soda fountain.

Required:
a. On a functional basis, record the transactions and adjustments in journal entry form for the year ended March 31, 1983.
b. Prepare the appropriate all-inclusive activity statement for the year ended March 31, 1983, on a functional basis.

(AICPA adapted)

Index

A

Account groups, 835–36
Accounting, definition, 834
Accounting entity, 37
Accounting Principles Board (APB),
  237
  Opinion No. 3, 153
  Opinion No. 6, 50 n
  Opinion No. 9, 625
  Opinion No. 11, 325
  Opinion No. 15, 198 n, 208 n
  Opinion No. 16, 10, 11 n, 13,
    41–42, 50–51, 130 n, 196 n,
    417 n
  Opinion No. 17, 130 n
  Opinion No. 18, 108, 131, 266,
    270–71, 272 n, 280, 332, 375,
    460, 467
  Opinion No. 21, 764
  Opinion No. 22, 40
  Opinion No. 23, 416
  Opinion No. 29, 241
  Statement No. 4, 37
Accounting research
  comprehensive example, 242
  process, 241–42
  source material, 239–40
  structure of authority, 236–39
Accounting Research Bulletin, 237
  No. 4, 560
  No. 51, 46 n, 262, 329–30
Accounting Series Release, 237
  No. 244, 216
Acquisition, 7, 182–83
  financial reports, 36
  offering procedures, 13–14
Administrator of estate, 784
Affiliated group, 150
Agency fund, accounting for, 903,
  918

Aggregative concept of partnership,
  610–11
AICPA; *see* American Institute of
  Certified Public Accountants
Algebraic solution in bilateral stock-
  holdings allocation, 460
American Institute of Certified
  Public Accountants (AICPA),
  237, 239
  Industry Audit Guides, 900
  Statement No. 1, 843, 845
  Statement of Position 78-10, 901,
    908, 920
  Statement of Position 80-2, 729
Annuity and life income fund,
  accounting for, 903, 918–20
APB; *see* Accounting Principles
  Board
Appropriations account, 836
Asset-liability elimination, 495–96

B

Bankruptcy insolvency, 741
Bankruptcy Reform Act of 1978,
  741–45, 752–53
  Chapter 11, 753–55, 758
Basket purchase, 9
Baskin, E., 21 n
Bavishi, V., 13 n
Baxter, George C., 486 n
Beneficiary, 789–90
Bilateral stockholdings, 457–76
  algebraic solution, 460
  allocation of net incomes to
    outside shareholder inter-
    ests, 458
  differential amortization, 466
  equity basis net income, 458–60,
    467
  intercompany profits on asset
    transfers, 462–65

Bilateral stockholdings—*Cont.*
  investment elimination entry, 468
  matrix applications for complex
    affiliations, 468–71
  parent company involved, 460–
    62
  parent company not involved,
    457–60
  purchase of shares in mutually
    related subsidiary, 466
  recording equity in affiliate's
    earnings, 466–68
  successive iteration, 458–60
  traditional allocation method,
    457–71
  treasury stock method, 471–76
Bittker, B. I., 24 n
Boatsman, J., 21 n
Bonus method of recording admission of new partner, 615, 665–
  71
Book values, 51
Bradley, M., 19 n
Branch accounting, 496–509
  account terminology, 497–98
  agencies, 497
  billing in excess of cost, 503–8
  branch current account, 498
  combined financial statements,
    499–503
  home office centralization, 510
  illustrative entries, 498–99
  reconciling adjustments, 508
  substitution principle, 501
  transshipments of merchandise,
    508–9
Budgetary accounting, 836–37, 840
Business combination
  accounting methods, 9–14
  closely held companies, 19–23
  criteria for classifying, 182–83

Business combinations—*Cont.*
   earnings per share analysis, 196–211
      changing conversion rates or exercise prices, 208–9
      contingent stock issuances, 209–10
      fully diluted earnings per share, 202–4
      involving affiliates, 204–8
      primary earnings per share, 198–204
      restatement of prior period earnings, 210
      traditional calculations, 197–98
   economic motivations, 4–5
   historical summaries, 193–96
   mechanisms for, 5–8
   negotiation of publicly traded companies, 14–19
   pooling of interests method of accounting, 4–14, 185–93
   purchase method of accounting, 9–13, 182–85, 189–93
   tax attribute carryovers, 26
   tax factors affecting, 23–26
   tax status criteria, 24–26
   type A, 24, 26
   type B, 24
   type C., 24, 26
Business failures, 740

C

Canada, accounting principles, 13
Capital grant, 838
Capital projects funds, 853–55
Cash exchange for common stock as payment in business combinations, 5–7
Cestui que trust, 790
Chapter 11 of Bankruptcy Reform Act, 753–55, 758
Choi, F., 13 n
Cities Service Co., 5
Closely held companies
   negotiation of business combination, 19–23
   payment method determination, 21–23
   valuation of, 20–21
Colleges and universities, 900–901, 921–27
Combined (group) financial statement, 152
   branch accounting, 499–503
Common stock equivalent, 198

Common stock exchange as payment in business combination, 6–7
Common stock warrants, 200–202
Confirmed income, 267
Conn, R., 19 n
Conoco, Inc., 5, 242–47
Consolidated balance sheet, 43–60
   adjustment entries, 37–60
   disposition of debt (credit) differentials, 50–53
   intercompany transactions other than parent-subsidiary, 54
   investment cost per share at book value of subsidiary stock, 44–48
   investment cost per share exceeds book value of subsidiary stock, 48–50
   treasury stock of subsidiary, 55–57
   unpaid subsidiary dividends at acquisition, 55
Consolidated earnings, 18
Consolidated financial statement, 37–42
   asset-liability elimination, 495–96
   bilateral stockholdings, 457–76
   branch accounting, 496–509
   changes in parent company's equity, 387–418
   cost method, 80–83
   criteria for inclusion, 38–39
   date of acquisition, 37–60
   determining cost of acquisition, 41–42
   differential amortization, 130–43
   entity theory, 486–91
   equity method, 80–83
   evaluation of, 40–41
   income tax considerations, 150–52
   intercompany bonds, 346–69, 496
   intercompany profit eliminations, 496
   intercompany transaction other than with subsidiary, 93–94
   investment elimination, 495
   multilevel affiliation, 446–57
   policy disclosure, 39–40
   postacquisition, 80–111
   preference interests, 346–79
   preferred stock, 369–79
   revenue-expense eliminations, 496
   working papers
      first year subsequent to acquisition, 84–89

Consolidated financial statement—*Cont.*
   working papers—*Cont.*
      second year subsequent to acquisition, 89–93
      trial balance, 491–94
Consolidated net income, 83, 95, 137, 267
   schedular calculation, 105–6
Consolidated statement of retained earnings, 83–84, 99
   schedular calculation, 106–7
Consolidated working paper, 45
Consolidation, 8, 24, 112
Continental Air, 4
Contingent stock issuances, 209–10
Cooper Industries, 4
Corporate affiliation, 36
   reasons for, 36–37
Corporate joint ventures, 107, 108
Corporate liquidation, 740–65
   assignment for benefit of creditors, 745–46
   realization and liquidation account, 760–65
   statement of affairs, 746–52
      annotations, 748–50
      contingent liabilities, 750–51
      extended usefulness, 751–52
      prepaid insurance, 751
      stockholders' equity, 750
      trustee's account, 755–60
   voluntary and involuntary, 740, 742
Corporate reorganization
   judicial remedies, 753–55
   nonjudicial remedies, 752–53
      composition settlement, 752–53
      creditor management committee, 753
      voluntary assignment, 753
Corpus of estate, 786, 794–96, 802
Cost accounting method, 80–83, 100–107, 157–59
   preferred stock investment in subsidiary, 378
County courts, 784
Crane, Judson A., 716 n
Credit differential, 49, 51, 130
   disposition, 51–53
Crouse-Hinds Co., 14
Currency exchange rate, 531–32
   current, 532
   direct quotes, 532
   free, 531
   future or forward, 532
   indirect quotes, 532
   multiple rate structure, 531, 549–50

Currency exchange rate—*Cont.*
  official, 531
  spot, 532, 541

D

Debt differential, 48, 51, 130
Debt service funds, 855–56
Deferred credit, 53
Deferred revenue, 839
Deficiency account, 748, 750
Descent and distribution, laws of, 784
Devise, 785
Devisee, 785
Differential amortization, 130–43, 157–59, 403–9, 451, 466
Differentials, accounting for, 577–82
Dilutive versus antidilutive conversions and exercises, 199–200
Direct costs, 41
Discount, 541, 543
Diversified company, 212
Dividends declared account, 85
Dividends payable and receivable, 55
Dodd, P., 19 n
Dome Petroleum, Ltd., 242–47
Donor, 789
Downstream sale, 263, 273, 274–82, 310
DuPont, 5

E

Earnings per share analysis, 196–211
  affiliates, 204–8
  changing conversion rates or exercise prices, 208–9
  fully diluted earnings per share, 202–4
  primary earnings per share, 198–202
  traditional calculations, 197–98
  two-tier method, 211
Economic entity, 37
  financial statements, 38
Economic Recovery Act of 1981, 239
Education for financial accounting practice, 236
End-of-period percentage ownership interest, 399–401
Endowment fund, accounting for, 903, 916
Enterprise funds, 858–69
Entitlement, 838, 839

Entity concept of partnership, 610–11
Entity theory of consolidated statements, 50 n, 486–91
  debit credit differentials, 487
  intercompany profit, 487
  minority shareholder interests, 487–88
Equity basis net income, 458–60
Equity insolvency, 741
Equity method of accounting, 80–83
  intercompany bonds, 347–50
  preferred stock investment in subsidiary, 378
Estate administration, 784–89
  bequests of personal property, 788–89
  claims against estate, 786–88
  inventory of assets, 785–86
Estate planning, 791–94
Estate tax, 793
Eurodollar market, 541 n
Eustice, J. S., 24 n
Exchange gains and losses, 530, 533, 538–39, 543, 547–48, 562
Exchange ratio negotiating range, 15–18
Executor, 784

F

FASB; *see* Financial Accounting Standards Board
Fair value accounting, 50–53
Fiduciary
  bequests of personal property, 788–89
  claims against estate, 786–88
  corporate reorganization, 755–65
  definition, 784
  dual bases of accountability, 794–801
    principle and income distinguished, 794–96
    special problems, 796–801
  estate administration, 784–85
  estate planning, 791–94
  inventory of assets, 785–86
  trust administration, 789–91
Fiduciary accounts and reports, 802–11
  accounting procedures and entry sequence for an estate, 802–6
  charge and discharge statement, 806–8
  closing entries, 808–9
  properties transferred to trustees, 809–11

Financial accounting practice, 236
Financial Accounting Standards Board, 236, 238–40
  Interpretation No. 2, 764
  Statement of Financial Accounting Concepts No. 1, 625 n
  Statement of Financial Accounting Concepts No. 4, 829, 901
  Statement of Financial Accounting Standards No. 32, 901
  Statement No. 8, 561 n, 562
  Statement No. 10, 11
  Statement No. 14, 212, 213
  Statement No. 16, 625
  Statement No. 18, 213
  Statement No. 21, 198, 213
  Statement No. 24, 213
  Statement No. 52, 530, 533, 542 n, 549, 562, 563, 565, 577
  Statement No. 55, 199
Financial Reporting Releases, 237
  No. 1, 238
First-in, first-out rule, 398
Fiscal entity, 834
Fixed assets, accounting for, 862–63
Foreign affiliate, 565
  accounting for differentials, 577–82
  accounting procedures for currency translation, 568–77
  branches, 588
  consolidating, 582–86
  financial statement disclosures, 588
  functional currency, 565
  highly inflationary economies, 566
  initial investment, 566–68
  intercompany profits, 588
  relevant exchange rates, 588
  reporting on, 590
Foreign currency financial statements, translation of, 530, 562–64
  consolidated statement of changes in financial position, 584–86
  consolidating foreign subsidiary, 582–84
  current-noncurrent method, 560–61
  current rate method, 562–63, 568–73
  differentials, accounting for, 577–82
  financial statement disclosures, 588–89
  foreign branches, 588

Foreign currency financial statements—*Cont.*
  functional currency, 564–66
  initial investment in foreign affiliate, 566–68
  monetary and nonmonetary method, 561
  relative exchange rates, 588
  remeasuring inventory valued using lower of cost or market, 586–88
  reporting on foreign affiliates, 590
  temporal method, 561–63, 573–77
Foreign currency transactions, 530, 532–50
  exchange gains or losses, 533, 538–39, 543
  exchange rates, 531–32
  forward contracts, 535–38, 539–49
  functional currency, 533
  hedging, 535–38, 539–40
  import/export transactions, 534–38
  measurement, 533, 562
  multiple exchange rates, 549–50
Forward exchange contracts, 532, 539, 541–43
  accounting procedures, 542–49
  characteristics of accounting categories, 54
  discount, 541
  hedging, 535–38, 539–49
  measurement, 539
  premium, 541
  spot and forward exchange rates, 541
Founder, 789
Fractional elimination of intercompany profits, 330–32
France, accounting principles, 13
Functional currency, 533, 563, 564–65
  remeasuring affiliates foreign currency, 573–77
Funds, accounting for
  capital project, 853–55, 868
  debt service, 855–56, 868
  enterprise funds, 858–69
    annual financial reports of state and local governments, 868–69
    general fixed assets, 862–63
    general long-term debt, 863, 868
    internal service funds, 859–60
    trust and agency funds, 861–62

Funds—*Cont.*
  general fund
    account groups, 835–36
    allotments and apportionments, 835
    budgetary accounting, 836–37
    comprehensive illustrative entries, 846–51
    expendable and nonexpendable, 834–35
    expenditure control, 841
    financial statements for, 845
    grants, entitlements and shared revenues, 838–39
    recording actual transactions, 840–42
    recording budget, 839–41
    recording encumbrances, 842
    reserves, 844–45
  nature of, 834
  nonbusiness organizations, 903–42
    financial statements, 920–42
    restricted funds, 909–12
    unrestricted funds, 903–9
  special assessment funds, 856–58
  special revenue funds, 851–53
Future rate of exchange, 632

G

General Electric Company, 15–18, 21–22
General Foods, 4
General long-term debt, 863, 868–69
General partnership, 107
Germany, accounting principles, 13
Gift tax, 792–93
Gonedes, N., 19 n
Good will, 51–52, 130
  partnership accounting method, 615, 665–71
Governmental accounting
  funds; *see* Funds, accounting for
  historical perspective, 828–30
  principles of, 830
Governmental Accounting, Auditing and Financial Reporting, 828
Governmental Accounting Standards Board (GASB), 829
Grant, 838
Grossman, S., 19 n

H

Halpern, P., 19 n
Harrison, W., 9 n, 625 n
Hart, O., 19 n

Haugen, R., 19 n
Hedging, 535–38, 539–40
  exposed asset condition, 546–48
  foreign currency commitments, 540
  forward exchange contracts, 535–38, 539–49
  net investment in foreign subsidiary, 540
Historical financial summaries, 193–96
Holding company, 36
Hudson's Bay Oil and Gas Company, 242
Hospitals, accounting for, 900, 901, 928–33

I

Income tax
  consolidated returns, 150
  deferral of taxes on intercompany profits, 325–29
  deferred taxes on undistributed subsidiary earnings, 150–52
  partnerships, 616–17
Incremental approach to consolidated net income, 95, 98, 137
Independent schools, accounting for, 929–42
Index to Accounting and Auditing Technical Pronouncements, 240
Industry Accounting Guide, 239, 240
Industry Audit Guides, 239, 240, 900–901, 907, 908, 912, 913
Insolvency, 741
  state legislation distinguished from federal, 741–42
Intercompany bond elimination, 496
Intercompany bonds, 346–69
  analysis of gain or loss, 351–53
  bond elimination, 357–67, 496
  entries and eliminations after date of purchase, 353–68
  entries and eliminations at date of purchase, 353–68
  equity method of accounting, 347–50
  interim purchases, 369
Intercompany profit on asset transfers
  bilateral stockholdings, 462–65
  deferral of income taxes, 325–29
  entity theory, 487
  fractional elimination, 330–33
  merchandise; *see* Intercompany profit on merchandise transfer

Intercompany profit on asset transfers—*Cont.*
  multilevel affiliation, 454–57
  multiple exchange rates, 588
  nondepreciable assets, 322–23
  plant and equipment; *see* Intercompany profit on plant and equipment
  pro rata allocation, 267, 269, 273, 353
  services, 323
Intercompany profit on merchandise transfer, 258
  beginning and ending inventories, 295
  consolidated net income calculation, 263–66, 294
  downstream sale, 263, 274–82
  effect of allocating all eliminated intercompany profits against majority stockholders, 294–95
  effect of parent carrying investment account on cost or modified equity basis, 296
  elimination in consolidated statement working paper, 273–96
  elimination principles for unconfirmed profit, 262–67
  income tax effects, 262
  inventory market adjustments, 261–62
  parent company entries, 270–73, 284–85
  pro rata allocation, 267, 269, 273
  relationship between investment account balance and net assets of subsidiary, 280–82, 289, 294
  relationship between value of minority interest and net assets of subsidiary, 287–89
  reported and confirmed income of affiliates, 267–70
  seller's gross, 260–61
  transportation costs, 261
  upstream sale, 263, 282
Intercompany profit on plant and equipment, 310–22
  confirmation of, 310–11
  consolidated net income, 319–21
  depreciation, 310–11, 316
  downstream transfers, 310
  income tax effects, 328–29
  parent company entries, 311
  relationship between
    investment account balance and net assets of subsidiary, 321–22

Intercompany profit on plant and equipment—*Cont.*
  relationship between—*Cont.*
    value of minority interest and net assets of subsidiary, 321
  upstream sale, 310–22
Intercompany profit elimination, 496
Interim purchases of subsidiaries, 145–49
Internal Revenue Code, Section 368, 24, 26
Internal service funds, 859–60
International operations
  currency exchange rates, 531–32
  exchange gains and losses, 538–39
  foreign currency transactions, 532–34
  forward exchange contracts, 539–49
  import/export transactions, 534–38
  multiple exchange rates, 549–50
InterNorth, Inc., 14
Intersegmental transfer pricing, 216–17
Inventory accounting
  beginning and ending inventory, 295–96
  eliminating intercompany profits, 273–96
  remeasuring using lower of cost or market, 586–88
Investment account balance, 141
Investment elimination, 495
Investment elimination entry, 44–50, 85–89

J–L

Japan, accounting principles, 13
Joint ventures, 107–11
  corporate, 107, 108
  general partnership, 107
  limited partnership, 107
  proportionate consolidation, 109–11
  real estate, 111
King, Thomas E., 271 n
Langetieg, T., 19 n
Larsen, K., 19 n
Lembke, Valdean C., 271 n
Letters of administration, 714
Letters testamentary, 784
Lewis, William Draper, 717 n
Limited partnership, 107

Liquidation
  corporate; *see* Corporate liquidation
  partnership; *see* Partnership liquidation
Living trust, 789
Loan fund, accounting for, 903, 916
Lorensen, Leonard, 561 n
Lower-of-cost or market rule, 261

M

Mandelker, G., 19 n
Marathon Oil Company, 14
Masulis, R., 19
Mautz, R. K., 212
Merchandise transfer, 258
  income tax effects, 262
  intercompany profits, 260
  transportation costs, 261
Merger, 7–9, 24, 182
Mesa Petroleum, 5
Minch, Roland, 476 n
Minority interest, 38, 43, 88, 267, 289
  eliminating intercompany inventory profit, 287, 289, 291
Mobil Corporation, 14
Modified accrual basis of accounting, 837
Modified functional elimination of intercompany profits, 332–33
Moonitz, Maurice, 486
Multilevel corporate affiliation, 36, 446
  chain control less than 50 percent, 451–54
  differential amortization, 451
  intercompany profit, 454–57
Multiple exchange rate, 549–50, 588

N–O

National Bankruptcy Act (1898), 741
National Council on Governmental Accounting (NCGA), 828, 833 n
  Statement 1, 828–30
  Statement 2, 838
Net present value, 4
Netherlands, accounting principles, 13
Nielsen, J., 19 n
Nonbusiness organizations, accounting for, 900–942
  authoritative pronouncements, 900–902
  distinguishing characteristics, 902

Nonbusiness organizations—*Cont.*
  financial statements, 920–42
  funds used, 903–20
Nonprofit organizations, account-
  ing for, 900, 901
Offering procedures, 13–14
Operating grant, 838
Orphan's court, 784
Oscar Mayer, 4

P

Parent company, 7, 36
  concept of consolidated state-
    ment, 43, 80
  entries for inventory profits, 270–
    73
  financial statement, 38, 152–53
Parent company equity changes,
    387–418
  adjust cost measurement, 398
  average carrying value, 398
  block purchases in open market,
    393–98
  differential amortization, 395–98,
    403–9
  dollar equity in subsidiary net
    assets, 411–13
  first-in, first-out rule, 398
  incremental purchases of subsidi-
    ary stock from public, 392–98
  interim subsidiary stock issue,
    418
  issuance of new subsidiary
    shares, 413–18
  new shares
    nonratably subscribed by major-
      ity and minority stockhold-
      ers, 417
    ratably subscribed, 417–18
    totally subscribed by parent
      company, 413–15
    totally subscribed by third
      parties, 415–17, 423–27
  partial sales of holdings of sub-
    sidiary, 398–409
  percentage ownership interests,
    409–11
  restructuring form of subsidiary
    stock transaction, 423–27
  sales of subsidiary stock to pub-
    lic, 398–409
  subsidiary repurchase of treasury
    shares, 418–21
  subsidiary stock transaction, 409–
    21
  unconfirmed profit on asset
    transfers, 421–23

Partnership, 107
  admission of new partner, 663–
    76
    bonus method of recording,
      665–71
    goodwill method of recording,
      665–71
    legal status of new partner,
      674
    with payment to existing part-
      ner, 671–74
    with payment to partnership,
      664–69
    tax basis of new partner, 674–
      76
  aggregative concept, 610–11
  agreement, 611–13
  allocating net income, 619–26
    order of distribution, 624
    prior years net income, 625
    relative capital investments,
      620–21
    services rendered, 623
    specific ratios, 620
  balance sheet, 627–28
  death of partner, 679–80
    legal status, 680
  entity concept, 610–11
  income statement, 626–27
  income tax considerations, 616–
    17
    tax basis of partner's interest,
      616
  interest
    average capital balances, 621–
      22
    beginning capital balance, 621
  partner's capital, statement of,
    627
  realignment of ownership, 662–
    80
    basic legal provisions, 662–63
  recording initial contributions,
    613–16
  retirement of partner, 676–79
    legal status, 680
    sale of interest to continuing
      partners, 677–79
    sale of interest to new partner,
      676–77
Partnership liquidation, 696–726
  comprehensive illustration, 721–
    26
  insolvent partnership, 715–21
    accounting analysis, 718–21
    all partners insolvent, 720–21
    basic rights, 715–18
    one solvent partner, 718–20

Partnership liquidation—*Cont.*
  installment payments, 704–15
    basic accounting problems,
      704–5
    cash predistribution plan, 712–
      15
    expenses and unrecorded
      liabilities, 111–12
    partners' loans, 708–11
    periodic computation of safe
      payments, 705–8
    schedule, 698–99
  simple, 697–704, 706
    basic distributive rights, 697–99
    expenses, 704
    partners' debit balances, 699–
      701
    partners' loans, 701–4
  solvency and insolvency, 696–97,
    705
Petri, E., 52 n, 476 n
Plant fund, accounting for, 903,
    912–15
Pooled investments, accounting for,
    916–18
Pooling of interests method of
    accounting, 9–14, 182–85, 189–
    93
  cost determination of acquired
    company, 41
Power of appointment, 790
Preferred stock, 369–79
  allocation of earnings, 369–73
  cost method of accounting, 378
  differentials and elimination
    entries, 373–78
  equity method of accounting, 378
  nonparticipative, noncumulative,
    373
Premium, 51
Primary earnings per share, 198–
    203, 205–6
  common stock equivalents, 198–
    99
  common stock warrants, 198–99
  dilutive versus antidilutive con-
    versions or exercises, 199–
    202
Principal of estate, 786, 794–96, 802
Probate court, 784
Probating will, 784
Proportionate consolidation, 109–11
Proprietary accounts, 840
Proprietary theory, 486
Purchase method of accounting, 9–
    13, 182–85, 189–93
  cost determination of acquired
    company, 41

Purchased preacquisition earnings, 400
Push down accounting, 53–54

Q–R

Quasi-external transactions between funds, 837
Real estate joint ventures, 111
Realization and liquidation account, 760–65
  accruals, 764
  cash discounts, 763–64
  depreciation and uncollectibles, 764
  favorable and unfavorable settlement of liabilities, 764–65
  sales and purchases, 763
  statement annotation, 761–63
Registration costs, 41–42
Regulation S-K, 237, 240
Regulation S-X, 237, 240
Reimbursements between funds, 837
Remainderman, 790
Reported net income, 98
Research in accounting, 236
  comprehensive example, 242–47
  process, 241–42
  source materials, 239
Residual approach to consolidated net income, 95, 98–99
Residual equity transfers, 837–38
Restricted funds, accounting for, 909–12
Revenue, 839
Revenue Act of 1971, 238
Revenue expense elimination, 496
Revised Uniform Principal and Income Act, 794, 795, 798, 799 n
Robinson v. *Security Co.*, 717 n
Rowley, Reed, 697 n
Ruback, R., 19

S

Safe payments in partnership liquidation, 705
Securities and Exchange Commission, 236, 237, 240
Segmental reporting, 211–19
  allocating common costs, 217
  example of, 218–19

Segmental reporting—*Cont.*
  identifying assets, 217, 219
  identifying significant segments of firm, 213–16
  intersegmental transfer pricing, 216
  measuring profitability, 217
  need for, 212–13
Severable assets, 22, 23
Shared revenue, 838, 839
Smiley, R., 19 n
Special assessment funds, 856–58
Special revenue funds, 851–53
Specific exchange ratio, 18–19
Speculative forward exchange contract, 541, 542, 549
Spinney, James C., 486 n
Spot rate of exchange, 532, 541
Staff Accounting Bulletin, 237
  No. 51, 411
Statement of changes in financial position, 153–55
Stickney, C., 52 n
Stock dividends, 143–45
Stock exchange ratio, 14–15
Subsidiary
  consolidated balance sheet, 36, 38–39, 43–60
  consolidated statements, 36, 38–39
  deferred taxes on undistributed earnings, 150–51
  foreign; *see* Foreign affiliate
  interim purchases, 145–49
  realignment of shareholder's equity, 143–45
Substitution principle, 501
Successive interaction in bilateral stockholdings, 458–60
Surrogate court, 784
Sweden, accounting principles, 13
Switzerland, accounting principles, 13
Synergistic value, 4–5, 15
Synergy, 5

T

Tax-free acquisitions, 24
Tax-free reorganizations, 23–24
Tax Reform Act of 1976, 791 n, 792
Testamentary trust, 789
Testamentary trustee, 789, 790
Testator, 784

Texas International Air, 4
Texas Probate Code, 785, 787
Times interest earned statistic, 10
Treasury stock, 13
  subsidiary, 55–57
Trend analysis, 193–96
Trial balance working paper, 84, 491–94
Trust administration, 789–94
Trust and agency funds, 861–62
Trustee's accounts, 755–60
Trustor, 789
Trusts inter vivos, 789
Two-class method of earnings per share calculation, 211

U

Udell, J., 19 n
Unallocated credit differential, 51, 130
Unallocated debt differential, 51, 130
Undivided interests, 108–11
Uniform bankruptcy laws, 741
Uniform Certified Public Accountant Examination, 494
Uniform Partnership Act, 610–12, 643–60, 679, 708, 717, 720
Unrestricted fund, 903–9
  assets and liabilities, 908–9
  designated funds, 907
  donated materials and services, 905–6
  expenses and expenditures, 908
  mandatory and nonmandatory transfers, 907
  pledges, 906
  revenues, 903–5
Upstream sale, 263, 273, 282–94, 310–22
Utah International, 15–18, 21–22

V–Z

Venturers, 107, 108, 110
Voluntary health and welfare organizations, 900, 901, 934–38
Welsch, G., 9 n, 625 n
Working papers, 45
  consolidated financial statements, 84–93, 157–59, 273–96
  trial balance, 491–94
Zlotkovich, C., 9 n, 625 n

This book has been set VIP, in 10 and 9 point Palatino, leaded 2 points. Unit numbers and chapter numbers are set in 24 and 36 point Helvetica Light. Unit titles and chapter titles are set in 20 and 18 point Helvetica Regular. The size of the type page is 28 by 46 picas.